Poole's Textbook on Contract Law

Poole's Textbook on
Contract Law

14th edition

ROBERT MERKIN QC

LLM (London), LLD (Cardiff)
Professor of Commercial Law
Exeter Law School,
University of Exeter

SÉVERINE SAINTIER

Maitrise, LLM, PhD
Associate Professor in Commercial Law
Exeter Law School,
University of Exeter

Earlier editions of this book were written by Professor Jill Poole

JILL POOLE

LLB, LLM, FHEA, FRSA, FCI Arb, Barrister
50th Anniversary Professor of Commercial Law and Head of Aston Law
Deputy Dean, Aston Business School,
Aston University

OXFORD
UNIVERSITY PRESS

Great Clarendon Street, Oxford, OX2 6DP,
United Kingdom

Oxford University Press is a department of the University of Oxford.
It furthers the University's objective of excellence in research, scholarship,
and education by publishing worldwide. Oxford is a registered trade mark of
Oxford University Press in the UK and in certain other countries

Eleventh edition 2012
Twelfth edition 2014
Thirteenth edition 2016

Impression: 1

Published in the United States of America by Oxford University Press
198 Madison Avenue, New York, NY 10016, United States of America

British Library Cataloguing in Publication Data
Data available

Library of Congress Control Number: 2019931964

ISBN 978–0–19–881698–0

Printed in Italy by L.E.G.O. S.p.A.

Dedicated to the memory of Professor Jill Poole: Scholar, teacher, and inspiration

ABOUT THE AUTHORS

Professor Robert Merkin QC

Robert Merkin is Professor of Law at the University of Exeter and Special Counsel to Duncan Cotterill. He has taught the Law of Contract for many years. Robert has written a number of texts and articles on contract, insurance, and arbitration. He is co-editor of the *Lloyd's Law Reports*. He was appointed Queen's Counsel (honoris causa) in 2015 and was awarded a higher doctorate by Cardiff University in the same year. In 2018 Robert became Honorary Life President of the International Association of Insurance Law (AIDA).

Robert Merkin and Jill Poole were colleagues at Cardiff for a number of years, and Robert worked with Jill on an informal advisory basis on earlier editions of both the *Textbook* and *Casebook*. He has co-edited the book *Essays in Memory of Professor Jill Poole: Coherence, Modernisation and Integration in Contract, Commercial and Corporate Laws*.

Dr Séverine Saintier

Séverine Saintier is Associate Professor in Commercial Law at the University of Exeter where she teaches contract, commercial, and French contract law. She has authored publications such as *Commercial Agency Law: A Comparative Analysis* and written a number of articles for leading journals including the *Journal of Business Law* and the *European Review of Private Law*. Séverine is co-author with Robert of the Privity chapter in *Essays in Memory of Professor Jill Poole*.

Professor Jill Poole LLB, LLM, FHEA, FRSA, FCI Arb, Barrister

Jill Poole was Deputy Dean, Head of Aston Law and 50th Anniversary Professor of Commercial Law, Aston Business School, Aston University. Before her appointment at Aston she was a lecturer at Cardiff Law School. She was co-author of *Contract Formation and Letters of Intent* and also authored *Casebook on Contract Law*, to be used alongside this textbook, and *Contract Law Concentrate*, a law revision and study guide. Jill also authored and co-authored a series of important articles on contract law, particularly remedies for breach.

PREFACE

Professor Jill Poole was taken from us in 2016 at a tragically young age. She left a rich legacy of published work, a superb Law School at Aston, a generation of students who were fortunate enough to receive the benefit of her teaching, and of course admiration and deep affection of everyone who worked with her. She was immensely proud of *Textbook on Contract Law*, and through the thirteen editions written by her she gradually refined and developed her presentation of the law. Her clarity of exposition and explanation resulted in her *Textbook* becoming in a relatively short period one of the most popular student works on the Law of Contract. The academic world owes Jill a great debt, and on a personal note we will both miss her wisdom and friendship.

When the publishers approached us to prepare a new edition of the *Textbook*, we felt privileged, delighted, and daunted. It was agreed within seconds that the work would be retitled *Poole's Textbook on Contract Law*, both in honour of her life and achievements and also in recognition of the fact that this book would, as far as possible, remain in her image. We have retained as much of her writings as is appropriate, given the rapid and extensive changes in the law since the last edition was completed in February 2016. We have also sought to emulate her approach, which she described in her preface to the thirteenth edition as 'training the intellect of the reader to be able to interpret and find solutions to practical business problems'. It has been a challenging task to maintain Jill's standards, and we hope that the resulting product is seamless in its style and content.

In preparing the present edition we were greatly assisted by a number of anonymous reviewers, both teachers and students, who pointed out to us where we might amend the text in the light of developments. We owe a particular debt to Adam Shaw-Mellors of Aston University who maintains the accompanying online resources, and to our Exeter colleague Dr Timothy J. Dodsworth who made a series of important suggestions as to how we could improve our analysis. We also wish to thank the team at Oxford University Press, particularly Sarah Stephenson and Alec Swann. Sarah has been incredibly supportive and patient in equal measure in extracting the various chapters from us. As Jill said in her last preface, 'the final published book doesn't just happen! It takes many months of work by a team of experts'. We can only but vouch for the veracity of that statement! We therefore also thank them for allowing us the opportunity to stand on the shoulders of a giant. Our respective families have, as ever, been supportive and have ensured that we stay grounded and do not get carried away with our delusions of adequacy.

In her final preface, Jill thanked all those tutors and students who had recommended and used the *Textbook*. We echo those thanks, and repeat her receptiveness to comments and questions from readers irrespective of their level of experience.

Rob Merkin: r.m.merkin@exeter.ac.uk
Séverine Saintier: s.saintier@exeter.ac.uk
School of Law, University of Exeter
November 2018

LATE NEWS

New and important cases have come through whilst the book was undergoing its production process. Whereas it was not possible, for obvious reasons, to incorporate them in the relevant chapters, given their importance, it is nevertheless crucial to flag those cases at this point of the book.

Wells v Devani [2019] UKSC 4: Interpretation of terms, Chapter 6

The Supreme Court unanimously held that an estate agency contract was valid even though the precise circumstances upon which commission was payable were not agreed. In doing so, the Supreme Court overturned the majority of the Court of Appeal decision ([2016] EWCA Civ 1106), which found that there could not be a legally binding contract when an essential term was missing. Lord Kitchin, (with whom Lord Wilson, Lord Sumption and Lord Carnwarth agreed) reiterated that in order to decide whether there was a binding contract between the parties, the court had to consider, objectively, whether the parties intended, through their words and conduct, to create a legally binding contract and whether they had agreed 'all the terms that the law requires as essential for that purpose' (at [17]). After reiterating the courts' general reluctance to find an agreement too vague or uncertain to be enforced when the parties have acted on their agreement (at [18]), Lord Kitchin stated that in the context of the conversation that took place between Mr Wells and Mr Devani, it was understood that Mr Devani would be entitled to a commission of 2% plus VAT. His Lordship added that this payment would become due on completion and would be payable from the proceeds of sale (at [19]). Lord Briggs gave a concurring judgment.

As remarked by the Supreme Court, the discussion over the payment of commission in the context of estate agency contracts is not new since 'the case before us is another in which the parties meant by their words and actions that the agent was engaged on the usual terms, that is to say that a commission payable not upon the introduction by Mr Devani of a prospective purchaser to Mr Wells, nor upon the exchange of contracts, but rather upon completion of the sale and then from its proceeds' (at [23]). In the circumstances, there was therefore no need for the court to imply a term. However, if it had been necessary, then his Lordship would have had no hesitation to imply a term that payment would fall due on completion of the purchase by a person whom Mr Devani had introduced (at [27]). Following *Marks and Spencer v BNP Paribas* [2015] UKSC 72, [2016] AC 742, this was necessary since 'to leave Mr Wells without any obligation to pay Mr Devani would be completely inconsistent with the nature of their relationship' (at [29]).

Bates v Post Office Ltd [2019] EWHC 606 (QB): Good faith and relational contracts, Chapter 1

This case involved group litigation of around 550 sub-post masters and the post office. The post office introduced a compulsory new payment system, which the claimants had to use. This system, following several defects, gave rise to unexplained losses and accountancy discrepancies. Litigation arose over the question of liability for such losses. Although not all sub-masters suffered in the same manner following the introduction of this new payment system, common issues were agreed for the group litigation to be as effective as possible. The first of these issues, which Fraser J describes as the most important aspect of this litigation, was whether the contracts between the sub-post masters and the post office were relational contracts and whether duties of good faith, fair dealing, transparency, co-operation, and trust and confidence were implied into the contract. On the issue of relational contracts, Fraser J clarified, after careful consideration, that such contracts do indeed exist in English law. But Fraser J did not stop there and after careful examination of the academic debate on this matter (at [702–720]) gave what he considered to be a non-exhaustive list of characteristics to be taken into consideration for contracts to be regarded as relational (at [725]).

1. There must be no specific express terms in the contract that prevents a duty of good faith being implied into the contract.
2. The contract will be a long-term one, with the mutual intention of the parties being that there will be a long-term relationship.
3. The parties must intend that their respective roles be performed with integrity, and with fidelity to their bargain.
4. The parties will be committed to collaborating with one another in the performance of the contract.
5. The spirits and objectives of their venture may not be capable of being expressed exhaustively in a written contract.
6. They will each repose trust and confidence in one another, but of a different kind to that involved in fiduciary relationships.
7. The contract in question will involve a high degree of communication, co-operation and predictable performance based on mutual trust and confidence, and expectations of loyalty.
8. There may be a degree of significant investment by one party (or both) in the venture. This significant investment may be, in some cases, more accurately described as substantial financial commitment.
9. Exclusivity of the relationship may also be present.

Fraser J added (at 725]) that 'No single one of the above list is determinative, with the exception of the first one. This is because if the express terms prevent the implication of a duty of good faith, then that will be the end of the matter'. On the facts, he considered that all those characteristics to be present in the contract between the parties and therefore held the contract to be of a relational nature. He, however, quickly added (at [726]) that 'finding that these contracts with the Post Office are relational, does not mean there will be automatic and widespread application of an implied duty of good faith to all commercial relationships'. This case confirms the authors' viewpoint aired in chapter 1 that good faith is here to stay.

Randgold Resources Ltd v Santam Ltd [2018] EWHC 2493 (Comm): Reinsurance and Contract (Rights of Third Parties) Act 1999, Chapter 11

This was a complex reinsurance dispute in which the policyholder sought a declaration that its insurers had a valid claim against reinsurers; the insurers were liable to the policyholder only if they had reinsurance cover. The reinsurance agreement contained a 'cut-through' clause under which the policyholder could make a direct claim against the reinsurers as long as the claim was covered by both the reinsurance and by the insurance. It was held that the policyholder could rely upon the Contracts (Rights of Third Parties) Act 1999.

The cut-through clause was a term for the benefit of the policyholder, and the parties to the contract had intended that it should be enforceable by the policyholder. Under the 1999 Act, the third party had the same right to enforce the term as the parties to the contract, and it was therefore possible for the policyholder to obtain a declaration in the same way as the reinsured, even though there was no subsisting dispute between the reinsured and the reinsurers.

Chudley v Clydesdale Bank plc [2019] EWCA Civ 344: Fraud, Chapter 16

The Bank agreed with a property developer, Arck, that it would open a segregated bank account into which investors would make payment, and that sums could be removed from the account only on the receipt of an unconditional undertaking by lawyers that the sums would be devoted to project costs. The scheme was fraudulent: sums were withdrawn by the developers without the provision of such an undertaking, and they were lost. Investors succeeded in a claim against the Bank. The Court of Appeal held that the Bank's undertaking to open the account and to hold the moneys in it in accordance with the terms of he undertaking was a binding contract, and that it was intended to be for the benefit of investors so that it could be enforced by them under the Contracts (Rights of Third Parties) Act 1999. The most important feature of the Court of Appeal's decision is its rejection of the view put forward in *Chitty on Contracts* that the requirement that the contract conferred a benefit on the third party (section 1(1)(b)) was always distinct from the requirement in section 1(3) that the third party should be identified by name, class or description, and that it was possible for the same term to satisfy both elements of the legislation.

Canary Wharf (BP4) T1 Ltd v European Medicines Agency [2019] EWHC 921 (Ch): Frustration and Brexit, Chapter 12

The court held that the 25-year lease between the parties would not be frustrated by Brexit. In a careful and considered review of the law on frustration, the honourable Marcus Smith J confirms the restrictive nature of which events will frustrate contracts.

NEW TO THIS EDITION

This case law list represents a selection but is by no means a comprehensive account of all the new case law included in this book:

- Ch. 1: Strengthened discussion of the impact of good faith generally as well as in relation to the nascent recognition of relational contracts following *Sheikh Tahnoon Al Nehayan v Kent* [2018].

- Ch. 4: Discussion of the impact of *MWB Business Exchange Centres Ltd v Rock Advertising Ltd* [2018] on the area of consideration.

- Ch. 6: Redeveloped chapter on interpretation of contract to accommodate key Supreme Court decisions of *Wood v Capita Insurance Services Ltd* [2017]; *MT Hojgaard A/S v E.ON Climate and Renewable UK Robin Rigg East Ltd* [2017]; and *BNY Mellon Corporate Trustee Services Ltd v LBG Capital No. 1 plc* [2016].
  Extended coverage of cases on implied terms including *Bou-Simon v BGC Brokers LP* [2018] and *Al Jaber v Al Ibrahim* [2018].
  New coverage of No Oral Modification clauses (NOM) following *Rock Advertising Ltd v MWB Business Exchange Centres Ltd* [2018].
  Discussion of the impact of *Goodlife Foods Limited v Hall Fire Protection Limited* [2018] on the assessment of whether a clause is onerous.

- Ch. 7: Discussion of various aspects of exclusion clauses to cover *African Export-Import Bank v Shebah Exploration and Production Co. Ltd* [2017] on dealing with someone else's standards terms of business. *First Tower Trustees Ltd and Intertrust Trustees Ltd v CDS (Superstores International) Ltd* [2018] and *Goodlife Foods Limited v Hall Fire Protection Limited* [2018].

- Ch. 8: Discussion of the impact of *MSC Mediterranean Shipping Co. SA v Cottonex Anstalt* [2016] on breach.

- Ch. 9: Clarification of the rule on wasted expenditure. Clarification, following *Globalia Business Travel SAU of Spain v Fulton Shipping Inc of Panama* [2017], on what happens for a benefit received.

- Ch. 10: Substantial rewrite of the chapter to accommodate the impact of *Morris-Garner v One Step (Support) Ltd* [2018] on the *Attorney General v Blake* principle.

- Ch. 13: Discussion of *Triple Seven MSN 27251 Ltd v Azman Air Services Ltd* [2018].

- Ch. 14: Discussion of *Hayward v Zurich Insurance Co. plc* [2016] on fraudulent misrepresentation and damages in the light of s. 3 Misrepresentation Act 67 with *First Tower Trustees Ltd v CDS (Superstores International) Ltd* [2018].

- Ch. 16: Substantial redeveloped illegality chapter following *Patel v Mirza* [2016].

GUIDE TO USING THE BOOK

Poole's Textbook on Contract Law includes a range of tools and features to help you to establish a well-rounded appreciation of the subject. Case-driven content and succinct explanations are combined with summaries, questions, and examples to allow you to gain a sound understanding of the theory and application of contract law principles. This guide shows you how to fully utilize your textbook to get the most out of your studies.

Chapter summaries

Each chapter starts with a list of key issues that will be discussed, so that you are aware of what will be covered and can check your understanding.

> **SUMMARY OF THE ISSUES**
>
> This chapter examines the process of determining v
> the parties.
>
> - The existence of agreement is determined object
>   ties' words and actions. However, the actual assump
>   the promise (offer) is made) are relevant in the sens
>   know, that an offer on these terms was not intended
>   principle has particular practical relevance where

Extracts

Short extracts from cases and legislation are highlighted for easy identification.

> In contracts you do not look into the actual intent in
> A contract is formed when there is, to all outward ap
> contract by saying: 'I did not intend to contract', if by
>
> It follows that the 'voluntary' (consensual) natu
> ent than real. This conclusion raises difficult the
> primacy of contractual obligations, as compared
> basis that contractual obligations are voluntarily

Case summaries

Summaries of the cases discussed appear in coloured font, so that you can easily pick out the salient facts and details.

> In *Gibson v Manchester City Council*, the council had
> Gibson was such a tenant and he applied for details
> 'may be prepared to sell the house to you' and invit
> he wished to buy. Mr Gibson did this, but the coun
> to whether there was already a concluded contract
> House of Lords held that there was no concluded co
> letter made it clear that the council did not intend to
> was not an offer that Mr Gibson had accepted; rath
> buy. Although Mr Gibson had made such an offer to

Questions

Some of the questions that students ask most frequently on various points of contract law have been selected to appear in these question boxes, together with clear and succinct answers and explanations.

> **? QUESTION**
>
> **Is the promise requesting performance of an**
>
> The identification of an advertisement as an off
> ate confusion (and many emails asking for assis
> contracts on contract law modules, there are rela
> vast majority of contracts are bilateral, i.e. they
> The contract will be bilateral if it is possible to
> attracts legal consequences, simply by making

Examples

Key points of law are illustrated by reference to everyday situations, so that you can see how the law operates in practice.

→ EXAMPLE

When a student goes into a shop to buy a new textbo[ok] the student do not discuss or express any terms rela[...] Nevertheless, if an important section of the book wa[s...] happy if he had no remedy against the retailer. On [...] book that is in the state in which a book of that des[...] standing is incorporated into the contract by means [...] a term derived from statute. Since this is a B2C con[...]

Key points

Points of particular significance are featured in key point boxes, so that you can check your understanding of these fundamental principles during learning and revision.

! KEY POINT

To extend to exclude liability in negligence, the c[...] expressly to negligence liability, e.g. by using the w[...] done, then effect will be given to this wording, an[d...] strict contractual liability *and* negligence liability, a[...]

If there is no express reference to negligence, but th[...] to cover negligence liability, the exclusion will no[t...] liability to which the clause could extend on the fact[s...]

Summaries

Some of the more complex principles are presented in summary boxes within chapters to provide additional clarification and to further aid the learning process.

⟳ SUMMARY

Pao On v Lau Yiu Long

1. The defendants request a promise from the clai[...] shares for one year).

2. This request is coupled with an understanding tha[t...] some form of protection (or indemnity) against a fall[...]

3. The claimants make the promise to retain the s[...]

Figures

Line diagrams offer visual representations of contractual relationships to help you to understand this often complex subject.

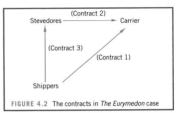

FIGURE 4.2 The contracts in *The Eurymedon* case

Further reading

The recommendations for further reading that appear at the end of each chapter will help you to broaden your understanding, and ensure that your study is efficient and well directed.

FURTHER READING

General on agreement and unilateral contracts
Adams and Brownsword, *Understanding Contract Law*, 5th [...]
Cartwright, *Formation and Variation of Contracts: The Agree[...] sory Estoppel* (Sweet and Maxwell, 2014).
Furmston and Tolhurst, *Contract Formation: Law and Pract[...] 2016).
Goodhart, 'Unilateral contracts' (1951) 67 LQR 456.

Poole's Textbook on Contract Law can be used as a stand-alone text or in conjunction with *Poole's Casebook on Contract Law*

Cases that are the subject of extended extracts in *Poole's Casebook on Contract Law* are highlighted in **bold and colour** for easy cross-referencing between the two texts.

The classic example of such offers is the offer of a rewar[d...] of some service, such as the apprehension of a criminal or[...] *Carlill v Carbolic Smoke Ball Co.* [1893] 1 QB 256 (the facts[...] ants sought to avoid having to pay the promised sum, al[...] influenza after using the smoke ball in the manner requeste[d...] no contract because there would otherwise have been a un[...] world. Bowen LJ rejected this argument, saying at p. 268:

GUIDE TO USING THE ONLINE RESOURCES

Poole's Textbook on Contract Law is accompanied by online resources providing students with ready-to-use learning resources:

 www.oup.com/uk/poole

Updates

This valuable resource allows you to access changes and developments in the law that have occurred since publication of the book. They allow you to keep up to date, while continuing to benefit from insightful analysis.

Guidance on answering problem-style questions

This advice on how to answer problem questions will stand you in good stead when you start your contract law course. It covers fundamental issues, such as organizing answers, using facts, and making statements about the law.

Self-test questions and answers

You can access a series of questions on each topic to test your knowledge and understanding, and then you can see the sample answers for reference.

Multiple-choice questions

300 multiple-choice questions, all with answers and feedback so that you can check and test your knowledge. All the feedback comes with references to the book so you know which sections to read if you need to revise a particular area.

OUTLINE CONTENTS

DETAILED CONTENTS

Part 4 Methods of policing the making of the contract   509

TABLE OF CASES

European Union

Court of Justice of the European Union (formerly European court of Justice)

International

Australia

Canada

TABLE OF LEGISLATION

National Legislation

New Zealand

United States

European Directives

European Regulations

International Instruments

Chapter 1

Introduction to the law of contract

SUMMARY OF THE ISSUES

- Contracts are legally enforceable agreements that represent a vehicle for planned exchanges. In our society, these exchanges are regulated by the principles of contract law in a way that is designed to meet the needs of society and should reflect the theoretical basis for the chosen regulatory approach. This chapter explains some of the main theories underpinning the development of English contract law and notes that, in order to be satisfactory, the theory must explain how the law has developed to the point at which it is today, as well as provide the basis for establishing how the law may develop in the future by indicating general principles capable of giving rise to specific rules.

- This chapter also examines the nature of contractual liability as a prelude to the more specific treatment of the components of that liability examined in subsequent chapters. Contractual obligations derive from agreements between the parties and it is this feature that distinguishes contractual liability from liability in tort. The relationship between contract and tort is considered, highlighting the fact that a set of facts may give rise to concurrent liability in contract and tort, and assessing the distinctions between such claims and remedies.

- The movement towards the globalization of contract law proved important in the latter stages of the twentieth century and this remains the case in the twenty-first century. This chapter therefore examines the various attempts to produce a set of harmonized principles, together with the impact of other international developments such as the growth in e-commerce and electronic communications, and the significance in a shrinking world of the principles of contract law applied in other jurisdictions.

- European directives have profoundly influenced the development of English contract law, especially in relation to consumer contracts. The most significant of these directives are noted and new developments highlighted for future reference. Perhaps the most important outcome of the implementation of these European directives has been the introduction of the concept of 'good faith' into English contract law. The debate surrounding the meaning and significance of this concept is outlined and briefly assessed. (See also the examination in the context of unfair contract terms in **Chapter 7**.) Recent case law assessing express duties to perform in good faith and whether there is an implied duty to act in good faith in commercial contracts is also explained and evaluated.

- This chapter also examines the Consumer Rights Directive in the context of the review of the consumer acquis (i.e. the body of European law and directives), and notes its implementation by means of the Consumer Rights Act 2015 and various statutory instruments.

»

- Finally, the issue of Brexit in the context of the relevance of English law in a globalized world must be considered. English law remains the law of choice for many contracting parties throughout the world. The commercial court's caseload is therefore very international in its nature, making English contract law an 'invisible export', a point emphasized in the Lord Chief Justice's Review of the Administration of Justice in the court (at para. 5.78) in 2008 (available at https://www.judiciary.uk/wp-content/uploads/JCO/Documents/Reports/report_lordchiefjustice_review_2008.pdf).

1.1 The role of contract

The central role of contract in our legal and economic systems is not accidental. It serves important purposes in society. Indeed, it appears that the device of contract is put to important uses in many diverse societies, and it would be wrong to assume that English contract law is the only model, or is of universal application. All societies require a vehicle through which *planned exchanges* can be made. Societies require methods of ordering existence so that such cooperation as is deemed necessary may take place. The role of planning embraces the need that people have to project reliable courses of action into the future. The idea of *exchange* includes not only 'one-off' contracts, but also long-term business relationships comprising perhaps many hundreds of individual contracts; it may also include interpersonal relationships, and even the individual's relationship with the state. There is a relationship of mutual support between societal stability, the idea of planning, and the existence of exchange. The ability to plan ahead is an important factor in creating stability, while a stable society, in which it can be predicted that exchanges will take place, is an essential ingredient of reliable planning.

For many readers, the only experience of contracting will be as an ultimate consumer, so that each contract made seems isolated and discrete. In that sort of situation, the planning element in contracts is not self-evident. The following example may therefore help.

→ EXAMPLE

When a student purchases a book in a shop or on a website, there is no doubt that the machinery by which the purchase is executed is a contract, but there is little sense of this contract being merely one link in a chain, since the student is the last link. A moment's consideration will reveal, however, that the particular contract of sale can be achieved only within a complex matrix of other contracts. If it is an academic textbook, it is likely to have been commissioned by a publisher from the authors. Both parties derive planning benefits from such a contract. The authors know that the time spent labouring on the book will be rewarded by publication and (hopefully) the payment of royalties on sales. The publisher is able to fill a gap in the list of books that it publishes, in the secure knowledge that it will have such a book to offer to booksellers after a certain period. Before the decision to go ahead with the book is made, the publisher's employees will have carried out some market research and a decision will have been reached on the price at which such a book will sell. The publisher will seek to meet that price target by making contracts with printers and binders that will keep costs at the estimates made when fixing the price of the book. The printers and binders will, in turn, make long-term contracts with their raw-material suppliers, so that they too may be sure that their costs remain within estimates. Finally, delivery services, wholesalers, and retailers will all be involved in the process of delivering the book to the ultimate consumer.

Businessmen do not assume that the link between authors and readers will be achieved by a catalogue of fortunate accidents: they plan every stage of the marketing of a book, and they achieve confidence in the planning by securing it with contracts. That planning will apply to other fields than books: getting the goods on the supermarket shelves; delivering oil and diesel through the pumps etc. Although the planning is crucial for all those relationships, the circumstances, i.e. the particular matrix of contractual relationships will differ. Yet, this *matrix of contractual relationships, against which any particular contract must be viewed, explains why the first instinct of contract lawyers is to seek to preserve an agreement under threat, since much more is at stake when one contract fails than only the relationship between the two contracting parties.*

Before continuing, it is essential to distinguish between the device of 'contracts', which has universal qualities, and 'the law of contract', which is the vehicle for adapting those universal qualities to the particular needs of a given society.

1.2 The role of contract law

If the role of the device of 'contracts' is to provide for confident planning of exchanges, the role of 'contract law' is to mould those planned exchanges to the particular society the law serves and to devise applicable principles that regulate the contractual relationship, e.g. deciding when a contract comes into existence, when it is deemed to be broken, and the consequences of such a breach. Thus, inevitably, English contract law reflects the politico-economic philosophy prevailing in this country. Contract principles tend to reflect society's changing political context, e.g. changing attitudes to the prevalence of contractual certainty or flexibility.

1.3 The nature of contractual liability

Contracts are legally enforceable agreements.

- To say that an agreement is 'legally enforceable' is merely a shorthand way of saying that it is an agreement to which the law gives its sanction, as opposed to a mere social arrangement, which exists outside the framework of the law and which is binding only in the sense of moral obligation or social convention.
- Liability for breach of contract is therefore liability for failure to keep to the terms of such an agreement.

This definition of contract implies (at least) three distinct fields of legal rules relating to contracts that are required in any contract law. There must be:

- rules relating to the formation and content of agreements;
- rules relating to the enforcement of agreements; and
- rules distinguishing those agreements that are legally enforceable from those that are not.

1.3.1 The essential ingredients of enforceability

The rules determining whether an agreement is to be regarded as enforceable are the subject of **Chapters 4** and **5**. They embrace three separate elements: consideration (**4.2**); intention (**5.1**); and form (**5.4**). Thus an agreement will be classed as a contract only if it satisfies the requirements of consideration, if the parties intend legal consequences to result from it, and if it meets any special rules of form or evidence that are applicable to this type of contract.

Consideration is a distinguishing feature of common law contract not found in civil law systems. *Consideration will be defined elsewhere* (see **4.2.1**) *as the action, inaction, or promise thereof by one party that induces the action, inaction, or promise of another.* Consideration for one promise may therefore be provided by another promise, and so a contract may be constituted out of nothing more than an exchange of promises. There are good functional reasons for the enforceability of promises that have induced the reliance of another, but it has sometimes been suggested that liability upon a promise that has not yet induced another's reliance is an unnecessary feature of the law. The reason for that suggestion is that where there has been no reliance, no harm will be caused by the failure to keep the promise. However, it would be dangerous to rest enforceability on reliance owing to the evidential difficulties of establishing it. The problem of the issue of reliance is best illustrated with the following example.

> **→ EXAMPLE**
>
> A promises to sell to B 100 tonnes of grain and B agrees to buy it. Before A commences delivery or B makes any payment, one of them backs out of the agreement. In such a case, it might be said that no harm will be done by the cancellation of the contract, since neither party has done anything in reliance on it. However, what if B has already agreed to resell the grain to C, or A has turned down the opportunity to sell the grain to D, on account of the contract A had with B?

Rather than put the parties to the proof of their reliance, the law assumes that promises have a tendency to induce reliance, and so liability attaches to the mere act of reciprocal promising. Contracts in which performance on both sides remains in the future are described as 'executory', and the binding nature of such agreements is an important element in the commercial value of the device of contract.

1.3.2 Agreement

The rules relating to the formation and the substance of agreements are covered, respectively, in **Chapters 2, 3**, and **6**. In defining contracts as being based on agreements, it is implicit that we are concerned with obligations that are consensually (or voluntarily) undertaken. Moreover, it follows from the description of consideration given above that agreements usually consist of reciprocal promises. It is important, however, to give an early warning about the limits of the notion of agreement.

- Not all undertakings are completely voluntary, as the law imposes certain obligations on those who enter particular types of agreement (see **6.4**). Thus the fact of entering the agreement may be voluntary, but the substance of the agreement can be dictated by law (e.g. undertakings as to the quality of goods sold).

- Not all agreements are consensual if by that term we are to understand a precise symmetry between the real intentions of the parties.

The law regards agreements as formed by a coincidence of *objectively ascertained* intentions—that is, what each party actually intended is irrelevant when, to all *outward appearances*, the parties are in agreement (see **2.1**).

1.3.3 Enforcement

Although we speak of the enforcement of contractual obligations, the paradigmatic remedy for breach of contract is compensation for non-performance rather than compulsion of the performance promised in the contract (see the text opening **Part 3** and see **Chapter 9**). Moreover, although in the field of criminal law the idea of 'law enforcement' involves the imposition of penalties for non-compliance, the law of contract denies any role to penalties or punishment in securing performance of contracts.

1.4 Theories of the law of contract

The law does not stand still. Changes in the law may result from judicial reasoning by reference to values where the courts perceive the need to make a choice concerning how the law should develop to meet a situation not previously encountered, or where the scope of a particular rule has not been precisely defined. Consistent development of the law, so that such changes 'fit' within the existing scheme of things, assumes that judges have a sense of what the scheme of things is. Thus an understanding of the theory of contract is essential to rational choices in developing the law and should provide students of law with criteria by which to assess the appropriateness of choices made. A satisfactory theory must explain how the law has developed to where it is today and must provide the basis for establishing how the law may develop in the future by indicating general principles capable of giving rise to specific rules. Dissatisfaction with theory may have been caused by the growing inability of classical theory, which has been the dominating theory, to account for some of the existing rules of the law of contract. The question remains whether there is any more satisfactory theory that can take its place.

The discussion in this section inevitably refers to the substance of the law, which is examined later in this book. Readers may therefore find it beneficial to return to this section after completing their study of the substantive law.

1.4.1 Classical theory

The roots of classical theory go back at least as far as the eighteenth century. English law has however not developed in an insular manner, since nineteenth-century commentators borrowed from the writings of French legal theorists, who, by 1804, had succeeded in embodying in the French Civil Code a highly individualist conception of contract. The parties were regarded as having the power and the unrestricted freedom to determine how their relationship was to be governed. This French approach, the product of the political liberalism of the eighteenth century, fell in with the economic liberalism of nineteenth-century England to produce an equally individualist theory of contract law in this country. Nevertheless, the realities of the process of adjudication meant that the substantive law was obliged to move away from a purely individualist or subjective approach to contract, so that the much-vaunted sanctity of individual autonomy in contracting, which made contract immune from judicial interference, was much more a theoretical ideal than a rule of law.

When we talk about the classical theory of contract today—see Fried, *Contract as Promise: A Theory of Contractual Obligation* (1st edn, Harvard University Press, 1981; 2nd edn, Oxford University Press, 2015)—we must consider a modified form of the theory, which has tried to account for the way in which the law has developed. *Nevertheless, at the core of this 'modern' classical theory is the binding nature of the promise that has been voluntarily made.*

The crucial element in contract, which marks it out from most other areas of the law of obligations, is that it is creative. It does not merely provide the means of resolving disputes that may arise when certain events happen; it provides the mechanisms whereby things can be made to happen. For early contract scholars, it was a crucial observable phenomenon that, without any reliance by either party, the law regarded the mutual exchange of promises as, without more, sufficient to create a binding obligation (see **4.2.1.1**).

Tort and restitution were obligations produced by a reaction to events, but contracts produced obligations as the result of the mere exercise of will in the form of promise. It was unsurprising, therefore, that promise became the core of the theory, since it appears to be the essential ingredient marking contract out as separate from the rest of the law of obligations. But why should the mere fact of promise (or voluntary undertaking) produce obligations?

1. A first explanation, which owes much to political liberal theory, is that there is a *moral obligation* inherent in promising, which is derived from the social convention of creating expectations by one's undertaking: Fried, *Contract as Promise*, pp. 14–17. The social convention came into being because the liberal ideal of respect for persons and property could be achieved only if reliable cooperation could be established. There is support for this idea in the rule that the measure of damages for breach of contract is the amount necessary to put the non-breaching party into the position in which they would have been had the contract been performed (see **9.2**), which is generally regarded as protecting that party's *expectation* under the contract (what the parties expected to gain from entering into the contract). We know that this protection of *expectation* is restricted by rules relating to remoteness (see **9.5.2**), mitigation (see **9.5.3**) and that it is not possible to recover for loss of *expectation* where that loss is too speculative (see **9.3.4**). However, a cogent argument can be made that these doctrines are no more than necessary limits to cope with procedural problems such as the fallibility of the means of proof and do not take away from the basic premise that the promisee's actual expectation is to be protected. A more serious objection arises out of the fact that the objectivization of contract apparent in the formation of contracts (see **2.1**) and in remedies for breach of contract (see **9.3**) appears to be more than procedural, and seems to substitute for the actual expectation a collective appraisal of what the expectation should have been.

2. A second explanation of the binding nature of promise, not entirely distinct from the first, derives from the liberal economic theories of the nineteenth century. *Here, individual autonomy is not the goal itself, but a pivotal tool in the achievement of the actual goal of maxi-*

mization of wealth to the greater good of all in society. Maximization of wealth is achieved by market exchanges, in which both, or all of the parties involved, count themselves as having benefited from the exchange that has taken place. Markets and contracts are therefore closely linked. Indeed, the concept of market depends upon the binding nature of bargains made in the market, so that the individual's promise is required to be binding for the market system to work. Without this, trust in the market will be undermined and, in consequence, market transactions will lose their appeal. Support for this version of classical theory can be found in the existing English rules relating to exemption clauses in genuinely freely negotiated contracts (see **7.1.2**). The purpose of such devices is said by economists to be to provide a mechanism whereby the parties may allocate the risks of the enterprise between them: if they are both wealth maximizers, they may be assumed to have allocated those risks in a mutually beneficial way. To refuse to enforce exemption clauses in such circumstances would be wrong, since the effect would be to reallocate the risk away from what the parties had calculated was mutually beneficial. Nevertheless, classical theory is ill-equipped to account for such intervention in freedom of contract as is provided e.g. by the Unfair Contract Terms Act (UCTA) 1977 and, in particular, the Consumer Rights Act 2015, Part 2 (see **7.5** and **7.6**). On the other hand, the recent trend to accept the parties' own allocation of the risks in the context of commercial contracts (see **7.5.5.2**) indicates a return to the basic principles of classical contracting in this sector.

It is not surprising that classical theory provides a coherent explanation of the rules of formation (**Chapter 2**). Promise is the essence of the theory. Promises create expectation and can do so only if clear lines of communication are established. These rules do no more than set out the means by which promises are made.

It is perhaps surprising that classical theory should cavil at the doctrine of consideration: Fried, *Contract as Promise*, pp. 28–39, especially at p. 35. After all, the paradigm of consideration is usually said to be the mutual exchange of promises. Perhaps the consideration doctrine is no more than a trace of the Protestant work ethic in the common law: a rule against getting something for nothing! More probably, it shows that the common law idea of contract is founded in economic rather than political liberalism: wealth maximization results from mutual exchange, and there is no exchange involved in gratuitous promising.

Beyond the rules relating to the formation of contracts, recent developments have evidenced a greater reliance on interpretation (or construction) of the express words in the contract as expressing the wills of the parties, albeit objectively ascertained, e.g. the interpretation (or construction) approach in the context of identifying frustrating events rather than reliance on the implication of a term (**Chapter 12**) and the approach to contractual interpretation adopted by the Supreme Court in *Arnold v Britton* [2015] UKSC 36, [2015] AC 1619 and *Wood v Capita Insurance Services Ltd* [2017] UKSC 24, [2017] 2 WLR 1095, [2017] AC (**6.5.4**).

There is no doubt that classical theory shaped the law in a crucial period of its development and that it draws attention to an important element in modern contract law: the binding nature of mutual promises. However, it cannot be regarded as an entirely satisfactory theory, since it probably reflects the fact that the politico-economic philosophy that inspired it is no longer the philosophy underlying our contemporary law. Nevertheless, the doctrine of binding precedent ensures that cases decided during the period when the classical concept of contract was at its height remain influential today, and classical theory continues to make a significant contribution to existing law.

Two separate perceptions generated the belief among many commentators that classical theory was unable to explain the entirety of modern contract law.

- *The first is that contract law is not merely a response to the exercise of will by the contracting parties. Contract law also responds to events, often by imposing an obligation generally regarded as nevertheless contractual, or by modifying an already existing obligation. In each case, the reaction of the law is independent of the will of the parties.* An example of this response to events may be found in the law relating to promissory estoppel (see generally **4.8**).

- *The second perception is that the limited empirical evidence available—see Beale and Dugdale (1975) 2 Brit J of Law & Soc 45—suggests that, in practice, business people do not behave in a manner consistent with the classical conception of contract. Linked to this is the timid, yet growing, acknowledgement of the category of commercial contracts, referred to as 'relational contracts', a category particularly linked to good faith* (see **1.6.3**).

1.4.2 Reliance-based theories

The most significant post-classical theory of contract is based on the notion that obligation results from the fact of reliance—and its most eloquent exponent has been Professor Atiyah: see especially (1978) 94 LQR 193. Both the practice of business people and some of the legal doctrines noted earlier (especially promissory estoppel) suggest that the important factor is not the promise made, but the fact of reliance on it. Promise remains important in providing evidence of what has been undertaken, but it is not the source of obligation. Even in the field of formation of agreements, in which classical theory is relatively secure, the analysis is sometimes improved by considering reliance as the source of obligation. This view is certainly a more rational explanation of the cases relating to what are known respectively as the 'battle of forms' (see **2.4.2.3**) and 'agreements to agree' (see **3.1.4.2** and **3.1.4.3**).

In general, it seems that our instinct of obligation (or its absence) lies not in the mere fact of promise, but in the quality of the reaction to the promise.

> ### ⇒ EXAMPLE
>
> A says to B: 'Let's go out for dinner. I'll pay for the meal; you buy the wine.' B agrees, and they arrange to meet at the restaurant. A does not keep the date, preferring to go to the cinema with C. It is almost universally accepted that A's behaviour should not be regarded as a breach of contract actionable in the courts.

For classical theory, that conclusion presents a problem, since there appears to be no difference in moral terms between this promise and a promise of a more commercial nature (e.g. to deliver goods for payment). The social convention of keeping promises applies equally to both. Neither is there an absence of exchange: A's promise is not gratuitous, and therefore appears to meet the wealth-maximizing criterion. Why, then, is it our first instinct that A's promise did not give rise to a contractual obligation? The answer appears to lie in the quality of our reaction to the promise, which involves weighing the extent and nature of the reliance placed upon it. Thus serious consequences are likely to result from the failure to deliver goods that have been promised in return for payment, but it is not easy to predict very serious consequences resulting from the failure to keep a dinner date. Notice, however, that our reaction is not in terms of what actually happened: it is a generalized reaction based upon what, in our experience, would normally be the case, or what would be reasonable in the circumstances. It seems clear, therefore, that in some circumstances reliance may provide a better explanation of the source of contractual obligations than does classical theory.

Nevertheless, it also seems that, like classical theory, reliance alone cannot account for the whole of the law of contract. First, there is the problem of wholly executory contracts, which are enforceable after the mere exchange of promises. Secondly, there is the problem of promissory estoppel, which, although a source of obligation, is only a qualified source: it does not create any new obligations where none existed previously (see **4.8.3.2**). How can reliance be the major source of obligation when the principal reliance-based doctrine does not itself create active obligations? In addition, reliance theory is unable to account for the court's intervention in the contract on grounds of reasonableness or public policy that does not derive from the dealings between the parties, but from a collective or community sense of what is right in the circumstances (see **Chapter 16**).

1.4.3 Protecting reasonable or legitimate expectations

This theory is similar to classical theory in seeing expectation as the essence of contract, but it goes beyond classical theory in recognizing that promise is not the only means of creating expectation. *Indeed, it assumes that, in many circumstances, society (through the courts) will regard one party's expectation as reasonably held and so deserving of protection irrespective of the will of the other party.* So some expectation will be created by promise, some by reliance, and some by other means, including perhaps the protection of certain classes within society and 'fairness'. The essence of this collective approach to contract and its basis in reasonable expectation is that it endeavours to be sufficiently flexible to account for most, if not all, observable instances of contractual obligation: see e.g. Reiter and Swan, 'Contracts and the protection of reasonable expectation', in *Studies in Contract Law* (Butterworths, 1980), pp. 1–23, and Steyn (1997) 113 LQR 433.

This theory rests heavily on the roles both of the device of contract and of contract law. Contract law, it was suggested earlier in this chapter, is the vehicle that adapts the device of contract, which is important for its facilitation of planned exchanges, to the need of a particular society. Classical contract law therefore reflected the use made of planned exchanges in the aggressively free enterprise society of the nineteenth century. It would not be surprising to find classical ideas of contract law unsatisfactory if the nature of society had itself changed from out-and-out free enterprise to a mixed economy. Today, the law does not strive only for allocative efficiency, as a free-market approach would prescribe, but also contains an element of distributive justice that cannot be explained in terms of market economics, such as good faith obligations. The law, whether it is a judicial creation or the creation of Parliament, attempts to redress the balance between the weak and strong elements in society, protecting the former against the latter. On the other hand, the very idea of a *mixed* economy means that where the functions of balance and protection are not required, the legal system must enable private ordering of exchange. Thus the law must assess the level of intervention required according to the type of contract confronting it. It is able to do so by amending the nature of what it deems to be a reasonable expectation according to the circumstances of the case.

The relevant circumstances to be consulted in evaluating what are the reasonable expectations in any given situation will include the nature of the parties, and especially their relative positions. However, they will also include the nature of the subject matter of the contract, the manner in which the contract was entered into, and relevant public policies of the society in which the contract was made. The result is that we should have general principles of the law of contract, but also specific rules tailored to particular types of contractual activity. This theoretical breaking down of contractual activity into distinct groups, to which distinct rules may apply because of the different assumptions that we make about what would be a reasonable expectation within each particular type of activity, is clearly reflected in more recent developments in the substantive law. Although there is still a common core of principles of contract law, many discrete areas of contractual activity have developed their own specialized rules. Employment contracts, contracts for the sale of goods, contracts made by consumers, contracts of insurance, and contracts of international trade are all examples of areas in which it is necessary to proceed from an understanding of the general law of contract to more specific rules relevant to the particular context alone.

> ## ⇨ EXAMPLE

In commercial contracts for the sale of goods, there is no blanket implied term guaranteeing the quality of goods sold, but there is such an implied term where the seller is selling 'in the course of a business': such terms are implied (imposed) through a statute, the Sale of Goods Act (SGA) 1979, s. 14(1) and (2). There is also a term imposing an obligation to provide goods of satisfactory quality in the consumer context (contracts between a trader and an individual consumer who is 'acting for purposes that are wholly or mainly outside that individual's trade, business, craft or profession'): Consumer Rights Act (CRA) 2015, s. 9 (see **6.4.2.4**). In the consumer context this is an entrenched 'right' and liability for its breach cannot be excluded or restricted: CRA 2015, s. 31. By comparison, in the context of a B2B (business to business or commercial) contract, this implied term about quality can be excluded by express words in the contract of sale where the buyer is also in business, provided that the exclusion is reasonable: UCTA 1977, s. 6(1A) (see **7.5.3.1**).

1.4.4 Formalism and realism

One further theory, which also reflects the practical distinction in approach to commercial and consumer contracts, merits some mention here. Adams and Brownsword, in 'The ideologies of contract' (1987) 7 LS 205; *Understanding Contract Law*, 5th edn (Sweet and Maxwell, 2007)—see also Brownsword, *Contract Law: Themes for the Twenty-First Century*, 2nd edn (Oxford University Press, 2006), ch. 7—argued that there are competing ideologies in the approach of the judiciary to contract cases. They believe that these competing ideologies assist both in explaining contract decisions and in predicting future decisions, although the ideologies lead to tensions in what Adams and Brownsword refer to as the contract 'rule book'.

- *Formalism* regards the rule book as a closed system of principles that are to be mechanically applied, and it is therefore divorced from the results in individual cases.
- However, most modern judges tend to adopt a *realist approach*, which may involve challenges to the rule book where it stands in the way of achieving justice. The realist approach can itself be broken down into:

(a) market-individualism; and

(b) consumer-welfarism.

The philosophy behind the *market-individualist* approach is essentially commercial and focuses on contract as the means to facilitate competitive exchanges. Therefore certainty is a vital influencing factor for market-individualists, who in this context seek to defend the reasonable assumptions of the parties. On the other hand, the *consumer-welfarist* approach is more interventionist (e.g. consumer protection), and focuses on questions of fairness and reasonableness. As a result, it is far more flexible and protectionist in its approach compared to market-individualism. As Brownsword states in *Contract Law: Themes for the Twenty-First Century*, at p. 137:

> Putting the contrast very generally, whereas the former ideology insists upon contractors being held to their freely agreed exchanges, the latter seeks to ensure a fair deal for consumer contractors and, more generally, to relieve against harsh or unconscionable bargains.

It is possible to identify these differing approaches in individual judgments and *ratios* of cases: see Adams and Brownsword, *Understanding Contract Law*. They also reflect—although not perfectly, since commercial certainty does not always prevail in commercial contracts—the growing distinction in the law between commercial and consumer contracts.

1.5 The relationship between contract and tort

English law maintains a fairly strict division between contract and tort, which represents one of the major divisions of legal classification between obligations voluntarily assumed and obligations imposed by law.

This distinction was explained by Jackson LJ in *Robinson v PE Jones (Contractors) Ltd* [2011] EWCA Civ 9, [2011] 1 AC 534, at [79]:

> Contractual obligations are negotiated by the parties and then enforced by law because the performance of contracts is vital to the functioning of society. Tortious duties are imposed by law (without any need for agreement by the parties) because society demands certain standards of conduct.

1.5.1 Overlap between contract and tort

The same factual situation may give rise to both contractual and tortious liability.

> **→ EXAMPLE**
>
> A student (A) arranges with a courier (B) to send his case of belongings to his university, paying in advance for the service to be provided. In the course of performance of this service, the case is placed in a van and, as the van goes round a sharp bend, the doors open and the case falls off the back of the van and into the river. A has a contract with B. There are reciprocal, voluntarily assumed obligations (A to pay; B to deliver the case undamaged). A may therefore ＞＞

bring an action for breach of contract against B. Alternatively, if A can prove negligence on B's part (which may not be difficult, since the assumption must be that it is not normal for a case to be lost in this way), A may sue in tort, since B will be in breach of a duty to take proper care of A's case. Thus the same facts may give rise to a claim either for breach of contract or for breach of a duty of care arising in tort.

At first sight, it may seem curious to regard the contractual obligation in this situation as superior to that arising in tort, since they are identical. *It is possible, however, because contractual obligations are agreed, to agree also to modify the nature of the obligation by contract, e.g. by inserting an exemption clause in the contract that limits or excludes B's liability* (see **Chapter 7**). In *Henderson v Merrett Syndicates Ltd* [1995] 2 AC 145, at p. 193, Lord Goff considered that 'the law of tort is the general law, out of which the parties can, if they wish, contract'. To this extent, Lord Goff acknowledges the superiority of contract since, in principle at least, it is possible by contract to exclude liability in tort.

Nevertheless, the potential for a contractual term to exclude liability is today seriously diminished. For example, a clause purporting to limit B's liability in the above example (a B2C contract or consumer contract) would now be subject to the CRA 2015, see s. 57 and the principles regulating unfair terms contained in ss. 65 and 66 (see **7.6.3**), and, if A had been another business, any exemption clause would be valid only if it were shown to be reasonable under the UCTA 1977, s. 2 (see **7.5.2**). Thus absolute freedom of contract, if it ever existed, has given way to a much more limited freedom, which must coexist with many rules of contract law that impose obligations on the parties and limit the substance of a contract.

1.5.2 The remaining significance of the division

Despite the blurring of the distinction between contract and tort that has taken place in recent years, it is easy to identify ways in which contract and tort remain separate.

- An obligation of positive performance at some time in the future can normally be created only by contract, even if some of the substance of that obligation will be defined by legal imposition.

- The standard of performance required under a contract is often strict in the sense that obligations must be completely and precisely performed (see **8.2.1.1**), while liability for the tort of negligence depends upon the claimant being able to prove that the defendant acted unreasonably.

1.5.2.1 The measure of loss recoverable

The traditional distinction between damages for breach of contract and damages for negligence was that, in the case of the former, damages for loss of profit might be recovered (see the text opening **Part 3**); in the latter case, lost profit (or pure economic loss) could not be recovered, and the claimant was limited to being restored to the position in which they were before the tort took place. However, it has been accepted for some time that a claimant bringing proceedings for breach of contract may claim wasted expenditure rather than lost profits in some circumstances (see **9.3.5**). If the claimant is unable to establish what the lost profit would have been, because it is too speculative, the claimant may even be forced to claim wasted expenditure (see **9.3.5.1**). Although English law has flirted with the converse rule—that a person bringing a claim in tort may recover expectation loss (or 'pure economic loss')—this has occurred only in limited circumstances (see **11.5.1**). Therefore, in this field at least, the notion that contract is the superior norm still prevails to some extent.

1.5.2.2 The remoteness of damage

In both contract and tort, damages may not be recovered for losses that are too remote (i.e. are regarded as too improbable to arise) a consequence of the breach of contract or breach of duty. In order to assess which damages are deemed not to be too remote and can therefore be claimed, the courts will apply a rule which is referred to as the test of remoteness. This rule, which can be analysed in economic terms, relates to the allocation of risks between the parties to the contract. Indeed, the rule is present in order to ensure that the defendant is aware, when making the contract, that he has to avoid causing certain losses that may occur following his breach. The defendant therefore bears the risk of losses which will flow from the breach he has committed. The remoteness test in contract is therefore based upon what is in the reasonable contemplation of the parties, what the parties can contemplate will happen following a breach. *It has been traditional to assert that this test of remoteness is stricter in relation to contract claims than it is in relation to claims in tort, in that the test in contract is one of reasonable contemplations, whereas the test in tort is reasonable foreseeability*: *Koufos v C Czarnikow Ltd, The Heron II* [1969] 1 AC 350. However, in *H. Parsons (Livestock) Ltd v Uttley Ingham & Co. Ltd* [1978] 1 QB 791, the members of the Court of Appeal were unable to agree whether there was any difference at all in the remoteness tests of contract and tort, or whether such difference as there was, lay not between contract and tort, but between expectation (profit) and reliance (physical) losses. It seems clear that, despite the references to a test based on 'assumption of responsibility' (a key element in establishing liability in the law of tort) in the speeches of Lords Hoffmann and Hope in *Transfield Shipping Inc. v Mercator Shipping Inc., The Achilleas* [2008] UKHL 48, [2009] 1 AC 61, a stricter test (or outcome) in contract must remain, since the assessment of risk is very different where the parties know each other through the contractual relationship because the parties will have negotiated and contracted for certain risks, something that cannot be done in tort. Subsequent case law indicates that the courts wish to restrict the approach in *The Achilleas* to limited instances and retain an allegiance to the traditional remoteness test in contract. More recently, the Court of Appeal in *Wellesley Partners LLP v Withers LLP* [2015] EWCA Civ 1146, [2016] CILL 3757, see **9.5.2.8**, held that where there was concurrent liability, the remoteness test determining recovery for economic loss should be the same—and it should be the contractual test because the parties to the contract had the opportunity to draw special circumstances to each other's attention when contracting and they were assumed to be contracting on the basis of recovery of only those losses that fell within their reasonable contemplations. This position should not alter on the basis that there was concurrent liability in tort.

1.5.2.3 The limitation of actions

Although, under the Limitation Act 1980, a standard limitation period of six years applies to claims both in contract (s. 5) and in tort (s. 2)—with the exception of personal injury cases in tort, for which the period is three years (s. 11), and in tort cases involving latent damage, for which it is three years from the date on which the damage was discoverable (s. 14A)—the time at which the limitation period begins to run varies. In contract, it begins to run at the time of breach (i.e. the time when the cause of action accrues). In tort, it does not begin to run until some damage occurs, because there is no cause of action up to this time. This is difficult to justify where there is concurrent liability, and a claim is brought in both contract and tort.

1.6 The globalization of contract law

There are a number of international influences on the principles of English contract law that have had a considerable impact on its development over recent years. These developments have, in the first place, meant that some changes to substantive principles have been necessary, e.g. to implement European legislation. In addition, English contract law needs to adapt to the demands of contracting in an electronic age, which is necessarily international. The growth of e-commerce poses considerable challenges for existing principles. To ensure that English law remains relevant and keeps up with technological development, the Law Commission launched a consultation on the electronic execution of documents (details can be accessed at https://www.lawcom.gov.uk/project/electronic-execution-of-documents/). Alongside these developments, there have been a number of projects aimed at the harmonization of contract and commercial law principles. Given the increasingly international dimension of contracting, it is seen as important to address the differences in principles and treatment of specific issues arising in contractual formation, performance, and breach.

1.6.1 Harmonized statements of principle

In the latter part of the twentieth century, there were a number of attempts to harmonize or produce statements of principles in an effort to rationalize the distinctions apparent between jurisdictions.

1.6.1.1 The Vienna Convention on Contracts for the International Sale of Goods (CISG)

In the context of international sales contracts, the United Nations Commission on International Trade Law (UNCITRAL) was responsible for the 1980 Vienna Convention on Contracts for the International Sale of Goods (CISG). As an international convention, this can have effect only if ratified by the country concerned. To date, the UK has not ratified the Vienna Convention, although it has been ratified by most other significant trading nations and now forms part of the legal principles applicable to international sales contracts within those jurisdictions, particularly many European jurisdictions. Its influence can be seen in the proposed Common European Sales Law Regulation (CESL).

1.6.1.2 The UNIDROIT Principles of International Commercial Contracts (PICC)

In 1994, UNIDROIT, the International Institute for the Unification of Private Law, produced its Principles of International Commercial Contracts (PICC) in an attempt to provide a uniform set of principles (or articles) that might be adopted for use in any jurisdiction. The intention is that these principles can be adopted by the parties as governing their contractual dealings. The principles are truly international, in the sense that the participants to the discussions who devised the principles come from a range of backgrounds, including common law, civil law, and socialist traditions: see Furmston (1996) 10 JCL 11. Those principles, in order to remain relevant, are regularly updated. A new edition of the PICC was issued in 2016. Those principles are freely accessible on the UNIDROIT website (https://www.unidroit.org/instruments/commercial-contracts/unidroit-principles-2016).

1.6.1.3 The Principles of European Contract Law (PECL)

At the same time as UNIDROIT published the PICC, the Lando Commission produced a set of contract law principles for Europe as the basis for a possible harmonization of contract and commercial law within the European Union (experience with the implementation of relevant European directives having highlighted the fundamental differences between the legal backgrounds in member states). These Principles of European Contract Law (PECL) were published in three parts, Parts 1 and 2 forming part of a single volume—Lando and Beale, *Principles of European Contract Law: Parts I and II* (Kluwer Law International, 2000)—and the third part published separately—Lando, *Principles of European Contract Law: Part III* (Kluwer Law International, 2003). As we shall see, there are many similarities between the PICC and PECL. However, neither have any legal force and their use was always dependent upon adoption by the parties. Both the PICC and PECL have been cited as examples of alternative approaches and how the law might develop; e.g. discussions of such principles are included in Law Commission Consultation Papers as a matter of course. It is therefore important that students should both be aware of their existence and have some exposure to examples of relevant articles in individual instances. For this reason, examples of some individual articles are referred to in this text.

1.6.1.4 The draft Common Frame of Reference (DCFR) and the Common European Sales Law (CESL)

In 1989 and 1994, the European Parliament adopted two resolutions advocating the creation of a European Code of Private Law as the most effective method to achieve harmonization and to complete the internal market. Following a preliminary draft produced in 1999 (Study Group for a European Civil Code, Academy of European Private Lawyers, *European Civil Code: Preliminary Draft* (1999)), the European Commission issued its action plan in February 2003: *A More Coherent European Contract Law*, COM (2003) 68 final. Seemingly backing away from the option of an imposed European contract code in favour of improving the coherence of existing instruments concerning contract law and promoting the wider use of standard contract terms across the European Union, the aim of the document was to produce a Common Frame of Reference for European Contract Law (CFR) or 'toolbox' (of fundamental principles, key definitions, and model provisions) to be used when revising existing legislation or producing new legislation covering contract law.

The Draft CFR (DCFR) was published in early 2009. The European Commission's intention was that the CFR should be a non-binding legal instrument that may be used on a voluntary basis and which would serve as a common source of inspiration or reference. The DCFR did not however receive a favourable response from the House of Lords in its twelfth report for the 2008–09 session published in June 2009: *European Contract Law: The draft common frame of reference*, HL Paper 95.

The impact of the draft CFR has been minimal, but the Scottish Law Commission has used the DCFR on several of its reports and discussion papers (Discussion Papers on Formation (DP 154), Interpretation (DP 147) amongst others).

The idea for a Common European Sales Law (CESL) was first aired in 2010, when the Commission issued a Green Paper, Com (2010) 348 final, setting out a broad range of policy options for

European Contract Law. This was followed in October 2011 with the publication of a proposal for a 'Common European Sales Law': *Proposal for a Regulation on a Common European Sales Law*, Com (2011) 635 final. This was seen as the 29th Law (the other twenty-eight being the laws of individual member states), which traders may choose to use to govern their cross-border sale and supply contracts (i.e. it is an optional instrument). The regulation covers digital sales, as well as those conducted traditionally, on and off the trader's premises and contained two separate systems of law applicable to B2C and B2B contracts (although there are size restrictions, the regime not being intended for contracts between two large businesses), which can be adopted by the parties. The CESL proposal was highly controversial in the UK. On 10 November 2011, the Law Commission published useful advice to the UK government and made comments on the proposal (An Optional Common European Sales Law: Advice and Problems Advice to the UK Government, available at http://www.lawcom.gov.uk/app/uploads/2015/03/Common_European_Sales_Law_Summary.pdf). The Law Commission concluded that, whereas 'there is a case for a new optional consumer code to cover distance selling across the European Union', it was not convinced 'that the current text always strikes the right balance' (s. 14). In consequence, the Law Commission concluded that developing CESL for commercial parties was not seen as a priority (s. 51).

In December 2014, when the EU Commission presented its Work Programme to the European Parliament, it became clear that the existing proposal for the CESL regulation was being withdrawn. Following this, policy-making moved to the problems of digitalization in contract law (Digital Single Market Strategy for Europe), part of which is to provide better access to online goods for consumers and businesses (Com (2015) 634 and COM (2015) 635, for which a new proposal is pending).

1.6.1.5 End note

In spite of, or perhaps because of, the current uncertainty over Brexit (see **1.6.2.3** for discussion of the impact)—and for now, as the UK is still a member of the European Union—this text still makes reference to the PECL provisions for academic and comparative interest. The selection of European and international-based text such as PICC is based on a desire to present some illustrative examples of different solutions and treatment.

Furthermore, where relevant and of interest, this book also highlights some decisions of Commonwealth courts, e.g. the High Court of Australia and the Supreme Court of Canada, and principles of substantive law, e.g. § 90 of the American Restatement of Contracts (2d), for the purposes of indicating how these jurisdictions have approached a particular issue or legal dilemma, e.g. alteration promises (see **4.8.6**) and privity (see **11.3.3** and **11.6.4**). It has become common practice for judges to refer to a range of sources as justifying their decisions. This factor alone is further evidence of the internationalization of contract law.

1.6.2 European directives and their implementation in English law

The European Union has introduced a number of measures, essentially in the field of consumer protection, as directives, which have required implementation by member states. These have had considerable influence on the law of consumer protection and, less directly, on general approaches to contracting. These directives were issued and implemented in a piecemeal way, which meant that the measures sometimes overlapped, e.g. the Distance Selling Directive and its implementing measure overlapped to some extent with the E-Commerce Directive 2000/31/EC. It also meant that consumers were required to search in a number of different legislative measures in order to determine the applicable law (known as the 'consumer acquis').

Until recently, the most significant directive in terms of general contract law was probably Directive 1993/13/EC on unfair terms in consumer contracts (implemented in English law as the Unfair Terms in Consumer Contracts Regulations 1999, SI 1999/2083; this history is discussed at **7.6.1**). Although the central importance of the Directive is its scope and challenge to the fairness of terms in consumer contracts, it also introduced the concept of 'good faith' as a principle of English contract law (see **1.6.2.3**). There have also been directives aimed at achieving an effective basis for e-commerce in the European Union—namely, the Electronic Signatures Directive 1999/93/EC (implemented in part by the Electronic Communications Act 2000 and in part by the Electronic Signatures Regulations 2002, SI 2002/318) and the E-Commerce Directive 2000/31/EC (implemented by the Electronic Commerce (EC Directive) Regulations 2002, SI 2002/2013). Other directives sought to ensure that, in the consumer context, there was an effective enforcement mechanism for these consumer protection measures, e.g. the Injunctions Directive 1998/27/EC (implemented by Part 8 of the Enterprise Act 2002).

Recent examples of important European legislation are the ADR Directive (alternative dispute resolution) (2013/11/EU) and the ODR Regulation (online dispute resolution) (524/2013), aimed at promoting the use of ADR schemes in disputes involving consumer complaints.

1.6.2.1 The Directive on Consumer Rights and its implementation

In this context of disquiet over the multiple and overlapping directives and inconsistencies in their implementation, in February 2007, the European Commission issued a Green Paper that set out various options for reform of the existing directives, and suggested areas that could be revised with a view to creating an improved framework for consumer protection and simplifying consumers' rights and responsibilities. This was followed in October 2008 by the publication of its proposal for a new Consumer Rights Directive: *Proposal for a Directive on Consumer Rights*, COM (2008) 614 final. This framework directive intended to repeal four existing European consumer directives—the Doorstep Selling Directive 85/577/EEC, the Unfair Terms in Consumer Contracts Directive 93/13/EEC, the Distance Selling Directive 97/7/EC, and the Consumer Sales and Guarantees Directive 1999/44/EC—and replace them with a single instrument. This proposal had a difficult time, and the Consumer Rights Directive (CRD) 2011/83/EU sought only to make amendments to the Unfair Terms and Consumer Sales and Guarantees Directives. In essence, the CRD produces a more combined legislative provision addressing only distance and off-premises selling in B2C contracts and, in particular, informational and withdrawal rights, and an extension of liability for misleading and aggressive practices in B2C contracts. It became a seriously curtailed version of the original proposal.

Despite the identified need for 'consumer law' to be presented in a single 'one-stop shop' legislative instrument, the UK government has implemented the CRD by means of a series of legislative provisions, including the Consumer Contracts (Information, Cancellation and Additional Payments) Regulations 2013, SI 2013/3134, the Consumer Rights Act 2015, and the Consumer Protection (Amendment) Regulations 2014, SI 2014/870 (see **1.6.2.2**). These legislative measures are discussed further below and at the relevant points of substance in this text.

The CRD required amendments to the distance-selling rules and implementation of these amendments is proposed via the Consumer Contracts (Information, Cancellation and Additional Payments) Regulations 2013, SI 2013/3134. These Regulations supersede the Distance Selling Regulations 2000, SI 2000/2334, and the Cancellation of Contracts Made in a Consumer's Home or Place of Work etc. Regulations 2008, SI 2008/1816.

The Consumer Rights Act 2015 covers consumer rights and remedies relating to the supply of goods, digital content, services, unfair terms law, and enforcement powers. In its first part, it collects the statutory implied terms in relation to goods and services in the sales and supply law into a separate regime of consumer terms as 'rights', and extends this protection to 'digital content' contracts, e.g. providing that goods will be of satisfactory quality, fit for the particular purpose, etc. These implied (or included) terms are presented as 'rights' that cannot be excluded or restricted, and consumers are given various remedies that they can enforce, e.g. an early right to reject, the right to repair or replacement, the right to a price reduction, and a final right to reject. The pre-existing law—i.e. the SGA 1979 and the Supply of Goods and Services Act (SGSA) 1982—remains applicable to B2B contracts (or any contract which is not covered by the scope of the CRA 2015) and (in the case of some provisions of the SGA) the pre-existing legislation also remains applicable to B2C contracts, which again calls into question a key objective of the legislation.

Part 2 of the Consumer Rights Bill covers unfair terms. The CRD was originally intended to repeal Directive 93/13; in fact, it made only minor amendments to it. However, the UK government has used this opportunity to revise and collect the law regarding enforceability of unfair terms in consumer contracts into the main consumer statute, i.e. the Consumer Rights Act. The Consumer Rights Act 2015 revokes and replaces the previous legislative regulation of unfair terms in consumer contracts—the UTCCR 1999—albeit that the tenure and much of the substance of the regulation remains the same. It follows that the CRA 2015 also restricts the application of UCTA 1977 to B2B exclusions (see the discussion at **7.5**).

1.6.2.2 The Unfair Commercial Practices Directive: the CPRs

Implementation of another important directive was required in the years intervening before the CRD—namely, the EU Unfair Commercial Practices Directive (UCPD) 2005/29/EC, which was implemented in the UK as the Consumer Protection from Unfair Trading Regulations 2008, SI 2008/1277 (the CPRs). The UCPD is a maximum harmonization directive, so that member states may not adopt measures that are more restrictive, i.e. that impose higher standards of consumer protection. This was confirmed in C-261/07 *VTB-VAB NV v Total Belgium NV* [2009] 3 CMLR 17.

The Directive is designed to combat unfair behaviour in B2C contracts by prohibiting certain marketing and selling practices. The CPRs, as introduced in 2008, prohibit traders in all sectors from engaging in unfair commercial (mainly marketing and selling) practices against consumers and set out rules that determine when commercial practices are unfair (reg. 3). Regulation 5 covers misleading actions (including false or deceptive information) and reg. 6 is aimed at misleading material omissions. Regulation 7 seeks to prohibit aggressive commercial practices involving harassment, coercion, or undue influence. The CPRs create various offences relating to these unfair commercial practices (enforceable by the Competition and Markets Authority (CMA) via the Enterprise Act 2002), but, as originally implemented, did not impact directly on 'the rules on the validity, formation and effect of a contract' in the common law or statute and, as originally implemented, did not provide individual consumers with the ability to claim damages in the event of infringements of the CPRs.

The Consumer Protection (Amendment) Regulations 2014, SI 2014/870 made amendments to the CPRs 2008 (Part 4A) to provide that where a trader has engaged in a 'prohibited practice' in relation to the product that forms the subject matter of a contract between that trader and a consumer and that prohibited practice is a significant factor in the consumer's decision to enter into the contract, the consumer has a range of possible civil rights to secure redress, including a right to unwind the contract within 90 days or a right to a discount, and a right to seek damages (see **14.1.2**). However, this extension will not allow civil liability across the entire scope of the CPRs, since misleading omissions and Sch. 1 practices do not appear to be covered.

Following a review of the fitness of European consumer law (Fitness Check of Consumer and Marketing Law and of the evaluation of the Consumer Rights Directive (Brussels, May 2017)), the European Commission concluded (A New Deal for Consumers, COM (2018) 183 final) that the protection for consumers across the EU was still very strong but nevertheless highlighted areas for improvement in relation to enforcement and digital rights. As the process is still ongoing, its potential impact for UK consumers is of course, as yet, unknown following the current process of the UK leaving the EU, otherwise known as Brexit.

1.6.2.3 Brexit and (consumer) contract law

It is clear that a significant amount of UK consumer contract law (business to consumer, B2C) derives from European law. In comparison, the impact of European law on commercial transactions (business to business, B2B) has been, in the words of Professor Goode, 'almost negligible' (Goode, *Commercial Law in the Next Millennium* (Sweet & Maxwell, 1998), 88). It is to be noted however that the Directive on Self-Employed (Commercial Agents) 1986/653/EC has a more general impact on agency law in the commercial context, and the Late Payment Directive 2000/35/EC has also been seen as an important measure having broader impact.

Yet, the impact of Brexit is nevertheless likely to be felt more substantively on consumer contract law. The European Union (Withdrawal) Bill provides that 'EU-derived domestic legislation . . . continues to have effect in domestic law on and after exit day' (s. 2(1)). Of course, uncertainty over the level of consumer protection nevertheless remains since the Bill also stipulates that in relation to the 'interpretation of retained EU law' (s. 6(1)), once the UK is out of the EU, the courts will not be bound by any such interpretation by the Court of Justice of the EU interpreting European texts and other EU-derived rules. What the level of consumer protection will be is therefore uncertain. The aforementioned green paper on modernizing consumer markets appears to highlight a commitment to retain the strong protective rules, but it is too early to say what will happen. Some predict a weakening in the light of the 'track record of distinctly non-protective interpretations' by the UK Supreme Court (Willett, 'Theorising consumer law' (2018) 77 CLJ 179–210, at 210).

Aside from the impact on the substantive law, there is also the question of the impact of Brexit on the rules to determine the governing law of contractual obligations (the Rome I Regulation (EC) No 593/2008) as well as its impact on English jurisdiction clauses in international commercial contracts (the recast Brussels I Regulation (Regulation (EU) No. 1215/2012)). There is no space to discuss this here; for an excellent discussion as to why English law is likely to remain the law of choice for many international contracts, see Clarke, Hooley, Munday, Sealy Tettenborn, and Turner, *Commercial Law: Text, Cases, and Materials* (Oxford University Press, 2017).

1.6.3 Good faith and English law: a difficult relationship

Unlike civil law jurisdictions, several common law jurisdictions, and numerous international texts, English law does not recognize any general concept of good faith in terms of negotiation, content, or performance of contracts. One of the difficulties of English law in relation to good faith, as will be seen, is the difficulty of defining the notion. This is not the place for an in-depth discussion of the issues and arguments over the pros and cons of the UK position (for an excellent discussion of the issues and arguments, see however Brownsword, *Contract Law: Themes for the Twenty-First Century*, 2nd edn (Oxford University Press, 2006), ch. 6). The discussion here is merely intended to give some background to the current debate and highlight that in spite of a difficult relationship, good faith obligations nevertheless continue to be inserted in commercial contracts. The discussion over the meaning, content, and application of the notion is therefore unlikely to disappear.

Although English law does not recognize a concept of good faith, it has, nevertheless, to use the words of Bingham LJ, 'developed piecemeal solutions in response to demonstrated problems of unfairness' or unconscionability, e.g. the regulation of exemption clauses (**Chapter 7**), the penalty rule (see **9.6**), duress and undue influence (**Chapter 15**), and the rule governing incorporation of onerous and unusual terms (see **6.3.1.4**). However, this is clearly not the same thing as adopting a general principle.

There has been some scepticism about the desirability of adopting a general principle of good faith in English contract law, e.g. Lord Ackner in *Walford v Miles* [1992] 2 AC 128, at p. 138 (discussed at **3.1.4.2**), who, in the context of negotiations, regarded such a concept as too vague and 'inherently repugnant to the adversarial position of the parties when involved in negotiations'. Commercial lawyers and members of the judiciary, concerned to ensure that England retains its primary role in the resolution of international commercial disputes, have worried about the inherent uncertainty of such a general concept and the restrictions that it may impose on commercial dealings. Of course, this may be to underestimate unduly the ability of the English courts to give effect to vague principles and notions. For example, it is accepted that English law gives effect to 'reasonable expectations' of the contracting parties, which some would argue can be equally difficult to identify with precision.

1.6.3.1 Good faith as an interpretative tool in the context of unfair terms

In this context, the explicit incorporation of the concept of good faith into English law in the context of the assessment of unfair terms in consumer contracts, initially under the Unfair Terms in Consumer Contracts (UTCCR) 1994, re-enacted in a modified form in UTCCR 1999, and now contained in Part 2 of the Consumer Rights Act 2015, s. 62(4) is of crucial importance. In *Director General of Fair Trading v First National Bank plc* [2001] UKHL 52, [2002] 1 AC 481, the House of Lords examined 'good faith' in the context of the UTCCR 1994, treating the concept as an overarching concept of 'fair and open dealing' requiring both procedural and substantive fairness in contracting. (Good faith is discussed further in relation to the unfair terms regime in consumer contracts at **7.6.4**.) It therefore appears that, in this context at least, English judges have experienced fewer difficulties with the concept than the sceptics anticipated. Given that the concept of good faith appears to be an integral element of European consumer protection, it is perhaps surprising that its significance has not been more substantial.

1.6.3.2 Good faith in contract law more generally

Good faith, although statutory for consumer contracts, is not confined to them and has emerged through court decisions in the context of commercial contracts. Although generalized common law good faith is more controversial, it has proved to be remarkably significant, especially in relation to the emerging notion of 'relational contracts'. Good faith raises different questions depending on the stage at which the concept arises, namely, in pre-contractual negotiations or in performance of contractual obligations.

In relation to the former, the issue first arose in *Walford v Miles* [1992] 2 AC 128, where Lord Ackner (at p. 138E), famously rejected the notion of an implied duty to negotiate in good faith in the following manner:

. . . the concept of a duty to carry on negotiations in good faith is inherently repugnant to the adversarial position of the parties when involved in negotiations. Each party to the negotiations is entitled to pursue his (or her) own interest, so long as he avoids making misrepresentations. To advance that interest he must be entitled, if he thinks it appropriate, to threaten to withdraw from further negotiations or to withdraw in fact, in the hope that the opposite party may seek to reopen the negotiations by offering him improved terms . . .

It is of course important to emphasize that in *Walford v Miles* the issue was whether there could be an implied duty to negotiate in good faith in the context of negotiations made expressly 'subject to contract'. Good faith arose again, as an issue, in the case of *Petromec Inc. v Petroleo Brasileiro SA Petrobras (No. 3)* [2005] EWCA Civ 891, [2006] 1 Lloyd's Rep 121. However, in this context, the court had to decide whether an express term to negotiate a contract in good faith could be enforced. The issue of good faith was therefore relevant in the wider context of 'agreements to agree'. As this wider context is not solely confined to good faith, to ensure a consistent and coherent understanding of the issues pertaining to 'agreements to agree', this this iteration of issue of good faith will therefore be dealt with in **Chapter 3 (3.1.4.2)**.

Turning to good faith, as an issue pertaining to the performance of contracts, some context is important. PECL and PICC contain a general principle requiring that the parties act in accordance with fair dealing and good faith (Art. 1:201 PECL, and Art. 1.7 PICC). This broad principle is applied in other articles throughout each set of principles. The concept is therefore seen as an essential underlying principle against which the parties' dealings are to be judged and in the light of which future principles will need to develop. As previously mentioned, good faith exists as a general principle, not only in civilian but also in several common law systems (see in particular the Canadian Supreme Court decision of *Bhasin v Hrynew* (2014) 2014 SCC 71, [2014] 3 SCR 495). Using this context, in *Yam Seng Pte Ltd v International Trade Corporation Ltd* [2013] EWHC 111 (QB), [2013] 1 CLC 662, [2013] 1 All ER (Comm) 1321, Leggatt J regarded the UK's rather unique position as 'swimming against the tide' (at [124]) and proposed to use implications of terms in fact to introduce a good faith obligation in English law. In the context of performance of the contract, good faith arises again in several guises.

1.6.3.3 Express provisions requiring 'good faith' in performance

The reluctance of the courts to embrace good faith as a concept has clearly not deterred businesses from inserting express good faith obligations (or obligations of the same ilk), which of course have to be couched in terms precise enough so that they can indeed apply as held in *Bristol Rovers (1883) Ltd v Sainsbury's Supermarkets Ltd* [2016] EWCA Civ 160 for an obligation to use 'reasonable endeavours' or in *Fujitsu Services Ltd v IBM* [2014] EWHC 752 (TCC) in relation to an obligation to 'have regard to'. The courts have however tended to adopt a narrow approach when construing express terms that impose a duty to act in good faith. In terms of content, in *Berkeley Community Villages v Pullen* [2007] EWHC 1330 (Ch), the contract stipulated that 'in all matters relating to this agreement the parties will act with utmost good faith towards one another and will act reasonably and prudently at all times'. With reference to the US position, Morgan J stated (at [97]) that this boiled down to the following three elements:

i. to observe reasonable commercial standards of fair dealing;

ii. to be faithful to the common purpose; and

iii. to be consistent with the justified expectations of the other contracting party.

Similarly, in *CPC Group v Qatari Diar Real Estate* [2010] EWHC 1535 (Ch), the contract stipulated that the parties 'shall both act in the utmost good faith towards each other in relation to the matters set out in this deed'. Vos J at [243,246], with reference to Australian law, stated that the content of the obligation was 'to adhere to the spirit of the contract . . . and to observe reasonable commercial standards of fair dealing and to be faithful to the agreed common purpose and to act consistently with the justified expectations of the parties'.

A similar interpretation was reached more recently in *Health & Case Management Ltd v The Physiotherapy Network Ltd* [2018] EWHC 869 (QB). In this case, the question was whether a covert use of data was a breach of a reciprocal obligation of good faith that the parties owed each other at all times (clauses 3.1 and 4.1). In order to answer in the positive, Nicklin J (at [128]) stated that a party could only be in breach of good faith if that party had acted in bad faith (at [109]) and that it was possible to act in bad faith without actually being dishonest (at [109]). Relying on *CPC Group v Qatari Diar Real Estate* and *Berkeley Community Villages v Pullen* for the content as reasserting the importance of the context as defined in Mid Essex, Nicklin J stated that any 'opportunistic, underhand or exploitative' intention will be a breach of good faith (at [129]). Interestingly, in this case, the contract also contained a confidentiality clause, but as it only restricted the disclosure of confidential information rather than restricting the actual use of that information, it could not help in this instance (at [106]). Far from being diminished, the express clause on good faith was therefore enhanced (at [129]). In this instance, good faith therefore came to the rescue. From such cases, it transpires that good faith remains rather limited to being an excluder of bad faith behaviour.

In terms of scope, express good faith obligations will be interpreted as they arise from the contract. Their impact is therefore limited since they cannot cut across other terms, unless expressly stipulated in the contract. In *Mid Essex Hospital Services NHS Trust v Compass Group UK and Ireland Ltd (t/a Medirest)* [2013] EWCA Civ 200, [2013] BLR 265, it was a term of the contract between the catering and cleaning supplier and the Trust that:

> The Trust and the Contractor will co-operate with each other in good faith and will take all reasonable action as is necessary for the efficient transmission of information and instructions and to enable the Trust . . . to derive the full benefit of the Contract.

The Trust had imposed various penalties on the supplier for service failures. Although the judge at first instance had interpreted this good faith provision in a long-term contract as imposing a general duty to cooperate in good faith, the Court of Appeal disagreed and construed the term narrowly so that there was no general obligation of this nature; instead, the term 'specifically focused upon the two purposes stated in the second half of that sentence' at [106]. The court considered that 'the content of a duty of good faith is heavily conditioned by its context', and in this context it meant that 'the parties will work together honestly endeavouring to achieve the two stated purposes': *per* Jackson LJ, at [112]. Beatson LJ emphasized the need to take care 'not to construe a general open-ended obligation such as good faith to cooperate . . . as covering the same ground as more specific provisions lest it cut across those more specific provisions' at [154]. In light of this narrow construction, the Court of Appeal found that the Trust was not in breach of the express good faith obligation.

Similarly, a narrow construction of a good faith obligation, restricted to the term to which it was attached, meant that it could not apply to control a termination clause in *TSG Building Services plc v South Anglia Housing Ltd* [2013] EWHC 1151 (TCC), [2013] BLR 484, 148 Con LR 228. In this case, the term required the parties 'to work together in the spirit of trust, fairness and mutual cooperation' within the scope of the parties' 'agreed roles, expertise and responsibilities' (i.e. cooperation in performance objectives). The contract was terminated by South Anglia under the terms of a termination clause, which provided that either party could give three months' notice to terminate without cause and at any time. TSG claimed, in the alternative, that exercising the termination clause was a breach of the 'good faith' clause or that there was an implied obligation of good faith that the contract could be terminated only if the terminating party was acting in good faith. The judge firmly rejected both arguments, i.e. the termination was valid. The express clause had to be narrowly construed and, as a matter of commercial common sense, it could not require South Anglia to act reasonably when invoking the termination provision. A general duty to act in fairness and mutual cooperation was unworkable in the context of the other contractual obligations, which imposed absolute standards. Finally, in *MSC Mediterranean Shipping Co. SA v Cottonex Anstalt* [2016] EWCA Civ 789, [2017] 1 All ER (Comm) 483, [2016] 2 Lloyd's Rep 494, [2016] 2 CLC 272, the Court of Appeal confirmed that good faith could not be invoked to regulate the decision of a victim of a repudiatory breach to end or affirm the contract. Such a right was not akin to a contractual discretion.

1.6.3.4 An implied duty requiring good faith in performance?

As mentioned earlier, terms can be implied into a contract (imposed) through statutes. It is also possible for the courts to imply terms on a case by case basis (implied terms in fact) if certain conditions are met (implied terms in their entirety are discussed in **Chapter 6** at **6.4**). This is what happened in *Yam Seng Pte Ltd v International Trade Corporation Ltd* [2013] EWHC 111 (QB), [2013] 1 CLC 662, [2013] 1 All ER (Comm) 1321, where Leggatt J stated, *obiter*, that a contract for a licence to distribute and supply branded goods contained an implied term of good faith in its performance. This implied term manifested itself so as to impose an obligation whereby one party was not *knowingly* to provide false information on which the other party was likely to rely. However, after noting the solitary position of the UK in rejecting a duty of good faith, Leggatt J nevertheless went further, at [119]–[154], in appearing to advocate a general implied term in fact (based on the presumed intentions of the parties) to perform in good faith in all commercial contracts on the basis of giving effect to the reasonable expectations of the parties, although accepting that the content of the duty would always depend on its context. Leggatt J had considered that such an implied duty of good faith was merely a test of whether 'the conduct would be regarded as commercially unacceptable by reasonable and honest people' (at [144]). In doing so, Leggatt J was clear that this was a logical step in the development of English law drawn from existing norms and it would not introduce a notion based on a civilian notion (at [131]). Such heretical thoughts have not been well received by the courts, not least because such a broad implication would undermine the necessary certainty required in commercial contracts and the primacy of English commercial law.

In *Mid Essex Hospital Services NHS Trust v Compass Group UK and Ireland Ltd (t/a Medirest)*, Jackson LJ was clear, at [105], that there was no general implied duty of good faith in English law and Beatson LJ sought to limit *Yam Seng* to its context. In *TSG Building Services plc v South Anglia Housing Ltd*, Akenhead J refused to accept the argument advocating an implied duty to act in good faith. Referring to *Yam Seng*, the judge stated, at [46], that he 'would not draw any principle from this extremely illuminating and interesting judgment which is of general application to all commercial contracts'. In any event, he could distinguish *Yam Seng* on the basis that implied obligations of honesty and fidelity were not at issue in the decision to terminate in *TSG Building Services*.

The question of 'fidelity to the bargain' was covered by the express good faith clause and there was no need for any implication, given that the parties had spelt out an express, albeit limited, good faith provision. Norris J, in *Hamsard 3147 Ltd (t/a Mini Mode Childrenswear) v Boots UK Ltd* [2013] EWHC 3251 (Pat), also restricted the possible field of application of *Yam Seng*, specifically to relational (long-term) contracts. He added, at [86]: 'I do not accept that there is to be routinely implied some positive obligation upon a contracted party to subordinate its own commercial interests to those of the other contracting party.' Similarly, in *Greenclose Ltd v NatWest Bank plc* [2014] EWHC 1156 (Ch), [2014] 2 Lloyd's Rep 169, [2014] 1 CLC 562, Andrews J (at [150]) confirmed that *Yam Seng* had very restricted application and did not lay down any general principle applicable to all commercial contracts:

> So far as the 'good faith condition' is concerned, there is no general doctrine of good faith in English contract law and such a term is unlikely to arise by way of necessary implication in a contract between two sophisticated commercial parties negotiating at arms' length. Leggatt J's judgment in *Yam Seng* . . ., on which Greenclose heavily relies, is not to be regarded as laying down any general principle applicable to all commercial contracts. As Leggatt J expressly recognized at [147] of that judgment, the implication of an obligation of good faith is heavily dependent on the context. Thus in some situations where a contracting party is given a discretion, the court will more readily imply an obligation that the discretion should not be exercised in bad faith or in an arbitrary or capricious manner, but the context is vital. A discretion given to the board of directors of a company to award bonuses to its employees may be more readily susceptible to such implied restrictions on its exercise than a discretion given to a commercial party to act in its own commercial interests.

As previously mentioned, this is particularly important in the context of termination where the issue of the use of an implied obligation of good faith requiring 'cooperation' in relation to termination resurfaced in *Ilkerler Otomotiv v Perkins Engines Co. Ltd* [2017] EWCA Civ 183, where the court, [at 30], distinguished the contract requirements in the contract for communication and cooperation defined in *Yam Seng* by Leggatt J (at [142]–[143]), which applied during the performance of the contract from the position where a party was seeking to exercise its rights in relation to termination. For Longmore LJ, to do so at the stage of termination 'would take one into a different realm altogether' (at [29]). Similarly, in *Monde Petroleum SA v Westernzagros Ltd* [2016] EWHC 1472 (Comm), it was decided that the reasoning of Socimer 'simply does not apply to the exercise of a contractual right of termination' (at [265]).

In *Myers v Kestrel Acquisitions Ltd* [2015] EWHC 916 (Ch), the court also rejected such a term, concluding that it had no power to introduce such a term merely to make the contract fairer where the contract was detailed and negotiated at arm's length by commercial parties. This accords with the approach taken by the Supreme Court in *Marks and Spencer plc v BNP Paribas Securities Services Trust Co. (Jersey) Ltd* [2015] UKSC 72, [2015] 3 WLR 1843, at [21]. In *MSC Mediterranean Shipping Co. SA v Cottonex Anstalt* [2016] EWCA Civ 789 [2017] 1 All ER (Comm) 483, [2016] 2 Lloyd's Rep 494, [2016] 2 CLC 272, Moore-Bick LJ went further by warning of the danger of having a 'general principle of good faith' as 'it would be invoked as often to undermine as to support the terms' (at [45]).

Is an extended duty of good faith to be implied specifically in relational contracts?

The rather lukewarm judicial reaction to *Yam Seng* appears particularly clear in its reluctance to embrace good faith in all contracts, let alone commercial ones. Yet, the position appears different in relation to a particular class of commercial contracts, what Leggatt referred to in *Yam Seng* as 'relational contracts', which, for Leggatt J require 'a high degree of communication, cooperation' and even involve expectations of 'loyalty' (at [142]). Indeed, even a fierce critic such as Norris J, in *Hamsard 3147 Ltd (t/a Mini Mode Childrenswear) v Boots UK Ltd* [2013] EWHC 3251 (Pat), appeared to embrace the idea of restricting the possible field of application of *Yam Seng* to relational (long-term) contracts.

Richard Spearman QC (sitting as Deputy Judge of the Chancery Division) in *Bristol Groundschool Ltd v Intelligent Data Capture Ltd* [2014] EWHC 2145 (Ch) embraced the notion of relational contracts and stated that it was possible to imply a general duty of good faith on the facts. The parties had a continuing business relationship over a period of ten years relating to artwork supplied by the defendant and used in the training manuals produced by the claimant. Under their contracts the claimant owned the copyright in this artwork. The parties' relationship deteriorated and proceedings were commenced alleging breach of contract and infringement of copyright. One of the issues was whether the claimant was in repudiatory breach of an implied general duty of good faith for accessing and downloading materials, without consent, from the defendant's computer system in order to develop its own software system for the defendant's artwork (in purported anticipation of a breach of contract by the defendant). The judge considered that there was a general duty of good faith implied into the parties' agreements because this was a relational contract of the type described by Leggatt J in *Yam Seng* and based on the evidence of the parties' relationship of trust. Nevertheless, it is important not to overstate the significance of this decision. Indeed, the judge appeared to consider that the Court of Appeal in *Mid Essex* had not disapproved of *Yam Seng* and had not focused on the general issue of the implied duty of good faith outside the categories explicitly mentioned by Leggatt J as accepted instances for such implication (i.e. as terms implied in law, such as duties of good faith implied by law into contracts of employment). This must in fact be doubted because the Court of Appeal in *Mid Essex*, particularly in the judgment of Jackson LJ, appears to state that outside of these accepted instances of terms implied in law, any duty of good faith would need to be included as an express term of the parties' agreement.

Nevertheless, *Bristol Groundschool* is important in adding to our understanding of how good faith will be interpreted. It 'extends beyond, but at the very least includes' honesty and the judge considered the test to be whether the conduct complained of 'would be regarded as "commercially unacceptable" by reasonable and honest people in the particular context involved'. The problem however is the lack of clear definition as to what such contracts are and why they are deserving of such an obligation. Similarly, in *D & G Cars Ltd v Essex Police Authority* [2015] EWHC 226 (QB), Dove J recognized an implied duty of honesty and integrity, although conceding that 'integrity' was different to 'good faith'. Integrity was considered to capture the requirements of fair dealing and transparency which were important in relational contracts. The claimant had a contract with the police for vehicle recovery and crushing. The claimant failed to crush a particular car and made use of it for its own purposes. The police authority terminated the recovery contract and the claimant complained that it was not entitled to do so. Although the recovery firm had not acted dishonestly, it had breached this implied duty of honesty and integrity in the context of this relational contract. Such decisions, together with *Yam Seng*, have been criticized for failing to define with precision what a relational contract is or why it is deserving of such a heightened notion of good faith (S. Saintier, 'The elusive notion of good faith in the performance of a contract: why still a bête noire for the civil and the common law?' [2017] JBL 441), a position is nevertheless slowly emerging (H. Collins, 'Is a relational contract a legal concept?' in S. Degeling, J. Edelman, and J. Goudkamp (eds.), *Contract in Commercial Law* (Thomson Reuters, 2016), 37–59). In *Sheikh Tahnoon Al Nehayan v Kent* [2018] EWHC 333 (Comm), [2018] EWHC 333 (Comm), Leggatt J further refined his position on relational contracts, stating that what was important was that the interests of the parties were 'inter-linked'. Although not fully fledged, the notion of 'relational contracts' nevertheless appears to have taken hold. Perhaps more important appears to be the recognition that such contracts are somewhat different from other commercial contracts. Indeed, in the context of contract interpretation, in *Globe Motors v TWR Lucas Verity Electric Steering Ltd* [2016] EWCA Civ 396, Beatson LJ stated at [65] that there was no special rule of interpretation to be applied to 'relational contracts', yet, when ascertaining the presumed intention of the parties in such contracts, he nevertheless added, at [67], that 'the courts may be more willing to imply a duty to cooperate, or, in the language used by Leggatt J in *Yam Seng PTE v International Trade Corp Ltd* [2013] EWHC 111 (QB) at [131], [142] and [145], a duty of good faith'.

The vision of Leggatt J in *Yam Seng* of implying 'good faith' in fact in most commercial contracts has not materialized. Although we are miles away from the antagonist attitude of *Walford v Miles* in the context of contract negotiation, good faith nevertheless remains limited to what Bingham LJ in *Interfoto Picture Library Ltd v Stiletto Visual Programmes Ltd* [1989] 1 QB 433 referred as being 'in essence a principle of fair and open dealing'. Although good faith is used by commercial parties as an express obligation in their contract, the manner in which it is interpreted by the courts nevertheless remains limited. The lukewarm judicial reception to implying a term in fact must of course be placed in the light of the reiteration by the Supreme Court in *Marks and Spencer plc v BNP Paribas Securities Services Trust Co. (Jersey) Ltd* [2015] UKSC 72, [2015] 3 WLR 1843, discussed at **6.4.2.3**, that it is possible to imply a term only where the implication is necessary to give business efficacy to the contract or so obvious that it goes without saying. These requirements are strict and it is only after the process of construing the express words is complete, that the question of whether there is any implied term will fall to be considered. *Yam Seng* was decided on the basis of the previous (now discredited) approach to terms implied in fact set out by Lord Hoffmann in *Attorney General of Belize v Belize Telecom Ltd* [2009] UKPC 10, [2009] 1 WLR 1988 and the broad view of contractual interpretation giving predominance to the commercial background and purpose of the contract which pre-dated the Supreme Court decision in *Arnold v Britton* [2015] UKSC 36, [2015] AC 1619 (see **6.5.3** and also Leggatt J's response to this in *Sheikh Tahnoon Al Nehayan v Kent* [2018] EWHC 333 (Comm)). It is clear that good faith, as a concept, has not disappeared.

MULTIPLE-CHOICE QUESTIONS

 Test your knowledge by trying this chapter's **multiple-choice questions**:
www.oup.com/uk/poole

FURTHER READING

General and theory

Adams and Brownsword, 'The ideologies of contract' (1987) 7 LS 205.

Adams and Brownsword, *Understanding Contract Law*, 5th edn (Sweet and Maxwell, 2007).

Atiyah, 'Contracts, promises and the law of obligations' in *Essays on Contract* (Oxford University Press, 1986) or (1978) 94 LQR 193.

Atiyah, 'The modern role of contract law' in *Essays on Contract* (Oxford University Press, 1986).

Baker, 'From sanctity of contract to reasonable expectations' [1979] CLP 17.

Brownsword, *Contract Law: Themes for the Twenty-First Century*, 2nd edn (Butterworths, 2006), chs. 5 and 6.

Burrows, 'Contract, tort and restitution: a satisfactory division or not?' (1983) 99 LQR 217.

Coote, 'The essence of contract' (1988) 1 JCL 91 and 183.

Eisenberg, 'Relational contracts' in Beatson and Friedmann (eds.), *Good Faith and Fault in Contract Law* (Oxford University Press, 1995).

Fried, *Contract as Promise: A Theory of Contractual Obligation* (1st edn, Harvard University Press, 1981; 2nd edn, Oxford University Press, 2015).

Gilmore, *The Death of Contract* (Ohio State University Press, 1986).

McKendrick, 'English contract law: a rich past, an uncertain future?' [1997] CLP 25.

Mitchell, 'Leading a life of its own? The roles of reasonable expectation in contract law' (2003) 23 OJLS 639.

Reiter and Swan, 'Contracts and the protection of reasonable expectation' in *Studies in Contract Law* (Butterworths, 1980).

Smith, *Contract Theory* (Clarendon Press, 2004).

Steyn, 'Contract law: fulfilling the reasonable expectations of honest men' (1997) 113 LQR 433.

Good faith

Carter, Courtney, 'Good faith in contracts: is there an implied promise to act honestly?' (2016) 75 CLJ 608.

Collins, 'Is a relational contract a legal concept?' in Degeling, Edelman, and Goudkamp (eds.) *Contract in commercial law* (Thomson Reuters, 2016), 37–59

Foxton, 'A good faith good bye: GR obligations and contractual termination rights?' [2017] LMCLQ 3, 339.

Granger, 'Sweating over an implied duty of good faith: *Yam Seng v ITC*' [2013] LMCLQ 418.

Hemsworth, 'The fate of GF in insurance contracts' [2018] LMCLQ 143.

Saintier, 'The elusive notion of good faith in the performance of a contract: why still a bête noire for the civil and the common law?' [2017] JBL 441.

Whittaker, 'Good faith, implied terms and commercial contracts' (2013) 129 LQR 463.

History

Atiyah, *The Rise and Fall of Freedom of Contract* (Oxford University Press, 1979).

Simpson, *A History of the Common Law of Contract* (Oxford University Press, 1987).

Lord Thomas, 'Keeping commercial law up to date' in Merkin and Devenney (eds.), *Essays in Memory of Professor Jill Poole* (Informa Law, 2018), ch. 1.

Contract law in practice

Beale and Dugdale, 'Contracts between businessmen: planning and the use of contractual remedies' (1975) 2 Brit J of Law & Soc 45.

Consumer Rights Act 2015

Cartwright, 'Redress compliance and choice: enhanced consumer measures and the retreat from punishment in the Consumer Rights Act 2015' [2016] CLJ 271.

Giliker, 'The consumer Rights Act 2015, a bastion of European Consumer Rights' (2017) 2 Legal Studies 78.

Samuels, 'The Consumer Rights Act 2015' [2016] JBL 159.

Whittaker, 'Distinctive features of the new consumer contract law' (2017) 133 LQR 47.

Willett, 'Re-theorising consumer law' (2018) CLJ 179.

Principles of international commercial contracts and uniform principles

Furmston, 'Unidroit general principles for international commercial contracts' (1996) 10 JCL 11.

Hobhouse, 'International conventions and commercial law: the pursuit of uniformity' (1990) 106 LQR 530.

UNIDROIT, *Principles of International Commercial Contracts* (UNIDROIT, 2010).

European directives and harmonization

Austen-Baker, 'Harmonization and contract in a globalized world' in Merkin and Devenney (eds.), *Essays in Memory of Professor Jill Poole* (Informa Law, 2018), ch. 4.

Bridge, 'Good faith in commercial contracts' in Brownsword, Hird, and Howells (eds.), *Good Faith in Contract* (Dartmouth, 1999).

Brownsword, '"Good faith in contracts" revisited' [1996] CLP 111.

Giliker, 'Examining English contract law in the light of Brexit—an end to the European dream?' in Merkin and Devenney (eds.), *Essays in Memory of Professor Jill Poole* (Informa Law, 2018), ch. 2.

Kenny, 'From the 2004 communication on European contract to the 2015 draft directive on the supply of digital content: harmonisation, unification or transformation of EU private law?' in Merkin and Devenney (eds.), *Essays in Memory of Professor Jill Poole* (Informa Law, 2018), ch. 3.

Lando, 'Principles of European contract law: an alternative to or a precursor of European legislation' (1992) 40 Am J of Comp Law 573.

Lando, *Principles of European Contract Law: Part III* (Kluwer Law International, 2003).

Lando and Beale, *Principles of European Contract Law: Parts I and II* (Kluwer Law International, 2000).

Twigg-Flesner, 'Deep impact? The EC Directive on unfair commercial practices and domestic consumer law' (2005) 121 LQR 386.

European contract: Draft Common Frame of Reference (DCFR)

Miller, 'The Common Frame of Reference and the feasibility of a common contract law in Europe' [2007] JBL 378.

Von Bar and Clive (eds.), *Principles, Definitions and Model Rules of European Private Law: Draft Common Frame of Reference (DCFR)* (Oxford University Press, 2010).

Whittaker, 'A framework of principle for European contract law?' (2009) 125 LQR 616.

Common European Sales Law (CESL)

European Commission, *Proposal for a Regulation on a Common European Sales Law (CESL)*, COM (2011) 635 final (October 2011).

Law Commission, *An Optional Common European Sales Law: Advantages and problems—Advice to the UK government* (November 2011).

Whittaker, 'The proposed "Common European Sales Law": legal framework and the agreement of the parties' (2012) 75 MLR 578.

Part 1

Formation

This part looks at the requirements to create a contract. A contract is a legally binding agreement and this has two elements: there must be an agreement which must be legally enforceable.

Chapter 2 examines the process by which an agreement has been reached between the parties. This raises the preliminary question of how we determine the existence of agreement. The law usually requires the existence of an offer and a corresponding acceptance. To be effective, any offer or acceptance must be properly communicated. The point at which a communication becomes effective is when it is received or when the communication is dispatched. **Chapter 2** examines the interrelationship of the various legal principles determining agreement, including the process for electronic communications.

Negotiating to reach agreement can be a protracted process and, on occasion, the parties may fail to reach agreement on *all* of the terms of their contract, or may agree to negotiate or deliberately to leave gaps in their agreement. **Chapter 3** examines the principles determining when an agreement is sufficiently certain to be capable of enforcement and what happens when no agreement is reached. It also examines mistakes that prevent the parties from reaching agreement and mistakes whereby the contractual document fails to reflect accurately what the parties agreed.

The factors determining the enforceability of agreements and promises are examined in **Chapters 4** and **5**—namely, the general requirement to provide consideration to enforce a contractual promise (**Chapter 4**), and the existence of an intention to create legal relations and specific requirements of form, such as writing, in order for an agreement to be legally binding (**Chapter 5**). The consideration requirement (**Chapter 4**) is relevant both to formation of a contract and to the enforceability of promises altering the terms of an existing contract (alterations). For ease of understanding both are examined together.

Chapter 2

Agreement

SUMMARY OF THE ISSUES

This chapter examines the process of determining whether an agreement has been reached between the parties.

- The existence of agreement is determined objectively on the basis of the impression given by the parties' words and actions. However, the actual assumptions made by the promisee (i.e. the person to whom the promise (offer) is made) are relevant in the sense that if the promisee knows, or ought reasonably to know, that an offer on these terms was not intended, that promisee cannot 'snap up' the offer. This legal principle has particular practical relevance where goods are advertised at dramatically reduced prices on retailers' websites in circumstances under which it is clear that there is no obvious special offer, e.g. a television set normally retailing for £499 that is advertised for sale on a website at £4.99.

- Traditionally, the objective evidence of agreement is the existence of an offer and corresponding acceptance. Although this approach has, on occasions, been criticized as artificial and inflexible, and the courts have found agreement in the absence of these traditional criteria, particularly where there has been performance (see **2.1.3**), such situations remain exceptional and the traditional approach remains the normal analysis.

- An offer is an expression of willingness to contract on the specified terms without further negotiation and must be distinguished from an invitation to treat (or invitation to negotiate). Generally, advertisements, displays in shop windows, displays on supermarket shelves, and invitations to tender are all classified as invitations to treat. However, some advertisements or invitations to tender may amount to offers and a retailer's website, whilst probably an invitation to treat, is not definitively so.

- An acceptance is a final expression of assent to the terms of the offer and must be made in response to that offer. The operation of the mirror-image rule (requiring that the acceptance must mirror the terms of the offer) has given rise to some practical difficulties in the form of the 'battle of (standard) forms'.

- Offer and acceptance must be properly communicated in order to be effective. The general rule is that actual communication is required. Actual communication is interpreted to mean that the communication has to reach the intended recipient. However, the dispatch rule is the general rule applicable to postal acceptances (i.e. a postal acceptance is treated as communicated when it is posted) and there is an implied waiver of the communication requirement in the case of most unilateral offers.

- An offer may be terminated by rejection, by counter-offer, by lapse of time, and in some circumstances by the death of the other party. An offer may also be terminated by revocation (withdrawal) of the offer before acceptance occurs. Generally, a revocation of an offer must be actually communicated (received) to be effective, but there are special rules applying to the question of whether it is possible to revoke a unilateral offer once performance has commenced (*Errington v Errington*) and with regard to the communication requirement for revocation of a unilateral offer (*Shuey v United States*).

2.1 Determining the existence of agreement: the objective approach

In order to be able to conclude that there is a contract giving rise to enforceable obligations, we must first identify the existence of a binding *agreement* between the parties.

It is the fact that the obligations are voluntarily agreed that distinguishes contract from other areas of law, such as tort, in which the obligations are imposed by law. However, although it is often said that, for an agreement to exist, there must be a *consensus ad idem* (or a 'meeting of minds'), this does not mean that, subjectively, the parties' intentions must coincide. The existence (and indeed the content) of an agreement, and whether that agreement was intended to be legally binding, are not determined on the basis of what the parties themselves thought or intended. Instead, the courts look at external evidence (what the parties said and did at the time) as objectively indicating the parties' intentions and ask whether, on the basis of this evidence, the reasonable person would say that the parties were in agreement. As Lord Denning stated in *Storer v Manchester City Council* [1974] 1 WLR 1403, at p. 1408:

> In contracts you do not look into the actual intent in a man's mind. You look at what he said and did. A contract is formed when there is, to all outward appearances, a contract. A man cannot get out of a contract by saying: 'I did not intend to contract', if by his words he has done so.

It follows that the 'voluntary' (consensual) nature of contractual liability may be more apparent than real. This conclusion raises difficult theoretical questions when seeking to justify the primacy of contractual obligations, as compared, for example, to tortious responsibility, on the basis that contractual obligations are voluntarily assumed. In addition, it makes it difficult to support contractual theories that rest on the premise of respect for contractual obligations as consensual and which therefore seek to resolve issues by reference to the parties' 'intentions' (discussed in **Chapter 1**). Such intentions must also be determined objectively and therefore may not correspond with actual intentions. For example, in *Moran v University College Salford*, The Times, 27 October 1993, an offer to study physiotherapy sent following a clerical error was binding.

Theoretical considerations apart, to determine the existence of a contract, the determination of whether the parties intended to be legally bound, and the determination of the contractual content have all been held to turn not on the parties' subjective intentions, but on the impression those parties have given by their words and actions. In the Supreme Court in *RTS Flexible Systems Ltd v Molkerei Alois Müller GmbH & Co. KG (UK Production)* [2010] UKSC 14, [2010] 1 WLR 753, at [45], Lord Clarke SCJ was clear that:

> Whether there is a binding contract between the parties and, if so, upon what terms depends upon what they have agreed. It depends not upon their subjective state of mind, but upon a consideration of what was communicated between them by words or conduct, and whether that leads objectively to a conclusion that they intended to create legal relations and had agreed upon all the terms which they regarded or the law requires as essential for the formation of legally binding relations.

As this statement makes clear, the objective approach also applies to determine whether the parties intended to be legally bound: see **Chapter 5**, Longmore LJ in *Maple Leaf Macro Volatility Master Fund v Rouvroy* [2009] EWCA Civ 1334, [2010] 2 All ER (Comm) 788, at [17], and Teare J in *Dhanani v Crasnianski* [2011] EWHC 926 (Comm), [2011] 2 All ER (Comm) 799, at [65] and [75].

The intentions of the parties on contractual content are also assessed by reference to objective criteria as stressed by the Privy Council in *Attorney-General of Belize v Belize Telecom Ltd* [2009] UKPC 10, [2009] 1 WLR 1988. Lord Hoffmann stated, at [16], that a court:

> is concerned only to discover what the instrument means. However, that meaning is not necessarily or always what the authors or parties to the document would have intended. It is the meaning which the instrument would convey to a reasonable person having all the background knowledge which would reasonably be available to the audience to whom the instrument is addressed: see *Investors Compensation Scheme Ltd v West Bromwich Building Society* [1998] 1 WLR 896, 912–913. It is this objective meaning which is conventionally called the intention of the parties . . .

The Supreme Court in *Marks and Spencer plc v BNP Paribas Services Trust Co. (Jersey) Ltd* [2015] UKSC 72, [2015] 3 WLR 1843, also explicitly accepted this principle, while impliedly criticizing and reformulating much of the remainder of Lord Hoffmann's judgment in *Belize*. Specifically, Lord Neuberger (at [21]) explained: 'If one approaches the question by reference to what the parties would have agreed, one is not strictly concerned with the hypothetical answer of the actual parties, but with that of notional reasonable people in the position of the parties at the time at which they were contracting.' Lord Clarke SCJ, delivering an agreed speech in the Supreme Court in *Rainy Sky SA v Kookmin Bank* [2011] UKSC 50, [2011] 1 WLR 2900, also recognized objectivity as the approach to contractual construction when he stated, at [14], that 'the ultimate aim of interpreting a provision in a contract . . . is to determine what the parties meant by the language used, which involves ascertaining what a reasonable person would have understood the parties to have meant' and this position was reaffirmed by the Supreme Court in *Arnold v Britton* [2015] UKSC 36, [2015] AC 1619, Lord Neuberger stressing (at [15]) the need to disregard any subjective evidence of party intentions.

From a pragmatic perspective, the objective approach is clearly preferable to a purely subjective approach, for a number of reasons, as follows.

- A subjective approach would create uncertainty. It would not be safe to rely on any promise if the promisor (i.e. the person making the promise) could later deny that they ever intended to make such a promise. Security of transactions is an essential characteristic of contract law.

- It would be totally impractical. As the parties may later say whatever suits their purpose at that time, in evidential terms it is clearly preferable to look only at what the parties said and did at the time of the agreement.

As Adams and Brownsword, in *Understanding Contract Law*, 5th edn (Sweet and Maxwell, 2007), at p. 48, have stated: 'To found contract on a subjective approach, therefore, would impede commerce, invite fraud, and unfairly defeat good faith reliance on the natural meaning of a promise.' The objective approach is a versatile tool. It applies equally when the alleged contract is entered into orally or in an informal setting such as in a pub or restaurant, as was the case in *Blue v Ashley* [2017] EWHC 1928 (Comm) (discussed in **Chapter 5**) and *MacInnes v Gross* [2017] EWHC 46 (QB) or, on the contrary when the parties are experienced commercial parties which deal at arm's length with lawyers as highlighted in *Rosalina Investments Ltd v New Balance Athletic Shoes (UK) Ltd* [2018 EWHC 1014 (QB).

2.1.1 The objective approach interpreted

Of course, the objective approach raises a further question: whose views determine the impression given? Steyn LJ, in *Trentham Ltd v Archital Luxfer Ltd* [1993] 1 Lloyd's Rep 25, at p. 27, said that 'the governing criterion is the reasonable expectations of honest men' or what *a reasonable person* has been led to believe the position to be. The classic statement of assessment by the 'reasonable man' is made by Blackburn J in *Smith v Hughes* (1871) LR 6 QB 597, at p. 607 (see **3.3.2.1**):

> If, whatever a man's real intention may be, he so conducts himself that a reasonable man would believe he was assenting to the terms proposed by the other party, and that other party upon that belief enters into the contract with him, the man thus conducting himself would be equally bound as if he had intended to agree to the other party's terms.

But who is the reasonable person for this purpose? In the context of contract formation and intention to be legally bound, the 'reasonable person' is judged in terms of the reasonable promisee to whom the words have been conveyed. For example, in *Bowerman v ABTA Ltd* [1996] CLC 451, the majority of the Court of Appeal held that the Association of British Travel Agents (ABTA) notice would reasonably have been read by a member of the public (in the position of the promisee) as containing an offer of protection. By comparison, in the context of contractual construction, the determination of content is necessarily going to reflect an objective evaluation of what both parties must have intended and generally seems to be based on the interpretation of an objective outsider who has the contextual knowledge of both a reasonable promisor and promisee. Lord Clarke SCJ in *Rainy Sky SA v Kookmin Bank* [2011] UKSC 50, [2011] 1 WLR 2900, quoting Lord Hoffmann in the *Investors Compensation Scheme case* [1998] 1 WLR 896, at p. 912, concluded that 'the relevant reasonable person is one who has all the background knowledge which would reasonably have been available to the parties in the situation in which they were at the time of the contract'. This principle was also affirmed by Lord Neuberger in *Arnold v Britton* [2015] UKSC 36, [2015] AC 1619, [15], citing Lord Hoffmann in *Chartbrook Ltd v Persimmon Homes Ltd* [2009] UKHL 38, [2009] 1 AC 1101, [14], with approval.

2.1.2 The residual subjective element

Of course, subjective intentions are relevant in the general sense that they may well coincide with the objectively ascertained intentions of the parties. However, does subjective intention have any other relevance?

Goff LJ, in the Court of Appeal in *The Leonidas D (Allied Marine Transport Ltd v Vale do Rio Doce Navegacao SA)* [1985] 1 WLR 925, at p. 936, explained the approach to determining formation in the following terms:

> [I]f one party, O, so acts that his conduct, objectively considered, constitutes an offer, and the other party, A, believing that the conduct of O represents his actual intention, accepts O's offer, then a contract will come into existence, and on those facts it will make no difference if O did not in fact intend to make an offer, or if he misunderstood A's acceptance, so that O's state of mind is in such circumstances irrelevant.

Whereas the conduct of the promisor ('O' in this statement) is judged objectively and what that promisor may subjectively have intended is irrelevant, the actual assumptions made by the promisee ('A' in this statement) are relevant where the promisee:

1. either knows, or

2. ought reasonably to know

that the promisor did not intend to make an offer (or did not intend to make an offer in those terms). It is only in this sense that subjective considerations are relevant to determining the existence of agreement.

There will therefore be no contract where the promisee actually knows that the promisor has no intention to contract with them on those terms. Peel, in *Treitel's The Law of Contract*, 14th edn (Sweet and Maxwell, 2015), [1-002], makes clear the reasoning for this exception when he states that the purpose of the objective approach is:

> to protect B [the promisee] from the prejudice which he might suffer as a result of relying on a false appearance of agreement. There is clearly no need in this way to protect a party who knows that the objective appearance does not correspond with reality.

It is equally clear that if it can be established that the promisee 'could not have been unaware' of the true position or 'ought reasonably to have known' the meaning intended by the promisor, then the promisee cannot 'snap up' (take advantage of) an error on the part of the promisor, or at least cannot snap up that error in English law where it relates to the terms of the offer. ('Snapping up' is discussed in the context of agreement mistake at **3.3.2.2**.) In the first instance decision in *Maple Leaf Macro Volatility Master Fund v Rouvroy* [2009] EWHC 257 (Comm), [2009] 1 Lloyd's Rep 475, Smith J explained that the burden of proving the promisees' subjective intentions (that they knew or ought reasonably to have known that the promisors had no intention to be bound) rested with the promisors. This burden would not be discharged where the promisee had 'simply formed no view one way or the other' as to whether the promisors intended to be bound. By comparison, in *Hartog v Colin and Shields* [1939] 3 All ER 566 (for the facts, see **3.3.2.2**), the evidence was established and it was held that, on the basis of the pre-sale negotiations, the claimant (offeree) could not reasonably have supposed that the offer contained the offeror's true intention as to the contract terms. At first sight, this decision is difficult to reconcile with that of the Court of Appeal in *Centrovincial Estates plc v Merchant Investors Assurance Company Ltd* [1983] Com LR 158 (for the facts, see **3.3.2.2**). It can be argued that, in *Centrovincial*, the defendants—the tenants—ought to have known of the claimants' mistake because the rent review clause indicated that in no circumstances should the rent fall when reviewed. Nevertheless, the Court of Appeal did not consider that the claimants had satisfied the necessary burden of proof on this issue, i.e. they had not shown that the defendants ought to have known of the mistake.

However, there is an important limitation on the relevance of subjective intentions in English law in that the promisee must know, or the promisee ought to know, that the promisor is making a mistake as to *the terms of the contract*, e.g. in the Singapore decision of *Chwee Kin Keong v Digilandmall.com Pte Ltd* [2005] 1 SLR(R) 502 (see **3.3.2**), the mistake related to a term—namely, the price of goods being sold on an Internet site—and the buyer ought reasonably to have known that this price was so low that the seller had made a mistake. If, on the other hand, the mistake relates to an ancillary (or collateral) matter, the subjective position of the promisee is irrelevant: *Smith v Hughes* (1871) LR 6 QB 597. In *Statoil ASA v Louis Dreyfus Energy Services LP, The Harriette N* [2008] EWHC 2257 (Comm), [2008] 2 Lloyd's Rep 685, [2009] 1 All ER (Comm) 1035 (see also **3.3.2.1** and **13.5.3**), Aikens J stated, at [88]:

> [I]f one party has made a mistake about a fact on which he bases his decision to enter into a contract, but that fact does not form a term of the contract itself, then, even if the other party knows that the first is mistaken as to this fact, the contract will be binding.

2.1.3 Traditional and non-traditional approaches to identifying agreement

The objective approach looks for external evidence of agreement, i.e. the words and conduct of the parties. Traditionally, agreement must be demonstrated by an unequivocal offer made by one party (the offeror) and by complete acceptance of that offer by the other party (the offeree). This neat approach is designed to promote certainty. However, it is artificial and inflexible, and may well ignore the reality of the situation by dictating that no agreement has been reached for purely technical reasons. As a result, there have long been instances of the courts either 'finding' the necessary offer and acceptance ('reasoning backwards'), or ignoring the traditional approach and simply recognizing the existence of agreement by means of other external evidence.

Lord Wilberforce, in *New Zealand Shipping Co. Ltd v A M Satterthwaite & Co. Ltd, The Eurymedon* [1975] AC 154 (for the facts, see **4.4.2**), admitted that it was a recognized practice to seek to 'find' the necessary offer and acceptance when he said, at p. 167:

> English law, having committed itself to a rather technical and schematic doctrine of contract, in application takes a practical approach, often at the cost of forcing the facts to fit uneasily into the marked slots of offer, acceptance and consideration.

This statement was later used by Lord Denning MR to support his view that, on occasion, a different approach to determining the existence of agreement was called for. In *Butler Machine Tool Co. Ltd v Ex-Cell-O Corporation (England) Ltd* [1979] 1 WLR 401, Lord Denning suggested that the circumstances as a whole (i.e. all of the documents and the parties' conduct) should be examined in an attempt to discover agreement. Although Lord Denning applied this approach in both *Butler Machine* and in the Court of Appeal in *Gibson v Manchester City Council* [1978] 1 WLR 520, the House of Lords in *Gibson* [1979] 1 WLR 294 (see the judgment of Lord Diplock at p. 297) made it clear that offer and acceptance remained the normal analysis, and applied that analysis to the facts before them (involving a contract said to have been entered into as a result of exchange of correspondence).

Of course, it does not follow that the House of Lords in *Gibson* was accepting that offer and acceptance was the *only* mechanism for determining the existence of a contract. Lord Diplock said, at p. 297, that 'there may be certain types of contract, though I think they are exceptional, which do not fit easily into the normal analysis of a contract as being constituted by offer and acceptance'.

2.1.3.1 In what circumstances might a different analysis of agreement be appropriate?

A distinction needs to be made between contracts formed by means of an exchange of communications (an offer and a corresponding acceptance) and contracts based on conduct. Steyn LJ, in *Trentham Ltd v Archital Luxfer Ltd* [1993] 1 Lloyd's Rep 25, at p. 27, considered that the traditional analysis would apply 'in the vast majority of cases' and specifically gave a contract alleged to be made by exchange of correspondence as an example of the application of this approach. However, he added that this 'is not necessarily so in the case of a contract alleged to have come into existence during and as a result of performance'. Agreement may be recognized to exist on the basis of the conduct of the parties (i.e. an executed agreement), despite the inability to analyse the performance in terms of offer and acceptance. Any contract formed by such performance requires conduct by both parties, and that conduct 'must generally be referable to the particular alleged contract': *Finmoon Ltd v Baltic Reefers Management Ltd* [2012] EWHC 920 (Comm), [2012] 1 CLC 813, *per* Eder J, at [26] and [30]. It is inherent in the nature of contracts based on conduct that it can be more difficult to pinpoint the precise time of formation; this has not prevented the courts from concluding that a contract exists: *Brogden v Metropolitan Railway Co.* (1877) 2 App Cas 666 (see **2.4.2.1**).

Nevertheless, it cannot be said that the decision in *Trentham* provides unqualified general support for any alternative analysis determining the existence of agreement, since the *Trentham* principle appears to be part of a more general policy-based approach to recognizing executed agreements wherever possible (see **3.1.3.3**). The Supreme Court noted in *RTS Flexible Systems Ltd v Molkerei Alois Müller GmbH & Co. KG (UK Production)* [2010] UKSC 14, [2010] 1 WLR 753, that performance did not always equate with a finding that there was a contract between the parties, although where there was agreement on all material terms, performance was an important factor in deciding whether a binding contract existed. In *Reveille Independent LLC v Anotech International (UK) Ltd* [2016] EWCA Civ 443, [2016] 166 Comm LR 79, a similar approach was followed to decide whether a party had accepted an offer through conduct even when it had requested that signature was the only method of acceptance possible. Cranston J held that performance by the offeree did amount to acceptance since in doing so, he had waived a prescribed method of acceptance by signature set out for its benefit and that this was not to the detriment of the offeror (at [44]).

There is clear acceptance in the UNIDROIT PICC of the fact that agreement can be reached without the traditional analysis of offer and acceptance, e.g. Art. 2.1.1 PICC (conduct sufficient to show agreement). Further, there are recognized situations in case law in which the offer and acceptance analysis does not work very well, and may come to be abandoned. These are situations that involve one or more third parties in the negotiating process (see *Clarke v Dunraven* [1897] AC 59), or instances in which an offer is made more generally than to a single, identified offeree (see *Wilkie v London Passenger Transport Board* [1947] 1 All ER 258), or instances in which the court is using the vehicle of contract to impose an obligation (see *Upton-on-Severn RDC v Powell* [1942] 1 All ER 220).

2.1.3.2 Conclusion

Although there are instances in English law in which the traditional offer and acceptance analysis has not been employed, the House of Lords in *Gibson* regarded them as 'exceptional' and this has since been confirmed by the Court of Appeal in *Tekdata Interconnections Ltd v Amphenol Ltd*, so that, for the purposes of application, the traditional offer and acceptance analysis should be the starting point.

2.2 The traditional approach: offer and acceptance

Determining the existence of agreement using offer and acceptance is inevitably a technical process. *There must be a valid and communicated offer and acceptance of that offer before any effective revocation (or withdrawal) of the offer occurs*. The analysis or application therefore involves two steps:

1. *Identification of the correspondence.* The first question to address is whether the offeror made an 'offer'. This involves an examination of what can constitute an offer (see **2.3**). Other questions then arise, such as: did the offeree accept that offer (and what is needed to constitute an acceptance—see **2.4**); or was the offer withdrawn before acceptance could occur (see **2.5**)?

2. *Does that correspondence satisfy the relevant communication rule, i.e. is it effective and when does it take effect?* It is necessary to determine whether the correspondence in question—be it offer, acceptance, or revocation—has been effectively communicated, since until such time it cannot take effect (see **2.3.3** and **2.4.5**). This involves:

   – identifying the applicable principle for communication, e.g. the general rule may apply and the communication may need to be actually communicated to the recipient;

   – then determining whether this in fact happened; and

   – if communication occurred, it may then be necessary to determine the precise point in time at which it occurred.

The interrelationship of the applicable principles will determine whether offer and acceptance (and hence agreement) have occurred. Adams and Brownsword, in *Understanding Contract Law*, 5th edn (Sweet & Maxwell, 2007), p. 49, likened this process to learning the rules of chess, i.e. it is necessary to learn the ways in which each piece (principle) can be moved and the impact that each move will have on the other pieces (principles) and the eventual outcome.

2.3 Offers and invitations to treat

2.3.1 Making the distinction

An offer is an expression of willingness to contract on the specified terms without further negotiation, so that it requires only acceptance for a binding agreement to be formed.

An offer must be distinguished from all other statements made in the course of negotiations towards a contract (so-called 'invitations to treat') since only an offer can translate into a contract by the fact of acceptance.

A technical definition of an invitation to treat would be restricted to statements indicating the maker's willingness to receive offers. However, the expression is commonly used to describe any negotiating statement falling short of an offer that furthers the bargaining process, e.g. 'Would you be interested in buying my car?' is an invitation to treat and not an offer. Such statements may take the form of attempts to stimulate interest, requests for the supply of information, or any other stage in the sometimes lengthy progress to agreement.

On many occasions, offers and invitations to treat are easily distinguishable. Yet, there are times when the distinction is more difficult. Indeed, one should not assume that correspondence described as 'an offer' will be considered as such. In practice, the courts look to the individual facts of each case in making the distinction, although there are recognized instances in which a communication is more likely to be regarded as only an invitation to treat (as to why this is so, see *Partridge v Crittenden* [1968] 1 WLR 1204 discussed at **2.3.2**).

The starting point for any determination of this issue must be that, in order to constitute an offer, the communication must be both:

- *sufficiently specific in terms of the main obligation and price to be capable of immediate acceptance; and*

- *made with an intention to be bound by the mere fact of acceptance (i.e. a definite promise to be bound).*

2.3.1.1 The language used

This intention to be bound by the mere fact of acceptance is determined objectively, so that it amounts to examining the language used.

In *Gibson v Manchester City Council* [1979] 1 WLR 294, the House of Lords examined the language of the correspondence between the parties in order to determine whether there was the necessary intention to be bound.

> In **Gibson v Manchester City Council**, the council had a policy of selling council houses to tenants. Mr Gibson was such a tenant and he applied for details. The city treasurer had replied that the council 'may be prepared to sell the house to you' and invited Mr Gibson to complete an application form if he wished to buy. Mr Gibson did this, but the council changed its policy, and the question arose as to whether there was already a concluded contract of sale between Mr Gibson and the council. The House of Lords held that there was no concluded contract because the language of the city treasurer's letter made it clear that the council did not intend to make a binding promise to be bound. The letter was not an offer that Mr Gibson had accepted; rather it was inviting Mr Gibson to make an offer to buy. Although Mr Gibson had made such an offer to buy, his offer had not been accepted at the time of the change of policy.

The decision in *Gibson* is normally contrasted with that of the Court of Appeal in *Storer v Manchester City Council* [1974] 1 WLR 1403, in which the court held that a binding contract had been concluded because the language used—namely, 'If you will sign the Agreement and return it to me, I will send you the Agreement signed on behalf of the [Council] in exchange'—indicated that it was the council's intention to be bound and therefore constituted an offer.

A further useful illustration is provided by the decision in *Harvey v Facey* [1893] AC 552, in which the claimants had asked the defendants whether they would sell a particular property and requested that the defendants telegraph their lowest price. The defendants' reply, stating that the lowest price was £900, was held not to constitute an offer, but to be only an indication of the minimum price *if* the defendants decided to sell. This case also illustrates that, in contracts for the sale of land, the courts will look for clear evidence that the process of negotiation is complete and that a definite promise to be bound is being made before they determine that there is an offer capable of being accepted. For example, in *Clifton v Palumbo* [1944] 2 All ER 497, the statement 'I am prepared to offer you my estate for £600,000' was held not to constitute an offer. This statement was part of a letter, which also stated that 'reasonable and sufficient time shall be granted to you for the examination and consideration of all the data and details necessary for the preparation of the Schedule of Completion'. The Court of Appeal unanimously held that these additional words meant, on a matter of construction, that the parties meant to enter into a formal purchase contract. The original letter could therefore not be an 'offer' capable of being accepted.

2.3.1.2 The context of the communication

In more general terms, the context in which the communication is made can affect whether it is interpreted as an offer or an invitation to treat. In *iSoft Group plc v Misys Holdings Ltd* [2003] EWCA Civ 229, unreported, 28 February 2003, a term of an agreement for the acquisition of a company provided that the vendor was to 'offer to sell' to the purchaser 'after-acquired competing businesses [a competing business acquired after the company in question] for fair market value and on fair and reasonable conditions'. The Court of Appeal considered that the parties, and the business community, could not reasonably have envisaged that this term amounted to an offer capable of acceptance, which could thereby become an *immediately binding* contract. The term required only that the vendor should indicate a willingness to sell for a fair market value. Similarly, in *Global Asset Capital, Inc. v Aabar Block S.A.R.L.* [2017] EWCA Civ 37, [2017] 4 WLR 163, an offer made 'subject to contract' clearly negated contractual intention. It has long been established that this formulation is the standard means of negativing a contractual intention in what might otherwise appear to be a clear offer.

2.3.2 Recognized instances of offer or invitations to treat

Case law has established recognized instances in which a particular communication is more likely to be regarded either as an offer or as an invitation to treat. These operate as a starting point for consideration by the courts, but it is quite possible that the normal principle may be found to be inappropriate, being at odds with the intention of the parties as revealed by the facts and the language used in a given situation.

2.3.2.1 Advertisements, brochures, and price lists

2.3.2.1.1 The general rule: advertisements, brochures, and price lists amount to invitations to treat

In *Partridge v Crittenden* [1968] 1 WLR 1204, the appellant had placed an advertisement indicating that he had certain wild birds for sale. It was an offence to offer such birds for sale. The advertisement did state a price, but gave no details about delivery or quantities available. On appeal, the appellant's conviction was quashed, because *the court held that the advertisement did not amount to an offer, but was merely an invitation to treat*. In the words of Lord Parker, there was 'business sense' in treating such an advertisement as no more than an invitation to treat.

This makes 'business sense' because construing such an advertisement as an offer would mean that the seller might find themselves unable to supply all those who replied to the advertisement (the 'limited stocks' argument). In *Grainger and Sons v Gough* [1896] AC 325, a wine merchant's catalogue and price list were considered to constitute no more than an invitation to treat on precisely that ground. If, however, the catalogue had been addressed to a limited group of customers or had made it clear that unlimited supplies were available, then, other things being equal, it might have been sufficiently specific to amount to an offer. In any event, it is possible to meet the 'limited stocks' argument by arguing that there is an implied term that the 'offer' is available only while stocks last. It can be avoided more explicitly by an express term to this effect.

2.3.2.1.2 The exception: where the advertisement is unilateral

A unilateral contract (discussed in detail at **2.6**)—or the so-called 'if' or 'reward' contract—is a contract under which one party (the promisor) binds itself to perform a stated promise upon performance of the requested act or condition by the promisee. However, the promisee gives no commitment to perform the act or condition, but rather is left free to choose whether to perform or not.

If a reward is advertised for the performance of a specified act, such as supplying information, that advertisement will constitute a unilateral offer, assuming that the language is sufficiently definite to be viewed as such. The acceptance of such an offer is the performance of that act, and it cannot be accepted by making a promise (which is the position in the case of bilateral contracts, such as simple sale of goods contracts).

In **Carlill v Carbolic Smoke Ball Co.** [1893] 1 QB 256, the defendant had placed an advertisement in which it promised to pay £100 to any person catching influenza after using its smoke ball remedy three times a day for two weeks. The advertisement stated that £1,000 had been placed in a separate bank account in order to meet any claims made. The claimant had caught influenza after using the smoke ball in the required manner, but the defendant denied any liability to pay £100. The Court of Appeal held that the advertisement constituted an offer since it requested performance of an act as the acceptance (using the smoke ball as directed and catching influenza). In addition, the Court of Appeal treated the deposit of money as an indication of a willingness to be bound by the terms of the advertisement, thereby confirming the intention to be legally bound. It followed that the £100 was payable.

Similarly, in **Bowerman v ABTA Ltd** [1996] CLC 451, the majority of the Court of Appeal held that an ABTA notice, which was displayed on the premises of an ABTA member travel agent, was intended to be read, and would reasonably have been read, as an offer (or promise) of ABTA protection. It requested the performance of an act as the acceptance, i.e. booking a holiday through an ABTA member.

A further illustration is provided by the facts in **O'Brien v MGN Ltd** [2001] EWCA Civ 1279, [2002] CLC 33, in which the advertisement in the *Daily Mirror* of a scratch card game with a prize of £50,000 was held to constitute an offer, which was accepted when those with winning scratch cards telephoned the hotline to claim their prize.

The fact that such advertisements are regarded as offers makes practical sense, since if a notice of a reward for performance of a particular act were to be regarded as an invitation to treat, the response (namely, performing the act) would be the offer that could be accepted or rejected at will. People offering a reward would therefore have the benefit of seeing the requested act performed and yet not be bound to pay the reward.

That an advertisement requesting performance of an act constitutes an offer can be seen in the US decision in *Lefkowitz v Great Minneapolis Surplus Store*, 86 NW 2d 689 (1957). Here, the advertisement was in the following terms: 'Saturday 9 a.m. sharp: 3 brand new fur coats, worth to $100. First come first served. $1 each.' This was held to be an offer. Such an advertisement requested performance of an act (being one of the first three customers on Saturday morning). Performance of this act constituted the acceptance and therefore entitled the customer to purchase one of these fur coats at this sale price.

However, if such an advertisement is to constitute an offer, it must be clear and definite in its terms and leave nothing open for negotiation. It may also need to relate to a limited quantity of the specified goods, as in *Lefkowitz*.

? QUESTION

Is the promise requesting performance of an act?

The identification of an advertisement as an offer or as an invitation to treat appears to generate confusion (and many emails asking for assistance). Despite the time devoted to unilateral contracts on contract law modules, there are relatively few unilateral contracts in practice. The vast majority of contracts are bilateral, i.e. they involve a promise in exchange for a promise. The contract will be bilateral if it is possible to respond to the initial promise, in a way that attracts legal consequences, simply by making a promise. On exchange of such promises, each party is bound, although performance of those promises will occur later. For example, I may promise to pay you £100 for your bicycle if you deliver it, with payment on delivery. You promise (agree) to sell and deliver your bicycle next Monday. We are bound on exchange of promises, although payment and delivery will not occur until 'next Monday'.

The fact that I have requested that you deliver the bicycle does not render this unilateral since it is possible to accept by promising to do this. The promise will be only requesting an act (and therefore will be unilateral) if it is possible to respond only by actually performing the act in question. This will be the case in reward scenarios: e.g. in *Carlill v Carbolic Smoke Ball Co.*, it would not have been possible to respond by *promising* to perform the requested act of using the smoke ball as directed and catching influenza; the act itself had to be performed to render the promise to pay enforceable. Similarly, if I promise to pay a reward of £50 to anyone who finds and returns my lost dog, it is not possible for you to claim this reward simply by promising to find and return the dog; performance of the act itself is essential.

The crucial question, therefore, is whether it is possible to accept by promising to perform (bilateral) or whether the only possible way to accept is by performing the requested act (unilateral).

2.3.2.2 Shop displays: shop windows or supermarket shelves

Shop displays are invitations to treat following *Fisher v Bell* [1961] 1 QB 394, which held that to display a flick-knife with a price marker in a shop window did not amount to commission of the offence of offering such a knife for sale.

In ***Pharmaceutical Society of Great Britain v Boots Cash Chemists (Southern) Ltd*** [1953] 1 QB 401, it was held that the display of goods on shelves in a self-service store did not amount to an offer of the goods for sale, so that no contract was formed merely by the customer removing the goods from the shelf.

It was a legal requirement that certain drugs and medicines could be sold only under the supervision of a registered pharmacist. Boots had introduced self-service stores where the cash desks were supervised by such a person. Therefore an offence was committed if any sale contract relating to these drugs and medicines was formed *before* the customer reached the cash desk, e.g. if the sale contract was formed when the goods were removed from the shelves, since there was no supervision at that point. It was held that no offence had been committed. The display of goods on supermarket shelves constituted an invitation to treat and not an offer, so that there was supervision at the point of sale.

2.3.2.2.1 Analysis of the Boots case

There is no consensus on what would constitute the offer by the customer, since although in *Boots* at first instance Lord Goddard appeared to consider that the offer was made when the goods were selected and put into the basket, there are strong grounds for arguing that the offer does not occur until the customer presents the goods to the cashier at the cash desk, thereby communicating a definite intention to be bound to the shopkeeper. The acceptance (on behalf of the shopkeeper) would appear to be the cashier's act of 'acceding to the sale', constituted by 'accepting the price' (see the judgments of Lord Goddard CJ and Somervell LJ in *Boots* before the Court of Appeal).

It appears to have been imperative to the future operation of self-service systems for the courts in the *Boots* case to conclude that the contract was made 'at the cash desk' and not before—so as to be able to conclude on the facts that Boots had committed no offence. The decision, that a display amounted to an invitation to treat, was justified on two grounds: (1) the shopkeeper's freedom of contract (by analogy with an ordinary shop); and (2) the unfortunate practical consequences considered to follow from the conclusion that a display constituted an offer.

1. The shopkeeper's freedom of contract

In an ordinary shop, such as a bookshop, the shopkeeper reserves the right to refuse to sell (subject to anti-discrimination legislation), and that option is exercised in each case by the cashier on the shopkeeper's behalf when the goods are presented for payment. In the self-service scenario, in order to achieve the objective of preserving the shopkeeper's freedom of contract (i.e. controlling acceptance), the court considered that the offer to buy must come from the customer. Accordingly, the offer could not be the shopkeeper's display of the goods.

On the other hand, it could be argued—see e.g. Unger (1953) 16 MLR 369—that the price of instituting a self-service system with its associated cost savings should be that the shopkeeper loses this freedom of contract and that it makes more sense to analyse the display as a standing offer, as in the case of the deckchairs in *Chapelton v Barry Urban District Council* [1940] 1 KB 532 (considered later in this section) and other displays over which further negotiation is not envisaged. The acceptance, and control of the contract, would then rest with the customer.

2. The practical consequences for customers if a display were held to amount to an offer

The courts in the *Boots* case appear to have assumed that if they found the display to be an offer, then the customer's acceptance would have been the act of removing the goods from the shelves. This would have been extremely inconvenient in a practical sense, since customers would not have been able to select goods from the shelves and put them in baskets or trolleys, but subsequently change their minds about the purchase.

However, this does not necessarily follow. If the display were to constitute an offer, the acceptance could occur much later, e.g. in the act of presenting the goods to the cashier: see the US case of *Lasky v Economy Grocery Stores*, 65 NE 2d 305 (1946). The argument is that, on this interpretation, there would be supervision before the contract is concluded, although arguably the pharmacist could not prevent such a sale if control over the conclusion of the contract (acceptance) were to rest with the customer. However, it would allow some flexibility prior to that time, since the shopkeeper could withdraw such an offer at any time before acceptance and customers would retain the ability to change their minds before their own act of acceptance.

? QUESTION

If there is a non-self-service counter inside a supermarket, where is the contract of sale made?

This point has arisen indirectly in the criminal law context where the goods in question have deliberately been priced at a lower price as a result of an arrangement between the customer

»

and the counter assistant, leading to a charge of theft. It has been assumed in such a case that the contract of sale occurs at the counter, although property in the goods would not pass until payment of the price at the cash desk: see e.g. Jackson (1979) 129 NLJ 775, at p. 777, interpreting comments in *Pilgram v Rice-Smith* [1977] 2 All ER 658. Jackson assumed that the customer was making an offer to *buy* the selected goods, e.g. a joint of meat, and that the assistant accepted that offer by marking up the goods with the applicable price. The important distinguishing factor is considered to be 'having dealt with another human agent'.

However, the correctness of this interpretation must be questioned. The point is unlikely to be litigated and supermarkets accept that customers will change their minds about selected products. It would seem that this 'transaction' is no different from any other **selection** of goods in a supermarket, e.g. putting a tin of baked beans into the shopping trolley, but later changing one's mind. The customer does not make an offer to buy until such time as the shopping is complete and the customer decides to check out. This position would also equate with the website shopping experience, i.e. it is possible to remove selected items from the cart at any time before the checkout process.

Note: The making of a sale contract (and so incurring a contractual obligation) and the passing of property (i.e. ownership) in the goods that are the subject of that contract may occur at different times. In a supermarket, the property in the goods does not pass until the price is paid: *Lacis v Cashmarts* [1969] 2 QB 400, at p. 407; *Davies v Leighton* (1979) 68 Cr App R 4, [1978] Crim LR 575.

Despite the decision in the *Boots* case, it is possible to imagine a situation in which the display of goods in a shop would amount to an offer, e.g. if it were made clear that the shopkeeper would be willing to sell to anyone paying the displayed price. On this basis, it is also possible to explain the conclusion in *Chapelton v Barry Urban District Council* [1940] 1 KB 532 that a display of deckchairs constituted an offer. It followed that the contract to hire the deckchair could already have been concluded before a ticket containing an exemption clause was issued. Accordingly, the exemption clause, which was not seen prior to the conclusion of the contract, was not incorporated into the contract. The clause could not protect the local council from liability when the deckchair collapsed, resulting in injury to the hirer. Thus there may have been policy reasons that explain why the display was treated as an offer in this case.

Similarly, in *Thornton v Shoe Lane Parking Ltd* [1971] 2 QB 163 (discussed at **6.3.1.3**), Lord Denning MR analysed automatic machines, e.g. vending machines, as constituting standing offers on the basis that as soon as the machine was activated there was no possibility of negotiation. The 'standing offer' approach also enables commercial sense to be realized by accepting the conclusion that, in a self-service petrol station, the customer accepts the garage's offer of petrol by putting petrol into the vehicle's petrol tank and is therefore liable to pay the amount shown on the pump: *Re Charge Card Services Ltd (No. 2)* [1989] Ch 497.

Modern shopping practices raise a further question: would a self-service checkout in a supermarket alter the traditional analysis? Is this position similar to an ordinary vending machine? It would seem that the traditional position must remain since it is the customer who is making the offer when presenting the goods to the self-service checkout and it is the machine that is accepting the customer's offer on behalf of the supermarket.

2.3.2.3 Websites

It would seem that websites are the electronic equivalent of displays, advertisements, or catalogues of products for sale. In English law, this should mean that, in general, a website constitutes an invitation to treat. From a practical perspective, this is important, since, as discussed earlier, the result is that the site provider will retain freedom to contract because the offer will come from the customer. The site provider can therefore avoid entering into contracts with online buyers in excluded jurisdictions. In addition, the provider's stock may be limited, and if the website is an invitation to treat so that customers make offers to buy, the provider can manage its stock and will not find itself bound to supply all those online buyers who seek to place orders. Regulation 12 of the Electronic Commerce (EC Directive) Regulations 2002, SI 2002/2013, may imply that a website will be treated as an invitation to treat since it provides that the customer's 'order *may be* the offer'. However, the language used is hardly conclusive on this point. In any event, the final say on the steps necessary for electronic contract formation will rest with the retailer, which is placed under a duty to provide details of the process (Electronic Commerce Regulations 2002, reg. 9(1), and might specifically state in its terms and conditions that a website is only an invitation to treat.

If the website does constitute an invitation to treat, the offer will presumably be made by the customer at the checkout stage when the customer clicks the relevant instruction to process the order. The retailer may, however, wish to provide all of the order and payment details, and provide for acceptance to be made by the customer (thereby ensuring that acceptance is received in the retailer's jurisdiction).

2.3.2.3.1 *Pricing mistakes on websites*

A particular problem for website providers is the inadvertent mispricing of goods. For example, in September 1999, Argos advertised Sony television sets on its website at £3 instead of £299. On New Year's Eve 2001, a particular camera was incorrectly advertised on the Kodak website at £100 instead of the actual price of £329. Kodak had sent customers an automated order confirmation stating that £100 would be charged to their credit cards. There was a similar incident in March 2003 when the Amazon website offered a pocket PC for sale at £7.32 instead of the retail price of £274.99, and a television normally retailing for £350 was displayed at a price of 49p on the Argos website during the August bank holiday weekend in 2005. In this context, the status of the website and whether a binding contract has been made will be highly relevant. If a website constitutes no more than an invitation to treat, mispricing will not result in the supplier having to fulfil a contract at the misquoted price.

The legal position might be different depending on what happened to individual customers: in the 1999 Argos incident, some orders were placed and also confirmed by Argos, while, on discovering the mistake, Argos advised other customers trying to place orders that there had been a mistake and that no orders could be accepted at the stated price. In the case of customers whose orders were not accepted or confirmed, there could be no binding contract of sale if the website constituted an invitation to treat. These online buyers would need to argue that the website was an offer, which would be a theoretical possibility only if performance of an act is requested (see **2.3.2.1**) and where it is clear that the stock is limited. Something similar to the factual scenario in *Lefkowitz v Great Minneapolis Surplus Store*, 86 NW 2d 689 (1957) would be required, e.g. a television set priced at £3 to the first ten online buyers after 6 a.m. GMT on Thursday 1 March. However, a normal sale of goods contract is bilateral, involving an exchange of promises and not the performance of an act.

2.3.2.3.2 *What about those customers whose orders had been confirmed and whose credit cards had been charged?*

It might be thought that the 'offers' of those whose orders had been confirmed and whose credit cards had been charged had been accepted by the retailer. However, there are two legal hurdles facing such customers.

The first difficulty facing those customers whose orders had been confirmed was the fact that Argos had made a very clear mistake as to the price term, which online buyers either knew, or ought reasonably to have known, had been made. This was surely the whole point of the attempts to secure the television sets at the bargain price; online buyers knew very well that a mistake had been made and were seeking to 'snap it up'. The case law establishes that there will be no binding contract in this situation: *Hartog v Colin and Shields* [1939] 3 All ER 566 (see **2.1.2** and **3.3.2**). In *Chwee Kin Keong v Digilandmall.com Pte Ltd* [2004] SLR(R) 594, the High Court of Singapore had indicated that suspicious pricing on an Internet site, when compared with the known market value of the goods, would lead to the conclusion that a person in the position of a reasonable prospective purchaser 'ought to have known' of the mistake and would therefore be seeking to snap it up (see **3.3.2**). This leaves open the possibility that it is not 'snapping up' where the goods are priced incorrectly, but not noticeably so, e.g. a television set at £200 instead of the normal retail price of £300. In addition, in the earlier example in which a television set is offered for £3 to the first ten online buyers, it is clear that a special offer was intended and that there is no mistake as to the price term.

Of course, if the website is not an 'offer' or if the acceptance does not come from the buyer, then acceptance comes from the retailer and the customer's so-called 'snapping up' offer can be rejected by the retailer on those terms. It is only the offeree's subjective position that is relevant and not that of the offeror (see **2.1.2**). However, it is the principle of seeking to take advantage to which the courts object and the balance has swung in favour of the retailer in any event by the practice of retailers delaying acceptance (see later in this section).

Secondly, an electronic confirmation of an order may be no more than this (reg. 11 of the Electronic Commerce (EC Directive) Regulations 2002 (SI 2002/2013)), i.e. it may not constitute an acceptance of the order, but serve only to identify and warn customers of orders placed unintentionally.

Increasingly, online retailers have complied with the duty to indicate to consumers 'in a clear, comprehensible and unambiguous manner . . . the different technical steps to follow to conclude the contract' (reg. 9(1)), so that the site provider's terms and conditions normally spell out precisely what action will constitute the acceptance. For example, terms and conditions may specify that acceptance will not occur, and a contract will not be formed, until the goods are dispatched (as was the case in the Argos incident of August 2005). It follows that the retailer can withdraw the advertisement prior to dispatch of the goods.

Finally, it should not be assumed that there is no liability on suppliers in this situation. First, there may be criminal liability since the Consumer Protection from Unfair Trading Regulations (CPRs), SI 2008/1277, e.g. reg. 5 (prohibiting a range of actions misleading consumers), make it a criminal offence to engage in such prohibited activities (see **1.6.2.2**). In addition, reg. 13 of the Electronic Commerce (EC Directive) Regulations 2002 allows for an action seeking damages for breach of statutory duty where, for example, the site provider has not complied with the reg. 9(1) requirement to indicate clearly, before an order is placed, the steps that will result in a concluded contract.

Until recently, however, there was no contractual liability or ability to obtain compensation with which to purchase the goods that had been denied at a misleading price. Following the Consumer Protection (Amendment) Regulations 2014, SI 2014/870, which added a new Part 4A to the CPRs (effective 1 October 2014), consumers now have a variety of rights to redress in this situation, e.g. the rights to unwind (the right to end the contract), to a discount, or to damages, and the ability to bring civil proceedings to enforce those rights.

2.3.2.4 Tenders

2.3.2.4.1 A request for tenders is normally an invitation to treat (inviting tenders)

The request for tenders (or quotations) is a common negotiating device for major commercial contracts. A company seeking to purchase a major item or service, such as a piece of equipment or some construction work, will invite tenders (or quotations) from those interested in supplying the goods or service sought. Such an invitation may be published generally or in a trade journal, or circulated to companies likely to be interested. In normal circumstances, the invitation for tenders is not treated as an offer, since the company issuing it may have criteria other than price that it wishes to take into account in awarding the contract. In that case, the tenders themselves are the first offers made—see *Spencer v Harding* (1870) LR 5 CP 561—and the person requesting the tenders has the freedom to determine which (if any) they will accept.

2.3.2.4.2 Exceptions in which the request can also constitute an offer (or promise)

There are, however, two situations in which the request to submit tenders (or bids) can *also* constitute an offer that, if accepted, will form a binding contract containing a specific promise.

1. An express contractual promise to accept the most competitive bid

Where the request for bids commits the person issuing the invitation to tender to accept the most competitive bid (either the highest or the lowest bid), that promise to accept the most competitive bid will result in a contractual obligation to do just that. There are *obiter* statements to this effect in *Spencer v Harding* (above) and the legal position was analysed in *Harvela Investments Ltd v Royal Trust Co. of Canada (CI) Ltd* [1986] AC 207.

> In **Harvela**, the vendors of a plot of land sought a 'single offer' for the whole plot from each of two interested parties, promising to accept the highest offer received. Both parties submitted bids, but while one merely stated a price that it was prepared to pay, the other stated both a concrete sum and a referential bid (i.e. '$101,000 in excess of any other offer'). The question for the House of Lords was which of the two bids was the higher. In one sense, the referential bid was indeed the higher offer, but such a conclusion is only possible when only one party makes such a bid. It would not be so if two (or more) bidders did.
>
> The House of Lords considered that allowing unrestricted use of referential bids risked undermining the competitive tendering process. The House of Lords therefore implied into the request for bids a stipulation that referential bids would not be accepted.

The unilateral contract: in *Harvela*, the House of Lords faced a conceptual difficulty in respect of the implied stipulation against referential bids, in that there was no contract immediately apparent into which that stipulation could be implied. It could not be implied into any eventual contract to buy the land, since such a term would be too late and would bind only one party. Lord Diplock overcame the problem by describing the tendering process as being governed by a unilateral contract (see **2.6**) under which:

- the invitation to submit tenders was a unilateral offer (promise) to accept the highest bid; and
- this offer was accepted by submitting the highest bid.

This analysis is equally useful where the party inviting bids has committed itself to accept the highest (or lowest) bid, but then sells the goods to a bidder who did not submit the highest (or

TABLE 2.1 Summary and comparison of *Spencer v Harding* and *Harvela*

	Main bilateral contract awarding goods or services	Unilateral contract based on the promise to accept most competitive tender
Invitation to tender	Invitation to treat	Offer promising to accept most competitive tender, e.g. lowest tender for work
Tenders	Each tender is an offer	Submitting lowest tender accepts the offer and results in a contract based on that promise
Requestor decides on successful tenderer	Acceptance of a tender results in a contract with that party by which it is awarded the work	If the party awarded the contract under the bilateral contract is not the lowest tenderer, awarding the contract under the main bilateral contract will breach the unilateral contract and entitle the lowest tenderer to damages to compensate for its loss

lowest) bid. As a general principle, English law does not recognize pre-contractual liability, i.e. it does not impose any liability on the person requesting the bids prior to the making of the contract to sell or to award work—and then, it imposes it only with the person who buys the goods or is awarded the work. To hold a party to its promise is to give effect to the bidder's reasonable expectations on the basis of reliance on the promise. Some legal analysis is therefore needed to define the conditions in which such a promise will be binding. The courts avoid recognition of 'pre-contractual' liability by creating a separate (unilateral) contract to enforce the promise to accept the highest (or lowest) bid in favour of that bidder.

Although there will be a unilateral contract with the highest (or lowest) bidder, the only remedy for breach of that promise to sell to the highest (or lowest) bidder will be an award of damages. The highest bidder will not be entitled to receive the goods or work that were bid or tendered for because this is determined by the separate bilateral contract (see *Spencer v Harding*, above). The judicial analysis of the aforementioned cases is summarized in **Table 2.1**.

2. A contractual obligation to consider tenders that conform to the bid conditions

Similarly, the unilateral contract device was employed in *Blackpool and Fylde Aero Club Ltd v Blackpool Borough Council* [1990] 1 WLR 1195 to impose an obligation to consider tenders (or bids) that conformed to bid conditions.

In *Blackpool*, the council ran an airport and granted a single concession to operate pleasure flights from the airport. The licence had been held by the claimant club, but when the concession came up for renewal, the council determined to invite competitive tenders for it. Tenders were to be submitted by 12 noon on a specified day. On that day, the council's letter box was not cleared between the time at which the claimant club posted its tender and the closing time for bids, with the result that the club's tender was not considered. The club claimed that the council was in breach of an implied obligation to consider all conforming tenders received before the deadline.

The Court of Appeal agreed. There was an implied unilateral offer (promise) to consider conforming bids, which was accepted by submitting such a bid.

Bingham LJ recognized that no one would go to the trouble and expense of preparing a tender and submitting it in time if that person thought that it would not even be considered. Therefore, in recognizing the implied unilateral contract based on an implied promise, the Court of Appeal was giving effect to these reasonable expectations and reliance on the part of those submitting tenders.

However, the court also stressed that the only contractual obligation was to *consider the bid*. Thus, as in the *Harvela* analysis, the only liability for breach of the contractual obligation to consider conforming tenders will be in damages (and it is likely that the damages award would compensate for wasted expenditure, or possibly damages for loss of the chance to be awarded the contract—see **9.3.5** and **9.3.4**). This analysis of an implied unilateral contract was accepted by the Court of Appeal in *Fairclough Building Ltd v Port Talbot Borough Council* (1992) 62 BLR 82, although the *Blackpool Aero Club* case was distinguished on its facts.

Although based on the same unilateral contract analysis, the *Harvela* and *Blackpool* scenarios can be distinguished since, whereas in *Harvela* the obligation forming the basis of the unilateral contract was an *express* promise to accept the highest bid, in *Blackpool Aero Club* the obligation to consider confirming tenders was *implied* from the circumstances—namely, the facts that only a limited number of contractors were invited to tender and that there was a detailed procedure to be followed for the submission of tenders. These factors were said to justify the implication of a promise to consider conforming tenders. Since these factors are hardly exceptional, it is likely that such an implication can be made in the vast majority of formal tendering situations, although, in general terms, it is difficult to establish the existence of an implied contract (see **5.2.2.3**).

In the *Blackpool* case Bingham LJ had considered argument relating to whether there should be a remedy in two specific situations: (i) if the council had opened the first tender it received and accepted it before the deadline for the submission of all tenders, or (ii) if the council had accepted a tender received well after the deadline. He considered that there could be no remedy in these situations would be out of line with the 'confident assumptions of commercial parties'—both the tenderers and the council. In the context of public sector contracts (with local authorities and government bodies), the courts appear willing to accept an implied obligation of greater scope than the obligation accepted in *Blackpool*—namely, an implied obligation to act fairly in the tendering process: *Harmon CFEM Facades (UK) Ltd v Corporate Officer of the House of Commons* (1999) 67 Con LR 1; *Pratt Contractors Ltd v Transit New Zealand* [2003] UKPC 83, [2004] BLR 143. The tendering and award of contracts by public sector bodies is subject to special legislative regulation (see e.g. the Public Contracts Regulations 2015, SI 2015/102, and the Utilities Contracts Regulations 2006, SI 2006/6), and this appears to distinguish these types of contract.

It was suggested by Lord Toulson in *Central Tenders Board v White (t/a White Construction Services)* [2015] UKPC 39, [2015] BLR 727, that Bingham LJ's references to accepting an earlier or a later offer despite the existence of a deadline, were influenced by the public sector context for the contract and that, although it was unnecessary to determine this on the facts of the *Central Tenders Board* case, 'if a private citizen had invited offers for the sale of some personal possession and set a deadline' it did not necessarily follow from *Blackpool*, 'that such a person would be barred by an implied contract from accepting an earlier offer [before the deadline expired] or a later offer [received after the deadline expired]'. *Blackpool* is, indeed, confined to recognizing a duty to consider conforming tenders. It does not prevent the award of a contract, outside the area of legislative regulation, to any party selected by the person inviting tenders.

2.3.2.5 Auctions

An advertisement that an auction is to be held is not an offer to hold it and a request for bids at an auction is generally no more than an invitation to treat—Harris v Nickerson (1873) LR 8 QB 286— even if the auction advertisement refers to lots being 'offered for sale': *British Car Auctions Ltd v Wright* [1972] 1 WLR 1519. Therefore each bid is an offer and acceptance occurs when the auctioneer indicates acceptance of a bid with the fall of the hammer: Sale of Goods Act (SGA) 1979, s. 57(2). *Harris v Nickerson* is authority for the principle that if an advertised auction fails to take place or if the lots advertised are withdrawn from the sale, since the advertisement was only an invitation to treat, the auctioneer will incur no liability.

2.3.2.5.1 Auctions without reserve

However, the position is different where an auction is advertised as being 'without reserve' (i.e. involving a promise to sell to the highest bidder and promising not to apply any reserve price or to allow the vendor to bid in order artificially to push up the price).

In *Warlow v Harrison* (1859) 1 E & E 309, the court dealt *obiter* with the question of whether the next highest bidder has any remedy where the owner successfully bids for the property at an auction without reserve. The court stated that there would be a remedy for breach of contract. The basis for this appears to be the implication of a unilateral contract based on the promise that it will be an auction without reserve.

- *This promise (that there will be no reserve) constitutes a unilateral offer.*
- *The unilateral offer is accepted by the highest genuine (bona fide) bidder at the auction.*

If the promise not to apply a reserve is broken, the auctioneer will be liable in damages to the highest genuine bidder who suffers loss. However, the highest genuine bidder will not be entitled to the property sold, because his offer has not been accepted by the fall of the auctioneer's hammer.

This analysis of *Warlow v Harrison* was applied by the Court of Appeal in *Barry v Davies (t/a Heathcote Ball and Co.)* [2000] 1 WLR 1962.

> **Barry v Davies** concerned the sale of two machines at an auction without reserve. The claimant was the only bidder for the two machines, worth about £14,000 each. The auctioneer withdrew the machines from the sale on the basis that the bids (of £200 for each machine) were too low. The claimant claimed damages representing the cost to purchase the machines elsewhere, less the amount of his auction bids.
>
> The Court of Appeal allowed this damages award (of £27,600) on the basis that there was a collateral (separate) contract between the auctioneer and the highest bidder whereby the auctioneer promised to sell to that bidder. The auctioneer had breached this contract by withdrawing the machines from the sale.

⟳ SUMMARY

This analysis means that the following is true of an auction without reserve.

1. There is a *bilateral contract selling the goods* to whoever makes the bid that the auctioneer accepts by the fall of the hammer. On this analysis, the advertisement of an auction without reserve (or requests for bids at such an auction) is an invitation to treat and each bid is an offer. The acceptance comes from the auctioneer. This contract determines the person who is entitled to the goods.

2. *The promise that the auction is 'without reserve' constitutes a unilateral offer (promise) to that effect, which is accepted by the highest genuine bidder.* If a reserve is applied and the goods withdrawn from the sale, or if the owner is permitted to bid and artificially pushes up the price, there is a breach of this unilateral contract, and the highest genuine bidder is entitled to be compensated by the payment of damages. That person is not, however, entitled to the goods, since this matter is governed by the bilateral contract of sale.

Is it possible to withdraw a bid at an auction without reserve?

Following *Barry v Davies*, it is clear that the unilateral offer is accepted only by the highest genuine bidder, and since this fact cannot be determined until the fall of the hammer or when the auctioneer withdraws the goods from the sale, it follows that a bid can be withdrawn until that point.

2.3.3 Communication of the offer

An offer does not take effect unless and until it is actually communicated to the offeree, and it is not possible for an offeree to accept unless the offeree had knowledge of the offer (see **2.4.4**). Thus the point of communication of the offer is important because it is only then that the offer can be accepted. This gives rise to the question of what will constitute 'actual communication' (which is also a question of relevance when considering acceptances and revocations). What, for example, would the position be if the offer letter (or email) were delivered to the offices of the offeree, but not immediately opened by the offeree? This issue is considered later in the chapter at **2.4.5.3** and **2.4.5.4**, but it is interesting to note that the Vienna Convention for the International Sale of Goods 1980 (CISG) has a 'receipt' rule for offers (Art. 15.1) and helpfully defines 'receipt' as occurring when an offer 'is made orally' to the offeree or is 'delivered by any other means to him personally, to his place of business or mailing address'; see also Art. 1.10 PICC, Art. 1:303 of the Principles of European Contract Law (PECL). Where a person has no mailing or business address, receipt will occur when the offer is delivered to that person's 'habitual residence'. Therefore 'receipt', in these contexts, does not require that the communication should actually have been read by the person to whom it is addressed.

However, it would not be possible to accept without knowledge of the offer, so that although an offer might be communicated without the offeree having read or listened to it, any acceptance of that offer would not then be given in exchange for the offer and so would be invalid as an acceptance (see further **2.4.4**).

2.4 Acceptance

2.4.1 Requirements for a valid acceptance

Acceptance is what turns a specific offer, made with the intention to be bound, into an agreement.

How do we identify whether such an acceptance has occurred? The general principles applying to acceptances are as follows.

- To constitute acceptance (and thus agreement), the offeree's unequivocal expression of intention and assent (by statement or conduct) must be made in response to, and must exactly match, the terms of the offer. This concerns the fact of acceptance, i.e. whether we can recognize the correspondence or action as a valid acceptance.

- The matching acceptance must be communicated to the offeror in order to be effective.

In simple consumer transactions, it is common that only one offer is made and acceptance is straightforward. No detailed negotiation of terms is involved. Taking the example of a sale in a self-service shop (see **2.3.2.2**), the customer takes a price-displayed item off the shelf and presents it to the cashier, thus making an offer to buy it for the displayed price. The cashier accepts the offer on behalf of the shop, payment is instantaneous, and terms as to quality are left to be implied under the Consumer Rights Act (CRA) 2015 (see **6.4.2.4**). The role of acceptance in this case is crucial, but without legal difficulty.

Commercial contracts, especially for non-standard goods, may be very different. Frequently more than one offer will be made before negotiations are complete, and the language of 'acceptance' may be used before a technical legal analysis would identify acceptance as having been made.

2.4.2 The mirror-image rule: identifying a valid acceptance

An acceptance must be unconditional and correspond with the exact terms proposed by the offeror.

2.4.2.1 Counter-offers

If, when responding in a form purporting to be an acceptance, the offeree alters the terms contained in the offer or adds a new term, the offeree's response will constitute a *counter-offer*. This counter-offer cannot constitute an acceptance of the original offer; instead, the following will apply.

- Because the counter-offer is itself an offer on the revised terms being made by the offeree, agreement will result only if there is acceptance of the counter-offer by the original offeror.

- The further effect of a counter-offer is to operate in the same way as a rejection—namely, to destroy the original offer, and so prevent the original offeree from changing its mind and accepting that original offer. This effect is clearly demonstrated in the case of *Hyde v Wrench* (1840) 3 Beav 334.

In *Hyde v Wrench*, A offered to sell land to B for £1,000. B replied, offering £950. Clearly, that was not an acceptance, but a counter-offer. A rejected the counter-offer of £950, whereupon B purported to accept the original offer of £1,000. A denied that any contract had been made and the court agreed. It was not open to B to revive A's offer unless A was willing to revert to those terms.

This counter-offer rule can lead to difficulty where the parties fail to notice discrepancies between the offer and the purported acceptance. This difficulty is illustrated by *Brogden v Metropolitan Railway Co.* (1877) 2 App Cas 666, in which a counter-offer was accepted by conduct.

In *Brogden*, the appellant had for some time supplied coal to the respondent company as and when required. The parties decided to enter into a more formal long-term agreement. After negotiations, a draft contract was drawn up by the respondent and sent to the appellant. The appellant filled in the name of an arbitrator, marked the draft as 'approved', and returned it to the respondent. In technical terms, the appellant's communication was a counter-offer, but the respondent's manager, being satisfied with the draft, merely put it in a file. He did not communicate his acceptance of the additions made. The parties then commenced performance under the agreement. Subsequently, a dispute arose in which it was questioned whether in fact any long-term contract had come into existence. The House of Lords held that the commencement of performance by the respondent, which had ordered and taken delivery of coal consistently with the terms of the alleged agreement, was acceptance by conduct of the appellant's counter-offer.

2.4.2.2 Identifying a counter-offer

A counter-offer that purports to accept, but in fact operates to reject, the original offer must be distinguished from a request for further information before the offeree decides whether to accept.

2.4.2.2.1 Requests for further information

If there is no more than a request for further information, the offer will remain available for acceptance. This can be seen in *Stevenson, Jacques and Co. v McLean* (1880) 5 QBD 346.

In **Stevenson**, the defendant had offered to sell at a price of '40s net cash per ton'. The claimants had replied, asking whether the defendant would accept '40 for delivery over 2 months, or if not, the longest limit you could give'. It was held that this reply did not operate to reject the defendant's offer, but was only an inquiry to determine whether there was any flexibility in the offer terms to allow for staggered delivery. Therefore it remained possible for the claimants to accept that offer.

? QUESTION

Is the response a counter-offer or a request for further information?

This is perhaps the most frequently asked student question in the initial weeks of study.

It is not too difficult to make the distinction between counter-offer and request for more information on the facts in *Stevenson v McLean*, since the claimants had not reached the stage at which they were purporting to accept, and their response could not be interpreted as sufficiently specific and definite to constitute a counter-offer. However, other cases may prove more difficult.

As indicated earlier, there are two key factors in making the distinction:

1. Is the offeree purporting to accept, but at the same time changing the terms (counter-offer), or is he trying to decide whether he can accept by seeking to negotiate on the offer terms (request for further information)?

2. How certain is the language used in the response? For example, A offers to sell B his car for £1,500. B replies 'I agree, but I'm only prepared to pay £1,400' (counter-offer). Compare this with the situation in which A offers to sell B his car for £1,500 and B replies by asking *whether A might be prepared to accept £1,400* (request for further information before deciding whether to accept).

2.4.2.3 The battle of forms

With the increasing use of often-conflicting standard terms of business, each party to a sale or supply contract will send its own terms in an effort to ensure that those terms and conditions prevail. The question in such a case is to determine whose terms govern in this 'battle of forms'. The problem is that if the traditional analysis of offer, counter-offer, and acceptance is applied, there may well be no contract at all, because of the absence of a matching offer and acceptance, or there may be a contract referable to the last set of terms to be sent before performance. In both situations, it is likely that neither party would have appreciated the legal effect. In a 'no contract' situation, there cannot be payment for goods or services supplied based on 'contract' terms since the contract does not exist. However, it may be possible to obtain payment for goods or services on a restitutionary basis (on the basis that otherwise the receiving party would be unjustly enriched by receiving goods without having to pay for them): *British Steel Corporation v Cleveland Bridge & Engineering* [1984] 1 All ER 504 (see **3.1.5**).

Despite the consequences that can result from the application of the traditional analysis, the courts have tended to follow it. For example, it was adopted by the majority of the Court of Appeal in *Butler Machine Tool Co. Ltd v Ex-Cell-O Corporation (England) Ltd* [1979] 1 WLR 401, although Lord Denning MR suggested a more radical approach.

In **Butler Machine**, the sellers sent a quotation for the supply of a machine to the buyers. This quotation was issued on the basis of the sellers' conditions, which were to 'prevail over any terms and conditions in the buyer's order', and which included a price variation clause. The buyers placed an order and their letter contained conflicting conditions that, in particular, contained no price variation clause (i.e. the buyers required a fixed-price contract). At the bottom of the buyers' order, there was a tear-off confirmation slip expressly subject to the buyers' terms, which the sellers completed and returned. The sellers claimed to be entitled to vary the contract price. The Court of Appeal rejected that claim on the basis that the sellers had expressly accepted the buyers' terms when they completed and returned the acknowledgement slip. In other words, the sellers had accepted the buyers' 'last shot'. The majority (Lawton and Bridge LJJ) analysed this last shot as a counter-offer that had been expressly accepted.

The 'last shot' invariably appears to be the significant document in determining who wins (or loses) the battle of forms because of the possibility of acceptance of this counter-offer by conduct, e.g. in *Tekdata Interconnections Ltd v Amphenol Ltd* [2009] EWCA Civ 1209, [2010] 1 Lloyd's Rep 357, [2009] 2 CLC 866 (noted at [2010] CLJ 230), there was a long-term contracting arrangement whereby the buyer would send purchase orders containing its own terms and conditions and the seller would acknowledge the purchase orders by sending an acknowledgement stating that its own terms and conditions (including an exemption clause) would prevail. Since the last shot was sent by the seller, acceptance of delivery by the buyer resulted in a contract on the seller's terms. Dyson LJ noted, at [25], that this approach 'has the great merit of providing a degree of certainty which is both desirable and necessary in order to promote effective commercial relationships'.

Acceptance of the 'last shot' by conduct prevailed again in *Trebor Bassett Holdings Ltd v ADT Fire and Security plc* [2011] EWHC 1936 (TCC), [2011] BLR 661. ADT had sent a quotation to design, supply, and install a fire suppression system, which referred to its 'attached' terms and conditions, although these were not in fact attached. These terms limited liability to £13,781. Trebor's purchase order referred to its own terms as having already been supplied and available on request. These terms contained no limitation. ADT had not objected to Trebor's terms or sought a further copy of them, but had instead commenced the work. Accordingly, the terms were governed by Trebor's 'last shot' and the total loss of £110 million could be recovered.

In the *Butler Machine* case, Lord Denning MR also considered that there was a contract based on the last shot (the buyers' terms), but he reached his conclusion using a very different approach. Lord Denning's approach involved separating the question of formation of a contract from the determination of its content, which is in direct conflict with the mirror-image rule that treats formation and content as interdependent. Lord Denning considered that a contract was formed where the parties were agreed on the material points even if there were conflicting terms in their forms. He then turned to the question of content and whose terms would govern, and stated, at p. 405:

> In some cases, the battle is won by the man who gets the blow in first. If he offers to sell at a named price on the terms and conditions stated on the back: and the buyer orders the goods purporting to accept the offer—on an order form with his own different terms and conditions on the back—then if the difference is so material that it would affect the price, the buyer ought not to be allowed to take advantage of the difference unless he draws it specifically to the attention of the seller. There are yet other cases where the battle depends on the shots fired on both sides. There is a concluded contract but the forms vary. The terms and conditions of both parties are to be construed together. If they can be reconciled so as to give a harmonious result, all well and good. If differences are irreconcilable—so that they are mutually contradictory—then the conflicting terms may have to be scrapped and replaced by a reasonable implication.

This approach has not generally found favour with the English courts, although in *GHSP Inc. v AB Electronic Ltd* [2010] EWHC 1828 (Comm), [2011] 1 Lloyd's Rep 432 Burton J purported to follow Lord Denning's 'formation and content' approach. Burton J had to determine which parties' standard terms of business prevailed when it seemed clear that neither party was prepared to contract on the others' terms. The defendant supplied pedal sensors for motor vehicles. The supply terms purported to exclude liability for consequential loss or damage and restricted liability to rectification or repair. The negotiations had revolved around the claimant's standard terms, which contained no limitation on liability, although it was clear that the defendant supplier was not prepared to contract without some cap on its liability. Negotiations to agree a cap on liability had not resulted in any agreement and any conduct was not referable to either set of standard terms. This posed a dilemma and the natural instinct might have been to hold that no contract had been concluded. However, both parties agreed that 'there was plainly a contract' between them (compare the position in *British Steel Corporation v Cleveland Bridge and Engineering Co. Ltd* [1984] 1 All ER 504—see **3.1.4.1**) and it was evident that, since the goods had been manufactured and supplied, there had been performance of this contract. Burton J's solution was to regard the terms of the contract as the implied terms in the Sale of Goods Act 1979 (see **6.4.2.4**), which would be implied in any event. It follows that the parties' own terms had no part to play. This seems an odd outcome, although it was the argument presented to the judge by both counsel.

If a party wishes to avoid contracting on the other's terms, it seems that it will need to make this explicitly clear, as the supplier did during negotiations in the *GHSP* case. It may be more problematic to achieve this result using the standard terms of business. For example, although in *Butler Machine* the sellers had tried to ensure that their terms were paramount by drafting a clause stating that their terms and conditions would prevail over those in the buyers' order, this proved ineffective in the face of their express acceptance of the buyers' counter-offer (the 'last shot'). The sellers had also claimed that their terms were in fact the last document, because in sending the acknowledgement slip they had again referred to their quotation. This argument failed because the Court of Appeal regarded this reference as relevant only to the issue of the price and not as an attempt to incorporate the sellers' standard terms of supply. Interestingly, however, Lawton LJ was equally clear in *Butler Machine*, at p. 406, that, in the absence of the express acknowledgement slip, the buyers would not have been taken to accept the sellers' terms through accepting physical delivery of the machine since, by that point, they had already made it explicitly clear through other correspondence that they were not accepting.

2.4.2.3.1 Recent case law and analysis of the global approach

Recent decisions have confirmed the position of the majority of the Court of Appeal in *Butler Machine*, while accepting that there may be some situations in which the traditional analysis would not apply. These instances appear to be confined to situations where the course of dealing between the parties indicates that they accepted a different position. The decision in *GHSP* may be one such situation.

In *Tekdata Interconnections Ltd v Amphenol Ltd* [2009] EWCA Civ 1209, [2010] 1 Lloyd's Rep 357, [2009] 2 CLC 866, although the Court of Appeal accepted the application of the traditional analysis (and acceptance by conduct of the last shot), Dyson LJ concluded, at [25]:

> it is not possible to lay down a general rule that will apply in all cases where there is a battle of the forms. It always depends on an assessment of what the parties must objectively be taken to have intended.

Nevertheless, he concluded that in a simple situation where 'A makes an offer on its conditions and B accepts that offer on its conditions and, without more, performance follows', the 'traditional offer and acceptance analysis' is correct and 'there is a contract on B's conditions'.

Longmore LJ, at [21], also explained:

> [A]lthough I am not saying that the context of a long term relationship and the conduct of the parties can never be so strong as to displace the result which a traditional offer and acceptance analysis would dictate, I do not consider the circumstances are sufficiently strong to do so in the present case. Indeed I think it will always be difficult to displace the traditional analysis in a battle of forms case, unless it can be said there was a clear course of dealing between the parties. That was never proved.

It follows that the Court of Appeal was not saying that a 'Denning contextual approach' would never be applicable, but that it was not the starting point for any analysis and would be difficult to establish on the facts. In particular, Longmore LJ appears to have been influenced by argument to the effect that whatever Lord Denning said in *Butler Machine Tool*, he actually applied a traditional analysis, i.e. that the acknowledgement slip had been expressly accepted by the seller.

The application of these principles was accepted as being the correct approach by Edwards-Stuart J in *Transformers & Rectifiers Ltd v Needs Ltd* [2015] EWHC 269 (TCC), [2015] BLR 336, 159 Con LR 33 at [42], although the factual issue was concerned with whether reasonable notice of each party's terms and conditions had been given (discussed at **6.3.1.2**), and by Coulson J in *Trebor Bassett Holdings Ltd v ADT Fire and Security plc* [2011] EWHC 1936 (TCC), [2011] BLR 661. In *Trebor*, Coulson J noted, at [154], that 'some care is needed' with 'the last shot doctrine' and that 'the court has to construe all the relevant communications'. Therefore the mere existence of a 'last shot' cannot determine the battle.

It remains the case in English law that Lord Denning's approach is not the starting point in instances of the battle of forms, and we shall have to go some way further down the road to judicial intervention in the process of contracting before the courts will construct a contract on behalf of the parties out of the conflicting terms and conditions in the various documents passing between them. The traditional approach in England remains different from the approach in other jurisdictions and in the drafts of harmonized principles, e.g. see § 2–207 of the US

Uniform Commercial Code (UCC) and Art. 19 CISG 1980. Section 2–207 UCC provides that in general if the parties' communications indicate that they intend to contract, any differences between the standard forms will not prevent contract formation, i.e. the second communication will be an acceptance and not a counter-offer. Any additional terms in the second communication which do not materially alter the offer will generally become terms unless the offer expressly limits acceptance to the offer terms or the additional terms are objected to within a reasonable time.

Article 2.1.22 PICC and Art. 2:209 PECL also all broadly accept that a contract is formed in a battle of forms situation unless one party has explicitly notified the other (either in advance or without delay) that it does not intend to be bound if there are conflicting terms. Where a contract is formed despite the conflicting terms, its content will comprise those terms that are common in substance, and the implication is that the courts will fill any gaps.

Each set of principles also contains a provision addressing 'modified acceptances', 'which do not materially alter the terms of the offer' (Art. 2.1.11 PICC and Art. 2:208 PECL). These Articles state the general rule—namely, that a modified acceptance is a counter-offer (i.e. a rejection and a new offer). However, 'modified acceptances' will be acceptances unless the offeror makes speedy objection to the discrepancy (PICC and PECL), or the offer expressly limited acceptance to the terms of the offer (PECL), or the offeree's acceptance was conditional upon the offeror's assent to the differing terms and the assent was not received within a reasonable time (PECL). Where there is such an acceptance, the terms of the contract will be the offer terms as modified by the acceptance.

Lord Denning's approach to formation of the contract—like the formulations in the US UCC, the Vienna Convention, the UNIDROIT PICC, and the PECL—placed great emphasis on material terms or terms that 'materially alter' the offer. This raises the question of identification of 'material terms' and hence 'material alterations'. Article 19(3) CISG 1980 defines 'material alterations', as does Art. 38(2) CESL. However, this definition is extremely broad and only the most trivial of alterations would be regarded as not materially altering the offer. In particular, if the response contains any changes to price, payment terms, delivery, liability, and any dispute mechanism, the response would constitute a rejection. There is some explanation of 'material' terms and modifications in the commentary to the UNIDROIT PICC and PECL, but the idea of a list as in Art. 19(3) CISG 1980 was expressly rejected by the PECL in favour of the retention of flexibility, given that any list could not be exhaustive. Instead, Art. 1:301(5) PECL contained a definition of 'material' as a matter that 'a reasonable person in the same situation as one party ought to have known would influence the other party in its decision whether to contract on the proposed terms or to contract at all'.

2.4.3 Failure to follow the prescribed method of acceptance: A valid acceptance nevertheless?

The offer may stipulate that the offeree is to respond using a particular method of communication or is to respond to a particular address. Where the offeree has failed to comply with the stipulated method for accepting prescribed by the offeror, it might be thought, on the basis of the mirror-image rule, that where the offeree uses a different method that 'acceptance' would be invalid. However, where the offeror has not made it clear that the stipulated method is mandatory and that no other will suffice, a pragmatic approach has been taken in the case law. Mirror-image is required where the prescribed method stipulation is mandatory, but not otherwise.

1. Explicit words are required in order for a stipulated method to be considered mandatory, e.g. an explicit statement that the prescribed method must be followed and that no other will suffice. In *Siemens Hearing Instruments Ltd v Friends Life Ltd* [2014] EWCA Civ 382, [2014] 2 P & CR 5, [2015] 1 All ER (Comm) 1068, the Court of Appeal held that the use of the word 'must', relating to a form of notice to exercise a break clause in a lease, meant that it was a mandatory requirement. Since the notice did not comply, it was an invalid notice.

2. In *Manchester Diocesan Council of Education v Commercial & General Investments Ltd* [1970] 1 WLR 241, Buckley J stated that where the offeror has not made it very clear that the stipulated method is mandatory and that no other will suffice, the method was permissive only and the following principles applied so that the acceptance might nevertheless be valid.

   – Any equally efficacious method of acceptance will be valid if it fulfils the purpose in prescribing the method. For example, if the offeror wants a quick response and prescribes acceptance by fax, then as long as this method is not mandatory, any acceptance that is just as quick as a fax acceptance will suffice.

   – Alternatively, if the method was prescribed in order to benefit the offeree, the offeree can waive (give up) a stipulation for its benefit and use a different method as long as this method does not disadvantage the offeror. In *Yates Building Co. Ltd v Pulleyn & Sons (York) Ltd* (1975) 119 SJ 370, the offer stipulated that the acceptance should be sent by registered or recorded post. This was intended to enable the offeree to prove that the acceptance had been posted (see **2.4.5.2**). Accordingly, the offeree could waive this requirement and take the risk of the ordinary post.

The facts of *Manchester Diocesan* are slightly unusual.

In **Manchester Diocesan**, it was the offeree who had required that the offer specify that the offeree's acceptance letter was to be sent to the particular address given in the tender. The intention was to ensure that there would be a binding acceptance on posting to the prescribed address (see more on the postal rule of acceptance at **2.4.5.2**). However, the claimant offeree had in fact sent the acceptance to the offeror's surveyor and not to the address specified in the offer. Buckley J held that since the stipulated method was intended to benefit the offeree, the offeree could waive compliance with this if the method used was no less advantageous to the offeror. On the facts, the method used was no less advantageous to the offeror since the acceptance had been actually communicated.

By comparison, in *Anglian Water Services Ltd v Laing O'Rourke Utilities Ltd* [2010] EWHC 1529 (TCC), [2011] 1 All ER (Comm) 1143, in the context of a provision for the giving of notices in relation to a construction contract, Anglian Water's solicitors had faxed the notice to Laing O'Rourke's solicitors, who had received it and passed it to the relevant individuals within Laing O'Rourke within the time limit. However, a clause in the contract stipulated that the notice would take effect 'when received at the last address notified by the party receiving the notice'—in this case, the construction company's (Laing O'Rourke's) offices. Edwards-Stuart J held that the contract required compliance with the terms of that clause since the commercial purpose of the stipulation in the clause was that all communications should be channelled through one particular office to ensure proper records and responses, and this was expressly linked by the clause to the timing of receipt at that place. It followed that compliance with this notice stipulation was the only way of judging that timing under the contract.

Whereas in *Manchester Diocesan* it was considered that there was no actual disadvantage in the circumstances in using the alternative method of communicating, the judge in *Anglian Water* assessed the operation of the clause, and issues of disadvantage, in the abstract, emphasizing the general application of the clause to all notices under the contract. There was clearly no disadvantage on the actual facts, but there might have been in other instances.

In *A Ltd v B Ltd* [2015] EWHC 137 (Comm), A Ltd sought to avoid an agreement to purchase cotton from B Ltd by arguing that, since it had not signed and returned a copy of the draft contract, it had not followed the prescribed method of communicating acceptance. In rejecting this argument, Phillips J held, following a similar comment by Longmore LJ in *Maple Leaf Macro Volatility Master Fund v Rouvroy*, at [15], that the insertion of a signature block (or space for a signature) in the draft contract did not mean that signature became a prescribed method of acceptance, even if the block was headed with the word 'Acceptance' and there was a request for the signed contract to be returned. In any event, the judge held that any signature prescription would have been to benefit B, as offeror, and B was free to waive, and had waived, this stipulation for its benefit.

? QUESTION

If an offer is sent by post, must the acceptance be sent by post?

No. The acceptance would not necessarily need to be sent by post unless the offeror had made it quite clear that acceptance by post was mandatory. That apart, where an offer is sent by post and the parties are at a distance, the post will be considered as *one* of the envisaged methods for a response—*Henthorn v Fraser* [1892] 2 Ch 27 (offer communicated by hand, but the parties were at a distance from one another)—but it need not be the only one. It will be necessary to consider the context and the evidence of the offeror's objectives in making the offer by post. For example, it may be clear from the terms of the offer that the offeror contemplates a quicker response, e.g. by email or fax, than is possible using the postal service.

2.4.4 Acceptance in response to the offer

The rule that acceptance must be made in response to the offer is a close relative of the principle requiring communication of an offer and also the principle that defines consideration as the price for which the promise of the other is bought. The fact that a claimant is not entitled to a reward when the performance of the act requested takes place in ignorance of the reward offer can be explained either in terms of an absence of consideration or in terms of an absence of agreement (see *R v Clarke* (1927) 40 CLR 227, at **4.2.1.1**), i.e. either the performance was not induced by the offer or the acceptance (which, in such a contract, is constituted by the performance of the requested act—see **2.6**) was not made in response to the offer.

However, it is clear from the decision in *Williams v Carwardine* (1833) 5 C & P 566, 172 ER 1101, that as long as the offeree did have knowledge of the offer and thus accepted in response to it, his motive in so doing is irrelevant. The decision in *Gibbons v Proctor* (1891) 64 LT 594 might be considered to be at odds with the principle that there must be knowledge of the offer in order to be able to claim the reward. However, this decision has been explained as turning on the particular requirements of the offer, which were that the information should be given to a particular person—namely, on the facts, Superintendent Penn. Although the information was initially given to another colleague at a time when there was no knowledge of the reward, the offeree had the necessary knowledge at the time when the information reached Superintendent Penn and the decision can therefore be interpreted as reflecting accepted principle.

The rule that acceptance must be in response to, and with knowledge of, the offer may leave parties without a contract, despite the fact that they are subjectively agreed on all matters, where they cannot objectively be shown to have gone through the process of agreement. If two parties both make offers to each other more or less simultaneously (i.e. before receiving the other's offer)—i.e. if they make cross-offers—then, even if the offers are made in identical terms, there is no contract. The offers may correspond, but there is no agreement, because there is no acceptance made in response to the other's offer: *Tinn v Hoffman* (1873) 29 LT 271. In practice, the apparent harshness of this rule is mitigated by the fact that any small act of performance by one party may well be regarded as acceptance by conduct and so may establish agreement (see **2.4.2.1**).

2.4.5 Communication of acceptance

The second general principle of acceptance is that the acceptance needs to be communicated to the offeror (in the sense of being actually received).

There are two important exceptions to this general rule:

1. implied waiver of the communication requirement in the case of unilateral contracts; and

2. acceptances by post, where the parties are necessarily not in each other's presence.

2.4.5.1 Implied waiver of the need to communicate acceptance in unilateral contracts

In a unilateral contract, performance of the act constitutes the acceptance and there is therefore no need to communicate the fact that you are *attempting to perform* that act. Authority for this principle is the decision in *Carlill v Carbolic Smoke Ball Co.* [1893] 1 QB 256 and, in particular, the statement by Bowen LJ at p. 270:

> In the advertisement cases it seems to me to follow as an inference to be drawn from the transaction itself that a person is not to notify his acceptance of the offer before he performs the condition, but if he performs the condition notification is dispensed with.

Bowen LJ gave the example of a reward for the return of a lost dog to a particular place. The acceptance is the act of returning the dog to that place and there is no need to communicate an intention to perform the act. Of course, the particular offer may expressly provide that communication is a necessary part of the acceptance (requested act), e.g. where there is a reward for supplying information. In addition, although it may not be necessary to communicate an intention to seek to perform the requested act, it may still be necessary at a practical level to communicate the fact of that performance in order to notify the offeror that the reward is being claimed. However, that is not part of the acceptance itself.

Waiver of the need to communicate acceptance also occurred in relation to an announcement promising to pay a guaranteed employment bonus to employees in *Dresdner Kleinwort Ltd v Attrill* [2013] EWCA Civ 394, [2013] 3 All ER 607. In *Carlill*, Bowen LJ had stated that, since notification of acceptance is required for the benefit of the offeror, the offeror could waive this and dispense with notice to himself. In these circumstances, Dresdner Kleinwort, the employer, had clearly dispensed with the need for any response to its offer to pay the bonus and it was therefore deemed to be accepted. Delivering an agreed judgment, Elias LJ noted, at [98], that 'it would be a wholly formal and unnecessary exercise' to have to positively accept the offer. In any event, the promise contained no disadvantage for the employees and nobody hearing the announcement would expect that an employee could benefit only if they were to positively accept the offer.

2.4.5.1.1 Silence in bilateral contracts

By comparison, in standard bilateral negotiations, the general rule is that the offeror cannot waive the need for communication and stipulate that silence will constitute acceptance. The authority for this is said to be the decision in *Felthouse v Bindley* (1862) 11 CB NS 869.

> In *Felthouse v Bindley*, an uncle and nephew had been negotiating the sale of the nephew's horse to his uncle, but they could not agree on the price. In the end, the uncle had written to the nephew, saying that if he heard no more he would assume that the nephew agreed to his proposal of a price of £30 15s. The nephew appears to have been satisfied with this arrangement, since he instructed an auctioneer to withdraw the horse in question from a sale. However, he did not communicate this fact to his uncle. When the auctioneer mistakenly sold the horse, the uncle sued him for conversion, claiming to be the owner of the horse under a contract with his nephew. The court did not accept his claim, stating at p. 875 as one of its reasons that 'the uncle had no right to impose upon the nephew a sale . . . unless he chose to comply with the condition of writing to repudiate the offer'.

As Miller (1972) 35 MLR 489 argued, the actual decision on the facts in *Felthouse v Bindley* appears to be incorrect, since neither of the grounds said to justify the silence principle applied on the facts.

1. Silence will often be equivocal, and the silence principle is said to protect offerees from contracts that they had no intention to accept. However, the nephew's conduct in instructing the auctioneer not to include the horse in the auction sale would appear to indicate that there was an intention to accept.

2. It would be difficult to argue that the problem was that the nephew had not communicated this intention to his uncle since, in imposing the silence requirement, the uncle had waived the need for that communication.

Nevertheless, the silence principle itself is valid and underpins the rules on inertia selling, i.e. where an offeror, without any previous course of dealing, seeks to force an offeree to reply in order to avoid the formation of a contract. In the case of such 'inertia selling' to consumers (where a company sends a product to a consumer that the consumer has not requested and then demands payment for the said product or return of that product), inertia selling constitutes an unfair commercial practice under the Consumer Protection from Unfair Trading Regulations 2008, SI 2008/1277 (CPRs) (reg. 27M inserted by the Consumer Contracts (Information, Cancellation and Additional Payments) Regulations 2013, SI 2013/3134, reg. 39). The consumer can treat the goods supplied as an unconditional gift and it is expressly provided that silence will not constitute consent (reg. 27M(3)(4)). The offeror trader may also commit an offence within the provisions of Part 3 of the Regulations.

Businesses can also be victims of such 'inertia selling' and are protected by the Unsolicited Goods and Services Act 1971.

2.4.5.1.2 *Exceptions*

However, it is certainly not the case that silence can never be acceptance. In some contexts—especially those in which there has been a continuing course of dealing—silence (or conduct) can be sufficient acceptance.

1. If there has been a course of dealing whereby the offeree has taken the benefit of services offered, the offeree's silence (or conduct) can constitute acceptance

If A operates a coal delivery (or window cleaning) round and regularly delivers two bags of coal to B or cleans B's windows, either collecting the money on delivery or leaving an invoice to be paid later, without any formal order being placed, B would be unable to deny the existence of a contract for coal actually delivered (or for the cleaning of his windows). B would be bound by his own silence, which would constitute a sufficient acceptance.

2. If it is the offeree *who is attempting to hold the* offeror *to the offeror's stipulation of silence, then the offeree's silence will constitute acceptance*

In *Felthouse v Bindley* (1862) 11 CB NS 869, the particular form of the action (against the auctioneer) seems significant. If the facts had been different and it had been the uncle who had refused to take delivery of the horse on the basis that there had been no communication of acceptance to him, the nephew should have been able to rely on the uncle's stipulation and his own silence as establishing the existence of the contract: see Peel, *Treitel's The Law of Contract*, 14th edn (Sweet and Maxwell, 2015), [2–046], and Miller (1972) 35 MLR 489. In this situation, the offeror would be bound by the offeree's silence, and arguably the basis for this would be estoppel (i.e. the fact that the offeror expressly formulated his offer so that silence should be acceptance and therefore cannot deny this position where the offeree has relied on it). The technical difficulty here is that in *Fairline Shipping Corporation v Adamson* [1975] QB 180, Kerr J held that this would amount to using the estoppel as a cause of action, which is not permitted in English law. However, it must be the case that the estoppel would operate to prevent the defendant (offeror) from raising lack of communication of the acceptance as a defence to the offeree's claim for payment.

3. If it were the offeree, rather than the offeror, who initiated the proposal that the offeree's silence would constitute acceptance

In *Re Selectmove Ltd* [1995] 1 WLR 474, at p. 478, Peter Gibson LJ suggested, in *obiter* comments, that an offeree would be bound by his silence where he has given an undertaking to speak:

> Where the offeree himself indicates that an offer is to be taken as accepted if he does not indicate to the contrary by an ascertainable time, he is undertaking to speak if he does not want an agreement to be concluded. I see no reason in principle why that should not be an exceptional circumstance such that the offer can be accepted by silence. But it is unnecessary to express a concluded view on this point.

On the facts in ***Re Selectmove Ltd***, the taxpayer had been in negotiations with the Inland Revenue over tax arrears. In August 1991, he had made an offer to the tax collector that he would pay future amounts as they fell due and arrears by monthly instalments commencing in February 1992. The collector indicated that he would have to seek approval for this proposal, but that he would advise the taxpayer if the proposal was unacceptable. There was no further communication between them until October 1991, when the Revenue demanded payment in full. The taxpayer argued that there was a binding agreement for the Revenue to accept payment by instalments. The Court of Appeal rejected this argument on the basis that the tax collector had no authority to commit the Revenue to the suggested contract.

However, it was accepted that the position may be different where the offeree does possess the necessary authority to contract. Any other position would defeat the legitimate expectations of the offeror. In addition, there can be no objection on policy grounds, since there is no question of a duty to speak being *imposed* by the offeror on the offeree. (If there had been the necessary authority and if the taxpayer had paid the arrears in accordance with the proposal, there might have been an issue of estoppel, since the proposal terms would then have been relied upon.)

4. If a party initiates a proposal and receives that proposal, but then does not respond for a lengthy period, this may be treated as acceptance in some circumstances

In *Rust v Abbey Life Assurance Co. Ltd* [1979] 2 Lloyd's Rep 334, the claimant had been negotiating with the defendant insurance company in relation to investing in property bonds. The claimant submitted an application for the bonds and sent a cheque for £91,600. The defendant allocated units in the fund and sent the claimant her policy. The claimant did nothing for seven months, but then sought the return of her money. The first ground for the decision was that there was a contract based on the fact that the defendant had accepted the claimant's offer. However, a second ground relates to the claimant having accepted the offer from the defendant through silence or acquiescence (see also Lord Steyn in *Vitol SA v Norelf Ltd, The Santa Clara* [1996] AC 800, 812, discussed at **8.4.2.1**).

Rust v Abbey Life was distinguished in *Cooper v National Westminster Bank plc* [2009] EWHC 3035 (QB), [2010] 1 Lloyd's Rep 490, in relation to an offer to settle a claim. The offeror bank had pressed this offer on the claimant, since it had credited his account with the settlement figure. The customer did not raise his dissatisfaction with the offer until eight months later. The bank sought to rely on *Rust v Abbey Life*, but the judge rejected this argument and held that it could not be inferred that the customer had accepted the bank's offer. The offer was disadvantageous to the customer and the bank must have realized that the customer would not have accepted it if given a free choice. By comparison, in *Rust v Abbey Life* it was clear that the claimant had applied for the bonds and had also paid for them.

Nevertheless, the circumstances may make it quite clear that the silence is not to be taken as acceptance or as involving any binding promise or variation.

For example, in **Northstar Land Ltd v Brooks** [2006] EWCA Civ 756, [2006] 2 EGLR 67, the claimant purchaser had served notice to complete following the exercise of an option to purchase land for development. This notice required completion on 2 January. However, the claimant later offered to extend the deadline for completion to 9 January in light of the Christmas and New Year break. On 2 January, solicitors for the defendants (vendors) were asked to agree to completion being deferred to 9 January. The solicitors stated that they would need to take instructions and would revert back. However, they did not do so. Having received no response, the claimant assumed that the completion date had been deferred and so did not complete on the scheduled date of 2 January. The Court of Appeal confirmed that there was no obligation on the vendors' solicitors to respond, so that the claim for specific performance had to fail.

2.4.5.2 **The postal rule of acceptance**

When the parties negotiate to a conclusion in each other's presence, there is little danger of uncertainty as to whether agreement has been reached, although recollections may differ as to its content if it has not been recorded. The general rule is that words of acceptance must not only be spoken, but must also be communicated to the offeror. Thus if words of acceptance are drowned by a loud noise, they must be repeated before the contract is concluded: see the judgment of Denning LJ in *Entores Ltd v Miles Far East Corporation* [1955] 2 QB 327.

However, when the parties are not in each other's presence, communication becomes a more critical issue, especially when the agency of a third party, such as the Post Office, or of a machine is involved. The law has developed a distinction of potentially fundamental importance between instantaneous and non-instantaneous communications. Instantaneous communications are treated more or less as if the parties were in each other's presence, whereas special rules apply to non-instantaneous communications.

2.4.5.2.1 *Acceptance and the risk of the post*

The problem with contract negotiation by post is that letters may either be delayed or lost. The central question is: who should bear this risk of loss or delay? In *Adams v Lindsell* (1818) 1 B & Ald 681, the defendants offered to sell wool to the claimants, asking for a reply 'in course of post'. The defendants' letter was misdirected, so that the claimants' reply was delayed beyond the normal course of post, and the defendants sold the wool to someone else. Nevertheless, the claimants had sent a letter of acceptance on the day on which the offer had been received and claimed that there was an enforceable contract. The court upheld that claim, and since this case the general rule has been that, where acceptance is communicated by post, the contract is formed as soon as the letter of acceptance is sent without need for it to reach the offeror. This rule applies even if the postal acceptance never arrives and the offeror is ignorant of the fact that an acceptance was posted: *Household Fire and Carriage Accident Insurance Co. Ltd v Grant* (1879) 4 ExD 216. In *Household Fire v Grant*, the postal acceptance never arrived, but the Court of Appeal held there to be a binding contract on posting. The postal rule therefore places the risk of loss or delay squarely on the offeror, since it follows that the offeror will be bound by a contract despite the non-receipt of an acceptance sent by post.

Attempts have been made to justify the rule on all kinds of grounds.

1. It is said that, without such a rule, offerees would never know whether a contract had been formed. In other words, if actual communication of a postal acceptance is required, the offeree would not be safe in relying on the acceptance until receipt of written notification that the acceptance had arrived, and such confirmation would also be necessary for the notification of the fact of receipt of the acceptance, and so on. Such a position was considered to be commercially inconvenient.

2. It has also been argued that the postal rule prevents offerees from speculating by posting an acceptance and then (if the market changes) withdrawing it by speedier means (e.g. telephone)—although see further the discussion on retraction (or overtaking) of a postal acceptance (**2.4.5.2.4**).

3. It could be argued that the offeror, unlike the offeree, will not be prejudiced by delays or loss in the post, since the offeror is expecting a response and will check if a reply is not received.

4. Alternatively, it is argued that if the offeror has indicated that use of the post is permissible, then it is the offeror who should bear the risks of that system. This last explanation is borne out by *Henthorn v Fraser* [1892] 2 Ch 27, in which it was made clear that the postal rule is applicable only where it was reasonable in all of the circumstances for the offeree to have used the post—as would most obviously be the case had the offer been sent by post.

The truth of the matter is almost certainly that whenever one of the risks of the use of the post materializes, whatever conclusion the court reaches will be harsh on one of the parties. The postal rule is no more than a rule of convenience adopted in the interests of certainty. The basic argument is that offerors should know the risks inherent in use of the post and can protect themselves if they so wish. Indeed, the fact that the postal rule can be avoided in practice is often used as a reason to justify its existence!

2.4.5.2.2 Criticisms of the postal rule

The postal rule has been the subject of much criticism.

- Where a postal acceptance has been lost in the post, the offeror may believe that, since no reply has been received, the offeree does not wish to accept. The offeror may therefore believe that there will be no question of breach if a contract relating to the same subject matter is made with someone else.

- A further criticism made by Bramwell LJ in a powerful dissent in *Household Fire and Carriage Accident Insurance Co. Ltd v Grant* (1879) 4 ExD 216 was that the operation of such a rule is arbitrary, since it does not apply to non-postal acceptances and since little conscious thought may have been given to the decision to communicate the acceptance using one form of communication rather than another, e.g. the post rather than hand delivery or acceptance by faxed letter. Bramwell LJ would therefore have preferred the ordinary rule of communication to apply equally to acceptance by post. The most significant part of his judgment is that in which he says that the harm he perceives in the postal rule 'will be obviated only by the rule being rendered nugatory by every prudent man saying "Your answer by post is only to bind if it reaches me"'.

2.4.5.2.3 Avoiding the postal rule

It is sensible, therefore, for the offeror to seek protection against the risks posed by the postal rule by stipulating that a particular means of acceptance (other than the post) is required, or by wording the offer to require actual communication of any acceptance. This is precisely what the offeror achieved in *Holwell Securities Ltd v Hughes* [1974] 1 WLR 155.

In *Holwell*, the defendant granted the claimant an option for the purchase of certain land, which was said to be exercisable by notice in writing to the defendant at a given address within six months. An option is no more than an offer, and although the claimant posted a letter accepting the offer in question within the six-month period, it failed to arrive. The Court of Appeal held that the option had not been validly exercised and, accordingly, there was no contract. The main finding was that the mere words 'notice in writing to' were sufficient to oust the postal rule. These words amounted instead to a stipulation that notice must reach the offeror, thus reinstating the general principle of actual communication.

It would seem relatively straightforward, in the light of this interpretation of what are fairly common words, to avoid the operation of the postal rule. For example, the words 'let me know your answer' may suffice as emphasizing the need for actual communication. It follows that the significance of the postal 'rule' as a practical principle may well be overstated. In his judgment, Lawton LJ (at 161B) referred to football pools coupons as an example of a familiar situation in which the postal rule is ousted.

Although *Holwell* provides authority for the fact that it is possible to oust the operation of the postal rule of acceptance by using *express* words, Lawton LJ also stated (at 161B) that the postal rule 'probably does not operate if its application would produce manifest inconvenience and absurdity', and he interpreted this to mean that the rule can be ousted if it is clear from the subject matter and the circumstances that the parties cannot have intended that there should be a binding agreement until there has been actual communication of an acceptance. This again provides ample scope for the avoidance of the postal rule in practice.

2.4.5.2.4 *Retraction of (or overtaking) a postal acceptance*

Is it possible to retract a postal acceptance before it reaches the offeror? In other words, could the offeree post an acceptance, but then change his mind and telephone the offeror to tell her that he does not want to accept and that the offeror should therefore disregard any acceptance letter?

There is no English case authority and a Scottish case—*Countess of Dunmore v Alexander* (1830) 9 S 190—is highly dubious authority, although it is sometimes cited in support of the conclusion that it is possible to overtake a postal acceptance. This Scottish case is of questionable authority because:

- the majority appear to be treating the letter being overtaken as an offer, and offers are revocable before they are communicated and accepted;
- the case is complicated by the fact that communications take place through an agent or intermediary; and
- it is not strictly speaking an 'overtaking' case, because both communications arrived at the same time.

Despite the absence of authority, there has been much academic discussion of this question of whether it is possible to overtake a postal acceptance. There are two opposing positions, as follows.

1. *It is not possible to retract (or overtake) a postal acceptance.* It might be assumed that if the postal rule is in fact a 'rule', then logic would dictate that it would not be possible to retract a postal acceptance, since it would be binding on posting. This conclusion is frequently supported by asserting that to allow any other conclusion would permit the offeree to be able to 'play the market', i.e. to accept an offer to purchase goods at one price and later to withdraw that acceptance by a quicker method if market conditions were to make the contract less profitable.

2. *It is possible to retract (or overtake) a postal acceptance where the offeror is not disadvantaged.* It can be argued that the postal 'rule' is nothing more than a rule of convenience to determine who should bear the risk of loss or delay in the post. As such, its operation should focus on the question of inconvenience, and it can be argued that, logically, any offeror will accept and act upon the communication received first (including taking action to sell the offered goods elsewhere), so that as long as a postal acceptance is retracted before any postal acceptance arrives, the offeror suffers no disadvantage: see Hudson (1966) 82

LQR 169. Not only does the offeror suffer no disadvantage, but it might equally be considered unreasonable for the offeror to rely upon a postal acceptance that he knows has been retracted. A further justification for allowing the offeree this latitude of retraction is the fact that the offeror can always oust the operation of the postal rule if he wishes by the use of express words requiring that the post should not be used or requiring actual communication of any acceptance sent by post.

2.4.5.3 Instantaneous methods of communicating and non-instantaneous messages

The post is very obviously a method of non-instantaneous communication, and therefore the law has recognized that there needs to be a principle to determine who should bear the risks of transmission. On the other hand, it is generally accepted that telephone negotiation is a form of instantaneous communication, so that the parties are treated as if in each other's presence and no contract will be formed unless the words of acceptance are clearly heard by the offeror ('the receipt rule'). A similar approach was taken to telex communications in *Entores Ltd v Miles Far East Corporation* [1955] 2 QB 327. On the facts of *Entores*, it was necessary to decide *where* the contract was formed in order to determine whether the contract was subject to English or Dutch law.

> In *Entores*, a Dutch company sent an offer by telex to an English company. The English company sent a counter-offer response by telex, and the Dutch company responded by telexing an acceptance of the counter-offer. The Court of Appeal held that the contract was made in England, where the acceptance was received.

By analogy with telex messages, an acceptance by fax has also been held to amount to an instantaneous communication that takes effect on receipt: *JSC Zestafoni Nikoladze Ferroalloy Plant v Ronly Holdings Ltd* [2004] EWHC 245 (Comm), [2004] 2 Lloyd's Rep 335, at [75] (the agreement was made in England, where the fax acceptance was received). Of course, the sender of a fax receives a message informing them that the message has been received, although it does not always follow that the fax communication has been received in its entirety—or legibly.

2.4.5.3.1 What if an instantaneous method is used, but the actual communication is non-instantaneous?

In *Entores*, Denning LJ had recognized that there were occurrences that could affect the instantaneous nature of the transmission, e.g. if the telephone or telex line were to go dead during transmission, but the offeree be unaware of this fact and think that the acceptance message had got through. If the offeror, knowing that a message was being sent, did not ask for it to be repeated, Denning LJ considered, at p. 333, that 'the offeror . . . is clearly bound, because he will be estopped from saying that he did not receive the message of acceptance. It is his own fault that he did not get it'.

⚙ SUMMARY

The principles in the judgment of Denning LJ as they apply to communication of acceptance by an instantaneous method can be summarized as follows.

- In general, the onus is on the communicator (offeree) to get his message through.

»

- If the line goes dead and the communicator (offeree) knows this, then the offeree must repeat the message and ensure that it is received.

- If the recipient (offeror) knows that a message is being sent and that it has not been received, but the offeree believes the message has got through, then the offeror must ask for the message to be repeated. If he does not do so, the offeror will not be able to deny that the acceptance was effectively received.

- If no one is at fault (i.e. the offeree believes the message got through and the offeror does not know that any message was being sent), then the acceptance will not have been communicated and there will be no contract.

That there are instances in which the actual communication would be non-instantaneous, despite the use of an instantaneous method of communication, was explicitly recognized in *Brinkibon Ltd v Stahag Stahl und Stahlwarenhandelsgesellschaft GmbH* [1983] 2 AC 34. Lord Wilberforce stated that messages are frequently sent by telex out of business hours, leaving messages stored until the following day. (The same can be said of fax communications and, nowadays, of business emails.) In such non-instantaneous cases, Lord Wilberforce stated, at p. 42, that:

> No universal rule can cover such cases: they must be resolved by reference to the intentions of the parties, by sound business practice and in some cases by a judgment where the risks should lie.

In effect Lord Wilberforce was saying that there is no rule for such cases. *However, a general principle appears to be identifiable—namely, that if the offeree has done all that he might reasonably be expected to do to get his message through, acceptance should take effect when the offeree might reasonably expect it to be communicated to the offeror.*

1. Communication to a business during office hours

It follows that if an acceptance has been communicated to a business during office hours, the offeree could reasonably expect the offeror to be monitoring (say) the fax machine and would expect communication to occur when the message was received by the machine. Accordingly, in this situation, communication to the machine would suffice as 'actual communication'. Authority for this principle is provided by:

- the decision in *The Brimnes* [1975] QB 929 (although the case itself concerned a notice of withdrawal rather than an acceptance); and

- comments by Lord Fraser in *Brinkibon Ltd v Stahag Stahl* that messages would be at the risk of the recipient if the recipient were to fail to man its telex (or fax) machine.

2. Communication to a business outside office hours

This issue was considered by Gatehouse J in *Mondial Shipping and Chartering BV v Astarte Shipping Ltd* [1995] CLC 1011. The judge suggested that receipt of a contractual notice should be deemed to occur at the start of the next working day if it was in fact received and stored outside normal working hours (in this case, the opening for business on the following Monday, since the message was sent and received at 23:41 on a Friday). Gatehouse J also indicated that he viewed this result as consistent with Lord Wilberforce's approach, which was to consider each case on its particular facts.

3. The meaning of 'ordinary business hours'

This raises a difficult question concerning the definition of 'ordinary business hours' and how this will be determined. In *The Brimnes* [1975] QB 929, a message received between 17:30 and 18:00 was considered to be received within 'ordinary business hours'. Blair J, in *Thomas v BPE Solicitors (a firm)* [2010] EWHC 306 (Ch), [2010] All ER (D) 306 (Feb), at [90], considered that an email sent at 18:00 was sent within office hours given the context of the parties' negotiations. This indicated that, on the basis of the previous emails, the transaction could have been completed that evening. In fact, the recipient had gone home at 17:45 on a Friday evening in late August and the office did not reopen until the following Tuesday because of the bank holiday. The issue arose again before Blair J in *Lehman Brothers International (Europe) (In administration) v Exxonmobil Financial Services BV* [2016] EWHC 2699 (Comm), [2017] 2 All ER (Comm) 959. In this instance, at the time Lehman Brothers went into administration, there was an outstanding sale and repurchase agreement under which the defendant had lent some funds to the claimant who, in return, had provided a portfolio of securities as collateral. Some securities were not sold and a dispute arose over how much was left owing under the contract which was governed by a standard form used internationally for such agreements, the GMRA 2000. The dispute over the valuation arose following disagreement as to the interpretation of the termination provisions of the GMRA 2000 and how those provisions were to apply in practice. The GMRA 2000 provided for a default notice to be given after 'an event of default'. The GMRA also provided for a default valuation notice which had to be given by the default valuation time, itself defined at 'the close of business' in the appropriate market. This also dictated a certain valuation method for the non-defaulting party. The source of the dispute arose when, on 22 September, the defendant sent a default valuation notice, through email, which arrived at the claimant's outside of business hours. As the GMRA 200 stipulated that this had to be received by 'close of business', the court therefore had to decide whether or not this had indeed been satisfied on the facts. After noting that 'modern commercial banks close at about 7 pm', Blair J stated that the notice had indeed been received 'before close of business on 22-09-2008' (at [156]. Blair J however was careful to state that his conclusion was 'limited to this case' (at [155]).

4. Messages left on telephone answering machines

Even these principles leave open some difficult questions, such as: when is there communication of an acceptance message left on a telephone answering machine?

- If we apply the general principle of what the offeree could reasonably expect, the conclusion might be that the message will not be communicated until actually played back, since anyone leaving a message should reasonably assume that, as the machine is switched on, the message will not be communicated immediately. (This ignores the practice of using an answering machine to screen calls.)

- On the other hand, Coote (1971) 4 NZULR 331 argued, by analogy with the postal rule, that where the machine appears to be working, in leaving the message the offeree has put the matter out of his control, so that this should be the point of communication. In addition, in inviting communication using this method, the offeror may be taken to have accepted the risk of being bound by an acceptance of which he has no knowledge. Such a position might be preferable for evidential reasons, since many machines will record the time of receipt of the message; it is also a good deal more convenient for the offeree, since it avoids the possibility of numerous repeat telephone calls.

2.4.5.4 Electronic means of communicating

The Consumer Contracts (Information, Cancellation and Additional Payments) Regulations 2013, SI 2013/3134, reg. 14, require a trader who enters into a distance contract concluded by electronic means to provide the consumer with certain specified information before the consumer concludes a contract. It follows that it is essential to identify the point of contracting, and this in turn will determine where the contract is concluded. It is vitally important to decide whether the postal rule ('the dispatch rule') or 'the receipt rule' applies to these communications, because this in turn will determine the place, and time, of contracting. A distinction exists between contracts made on a retailer's website and contracts made exclusively by the exchange of email messages. Whereas the Electronic Commerce (EC Directive) Regulations 2002, SI 2002/2013, apply to website contracting, their application is expressly excluded from applying to contracts made exclusively by exchange of emails (regs. 9(4) and 11(3)).

2.4.5.4.1 Email

First, it is important to appreciate that on the facts, it may be the case that, despite the use of email communications during the negotiation stage, the parties did not intend there to be a binding contract reached by the exchange of emails: e.g. *Pretty Pictures v Quixote Films Ltd* [2003] EWHC 311 (QB), in which a signed written contract was contemplated by the parties.

Email acceptance messages raise complex questions, since the expression 'electronic mail' may suggest that they are a replacement for posted letters of acceptance, so that the postal rule should apply. Those who support this view argue that the sender of the message puts it out of their control by pressing the 'send message' key (although there are limited possible ways in which to recall an email message). If the postal rule applied, the email contract would be binding at the moment when the message of acceptance is sent. This would be important, assuming that the customer makes the offer, for suppliers of goods or services who send acceptances by email, since the contract would then be formed in the jurisdiction of that seller or supplier.

However, this view was not supported in *obiter* comments by Blair J in *Thomas v BPE Solicitors (a firm)* [2010] EWHC 306 (Ch), [2010] All ER (D) 306 (Feb). Instead, the judge considered, at [86], that where contracts are made by exchange of email the receipt rule applies (by analogy with the telex case law and *Entores v Miles Far East Corporation* [1955] 2 QB 327). Responsibility for getting the message through to its destination should lie with the communicator. This approach is also supported by the decision of the High Court of Singapore in *Chwee Kin Keong v Digilandmall.com Pte Ltd* [2004] SLR(R) 594, at [97]–[99], on the basis that the receipt rule has greater global acceptance and because email is in some respects very different from a postal communication. In addition, Andrews J in *Greenclose v National Westminster Bank plc* [2014] EWHC 1156 (Ch), [2014] 2 Lloyd's Rep 169, [2014] 1 CLC 562, at [138] and [140], was also clear that 'e-mail is not subject to the postal acceptance rule. It is a form of near instantaneous communication' and therefore must be actually communicated.

Nevertheless, there are two obvious problems with the receipt solution:

- If the customer makes the offer and the supplier accepts, the contract will be formed in the customer's jurisdiction (the place of receipt of the acceptance), which may suit the customer, but will be too risky for suppliers.

- What is meant by 'receipt' or 'actual communication'? Is it communication to the mail server, to the computer, or when the acceptance message is actually read? This may depend on the terms of the offer, e.g. they may indicate that the sender is expected to ensure that the recipient knows about the message (*Greenclose Ltd v National Westminster Bank plc*).

As mentioned at **2.3.3**, the CISG 1980, UNIDROIT PICC, and PECL all adopt a definition of 'receipt' to assist with certainty, and a similar rule might be usefully devised to cover electronic communications if the receipt principle is adopted. Expert evidence would be required to identify this point in time. In *Thomas v BPE Solicitors (a firm)*, Blair J treated an email sent at 18:00 as effective when received in the inbox at around 18:00, since, on the facts, it was then available to be read by the recipient. Although a similar position was reached by Blair J in *Lehman Brothers International (Europe) (In administration) v Exxonmobil Financial Services BV*, it is nevertheless clear that a purposive and contextual interpretation remains the norm.

2.4.5.4.2 Website (or Internet) contracting

Internet contracting (i.e. offer and acceptance at the website, also discussed at **2.3.2.3**) is instantaneous, so that the receipt rule should apply. The Electronic Commerce (EC Directive) Regulations 2002, SI 2002/2013, apply to such contracts. In practical terms, the transmission of messages is controlled by clicking on various responses to messages. The online buyer initially clicks on a 'checkout' or 'send order' button. The retailer then checks stock availability and will usually confirm this by a message displayed on the screen. This is not intended to constitute acceptance, because it is clear to the customer that further action on their part is required by entering credit or debit card details. Only after these details have been transmitted and accepted does the retailer send a message confirming that the order has been received. This is unlikely, however, to be regarded as the retailer's acceptance, which is often expressly delayed until the dispatch of the goods themselves. It may be interpreted as an offer, leaving it to the customer to accept by confirming (and thereby ensuring that the contract is made in the retailer's jurisdiction, where the acceptance is received).

Although what constitutes the acceptance is not identified in the E-Commerce (EC Directive) Regulations 2002, reg. 11(2) does provide that, unless the parties are businesses and agree otherwise, the order and the acknowledgement of receipt of order 'will be deemed to be received when the parties to whom they are addressed are able to access them'. This appears to confirm that the receipt rule is appropriate in this context, and that receipt will occur when the message has been downloaded from the server and is therefore capable of being accessed by the addressee. This approach receives explicit support in the decision of the High Court of Singapore in *Chwee Kin Keong v Digilandmall.com Pte Ltd* [2004] SLR(R) 594, at [101], although Blair J in *Thomas v BPE Solicitors (a firm)* [2010] EWHC 306 (Ch), [2010] All ER (D) 306 (Feb), at [86], limited his conclusions on the receipt rule by noting that this was the position 'at least where the parties are conducting the matter by email'.

Logically, the receipt principle ought to apply equally to the order, acknowledgement of the order, and to whatever constitutes the acceptance communication in email or website contracting.

2.4.5.4.3 Conclusion

Although the Electronic Commerce (EC Directive) Regulations, which accept the receipt rule, do not apply to email contracting, it would be very strange if the 'receipt' rule were to apply to Internet contracting and to all email correspondence apart from email acceptances, so that it seems preferable for the receipt rule to be adopted generally in this context.

2.5 Termination of offers

To be capable of acceptance, an offer must not only be specific and have been made with the intention of being bound (see **2.3.1**), but must also be current. Acceptance made after an offer has ceased to be valid is ineffective to form a contract. This section examines the means by which offers terminate so that they are no longer available for acceptance.

2.5.1 Lapse of time

Where an offer is left open indefinitely, there may come a time when the offeree can no longer accept.

In *Ramsgate Victoria Hotel Co. Ltd v Montefiore* (1866) LR 1 Ex 109, the defendant had applied for shares in the claimant company in early June 1864. Shares were allotted to him in late November 1864. The defendant refused to pay for the shares, although he had not withdrawn his application at the time when the shares were allotted. It was held that he was not obliged to go through with the purchase of the shares. The company's response to the defendant's offer had not been made within a reasonable time.

It is not possible to give any indication of what is a reasonable time, which will be a question of fact in each case. Where the offer is expressly stipulated to be open for a limited period ('a firm offer'), the offer will automatically lapse at the end of this fixed period.

2.5.2 Death

The death of either party may terminate an offer, although the English authorities are far from clear as to the precise circumstances in which an offer will lapse on death.

2.5.2.1 Death of the offeror

Where the contract is for the performance of a personal service by the offeror, which depends upon some skill that is exclusive to the offeror, the offeror's death automatically terminates the offer. Thus an offer by a concert pianist to perform at a concert could not be accepted after the death of the pianist.

However, where the subject matter is something available in an open market, there is no difficulty about obtaining substitute performance of what had been offered. Then the issue is whether the executor of the dead offeror's estate should have to arrange such substitute performance. The orthodox view is that the burden should not fall upon the executor, provided that notice of the death of the offeror has been given to the offeree, so that in the case of an offer to give a guarantee, it has been held that an offeree cannot accept it after he has been informed of the death of the offeror: *Coulthart v Clementson* (1879) 5 QBD 42. But where the offeree has no notice of the death of the offeror at the time when the acceptance is made, the deceased's estate will be bound. There are *obiter dicta* to this effect in *Bradbury v Morgan* (1862) 1 Hurl & C 249.

2.5.2.2 Death of the offeree

Although there are *obiter* statements in *Reynolds v Atherton* (1921) 125 LT 690 suggesting that, in the situation of the death of the offeree, the offer ceases to be an offer at all, the position is probably that the offeree's representatives can accept the offer if it is of a non-personal nature.

2.5.3 Revocation

An offer may be expressly terminated (or revoked), or the revocation may occur by implication, e.g. where the response to the offer is a counter-offer: *Hyde v Wrench* (1840) 3 Beav 334 (see **2.4.2.1**). In addition, an offer may be impliedly revoked by the offeror making a second offer. The decision in *Pickfords Ltd v Celestica Ltd* [2003] EWCA Civ 1741 provides authority for the fact that where A makes an offer to B (the first offer, or price quotation) and then makes a second (differing) offer without expressly revoking the first, the second offer may automatically revoke the first if, in making the second offer, the offeror 'clearly indicates an intention . . . to withdraw the first offer'. This can be compared with the situation in which B asks for a second (additional) quotation based on different facts, e.g. a fixed-price quotation. In this situation, B has a choice between the two offers or quotations, because the second quotation was requested and provided on the basis of providing greater choice rather than rejecting the original offer.

2.5.3.1 Express revocation of an offer

In negotiations towards a bilateral contract, the general rule is that the offeror is free to withdraw the offer at any time before acceptance: *Offord v Davies* (1862) 12 CB NS 748. It follows that revocation of an offer after the time of acceptance is ineffective.

2.5.3.2 'Firm offers'

It is not uncommon for an offer to be expressed as 'open' for a given period of time. It follows that the offer cannot be accepted once that period has elapsed (see **2.5.1**). It might also be thought that the offeror is promising that he will not revoke the offer within that period of time. However, this is no more than a pre-contractual promise, and English law is clear that such a promise is no different from any other promise and is unenforceable unless supported by separate, valuable consideration (e.g. such as an option to purchase: see *Holwell Securities Ltd v Hughes* [1974] 1 WLR 155). *Routledge v Grant* (1828) 4 Bing 653 provides authority for the fact that a firm-offer promise is freely revocable in English law unless supported by consideration.

> In *Routledge v Grant*, the defendant offered to take a lease of premises belonging to the claimant, at the same time promising to hold his offer open for six weeks. After only three weeks, the defendant purported to revoke this offer, while at the end of the six weeks the claimant purported to accept it. The court held that there was no contract. In the absence of consideration to support the promise to keep the offer open for a specified period, the offer may be withdrawn at any time, even before expiry of that period.

2.5.3.3 A critique of the firm offer rule in English law

The English rule on firm offers is not accepted by most other legal systems. Even most US states, the contract law of which is derived from English law, have abandoned the rule, at least in the case of firm offers made by those in business in relation to potential sales of goods:

see US UCC § 2–205. Since the firm offer is a valuable tool in forward planning, especially where a developer wishes to be able to rely on prices quoted by potential subcontractors when tendering for a major contract, it might be thought desirable for the English rule to be abandoned so that it would not be possible to revoke such an offer during the period stated. Article 2.1.4 PICC and Art. 2:202 PECL provide that an offer cannot be revoked if it states a fixed time for acceptance, and it is clear from the commentary to PECL that this would cover the firm offer.

Such a reform of English law might be achieved simply by identifying a very small reciprocal benefit to the offeror in making the firm offer promise, such as might amount to consideration under the approach adopted in the context of alteration promises to pay more in *Williams v Roffey Bros. & Nicholls (Contractors) Ltd* [1991] 1 QB 1 (described as a 'practical' or 'factual' benefit—see **4.4.4**). There might, for example, be some factual benefit to the offeror in having an identified offeree carefully considering his offer, even if it may not be converted into the benefit of an actual contract. However, the *Williams v Roffey Bros.* principle *cannot be applied in this context* because it applies only to promises altering *existing* contracts (see **4.4.4**).

2.5.3.4 Communication of a revocation

In all types of negotiation, whether instantaneous or not, revocation is ineffective until actually communicated to the offeree, and until that time the offer is open for acceptance.

2.5.3.4.1 A revocation must be actually communicated and the postal rule of acceptances does not apply to revocations of offers

The fact that the postal rule applies in the case of acceptance (see **2.4.5.2**), but does not apply in the case of revocation (see **2.5.3**), means that the courts must pay close attention to the timing of communications.

If a letter of acceptance is posted after a letter of revocation has been posted, but before that revocation is received, the acceptance will be effective to form a binding contract, although it was dispatched after the revocation. This was exactly what happened in *Byrne and Co. v Van Tienhoven and Co.* (1880) 5 CPD 344.

> In **Byrne**, a letter of revocation of an offer was sent from Cardiff to New York on 8 October. Acceptance of the original offer was telegraphed on 11 October from New York to Cardiff, before the letter of revocation had arrived. The court held that a contract had come into existence on 11 October (the postal rule also applying to acceptances by telegram), because the revocation was ineffective until communicated to the offeree.

A further example is provided by the facts of *Henthorn v Fraser* [1892] 2 Ch 27, in which the revocation of an offer posted at 12 noon did not reach the offeree until 5 p.m. However, since the offeree posted the acceptance at 3.50 p.m., there was a binding contract from that time. The revocation has to be communicated in order to be effective and was therefore too late.

The UNIDROIT PICC and the PECL both contain potentially useful provisions that aim to protect the offeree against intervening revocation in the case of postal acceptances, given that both sets of principles apply the receipt rule to postal acceptances. Although an acceptance is not effective until it reaches the offeror (Art. 2.1.6(2) PICC, Art. 2:205 PECL), the offeror can revoke only if the revocation reaches the offeree before he has dispatched (sent) his acceptance (Art. 2.1.4(1) PICC, Art. 2:202 PECL).

2.5.3.4.2 *Revocation of unilateral offers made to the whole world*

There is a special rule applicable in the case of revocations of unilateral offers made to the whole world in which the offerees are necessarily unidentified, so that actual communication of a revocation to individual offerees cannot occur: *Shuey v United States*, 92 US 73 (1875) (discussed at **2.6.4**).

2.5.3.4.3 *The revocation need not be authorized by the offeror, provided that the offeree ought reasonably to believe it*

In **Dickinson v Dodds** (1876) 2 Ch D 463, the defendant had offered to sell a house to the claimant and had promised to leave the offer open for three days, although the claimant had given no consideration for the promise. The claimant had decided to accept the offer, but had taken no steps to communicate his decision to the defendant, when he was informed by Berry, an apparently reliable person, that the defendant had agreed to sell the property to a third party. The claimant then attempted to communicate his acceptance to the defendant and claimed that there had been no effective revocation of the offer before his communication of acceptance.

The Court of Appeal held that the manner of communication of the revocation was irrelevant, provided that the claimant knew that the defendant no longer intended to sell the property to him by the time his purported acceptance was made.

This conclusion means that an offeree will have to decide whether to believe revocation information that is communicated by a third party. There is a risk that the source is unreliable and the information is incorrect. The safest course of action, if possible, will be for the offeree to check directly with the offeror in such circumstances.

2.6 Unilateral contracts

A unilateral contract is a contract under which one party (the promisor) binds itself to perform a stated promise upon performance of a stated act by the promisee, but under which the promisee gives no commitment to perform the act and instead is left free to choose whether to perform or not. This kind of bargain is outside the standard contracting situation, usually described as 'bilateral' or 'synallagmatic', in which there are two identified contracting parties who exchange promises and are both bound from the moment of that exchange.

Unilateral contracts are sometimes referred to as 'if contracts', since they take the form of the following well-known example first cited in *Great Northern Railway Co. v Witham* (1873) LR 9 CP 16: 'If you will go to York, I will give you £100.' Examples of unilateral contracts are option contracts, estate agency contracts, and reward contracts (which can include rewards for information, for the return of property, and for collecting tokens in an advertising promotion). A recent commercial example occurred when an issuer of loan notes made an offer to each member of a class of noteholders, promising a cash payment in proportion to the notes that each member held if they were to cast their individual vote so as to appoint a valid proxy who voted in favour of a resolution for financial restructuring and the resolution was passed. If the noteholders performed the requested act and the resolution was passed, the issuer was obliged to pay: *Azevedo v Imcopa Importação, Exportaação e Indústria de Olêos Ltda* [2013] EWCA Civ 364, [2015] QB 1, [38]). In *Vehicle Control Services Ltd v Revenue & Customs Commissioners* [2013] EWCA Civ 186, [2013] RTR 24, the issuing of a parking permit to a motorist was held to constitute a unilateral offer to permit the motorist to park in the designated area on the basis of the terms and conditions of the parking scheme, and motorists accepted this offer when first parking their cars in this designated area.

Unilateral contracts can be explained in terms of offer and acceptance, but sometimes only with difficulty. It was in the context of just such a contract that Lord Wilberforce commented upon the artificiality of the offer and acceptance analysis in *The Eurymedon* [1975] AC 154 (see **2.1.3**).

2.6.1 Unilateral offer

There are two different types of unilateral offer.

2.6.1.1 A unilateral offer (requesting performance of an act) may be made to an identified individual

In *Great Northern Railway Co. v Witham* (1873) LR 9 CP 16, the defendant argued that a unilateral offer (promise requesting performance of an act in exchange) could not result in a contract, because there was no reciprocity from the promise, i.e. only the promisor is bound when this promise is made. That argument was roundly rejected by the court, which saw such offers as a matter of everyday practice.

2.6.1.2 Alternatively, the offer may be made to the public at large, or to a particular class of persons

The classic example of such offers is the offer of a reward in return for the performance of some service, such as the apprehension of a criminal or the finding of lost property. In *Carlill v Carbolic Smoke Ball Co.* [1893] 1 QB 256 (the facts are given at **2.3.2.1**), the defendants sought to avoid having to pay the promised sum, although the claimant had caught influenza after using the smoke ball in the manner requested, by saying that there could be no contract because there would otherwise have been a unilateral contract with the whole world. Bowen LJ rejected this argument, saying at p. 268:

> It is not a contract made with all the world. There is the fallacy of the argument. It is an *offer* made to all the world; and why should not an offer be made to all the world which is to ripen into a contract with anybody who comes forward and performs the condition? It is an offer to become liable to anyone who, before it is retracted, performs the condition, and, although the offer is made to the world, the contract is made with that limited portion of the public who come forward and perform the condition on the faith of the advertisement.

This authority was relied on by the majority of the Court of Appeal in *Bowerman v ABTA Ltd* [1996] CLC 451, in deciding that an ABTA notice, displayed by travel agents and containing a promise to reimburse the cost of holidays when ABTA members ceased to operate, constituted an offer to customers that was accepted by anyone booking a holiday with an ABTA member.

2.6.2 Acceptance and consideration in the unilateral contract

Acceptance must be made *in response to* the offer (see **2.4.4**). This principle has particular application in the context of unilateral offers made to the whole world, such as offers of rewards, and much of the case law is concerned with these offers. The requested act must be carried out in response to the offer of a reward, so that there can be no acceptance where there was no knowledge of the offer.

The general rule is that, in unilateral contracts, performance of the requested act constitutes both the acceptance and the consideration to support the offeror's promise to pay the reward. Thus, in *Daulia Ltd v Four Millbank Nominees Ltd* [1978] Ch 231, at p. 239, Goff LJ said: '[T]he true view of a unilateral contract must in general be that the offeror is entitled to require full performance of the condition which he has imposed and short of that he is not bound.'

However, there is an argument—see Winfield, *Pollock's Principles of Contract*, 13th edn (Stevens, 1950), p. 19, adopted by the Law Revision Committee in its Sixth Interim Report in 1937, Cmnd 5449—which suggests that, for some purposes, acceptance may be constituted by commencing performance of the stipulated act, so that any attempt to revoke the offer after the commencement of performance will be too late (see **2.6.3.2**). It follows that both parties are bound on acceptance. But no reward would be payable until the complete performance of the act, since, until that time, the consideration for the promise of the reward will not have been provided. There are considerable difficulties in accepting this analysis, which are discussed at **2.6.3.2**.

2.6.3 Revocation

Revocation presents particular difficulties in the case of offers of unilateral contracts owing to the fact that acceptance in a unilateral contract is constituted by performance of the act requested in the offer promise. It follows that, in theory, it would be open to the offeror to revoke the offer at any time before completion of that performance, even where the offeree had gone to effort or expense in attempting performance, since the revocation would have occurred before the moment of acceptance (see **2.5.3**).

It has however long been recognized that application of the normal rule in this situation can cause hardship and injustice. Nevertheless, attempts to overcome the rule have run into conceptual difficulties. It is generally accepted that it would be desirable for the power to revoke to be lost once the offeror has notice that an offeree has unequivocally embarked upon performance. Loss of the power to revoke would not affect the rule that acceptance is constituted only by full performance of the act requested in the offer. There are *dicta* to that effect from Goff LJ in *Daulia Ltd v Four Millbank Nominees Ltd* [1978] Ch 231. This position was also affirmed by the Court of Appeal in *Soulsbury v Soulsbury* [2007] EWCA Civ 969, [2008] 2 WLR 834, in relation to a promise of £100,000 on the death of an ex-husband in exchange for the ex-wife refraining from enforcing a county court order in her favour. The Court of Appeal considered that once the ex-wife acted on this promise by not suing to enforce the maintenance order, the promise could no longer be revoked. However, if she were to give up and sue for the maintenance, then clearly she would not have accepted and could not claim the £100,000. (See the discussion of this unilateral contract by Longmore LJ at [48]–[50].)

The difficulty is in finding a conceptual explanation for such a principle.

2.6.3.1 Promissory estoppel

Perhaps the most obvious explanation lies in the doctrine of promissory estoppel (see **4.8.2**), since it is not difficult to identify, in the context of a unilateral contract, the elements needed for promissory estoppel—namely, a representation that the offer would be held open long enough for performance to be completed and a reliance by the other party on that representation.

> In ***Errington v Errington and Woods*** [1952] 1 KB 290, a father had bought a house for his son and daughter-in-law to live in, promising that although the house and accompanying mortgage were in his name, he would transfer the house to their names once they had paid all of the mortgage instalments. The father died and the son left the daughter-in-law, who continued to live in the house and to pay the instalments. The question arose whether the daughter-in-law could be forced to surrender possession of the house.

Denning LJ said, at p. 295:

> The father's promise was a unilateral contract—a promise of the house in return for their act of paying the instalments. It could not be revoked by him once the couple entered on performance of the act but it would cease to bind him if they left it incomplete and unperformed . . . They have acted on the promise and neither the father nor his widow, his successor in title, can eject them in disregard of it.

There is a hint in the passage quoted that Denning LJ viewed the inability to revoke the promise as based on estoppel, since, after identifying the father's promise (the representation requirement as defined earlier), he referred expressly to the fact that the couple had acted on the promise (the reliance requirement on that promise). In many cases, however, such an analysis will not work, because there is no pre-existing legal relationship and because, in English law, the doctrine cannot currently be used to found a cause of action (see **4.8.3.2**).

2.6.3.2 Acceptance upon commencement

An alternative explanation is to question the usual rule that, in unilateral contracts, acceptance and consideration are synonymous and simultaneous (see **2.6.2**). Instead, it is argued that acceptance in a unilateral contract can occur by commencing performance of the requested act, although there is no entitlement to the reward until the consideration (full performance of the act) has been supplied.

However, the main difficulty with such a simple rule is that, pending complete performance of the requested act, it has always been accepted that an offeree is entirely free to decide whether or not to perform, and indeed is free to commence performance and then stop before completion without fear of any penalty other than the loss of the opportunity to earn the promised reward. (This was expressly confirmed by Longmore LJ in *Soulsbury v Soulsbury* [2007] EWCA Civ 969, [2008] 2 WLR 834, at [48]–[50].) If acceptance were to be constituted by starting performance, the offeree would be obliged to complete performance or face a claim for breach of contract. To tie the offeree in by such a rule would be to defeat one of the objects of the unilateral contract, which is to avoid the need for initial reciprocity inherent in the consideration doctrine as it is applied to bilateral contracts. ('Unilateral' means that only one party is bound, the offeror on the giving of the promise; the offeree, not promising anything is never bound.)

2.6.3.3 **The collateral contract**

A third explanation rests on the identification of two contracts in such cases:

1. the main unilateral contract, with acceptance and consideration furnished in the ortho-dox way by performance of the act stipulated in the offer, and under which, until complete performance of the act, no reward would be payable; and

2. an additional collateral (or ancillary) unilateral contract, which consists of an offer (implied promise) not to revoke the main offer once the offeree has commenced perfor-mance of the stipulated act, which offer would be accepted by that act of commencing this performance—see McGovney (1914) 27 Harv LR 644, at p. 659. There would then be an enforceable promise to keep open the main offer (and not to revoke). There is no real conceptual difficulty with this explanation, since commencing performance can be the consideration for the collateral contract not to revoke because it is the performance impliedly requested in the offer.

However, this explanation is highly artificial and bears no resemblance to the manner in which unilateral offers are in fact made. It also possesses one significant drawback—namely, that this mechanism will not actually prevent revocation of the main unilateral offer. It means only that there will be a breach of the collateral contract, for which the remedy would be damages. Nevertheless, more recent developments in respect of implied contracts—see e.g. *Harvela Investments v Royal Trust Co. of Canada Ltd* [1986] AC 207 and *Blackpool and Fylde Aero Club v Blackpool Borough Council* [1990] 1 WLR 1195 (discussed at **2.3.2.4**)—may lend support to the 'two contract' approach as the solution to the conceptual dilemma.

Furthermore, there is clear support in the case law for the 'two contract' approach to revoca-tion since both the House of Lords in *Luxor (Eastbourne) Ltd v Cooper* [1941] AC 108 and the Court of Appeal in *Daulia v Four Millbank Nominees* [1978] Ch 231 considered the question of whether revocation was possible by first deciding whether there was an implied promise not to revoke once performance had commenced. The existence of such an implied promise acts as the basis for the collateral unilateral contract. On the facts, no such promise could be implied in *Luxor v Cooper* since the context envisaged an offer that should be freely revocable until completion of the sale.

> *Luxor v Cooper* involved an estate agency contract on terms under which the agent was to be paid £10,000 on completion of the sale of two cinemas to a purchaser for at least £185,000. Although such a purchaser was found, the sale did not take place. The House of Lords refused to imply a term to the effect that the owners had undertaken not to prevent the sale (i.e. there was no implied promise not to revoke) on the basis that the terms of the offer made it clear that it was to be freely revocable at any time before completion.

2.6.3.4 **Conclusion**

None of the above explanations is entirely satisfactory. It is likely that future courts will con-tinue being reticent to explain why they are prepared to hold that a unilateral offer can no longer be revoked once performance has commenced.

Nevertheless, despite the difficulties in legal analysis, it seems fairly safe to predict that the courts will continue to find offers of unilateral contracts to be irrevocable after performance has begun. However, there will be instances in which the offer may make it clear that the parties intended that revocation might occur at any time before complete performance of the act, as in *Luxor (Eastbourne) Ltd v Cooper* [1941] AC 108, so that the principle cannot be stated in all-embracing terms. In *Schweppe v Harper* [2008] EWCA Civ 442, [2008] BPIR 1090, the Court of Appeal was clear that instances in which the right to revoke is reserved, e.g. as in *Luxor v Cooper*, should be rare.

In *Schweppe v Harper*, at [46], Waller LJ made the following comment in the context of passages from *Chitty on Contracts*, which clearly support the 'acceptance' on commencement approach:

> Where there is an offer to pay for the performance of a certain task, part performance can produce a contract under which that offer cannot be withdrawn. That should be the more so where there has not only been part performance but there is a real benefit being accepted by the offeror from that part performance. In such a case the court should be reluctant to find that the offeror has reserved a right to withdraw the offer after part performance.

This suggests that part performance constitutes acceptance of the contract. However, the true motivation is to prevent revocation, particularly because it would defeat the reasonable expectations of the offeree once there has been part performance that has conferred a benefit on the offeror. On the other hand, there are other ways of recognizing enrichment and reimbursing for performance short of imposing acceptance—and hence an obligation on the offeree to perform. In addition, the acts that will constitute 'starting to perform' or acts of 'part performance' in any context are by no means clear.

2.6.4 Communication of revocation of a unilateral offer

In relation to offers made to the whole world, there are particular problems in applying a rule that states that a revocation of an offer must be communicated to the offeree, since the offerees will be unidentified. Practical considerations would therefore suggest that it would be appropriate to follow the approach taken in the American case of *Shuey v United States*, 92 US 73 (1875). In this case, it was held to be sufficient that the 'same notoriety be given to the revocation that was given to the offer'. Therefore, if the same channel is used and the same level of publicity achieved, the fact that an individual offeree has not seen the revocation would be irrelevant.

2.6.5 The unilateral contract device

The typical unilateral contract is usually regarded as being the offer of a reward for the performance of some service—see *R v Clarke* (1927) 40 CLR 227—or the repeat option for the supply of goods provided in a long-term contract to deliver goods as and when ordered—see *Great Northern Railway Co. v Witham* (1873) LR 9 CP 16. These functions are well known and well documented, and require no further comment.

In addition to these typical functions, as we have seen throughout this chapter (e.g. at **2.3.2.4**), unilateral contracts are sometimes used by the courts to manipulate the facts of situations of negotiation into binding contracts where instinct suggests that a contractual relationship exists, but the facts do not lend themselves to a conventional analysis of a bilateral contract. Two House of Lords cases will serve to illustrate the point, as follows.

2.6.5.1 *The Eurymedon*

The facts of *New Zealand Shipping v Sattherthwaite (The Eurymedon)* [1975] AC 154 are related elsewhere (see **4.4.2** and **11.6.4**). The essential point is that the court found a contract to exist between a shipper and a stevedore even though the two had not dealt directly with each other, but each had a separate contract with the carrier. Lord Wilberforce explained the existence of the contract between shipper and stevedore in the following way, at pp. 167–8:

> The bill of lading brought into existence a bargain initially unilateral but capable of becoming mutual, between the shippers and the stevedore, made through the carrier as agent. This became a full contract when the stevedore performed services by discharging the goods. The performance of these services for the benefit of the shipper was the consideration for the agreement by the shipper that the stevedore should have the benefit of the exemptions and limitations contained in the bill of lading.

There is little doubt that this analysis owes more to the court's legitimate desire at that time—before the Contracts (Rights of Third Parties) Act 1999 (see **11.4**)—to avoid the doctrine of privity of contract than it does to any genuine description of the nature of the negotiations between the three parties.

2.6.5.2 *Harvela Investments Ltd v Royal Trust Co. of Canada*

In *Harvela Investments Ltd v Royal Trust Co. of Canada* [1986] AC 207 (see **2.3.2.4**), Lord Diplock adopted a 'two contract' analysis in order to 'create' a contract comprising a promise to accept the highest offer received (and into which could be implied a term ruling out the adoption of a referential bid).

It seems highly probable that the implication of such unilateral contracts will continue as a pragmatic means of solving existing deficiencies in English contract law.

MULTIPLE-CHOICE QUESTIONS

 Test your knowledge by trying this chapter's **multiple-choice questions**:
www.oup.com/uk/poole

FURTHER READING

General on agreement and unilateral contracts

Adams and Brownsword, *Understanding Contract Law*, 5th edn (Sweet and Maxwell, 2007).

Cartwright, *Formation and Variation of Contracts: The Agreement, Formalities, Consideration and Promissory Estoppel* (Sweet and Maxwell, 2014).

Furmston and Tolhurst, *Contract Formation: Law and Practice*, 2nd edn (Oxford University Press, 2016).

Goodhart, 'Unilateral contracts' (1951) 67 LQR 456.

Graw, 'Puff, Pepsi and "that plane": the John Leonard saga' (2000) 15 JCL 281.

Morgan, 'Formation of contract', in *Great Debates in Contract Law*, 2nd edn (Palgrave Macmillan, 2015), ch. 1.

Saprai, 'Balfour v Balfour and the separation of contract and promise' (2017) 37(3) Legal Studies 468.

Simpson, 'Quackery and contract law: the case of the *Carbolic Smoke Ball*' (1985) 14 JLS 345.

Approach to identifying existence of agreement

De Moor, 'Intention in the law of contract: elusive or illusory?' (1990) 106 LQR 632.

Offers and invitations to treat

Adams and Brownsword, 'More in expectation than hope: the *Blackpool Airport case*' (1991) 54 MLR 281.

Jackson, 'Offer and acceptance in the supermarket' (1979) 129 NLJ 775.

McKendrick, 'Invitation to tender and the creation of contracts' [1991] LMCLQ 31.

Montrose, 'The contract of sale in self-service stores' (1954) 4 Am J Comp Law 235.

Phang, 'Tenders and uncertainty' (1991) 4 JCL 46.

Scott, 'The auction house: with or without reserve' [2001] LMCLQ 334.

Unger, 'Self-service shops and the law of contract' (1953) 16 MLR 369.

Acceptance

McKendrick, 'The battle of the forms and the law of restitution' (1988) 8 OJLS 197.

Miller, '*Felthouse v Bindley* revisited' (1972) 35 MLR 489.

Mitchell and Phillips, 'The contractual nexus: is reliance essential?' (2002) 22 OJLS 115.

Morgan, 'Battle of the forms: restating the orthodox' [2010] CLJ 230.

Rawlings, 'The battle of forms' (1979) 42 MLR 715.

Effective communication

Capps, 'Electronic mail and the postal rule' (2004) 15 ICCLR 207.

Coote, 'The instantaneous transmission of acceptances' (1971) 4 New Zealand UL Rev 331.

Evans, 'The Anglo-American mailing rule' (1966) 15 ICLQ 553.

Gardner, 'Trashing with Trollope: a deconstruction of the postal rules in contract' (1992) 12 OJLS 170.

Lee, 'The contract formation under the caveat emptor rule: assessing its utility' in Merkin and Devenney (eds.), *Essays in Memory of Professor Jill Poole* (Informa Law, 2018), ch. 6.

Hudson, 'Retraction of letters of acceptance' (1966) 82 LQR 169.

Mik, 'The effectiveness of acceptances communicated by electronic means, or—does the postal acceptance rule apply to email?' (2009) 26 JCL 68.

Mik, 'The *un*importance of being "electronic" or—popular misconceptions about "Internet contracting"' (2011) 19 Int J Law Info Tech 324.

Nolan, 'Offer and acceptance in the electronic age' in Burrows and Peel (eds.), *Contract Formation and Parties* (Oxford University Press, 2010).

Chapter 3

Agreement problems

SUMMARY OF THE ISSUES

This chapter examines two issues.

1. Certainty: those principles determining when an agreement is sufficiently certain to be capable of enforcement and asks whether there can be any liability in the absence of agreement; and

2. Agreement mistakes: mistakes preventing agreement or which result in a contractual document failing to reflect accurately what the parties agreed.

• For the former, as a general principle, it is for the parties to make their agreement and to ensure that the terms are sufficiently certain to be enforced. The courts will consequently generally refuse to fill any gaps and an uncertain agreement will be void. However, this must be balanced with the need to avoid the parties using allegations of uncertainty to escape from bad bargains, especially where the alleged uncertain agreement has been executed, i.e. performed. Therefore, in practice, the courts may rescue an agreement if some objective evidence is available to fill the gaps. The courts use commercial practice and previous performance to determine the meaning of vague terms so that the meaning represents the obvious intentions of the parties. If no such evidence exists, there will be no contract.

• Alternatively, if an uncertain clause is meaningless, as opposed to still to be agreed, it may be possible to remove that clause and enforce the remaining terms of the agreement.

• Agreements for the parties to agree a matter in the future ('agreements to agree') such as the price, will generally lack the necessary certainty. If nothing is said as to price, then statute may imply a reasonable price. If the parties have provided a mechanism for fixing the price and that mechanism operates, there is no certainty problem. However, where such a mechanism for fixing the price breaks down, the courts will need to decide whether the mechanism is integral and essential for fixing the price, and whether any of the parties is at fault in relation to this breakdown.

• If there is uncertainty and no contract results, in some circumstances there may nevertheless be an obligation to pay the reasonable value for requested performance that has been received, on the basis that otherwise the recipient would be unjustly enriched (i.e. a *quantum meruit* claim).

• For the latter, a formation (agreement) mistake will occur where one or both of the parties allege that they made a fundamental mistake that prevents agreement. However, the doctrine of mistake is very narrow; in part, this is because of the effect on third parties of a finding that the agreement is void. In particular, the mistake must be a mistake as to terms, as opposed to a mistake as to a collateral matter.

• The parties may be at cross-purposes, so that objectively there is no agreement. A contract will be void only if there is no element of fault, i.e. if such a mistake was not provoked by, or the responsibility of, one of the parties.

• Following the House of Lords' decision in *Shogun Finance Ltd v Hudson*, in the case of unilateral mistakes as to identity, the law distinguishes between contracts concluded via written documents

»

and contracts made in face-to-face dealings. Where the contract is made via written documents, identity is important to the decision to contract, so that the offer made to the party named in the writing can be accepted only by that named person. It follows that a rogue will acquire no title (ownership) under such a contract and the mistaken party can recover the property. However, where a contract is concluded via face-to-face dealings, there is a presumption of an intention to contract with the person physically present. Such a contract will therefore not be void, but will be voidable for the fraudulent misrepresentation as to identity. The result is that the innocent third party purchaser can keep the goods where the contract is voidable.

• Mistakes in transcribing the parties' agreement can be rectified to conform to that agreement, but the circumstances in which this can happen are tightly circumscribed.

• The defence of *non est factum* ('not my deed') is rarely available if (a) a party can show that they were unable, through no fault of their own, to understand the effect of the document being signed, and (b) that the actual document signed is fundamentally different in nature from the document that the party believed it was signing.

General background

Despite the apparent existence of agreement between the parties, the agreement may be void as a contract (automatically of no effect from the very beginning) owing to uncertainty in its terms, or because the parties have made a fundamental mistake as to a term of the agreement.

However, because the effect of a contract being void is so drastic:

• the courts have limited the circumstances in which an allegation of mistake will lead to this result on the basis that mistake is not to be used as an excuse to escape from bad bargains and should not detract from the core principle of the security of transactions; and

• the courts have employed the same approach in the context of curable uncertainty. They are keen, recognizing the need for precision in business contracts, to find a concluded contract despite allegations of uncertainty as long as they are able to determine the meaning of vague terms or resolve a problem of a missing term. This is particularly the case where the agreement in question has been executed by the parties. As Lord Tomlin stated in *Hillas & Co. Ltd v Arcos Ltd* (1932) 147 LT 503, at p. 512, the purpose is to ensure that 'the dealings of men may so far as possible be treated as effective, and that the law may not incur the reproach of being the destroyer of bargains'.

3.1 Certainty of agreements

3.1.1 Background

More complex than the issue of the existence of an agreement is the problem raised where the existence of an agreement in formal terms is not disputed, but one party alleges that either:

• important terms have not been agreed upon; or

• a term is, or terms are, too vague, so that the contract is unenforceable.

In practice, there is considerable overlap between these possibilities, since if an essential term is omitted, the agreement will necessarily be vague, and if certain terms are vague, in the sense that their meaning is unclear, this will lead to uncertainty as to the meaning of what has been agreed.

This is clearly an area in which there is at least potential for conflict between the relational nature of contracting and the once-and-for-all focus inherent in judicial intervention in contracts. In the words of Lord Wright in *Hillas & Co. Ltd v Arcos Ltd* (1932) 147 LT 503, at p. 516, it is accepted that when business people make 'big forward contracts for future goods over a period . . . in general in such contracts it must be impossible . . . to specify in advance all the details of a complicated performance'. Consequently, parties sometimes leave trivial details to be worked out later, or in long-term contracts leave the price to be agreed from time to time, or otherwise consciously leave gaps in their agreements because the information and transaction costs of negotiating an agreed allocation of any particular risk are out of proportion to the likelihood of the risk maturing. Sometimes, as a safety net, they put in an arbitration clause for the resolution of matters that cannot be worked out amicably between them. In nearly all cases, they rely on their goodwill at the time of contracting and their mutual interest in maintaining the relationship (which almost certainly extends beyond the individual contract in question) to iron out any problems not covered by the agreement.

It is possible that loosely drafted contracts may be some way into performance before this vagueness or lack of provision is appreciated or considered an issue. At that point, any court that becomes involved will be left with an invidious task. If asked to enforce the agreement between the parties where they have left some matters deliberately unspecific, the court may feel that it has nothing tangible to enforce. Yet if there has been more than trifling performance by one or both of the parties, it is a drastic step to say that the supposed terms are too vague for there to be any real agreement and thus to conclude that there is no contract.

3.1.2 The approach of the courts

The task of the court is to walk the narrow line between:

- writing the parties' agreement for them (which is generally viewed as beyond the judges' power and an infringement of freedom of contract); and

- maintaining the contract by construing it to spell out what the parties would reasonably understand it to mean, through the implication of terms that are deemed necessary to the workability of the contract and reflect the perceived intentions of the parties. (On the implication of terms, see generally **6.4**.)

In *Hillas & Co. Ltd v Arcos Ltd* (1932) 147 LT 503, Lord Wright made it clear that the role of the court (at least where there has already been some performance) is to preserve the contract whenever possible. He stated, at p. 514:

[T]he court is [not] to make a contract for the parties . . . except in so far as there are appropriate implications of law, as for instance, the implication of what is just and reasonable to be ascertained by the court as a matter of machinery where the contractual intention is clear but the contract is silent on some detail. Thus in contracts for future performance over a period, the parties may neither be able nor desire to specify many matters of detail . . . Save for the legal implication I have mentioned, such contracts might well be incomplete or uncertain.

Much depends upon the facts of each case. However, the general principle can probably be stated as follows: to be enforceable as a contract, an agreement must be sufficiently precise (taking into account the whole context of the negotiations) for the court to be confident that it is recognizing and giving effect to the contract as it would be reasonably understood through construing the document to reveal the parties' actual intentions—objectively ascertained, of course (see **2.1**)—rather than any imputed to them by the court itself. The problem, ironically, is that this principle is itself vague and involves a considerable amount of judicial discretion.

3.1.3 Agreements in which essential terms are vague

3.1.3.1 Ambiguity

In *Raffles v Wichelhaus* (1864) 2 Hurl & C 906, 159 ER 375, the level of ambiguity was such that there could be no agreement between the parties.

> The claimant had promised to sell and deliver to the defendants 125 bales of cotton at a given price 'to arrive ex *Peerless* from Bombay'. There were two ships called *Peerless*; one left Bombay in October, while the other left Bombay in December. When the defendants refused to accept the claimant's cotton, which had been shipped on the December ship, the claimant brought an action against the defendants alleging breach of contract. The defendants alleged that they understood the ship in the agreement to be the ship sailing in October. At the time of contracting, the fact that there were two ships of this name sailing from Bombay within this time period seems not to have been known by either party. The court found for the defendants.

Understanding the case is not easy, since the court gave no reason for its decision. The case is cited by some as one of the last vestiges of a subjective approach to intention (see **2.1**). The real intentions of the parties (assuming that the court had discovered their real intentions) did not coincide, so that there never was any agreement. Equally, however, a reasonable person (or objective bystander) in the defendants' shoes would have had no way of knowing from the words used by the parties which of the two ships was intended. Lord Phillips MR, in *Great Peace Shipping Ltd v Tsavliris Salvage (International) Ltd* [2003] EWCA Civ 1407, [2003] QB 679, at [29], treated *Raffles v Wichelhaus* as a case of latent ambiguity (an ambiguity that is not immediately apparent, but is revealed, when at a later stage, it is clear that the parties were always at cross purposes) and, on the facts, the court in *Raffles* also recognized this ambiguity. This type of ambiguity could not, in this case, be resolved by resort to any objective standard. The court was therefore left with no alternative other than to conclude that there was no contract.

3.1.3.2 The objective basis for determining the meaning of terms

Even where there is no total ambiguity, it must be possible to ascertain a meaning that would satisfy the objective bystander.

> In *Scammell & Nephew Ltd v Ouston* [1941] AC 251, the House of Lords was faced with an agreement to purchase a van on 'hire purchase terms', but details of these hire purchase terms—such as amount of any deposit, and the amount and frequency of repayments—had not been agreed. The House of Lords considered that there were so many possible interpretations of this expression that it was impossible to say which one the parties had intended.

However, it is equally clear that where a court can resort to clear commercial practice or to previous dealings between the parties in order to ascertain the meaning of a particular contractual expression, it will do so, thereby giving effect to what must have been the 'obvious' intentions of the parties. For example, in *Scammell v Ouston*, at p. 273, Lord Wright referred to the example of a sale contract 'on cif [cost, insurance, and freight] terms', which he regarded as having 'a definite and complete meaning under the law merchant'. By contrast, there are a number of different meanings of a contract made on 'fob' ('free on board') terms.

The need for some objective basis on which to determine the terms of the contract is essential.

In *Baird Textile Holdings Ltd v Marks & Spencer plc* [2001] EWCA Civ 274, [2002] 1 All ER (Comm) 737 (see **4.8.3.1**), the alleged term was that Marks & Spencer would acquire garments from Baird 'in quantities and at prices which in all the circumstances were reasonable', but there were no objective criteria for assessing any reasonable quantity or price. The Court of Appeal held that it could not make an agreement for the parties in the absence of any objective basis for determining its terms.

The existence of evidence as to the recognized meaning of 'fair and reasonable specification' was regarded as one of the factors rescuing an option in *Hillas and Co. v Arcos Ltd* (1932) 147 LT 503.

The claimants had agreed to buy '22,000 standards of softwood goods of fair specification' from the defendants during the 1930 season and had also been granted an option to enter into a contract 'to purchase 100,000 standards for delivery during 1931'. The option clause did not specify the kind, size, or quality of goods to be supplied. The claimants made a valid exercise of the option, but the defendants had already sold their entire season's production of timber and so claimed that there was no option contract because it was too vague to be enforceable. However, the House of Lords held that the option contract was complete and binding by implication from the terms of the 1930 contract, which had already been performed, and by expert evidence regarding recognized commercial practice in interpreting 'fair specification'.

The option clause had been part of what the claimants had paid for and to have found it unenforceable as being too vague would have been to deprive the claimants of part of their bargain. Therefore the preferable course was clearly to rescue this agreement, if at all possible.

The Court of Appeal in *Durham Tees Valley Airport Ltd v bmibaby Ltd* [2010] EWCA Civ 485, [2011] 1 All ER (Comm) 731, [2011] 1 Lloyd's Rep 68, also considered that there was sufficient evidence of the core obligations for a commercial agreement to be sufficiently certain.

The contract required the airline to base and fly two aircraft from a particular airport over a ten-year term. When the airline shut its base at the airport, the claimant sought damages. The Court of Appeal held that the agreement was not void for uncertainty since it contained sufficient terms to enable a court to give the agreement a practical meaning and to determine whether the airline was in breach. It was not necessary for the contract to specify a minimum number of flights or passengers. It followed that the alleged implied term (to operate from the airport in a manner that was reasonable in all of the circumstances) did not need to be found. The express terms sufficed. Toulson LJ stated, at [88]:

Where parties intend to create a contractual obligation, the court will try to give it legal effect. The court will only hold that the contract, or some part of it, is void for uncertainty, if it is legally or practically impossible to give to the agreement (or that part of it) any sensible content. (See *Scammell v Dicker* [2005] EWCA Civ 405, [2005] 3 All ER 838, para. 30, *per* Rix LJ.)

3.1.3.3 The significance of performance

The other significant factor in *Hillas and Co. v Arcos Ltd* (1932) 147 LT 503 was the fact that part of the contract, relating to supply in the 1930 season, had already been performed and, in general, *case law suggests that there is a reluctance to come to the conclusion that there is no valid agreement where there has been performance.* After all, if the parties have managed to perform an apparent agreement, it would appear odd if a court were to conclude that it is too vague to be capable of performance.

The importance of the 'executed agreement' factor in influencing the decision of courts was recognized by Cohen LJ in *British Bank for Foreign Trade Ltd v Novinex Ltd* [1949] 1 KB 623, at pp. 629–30, quoting Denning J, the judge at first instance. It was also more fully articulated in *Trentham Ltd v Archital Luxfer Ltd* [1993] 1 Lloyd's Rep 25, at p. 27, when Steyn LJ stressed that where both parties have partly or fully performed the apparent agreement, it will be 'unrealistic' to argue that an apparent agreement is void for vagueness or uncertainty. He added that 'the fact that the transaction is executed makes it easier to imply a term resolving any uncertainty, or, alternatively, it may make it possible to treat a matter not finalized in negotiations as inessential'. There is a similar comment concerning performance of a commercial contract and certainty of terms in the first instance judgment of Andrew Smith J in *Maple Leaf Macro Volatility Master Fund v Rouvroy* [2009] EWHC 257 (Comm), [2009] 2 All ER (Comm) 287, [2009] 1 Lloyd's Rep 475, at [235].

However, it must be clear from the decision in *British Steel Corporation v Cleveland Bridge & Engineering Co. Ltd* [1984] 1 All ER 504 (see **3.1.4.1**) that this 'executed factor' will enable a court to avoid a conclusion of vagueness or uncertainty only where there is sufficient agreement on essential terms. In this case, the parties entered into negotiations for the manufacture of steel nodes by the claimant. Before all the terms had been finalized, the defendant asked the claimant to start the manufacture of the nodes. No formal contract was ever concluded when the claimant had delivered all but one node. On that basis, Robert Goff J had concluded that there was too much that had yet to be agreed on the facts. It is therefore a question of degree and, despite performance, much will turn on whether important material terms have still to be agreed. In 'Contract law: fulfilling the reasonable expectations of honest men' (1997) 113 LQR 433, at p. 435, Lord Steyn, writing extrajudicially, explained:

> The greater the evidence of reliance, and the further along the road towards implementation the transaction is, the greater the prospect that the court will find a contract made and do its best, in accordance with the reasonable expectations of the parties, to spell out the terms of the contract.

The finding of 'contract' or 'no contract' makes the difference between the ability to rely on the contract terms, e.g. price and liquidated damages clause, or to resort to a possible restitutionary remedy, i.e. reasonable value of the performance assuming that a *quantum meruit* is available.

In *RTS Flexible Systems Ltd v Molkerei Alois Müller GmbH & Co. (UK Production)* [2010] UKSC 14, [2010] 1 WLR 753, [2010] Bus LR 776, the parties had entered negotiations for the manufacture of automated packaging machinery by the claimants. Work had initially been undertaken under a letter of intent (or intention to contract, hence 'subject to contract') and had continued after this expired, although some issues remained unresolved. The Supreme Court had to determine whether a contract had come into existence. It held that even if certain terms had not been finalized, where an objective appraisal of the parties' words and conduct led to the conclusion that they had not intended agreement on the terms outstanding to preclude agreement, but had reached agreement on all terms of 'economic significance', and where work had begun and there had been performance on both sides, it was possible to conclude that there was a legally binding agreement that was sufficiently certain. The conduct of the parties, including the fact that there had been 'substantial works carried out', led to the conclusion that the parties were proceeding with a contract on the basis of all the essential terms they had agreed. It followed that one of these agreed essential terms, the liquidated damages clause, was applicable.

Lord Clarke explained in *RTS* that the Supreme Court saw no conflict in the different outcomes in *Trentham v Architel Luxfer* (where a contract was found to exist) and the *British Steel* case (where no contract was found to exist). At [54], he said:

> Each case depends upon its own facts. We do not understand Steyn LJ [in *Trentham*] to be saying that it follows from the fact that the work was performed that the parties must have entered into a contract. On the other hand, it is plainly a very relevant factor pointing in that direction. Whether the court will hold that a binding contract was made depends upon all the circumstances of the case, of which that is but one. The decision in the *British Steel* case was simply one on the other side of the line. Robert Goff J was struck by the likelihood that parties would agree detailed provisions for matters such as liability for defects and concluded on the facts that no binding agreement had been reached.

In addition, the Supreme Court noted at [53] that, in the *British Steel* case, 'one set of terms provided no limit to the seller's liability for the delay and the other excluded such liability altogether'. The conclusion that there was no contract was hardly surprising!

In terms of the facts in *RTS Flexible*, Lord Clarke concluded, at [61]:

> The striking feature of this case which makes it very different from many of the cases which the courts have considered is that essentially all the terms were agreed between the parties and that substantial works were then carried out and the agreement was subsequently varied in important respects. The parties treated the agreement of 25 August as a variation of the agreement that they had reached by 5 July. Nobody suggested in August that there was no contract and thus nothing to vary. It was not until November, by which time the parties were in dispute, that points were taken as to whether there was a contract.

This enables the decision of the Court of Appeal in *Whittle Movers Ltd v Hollywood Express Ltd* [2009] EWCA Civ 1189, [2009] CLC 771 (see **3.1.5**), to be explained, since although performance had commenced there could be no contract, because the parties were still negotiating on important terms.

The Supreme Court in *RTS Flexible* also concluded that there was a contract despite the fact that a draft during negotiations had provided that the proposed contract could not take effect until formal documents had been executed—and this had not occurred. A similar provision in *Whittle* was a ground for concluding that there was no contract.

3.1.3.4 Severing meaningless clauses

Where a particular inessential term is vague, it may be possible to sever (remove) that term and enforce the rest of the agreement.

In **Nicolene Ltd v Simmonds** [1953] 1 QB 543, the agreement in question referred to acceptance as being on 'the usual conditions of acceptance' when there were no such 'usual conditions of acceptance'. The claimants, the buyers in the case, sought damages for breach of contract by the seller, and the seller argued that no contract had been concluded because of the uncertainty as to this term. However, the Court of Appeal rejected this argument, holding that, because this clause was meaningless, it could be severed from the rest of the agreement. Denning LJ expressly distinguished a meaningless clause (capable of being severed) from a clause on which agreement had not yet been reached (see **3.1.4**).

There is a discernible policy objective in this decision—namely, that without the application of severance in such circumstances, a party would be able to insert a meaningless clause in order to allow for a later escape route from the contract.

3.1.4 Agreements in which essential terms are missing

3.1.4.1 The general principle

Thus, as we have seen, as a general principle there needs to be agreement on all important terms or the agreement will be too uncertain to be enforceable. If important matters have yet to be agreed between the parties, the assumption must be that the parties are still negotiating and do not yet intend to be legally bound.

In **British Steel Corporation v Cleveland Bridge & Engineering Co. Ltd** [1984] 1 All ER 504, negotiations were entered into in anticipation of concluding a contract whereby the claimants would manufacture steel nodes for the defendants. Although all of the elements of the contract had not been agreed, both parties confidently expected that a contract would result. The defendants requested the claimants to commence the work before complete agreement was reached. However, agreement was never reached on some matters and no formal contract was concluded. The claimants had delivered all but one of the steel nodes and so sued the defendants for the value of the nodes on the basis of a *quantum meruit* (reasonable value). The defendants counterclaimed for breach of contract. Robert Goff J found that so much remained to be agreed (such as price, delivery dates, and liability for consequential loss and delay) that it was 'very difficult to see' how a contract had been formed. Accordingly, there could be no counterclaim for breach of contract.

The judge clearly considered that the defendants were largely responsible for the failure to agree. To have found a contract in the circumstances might have exposed the claimants to an action for breach of contract by the defendants, penalizing the claimants for something that, in the judge's view, was not their fault. However, it was held that the claimants could recover on a *quantum meruit* for the value of the nodes delivered because the defendants would otherwise have been unjustly enriched at the claimants' expense (see **3.1.5**).

3.1.4.2 Agreements to agree

If a matter is left to later agreement between the parties, then it will lack the necessary certainty.

In **May & Butcher v R** [1934] 2 KB 17, an agreement had been made for the sale of surplus war equipment to the claimants, the price being left to be agreed between the parties 'from time to time'. The parties were unable to agree, and the claimants sought to enforce the agreement at a 'reasonable price' to be determined by the court. The House of Lords refused to do this.

The point was not articulated as part of the reasoning, but there can be little doubt that the court's conclusion that no contract had come into existence was made much easier by the fact that no performance under the agreed terms had taken place.

In *Barbudev v Eurocom Cable Management Bulgaria EOOD* [2012] EWCA Civ 548, [2012] 2 All ER (Comm) 963, as a matter of construction, a side letter offering investment on 'terms to be agreed' was held not to constitute a legally enforceable contract, since it did not address essential terms for such an agreement; instead, it was an unenforceable agreement to agree.

However, this must be distinguished from situations where what appears to be a matter left open for later agreement may not be. In *Bell Scaffolding (Aust) Pty Ltd v Rekon Ltd* [2006] EWHC 2656 (TCC), [2007] CILL 2405, the judge concluded that a reference to 'agreed prices' was a reference to the claimant's price list. It did not mean 'prices to be agreed' and could therefore be clearly distinguished from an agreement to agree.

A further example of the reluctance of the English courts to enforce these 'agreements to agree' where there has been no performance under the terms of the alleged contract is provided by the decision of the House of Lords in *Walford v Miles* [1992] 2 AC 128.

> In **Walford v Miles**, the parties, negotiating for the sale and purchase of a business, had entered into a 'lock-out agreement', the purported effect of which was to prevent the respondent prospective sellers from negotiating with anyone other than the appellants. Negotiations were unsuccessful and, after a time, the respondents decided to sell to a third party. The appellants then brought an action for breach of the 'lock-out agreement'. The agreement was found to be unenforceable.

According to Lord Ackner, the fatal weakness of the agreement was that it was indefinite in length. It was a bare agreement to negotiate and therefore without legal force.

The House of Lords rejected the argument that such an agreement could be made sufficiently certain because there was an implied duty placed on a party who had agreed to a lock-out to negotiate in good faith with the other party in order to reach agreement. Such a position was regarded as 'irreconcilable with the adversarial nature of the parties when involved in contract negotiations': *per* Lord Ackner at p. 138.

More recently, in *Shaker v Vistajet Group Holdings SA* [2012] EWHC 1329 (Comm), [2012] 2 All ER (Comm) 1010, [2012] 2 Lloyd's Rep 93, the court had to decide whether an agreement to agree was enforceable. In this instance, the agreement was to proceed in good faith and to use reasonable endeavours to agree the Transaction Documents and obtain written confirmation from the financing party in relation to an agreement. Teare J, at [7], explained why agreements to agree are unenforceable in English law:

> The reason for such unenforceability is that there are no objective criteria by which the court can decide whether a party has acted unreasonably and that a duty to negotiate in good faith is unworkable because it is inherently inconsistent with the position of a negotiating party.

Nevertheless, the House of Lords in *Walford v Miles* had concluded that, had the 'lock-out agreement' stipulated a period of time during which exclusive negotiations were to take place, it would have been enforceable, because the element of uncertainty would have been removed. Lord Ackner's *dictum* to this effect was followed by the Court of Appeal in *Pitt v PHH Asset Management Ltd* [1994] 1 WLR 327, in relation to a 'lock-out' agreement for a two-week period. In the case of enforceable 'lock-out agreements', the remedy for breach will focus on the purchaser's wasted costs (see **9.3.5**), and since the transaction may not have proceeded in any event, the measure of damages might be restricted to the additional costs wasted as a result of the vendor's breach of the 'lock-out'.

3.1.4.2.1 *Express provisions requiring parties to negotiate in good faith or to use reasonable endeavours*

It is important to bear in mind that the decision in *Walford v Miles* [1992] 2 AC 128, that there could be no *implied* duty to negotiate in good faith, was made in the context of negotiations that were expressly made 'subject to contract'. Unlike in *Walford v Miles*, in which the argument had been to *imply* a duty to negotiate in good faith, in *Petromec Inc. v Petroleo Brasileiro SA Petrobas (No. 3)* [2005] EWCA Civ 891, [2006] 1 Lloyd's Rep 121, the Court of Appeal had to consider whether the courts should enforce an *express provision in a commercial contract* requiring the parties to negotiate in good faith in respect of the cost of certain contractual extras. The arguments against such recognition, based on *Walford v Miles*, were that the obligation was no more than an agreement to agree, so that it was too uncertain to be enforced and it was difficult or impossible to say whether any termination of negotiations was the result of bad faith. Walford was therefore distinguished by Longmore LJ in *Petromec*. The court held that it was not bound by *Walford v Miles* on the basis that in *Petromec*, the agreement contained an express term to negotiate in good faith and that, on the contrary, in *Walford v Miles* 'there was no concluded agreement at all since everything was "subject to contract", there was moreover, no express agreement to negotiate in good faith' (at [120]). As a result, an express obligation to negotiate in good faith would be enforceable as otherwise it would be 'a strong thing to declare unenforceable, a clause which the parties have deliberately and expressly entered' (at [121]).

The Court of Appeal—see, in particular, the judgment of Longmore LJ at [115]–[121]—reached the following conclusions.

1. That this was an agreement to agree was irrelevant, since this was an obligation contained in an agreement that was itself legally enforceable.

2. It would be relatively easy to determine the actual costs in question and therefore it ought not to be difficult to determine what the result of good faith negotiations would be. This disposed of the argument that it could never be known whether agreement would have been reached and what its terms would have been, so that it would have been impossible to assess loss caused by breach of the obligation.

3. Although 'bad faith' withdrawal from negotiations (and hence identification of a breach of such a duty) was 'somewhat elusive' as a concept, this case could be clearly distinguished from *Walford v Miles* in which there had been no concluded agreement between the parties, in which all negotiations were 'subject to contract', and in which there was no express undertaking to negotiate in good faith. Here, the express agreement to negotiate was contained in a complex commercial agreement reached between the parties, and it would defeat the expressed intentions and reasonable expectations of the parties to deny the enforceability of that express obligation.

On the facts, however, it was held that there had been no breach of the obligation to negotiate in good faith.

The second point above is significant in terms of the ability to accept an express provision to negotiate in good faith, i.e. it must be possible for the court to conduct the exercise of fixing the cost or price in question. In *Shaker v Vistajet Group Holdings SA* [2012] EWHC 1329 (Comm), [2012] 2 All ER (Comm) 1010, [2012] 2 Lloyd's Rep 93, at [17], in the context of an agreement to use reasonable endeavours to agree, Teare J distinguished *Petromec* on the basis that, in that case, there were objective criteria by which to assess the extra costs in the absence of agreement. In *Shaker*, however, there were no objective criteria by which to judge whether there had been 'reasonable endeavours'. This emphasis on the need for objective criteria reflected Teare J's earlier judgment in *Dhanani v Crasnianski* [2011] EWHC 926 (Comm), [2011] 2 All ER (Comm) 799, in which he had held that since a signed letter and term sheet contained no indication of any objective criteria by reference to which agreement was to be reached on those matters that had not been agreed, it constituted an unenforceable agreement to agree on the exact structure of the funding to be provided. Further reference to 'objective criteria' can be found in *Dany Lions Ltd v Bristol Cars Ltd* [2014] EWHC 817 (QB), [2014] 2 All ER (Comm) 403, [2014] Bus LR D11 (see also **13.2.1**) there was an agreement to settle a dispute in relation to a contract concerning a vintage car which BC Ltd was unable to perform. This provided that DL Ltd was to use reasonable endeavours to enter into a reconditioning contract with a specialist restorer. Andrews J held that this settlement agreement was not legally binding because they were important matters left open for negotiation and there were no objective criteria to determine whether it was reasonable for DL Ltd to agree or refuse to agree any particular terms proposed. Although it is therefore a matter of context and fact as to whether the clause will be sufficiently certain to be valid, in the more recent case of *Astor Management AG v Atalaya Mining plc* [2017] EWHC 425 (Comm), [2017] 1 Lloyd's Rep 476, Leggatt J (as he then was) reiterated that the '*role of the court in a commercial dispute is to give effect to what the parties have agreed*' (at [64], emphasis added) even when the contractual provisions in question 'are cast in very open-ended language' (at [65]). In this case, the court agreed that the clause requiring a party to agree to use reasonable endeavours to obtain a particular form of finance referred to as a 'senior debt facility' (an agreement to agree) was valid, although, on the facts, it had not been breached. Leggatt J added that 'far from being exceptional, it should almost always be possible to give sensible content to [such an undertaking]' (at [67]). To do so 'is a question of fact which a court can perfectly well decide to do' (at [67]). Furthermore, the 'difficulty of proving a breach of a contractual obligation is not . . . a reason to hold that there is no obligation' (at [67]). Nor did the court find that as an alternative there was an implied obligation of good faith (at [97]–[99]). A similar emphasis on the duty of the court to try to give effect to the parties' intention can also be seen in Mrs Justice Rose's judgment in *Associated British Ports v Tata Steel UK Ltd* [2017] EWHC 694 (Ch), [2017] 2 Lloyd's Rep 11 (at [26–35]).

In relation to the third point in *Petromec*, that of the recognition of an obligation to negotiate in good faith, the general acceptance of such express clauses appears to be confirmed by Leggatt J in *Knatchbull-Hugessen and others v SISU Capital Ltd* [2014] EWHC 1194 (Comm), where he stated that it is now 'generally accepted that [a contract] may impose an obligation on one or both parties to conduct negotiations in good faith' (at [23]). He then added, for the avoidance of doubt, that in the event of breach of such a clause, cost and expenses can be recovered if the negotiations are cut short (at [23]). The *Knatchbull-Hugessen* case however raised the issue of *implying* a term that would extend an express obligation to negotiate in good faith beyond the agreed six-months exclusivity period. This was rejected as contrary to the express parties' intention (at [28]). It is however clear that such an obligation can only be accepted if expressly provided. Moreover, as reiterated more recently in *Rosalina Investments Ltd v New Balance Athletic Shoes (UK) Ltd* [2018] EWHC 1014 (QB), the courts are bound by the restrictions of *Petromec*. Indeed, as was made clear by May J in this case, this cannot therefore be used as a tactic by one party to argue that a contract has come to existence (at [52]).

Thus, although English law does not recognize a general (or implied) duty to negotiate in good faith—see comments by Lord Steyn (1997) 113 LQR 433, at p. 439—it will clearly be prepared to recognize an express provision in a concluded contract to negotiate in good faith or other similar open-ended clauses such as use reasonable endeavours to reach a particular issue where there are clear objective criteria on which to make the calculation in question. This position may usefully be compared with the recognition of a duty to negotiate in good faith in other jurisdictions, such as Germany, and the provisions of attempted codifications of contractual principles (see **1.6.1**) and through an international lens. Article 2:301 of the Principles of European Contract Law (PECL) is in the same terms, as is Art. 2.1.15 of the UNIDROIT's Principles of International Commercial Contracts (PICC). A contract to negotiate in good faith is also recognized in the United States: see *Channel Home Centers Division of Grace Retail Corporation v Grossman*, 795 F 2d 291 (1986).

3.1.4.3 Agreements to agree a price: The significance of performance

In English law, even where there is only an agreement between the parties to agree a price, it seems that the courts will enforce that agreement if at all possible once performance has begun.

In *Foley v Classique Coaches Ltd* [1934] 2 KB 1, the parties had made an agreement for the supply of the defendants' petrol requirements, at a price to be agreed from time to time. The contract included an arbitration clause and was linked to a deal whereby the defendants purchased a parcel of land from the claimant. Performance continued without incident for three years before the defendants argued that this contract was unenforceable because the price clause was uncertain. The Court of Appeal found that the agreement was enforceable, the defendants having to pay a 'reasonable price' for petrol supplied. What was reasonable in the circumstances might be determined, if necessary, by arbitration.

In part, it seems that it was the fact of actual performance, including the conveyance of the parcel of land and the danger of depriving the claimant of one important element of the bargain, which persuaded the Court of Appeal. It is interesting to note that the court did not allow the decision of the House of Lords in *May and Butcher v R* [1934] 2 KB 17 (see **3.1.4.2**) to dissuade it from reaching this conclusion. It seems, therefore, that uncertainty as to price is not as a matter of law always fatal to an agreement; rather, it is a question of construction of the contract in each case. The most obvious distinguishing feature between the two cases, however, is the lack of performance in one and the substantial performance in the other.

It is also clear that, as long as there is initial agreement on the price in a continuing contract, the contract is sufficiently certain.

In *Mamidoil-Jetoil Greek Petroleum Co. SA v Okta Crude Oil Refinery (No. 1)* [2001] EWCA Civ 406, [2001] 2 Lloyd's Rep 76, the fee for the first two years of a ten-year contract was fixed at the outset. The fee for the remaining eight years of the term was left to be fixed, although the evidence was that agreement had in fact been reached for four of these years. On this basis, the Court of Appeal rejected the argument that there was an 'agreement to agree' the fee so that the agreement was uncertain. Instead, the court held that, in the event of a failure to fix the fee in the latter years of the term, a term would be implied allowing for a reasonable fee to be fixed.

This decision represents a practical recognition of the fact that, in the case of continuing contracts, it may not be practical or feasible to fix all matters at the outset of the contractual term. There was a sufficiently certain contract at the outset and, on that basis, 'the courts will seek to make it work': *per* Rix LJ, at [73]. This point was also approved in *Bell Scaffolding (Aust) Pty Ltd v Rekon Ltd* [2006] EWHC 2656 (TCC), [2007] CILL 2405 (see **3.1.4.2**), in that although it was envisaged that the prices in the price list might change over time, those prices would remain as the applicable prices until a new agreement was reached and the court 'would strive to preserve the contract once there had been performance': *per* Ramsey J, at [89].

3.1.4.4 Mechanisms for determining the price

3.1.4.4.1 No mechanism for fixing the price

Section 8 of the Sale of Goods Act (SGA) 1979 provides:

> (1) The price in a contract of sale may be fixed by the contract, or may be left to be fixed in a manner agreed by the contract, or may be determined by the course of dealing between the parties.
>
> (2) Where the price is not determined as mentioned in subsection (1) above the buyer must pay a reasonable price.

In *May and Butcher v R* [1934] 2 KB 17, Lord Dunedin suggested that s. 8(2) (then SGA 1893)—and the ability to fix a reasonable price—applies *only* where the contract is silent as to price and does not apply where a price-fixing mechanism has failed to work. Such an interpretation reflects the words of s. 8, but seems to be unduly narrow and to fly in the face of logic. To say nothing at all about price is surely less certain than to attempt to make a flexible provision, which takes into account the changing value of money through time.

For a more recent application of the validity of an agreement to agree under the SGA 1979 we can cite *Hughes v Pendragon Sabre Ltd (t/a Porsche Centre Bolton)* [2016] EWCA Civ 18, [2017] 1 All ER (Comm) 173, where it was held that a collateral contract for the sale of a Porsche had been created even though there was no price, specification of the car, or a delivery date.

The same term imposing a reasonable price or charge in the absence of an express provision or express mechanism for fixing the charge also applies in relation to a contract to supply a service (Supply of Goods and Services Act (SGSA) 1982, s. 15 (B2B—business to business) and the Consumer Rights Act (CRA) 2015, s. 51 (B2C—'trader' to 'consumer')). It is interesting that s. 8 SGA 1979 applies in both contexts and there is no separate treatment in the CRA 2015. The result is that some provisions of the SGA 1979 remain of relevance to consumers.

3.1.4.4.2 The price-fixing mechanism fails to work

1. The principle in *Sudbrook Trading Estate Ltd v Eggleton*

May and Butcher v R [1934] 2 KB 17 was distinguished in *Sudbrook Trading Estate Ltd v Eggleton* [1983] 1 AC 444.

> In **Sudbrook Trading v Eggleton**, a lease contained an option to purchase the land in question at a price to be agreed by two valuers, one to be nominated by each party. The lessors refused to appoint a valuer and claimed that the option clause was unenforceable because the price term was uncertain. The House of Lords refused to find the clause unenforceable and held that if the parties have provided sensible, but subsidiary and non-essential, machinery for fixing a fair price, and that machinery had for some reason broken down, then the court should attempt to take the place of that machinery by identifying a fair and reasonable price.

Lord Diplock's speech distinguishes this position from a case in which an individual is specifically named in the clause as being given the responsibility to determine the important matter, in which case the contract would be frustrated if that person were then unable to make a determination through no fault of either of the parties, e.g. as a result of the death of the person named.

No doubt their Lordships were influenced in their conclusion that this clause was inessential by the fact that there had been considerable performance of the main contract and there would be a danger of the lessee being deprived of an important part of its bargain had a contrary result been reached. Lord Fraser stressed that although it might appear logical for the courts to refuse to substitute their own machinery for that provided by the parties, such a practice would be commercially inconvenient, because the inevitable consequence would be that such an agreement would be void. He also highlighted the fact that it was the lessors who, in not making the appointment, were preventing the machinery from operating, thereby depriving the lessees of this benefit.

2. Limiting the principle in *Sudbrook v Eggleton*

Sudbrook Trading Estate Ltd v Eggleton [1983] 1 AC 444 was distinguished by the Court of Appeal in *Gillatt v Sky Television Ltd* [2000] 1 All ER (Comm) 461, in the context of an argument to enforce a single payment provision. The Court of Appeal in *Gillatt* had no incentive to substitute its own machinery, since the agreement itself would not be rendered void. In addition, the party requesting the court to substitute its own machinery had the ability (but had failed) to make the necessary appointment itself.

In **Gillatt**, Sky had acquired shares in Tele-Aerials Satellite Ltd (TAS) by an agreement that provided (in clause 6) that if Sky were to sell or dispose of this shareholding, Sky would pay Mallard Ltd '55 per cent of the open market value of such shares . . . as determined by an independent chartered accountant'. Mallard Ltd had subsequently assigned (transferred) this right to Gillatt. Sky later transferred its shares to a wholly owned subsidiary, and Gillatt claimed to be entitled to the payment under clause 6. The trial judge accepted that the value of the shares had to be determined within a reasonable time after the sale of the shares. However, neither Gillatt, nor Sky, nor Mallard had taken any steps to appoint the independent accountant to determine the value of the shares and, since a reasonable time had elapsed, it was no longer possible to do so. Gillatt argued that this requirement to appoint an independent accountant to determine the value of the shares was intended only as a description of the machinery to be applied if there were any dispute between the parties and was not an essential precondition to the existence of any entitlement under the clause. This argument relied on *Sudbrook* as authority to support the principle that 'where the machinery is not essential, if it breaks down for any reason the court will substitute its own machinery'.

However, the Court of Appeal reached the following conclusions:

1. The valuation requirement in *Gillatt* was both integral and essential, and the clause did not contain any other objective criteria in order to determine the value of the shares because there was no definition of 'open market value' (despite the fact that there were many ways of calculating this). This indicated that the parties had agreed to leave this to the independent chartered accountant, and it was the duty of the court to give effect to this intention rather than to make its own valuation.

2. This was also not a case involving a breakdown of the contractual machinery, since neither party had attempted to make the necessary appointment.

It had also been thought that, where a particular person was not named in the clause, that machinery was more likely to be regarded as non-essential on the basis that a decision to name a person indicated that this machinery was regarded as essential because certain skills, which this individual possessed, were required by the parties. This was strongly argued by counsel for Mr Gillatt, but was not regarded as significant by the Court of Appeal in the light of the other evidence. More fundamentally, it is clear that the principle in *Sudbrook* cannot be relied upon in the absence of any evidence of objective criteria intended by the parties to be used in determining the price: *Gillatt v Sky Television Ltd* and *Baird Textile Holdings Ltd v Marks & Spencer plc* [2001] EWCA Civ 274, [2002] 1 All ER (Comm) 737 (see **3.1.3.2**).

It would also appear that the principle in *Sudbrook* (where the court will attempt to fix a price) will in future be confined to cases in which the breakdown in the machinery is attributable to the fault of one of the parties in not cooperating and that party is now citing this breakdown as the basis for the allegation that the contract is void, as opposed to arguing for a substitute mechanism because the original mechanism has failed. This is a matter of policy based on the argument being employed—i.e. in *Sudbrook*, the party claiming that the contract was void was the party who had caused the failure of the original machinery, and the court was clearly reluctant to support such a practice by accepting this conclusion. Similar policy arguments prevailed in *Gillatt*, in which a party who had not activated the original machinery was asking the court to override what the parties had agreed and to substitute something different. Not surprisingly, the court refused to accede to this request.

Gillatt v Sky Television was followed by the Court of Appeal in *Infiniteland Ltd v Artisan Contracting Ltd* [2005] EWCA Civ 758, [2006] 1 BCLC 632, in preference to *Sudbrook Trading Estate v Eggleton* because (a) the machinery for price adjustment was considered to be essential, and (b) it had not broken down, since, as in *Gillatt*, it had failed to operate owing to the failure of the party seeking the adjustment to operate the machinery provided for in the clause. Infiniteland, as the purchaser, was required by the clause to produce a calculation of net asset value as the first step in the procedure and it had failed to do so. Chadwick LJ stated, at [59]:

I can see no reason, in principle, why a party, say 'A', who chooses not to allow the contractual machinery to operate should be able to ask the court, nevertheless, to enforce the contract against the other party, say 'B'. It is no answer, in such a case, to say that the machinery is non-essential. It is the machinery upon which the parties agreed when they made their bargain. A cannot be heard to insist on the agreed machinery—as a defence to a claim made against him—if it is he who has not allowed it to operate. But, equally, as it seems to me, in such a case A cannot insist on imposing on B other machinery to which B has never agreed. B is not to be denied the benefit of the machinery to which he has agreed—in resisting a claim made against him—by A's unilateral refusal to allow that machinery to operate.

⚙ SUMMARY

It is quite common for a contract to leave certain matters (obligations) to be agreed upon at a later date. Such 'agreements to agree' as they are referred to come in various guises, e.g. an obligation to negotiate in good faith (or use reasonable endeavours), or an agreement on the price of the subject matter of the contract to be decided in the future. Regardless of what it is that is left to be agreed, the main question is whether such agreements are sufficiently certain to be enforceable. As remarked by Justice Cranston for the Court of Appeal in *Hughes v Pendragon Sabre Ltd (t/a Porsche Centre Bolton)*, in modern times, the courts are, as a matter of general

»

principle, readier to find a contract even when elements are missing (at [30]). It seems that the important elements for deciding that an agreement to agree is enforceable are the clarity of terms and the intention of the parties: where the parties have made use of clear means by which to ascertain the terms to be agreed.

3.1.5 Recovery where a contract fails to materialize

As was seen in *British Steel Corporation v Cleveland Bridge and Engineering* [1984] 1 All ER 504 (see **3.1.4.1**), even where the court concludes that no agreement was reached between the parties because essential terms are missing, it may still be prepared to order that the recipient should pay a sum to cover the reasonable value of the performance received where that performance was requested by that party. The basis for this award is restitution—namely, that to allow the recipient to retain the promised performance would result in that party being unjustly enriched at the expense of the performing party.

The Court of Appeal, in *Whittle Movers Ltd v Hollywood Express Ltd* [2009] EWCA Civ 1189, [2009] CLC 771, expressly considered that courts should 'not strain to find a contract' where the parties were still negotiating as to terms, but some performance had commenced. A restitutionary solution was the appropriate response.

3.1.5.1 Generally no recovery for expenses incurred during the negotiation process

However, this possibility of recovery does not apply generally to expenses incurred during the negotiation process in preparation for the contract. This was made clear in the decision of Rattee J in *Regalian Properties plc v London Dockland Development Corporation* [1995] 1 All ER 1005. The judge stated that, in the absence of an express contractual undertaking to cover such costs, the words 'subject to contract' made it clear that each party was free to withdraw from negotiations at any time and that each party incurred pre-contractual costs at its own risk: see also *Benourad v Compass Group plc* [2010] EWHC 1882 (QB). In addition, it was possible to distinguish *British Steel Corporation v Cleveland Bridge* on the basis that, in that case, the claimants had sought to recover for the 'accelerated performance of the anticipated contract' where that performance had been requested by the defendants, whereas in *Regalian*, the claimants had incurred expenses in the form of payment of professional fees for designs to enable them *to obtain and perform the contract*. There was therefore not the same benefit to the defendant.

On the facts in *Regalian*, the judge also found that the contract did not materialize because of the failure to agree on the price and not, as had been alleged by the claimants, because the defendant decided to abandon the project. Rattee J did not deal with the position in which the negotiations were not 'subject to contract' and in which they broke down because of the unilateral decision by one party to abandon the project. However, in *Countrywide Communications Ltd v ICL Pathway Ltd* [2000] CLC 324, there was fault.

3.1.5.2 Exceptional cases in which it is possible to recover for expenses incurred in anticipation of a contract that does not materialize: *Countrywide Communications*

The claimant in ***Countrywide Communications Ltd v ICL Pathway Ltd*** [2000] CLC 324 had carried out public relations (PR) work in connection with a successful bid that had been made by the defendant to supply a system for the payment of benefits. The claimant had been assured that it would be appointed if the bid were to succeed, but on the success of the bid, the defendant appointed another consultancy.

> It was held that the claimant was entitled to payment (£38,370) for the time that it had spent and to cover its costs on the basis that (a) there was fault on the part of the defendant, and (b) the services in question were of benefit to the defendant.

The judge, Nicholas Strauss QC, stressed that this did not allow for any general recovery of costs incurred in tendering or preparing for a hoped-for contract—although see *Blackpool and Fylde Aero Club v Blackpool Borough Council* [1990] 1 WLR 1195 (at **2.3.2.4**), in which an obligation to consider conforming tenders was implied and, in the event of breach of this promise, contractual damages would be available that might be based on loss of chance or wasted expenditure.

The judge in *Countrywide Communications*, at p. 349, identified a number of factors to consider in deciding whether it was possible on a particular set of facts (referred to as 'exceptional cases') to recover for expenditure incurred in anticipation of a contract that did not materialize. These factors comprised:

1. whether the services were of a kind that would normally be given free of charge;

2. the terms in which the request to perform the services was made, which may be important in establishing the extent of the risk (if any) that any claimants may fairly be said to have taken that such services would, in the end, be unrecompensed (being linked to the issue of whether the parties were expressly or impliedly negotiating 'subject to contract', or whether one party had given an assurance that it would not withdraw in these circumstances);

3. whether the services were of real benefit to the defendant, so that he could be said to be unjustly enriched at that claimant's expense (clearly important in light of *Regalian Properties plc v London Dockland Development Corporation* [1995] 1 All ER 1005, although Denning LJ in *Brewer Street Investments Ltd v Barclays Woollen Co. Ltd* [1954] 1 QB 428 had regarded the fact that the services were requested as being a benefit in itself); and

4. the circumstances in which the contract failed to materialize (i.e. any fault on the part of the defendant, so that the circumstances are outside the risk undertaken by the claimant).

In addition, the judge stressed that recovery was unlikely if the expense was not incurred in the course of providing services requested by the defendant and that the weight to be given to each of these factors would vary from case to case.

3.1.5.3 Conclusion

Although English law does not expressly recognize any general duty of good faith in contract negotiations, there are nevertheless clear indicators here of some recognition of principles of fair dealing through the use of restitutionary principles to recompense a party who has performed services at the request of the other party, where that party has been expressly led to believe that it will be awarded the contract to which those services relate.

3.2 Agreement mistake

By 'agreement mistake', we mean that one or both of the parties made a fundamental mistake relating to the terms of the contract (i.e. an 'offer and acceptance' mistake), which prevents the formation of an agreement, although the parties may well subjectively believe that they are in agreement. Peel, in *Treitel's The Law of Contract*, 14th edn (Sweet and Maxwell, 2015), [8-001], refers to these mistakes as 'negativing consent'.

There is another category of mistake in English law that does not relate to the issue of reaching agreement. This occurs where both parties do not deny that they reached agreement, but allege that this agreement is impossible to perform because they both made a fundamental mistake (see common or shared mistake, in **Chapter 13**).

3.2.1 The doctrine of mistake in English law

It has been argued that English law really knows no independent doctrine of mistake and that those cases in which apparent mistake has resulted in a contract being set aside involve the application to the particular situation of established rules of the law of contract, such as the rules of offer and acceptance. While the rules of offer and acceptance play an increasingly important role, there is evidence of identifiable principles relating to mistake, although such a doctrine of mistake is nevertheless extremely limited.

Indeed, much of what passes for mistake can be explained in terms of other rules of English law that have been dressed up in language borrowed from the civil law and which are arguably inappropriate to the common law conception of contract. The reason for this civil law influence appears to be that the writing of systematic legal treatises began in France much earlier than it did in England and that, at the end of the eighteenth century and the beginning of the nineteenth century, the writings of the celebrated French lawyer, Pothier, gained a certain currency in England. The transference of the notion of mistake from one legal system to the other was misguided, however, since French law at the time was committed to a much more subjective approach to the formation of contracts than ever prevailed in England.

3.2.2 The effect of mistake on a contract

One reason for the limited doctrine of mistake in English law is that where mistake operates, it usually makes the contract void, i.e. there is no contract and the law takes the view that there never has been a contract. The wider impact of this conclusion is such that the courts appear to have been unwilling to extend the mistake doctrine.

The fact that the contract is void is of fundamental importance in the context of sale of goods: if no contract ever existed, title to the property (i.e. ownership rights, and the ability to transfer ownership and possession), which is the subject matter of the sale, cannot have passed between seller and buyer (on this and the wider consequences in the context of the Sale of Goods Act 1979, see Tettenborn, 'Transfer of chattels by non-owners: still an open problem' (2018) 77 CLP 151–78). By contrast, if a sale of goods contract is voidable (i.e. valid until set aside), as for example in the case of a contract induced by misrepresentation (see generally **Chapter 14**), title does pass.

It is the fact that title does not pass under contracts that are void for mistake that has made mistake an attractive doctrine to claimants, but has left the courts uneasy about its application.

3.2.2.1 The effect if the contract is void for mistake

Where a contract is void for mistake, the seller has not lost title to the goods in question and is therefore entitled to the return of the actual goods, or their monetary equivalent, by virtue of possessing rights of ownership. If the contract is void and the goods have passed out of the hands of the original buyer into the hands of a third party who knows nothing of the dealings between seller and buyer (known as an 'innocent' third party), the seller is nevertheless entitled to the return of the goods because it is the seller who retains title.

However, if the contract were merely voidable (liable to be set aside by the remedy of rescission) and, before the time of the seller's claim, the buyer had disposed of the goods to an innocent third party, the third party would be protected from recovery of the goods by the original seller because rescission is a personal remedy and not available against a third party.

3.2.2.2 Two 'innocent' parties

It is true that both the original seller and the third party into whose hands the goods have passed are 'innocent', so that it is unfortunate that either should suffer. Nevertheless, it is generally considered that the original seller is in a better position to guard against mistake than the third party, who played no part in the transaction between seller and buyer. It would be somewhat harsh, therefore, for the third party to be the person who suffers. However, this will be the inevitable result where the original seller retains title to the goods because the contract was void. It is probably for this reason that, traditionally, the English courts have been unwilling to extend the doctrine of mistake beyond its narrow bounds and have generally preferred to avoid the conclusion that the contract is void for mistake—although see the impact of policy and contextual considerations in *Shogun Finance Ltd v Hudson* [2003] UKHL 62, [2004] 1 AC 919.

3.3 Types of mistake negativing agreement

Agreement mistakes occur where, despite what one or other party may assert, it is impossible to identify objective evidence of agreement from what has passed between the parties (see **2.1**). For that reason, these mistakes are sometimes called 'mistakes negativing consent'. Problems occur when one of the parties asserts that an agreement exists on the basis of the terms as *that party* understood them. Cases fall into two categories:

1. those in which the parties are genuinely at cross-purposes, so that each party makes a mistake, but the mistakes are different (see **3.3.1**); and

2. unilateral mistakes, in which only one party is mistaken, but the other either knows (or ought to know) of the mistake (see **3.3.2**).

Instances of either type of mistake being claimed successfully are comparatively rare. The conclusion must consequently be that, in this context, mistake is a very narrow doctrine unlikely to afford relief in the majority of cases.

3.3.1 Cross-purposes mistake

Mistakes in which the parties are at cross-purposes are sometimes referred to as 'mutual mistakes', although care must be taken with this expression because it has also been used, especially by nineteenth-century courts, to describe shared or common mistakes. (In the case of shared or common mistake, the parties do not deny that they reach agreement, but it is alleged that the contract is impossible to perform because both parties entered into the contract on the basis of the same fundamental mistaken assumption (see **Chapter 13**).

In the case of mutual or cross-purposes mistakes, the problem is that although one or both parties may assert that a contract exists, each on terms favourable to that party, on an objective interpretation it is impossible to resolve the ambiguity over what was agreed, so that the only possible conclusion is that there is no contract. In fact, when stated in this way, it is clear that the rule is not peculiar to the law on mistake. It is the same rule examined in relation to the formation of agreements and certainty of terms (see **2.1** and **3.1.3.1**). Thus the famous old case of *Raffles v Wichelhaus* (1864) 2 Hurl & C 906 (two ships named *Peerless* sailing from Bombay) has been treated as an instance of cross-purposes mistake (see **3.1.3.1** for a full discussion).

In **Scriven Bros. and Co. v Hindley and Co.** [1913] 3 KB 564, two lots taken from the cargo of a single ship were put up for sale by auction. Inspection would have revealed that one was hemp and one was tow, but the auction catalogue did not reveal this. The lots carried the same shipping marks, and the custom of the trade was that different cargoes would not normally have the same marks. The buyers bid for both lots, having inspected the hemp, but not the tow, in the mistaken belief that both lots were hemp. The buyers had therefore agreed to pay well over the market price for the lot that was tow. The sellers brought an action against the buyers to recover the price of the tow, and the buyers alleged that they had not agreed to buy the tow and that a mistake had been made.

After considering the evidence, the court allowed the defendants to avoid the contract on the basis that there had been no agreement. Both parties' interpretations were equally plausible in an objective sense.

A reasonable person in the position of the defendant buyers would reasonably have concluded that the lots being sold with the same shipping marks were the same and the evidence was that the auctioneer realized only that the defendants had made a mistake as to the value of the goods being sold, but would not have realized that the defendants thought both lots were hemp. Since it was impossible to say what should have been understood from the lots on display, the decision that there was no contract is justifiable.

3.3.1.1 The objective test

Thus the courts apply the objective test to the question of the existence of agreement and ask whether one party's interpretation is more reasonable than the other's.

Smith v Hughes (1871) LR 6 QB 597 (see **3.3.2.1**), the leading case on the meaning of objectivity, involved an allegation of cross-purposes mistake, but the court concluded that since, on an objective assessment, there was symmetry between what was offered and what was accepted, the contract should be upheld.

In **Smith v Hughes**, the claimant offered to sell oats to the defendant. On delivery, it was discovered that the oats were 'new' and thus of no use to the defendant, who required 'old' oats (i.e. the previous season's oats). The defendant then refused to pay, claiming that the contract was void for mistake. The court rejected this defence. The mere fact that one party had deluded himself into entering into a contract that was of no advantage to him did not enable the court to say that there was no contract in the absence of any express mention by the defendant that he required 'old' oats.

3.3.1.2 A fault doctrine?

It is difficult in relation to these cases to resist the inference that the courts sometimes (although not always) apply an unarticulated fault doctrine. Where a genuine situation of cross-purposes is seen to exist and one party is seen as responsible for provoking the mistake, the court will decide in favour of the other party. Depending on the facts and which party is seeking enforcement, this may involve a finding that there was a contract or that there was no contract.

> In **Scriven Bros. and Co. v Hindley and Co.** [1913] 3 KB 564, the auctioneer who sought to enforce the contract had provoked the mistake by failing to make clear the distinction between the bales of hemp and tow, although they had the same shipping marks, and by producing a catalogue that was unclear and misleading.

The court refused to enforce the contract at the request of the auctioneer, Lawrence J stating (at p. 569):

> [I]t was peculiarly the duty of the auctioneer to make it clear to the bidder . . . which lots were hemp and which lots were tow . . . [A] contract cannot arise when the person seeking to enforce it has by his own negligence, or by that of those for whom he is responsible, caused, or contributed to cause, the mistake.

Of course, the defendants had not investigated both lots, but the court recognized that the defendants owed no *duty* to examine the samples of tow.

The decision to enforce the alleged contract in *Smith v Hughes* (1871) LR 6 QB 597 can be explained in similar terms. The party seeking to resist enforcement of the contract (the buyer) had contributed to, or provoked, the mistake by not indicating clearly that 'old' oats were required and could not then be heard to say that there was no contract. The court therefore held that there was a contract.

Similarly, in *Tamplin v James* (1880) 15 Ch D 215, the defendant clearly misunderstood the offer that he accepted. He thought he was buying an inn and adjoining gardens of a property well known to him. In fact, the sale particulars were clear that the gardens were not included in the property on offer, but the defendant had not bothered to examine these particulars and so was at fault. It followed that, objectively, there was agreement, and at first instance Baggallay LJ granted specific performance (i.e. an order enforcing performance of the contract in accordance with its terms) against the defendant, saying, at pp. 217–18:

> [W]here there has been no misrepresentation, and where there is no ambiguity in the terms of the contract, the defendant cannot be allowed to evade the performance of it by the simple statement that he has made a mistake. Were such to be the law the performance of a contract could rarely be enforced upon an unwilling party who was also unscrupulous.

The claimant was unaware of the mistake being made by the defendant and, if specific performance had been refused, would have been forced to find another buyer as a result of the reckless conduct of the defendant buyer.

3.3.2 Unilateral mistake

In some situations, it is said that only one of the parties is mistaken. However, as can be seen from the discussion of the case law concerning cross-purposes mistake (at **3.3.1**), this is in fact no more than another way of saying that one party's understanding and the objectively observed agreement coincide, and the other party's understanding is out of line.

In such circumstances, the objectivity principle determines that there is a contract on the objectively observed terms, which will be enforced by the courts. However, the courts will ignore the objectivity principle where it appears that the party whose understanding coincides with the objective agreement was aware that the other party was labouring under a mistake and failed to draw the attention of that other to that mistake. Indeed, the courts will go further and assume that a party is aware of the other's mistake where a reasonable person in that party's place would have been so aware. For example, in *Chwee Kin Keong v Digilandmall.com Pte Ltd* [2005] 1 SLR(R) 502, at [38], the Singapore Court of Appeal considered that a buyer of goods on an Internet site that were priced 'so absurdly low in relation to [their] known market value . . . ought reasonably to have known' that the seller was making a mistake.

This very limited mistake doctrine of unilateral mistake applies where:

1. one party is genuinely *mistaken as to a term of the contract* and the mistake is one without which that party would not have entered into the contract;

2. that mistake ought reasonably to have been known to the other party; and

3. the mistaken party is not in any way at fault.

3.3.2.1 It must be a mistake as to term, rather than a mistake as to a collateral matter

If the mistake does not relate to a term of the contract, but affects a so-called 'collateral' matter, such as a quality of the subject matter or a fact on which the decision to enter the contract was based, it will not prevent agreement, because it is not a mistake relating to what has been offered and accepted.

In *Smith v Hughes* (1871) LR 6 QB 597 (see **3.3.1.1**), in the absence of an express stipulation for 'old' oats, whether the oats supplied were 'old' or 'new' was only a collateral matter concerning a quality of the oats.

In *Statoil ASA v Louis Dreyfus Energy Services LP, The Harriette N* [2008] EWHC 2257 (Comm), [2008] 2 Lloyd's Rep 685, [2009] 1 All ER (Comm) 1035 (see also **2.1.2** and **13.5.3**), Aikens J stated, at [88], and expressly relying on *Smith v Hughes*:

> [I]f one party has made a mistake about a fact on which he bases his decision to enter into a contract, but that fact does not form a term of the contract itself, then, even if the other party knows that the first is mistaken as to this fact, the contract will be binding.

The mistake related to the date of discharge of the cargo, which was erroneously thought to have been completed on 13 October (so ending the laytime), when it had not occurred until 24 October. This mistake influenced a compromise agreement (agreement to settle a dispute) covering the amount of demurrage (freight) that was payable under the contract of sale, but it was not a term of the agreement. The judge compared this with the position in the decision of the Court of Appeal in Singapore in *Chwee Kin Keong v Digilandmall.com Pte Ltd* [2005] 1 SLR(R) 502 (see **3.3.2**), in which the mistake related to the price *term* of goods on an Internet site.

3.3.2.2 The difficulty of meeting the requirements for an operative unilateral mistake

Examples of all of the conditions being met are rare.

In *Hartog v Colin and Shields* [1939] 3 All ER 566, the defendants offered to sell the claimants certain hare skins at 10¼d per pound. In fact, the defendants intended to sell at the same price per piece. The trade custom was to sell by the piece, and there were about three pieces to the pound, so that the defendants' offer was at about one-third of the normal price. The claimants claimed to have accepted the offer so that there was a binding agreement based on the contract price as mistakenly offered. They claimed to be entitled to damages when the defendants failed to perform. The court found for the defendants. Singleton J made it clear that the crucial element for any defendant to establish was that the other party must have realized the mistake. In other words, a party cannot 'snap up' an offer when that party is aware or ought to have been aware that the other has made a mistake relating to the offer terms.

This is the recognition of a principle of fair dealing in contractual negotiations in English law that prevents a party taking advantage of an obvious error by the other party (see also the discussion of mispricing on websites at **2.3.2.3**).

However, in many instances, the impact of the mistake will be much less clear, in which case the mistaken party may find it impossible to satisfy the burden of proof. This occurred in *Centrovincial Estates plc v Merchant Investors Assurance Co. Ltd* [1983] Com LR 158.

The defendants were tenants of offices with an annual rental of £68,320, subject to review from 25 December 1982. The rent review clause provided that, on that date, the rent should be increased to the current market rental value, as agreed between the parties, and in no circumstances should the rent be lower than the figure payable immediately before the review. Agreement was reached on a figure of £65,000 before the claimants realized that they had made a mistake, since they claimed that they had intended to propose a figure of £126,000.

The Court of Appeal refused to grant a declaration to the effect that there was no legally binding agreement on the figure of £65,000, on the ground that it had not been established that the defendants knew or ought reasonably to have known of the claimants' error when they reached agreement on the figure of £65,000.

The court appears to have considered it was 'at least arguable' that the defendants considered that the rent might be reduced, despite the existence of the proviso in the rent review clause.

3.3.3 Unilateral mistake: Mistake as to identity

The situation in which unilateral mistake has most often been relied upon is that of mistake as to identity. It is nearly always the case that the mistake as to identity has been provoked by conduct on the part of the other party that amounts to fraudulent misrepresentation (see **14.4.1.1**). The disadvantage of a claim based on misrepresentation is that its effect is to make the contract merely voidable, and since rescission is a purely personal remedy, it may be sought only against the person making the representation. However, in cases of mistake as to identity, the usual situation is that property is acquired and immediately resold to a third party by the dishonest party (the 'rogue') who then disappears, making the misrepresentation remedy worthless and leaving the original owner trying to recover the property from the third party (see **Figure 3.1**).

Thus the mistaken party (MP) is induced by the rogue (R) to transfer possession of goods under a contract. R immediately resells the goods to a third party who knows nothing of the fraudulent inducement and so is an 'innocent third party purchaser' (ITP).

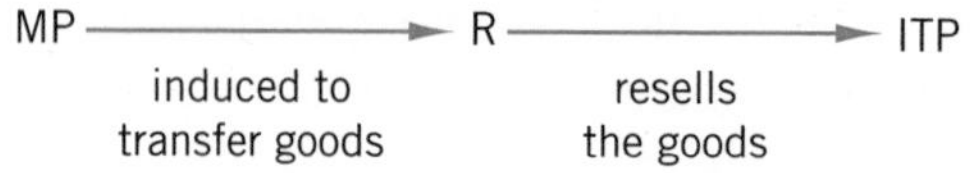

```
MP ─────────────▶ R ─────────────▶ ITP
      induced to          resells
     transfer goods       the goods
```

FIGURE 3.1 Mistake of identity

If the contract between MP and R is void for mistake as to identity, R will not have acquired any title to pass on to the ITP, so that MP can recover the goods from the ITP or sue the ITP for damages in the tort of conversion. However, if the contract between MP and R is merely voidable for the fraudulent misrepresentation, R will have obtained title to the goods which R can pass on to the ITP. Since MP's remedy is a personal remedy of rescission (setting aside the contract) as against R, it is lost once an ITP purchases the goods: s. 23 of the Sale of Goods Act (SGA) 1979. The goods cannot then be recovered from the ITP.

The result is that the courts are faced with having to decide which of two 'innocent parties' should suffer as a result of the fraud by the rogue: if mistake can be proved, the contract is void (see 3.2.2), and the original owner will succeed in recovering the property from the third party, even where that third party may be wholly innocent.

In order to avoid this conclusion, Lord Denning suggested that the effect of mistake as to identity *ought to be* to make the contract voidable—see *Lewis v Averay* [1972] 1 QB 198—on the basis that the innocent third party is generally more 'innocent' than the mistaken party and in need of greater protection. This suggestion has its attractions and had been recommended by the Law Reform Committee in its *Twelfth Report on Transfer of Title to Chattels* (Cmnd 2958, 1966), para. 15. However, Lord Denning was a lone voice, and instead the courts relied upon a policy of restricting the circumstances in which a contract would be void for mistake as to identity by adopting a complicated distinction between 'true mistakes as to identity' and 'mistakes as to attributes', which can be said to represent the distinction between mistakes as to terms and collateral matters in the context of identity (see *Smith v Hughes* and discussion at 3.3.2.1). A mistake as to attributes, e.g. creditworthiness, was not regarded as sufficiently fundamental to render the contract void. Thus the approach was to take a very limited interpretation of 'identity' as a term of the contract. In addition, a mistake as to identity had to be crucial to the decision to contract. Although in *Cundy v Lindsay* (1878) 3 App Cas the House of Lords had held identity to be crucial where a contract had been concluded by written correspondence, in situations in which the contract was made face-to-face, the presumption was that identity was not crucially important to the parties who intended to deal with the person physically present, whoever that was. This accorded with the central policy objective of protecting third parties. Even in this context however, there were apparently irreconcilable decisions that appeared to turn on whether the court in question had presented the identity question as an 'offer and acceptance' analysis, i.e. MP intended to offer the goods for sale to the person whose identity was assumed by R, rather than to R. Accordingly, R could not accept the offer.

It had been hoped that the House of Lords, in *Shogun Finance Ltd v Hudson* [2003] UKHL 62, [2004] 1 AC 919, would inject some clarification and certainty into the law on mistake as to identity by resolving these apparent inconsistencies in approach, e.g. by introducing a general principle that 'mistake' as to identity rendered the contract voidable, so abolishing the identity/attributes distinction and the emerging distinction between face-to-face and written contracting. However, if anything, the split decision of the House of Lords in terms of result—and, to some extent, in terms of analysis—has added to the complexity of the applicable law and reinforced arbitrary distinctions of principle.

In order to identify and evaluate the decision in *Shogun Finance Ltd v Hudson*, it is vital to appreciate the state of the law immediately prior to the decision.

3.3.3.1 Testing the fundamental importance of identity: The face-to-face case law prior to the decision in *Shogun Finance v Hudson*

In a face-to-face situation, in which the parties negotiate in each other's physical presence, the actual decision to sell does not normally rest on the question of the identity of the buyer. It is the decision to allow the goods to be taken away on credit that will be influenced by the attributes of the buyer, but this is a collateral issue. Accordingly, in face-to-face situations, the courts generally concluded that the contract was not void for mistake as to identity because of the presumption that the parties intended to deal with the person physically present.

There has always been a recognized exception to this position in face-to-face contracts in which identity can be shown to be crucial—namely, where the intention is to contract with a particular company and the contract purports to be made by a person on behalf of that company (a so-called 'bogus official'), but that person has no such authority to act: *Hardman v Booth* (1863) 1 H & C 803, 158 ER 1107. In such situations, the clear intention is to deal with *another* person, i.e. the company, so that no personal contract can be concluded with the rogue official.

However, this apart, in face-to-face contracting it is generally presumed that identity is not crucial to the decision to contract.

In **Phillips v Brooks Ltd** [1919] 2 KB 243, a rogue went into a jewellery shop and examined some jewellery. He wrote out a cheque for some pearls and a ring, and announced that he was Sir George Bullough, giving an address in St James's Square. He was allowed to take a ring without paying for it after the claimant had checked that the name and address tallied. The court was unwilling to allow the claimant to recover the ring from the third party to whom it had been pledged, since in its view the contract was not void. The claimant had intended to contract with the person who had been present in the shop. It was a judgement as to creditworthiness, rather than the person's identity, which had persuaded the claimant in this case to allow the contract to proceed on credit terms.

The same rationale explains *Lewis v Averay* [1972] 1 QB 198.

The claimant had advertised his car for sale. The rogue offered to buy it. He said that he was the well-known actor, Richard Greene, and wrote out a cheque, signing it 'R. A. Green'. The claimant was unwilling to allow him to take the car away until the cheque had cleared, but the rogue showed him an official pass for Pinewood Studios with his photograph on it in the name of 'Richard A. Green'. At that point, the claimant allowed the rogue to take the car and the log book. The rogue sold the car to the defendant (an innocent purchaser). The rogue's cheque proved to be worthless, but the claimant was unable to recover the car from the defendant.

Lord Denning's reasoning in the case has already been explained (see **3.3.3**). Megaw LJ proceeded by a more orthodox analysis to reach the same conclusion. Megaw LJ felt that the claimant had not been concerned about the identity of the person with whom he was dealing. He had been misled by the rogue into believing that he was dealing with a person of substance, but this was merely a mistake as to creditworthiness. Phillimore LJ considered, at p. 208D, that this case was 'on all fours with *Phillips v Brooks*'.

3.3.3.1.1 *Case analysis*

In both *Phillips v Brooks Ltd* [1919] 2 KB 243 and *Lewis v Averay* [1972] 1 QB 198, the presumption of an intention to contract with the person physically present had not been rebutted. In addition, in both cases it can be argued that the decision to contract had already been made before the issue of identity was raised, and in neither case was the sale 'called off' when the purchaser proposed to pay on credit. In both cases, it is therefore possible to argue that, at the point at which the question of identity was raised, it related only to the issue of creditworthiness prior to the decision to allow the person present to take the goods away on credit before the cheque payment had cleared.

This was often the basis used to explain and distinguish the decision of the Court of Appeal in *Ingram v Little* [1961] 1 QB 31, i.e. based on the argument that the claimants had made it clear at the outset that they were not prepared to let the car be taken away before the cheque had cleared and that they had changed their minds only after checking identity. On this reasoning, it was at least arguable, even in face-to-face contracts, that if the rogue were to introduce himself at the outset as someone else, this might make identity crucial to the decision to contract. Yet, all three cases appear essentially to turn on a judgement about ability to pay and creditworthiness, and so ought to have reached the same basic conclusion on the effect of the mistake. In any event, the reports of *Phillips v Brooks Ltd* are ambiguous as to the precise point at which the rogue mentioned that he was Sir George Bullough.

> In *Ingram v Little*, two spinster sisters had negotiated for the sale of their car to a rogue masquerading as someone named 'Hutchinson'. At first, they would not accept his cheque, but they later relented, having checked the name, initials, and address that he had given them against a telephone directory entry. They then allowed him to take the car away immediately, and later sought to recover it from the innocent third party to whom it had been sold. The majority in the Court of Appeal appear to have been satisfied that the claimant had intended to deal with the person the rogue had pretended to be rather than with whoever was present before her.

In the light of the very limited check on his identity made by the claimants, this decision is a little surprising. The reasoning rested on concluding that the offer to sell had been made only to the *real* Hutchinson, so that only *he* could accept it. However, this offer and acceptance analysis presupposes the fundamental importance of identity to the decision to contract when this had to be established separately. In other words, the offer will be made to the real Hutchinson only if that identity was so important to the decision to contract that it became a part of the offer terms that only the *real* Hutchinson could accept.

> For example, in *Boulton v Jones* (1857) 27 LJ Ex 117, the defendant sent an order for goods to Brocklehurst. Brocklehurst had sold his business, including current stock, to the claimant, his former foreman. The claimant supplied the goods, but the defendant was unwilling to pay for them on the basis that he had ordered from Brocklehurst because he had a set-off (a credit) against him. The court found for the defendant because it was not open to the claimant to substitute himself for the original offeree without first informing the offeror (which would amount to making a counter-offer). The identity of the contracting party was vitally important to the defendant because of the existence of the right of set-off and the claimant was aware that the defendant intended to deal with his predecessor. Accordingly, the claimant could not accept an offer that he knew was intended for another.

On these facts, it was clear that identity was vital to the terms on which the offer was placed, but in other cases this fact may be less obvious.

In *Lewis v Averay, Ingram v Little* was treated as anomalous. Lord Denning considered the 'material facts' in all three cases to be 'quite indistinguishable'. It may be that the decision is explicable as one based on policy in that, in normal circumstances, where an allegation of mistaken identity is made, the courts are concerned to protect the innocent third party purchaser who acquired the goods from the rogue. However, in *Ingram v Little*, that innocent third party was a car dealer, and the Court of Appeal may have felt more sympathy towards the elderly claimants.

The majority of the Court of Appeal in *Shogun Finance Ltd v Hudson* [2001] EWCA Civ 100, [2002] QB 834, rejected an argument based on the application of the presumption that a contracting party intends to contract with the person in front of them in face-to-face negotiations (in this case, the contract between the rogue and the finance company had been entered into at the premises of a car dealer). The majority reached their conclusion on the basis that the car dealer was not acting as agent for the finance company, so that this was not a face-to-face contract. However, more generally, the majority also considered that the face-to-face presumption applied only to oral contracts, whereas the contract in question was written. There was a strong dissent from Sedley LJ, who considered that the presumption applied so that the finance company had contracted with the rogue.

The majority decision of the Court of Appeal in *Shogun Finance v Hudson* also adopted the offer and acceptance analysis that had been used by the majority of the Court of Appeal in *Ingram v Little*, i.e. focusing on the question: 'To whom should the offeree (the rogue) reasonably have interpreted the offer as having been made?' Sedley LJ advocated that Parliament should look at this area of the law because development at common law was effectively curtailed by the decision of the House of Lords in *Cundy v Lindsay* (1878) 3 App Cas 459. Therefore, before examining the decision of the House of Lords on appeal in *Shogun Finance v Hudson*, it is first necessary to examine the earlier decision of the House in *Cundy v Lindsay* and the limitations that it imposed.

3.3.3.2 The decision of the House of Lords in *Cundy v Lindsay*

This decision is authority for the fact that, where the parties negotiate at a distance, it may be easier to establish an identity mistake and that identity was of crucial importance because the identity of the person placing an order has to be known in order to dispatch the goods. To put it in terms of offer and acceptance: the offer must be made to the person named on the written order form, so that only *that* person can accept.

In *Cundy v Lindsay* (1878) 3 App Cas 459, the rogue set up business under the name 'Blenkarn' at 37 Wood Street. A very respectable company called Blenkiron and Co. traded at 123 Wood Street. The rogue ordered goods from the claimants, making his signature appear as though it read 'Blenkiron'. The claimants sent the goods without payment to 'Blenkiron and Co.' at the rogue's address, and the rogue sold them to the defendants, innocent purchasers. The success of the claimants' plea of mistake, and thus their ability to recover the goods from the defendants, depended upon whether they intended to deal with whichever firm traded at 37 Wood Street or whether they intended to deal specifically with Blenkiron and Co. The House of Lords held that the claimants intended to deal with Blenkiron and Co. so that the contract was void for mistake.

The consequence of the finding that the contract was void for mistake as to identity was that it was the defendants, as innocent third party purchasers, who suffered the loss, because they were found to have converted goods (tort of conversion) to which they had no title.

It seems a reasonable inference from the facts that the claimants intended to deal with a particular firm by name, rather than to deal with an address, which would be of no great significance to them. However, this gives rise to the question of why the name of the firm would be important to them. It may well be because they thought they were dealing with the respectable Blenkiron and Co., which was likely to pay for the goods supplied on credit. The decision may also be questionable because of the emphasis placed on the need for a subjective meeting of minds in the speeches in the House of Lords.

Nevertheless, the analysis of their Lordships that the claimants intended to contract with Blenkiron and Co., as named in the written document, was subsequently relied upon to underpin the decision of the majority of the House of Lords in *Shogun Finance v Hudson* [2003] UKHL 62.

3.3.3.3 Mistaking one existing person for another

The decision in *Cundy v Lindsay* (1878) 3 App Cas 459 illustrates the principle that, in order to render the contract void, any mistake must involve the mistaken party mistaking the rogue for another *existing entity*. It was key that the claimants knew that there was a reputable firm named Blenkiron and Co. operating from Wood Street; otherwise, the use of any fictitious name might suffice. However, and ironically, it is the fact that they had heard of Blenkiron and Co. that provides evidence to support the conclusion that the decision to contract may have been motivated by considerations of creditworthiness. As Lord Denning noted in *Lewis v Averay* [1972] 1 QB 198, it is very difficult to distinguish a person's identity from his attributes (referring to it as a 'distinction without a difference'); indeed, a person may be identified by means of his attributes, e.g. 'the wife of Van der Borgh' in *Lake v Simmons* [1927] AC 487.

Nevertheless, it is clear that the mistake must relate to another existing entity—and *an offer cannot be made to a non-existent person.*

In **King's Norton Metal Co. Ltd v Edridge, Merrett and Co.** (1897) 14 TLR 98, a rogue, named Wallis, established a bogus business called 'Hallam and Co.' and had written to the claimants on headed paper depicting a large factory, suggesting that it was a well-established and thriving firm. The claimants supplied goods to Hallam and Co. on credit. These goods were immediately sold to the defendants, innocent purchasers. The claimants claimed that the contract was void for mistake and sought to recover the goods from the defendants. The Court of Appeal rejected their claim. The claimants had intended to deal with the writer of the letter, whoever that was. In order for a mistake as to identity to operate, one existing entity had to be mistaken for another existing entity. There was only one existing identity here (the rogue using an alias) and the claimants must have intended to deal with that person.

In fact, the mistake made by the claimants was as to the writer's ability or willingness to pay for the goods. In other words, it was merely a mistake as to creditworthiness, or an error of judgement, which consequently should not negative agreement.

3.3.3.4 The decision of the House of Lords in *Shogun Finance Ltd v Hudson*

The decision of the House of Lords in *Shogun Finance v Hudson* [2003] UKHL 62, [2004] 1 AC 919, is striking in terms of the differences in approach adopted by the majority and the minority—and even within the majority speeches.

The rogue had visited a Mitsubishi motor dealer and expressed an interest in purchasing a Mitsubishi Shogun. The rogue had then identified himself as 'Mr Dulabh Patel', and had produced Mr Patel's stolen driving licence as proof of his identity and address. The dealer had agreed the price for the car (£22,500) and had then faxed a copy of the proposed hire purchase agreement to the claimant finance company, together with a copy of the driving licence. This agreement named Mr Patel as the customer, but the rogue had signed it by forging Mr Patel's signature. The finance company carried out the usual checks on credit rating and approved the finance. As a result the dealer allowed the rogue to take away the vehicle. The rogue then sold the vehicle to the defendant for £17,000 and disappeared.

When the finance company brought a claim against the defendant for damages in the tort of conversion, the defendant claimed that he had acquired good title under s. 27 of the Hire Purchase Act 1964, because the rogue was a 'debtor' under the terms of that section and so could pass good title to the defendant. The majority of the Court of Appeal had held that the rogue was not a 'debtor' because the hire purchase agreement had been made with the real Mr Patel, who was named in the written document. The real Mr Patel could not be liable on that agreement, because his signature had been forged. The majority also rejected the defendant's alternative argument that the dealer had acted as agent for the finance company, so that this was a face-to-face contract made between the finance company and the rogue, and to which the presumption applied. The House of Lords dismissed the appeal by a majority of three to two, Lords Nicholls and Millett dissenting. The majority held that there was a written agreement made between the finance company and the rogue, which was a nullity because Mr Patel's signature had been forged.

The result on these facts was that, contrary to the traditionally assumed policy on this matter, the innocent third party purchaser was not protected. This appears to be because the majority of the House of Lords relied heavily on a different policy argument—namely, the primacy of written documents and the prevention of identity fraud, i.e. to have gone behind the writing and the named parties in the writing was considered to be dangerous practice, and would expose the finance company to the dangers of fraud by those who were able to steal identity and assume the identity of that other.

3.3.3.4.1 Majority: Lord Hobhouse

Lord Hobhouse considered that the question arising for determination related only to the construction of the written hire purchase agreement rather than the law as to mistake as to identity. He applied the parol evidence rule (see **6.2.1**) and concluded that, since the written contract named Mr Patel, it was the named Mr Patel who had made the offer to take the vehicle on hire purchase terms. It followed that the acceptance related only to that offer. It was not possible to go outside the terms of the written document. Lord Walker also purported to agree with the speech of Lord Hobhouse.

3.3.3.4.2 Majority: Lords Phillips and Walker

Lord Phillips focused on the 'offer and acceptance' analysis in mistake as to identity cases (i.e. the question of agreement), and reaffirmed the distinction in the previous case law between face-to-face contracting and contracting via written correspondence, so that, in face-to-face contracting, there is a presumption that the offer is intended to be made only to the person physically present and only that person can accept it, whereas in contracts made by means of written documents, such as the present case, the offer and acceptance questions were determined solely by focusing on those written terms. Accordingly, Lord Phillips came to the same overall conclusion as Lord Hobhouse, whilst expressly maintaining the face-to-face presumption for non-written contracts.

3.3.3.4.3 Lords Nicholls and Millett (dissenting)

In the dissenting speeches, the distinction between written and face-to-face contracting was considered to be arbitrary, and their Lordships favoured a policy approach that protected the innocent third party purchaser since, according to Lord Nicholls, at [35], '[t]he loss is more appropriately borne by the person who takes the risks inherent in parting with his goods without receiving payment', and according to Lord Millett, at [82]:

> It is surely fairer that the party who was actually swindled and who had an opportunity to uncover the fraud should bear the loss rather than a party who entered the picture only after the swindle had been carried out.

Not surprisingly, therefore, given this policy approach, the minority concluded that the contract was voidable. They follow a two-step analysis, which separated the contract formation and consideration of the fraud. On the view of the minority, there was a contract in existence between the finance company and the rogue, based on the presumption that you intend to contract with the person with whom you are 'dealing'. The fraud would render such a contract voidable.

3.3.3.5 Analysis

The real distinction in the approaches is between reliance on objective determination of agreement via offer and acceptance (the 'offer and acceptance' analysis) and reliance upon the fraud that induced a mistake. However, identity must be crucially important in order for the rogue offeree to know that the offer is intended for someone else so that the rogue offeree cannot accept it. Equally, the offeror must consider that the identity of the offeree is so important that the offer is made only to the 'real' offeree. The difficulty is that the cases do not provide a satisfactory answer to determine this and the analysis tends to be circular. The results in the face-to-face cases should remain true, i.e. identity was not the vital factor, because the decision to contract was not affected by any mistake, but only the decision to let the goods be taken away on credit. (This may be the accepted position of all members of the House of Lords, albeit that Lord Hobhouse does not consider this case law to be relevant on the facts.) The difficulty in *Shogun Finance v Hudson* [2003] UKHL 62 is that, in the context of the hire purchase agreement, the offer has to be made to the person named in the document, making it difficult to argue that someone else was the intended contracting party. However, the facts require a different approach, since had the rogue handed over counterfeit cash for the Mitsubishi car, the contract to sell the car would have been made between the dealers and the rogue. Shogun Finance would inevitably make decisions on whether to agree hire purchase terms based on the credit rating of a named individual, and it is the fact that the name carries with it a credit rating that is significant, rather than the 'identity' of the person named in the written document. Therefore what is needed is some coherent principle to determine when identity is important to the decision to contract. The alternative approach is to conclude that, apart from factual scenarios such as that in *Boulton v Jones* (1857) 27 LJ Ex 117, identity is rarely important to *the decision to contract*, but only to the credit terms—and therefore to conclude that it is the fraud that is important, rather than the existence of agreement on an offer and acceptance analysis.

3.3.3.5.1 The fault question

It is interesting to consider whether there is any residual 'fault' question after the decision of the House of Lords in *Shogun Finance v Hudson* [2003] UKHL 62.

The position prior to *Shogun* was that the claimant had to show that it was not at fault by demonstrating that reasonable steps were taken to check the identity of the person with whom the claimant was dealing. This was considered to provide an alternative explanation of the 'face-to-face' case law. For example, in *Phillips v Brooks Ltd* [1919] 2 KB 243 (see **3.3.3.1**), merely to have checked in a directory that Sir George Bullough lived at the address given did not establish that the man in the jewellery shop was in fact Sir George Bullough. This would not explain the different conclusion on the effect of the mistake in *Ingram v Little* [1961] 1 QB 31, in which the claimants had checked that the person, whose identity the rogue had assumed, lived at the address given, but no more. In *Lewis v Averay* [1972] 1 QB 198, checking the pass to Pinewood Studios, displaying a photograph of the rogue, ought arguably to be regarded as reasonable steps to confirm identity, since there is then a connection between the identity claimed and the evidence to establish that the person in question has that identity. This would seem to be fairly typical as a means of checking identity. However, on the facts, the Court of Appeal regarded this as insufficient.

On this basis, it might be considered that the dissenting view of Sedley LJ in the Court of Appeal in *Shogun Finance Ltd v Hudson* [2001] EWCA Civ 1000, [2002] QB 834 (see **3.3.3.1**) has much to recommend it, since although the claimants carried out a credit check for the person named on the driving licence, they did not check that the person before them was in fact the licence holder.

It is more likely, however, that fault is irrelevant where the contracting is achieved on the basis of written documents. The House of Lords in *Cundy v Lindsay* (1878) 3 App Cas 459 (see **3.3.3.2**) did not even consider any requirement to check identity. At the time, such a check might have considerably delayed the process of reaching agreement because communications at a distance could not be achieved via instantaneous methods. Of course, nowadays, no such argument could be sustained, and it would seem to be appropriate practice to carry out some sort of check before dispatching goods on credit. Inevitably, however, this may necessarily be a credit check rather than a true check to establish identity.

The majority of the House of Lords in *Shogun Finance v Hudson* was keen to protect lending and credit bodies which carried out a traditional identity check of asking to see an identity document, but which were happy to allow a £22,500 car to be taken away on the basis of a driving licence and a signature that resembled that of the licence holder. By comparison, in the Court of Appeal, Sedley LJ had expressed dissatisfaction with the checks carried out by the finance company, given the value of the transaction, and had concluded, at [12], that 'if there was ever a seller who ought to be treated as having assumed the risk of loss, it was . . . the present claimants'. That said, the innocent third party purchaser had purchased a car worth £22,500 for £17,000, but would have felt reasonably confident, since the seller had both the car and the relevant paperwork. The fraud in *Shogun Finance* would clearly have been more difficult to achieve with photographic identity which is now possible in the case of both driving licences and passports.

3.3.3.6 Conclusion

1. The decision in *Shogun Finance v Hudson* [2003] UKHL 62, which had been so eagerly awaited, proved to be a huge disappointment in terms of clarifying the applicable principles to determine when a contract will be void for mistake. Contracts made in writing are likely to be void and contracts made face-to-face are likely to be voidable. However, to the parties, it might appear far from clear whether the contract is face-to-face or written, e.g. the dealings with the car dealer in *Shogun Finance*, followed by the making of a written hire purchase contract with the finance company. A customer might well consider that the contract was made with the dealer, although the agency argument was rejected in that case.

2. It appears that there will be no contract with the rogue where the real intended party is named in a written document. However, where the parties contract in a face-to-face situation, the contract is likely (and even almost certain) to be voidable for fraud. The answer for lenders and vendors is therefore to insist on a written contract whenever this is practical, but there seems no obvious method of protection available to innocent third party purchasers, although some checks may be possible where pressures of time permit. The significance, or otherwise, of any degree of fault on the part of the mistaken party or the innocent third party purchaser should have greater significance in determining which of these two innocent parties should suffer the loss caused by the actions of the rogue.

3. Arguably the void/voidable distinction is not the most appropriate one, since it is an 'all or nothing' approach, i.e. either the contract is void for mistake so that the mistaken party can recover the goods (and the innocent third party purchaser suffers the loss), or the contract is voidable for fraud so that the innocent third party can keep the goods (and the mistaken party suffers the loss). An alternative suggestion of apportioning the loss between these two innocent parties in accordance with their respective degrees of fault was suggested by Devlin LJ in *Ingram v Little* [1961] 1 QB 31 and would be similar to the apportionment of losses having an extrinsic cause seen in the Law Reform (Frustrated Contracts) Act 1943 (discussed at **12.7.2**). However, this solution did not find favour when it was considered by the Law Reform Committee, in its *Twelfth Report on Transfer of Title to Chattels* (Cmnd 2958, 1966). The reason given was that apportionment was considered to leave too much to judicial discretion and was too complex, thereby leading to uncertainty.

3.4 Mistakes in documents

- The remedy of rectification of a written document may be available in some limited instances and on strict conditions in which a transcription mistake (by one or both parties) has been made in recording the parties' oral agreement in writing (see **3.4.1**).

- Another type of mistake relating to a document may raise the question of the applicability of the plea of *non est factum*. It is important to appreciate that this plea will be applicable only in exceptional cases. It involves a party asserting that, although a document contains that party's signature, it is not the document that the party thought they were signing, so that it should not bind them (see **3.4.2**). This plea of *non est factum*, although in one sense reflecting a mistake by the party signing, also bears some relationship to fraud (see **14.4.1.1**).

3.4.1 Rectification

Rectification was defined earlier as providing a remedy where there has been a simple transcription mistake in recording an oral agreement in writing (on a critical analysis of the law of rectification, see Davies, 'Rectification versus interpretation: the nature and scope of the equitable jurisdiction' (2016) 75 CLJ 62–85).

Peter Gibson LJ in *Swainland Builders Ltd v Freehold Properties Ltd* [2002] EWCA Civ 560, 2 EGLR 71, at [33] set out the necessary requirements for the party seeking rectification as follows:

(1) the parties had a common continuing intention, whether or not amounting to an agreement, in respect of a particular matter in the agreement to be rectified,

(2) there was an outward expression of accord;

(3) the intention continued at the time of the execution of the instrument sought to be rectified;

(4) by mistake, the instrument did not reflect that common intention

Approved by Lord Hoffmann in *Chartbrook Ltd v Persimmon Homes Ltd* [2009] UKHL 38, [2009] 1 AC 1101, (at [48]), those factors were further refined in *Daventry District Council v Daventry and District Housing Ltd* [2011] EWCA Civ 1153, [2012] 1 WLR 1333, [2012] Bus LR 485, at [80], Etherton LJ set out the requirements for rectification, following the decision in *Chartbrook Ltd v Persimmon Homes Ltd* [2009] UKHL 38, [2009] 1 AC 1101, as:

(1) [T]he parties had a common continuing intention, whether or not amounting to an agreement, in respect of a particular matter in the instrument to be rectified; (2) which existed at the time of execution of the instrument sought to be rectified; (3) such common continuing intention to be established objectively, that is to say by reference to what an objective observer would have thought the intentions of the parties to be; and (4) by mistake the instrument did not reflect that common intention.

3.4.1.1 The operation of the doctrine

3.4.1.1.1 Rectification is normally available only when the document said to incorporate the agreement fails to reproduce the common intentions of the parties

In **Joscelyne v Nissen** [1970] 2 QB 86, a daughter owned a house, which was also occupied by her parents. Her father had agreed to transfer his car-hire business to her and, in return, she had agreed to pay him a weekly sum and to pay household expenses, including the gas, electricity, and coal bills, and the cost of a home help. However, the eventual written agreement referred to the payment of the weekly sum and that the daughter was to 'discharge all expenses in connection with the whole premises'. Following a dispute, the daughter had stopped paying the fuel bills and costs of home help. The father sought rectification of the document containing their agreement to make explicit their original intention that such bills should be paid by the daughter.

The court was satisfied that the father's version of the agreement did reflect what had actually been agreed between the parties. Indeed, the daughter's defence focused more on pursuing a legal argument against rectification (see below) than on denying the terms of this agreement. The contract was rectified.

The most difficult obstacle confronting a claimant seeking rectification is to prove that the document does not truly reflect what was agreed. Courts are understandably reluctant to change the terms of a written agreement, since in the great majority of cases the contractual document is the most secure evidence that there is of what was agreed by the parties (often referred to as representing 'the cogent evidence of the parties' intention'). In *Joscelyne v Nissen*, the Court of Appeal stated that 'convincing proof' would be required to counteract that 'cogent evidence', indicating that, by this expression, it intended a high burden of proof to fall on any claimant. The burden of proof was explained in similar terms by Brightman LJ in *Thomas Bates & Son Ltd v Wyndham's (Lingerie) Ltd* [1981] 1 WLR 505, at p. 521, and by Peter Gibson LJ in *Swainland Builders Ltd v Freehold Properties Ltd* [2002] 2 EGLR 71, at p. 74.

Lord Hoffmann in *Chartbrook Ltd v Persimmon Homes Ltd* [2009] UKHL 38, [2009] 1 AC 1101, at [60], stated that evidence of the continuing common intention had to be assessed objectively, i.e. in terms of whether a reasonable observer would consider there to be such an intention and not what the parties later claim their intention to have been. In other words, it was necessary to show a prior consensus that differed from the objective meaning of the formal contract and that, for this purpose, the prior consensus would have the meaning that a reasonable observer would have given to it, rather than the meaning that one or both of the parties would have considered to apply.

This objective approach was applied and explained by the majority of the Court of Appeal in *Daventry District Council v Daventry and District Housing Ltd* [2011] EWCA Civ 1153, [2012] 1 WLR 1333, [2012] Bus LR 485 (commented by Morgan, 'Rectification: is it broken? Common mistake after Daventry' [2013] RLR 1).

> The council and the housing association had negotiated for the transfer of the council housing stock and staff to the housing association. The initial non-binding prior accord provided for the housing association to cover the cost of the deficit in the pension fund of the council's housing staff who were transferred to the housing association. However, the contract provided for the council to cover the deficit. Whereas the council's negotiator did not notice this, the housing association's negotiator knew that the council believed that the housing association was to cover the deficit but said nothing. The housing association's negotiator also did not inform the housing association so that the association was also unaware of the mistake. The council sought rectification, arguing that there had been a mistake so that the agreement should reflect the initial prior accord.
>
> The Court of Appeal had to consider whether there was the necessary continuing intention. The majority held (Etherton LJ dissenting) that the claimant council was entitled to rectification based on mutual mistake, i.e. that the council and the housing association both believed that the final contract they had signed gave effect to the prior accord and they had been in agreement on that accord. Given the unconscionability on the part of the housing association's negotiator who was aware that the parties' agreement was not reflected in the final contract terms, the majority considered that rectification was not unfair to the association.

The test applied to determine whether there was a 'continuing common intention' was whether, on an objective assessment, the housing association had informed the council that it intended to contract on a different basis from the position set out in the accord. Lord Neuberger considered that the hypothetical observer would not have concluded that the association was departing from the prior accord (at [213]); only that it was making a mistake and therefore that there was a continuing common intention. However, Etherton LJ, dissenting, explained the policy justification for the objective approach (at [85]–[89]) but considered that an objective assessment would lead to the conclusion that, by the final contract, the housing association had indicated to the council that it intended to contract on a different basis.

There is some evidence that Toulson LJ and Lord Neuberger MR were not entirely convinced with the formulation of the *Chartbrook* objective test, Toulson LJ expressing 'misgivings', and Lord Neuberger stating that it was 'not without difficulties'. The issues were set out by Leggatt J in *Tartsinis v Navona Management Company* [2015] EWHC 57 (Comm), in the context of determining whether a price mechanism under a share transfer agreement reflected the intention of the parties. Leggatt J (in *obiter* comments) had 'difficulty with this statement [i.e. *Chartbrook* and *Daventry*] of the test', although the judge accepted that despite 'very real misgivings', he would have been bound to follow it (at [99]). He stated (at [90]): 'It is one thing to say that a contract should not be rectified just because both parties privately intend it to bear a meaning different from its meaning objectively ascertained. It is quite another thing, however, to say that a contract should be rectified to conform to what a reasonable observer would have understood the parties previously to have agreed, irrespective of the parties' own understanding.' Thus, the criticism is that the *Chartbrook* approach involves giving precedence, in the form of the wording of the final contract via rectification, to an interpretation (that of the hypothetical reasonable observer) of a prior 'accord' that at least one of the parties did not agree with. As Leggatt J put it (at [92]): 'the effect is to treat the objective meaning of communications which were not intended to be legally binding as superior to the objective meaning of the document intended to record the parties' final agreement and to allow the former to displace the latter'.

The *Daventry* test was, however, applied in *Liberty Mercian Ltd v Cuddy Civil Engineering Ltd* [2013] EWHC 2688 (TCC), [2014] 1 All ER (Comm) 761, [2014] BLR 179. It was argued that a contract should be rectified to reflect the fact that a mistake had occurred in naming the defendant because an earlier letter of intent indicated that the party should have been the Cuddy Group. However, Ramsey J considered that there was no continuing common intention and the objective observer would have concluded that it was the intention of the parties that the contractor should change from Cuddy Group to the defendant. By comparison in *DS-Rendite-Fonds NR. 106 VLCC Titan Glory GmbH & Co. v Titan Maritime SA* [2013] EWHC 3492 (Comm), Hamblen J considered (at [79] and [80]), that the equity for granting rectification was clear: the parties were both subjectively and objectively agreed; there was a common continuing intention with respect to the payment of the minimum hire; it had been outwardly expressed and continued to the date of the agreement, albeit that due to a drafting error the agreement document did not reflect that common intention. In *Milton Keynes BC v Viridor (Community Recycling MK) Ltd (No 2)* [2017] EWHC 239 (TCC), [2017] BLR (QBD) TCC, the argument that there was no common continuing intention since the contract had been subject to 'minor tweaks' was rejected and rectification granted.

3.4.1.1.2 If all of the objective evidence is that the parties did agree in the terms used in the document, rectification will not be ordered on the basis that the claimant misunderstood the meaning of the words used

In *Frederick E. Rose (London) Ltd v William H. Pim Junior & Co. Ltd* [1953] 2 QB 450, the claimants were asked by a third party to supply 'Moroccan horse beans described as "feveroles"'. The claimants did not know what feveroles were and asked the defendants, who said that they were simply horse beans. The claimants therefore entered into a contract to purchase the requisite number of horse beans from the defendants. The claimants then discovered that 'feveroles' were a superior type of horse bean, and the buyers of these 'feveroles' sought damages from the claimants. The claimants sought rectification of their agreement with the defendants. However, the Court of Appeal refused rectification on the basis that the contract, as written down, reflected what had been agreed orally. (In fact, both parties had mistakenly thought that 'feveroles' were the same as horse beans, but on the facts there was no remedy in mistake: see **13.4.1.3**).

The difficulty with this 'objective approach' is that it raises the question of the boundaries between contract interpretation and rectification. As highlighted by Lord Neuberger in the decision of the Supreme Court in *Marley v Rawlings* [2014] UKSC 2, [2014] 2 WLR 213, at [40], the question is not merely 'academic'. Indeed, his Lordship added:

> if it is a question of interpretation, then the document in question has, and has always had, the meaning and effect as determined by the court, and that is the end of the matter. On the other hand, if it is a question of rectification, then the document, as rectified, has a different meaning from that which it appears to have on its face, and the court would have jurisdiction to refuse rectification or to grant it on terms (eg if there had been delay, change of position, or third party reliance).

The issue has attracted considerable academic interest as well as extra-judicial discussion and for some clearly poses a threat to the very existence of rectification (Davies (2016) 75(1) CLJ 62–85). Whether the courts will resume the primacy of rectification, only time will tell.

3.4.1.2 Rectification if the contractual document fails to record accurately the intentions of only *one* party

There were authorities, culminating in *A. Roberts & Co. Ltd v Leicestershire County Council* [1961] Ch 555, which suggested that even where the document failed to record the intentions of only *one* of the parties, rectification might be available. However, those authorities were largely overruled by *Riverlate Properties Ltd v Paul* [1975] Ch 133, in which a lessor had made a mistake in drafting a document containing a proposed lease and subsequently sought to amend it in a way that would have increased the burden on the lessee. The Court of Appeal refused to rectify the lease in those circumstances since, at the time of contracting, the lessee did not know about the lessor's mistake, still less had there been any kind of sharp practice.

The significance of these factors was made clear in *Thomas Bates & Son Ltd v Wyndham's (Lingerie) Ltd* [1981] 1 WLR 505.

> Tenants had taken a lease from the claimants on two previous occasions and, on each occasion, an option for renewal in the lease contained a price term leaving the matter to be agreed between the parties, or to be fixed by arbitration. A further lease omitted provision for arbitration in the event of any dispute over fixing the rent: a fact noted by the tenants, but not drawn to the attention of the claimants who then sought rectification of the lease after it had been executed. The Court of Appeal dismissed the tenants' appeal against the trial judge's order for rectification. *Rectification would be allowed even where the mistake was one-sided, provided that the other party knew of the mistake, but failed to draw it to the attention of the mistaken party, and provided that there was some inequitable benefit to the party conscious of the other's mistake (not necessarily amounting to sharp practice). A. Roberts & Co. Ltd v Leicestershire County Council* was good law because it rested on precisely this principle.

This line of authority was considered again in *Commission for the New Towns v Cooper (GB) Ltd* [1995] Ch 259. Stuart-Smith LJ suggested that rectification in the one-sided mistake cases turned upon the existence of 'unconscionable conduct'. *This, in turn, raised the subsidiary question of whether rectification could ever be granted in such circumstances if the party seeking to rely upon the terms as written did not know of the other's mistake.*

Stuart-Smith LJ was satisfied that the existence of unconscionable conduct would be established if it could be shown that a party intended the other to be mistaken and so conducted himself as to divert that other's attention from discovering the mistake. Stuart-Smith LJ was also satisfied that, in such circumstances, the suspicion that the other may indeed be mistaken would be sufficient to amount to actual knowledge of the mistake. In so deciding, he relied upon the classification of knowledge of Peter Gibson J in *Baden v Société Générale pour Favoriser le Développement du Commerce et de l'Industrie en France SA (1982)* [1993] 1 WLR 509, at pp. 575–6, which treats 'wilfully shutting one's eyes to the obvious' as actual knowledge.

Rectification was ordered on this basis in *Hurst Stores & Interiors Ltd v ML Europe Property Ltd* [2004] EWCA Civ 490, [2004] BLR 249. A final version of a statement of account was different from all previous versions seen by the parties and did not reflect the agreement that the parties had reached on the basis for the valuation of certain works. The project manager for the construction company had signed this final version of the statement without the difference being drawn to his attention. The Court of Appeal held that the employer's construction manager, who had prepared the final document, had actual or 'shut-eye' knowledge of this mistake, so that rectification was appropriate. By comparison, the Court of Appeal in *George Wimpey UK Ltd v VI Components Ltd* [2005] EWCA Civ 77, [2005] BLR 135, rejected a claim for rectification based on unilateral mistake concerning the formula for the calculation of an extra payment because there was insufficient evidence of actual knowledge of the mistake (even on the extended definition of actual knowledge in *Baden v Société Générale*) or that the vendor had failed to draw the purchaser's attention to the last-minute change to this formula. The Court of Appeal stressed the exceptional nature of the jurisdiction in *Commission for the New Towns* to rectify a contract on the basis of unilateral mistake and the considerable contracting experience of this purchaser when compared with that of the vendor.

In general terms, it will be extremely difficult to succeed in proving both the requirement of actual knowledge and unconscionable conduct on the part of the other party, so that rectification based on unilateral mistake will be rare. For example, the argument was rejected in *Liberty Mercian Ltd v Cuddy Civil Engineering Ltd* [2013] EWHC 2688 (TCC), [2014] 1 All ER (Comm) 761, [2014] BLR 179 (see also **3.4.1.1**), because although the claimant mistakenly believed that the defendant was the same as the Cuddy Group, there was no evidence of actual knowledge or wilful blindness on the part of the defendant. In *Rowallan Group Ltd v Edgehill Portfolio No. 1 Ltd* [2007] EWHC 32 (Ch), [2007] NPC 9, at [14], Lightman J reiterated the conclusion in *George Wimpey*:

> that the remedy of rectification for unilateral mistake is a drastic remedy, for it has the result of imposing on the defendant to the claim a contract which he did not, and did not intend to, make. Accordingly, the conditions for the grant of such relief must be strictly satisfied.

The judge spelled out the need to establish that the defendant had actual knowledge of the claimant's mistake, which included 'wilfully shutting one's eyes to the obvious and wilfully and recklessly failing to make such inquiries as an honest or reasonable man would make'. However, he noted, at [15]:

> [I]f the Defendant intended that the Claimant should be mistaken in this regard and deliberately set about diverting the Claimant's attention from discovering the mistake, it is unnecessary that the Claimant actually knew that the Claimant was mistaken: it is sufficient that the Defendant merely suspected that it was so.

On the facts, however, the defendant had no actual knowledge of factors influencing the making of the amendment, and there was no reason why the defendant should have known of the mistake or suspected it. It was therefore, to use the judge's words, a 'hopeless case'.

3.4.1.3 Rectification where the contract contains an entire agreement clause

The fact that a written contract contains an entire agreement clause (a clause that states that the agreement between the parties is solely what is in the written contract) (see **6.2.1.4**) does not prevent rectification where it is claimed that the written document does not represent the parties' common continuing intention: *Surgicraft Ltd v Paradigm Biovices Inc.* [2010] EWHC 1291 (Ch). In that case, the judge explained, at [73], that:

[The purpose of the entire agreement clause] was to limit possible contractual claims arising from dealings outside the contract. A claim for rectification is quite different: it proceeds on the basis that the parties have made a mistake in expressing their true agreement, a mistake which infects [an entire agreement clause] as much as any other aspect of the agreement.

Similarly, in *Milton Keynes BC v Viridor (Community Recycling MK) Ltd (No 2)* [2017] EWHC 239 (TCC), [2017] BLR (QBD) TCC, the honorary Mr Justice Coulson, at [77] rejected the argument that the existence of the entire agreement clause is 'a factor militating against the rectification of the contract'.

3.4.2 The plea of *non est factum*

The Latin phrase *non est factum* literally means 'it is not my deed'. As a rule of the law of contract, it affords a defence to a party against whom a claim is brought in reliance upon a signed written agreement, where that party is able to show that they were unaware of the true meaning of the document when signing it. It is a very limited exception to the rule that a person's signature on a document irrevocably binds the person to its contents (see **6.2.2**).

The rule developed at a time when adult literacy was far from commonplace: *Thoroughgood's Case* (1584) 2 Co Rep 9a. The classic example of the operation of the rule is *Lewis v Clay* (1897) 67 LJ QB 224.

The claimant in *Lewis v Clay* asked the defendant to witness some deeds for him. He showed the defendant some papers, over which he held a piece of blotting paper with a number of holes cut in it, his explanation being that the content of the deeds must remain private. The defendant signed in the spaces. In fact, the papers were promissory notes made out to the claimant to the value of £11,000. It was found as a fact that the defendant had not been negligent and he was therefore able to resist the claimant's action.

Later, the advent of universal education and general adult literacy put the continued existence of the rule in doubt. The matter eventually came before the House of Lords in *Saunders v Anglia Building Society* (also known as *Gallie v Lee*) [1971] AC 1004.

An elderly aunt intended to give her house to her nephew, so that he could use it as security for a loan, on condition that she was allowed to remain living there. A friend of the nephew, known to be assisting him in obtaining a loan, asked her to sign a document, which the friend said was a deed of gift of the house to the nephew. The aunt had broken her glasses and so signed without reading the document, which turned out to be a deed conveying the house to the friend. The friend then mortgaged the property, but defaulted on the payment of the mortgage instalments, so that the building society sought possession of the house. The House of Lords declined to abolish the plea of *non est factum*, but considered that the aunt's plea failed on these facts.

The narrow *ratio* of their Lordships' decision is that the difference between what the aunt signed and what she thought she was signing was not so great as to establish beyond doubt that she did not consent to it. She thought that she was signing a document transferring ownership of the house, which is precisely what she signed. Thus the *non est factum* defence is not available except in cases in which 'the transaction which the document purports to effect is essentially different in substance or in kind from the transaction intended': *per* Lord Wilberforce, at p. 1026. Their Lordships did, however, consider the extent of the rule. Lord Wilberforce thought it would be rare today for a literate adult to succeed in a plea of *non est factum*. In the case of those who were illiterate, or blind, or lacking in understanding, the position was less clear. According to Lord Wilberforce, at p. 1027:

> The law ought . . . to give relief if satisfied that consent was truly lacking but will require of signers even in this class that they act responsibly and carefully according to their circumstances in putting their signature to legal documents.

Therefore if the signatory is careless in signing the document the plea of *non est factum* will not be available. Carelessness would be established by not wearing reading glasses or by signing a document in blank—or leaving blanks to be filled in later: *United Dominion's Trust Ltd v Western* [1976] QB 513 and *C F Asset Finance Ltd v Okonji* [2014] EWCA Civ 870, [2014] ECC 23, [2014] CTLC 218.

That the plea of *non est factum* has been severely restricted by the decision in *Saunders v Anglia Building Society* was confirmed by the peremptory dismissal of the plea by the Court of Appeal in *Avon Finance Co. Ltd v Bridger* [1985] 2 All ER 281—and evidence of the continued judicial reluctance to invoke the doctrine can be seen in the decision in *Norwich and Peterborough Building Society v Steed (No. 2)* [1993] Ch 116. Remedies may nevertheless be available in a *non est factum* scenario, depending on the facts, based on misrepresentation (see **Chapter 14**) or undue influence (see **15.2**). However, misrepresentation and undue influence render the contract voidable, which is a less drastic a remedy and offers some protection for third parties. The bars to rescission may, however, operate in relation to a voidable contract (see **14.5.2**).

There is a rare recent instance (described by the judge as 'exceptional facts') in which the doctrine was invoked successfully in the context of a fraud perpetrated against the employee defendant, who was led to believe that he was merely witnessing the signatures of others, rather than signing as the guarantor of the lease of the company that employed him: *Trustees of Beardsley Theobalds Retirement Benefit Scheme v Yardley* [2011] EWHC 1380 (QB). There were, however, also successful defences to enforcement based on undue influence and fraudulent misrepresentation on these facts.

MULTIPLE-CHOICE QUESTIONS

Test your knowledge by trying this chapter's **multiple-choice questions**:
www.oup.com/uk/poole

FURTHER READING

Agreements to agree

Brown, 'The contract to negotiate: a thing writ in water' [1992] JBL 353.

Buckley, '*Walford v Miles*: False certainty about uncertainty—an Australian perspective' (1993) JCL 58.

Neill, 'A key to lock-out agreements?' (1992) 108 LQR 405.

Steyn, 'Contract law: fulfilling the reasonable expectations of honest men' (1997) 113 LQR 433.

Failure of anticipated contracts to materialize

Ball, 'Work carried out in pursuance of letters of intent: contract or restitution?' (1983) 99 LQR 572.

Barker, 'Coping with failure: reappraising pre-contractual remuneration' (2003) 19 JCL 105.

McKendrick, 'Negotiations "subject to contract" and the law of restitution' [1995] RLR 100.

Agreement mistake

General

Brownsword, 'New note on the old oats' (1987) 131 SJ 384.

Simpson, 'Contracts for cotton to arrive: the case of the two ships *Peerless*' (1989) 11 Cardozo L Rev 287.

Spark, *Vitiation of Contracts: International Contractual Principles and English Law* (Cambridge University Press, 2013).

Identity

Chandler and Devenney, 'Mistake as to identity and the threads of objectivity' (2004) 1 JOR 7.

Macmillan, 'Mistake as to identity clarified?' (2004) 120 LQR 369.

Macmillan, 'Rogues, swindlers and cheats: the development of mistake of identity in English contract law' [2005] CLJ 711.

McLauchlan, 'Mistake of identity and contract formation' (2005) 21 JCL 1.

Tettenborn, 'Transfer of chattels by non-owners: still an open problem' (2018) CLJ 151.

Rectification

Davies, 'Rectifying the course of rectification' (2012) 75 MLR 412.

Davies, 'Rectification versus interpretation: the nature and scope of the equitable jurisdiction' (2016) CLJ 62.

Dawson, 'Interpretation and rectification of written agreements in the commercial court' (2015) 131 LQR 344.

Etherton, 'Contract formation and the fog of rectification' [2015] CLP 1.

Leggatt, 'Making sense of contracts: the rational choice theory' (2015) 131 LQR 454.

McLauchlan, 'The "drastic" remedy of rectification' (2008) 124 LQR 608.

McLauchlan, 'Commonsense principles of interpretation and rectification' (2010) 126 LQR 8.

McLauchlan, 'Refining rectification' (2014) 130 LQR 83.

Morgan, 'Rectification: is it broken? Common mistake after *Daventry*' [2013] RLR 1.

Patten, 'Does the law need to be rectified? *Chartbrook* revisited', Chancery Bar Association Annual Lecture (2013), http://www.chba.org.uk/for-members/library/annual-lectures/does-the-law-need-to-be-rectified-chartbrook-revisited.

Toulson, 'Does rectification require rectifying?' TECBAR Annual Lecture, 31 October 2013, https://www.supremecourt.uk/docs/speech-131031.pdf.

Chapter 4

Enforceability of promises: consideration and promissory estoppel

4

SUMMARY OF THE ISSUES

Chapters 4 and 5 examine the necessary criteria to establish the existence of a binding contract—namely, that:

1. either there is consideration to support the promise that is sought to enforce or that promise is contained in a deed (Chapter 4); and

2. there is an intention to be legally bound (Chapter 5).

English law generally enforces bargains and not gratuitous promises. Accordingly, a promise will be unenforceable unless it is contained in a deed (indicating that the promise is taken seriously) or is supported by consideration. 'Consideration' means an act or a promise given in exchange for the promise (i.e. the price for which the other's promise was bought).

• Consideration need not be adequate, but must be sufficient, meaning that the courts will not examine whether what has been given in exchange is of equivalent value. But some acts or promises are not recognized in law as good consideration, e.g. past consideration, performance of an existing legal duty.

• In addition, consideration is also required to support a promise to alter an existing contract; therefore, simply performing the existing contractual duty was not recognized as a good consideration because there was no fresh benefit or detriment to support the new alteration promise. However, in the context of an alteration promise to pay more, the Court of Appeal in *Williams v Roffey Bros.* held that consideration to support an alteration promise would exist where *factual* benefits arose to the promisor from the making of the alteration promise and this amounted to consideration.

• This contrasted with the House of Lords decision in *Foakes v Beer*, in the context of alteration promises to pay less. In this case, factual benefit to a creditor arising from a promise to accept part payment in full satisfaction and not to sue for the balance was not considered sufficient. Fresh consideration was held to be required. The result is a discrepancy in the treatment of different alteration promises, since an alteration promise to pay more may be supported by consideration (factual benefit to the promisor), whereas factual benefit cannot suffice as the consideration to support an alteration promise to accept less. In *MWB Business Exchange Centres Ltd v Rock Advertising Ltd* [2016] EWCA Civ 553, [2016] 2 Lloyd's Rep 391, the Court of Appeal distinguished *Foakes* and *Selectmove* (Arden LJ at [84–85] and »

Kitchin LJ at [48]). This decision was reversed on a different ground by the Supreme Court, [2018] UKSC 24. Sumption JSC acknowledged, at [18] that the issue was 'a difficult one' and that the area was 'probably ripe for re-examination'.

• Where an alteration promise is not supported by consideration, that promise may nevertheless be binding (although not the same binding effect as where consideration is present) on the basis of the doctrine of promissory estoppel. This estoppel is based on reliance and prevents a promisor from going back on their promise where that would be inequitable in the circumstances in which the promisee has relied upon that promise. Promissory estoppel in English law operates only as a defence and cannot create a cause of action. A more flexible approach to estoppel exists in Australia, and this has led to academic arguments supporting the use of the Australian approach in English law. The future of consideration and its relationship with the doctrine of estoppel remains interesting.

4.1 Introduction

In **Chapter 1**, a contract was defined as a legally enforceable agreement (see **1.3**). We have already considered the process of finalizing agreement (see **Chapter 2**), and problems relating to uncertain terms and agreement mistakes, which may result in the agreement having no effect (see **Chapter 3**). Later, we shall also be examining factors that may vitiate (e.g. destroy) consent and which relate to the actual making of the agreement, such as misrepresentation (see **Chapter 14**), duress and undue influence (see **Chapter 15**).

It is an implicit assumption of the definition, however, that not all agreements are contracts. There must therefore be a body of legal rules by which it is possible to determine whether or not an agreement amounts to a contract. This chapter and **Chapter 5** examine the principles determining the circumstances in which an agreement will be treated as enforceable (i.e. treated as a legally binding contract).

The major indicator of enforceability adopted by the common law was that of mutual exchange of (at the very least) promises of value. In the terminology of the law, where a promise in an agreement was given in return for something of value (including another promise), the first promise was given for *consideration* and could be enforced by legal action. A promise given without consideration (gratuitous promise) was unenforceable unless made in a deed. The formal requirements for a deed are contained in s. 1 of the Law of Property (Miscellaneous Provisions) Act 1989 and are discussed at **5.4.2**. It used to be said that a deed needed to be 'signed, sealed, and delivered'. The requirement for a seal has been formally abolished and it now suffices that it is a signed and attested (witnessed) document containing promises, which is clearly intended to be a deed on its face and to bind the persons signing.

4.1.1 The debate about the consideration requirement

It is easy to understand how consideration became the cornerstone of contracts at common law since those seeking to make promises enforceable could avoid quite considerable formality simply by providing evidence of an exchange of things of value. However, consideration has also frequently been the source of much academic debate for the following reasons.

1. Many other legal systems have efficient and just rules of contract law without any requirement of consideration as a precondition of enforceability.

2. Some agreements that are acknowledged to satisfy the requirement of consideration are said nevertheless to be unenforceable, because either:

   (a) the court is unwilling to believe that the parties ever intended that they should be enforced by legal action (see Chapter 5 on the intention to create legal relations); or

   (b) the court is not satisfied that there is adequate evidence of the alleged agreement (see 5.4 on formalities requirements).

In consequence, some have suggested that the requirement of consideration should be abandoned since the task of sorting enforceable from unenforceable agreements is already achieved by principles requiring that an intention to create legal relations be established and by essential formalities for certain types of contract. (Intention is recognized as the applicable criterion in the Principles of European Contract Law, or PECL, Arts. 2:101 and 2:102.) Article 3.1.2 of the UNIDROIT's Principles of International Commercial Contracts (PICC) makes it clear that the only requirement for a contract is agreement. In determining whether there is agreement, Art. 2.1.2 provides that intention to be bound is regarded as relevant. Article 3.1.2 expressly excludes consideration or the continental requirement of 'cause' as requirements of enforceability. This position is also reflected, at least in the context of alteration promises, in the approach of the Court of Appeal of New Zealand in *Antons Trawling Co. Ltd v Smith* [2003] 2 NZLR 23, in which Baragwanath J, giving the judgment of the court stated, at [93]:

> *The importance of consideration is as a valuable signal that the parties intend to be bound by their agreement, rather than an end in itself.* Where the parties who have already made such intention clear by entering legal relations have acted upon an agreement to a variation, in the absence of policy reasons to the contrary they should be bound by their agreement.

Yet, others, such as Williston in the United States, have suggested that principles determining intention to create legal relations and evidential formality are themselves redundant, since the consideration doctrine (the 'test of bargain') embraces such functions: see Hepple [1970] CLJ 122.

Nevertheless, the orthodox view remains that intention to create legal relations, consideration, and (in some cases) evidential formality are *all* essential ingredients of enforceability: see *Edmonds v Lawson* [2000] QB 501 (discussed at **5.3**).

4.1.2 Is the promise supported by consideration?

The terminology changes in this chapter because the question focuses on enforceability of promises rather than on the making of agreements. The presence or absence of consideration to support a promise will become an issue where the promise has not been performed and it is sought to enforce it (i.e. to sue for its breach). The person seeking to enforce the promise is (ignoring third party questions for the present time) the person to whom the promise was made. This person is the *promisee*. The person making the promise is the *promisor*.

→ **EXAMPLE**

In a sale of goods (a contract by the exchange of promises), the seller (S) has promised to deliver the goods and the buyer (B) has promised to pay for them on delivery.

1. S, in breach of its promise, fails to deliver and B wants to sue for breach. In relation to the delivery promise, S is the promisor and B is the promisee who is now seeking to enforce that promise, and B therefore needs to show that it has provided consideration to support S's promise. B can do this since B promised to pay for the goods on delivery.

2. However, what if B is the party in breach? S has delivered the goods and B has failed to pay for them, in breach of its promise to do so. S is seeking to enforce B's promise, so this time S is the promisee and B is the promisor. S can demonstrate the necessary consideration to support B's promise, since S promised to deliver the goods.

4.1.3 Formation and alteration promises

A formation promise is a promise made where there is no existing contract between the parties and it is sought to create one. Formation promises must therefore be distinguished from alteration promises, where a party (or parties) to an existing contract seeks to alter (vary) its terms.

As a general rule, both types of promise must be supported by consideration for the promise to be enforceable (assuming that it is not contained in a deed). However, a more relaxed approach to the enforceability of alteration promises can be detected because either:

1. it is easier to find consideration to support some alteration promises (i.e. in some circumstances, it can take the form of a factual benefit to the promisor *Williams v Roffey Bros.*, discussed at **4.4.4**, which arises from the making of the alteration promise); or

2. despite the absence of consideration, the doctrine of promissory estoppel operates as a defence to prevent the promisor from going back on its promise (discussed at **4.8**).

Arguably, a more relaxed approach *should* be taken to enforcing alteration promises that were freely made as a response to circumstances as consideration will already have been provided to achieve a binding contract between these parties (formation consideration).

It is not always difficult to identify consideration to support a formation promise since all sorts of trivial exchanges have sufficed. However, the law takes a strict approach to some acts or promises that it generally considers to be insufficient as consideration.

4.2 Identifying consideration

4.2.1 Definitions of consideration: benefit/detriment or the price for which the promise of the other is bought

Traditionally, consideration is said to exist when the law accepts that there is a demonstrable *benefit and/or a detriment*. In *Currie v Misa* (1875) LR 10 Ex 153, at 162, Lush J stated that '[a] valuable consideration, in the sense of the law, may consist either in some right, interest, profit or benefit accruing to the one party, or some forbearance, detriment, loss or responsibility, given, suffered, or undertaken by the other'. The act or promise said to constitute the consideration may be both a detriment to the promisor and a corresponding benefit to the promisee; it is, however, unnecessary to have both benefit and detriment, as made clear by Lush J.

Modern English law has largely abandoned the benefit/detriment analysis, preferring the definition of consideration provided by Sir Frederick Pollock—in Sir Percy Winfield (ed.), *Pollock's Principles of Contract*, 13th edn (Stevens, 1950), p. 133—to the effect that consideration is constituted by 'an act or forbearance of one party, or the promise thereof', being 'the price for which the promise of the other is bought' (introducing the notion of exchange). This statement was adopted by Lord Dunedin in *Dunlop Pneumatic Tyre Co. Ltd v Selfridge & Co. Ltd* [1915] AC 847.

It is important to be familiar with both formulations, not only because some of the cases still use the language of benefit and detriment, but also because some sub-rules of the doctrine of consideration owe their existence to the traditional formulation (see 4.3). The continuing influence of the language of benefit and detriment is clear in *Williams v Roffey Bros. and Nicholls (Contractors) Ltd* [1991] 1 QB 1, which caused a thorough re-evaluation of the doctrine of consideration (see especially **4.4.4** and **4.6.1**). However, when analysing in a contemporary problem whether consideration exists in an agreement, it would be much better to rely on the notion of exchange.

The essential test is whether what is provided by the one party (be it action, inaction, or merely a promise thereof) induced the action, inaction, or promise of the other.

4.2.1.1 Acts or promises given in exchange: the bilateral/unilateral distinction

Consideration is defined both in terms of acts done (or not done) and in terms of promises; the other's promise can therefore be 'bought' in two ways.

Contract's great value as a commercial device is that it allows liability on an obligation even where performance on both sides remains in the future (see **1.3.1**). It is in this facility that the strength of contract as an instrument of planning lies.

4.2.1.1.1 Bound on the exchange of promises

In a bilateral contract, consideration is provided by the exchange of promises.

The classic example of consideration involving an exchange of promises is a contract for the sale of goods, under which the seller agrees to deliver the goods at some time in the future and the buyer agrees to pay for them either on delivery or by some credit arrangement. At the time of the agreement, neither side has done anything towards the performance of the promises made, but the agreement still has contractual force. Both parties have subjected themselves to a potential claim for breach of contract in the event that they fail to perform and, in this sense, there is a clear benefit or detriment at the time that the promises are given. This type of consideration is described as *executory*.

If the seller fails to deliver, the buyer has a claim for breach of contract (i.e. the delivery promise), since this promise is supported by the buyer's consideration (i.e. the buyer's promise to pay on delivery). The contract exists from the moment of the exchange of the promises, although performance occurs later.

4.2.1.1.2 Consideration as the performance of the requested act

Where consideration consists of an exchange of a promise for an act, it is described as *executed*. This type of contract is a unilateral contract (see **2.6**), e.g. a promise of a reward *in exchange* for the act of supplying certain information, as in *R v Clarke* (1927) 40 CLR 227.

In **R v Clarke**, the government of Western Australia had offered a reward for information leading to the arrest of certain criminals. Clarke gave information that led to a conviction and sued to recover the reward, although he admitted that, at the time of giving the information, his only motive had been to clear his own name. It was held that he was unable to recover.

The case is usually described as an example of the need to know about an offer before being able to accept it. Clarke, however, had seen the reward offer, but had forgotten about it. The better view may therefore be that his action was not induced by the promise of reward and therefore consideration was absent. The element of exchange is vital.

Executed consideration consists of a promise followed by an act. Care must be taken to distinguish the situation in which an act is followed by a promise, which does not amount to consideration (see **4.3.3**: past consideration).

4.2.1.2 Consideration must be distinguished from the motive for the making of the promise

The exchange theory of consideration also requires the giving, in exchange for a promise, of something of value, so that mere motive in making a promise, unattached to any element of value, is not sufficient consideration.

In **Thomas v Thomas** (1842) 2 QB 851, 114 ER 330, the testator, a dying man, had expressed the wish to the executors of his will that his wife should be able to live in his house for as long as she should wish to do so and for as long as she remained a widow. There was, however, no provision to that effect in his will. Wishing nevertheless to comply with the testator's intentions, the executors promised the house to the widow 'in consideration of such desire'. Nevertheless, the executors later refused to let her stay in the house and she was ejected. The court was unanimous in its view that, whatever the moral obligation, in such a situation the mere motive of satisfying the wishes of the deceased testator could not constitute consideration on the part of the executors.

In addition, satisfying the testator's desire could not be consideration to support the executors' promise enabling the widow to enforce their promise, since consideration had to move from (be supplied by) the promisee (the widow), and this was not consideration supplied by the promisee (the widow).

4.2.2 Does consideration need to 'move from the promisee'?

In *Thomas v Thomas* (1842), it was interpreted that the consideration to support a promise had to move from (i.e. be supplied by) the promisee—a point itself interpreted to mean that the consideration had to *move* from the claimant or person enforcing the promise. However, if adopted, this interpretation would prevent a third party from enforcing a promise. The Contracts (Rights of Third Parties) Act 1999 now provides for third party enforcement in certain circumstances and it is clear that, in light of this legislative measure and comments by the Law Commission in its report *Privity of Contract: Contracts for the benefit of third parties* (Cm. 3329, 1996), Part VI, consideration need not be provided by a claimant (see **11.2.1**). However, consideration to support a promise must be supplied **by the promisee** if the promise is to be enforceable, i.e. by the person to whom the promise was made.

4.2.3 Consideration need not move to the promisor

Consideration may be provided where the promisee suffers a detriment at the request of the promisor but this confers no corresponding benefit on the promisor. This can occur where the promisee enters into a contract with a third party at the request of the promisor.

In **Hunt v Optima (Cambridge) Ltd** [2014] EWCA Civ 714, [2015] 1 WLR 1346, Optima sold flats to purchasers and Strutt & Parker (S&P), who were employed by Optima for this purpose, issued architects' certificates attesting to the satisfactory construction of the flats. The certificates were received by the purchasers of the flats after exchange of contracts and execution of the leases on the flats. The Court of Appeal rejected claims based on breach of warranty in relation to the certificate but S&P had argued that if there was such a warranty it would not have been supported by consideration on the part of the purchasers who had already agreed to purchase the flats when they received the certificates, i.e. that any consideration would be past (see **4.3.3**). Christopher Clarke LJ (at [81]) rejected this argument on the basis that if the certificates had amounted to contractual promises, in exchange for promising to pay the price, there was a promise to convey the flat and to produce the certificate. The issue of the certificate did not involve any subsequent act. In addition, it was immaterial that consideration from the purchasers did not move to S&P in exchange for any certificate promise since the requirement was only that it needed to move from the purchasers (as promisees). (The decision of the Court of Appeal was that purchasers who received their certificates after completion would not have relied upon any negligent statement in the certificate when committing to the purchase and so had no cause of action based on the tort of negligent misstatement.)

The operation of credit cards provides a good illustration of consideration not moving to the promisor. The card issuer promises the retailer, who accepts payment using the card, that the retailer will be paid. The retailer's consideration for this promise is the retailer's promise to supply the goods purchased to the buyer/card holder (*Re Charge Card Services Ltd* [1987] Ch 150, affirmed [1989] Ch 497).

4.3 Consideration must be sufficient, but need not be adequate (equivalent)

4.3.1 Need not be adequate (equivalent)

Once something of value can be shown to exist, the court makes no inquiry into whether the thing offered is a genuine equivalent of the promise made.

At some early point in its history, the doctrine of consideration might have developed as a means to police bargains between parties, requiring the exchange of things of equivalent value. As such, it would have been part of the law's armour against duress and fraud (see **4.4.4** and **Chapter 15**). But, the doctrine of freedom of contract, and no doubt the mere practical difficulty of proving equivalence, intervened to prevent such a development. There is no investigation of whether the value given in return for the promise is any real benefit to the promisor or any real detriment to the promisee, let alone of whether the promises exchanged are of equivalent value. All that is required is that actual value be given. Thus, in *Thomas v Thomas* (1842) 2 QB 851, 114 ER 330, the widow to whom the house was promised had in turn promised to pay £1 per annum as ground rent, and to maintain the property in good and tenantable repair. This return promise was found to be of actual value and thus to amount to sufficient consideration. This rule finds frequent expression in the provision in leases for peppercorn rents.

In the consumer context, however, it may be possible for the adequacy of the price to be assessed and the term may be held to be not binding on the consumer. Section 64 of the Consumer Rights Act (CRA) 2015 provides that in a contract to which the Act applies (B2C—between a 'trader' and a 'consumer'), although it is not generally possible to assess the appropriateness (level) of the price payable compared with what is supplied, the price may be assessed for fairness where the term in question is not presented in a way that satisfies the requirements of transparency and prominence. It follows that in this context a court will first need to consider whether the price term is transparent and prominent. It may not be so if the price appears in the small print, in which case and it would then be possible to assess the price term for fairness under the provisions of Part 2 of the Act.

The language of s. 64 differs from its predecessor (reg. 6(2) UTCCR 1999, SI 1999/2083) which provided that the price term could only be assessed for fairness if it was not expressed in 'plain and intelligible language'. However, this was found to be easily satisfied (*Office of Fair Trading v Abbey National plc* [2009] UKSC 6, [2010] 1 AC 696 (the 'bank charges' case)). The subsequent decision of the European Court of Justice (ECJ) in Case C-26/13, *Kásler v OTP Jelzálogbank Zrt* [2014] Bus LR 664, [2014] 2 All ER (Comm) 443, confirmed that the European legislation required more than formal grammatical clarity and intelligibility. There was a requirement of transparency which had to be understood in a broad sense (at [72]) given the consumer's possible position of weakness in the relationship. In particular, the term needed to be set out with such transparency that average consumers would be in a position to evaluate the consequences of the application of the term for them (at 74]). This change in emphasis may therefore lead to greater intervention on behalf of consumers (in the context of B2C—trader to consumer—contracts).

4.3.2 Sufficiency: something of value in the eyes of the law

Consideration must be something that the law is prepared to accept as having some value. Trivial acts *can* amount to valid consideration provided that the law recognizes them as such.

Chappell & Co. Ltd v Nestlé Co. Ltd [1960] AC 87 involved a promotional scheme for a brand of chocolate whereby records of a song were offered to the public for 1s. 6d. (7.5p) and three chocolate wrappers, whereas the normal price was 6s. 6d. (32.5p). Manufacture and sale of the records constituted a breach of copyright in the song unless royalties were paid to the copyright owners, who in this case were the claimants. Under a statutory scheme, a copyright owner was not entitled to object if informed and paid a royalty of 6.25 per cent of the ordinary retail selling price. The defendant gave notice, stating the ordinary retail selling price to be 1s. 6d., and the claimants objected.

The House of Lords took the view that whether the chocolate wrappers were part of the price paid depended upon whether they were part of the consideration for the sale of the records to the public. A minority of their Lordships found evidence of motive in the promotional scheme, but not consideration. Lord Reid, making the leading speech for the majority, conceded that the wrappers could not be seen as either benefit or detriment in one sense: the chocolate company threw them away as soon as they received them, and no doubt the consuming public would have thrown them away too but for the offer. However, what mattered was that the company saw fit to require the delivery of the wrappers in exchange for its delivery of the record. The company's motive for so doing was of no interest to the court, but the requirement of exchange nevertheless demonstrated the existence of consideration.

This minimalist approach of finding a benefit in *Chappell v Nestlé* was again evident in *Williams v Roffey Bros.* [1991] 1 QB 1 (the facts are given at **4.4.4**). In *Roffey*, the Court of Appeal had to decide whether a promise to pay more money to achieve performance under an existing contract was enforceable, despite the fact that the claimant had apparently given nothing additional in return for this promise. The Court of Appeal was willing to find consideration, despite its absence on a legal and objective analysis, in the subjective (factual) benefit to the promisor arising from making the promise. Detriment was not a required part of the equation—and this position has subsequently been confirmed by the recognition of consideration only in the form of benefit in *Edmonds v Lawson* [2000] QB 501. Thus, the definition of consideration in *Chappell v Nestlé* and in *Williams v Roffey Bros.* may be regarded as coinciding with Sir Frederick Pollock's definition of consideration as 'the price for which the promise of the other is bought' (see **4.2.1**), provided that it is realized that 'price' here means anything of actual subjective value to the promisor.

We must turn to the test by which the courts determine whether something is of sufficient value to amount to consideration. It appears to embody elements of both law and fact. Mere sentiment cannot constitute consideration, and consideration cannot involve a promise to give up a right which is not possessed: see *White v Bluett* (1853) 23 LJ Ex 36, in which a son's promise not to complain about his father's distribution of his property could not be consideration because the son had no right to complain. However, subject to these legal limitations, it seems that anything may be of sufficient value to amount to consideration if the party receiving it regards it at the time as a sufficient inducement to give their (return) promise, which is essentially a factual test. This idea of mutual inducement as the most basic kind of exchange is at the heart of the majority opinion in *Chappell v Nestlé*, and many of the more difficult English cases on consideration fit more comfortably with that analysis than with any other.

4.3.3 Past consideration: the necessity for exchange

It was suggested at 4.2.1.1 that where it is alleged that a contract exists on the basis of an act followed by a promise, the courts will not enforce such a promise. In such cases, the consideration is described as 'past', and the rule is easily explained by the theory of exchange, since the act is not given in exchange for the promise.

> **→ EXAMPLE**
>
> I am drowning in a lake. You rescue me. I *then* promise to pay you £100 for your trouble. The only consideration that you have provided is your act of rescuing me, but that act cannot be a good consideration, because it pre-dates my promise and is therefore not given in exchange for that promise.

The past consideration rule is well illustrated by the classic case of *Roscorla v Thomas* (1842) 3 QB 234, 114 ER 496.

The claimant had negotiated the purchase of a horse from the defendant for a given price. When the negotiations had been completed and agreement reached, the defendant assured the claimant that the horse was sound and free from vice. The horse failed to match that description and the issue was whether any enforceable warranty (i.e. promise) had been given that the horse was sound. As this express warranty was given *after* the making of the contract, it could therefore not be the consideration to support the promise to buy, because it was not given in exchange for that promise.

Re McArdle [1951] Ch 669 provides a further illustration of the past consideration rule.

The children of a family were, under their father's will, entitled to a house after their mother's death. During the mother's lifetime, one of the married children lived in the house and his wife paid for several improvements to be made. Subsequently, all of the children signed a document in which they promised that the wife should be repaid £488 out of the estate for the work done. This promise was held to be unenforceable because the work amounted to past consideration. The work had been executed before the promise was made and therefore had not been given in exchange for the promise.

4.3.3.1 Sidestepping past consideration: the 'previous request' device

A device can be used to avoid (or sidestep) the past consideration rule when it can be said that there was an understanding that goods or services were to be paid for, but no express agreement had been reached as to the amount payable before the time for performance. In such cases, a subsequent promise to pay a stated sum might well appear to be past consideration. However, it would be undesirable as a matter of policy for such understandings not to be enforceable, not least because many professional people, such as accountants and solicitors, operate on the basis that their services are to be paid for, but that the precise fee will not be invoiced until after performance.

This device is therefore not an exception to the past consideration rule but merely a way of reinterpreting the factual situation in order to sidestep that rule. Using this 'device', the subsequent promise to pay is no more than quantification and evidence of an obligation to pay, which had already arisen by virtue of a simple contract between the parties. As we saw in **Chapter 3**, under s. 8(1) Sale of Goods Act 1979 it is perfectly possible, in a sale of goods contract, for the price to be left unspecified at the formation stage and fixed at a subsequent date.

In *Pao On v Lau Yiu Long* [1980] AC 614, at p. 629G, Lord Scarman provided the following definition of the conditions for operation of the previous request device:

The act must have been done at the promisor's request: the parties must have understood that the act was to be remunerated either by a payment or the conferment of some other benefit: and payment, or the conferment of a benefit, must have been legally enforceable had it been promised in advance.

Pao On v Lau Yiu Long extended the scope of this device to apply not only to requested acts, but also to situations in which the making of a promise is requested.

⟳ SUMMARY

1. I request that you perform an act (or make a particular promise).
2. That request carries with it an *implied promise to pay* (the promise).
3. The act is performed (or requested promise made).
4. There is a *later express promise* that fixes the amount of the reward (a reward promise).

Performing the act (step 3) can be good consideration to support the earlier implied promise to pay (step 2) because the act comes after that promise and is performed in exchange for that implied promise.

The earliest example of recognition of this device is *Lampleigh v Brathwait* (1615) Hob 105, 80 ER 255.

Brathwait had killed a man and asked Lampleigh to intercede with the King to obtain a pardon. Lampleigh did as he was asked and was successful in obtaining the pardon. Brathwait *then* promised him £100. There is no doubt that Lampleigh's performance was executed before the promise was made, but the court said that the fact that the service had been requested meant that the promise was nevertheless supported by consideration—namely, the performance by Lampleigh.

In making the request, Brathwait must be taken impliedly to have promised to pay for the service rendered and, in relation to that promise, consideration was not past. The later express promise merely fixed the amount of the reward.

This explanation of *Lampleigh v Brathwait* was put forward in *Re Casey's Patents* [1892] 1 Ch 104, at pp. 115–16, by Bowen LJ:

Even if it were true . . . that a past service cannot support a future promise, you must look at the document and see if the promise cannot receive a proper effect in some other way. Now, the fact of a past service raises an implication that at the time it was rendered it was to be paid for, and, if it was a service which was to be paid for, when you get in the subsequent document a promise to pay, that promise may be treated either as an admission which evidences or as a positive bargain which fixes the amount of that reasonable remuneration on the faith of which the service was originally rendered.

4.3.3.2 Does the previous request device apply on the facts?

There are two core requirements.

1. Was there a request to perform the act or make the promise?
2. Can it be said that this request carries with it an implied promise to pay or compensate?

In addressing these questions—and particularly the second one—it is helpful to distinguish commercial and domestic agreements, since there is some evidence that a court may be more willing to imply a promise to pay from a request in a commercial relationship than in a domestic one, and even to imply the request itself in the commercial context, although not the domestic.

In *Re McArdle* [1951] Ch 669 (for facts, see **4.3.3**), a domestic situation, the court did not find any implied promise to pay dating back from before the time when the work was done. There could be no earlier implied promise to compensate because there had been no request by the promisors that the work be carried out. Further, if the context is domestic, even where a request can be found, it will inevitably be more difficult to argue that the request carries with it an implied promise to pay for the services. If I ask my neighbour to help me to take out my rubbish for the rubbish collection, although I have made a request, no remuneration is expected for this service, in the absence of some express promise to this effect.

In a commercial context, however, where there is a request of some kind, it is much easier to establish an implied promise to pay for the services simply because, in this context, people do not generally do something for nothing.

Re Casey's Patents [1892] 1 Ch 104 is an example of the commercial context. A manager promoted a particular invention for the owners of the patent rights for a two-year period. The owners then promised him a share in those rights in consideration for his previous services for them. It was alleged that the promise was unenforceable as being supported only by past consideration. In finding the promise to be enforceable, Bowen LJ found evidence on which to base the implication of a promise to pay in the circumstances of the case: the manager must always have assumed that his work would be remunerated in some way. The subsequent promise therefore merely fixed the form of that remuneration.

The facts of *Pao On v Lau Yiu Long* [1980] AC 614 provide a further example of the implication of a promise to pay (or to indemnify) arising from a request in the context of a commercial contract.

> *Pao On v Lau Yiu Long* concerned the enforceability of a promise of indemnity in favour of the claimants, which had been made by the defendants, the majority shareholders in the Fu Chip Investment Company. This indemnity document referred to the main agreement between the Fu Chip Company and the claimants, whereby the latter had promised not to sell 60 per cent of their shares in Fu Chip before 30 April 1974. It was clear that the claimants' promise in the main agreement had been made at the request of the defendants, who wished to ensure the stability of the market price for shares in Fu Chip. The Privy Council considered that the promise had been made on the understanding that the claimants were to be compensated by the defendants for agreeing to this restriction on their ability to sell their shares. Accordingly, the claimants' promise in the main agreement, whereby they promised to retain the shares, constituted a valid consideration for the defendants' implied promise to compensate them. The later indemnity promise merely fixed the nature of that protection.

Lord Scarman, giving the judgment of the court at p. 634, laid great stress upon the fact that this case involved businessmen bargaining at arm's length:

> It seems clear, therefore, that where the whole arrangement is couched in terms of commercial exchange, the courts may be more willing to interpret circumstances as amounting to a request to perform a service, despite the absence of anything as express between the parties, and they may be more willing to find that the request carries with it an implied promise to pay.

⚙ SUMMARY

Pao On v Lau Yiu Long

1. The defendants request a promise from the claimants (i.e. the claimants will retain their shares for one year).

2. This request is coupled with an understanding that the defendants were to give the claimants some form of protection (or indemnity) against a fall in the value of those shares in this period.

3. The claimants make the promise to retain the shares for a year.

4. The defendants give the indemnity promise fixing the exact protection.

In relation to the defendants' promise to give an indemnity (step 2), the claimants' promise (step 3) is not past consideration.

4.3.3.3 Consideration distinguished from conditions imposed upon the recipients of gifts

This distinction can be difficult to explain. Peel, in *Treitel's The Law of Contract*, 14th edn (Sweet and Maxwell, 2015), [3-011], argues that, in *Carlill v Carbolic Smoke Ball Co. Ltd* [1893] 1 QB 256, the consideration provided by the claimant was her use of the smoke ball as directed by the defendants. The need to catch influenza is interpreted as only a condition enabling her to enforce the promise. This may be because catching influenza cannot be controlled directly by the claimant and therefore cannot be seen as something of value provided by the claimant. Similarly, in *Thomas v Thomas* (1842) 2 QB 851, 114 ER 330 (discussed at **4.2.1.2**) the requirement that the widow should remain a widow and not remarry was a condition entitling her to enforce the promise and not the consideration to support the testator's promise to leave her his house.

These examples of conditions are very different in nature from the requirement to supply three chocolate wrappers in *Chappell & Co. Ltd v Nestlé Co. Ltd* [1960] AC 87 (for facts, see **4.3.2**). The House of Lords rejected an argument to the effect that the wrappers were not part of the consideration, but merely a condition for the supply of the record for 1s. 6d. As Lord Reid stated, the wrappers were supplied by the applicant at the request of the defendants and were of benefit (albeit in the loosest sense of this word) to the defendants. However, in the case of conditional gifts, there is no direct benefit to the requestor from performance of the condition entitling the party to enforce the promise, e.g. catching influenza or remaining a widow.

This distinction may be considered largely redundant if the *Chappell v Nestlé* approach to the definition of consideration is adopted, i.e. if the consideration to support a promise consists of whatever has been requested in exchange by the promisor. On this basis, catching influenza (*Carlill*) OR remaining a widow (*Thomas*) would be part of the consideration to support the promise rather than a condition or entitlement to enforce it, since these acts are part of the *requested exchange*.

4.3.3.4 Genuine exception for negotiable instruments

A negotiable instrument, such as a cheque for instance, is a document containing a promise of payment. When the document (cheque) is transferred to the transferee (the person who will cash the cheque), this gives the transferee for value a right to enforce the promise of payment against the promisor (the person who signed the cheque) free of any defences that would have been available to the promisor against the transferor (see **11.5.4**).

Section 27(1) of the Bills of Exchange Act 1882 provides that valuable consideration for a bill of exchange may be constituted either by consideration, as normally defined in contract law, or by 'an antecedent debt or liability' (s. 27(1)(b)). Goods or services may have been supplied, and these goods or services are paid for by cheque. The consideration for the promise of payment contained in that cheque would be past consideration were it not for the statutory exception in s. 27(1). This is because the cheque is used as payment to satisfy an existing debt, albeit that the debt may have just been created (e.g. employing a cleaner and writing a cheque in payment).

4.4 Performance of existing duties

Traditionally, in most circumstances, the performance of an existing duty cannot be consideration for a further promise. In terms of our definition of consideration, the reason is relatively clear: where I am already under a legal duty to perform an act or to make a promise, I cannot be said to have been induced to do that thing by the further promise made by another, since the obligation to do it already existed.

It is traditional to subdivide the rule into three different types of case:

(a) *performance of a duty imposed by law;*

(b) *performance of an existing contractual duty owed to a third party;* and

(c) *performance of an existing contractual duty owed to the promisor* (the context for which will necessarily be a promise to alter an existing contract between the parties).

Performance of a duty imposed by law (a) and performance of an existing contractual duty owed to the promisor (c) have traditionally been regarded as insufficient to act as consideration for a fresh promise. Performance of a contractual duty owed to a third party (b), however, has long been recognized as an exception, presumably because of the involvement of the third party, although no single justification for this exception has been accepted.

The strictness of this refusal to accept performance of existing duties as consideration to support fresh promises has been mitigated in two ways, as follows.

1. **Going beyond the duty**

    The courts have been willing to find additional benefit or detriment in actions that go beyond the legal duty (a) or existing contractual duty owed to the promisor (c).

2. **The *Roffey* principle**

    As a result of *Williams v Roffey Bros.* [1991] 1 QB 1, it may be possible to avoid the restrictive outcome in category (c)—i.e. performance of an existing contractual duty owed to the promisor—where there is a factual (or practical) benefit to the promisor arising from the making of a promise to pay more money to secure performance of an existing duty owed to that promisor. This is not, however, the same thing as saying that the 'promisee's performance' itself generates the consideration, as is the case in category (b) cases. As will be seen, it is the *promisor's* promise to pay more that provides the consideration (factual benefit to the promisor) in the category (c) case.

4.4.1 Performance of a duty imposed by law: category (a)

The leading case in the area of public duties is *Collins v Godefroy* (1831) 1 B & Ad 950, 109 ER 1040.

> The claimant was promised payment in return for his undertaking to give expert evidence at a trial at which he was, in any case, obliged to attend to give evidence because he had been summoned by subpoena. In those circumstances, the promise of payment was unenforceable because the claimant had given no consideration for it. He was under an existing duty imposed by law to attend the trial and, accordingly, had done no more than he was already legally obliged to do.

A more modern statement of the rule was given by the House of Lords in *Glasbrook Brothers Ltd v Glamorgan County Council* [1925] AC 270, although on the facts their Lordships considered that there was consideration because the police had gone beyond the scope of the duty imposed by law.

> *Glasbrook Brothers Ltd v Glamorgan County Council* involved a claim by a local authority to recover payment for the provision of police to guard a mine during a strike. The defendants argued that the police were charged with a duty imposed by law to guard the mine as part of their general duty to keep the peace, to prevent crime, and to protect persons and property from criminal injury. However, at the time of the strike, the colliery owners had insisted on a greater level of manning than the local police had deemed necessary. The House of Lords, by a bare majority, decided that the only duty on the local authority was to provide such policing as was considered necessary by the police authority.

Provision of policing beyond what was deemed necessary was not therefore performance of an existing duty and could amount to consideration for a promise to pay for the service provided. This matter is now governed by s. 25 of the Police Act 1996, which provides for payment where 'special police services' are requested, although the principles to determine whether the services are 'special' relate to the scope of the duty of the police and whether the services requested go beyond this.

> In *Leeds United Football Club v Chief Constable of West Yorkshire* [2013] EWCA Civ 115, [2013] 3 WLR 539, the Court of Appeal regarded policing of areas in the immediate vicinity of the football club, but outside the club's property, as not going beyond normal policing duties to maintain law and order and protect public property.

However, in *Ward v Byham* [1956] 1 WLR 496, the majority of the Court of Appeal found consideration in actions that they considered to go beyond the scope of the duty owed by law.

> The father of an illegitimate child agreed to pay the mother £1 per week to maintain the child, provided that the mother was able to show that the child was 'well looked after and happy', and that the child was allowed to choose for herself whether to live with her mother or to carry on being cared for by a neighbour of the father's. The child went to live with the mother, but the father stopped the payments when the mother married.
>
> The Court of Appeal treated the case as one of performance of an existing duty because the mother was under a statutory duty to look after the child properly. The majority of the Court of Appeal, Morris and Parker LJJ, while acknowledging that the mother did owe an existing duty, found 'ample consideration' for the promise in the mother's undertakings to keep the child happy and to allow her to choose where to live. On the other hand, Denning LJ would have enforced the promise of maintenance on the basis that he considered that a promise to perform an existing duty could be a good consideration where, as here, there was a factual benefit to the father in securing that performance.

The approach of the majority did not attack traditional orthodoxy (i.e. that there is no legal benefit or detriment in performing an existing duty), since it involved identifying additional benefit or detriment in law through actions or promises outside the scope of the duty owed in law. Denning LJ's approach was considerably more radical, since it involved recognising benefits in fact rather than in law. Nevertheless, in *Williams v Williams* [1957] 1 WLR 148, at p. 151, Denning LJ repeated his argument that 'a promise to perform an existing duty is, I think, sufficient consideration to support a promise, so long as there is nothing in the transaction which is contrary to the public interest'. For example, to enforce a promise such as that in *Collins v Godefroy* would clearly be contrary to the public interest.

4.4.2 Performance of an existing contractual duty owed to a third party: category (b)

The performance of an existing contractual duty owed to a third party may be consideration for a promise.

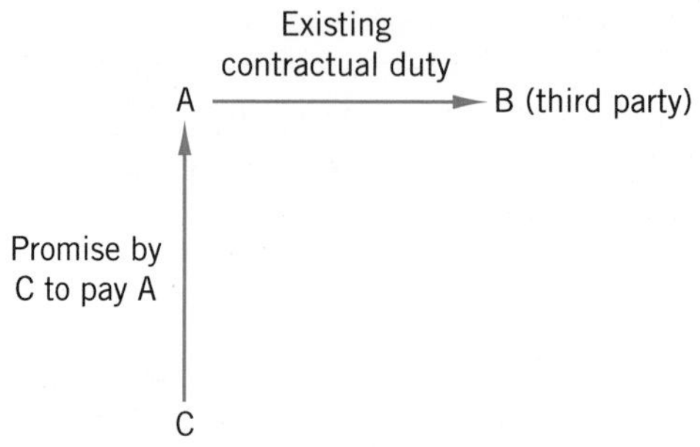

FIGURE 4.1 Performance of a contractual duty to a third party as consideration for a promise

→ EXAMPLE

If A owes an existing contractual duty to B, A can use the performance of this duty to B (or their promise to perform it) as consideration to support a promise by C to pay A a sum of money. (In relation to the contract A/C, B is clearly a third party.) A's performance of the contract A/B can provide the consideration for a promise made by C (see **Figure 4.1**).

Early evidence of this exception may be found in *Scotson v Pegg* (1861) 6 Hurl & N 295, 158 ER 121.

In *Scotson v Pegg*, A entered into a contract with B to deliver coal to C. C then said to A that if A would deliver the coal to him, C would unload the coal at a fixed rate per day. C failed to keep his promise and, in response to legal action by A, claimed that his promise was unsupported by consideration since A was already bound by his contract with B to deliver the coal to C. C was nevertheless found liable, and the court expressed the view that performance of an existing contractual duty owed to a third party (i.e. owed to B since the contract in question was the contract A/C) might be consideration for a separate promise (i.e. a promise by C).

It is not clear, however, whether this was the basis of the decision, or whether, on account of facts not disclosed in the report, A's promise to C carried an extra burden by comparison with his promise to B.

Further support for the existence of this exception is in *Shadwell v Shadwell* (1860) 9 CB NS 159, 142 ER 62, in which a nephew had supplied consideration to support a promise to pay him £150 annually if he were to marry his fiancée, whom he was under an existing contractual duty to marry because 'breach of promise to marry' actions existed at this time. However, this decision is of doubtful authority on several grounds, including a possible absence of intention to create legal relations (see **5.2.1**), since it was a family agreement and because the majority placed reliance on finding detriment to the nephew and a benefit to the uncle as a result of the nephew's marriage.

Whatever the authority of the earlier cases, the exception was subsequently confirmed by two Privy Council decisions, which are generally accepted as representing English law on this question. In *New Zealand Shipping Co. Ltd v A. M. Satterthwaite & Co. Ltd, The Eurymedon* [1975] AC 154, at p. 168, Lord Wilberforce, giving the majority opinion, said:

An agreement to do an act which the promisor is under an existing obligation to a third party to do, may quite well amount to valid consideration and does so in the present case: the promisee obtains the benefit of a direct obligation which he can enforce. This proposition is illustrated and supported by *Scotson v Pegg* . . . which their Lordships consider to be good law.

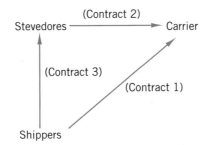

FIGURE 4.2 The contracts in *The Eurymedon* case

In *The Eurymedon*, the carrier of goods had, by contract, validly limited its liability to the shipper of the goods (contract 1). It was the carrier's responsibility to procure a stevedore to unload the goods (contract 2), but the court found that the stevedores enjoyed a quite independent contract with the shippers (contract 3) (on which aspect of the case, see 2.6.5.1 and 11.6.4). (See Figure 4.2.)

1. Contract 1 was the main contract between the shippers and the carrier whereby the carrier, their servants, agents, and independent contractors had the benefit of the exemption clause (the 'Himalaya clause').

2. Contract 2 was the contract whereby the carrier employed the stevedores to unload the goods at their destination.

3. Contract 3 needed to be 'created' by the court in order to make the promise of exemption in Contract 1 directly enforceable by the stevedores.

In order to establish that the promise of exemption was enforceable by the stevedores, it had to be shown that they had provided consideration to support it. The only action of the stevedores that could constitute consideration was their act of unloading the goods, and this was a duty that they were already bound by their contract with the carrier (contract 2) to perform.

The Privy Council considered that the performance of this contractual duty (contract 2) owed to the carrier, a third party in relation to contract 3 between the shippers and stevedores, was a good consideration for the shippers' promise of exemption (contract 3).

In *Pao On v Lau Yiu Long* [1980] AC 614 (for facts see 4.3.3.2), the Privy Council followed *The Eurymedon* on the question of consideration and performance of a duty owed to a third party. The Privy Council held that the claimants had provided consideration for the promise of indemnity given by the defendants, the majority shareholders, by promising to perform their existing contractual duty to the Fu Chip Company to retain 60 per cent of their shares. The case is therefore significant as an example of a situation in which *promising* to perform an existing duty owed to a third party was held to constitute a valid consideration.

4.4.3 The basis of the 'pre-existing duty' rule and the justification for the exception

The main interest in *Pao On v Lau Yiu Long* [1980] AC 614 may lie in the discussion by Lord Scarman of the purpose of the 'pre-existing duty' rule. Although the court was not prepared to commit itself to any particular view, it appeared sympathetic to the idea that the 'pre-existing duty' rule might be based in the prevention of duress by contracting parties against those to whom they owed contractual obligations: see *Pao On* at p. 634 (see also 4.4.4).

Accordingly, it might be thought that, in the case of promises by third parties, the risk of such coercion would be considerably diminished so that no such public policy need for the rule would exist in such a case. The Privy Council, however, went further, Lord Scarman stating at pp. 634C–D:

> Where businessmen are negotiating at arm's length it is unnecessary for the achievement of justice, and unhelpful in the development of the law, to invoke such a rule of public policy . . . If a promise is induced by coercion of a man's will, the doctrine of duress suffices to do justice.

In fact, the *Pao On* case was an important stage in the development of a doctrine of economic duress (see 15.1.2), which made the possibility of success in a claim based on duress much greater. For this reason, Lord Scarman's argument above was broad enough in scope to apply not only to pre-existing duties as consideration for third party promises, but also to the pre-existing duty cases (categories (a) and (c) at **4.4.1** and **4.4.4**), in which traditionally there has been said to be no consideration.

This proposal had already been made by Denning LJ in *Williams v Williams* [1957] 1 WLR 148, at p. 151 (see **4.4.1**), when he stated that performance of existing duties should be a good consideration 'so long as there is nothing in the transaction which is contrary to the public interest'. The development of the modern doctrine of economic duress has since been accepted as justification for a more liberal interpretation of the consideration requirement, but only in the context of category (c) cases—*Williams v Roffey Bros.* [1991] 1 QB 1 (see 4.4.4)—and even this has been limited further by denial of the application of this more generous interpretation in the context of alteration promises to accept less (*Roffey* involved an alteration promise to pay more).

4.4.4 Performance of a contractual duty owed to the promisor: category (c)

The traditional principle is that performance of an existing contractual duty cannot be consideration for a further promise from the party to whom the existing duty is owed, since there is no additional legal benefit or detriment.

The leading case was *Stilk v Myrick* (1809) 2 Camp 317, 170 ER 1168.

A crewman had contracted to work a vessel on a voyage for a fixed sum, promising to do anything needed in all of the emergencies of the voyage. During the voyage, two men deserted. The master offered extra payment to those remaining if they would work the ship home; on arrival, the master refused to pay. The promise of extra payment was unenforceable, because desertion of crewmen was an emergency of the voyage, so that there was already a duty to the employer to work the ship home in such a case. Therefore there was no consideration for the promise of further payment.

Most commentators accept that there is a considerable element of policy in the decision: to have enforced the promise was perceived to have been to risk exposing ships' masters to blackmail by the crew as a way to obtain higher wages when far from England. Indeed, this was stated to be the *ratio* for the decision in Espinasse's report of *Stilk v Myrick* at (1809) 6 Esp 129, 170 ER 851, and although Espinasse was not regarded as the most reliable of reporters, the need to prevent extortion is a clear factor in both reports. Therefore, in *Stilk v Myrick*, the doctrine of consideration seems to have performed the function of a rule to prevent economic duress (see **15.1.2**).

In order to avoid this restrictive interpretation of the performance of an existing duty owed to the promisor as insufficient consideration, the courts sought to find additional contractual performance in order to be able to conclude that there was the necessary additional benefit or detriment to render the promise enforceable: *North Ocean Shipping Co. Ltd v Hyundai Construction Co. Ltd, The Atlantic Baron* [1979] QB 705. In this case, the defendant, a shipbuilding company, agreed to build a tanker for the claimant at a fixed price, to be paid in five instalments. The defendant agreed to open a letter of credit to provide security for the repayment of the instalments in case of default in the performance of the contract. The claimant promised to pay an additional 10 per cent in the instalments when the US dollar was devalued and asked the defendant to make a corresponding increase in the letter of credit. It was found that in agreeing to increase the letter of credit, the claimant had undertaken an additional contractual obligation that rendered it liable to an increased detriment. This therefore constituted consideration for the promise by the claimant to increase the instalment payments. It followed that the scope of the original contractual duty was therefore also important in determining the existence of consideration, e.g. the more limited the scope of that duty, the easier it was to demonstrate that the promisee had gone beyond the scope of the duty and provided consideration.

Subsequently, however, in *Williams v Roffey Bros. & Nicholls (Contractors) Ltd* [1991] 1 QB 1, whilst accepting the need to find consideration to support an alteration promise, the Court of Appeal considered that the consideration could be found in the form of a factual (or practical) benefit arising to the promisor from making the promise, despite the fact that the promisee had done no more than he was already contractually bound to do under the terms of the existing contract. This decision does *not* provide that performance of an existing contractual duty is the consideration to support a fresh promise, but it *does* mean that the fresh promise may well be enforceable where the promisee has done nothing more in exchange than perform his existing contractual duty. On this basis, it is possible (in one sense, at least) to reconcile this decision with the principle in *Stilk v Myrick*. Indeed, the Court of Appeal in *Roffey* denied that its decision had overruled *Stilk v Myrick*. Glidewell LJ preferred to describe his approach as being to 'refine and limit the application of that principle' at [16B]. That said, the net effect of *Roffey* must be to diminish the impact of the authority of *Stilk v Myrick*, since it is clear that, in that case, there were factual benefits to the master and shipowner in ensuring that the ship was sailed home whilst short-handed. The only sensible distinction between the cases rests on the context for extortion in *Stilk v Myrick* and the finding in *Williams v Roffey Bros.* that the promise was not extracted by duress (extortion or threats).

The defendants in **Williams v Roffey Bros.** were main contractors on a building contract, and they identified that the claimants, who were subcontractor carpenters on the job, were in financial difficulty and at risk of not completing the work. Had the claimants failed to complete the work, the defendants would have become liable to the building owner under an agreed damages clause (see **9.6**). The defendants therefore took the initiative to avoid the problem, by offering more money for the job to be completed on time. The claimants accepted that offer and then, when the additional payment was not made as promised, sought damages, relying on the promise to pay more as being an enforceable promise.

The problem confronting the claimants, arising out of *Stilk v Myrick*, was that they had given nothing in return for the promise of extra payment other than the performance that they had undertaken to provide under the original contract. However, the commercial sense of the agreement was that the promise should be enforceable—not having been extracted as a result of duress (see **15.1.2.3**)—and this view prevailed with the Court of Appeal.

Although no single majority emerges from the three judgments in the Court of Appeal, three strands of reasoning can be identified, as follows.

1. The policy element in *Stilk v Myrick*, which resulted in the consideration doctrine being applied in a very strict and formal way, is no longer present because of the emergence of the doctrine of economic duress, which allows for a more substantive appraisal of potentially unconscionable contracts (see **15.1.2**). Thus the decision represents a relaxation of the strictness of the rules to identify consideration in the absence of evidence of duress (which would render the promise otherwise unenforceable).

2. The necessary consideration in a commercial case of this kind might be constituted by a factual (practical) benefit to the promisor, if the promisor were in fact induced to make the promise by the benefit that *he perceived himself* to be receiving. There was a real (factual) benefit to the defendants in *Roffey Bros.* in avoiding having to pay the sums due under the main contract in the event of late completion, and so the avoidance of the risk of breach by the subcontractors clearly induced the defendants to make their promise. In addition, the defendants achieved a further factual benefit by avoiding the difficulties of finding another subcontractor to complete the carpentry work. They avoided the risk of breach by the subcontractors.

3. By analogy with the second category of pre-existing duty cases—i.e. category (b), under which performance of a duty owed to a third party may be consideration for a contract with a separate promisor (see **4.4.2**)—no further consideration is required for the modification of an existing contract provided that there is sufficient evidence of an intention that the alteration be legally binding.

Arguments 2 and 3 are conceptually very different, but it would be wrong to make much of this in light of the ease with which a court may find a factual benefit if it so requires; consequently, the two arguments are functionally very closely related.

Although some doubts have been cast upon interpretations of *Williams v Roffey Bros.*, which have proposed a very wide scope for the *ratio* of the case, it has not been suggested that the *ratio* is in any sense unreliable. Indeed, in distinguishing *Williams v Roffey Bros.* by restricting it to the context of extra payment for the originally agreed amount of work (so-called 'promises to pay more'), two differently constituted Courts of Appeal appear to have accepted the correctness of the decision in this respect: see *Re Selectmove Ltd* [1995] 1 WLR 474 and *Re C (a debtor)* [1996] BPIR 535, The Times, 11 May 1994. More recently, it appears to have been accepted (albeit *obiter*) by Teare J in *Horwood v Land of Leather Ltd (in administration)* [2010] EWHC 546 (Comm), [2010] 1 CLC 423. The judge was prepared to recognize practical benefit in the form of an agreement to pay a debt in instalments. This was regarded as a commercial benefit in that it provided some reassurance that the existing credit note of $900,000 would be paid. Teare J noted, at [41]:

> [A]lthough counsel for the Claimants contended that this could not properly be regarded as a practical benefit the court should be slow to say that that which a business man says is a benefit is not: see *Williams v Roffey Bros* at p. 21E–H *per* Purchase LJ.

Nevertheless, the artificial nature of the consideration has increasingly meant that the decision has been subjected to some criticism. In *South Caribbean Trading v Trafalgar Beheer BV* [2004] EWHC 2676 (Comm), [2005] 1 Lloyd's Rep 128, Colman J (*obiter*) considered that doing no more than the promisee was already contractually bound to do under the terms of its contract with the promisor should not constitute a sufficient consideration: *Stilk v Myrick*. He added, at [108]:

> But for the fact that *Williams v Roffey Bros.* was a decision of the Court of Appeal, I would not have followed it. That decision is inconsistent with the long-standing rule that consideration, being the price of the promise sued upon, must move *from* the promisee . . . Lord Justice Glidewell substituted for the established rule as to consideration moving from the promisee a completely different principle—that the promisor must by his promise have conferred a benefit on the other party. Lord Justice Purchas, at pp. 22–23 clearly saw the nonsequitur but was 'comforted' by observations from Lord Hailsham LC in *Woodhouse AC Israel Cocoa Ltd v Nigerian Product Marketing Co. Ltd* [1972] AC 741 at pp. 757–758. Investigation of the correspondence referred to in those observations shows that the latter are not authority for the proposition advanced 'with some hesitation' by Lord Justice Purchas.

Despite this, Colman J concluded (at [109]) that he would have been bound to follow *Williams v Roffey Bros.* since it 'has not yet been held by the House of Lords to have been wrongly decided', although *Roffey* and a finding that factual benefit to the promisor enabled the promise to be enforceable could be avoided where there was evidence of duress.

It seems unlikely that, at this stage, the Supreme Court would unravel the *Roffey* principle. Indeed, although in terms of strict principle it must be considered as a 'creative' decision, the principle is nevertheless in line with the result sought to be achieved in respect of the enforceability of alteration promises. The only possibility of any higher intervention would seem to depend on acceptance of a wider principle of estoppel to replace *Roffey* as the basis of enforcement of alteration promises—or, even more radically, enforceability based on reliance alone (see the discussion of these possibilities at **4.7.3**).

The conclusion must therefore be that, at least in the context of alteration promises to pay more, consideration can be found in the factual benefit to the promisor arising from the alteration promise to pay more. In this situation, therefore, it should not be too difficult to establish the existence of a binding variation (or alteration promise), given that it appears that factual benefit is judged subjectively and it is unlikely that anyone would promise more to secure a result unless they were subjectively to consider this to be in their best interests.

4.4.4.1 *Roffey* consideration and the relationship with duress

In *Williams v Roffey Bros.*, Glidewell LJ had sought to state the applicable legal principles in the following proposition.

1. If A has entered into a contract with B to do work for, or to supply goods or services to, B in return for payment by B, and

2. at some stage before A has completely performed his obligations under the contract B has reason to doubt whether A will, or will be able to, complete his side of the bargain, *and*

3. B thereupon promises A an additional payment in return for A's promise to perform his contractual obligations on time, and

4. as a result of giving A his promise, B in practice obtains a benefit or obviates a disbenefit, and

5. B's promise is not given as a result of economic duress or fraud on the part of A, then

6. the benefit to B is capable of being consideration for B's promise, so that the promise will be legally binding.

This can be interpreted as a single 'integrated principle' whereby the existence of duress in this alteration context will prevent a conclusion that there is consideration for the alteration promise despite the existence of factual benefits. In other words, absence of duress may be seen as a qualifying condition for such a conclusion. However, this poses a conceptual difficulty since duress is a vitiating factor and it might be argued that, unless there is a binding contract in principle (i.e. consideration exists), there is no contract to set aside for duress. It follows that, logically, the existence of consideration should be determined first and only then should the question of duress arise. In practice, the opposite approach seems to apply, i.e. duress is ruled out and then consideration can be found in the form of practical benefits resulting from an alteration promise that was freely given. In addition, the 'integrated analysis' does not fit easily with any arguments suggesting that duress has replaced consideration as the key requirement to determine the enforceability of an alteration promise (or at least an alteration promise to pay more).

Adam Opel GmbH v Mitras Automotive Ltd [2007] EWHC 3205 (QB), [2008] Bus LR Digest D55 (reporting the economic duress paragraphs only), was a clear case of economic duress in the context of an alteration promise to pay more. In this case, Mitras was the sole supplier of a particular type of van bumper mounts for Opel. Following a redesign of their van, Opel, which no longer needed the van bumper supplied by Mitras gave them notice that the contract to supply was to be terminated in six months' time. Upon the notice, Mitras had sought an immediate increase in the price to be paid during the notice period and had threatened to suspend supplies if this was not agreed. The buyer, Opel, had no realistic choice other than to agree or its production would have come to a halt within days. When the notice period ended, the buyer sought repayment, arguing both that the promise to pay more was unenforceable because it was made under duress and that there was no consideration.

The judge, David Donaldson QC, sitting as a deputy High Court judge, focused on the duress argument and had no difficulty concluding that there was duress so that the agreement to pay more was voidable. He added, at [42]:

> The law of consideration is no longer to be used to protect a participant in such a variation. That role has passed to the law of economic duress, which provides a more refined control mechanism, and renders the contract voidable rather than void.

Quite apart from the terminology problems with the use of the word 'void' to explain absence of consideration when 'unenforceable' is far preferable, the judge seemed to treat economic duress as a first hurdle. Having identified economic duress, he concluded at [43], without more, that it necessarily followed that 'GMR cannot rely on absence of consideration, whether as a supplement or an alternative to economic duress'. The judge did not, however, make clear whether (i) duress prevents *Roffey* consideration on the integrated analysis of Glidewell LJ, or (ii) there is in fact *Roffey* consideration for the alteration promise, but it does not matter given the finding of economic duress.

If duress is the central concept, it is difficult to reconcile with Glidewell LJ's single test of consideration with its integrated requirement of *absence* of duress.

4.5 Alteration promises

4.5.1 The consideration requirement

As we can see from the discussion of contractual duties owed to the promisor (**4.4.4**), the role of consideration is not limited to the initial formation of contracts. Agreements between contracting parties not to continue with the contract, or to change (or alter) its terms, are normally unenforceable unless themselves contracts: see e.g. *The Hannah Blumenthal* [1983] 1 AC 854. It follows that consideration is also required to support an alteration promise: *Stilk v Myrick* (1809) 2 Camp 317, 170 ER 1168, *Williams v Roffey Bros.* [1991] 1 QB 1, and *Foakes v Beer* (1884) 9 App Cas 605.

In practice, what happens may be very different. Parties on very good terms and who regularly contract with each other may be willing to uphold non-contractual variations and terminations of contracts. The problem with relying on the good relationship between the parties rather than on a legally enforceable agreement is that unforeseen circumstances may intervene to sour the good relationship or to make its impact irrelevant, e.g. where the original party is replaced by a trustee in bankruptcy, who is under a legal obligation to insist on strict legal rights.

4.5.2 Termination

As far as the termination of agreements is concerned, it is fairly easy to establish consideration in those cases in which the contract is wholly or partially executory, i.e. those in which both parties still have some or all of their performance under the agreement left to execute. In this situation, if both parties give up their right to receive the remaining performance from the other party (so-called 'mutual release'), then there is in that fact an exchange amounting to consideration. It does not matter that the performances outstanding are disproportionate, since the rule that consideration must be sufficient but need not be adequate (see **4.3.1**) prevents examination of the equivalence of the exchange.

The Court of Appeal in *Compagnie Noga D'Importation et D'Exportation v Abacha (No. 4)* [2003] EWCA Civ 1100, [2003] 2 All ER (Comm) 915, was able to avoid the application of the principle in *Stilk v Myrick* (that performance of an existing contractual duty cannot be a good consideration for a fresh promise of payment) by concluding that there had been rescission (or termination) of an earlier agreement, followed by a new agreement ('replacement'), rather than an unenforceable variation of the original agreement. It had been alleged that the new agreement of 16 August was unenforceable since it was not supported by any fresh consideration. However, the Court of Appeal held that an earlier agreement between the parties of 13 August, under which both had unperformed obligations, had been terminated by mutual release and the obligations under it had ended. This mutual release and the mutual promises in the new agreement were construed as the consideration for the new agreement of 16 August.

This construction, and the ability to identify mutual release and mutual promises, is illustrated further in the 'coffee substituted for tea' example below (see **4.5.3**).

Difficulties arise, however, where one party has performed fully. In this situation, a release of the other party resembles a one-sided variation and requires further consideration for it to be binding under existing contract principles.

4.5.3 Variation (or alteration)

Variation of the terms of a contract presents greater difficulty. A variation intended to be advantageous to both sides is automatically supported by consideration, since there is a mutual exchange of benefits (see **4.2.1**). Sometimes, what appears at first to be a one-sided variation can nevertheless, when properly analysed, be brought within the consideration doctrine. Consider the following example.

> **→ EXAMPLE**
>
> A agrees to sell to B ten packets of biscuits, ten packets of tea, and ten loaves of bread for £40. Before either party has performed, B asks A to substitute five jars of coffee for five of the packets of tea. A agrees, saying that the price will remain the same. Is the variation enforceable?
>
> It might seem that the variation lacks consideration, since A is to perform something other than what was first agreed, while B is to pay only what was originally asked. However, if the variation is seen as a two-stage (rather than single-stage) process, it is possible to discern consideration for the change being made.
>
> 1. The first stage is that at which B agrees not to receive five packets of tea, in return for which A agrees not to receive whatever proportion of the total price is represented by the five packets. That stage represents one contract.
>
> 2. A then agrees to supply five jars of coffee, in return for which B agrees to pay whatever balance brings the total price back to £40. This is a second contract, and the variation is thereby enforceable.
>
> Following the rule that consideration must be sufficient but need not be adequate, the court does not have to consider whether a packet of tea is in fact worth the same as a jar of coffee.

Where, however, a variation benefits only one of the parties, some consideration additional to that of the original contract has traditionally been regarded as necessary for the variation to be binding. The Court of Appeal in *Williams v Roffey Bros.* [1991] 1 QB 1 (see **4.4.4**) confirmed the need for consideration to support an alteration (variation) promise, albeit making it easier to identify that consideration in some circumstances.

4.6 Alteration promises to pay more and alteration promises to accept less

Problems over consideration in contract variation cases are of two kinds:

1. one party wishes to obtain more money or greater reward than was originally agreed from the other party, whilst providing the same performance (the enforceability of the other's promise to pay more); or

2. one party wishes to obtain the agreed performance from the other party, while giving something less than was agreed in return (the enforceability of the other's promise to accept less).

4.6.1 Promises to pay more

The decisions of *Stilk v Myrick* (1809) 2 Camp 317, 170 ER 1168, and *Williams v Roffey Bros.* [1991] 1 QB 1 provide authority for the fact that such a promise must be supported by fresh consideration if it is to be enforceable by the promisee, and the fact that the promisee has rendered the performance originally required of him by the terms of the contract is insufficient to constitute that fresh consideration. However, as discussed at **4.4**, there appear to be two ways in which that fresh consideration can be provided, as follows.

1. It is possible to demonstrate that the promisee has gone beyond the scope of the original contractual duty and has thereby provided an additional benefit and/or incurred additional detriment: *North Ocean Shipping Co. Ltd v Hyundai Construction Co. Ltd, The Atlantic Baron* [1979] QB 705.

2. It is possible to find the necessary consideration in the fact that the promise gives rise to a factual benefit for the promisor: *Williams v Roffey Bros.* (This consideration is generated by the alteration promise itself and does not move from the promisee, who has done no more than they were contractually bound to do under the contract. Thus this consideration can involve factual benefit to the promisor without any corresponding additional *legal* detriment to the promisee—although there will be a factual detriment in performing the contractual duty already owed.)

The result is that consideration may be relatively easy to establish in the context of such an alteration promise, assuming that the promise was freely given and that factual benefits are determined subjectively.

4.6.2 Promises to accept less

Promises to accept less than is owed under the existing contract have long troubled English courts. The problem is easily illustrated.

> ### → EXAMPLE
>
> A sells his book to B for £10, payable next Tuesday; on Tuesday, B does not have £10, but offers £8, which A accepts, promising (expressly or impliedly) that he will not seek to recover the remaining £2 from B. However, A later seeks to recover the balance of £2. Is A's promise (to accept £8 in place of £10 and not to sue for the £2 balance) enforceable?

4.6.2.1 The need to supply fresh consideration

In *Pinnel's Case* (1602) 5 Co Rep 117a, it was held that a promise to accept less and not to sue for the balance (such as that made by A) was unenforceable unless B (as promisee) gave some new consideration for it. If B only performed a part of the existing obligation to repay the debt, that was insufficient to support the promise to accept less, since B was doing no more than B was already bound to do.

The rule in *Pinnel's Case* was confirmed by the House of Lords in *Foakes v Beer* (1884) 9 App Cas 605.

In **Foakes v Beer**, Dr Foakes was liable on a judgment debt to Julia Beer, and it was agreed that if the judgment debt sum were to be repaid by agreed instalments, then Julia Beer would not take any proceedings on the judgment. The judgment debt sum was repaid, but Julia Beer claimed the interest on that judgment debt. The House of Lords considered that any promise by Julia Beer not to take any further proceedings on the judgment (e.g. by seeking interest) was not supported by consideration, since Dr Foakes had done no more than he was already contractually bound to do. Accordingly, such a promise was unenforceable.

4.6.2.2 Finding the fresh consideration or other basis for enforceability of the alteration promise to accept less

However, provided that something was given, the court is not entitled to inquire whether what was given was equal in value to the promise made (see **4.3.1**). For example, the courts accepted that payment in kind ('a horse, a hawk or a robe'), if accepted by the creditor, could constitute the necessary consideration: *Pinnel's Case* (1602) 5 Co Rep 117a. In addition, if additional benefit were to be conferred and/or detriment suffered, that would also constitute consideration for a promise to accept less, e.g. payment in advance at the creditor's request— *Pinnel's Case*—or at a different place at the creditor's request—although not if simply to suit the debtor, because there would be no additional benefit or detriment: *Vanbergen v St Edmund Properties* [1933] 2 KB 223.

Promises to accept less are also enforceable either if they are part of a composition agreement—e.g. agreement amongst all of the creditors of a particular debtor to accept a certain percentage of their debts in full satisfaction: *Cook v Lister* (1863) 13 CB (NS) 543, 143 ER 215—or if the part payment is made by a third party as agent for the debtor and accepted, as such, in full settlement: *Hirachand Punamchand v Temple* [1911] 2 KB 330. In this case, Lieutenant Temple had borrowed money from the claimants, but the claimants had cashed a draft for a smaller sum sent by the lieutenant's father (the third party to the debt contract) in full satisfaction of his son's debt. The Court of Appeal held that the claimants could not then sue Lieutenant Temple for the balance. In this context, payment by the third party provides the consideration for the discharge of the debtor. As a result, following 'acceptance of that money by the claimant the full knowledge of the terms on which it is offered . . . the debt is absolutely extinguished' (Fletcher Moulton LJ at 340). For a more recent illustration of this principle, see *Bracken v Billinghurst* [2003] EWHC 1333 (TCC), [2004] TCLR 4, where consideration was found to exist on the facts. In this instance, the creditor had cashed a cheque issued by a third party, the cheque having been offered in full and final settlement of a debt. Following the principle of *Hirachand*, the debtor had a complete defence to the creditor's claim for summary judgment on the debt, since the cashing of the cheque amounted to acceptance of the third party offer. It is important to note that the principle of *Hirachand* must be distinguished from part payment by a debtor where the funds have been secured as a loan from a third party. This is a direct part payment by the debtor: see *Treasure & Sons Ltd v Dawes* [2008] EWHC 2181 (TCC).

The basis for these last two exceptions seems to be that it would be a fraud (on the other creditors or on the third party) to go back on the promise. However, in both *Hirachand Punamchand v Temple* and *Bracken v Billinghurst*, in the context of part payment by a third party, it was also considered that the debt was extinguished by the agreement with the third party to accept a smaller sum and so could not be revived for the purposes of suing the debtor for the balance on the debt.

4.6.2.3 Can factual benefit constitute the fresh consideration in the context of alteration promises to accept less?

In *Foakes v Beer* (1884) 9 App Cas 605, at p. 622, Lord Blackburn expressed some dissatisfaction with the conclusion that, since payment of a smaller sum provided no additional benefit/detriment, it did not extinguish the debt, so that the creditor could sue for the balance, arguing:

> All men of business . . . do every day recognise and act on the ground that prompt payment of a part of their demand may be more beneficial to them than it would be to insist on their rights and enforce payment of the whole. Even where the debtor is perfectly solvent, and sure to pay at the last, this is often so. Where the credit of the debtor is doubtful it must be more so.

Such a reasoning recognizes that there may be a factual benefit in promising to accept less. Indeed, promises to accept less might seem to be no different in their nature from promises to pay more for the same performance, as in *Williams v Roffey Bros.* [1991] 1 QB 1: see Carter, Phang, and Poole (1995) 8 JCL 248 and *Musumeci v Winadell Pty Ltd* (1994) 34 NSWLR 723; although compare O'Sullivan (1996) 55 CLJ 219.

If *Williams v Roffey Bros.* had been held to be applicable to such promises, consideration might more easily have been found (arising from the factual benefit to the promisor) in a promise to accept less than the sum owed and promising not to claim for the balance. Nevertheless, in two cases heard by the Court of Appeal concerning promises to accept less, the Court of Appeal decision in *Williams v Roffey Bros.* has been rejected in favour of adherence to the old-established authority of the House of Lords in *Foakes v Beer* (not cited to the Court of Appeal in *Williams v Roffey Bros.*). In *Re C (a debtor)* [1996] BPIR 535, The Times, 11 May 1994, Bingham MR, speaking for the whole court, simply did not accept that, in the face of *Pinnel's Case* (1602) 5 Co Rep 117a and *Foakes v Beer*, the *Williams v Roffey Bros.* approach could be extended to promises to accept less than contractually owed. In *Re Selectmove Ltd* [1995] 1 WLR 474, however, Peter Gibson LJ (*obiter*) was clearly reluctant in conceding that he and the Court of Appeal were bound by the decision of the House of Lords in *Foakes v Beer*, and it seems that he might otherwise have reached a different conclusion. In *Birmingham City Council v Forde* [2009] EWHC 12 (QB), [2009] WLR 2732, at [89], Christopher Clarke J noted that *Re Selectmove* had not actually cast any doubt on *Williams v Roffey*.

Re Selectmove and *Re C (a debtor)* both involved debts to public bodies rather than variation of commercial contracts. Nevertheless, in the face of the doctrine of precedent, they clearly restrict further extension of *Williams v Roffey Bros.*, and have led to an unfortunate distinction, in terms of applicable principle and resultant enforceability, between contractual variations involving a promise to pay more and those contractual variations involving a promise to accept less. This distinction between the two promises can be seen as 'arbitrary'. Indeed, the promise to accept less could be seen as, in effect, equivalent for the creditor to waive its rights to the payment of the debt in full. This distinction was also implicitly accepted by the Court of Appeal in *Collier v P. & M. J. Wright (Holdings) Ltd* [2007] EWCA Civ 1329, [2008] 1 WLR 643 (see **4.8.2.2**), *per* Arden LJ at [3], in which *Roffey* was assumed to be inapplicable in the context of an alteration promise to accept less. It is important to stress at this point that *Collier* is not an actual decision applying promissory estoppel and only a finding that there was an arguable defence of promissory estoppel. Crucially however, the distinction between the two promises was treated as illogical by Arden LJ in the Court of Appeal in *MWB Business Exchange Center Ltd v Rock Advertising* [2016] EWCA Civ 553, [2016] 2 Lloyd's Rep 391 ([at 79]), and her

Ladyship concluded that 'the principle that a benefit can in law be consideration for a promise must logically apply whatever the nature of the contract' (at [84]). Kitchin LJ (at [49]) approved of Arden LJ's judgment on this.

It is as well to note that *Foakes v Beer* was not applied in one first instance decision in which factual benefit was recognized in the context of paying less.

In *Anangel Atlas Compania Naviera SA v Ishikawajima-Harima Heavy Industries Co. Ltd (No. 2)* [1990] 2 Lloyd's Rep 526, the claimants had contracted to purchase a ship built by the defendants. The world shipping market fell into recession and the claimants discovered that the defendants were offering more advantageous terms to other clients. They sought and obtained the defendants' agreement that they should be accorded 'most favoured customer' status, so that in all respects, including price and terms of payment, they would be treated as favourably as any other customer. They subsequently sought to enforce this agreement, alleging that another customer had paid a lower price on more favourable payment terms. The defendants argued that the agreement was not supported by consideration. There was no suggestion that the claimants' request for more favourable terms constituted economic duress. *Foakes v Beer* was not referred to in the judgment, but the practical effect of the agreement was to allow the claimants to pay less than the sum originally agreed (albeit that it involved direct enforcement of a promise). By enforcing this agreement in express reliance on *Williams v Roffey Bros.* and the notion of factual or subjective benefit, Hirst J seems to have avoided the problem posed by *Foakes v Beer*.

One must expand on *MWB Business Exchange Centres Ltd v Rock Advertising Ltd* [2016] EWCA Civ 553, [2016] 2 Lloyd's Rep 391. In this case, through a licence agreement, MWB had rented out serviced offices to Rock Advertising. Rock Advertising, who accumulated significant arrears of licence fees, claimed to have entered into an oral agreement with MWB defining a revised schedule upon which the arrears would be repaid. As the contract contained a no oral variation clause (NOM) (a clause which prevents the parties from modifying the contract orally), the issues at hand were whether the variation agreement was valid and whether the NOM was legally effective (see **6.2.1.5**). On the question of the variation, the Court of Appeal accepted that part payment of a debt was not itself consideration, in the context of the creditor agreeing to accept less money. But, the court nevertheless accepted that the promisor obtained a practical benefit since MWB had a better chance of recovering the amount due and it was better to have a unit occupied than being left empty (the alternative to not agreeing a revised payment schedule was for Rock to be ejected). For Kitchin LJ, this additional practical benefit 'went beyond the advantage of receiving a prompt payment of part arrears' and was therefore 'good consideration' (at [48]). Similarly, Arden LJ emphasized that the benefit went 'over and above the mere fact of accommodating the debtor' (at [87]). This allows the court to carve out an exception to *Foakes v Beer* and appears to collapse the distinction between promises to pay more and promises to pay less (on doubts whether the Court of Appeal satisfactorily reconciled its position with that of *Foakes* see Shaw-Mellors and Poole [2016] JBL 696). The substantive judgments of Arden and Kitchin LJJ (Arden LJ at [46]–[49] and Kitchin LJ at [77]–[90]) highlight the increasingly pressing need to re-examine *Foakes v Beer* and the artificial distinction. Although much hope was placed on the Supreme Court in *Rock Advertising* ([2018] UKSC 24) to clarify the situation, this has not happened. Reversing the decision on a different ground and focusing on the issue of the no-oral modification clause (discussed in **Chapter 6**), Sumption JSC (with whom Lady Hale, Lord Wilson, and Lord Loyd-Jones agreed, Lord Briggs dissenting) stated that it was therefore 'unnecessary to deal with consideration' and even 'undesirable to do so' (at [18]). Recognizing the difficulty of the issue, Lord Sumption's added, *obiter*, that the current state of the law on the issue of practical benefit was 'ripe for re-examination' and that this would likely involve re-examining *Foakes v Beer*, but this 'should be before an enlarged panel of the court' (at [18]). Yet, Sumption JSC nevertheless appears to disapprove of the Court of Appeal's findings on the practical benefit by stating that such expectations were not 'of contractual value' (at [18]). This seems to highlight some remaining reluctance of the highest court to go against the clear authority of *Foakes v Beer*. Until that is done, however, the law governing the enforceability of alteration promises remains extremely complicated, but alive as considered again in *Simantob v Yacob Shavleyan t/a Yacob's Gallery* [2018] EWHC 2005 (QB).

⚙ SUMMARY

1. *Williams v Roffey Bros.* applies to alteration promises to pay more money so that (given the absence of economic duress) if there is a factual (or practical) benefit to the promisor arising from the promise, consideration to support that alteration promise can be found.

2. However, in stating that *Foakes v Beer* must apply to alteration promises to accept less, *Re Selectmove* and *Re C (a debtor)* have ruled out the possibility of finding consideration from a factual benefit to a creditor in agreeing to accept a smaller sum in full satisfaction. This is to be contrasted with the position of the Court of Appeal in *MWB Business Exchange Centres Ltd v Rock Advertising Ltd* reversed on a different ground.

3. It will therefore be necessary to look elsewhere for the consideration to support a promise to accept less (see discussion above), or, in the absence of consideration, the promise may have limited enforceability if the defence of promissory estoppel can be invoked.

4.7 Conclusions: the future of consideration

Although consideration appears to be firmly established in a central role in the English law of contract, and indeed appears to be an important element that distinguishes the common law contract from its continental civilian cousin, it would be wrong to conclude this section without acknowledging that, for much of the past century, consideration has been under attack from various quarters.

4.7.1 The reform agenda

In 1937, the Law Revision Committee—see its Sixth Interim Report (Cmd 5449, 1937) and (1937) 1 MLR 97—recommended a number of amendments to the detailed rules. Some of these proposals would have wrought a major change in the law of England and Wales and could not be achieved without parliamentary intervention. For example, it was proposed that a promise in writing should be enforceable even if not supported by consideration. It was also proposed that 'an agreement to accept a lesser sum in discharge of a larger sum shall be deemed to have been made for valuable consideration' (although the full debt would revive if the smaller sum were not paid). The courts have addressed this issue, although not in a way that provides for recognition of part payment as consideration (see **4.8**). Performance of an existing duty was also to be 'deemed to have been made for valuable consideration'. We have seen that the courts have found ways of finding this valuable consideration in going beyond the duty and in recognition of factual benefits in *Williams v Roffey Bros.* [1991] 1 QB 1. Other proposals have also been at least partially achieved as a result of the continuing internal dynamism of the common law, e.g. the rule that promisors in unilateral contracts should not be allowed to revoke once a promisee has started to perform (see **2.6.3**).

A more radical proposal was based on reliance as justifying enforcement, i.e. if the promisor knows, or reasonably should know that a promise will be relied on by the promisee, it was proposed that the promise should be enforced as long as the promisee had altered their position to their detriment. This proposal received strong support from Professor Atiyah.

4.7.2 Professor Atiyah and the argument that enforceability should turn on reliance

Professor Atiyah argued that there are historical grounds for saying that consideration is not the sole test used by the courts to determine whether a promise shall be enforceable and that, where justice required, the courts have enforced promises on the basis of reliance by the promisee: see Atiyah, 'Consideration in contracts: A fundamental restatement', in *Essays in Contract Law* (Oxford University Press, 1986). Such a notion, as we shall see (see **4.8.6.2**), is consistent with developments in the United States.

More recently, the Court of Appeal of New Zealand in *Antons Trawling Co. Ltd v Smith* [2003] 2 NZLR 23 has accepted the existence of a binding variation to an employment contract based purely on the existence of reliance on the alteration promise, without seeking to rely on the principle of factual benefit in *Williams v Roffey Bros.* [1991] 1 QB 1. It will be interesting to see how this reliance principle develops, but it is important to appreciate that it is more limited than Professor Atiyah's argument for enforceability of *all* promises based on reliance. The *Antons Trawling* principle is limited to alteration promises (or modifications to existing contracts).

4.7.3 The special position and treatment of alteration promises

The decision in *Williams v Roffey Bros.* [1991] 1 QB 1 highlights the pragmatic approach to finding consideration that some courts are prepared to take in order to hold a particular promise to be binding in the light of the general context in which it was made. There was always likely to be a gradual progression away from the technical analysis of benefit and detriment towards the more impressionistic notion of inducement, thereby allowing the judges greater freedom to decide according to the flavour of the transaction whether agreements and promises should be treated as binding. Lord Wilberforce pointed the way forward in *The Eurymedon* [1975] AC 154 (see **4.4.2**), at p. 167, where he said of the transaction in dispute:

> If the choice, and the antithesis, is between a gratuitous promise, and a promise for consideration . . . there can be little doubt which, in commercial reality, this is. The whole contract is of a commercial character, involving service on one side, rates of payment on the other, and qualifying stipulations as to both. The relations of all parties to each other are commercial relations entered into for business reasons of ultimate profit. To describe one set of promises, in this context, as gratuitous, or *nudum pactum*, seems paradoxical and is *prima facie* implausible. It is only the precise analysis of this complex of relations into the classical offer and acceptance, with identifiable consideration, which seems to present difficulty.

More particularly, it has long been considered that the need to establish consideration to support alteration promises may be too strict a requirement and may fail to reflect the commercial realities of such alteration promises. This is evidenced in the development of the doctrine of promissory estoppel and, in 1977, Professor Reiter (1977) 27 Uni Toronto LJ 439, at p. 507, stated that insistence on the need to establish consideration in this context failed to recognize:

> the illogicality of equating modifying with originating promises or to see that, insofar as consideration serves to exclude gratuitous promises, it is of little assistance in the context of on-going, arms-length, commercial transactions where it is utterly fictional to describe what is being conceded as a gift, and in which there ought to be a strong presumption that good commercial 'considerations' underlie any seemingly detrimental modification.

In the immediate aftermath of the decision in *Williams v Roffey Bros.*, there appeared to be clear evidence of such a practice and the pragmatic nature of the decision, if not its technical basis, was warmly welcomed: see Adams and Brownsword (1990) 53 MLR 536. The only issue at that time appeared to lie in assessing just how much the foundations of the doctrine of consideration had been shaken by this important decision.

The variety of reasons given for enforcing the promise of extra payment (see **4.4.4**) makes it possible to identify both a narrow and a wide principle emanating from the decision. At the narrowest, it seems that the law relating to binding alterations of contracts has changed, so that a post-contractual promise relating to the main agreement (other than a promise to accept as full payment an amount less than the originally agreed price) will be enforced, subject to proof of the necessary intention and the absence of duress. In *Dresdner Kleinwort Ltd v Attrill* [2013] EWCA Civ 394, [2013] 3 All ER 607, at [80], Elias LJ stated that he 'would start from the premise ... that where a term is being introduced into a pre-existing contractual relationship, there will be a very strong presumption that it is intended to be legally binding'. (In *Dresdner*, the pre-existing relationship was an employment relationship and the alteration promise concerned a promise to pay a guaranteed employment bonus to employees: see **5.2.2**.)

However, a broader argument based on *Roffey* is possible. It may also be argued that, on the basis of this decision, other areas of the law of contract, in which the requirement of consideration may be said to be simply 'technical', might no longer prove troublesome, because the identification of a 'factual benefit' is always possible when the commercial context makes it implausible for the promise not to be regarded as binding: see e.g. Coote (1990) 3 JCL 23, who argued that nobody would promise to pay more to achieve performance unless they were to regard such a promise as beneficial to them—no one would 'throw good money after bad'.

Of course, *Williams v Roffey Bros.* is confined to the context of alteration promises. All three members of the Court of Appeal made it clear that they believed the particular context, which so influenced their reasoning, to be distinct from that of the formation of initial contracts. Accordingly, this principle will not be of any assistance in the context of the rule that a promise to keep an offer open is binding only if it is supported by consideration (see **2.5.3.2**). Consequently, it would have been impossible to argue that the result of *Williams v Roffey Bros.* would be that the doctrine of consideration would be abandoned altogether. Indeed, it would have been astonishing if such an interpretation were to have been suggested. There is no reason to think that English law should suddenly wish to make all gratuitous promises enforceable. The restrictive comments of the Court of Appeal in this important case were clearly designed to bring home the point that the doctrine of consideration remains central to mainstream contracts, and the decision reinforces the need to find consideration, albeit making it easier to establish in the context of promises to pay more. The Court of Appeal was at pains to stress this and would not otherwise have had to go to such lengths to identify the required consideration. Nevertheless, in *Anangel Atlas Compania Naviera v Ishikawajima-Harima Heavy Industries Co. Ltd (No. 2)* [1990] 2 Lloyd's Rep 526, at p. 545, Hirst J rejected the argument that *Williams v Roffey Bros.* 'should be read as having only a very narrow ambit', although even in that context the judge was not prepared to extend the *ratio* beyond the question of variation of an existing contract.

In subsequent cases—*Re Selectmove Ltd* [1995] 1 WLR 474 and *Re C (a debtor)* [1996] BPIR 535, The Times, 11 May 1994—the Court of Appeal sought to place a limit on the scope of the *Roffey ratio*, and these decisions appear to indicate that the courts are reluctant to abandon traditional rules of consideration, at least as far as release from debts is concerned. This of course must be appreciated in the light of the Court of Appeal decision in *Rock Advertising Ltd* (as discussed earlier at **4.6.2.3**),

More generally, it is as well to end this discussion of the impact of *Williams v Roffey Bros.* with a note of caution about the developments arising out of it. Although the tone of the preceding analysis may have been to regard these developments as beneficial, any benefit is achieved at a price. The traditional consideration rules had the virtue of simplicity and the absence of difficult judgmental issues. The *Roffey* principle invests the judges with an enormous discretion over such cases, especially in ascertaining intention and in determining whether threats amount to economic duress (see **15.1.2**), and it is important to consider whether there is, or should be, any *objective* evaluation of whether a benefit can be said to be a factual benefit where it is of *subjective* benefit to the party seeking to enforce an alteration promise to pay more.

In addition, since the decision in *Re Selectmove*, which limited the application of the *Roffey* principle to alteration promises to accept more, developments since the 1950s in the field of promissory estoppel will continue to be of relevance (see **4.8.2**). Much of the academic argument—such as Chen-Wishart, 'Consideration: Practical benefit and the Emperor's new clothes', in Beatson and Friedmann (eds.), *Good Faith and Fault in Contract Law* (Oxford University Press, 1995), and Hird and Blair [1996] JBL 254—has focused on arguments that, because of the technical difficulties in rationalizing the decision in *Williams v Roffey Bros.*, the preferable approach to ensure the enforceability of alteration promises would be to adopt a flexible concept of estoppel, as in the High Court of Australia: see *Waltons Stores (Interstate) Ltd v Maher* (1988) 164 CLR 387 and *Commonwealth of Australia v Verwayen* (1990) 170 CLR 394 (discussed at **4.8.6.1**). This approach involves a fundamental shift of emphasis away from the consideration doctrine towards a more limited enforceability by means of the estoppel doctrine (see **4.8.6**). Alternatively, it may be preferable to follow the lead given by the Court of Appeal of New Zealand in *Antons Trawling Co. Ltd v Smith* [2003] 2 NZLR 23 (discussed at **4.7.2**) and simply recognize that reliance alone is sufficient to justify enforcing an alteration promise.

In **Antons Trawling Co. Ltd v Smith**, the claimant, master of one of the defendants' fishing vessels, claimed that he had been promised a 10 per cent share of any additional fishing quota allocated to the defendants if he were able to demonstrate that there were sufficient fish to justify the government setting a larger quota. The government set a larger quota and, when the claimant sought to claim the promised 10 per cent of the fish caught under the additional quota, the defendants claimed that he had not supplied any consideration to support their promise, since it required him to do no more than was already required of him under the terms of his contract to explore for fish.

The Court of Appeal of New Zealand held that where an alteration promise had been acted upon, in the absence of policy reasons to the contrary, the parties should be bound by the alteration, since it was clear that the variation promise was intended to be acted upon and there was an intention to be legally bound by it.

Of course, the claimant still needed to show that he had acted on the promise and performed the task entitling him to the benefit of the alteration promise, i.e. to establish the existence of fish in sufficient commercial quantities ('the existence of a commercial fishery'). He had achieved this only in respect of one part of the larger quota.

Although this principle applies only to alteration promises, it has the potential to allow for the enforceability of *all* alterations promises (promises to pay more and promises to accept less), and so would eliminate the artificial and technical restrictions inherent in the current English law, along with the artificiality of the courts' refusal to extend the principle in *Roffey* to alteration promises to accept less. Whether *Rock Advertising Ltd* (discussed at **4.6.2.3**) is the precursor of change, only time will tell.

4.8 Absence of consideration and the defence of promissory estoppel

4.8.1 The development of the estoppel doctrine

Towards the end of the nineteenth century, the courts developed a doctrine of equitable estoppel in order to prevent injustice arising when one party (A) agrees to forgo his strict legal rights under the contract and this induces the other party (B) to rely on this position, but A then goes back on the arrangement and seeks to enforce his strict rights.

> **→ EXAMPLE**
>
> In the context of the part-payment example described earlier (see **4.6.2**), B will have relied upon A's promise to accept £8 in full satisfaction of the £10 debt and may have spent the £2 balance. A is now seeking to enforce the original contract terms and to reclaim the £2 balance, claiming that any promise to forgo the balance is not supported by fresh consideration from B. In some circumstances, B could now rely on the doctrine of promissory estoppel (see *Central London Property Trust Ltd v High Trees House Ltd* [1947] KB 130, at **4.8.2.1**) to suspend A's ability to recover this balance.

The application of the equitable estoppel doctrine meant that one-sided variations of contract might be *enforceable* in some circumstances despite the absence of consideration to support them. The best example of the operation of the doctrine is the leading case of *Hughes v Metropolitan Railway Co.* (1877) 2 App Cas 439.

In ***Hughes v Metropolitan Railway Co.***, a lease contained a covenant requiring the lessee to repair if the lessor gave notice. Hughes, the lessor, gave notice requiring repair within six months. The railway company, the lessee, responded by offering to sell back to the lessor the company's remaining interest in the property under the lease. Negotiations continued for some two months, before breaking down. Hughes subsequently claimed to be entitled to possession of the property on the basis that, since the lessee company had failed to carry out the required repairs within six months of the original date of the notice requiring repair, the lease had been forfeited. The company claimed that there was a tacit understanding (or an implied promise) that the repairs need not be carried out if the negotiations were to come to a successful conclusion and that, in the meantime, the period of notice would not start to run. In the House of Lords, the existence of that implied promise was not really in doubt. Nevertheless, it was unsupported by consideration and therefore arguably unenforceable. However, the House of Lords refused to accept that argument.

The basis of their Lordships' decision in *Hughes* is contained in the following, now famous, passage from the speech of Lord Cairns LC, at p. 448:

> It is the first principle upon which all Courts of Equity proceed, that if parties who have entered into definite and distinct terms involving certain legal results . . . afterwards by their own act or with their own consent enter upon a course of negotiations which has the effect of leading one of the parties to suppose that the strict rights arising under the contract will not be enforced or will be kept in suspense or held in abeyance, the person who might otherwise have enforced those rights will not be allowed to enforce them where it would be inequitable, having regard to the dealings which have thus taken place between the parties.

Thus it is accepted that there is, in the name of equity, a doctrine that makes certain promises enforceable despite the absence of consideration. However, the nature and exact limits of this doctrine remain unclear. It should be noted that, in many of the cases discussed in the following sections, the expression 'promissory estoppel' is used, rather than 'equitable estoppel'. The change in terminology came about because of developments in the law starting in 1947. Those developments are discussed next.

4.8.2 The development of promissory estoppel

In the 1940s, the equitable doctrine established in *Hughes v Metropolitan Railway Co.* (1877) 2 App Cas 439 was taken in a direction in which, some would argue, it had not been intended to operate.

4.8.2.1 The extension of the doctrine: promissory estoppel and *High Trees House*

Some years prior to the more direct attempt to enforce alteration promises in *Williams v Roffey Bros.* [1991] 1 QB 1, the courts had made a limited attack upon the rule in *Foakes v Beer* (1884) 9 App Cas 605 that, in the absence of consideration, a part-payment promise was unenforceable. Rather than focusing on the identification of consideration, this attack focused on the question of enforceability based on reliance on the promise. The attack was led by Denning J in *Central London Property Trust Ltd v High Trees House Ltd* [1947] KB 130. In *High Trees*, Denning J suggested in an *obiter dictum* that where the conditions of promissory estoppel were satisfied, a creditor could not go back on a promise to accept less (and not to sue for the balance) where it would be inequitable to do so despite the absence of consideration to support the promise.

In *High Trees*, the tenant company was a subsidiary of the landlord company. The property in question was a block of flats over which the defendant tenant company had a 99-year lease, for which it paid a rent of £2,500 per year. At the outbreak of the Second World War, many of the flats remained vacant and the tenant company was unable to pay the full rent. The landlord company agreed to halve the rent (to £1,250 per year), and the tenant company paid that amount from 1940 onwards. By the beginning of 1945, the flats were fully let again. The landlord company was in receivership. The receiver believed that the company was entitled to arrears of rent for the whole period of the war, but brought a test case claiming full rent for the last two quarters of 1945.

Denning J, relying on **Hughes v Metropolitan Railway Co.** (1877) 2 App Cas 439, said that, as a result of the equitable doctrine of estoppel, 'a promise to accept a smaller sum in discharge of larger sum, if acted upon, is binding notwithstanding the absence of consideration'. He noted with some satisfaction that his interpretation of the authorities achieved that which had been recommended by the Law Revision Committee in 1937—namely, that a creditor's promise to accept part payment as full settlement should be binding.

Since the landlord company had sought only the rent for the last two quarters of 1945, this was held to be recoverable. Any estoppel had come to an end so that there was no difficulty in reverting to performance of the strict legal rights under the contract for the period covered by the claim. Denning J's comments concerning the rent for the period of the war when the flats could not be fully let and the identification of an estoppel as operating in that period are therefore only *obiter*.

4.8.2.2 Assessment of the *High Trees House* decision

There were two difficulties getting to accept the operation of the doctrine of equitable estoppel in the context of part-payment situations.

1. **The authority of *Foakes v Beer***

   It had previously been thought that there were clear authorities against the enforceability of alteration promises to accept less than the debt owed in the absence of fresh consideration to support that promise. In *Foakes v Beer* (1884) 9 App Cas 605, the House of Lords refused to enforce a promise not to seek interest on a debt when the promise was given without consideration (see **4.6.2.1**) and *Foakes v Beer* was decided only seven years after *Hughes v Metropolitan Railway Co.* (1877) 2 App Cas 439, without reference being made to that earlier decision. Although it can be argued that estoppel must be pleaded before the court may rely on it, it seems inconceivable that counsel in *Foakes v Beer* would have overlooked the decision in *Hughes* had counsel considered it relevant. In fact, *Hughes* deals with a different issue from that which arose in *Foakes v Beer* and in *Central London Property Trust Ltd v High Trees House Ltd* [1947] KB 130. In *Hughes*, the principle was that, having implied that the tenant did not need to comply with the obligation to repair, the landlord could not treat the failure to comply as a breach of contract and forfeit the lease. By comparison, in *Foakes v Beer* and *High Trees*, the issue was whether the creditor (promisor) could change its mind and insist on performance of the contract in accordance with its terms, i.e. there was no question of the creditor alleging that the debtor was in breach of contract in complying with the amended terms.

   Unsurprisingly, courts are still reluctant to disregard the House of Lords' authority of *Foakes v Beer* as the starting point where it is relevant on the facts: see *Re Selectmove Ltd* [1995] 1 WLR 474 and *Collier v P. & M. J. Wright (Holdings) Ltd* [2007] EWCA Civ 1329, [2008] 1 WLR 643, in which the Court of Appeal applied *Foakes v Beer* in the context of an agreement by a creditor with a joint debtor whereby the creditor had agreed to accept only the proportionate share from that debtor and not to sue him for the remainder of the debt. We have seen that this reluctance was weakened following the Court of Appeal's decision in *MWB Business Exchange Centres Ltd v Rock Advertising Ltd*. Although the decision was reversed on different grounds by the Supreme Court, the need to clarify the whole area was nevertheless noted.

2. *Jorden v Money* **and the restriction of estoppel to representations of existing fact**

The other major obstacle to the decision in *High Trees* was *Jorden v Money* (1854) 5 HL Cas 185, in which the House of Lords determined that the common law estoppel principle (which prevents a person from going back on a statement made once it has been relied upon) applied only to misrepresentations of *existing* fact; it did not apply to promises of *future* conduct, such as a promise not to sue for the balance of a debt. However, this objection applies equally to *Hughes v Metropolitan Railway Co.* If that case is accepted as a valid exception to the rule in *Jorden v Money*, there would appear to be no reason why the *High Trees* case could not also be an exception.

It is possible to explain away these inconsistencies by ingenious arguments, as Denning J did in the *High Trees* case itself, resorting respectively to 'the fusion of law and equity' (by allowing at common law the application of equitable principles, at pp. 134–5) and an absence of intention to be legally bound. Nevertheless, the truth of the matter appears to be that, as originally conceived in *Hughes v Metropolitan Railway Co.*, equitable estoppel was not intended to apply to variations of price unsupported by consideration. Once, however, Bowen LJ had stated in *Birmingham and District Land Co. v LNW Railway Co.* (1888) 40 Ch D 268 that the doctrine was not limited to forfeiture cases, but applied to all variations of contractual rights, no meaningful distinction could be made between price terms and any others—although, from the reasoning in *Re C (a debtor)* [1996] BPIR 535, The Times, 11 May 1994, it appears that Sir Thomas Bingham MR would not agree. Denning J exploited this fact to the full by extending the equitable estoppel doctrine to its logical conclusion. Nevertheless, in both *Tool Metal Manufacturing Co. Ltd v Tungsten Electric Co. Ltd* [1955] 1 WLR 761, *per* Lord Tucker at p. 784 (see **4.8.5.1**) and *Woodhouse A. C. Israel Cocoa Ltd v Nigerian Produce Marketing Co. Ltd* [1972] AC 741, *per* Lord Hailsham at p. 758 (see **4.8.3.1**), the House of Lords expressly reserved the question of the existence, or at least the extent, of the doctrine.

4.8.3 The requirements for promissory estoppel to operate

4.8.3.1 A clear and unequivocal representation

The doctrine operates only where there is a clear and unequivocal representation that strict rights will not be enforced. In *Woodhouse A. C. Israel Cocoa SA v Nigerian Produce Marketing Co.* [1972] AC 741, at p. 756, Lord Hailsham said:

> The meaning is to exclude far-fetched or strained, but still possible, interpretations, while still insisting on a sufficient precision and freedom from ambiguity to ensure that the representation will . . . be reasonably understood in the particular sense required.

The promissory estoppel representation may need to have 'at least as much precision as would be needed for a variation of the contract': *per* Lord Pearson, at p. 762. In *Kim v Chasewood Park Residents Ltd* [2013] EWCA Civ 239, [2013] HLR 24, the claimants had a 125-year lease in a block of 97 flats. Under the terms of the lease, they had to pay ground rent and a service charge. The landlord of the block of flats was a building society which had a 999-year head-lease (or reversion). The building society offered to sell the head-lease to the leaseholders. A residents' association, in charge of the negotiations with the building society, therefore wrote to the leaseholders to gauge their interest in the purchase of the reversion. The association therefore wrote a letter indicating a list of the benefits of the purchase, one of which was that there was 'no ground rent to pay'. The Court of Appeal held that a reference in the letter to 'no ground rent to pay' relating to a possible purchase of the reversion was not a clear representation for the purpose of inducing the tenants to support the purchase; rather, it highlighted only a potential benefit that might arise. Accordingly, the statement could not form the basis for any estoppel.

Further, it seems that what is required is that only one reasonable meaning should be apparent from the representation made. In *Baird Textile Holdings Ltd v Marks & Spencer plc* [2001] EWCA Civ 274, [2002] 1 All ER (Comm) 737, a claim based on estoppel failed because the alleged representation was considered to be no more than a bare assurance and insufficiently certain.

Nevertheless, it is apparent from *Hughes v Metropolitan Railway Co.* (1877) 2 App Cas 439 that if there is a sufficiently clear and unequivocal representation, it need not be express, since in that case the representation was implied from the conduct of the lessor.

4.8.3.2 The doctrine operates as a defence and not as a cause of action

The major limitation on the promissory estoppel doctrine in English law is that it cannot be used to found a cause of action, i.e. it may not be used in legal proceedings brought to force someone to uphold a promise. It can be used only to prevent someone from going back on their promise and insisting on enforcement of their strict rights.

> In *Combe v Combe* [1951] 2 KB 215, during divorce proceedings, the husband had promised to pay the wife a certain sum by way of maintenance. The wife gave no reciprocal promise to refrain from applying to the court for maintenance, so that (unusually) the husband's promise was not supported by consideration. The wife attempted to enforce the promise on the basis of 'promissory' estoppel, but her claim was refused by the Court of Appeal.

In *Combe v Combe*, at pp. 219–20, Denning LJ said of promissory estoppel:

> Much as I am inclined to favour the principle . . . it is important that it should not be stretched too far, lest it should be endangered. That principle does not create new causes of action where none existed before . . . The doctrine of consideration is too firmly fixed to be overthrown by a side-wind. Its ill-effects have been largely mitigated of late, but it still remains a cardinal necessity of the formation of a contract, though not of its modification or discharge.

There are two separate points being made in this statement, as follows.

4.8.3.2.1 *Promissory estoppel does not give rise to a cause of action*

In *Baird Textile Holdings Ltd v Marks & Spencer plc* [2001] EWCA Civ 274, [2002] 1 All ER (Comm) 737, Jacob LJ considered that 'an estoppel inherently must be raised by way of riposte' once the claimant has pleaded its case in order to argue that the claimant is prevented from pursuing that claim. It does not give rise to a cause of action in itself.

This limitation is sometimes expressed in the maxim that equitable or promissory estoppel is 'a shield not a sword': *per* Birkett LJ in *Combe v Combe* [1951] 2 KB 215. As an image, the expression makes the point quite well, but it should not lead to the mistaken belief that the doctrine is available only to defendants and not to claimants. Promissory estoppel cannot found a cause of action where none would otherwise exist, but it may be used by a claimant in support of a cause of action that has an independent existence. Thus if, in *Hughes v Metropolitan Railway Co.*

(1877) 2 App Cas 439, the lessor had actually retaken possession of the property and, upon breakdown of negotiations, the lessee had sued to regain possession, the lessee would still have been able to rely on equitable estoppel to defeat the lessor's defence based on the lessee's failure to repair, since the cause of action would be based not on the implied promise to defer the time for repair, but on the right under the original lease to occupy the premises undisturbed for the agreed period.

The future of this limitation on promissory estoppel in English law is the subject of much debate in light of comments made by Glidewell and Russell LJJ in *Williams v Roffey Bros.* [1991] QB 1 suggesting that, had promissory estoppel been pleaded, they might have been prepared to reconsider the limitation. *Roffey* involved seeking to enforce a promise to pay more, and this would have involved attempting to use promissory estoppel as a cause of action had it in fact been pleaded. In addition, no such limitation was imposed by the High Court of Australia in *Waltons Stores (Interstate) Ltd v Maher* (1988) 164 CLR 387 (discussed at **4.8.6.1**), in the context of a claim based on estoppel. In *Baird Textile Holdings Ltd v Marks & Spencer plc* [2001] EWCA Civ 274, [2002] 1 All ER (Comm) 737, there was an unsuccessful attempt to rely on the *Waltons Stores* general category of estoppel as a cause of action. However, the judgments disclose that the rejection of this argument might be reconsidered in the future if an appropriately argued case were to arise for determination by the Supreme Court (see **4.8.6.3**).

4.8.3.2.2 *Promissory estoppel applies only in the context of alteration promises and does not do away with the need to establish consideration to support formation promises*

In *SmithKline Beecham plc v Apotex Europe Ltd* [2006] EWCA Civ 658, [2007] Ch 71, Jacob LJ, with whose judgment Morritt C and Moore-Bick LJ agreed, stated that an estoppel could not be used to create a legal relationship, citing *Baird Textile Holdings Ltd v Marks & Spencer plc* [2001] EWCA Civ 274, [2002] 1 All ER (Comm) 737, as an example of an unsuccessful attempt to create a legal obligation where none existed before.

Thus promissory estoppel in English law is not intended to replace the consideration requirement on the formation of a contract. In *Brikom Investments Ltd v Carr* [1979] QB 467, at p. 486D, Roskill LJ stressed the danger of using promissory estoppel to abolish consideration by making it easier for promises to be binding when he stated that 'it would be wrong to extend the doctrine of promissory estoppel, whatever its precise limits at the present day, to the extent of abolishing in this backhanded way the doctrine of consideration'.

4.8.3.3 Reliance and the fact that it must be inequitable to go back on the promise

The promissory estoppel doctrine depends upon some act of reliance by the promisee before it operates. There are those who believe that reliance demands that the promisee must have been induced by the promise to have acted to their detriment in some way (based arguably on the doctrine of strict estoppel, where such a requirement exists). Such a definition is suspiciously reminiscent of now outmoded definitions of consideration (see **4.2.1**) and may arise out of a confusion with proprietary estoppel, under which there is a requirement of detrimental reliance in response to a representation or encouragement by a property owner that a non-owner either has, or will acquire, an interest in the property: *Crabb v Arun District Council* [1976] Ch 179, *Gillett v Holt* [2001] Ch 210, and *Thorner v Major* [2009] UKHL 18, [2009] 1 WLR 776. Proprietary estoppel, unlike promissory estoppel, does give rise to a cause of action in English law to protect this property interest, and this may result in the court ordering the property to be conveyed or determining that there is a right to occupy for life in order to give effect to the estoppel.

In fact, it is not easy to see that the promisees in either *Hughes v Metropolitan Railway Co.* (1877) 2 App Cas 439 or *Central London Property Trust Ltd v High Trees House Ltd* [1947] KB 130 acted to their detriment, other than that they acted in accordance with the subsequent promise rather than the original contract. The suspension of the strict rights under the contracts was, on the contrary, a benefit to the promisees in both cases. Equally, in *Collier v P. & M. J. Wright (Holdings) Ltd* [2007] EWCA Civ 1329, [2008] 1 WLR 643 (see **4.8.2.2**), the debtor had acted on the promise which was beneficial to him but Arden LJ concluded that a triable issue based on promissory estoppel had been established.

The reliance requirement for the operation of the doctrine of promissory estoppel was formulated so as to require the promisee to have 'altered his position' in reliance on the promise. In *E. A. Ajayi v R. T. Briscoe (Nigeria) Ltd* [1964] 1 WLR 1326, Lord Hodson interpreted this expression to mean that the promisee's position had to be altered in a detrimental way. However, in *W. J. Alan & Co. Ltd v El Nasr Export and Import Co.* [1972] 2 QB 189, Lord Denning MR (at p. 213F) stated that he could find no support in the authorities for the view that there must be a detriment, and that all that was required was that the promisee must have 'conducted his affairs on the basis' of the promise so that 'it would not now be equitable to deprive him of its benefit'. Lord Denning therefore interpreted 'altered his position' to mean that the promisee 'must have been led to act differently from what he otherwise would have done' (at p. 213H).

The one sense in which detriment is relevant to the doctrine is that there would be a detriment if the original contract were to be enforced paying no attention at all to the subsequent representation or promise. Here, however, the sense of 'detriment' is nowhere near the same as that used in the context of defining consideration. It does no more than contribute to the sense of justice inherent in the requirement that enforcement of the strict rights under the contract be 'inequitable' in the circumstances. Indeed, it may be that even the requirement of reliance is no more than the most likely way of demonstrating inequity and is not in itself sufficient to trigger the promissory estoppel doctrine. In *Virulite LLC v Virulite Distribution Ltd* [2014] EWHC 366 (QB), [2015] 1 All ER (Comm) 204, Stuart-Smith J explained (at [121]) that '[w]hat is required is that a party's acts (or desisting from acting) should make it inequitable for the representor thereafter to enforce his legal rights inconsistently with the representation'.

In *Société Italo-Belge pour le Commerce et l'Industrie SA v Palm & Vegetable Oils (Malaysia) Sdn Bhd, The Post Chaser* [1982] 1 All ER 19, Robert Goff J had also insisted that the only requirement was that inequity be demonstrated. He said, at p. 27:

> But it does not follow that in every case in which the representee has acted or failed to act, in reliance on the representation, it will be inequitable for the representee to enforce his rights, for the nature of the action, or inaction, may be insufficient to give rise to the equity, in which event a necessary requirement stated by Lord Cairns LC for the application of the doctrine would not have been fulfilled.

In this case, the promisees did rely on the representation made, but the promisors withdrew the suspension of strict rights very soon afterwards and before any real harm had been done, so that in the particular circumstances the judge found that it would not be inequitable to enforce the strict rights (and that the promisors could therefore go back on their representation despite the fact that it had been acted upon).

These comments reflect what must be the functions of reliance as a requirement. One function must be evidential: the existence of reliance tends to confirm that the promise was made and was taken seriously. A second function reflects the statement by Lord Cairns LC in *Hughes v Metropolitan Railway Co.*, at p. 448 (see **4.8.1**), that the doctrine applies to prevent the enforcement of strict rights where to enforce them 'would be inequitable having regard to the dealings which have thus taken place between the parties'. In other words, as indicated by the comments in *The Post Chaser*, the fact of reliance is at least one element to be taken into account in assessing whether enforcement would, in all of the circumstances, be inequitable. Where the reliance is detrimental, it should be easier to establish that it would be inequitable to allow the promisor to go back on the promise.

4.8.4 Duress against creditors: is it inequitable to go back on an alteration promise to accept less where that promise was extracted as a result of the exercise of duress?

It has already been suggested that a probable reason for the rule that consideration cannot be provided by the performance of an existing duty is the fear of duress by debtors against creditors (see **4.4.4**). The decision in *Central London Property Trust Ltd v High Trees House Ltd* [1947] KB 130 results in the enforcement (albeit in a limited sense) of a promise to accept a smaller sum in full satisfaction for a larger sum owed. However, particularly in times of financial difficulty, it may be the case that the promise to accept less may have been obtained as a result of duress. This problem was confronted in *D. & C. Builders Ltd v Rees* [1966] 2 QB 617, in which the debtor exploited the straitened circumstances of the creditor to extort a promise to accept immediate part payment of the debt in final settlement (the evidence was that the debtor's wife was aware of the creditor's circumstances). The claimant creditor then claimed the balance, and the question facing the Court of Appeal was whether there was a binding promise to accept less than the debt owed in full satisfaction of the debt. Lord Denning MR (who was in a minority on this reasoning, but not in the result in the case) found for the claimant creditor by relying on the statement of the doctrine by Lord Cairns LC in *Hughes v Metropolitan Railway Co.* (1877) 2 App Cas 439. Lord Denning MR said, at p. 625:

> The creditor is only barred from his legal rights when it would be *inequitable* for him to insist upon them . . . Where there has been a *true accord* . . . then it is inequitable for the creditor afterwards to insist on the balance . . . In the present case, on the facts as found by the judge, it seems to me that there was no true accord. The debtor's wife held the creditor to ransom.

In simple terms, there is nothing inequitable about not enforcing such a promise when the promise was obtained by duress. This approach matches that of Lord Scarman in *Pao On v Lau Yiu Long* [1980] AC 614, who said that there was no harm in allowing consideration to be constituted by performance of an existing duty, provided that there was protection against duress (see **4.4.3**). Similar reasoning was used to justify a more liberal approach to the doctrine of consideration in *Williams v Roffey Bros.* [1991] 1 QB 1 (see **4.4.4**). Of course, it follows that it is necessary to be able to make a clear distinction between pressure or threats that constitute duress and instances in which there is no such pressure (see **15.1.2.3** for further discussion of the scope of economic duress).

4.8.5 The effect of promissory estoppel: suspending or extinguishing the strict legal rights?

Where an alteration promise to accept less is supported by fresh consideration or is otherwise enforceable (see **4.6.2.2**), the promise is binding for all time. This is a higher level of enforcement than is possible using the doctrine of promissory estoppel, so that the fact that the courts have limited the application of the decision of the Court of Appeal in *Williams v Roffey Bros.* [1991] 1 QB 1 to promises to pay more is extremely significant: *Re Selectmove Ltd* [1995] 1 WLR 474. The *Williams v Roffey Bros.* (factual benefit) approach to the identification of consideration would have rendered the equitable doctrine of promissory estoppel largely redundant in this context. Such a result might have been preferable since, if supported by consideration, a promise is legally enforceable for all time, whereas the effect of promissory estoppel appears to be more limited. In particular, it would seem that the doctrine operates only to suspend legal rights and not to extinguish them, so that it may be possible in the future to go back on a promise to accept less despite the operation of the doctrine of promissory estoppel. In *Hughes v Metropolitan Railway Co.* (1877) 2 App Cas 439, such a consequence was inevitable since it was impossible in the factual context to extinguish the property owner's right to have the property repaired. All that was in issue was the date by which the lessee needed to have complied with the duty to repair. In *Central London Property Trust Ltd v High Trees House Ltd* [1947] KB 130 (see **4.8.2.1**), the promissory estoppel that Denning J found to exist on the facts was stated to operate only for as long as the wartime conditions prevailed. The right to enforce the strict rights under the contract was revived once those conditions ceased to exist. However, the implication must be that it might well be considered inequitable to end the estoppel within the time period specified in the representation, e.g. if the landlord in *High Trees* had sought to revive its strict legal rights before the bombing had stopped. If the term of the lease had ended before the bombing had stopped, technically it would seem possible to say that the strict legal rights to the balance on the rent had been extinguished.

Ogilvy v Hope Davies [1976] 1 All ER 683 provides an example of a situation in which it was held to be inequitable to allow the vendors of property to insist on the strict date for completion and this operated as a permanent waiver on the particular facts. In *Ogilvy* the vendors of the property were selling it as trustees, but failed to supply the purchaser with their own deed of appointment. This was required before the purchaser could make requisitions on title and, on 15 August (15 days before the completion date), the vendors led the purchaser to believe that all of the requisitions should be held up until they could be made comprehensively. Given that time was short when this statement was made and the deed was not in fact delivered until 20 August, the purchaser was entitled to assume that completion by 30 August would not be possible. It was inequitable, given the time period, to go back on that representation before 30 August. In this sense, the completion date of 30 August was *permanently waived* and the vendors could not claim for any losses incurred as a result of the delayed completion.

In *Virulite LLC v Virulite Distribution Ltd* [2014] EWHC 366 (QB), [2015] 1 All ER (Comm) 204, the promisor represented that a sum due in accordance with the contract terms did not need to be paid until the approval of a third party had been obtained. This representation had been relied upon (with attempts being made to secure the third party approval) and it was held to be inequitable to go back on it, and insist on the payment in accordance with the time limit set for the payment, until that approval had been obtained. It followed that non-payment could not be used as a ground to terminate the contract. This is similar to *Hughes* in terms of the nature of the representation. The judge stressed, at [122], that the critical issue was 'whether it is inequitable in all the circumstances for the representor to enforce his rights inconsistently with the representation' and added that all the circumstances 'will include, but are not limited to, the precise terms of the representation, how the representee has responded to the representation, and whether it remains possible for the representee to comply with his original obligation'. The representation in *Hughes v Metropolitan Railway* was described as being 'in the nature of an open-ended forbearance' which suspended the ability of the representor 'to rely on the underlying contractual obligation and any breach of it until reasonable notice is given that brings the period of suspension to an end. When the period of suspension is ended, the representor will be allowed to rely upon the underlying contractual obligation as from that date, but he is generally not entitled to enforce the obligations as if they had been in full force during the period of suspension.' It follows that it is the general right that is suspended while the estoppel operates and in *High Trees* this was held to be until the early part of 1945, although the full rent was claimed only for the last two quarters of 1945.

The reference in *Virulite* to *Hughes* as a case involving an 'open-ended forbearance' should not be interpreted too literally. In *Dunbar Assets plc v Butler* [2015] EWHC 2546 (Ch), [2015] All ER (D) 138 (Sep) the alleged representation was that Dunbar would postpone 'indefinitely' any enforcement action under guarantees given by Mr Butler for loans taken out by two property development companies if Mr Butler continued to manage the development companies. The judge held that despite the indefinite nature of the alleged postponement, it could not reasonably be interpreted to mean that Mr Butler could unilaterally prevent the taking of enforcement action by his continuing to undertake work on the developments even if Dunbar made it clear that it was not required. It could only be understood as operating for the duration of the agreement and could be brought to an end by reasonable notice. On the facts Mr Butler had ceased to manage the development companies in the autumn of 2013 and the notice had been served in September 2013.

As Stuart-Smith J recognized in *Virulite*, 'there is scope for confusion in the use of the terms 'suspensory' and 'extinguishing' in this context, since 'a representation may be revocable, and in that sense suspensory, while effectively extinguishing the representor's right to rely upon his contractual rights during the period of suspension'. The judge then drew a distinction based on the terms of the particular representation between an 'open-ended forbearance' and 'a promise not to enforce until a particular date is reached or a particular set of circumstances prevails' since this determines whether it is inequitable to allow the strict rights to revive.

Such a distinction does exist but it might be better explained as follows. An 'open-ended forbearance' in the single debt context allows more time to pay the balance but the contractual right to receive payment of the full sum does not go away. Depending on the terms of the representation, it can be revived at any point in the future. In this sense the strict legal rights are suspended for the time being, but they are not extinguished for all time. However, where the debt involves continuing periodic payments (such as rent or individual compensation payments) and the representation relates to a promise to forgo part or all of these payments for a set period or while certain circumstances prevail, the representation makes it clear that while the full future rent or royalty payment amounts can be revived (the strict rights for the future), it is not possible to go back and claim the balance on the part payments made while the terms of the representation (and the estoppel based on it) prevailed. In this sense the rights in relation to these individual period payments are extinguished.

Thus, in *Tool Metal Manufacturing Co. Ltd v Tungsten Electric Co. Ltd* [1955] 1 WLR 761, it was assumed that, after termination of the suspension, the appellants were not entitled to claim for royalty compensation that would otherwise have been payable during the period of suspension of the right to receive the royalty payments. Moreover, in the leading case of *Central London Property Trust Ltd v High Trees House Ltd* [1947] KB 130 (see **4.8.2.1**), there are *obiter dicta* of Denning J to the effect that periodic payments of rent that had fallen due during the period of suspension of rights could not be recovered once the suspension of rights had come to an end.

Statements made by Lord Denning in *Brikom Investments Ltd v Carr* [1979] QB 467, at pp. 484–5, might suggest that he believed that, in some circumstances, it might be impossible for the promisor to go back to the strict rights under the contract. He made a statement to similar effect in *D. & C. Builders Ltd v Rees* [1966] 2 QB 617, at p. 624, suggesting that promissory estoppel might operate to extinguish legal rights. These comments can be explained if Lord Denning was referring to individual periodic payments, such as the rental payments during the bombing of London in the *High Trees* case and the compensation payments during the Second World War in the *Tool Metal* case.

Equally, statements by Arden LJ in *Collier v P. & M. J. Wright (Holdings) Ltd* [2007] EWCA Civ 1329, [2008] 1 WLR 643, at [39] and [42], suggesting in the context of a single debt obligation that 'promissory estoppel has the effect of extinguishing the creditor's right to the balance of the debt' must be greeted with caution. The position would depend on the nature of the representation. Moreover, the reliance on *obiter* statements of Denning J in *High Trees* suggest that Arden LJ may have been referring to the balance on the rental payments during the war (the arrears) as having been extinguished since Denning J was equally clear that the general right to full rent revived when the bombing stopped (and considered this to be the early part of 1945).

Any attempt to treat promissory estoppel as extinguishing rights in a more general sense would elevate the effect of promissory estoppel to the equivalent of consideration and would then represent a direct and immediate challenge to *Foakes v Beer* (1884) 9 App Cas 605, since the two could not stand together. As mentioned earlier, *Collier* is not an actual decision applying promissory estoppel and only a finding that there was an arguable defence of promissory estoppel, the best advice may be to treat these comments as 'unfortunate'. In *Virulite* Stuart-Smith J appears to consider that the judgment of Arden LJ in *Collier* may be an example of his identified confusion in the use of the terms 'suspensory' and 'extinguishing'. Extinguishing should be interpreted to mean that the balance on the debt is gone forever and cannot be revived. This should apply only to payments due in the period of the suspension (or estoppel) and not to the general right itself.

As yet the enforceability of joined promises, both not to enforce strict rights and not to withdraw that first promise, has not been tested in the courts.

4.8.5.1 Giving notice to revive the strict legal rights

The ability to require performance in accordance with the contractual terms may be revived by the giving of reasonable notice to the promisee but this will be effective only if it is no longer inequitable to go back on the terms of the promise or representation.

In ***Tool Metal Manufacturing Co. Ltd v Tungsten Electric Co. Ltd*** [1955] 1 WLR 761, the respondents were bound to pay royalties to the appellants under an agreement made in 1938 for the import, manufacture, use, and sale of hard metal alloys. They were also to pay compensation if the material manufactured were to exceed a stated volume. At the outbreak of the Second World War, the appellants agreed to suspend the right to compensation. In 1945, the appellants claimed to have revoked that suspension and to be entitled once more to receive it from June 1945. That claim failed on the basis that reasonable notice needed to be given in order to resume the strict legal rights under the contract. In the later case, this earlier court action was held by the House of Lords to be sufficient notice to the respondents of termination of the suspension of the right to compensation.

4.8.6 Conclusion: the future of promissory estoppel and the Australian use of estoppel to prevent unconscionable conduct

Despite doubts expressed about the scope of the doctrine in decisions of the highest court—*Tool Metal Manufacturing Co. Ltd v Tungsten Electric Co. Ltd* [1955] 1 WLR 761, *per* Lord Tucker at p. 784, and *Woodhouse A. C. Israel Cocoa Ltd v Nigerian Produce Marketing Co. Ltd* [1972] AC 741, *per* Lord Hailsham at p. 758—and fears that it might abolish in a backhanded way the doctrine of consideration (see **4.8.3.2**), promissory estoppel appears now to be well established as a doctrine of English law. Suggestions that it might become largely redundant by virtue of developments in relation to consideration (see **4.7.3**), which avoid the restriction afflicting promissory estoppel (i.e. that it cannot be used as a cause of action), have subsided as a result of the continuing significance of the decision of the House of Lords in *Foakes v Beer* (1884) 9 App Cas 605. The possibility that the Australian lead might be followed to develop a broader category of estoppel in English law has failed to materialize.

4.8.6.1 *Waltons Stores v Maher*

In the Australian courts, a general category of estoppel has been used to prevent unconscionable conduct. This estoppel has been utilized in circumstances under which there was no pre-existing relationship between the parties and in order to enforce a (albeit implied) promise directly.

> In *Waltons Stores (Interstate) Ltd v Maher* (1988) 1 64 CLR 387, negotiations had taken place between the respondent and the appellant, whereby the respondent was to demolish an existing building on land it owned and then build a new building, in accordance with the appellant's specifications. The new building would then be leased to the appellant. The respondent thought that the agreement needed only to be executed and that this was to take place. The respondent therefore began the work of demolition. The appellant failed to execute the agreement, but did not inform the respondent until a considerable amount of the work had taken place.
>
> The respondent argued that the appellant was estopped from going back on its implied promise to complete the contract. The appellant argued that estoppel could not operate because there was no pre-existing legal relationship and because estoppel could not be used in this way, i.e. as a cause of action.
>
> The High Court of Australia held that the appellant knew that the respondent was exposed to a detriment in acting in reliance on the representation that the contract would be executed and it was unconscionable to act in a way that encouraged that detriment. Accordingly, the appellant was estopped from denying that it was bound.

The decision in *Waltons Stores* (and hence this estoppel) is based on preventing 'detrimental reliance', and so it would not be appropriate, in this form, in cases in which there was no detriment, such as *Central London Property Trust Ltd v High Trees House Ltd* [1947] KB 130.

In addition, the estoppel will not necessarily lead to full enforcement of the promise. The remedy available will be limited to the 'minimum equity needed to avoid the detrimental reliance'; see also the support for the 'minimum equity' principle in *Commonwealth of Australia v Verwayen* (1990) 170 CLR 395. Since the estoppel in *Waltons Stores* protects against detrimental reliance through the unconscionable conduct of a promisor, it might be thought that reliance damages (damages to compensate the loss suffered when relying on the promise or representation) would be the appropriate remedy rather than fulfilling the promisee's expectations, although there could be no universal rule: see Robertson, 'Reliance and expectation in estoppel remedies' (1998) 18 LS 360. However, in *Giumelli v Giumelli* (1999) 163 ALR 473—see Edelman (1999) 15 JCL 179—the High Court of Australia took the view that this estoppel is not based solely on a requirement of detrimental reliance. The court therefore suggested that, prima facie, the expectation measure (damages which puts the claimant in the position they would have been in had the promise been fulfilled) was appropriate in order to ensure that the promise is fulfilled: see also Cooke (1997) 17 LS 258. Only in instances of detrimental reliance would a reliance-based remedy be appropriate.

There are signs, therefore, of an even greater relaxation of this 'estoppel' in the Australian courts, although further clarification is required on the details and the theoretical underpinning for this doctrine. In particular, if the basis for this equitable intervention is the existence of 'unconscionable conduct', it will be necessary to provide sufficient scope in this definition to justify intervention in scenarios typically covered by promissory estoppel. In the context of proprietary estoppel, the English House of Lords expressly rejected unconscionability as the basis for raising that estoppel in the absence of a proprietary claim—*Cobbe v Yeoman's Row Management Ltd* [2008] UKHL 55, [2008] 1 WLR 1752—which may present difficulties. There are other specific dangers associated with a general estoppel, since it will inevitably be uncertain and may cause problems in its application. However, even the Australian courts deny the existence of a single unified estoppel, while effectively merging the existing estoppels to such an extent that this is the inevitable conclusion.

4.8.6.2 Other examples of limited direct enforcement

The American Restatement (2d) Contracts (1979), § 90(1), also recognizes that promissory estoppel may give rise to a cause of action and gives the courts a discretion to determine the appropriate remedy:

A promise which the promisor should reasonably expect to induce action or forbearance on the part of the promisee or a third person and which does induce such action or forbearance is binding if injustice can be avoided only by enforcement of the promise. *The remedy granted for breach may be limited as justice requires.* [Emphasis added.]

4.8.6.3 The possibilities for relaxation of the strict requirements for promissory estoppel in English law

In *Williams v Roffey Bros.* [1991] 1 QB 1, both Glidewell and Russell LJJ raised the possibility that estoppel might have been pursued as an argument on the facts. Counsel for the claimant clearly considered that, since the claimant was seeking direct enforcement of a promise to pay more, an argument based on factual benefit was more likely to succeed than an argument based on estoppel as giving rise to a cause of action. However, Russell LJ (at p. 17H) commented that he would have 'welcomed' such an argument based on estoppel. It must be noted, however, that this was a very pragmatic Court of Appeal and that another Court might not be willing to entertain an argument that appears to conflict so directly with *Combe v Combe* [1951] 2 KB 215.

Indeed, *Combe v Combe* was relied upon by the Court of Appeal in *Baird Textile Holdings Ltd v Marks & Spencer plc* [2001] EWCA Civ 274, [2002] 1 All ER (Comm) 737, in reaching its conclusion that Baird could not successfully argue that there was an estoppel that gave it a right to require Marks & Spencer to continue to place orders for garments (the estoppel argument also failed because of the uncertainty of any representation: see **4.8.3.1**). Counsel for Baird argued that *Waltons Stores (Interstate) Ltd v Maher* (1988) 1 64 CLR 387 could be relied upon in order to create a cause of action. The argument was rejected on the basis that English law had not yet reached this position, although it was conceded that such an argument might succeed in a future case before the House of Lords. However, the actual decision in *Waltons Stores* might not provide strong authority for the use of a promissory estoppel as a cause of action. Mance LJ considered that *Waltons Stores* was a decision relating to formalities, i.e. there was agreement, but it had not been executed. Given the existence of agreement, he considered that using estoppel in this situation might not constitute 'giving a cause of action in itself'; rather, it had operated in *Waltons Stores* to prevent Maher from objecting to the binding nature of what was an agreed lease.

MULTIPLE-CHOICE QUESTIONS

Test your knowledge by trying this chapter's **multiple-choice questions**:
www.oup.com/uk/poole

FURTHER READING

General and reform

Atiyah, 'Consideration: a restatement', in *Essays on Contract* (Oxford University Press, 1986).

Coote, 'Consideration and variations: a different solution' (2004) 120 LQR 19.

Coote, 'Variations sans consideration' (2011) 27 JCL 185.

Treitel, 'Consideration: a critical analysis of Professor Atiyah's fundamental restatement' (1976) 50 Aust LJ 439.

Treitel, 'Agreements to vary contracts' in *Some Landmarks of Twentieth-Century Contract Law* (Clarendon Press, 2002).

Roffey and existing duty and contract modification

Adams and Brownsword, 'Contract, consideration and the critical path' (1990) 53 MLR 536.

Arzandeh and McVea, 'Refining consideration: RIP *Foakes v Beer*' [2017] LMCLQ 1, 7.

Capper, 'Consideration in the modification of contracts' in Merkin and Devenney (eds.), *Essays in Memory of Professor Jill Poole* (Informa Law, 2018), ch. 7.

Carter, Phang, and Poole, 'Reactions to *Williams v Roffey*' (1995) 8 JCL 248.

Chen-Wishart, 'Consideration: practical benefit and the emperor's new clothes' in Beatson and Friedmann (eds.), *Good Faith and Fault in Contract Law* (Oxford University Press, 1995).

Chen-Wishart, 'A bird in the hand: consideration and contract modification' in Burrows and Peel (eds.), *Contract Formation and Parties* (Oxford University Press, 2010), ch. 5.

Coote, 'Consideration and benefit in fact and in law' (1990) 3 JCL 23.

Davies, 'Varying contracts' (2016) 75(3) CLJ 455.

Giancaspro, 'Practical benefit: an English anomaly or a growing force in contract law?' (2013) 30 JCL 12.

Halson, 'Opportunism, economic duress and contractual modifications' (1991) 107 LQR 649.

Hird and Blair, 'Minding your own business: *Williams v Roffey* re-visited—consideration reconsidered' [1996] JBL 254.

Morgan, 'Contracting for self-denial: on enforcing "no oral modification" clauses' (2017) 76(3) CLJ 589.

O'Sullivan, 'In defence of *Foakes v Beer*' (1996) 55 CLJ 219.

O'Sullivan, 'Unconsidered modification' (2017) 133 LQR 191.

Shaw-Mellors and Poole, 'Contractual variations and promises to accept less: pragmatism in the Court of Appeal' [2016] JBL 696.

Promissory estoppel

Cooke, 'Estoppel and the protection of expectations' (1997) 17 LS 258.

Denning, 'Recent developments in the doctrine of consideration' (1952) 15 MLR 1.

Denning, *The Discipline of Law* (Butterworths, 1979).

Duthie, 'Equitable estoppel, unconscionability and the enforcement of promises' (1988) 104 LQR 362.

Edelman, 'Remedial certainty or remedial discretion in estoppel after *Giumelli*' (1999) 15 JCL 179.

Halson, 'The offensive limits of promissory estoppel' [1999] LMCLQ 256.

McFarlane, 'Promissory estoppel and debts' in Burrows and Peel (eds.), *Contract Formation and Parties* (Oxford University Press, 2010), ch. 6.

Robertson, 'Reliance and expectation in estoppel remedies' (1998) 18 LS 360.

Shaw-Mellors, 'Estoppel and promises: the importance of coherence, rationalisation and adhering to basic principles' in Merkin and Devenney (eds.), *Essays in Memory of Professor Jill Poole* (Informa Law, 2018), ch. 8.

Spence, *Protecting Reliance: The Emergent Doctrine of Equitable Estoppel* (Hart Publishing, 1999).

Thompson, 'Representation to expectation: estoppel as a cause of action' [1983] CLJ 257.

Chapter 5

Intention to be legally bound, formalities, and capacity to contract

5

SUMMARY OF THE ISSUES

- To be enforceable as a contract, the parties must have an intention to be legally bound (known as an intention to create legal relations). This is judged objectively through the use of the following two presumptions that are capable of being rebutted. Clear evidence is required to do so.

- In relation to social or domestic agreements, it is presumed that there was no intention to be legally bound. This position appears to be a matter of public policy, but the presumption is not irrebuttable. However, it is unlikely to be rebutted in the absence of clear reliance, certainty of terms, and evidence of the seriousness of the promise.

- In relation to commercial agreements, it is presumed that the parties intended to be legally bound unless there are clear words indicating the absence of a promise or that the parties have agreed to be bound in honour only.

- In addition to the requirement to establish an intention to create legal relations, a promise will, in general terms, be unenforceable unless it is contained in a deed or is supported by consideration. (The requirements for a deed or consideration were discussed in **Chapter 4**.) Some contracts require particular formalities to be binding, and **Chapter 5** outlines some examples of these and the consequences of non-compliance with the formality requirements.

- The chapter concludes with a brief discussion of the capacity rules in contract (i.e. a party's ability in law to contract) and the effect of incapacity on a contract. The capacity rules, as a general rule, also have the effect of rendering the contract unenforceable, at least for the party affected by the lack of capacity. This part of the chapter focuses, in particular, on contracts made by minors (persons under 18 years of age).

- Minors have the capacity to make contracts for 'necessaries' and may be bound by certain contracts unless they are repudiated. Other contracts entered into by minors are invalid unless ratified on reaching the age of 18. The Minors' Contracts Act 1987 contains provisions allowing the court to order restitution of property to the other contracting party.

- The ability to contract of those lacking capacity owing to 'an impairment of, or a disturbance in the functioning of, the mind or brain' is governed by the provisions of the Mental Capacity Act 2005. These provisions include the fact that a person so lacking capacity must pay a reasonable price for 'necessaries'.

»

- Companies and limited liability partnerships (LLPs) are separate legal persons. Whereas statute provides that an LLP has unlimited capacity, the capacity of a company is dictated by its constitution, although statute protects innocent third parties where the company acts *ultra vires* (i.e. beyond its powers).

5.1 Intention to be legally bound: the context

It is generally accepted that legal systems must have some means of identifying those agreements that outwardly appear to qualify as contracts, but which are regarded as being beyond the reach of legal remedies. In essence, therefore, the concept of 'intention to create legal relations' is used by the courts as a device to enable them to deny enforceability to those agreements that they consider should not be legally binding such as trivial family arrangements.

→ EXAMPLE

Tom is a 19-year-old student, living at home with his parents during the holidays. He has no money and approaches his father, Dick, for an allowance. Dick says that if Tom will clean the family car once a week, do the shopping, and keep the garden tidy, he will give him £30 per week. Tom agrees. Not many people would disagree with the conclusion that, despite the outward appearance of agreement and consideration (a promise to do the various odd jobs about the house in exchange for a promise to pay an allowance), this arrangement should not be regarded as a contract, in the sense that the courts ought to be unwilling to enforce trivial family agreements.

For much of the nineteenth century, the period of development of modern contract law, the underlying theory (as discussed at **1.4.1**) was that contracts were built upon the will of the parties. Unsurprisingly, therefore, the test for identifying those contracts beyond the reach of the law was framed in terms of whether the parties intended legal relations (or intended to be bound in law). Nevertheless, today it is accepted that reference to the parties' intentions may be no more than a convenient short way of describing a test that is rather more complex than that. In fact, it is notoriously difficult to prove intention, since there is often no objective evidence that may be produced as conclusive proof. If every party seeking a legal remedy under a contract were to be put to the burden of establishing that both parties positively intended legal consequences to follow from their agreement, it would be a major stumbling block to the formation of valid contracts and commercially inefficient. For this reason, the law has had to accept a much more restricted test of intention.

5.2 Presumed intention

The conventional view of intention to create legal relations is that agreements are categorized into two general types: (a) social/domestic agreements and (b) commercial agreements. For each type there is a corresponding presumption.

For social/domestic agreements, the presumption is that there is no such intention to create legal relations; for commercial agreements, the presumption is that such an intention exists. One difficulty with this otherwise straightforward scheme lies in the nature of presumptions, which are technical devices of the law of evidence. A presumption may be displaced by any actual evidence to the contrary. Such a precarious status is inconsistent with the role that the particular presumptions are called upon to play in relation to intention to create legal relations, which is precisely to avoid instability in contracts caused by parties finding it too easy to deny liability by denying the relevant intention.

From the cases that are discussed below, it will be apparent that, in this particular context, the presumptions are by no means easily displaced and, indeed, it may seem that they are at times impossible to displace. The true situation seems to be that the term 'presumption' is not being used in its technical evidential sense here. Rather, when we say that intention is presumed in relation to commercial agreements, we mean that a reasonable person in this situation would have expected legal consequences to flow from this agreement: see the discussion at **2.1** of the objective test for determining intention to be legally bound, citing *Maple Leaf Macro Volatility Master Fund v Rouvroy* [2009] EWCA Civ 1334, [2010] 2 All ER (Comm) 788, *Dhanani v Crasnianski* [2011] EWHC 926 (Comm), [2011] 2 All ER (Comm) 799, and *RTS Flexible Systems Ltd v Molkerei Alois Müller GmbH & Co. KG (UK Production)* [2010] UKSC 14, [2010] 1 WLR 753, *per* Lord Clarke SCJ at [45]. In the absence of some reason of policy against it, the court will enforce that reasonable expectation. Equally, when we say that there is a presumption of an absence of intention to create legal relations in social or domestic agreements, we mean that the reasonable expectation is that no legal consequences would flow from the agreement. Recognizing reasonable expectations from the context also seems to be the basis for the decision in *Edmonds v Lawson* [2000] QB 501 (discussed at **5.3**), in which the presumptions were not applied.

The presumptions are simple and can be rebutted, placing the burden of proof on the party seeking to establish the opposite. To do so may be very difficult; in legal terms, the burden of proof is very high.

There is also a clear policy dimension. The rule of presumed absence of intention is really based on a judicial policy of unwillingness to interfere in domestic disputes (sometimes referred to as 'freedom *from* contract'). In the words of Atkin LJ in the leading case of *Balfour v Balfour* [1919] 2 KB 571, at p. 579: 'In respect of these promises each house is a domain into which the King's writ does not seek to run.' By comparison, the inference is that the effectiveness of contracting as a mechanism for planned exchanges in the commercial context would be seriously undermined if there were no assumption of an intention to be legally bound in the case of commercial contracts.

5.2.1 Social and domestic arrangements

The law relating to intention to create legal relations is most difficult in the case of non-commercial agreements. The difficulty stems partially from difficulties in identifying social and domestic arrangements, and partially from the desire to be able to enforce certain agreements even if they are social or domestic in character.

5.2.1.1 Husband and wife

The key authority is *Balfour v Balfour* [1919] 2 KB 571.

The husband worked overseas and it became clear that, for reasons of health, his wife could no longer live where he worked. On a return trip to England, they agreed that he would return overseas, while she stayed in England, and that he would pay her £30 per month for her living expenses. Subsequently, they became estranged and the wife sued to enforce the promise of financial support. The Court of Appeal held that the promise was not legally enforceable because there had been no intention to create legal relations.

There is no doubt, as subsequent cases have shown—see *Merritt v Merritt* [1970] 1 WLR 1211—that if the maintenance agreement had been made upon the breakdown of the marriage, rather than prior to it when the relations between the parties were entirely amicable, the agreement would have been enforceable even though entered into between husband and wife: see also *Soulsbury v Soulsbury* [2008] EWCA Civ 969, [2008] 2 WLR 834, *per* Ward LJ at [35]. It is not disputed that legal relations are intended in the latter situation because the fact of the breakdown takes the agreement outside the sphere of domestic arrangements. In *Merritt v Merritt*, at p. 1213, Lord Denning MR stated:

> It is altogether different when the parties are not living in amity but are separated, or about to separate. They then bargain keenly. They do not rely on honourable understandings. They want everything cut and dried. It may safely be presumed that they intend to create legal relations.

Nevertheless, it will still be necessary for the language of a promise made on separation to be sufficiently certain for it to be enforced. In *Gould v Gould* [1970] 1 QB 275, a separating husband's promise of payment 'so long as I can manage it' was not sufficiently certain to rebut the normal presumption of no intention to be legally bound.

These cases are further examples of the way in which many potential contractual rights crystallize at the time of formation of the agreement and cannot be affected by subsequent events. In *Balfour v Balfour*, the only relevant intention was that existing at the time of making the agreement, and the fact that subsequently the marriage had broken down could not change it from being beyond the scope of the law.

Balfour v Balfour highlights a desire to prevent the courts from being flooded with litigation concerning domestic agreements (see e.g. Atkin LJ's statement at p. 579 that 'the small Courts of this country would have to be multiplied one hundredfold if these arrangements were held to result in legal obligations').

5.2.1.2 Rebutting the presumption

In the case of the presumption against intention to create legal relations, it is unlikely that the courts would find any express statement of the parties to be conclusive, since it is here that the policy element of the doctrine is at its strongest. Thus, in the example of Tom and Dick (see **5.1**), it is unlikely that we would be any happier about the legal enforceability of their agreement had it contained a clause stating that it was intended to create legal relations. The policy against judicial intervention in such agreements would still prevail. Nevertheless, the courts have been willing to find social/domestic agreements enforceable in some cases, although it is not always easy to identify the evidence that caused the presumption to be rebutted. *Factors such as certainty of terms, seriousness, and reliance appear to be important.*

An instructive case involving the question of intention to create legal relations between *parent and child* is *Jones v Padavatton* [1969] 1 WLR 328.

In *Jones v Padavatton*, the claimant sought to persuade her daughter to take up a new career by offering to pay her fees and to provide her with a living allowance while she pursued studies to become a barrister. The claimant also bought a house, in which the daughter had rooms, the rest being let to tenants. Eventually, after more than one unsuccessful attempt at the examinations, mother and daughter fell out, and the mother sought to evict the daughter from the house. The majority of the Court of Appeal (Danckwerts and Fenton Atkinson LJJ) found that the daughter had no right to stay in the house because there was no enforceable contract between her and her mother. The majority relied on the speech of Atkin LJ in *Balfour v Balfour* [1919] 2 KB 571 in concluding that this was a domestic agreement and that the presumption of no intention to create legal relations had not been rebutted.

Although there was clear reliance by the daughter on the mother's promise, the terms of their arrangement were regarded as not being sufficiently certain. Salmon LJ agreed with the overall conclusion of the majority, but for different reasons. Salmon LJ considered that when the agreement was entered into, it was intended to have contractual force, emphasizing the daughter's reliance on the promise by giving up her secure and lucrative career. However, this agreement was only to last for a reasonable period of time and he felt that this period had elapsed, so that the mother was entitled to possession of the house.

There is much to commend the reasoning of Salmon LJ in this case. It suggests that while families' trivial agreements are beyond the scope of the law, when families come to agreements that will have a serious impact on the lives of their members, they are as entitled to the remedies of the courts as everybody else. An example is provided by *Granatino v Radmacher* [2010] UKSC 42, [2011] 1 AC 534, which concerned a prenuptial agreement between husband and wife as to ownership of assets. Baroness Hale stated, at [142]:

> There is nothing to stop a husband and wife from making legally binding arrangements, whether by contract or settlement, to regulate their property and affairs while they are still together (type (a) agreements). These days, the commonest example of this is an agreement to share the ownership or tenancy of the matrimonial home, bank accounts, savings or other assets. Agreements for housekeeping or personal allowances, however, might run into difficulties.

This suggests that the agreement in *Balfour v Balfour* was not sufficiently serious for these purposes, since it was an agreement for housekeeping.

Other cases also seem to support the idea that where the subject matter of the dispute is more than trivial, the courts will be more willing to find the requisite intention in order to ensure that a contractual remedy will be available. For example, *Parker v Clark* [1960] 1 WLR 286 concerned an agreement between family members.

The defendants, an elderly couple, agreed with another couple (their niece and her husband, who were some years younger than them) that if the younger couple would sell their home and move in with them, sharing household expenses, the defendants would leave their house to the niece, her sister, and daughter. The younger couple, the claimants, sold their own home and moved in with the older couple. However, the two couples later fell out and the claimants were told to find alternative accommodation. They sought damages for breach of contract. Devlin J held that the language of the correspondence, the surrounding circumstances, and the precise details governing the arrangement indicated that the parties intended to create legal relations.

The presumption normally applicable in domestic arrangements had, in this case, been rebutted. In particular, the judge could not believe that the claimants would have taken the drastic step of selling their own house without the security of a legal right to live in the home of the other couple. On these facts, there was seriousness, certainty of terms, and reliance.

By comparison, it may be unlikely that an arrangement between family members, friends, or work colleagues to share prizes or competition winnings would be sufficient to rebut the presumption of no intention to be legally bound in the absence of a written document recording the terms of the arrangement and thereby indicating the seriousness of the parties' intent: *Wilson v Burnett* [2007] EWCA Civ 1170, (2007) 151 SJLB 1399, in which there was no binding agreement to share bingo winnings; although compare *Simpkins v Pays* [1955] 1 WLR 975, in which there was a coupon containing forecasts by each of the three parties who lived in the same house and evidence of agreement whereby they would share any winnings. In the latter case, the claimant had established that the parties contemplated legal consequences.

5.2.1.3 Intention and reasonable expectation

The view that social and domestic agreements are enforceable where they have a serious impact on the parties is problematic as it is not entirely consistent with what the judges say they are doing. Moreover, the orthodox language of intention appears to be based on a legal fiction, in that few (if any) parties turn their minds at the time of forming such agreements to the question of whether legal rights are being created. This is hardly surprising, since such agreements are entered into in confident anticipation of continued good relations. It would be undesirable if the nobler feelings of parties to serious social or domestic agreements were to become an impediment to legal recourse in situations in which their good relations have broken down. For this reason, the courts must put themselves in the place of the parties at the time of the agreement and ask whether it would have been reasonable to expect legal relations to result from the agreement in the undesirable event of amicable relations ending. In this way, it is possible to avoid the 'rose-tinted' view of the parties at the time of making the agreement. Unsurprisingly, therefore, the courts' willingness to find intention increases the more serious the promises made in the agreement, the more precisely they are expressed, and the greater the reliance on the agreement.

5.2.1.4 Policy considerations and agreements to provide lifts to work

We have seen that policy considerations can be important in the social or domestic context (**5.2.1.1**). For instance, in *Balfour v Balfour* [1919] 2 KB 571 there is clear recognition of a desire to prevent the courts from being flooded with litigation concerning domestic agreements (see e.g. Atkin LJ's statement at p. 579 that 'the small Courts of this country would have to be multiplied one hundredfold if these arrangements were held to result in legal obligations').

In relation to agreements to provide lifts to work, the basic policy objective and the inevitable 'hazards of everyday life' were such that there was no intention to create legal relations: *Coward v Motor Insurers' Bureau* [1963] 1 QB 259, at 271 (the main question in this case was to know whether Coward, who received a daily lift to the factory by a co-worker was being carried 'for hire or reward under s. 36 of the Road Traffic Act 1930'). However, the broader social need to ensure that such passengers are nevertheless covered by insurance appears to have led the House of Lords in *Albert v Motor Insurers' Bureau* [1972] AC 301 to conclude that, in this instance, there was an intention to create legal relations (based on a finding that it was a business arrangement and therefore subject to the presumption applicable to commercial contracts).

The determination of contractual intention may even turn on the precise question before the court: see Hedley (1985) 5 OJLS 391, who claimed that the question in *Coward v MIB* was whether a driver could be compelled to carry others in future (an executory arrangement), whereas in *Albert v MIB* the issue was whether there was an obligation to pay for services rendered (i.e. an executed arrangement). Thus the courts may be unwilling to declare that there is no contractual intention when faced with a question reflecting the existence of an executed social or domestic agreement.

5.2.2 Commercial agreements

It was suggested earlier (see **1.1**) that one of the main economic purposes of contracts is to stimulate exchange. It would be undesirable, therefore, for the requirement that there must be an intention to create legal relations to become a further hurdle in the way of a party seeking to enforce a commercial contract. For this reason, the presumption that intention exists in such contracts is extremely difficult to displace—see the arguments attempted unsuccessfully in *Dresdner Kleinwort Ltd v Attrill* [2013] EWCA Civ 394, [2013] 3 All ER 607, in relation to an announcement of a guaranteed employment bonus—so that only a party with solid evidence of a contrary intention would risk litigation.

5.2.2.1 Advertising: advertising gimmick or promissory statement?

For commercial agreements, advertisers may seek to rely on an absence of intention to create legal relations to avoid being held to the exact words of advertisements. If a beer producer chooses to promote its product by claiming that it enables those who drink it to achieve impossible feats beyond the reach of ordinary mortals, it is no doubt seen by reasonable people as a joke and not as a serious claim to be elevated into a contractual promise or as having any legal consequences. Such a statement is a mere advertising gimmick, or 'puff'. Nevertheless, it may be possible to establish that an advertisement amounts to a promise because, on the facts, there is evidence of an intention to be legally bound. This is what happened in *Carlill v Carbolic Smoke Ball Co.* [1893] 1 QB 256 (for facts, see **2.3.2.1**). The fact that the advertisement stated that the company had placed £1,000 in a specific bank account as proof of its sincerity led the Court of Appeal to conclude that there was an intention to be bound by the promise.

A similar argument of no intention to be bound in relation to an Association of British Travel Agents (ABTA) notice of protection was rejected by the majority of the Court of Appeal in *Bowerman v ABTA Ltd* [1996] CLC 451.

> The claimants had booked a holiday through a tour operator, which was a member of ABTA. The tour operator had become insolvent and the question that arose for decision was whether the ABTA notice displayed on the premises of the tour operator amounted to a binding offer of protection, so that customers were entitled to be reimbursed the full cost of the holiday.
>
> The majority of the Court of Appeal (Waite and Hobhouse LJJ) rejected an argument that this notice was non-promissory and therefore not binding. The majority considered that the notice was intended to be read, and would reasonably be read by customers, as constituting a binding offer that a customer could accept by booking a holiday with the tour operator.

Hobhouse LJ stated, at p. 461, that the document 'is clearly intended to have an effect on the reader and to lead him to believe that he is getting something of value'. He added that, given this reasonable interpretation by the public, ABTA could not deny that it intended to accept any legal obligation to the customer or say that it was not making any promise. If ABTA had wished to deny legal effect, it should have done so by the use of express words to this effect. However, as Hobhouse LJ recognized, at p. 464, from a commercial perspective, ABTA would not have wished to do this, because:

> To have included such words would have destroyed the value of the document in the eyes of the public and nullified the very effect which ABTA intended it to, and which it did, achieve—to induce the public to book with and entrust their money to ABTA members.

This approach can be compared with the denial of legal effect contained in the dissenting judgment of Hirst LJ, who considered that this was a non-promissory notice intended only to reassure the public. He placed emphasis on the language used as indicating a lack of contractual commitment and considered that this position was supported by the decision of the Court of Appeal in *Kleinwort Benson v Malaysia Mining Corporation Bhd* [1989] 1 WLR 379 (see **5.2.2.2**).

These cases indicate that whether a particular advertisement is regarded as promissory and as intended to have legal effects will depend upon the particular facts, and it seems that the 'promissory hurdle' must be overcome before the presumption of an intention to be legally bound will apply in the commercial context.

As the difference of opinion in *Bowerman* illustrates, judges may be in total agreement about the law applicable, but unable to agree upon its application to the facts. A similar difference of opinion occurred in the House of Lords in *Esso Petroleum Co. Ltd v Commissioners of Customs and Excise* [1976] 1 WLR 1.

> The company had organized a promotion in conjunction with the 1970 World Cup, whereby purchasers of four gallons of petrol received a free 'World Cup coin'. It was sought to recover purchase tax on the coins on the ground that they had been produced for general sale. In the House of Lords, one argument was that the coins could be 'for sale' only if there was an intention to create legal relations in respect of the transfer of the coins between garage proprietors and customers purchasing petrol. Lords Simon and Wilberforce considered that there was such an intention, relying on the business context and the large commercial advantage that Esso expected to derive from the scheme. Viscount Dilhorne and Lord Russell came to the opposite conclusion, relying on the language of the offer, the trivial value of the coins, and the fact that it was unlikely that any motorist denied a coin would bring an action in the belief that a legal remedy was available.

5.2.2.2 Comfort letter or guarantee?

The question of intention to create legal relations in commercial agreements was considered in *Kleinwort Benson Ltd v Malaysia Mining Corporation Bhd* [1989] 1 WLR 379 in relation to a 'letter of comfort'.

> The claimant bank agreed to make a loan facility available to M, a wholly owned subsidiary of the defendants. In the course of the negotiations, the defendants had provided a 'letter of comfort', containing the key sentence: 'It is our policy to ensure that the business of M is at all times in the position to meet its liabilities to you under the above arrangements.' When the tin market collapsed, M ceased trading and went into liquidation without paying its very considerable debt to the claimant bank. The bank

sued the defendants, claiming that this sentence in the 'letter of comfort' was a contractual promise, which had been broken.

At first instance in *Kleinwort Benson*, the judge had approached the question of whether there was a contractual promise by considering whether there was an intention to create legal relations. He had applied the presumption applicable to commercial agreements in concluding that there was. However, the Court of Appeal considered that the correct approach was first to consider whether, on the construction of the statement, it was promissory in its nature. On these facts, the particular statement was no more than a statement of present intention and not a promise about the future conduct of the defendants. Therefore it had no contractual force.

In coming to this conclusion, Gibson LJ for the Court of Appeal noted the fact that the parties had been unable to agree upon more formal security, and that the notion of a comfort letter was known by both sides to describe a document by which the defendants gave comfort to the claimants (at 391F) 'by assuming, not a legal liability to ensure repayment of the liabilities of the subsidiary, but a moral responsibility only'.

5.2.2.3 Rebutting the presumption in the context of commercial agreements: 'honour clauses' and other express statements denying enforceability

As was indicated in the decision of the majority in *Bowerman v ABTA Ltd* [1996] CLC 451 (see **5.2.2.1**) and assuming the necessary promissory statement, a presumption of intention to create legal relations will arise in relation to commercial agreements. However, this presumption may be rebutted by express words denying that the agreement is to have legal consequences and to be enforceable in the courts by stating that it is 'binding in honour only'. For example, football pools coupons contained such a statement: see *Jones v Vernon's Pools Ltd* [1938] 2 All ER 626. The leading case accepting the validity of such honour clauses is *Rose & Frank Co. v J. R. Crompton & Bros. Ltd* [1925] AC 445.

The claimants in **Rose & Frank Co. v J. R. Crompton & Bros. Ltd** were to be the defendants' agents to sell a certain kind of paper in the United States, and the document setting out the agency agreement contained a term usually referred to as the 'honourable pledge clause'. It purported to provide that the agreement was to be viewed as a definite expression of intention, but not as a formal or legal agreement subject to the jurisdiction of the courts. The parties continued their relationship for some time and, from time to time, the claimants would place a specific order, which was met by the defendants. The defendants then suddenly announced that they would fulfil no more orders and the claimants sued to enforce the general agency agreement. The House of Lords upheld the 'honourable pledge clause', effectively saying that, in the main agency agreement, there was no intention to create legal relations and no legally binding contract.

On this basis, there could therefore be no obligation on the claimants to place orders and no obligation on the defendants to fulfil those orders. However, their Lordships treated actual transactions under this agency agreement as giving rise to 'ordinary legal rights', so that there was an obligation to deliver goods where orders had been accepted and there was an obligation to pay for those goods on delivery.

The presumption of intention can be seen as having been rebutted by the express clause in the agreement, but there is some logical difficulty about this view, since ironically it would seem that the clause could have no legal force if the agreement in which it was contained were found not to be a contract.

5.2.2.3.1 The burden of proof

It might seem that there is little difference between the approach adopted in respect of intention to create legal relations in *Rose & Frank Co. v J. R. Crompton & Bros. Ltd* [1925] AC 445 and that adopted in *Kleinwort Benson Ltd v Malaysia Mining Corporation Bhd* [1989] 1 WLR 379. However, although it was said to be of no practical significance in the outcome of the case, the Court of Appeal in *Kleinwort Benson* suggested that, in its approach of relying simply on the construction of the words used, the onus of proof lay on the claimants to show that the letter of comfort should be treated as a contractual promise. However, where the promise is clear, in relation to a commercial contract, the onus is on the party seeking to rebut the presumption that there is an intention to create legal relations to show that the contract is unenforceable. Thus there is a difficult distinction between:

1. clauses stating that commercial agreements will not be legally enforceable (where the burden of proof is on the party denying legal enforceability to rebut the normal presumption of intention to create legal relations); and

2. statements in commercial agreements that are non-promissory in nature and so without legal force (where the burden of proof is on the party asserting that the statement is promissory and therefore has legal force because of the operation of the presumption in the commercial context).

It is perhaps for this reason that the decision in *Kleinwort Benson* has been criticized in some quarters, because it makes it all too easy to avoid legal responsibilities in the commercial context by establishing that statements are non-promissory: see *Banque Brussels Lambert SA v Australian National Industries Ltd* (1989) 21 NSWLR 502, noted by Tyree (1989–90) 2 JCL 279.

5.2.2.3.2 Implied agreements in the commercial context

Where it is alleged that an *implied* agreement has been reached, as was the case in *Baird Textile Holdings Ltd v Marks & Spencer plc* [2001] EWCA Civ 274, [2001] 1 All ER (Comm) 737, then, despite the commercial context, it is for the party alleging that there is a contract to establish the necessary intention to create legal relations: *Modahl v British Athletics Federation* [2002] 1 WLR 1192 and *Assuranceforeningen Gard Gjensidig v International Oil Pollution Compensation Fund* [2014] EWHC 3369 (Comm), [2014] 2 CLC 699, at [98] in relation to an alleged hybrid agreement, i.e. based partly on implication from conduct and a combination of meetings and communications.

As Mance LJ stated in *Baird Textile*, at [61]:

> An intention to create legal relations is normally presumed in the case of an express or apparent agreement . . . it is otherwise when the case is that an implied contract falls to be inferred from parties' conduct . . . It is then for the party asserting such a contract to show the necessity for implying it.

An intention to be legally bound was not established on the facts, since the evidence pointed towards a deliberate decision not to enter into any express contract to maintain flexibility in the commercial relationship.

5.2.2.3.3 Difficulties with evidence of contractual intent

In many cases, direct evidence of intention will not be available and the courts must draw such implications as they may from the surrounding circumstances.

The willingness to examine the wider background and circumstances to determine promissory statements and contractual intention is evident in the decision of the majority of the Court of Appeal in *Bowerman v ABTA Ltd* [1996] CLC 451. However, this is in marked contrast to the approach adopted by Hirst LJ (dissenting), who limited his evaluation to the wording of the document and concluded that the words used were non-promissory. The approach adopted can therefore be pivotal in the evaluation of intention.

In both *Rose & Frank Co. v J. R. Crompton & Bros. Ltd* [1925] AC 445 and *Kleinwort Benson Ltd v Malaysia Mining Corporation Bhd* [1989] 1 WLR 379, a document existed that, on its face, indicated an apparent absence of legal intention, respectively in the 'honourable pledge clause' and the designation of the document containing the relevant assurances as a 'comfort letter'. This evidence is fairly conclusive. Frequently, it seems that a decision on the question of intention to create legal relations is a cloak for a more pressing question of policy. In *Ford Motor Co. Ltd v AUEFW* [1969] 2 QB 303, the court was faced with the question of whether a collective bargaining agreement between management and the trade union was legally binding. The matter was clearly commercial and so the burden lay on the union, which sought to deny contractual intention. The court found in the union's favour. In so doing, it relied on evidence from industrial relations experts, which was general rather than relevant to the particular agreement. Thus the actual intentions of the parties seem to have been less relevant than the court's view that it was desirable as a matter of policy to keep such agreements out of the courts. The matter is now governed by s. 179 of the Trade Union and Labour Relations (Consolidation) Act 1992, which reverses the presumption otherwise prevailing in commercial cases.

5.3 A contextual approach

In *Edmonds v Lawson* [2000] QB 501, the Court of Appeal considered the question of intention to create legal relations in relation to a claim by a pupil barrister that her pupillage constituted a contract of employment for the purposes of the National Minimum Wage Act 1998. This decision was potentially of great significance to the operation of the pupillage system. The judge at first instance had found for the claimant, having concluded that there was an intention to create legal relations in relation to an offer of pupillage because it was a business (commercial) arrangement. However, the Court of Appeal, while holding that there was an intention to create legal relations and hence a binding contract, held that the pupillage was not a contract of apprenticeship (pupils are not 'workers'), so that pupil barristers were not covered by the legislation.

The Court of Appeal's approach is interesting in that it was far from clear which presumption should apply to the agreement. It is arguable that it was not commercial, since pupils are not paid, but should such an agreement be classified as social or domestic? Rather than being bound by such constraints, the court focused on the specific context to determine whether, objectively, there was the necessary contractual intention to be legally bound. In particular, it seems that the court was focusing on the seriousness of the arrangement for all of the parties concerned as indicating that necessary intent. The court emphasized the process leading up to the making of an offer of pupillage and the benefit of recruiting the ablest pupils who might later go on to be considered for tenancy. Lord Bingham CJ specifically stressed, at p. 515, that whether either the pupil or chambers would sue in the event of default made no difference to the conclusion on the question of whether there was the necessary intention to be legally bound.

5.3.1 Conclusion

Difficulties can exist in identifying the type of contract for the purposes of the application of the presumptions. *Edmonds v Lawson* [2000] QB 501 is a good illustration of the fact that, on occasions, it can be difficult to make a clear identification of a contract as either commercial or social/domestic, and the very existence of the presumptions can force an artificial classification that fails to reflect the realities of the contractual context. It is the nature of and context for the agreement that should determine, rather than the identity of the parties to that agreement. A good example of this can be seen in *Snelling v John G. Snelling Ltd* [1973] 1 QB 87 (discussed at **11.7.2**), which involved a business agreement between brothers. In such a commercial agreement, the presumption in favour of an intention to create legal relations will operate.

Context is therefore particularly relevant, especially when negotiations take place in an informal setting such as in a pub as in *Blue v Ashley* or a restaurant as in *MacInnes v Gross* [2017] EWHC 46. The informality of setting alone is not sufficient a reason to regard that there is no contract as Leggatt J made clear in *Blue v Ashley* (at [81]). In fact, the setting and context in *Blue v Ashley* were sufficiently important for them to be commented upon. Indeed, Leggatt J remarked that the setting, in a pub where copious amount of alcohol had been consumed was unusual. Yet, in this context, 'while this might be true in the case of an ordinary businessman, Mr Ashley is not an ordinary businessman but is someone who adopts an "unorthodox approach to taking business decisions in informal settings while consuming substantial amounts of alcohol"' (at [81]). The setting of the pub together with the purpose of the meeting were therefore important elements in the particular circumstances to show that in spite of the informal setting, the meeting was not merely a social engagement but a commercial one (at [81–84]). However, on the facts, the claim that a contract was created was rejected as lacking seriousness.

Context—specifically the context of an existing employment relationship—was also important to the Court of Appeal when it rejected an argument that the presumption should be rebutted on the facts in *Dresdner Kleinwort Ltd v Attrill* [2013] EWCA Civ 394, [2013] 3 All ER 607 (see also **2.4.5.1**).

5.4 Formalities: unenforceability by defect of 'form'

5.4.1 Introduction

Where the law states that a contract is enforceable only if recorded in a particular way, the rule is described as a requirement of form.

It is one of the commonest misconceptions of contract law among lay people that contracts are enforceable only if in writing. It is true that the job of the courts, and of lawyers advising clients, would be much easier if we were to insist that all contracts be put in writing. If we pause and consider the implications of this, it will soon be realized, however, that this would mean that each time anyone bought a loaf of bread or a drink in a pub, they would be obliged to countersign an invoice. There would be an intolerable burden on daily consumer intercourse. For that reason, the general rule is that there is no formal requirement that contracts be made in writing and the parties are left to their own good sense as to whether written evidence is necessary. For a discussion as to the impact of this in relation to the parties choosing specified formalities to be observed for a variation, see **6.2.1.5**.

In commercial dealings, written evidence is almost inevitably available, but for the most part that is a matter of choice, not a matter of law. Where complex obligations of great value are undertaken on each side, so that any dispute may involve liability for very large sums of money, parties will inevitably choose to keep an accurate record of their agreement (and see **3.4.1** on the rectification of written agreements).

In the seventeenth century, the law required a large number of contracts to be made in writing. Today, it may generally be said that the law insists on writing only where the subject matter or nature of the contract requires either absolutely certain evidence or some cautionary element to bring home to one of the parties the seriousness of the legal agreement being entered into. Thus some consumer credit, hire purchase, and distance selling agreements (defined in **5.4.2.2.3**) require a particular form of writing and subject parties to informational duties as a means of protecting consumers. In recent years, there has been a growth in the formality requirements in the consumer context, with a view to increasing the level of protection for consumers: see, in particular, European directives such as the Consumer Rights Directive (CRD) 2011/83/EU and its implementation in English law by means of the Consumer Contracts (Information, Cancellation and Additional Payments) Regulations 2013, SI 2013/3134 and now of course Part 1 of the Consumer Rights Act (CRA) 2015.

There are differing consequences for non-compliance with formalities, e.g. the contract may be void, ineffective, unenforceable, or the effect may be to deprive the transaction of the consequences that would normally follow.

5.4.2 Instances in which there are requirements of form in English law

Requirements of form are of four types:

1. contracts required to be made by deed (see **5.4.2.1**);
2. contracts required to be in writing (see **5.4.2.2**); and
3. contracts required to be evidenced in writing (see **5.4.2.3**).
4. in relation to e-commerce, contracts requiring electronic signature (**5.4.2.4**).

5.4.2.1 Contracts required to be made by deed

The common law made provision for a particularly formal kind of legal writing by means of the document made under seal (a deed). Deeds must still be made in accordance with certain formal requirements, as set out in s. 1 of the Law of Property (Miscellaneous Provisions) Act 1989, although the need for a seal was abolished by s. 1 of that Act. These include the require-ment of properly attested signature and delivery (s. 1(3)). Although the word 'deed' does not need to be used in the document, it must be clear on the face of the document that the parties intended the document to have this extra status of formality (s. 1(2)).

The most common transaction that must be made in the form of a deed is the conveyance of a legal estate in land, e.g. a lease for more than three years (see ss. 52 and 54 of the Law of Property Act 1925). A deed is also the means by which to make enforceable a gratuitous promise that otherwise would have no legal effect (see **4.1**): if there is a deed, there is no requirement to plead and establish the existence of consideration. A further advantage is that a longer limitation period applies to a contract made in a deed—12 years from the date of the breach of contract, under s. 8(1) of the Limitation Act 1980—whereas the period applicable to a simple contract (i.e. not contained in a deed) is six years (s. 5(1) of the Limitation Act 1980). Although this form of enforceable promise is not often used for commercial transactions, there can be tax reasons that dictate its use, e.g. covenants to make gifts to charity.

5.4.2.1.1 *Corporate deeds*

Where a deed is required in the corporate context, s. 46 of the Companies Act (CA) 2006 provides for a document to be validly executed by a company if duly executed and delivered as a deed. Delivery is presumed to occur on execution unless it is clear that this was not the intention, e.g. if the intention was to sign and hold the deed until satisfaction of an outstanding condition.

To be validly executed as a deed (CA 2006, s. 44) the company document must be in writing and accord with the signature requirements set out in that section. The CA 2006 provides for signature by either two directors, by a director and a company secretary, or by one director in the presence of a witness who attests the signature. Alternatively, the company's common seal may be affixed to the document if the company has elected to retain a seal (CA 2006, s. 45).

5.4.2.2 **Contracts required to be made in writing**

Some contracts must be made in writing. The most important ones are: contracts for the sale or disposition of an interest in land; consumer credit agreements; distance selling contracts; marine insurance contracts; and bills of exchange.

5.4.2.2.1 *Contracts for the sale or disposition of an interest in land*

Such contracts must be made in writing, signed by both parties (as to signature, see the discussion of electronic signatures at **5.4.2.4**) pursuant to the Law of Property (Miscellaneous Provisions) Act 1989, s. 2.

Section 2 of the Law of Property (Miscellaneous Provisions) Act 1989

(1) A contract for the sale or other disposition of an interest in land can only be made in writing and only by incorporating all the terms which the parties have expressly agreed in one document or, where contracts are exchanged, in each.

Case law determines which transactions fall within s. 2 and whether or not the requirements of s. 2 are satisfied.

Transactions falling within s. 2

The grant of an option to purchase land falls within the scope of the section, but its exercise does not and so need not be signed by both parties: *Spiro v Glencrown Properties Ltd* [1991] Ch 537. An agreement made not to enter into negotiations with any rival purchaser for a period of time (a 'lock-out' agreement) is not a disposition of an interest in land and so does not fall within the scope of s. 2(1): *Pitt v PHH Asset Management Ltd* [1994] 1 WLR 327 and *Dandara Holdings Ltd v Co-operative Retail Services Ltd* [2004] EWHC 1476 (Ch), [2004] 2 EGLR 163. A contract where the consideration, or part of it, is the actual disposition of an interest in land rather than an agreement to dispose of the interest does not fall within s. 2: *Keay v Morris Homes (West Midlands) Ltd* [2012] EWCA Civ 900, [2012] 1 WLR 2855, at [8]. In *Rollerteam Ltd v Riley* [2016] EWCA Civ 1291, [2017] 2 WLR 870, the Court of Appeal, after reviewing the case law on s. 2, clarified the situations where s. 2 applies or not. In this case, which involved a settlement agreement over a dispute on a family business, it was held that s. 2 applied only to executory *contracts* for the future sale or other disposition of an interest in land, and not to a contract which itself effects such a disposition. In other words, s. 2 does not apply to leases, mortgages and charges, or, in this instance, the settlement agreement. Performance of the settlement agreement constituted both the performance of the contract and the consideration and therefore could not be covered by s. 2.

Satisfying the requirements of s. 2

Incorporation of the terms following s. 2 of the 1989 Act is achieved by setting them out in the contract document or by reference to another document (s. 2(2)). In *Record v Bell* [1991] 1 WLR 853, it was held that where incorporation is alleged to have been achieved by reference to another document, to be effective for the purposes of s. 2 the contract of sale that both parties have signed must refer to and identify that other document.

Each party must sign a document incorporating the terms, although it need not be the same document that bears both signatures, especially where there is to be an exchange of contract documents (s. 2(3)). It is clear that, where the terms of a secondary document are to be incorporated, it is the principal document that needs to be signed. In *Firstpost Homes Ltd v Johnson* [1995] 1 WLR 1567, the document, that it was claimed contained the contract between the parties referred to an attached plan. The purchaser signed the plan, but not the principal document, and the Court of Appeal found that the requirements of s. 2 were not satisfied.

In the Matter of Stealth Construction Ltd, sub nom Green (Liquidator of Stealth Construction Ltd) v Ireland [2011] EWHC 1305 (Ch), [2012] 1 BCLC 297, the judge suggested that an exchange of emails may also, in some circumstances, satisfy the requirements of s. 2. However, the emails would need to refer to all of the terms that had been agreed orally—specifically terms relating to price—and had to point to binding obligations being undertaken. In *Marlbray Ltd v Laditi and another* [2016] EWCA Civ 476, [2017] 1 WLR 5147, the Court of Appeal held that a contract signed by a husband on behalf of his wife but without her authority was nevertheless valid as it satisfied the requirements of s. 2. This was possible, on the interpretation of the contract in this contract which stipulated 'where two or more persons constitute the Purchaser all obligations contained in this Agreement on the part of the Purchaser shall be joint and several obligations on the part of such persons'. In this context, the court considered that there was no reason why the several obligations of the husband should not be binding upon him.

Failure to comply with the s. 2 requirements

A purported contract made in contravention of these rules would be without effect. Protections exist through rectification, collateral contract, proprietary estoppel, and constructive trust.

5.4.2.2.2 Consumer credit agreements

Other important contracts required to be made in a particular form of writing are consumer hire purchase and credit sales agreements, which are regulated agreements under the Consumer

Credit Act (CCA) 1974, s. 60. Such contracts must be in the form prescribed by regulations (s. 61(1)(a)). This means that the express terms must be set out in a prescribed order and various notices given, e.g. the notice of the right to cancel during the 'cooling-off period'. This document must be signed by both parties 'in the prescribed form' (which has been held to include electronic signature, i.e. clicking on the 'I accept' button so as to generate a document containing the typed name: *Bassano v Toft* [2014] EWHC 377 (QB), [2014] ECC 14, [2014] Bus LR D9). A copy must be supplied to the debtor. There are also certain prescribed informational requirements.

Failure to comply with the formalities set out in the legislation may not be fatal to such an agreement, but it will require a court order if the agreement is to be enforced (CCA 1974, s. 65(1)), and such an order will not be issued if the consumer did not sign the agreement, or did not receive a copy of the agreement or notice of his right to cancel.

5.4.2.2.3 *Distance selling contracts*

The Consumer Contracts (Information, Cancellation and Additional Charges) Regulations 2013, SI 2013/3134, came into force on 13 June 2014 and apply to contracts entered into on or after that date. These Regulations implement the Consumer Rights Directive (CRD) 2011/83/EU, which repealed and replaced the European Distance Selling Directive 97/7/EC. The previous law, which implemented that Distance Selling Directive, is contained in the Consumer Protection (Distance Selling) Regulations 2000, SI 2000/2334, as amended by the Consumer Protection (Distance Selling) (Amendment) Regulations 2005, SI 2005/689, and this will continue to apply to contracts entered into before 13 June 2014. The CRD also repealed the Doorstop Selling Directive 85/577/EC, protecting consumers in respect of contracts negotiated away from business premises. It follows that the Cancellation of Contracts made in a Consumer's Home or Place of Work etc. Regulations 2008, SI 2008/1816, are also superseded by the 2013 Regulations for contracts entered into on or after 13 June 2014.

The new Regulations strengthen consumer rights in relation to distance sales, e.g. the seven-day cooling-off period is extended to 14 days and there is an extended definition of a distance sale, thereby extending the scope of the consumer protection.

The 2013 Regulations apply to consumer contracts between a consumer and a trader (defined in reg. 4) other than those consumer contracts that are excluded by reg. 6. Part 2 details the information that must be supplied to the consumer prior to the conclusion of the contract (the so-called 'informational requirements') and extends these requirements to on-premises (Sch. 1 information), off-premises, and distance contracts (Sch. 2 information). Distance contracts can include contracts concluded by electronic means and contracts that commence with a telephone call. The information that is required to be made available, and which can include cancellation rights, is stated to be 'treated as included as a term of the contract'. Regulations 12 and 16 impose a requirement on the trader to provide the consumer with a copy of the signed contract or a confirmation of the contract within a reasonable time after the contract is concluded. A failure to give notice of the right to cancel may also constitute an offence in an off-premises contract (regs. 19–26).

Provisions covering the right to cancel in a distance or off-premises contract are contained in Part 3 of the 2013 Regulations.

5.4.2.2.4 *Marine insurance contracts*

By ss. 21–24 of the Marine Insurance Act 1906, a contract of marine insurance will not be admitted in evidence unless contained in a document (a policy) signed by the insurer. Thus the whole contract must be in writing.

This is not strictly a condition of validity of such a contract, but only of its admissibility in evidence in trial proceedings. In fact, the contract itself is regarded as formed by assent given before the policy is drawn up. However, inadmissibility in evidence may be an insurmountable obstacle to enforcement.

5.4.2.2.5 *Bill of Exchange*

A bill of exchange must be in writing and signed (ss. 3(1) and 17(2) of the Bills of Exchange Act 1882). It is therefore an instrument. A typical example of a bill of exchange is a cheque (see **11.5.4**). A bill of exchange is an instrument which contains an unconditional promise of payment to the holder of the bill by the issuer of the bill. The main advantage of a bill of exchange is that it is freely transferable to a third party and thus can be used to make unconditional payment. There is no better example of a negotiable instrument than a £5 note. It contains a promise by the Bank of England to pay whosoever happens to be in possession of the note at the time. If the instrument is not in writing, it will not be a bill of exchange and the usual characteristics of that instrument will be lost, e.g. negotiability.

5.4.2.3 **Contracts required to be evidenced in writing**

Contracts of guarantee are required to be evidenced in writing (Statute of Frauds 1677, s. 4). There must be 'some memorandum or note thereof' in writing, which is signed by the party to be charged. A guarantee is defined by s. 4 as a 'promise to answer for the debt, default or miscarriage of another person'. In other words, there is a promise by one person to meet the liabilities of another should that other become liable and fail to pay. It follows that it is considered appropriate to protect against alleged purely oral commitments to guarantee.

The definition of a guarantee is important because the formality rule is said not to apply to contracts of indemnity. Contracts of indemnity are defined as promises to pay for another whether or not there is liability on that other. Thus, in the case of indemnities, the guarantor is taking on primary liability, whereas s. 4 applies only where the guarantor takes on secondary liability. However, this distinction has been subject to severe criticism—see *Yeoman Credit Ltd v Latter* [1961] 1 WLR 828—and appears illogical in policy terms.

The s. 4 requirement continues to offer protection. In *Carlton Communications plc v The Football League* [2002] EWHC 1650 (Comm), 1 August 2002, it was claimed that Carlton and Granada, as shareholders of the parent company of ONdigital plc, were liable under an alleged guarantee for ONdigital's liabilities under a contract with the Football League. This argument failed because: (i) there was no such guarantee, only a statement in a bid document that was 'subject to contract'; (ii) there was no authority to give such a guarantee; and (iii) even if there had been a guarantee, it would have been unenforceable under s. 4 of the Statute of Frauds 1677 because of the lack of a written document containing an unequivocal guarantee.

However, a party may not seek to deny a guarantee by relying on s. 4 if there is clear written evidence of the guarantee. In *Golden Ocean Group Ltd v Salgaocar Mining Industries PVT Ltd* [2012] EWCA Civ 265, [2012] 1 WLR 3674, the Court of Appeal confirmed that the s. 4 requirements were satisfied in relation to a guarantee where the parties had been negotiating by email and had finally reached agreement on the basic terms of a charterparty and guarantee, but subsequent emails refining the detailed terms of the charterparty had stopped making express reference to the guarantee. It was alleged that s. 4 would be satisfied only if there were express reference made in later documents. The Court of Appeal considered that the conclusion of commercial contracts—particularly charterparties—by means of such a sequence of communications was 'entirely commonplace': *per* Tomlinson LJ at [22]. Since the last emails in the sequence had referred impliedly to those earlier in the process, there was a sufficient agreement for a guarantee. The guarantee did not need to be in a separate document or in ampler terms. In addition, although the final email was not of itself the contract of guarantee, the broker's signature on that document, assuming the broker's authority, authenticated the contract of guarantee contained in the sequence of emails.

In *J. Pereira Fernandes SA v Mehta* [2006] EWHC 813 (Ch), [2006] 1 WLR 1543, the question was whether an email could satisfy the requirements of s. 4.

> Mehta was a director of a company that had failed to pay for goods supplied by the Portuguese company. To settle the matter, Mehta had sent an email offering a personal guarantee of £25,000 and repayment terms. The body of the email did not mention Mehta's name and there was no signature at the bottom. However, the service provider automatically indicated the email address of the sender in the email header of all messages sent and received. It was held that although (i) the email constituted a written memorandum of the guarantee for the purposes of s. 4 because it was in writing, the terms were clear and the evidence was that this offer had been accepted orally, (ii) it could not satisfy the s. 4 requirements because the email contained no signature. The name of the sender inserted at the end of the body of the text would constitute a signature if it were clear that it had been inserted to give authenticity to the guarantee commitment, but the automatic insertion of the email address would not clearly be intended to operate as a signature, in the absence of evidence to the contrary, and could not suffice for these purposes because it was merely an 'incidental' inclusion. It followed that the guarantee was unenforceable.

The decision in *Mehta* seems correct on the facts and has contributed to some degree of clarity in relation to electronic contract formation, since it is quite clearly the case that emails can satisfy any requirement for writing. It also provides guidance on the form needed to satisfy any signature requirement.

The policy underlying s. 4 of the Statute of Frauds was confirmed by the House of Lords in *Actionstrength Ltd v International Glass Engineering SpA* [2003] UKHL 17, [2003] 2 AC 541, in which a claim based on estoppel was made in an attempt to avoid the s. 4 formality requirement.

> The case concerned an alleged oral agreement between the claimant (which was providing labour for International Glass) and Saint-Gobain Glass (for whom International Glass was building a factory) that, in consideration of the claimant not withdrawing its labour from the site, Saint-Gobain would attempt to persuade International Glass to pay the claimant in full and on time, and failing this Saint-Gobain would withhold sums due to International Glass to pay the claimant directly. When the claimant sought to rely on this alleged oral agreement, Saint-Gobain claimed that the agreement amounted to a guarantee and was unenforceable, since the s. 4 formalities had not been complied with. In response, the claimant argued that Saint-Gobain was estopped from relying on s. 4 once the claimant had acted to its detriment on the faith of Saint-Gobain's oral promise.
>
> The House of Lords could find no evidence for any estoppel because there was no evidence that Saint-Gobain had represented either that there was a guarantee or that the absence of writing would not be a problem. The only representation was the oral agreement, which was unenforceable in accordance with s. 4. In any event, their Lordships considered that to allow an argument based on estoppel would be inconsistent with the statute and would undermine its purpose. It would always be the case that the party seeking to enforce a guarantee would have performed first and would have acted to its detriment on the faith of the promise in the guarantee. Section 4 could not be defeated by an argument that the unenforceable oral promise in the guarantee amounted to an enforceable estoppel.

However, their Lordships considered that some estoppels might prevent reliance on the statutory formalities, e.g. if there were a representation that the statute would not be invoked or that the guarantee would be confirmed in writing.

5.4.2.4 Electronic signatures and the implications of e-commerce

5.4.2.4.1 Recognition of electronic signatures

Electronic signatures were given legal recognition by s. 7 of the Electronic Communications Act 2000 (implementing aspects of the Electronic Signatures Directive 1999/93/EC, OJ L 13/12 of 19-1-2000). The Act was recently amended in part by the eIDAS Regulations 2016 (the Electronic Identification and Trust Services for Electronic Transactions Regulations 2016, (SI 2016/696)). Section 7(1) refers to the admissibility of an electronic signature 'incorporated into or logically associated with a particular electronic communication or particular electronic data' and 'certification by any person of that signature', as evidence of the authenticity or integrity of the communication or data. In other words, an electronic signature may fulfil the same function as a hand-written signature in relation to electronic communications. This is vitally important for the effectiveness of internet contracting. Following the eIDAS Regulations, s. 7(2)(b) also states that the person must be intending to purports to be used by the individual creating it to sign. Authenticity is explained in s. 15(2) as relating to questions of whether the communication comes from that person, whether the communication is 'accurately timed and dated', and whether it is intended to have legal effect. To ensure that the current rules remain relevant, the Law Commission is currently looking at the rules pertaining to the electronic execution of documents (see https://www.lawcom.gov.uk/project/electronic-execution-of-documents/).

The decision in *J. Pereira Fernandes SA v Mehta* [2006] EWHC 813 (Ch), [2006] 1 WR 1543 (see **5.4.2.3**) has clarified the fact that signature can occur by including the sender's name in the email text, provided that it is clear that the name was intended to operate as a signature.

5.4.2.4.2 Facilitating the effectiveness of e-commerce

Section 8 of the Electronic Communications Act 2000 gives the Secretary of State the power by statutory instrument to remove restrictions in any other legislation that impede the effectiveness of electronic commerce (e.g. formalities, such as deeds or other writing, or a requirement that the post be used). In addition, Art. 9(1) of the E-Commerce Directive 2000/31/EC (as implemented by the Electronic Commerce (EC Directive) Regulations 2002, SI 2002/2013, see **2.4.5.4**) provides that EU member states must ensure that their legal systems allow contracts to be concluded by electronic means, and that this means ensuring that any legal requirements that apply to the contractual process 'neither create obstacles for the use of electronic contracts nor result in such contracts being deprived of legal effectiveness and validity on account of their being made by electronic means'. Article 9(2) provides for various exceptions; in particular, Art. 9(2)(a) allows for exemptions in relation to 'contracts that create or transfer rights in real estate except for rental rights'. The problem with this is that it does not appear to exempt leases, so that leases may need to be capable of being created or transferred electronically. There is also an exemption in Art. 9(2)(c) for 'contracts of suretyship granted and on collateral securities furnished by persons acting for purposes outside their trade, business or profession', which would take some guarantees outside the electronic requirements. However, the provision specifies that the exemption will apply only if the guarantor was 'acting outside their trade, business or profession'. Therefore business guarantees will also need to be capable of being effected electronically.

5.5 Contractual capacity

Contractual capacity (the ability to enter into legally binding agreements) is governed by principles which aim to balance the interests of those who are considered to need protection (in the form of a denial of capacity and hence the ability to contract) and the persons or firms who contract with them without knowledge of the relevant impediment.

5.5.1 The capacity of individuals

The contractual capacity's paradigm is embodied in the adult of sound mind, and any deviation from that state is cause to question a party's capacity to contract.

5.5.1.1 Mentally impaired and intoxicated persons

5.5.1.1.1 Persons lacking capacity under the Mental Capacity Act

The Mental Capacity Act 2005 provides that a person lacks capacity if he is 'unable to make a decision for himself in relation to the matter' at the time that the contract is made (s. 2(1)). It does not matter whether the mental impairment is permanent or temporary (s. 2(2)). Section 3(1) describes the impairment in terms of the inability:

(a) to understand the information relevant to the decision,

(b) to retain that information,

(c) to use or weigh that information as part of the process of making the decision, or

(d) to communicate his decision (whether by talking, using sign language, or any other means).

The mentally impaired person remains liable to pay a reasonable price for 'necessaries' (s. 7(1)), which are defined as goods or services 'suitable to a person's condition of life and to his actual requirements at the time when the goods or services are supplied' (s. 7(2)): see also the Mental Capacity Act 2005 Code of Practice, para. 6.58, and the discussion of 'necessaries' for minors' contracts at **5.5.1.2**.

5.5.1.1.2 Vulnerable adults with capacity under the Mental Capacity Act

DL v A Local Authority [2012] EWCA Civ 253, [2012] MHLO 32 highlights the limitations of the Mental Capacity Act. In this Court of Appeal judgment, MacFarlane LJ clarified that the Mental Capacity Act is aimed solely at those that are legally lacking in capacity. He added, at [1], that for those 'vulnerable adults' that fall outside of the scope of the Mental Capacity Act, there could be a risk of falling within a 'jurisdictional hinterland'. Consequently, he concludes, at [77], that further protection is needed whenever the Mental Capacity Act does not apply and is provided through the 'inherent jurisdiction' of the courts.

The case concerned an elderly couple, Mr and Mrs L and their adult son DL. Whilst Mr and Mrs L were partially disabled, they were deemed to have capacity under the Mental Capacity Act. It is alleged that DL was physically and emotionally abusive towards his parents, controlling their freedom, both outside and within their own home, restricting social contacts, and taking control of their finances. Because Mr and Mrs L had capacity, it was claimed by DL that his parents fell outside the scope of the Mental Capacity Act and that therefore their decision-making could not be challenged. MacFarlane LJ, making specific reference to the issue of abuse of vulnerable adults, held, at [56], that where the Mental Capacity Act did not apply, inherent jurisdiction of the courts would provide a 'safety net' for vulnerable adults. Thus, common law principles regarding coercion and undue influence would be considered.

The court did not provide a definition of the 'vulnerable adult'. This omission creates some uncertainty regarding who is protected by the 'safety net' of inherent jurisdiction. Further case law may be required to determine this point fully, but it appears that vulnerable adults include all those at risk, be it because of an inherent vulnerability or due to external circumstances.

5.5.1.1.3 Intoxicated persons, and those whose understanding and awareness is otherwise impaired

Where a person does not fall within the Act's definition for mental impairment, it can however be shown that, at the time of contracting, the person was incapable of understanding the nature of the actions in question or was intoxicated—*Matthews v Baxter* (1873) LR 8 Ex 132—*and* the other contracting party knew or ought to have known of this at the relevant time—see *Imperial Loan Co. v Stone* [1892] 1 QB 599—the contract will be voidable (capable of being set aside by that party) subject to the usual rule concerning 'necessaries'. Where the other party does not know, nor ought to have known, of the mental impairment at the time of contracting, the contract will be binding and enforceable: *Hart v O'Connor* [1985] AC 1000 (elderly man suffering from dementia). It is, however, questionable if this Privy Council decision, whereby 'the validity of a contract entered into by a lunatic who is ostensibly sane is to be judged by the same standards as a contract by a person of sound mind, and is not voidable by the lunatic or his representatives by reason of "unfairness" unless such unfairness amounts to equitable fraud', would be decided in this manner today. Instead, it is likely that capacity, or lack thereof of, of the person suffering from dementia, would first be determined. Then, if the person with dementia was deemed legally capable, then vitiating factors would fall to be considered.

5.5.1.2 Minors

A minor is a person under 18 years of age. Contracts by minors are governed by a mix of common law and statutory rules, particularly the Minors' Contracts Act 1987.

A contract made by a minor is not void, and although the minor is not normally bound, the other party will be. There are, however, some exceptions to this principle, in which the minor will be bound:

- contracts for necessaries;
- contracts that are binding on the minor *unless* repudiated by the minor before they reach the age of 18, or within a reasonable time of doing so (these might be referred to as 'voidable' contracts); and
- where the minor ratifies a non-binding contract on attaining their majority.

5.5.1.2.1 Contracts for necessaries

A minor must pay a reasonable sum for necessaries, defined by s. 3(3) of the Sale of Goods Act (SGA) 1979 as 'goods suitable to the condition in life of the minor . . . and to his actual requirements at the time of the sale and delivery'.

Necessaries are more than only what may be needed to keep body and soul together, and reflect a minor's 'condition in life'. The classic case is *Nash v Inman* [1908] 2 KB 1.

> The defendant, while still a minor, purchased clothing, including 11 fancy waistcoats, from the claimant. It was established that he already had a supply of clothing sufficient for his condition in life, and so the clothing purchased could not be regarded as necessaries.

The case illustrates the two difficulties inherent in the rule:

- the court has to make invidious judgments about what is appropriate to any particular 'condition of life'; and
- more seriously, a salesperson may well be unable to judge, when confronted with a minor wishing to make a purchase, whether the good in question is a 'necessary' in the case of the particular minor.

The Law Commission once suggested that the concept of necessaries should be abandoned and replaced with a more narrowly defined concept of necessities: see Law Commission, *Minors' Contracts*, Working Paper No. 81 (1982). This suggestion was not pursued by the final report: Law Commission, *Law of Contract: Minors' Contracts*, Law Com. No. 134 (1984).

Contracts of employment, of apprenticeship, or for instruction are also treated as contracts for necessaries. They are binding on minors unless more burdensome than beneficial: *Doyle v White City Stadium* [1935] 1 KB 110 and *De Francesco v Barnum* (1890) 45 Ch D 430.

> In *De Francesco v Barnum*, the claimant brought an action for an injunction to prevent wrongful interference with his contract (under seal) with a minor who was apprenticed to him as a stage dancer. The contract provided that the girl was not to be paid unless actually employed by the apprentice master and that she should not accept other employment without his consent. The girl took alternative employment with the defendant and the claimant's action to restrain this interference in the contract of apprenticeship failed because the contract was invalid as unduly burdensome.

The rule is that such terms must not be out of proportion to the benefit accruing to the minor.

In what is known as the 'Wayne Rooney case', *Proform Sports Management Ltd v Proactive Sports Management Ltd* [2006] EWHC 2903 (Ch), [2007] Bus LR 93, the judge considered that the general rule applied rather than the exceptions, so that the minor (Rooney) was not bound.

> At the age of 15 (i.e. when a minor), Wayne Rooney had entered into a player representation agreement with the claimant whereby the claimant company was to act as his executive agent and represent him. Rooney could not become a professional footballer until he reached the age of 17 (under the Football Association Rules), but was employed as a trainee. The claimant alleged that the defendant had also entered into a player representation agreement with Rooney whilst its contract was still operating. The claimant therefore brought an action against the defendant for unlawful interference with and/or procuring the breach of its contract with Rooney.
>
> The judge held that: (a) the agreement was not enforceable against Rooney, because he was a minor and the general rule was that contracts were voidable at his option; and (b) the contract was not analogous to a contract for necessaries and could not be analogous to a contract of apprenticeship, education, or service (which would generally be enforceable against a minor), since Rooney was already with a football club and could not yet become a professional footballer. Therefore the contract with the agent did not enable him to earn a living or to advance his skills. It followed that the defendant could not be liable for the tort of inducing the breach of contract since this contract was voidable at Rooney's option.

5.5.1.2.2 Contracts valid unless repudiated at majority

Certain contracts made by minors are voidable, but become valid when the minor attains majority unless repudiated before or at that time.

The rules governing these contracts are unaffected by the Minors' Contracts Act 1987 and continue to be governed by the common law rules. The most common types of contract within this category are contracts to acquire shares in a company or an interest in land. In each case, what is acquired is an enduring benefit to which certain obligations attach. To be effective, the repudiation must be accompanied by a surrender of the interest in question: see *North Western Railway v McMichael* (1850) 5 Ex 114. The contract must be repudiated either before attaining majority or within a reasonable time of attaining majority, although what is a reasonable time is a question of fact in each case: see *Edwards v Carter* [1893] AC 360. Money paid is not recoverable in such a case, except where there has been a total failure of consideration: see **Steinberg v Scala (Leeds) Ltd** [1923] 2 Ch 452.

5.5.1.2.3 Contracts ratified on majority

Despite the general rule that other contracts are not binding on the minor, since the rule exists to protect minors and not to prevent contracts, the minor can choose to ratify the contract, expressly or impliedly, on reaching the age of 18.

5.5.1.2.4 Unenforceable contracts and the passing of the minor's property

Contracts that are not for 'necessaries' and not validated are unenforceable against the minor, although they are binding on the other party. Nevertheless, property may pass from the minor to the other party: *Chaplin v Leslie Frewin (Publishers) Ltd* [1965] 3 All ER 764. Moreover, the minor may not recover property or money that has passed under an unenforceable contract, except in circumstances under which such recovery would be available to a person of full contractual capacity, such as total failure of consideration.

By contrast, there is the possibility of recovering property, which has passed under the unenforceable contract from the other party to the minor.

5.5.1.2.5 Restitutionary remedy against minors

Section 3 of the 1987 Act may provide assistance where a trader has supplied goods to a minor on credit, but the trader is unable to obtain payment because the contract is unenforceable by virtue of the minor's age. (Of course, minors are not able to acquire a credit card, so that the practical instances of acquiring goods on credit may be extremely limited.)

Under s. 3(1), the court may order the minor to return the property acquired if it is just and equitable to do so. 'Property' is not defined in this section and so it is not clear whether it includes money obtained under such a contract. However, s. 3(1) applies to property acquired or any property representing it, and if property acquired has been converted into something else, it is likely to have been converted into money. If that may be recovered under the Act, it would be strange if money acquired directly could not be. Another difficulty with the notion of property representing property acquired under the contract is where the proceeds are money and that money has been paid into a bank account from which withdrawals have been made, or where other goods have been purchased, the value of which is greater than merely the proceeds of the property originally acquired.

5.5.1.2.6 *Misrepresentation of age*

A problem arises where the minor represents that he is of full age. The law's policy of protecting minors still applies, so that the contract is unenforceable. To allow the minor to take advantage of their own wrongdoing would be undesirable. A rule of equity therefore requires the minor to restore goods acquired. The same rule cannot provide for the repayment of money loaned.

> In *R. Leslie Ltd v Sheill* [1914] 3 KB 607, the defendant, when still a minor, had borrowed £400 from the claimant moneylenders, but had misrepresented that he was of the age of contractual capacity. The claimants brought an action to recover the principal sum and interest. The claimants were unable to obtain restitution because that would have been equivalent to enforcing the contract, which was not possible.

Where goods are acquired and sold, the proceeds of sale may be recovered by a tracing remedy (the essence of 'tracing' is to allow the claimant to trace not just her own property but also the money or other proceeds received from the sale of that property as long as it can be identified as such): *Stocks v Wilson* [1913] 2 KB 235.

5.5.2 Companies incorporated under the Companies Act and limited liability partnerships

5.5.2.1 A company incorporated under the Companies Act

A company incorporated under the Companies Act 1985 has separate corporate personality, i.e. it is a legal entity independent of the identity of its respective members: see *Salomon v A. Salomon & Co. Ltd* [1897] AC 22. (This can be compared with general partnerships, which have no separate legal capacity and whose contracts are governed by general agency principles.) The capacity of the company to contract is therefore a separate question to the capacity of the individual owners or directors to bind the company when making contracts.

A company that acts outside the limitations of its constitution is acting *ultra vires* (outside its capacity). Section 31 of the Companies Act 2006 provides that unless the company's constitution (articles of association) specifically restrict the company's objects, these objects will be unrestricted, and s. 39 of the Companies Act 2006 removes the possibility for *ultra vires* in the external sense by stating that the validity of a company's acts is not to be questioned on the ground of lack of capacity because of anything in the articles. Section 40 of the Companies Act 2006 protects persons 'dealing with a company in good faith' who need not be concerned about whether the directors are acting within the terms of the company's constitution. Such contracts will be valid and enforceable. *Ultra vires* is therefore likely to have any relevance only in terms of the internal relationship between the shareholders and the company (s. 40(4) and (5)).

5.5.2.2 Limited liability partnerships

Limited liability partnerships (LLPs) are bodies corporate under s. 1(2) of the Limited Liability Partnerships Act 2000, i.e. they have separate legal personality and they also have unlimited capacity (s. 1(3)). The power of members to bind the LLP is governed by agency principles (s. 6 of the Limited Liability Partnerships Act 2000).

MULTIPLE-CHOICE QUESTIONS

 Test your knowledge by trying this chapter's **multiple-choice questions**:
www.oup.com/uk/poole

FURTHER READING

Intention to be legally bound

Brown, 'The letter of comfort: placebo or promise?' [1990] JBL 281.

Freeman, 'Contracting in the haven: *Balfour v Balfour* revisited' in R. Halson (ed.), *Exploring the Boundaries of Contract* (Ashgate, 1996).

Hedley, 'Keeping contract in its place: *Balfour v Balfour* and the enforceability of informal agreements' (1985) 5 OJLS 391.

Hepple, 'Intention to create legal relations' [1970] CLJ 122.

Keyes and Burns, 'Contract and the family: wither intention' (2002) 26 Melbourne University Law Review 577.

Klass, 'Intent to contract' (2009) 95 Virginia Law Review 1437.

Saprai, '*Balfour v Balfour* and the separation of contract and promise' (2017) 37(3) Legal Studies 468.

Formalities

Robertson, 'The Statute of Frauds, equitable estoppel and the need for "something more"' (2003) 19 JCL 173.

Content, interpretation, performance, and breach

Part

2

A bilateral contract's essence is the existence of obligations owed by each contracting party to the other. Much litigation involves questions relating to the performance as well as the construction of the obligations created by the contract.

- Has a relevant pre-contractual statement become one of the 'promises' of the contract? (**6.1**)

- Are the parties subject to obligations other than those expressed in the terms of their agreement? (**6.4**)

- What standard of performance is demanded? (**8.2.1.1**)

- How is a particular obligation to be interpreted? (**6.5**)

- What are the consequences of breach of the terms of the contract? (**8.4.2**)

- Is it possible to avoid the consequences of breach? (**Chapter 7**)

All these questions are examined in **Part 2** (**Chapters 6–8**).

A further relevant consideration when examining whether it is possible to avoid the consequences of breach is

- What happens to the parties' obligations if, after the contract is made, some event occurs that is outside the control of the parties, but which makes further performance impossible? Does this provide an excuse for non-performance?

This question relates to the doctrine of frustration (**Chapter 12**). This concerns the question of the contractual allocation of risk and how the law responds to impossibility. The discussion is therefore deferred until examining impossibility in general (**Chapters 12** and **13**).

Chapter 6

Content of the contract and principles of interpretation

SUMMARY OF THE ISSUES

6

This chapter's purpose is twofold: (1) to examine how the terms of the parties' agreement are identified, i.e. how we identify the contractual promises to be performed and (2) to assess how the courts interpret the meaning of those terms.

- The first issue relates to the status of statements made prior to the conclusion of the contract and why this matters. Have those statements been incorporated as contractual terms, or are they misrepresentations (false statements of fact inducing the contract: see **Chapter 14**)? This depends on the parties' intentions, objectively ascertained, and on whether the parties intended that any binding promise was being made as to the truth of the statement. The courts have developed a number of guidelines to assist in determining the parties' intentions.

- If the alleged contract is in writing, the issues relate to whether that writing represents the parties' contract in its entirety or whether there are also other oral or written terms. The parol evidence rule provides that, where the contract is written, that writing represents the complete contract. However, this rule can be sidestepped by defining the contract as partly written and partly oral. Alternatively, any oral terms can take effect as a collateral contract, which is separate from any written contract to which the parol evidence rule applies. Nevertheless, entire agreement clauses are a common feature of contracts. Such clauses generally provide that the parties have not relied on any term (contractual promise) that is not contained in the written contract. Therefore entire agreement clauses prevent arguments that there are oral terms and/or that a collateral contract exists.

- Terms must be incorporated into the contract (and establishing incorporation is the first requirement to be able to rely on an exemption clause: see **Chapter 7**). Incorporation can be achieved by signature or by notice. Reasonable steps must be taken to bring the existence of the term to the other party's attention *before or at the time of contracting*, and the term in question must be contained in a document that would be expected to contain contractual terms. If the term is onerous or unusual, a higher standard of incorporation is required. Alternatively, if, for example, notice has been given too late on this occasion, it may still be possible for a term to be incorporated on the basis of a consistent course of dealing between the parties or on the basis of their common understanding.

- Terms may be implied into contracts from custom, by statute, e.g. terms imposing obligations on sellers of goods contained in the Sale of Goods Act (SGA) 1979 and the Consumer Rights Act (CRA) 2015, or by the courts. Courts imply terms in fact, i.e. to give effect to the intentions of notional ≫

reasonable people in the position of the parties at the time they contracted where the term in question satisfies the test of business necessity or 'obviousness' recently reasserted by the Supreme Court in *Marks & Spencer plc v BNP Paribas Securities Services Trust Co. (Jersey)*. By comparison, some terms are implied in law into all contracts of a particular type as a 'necessary incident' of that category of contracts.

• The interpretation of contracts is of considerable practical importance and the applicable principles are contained in a series of decisions, including the decisions and analyses of the House of Lords and Supreme Court, beginning with *Chartbrook Ltd v Persimmon Homes Ltd*, through *Rainy Sky SA v Kookmin Bank*, *Arnold v Britton* and culminating in *Wood v Capita Insurance Services Ltd*. Much has been written on the apparently different approaches and emphases between individual judges in these cases and between the cases themselves, although it has since been said by Coulson J in *HSM Offshore BV v Aker Offshore Partner* [2017] EWHC 2979 (TCC) that there was little merit in attempting 'to exploit certain fine linguistic differences between the various judgments'. In his view 'they all point in the same general direction. What matters is the objective meaning of the language, to be derived from the natural or usual meaning of the words used, when seen against the background/context of the contract; where there are rival interpretations, one test is to consider which interpretation is more consistent with business common sense' (at [165]).

The starting point is to identify the parties' intentions objectively, by reference to what a reasonable person having all the relevant background knowledge ('factual matrix') would understand the words to mean. This involves focusing on the words chosen and their natural meaning *in relation to their use*—which includes other terms, the purpose underpinning this term and this contract, as well as 'commercial common sense'. The critical tension is between the natural meaning of the words that the parties chose to use (or a strict literal meaning) and a more purposive interpretation which would make commercial common sense but can be accused of rewriting the contract to account for imprudence in bargaining. Where the words used are ambiguous, commercial common sense should prevail (*Rainy Sky SA v Kookmin Bank*). The most recent iteration of the Supreme Court on this, *Wood v Capita Insurance Services Ltd* emphasizes both contextualism and language used in the written terms.

6.1 Pre-contractual statements: terms or mere representations?

6.1.1 Introduction

The important question here is whether pre-contractual statements (which are often oral) have become terms of the contract.

Pre-contractual statements are of three types:

- puffs;
- represpresentations; or
- terms.

The most common type of puff is the advertising gimmick. Puffs are statements that give rise to no legal consequences. They are statements that are not meant to be taken literally and by which there is no intention to be legally bound (see **5.2.2.1**). *Carlill v Carbolic Smoke Ball Co.* [1893] 1 QB 256 is an example of an advertising gimmick in which the statement was more than a puff, because there was evidence of an intention to be bound in the statement that the company had deposited £1,000 with its bank.

6.1.2 Why distinguish representations and terms?

The basic distinction between a representation and a term is that a term involves a promise as to the truth of the statement, whereas a representation involves no such promise as to truth, although the statement in question does induce the making of the contract.

Both representations and terms give rise to legal consequences if the representation is false (misrepresentation, discussed in **Chapter 14**) or if the term is broken (breach of contract, discussed in **Chapter 8**). *It is significant, however, that the legal consequences for misrepresentation and breach of contract are not the same.*

Before the mid-1960s, the distinction between representations and terms was vitally important because the remedy of damages for misrepresentation could be obtained only if the misrepresentation was fraudulent. Therefore it was often vital to establish that a false pre-contractual statement was a term. However, since the House of Lords' decision in *Hedley Byrne & Co. Ltd v Heller & Partners Ltd* [1964] AC 465 (see **14.4.3.1**), and under the Misrepresentation Act 1967, damages are available for non-fraudulent misrepresentations.

Nevertheless, there is still a distinction between a claim for misrepresentation and one for breach of contract in relation to both the ability to claim damages and the measure of those damages.

6.1.2.1 The ability to claim damages

An automatic right to claim damages arises on proof of a breach of a term of the contract (see **8.4.1**), whereas damages for misrepresentation for B2B (business to business) (i.e. outside the Consumer Protection from Unfair Trading Regulations (CPRs) 2008, SI 2008/1277 regime) may be *claimed* only on proof of fault (i.e. where the statement maker was fraudulent or negligent in making the statement). Damages cannot be *claimed* for innocent misrepresentation, although for B2B (and where the CPRs do not apply in the consumer context) they may be awarded at the discretion of the court, under s. 2(2) of the Misrepresentation Act 1967 (see **14.6.5**).

For B2C (business to consumer) contracts where the CPRs apply (see discussion at **14.1.2**), there may be *a right to claim damages from the trader* in respect of the 'prohibited practice', i.e. a misleading action or statement, but only in limited circumstances. The consumer must have incurred financial loss or have 'suffered alarm, distress or physical inconvenience or discomfort' in consequence of the prohibited practice (although this does not include financial loss alleged to be the difference between the price paid and the market price of the product affected) (reg. 27J CPRs 2008), and such damages must have been reasonably foreseeable at the time of the prohibited practice for there to be recovery. The trader also has a defence (reg. 27J(5)) in certain circumstances as long as it can prove it took all reasonable precautions and exercised due diligence to avoid the prohibited practice occurring.

6.1.2.2 The different measure of damages

The most important distinction, however, remains the different measure of damages. In case of a breach of contract, the normal measure of damages will be the expectation measure, i.e.

the claimant is put into the position in which the claimant would have been, had the contract been properly performed, i.e. had the breach not occurred (see **9.2**). However, the measure of damages for misrepresentation is tortious, i.e. it aims to put the claimant into the position in which the claimant would have been had the contract not been made (see **14.6**).

The ability to recover for losses (the remoteness rule) is also very different, at least in terms of comparing typical claims. The applicable remoteness rule for a claim for breach of contract—*Hadley v Baxendale* (1854) 9 Exch 341 (see **9.5.2**)—is much stricter, because the loss in question must be within the reasonable contemplation of the parties when they made the contract as the probable result of its breach and/or that the breaching party has 'assumed responsibility for that loss': *Transfield Shipping Inc. v Mercator Shipping Inc.* [2008] UKHL 48, [2009] 1 AC 61 (see **9.5.2.7**). The remoteness rule for fraudulent misrepresentation—and, under s. 2(1) of the Misrepresentation Act 1967, for negligent misrepresentation—is considerably more generous (although controversial for negligent misrepresentation) from the perspective of the misrepresentee, since all direct losses suffered by that party, regardless of foreseeability, are recoverable (see **14.6.2.1** and **14.6.4.1**). For consumers, where the CPRs 2008 apply, it is possible to recover distress damages in certain limited circumstances (by comparison, see **9.5.4** for the limited recovery of this head of damages in a breach of contract claim). However, any damages available under s. 2 of the Misrepresentation Act 1967 will not be available to a consumer where that consumer has a right to redress under the CPRs 2008.

The difference between the contractual measure and the measure in either the tort of deceit or when seeking damages under s. 2(1) of the Misrepresentation Act 1967 may be important where there are a number of consequential losses resulting from the making of a false pre-contractual statement. In such circumstances, and despite the need to plead fault in relation to a misrepresentation claim, recovery of damages for misrepresentation may be preferable to seeking to recover in a claim for breach of contract, where such losses may be too remote to be recovered.

6.1.3 Making the distinction between representations and terms

The test of whether a representation has become a term is very imprecise. It is essentially a question of the statement maker's intention, as objectively judged: see **2.1** and Lightman J in *Inntrepreneur Pub Co. v East Crown Ltd* [2000] 2 Lloyd's Rep 611, at p. 615.

> **! KEY POINT**
>
> Was it the statement maker's intention to make a binding promise as to the truth of their statement so that, if the statement were inaccurate, it would result in automatic breach of the contract? See *Heilbut, Symons and Co. v Buckleton* [1913] AC 30.

Another way of putting this question is to ask whether the statement maker's intention was to guarantee the truth of their statement.

The problem is that there is often very little external evidence from which to identify this intention. In addition, there is an added complexity in the case law, because a statement can also amount to a contractual promise on the basis that it is a collateral warranty, i.e. a promise that reasonable care and skill has been exercised, as opposed to a guarantee of a particular result.

6.1.3.1 The guiding principles to assist in determining intention

Although the existence of the intention necessary for a statement to be incorporated into the contract as a term is regarded as a question of fact, some guiding principles emerge from examination of the cases.

First, where the agreement between the parties is reduced into writing soon after the statement was made and the statement is not part of the writing, there is, unsurprisingly, presumption that the statement was not intended to be part of the contract: *Heilbut, Symons and Co. v Buckleton* [1913] AC 30. In *Inntrepreneur Pub Co. v East Crown Ltd* [2000] 2 Lloyd's Rep 611, at [10], Lightman J went as far as referring to this as a *'prima facie* assumption . . . that the written contract includes all the terms the parties wanted to be binding between them'. Lightman J also stressed that 'the longer the interval' between the statement and the contract, 'the greater the presumption must be that the parties did not intend the statement to have contractual effect'.

However, this 'presumption' can be rebutted by reference to specific guidelines. The guidelines are a helpful starting point, but, as Lord Moulton warned in *Heilbut, Symons and Co. v Buckleton* at pp. 50–1, they cannot be decisive on the question of the parties' intentions:

[T]hey cannot be said to furnish decisive tests, because it cannot be said as a matter of law that the presence or absence of those features is conclusive of the intention of the parties. The intention of the parties can only be deduced from the totality of the evidence and no secondary principles of such a kind can be universally true.

6.1.3.2 Accepting responsibility or advising on verification

If the statement maker accepts responsibility for the truth of a statement, the statement is likely to be regarded as a term, because in accepting responsibility the statement maker is guaranteeing its truth: *Schawel v Reade* [1913] 2 IR 81 (the claimant stopped examining a horse when told by the defendant that the horse was sound and that there was no need to continue the examination). Yet, if the statement maker asks or advises the other to check the reliability of the statement, e.g. by recommending that a survey be carried out or that the accounts be examined, that statement should be interpreted as a representation, because in such circumstances that person cannot be making a binding promise that the statement is true: *Ecay v Godfrey* (1947) 80 Lloyd's Rep 286 (the defendant who, was selling a motor cruiser to the claimant, had asked the claimant if he would be having the motor cruiser surveyed, so that the defendant could not be accepting responsibility for its condition).

6.1.3.3 The 'importance attached' test

If it is made clear that the statement was so important to the recipient that the recipient would not have contracted had that statement not been made, that statement is likely to be interpreted as a term (or binding promise that the statement is true). It is not merely a matter of the importance of the statement to the recipient; it must also be the case that this importance is clear to the statement maker before the statement is made, either because the recipient expressly makes the importance clear or because its significance is clear from the circumstances of contracting.

In **Bannerman v White** (1861) 10 CB NS 844, the defendant asked whether sulphur had been used in the production of hops that he was considering buying, stating that he was not interested in buying them if it had. He was assured that no sulphur had been used. However, the hops were found to contain sulphur and the defendant claimed to be entitled to reject them, arguing that this amounted to a breach of term (i.e. breach of contract). His argument prevailed. Without the false statement, there would have been no contract. This meant that the statement was not merely a pre-contractual inducement, but amounted to a description of the subject matter of the sale and was thus a term.

6.1.3.4 The statement maker's special knowledge of the subject matter

Where the statement maker has special knowledge of the contract's subject matter, or holds herself out as having such knowledge, the courts may be more willing to treat the statement as a term of the contract. A party may hold herself out as having special knowledge by suggesting that there is no need to check the accuracy of the statement made: *Schawel v Reade* [1913] 2 IR 81. Thus the guidelines can overlap in terms of pointing to the same outcome.

The relevance of special knowledge is clear when contrasting two cases in which material facts about second-hand cars were falsely stated.

In *Oscar Chess Ltd v Williams* [1957] 1 WLR 370, a private seller represented his car to be a 1948 Morris. It was, in fact, a 1939 version of the same model, worth substantially less. The statement of the car's age was held not to be a term. The private seller had no special knowledge and had relied on the registration book for his belief. In addition, the buyers in this case were car dealers and were thus in at least as good a position to discover the truth of the statement. Therefore the private seller did not assume any personal responsibility for the statement.

By contrast, in *Dick Bentley Productions Ltd v Harold Smith (Motors) Ltd* [1965] 1 WLR 623, a car dealer stated that a car had an engine that had done only 20,000 miles. This was, in fact, untrue. The buyer sought damages alleging breach of contract. The statement as to mileage was treated as a term.

The apparent distinction between the cases is the status of the person making the representation. A private seller did not have the special knowledge that indicated an intention that the statement be treated as a contractually binding promise, but a car dealer did.

It was argued in *Pritchard v Cook & Red Ltd* (see **6.1.3.4**) that the defendant in that case was selling in a personal capacity and that *Oscar Chess v Williams* therefore applied to any statements made. However, the Court of Appeal distinguished *Oscar Chess* on the basis that, in that case, the seller had indicated that his statement was derived from the registration book, so that he could not be taking personal responsibility for it. In *Pritchard v Cook & Red Ltd*, the defendant had clearly taken personal responsibility for the manufacturer's specification by copying it onto his own paper and not issuing a disclaimer.

6.1.4 Collateral warranties

Prior to the time when damages were available in cases of non-fraudulent misrepresentation, it was frequently argued that a non-fraudulent pre-contractual statement was a term giving rise to liability in damages on the basis that it was a 'collateral warranty'. Whereas a statement is normally classified as a term on the basis that the intention is to guarantee the truth of the statement, the 'collateral warranty' is an implied promise that reasonable care and skill has been employed in making the statement. Such a promise will most frequently be implied where the statement in question is a forecast, made by an expert or other person with special knowledge of the subject matter. It follows that the courts have been able to treat such forecasts as contractual terms and impose liability in breach where the promise is broken (i.e. where there has been a failure to exercise reasonable care and skill).

In *Heilbut, Symons and Co. v Buckleton* [1913] AC 30, the House of Lords had stated that the courts should not be quick to find such collateral warranties and that there must be clear evidence of an intention that the statements made should have contractual force. Despite these strictures, the courts found the collateral warranty to be a useful device for achieving what they believed to be a just result, particularly in the period before damages for negligent misrepresentation became available. In *Dick Bentley Productions Ltd v Harold Smith (Motors) Ltd* [1965] 1 WLR 623 (see **6.1.3.4**), the Court of Appeal held that the car dealer's statement amounted to a collateral warranty, giving rise to a remedy of damages, because reasonable care and skill had not been taken in making the statement about the car's mileage. It was therefore a term on this basis.

In **Esso Petroleum Co. Ltd v Mardon** [1976] QB 801, the Court of Appeal held that a forecast by a person with 40 years' experience of the potential throughput of a petrol station, which was intended to induce the defendant to take a tenancy of that petrol station, amounted to a collateral warranty that the forecast had been given using reasonable care and skill. The Court of Appeal also held that the forecast amounted to a negligent misstatement (see **14.4.3.1**).

Thus when a person with special knowledge of the subject matter makes a statement, that statement is likely to be interpreted as a contractual promise on the basis that it constitutes a collateral warranty rather than because it can be said to be a guarantee of truth or result.

6.1.5 Conclusion

It is difficult to predict with absolute certainty which pre-contractual statements will be incorporated as terms and which will be regarded only as representations, since the application of these guidelines does not always lead to the predicted result, and it is submitted that this is because the courts have generally tended to focus on only *one* of these guidelines instead of applying them all to a particular set of facts. To illustrate: although the statement in *Dick Bentley Productions Ltd v Harold Smith (Motors) Ltd* [1965] 1 WLR 623 (see **6.1.3.4**) was held to amount to a term because of the special knowledge of the statement maker, it was also the case that the buyer had made it clear that he wished to purchase a 'well vetted' car, so that the 'importance attached' test would also appear to have been satisfied.

It is hard to resist the conclusion that the courts enjoy the element of discretion that the current vague guidelines provide and would not like to see them replaced by anything more certain.

However, for B2C contracts, there is some certainty of classification in contracts for the supply of goods at a distance. The pre-contract information required to be supplied in contracts to supply goods made at a distance by regs. 9, 10, or 13 of the Consumer Contracts (Information, Cancellation and Additional Charges) Regulations 2013, SI 2013/3134 and set out in para. (a) of Schs 1 and 2 (relating to the main characteristics of the goods) is expressly stated to be included as terms of the contract within s. 11 Consumer Rights Act (CRA) 2015 (i.e. goods to be as described, s.11(4) CRA 2015). Further, s. 12 CRA 2015 provides that any *other* pre-contract information supplied by the trader under regs. 9, 10, or 13 and falling within Schs 1 or 2, is also 'to be treated as included as a term of the contract'.

6.2 Written contracts

6.2.1 The parol evidence rule

If a contract is wholly in writing, there is no difficulty in ascertaining its express terms—although there may be difficulties interpreting them (see discussion at **6.5**). However, despite the existence of a written document, one party may allege that this is not the whole contract and that there is either some orally agreed term or a term in some other written document. Thus the allegation is that this first written document does not contain the entire contract.

> ! **KEY POINT**
>
> The parol evidence rule states that *if the contract is written*, then that writing is the whole contract and the parties cannot adduce extrinsic evidence—and especially oral evidence—to 'add to, vary or contradict that writing': *Henderson v Arthur* [1907] 1 KB 10.

A related rule prevents, generally, use of extrinsic evidence of negotiations and subsequent conduct to prove the meaning of words used in a written contract (see **6.5.5**).

In disallowing any terms other than those recorded in writing, the parol evidence rule contributes greatly to contractual certainty, since others can rely on the written document as representing the entire agreement between the parties. The parol evidence rule was relied on by Lord Hobhouse in *Shogun Finance Ltd v Hudson* [2003] UKHL 62, [2004] 1 AC 919 (discussed at **3.3.3.4**) as the basis for concluding that it was not possible to go outside the terms of the written offer of the hire purchase contract.

Nevertheless, contractual certainty can be achieved at the expense of apparent justice, since it may be clear that further terms have been agreed, but have not been included in the writing. In consequence, the courts developed a series of exceptions to the rule, to the extent that it can no longer be said that the general rule is that extrinsic evidence is inadmissible to prove further terms (unless the contract contains an entire agreement clause: see **6.2.1.4**). The parol evidence rule applies only to express terms and does not operate to prevent the implication of terms into the contract (see **6.4**). Neither does it operate to prevent proof by extrinsic evidence of such defects in the contract as mistake (see **Chapter 3**) and misrepresentation (see **Chapter 14**).

Thus, in addition to parol evidence being admitted to imply terms, it can also be admitted in the following situations.

6.2.1.1 Rectification

Rectification is an equitable remedy that allows a document to be revised where there has been a transcription mistake in recording in writing the terms of a previous oral agreement (see **3.4.1**). Rectification could not apply without the existence of an exception to the parol evidence rule, since extrinsic evidence must be introduced to prove the content of the original oral agreement.

6.2.1.2 Contracts partly written and partly oral

If it is held that the contract was intended to be partly written and partly oral, this necessarily means that it is not a wholly written contract and therefore the parol evidence rule does not apply. It is perfectly permissible to introduce extrinsic evidence of oral terms to determine whether the contract is a contract wholly in writing to which the parol evidence rule applies. This means that the parol evidence rule has little substance, since it can always be avoided by introducing evidence of oral terms and concluding that the contract is not a written one. This led Professor Wedderburn [1959] CLJ 58, at 60 to conclude that in the light of the limits upon the rule, it is no more than a 'self-evident tautology'.

In *J. Evans & Son (Portsmouth) Ltd v Andrea Merzario Ltd* [1976] 1 WLR 1078, the parties had been doing business together for some time. The claimants shipped goods on trailers with the defendants, the trailers always being stored below deck on the ship. The defendants wanted to change to container transport, and the claimants would agree to the change only if the containers were also shipped below deck. The defendants gave an oral assurance to that effect. However, the written contract purported to allow the defendants complete freedom in the handling and transportation of the goods. One container was stored on deck and, while in transit, fell into the sea.

The Court of Appeal had no doubt that there had been a breach of contract. As Roskill LJ stated at p. 1083E, where the contract is partly written and partly oral, '[t]he court is entitled to look at and should look at all the evidence from start to finish to see what the bargain was that was struck between the parties'.

Having accepted evidence that there was an oral term (promise) that the goods would be shipped below deck, the Court of Appeal also held that the oral term overrode the inconsistent written contractual term which allowed the defendants complete freedom in determining transportation of the goods. The Court of Appeal took a similar approach in *Couchman v Hill* [1947] KB 554, where an oral assurance that a heifer was 'unserved' was held to override an exemption printed in the auctioneers' catalogue that there was to be no responsibility for the correct description, or any fault or defect in a lot. More recently in *Thinc Group v Armstrong* [2012] EWCA Civ 1227, the Court of Appeal held that an oral assurance given to two financial advisers, whom the financial services company was seeking to recruit, overrode subsequent express written terms in the employment contract. The assurance related to an upfront payment that the company promised could be reclaimed *only* if the advisers were to leave within three years (and so not if their contracts were terminated by the company). However, the contract provided for this sum to be repayable on various repayment events, including termination by the company. To allow the written contract to prevail would be a wholly unreasonable construction and undermine the basis on which the advisers had agreed to contract.

6.2.1.3 Collateral contracts

The courts have also been willing to allow the use of collateral contracts to sidestep the parol evidence rule. *The parol evidence rule will apply to the written contract, but where there is an oral promise that exists in parallel, the court may conclude that the oral promise is enforceable as a second (or collateral) oral contract. The promise can be enforceable as a contract since the consideration for the promise is the making of the main written contract. Since this collateral contract is a separate oral contract, the parol evidence rule cannot apply to it.*

In theory, such a contract will be found to exist only if the promise it is alleged to contain is independent of the subject matter of the major contract: *Mann v Nunn* (1874) 30 LT 526. Equally, a collateral contract cannot contradict the terms of the major contract: *Henderson v Arthur* [1907] 1 KB 10. Nevertheless, the courts have not allowed these limitations to restrict the operation of this device as a means of avoiding the parol evidence rule.

In *City and Westminster Properties (1934) Ltd v Mudd* [1959] Ch 129, a representation was made that a landlord would not enforce a covenant in a lease preventing the tenant from residing in the premises.

The tenant would not have entered into the contract without that assurance. The oral assurance was held to be a contractual promise (on the basis of the 'importance attached' test). The court found this promise to have been incorporated in a separate collateral contract, overriding the inconsistent covenant against residence contained in the main contract.

Lord Denning, in the Court of Appeal in *J. Evans & Son (Portsmouth) Ltd v Andrea Merzario Ltd* [1976] 1 WLR 1078, concluded that the oral assurance that goods would be shipped only below deck constituted a separate collateral contract inducing the written contract and that the oral term of the collateral contract overrode the inconsistent term of the main written contract, which had allowed the defendants complete freedom in the handling and transportation of the goods.

6.2.1.4 The effect of an entire agreement clause

It should be possible to avoid the kind of argument that prevailed in *City and Westminster Properties (1934) Ltd v Mudd* [1959] Ch 129 and in *J. Evans & Son (Portsmouth) Ltd v Andrea Merzario Ltd* [1976] 1 WLR 1078 by inserting what is known as an 'entire agreement clause' in the written agreement.

> **! KEY POINT**
>
> An entire agreement clause states that the document is intended and agreed to contain the entirety of the contract between the parties, and each party acknowledges that it has not relied upon any promise or undertaking in entering into the agreement that is not expressly contained in the written document.

Inserting such a clause ought to be sufficient to indicate the parties' intentions on the matter—namely, that the contract is a purely written contract to which the parol evidence rule applies, so that it is not possible to adduce evidence of alleged oral terms to add to, vary, or contradict the written document. The effectiveness of such a clause in giving effect to the parties' intentions that the written document represents the totality of the parties' contractual promises was acknowledged by Lightman J in *Inntrepreneur Pub Co. v East Crown Ltd* [2000] 2 Lloyd's Rep 611.

> The claimant sought to enforce a covenant in a lease for a public house against the defendant. By the terms of this covenant, the defendant had agreed to purchase its supply of beer from the claimant (a 'beer tie'). The defendant alleged that a collateral warranty had been given by the claimant whereby it had agreed to release the tie by 28 March 1998, so that there was no such tie in existence after this date. One of the defences of the claimant to this allegation was that the contract contained an entire agreement clause, which prevented the defendant from relying on the alleged collateral warranty.
>
> Lightman J held, following *Deepak Fertilisers and Petrochemical Corporation v Davy McKee (London) Ltd* [1999] 1 Lloyd's Rep 387, that even if a collateral warranty could be established, it was deprived of legal effect by the entire agreement clause. The clause made it clear that the terms to which the parties had agreed were only those contained in the written agreement.

Lightman J stated, at p. 614, that:

> [A]ny promises or assurances made in the course of the negotiations (which, in the absence of such a clause, might have effect as a collateral warranty) shall have no contractual force save in so far as they are reflected and given effect in that document.

The clause precluded a party to a written agreement:

> from threshing through the undergrowth and finding, in the course of negotiations, some (chance) remark or statement (often long forgotten or difficult to recall or explain) upon which to found a claim . . . to the existence of a collateral warranty.

The basis of enforcement of entire agreement clauses was explained by Longmore LJ in *North Eastern Properties Ltd v Coleman* [2010] EWCA Civ 277, [2010] 1 WLR 2715, [2011] 1 P & CR 3, at [82]: 'If the parties agree that the written contract is to be the entire contract, it is no business of the courts to tell them that they do not mean what they have said.' It is therefore a matter of construing the clause in question, although most are very explicit as regard the terms of the contract. In *Axa Sun Life Services plc v Campbell Martin Ltd* [2011] EWCA Civ 133, [2012] Bus LR 203, [2011] 1 CLC 312 (discussed at **7.5.5.2.2**), at [64], Stanley Burnton LJ noted that the advantage of an entire agreement clause is that it 'gives both sides certainty as to the terms of their contract', although recognizing that it was likely to be more beneficial for the party that had drafted it.

An entire agreement clause is more effective than labelling any pre-contract negotiations as 'subject to contract', since it has been held that the latter form of wording will not prevent a collateral contract from being agreed: *Business Environment Bow Lane Ltd v Deanswater Estates Ltd* [2007] EWCA Civ 622, [2007] L & TR 26, [2007] NPC 79. It was also made clear in response to argument by counsel, although it may seem obvious, that an entire agreement clause, however drafted, does not exclude such implied terms as may be applicable to the particular contract: *per* Teare J in *Great Elephant Corporation v Trafigura Beheer BV, The Crudesky* [2012] EWHC 1745 (Comm), [2012] 2 CLC 505, [2013] 1 All ER (Comm) 415, provided that the implied terms satisfy the requirements for implications of term as recently reiterated in the Court of Appeal in *JN Hipwell and Son v Szurek* [2018] EWCA Civ 674, [2018] L & TR 15.

Such clauses are not a complete panacea for contract drafters, since a simple entire agreement clause as such does not extend to prevent a claim for misrepresentation because it is merely a denial of contractual force (see e.g. *Barclays Bank plc v Unicredit Bank AG* [2014] EWCA Civ 302, [2014] 2 All ER (Comm) 115, [2014] 1 CLC 342, [13] and [28]). Equally, in *Thinc Group v Armstrong* [2012] EWCA Civ 1227 (for facts, see **6.2.1.2**), the contract contained a 'no reliance clause' relating to prior representations, but it was held that this did not extend to exclude the possibility of relying on a collateral warranty.

However, modern clauses are frequently more complex and extend to forms of wording that may be interpreted as preventing the operation of any collateral warranty *and* excluding or limiting liability for misrepresentation. Clauses which exclude or limit liability for misrepresentation in a consumer contract are subject to scrutiny as potential 'unfair terms' in accordance with s. 62 CRA 2015. In a commercial contract, a clause that covers misrepresentations is liable to be treated as enforceable on the basis that it merely set out the terms of the parties' bargain. These clauses are discussed in more detail at **14.7.2**.

6.2.1.5 'No oral modification' clause

This type of clause has an effect similar to that of an entire agreement clause, and indeed, as remarked, at [14], by Sumption JSC in *Rock Advertising Ltd v MWB Business Exchange Centres Ltd* [2018] UKSC 24, the two 'are commonly coupled'. An entire agreement clause precludes consideration of any material other than the contract itself, and a 'no oral modification' (NOM) clause prevents any variation to the contract unless the variation is in writing. Whereas entire agreement clauses have been accepted for some time, the same could not however be said about NOM clauses until *Rock Advertising Ltd v MWB Business Exchange Centres Ltd*. In this case, the wording of a contractual licence for the occupation of offices provided that: 'This Licence sets out all of the terms as agreed between MWB and Licensee. No other representations or terms shall apply or form part of this Licence. All variations to this Licence must be agreed, set out in writing and signed on behalf of both parties before they take effect.'

A conversation took place between the parties as to how arrears of licence fees should be dealt with, and the trial judge found that there had been a concluded oral agreement to defer payment and to spread the arrears over future payments, but he further held that the NOM clause negatived the oral agreement. The decision was overturned by the Court of Appeal [2017] QB 604. The conceptual question for the Supreme Court was whether a NOM clause was overridden by a subsequent oral agreement varying the terms of the primary agreement, the argument being that by reaching an oral modification the parties necessarily intended not to be bound by the NOM. The Supreme Court agreed with the trial judge and ruled that the variation was invalid. In doing so, the Supreme Court formally recognizes NOM, interestingly, after considering what is happening in other jurisdictions and with reference to international texts (see Lord Sumption at [7]–[8] and 13]). In Lord Sumption's words, 'there is no conceptual inconsistency between a general rule allowing contracts to be made informally and a specific rule that effect will be given to a contract requiring writing for a variation' (at [15]), and that a later oral agreement did not demonstrate an intention no longer to be bound by the no oral agreement clause. He added that what the parties had agreed was 'not that oral variations are forbidden, but that they will be invalid'. In consequence, 'the mere fact of agreeing to an oral variation is not therefore a contravention of the clause. It is simply the situation to which the clause applies' (at [15]). Lord Sumption also disagreed with the argument of the Court of Appeal that this would go against party autonomy (as per Kitchin LJ at [34]). Lord Sumption disagreed in the strongest term stating that this was a 'fallacy' (at [11]). He added that 'party autonomy operates up to the point when the contract is made, but thereafter only to the extent that the contract allows'. After noting that under English rules many statutes prescribe a particular form of agreement, his Lordship therefore concluded that 'there is no principled reason why the parties should not adopt the same principle by agreement' (at [11]). Finally, Lord Sumption even covered the issue of guarding against 'the risk that a party may act on the contract as varied, for example by performing it and then find itself unable to enforce it' (at [16]). His lordship simply stated that the 'safeguard against injustice lies in the various doctrines of estoppel' (at [16]).

Lord Sumption's very pragmatic analysis was agreed with by Lady Hale and Lords Wilson and Lloyd-Jones. Lord Briggs however took a different approach, holding that it was perfectly open to parties who had agreed to no oral variations to change their minds and remove that clause orally, but that on the facts it could not be implied from the oral agreement that they had chosen to do so. Lord Briggs rejected the suggested analogy between entire agreement clauses and NOM clauses even though the parties themselves appear to have thought otherwise given the drafting of the contract.

6.2.2 The effect of signature

6.2.2.1 Bound by signature in the absence of fraud or misrepresentation

In *L'Estrange v E. Graucob Ltd* [1934] 2 KB 394, at p. 403, Scrutton LJ stated:

> When a document containing contractual terms is signed, then, in the absence of fraud, or, I will add, misrepresentation, the party signing it is bound, and it is wholly immaterial whether he has read the document or not.

This rule is an important buttress of contractual certainty and is a reflection of the objective approach to contract formation, since if the parties sign a document, they are objectively to be taken to be agreeing to its terms. However, its unbending application has sometimes appeared to cause hardship in the consumer context.

In *L'Estrange v E. Graucob Ltd*, the claimant had bought a cigarette vending machine from the defendants. She had signed the defendants' order form, which contained a broad exemption from liability in very small print on poor-quality paper. It was held that because the claimant had signed the written document, she was bound by its terms, including the exemption, although she had not read it.

Signature will not bind where it was fraudulently obtained or obtained as a result of a misrepresentation as to the effect of what was being signed. For example, in *Curtis v Chemical Cleaning and Dyeing Co.* [1951] 1 KB 805, the receipt for a wedding dress excluded all liability for damage, but the assistant had misrepresented its effect by asserting that liability was limited to damage to beads and sequins. The signature was not binding. The decision was consistent with *L'Estrange v Graucob Ltd*, in which it had been suggested that the strict approach to signed documents would not apply where the party claiming not to be bound was misled.

In *Peekay Intermark Ltd v Australia and New Zealand Banking Group Ltd* [2006] EWCA Civ 386, [2006] 2 Lloyd's Rep 511, [2006] 1 CLC 582, an argument based on misrepresentation seeking to avoid being bound by the signed writing failed (for discussion of the misrepresentation argument, see **14.2.2.4**).

An experienced customer had signed an investment contract without reading it on the basis that he claimed to have relied on an informal description of the product given over the telephone. The question for the court related to whether there had been a misrepresentation that had induced the contract, and whether that misrepresentation operated despite the existence of the signature to the conflicting terms describing the product in the written document. The judge at first instance had considered that there was a misrepresentation and that it prevailed, since the investor was entitled to assume that the terms in the writing made no material change to the product described orally. However, the Court of Appeal disagreed, stressing the fact that the true position appeared clearly on the face of the signed written document and that the investor had not been induced by any misrepresentation concerning the nature of the investment product. By signing, whilst failing to read the final terms and conditions, the claimant was taking the risk that the final contract terms would not be to his liking.

In any event, there was an entire agreement clause—a risk disclosure statement—placing the burden on the investor to satisfy himself of the nature of the transaction and the risk exposure, and this prevented him later seeking to deny this by raising allegations of misrepresentation (see **14.7.2.2**).

Moore-Bick LJ reinforced, at [43], the significance of the principle in *L'Estrange v Graucob*, describing it as:

an important principle of English life which underpins the whole of commercial life; any erosion of it would have serious repercussions far beyond the business community. Nonetheless, it is a rule which is concerned with the content of the agreement rather than its validity. Accordingly . . . the contract may be rescinded if one party has been induced to enter into it by fraud or misrepresentation.

On these facts, there was no such actionable misrepresentation.

6.2.2.2 Other limitations on the principle that signature binds

Other limitations on the principle in *L'Estrange v E. Graucob Ltd* [1934] 2 KB 394 are as follows:

1. Statute now regulates exemption clauses and, specifically, unfair terms in consumer contracts: see the Unfair Contract Terms Act (UCTA) 1977 for B2B contracts (see **7.5**), and Part 2 of the CRA 2015 for B2C contracts (see **7.6**).

2. The document that is signed must be a document that would be expected to contain contractual conditions. In *Grogan v Robin Meredith Plant Hire* [1996] CLC 1127, signing a time sheet containing clauses could not amount to a binding variation of the employment contract terms because a time sheet was not a document that might be expected to contain such clauses.

6.2.2.3 Electronic signatures

For electronic communications, signature includes an electronic signature under s. 7 of the Electronic Communications Act 2000 as amended (discussed at **5.4.2.4**).

6.3 Oral contracts: incorporation of written terms

The law on the question of incorporation of terms has evolved almost entirely through litigation in respect of clauses excluding or limiting liability (see **Chapter 7**), especially those contained in standard-form contracts. Nevertheless, the principles are equally applicable to all express terms. In relation to exclusion and limitation clauses, the law on incorporation of terms is less crucial than it once was because other means of control of such devices now exist, i.e. statutory controls (see **7.4**), which make it less important for a claimant to establish that the clause in question was not part of the agreement. However, analysis of this kind was used in *Interfoto Picture Library Ltd v Stiletto Visual Programmes Ltd* [1989] 1 QB 433 to exclude a clause that purported to impose a severe penalty for late performance, on the basis that it had not been incorporated into the contract because it had not been fairly and reasonably brought to the other party's attention (see **6.3.1.4**).

In addition, any statements that it is claimed have been incorporated as terms must be made prior to the conclusion of the contract, and it is for this reason that the rules of offer and acceptance are important in this context (see **Chapter 2**). Incorporation can be achieved as follows:

- by signature (discussed at **6.2.2** in relation to signature to a written contract, but a signature could equally appear on a written document alleged to be incorporated into an oral contract);
- by reasonable notice;
- on the basis of a consistent course of dealing; or
- on the basis of the common understanding of the parties.

A pre-contractual statement can also be incorporated as a term of the contract by means such as the 'importance attached' test and the collateral contract device (see **6.1.3.3** and **6.2.1.3**).

6.3.1 Incorporation of written terms into an oral contract: reasonable notice

It is difficult to establish precisely what terms have been agreed by the parties to an *oral* contract. It may be alleged that terms on unsigned written documents (e.g. on a ticket or order form) are incorporated as terms of an oral contract. For such terms to be effectively incorporated:

1. they must be set out in a document that would be expected to contain contractual terms; and

2. reasonable notice of the existence of the terms must have been given before or at the time of contracting.

6.3.1.1 A contractual document

In *Chapelton v Barry Urban District Council* [1940] 1 KB 532, the claimant obtained tickets for the hire of deckchairs from the deckchair attendant. He did not notice that the tickets contained a clause purporting to exempt the council from any liability for accidents or damage arising from the hire of the deckchairs. The Court of Appeal held that this term on the ticket could not be relied on by the council, since the ticket was a mere voucher or receipt for money paid rather than a contractual document.

There are two important factors to bear in mind when seeking to assess whether a written document, such as a ticket, constitutes a contractual document:

1. the fact that a ticket or other document is called a receipt is not conclusive of the fact that it is non-contractual; and

2. the time of the making of the contract appears to be important, since a document can constitute a contractual document only if it is delivered before the contract is formed.

On the facts in *Chapelton*, there was a binding contract when the deckchair was removed from the pile (the pile of deckchairs constituted a standing offer, which was accepted when a customer removed a deckchair from the pile). Since the ticket was not part of this contractual process and might be obtained some time later, it could only be a receipt for money paid. Of course, if the ticket were always obtained from the attendant before selecting and removing the deckchair, it would be a contractual document and its terms duly incorporated. (On the facts of *Chapelton*, the attendant happened to be standing near the pile of deckchairs so that the ticket was obtained at that time, but the Court of Appeal stressed that this might not have been the case, and hirers of deckchairs might have sat on the chair for some time before the attendant came to issue the ticket and collect their money.) This sort of distinction is unhelpful in terms of determining the terms of a contract.

Thus it is recognized that some documents record performance of an existing contractual obligation rather than forming part of the making of the contract and evidencing its terms. Such documents are not regarded as contractual documents, essentially because the contract has already been made. In *Grogan v Robin Meredith Plant Hire* [1996] CLC 1127, it was stated that invoices, time sheets, or statements of account are not normally documents forming part of the making of a contract. However, it is possible that, rather than recording the existence of a contract, a particular invoice constitutes the offer to contract, and clearly, in these circumstances, that invoice would be a contractual document, e.g. the delivery note in *Photolibrary Group Ltd (t/a Garden Picture Library) v Burda Senator Verlag GmbH* [2008] EWHC 1343 (QB), [2008] 2 All ER (Comm) 881 (discussed at **6.3.1.3** and **6.3.1.4.1**) was held to constitute an offer. In addition, in *Transformers & Rectifiers Ltd v Needs Ltd* [2015] EWHC 269 (TCC), [2015] BLR 336, at [42], it is clear that the suggestion that terms can appear in 'other documents such as invoices', as opposed to contractual documents, is based on a restricted definition of what constitutes a 'contractual document'. The judge recognized that if 'the other document' followed the conclusion of a contract it 'may be too late', whereas it can be argued that it will constitute a 'contractual document' where notice of its existence is given in time.

6.3.1.2 Reasonable notice of the existence of the terms
6.3.1.2.1 What is meant by 'reasonable notice'?

The question is whether reasonable notice (in an objective sense) of the *existence* of the terms was given to the offeree before the time of accepting the offer. However, importantly, the offeree does not need actual subjective knowledge of the detail of the terms in question.

If the person receiving the ticket (or other written document) knows that it contains writing, that person will be bound by the terms contained in the document, provided that it is a contractual document and provided that it is common knowledge that such writing contains terms and conditions: *per* Mellish LJ in *Parker v South Eastern Railway* (1877) 2 CPD 416. Nowadays, it is common knowledge that tickets and similar documents generally do contain such conditions, and the test is therefore whether sufficient notice of the conditions has been provided to people in general: *Thompson v London, Midland and Scottish Railway* [1930] 1 KB 41. No account is taken of the fact that the individual claimant is illiterate or unable to understand the language in which the terms are drafted, at least where this factor is not known to the party supplying the ticket or other document: *Geier v Kujawa Weston and Warne Bros. (Transport) Ltd* [1970] 1 Lloyd's Rep 364.

6.3.1.2.2 Can there be incorporation by reference? Is this reasonable notice?

Terms can be incorporated by reference to another document in which they are found. In *Thompson v London, Midland and Scottish Railway* [1930] 1 KB 41, the face of the ticket said 'see back'; on the back, it stated that the ticket was issued subject to conditions set out in the timetables, available for purchase at 6d. These conditions were held to be incorporated. Although this is an extreme case, because the timetables were extremely bulky and relatively expensive to purchase, the principle of incorporation by reference remains a valid one. This point is neatly illustrated by the facts and decision in *O'Brien v MGN Ltd* [2001] EWCA Civ 1279, [2002] CLC 33 (discussed at **6.3.1.4.1**), where the newspaper's rules governing scratch-card games were held to be incorporated into the contract, although these rules had not been published in full in the newspaper on the day in question. It was sufficient that the scratch card made reference to the existence of the rules that had been published in back issues of the newspaper or could be obtained, on request, from the newspaper's offices. Indeed, it is common commercial practice to make reference to the existence of full terms and conditions contained in a separate document and obtainable on request: *Rooney v CSE Bournemouth Ltd (t/a CSE Citation Centre)* [2010] EWCA Civ 1364, (2010) 107(25) LSG 17.

Whether a reference to a website would suffice as incorporation by reference arose for decision in *Impala Warehousing & Logistics (Shanghai) Co. Ltd v Wanxiang Resources (Singapore) Pte Ltd* [2015] EWHC 811 (Comm), [2015] 2 All ER (Comm) 234.

The parties had entered into a warehousing agreement. When a dispute arose between them, the respondent Singaporean trading company sought to bring proceedings in the Chinese courts seeking delivery of goods that it claimed to own. Impala then sought an interim anti-suit injunction from the English courts to stop these proceedings on the basis that the warehousing agreement had been made on Impala's terms and conditions which contained an exclusive jurisdiction clause making the English courts the forum for any disputes. The question was whether these terms and conditions had been incorporated into the warehousing agreement. The warehouse certificate contained a statement on the first page that all disputes arising were subject to Impala's terms and conditions and made reference to additional terms on the back of this page. The reverse of the page made reference to the latest applicable terms and conditions as being posted on the company's website. Was this sufficient incorporation by reference, particularly since there were three different sets of terms and conditions on the website, only one of which governed warehousing?

Teare J (in earlier proceedings for an interim anti-suit injunction, [2015] EWHC 25 (Comm)) had considered that since standard terms and conditions are frequently found on websites, the reference to the website was sufficient incorporation of those terms—and he did not consider the website confusing. This analysis was accepted by Blair J when concluding that the respondent had notice of Impala's terms and issuing the anti-suit injunction.

However, the terms must be displayed somewhere or be accessible for incorporation by reference to succeed. In *Sterling Hydraulics Ltd v Dichtomatik Ltd* [2006] EWHC 2004 (QB), [2007] 1 Lloyd's Rep 8, a faxed acknowledgement of the purchase order stated only that delivery was 'based on our General Terms of Sale'. A blank page 2 should have contained the seller's terms and conditions. When the goods supplied proved defective, the seller claimed that the contract incorporated its standard terms and conditions containing exemption clauses. However, the judge held that these terms had not been incorporated. The difficulty was not with the words of reference to standard terms to be found elsewhere, but with the failure to make a copy of these terms available at all, since this did not amount to 'adequate notice'; see also *J. Murphy & Sons Ltd v Johnston Precast Ltd* [2008] EWHC 3024 (TCC). Similarly, in *Transformers & Rectifiers Ltd v Needs Ltd* [2015] EWHC 269 (TCC), [2015] BLR 336, the claimant's purchase order made did not mention that there were terms and conditions on the reverse. When the defendant received the purchase order it sent an acknowledgement referring to its terms and conditions and stated that copies were available on request, although no request had been made. The judge held that for the terms to be validly incorporated by notice, the counter-offer acknowledgement had to refer on its face to the conditions, and where they were not a standard form in a particular industry, they needed to be printed on the reverse together with a statement on the face of the acknowledgement indicating that it was subject to the conditions on the back. The alternative, if the terms were not printed on the reverse, would be to send a separate copy and make it clear that these were the only terms and conditions upon which the party was willing to contract. The judge concluded that neither party's terms had been incorporated.

6.3.1.3 Before or at the time of contracting

Reasonable notice must be given 'in time', i.e. before or at the time of contracting. It is for this reason that the principles of offer and acceptance are important in this context.

In *Olley v Marlborough Court Ltd* [1949] 1 KB 532, a hotel sought to exclude its liability for the loss of valuable personal possessions by a guest at the hotel by reference to an exclusion notice on the back of the hotel bedroom door. However, the contract had been made at the hotel reception desk before the offeree had any possible means of knowing about the purported exclusion of liability. The court therefore found the notice to be ineffective, because it was too late to be incorporated as a term of the contract.

Similarly, in *Grogan v Robin Meredith Plant Hire* [1996] CLC 1127, the agreement for the hire of a driver and machine was made over the telephone, whereas the Contractors' Plant Association Conditions were not introduced until two weeks later, when the driver presented his time sheet referring to the work as being undertaken on the basis of these conditions. The Court of Appeal held that this notice was too late.

In *Photolibrary Group Ltd (t/a Garden Picture Library) v Burda Senator Verlag GmbH* [2008] EWHC 1343 (QB), [2008] 2 All ER (Comm) 881 (discussed at **6.3.1.4**), terms on a delivery note supplied with various photographic transparencies were considered to be incorporated, since this delivery, accompanied by the delivery note, was analysed as an offer that was accepted by the receipt of the transparencies.

The particular contract therefore must be examined to determine the contract formation process and the point at which the terms are delivered or referred to, a point well illustrated by 'the ticket cases'.

In *Parker v South Eastern Railway* (1877) 2 CPD 416, the railway company operated a left-luggage office in which the claimant left a bag, paying the required fee and receiving a ticket in return. On the ticket were the words 'See Back'; on the back was a clause purporting to limit the company's liability in the case of lost luggage to £10. The claimant's bag was lost; its contents were worth more than £10. The court found the clause on the ticket sufficient to limit the company's liability as stated. Mellish LJ took the view that printing on a ticket would be incorporated into a contract provided that a reasonable person would appreciate that there was writing containing conditions on the ticket.

In *Thornton v Shoe Lane Parking Ltd* [1971] 2 QB 163, Lord Denning explained the process of offer and acceptance in ticket cases so that the result could coincide with the position in *Parker v South Eastern Railway* and other nineteenth-century ticket cases in which incorporation was achieved. Lord Denning considered that the issue of the ticket is the offer, and that acceptance occurs when the customer takes the ticket and retains it without objection. On this basis, there is incorporation in time of any terms printed on the ticket. Lord Denning acknowledged that this interpretation was based on a 'fiction', because it assumes that the customer will examine the ticket and decide whether to accept the terms or return it without incurring any liability.

In *Thornton v Shoe Lane Parking Ltd*, there was a notice at the entrance to a barrier-operated car park stating that parking was to be 'at owner's risk'. An automatic barrier controlled entry to the car park. When the motorist drove up to the barrier, a machine dispensed a ticket. This ticket stated that it was 'issued subject to conditions displayed on the premises'. Inside the car park there was a notice excluding liability for personal injury to customers.

The Court of Appeal held that the exemption on the ticket was too late, because the contract for the use of the car park was concluded when the motorist drove up to the barrier and activated the machine.

Lord Denning said that he was not prepared to apply the nineteenth-century ticket cases in for a ticket issued by an automatic machine. Instead, he stated that the machine is making a standing offer, which the customer accepts when they do whatever is required to activate the machine, e.g. by putting money into a slot. The net effect of this analysis was that anything on the ticket dispensed by the machine would not be incorporated because it would be too late. This standing offer is similar to the offer represented by the pile of deckchairs in *Chapelton v Barry Urban District Council* [1940] 1 KB 532 and explains why that ticket was only a receipt for money paid. Notice of the ticket was too late and it could not be seen as a document that was part of the contract formation process.

6.3.1.4 The stricter approach for onerous or unusual terms

In *Thornton v Shoe Lane Parking Ltd* [1971] 2 QB 163, the notice at the entrance ('parking at owner's risk') was in time, but it was construed as not extending to exempt the car park from liability in respect of personal injury. This was because personal injury was said to be an unusual liability to exclude in these circumstances and therefore needed to be drawn to the customer's attention in explicit terms to be incorporated. Lord Denning considered, at p. 170, that '[i]n order to give sufficient notice, it would need to be printed in red ink with a red hand pointing to it, or something equally startling'; see also *J. Spurling Ltd v Bradshaw* [1956] 1 WLR 461.

This approach involves applying different standards of incorporation to different terms, and it was adopted by the Court of Appeal in *Interfoto Picture Library Ltd v Stiletto Visual Programmes Ltd* [1988] QB 433.

> The term in question involved a holding fee of £5 per day plus VAT per transparency for their late return. The defendants did not use the transparencies, forgot about them until they returned them late over a month later. The claimants sent an invoice for the payment of the holding charge of £3,783.50. The Court of Appeal regarded the clause relating to the holding charge as particularly onerous and unusual (due to the cumulative effect of the fee), and argued that such a clause would not be regarded as fairly and reasonably brought to the notice of the other party 'unless it was drawn to his attention in the most explicit way'. However, whereas Dillon LJ concluded that for this reason the clause was not incorporated, Bingham LJ considered that, although it was incorporated, it could not have any effect in the circumstances of the case.

Such unusual or onerous terms might need to be presented in a large-size print or be placed in a box in a written document to satisfy this higher standard of incorporation.

? QUESTION

What is the position if the argument relates to an alleged onerous or unusual term in a *signed* document that has not been sufficiently brought to the other's attention before signature?

In *Ocean Chemical Transport Inc. v Exnor Craggs Ltd* [2000] 1 All ER (Comm) 519, the Court of Appeal considered whether the *Interfoto* test had to be applied even where the other party had signed to acknowledge the terms. The Court of Appeal suggested that, in light of the principle in *L'Estrange v E. Graucob Ltd* [1934] 2 KB 394, that this would be the position only in an extreme case in which 'a signature was obtained under pressure of time or other circumstances' *and* in which the clause was particularly onerous or unusual in relation to the contract. In *Do-Buy 925 Ltd v National Westminster Bank plc* [2010] EWHC 2862 (QB), at [91], on reviewing the authorities, the judge noted that it was undecided whether the *Interfoto* principle could ever apply to a signed contract. However, where the case was not an 'extreme one', there was no reason to depart from the principle in *L'Estrange*. In any event, it would seem that there are other more appropriate contractual doctrines to call in aid in such a situation, such as duress and undue influence, or even the plea of *non est factum*.

6.3.1.4.1 The difficulties associated with this higher standard test for incorporation

1. Must the particular clause be onerous or unusual, or must it be an onerous or unusual version of a clause of this type?

This question was answered differently by the members of the Court of Appeal in *AEG (UK) Ltd v Logic Resource Ltd* [1996] CLC 265.

(a) The majority: Hirst and Waite LJJ

The majority held that, in a purchase contract to supply goods for export, a clause that stated that the purchaser was to return defective goods at his own expense was an onerous *and* unusual term, and would be incorporated only if 'fairly and reasonably brought to the attention' of the purchaser.

(b) Hobhouse LJ (dissenting)

Hobhouse LJ's dissenting judgment was because this type of clause was commonly found in printed conditions. Hobhouse LJ considered, at p. 277, that the correct approach would be to consider 'the kind of clause' in issue and whether a particular clause was onerous or unusual only in relation to this kind of clause. He considered it wrong to apply the test in *Interfoto Picture Library Ltd v Stiletto Visual Programmes Ltd* [1988] QB 433 to the specific terms of the particular clause in question, on the basis that this amounted to 'completely distorting the contractual relationship between the parties and the ordinary mechanisms of making contracts'. He therefore distinguished both *Interfoto*, which was described as 'an extortionate clause', and *Thornton v Shoe Lane Parking Ltd* [1971] 2 QB 163, in which the clause related to personal injuries, as something totally different from the subject matter of a car parking contract.

This significant difference in *AEG (UK) Ltd v Logic Resource Ltd* between the approach of the majority and Hobhouse LJ (dissenting) was resolved by the Court of Appeal in *Ocean Chemical Transport Inc. v Exnor Craggs Ltd* [2000] 1 All ER (Comm) 519. Evans LJ (with whose judgment the other members of the Court of Appeal agreed) stated, at [47]:

> It seems to me that the question of incorporation must always depend upon the meaning and effect of the clause in question. It may be that the type of clause is relevant. It may be that the effect of the particular clause in the particular case is relevant.

Thus Evans LJ rejected the approach of Hobhouse LJ in *AEG v Logic Resource* and required the *particular* clause to be unusual or onerous rather than the type of clause. A similar view was reached in *Goodlife Foods Limited v Hall Fire Protection Limited* [2018] EWCA Civ 1371 (for facts, see **7.5.2**), where Coulson LJ stated that 'the mere fact that the clause in question is a limitation or exclusion clause does not of itself mean that it is onerous or unusual. Everything turns on the context' (at [35]).

In *Kaye v Nu Skin UK Ltd* [2012] EWHC 958 (QB), [2012] CTLC 69, the question was whether a particular version of an arbitration clause in a distribution agreement between English parties was onerous or unusual so that it needed to be fairly and reasonably brought to the attention of the other party. Arbitration clauses are a common type of clause, although this one required disputes to be resolved by binding arbitration in the US state of Utah. The judge held that this was not so onerous that it should specifically have been brought to the other party's attention. Accordingly, it had been incorporated.

2. Must the clause be onerous or *unusual, or both onerous* and *unusual?*

The circumstances in which the higher standard of incorporation is called for require either that the clause in question should be onerous **or** unusual—albeit that, on the facts in *AEG (UK) Ltd v Logic Resource Ltd* [1996] CLC 265, the clause in question satisfied both elements of this test. This fact has not deterred statements such as that of Rix LJ (with whose judgment Mummery and Peter Gibson LJJ agreed) in *HIH Casualty & General Insurance Ltd v New Hampshire Insurance Co.* [2001] EWCA Civ 735, [2001] 2 Lloyd's Rep 161, at [22], requiring that the clause in question be both unusual *and* onerous. If the application of the higher standard turns on the type of clause, then the type of clause should be both unusual and an onerous version of the type of term. However, on the basis of the decision in *Ocean Chemical Transport Inc. v Exnor Craggs Ltd* [2000] 1 All ER (Comm) 519, in which it is the particular clause that needs to be assessed, it would seem that either requirement ought to suffice, and an examination of the early authorities indicates that these requirements are viewed as alternatives.

3. Establishing that the clause is onerous or unusual

As the interpretation question in point 1 above has now been resolved, the real difficulty with this difference in the standard to achieve incorporation is to decide whether *in fact* a clause is onerous or unusual, so that the higher standard of incorporation is required. This is a question of fact in each case, and there is often little agreement between individual judges over whether the higher test needs to be satisfied.

> In **O'Brien v MGN Ltd** [2001] EWCA Civ 1279, [2002] CLC 33, the majority (Hale and Potter LJJ) considered that there was nothing onerous or unusual in rule 5 of the newspaper's rules governing the operation of the scratch-card game, whereas Evans LJ clearly considered that this term needed to be given greater prominence (in part because he seems to have considered that it was a matter of chance whether a person had access to the rules). Rule 5 provided that where more prizes were claimed than were available, the prize would be awarded on the basis of a simple draw. The majority considered the rule to be sensible in the circumstances and was able to distinguish *Interfoto Picture Library Ltd v Stiletto Visual Programmes Ltd* [1988] QB 433 (in which the clause imposed an additional burden on the defendants) and *Thornton v Shoe Lane Parking Ltd* [1971] 2 QB 163 (in which the clause sought to exclude liability for personal injuries). Hale LJ stated (at [21]) that this clause 'merely deprives the claimant of a windfall for which he has done very little in return'.

In any event, as Hale LJ stated in *O'Brien v MGN*, at [23]:

> [T]he words 'onerous or unusual' are not terms of art. They are simply one way of putting the general proposition that reasonable steps must be taken to draw the particular term in question to the notice of those who are bound by it and that more is required in relation to certain terms than to others depending on their effect.

This is a common-sense statement of the principle, but fails to assist with the problem of certainty and predictability on such an important question as the incorporation of contractual terms, and is unlikely to resolve difficulties in drafting standard terms. However, there are signs of good sense: e.g. in *Shepherd Homes Ltd v Encia Remediation Ltd* [2007] EWHC 70 (TCC), [2007] BLR 135, a limitation of a construction contractor's liability to the contract price could not be said to be onerous or unusual. Generally speaking, the scope of terms that are regarded as 'usual terms in the trade' will tend to reduce the scope for argument that the term in question is onerous. The onerous or unusual argument was rejected in *Photolibrary Group Ltd (t/a Garden Picture Library) v Burda Senator Verlag GmbH* [2008] EWHC 1343 (QB), [2008] 2 All ER (Comm) 881 (discussed at **6.3.1.3**), on the basis that the facts were similar to those in *Interfoto* (photographic transparencies), since there was a substantial course of dealing between the parties based on the terms in the delivery notes that set fees for loss of the transparencies.

Since the fees set for loss were quite normal in the business, they could not be regarded as in any way unusual.

In *Allen Fabrications Ltd v ASD Ltd (t/a ASD Metal Services and/or Klockner & Co. Multi Metal Distribution)* [2012] EWHC 2213 (TCC), the judge rejected an argument that a clause 'abrogates statutory rights'—e.g. excluded or restricted liability under s. 14(2) of the Sale of Goods Act (SGA) 1979 or for personal injury under the Occupiers Liability Act 1957—means that it must necessarily be onerous or unusual. Notably, however, the judge added that if there was knowledge that an onerous clause (or clauses of the same type) was present in the contractual document, although it might not have been actually read, then additional notice was not necessary. As he acknowledged, at [63], 'in such a case, what will constitute bringing the clause fairly and reasonably to the attention of the other party is likely to be little more than what is necessary in respect of the conditions as a whole'. Adopting a similarly common-sense approach, and confirming the first instance decision ([2017] EWHC), in *Goodlife Foods Limited v Hall Fire Protection Limited* [2018] EWCA Civ 1371, Coulson LJ stated that to decide whether the clause was particularly onerous or unusual had to be done 'in the context of the contract as a whole' (at [36]). On the facts, although the clause was 'wide-ranging' (at [47]), it was neither particularly onerous or unusual. On the issue of notice, the court also confirmed the first instance decision by stating that the clause, far from being 'buried away in a raft of small print', was 'referred to on the front of the quotation and which were printed in clear type' (at [53]). Moreover, after noting that 'its potentially wide-reaching effect was expressly identified at the very start of those same conditions' (at [53]), Coulson LJ mentioned that the warning was 'cast in almost apocalyptic terms' (at [53]). In his words, 'if that did not alert them to the effect of clause 11, nothing would have done' (at [53]). Continuing with a very pragmatic common-sense approach, Coulson LJ also took into consideration the fact that Goodlife took over a year to consider Hall Life's quotation, that there was no suggestion that 'they did not read or understand the terms' (at [54]), and that this period was more than enough to 'take advice' (at [54]). In consequence, 'it would be commercially unrealistic to say that clause 11 was not fairly and reasonably brought to the attention of Goodlife' (at [55]).

6.3.1.5 Internet contracts and reasonable notice

Before leaving this section, it is important to consider the question of incorporation of terms for contracts concluded on the Internet. Surprisingly, in spite of the existence of texts dealing with internet-related contracting (the EC Directive on Electronic Commerce 2000), such texts do not contain substantive provisions dealing with the incorporation of terms (Wang, 'The incorporation of terms into commercial contracts: a reassessment in the digital age' [2015] JBL 87–119, at 88). The common law rules will therefore continue to apply. In consequence, a supplier will need to ensure that the customer had reasonable notice of applicable terms and conditions *before contracting*. Normally, this will be achieved by requiring the customer to click on an icon to signal agreement to the terms and conditions that are displayed (but which are seldom read) before the contract is concluded.

6.3.2 Consistent course of dealing

Even if notice of the terms was not given on the particular occasion, where the parties deal with each other on a regular basis on standard terms and conditions, the terms may be incorporated into the particular contract on the basis of a previous course of dealing between the parties: Hardwick Game

Farm v Suffolk Agricultural Poultry Producers Association [1969] 2 AC 31. Nevertheless, the party seeking to rely on a course of dealing for the incorporation of terms will have to sustain the burden of proving that the course of past conduct has been *sufficiently consistent* to give rise to the implication that, in similar circumstances, the same contractual result will follow.

In **McCutcheon v David MacBrayne Ltd** [1964] 1 WLR 125, the claimant had used the defendants' ferry service for his car on several occasions in the past. Sometimes he had been asked to sign a note containing an exclusion clause, but sometimes not. On the occasion in question, the ferry sank and no note had been signed. The defendants could not rely on the course of dealing to incorporate an exclusion clause into the contract, since the course of dealing was inconsistent.

In **Petrotrade Inc. v Texaco Ltd** [2000] CLC 1341, the contract was entered into by telephone and basic terms agreed. Subsequently, a telex was sent, which contained Petrotrade's standard terms, including a clause providing for payment to be made without deduction or set-off. It was alleged that these terms were incorporated on the basis of the previous dealings between the parties. The Court of Appeal found that, over the 13 months prior to this contract, there had been five other contracts between the parties for the sale of the same or similar products by Petrotrade and in which the transactions had been confirmed on the same terms, including this no set-off clause. Accordingly, given this previous course of dealing, both parties made the agreement on the basis that the contract would again be subject to these terms.

Similarly, in **Balmoral Group Ltd v Borealis (UK) Ltd** [2006] EWHC 1900 (Comm), [2006] 2 Lloyd's Rep 629, [2006] 2 CLC 220 (discussed further at **7.5.5.2.2**), the course of dealing was established, although this was despite the fact that the number of prior orders had been small and for very different goods. On the facts, a strong reason for accepting that a course of dealing was established was the fact that Borealis had made it plain, from the very beginning of the relationship, that it was only willing to contract on their own terms and that those terms were known (at [362]–[363]).

However, incorporation based on a course of dealing was rejected in *Capes (Hatherden) Ltd v Western Arable Services Ltd* [2009] EWHC 3065 (QB), [2010] 1 Lloyd's Rep 477, on the basis that the course of dealing consisted of only four contracts in the same year for the sale and purchase of a crop on a particular agricultural standard form, and the relevant contract notes supplied on previous occasions had not been noticed, nor had there been a requirement to sign them or to acknowledge receipt. In addition, the contracts that were alleged to incorporate these terms by course of dealing were for a different crop, and there had been an interval of five months between that series of contracts and the current ones. The judge concluded that this was borderline, but that an impartial observer could not have concluded that the parties had reached a common understanding that this standard form applied to the contracts in question.

In **Transformers & Rectifiers Ltd v Needs Ltd** [2015] EWHC 269 (TCC), [2015] BLR 336, the parties' relationship extended over 20 years and orders had been placed on an almost weekly basis. Sometimes the purchase orders were sent by post and in the case of these purchase orders the terms were printed on the back. However, the claimant had failed to use a consistent form of dealing because the majority of the purchase orders had been sent by fax or email and the terms and conditions had not been included with these orders. Following this inconsistency it was unclear to a reasonable person that they intended to rely on those terms.

The decisions in course of dealing cases turn on their particular facts, but it should be easier to establish the necessary consistency in the course of dealing between commercial parties (as in *Petrotrade v Texaco* and *Balmoral v Borealis*) than as against a consumer. For example, in *Hollier v Rambler Motors (AMC) Ltd* [1972] 2 QB 71, it was held that a garage's standard terms were not incorporated into a repair contract with a customer because there was not a consistent course of dealing between the parties using these terms. The customer had used the garage for repairs on only three or four occasions in a five-year period.

6.3.3 Common knowledge

In very limited circumstances, the courts may be willing to incorporate a term into a contract without actual notice and without any prior course of dealing. The courts will incorporate terms in these circumstances only where there is some common basis shared by the parties that justifies the presumption that the parties have a common understanding that the terms will apply. The common basis will usually be supplied by the fact that both parties belong to and are familiar with the terms of a particular trade, and indeed the terms in question may need to be standard conditions issued by a trade association.

An example of incorporation in this form can be found in *British Crane Hire Corporation Ltd v Ipswich Plant Hire Ltd* [1975] QB 303.

> The case involved a clause in a standard-form hire contract between two businesses, which were both in the plant hire business. Although notice was given too late in relation to the particular contract, the terms were held to be incorporated because both parties knew of these printed conditions, which were in common use in the plant hire business.

British Crane Hire can usefully be compared with *Grogan v Robin Meredith Plant Hire* [1996] CLC 1127, in which the judge rejected such an argument, and appeared to regard the terms in question as not being used so frequently and commonly as to be common knowledge within the industry. This seems doubtful in view of the decision in *British Crane Hire* (because the decision relates to the same set of standard terms), and the significant distinguishing factor may be the fact that the parties in *Grogan* were not operating in the same business: only one party was in the business of hiring plant; the other party laid pipes.

British Crane Hire was also distinguished in *Scheps v Fine Art Logistic Ltd* [2007] EWHC 541 (QB), partly, it seems, on the basis that the parties were not in exactly the same business.

> The claimant engaged the defendant to collect and store a sculpture. The sculpture went missing while being stored. The defendant alleged that the agreement with the claimant incorporated the defendant's standard terms and conditions, limiting its liability to a fixed figure. It alleged, relying on *British Crane Hire v Ipswich*, that these standard terms were common knowledge in the transport and storage business, so that the claimant, who had considerable experience of arranging for transport of such works of art, must have been aware of it.
>
> Teare J held that the terms were not incorporated, since (i) the defendant had not provided the claimant with a copy of these terms or with a document referring to them (see *Sterling Hydraulics Ltd v Dichtomatik Ltd* [2006] EWHC 2004 (QB), [2007] 1 Lloyd's Rep 8, discussed at **6.3.1.2.2**), and (ii) there was no evidence that the claimant had any particular knowledge of them. *British Crane Hire v Ipswich* was distinguished, the judge noting, at [24], that, in that case, '[b]oth parties to the hiring contract were in business of hiring out cranes'. Teare J also stressed the fact that the parties in *British Crane Hire* were of equal bargaining power, traded upon similar terms derived from the Contractors Plant Association form, and had in fact traded on two occasions in the immediate past on this basis. In that case it was therefore possible to 'readily conclude that the defendants intended to trade on the claimants' terms'.

6.4 Implied terms

6.4.1 Introduction

In many contracts, although the main primary obligations are contained in express terms, the parties do not express all of the primary obligations or do not provide for every eventuality.

The implication of terms might be considered controversial, since it can amount to filling the gaps in the contract, and this can give the impression that the courts are making the contract for the parties (see **3.1.1**) and/or interfering with contractual certainty, i.e. the ability to rely on the express terms of the contract as representing the parties' agreement without the risk of any 'extra' terms. However, the courts have traditionally justified the implication of terms to fill gaps on the basis of giving effect to the deemed intentions of the parties and/or on the basis of 'necessity' (reflecting what 'should be there'). Statute implies terms in some circumstances to give effect to policy objectives, e.g. the sale of goods legislation implies terms in favour of buyers as a protection device.

> **→ EXAMPLE**
>
> When a student goes into a shop to buy a new textbook or orders a copy online, the retailer and the student do not discuss or express any terms relating to the quality of the book to be sold. Nevertheless, if an important section of the book was missing, the student would be less than happy if he had no remedy against the retailer. On the contrary, what is being sold must be a book that is in the state in which a book of that description would normally be. That understanding is incorporated into the contract by means of an implied term—in the particular case, a term derived from statute. Since this is a B2C contract of sale between a 'trader' ('a person acting for purposes relating to that person's trade, business, craft or profession') and a 'consumer' ('an individual acting for purposes that are wholly or mainly outside that individual's trade, business, craft or profession'), the CRA 2015 applies and s. 9 of that Act imposes a term that the quality of the goods is satisfactory (see **6.4.2.4**).

6.4.1.1 Implication of terms to fill gaps in the express terms where the implication is based on strict necessity

The general position is that the courts imply terms in some cases to fill gaps in the express terms, i.e. as a process of addition. Such terms are implied as a matter of necessity and on a 'one-off' basis to reflect what must have been the parties' objective intentions. These terms implied in fact are traditionally implied to give business efficacy to the contract (to render it workable) or on the basis that the term would be considered by reasonable people in the position of both parties to be 'so obvious' that it went without saying (the so-called 'officious bystander test' for the implication of terms in fact).

This general position was, however, considered by legal academics and judges alike to have been altered by the decision in *Attorney-General of Belize v Belize Telecom Ltd* [2009] UKPC 10, [2009] 1 WLR 1988, where Lord Hoffmann had considered that the implication of terms in fact was not a process of 'addition' but rather involved a process of construction of the whole contract to give effect to the objectively assessed intentions of the parties, i.e. the implied terms were not 'added' but existed all along as reflecting imputed party intention. Lord Hoffmann specifically rejected the use of the previous 'business efficacy' and 'obviousness' tests as the basis for implication of terms in fact, although subsequent case law appeared to reintroduce elements of business efficacy by stressing the need for the term to be necessary 'to make the contract work'.

However, the Supreme Court in *Marks & Spencer plc v BNP Paribas Securities Services Trust Co. (Jersey) Ltd* [2015] UKSC 72, [2015] 3 WLR 1843, [2016] AC 742, has now explained that Lord Hoffmann's judgment in *Belize Telecom* had not diluted the requirements for terms implied in fact. Lord Neuberger was clear, at [24], that 'the law governing the circumstances in which a term will be implied into a contract remains unchanged following *Belize Telecom*'. Lord Neuberger also explained (at [26]) that Lord Hoffmann's single process of construction 'could obscure the fact that construing the words used and implying additional words are different processes governed by different rules'. It follows, as emphasized by Lord Neuberger at [28], that we are back to the position before *Belize Telecom* involving two separate steps. As a first step the courts construe the *express* terms of the contract to identify the intentions of the parties through interpretation of the words they have used (see the discussion at **6.5** for these principles). This is very different to the separate exercise attempting to fill the gaps in those words by implication of terms, albeit that both are about 'determining the scope and meaning of the contract' (see the discussion at **6.4.2.3**).

6.4.1.2 Implication of terms irrespective of the parties' intentions to secure a policy objective/protection for a category of contracting parties

Some terms are implied irrespective of the intentions of the parties: so-called 'terms implied in law' (see **6.4.2.2**).

In the example above (at **6.4.1**) of the sale of a book, the obligation to meet a certain quality standard is said to derive from an implied term, but it may not be certain that the retailer intended such a term. Indeed, it may be more honest simply to say that, in that situation, a positive obligation of the law of contract is imposed on the seller, whatever his intentions: see Stephenson LJ in *Mears v Safecar Securities Ltd* [1983] QB 54. The notion of an *imposed* obligation is all the more persuasive because, in our example involving the buyer as an individual consumer, it will be impossible for the seller to exclude or restrict liability for the obligation since this quality obligation is an entrenched consumer right (CRA 2015, s. 31, and see **7.6.4**). This leaves open the question of the basis on which terms are imposed on the parties, i.e. the so-called 'policy' question. Whatever the conceptual basis of implied terms of this type, in practice the courts have inevitably been drawn into seeking to ensure that contracts of a recognizable and frequently occurring type conform to general (reasonable) expectations of what obligations such contracts should contain.

6.4.1.3 Limitations on the ability to imply terms

While the courts today may be more willing to imply terms than they once were, there are nevertheless important limits on their ability to make such an implication.

1. The courts should not make a contract for the parties when this would amount to amending the meaning that would reasonably be put on the contract terms in the contractual context. It follows that express terms take precedence and the courts should not imply a term that is at odds with the express terms agreed by the parties (*BP Refinery (Westernport) Pty Ltd v Shire of Hastings* (1977) 180 CLR 266, *per* Lord Simon at pp. 282–3, see **6.4.2.3**). However, where the exact scope of an express term leaves some latitude in its application (such as in the form of a discretion), it may be narrowed or widened by an implied term: *per* Browne-Wilkinson V-C in *Johnstone v Bloomsbury Health Authority* [1992] 1 QB 333, at pp. 350–1).

Part 2

Content, interpretation, performance, and breach

2. The omission giving rise to the need for an implied term may be the result of oversight, or represent a deliberate decision (and this in turn may be because the parties agree to assume a particular risk by omission in the knowledge that they will not agree on the matter in question). Therein lies the dilemma for the courts, particularly when faced with a detailed commercial contract, when facing an argument for the implication of a missing term. Accordingly, the courts should be careful not to cross the line and 'write the parties' contract' for them with the benefit of hindsight: Lord Wright in *Hillas & Co. Ltd v Arcos Ltd* (1932) 147 LT 503 (see **3.1.2**). This point was recently reasserted by Asplin LJ for the Court of Appeal in *Robert Bou-Simon v BGC Brokers LP* [2018] EWCA Civ 1525 when she stated, at [12], that 'it is not appropriate to apply hindsight and to seek to imply a term in a commercial contract merely because it appears to be fair or because one considers that the parties would have agreed it if it had been suggested to them'. The time of assessment is therefore always the time of formation and is assessed objectively: 'a term will be implied if a reasonable reader of the contract, knowing all its provisions and the surrounding circumstances, would understand it to be implied is quite acceptable, provided that (i) the reasonable reader is treated as reading the contract at the time it was made', per Lord Neuberger in *Marks and Spencer*, at [23].

3. It must be possible to formulate any term implied by the courts with sufficient precision for the court to be able to give effect to it: *Shell UK Ltd v Lostock Garage Ltd* [1976] 1 WLR 1187 and *Durham Tees Valley Airport Ltd v bmibaby Ltd* [2009] EWHC 852 (Ch), [2009] 2 All ER (Comm) 1083, at first instance, although the Court of Appeal held that it was unnecessary to imply a term because the express terms were sufficiently certain to be enforceable (see **3.1.3.2**). In *Torre Asset Funding Ltd v Royal Bank of Scotland plc* [2013] EWHC 2670 (Ch), (2013) 157(35) SJLB 41, Sales J also reinforced the requirement that any proposed implied term had to be capable of being defined with sufficient precision to give reasonable certainty of operation. The inability to achieve this certainty of drafting can be a major stumbling block particularly when seeking to imply terms in fact.

6.4.2 Methods by which terms are implied

Terms may be implied by:

- custom or as a result of trade usage or business practice;
- the courts—either by implication into the particular contract on the basis that it is necessary to give the contract commercial or practical coherence and so reflect party intention, as objectively determined (terms implied in fact), or by implication into all contracts of a particular type on the basis that the term is a necessary incident of that type of contract (terms implied in law); or
- statute—into contracts of certain types, irrespective of party intention or wishes.

6.4.2.1 Terms implied by custom or trade usage

Terms may be implied on the basis of an established custom or usage of the relevant trade, unless such a term would be inconsistent with an express contractual term. For a term to be implied by custom, the term must be clearly established and 'notorious', i.e. well known within the trade context. In *Hutton v Warren* (1836) 1 M & W 466, the court implied a term into an agricultural lease that, upon quitting, tenants were entitled to an allowance for seed and labour, on the basis of a custom that was said to be incorporated into all such contracts.

It was once thought that such terms were incorporated by virtue of what it might be assumed in all of the circumstances must have been the intention of the parties, treating them as a species of term implied in fact. Today, the incorporation of customary terms, especially those in general use in a particular trade, may owe more to the courts' desire to regulate the content of contracts by encouraging the use of standardized terms. Such an approach would be more closely akin to that of terms implied in law.

> In **British Crane Hire Corporation Ltd v Ipswich Plant Hire Ltd** [1975] QB 303 (see also **6.3.3**), for example, the Court of Appeal held that the contract was subject to terms not made available to the offeree before the time of contracting. These terms were a version of the 'Contractors' Plant Association' terms that were customarily used in the particular trade and with which both parties would have been familiar, since they were both in the plant hire business.

6.4.2.2 Terms implied in law

Terms implied in law do not depend upon any intention imputed to the parties. They consist of legal obligations generally imposed on one of the parties in a common contractual relationship, without reference to the particular circumstances. Some legal obligations are imposed by the courts and some, although originally imposed by the courts, have now been given statutory force.

⏳ SUMMARY

Terms implied in law must be:

1. implied as a matter of policy into all contracts of a particular type;

2. a 'necessary incident' of this type of contract, i.e. necessary because of the contract's subject matter; and

3. a reasonable term to imply.

The Court of Appeal in *Crossley v Faithful & Gould Holdings Ltd* [2004] EWCA Civ 293, [2004] 4 All ER 447, [2004] ICR 1615 (Dyson LJ, at [36]) went so far as to suggest that the decision to imply a term in law rested on questions of 'reasonableness, fairness and the balancing of competing policy considerations' rather than 'necessity'.

Lord Denning MR described the process of implication of terms in law in *Shell UK Ltd v Lostock Garages Ltd* [1976] 1 WLR 1187. He said that it occurs in all common contractual relationships, such as seller and buyer, master and servant, landlord and tenant, and so on. He continued, at p. 1196:

> In such relationships the problem is not solved by asking: what did the parties intend? Or, would they have unhesitatingly agreed to it, if asked? It is to be solved by asking: has the law already defined the obligation or the extent of it? If so, let it be followed. If not, look to see what would be reasonable in the general run of such cases . . . and then say what the obligation shall be.

The basis for the implication of terms in this way appears to be the desire to regulate certain common types of contract. It is done so that one party does not take unfair advantage of another and so that adequate protection is given to both parties even when, as is often the case with such common contracts, little time is spent on detailed negotiation of the terms. Thus the common contracts have taken on standard content by implication of terms in law. The finding of a term in one case may be binding in terms of precedent in subsequent cases. Such a position would be inconceivable in the case of terms implied in fact.

The leading case on terms implied in law (i.e. involving legal obligations imposed on a contracting party by the courts) is *Liverpool City Council v Irwin* [1977] AC 239.

> The council let flats and maisonettes in a tower block to tenants. The lifts and rubbish chutes of the tower block constantly broke down. The tenancy agreement imposed certain obligations on tenants, but was silent about the obligations of the council to maintain the building. The tenants withheld their rent in protest at the council's failure to maintain the building properly. The council brought an action to obtain possession and the tenants counterclaimed for breach of an implied obligation to keep the block in proper repair.
>
> The House of Lords was prepared to imply, as a necessary incident of all tenancy agreements in which the tenants are granted the use in common of stairways, corridors, lifts, etc., an obligation on the landlord 'to take reasonable care to keep in reasonable repair and usability' the common parts (*per* Lord Wilberforce at p. 256G).

Lord Wilberforce suggested that the test was one of necessity. Lord Scarman in *Tai Hing Cotton Mill Ltd v Liu Chong Hing Bank Ltd* [1986] AC 80, at p. 107, and Lord Bridge in *Scally v Southern Health and Social Services Board* [1992] 1 AC 294, at p. 307, both refer to terms that are a 'necessary incident' of a 'definable category of' contractual relationship. Lord Bridge's formulation was warmly approved by Lord Woolf in *Spring v Guardian Assurance plc* [1995] 2 AC 296.

Despite this unfortunate parallelism of language, 'necessary on the facts' (terms implied in fact) and 'necessary incident of a definable category of contractual relationship' (terms implied in law) must have different meanings. The notion of 'necessary incident' draws upon a much wider set of criteria to determine its meaning and it must be supposed that, ultimately, terms implied in law on the basis of being a necessary incident of such contracts are founded upon reasonable expectation. Lord Woolf's short speech in *Spring v Guardian Assurance plc* provides an excellent demonstration of the implication of a term under this rule. He refers expressly to what is 'normal practice' in contracts of the particular kind and to the fact that it would not be right to expect the party to enter into an engagement of that kind except on the basis of the proposed implied term. This is very much the language of reasonable expectation, which was also the terminology employed by the House of Lords in *Equitable Life Assurance Society v Hyman* [2002] 1 AC 408, although the reasonable expectation in the case of terms implied in law embraces much broader contextual considerations than might be applicable for terms implied in fact on a one-off basis based on the reasonable expectations of 'notional reasonable people'. The implication of a term in law in *Scally v Southern Health and Social Services Board* was also based on 'wider considerations' outside the context and presumed intentions of reasonable people in the position of the parties.

It is difficult to know what these broader 'expectations' and 'considerations' might include: see Peden (2001) 117 LQR 459, and the suggestion that the courts take into account general issues of fairness and the impact on the parties of implication of the alleged term. Peden's comments were specifically relied upon by Dyson LJ in the Court of Appeal in *Crossley v Faithful*

& Gould Holdings Ltd [2004] EWCA Civ 293, [2004] 4 All ER 447, [2004] ICR 1615, (at [36]) in reaching the conclusion that it was better to focus on questions of 'reasonableness, fairness and the balancing of competing policy considerations' rather than the 'elusive concept of necessity'. In *Geys v Société Générale* [2012] UKSC 63, [2013] 1 AC 523, at [56], Lady Hale referred to Dyson LJ's statement in *Crossley* and added: 'There is much to be said for that approach, given the way in which [terms implied in law] have developed over the years.'

On the facts in *Crossley*, the Court of Appeal rejected an argument for an implied term that an employer should take reasonable care of an employee's economic well-being (by advising the employee of the financial consequences of early retirement). Unsurprisingly, such a term was considered to involve too large an extension of the law in this area, and to place an unfair and unreasonable burden upon employers. It is clearly much wider than the terms implied in *Mahmud v Bank of Credit and Commerce International SA (in liquidation)* [1998] AC 20 (implied term that employer would not conduct a dishonest or corrupt business) and in *Scally* (all employees in a certain category had to be notified of their entitlement to certain benefits), and needed to be more closely confined by the factual scenario.

6.4.2.3 Terms implied in fact: adding terms, after the construction of the express terms, as a matter of necessity to ensure that the particular contract does not lack commercial or practical coherence

Terms are implied in fact on the basis of an intention imputed to the parties from the actual circumstances as a process of addition of terms to ensure that, in the words of Lord Neuberger in *Marks and Spencer v BNP Paribas Securities Services Trust Co. (Jersey) Ltd* [2015] UKSC 72, [2015] 3 WLR 1843, [2016] AC 742, at [21], *the particular contract does not lack 'commercial or practical coherence', i.e. to make this contract work.* Thus there is no question of imposing a legal obligation. However, again, in the words of Lord Neuberger in *Marks and Spencer*, at [28], 'it is only after the process of construing the express words is complete that the issue of an implied term falls to be considered'. The courts will therefore start from a default position that the courts should not interfere with the parties' bargain as it is expressed. Indeed, in *Attorney-General of Belize v Belize Telecom Ltd* [2009] UKPC 10, [2009] 1 WLR 1988, Lord Hoffmann explained, at [17], that where there was no express term governing the event: 'The most usual inference . . . is that nothing is to happen. If the parties had intended something to happen the instrument would have said so.' This was considered to be the position on the facts in *Mediterranean Salvage and Towage Ltd v Seamar Trading and Commerce Inc., The Reborn* [2009] EWCA Civ 531, [2010] 1 All ER (Comm) 1, [2009] 1 CLC 909, in relation to the question whether a term should be implied into a charterparty that the charterer must nominate a safe berth at which the vessel was to be loaded. Lord Clarke MR stated at [11] 'if the parties had intended the charterers to warrant the safety of a loading berth, they could and would have said so, as is very common in voyage charterparties'.

Moreover the courts should not be using this process to introduce terms to make the contract either fairer or more reasonable. Lord Cross, in *Liverpool City Council v Irwin* [1977] AC 239, at p. 258, had also been clear that:

> What the court is being in effect asked to do is to rectify a particular—often a very detailed—contract by inserting in it a term which the parties have not expressed. Here it is not enough for the court to say that the suggested term is a reasonable one the presence of which would make the contract a better or fairer one; it must be able to say that the insertion of the term is necessary.

This represented a firm rebuke of Lord Denning MR who, in the Court of Appeal in the *Liverpool City Council v Irwin* case, had suggested that a term might be implied where it was just and reasonable in the circumstances. Such a test was firmly rejected on appeal to the House of Lords.

The Court of Appeal in *Dear v Jackson* [2013] EWCA Civ 89, [2014] BCLC 186, had to correct an approach at first instance that had come perilously close to reintroducing 'reasonableness' under the guise of contractual construction. It had been argued that a term that certain shareholders could appoint a director and secure his reappointment would be undermined by the provision of the articles, which allowed the directors to remove any other director. The decision at first instance—[2012] EWHC 2060 (Ch)—implied a term preventing the exercise of the power of removal on the basis of correcting a meaning that the reasonable person would not have understood the contract to have. The Court of Appeal rejected this approach as involving a rewriting of the parties' agreement on the basis of applying a 'sensible or reasonable commercial result'. This was not a proper basis for the implication of terms. Instead, the implication of a term can occur only where the term is considered to be a necessary inclusion in the contract. The matter has now firmly been clarified by the Supreme Court in *Marks and Spencer v Paribas* when Lord Neuberger stated (at [21]) 'a term should not be implied into a detailed commercial contract merely because it appears fair'.

6.4.2.3.1 *The test for implication of terms in fact*

The necessary conditions to imply a term in fact were summarized by Lord Simon in *BP Refinery (Westernport) Pty Ltd v Shire of Hastings* (1977) 180 CLR 266, at pp. 282–3:

> (1) [I]t must be reasonable and equitable; (2) it must be necessary to give business efficacy to the contract, so that no term will be implied if the contract is effective without it; (3) it must be so obvious that 'it goes without saying' (4) it must be capable of clear expression; (5) it must not contradict any express term of the contract.

To imply a term in fact, the term has to satisfy either the 'officious bystander' test or the 'business efficacy' test.

1. *The 'officious bystander' test*

The 'officious bystander' test derived from *Shirlaw v Southern Foundries (1926) Ltd* [1939] 2 KB 206, at p. 227, where MacKinnon LJ expressed it as follows:

> Prima facie that which in any contract is left to be implied and need not be expressed is something so obvious that it goes without saying; so that, if, while the parties were making their bargain, an officious bystander were to suggest some express provision for it in their agreement, they would testily suppress him with a common 'Oh, of course!'

This 'officious bystander' test imposed a very strict standard for the imposition of terms—*per* Lord Wilberforce in *Liverpool City Council v Irwin* [1977] AC 239—and attempts to imply terms on this basis often failed because while, objectively judged, one of the parties would clearly have assented to the term if it had been proposed, the same could not unquestionably be said of the other party.

In **Shell UK Ltd v Lostock Garage Ltd** [1976] 1 WLR 1187, the petrol company had introduced a subsidised support scheme that was available to selected tied garages, including two of the defendant's competitors, but not to the defendant's garage. When the defendant broke the tie agreement by obtaining petrol from another petrol company, Shell sought an injunction and damages for breach of contract. In its defence, the defendant claimed that Shell was in breach of an implied obligation that it would not discriminate abnormally against the defendant in favour of competing and neighbouring garages.

The majority of the Court of Appeal refused to imply such a term on the basis that it was not a necessary term.

Another reason why the suggested term was not implied in the *Shell* case was that it could not 'be formulated with sufficient precision', and this would seem to be an inherent problem with terms implied in fact.

2. The 'business efficacy' test

The 'business efficacy' test provides for the courts to imply a term with the object of giving the transaction such efficacy as, objectively judged, both parties must have intended that it should have.

In **The Moorcock** (1889) 14 PD 64, the claimants had agreed with the defendants that the claimants' ship should load and unload at the defendants' wharf on the Thames. Both parties knew that the ship would settle on the riverbed at low tide, but the defendants had not expressly guaranteed the good condition of the riverbed. The ship was damaged while at the wharf when it settled on hard ground rather than on mud. The question was whether there was an implied term in the contract to take reasonable care to see that the berth at the wharf was safe. The court found such a term to exist.

Bowen LJ said, at p. 68:

An implied warranty, or as it is called a covenant in law, as distinguished from an express contract or express warranty, really is in all cases founded upon the presumed intention of the parties, and upon reason. The implication which the law draws from what must obviously have been the intention of the parties, the law draws with the object of giving efficacy to the transaction and preventing such a failure of consideration as cannot have been within the contemplation of either side.

In other words, the term was implied because, without it, the contract could not be performed as the parties must have intended or it was being implied to make the contract work.

Equitable Life Assurance Society v Hyman [2002] 1 AC 408 is an example of a term 'implied in fact' prior to *Belize*. On the facts, the Society had issued retirement 'with profit' policies with a guaranteed annuity rate. When the general annuity rate fell, the policy became too expensive to honour. Following from this, the Society therefore adopted a policy of declaring a lower final bonus on such policies, relying on a provision in the Society's articles of association giving directors an absolute discretion in relation to the amount of bonus. The House of Lords affirmed the Court of Appeal's decision which held such a policy to be invalid. The House of Lords held that it was necessary to imply a term, restricting the discretion of the Society's directors to award lower final bonuses, to ensure that there was no conflict with the reasonable expectations of the parties. When the 'with-profits' policies had been issued, both parties would have assumed that the purpose was to protect policyholders against a fall in market annuity rates and this was a positive selling point when the Society marketed these policies. The effect of the proposed action by the directors would have been to deprive the guarantee in such a policy of any substantial value. On this basis, the implication of such a term was strictly necessary.

This 'two-pronged' approach was challenged in *Attorney-General of Belize v Belize Telecom Ltd* [2009] UKPC 10, [2009] 1 WLR 1988, at [27], by Lord Hoffmann who rejected the use of these tests and reformulated the overall approach as a single test of construction of the terms, i.e. rather than adding terms, the implication process involved recognition of terms that must already exist if the contract was to have the meaning that a reasonable person would take it to have. Lord Hoffmann therefore concluded that these tests were:

best regarded, not as a series of independent tests which must each be surmounted, but rather as a collection of different ways in which judges have tried to express the central idea that the proposed implied term must spell out what the contract actually means, or in which they have explained why they did not think that it did so.

This lead to some confusion in the law.

The 'more expansive approach' in *Belize Telecom* must, however, be seen in the light of the Supreme Court in *Marks & Spencer plc v BNP Paribas Securities Services Trust Co. (Jersey) Ltd* [2015] UKSC 72, [2015] 3 WLR 1843, [2016] AC 742, and the original officious bystander and business efficacy tests have been given unconditional re-acceptance as the correct tests to apply when implying terms in fact. The Supreme Court also explicitly rejected Lord Hoffmann's construction approach to the implication of terms.

The question on the facts was whether Marks & Spencer could recover rent from its former landlords which covered the period after the break date in its lease and the end of the rent quarter in which it fell. In July 2011 Marks & Spencer served a valid break notice of six months, had paid the December quarter's rent in full and on time, and had also paid the break premium (equivalent to one year's rent). Having validly exercised the break, the retailer then demanded repayment of the rent relating to the post-break period (i.e. between 24 January–24 March 2012). However, since there was no express term in the lease which entitled Marks & Spencer to this repayment, they needed to argue for such a term to be implied. The Supreme Court refused to imply such a term since it was well established that rent paid in advance could not be apportioned on a time basis and a different intention was not clearly established on the facts. A term would only be implied into a detailed commercial contract if it was necessary to give business efficacy to the contract or was so obvious that its implication went without saying.

The decision is of particular significance because the Supreme Court took the opportunity to explain the law on implied terms in fact and, in so doing, broadly accepted the tests of business efficacy or obviousness (set out earlier in this section) as explained in *BP Refinery (Westernport) Pty Ltd v Shire of Hastings* (1977) 180 CLR 266, *per* Lord Simon at pp. 282–3. Lord Neuberger (giving the leading judgment, with which Lord Sumption and Lord Hodge agreed) added some further explanation:

21 . . . It could be dangerous to reformulate the principles, but I would add six comments on the summary given by Lord Simon in the *BP Refinery* case . . . First, in *Equitable Life Assurance Society v Hyman* [2002] 1 AC 408, 459, Lord Steyn rightly observed that the implication of a term was 'not critically dependent on proof of an actual intention of the parties' when negotiating the contract. If one approaches the question by reference to what the parties would have agreed, one is not strictly concerned with the hypothetical answer of the actual parties, but with that of notional reasonable people in the position of the parties at the time at which they were contracting. Secondly, a term should not be implied into a

detailed commercial contract merely because it appears fair or merely because one considers that the parties would have agreed it if it had been suggested to them. Those are necessary but not sufficient grounds for including a term. However, and thirdly, it is questionable whether Lord Simon's first requirement, reasonableness and equitableness, will usually, if ever, add anything: if a term satisfies the other requirements, it is hard to think that it would not be reasonable and equitable. Fourthly, as Lord Hoffmann I think suggested in *Attorney General of Belize v Belize Telecom Ltd* [2009] 1 WLR 1988, para 27, although Lord Simon's requirements are otherwise cumulative, I would accept that business necessity and obviousness, his second and third requirements, can be alternatives in the sense that only one of them needs to be satisfied, although I suspect that in practice it would be a rare case where only one of those two requirements would be satisfied. Fifthly, if one approaches the issue by reference to the officious bystander, it is 'vital to formulate the question to be posed by [him] with the utmost care', to quote from *Lewison, The Interpretation of Contracts* 5th ed (2011), p 300, para 6.09. Sixthly, necessity for business efficacy involves a value judgment. It is rightly common ground on this appeal that the test is not one of 'absolute necessity', not least because the necessity is judged by reference to business efficacy. It may well be that a more helpful way of putting Lord Simon's second requirement is, as suggested by Lord Sumption JSC in argument, that a term can only be implied if, without the term, the contract would lack commercial or practical coherence.

Lord Neuberger then proceeded to reject the single test of construction (or interpretation) adopted by Lord Hoffmann in *Belize Telecom* and to emphasize that the previous tests of business efficacy and obviousness had not been diluted so that the law remained unchanged, despite Lord Hoffmann's attempts to reformulate principles. Lord Neuberger also concluded that construction of the express words and implication of terms were two distinct and sequential steps, albeit that some of the same factors will be relevant to both processes. He considered:

> 28 In most, possibly all, disputes about whether a term should be implied into a contract, it is only after the process of construing the express words is complete that the issue of an implied term falls to be considered. Until one has decided what the parties have expressly agreed, it is difficult to see how one can set about deciding whether a term should be implied and if so what term. This appeal is just such a case. Further, given that it is a cardinal rule that no term can be implied into a contract if it contradicts an express term, it would seem logically to follow that, until the express terms of a contract have been construed, it is, at least normally, not sensibly possible to decide whether a further term should be implied . . . [T]he express terms of a contract must be interpreted before one can consider any question of implication.
>
> 29 In any event, the process of implication involves a rather different exercise from that of construction. As Bingham MR trenchantly explained in the *Philips* case [*Philip's Electronique Grand Public SA v British Sky Broadcasting Ltd*] [1995] EMLR 472, 481:
>
>> The courts' usual role in contractual interpretation is, by resolving ambiguities or reconciling apparent inconsistencies, to attribute the true meaning to the language in which the parties themselves have expressed their contract. The implication of contract terms involves a different and altogether more ambitious undertaking: the interpolation of terms to deal with matters for which, *ex hypothesi*, the parties themselves have made no provision. It is because the implication of terms is so potentially intrusive that the law imposes strict constraints on the exercise of this extraordinary power.

It appears therefore that Lord Hoffmann's jurisprudential legacy has been subjected to attack in relation to remoteness of damage (and the test of 'assumption of responsibility', see **9.5.2.7**) and has been more directly and expressly challenged in relation to implied terms in fact. Lord

Neuberger phrased the attack in polite words by concluding (at [31]) that Lord Hoffmann's 'observations [in *Belize Telecom*] should henceforth be treated as a characteristically inspired discussion rather than authoritative guidance on the law of implied terms'. Nevertheless, the net conclusion is that the construction process for the implication of terms has been rejected. It is worth noting that although Lord Carnwath agreed that the argument for an implied term should be rejected, he would have been happy (at [74]) to accept the principles in *Belize Telecom* as having continued authority and regarded it as 'a valuable and illuminating synthesis of the factors which should guide the court' when considering whether to imply a term in fact.

The Supreme Court's strict position in *Marks & Spencer plc v BNP Paribas Securities Services Trust Co. (Jersey) Ltd* [2015] UKSC 72, [2016] AC 742 is followed in a wide array of cases: *Co-Operative Bank plc v (1) Hayes Freehold Ltd (In Liquidation)* [2017] EWHC 1820 (Ch); *Gard Shipping AS v Clearlake Shipping Pte Ltd* [2017] EWHC 1091 (Comm); *Irish Bank Resolution Corp. Ltd (In Special Liquidation) v Camden Market Holdings Corp.* [2017] EWCA Civ 7, *One Fish Co. Ltd v Iceland Foods Ltd* [2017] EWHC 3366 (Comm), (at [31]–[37]). In *Stevensdrake Ltd (t/a Stevensdrake Solicitors) v Stephen Hunt* [2017] EWCA Civ 1173, after referring to *Marks & Spencer* as 'the proper approach for the implication of terms' (at [48]), Hamblen LJ with whom Briggs LJ agreed, refused to imply a term where to do so would conflict with another, express, term of the contract (at [44]–[57]). The case of *Teekay Tankers Ltd v STX Offshore and Shipbuilding Co. Ltd* [2017] EWHC 253 (Comm), [2017] 1 Lloyd's Rep 387 reiterates that a term cannot be implied merely so as to complete a contract for the parties and rescue their bargain in circumstances where the relevant agreement amounts to no more than an 'agreement to agree'. This is so even though the parties themselves intended the agreement to be binding.

The strict position is further reinforced in two recent decisions by the Court of Appeal involving loans. In *Al Jaber v Al Ibrahim* [2018] EWCA Civ 1690, [2018] WLR(D) 46, the defendant borrowed US$30m to create an Arabic-language 24-hour satellite broadcasting service to rival Al Jazeera in 2001. The loan was agreed orally. Claims for repayment for the loan was made in 2015 when the claimant sought the debt itself as well as interests, which it was claimed was covered by an implied term. After confirming that the test for implying a term in fact was that set out in *Marks and Spencer v PNB Paribas*, the court dismissed the claim. Simon LJ noted (at [35]) that, although it was clear that the claimant had expected 'some benefit' from the transaction, it was nevertheless not defined precisely 'how they might do so'. As 'the first claimant would have been as content to have been rewarded with a share of the equity in Al-Arabiya as he would have been by the payment of interest' (at [36]), in consequence, 'implying a term that interest was due an implied term for the payment of interest was (a) not necessary to give business effect to the agreement, nor (b) so obvious that it went without saying, nor (c) such that the loan would lack commercial or practical consequence without the term, per Lord Sumption's coda referred to by Lord Neuberger in the *Marks & Spencer* case at [21]' (at [35]). In *Bou-Simon v BGC Brokers LP* [2018] EWCA Civ 1525, a similarly strict approach was followed in relation to a loan agreement to a partner. In February 2012, Mr Bou-Simon had joined BGC, a firm of brokers, as an employee with the clear understanding that he would become a partner. At the same time, the parties entered into a loan of £336,000. Under the terms of the agreement, the loan would be repaid from Bou-Simon's partnership distribution (clause 1). Under the same clause, should Bou-Simon cease to be a partner, any unpaid amount would be written off only if Bou-Simon served at least the full initial period as defined in the employment contract, namely four years. Clause 2 added that BGC was entitled to recall the loan to become immediately due if there was a material impairment to Bou-Simon's creditworthiness. Mr Bou-Simon resigned from BGC in June 2013. BGC sought to recover the loan plus interest on the basis of an implied term that

Bou-Simon failed to serve the full term of the initial period. Reversing the position of the High Court, Asplin LJ giving the leading judgment (with whom Singh and Hickinbottom LJJ agreed) for the Court of Appeal unanimously found no such implied term as it was neither necessary to give business effect nor obvious and the agreement did not lack commercial coherence (at [18]). Finally, it is worth pointing out the *obiter* remarks made by Asplin and Singh LJ on the issue of the potential impact of deleted words when implying terms. Both Asplin and Singh LJ emphasized that, in this context, the issue was different from that of the context of construction of terms (discussed at **6.5**). Asplin LJ stated that deletions of words 'are unlikely to be relevant to the process of implication' aside from 'very unusual circumstances' or 'where deletions have been relevant to the process of interpretation in the first place' (at [32]). Singh LJ however stated that he 'saw force in the suggestion in Lewison, *The Interpretation of Contracts* (6th edn), that "the consideration of deleted words may negative the implication of a term in the form of deleted words"' (at [36]). He added that 'This is because what would be admitted in that scenario is the *fact* that the same words which it is now argued should be implied into a contract had been deleted by the parties. It seems to me that fact could well have a bearing on the question whether the test for implication of a term into a contract has been met' (at [36]). He went on to say that 'I would not necessarily accept that, in the context of implied terms, there is a threshold requirement that there must be an ambiguity in the contract before deleted words could be admissible' (at [36]). It is perhaps appropriate to end those remarks with Singh LJ's comment that the issue is therefore 'not straightforward' (at [36]).

⟳ SUMMARY

Terms implied in fact must be:

1. implied on a 'one-off' basis into this particular contract after the express words of the parties have been interpreted;

2. based on necessity and to give 'business efficacy' (commercial or practical coherence) to the contract and/or on the basis that the term is so obvious that its implication goes without saying;

3. as reflecting the intentions of notional reasonable people in the position of the parties at the time when they contracted.

6.4.2.4 Terms imposed by statute

Certain obligations, which were at one time imposed by the courts, have now been given statutory force. Most important among these are terms relating to quality in sale or supply of goods contracts, and those relating to the standard of performance in contracts for services. Since the CRA 2015, there are separate statutory regimes for consumer contracts falling within the scope of that Act, and those contracts which fall outside it. To fall within the CRA regime, the contract must involve 'an agreement between a trader and a consumer for the trader to supply goods, digital content or services' (s. 1) where a trader is defined as 'a person acting for purposes relating to that person's trade, business, craft or profession' (s. 2(2)) and a consumer is defined as 'an individual acting for purposes that are wholly or mainly outside that individual's trade, business, craft or profession' (s. 2(3)).

Contracts which fall outside the CRA will therefore include B2B contracts and instances where an individual consumer is contracting for business purposes, e.g. a sole practitioner chiropodist contracting for the purchase of equipment to use in her business, as well as instances of private sales (C2C—consumer to consumer). The implied obligations for contracts falling outside the CRA 2015 can be found in the SGA 1979 (sales) and the Supply of Goods and Services Act (SGSA) 1982 (transfer of goods, hire and services) so that the applicable legislation turns on the type of contract involved—although the obligations relating to goods are similar. By comparison, the CRA uses the expression 'supply of goods' (s. 3(4)) in the consumer context to cover sales of goods, the hire of goods, and contracts for the transfer of goods.

The CRA does not use the term 'implied' for these obligations but refers to the fact that these terms are included. The end result is, however, the same, i.e. the terms are included even where they are not expressly stated by the parties. In addition, the overall effect of the included terms is the same as the terms in the SGA 1979 and SGSA 1982 which previously applied to all sale and supply contracts regardless of the status of the buyer as a consumer or not. It is sensible to begin our discussion there, albeit that the default position will be the CRA 2015 in any such contract between a trader and an individual (i.e. the trader has the burden of disproving the fact that the individual is a consumer for the purposes of the Act, s. 3(4)). 'Goods' are defined by the CRA as meaning 'any tangible moveable items' (although not water, gas, and electricity unless 'they are put up for supply in a limited volume or quantity').

6.4.2.4.1 *Implied terms where the CRA 2015 does not apply*

1. *The quality obligation in B2B sale of goods contracts*

The SGA 1979 defines a contract for the sale of goods as 'a contract by which the seller transfers or agrees to transfer the property in goods to the buyer for a money consideration, called the price' (s. 2(1) SGA 1979). (There is a distinction in this context between contracts whereby property on goods is transferred but this is not the primary purpose of the contract. Such contracts are discussed below (contracts for work and materials, point 4) and are covered by the SGSA 1982.)

Where the CRA does not apply to the sale of goods contract, the SGA 1979, s. 14(2), provides:

> *Where the seller sells goods in the course of a business*, there is an implied term that the goods supplied under the contract are of satisfactory quality. [Emphasis added]

For s. 14(2) (quality) and (3) (fitness for purpose, see below) to apply, the seller must sell 'in the course of a business'. In *Stevenson v Rogers* [1999] 2 WLR 1064, it was argued that the sale of a trawler by a fisherman was not 'in the course of a business', so that there was no implied term as to quality. However, the Court of Appeal held that a sale would be in the course of a business unless it were a purely private transaction outside the scope of *any business* carried on by the seller. It followed that the sale of the trawler could be an incidental part of the seller's business. The Court of Appeal also rejected the argument that the fisherman could not be conducting the sale 'in the course of a business' unless he was involved in selling trawlers on a regular basis. It followed that there was such an implied term in this contract. (It follows that there is no satisfactory quality obligation in private sales between two individual consumers where neither is acting in the course of a business.)

The Act then defines satisfactory quality as meaning that the goods 'meet the standards that a reasonable person would regard as satisfactory, taking account of any description of the goods, the price (if relevant) and all the other relevant circumstances' (s. 14(2A)). Quality of goods includes 'their state and condition', as well as matters such as fitness for all of the purposes for which goods of the kind in question are commonly supplied, appearance and finish, freedom from minor defects, safety, and durability (s. 14(2B)).

However, s. 14(2C) provides that:

> The term implied by subsection (2) . . . does not extend to any matter making the goods unsatisfactory—
>
> (a) which is specifically drawn to the buyer's attention before the contract is made,
>
> (b) where the buyer examines the goods before the contract is made, which that examination ought to reveal, or
>
> (c) in the case of a contract for sale by sample, which would have been apparent on a reasonable examination of the sample.

2. Fitness for a particular purpose in B2B sales of goods contracts

Under s. 14(3), again where the seller sells goods in the course of a business, where the buyer makes known to the seller a particular (as opposed to the common) purpose for buying the goods in question, there is a further implied term that the goods must be fit for that particular purpose.

3. Other implied terms in B2B sale of goods contracts

Section 13(1) of the SGA 1979 implies a term into *a contract for the sale of goods by description* that the goods will correspond with the description.

What is meant by 'a contract for the sale of goods by description' to which s. 13(1) applies? In *Harlingdon & Leinster Enterprises Ltd v Christopher Hull Fine Art Ltd* [1992] 1 QB 564, the Court of Appeal held that the sale of a painting as a 'Gabriele Münter' was not a sale by description. For a sale to be by description, that description had to be influential in the sale, so that it became a contractual term, and it would be extremely difficult to establish a common intention that the description should be a term of the contract where the party had not shown that it had relied on that description. Since the buyer was a specialist dealer and had inspected the painting before buying, it could not be said to be within the parties' reasonable contemplations that the buyer was relying on that description. Thus the Court of Appeal preserved the distinction between terms and representations (see **6.1.2**).

However, *Beale v Taylor* [1967] 1 WLR 1193 demonstrates that where a buyer has reasonably relied on a description, there will be a sale by description despite the fact that the buyer has inspected the goods. The defendant had offered his car for sale and described it as a 'Herald, convertible, white, 1961'; the claimant had examined the car and then purchased it. However, the car was in fact made up of two halves of different cars, which had been welded together, and although one half could be dated as 1961, the other half was older. The Court of Appeal considered that this was a sale by description of a '1961 Herald'—although compare *Oscar Chess Ltd v Williams* [1957] 1 WLR 370 (discussed at **6.1.3.4**), in which the statement as to a car's age was treated as a representation rather than a term as to description, possibly because the buyer was a garage rather than a private buyer.

In addition to applying in the context of B2B contracts, s. 13 SGA 1979 will continue to apply to private sales since there is no requirement (compare s. 14(2) and (3)) that the seller be selling in the course of a business for this section to apply.

Section 15(2) of the SGA 1979 implies a term into a contract for sale by sample that 'the bulk will correspond with the sample in terms of its quality' and that 'the goods will be free from any defect, making their quality unsatisfactory, which would not be apparent on reasonable examination of the sample'.

There are also implied terms that the seller has title to the goods (s. 12(1)), and that the seller has disclosed all charges and encumbrances known to the seller, but not known to the buyer (s. 12(4)).

There is a further implied term that the goods are free from any undisclosed encumbrances and that the buyer will otherwise enjoy quiet possession of the goods (s. 12(2)).

4. Contracts for work and materials in the B2B context

Contracts for work and materials are contracts in which the provision of 'work' or a service is the central object, but the contract also involves an incidental supply of materials (goods). Examples would be contracts to service or repair vehicles where new parts are used, or a contract to install central heating or a new bathroom where there is work ('labour'), but also a transfer of ownership of goods, e.g. the radiators, new bath or shower, etc.

(a) **Goods or materials**

Similar implied terms to those relating to the goods in a sale of goods contract are implied into contracts for work and materials by the provisions of the SGSA 1982, which deal with contracts for the transfer of property in goods. Thus s. 3(2) implies a term relating to the transfer of goods by description, s. 4(2), satisfactory quality if supplied in the course of a business, and s. 4(4) and (5), reasonably fit for a particular purpose made known prior to transfer.

(b) **The work (service) element**

The implied term applicable is that contained in SGSA 1982, s. 13 (contract for the supply of services), to be discussed shortly (at point 6).

5. Contracts for the hire of goods in the B2B context

There are similar implied terms relating to the goods that are the subject of the hire (defined by SGSA 1982, s. 6): see s. 8(2) (description), s. 9(2) (satisfactory quality), s. 9(4) and (5) (reasonably fit for the purpose), and s. 10(2) (sample).

6. Contracts for the supply of services: standard of performance in the B2B context

Under s. 13 of the SGSA 1982, there is an implied term that the supplier of services will carry out the service with reasonable care and skill. This standard is different from that applying to the sale or supply of goods. In the case of the latter, the obligation to meet the required standard is absolute and it will not be a defence to a claim of breach of the implied term of, for example, satisfactory quality that the seller did its best to supply goods of that quality. In the case of the supply of services, however, the performance obligation will be met if the person performing the services uses reasonable care and skill. There is no guarantee that a particular result will be achieved (see **8.2.1.1**).

6.4.2.4.2 Included terms where the CRA 2015 applies

As noted above that sales, hire, and work and materials contracts all involve the 'supply of goods, digital content or services' for the purposes of the legislation (s. 3(4)) and that the Act will apply only where this contract is between a 'trader' and a 'consumer' (as defined by s. 2(2) and (3)). The Act specifically recognizes various consumer rights in any supply contract relating to the goods supplied and provides for the consumer to enforce these rights in various ways (see **8.4.2.3**). The rights relate to the goods being of satisfactory quality, the goods being fit for any particular purpose that the consumer makes known to the trader, the goods matching the description, the goods matching a sample or any model seen or examined, and the trader's right to supply the goods and so transfer ownership, etc. See **Table 6.1** for description of equivalent provisions of the SGA and CRA.

TABLE 6.1 Comparison of statutory terms in B2B and B2C contexts

SGA 1979 (sale of goods) and SGSA 1982 (transfer of goods, hire and supply of service)	CRA 2015 provisions
s.12 SGA: Seller's right to sell (title) sale of goods s. 2 SGSA (transfer of goods) s. 7 SGSA (hire)	s. 17 CRA: Trader to have the right to supply goods
s. 13 SGA: Sale by description s. 3 SGSA (transfer of goods) s. 8 SGSA (hire)	s. 11 CRA: Goods to be as described
s. 14(2) SGA: Satisfactory quality where sale in the course of a business s. 4(2) SGSA (transfer of goods) s. 9(2) SGSA (hire)	s. 9 CRA: Goods to be of satisfactory quality
s. 14(3) SGA: Fitness for purpose where sale in the course of a business s. 4(4)(5) SGSA (transfer of goods) s. 9(4)(5) SGSA (hire)	s. 10 CRA: Goods to be fit for a particular purpose
s. 15 SGA: Sale by sample s. 5 SGSA (transfer of goods) s. 10 SGSA (hire)	s. 13 CRA: Goods to match a sample s. 14 CRA: Goods to match a model seen or examined
s. 13 SGSA: Supply of service with reasonable care and skill	s. 49 CRA: Supply of a service with reasonable care and skill

There is an additional s. 15 CRA 'right' whereby if installation of goods by or on behalf of the trader forms part of the contract for their supply, e.g. the shower to be installed by the plumber or the retailer's subcontractor plumber, an incorrect installation means that the goods will be treated as not conforming to the contract and the consumer's remedies apply in relation to the goods, with the exception of the short-term right to reject.

Similar rights apply to contracts involving the supply of digital content. The digital content must conform with these obligations relating to goods (Part 1, Chapter 3, CRA 2015). Section 16 CRA 2015 also provides that where the contract for the supply of goods includes digital content (e.g. if the digital content is supplied on a disk), if the digital content does not conform to the contract, the goods will be treated as not conforming.

There are also consumer rights relating to service contracts (services other than a contract of employment or apprenticeship), which include terms relating to the duty to perform the service with reasonable care and skill, and reasonable price and time (Part 1, Chapter 4, CRA 2015).

In broad terms, these CRA terms (or 'consumer rights') cannot be excluded or restricted (ss. 31, 47, and 57).

6.5 Principles determining how to interpret contracts

6.5.1 Introduction

Contractual obligations, once recognized as such, will need to be interpreted (or the contract 'construed') to work out precisely what the parties have undertaken to do. This process of interpreting the express words contained in the contract is the first step process identified by the

Supreme Court in *Marks & Spencer plc v BNP Paribas Securities Services Trust Co. (Jersey) Ltd* [2015] UKSC 72, [2015] 3 WLR 1843, [2016] AC 742. The Supreme Court also explained that the approach of Lord Hoffmann in *Attorney-General of Belize v Belize Telecom Ltd* [2009] UKPC 10, [2009] 1 WLR 1988, which had treated the implication of terms in fact as part of a single contractual interpretation, could not be sustained (see **6.4.2.3**).

The process of construction (or interpretation) of the words used in the contract is also the basis upon which decisions are made concerning the application of doctrines of mistake (see **3.2.1** and **Chapter 13**) and frustration (**Chapter 12**). Exemption clauses need to be construed to determine whether they cover the loss or liability which it is sought to exclude or restrict (see **7.3**). It is difficult therefore to understate the importance of contractual construction to contemporary English contract law.

The basic rule is that the court must find the intention of the parties. This intention is determined objectively (see **2.1**). According to Lord Clarke in the Supreme Court in *Rainy Sky SA v Kookmin Bank* [2011] UKSC 50, [2011] 1 WLR 2900, at [14]: '[T]he ultimate aim of interpreting a provision in a contract . . . is to determine what the parties meant by the language used, which involves ascertaining what a reasonable person would have understood the parties to have meant.'

In the past, the context for this assessment was limited to what was said within the 'four corners' of the contract, the so-called 'textualism' paradigm of interpretation. Traditionally, it was considered that, as a result of the parol evidence rule, the courts were, in general terms, limited in the search for intention to consideration of the contract document alone and had to 'construe the document according to the ordinary grammatical meaning of the words used therein': *Lovell & Christmas Ltd v Wall* (1911) 104 LT 85, *per* Cozens-Hardy MR at p. 88. In particular, as a general rule, it has long been considered that it is not possible to have regard to the parties' negotiations or subsequent conduct, although it has always been possible to go outside the document where the words had a particular technical meaning.

6.5.2 The broader context: *West Bromwich*

However, successive decisions of the House of Lords, and now the Supreme Court, have accepted that a broader context is appropriate, the so-called 'contextual' paradigm. In *Investors Compensation Scheme Ltd v West Bromwich Building Society* [1998] 1 WLR 896, Lord Hoffmann reformulated the principles to provide for a more contextual (or purposive) approach and to ensure that the interpretation of commercial contracts reflected commercial common sense. Lord Hoffmann listed the applicable legal principles, at pp. 912H–913E, as follows:

(1) Interpretation is the ascertainment of the meaning which the document would convey to a reasonable person having all the background knowledge which would reasonably have been available to the parties in the situation in which they were at the time of the contract.

(2) The background was famously referred to by Lord Wilberforce as the 'matrix of fact'. Subject to the requirement that it should have been reasonably available to the parties and to the exception to be mentioned next, it includes *absolutely anything* which would have affected the way in which the language of the document would have been understood by a reasonable man.

(3) The law excludes from the admissible background the previous negotiations of the parties and their declarations of subjective intent. They are admissible only in an action for rectification. The law makes this distinction for reasons of practical policy and, in this respect only, legal interpretation differs from the way we would interpret utterances in ordinary life.

(4) The meaning which a document . . . would convey to a reasonable man is not the same thing as the meaning of its words. The meaning of words is a matter of dictionaries and grammars; the meaning of the document is what the parties using those words against the relevant background would reasonably have been understood to mean. The background may not merely enable the reasonable man to choose between the possible meanings of words which are ambiguous but even . . . to conclude that the parties must, for whatever reason, have used the wrong words or syntax . . .

(5) The 'rule' that words should be given their 'natural and ordinary meaning' reflects the commonsense proposition that we do not easily accept that people have made linguistic mistakes, particularly in formal documents. On the other hand, if one would nevertheless conclude from the background that something must have gone wrong with the language, the law does not require judges to attribute to the parties an intention which they plainly could not have had. [Emphasis added]

This decision has created considerable academic and judicial discussion over the extent of the impact of Lord Hoffmann's five principles and whether they really were a recalibration or simply the continuation of existing principles of interpretation—the so-called battle between the 'textualism' and the 'contextualism' paradigms (for criticism of this discussion as a waste of time, see Coulson J in *HSM OffShore BV v Aker Offshore Partner Ltd* [2017] EWHC 2979 (TCC), at [165]). The discussion culminated in the *Wood v Capita Insurance Services Ltd* [2017] UKSC 24, [2017] 2 WLR 1095, [2017] AC 765, where Lord Hodge, speaking for the entire Supreme Court, stated that the process of interpretation was a 'unitary exercise' and that 'textualism' and 'contextualism' were therefore not conflicting paradigms (at [11]) (see **6.5.4**).

The first principle (see above) is undoubtedly correct and has been accepted as the starting point in a succession of decisions by the highest courts: *Bank of Credit and Commerce International SA v Ali* [2001] UKHL 8, [2001] 2 WLR 735, per Lord Clyde at [78]; *Attorney-General of Belize v Belize Telecom Ltd* [2009] UKPC 10, [2009] 1 WLR 1988, [2009] Bus LR 1316; *Chartbrook Ltd v Persimmon Homes Ltd* [2009] UKHL 38, [2009] 1 AC 1101; *Rainy Sky SA v Kookmin Bank* [2011] UKSC 50, [2011] 1 WLR 2900; *Arnold v Britton* [2015] UKSC 36, [2015] AC 1619; and most recently in *Wood v Capita Insurance Services Ltd* [2017] UKSC 24, [2017] 2 WLR 1095, [2017] AC 765.

The second and fourth principles (see above) give rise to more controversy. It is accepted that background knowledge or context has a part to play in interpretation and that it is possible to look beyond a very literal interpretation of the words used. However, the courts have taken time to determine the relationship between the natural meaning of the words used set against that context (or 'matrix of fact') and a purposive approach to interpretation which favours giving effect to commercial common sense. Lord Hoffmann's reference in *West Bromwich* to the 'matrix of fact' as including '*absolutely anything* which would have affected the way in which the language of the document would have been understood by a reasonable man' proved to be an initial source for debate. In *Bank of Credit and Commerce International SA v Ali* [2001] UKHL 8, [2001] 2 WLR 735, Lord Hoffmann took the opportunity, at [39], to explain what he meant by these words:

I did not think it necessary to emphasise that I meant anything which a reasonable man would have regarded as relevant. I was merely saying that there is no conceptual limit to what can be regarded as background. It is not, for example, confined to the factual background but can include the state of the law . . . I was certainly not encouraging a trawl through 'background' which could not have made a reasonable person think that the parties must have departed from conventional usage.

Nevertheless, *West Bromwich* was considered to highlight a distinct trend in the case law away from a tight literal construction of the words used and in favour of interpretation which reflected business common sense. As Lord Diplock stated in *Antaios Cia Naviera SA v Salen Rederierna AB, The Antaios* [1985] AC 191, at p. 201: 'If detailed semantic and syntactical analysis of words in a commercial contract is going to lead to a conclusion that flouts business common sense, it must yield to business common sense.' In other words, if the contract, as construed applying ordinary language and rules of syntax, would lead to an unreasonable result, the assumption had to be that the parties could not have intended it. This approach is similar to the much-criticized approach of the House of Lords in *Schuler v Wickman Machine Tool Sales Ltd* [1974] AC 235 (discussed at **8.5.3.2**). Yet, in *Kudos Catering (UK) Ltd v Manchester Central Convention Complex Ltd* [2013] EWCA Civ 38, [2013] 2 Lloyd's Rep 270, the Court of Appeal applied the approach in *Schuler v Wickman* and concluded that a clause in a catering services agreement (hidden away in a section dealing with indemnities and insurance), which purported to exclude all liability for direct loss (profits) and all indirect or consequential loss, did not reflect the parties' commercial intentions, since it could potentially result in there being no sanction for a refusal to perform. Accordingly, the Court restricted the operation of the clause to defective performance, as opposed to a refusal to perform, and justified its action, amongst other things, on the basis of the presentational positioning of the clause (see especially [28]–[29], *per* Tomlinson LJ with whom McCombe and Laws LJJ specifically agreed).

In *Mannai Investments Co. Ltd v Eagle Star Life Assurance* [1997] AC 749, at p. 771, Lord Steyn commented:

> In determining the meaning of the language of a commercial contract, and unilateral contractual notices, the law therefore generally favours a commercially sensible construction. The reason for this approach is that a commercial construction is more likely to give effect to the intention if the parties. Words are therefore interpreted in the way in which a reasonable commercial person would construe them. And the standard of the reasonable commercial person is hostile to technical interpretations and undue emphasis on niceties of language.

The *Investors Compensation Scheme* approach to contractual interpretation is open to criticism on a number of grounds, but in particular, because of its vagueness, it has inevitably led to the much-dreaded uncertainty in the context of commercial contracts, especially for third parties. There is clearly no universal understanding, even among commercial judges, of what will constitute 'business common sense'. In addition, as noted by Sir Christopher Staughton [1999] CLJ 303, at p. 307, the need to examine the matrix of facts when determining contractual interpretation means that '[i]t is hard to imagine a ruling more calculated to perpetuate the vast cost of commercial litigation'. This prediction has proved to be correct, with a significant number of cases before the commercial courts over subsequent years involving issues of contractual construction and the application of the *West Bromwich* principles to the facts.

The critical issue, however, must be whether the natural meaning of the words used in context will yield to commercial common sense in all cases—or whether commercial common sense is merely *a* background factor (along with all others, such as the parties' contractual purpose) to determine the natural meaning of the parties' chosen words. Much of the language used in Lord Hoffmann's fourth principle in *West Bromwich* suggests that he may have envisaged the latter approach rather than the former, at least in instances where the natural meaning of the words used is unambiguous. Nevertheless, it is clear that he also contemplated using background to conclude that the parties had used 'the wrong words or syntax' and this may have had the effect of lending support to arguments giving effect to the predominance of commercial common sense.

6.5.3 The primacy of the natural meaning of the words used: *Arnold v Britton*

Recent decisions have expressed disquiet at any approach which gave predominance in interpretation to giving effect to 'commercial common sense'. For example, Moore-Bick LJ explained the dangers in *Procter & Gamble Co. v Svenska Cellulosa Aktiebolaget SCA* [2012] EWCA Civ 1413, at [22]:

> [T]he starting point must be the words the parties have used to express their intention and in the case of a carefully drafted agreement . . . [T]he court must take care not to fall into the trap of re-writing the contract to produce what it considers to be a more reasonable meaning.

The same point was made by Aikens LJ in *BMA Special Opportunity Hub Fund Ltd v African Minerals Finance Ltd* [2013] EWCA Civ 416 and by the Court of Appeal in *Dear v Jackson* [2013] EWCA Civ 89, [2014] BCLC 186. It has now been confirmed as critical by the Supreme Court in *Arnold v Britton* [2015] UKSC 36, [2015] AC 1619 and again most recently in *Wood v Capita Ltd* [2017] UKSC 24, [2017] 2 WLR 1095, [2017] AC 765 (see **6.5.4**).

In *Arnold v Britton* [2015] UKSC 36, [2015] AC 1619, the Supreme Court was required to interpret service charge provisions in leases of chalets at a caravan park on the Gower Peninsula which had been granted at a time of high inflation in the late 1970s and 80s. Each lease contained a clause requiring the lessee to pay a fixed service charge and provided for this to increase at a compound rate. A typical clause required the lessee:

> To pay to the lessors without any deductions in addition to the said rent a proportionate part of the expenses and outgoings incurred by the lessors in the repair, maintenance, renewal and the provision of services hereafter set out the yearly sum of £90 and VAT (if any) for the first three years of the term hereby granted increasing thereafter by ten pounds per hundred for every subsequent three year period or part thereof.

The compounding of the amount of the annual increase would have resulted in a charge of over £500,000 per annum by the end of the 99-year term. The lessees therefore argued that this could not have been the intention of the provision and that the clause should be read as limiting their contribution to paying a proportionate part of the reasonable expenses incurred by the lessors subject to a cap of the fixed amount increasing after the first year on a compound basis. The lessors argued that the clause required payment of the fixed term as drafted. The lessors succeeded in securing a declaration to this effect from the High Court on the basis that the lessees' interpretation involved rewriting the clause.

The Court of Appeal upheld this decision and the Supreme Court agreed (Lord Carnwath JSC dissenting), rejecting the appeal by the lessees. The majority considered that nothing had gone wrong with the drafting of the clause and it was not ambiguous. In addition, they were able to find commercial justifications for it in the form of the certainty provided to both parties through a fixed rate charge. Inflation had been rampant at the time when the majority of the leases had been granted in the late 1970s, and often at a rate over 10 per cent, so that fixing a 10 per cent compound escalation was not absurd at the time when the leases were granted on these terms. It had merely proved to be imprudent over time.

Lord Neuberger (with whom Lord Sumption JSC and Lord Hughes JSC agreed), giving the lead judgment, set out seven factors, four of which (at [17]–[20]) are significant in terms of the general approach to interpretation.

The first factor emphasized 'the language of the provision which is to be construed' as the starting point to identify the intended meaning through the eyes of the reasonable reader since the parties had control over the choice of words used. Lord Neuberger then explained that the less clear the words are, the more ready the court will be to depart from their natural meaning. However, that would not justify a search for drafting errors to justify a departure from the natural meaning of the words. The third factor was that 'commercial common sense' was not to be invoked retrospectively and was relevant only to the assessment of how the words would have been interpreted by reasonable people in the position of the parties at the date the contract was made. In particular, the fact that the contract had worked out badly for one or both of the parties would not be a reason to depart from the natural meaning of the words. Lord Neuberger made express reference to *Schuler v Wickman* and the observations of Lord Diplock in *The Antaios* (see **6.5.2**) and stated that these needed to be read in this light. Fourthly, it was not the function of interpretation to relieve the parties from the consequences of an imprudent bargain. Lord Neuberger emphasized (at [20]) that:

> The purpose of interpretation is to identify what the parties have agreed, not what the court thinks they should have agreed . . . [W]hen interpreting a contract a judge should avoid re-writing it in an attempt to assist an unwise party or to penalise an astute party.

This decision is clear in emphasizing the starting point for interpretation as being the language the parties have chosen. If this language is clear and unambiguous the courts will not interfere with the words chosen in the parties' bargain. It follows that the clause should be interpreted in accordance with 'commercial common sense' only in instances of ambiguity or clear drafting problems—and not simply because one of the parties objects to the outcome of the natural meaning of a clause. A similar position has now been reached in *Wood v Capita Insurance Services Ltd* [2017] UKSC 24, [2017] 2 WLR 1095, [2017] AC 765.

6.5.4 Interpretation as a 'unitary exercise': *Wood v Capita*

In *Wood v Capita Insurance Services Ltd*, the Supreme Court was required to interpret an indemnity clause (clause 7.11) in a contract for the sale and purchase of shares in a specialist insurance broking company. The clause covered 'all actions, proceedings, losses, claims, damages, expenses and liability suffered or incurred' only if such losses were sustained 'following and arising out of claims or complaints registered with the FSA' or other regulators. Shortly after purchasing the company and following concerns raised by some employees about the company's sale process, an internal review was carried out and revealed that some telephone operators had indeed misled customers. The company therefore informed the FSA and the customers affected were compensated. Capita then sought to rely on the indemnity clause to recoup their loss. The Court of Appeal, overturning the High Court, held that the indemnity clause did not cover Capita's losses since they were not incurred following 'claims or complaints registered with the FSA' since the company had referred itself to the FSA. Lord Hodge, speaking for the Supreme Court as a whole, upheld the Court of Appeal's decision.

The buyer's main argument in his application for leave to appeal to the Supreme Court was that the Court of Appeal had paid too much attention to the words of the documents and too little attention to the factual matrix, hereby highlighting the aforementioned battle between 'textualism' and 'contextualism'. This was dismissed by Lord Hodge in no uncertain terms, stating, at [9] and [14] that *Rainy Sky* and *Arnold* were 'saying the same thing'. The relevant passages are [8]–[15]. Lord Hodge reiterated, at [10], that the role of the court was 'to ascertain the objective meaning of the language which the parties have chosen to express their agreement'. He added that this was not 'a literalist exercise focused solely on a parsing of the wording of the particular clause' and that on the contrary the court had to 'consider the contract as a whole and, depending on the nature, formality and quality of drafting of the contract, give more or less weight to elements of the wider context in reaching its view as to that objective meaning'. Lord Hodge emphasized at [11] that 'interpretation is . . . a unitary exercise' which [at 12] 'involves an iterative process by which each suggested interpretation is checked against the provisions of the contract and its commercial consequences are investigated'. In consequence, his Lordship concluded (at [13]) that 'textualism' and 'contextualism', far from being 'conflicting paradigms', are in fact 'tools to ascertain the objective meaning of the language which the parties have chosen to express their agreement'. Lord Hodge's position is therefore clear: both context (or factual matrix) and the written contractual content are of relevance, and the extent of that relevance will in part depend on the nature of the contract and its parties. Decisions post *Wood* have been at pains to emphasize a similar position, not least the Supreme Court itself in *MT Hojgaard A/S v E.ON Climate and Renewable UK Robin Rigg East Ltd* [2017] UKSC 59, [2017] Bus LR 1610. Perhaps Coulson J's words (at [165]) in *HSM Offshore BV v Aker Offshore Partner Ltd* [2017] EWHC 2979 (TCC), summarize the situation perfectly: 'The rules of construction are now well-known: there have been a plethora of cases in the House of Lords and the Supreme Court in recent years in which the relevant rules have been set out, including *Chartbrook Ltd v Persimmon Homes Ltd* [2009] UKHL 38; *Rainy Sky SA v Kookmin Bank* [2011] UKSC 50; *Arnold v Britton* [2015] UKSC 36; and *Woods v Capita Insurance Services Ltd* [2017] UKSC 24. Although some practitioners and legal commentators with nothing better to do have sought to exploit certain fine linguistic differences between the various judgments, in my view they all point in the same general direction. What matters is the objective meaning of the language, to be derived from the natural or usual meaning of the words used, when seen against the background/context of the contract'.

6.5.4.1 Linguistic mistakes: has something gone wrong with the language?

Chartbrook Ltd v Persimmon Homes Ltd [2009] UKHL 38, [2009] 1 AC 1101, concerned an agreement for the development of land. Persimmon was required to obtain planning permission and would carry out the construction. It would then use the proceeds of sale to pay Chartbrook a price for the land based on the total land value and an 'additional residential payment' (ARP), which was defined in the contract. The parties' dispute arose because they gave different interpretations to the ARP and its calculation. Chartbrook claimed that it had been underpaid.

At first instance and in the Court of Appeal, the APR definition was interpreted on the basis of ordinary rules of syntax, since 'the words made sense on their own'. However, the House of Lords allowed the appeal by Persimmon on the basis that the context and background indicated that 'something must have gone wrong with the language' (*per* Lord Hoffmann), although accepting that a court did not easily accept that linguistic mistakes were made in formal documents. An interpretation based on the ordinary rules of syntax made no commercial sense and would not accord with what a reasonable person, having all of the background knowledge that would have been available to the parties, would have understood the parties to have meant. Thus the House of Lords was able to correct this 'error' through interpretation without having to resort to a claim for rectification.

It was accepted that it is by no means the case that something will have 'gone wrong with the language' in all cases. In fact, it is quite rare (for a recent example, see *BNY Mellon Corporate Trustee Services Ltd v LBG Capital No. 1 plc* [2016] UKSC 29, [2017] 1 All ER 497). In many instances, there will be no doubt as to the ordinary meaning of the words used. Where the intended meaning is clear, it is not a basis for courts to adjudicate between parties about the commercial good sense of different meanings and interpretations of terms just because a particular term seems generous on the natural meaning interpretation: *Ing Bank NV v Ros Roca SA* [2011] EWCA Civ 353, [2012] 1 WLR 472, [2012] Bus LR 266, and *Pink Floyd Music Ltd v EMI Records Ltd* [2010] EWCA Civ 1429, [2011] 1 WLR 770, *per* Lord Neuberger MR at [20]:

> 20 [A]s Lord Hoffmann also made clear in *Investors Compensation* [1998] 1 WLR 896, there is a difference between cases of ambiguity, which may result in giving the words a meaning they can naturally bear, even if it is not their prima facie most natural meaning, and cases of mistake, which may result from concluding that the parties made a mistake and used the wrong words or syntax. However, he emphasised the court does 'not readily accept that people have made mistakes in formal documents'—*Chartbrook* [2009] 1 AC 1101, para 23. He also pointed out in paragraph 20, that, as the court, and therefore the notional reasonable person, cannot take into account the antecedent negotiations, the fact that the natural meaning of the words appears to produce 'a bad bargain' for one of the parties or an 'unduly favourable' result for another, is not enough to justify the conclusion that something has gone wrong. One is normally looking for an outcome which is 'arbitrary' or 'irrational', before a mistake argument will run.

It is clear from *Wood v Capita* that the 'factual background' retains relevance in the interpretation process (see also *Astex Therapeutics LTD v Astrazeneca AB* [2017] EWHC 1442 (Ch) at [87]), subject to the clear statement of principle in *Arnold* that this must not be permitted to facilitate a departure from the clear meaning of the words used. This much is illustrated by the affirmation of the decision in *Deutsche Trustee Company Limited v Cheyne Capital (Management) UK (LLP)* [2015] EWHC 2282 (Ch) on appeal by the Court of Appeal ([2016] EWCA Civ 743), with the court placing clear emphasis on the fact that the natural and ordinary meaning of the words of the relevant clause was clear and unambiguous. Indeed, as reiterated by Lord Hodge in *Wood v Capita* at [41], even if the clause was, for Capita, 'a poor bargain', 'it is not the function of the court to improve their bargain'. It will be increasingly difficult to identify a 'linguistic mistake', as opposed to a bad bargain, and it is arguable that linguistic mistakes are more appropriate in many instances as a claim for rectification.

6.5.4.2 Language having more than one potential meaning

The Supreme Court in *Rainy Sky SA v Kookmin Bank* [2011] UKSC 50, [2011] 1 WLR 2900, held that if a contract uses clear and unambiguous language, then the court has to apply it, however surprising, unlikely, or unreasonable the effect of that language might be and this accords with the Court's subsequent approach in *Arnold v Britton*. However, in *Rainy Sky* the Supreme Court held that where a clause is reasonably capable of bearing more than one possible meaning, the court could prefer the construction that better accords with the overall objective of the contract or was consistent with business common sense.

Rainy Sky SA v Kookmin Bank concerned the interpretation of the terms of refund guarantees (advance payment bonds). These had been issued by the bank in relation to six shipbuilding contracts to guarantee the instalments of the price being paid to the shipbuilders in the event of various default events specified in the shipbuilding contract. The terms of the advance payment bonds involved a promise (para. 3) to pay the buyer 'all such sums due to you under the Contract', and this was expressed to be 'in consideration of your agreement to make the pre-delivery instalments under the contract'. The shipbuilder became insolvent after instalments had been paid and the buyers sought to enforce the advance payment bonds. The bank rejected these claims on the basis that they had not undertaken to guarantee payment of refunds if the default event was the builder's insolvency. Insolvency was an event that triggered immediate repayment under the terms of the shipbuilding contract itself.

The Supreme Court held that the terms of the contract were relevant to the construction of the bonds and, although para. 3 was capable of two meanings, the buyer's construction was preferable, since it was consistent with the commercial purpose of the advance payment bonds. The builder's insolvency was the situation for which the bonds were most likely to be needed.

The difficulty with the modern approach, prior to *Wood v Capita*, was in setting out exactly how much weight could be placed on the wider context and factors such as 'commercial common sense' in determining ambiguity. There was some confusion as to what the rules were, and first instance judges emphasized different things. *Wood v Capita* is therefore of crucial importance for effectively summarizing the law as follows:

11. Interpretation is, as Lord Clarke stated in *Rainy Sky* (para 21), a unitary exercise; where there are rival meanings, the court can give weight to the implications of rival constructions by reaching a view as to which construction is more consistent with business common sense. But, in striking a balance between the indications given by the language and the implications of the competing constructions the court must consider the quality of drafting of the clause (*Rainy Sky* para 26, citing Mance LJ in *Gan Insurance Co Ltd v Tai Ping Insurance Co Ltd (No. 2)* [2001] 2 All ER (Comm) 299 paras 13 and 16); and it must also be alive to the possibility that one side may have agreed to something which with hindsight did not serve his interest: *Arnold* (paras 20 and 77). Similarly, the court must not lose sight of the possibility that a provision may be a negotiated compromise or that the negotiators were not able to agree more precise terms.

12. This unitary exercise involves an iterative process by which each suggested interpretation is checked against the provisions of the contract and its commercial consequences are investigated . . . To my mind once one has read the language in dispute and the relevant parts of the contract that provide its context, it does not matter whether the more detailed analysis commences with the factual background and the implications of rival constructions or a close examination of the relevant language in the contract, so long as the court balances the indications given by each.

13. Textualism and contextualism are not conflicting paradigms in a battle for exclusive occupation of the field of contractual interpretation. Rather, the lawyer and the judge, when interpreting any contract, can use them as tools to ascertain the objective meaning of the language which the parties have chosen to express their agreement. The extent to which each tool will assist the court in its task will vary according to the circumstances of the particular agreement or agreements. Some agreements may be successfully interpreted principally by textual analysis, for example because of their sophistication and complexity and because they have been negotiated and prepared with the assistance of skilled professionals. The correct interpretation of other contracts may be achieved by a greater emphasis on the factual matrix, for example because of their informality, brevity or the absence of skilled professional assistance. But negotiators of complex formal contracts may often not achieve a logical and coherent text because of,

for example, the conflicting aims of the parties, failures of communication, differing drafting practices, or deadlines which require the parties to compromise to reach agreement. There may often therefore be provisions in a detailed professionally drawn contract which lack clarity and the lawyer or judge in interpreting such provisions may be particularly helped by considering the factual matrix and the purpose of similar provisions in contracts of the same type.

For a recent application of a pragmatic application of the 'commercial common sense', one need look no further than the recent Supreme Court decision on NOM, *Rock Advertising v MWB Exchange* [2018] UKSC 24 (discussed at **6.2.1.5**).

6.5.5 Pre-contractual negotiations

6.5.5.1 The exclusionary rule

Prenn v Simmonds [1971] 1 WLR 1381 is authority of the House of Lords for 'the exclusionary rule', i.e. there is to be no recourse to pre-contractual negotiations to explain the meaning that the parties must be taken to have intended for their contractual document.

- Lord Wilberforce said that 'such evidence is unhelpful', because only when the contract is finally made is there a consensus and, until that time, the parties' respective intentions may change or be refined. There can be no guarantee, therefore, that an intention appearing during negotiations has remained constant until the time of contracting.

- In such circumstances, it is thought safer to rely on the words of the document alone, since statements made in pre-contract negotiations will be necessarily more subjective.

- There is a further argument that admission of such evidence would lead to uncertainty and unpredictability in terms of interpretation, which would add to the costs involved in any dispute and litigation.

- It is also argued that if negotiations are not excluded, there would be an adverse effect on third party rights, i.e. third parties taking an assignment of the contract or relying upon it as security could not be safe in making assumptions as to meaning without knowing what had taken place during these negotiations between the original parties.

6.5.5.2 Should 'the exclusionary rule' be reconsidered and pre-contractual negotiations become admissible as an aid to construction?

The UNIDROIT Principles of International Commercial Contracts (PICC, Art. 4.3) permits reference to prior negotiations when determining the 'common intention of the parties', so it might be thought that a similar approach should be acceptable in English law. Lord Nicholls, in his Chancery Bar Lecture 'My Kingdom for a horse: the meaning of words' (2005) 121 LQR 577, was critical of the non-admissibility of evidence of pre-contractual negotiations, considering this evidence to be inadmissible only if 'unhelpful', and that it would only be 'unhelpful' where the evidence merely illustrates separate positions and aspirations of the negotiating parties. However, if the evidence was that the parties had reached some agreement during the negotiations regarding the meaning of a word or phrase or of a particular clause, then evidence of this would be helpful as, to use the words employed by Lord Nicholls at p. 583, 'the best evidence of all'.

The more general question of whether the 'exclusionary principle' should be abandoned came before the House of Lords in *Chartbrook Ltd v Persimmon Homes Ltd* [2009] UKHL 38, [2009] 1 AC 1101 (see **6.5.4.1**). The House of Lords, having found in favour of Persimmon on the construction issue, made *obiter* observations as a response to an argument that account should be taken of the pre-contractual negotiations, particularly two letters that Persimmon claimed supported its interpretation of the agreement. The main ground discussed for permitting such evidence to be admissible was that, in some cases, such evidence would clearly be 'helpful' and 'relevant'. Lord Hoffmann put it thus, at [32]:

> Among the dirt of aspirations, proposals and counterproposals there may gleam the gold of a genuine consensus on some aspect of the transaction expressed in terms which would influence an objective observer in construing the language used by the parties in their final agreement. Why should the court deny itself the assistance of this material in deciding what the parties must be taken to have meant?

His Lordship considered that since 'the rule of inadmissibility has been established for a very long time' and by a consistent line of authority, and, at [41], 'there is no clearly established case for departing from the exclusionary rule', the fact that the rule might mean that 'parties are sometimes held bound by a contract in terms which, upon a full investigation of the course of negotiations, a reasonable observer would not have taken them to have intended' could be 'justified in the more general interest of economy and predictability in obtaining advice and adjudicating disputes', absent any empirical evidence pointing in the opposite direction. In any event, there were 'the safety nets' of rectification and estoppel by convention, i.e. the parties may claim that, as a result of a mistake, the final contract does not represent their common intention as to the meaning that they intended their agreement to have (discussed at **3.4.1**). Alternatively, if the parties have negotiated an agreement upon a common assumption that particular words will bear a certain meaning, then estoppel may operate to prevent a claim that the words should be given a different meaning.

However, Lord Hoffmann was clear that although the exclusionary rule excluded evidence of pre-contractual negotiations for the purpose of interpreting the parties' intended meaning, such evidence was not thereby excluded if it were sought to be introduced for other purposes, e.g. to establish that an objective fact that might be relevant as background (or as part of the factual matrix) was known to the parties—see *Estor Ltd v Multifit (UK) Ltd* [2009] EWHC 2565 (TCC), [2010] CILL 2800, in which the court used pre-contractual information to identify the parties to the contract on this basis—and clearly such evidence was admissible to support a claim for rectification or estoppel; indeed, this was frequently used by parties to bring the excluded pre-contractual evidence before the court. This evidence was not an exception to the rule, but rather it operated outside the rule. This was also confirmed by the Supreme Court in *Oceanbulk Shipping and Trading SA v TMT Asia Ltd* [2010] UKSC 44, [2011] 1 AC 662, at [39], where Lord Clarke noted:

> Trial judges frequently have to distinguish between material which forms part of the pre-contractual negotiations which is part of the factual matrix and therefore admissible as an aid to interpretation and material which forms part of the pre-contractual negotiations but which is not part of the factual matrix and is not therefore admissible. This is often a straightforward task but sometimes it is not.

It follows that whereas objective facts communicated in pre-contractual negotiations are part of the factual matrix and are therefore admissible, anything subjective in those same pre-contractual negotiations is inadmissible.

In *Chartbrook*, Baroness Hale concluded that '[i]n the end abolition may be the only workable legislative solution', but in the meantime the courts could determine in which cases such evidence is 'helpful', possibly by looking at whether, in terms of the law of rectification, a 'consensus' had been reached in the negotiations. If there were no consensus, then the evidence of the negotiations would necessarily be 'unhelpful'. There is something superficially attractive in this solution, assuming that it is intended to apply beyond rectification cases. However, it is less attractive when the position of third parties is considered, since they are unlikely to have knowledge of prior negotiations, let alone of whether those negotiations reached any consensus on the meaning of particular words or phrases.

Chartbrook has led to a growing relationship between principles of construction and the remedy of rectification in how cases are pleaded: see **3.4.1** and *Oceanbulk Shipping and Trading SA v TMT Asia Ltd*, at [45], where Lord Clarke noted that they are 'closely related'. The evidence of pre-contractual negotiations can be put before a court by inserting a claim for rectification and, as Baroness Hale admitted in *Chartbrook*, it is then difficult to put this evidence entirely from the mind for other purposes.

In *Dean & Dean Solicitors (a firm) v Dionissiou-Moussaoui* [2011] EWCA Civ 1331, at [20], Stanley Burnton LJ summarized the relationship:

> If a document is contractual, then in the absence of a plea of rectification, or an allegation that it has been replaced or revoked by a subsequent agreement, the role of the court is to construe the document. If it is alleged that the written agreement mistakenly failed to reflect an anterior oral agreement, so that the written agreement falls to be rectified, that earlier oral agreement must be clearly pleaded and proved. In the absence of a plea of rectification, communications preceding the written agreement may provide context and background, but they cannot be substituted for the terms of the written agreement itself.

6.5.6 Prior contracts

It is accepted that evidence of prior contracts, as opposed to prior contractual negotiations in this contract, is always admissible: *HIH Casualty & General Insurance Ltd v New Hampshire Co.* [2001] EWCA Civ 735, [2001] 2 Lloyd's Rep 161, at [83], and *KPMG LLP v Network Rail Infrastructure Ltd* [2007] EWCA Civ 363, [2007] Bus LR 1336.

6.5.7 Deleted words in contracts and documents

In *Mopani Copper Mines plc v Millennium Underwriting Ltd* [2008] EWHC 1331 (Comm), [2008] 2 All ER (Comm) 976, [2008] 1 CLC 992, at [120], Christopher Clarke J considered that where there was ambiguity in the words that remained in a document, it was legitimate to look at deleted words in a document to determine from the fact of deletion what the parties had decided that they had *not* agreed. Equally, deleted words in a printed document or form may resolve the ambiguity of a neighbouring paragraph that remains. This principle is said not to offend the 'exclusionary principle' relating to pre-contractual negotiations. However, in *Health & Case Management Ltd v The Physiotherapy Network Ltd* [2018] EWHC 869 (QB), Mr Justice Nicklin stated that even though deleted words are admissible 'in principle', he added that 'some caution needs to be adopted in determining what assistance can really be derived from the deletion of certain words from a subsequent contract' (at [72]). On the facts, the deletion played no material significance to the meaning of the clause.

6.5.8 The relevance of other documents

From the above, it should be clear that the courts will usually restrict themselves to interpreting the contract in the light of the documents exchanged between the parties. However, in certain limited circumstances, the content of other documents may well be relevant, such as the FSA's regulatory policy as illustrated by *BNY Mellon Corporate Trustee Services Ltd v LBG Capital No. 1 plc* [2016] UKSC 29, [2017] 1 All ER 497. In this case, which involved the construction of a trust deed which governed the terms of a negotiable instrument, Lord Neuberger (with whom Mance and Toulson LJJ agreed) stated (at [30]) that, in this case, it accorded with 'good sense' to take into account 'the general thrust and effect of the FSA regulatory material published in 2008 and 2009'.

6.5.9 Subsequent conduct is generally inadmissible

Authority for the principle that subsequent conduct is generally inadmissible can be found in the decision in *James Miller & Partners Ltd v Whitworth Street Estates (Manchester) Ltd* [1970] AC 572. This is because conduct of a party after making the contract does not assist in objectively identifying the meaning that the parties attributed to particular words at the time that they made the contract. Subsequent conduct by one party may, however, provide the basis for an estoppel: *per* Viscount Dilhorne at p. 611.

MULTIPLE-CHOICE QUESTIONS

Test your knowledge by trying this chapter's **multiple-choice questions**:
www.oup.com/uk/poole

FURTHER READING

Morgan, *Great Debates in Contract Law,* 2nd edn (Palgrave Macmillan, 2015), ch. 4.

Content

Bradgate, 'Unreasonable standard terms' (1997) 60 MLR 582.

Peel, 'Terms implied in fact' (2016) 132 LQR 531.

Kramer, 'Implication in fact as an instance of contractual interpretation' [2004] CLJ 384.

Law Commission Report No. 154, *Law of Contract: The Parol Evidence Rule* (Cmnd 9700, 1986).

Macdonald, 'Incorporation of contract terms by a "consistent course of dealing"' (1988) 8 LS 48.

Macdonald, 'The duty to give notice of unusual contract terms' [1988] JBL 375.

Macdonald, 'The emperor's old clauses: unincorporated clauses, misleading terms and the Unfair Terms in Consumer Contracts Regulations' (1999) 58 CLJ 413.

McCaughran, 'Implied terms: the journey of the man on the Clapham omnibus' [2011] CLJ 607.

Peden, 'Policy concerns behind implication of terms in law' (2001) 117 LQR 459.

Peden and Carter, 'Incorporation of terms by signature: *L'Estrange* rules!' (2005) 21 JCL 96.

Wedderburn, 'Collateral contracts' [1959] CLJ 58.

Implied terms

Davies, 'Contract formation and implied terms' (2018) 77(1) CLJ 22.

Goh, 'Lost but found again: the traditional tests for implied terms in fact' [2016] JBL 231.

Kennedy, 'Unnecessary complications' [2016] LMCLQ 90.

Peel, 'Terms implied in fact' (2017) 132 LQR 531.

Interpretation

Andrews, 'Interpretation of contract and commercial common sense: do not overplay the useful criterion' (2017) 76(1) CLJ 36.

Calnan, *Principles of Contract Interpretation* (Oxford University Press, 2013).

Carter and Courtney, 'Unexpressed intention and contract construction' (2017) 37(2) OJLS 326.

Davies, 'The meaning of commercial contracts' in Davies and Pila (eds.), *The Jurisprudence of Lord Hoffmann* (Hart Publishing, 2015).

Gee, 'The interpretation of commercial contracts' (2001) 117 LQR 358.

Grabiner, 'The iterative process of contractual interpretation' (2012) 128 LQR 41.

Havelock, 'The "unitary exercise" of contractual interpretation' (2017) 76 LQR 486.

Havelock, 'Some fallacies concerning the law of contract interpretation: a reply to Prof Laughlan' [2018] LMCLQ 40.

Kramer, 'Common sense principles of contract interpretation (and how we've been using them all along)' (2003) 23 OJLS 173.

McKendrick, 'The legal effect of an Anti-oral Variation clause' (2017) 32 Journal of International Banking Law and Regulation 439.

McLaughlan, 'Continuity not change in contract interpretation?' (2017) 133 LQR 546.

McLaughlan, 'Some fallacies in contract interpretation' [2017] LMCLQ 506.

McMeel, 'The rise of commercial construction in contract law' [1998] LMCLQ 382.

McMeel, 'Prior negotiations and subsequent conduct: the next step forward for contractual interpretation?' (2003) 119 LQR 272.

McMeel, *The Construction of Contracts: Interpretation, Implication and Rectification*, 3rd edn (Oxford University Press, 2017).

Morgan, 'Contracting for self-denial: on enforcing "No oral Modification" clauses' (2017) 76 CLJ 589.

Lord Nicholls, 'My kingdom for a horse: the meaning of words' (2005) 121 LQR 577.

O'Sullivan, 'Unconsidered modification' (2017) 133 LQR 191.

Shmilovits, 'Amending a contract contrary to its provisions' [2016] LMCLQ 363.

Shmilovits, 'Testing the limits of interpretation' [2016] LMCLQ 20.

Staughton, 'How do the courts interpret commercial contracts?' [1999] CLJ 303.

Chapter 7

Exemption clauses and unfair contract terms

SUMMARY OF THE ISSUES

- An exemption clause seeks either to exclude a party's liability for breach or to limit that liability to a specified amount. Exemption clauses may alternatively seek to exclude or limit the remedies that would otherwise be available for breach, or seek to deny that any breach of contract or breach of a duty of care has arisen.

- Although such clauses have benefits, especially in commercial contracts, in allocating risks between the parties and avoiding duplicate insurance cover, both the courts and Parliament have nevertheless sought to control their use.

- To be enforceable, the exemption clause must:
    1. be incorporated as a term;
    2. cover the loss that has occurred in the circumstances in which it occurred; and
    3. not be rendered unenforceable by the applicable legislation—the Unfair Contract Terms Act (UCTA) 1977 for B2B (business to business) contracts, and Part 2 of the Consumer Rights Act 2015 for B2C 'trader' and 'consumer' contracts. The Consumer Rights Act has a broader scope of application since it regulates unfair terms generally (with the exception of so-called 'core terms'). The UCTA 1977 only regulates exemption clauses (as defined by the Act, see **7.5.1.2**).

- Incorporation of terms was considered at **6.3**. This chapter examines the question of construction of the clause, and the legislative regulation of exemption clauses and unfair terms.

- Prior to the first piece of legislative regulation of exemption clauses (i.e. UCTA 1977), the courts construed exemption clauses very strictly to protect consumers (who were then—and until the Consumer Rights Act (CRA) 2015—also covered by UCTA 1977). Such a strict approach is no longer necessary, because the CRA 2015 can fulfil this purpose, and nowadays clauses are construed on their natural and ordinary meaning to see if they cover what has happened. Some of the restrictive construction devices may still be relied upon, e.g. negligence construction, but the courts are increasingly willing to adopt a less technical and more contextual approach to such construction, reflecting the general approach to contractual interpretation (see **6.5**).

- For B2B, UCTA 1977 will render the clause in question either totally unenforceable in the circumstances or enforceable only if shown to be reasonable. The applicable outcome is determined by the liability that it is sought to exclude or limit and, on occasion, by the type of loss that has occurred.

»

- For B2C, CRA 2015 Part 2 provides regulation of unfair terms in consumer contracts. A term is unfair if 'contrary to the requirement of good faith it causes a significant imbalance in the parties' rights and obligations arising under the contract' to the detriment of the consumer.

7.1 Introduction

7.1.1 Control of the substantive content of contracts

This chapter focuses on the regulation of 'substantive unfairness' in contracts. The parties' ability to control the content of their contracts is therefore not unrestricted, and both the courts and Parliament—to implement European directives—have interfered to prevent the inclusion and use of terms that are regarded as 'unfair'.

Clauses that purport to exclude or to limit liability for breach of contract are the most common form of what are referred to in this chapter as 'exemption clauses'. It is important to note that exemption clauses come in many different forms (see **7.1.3.1**); the applicable rules nevertheless remain generally the same.

The 'restraint of trade' doctrine and measures controlling anti-competitive agreements (discussed in **Chapter 16**) are further examples of the possible control of the content of contracts. This control is based both on reasonableness as between the parties and broader considerations of public policy, i.e. what is reasonable in the public interest. There may also be a broader doctrine of unconscionability—based on the principle in *Fry v Lane* (1888) 40 Ch D 312 (discussed at **15.3.4**)—that will affect contractual content. Finally, the 'penalty rule' and rules governing relief from forfeiture (discussed at **9.6**) also represent an attempt to regulate contractual content.

7.1.2 Standard-form contracts and exemption clauses

Since classical contract law saw contractual liability as something created by the operation of the will of the parties, rather than as liability imposed by law, it was inevitable that the classical law should accept the power of the parties to modify as they saw fit the nature of the liability created. Thus, while the usual result of the breach of a promise, which had been duly incorporated in a valid contract, was, at the very least, to create a secondary obligation to pay damages in compensation for any loss suffered (*Photo Production Ltd v Securicor Transport Ltd* [1980] AC 827, per Lord Diplock at p. 849), it was open to the parties to agree to contractual 'promises' that did not have this usual result. The more common means of modifying the usual liability were to exclude any obligation to pay compensation or to limit the amount of compensation payable.

Such exemption clauses are not necessarily bad and the classical law was not excessively naive in allowing parties to abdicate all responsibility for their promises. The classical law *assumed* (in a way that today might be frequently challenged) that all parties to contractual negotiations would bargain freely, would be best placed to know their own interests, and would agree to such terms *only* if some, not necessarily immediately apparent, benefit would accrue from so doing. These assumptions remain valid where the parties do in fact deal with each other on an equal footing. *In that situation, typified by the commercial contract, the exemption clause is an important device for allocating the risks of the contract between the parties.*

> → **EXAMPLE**
>
> Imagine a contract for the supply of machinery that depends upon the availability of raw materials from abroad. Both parties know that there is a slight risk that the usual, low-cost supplier will be slow to supply because of the unstable political conditions in its country. Alternative supplies are available at much higher costs. The seller of the machinery may quote two prices: let us say £2,500 for a guaranteed delivery date, by using the high-cost raw materials; let us say £1,500 using the low-cost raw materials, but subject to an exclusion of liability for late delivery. The buyer may then choose which contract is preferable, knowing that the seller will not agree to bear the risk of late delivery if the cheaper contract is chosen.

There is no reason for the law to interfere with this use of exemption clauses and, indeed, to do so would undermine the economic basis of the parties' agreement.

Nevertheless, it is generally accepted today that there are situations in which exemption clauses are not freely negotiated, at which point the law may seek to interfere. These situations usually involve standard-form contracts: contracts entered into on the basis of a standard set of contractual terms contained in a document drawn up by one of the parties (think of your contract with your phone provider). Standard-form contracts (or contracts of adhesion) are not necessarily bad. They represent the reaction of lawyers to the increase in contractual activity engendered by the Industrial Revolution. As goods were mass produced, it became much more convenient to use standardized contracts ('mass produced' contracts), since the circumstances of sales were normally very similar to one another, meaning that the costs of individual drafting could be avoided. It became normal practice to include one or more exemption clauses in such standardized contracts. Sometimes, the inclusion of these clauses reflected the practice of a particular trade in the allocation of risks between buyers and sellers, and so was entirely legitimate. Standard-form contracts, however, present little choice to the party who has not drawn up the document (especially if that person is a consumer). If that person wants the product, they may have to accept the terms drawn up by the other party; if the terms are unacceptable, that person will be resigned to not obtaining the product from this source.

Thus standard-form contracts may be used to *impose* an exclusion or limitation of liability that has not been negotiated and for which the person whose normal contractual rights are diminished has received no alternative benefit. *The imposition of such exemption clauses may be particularly harmful in consumer contracts, in which the disequilibrium between the bargaining positions of the parties may be substantial and where the consumer may have no alternative but to accept the terms if such exemptions are commonplace throughout the particular industry, as is often the case. If the clauses are not negotiated, this has increasingly been taken as a justification for intervention.* Accordingly, judicial attitudes to exemption clauses have hardened over the last hundred years, although it is still the case that individually negotiated contracts containing exemption clauses are generally assumed not to be harmful.

The attitude to standard-form contracts may be summarized by reference to the speech of Lord Diplock in the House of Lords in *Schroeder Music Publishing Co. Ltd v Macaulay* [1974] 1 WLR 1308 (p 1316).

- Standard-form contracts used for convenience to express common commercial agreements, and which do so in terms normal to such contracts, are presumed to be fair and reasonable.

- Standard-form contracts in consumer transactions, and in other situations in which one party is said to have no alternative but to contract on the terms offered if that person is to contract at all, are not presumed to be fair and reasonable; rather, they are viewed as the product of the superior bargaining position of one of the parties.

The courts often suspect that that superior bargaining position is being exploited at the cost of the other party, and for that reason will do everything in their power to avoid the consequences of such clauses. That position has been reinforced by legislation (see **7.4**).

7.1.3 Types and nature of the exemption clause

7.1.3.1 Types of exemption

It would be impossible, and fruitless, to catalogue every known type of exemption clause. The wit and invention of contracts' draftsmen were fuelled by the courts' attempts to control such clauses, and resulted in the regular discovery of new and ingenious forms of exemption clause, to which the courts subsequently had to react.

- Most common are the clauses purporting to exclude liability completely for part at least of what would otherwise be included in the contractual undertaking (e.g. excluding liability for consequential losses), and those clauses limiting liability to a particular sum (e.g. the price payable under the contract).

- Other common forms are those that limit the remedy available either by imposing a short time limit during which claims for breach must be made, or by imposing onerous conditions on obtaining the remedy (such as payment of costs of transport of defective goods to and from the supplier's place of business).

- More difficult to control are clauses that, rather than exempting liability for breach, purport to modify the performance obligation, so that no breach occurs (see the discussion at **7.5.3.2** of terms that modify expected contractual obligations) or purport to deny any actionable misrepresentation in relation to pre-contractual statements which induced the contract, i.e. non-reliance clauses (discussed at **14.7.2.1**).

7.1.3.2 The nature of exemption clauses

It is possible, and arguably more logical, to treat an exemption clause like any other term of the contract, so that it operates to define the obligations of the parties. This was the approach adopted by Lord Diplock in *Photo Production Ltd v Securicor Transport Ltd* [1980] AC 827. However, the generally accepted view is that such clauses may operate as a defence to the liability that would otherwise exist. This is artificial in that it involves construing all of the other terms of the contract to identify the contractual obligations and duties owed, and then separately considering whether the exemption clause operates to exclude or limit that liability.

7.1.3.3 Exemption clauses as defences to liability

There is no rule or doctrine whereby an exemption clause is declared unenforceable simply because it is unfair or unreasonable: *Photo Production Ltd v Securicor Transport Ltd* [1980] AC 827 (see **7.3.3**). For many years, therefore, the courts' hostility to such clauses found expression in the application, often in strict or strained terms, of devices of the general law of contract to the particular problem of exemption clauses. In theory, they are still applicable despite the enactment of statutory controls on certain exemption clauses; in practice, in many instances, the courts adopted a more realistic and less artificial approach to the application of these devices following more direct means of control where these are available. However, more recently, there is a tendency to rely upon the principle in *Interfoto Picture Library Ltd v Stiletto Visual Programmes Ltd* [1989] QB 433, requiring a higher standard of incorporation for certain exemption clauses considered to be onerous or unusual (discussed at **6.3.1.4**).

Generally, to be able to rely upon an exemption clause as a defence to liability, the party seeking to rely upon the clause has the burden of establishing that the exemption clause was incorporated and covers the liability that has occurred in the circumstances in which it occurred. The enforceability of the clause can then only be defeated if the clause is rendered unenforceable by statute.

7.2 Incorporation

The law on incorporation of written terms (see **6.2.2** and **6.3**) has developed almost exclusively through judicial attempts to avoid the impact of exemption clauses.

In the absence of signature, any clause not reasonably brought to the notice of the offeree before the time of acceptance of the offer (and thus the making of the contract) is not incorporated into the contract: see e.g. *Thornton v Shoe Lane Parking Ltd* [1971] 2 QB 163 (see **6.3.1.3**). Through this principle, there can be no reliance upon contract terms contained in orders or invoices where reasonable notice of their existence was not given to the contracting party when entering the agreement, *although it does not follow that the other party needs to have read these documents or to know of the terms.* Furthermore, a higher degree of notice is required for unusual or onerous terms to prevent reliance on terms not 'fairly and reasonably' brought to the attention of the other party: *Interfoto Picture Library Ltd v Stiletto Visual Programmes Ltd* [1989] QB 433 (see **6.3.1.4**). Notably, in *Interfoto*, Bingham LJ considered (at p. 439F) this to be an aspect of English law developing 'piecemeal solutions to demonstrated problems of unfairness' in a way that achieved the same result as the doctrine of good faith (or 'fair and open dealing') in other jurisdictions.

7.3 Construction

7.3.1 Devices of interpretation

At one time, construction was the final mechanism open to a court that sought to protect the consumer from the consequences of an exemption clause in a contract. On occasions, therefore, there is clear evidence of rather strained and artificial constructions of such clauses particularly in the consumer context, the classic example being the Court of Appeal's decision in *Hollier v Rambler*

Motors (AMC) Ltd [1972] 2 QB 71 on the interpretation of the following clause: 'the company is not responsible for damage caused to customers' cars on the premises'. The court held unanimously that the clause did not exclude liability for negligence (and therefore the company was liable for damages to the owner of the car) but instead was to be read as a statement of fact in the nature of a warning (see Salmon LJ at pp. 81G, 82E; and Stamp LJ at p. 83C–D). Such artificial interpretations are no longer required as such clauses are regulated by statutory provisions and the basic construction test propounded by Lord Bridge in *George Mitchell (Chesterhall) Ltd v Finney Lock Seeds* [1983] 2 AC 803, at p. 811, is that the clause is to be construed on its natural and ordinary meaning to see if it covers what has happened. The House of Lords recognized that strict construction should not be 'strained construction': *per* Lord Wilberforce in *Ailsa Craig Fishing Co. Ltd v Malvern Fishing Co. Ltd* [1983] 1 WLR 964, approved by Lord Bridge in *George Mitchell (Chesterhall) Ltd v Finney Lock Seeds Ltd*. Although this approach was overturned on appeal in *Kudos Catering (UK) Ltd v Manchester Central Convention Complex Ltd* [2013] EWCA Civ 38, [2013] 2 Lloyd's Rep 270 (discussed at **6.5.2**), and the scope of an exclusion clause interpreted so as to give effect to what 'must have been the parties' commercial intentions', *Kudos* must now be read in light of the approach to contractual interpretation adopted by the Supreme Court in *Arnold v Britton* [2015] UKSC 36, [2015] AC 1619, and *Wood v Capita* [2017] UKSC 24, [2017] AC 117 discussed at **6.5.4**. Exclusion clauses follow the same rules as contractual interpretation as recently reinforced in *Interactive E Solutions JLT v O3B Africa Ltd* [2018] EWCA Civ 62, [2018] BLR 167 (at [14]). Yet, the courts still can use a number of interpretation devices to fit the construction to the context of the contract. The interpretation can therefore be strict, particularly for a consumer contract where the courts wish to protect the consumer.

7.3.1.1 The courts will not imply any exemption greater than that contained in the words used

In *Andrews Bros. (Bournemouth) Ltd v Singer & Co. Ltd* [1934] 1 KB 17, the claimants contracted to purchase 'new' cars from the defendant company. A contractual clause excluded 'all conditions, warranties and liabilities implied by statute, common law or otherwise'. One of the cars had done a substantial mileage and was clearly not 'new'. The exclusion clause did not protect the defendant, since it excluded implied terms (the relevant one in this context was s. 13 SGA 1893 of goods to match their description, while the requirement that the cars be 'new' was an express term of the contract.

7.3.1.2 Clauses are construed *contra proferentem*

Where the meaning of an exemption clause is ambiguous, that ambiguity will be resolved against the party seeking to rely on the clause (the *proferens*), the courts adopting a meaning unfavourable to that party. Although this rule rests on the existence of ambiguity in the meaning of the exemption clause, the courts have been resourceful in finding such ambiguity to cut down the impact of a clause.

> In **Houghton v Trafalgar Insurance Co. Ltd** [1954] 1 QB 247, a car insurance policy did not give protection to cover damage occurring when the car was conveying 'any load in excess of that for which it was constructed'. An accident occurred when the car, designed to carry five people, was carrying six. The Court of Appeal considered that 'load' was ambiguous and construed it against the insurers to limit it to excess weight rather than excess passengers. It followed that there was valid insurance in place.

The *contra proferentem* rule is expressly applicable to consumer contracts in the Consumer Rights Act (CRA) 2015, s. 69:

> If doubt about the meaning of a written term, the interpretation which is most favourable to the consumer shall prevail.

However, this principle is excluded from operation in respect of pre-emptive challenges to clauses in standard forms by the Competition and Markets Authority (CMA) or other 'qualifying bodies' (CRA 2015, s. 69(2) and see the discussion of pre-emptive challenges at **7.6.8**).

7.3.1.3 Negligence construction: exclusion clauses

In a particular example of the operation of the contra proferentem *rule, the courts' policy is to limit the scope of exclusion clauses (as opposed to limitation clauses) by restricting the scope of the exclusion.* In particular, the courts have shown themselves unwilling to extend the scope of an exclusion clause to liabilities other than contractual (unless it is expressly stated to cover them), thereby ensuring that the claimant has an alternative remedy in tort to which the clause does not apply.

For purported exemptions from liability for negligence, this policy is given effect in the test proposed by Lord Morton in *Canada Steamship Lines v The King* [1952] AC 192, at p. 208:

> (ii) If the clause contains language which expressly exempts the person in whose favour it is made (hereafter called 'the *proferens*') from the consequence of the negligence of his own servants, effect must be given to that provision . . .
>
> (iii) If there is no express reference to negligence, the court must consider whether the words are wide enough, in their ordinary meaning, to cover negligence on the part of the servants of the *proferens* . . .
>
> (iv) If the words used are wide enough for the above purpose, the court must then consider whether 'the head of damage may be based on some ground other than that of negligence' . . . The 'other ground' must not be so fanciful or remote that the *proferens* cannot be supposed to have desired protection against it; but subject to that qualification . . . the existence of a possible head of damage other than that of negligence is fatal to the *proferens* even if the words are *prima facie* wide enough to cover negligence on the part of his servants.

Before explaining this construction device, two issues must be considered.

1. First, a note of caution on the application of these construction principles. In the speeches of the House of Lords in *HIH Casualty & General Insurance Ltd v Chase Manhattan Bank* [2003] UKHL 6, [2003] 1 All ER (Comm) 349, their Lordships confirmed that Lord Morton's guidelines would need to be read in light of the more contextual approach to contractual interpretation consequent on the principles developed in *Investors Compensation Scheme Ltd v West Bromwich Building Society* [1998] 1 WLR 896 (discussed at **6.5.2**). This can be linked to the need to reflect 'the presumed intentions of the parties': see *Greenwich Millennium Ltd v Essex Services plc* [2014] EWCA Civ 960, [2014] 1 WLR 3517, per Jackson LJ at [94], stating that *Canada Steamship* is based on the presumed intentions of the parties which must reflect the commercial context of the contract. It followed that: '[I]n the case of a construction contract a failure by the indemnitee to spot defects perpetrated by its contractor or subcontractor should not ordinarily defeat the operation of an indemnity clause even if that clause fails expressly to encompass damage caused by the negligence of that indemnitee.' This decision needs to be read following the subsequent decision of the Supreme Court in *Arnold v Britton* [2015] UKSC 36, [2015] AC 1619 (see **6.5.3**) and *Wood v Capita Insurance Services Ltd* [2017] UKSC 24; [2017] AC 117 (see **6.5.4**) reiterating the unitary process of contract interpretation. What is clear, however, is the fact that Lord Morton's guidelines are no more than guidelines and are not to be applied mechanistically (*Lictor Anstalt v MIR Steel UK Ltd* [2012] EWCA Civ 1397, [2013] 2 All ER (Comm) 54, [2013] CP Rep 7,

per Rimer LJ, at [35]). In *Lictor Anstalt* the Court of Appeal held that the guidelines did not produce an automatic result; rather, the role of the court is to interpret the contract in the context in which it was made. In the same vein, the most recent doubt arises from the Court of Appeal in *Persimmon Homes Ltd v Ove Arup & Partners Ltd* [2017] EWCA Civ 373, [2017] BLR 417. Jackson LJ, with whom Moylan and Beatson LJJ agreed, noted that the aforementioned passage of Lord Morton in Canada Steamship had been the object of a 'long running debate . . . over the last 66 years' (at [55]) and the question therefore arose as to 'the extent to which it is good law' (at [55]). His lordship continued: 'my impression is that, at any rate in commercial contracts, the Canada Steamship guidelines (in so far as they survive) are now more relevant to indemnity clauses than to exemption clauses' (at [56]) (an indemnity clause is a clause whereby a party undertakes to indemnify the other for a certain type of loss the other will suffer). In consequence, they were 'of very little assistance in the present case' (at [59]). Moylan LJ emphasized that in such contracts, the most important element is the allocation of risks. His lordship stated that 'in major construction contracts, the parties commonly agree how they will allocate the risks between themselves and who will insure against what. Exemption clauses are part of the construction apparatus for distributing risk' (at [57]). He then concluded that 'there is no need to approach such clauses with horror or with a mindset determined to cut them down. Contractors and consultants who accept large risks will charge for doing so . . . contractors and consultants who accept lesser degree of risk will presumably reflect that in the fees which they agree' (at [57]). This appears consistent with the prevailing approach to interpretation generally (see the discussion of *Wood v Capita*, **6.5.4**). The position of allocation of risk is particularly important where there are insuring provisions in the contract, and the general assumption will be that if party A is required to insure on behalf of both party A and party B against loss, then the agreement by implication means that party A is required to look to the insurers if a loss occurs and has no claim against party B, as illustrated in *Gard Marine and Energy Ltd v China National Chartering Co. Ltd* [2017] UKSC 35, [2017] 1 WLR 1793. Therefore the guidelines do not have the status of a set of rigid rules and are not to be applied in a way that would produce a result at odds with the parties' intentions in relation to the relevant background. Nevertheless, it remains that clear words will be required to exclude a person's liability for the consequences of their own negligence and the starting point must be the words the parties have used.

2. Further, to understand Lord Morton's guidelines, it is necessary to appreciate what is meant by 'liability' in negligence in this context. Contractual obligations require one of two standards of performance (discussed at **8.2.1.1**), so that either:

   – contractual liability may be strict (absolute obligations); or
   – contractual liability may be qualified (obligations imposing a qualified contractual duty to exercise reasonable care and skill).

Negligence liability, for the purposes of exemption clauses, will include breach of a duty of care in tort, but also includes breach of these qualified contractual obligations, i.e. obligations imposing a contractual duty to exercise reasonable care and skill such as those found in s. 13 of the Supply of Goods and Services Act 1982.

The *Canada Steamship* principle embodies the basic judicial policy of limiting the scope of *exclusion* clauses by restricting their operation so that, generally, they exclude only strict contractual liability.

> **! KEY POINT**
>
> To extend to exclude liability in negligence, the clause in question would need to extend expressly to negligence liability, e.g. by using the word 'negligence' or a synonym. If this is done, then effect will be given to this wording, and the exclusion clause will exclude both strict contractual liability *and* negligence liability, as relevant.
>
> If there is no express reference to negligence, but the words used in the clause are wide enough to cover negligence liability, the exclusion will not cover negligence liability if some other liability to which the clause could extend on the facts, such as strict contractual liability apply.

The classic example of the application of this rule of construction is *White v John Warwick & Co. Ltd* [1953] 1 WLR 1285.

> The claimant was injured when the saddle on a bicycle hired from the defendants tipped and he fell on the road. The contract of hire exempted the defendants from liability for any personal injuries to the hirers of bicycles, but made no express mention of negligence liability. Without the clause, the claimant might have succeeded against the defendants either for breach of contract or for the defendants' negligence. (There was a breach of the strict contractual obligation to supply a bicycle fit for the purpose and also liability in negligence owing to the failure to take care to ensure that the bicycle supplied was safe.) Since both types of liability had arisen on the facts, the Court of Appeal held that the exemption clause was effective to exclude liability in contract only, so that the claimant's action in negligence succeeded despite the clause.

Although the *Canada Steamship* test is a rule of construction, so that each case is treated on its particular facts, some common threads emerge.

7.3.1.3.1 *Negligence expressly mentioned*

In accordance with Lord Morton's first test in *Canada Steamship Lines v The King* [1952] AC 192, to exclude liability for negligence as well as liability for breach of contract, express words ('negligence' or a synonym of negligence) must be used: see e.g. *Monarch Airlines Ltd v London Luton Airport Ltd* [1997] CLC 698, in which the words 'neglect or default' extended to exclude liability for negligence and breach of statutory duty. It might be considered sensible therefore for the drafter to extend the scope of the exclusion clause to cover liability in negligence in express terms. However, as Steyn LJ made clear in *E. E. Caledonia Ltd v Orbit Valve Co. plc* [1994] 1 WLR 1515, at p. 1523, it might not make commercial sense to insert such a reference, because it would tend to frighten off the other party. Thus, '[o]missions of express reference to negligence tend to be deliberate'.

Since the courts' policy is to require very clear words indeed before permitting a party to avoid liability for the consequences of their own negligence, a strict interpretation is evident both in relation to express references to negligence and whether the clause is capable, on the basis of the words used, of applying to negligence liability. An example is provided by the Court of Appeal decision in *E. E. Caledonia Ltd v Orbit Valve Co. plc*.

> The claimants made a payment to the estate of an engineer following his death in a fire on the claimants' oil platform. The claimants sought to recover this payment from the defendants (the engineer's employers) under the terms of an indemnity. The indemnity applied in respect of any claim, demand, cause of action, loss, expense, or liability arising from the death of such an employee in the performance

of the contract. The death had been found to be the result of the claimants' negligence and a result of their breaches of health and safety regulations (i.e. breach of statutory duty, so that liability was strict). The Court of Appeal held that the indemnity did not expressly cover negligence and that very clear words would be required in order for it to operate to protect a party from the consequences of that party's own negligence. Furthermore, because there was another liability (breach of statutory duty), the indemnity could not extend to cover the negligence. (On the facts, the Court of Appeal also held that the indemnity did not cover the breach of statutory duty, because it amounted to a provision allocating full responsibility to each party for the consequences of its own actions.)

7.3.1.3.2 *Negligence the only liability on the facts*

Although not discussed by Lord Morton in *Canada Steamship Lines v The King* [1952] AC 192, it was held that an exemption clause must be construed to cover negligence liability, despite the absence of any express reference to negligence, if the clause's words are wide enough to cover negligence and negligence is the only liability that arises on the facts. (This would appear to follow from Lord Morton's point (iv) quoted above—see **7.3.1.3**.)

In **Alderslade v Hendon Laundry Ltd** [1945] 1 KB 189, the claimant sent items to the laundry that were not returned. The contract contained a clause restricting recovery for lost items to 20 times the laundering charge. Since the laundry's only liability for lost items lay in negligence (breach of a duty to take care), the limitation clause was redundant unless applicable to such liability. Therefore the Court of Appeal held that the defendant was able to rely on the clause to limit its liability.

In *Macquarie Internationale Investments Ltd v Glencore (UK) Ltd* [2008] EWHC 1716 (Comm), [2008] 2 CLC 223, whilst Walker J accepted the contextual approach to construction of exemption clauses in *HIH Casualty & General Insurance Ltd v Chase Manhattan Bank* [2003] UKHL 6, [2003] 1 All ER (Comm) 349, his finding that the clause was intended to cover negligence also matched the application of the *Canada Steamship* principles, since although negligence was not used explicitly, the words were wide enough to cover negligence and it was the only envisaged liability on the facts.

7.3.1.4 **The construction of limitation clauses**

Generally, the approach of the courts to limitation clauses, as opposed to total exclusion clauses, has been more generous and such clauses tend to be construed more favourably. In particular, to limit liability for negligence, the test is only that the clause should be 'most clearly and unambiguously expressed': *per* Lord Wilberforce in *Ailsa Craig Fishing Co. Ltd v Malvern Fishing Co. Ltd* [1983] 1 WLR 964, at p. 966.

Lord Wilberforce set out, at p. 966H, the basis for this favourable treatment:

Clauses of limitation are not regarded by the courts with the same hostility as clauses of exclusion: this is because they must be related to other contractual terms, in particular to the risks to which the defending party may be exposed, the remuneration which he receives, and possibly also the opportunity of the other party to insure.

This distinction in treatment was subsequently endorsed at the highest level, e.g. by Lord Bridge in *George Mitchell v Finney Lock Seeds* [1983] 2 AC 803, at p. 814, by Steyn LJ in *E. E. Caledonia Ltd v Orbit Valve plc* [1994] 1 WLR 1515, at p. 1521, and by Evans LJ in *BHP Petroleum v British Steel* [2000] 2 All ER (Comm) 133, at p. 143. However, there are a large number of assumptions made about the circumstances in which limitation amounts are determined. It may be that more favourable treatment should be given at the stage of legislative regulation (and, in particular, the reasonableness/fairness and circumstances of drafting the clause), rather than at the construction stage. It is also possible to envisage a position in which the limitation amount is drafted at such a low figure that it is not substantially different in effect from a total exclusion clause: see e.g. comments by the High Court of Australia in *Darlington Futures Ltd v Delco Australia Pty Ltd* (1986) 161 CLR 500. It would be sensible, therefore, to avoid any blanket rule applicable to limitation clauses and to leave examination of such clauses to the context of the legislation.

7.3.1.5 Inconsistent with an oral undertaking

If the exemption clause is inconsistent with an oral undertaking given before or at the time that the contract was made, the exemption clause will be overridden and will not apply on the facts: see *J. Evans & Son (Portsmouth) Ltd v Andrea Merzario Ltd* [1976] 1 WLR 1078 (discussed at **6.2.1.2**), in which an oral undertaking that the goods would be stored below deck overrode the inconsistent printed conditions that would have rendered the oral promise illusory; see also *Couchman v Hill* [1947] KB 554.

In *Mendelssohn v Normand Ltd* [1970] 1 QB 177, a car park attendant had expressly promised to lock a car after parking it. This was considered to amount to an implied promise by the attendant to see that the contents of a car were safe, and the Court of Appeal held that this implied promise took priority over a printed exemption that was inconsistent with it.

7.3.2 Fraud or misrepresentation

As discussed at **6.2.2.1**, a party will be unable to rely on an exemption clause if that person has induced the other party to enter the contract by misrepresenting, fraudulently or otherwise, the meaning and effect of the clause.

In *Curtis v Chemical Cleaning and Dyeing Co.* [1951] 1 KB 805, the defendants sought to rely on a clause exempting liability for 'any damage, however arising', which had been represented to the claimant as only excluding liability for particular risks—namely, the beads and sequins on the wedding dress. The Court of Appeal held that the defendants could not rely on the clause to avoid liability when the dress was returned with a stain that had appeared during cleaning, since that was a different type of damage from that covered in their representation to the claimant concerning the scope of the clause.

7.3.3 Fundamental breach

In the 1950s, it was suggested that, *as a matter of law*, the courts would not allow an exemption clause to exclude or limit liability for a breach that deprived the non-breaching party of the main performance due to the party under the contract. The authority for such a rule was never very clearly explained, and such interference with the intentions of the parties as expressed in their contract was out of character for the common law. In *Suisse Atlantique Société d'Armement Maritime SA v NV Rotterdamsche Kolen Centrale* [1967] 1 AC 361, the House of Lords attempted to put an end to this alleged rule of law.

Suisse Atlantique Société d'Armement Maritime SA v NV Rotterdamsche Kolen Centrale involved the charter of a ship for two years' consecutive voyages between the United States and Europe. The owners were to be paid according to the number of voyages made. Eight round trips were made in all and the owners alleged that, but for breach of the terms of the contract relating to loading and unloading, a further six trips could have been made. The charterers said that the owners' damages were limited by a clause fixing compensation for delay to $1,000 per day. The owners claimed not to be bound by that clause, because the charterers had committed a fundamental breach of the contract.

Viscount Dilhorne said, at p. 392:

> In my view, it is not right to say that the law prohibits and nullifies a clause exempting or limiting liability for a fundamental breach or breach of a fundamental term. Such a rule of law would involve a restriction on freedom of contract and in the older cases I can find no trace of it.

There can be little doubt that the other members of the House of Lords agreed with this statement and intended their remarks to be consistent with it. Nevertheless, their attempt to bury the fundamental breach doctrine was not entirely successful, since their remarks were strictly *obiter* given the conclusion that the clause in question was not an exemption clause at all, but a liquidated damages clause (see **9.6.2.2**). Moreover, several passages in their Lordships' speeches suggested that there might be a residual rule of law applicable in the case of fundamental breach, e.g. Lord Reid suggested that an election to treat a contract as repudiated caused the whole contract to cease to exist, including the exclusion clause, so that it would be ineffective to exclude loss.

The House of Lords was given a further opportunity to clarify the law in *Photo Production Ltd v Securicor Transport Ltd* [1980] AC 827. This time, there could be no doubt that the issue of the effect of fundamental breach on an exemption clause was squarely raised.

In *Photo Production Ltd v Securicor Transport Ltd*, the contract required Securicor to make patrol visits at night and at weekends to the premises of Photo Production. The contract contained a clause exempting Securicor from liability for the acts of its employees, unless such acts could have been prevented by due diligence on the part of Securicor, and exempting Securicor from liability for loss caused by fire unless the loss was solely attributable to the negligence of a Securicor employee acting within the course of their employment. One night, the duty patrolman deliberately started a fire and, although it was not found that his intention was to destroy the factory, his action caused a loss of £615,000.

The House of Lords said that the question of whether an exemption clause applied in the case of a very serious or 'fundamental' breach was no more than a question of the proper construction of the particular clause. It found that, in this case, the clause was drafted in such terms that liability was, in fact, excluded. The decision was justified on the basis that this was a commercial contract between parties in equal bargaining positions and the clause was therefore a risk allocation provision placing the burden of insurance on Photo Production.

The last vestiges of the fundamental breach rule of law were demolished by a careful analysis of the effect of a breach of condition or a serious breach of an innominate term (what is referred to as a repudiatory breach allowing the victim to terminate the contract and claim damages), since the House of Lords (*per* Lord Diplock) took the view that repudiatory breach and fundamental breach were one and the same thing. The effect of such a breach is to give the non-breaching party the option of treating the contract as repudiated (discussed at **8.4.2**), so that future primary obligations are discharged and do not need to be performed. However, the contract itself does not come to an end. The secondary obligations (e.g. to pay damages for loss caused by breach) remain in existence, as does any exemption clause. The ending of the primary obligations did not indicate the ending of *all* obligations.

The facts of *Photo Production* pre-dated the Unfair Contract Terms Act (UCTA) 1977, although the Act had been passed by the time the case reached the House of Lords. Lord Wilberforce indicated what he believed should be the policy of the common law towards exemption clauses after the passing of the Act, saying, at p. 843D:

> It is significant that Parliament refrained from legislating over the whole field of contract. After this Act, in commercial matters generally, when the parties are not of unequal bargaining power, and when risks are normally borne by insurance, not only is the case for judicial intervention undemonstrated, but there is everything to be said, and this seems to have been Parliament's intention, for leaving the parties free to apportion the risks as they think fit and for respecting their decisions.

7.3.4 Conclusion

The position at common law is that the only control exercised by the courts over the use of exemption clauses duly incorporated into the contract is to determine whether, as a matter of construction, they apply to the breach in question. The only significance of a fundamental breach is that clear words will be required if the clause is to cover such a breach. However, in *Astrazeneca UK Ltd v Albermarle International Corporation* [2011] EWHC 1574 (Comm), *obiter* (at [301]), Flaux J rejected the approach that had been taken earlier by the judge in *Internet Broadcasting Corporation Ltd (t/a NETTV) v Mar LLC (t/a MARHedge)* [2009] EWHC 844 (Ch), [2010] 1 All ER (Comm) 112, [2009] 2 Lloyd's Rep 295, as 'heterodox and regressive'. The judge in *MARHedge* had stated that there was a strong presumption against an exemption clause being construed to cover a deliberate repudiatory breach. Flaux J considered that this risked a return to the doctrine of fundamental breach that had been rejected in *Suisse Atlantique Société d'Armement Maritime SA v NV Rotterdamsche Kolen Centrale* [1967] 1 AC 361 and in *Photo Production Ltd v Securicor Transport Ltd* [1980] AC 827. Instead, for Flaux J (at [301]), the correct test 'was one of construing the clause, albeit strictly, but without any presumption'. The clause in *Astrazeneca* provided that '[n]o claims by [AZ] of any kind, whether as to the products delivered or for non-delivery of the products' could be accepted. Flaux J considered (at [301]) that this clause was 'sufficiently clearly worded to cover any breach of the delivery obligations, deliberate or otherwise'.

7.4 Statutory control of exemption clauses: an overview

7.4.1 The Unfair Contract Terms Act 1977

The enactment of UCTA 1977 introduced a major addition to the mechanisms for controlling exemption clauses. The power to override exemption clauses had been introduced in the case of implied terms in the sale of goods by the Supply of Goods (Implied Terms) Act 1973—now s. 55 of the Sale of Goods Act (SGA) 1979. The 1977 Act, however, applies more extensive controls to a wide range of categories of contract, so that, for contracts within the scope of the Act, for the first time the courts had a general and direct means of control of the use of exemption clauses.

Since the CRA 2015, UCTA 1977 (and s. 55 SGA 1979) applies only in relation to the regulation of exemption clauses in B2B contracts. In the B2B context, the application of UCTA 1977 may render an exemption clause either totally unenforceable, or unenforceable unless shown to be reasonable.

7.4.2 Regulation of unfair terms in consumer contracts: the Consumer Rights Act 2015, Part 2

Prior to the CRA 2015, the statutory regime of control of exemption clauses was introduced by European Directive 93/13/EC on Unfair Terms in Consumer Contracts, which was implemented in the Unfair Terms in Consumer Contracts Regulations (UTCCR) 1999 (replacing the original implementing Regulations of 1994, SI 1994/3159).

The changes brought by the CRA 2015 were designed primarily to separate the regulatory treatment of B2B exemption clauses from the broader (and previously overlapping) regulatory treatment of unfair terms in consumer (B2C) contracts. CRA 2015 Part 2 therefore incorporates the consumer law governing exemption clauses and unfair terms in its single consumer law regime and revokes the 1999 Regulations. In the CRA 2015, where there are differences compared to the law in the UTCCR, these are largely the product of recommendations made by the Law Commission (**7.4.3**), e.g. the removal in the CRA of any distinction between negotiated and not individually negotiated terms. The CRA 2015 also makes necessary amendments to UCTA 1977 to exclude references to consumer law. The result is separate regimes for the enforceability of exemption clauses, with UCTA 1977 (as amended) governing B2B contracts only.

Generally, CRA 2015 Part 2 provides that 'unfair terms' in a contract concluded between a 'trader' and a 'an individual consumer who is acting for purposes that are wholly or mainly outside that individual's trade, business, craft or profession' will not be binding on the consumer (CRA 2015, s. 2(2) and(3)). This regime extends beyond exemption clauses to 'unfair terms' generally whilst, in certain circumstances, excluding specified 'core' terms from the scope of assessment for unfairness.

7.4.3 The Law Commission's recommendations for reform as a prelude to the Consumer Rights Act 2015

Prior to the CRA 2015, there were therefore two potentially overlapping pieces of legislation which could apply to the regulation of terms, i.e. UCTA 1977 and the 1999 Regulations. The Law Commission, in its report *Unfair Terms in Contracts*, Law Com. No. 292 (Cm. 6464, February 2005), proposed a single unified regime to replace UCTA 1997 and the 1999 Regulations in relation to consumer contracts which covered 'unfair terms', i.e. not merely exemption clauses. This consumer regime was to extend to negotiated terms, as well as standard or non-negotiated terms, and was to alter the burden of proof that existed under the 1999 Regulations, so that the business would have the burden of showing that a term was fair and reasonable where the term was detrimental to the consumer (unless a pre-emptive challenge by the regulator occurred, when that body would have the burden of establishing that the term was unfair). It was recommended that this general provision would not apply to a term that defined the main subject matter of a consumer contract, as long as the term was transparent and substantially the same as the definition that the consumer reasonably expected (an interesting legislative inclusion of reasonable expectations, although one that it was predicted would inevitably give rise to case law). Of particular significance was the clarity proposed through express recognition that terms that are unenforceable under UCTA 1977, s. 2(1) (death or personal injury resulting from negligence: see **7.5.2**) and the old s. 6(2) UCTA 1977 (exclusion or limitation of liability for breaches of basic obligations in the sales legislation as against a consumer, e.g. satisfactory quality: see **7.5.3.1**), were to remain unenforceable. Although it was technically possible to establish that such terms were unfair under the 1999 Regulations, such terms were not automatically unfair.

In the business context, the report distinguished between 'small businesses' and other businesses. 'Small businesses' were considered to warrant protection that should not be extended to other B2B contracts. While it was commendable to wish to protect such businesses, there were difficulties in deciding where to draw the line, and the Law Commission's draft Bill contained complex definitions of 'small businesses' in an attempt to avoid the difficulties encountered in other areas of law in ensuring that 'small businesses' are, in fact, 'small'. (Interestingly, the Small Business, Enterprise and Employment Act 2015, s. 33, does contain a definition of small (and micro) businesses, albeit for a different purpose.)

The approach to other B2B contracts was non-interventionist, reflecting the approach to reasonableness in commercial contracts under UCTA 1977 (see the discussion at **7.5.5.2**). The old s. 6(3) UCTA 1977 protection, against exemptions of the implied obligations under sales law if the term is not shown to be reasonable, was not contained in the Law Commission's draft Bill and instead it was proposed that such a term in a B2B contract would have to be shown to be fair and reasonable only if one business were to deal on the other's written standard terms of business.

The Law Commission proposed a test of whether the clause was 'fair and reasonable', which referred to the need to take into account 'the extent to which the term is transparent' (defined in presentational terms) and 'the substance and effect of the term, and all the circumstances existing at the time it was agreed' (substantive and procedural fairness and reasonableness). In examining this second aspect of the test, any court was to have regard to an extensive list of factors.

The Law Commission report contained a draft Bill but, while the government accepted the Law Commission's recommendations in principle, any reform was put on hold for two reasons: because of the pending European Union's review of the *consumer acquis* and implementation of the European Consumer Rights Directive (CRD) 2011/83/EU, and because of the growing concern about the implications of the Supreme Court decision in *Office of Fair Trading v Abbey National plc* [2009] UKSC 6, [2010] 1 AC 696 (see **7.6.2.4**), the scope of the existing legislation, the 1999 Regulations, and the lack of clarity concerning the definitions of core and ancillary terms in those Regulations. In May 2012, the then Department of Business, Innovation and Skills (BIS) asked the Law Commission to review and update the recommendations in the 2005 Report. This was done in the Issues Paper *Unfair Terms in Consumer Contracts: A New Approach?* (July 2012), followed by a consultation. In March 2013, the Law Commission issued the document *Unfair Consumer Contracts: Advice to Department for Business, Innovation and Skills* (March 2013).

The draft Consumer Rights Bill 2013 (Cmnd 8657, June 2013) and, with some amendments, the Consumer Rights Bill (Bill 161, 2013–14) was presented to Parliament in January 2014. Enactment of this legislation resulted in the recognition of entrenched rights for goods supplied to consumers, i.e. satisfactory quality and fitness for purpose etc. cannot be excluded or restricted (e.g. CRA 2015, s. 31), and the provisions relating to the regulation of unfair terms in consumer contracts were enacted as a single coherent regime (CRA 2015, Part 2). There are now separate legislative regimes for B2B contracts (i.e. an amended UCTA 1977) and B2C contracts (i.e. the Consumer Rights Act 2015).

The Law Commission proposals relating to small businesses were not part of the recent reform and the division between the commercial and consumer may arguably place small businesses at a disadvantage. This may explain why the government has subsequently consulted on the need for regulation to protect small businesses (BIS, *Purchasing Goods and Services: Protection of small business* (March 2015)). The government's response (BIS, Protection of Small Businesses when Purchasing Goods and Services, (February 2016)) highlighted the need for further consultation especially for micro businesses (para. 3.17). In response to the concern expressed by small businesses that it was difficult to find out their rights when purchasing goods and services (para. 3.20), the government set up, in December 2017, the office of a Small Business Commissioner, which will have a particular focus on payment practices.

7.5 The Unfair Contract Terms Act 1977—B2B contracts

7.5.1 The scope of the Act

7.5.1.1 Business liability

UCTA 1977 applies (subject to certain exceptions) in the case of both contract and tort to 'business liability', which means liability for things done or to be done in the course of a business, and liability arising from the occupation of business premises (UCTA 1977, s. 1(3)). 'Business' is given a broad definition by the Act (UCTA 1977, s. 14), so that it embraces not only the normal meaning of commercial activity, but also the professions, government departments, and local or public authorities.

7.5.1.2 Clauses covered by the Act: s. 13

It must be stressed that UCTA 1977 does not provide a general power to strike out any term that the court considers to be unreasonable or unfair. Its main targets are exemption clauses, i.e. clauses excluding or limiting liability. This definition is extended by s. 13(1) to include clauses making the enforcement of liability subject to compliance with a condition, clauses excluding or limiting any right or remedy that would otherwise be available, and clauses restricting or excluding rules of evidence or procedure.

In *Stewart Gill Ltd v Horatio Myer & Co. Ltd* [1992] 1 QB 600, the Court of Appeal held that a 'no set-off' clause, which purported to prevent the buyer from exercising a 'right' to set off its claims and so withhold payment against the price due to the seller, fell within s. 13(1) as a clause that purported to restrict rights or remedies that would otherwise be available. It therefore fell within the ambit of UCTA 1977.

The 1977 Act also applies to clauses that purport to modify the expected contractual obligation or duty, rather than to exempt liability for breach (UCTA 1977, s. 13(1)).

In *Smith v Eric S. Bush* [1990] 1 AC 831, the House of Lords held that a disclaimer clause in a mortgage valuation stipulating that the valuation was provided without any acceptance of responsibility fell within s. 13(1) because it purported to prevent any duty of care from arising.

7.5.1.3 Clauses and contracts that are not covered by the Act

The 1977 Act does not, however, apply to arbitration clauses (UCTA 1977, s. 13(2)), or to international supply contracts, as defined by UCTA, s. 26(4). Certain other important categories of contract are excluded from the scope of the major provisions of the Act, i.e. contracts of insurance, contracts relating to interests in land, contracts relating to intellectual property, contracts relating to companies (whether or not incorporated), contracts relating to securities, and certain passenger rights for bus and coach transport. Various types of maritime contracts, i.e. contracts of marine salvage, charterparties, and contracts of carriage of goods by sea, are excluded from all provisions with the exception of s. 2(1) (liability in negligence for death or personal injury). The provisions dealing with exclusions or restrictions of liability in negligence (s. 2(1) and (2)) do not apply to employment contracts in the B2B context.

7.5.2 Liability for negligence: s. 2

'Negligence' is defined by the 1977 Act as breach of an obligation to take reasonable care or to exercise reasonable skill arising out of the express or implied terms of a contract, i.e. qualified contractual liability (see **8.2.1.1**), or existing as a common law duty (i.e. in tort) or arising out of the Occupiers' Liability Act 1957 (UCTA 1977, s. 1(1)).

Many obligations arising out of contracts are strict. That is to say, the standard of performance demanded is not merely to take reasonable care or to exercise reasonable skill in attempting to achieve the purpose of the contract; rather, the party performing can avoid breach only by actually achieving that purpose. Therefore exemption clauses relating to such contractual terms are not subject to the controls applying to clauses that purport to exclude or limit liability for 'negligence' contained in s. 2 of the Act—although they may be subject to other controls relating to attempts to exclude or limit contractual liability (discussed at **7.5.3**).

Nevertheless, some contractual obligations are not strict. Where the achievement of the result is dependent to some appreciable extent on factors beyond the control of the person providing the service, it would be nonsensical to *guarantee* that the result will be achieved (see **8.2.1.1**). Thus lawyers cannot guarantee that their clients will escape conviction when prosecuted; they can only undertake to use reasonable skill in carrying out legal services. Breach of such obligations is what is meant by 'negligence' liability in relation to contracts, and exemption clauses relating to such liability are governed by UCTA 1977, s. 2.

Section 2 of the 1977 Act provides:

(1) A person cannot by reference to any contract term or to a notice given to persons generally or to particular persons exclude or restrict his liability for death or personal injury resulting from negligence.

(2) In the case of other loss or damage, a person cannot so exclude or restrict his liability for negligence except in so far as the term or notice satisfies the requirement of reasonableness.

⌁ SUMMARY

In the B2B context, section 2(1) renders totally unenforceable any exclusions and limitations of liability for death or personal injury caused by negligence.

»

Section 2(2) provides that liability for other loss or damage (i.e. other than death or personal injury) resulting from negligence may be excluded, provided that the contract term or notice satisfies the requirement of reasonableness (see **7.5.5**). 'Other loss or damage' includes property damages and financial loss, e.g. as in *Smith v Eric S. Bush* [1990] 1 AC 831, in which the loss was financial loss following a negligent survey.

Goodlife Foods Ltd v Hall Fire Protection Ltd [2017] EWHC 767 (TCC), [2017] BLR 389, provides an illustration of the courts' willingness to sever part of an exclusion clause purporting to exclude liability for death or personal injury resulting from a party's own negligence from the rest of the particular clause. In 2002, Goodlife, a producer of frozen food, contracted with the defendant for the installation of a fire protection system for their factory at a cost of £7,490. In 2012, a fire caused substantial damage to property and the business to be interrupted causing substantial loss to the claimants. Goodlife was statute-barred from suing in breach of contract and therefore sued for negligence, alleging that the fire should have been prevented by the fire suppression system. The defendant claimed protection of clause 11 of the contract, which excluded any claim in negligence. Goodlife however argued that the clause, which purported to exclude liability for death and personal injury was invalid under s. 2(1) UCTA. To the question of severance, Judge Stephen Davies simply stated 'where a case seeks to exclude liability for death or personal injury and also liability for other kinds of loss or damage, the former can simply be excised and the remainder upheld as reasonable if appropriate to do so' (at [69]). On the facts, the rest of the clause was held to be valid as it was reasonable. The case went to appeal but solely on the reasonableness issue (discussed at **7.5.5**), which was upheld by the Court of Appeal ([2018] EWCA Civ 1371).

7.5.3 Contractual liability

In the case of attempted exemptions of strict contractual obligations (i.e. obligations that must be performed completely and precisely to an absolute standard), the 1977 Act contains two sets of provisions.

- There are specific provisions designed to deal with attempts to exclude or limit liability for breaches of the implied obligations relating to the goods in sale and supply contracts (UCTA 1977, ss. 6 and 7).

- There is also a general provision that may apply to attempts to exempt from liability for breaches of strict contractual obligations, but this will be applicable only if the qualifying condition is met (UCTA 1977, s. 3).

7.5.3.1 The sale or supply of goods

The Act contains special provisions that apply to clauses purporting to exempt liability for breach of the terms relating to the goods that are implied by statute into commercial contracts for the sale or supply of goods (see **6.4.2.4**).

Section 6 applies to implied terms in the sale of goods and hire-purchase of goods (UCTA 77, s. 6(1)). This section applies to all liability and not merely that incurred in the course of a business (UCTA 1977, s. 6(4)). However, the important implied terms of quality in s. 14 of the SGA 1979 arise only in the case of sales made in the course of a business. Sale and hire-purchase contracts are not the only contracts under which title to goods may pass (e.g. work and materials contracts, such as a building contract under which goods are to be incorporated into the finished structure as part of the contract performance: see **6.4.2.4**). Section 7 of UCTA 1977 therefore governs attempted exemptions of liability for breach of similar terms as implied in such types of contracts (the Supply of Goods and Services Act 1982 implies terms similar to those of the 1979 Act into contracts for the supply of goods).

7.5.3.1.1 *Title*

- For a sale of goods contract, the implied condition that the seller has or will have the right to sell the goods (SGA 1979, s. 12) cannot, in any circumstances, be excluded by reference to a contract term (UCTA 1977, s. 6(1)(a)).

- Section 6(1)(b) of the 1977 Act provides that breach of s. 8 of the Supply of Goods (Implied Terms) Act 1973 (relating to the transfer of goods in a hire-purchase contract) cannot, in any circumstances, be excluded by reference to a contract term (UCTA 1977, s. 6(1)(b)).

- Section 7(3A) of the 1977 Act provides that liability for breach of s. 2 of the Supply of Goods and Services Act 1982 (relating to the transfer of goods in a work and materials contract) cannot be exempted (Supply of Goods and Services Act 1982, s. 17(2)).

- However, liability for breach of s. 7 of the 1982 Act (implied obligation concerning the right to transfer possession of goods in a hire contract) can be exempted, but only if the clause satisfies the reasonableness requirement (UCTA 1977, s. 7(4)).

7.5.3.1.2 *Description, satisfactory quality, and fitness for purpose*

- In the case of attempts to exempt liability for breaches of ss. 13–15 of the SGA 1979 in commercial contracts (covering sale by description, satisfactory quality, fitness for purpose, and sale by sample), s. 6(1A)(a) provides that this liability can be excluded or restricted only where the exemption clause satisfies the requirement of reasonableness.

- In the case of attempts to exempt liability for breaches of ss. 9–11 of the 1973 Act in hire-purchase contracts (covering sale by description, satisfactory quality, fitness for purpose, and sale by sample), s. 6(1A)(b) provides that this liability can be excluded or restricted only where the exemption clause satisfies the requirement of reasonableness. There is a further similar provision in relation to attempts to exclude the same obligations relating to description, satisfactory quality, fitness for purpose, and correspondence with sample in contracts for work and materials, i.e. these obligations cannot be excluded or restricted except in so far as the clause in question is shown to be reasonable (UCTA 1977, s. 7(1A)).

7.5.3.2 **Section 3: general contractual liability**

Section 3 of the 1977 Act applies to breaches of strict contractual obligations, other than the implied goods obligations covered by ss. 6 and 7, but only if one party deals on the other party's written standard terms of business.

7.5.3.2.1 Dealing on the other's written standard terms of business

The expression 'written standard terms of business' is not defined in the 1977 Act. Many contracts are in standard form and s. 3 is clearly intended to apply to such contracts. It has not been clear, however, how much 'individualization' of such standard forms is permitted before the section ceases to apply. For example, many standard forms leave blanks in the clauses relating to quantity and to price, which must be filled in for each particular contract.

The policy behind the Act ought to mean that such standard forms are still within the meaning of the section, and in *Yuanda (UK) Co. Ltd v WW Gear Construction Ltd* [2010] EWHC 720 (TCC), [2011] Bus LR 360, [2011] 1 All ER (Comm) 550, at [21], Edwards-Stuart J concluded that:

> [T]he conditions have to be standard in that they are terms which the company in question uses for all, or nearly all, of its contracts of a particular type without alteration (apart from blanks which have to be completed showing the price, name of the other contracting party and so on).

He added, at [22]: 'In my view, it is the essence of such terms that they are not varied from transaction to transaction.'

The question of what constitutes written standard terms was considered at length by Judge Thayne Forbes, acting as an official referee in the High Court, in *Salvage Association v CAP Financial Services Ltd* [1995] FSR 654.

> There were two contracts. The first contract was contained in a document produced in advance by the defendants and these conditions were accepted without any attempt to renegotiate any of them. The defendants argued that they would have been willing to renegotiate, but the judge did not allow this to deflect him from finding that this contract was concluded on the defendants' written standard terms of business. The second contract took as its point of departure the first, but was further negotiated and, seemingly, amendments were made. Whether this amounted to a standard-form agreement was a question of fact, taking into account the degree of negotiation and variation, and alternatively the degree of imposition of terms, in light of the relative bargaining power of the parties. In this case, the second contract had moved sufficiently away from the original written standard terms of business for s. 3 not to apply.

Thus, although the existence of negotiations is not a relevant consideration (a point subsequently confirmed in *Yuanda v WW Gear Construction*), the extent of any negotiation will be. In *St Albans City and District Council v International Computers Ltd* [1996] 4 All ER 481, the defendants had submitted their standard form for negotiation. At first instance—[1995] FSR 686—Scott Baker J considered that if the terms are amended as a result of negotiations, assuming that the amendments were *not too substantial*, the contract could remain as standard form as long as there was no negotiation over the 'relevant exempting terms'. The Court of Appeal held, affirming Scott Baker J's decision on this point, that the local authority had contracted on the defendants' written standard terms of business because the standard form 'remained effectively untouched'. In *Watford Electronics Ltd v Sanderson CFL Ltd* [2000] 2 All ER (Comm) 984, at first instance, the judge applied a test of whether there had been a 'material variation' to the standard form. The form had been altered to add a clause committing the defendant to use its best endeavours to allocate appropriate resources to the project. The judge held that this amendment was no more than a vague and unenforceable obligation, so that the standard term had not been varied, and even if the amendment had been enforceable, it would have to be considered against the totality of the standard conditions that otherwise remained unaltered.

In *Yuanda (UK) Co. Ltd v WW Gear Construction Ltd*, at [24], as in *St Albans*, the judge laid particular emphasis on 'the extent and nature of any agreed alterations to the "standard terms" made as a result of the negotiations between the parties'. Edwards-Stuart J concluded, at [26], that '[i]f there is any significant difference between the terms proffered and the terms of the contract actually made, then the contract will not have been made on one party's written standard terms of business'. The test therefore appears to be one of 'significant difference', although in application the judge started from the conclusion that the alterations were material and not 'insignificant'. His conclusion that the contract was not made on 'the other's written standard terms of business' was supported by the fact that nearly all of some 30 contractors on the project had negotiated amendments to the terms proffered, so that none of the contracts could be said to be made on 'standard' terms.

More recently, in *African Export-Import Bank v Shebah Exploration and Production Co. Ltd* [2017] EWCA Civ 845, [2018] 1 WLR 487, the Court of Appeal reviewed once again the authorities on the question of when a party will be regarded as dealing on the other's written standard terms of business for the purpose of s. 3. The issue on the facts arose because an industry model form had been used as the basis on which the relevant transaction had proceeded, which gave rise to the question whether that industry model could be said to represent the standard terms of one of the parties to the transaction. Longmore LJ highlighted four elements to be established for the purpose of bringing s. 3 (and, in turn, the requirements of the s. 11 reasonableness test) into play, namely: (i) the term is written; (ii) the term is a term of business; (iii) the term is part of the other party's standard terms of business; and (iv) the party is dealing on those written standard terms of business (at [18]).

Longmore stated that the first two of these requirements would usually attract 'little controversy' (at [19]). The third requirement necessitated that it be shown that 'the other party habitually uses those terms' (with it not being enough that 'he sometimes does and sometimes does not'), which meant it was not sufficient to show that a model form had, on the occasion in question, been adopted (at [20]).

Requirement (iv) raised the question to what extent a party would be dealing on the other's standard terms where there had nonetheless been an element of negotiation between the parties pursuant to those terms to the effect that some, but not all, standard terms were relevant to the specific transaction in issue. After a review of the relevant authorities, Longmore LJ concluded (at [25]): 'it is relevant to inquire whether there have been more than insubstantial variations to the terms which may otherwise have been habitually used by the other party to the transaction. If there have been substantial variations, it is unlikely to be the case that the party relying on the Act will have discharged the burden on him to show that the contract has been made "on the other's written standard terms of business".'

The court concluded that the relevant transaction had not been on one party's standard terms and so s. 3 of UCTA was not engaged. In particular, no sufficient evidence had been adduced as to the use of the model form being one that could be described as being on *standard* terms (such evidence, in the court's view, not being difficult to obtain if true (at [33])). In any event, the fact of detailed negotiations between the parties (including some 'substantial' amendment to the model form used) rendered it impossible to say any standard terms of business had been used on the facts (at [35]).

From the above, the application of the UCTA 1977 will turn on whether the contract was made on 'the other's written standard terms of business'. Nevertheless, in its second report, preceding UCTA 1977, the Law Commission had made a deliberate decision not to recommend a definition of 'written standard terms of business', on the basis that any definition would provide businesses with the ability to draft to avoid it: Law Commission, *Exemption Clauses*, Law Com. No. 69 (1975), para. 157. It is probably a mistake, however, to allow for as much judicial uncertainty on this matter. There are also potential problems in the requirement that the standard terms be 'written' in light of the nature of electronic contracting and the requirements of the Electronic Communications Act 2000. The Law Commission's 2005 report *Unfair Terms in Contracts*, Law Com. No. 292 (Cm. 6464, 2005), determined to preserve these definitional difficulties by retaining this as the qualifying condition for regulation of general contractual liability for B2B contracts (see paras **4.45–4.57**), on the basis that this test 'is as good as any that can be achieved'. This conclusion would seem to be correct, but it does preserve the significance of the existing jurisprudence on the subject.

7.5.3.2.2 *The s. 3 test*

Where a party deals on the other's standard terms, that other may not exclude or limit its liability for breach of contract by means of a term in the contract except in so far as the term satisfies the requirement of reasonableness (UCTA 1977, s. 3(2)(a)). (The 'reasonableness' requirement is considered at **7.5.5**.)

7.5.3.2.3 *The scope of s. 3*

Generally, exemption clauses operate to exclude or limit liability for breach. However, careful drafting of a contract may result in the performance obligation being such that a performance that might normally be regarded as defective does not amount to breach at all. In this case, it is said that the term defines the performance obligation, rather than simply exempting liability for breach. Section 13 extends the scope of UCTA 1977 to cover such clauses, but only in respect of s. 2 and ss. 6 and 7. Nevertheless, s. 3 makes specific reference to clauses that purport to deny the basic performance obligation.

By s. 3(2)(b) of the 1977 Act, a party may not claim to be entitled:

(i) to render a contractual performance substantially different from that reasonably expected of him; or

(ii) . . . to render no performance at all,

except in so far as the contract term satisfies the requirement of reasonableness.

Of course, this control applies only in the case of contracts in which one party deals on the other's written standard terms (UCTA 1977, s. 3(1); see **7.5.3.2.1**).

Section 3(2)(b)(i) assumes that it is possible to identify a performance that is reasonably to be expected. For example:

- The contract might be of a recognized and standardized type.

→ EXAMPLE

A contract for the provision of domestic decorating services is rarely negotiated in detail. In particular, it is unlikely that the parties will discuss measures to be taken to protect existing decoration, which is not to be replaced; rather, the customer will assume that the decorator will take reasonable care to avoid damage to existing decorations, and such a term would normally be implied in law (Supply of Goods and Services Act 1982, s. 13). If the decorator's order form, which was signed by the customer, were to include a term making protection of existing decorations the responsibility of the customer, such a term would have defined the contractual obligations in a way other than would generally have been expected.

»

Section 3(2)(b)(i) does not say that it is not permitted to redefine the contractual obligations in such a way; it merely says that it is not permitted unless reasonable. This test might be satisfied relatively easily in such a case by showing that the customer was fully aware of the effect of the clause and possibly by showing that the price charged was lower than would be charged if it were the decorator's contractual responsibility to take such precautions.

- Alternatively, there may be a conflict between the apparent main purpose of the contract and the performance that one party is entitled to tender under the terms contained in the fine print of the agreement.

In *AXA Sun Life Services plc v Campbell Martin* [2011] EWCA Civ 133, [2012] Bus LR 2013, [2011] 1 CLC 312, at [50], Stanley Burnton LJ noted that it was not clear how s. 3(2)(b)(i) should operate, but he thought it was:

principally aimed at the small print that entitles a party to a contract to provide something other than that defined by the principal terms of the contract, as where a holiday company reserves the right to substitute a hotel or resort for that specified in the main part of the contract.

Given the wording of the paragraph, he also thought that it would be necessary to consider both the performance that was reasonably expected and that defined by the contract. Under s. 3(2)(b)(i) of the 1977 Act, assuming that the qualifying condition of s. 3(1) is met, the issue would be whether the clause is unreasonable in allowing changes to be made unilaterally from what had apparently been agreed under the main provisions of the contract.

Section 3(2)(b)(ii) is something of a red herring. If one party is defined by the contract as being under no obligations at all, the contract must surely fail for want of consideration (see **4.3**). Where the absence of obligation affects only part of the contract, it can be dealt with under s. 3(2)(b)(i).

7.5.4 Secondary contracts

Section 10 of UCTA 1977 is intended to prevent the evasion of the provisions of the Act by means of a secondary contract. Since the main provisions of the Act are concerned with terms in contracts that exclude or restrict liability arising under those contracts, it was feared that imposing such exclusions and restrictions by means of separate contracts might thwart the purpose of the Act. Section 10 attempts to close that loophole. A typical situation addressed by this provision would be where a maintenance contract, entered into in connection with the purchase of goods, purports to exclude or restrict rights arising under the purchase contract. In *Tudor Grange Holdings Ltd v Citibank NA* [1992] Ch 53, at p. 67C, Browne-Wilkinson VC held that s. 10 applies only to 'attempts to evade the Act's provisions by the introduction of such an exemption clause *into a contract with a third party*' (emphasis added). Consequently, in terms of the situation just described, s. 10 would apply where the maintenance service contract that provides the vehicle for the exemption clause is entered into with a party other than the supplier of the goods; it does not apply where the supplier is also the principal party to the maintenance agreement. This is important since, had s. 10 applied in the case of secondary contracts between the original parties, it would have left open the possibility for challenges to compromises or settlements, which would have been most undesirable in policy terms.

7.5.5 The 'reasonableness' requirement: s. 11

The reasonableness requirement under the 1977 Act is highly, and unnecessarily, complex. Moreover, although the policy objective was always fairly clear for consumer contracts when, prior to the CRA 2015, the 1977 Act also applied to B2C contracts, this was not so clear for B2B contracts, for which discernible differences in policy were identified in the case law in the early years: see Adams and Brownsword (1988) 104 LQR 94. A much clearer and consistent policy for B2B contracts can however be detected in more recent case law (for an example of the relation between non-reliance clauses and the Misrepresentation Act 1967, discussed at **14.7.2.2**): see *First Tower Trustees Ltd and Intertrust Trustees Ltd v CDS (Superstores International) Ltd* [2018] EWCA Civ 1396, especially Leggatt LJ at [101] and [104]).

It is important to appreciate at the outset that the reasonableness requirement is not always the applicable test under the Act (see e.g. UCTA 1977, s. 2(1)) and the temptation to apply it to all clauses must therefore be resisted.

Section 11(1) defines the test for determining reasonableness as whether the term is a fair and reasonable one to have been included in light of circumstances known (or circumstances that ought to have been known) to the parties at the time of contracting. The court may therefore not take into account subsequent events, and in particular the actual effect of breach, in determining whether the exemption clause was reasonable. Under UCTA 1977, s. 11(1), the courts may consider circumstances that should have been in the contemplation of the parties at the time of contracting. If a particularly serious breach has occurred, a court could hold that the parties should have realized the possibility of such a serious breach and may then find that it was unreasonable at the time of contracting to exclude liability for such consequences.

Under s. 11(5) the burden of proving reasonableness lies on the party seeking to rely on the exemption clause.

7.5.5.1 The approach to assessing reasonableness

In *George Mitchell (Chesterhall) Ltd v Finney Lock Seeds Ltd* [1983] 2 AC 803, Lord Bridge set out the approach to be taken by the courts in assessing reasonableness. Although Lord Bridge rejected the notion that such a decision was 'an exercise of discretion', he accepted, at p. 816A, that the courts 'must entertain a whole range of considerations, put them in the scales on one side or the other, and decide at the end of the day on which side the balance comes down'.

Consequently, each case must necessarily turn on its own particular facts, so that cases have limited significance in terms of their precedent value. In *Phillips Products Ltd v Hyland* [1987] 1 WLR 659, the Court of Appeal made this clear. Slade LJ, speaking for the whole court, at pp. 668–9, said:

> The question for the court is not a general question whether or not condition 8 is valid or invalid in the case of any and every contract of hire entered into between a hirer and a plant owner who uses the relevant CPA conditions. The question was and is whether the exclusion of Hamstead's liability for negligence satisfied the requirement of reasonableness imposed by the Act, in relation to *this particular contract* . . . It is important therefore that our conclusion on the particular facts of this case should not be treated as a binding precedent in other cases where similar clauses fall to be considered but the evidence of surrounding circumstances may be very different. [Emphasis original.]

The significance of this denial of precedent value for judicial decisions on the reasonableness of exemption clauses soon became apparent when the same clause was treated quite differently (in a different fact situation by a differently constituted Court of Appeal) in *Thompson v T. Lohan (Plant Hire) Ltd* [1987] 1 WLR 649.

In *Cleaver v Schyde Investments* [2011] EWCA Civ 929, [2011] 2 P & CR 21, at [55], Longmore LJ made it clear that it is not a question of whether the clause is generally reasonable, but of whether it is a reasonable clause made between these parties in the circumstances in which the contract was made. It is therefore preferable to speak of a clause being 'unenforceable' if it is unreasonable on the application of the reasonableness test in UCTA 1977, rather than referring to it as void.

7.5.5.1.1 *The role of appellate courts*

In *George Mitchell (Chesterhall) Ltd v Finney Lock Seeds Ltd* [1983] 2 AC 803, at p. 816B, Lord Bridge also explained that, in light of the essentially fact-based exercise undertaken by the courts, and on the basis that the court at first instance will have heard all of the evidence and witness statements relevant to the factors, 'the appellate court should treat the original decision with the utmost respect and refrain from interference with it unless satisfied that it proceeded upon some erroneous principle or was plainly and obviously wrong'. The position was recently reiterated by Lewison LJ in the Court of Appeal in *First Tower Trustees Ltd and Intertrust Trustees Ltd v CDS (Superstores International) Ltd* [2018] EWCA Civ 1396 (at [75]) when he stated 'whether a clause passes the test of reasonableness is an evaluative judgment for the trial judge. An appeal court should be slow to interfere'.

Watford Electronics Ltd v Sanderson CFL Ltd [2001] EWCA Civ 317, [2001] 1 All ER (Comm) 696, and *Regus (UK) Ltd v Epcot Solutions Ltd* [2008] EWCA Civ 361, [2009] 1 All ER (Comm) 586, are rare examples of cases in which the Court of Appeal overturned a first instance finding on reasonableness.

7.5.5.2 **Factors relevant in the assessment of reasonableness**

7.5.5.2.1 *Factors identified by the legislation*

- Under UCTA 1977, s. 11(4), there is a special test stated to be applicable to limitation clauses (i.e. clauses restricting liability to a specified sum of money). In such cases, the court must have particular regard to whether the party seeking to limit its liability could expect to have resources available to meet such liability should it arise, and to the extent to which it was possible for that party to have obtained insurance cover for such liability. The cost and availability of insurance has been applied more generally as a factor: e.g. in *Photo Production Ltd v Securicor Transport Ltd* [1980] AC 827 (see **7.3.3**), the House of Lords stressed that the cost of the patrolling service was modest and that it was reasonable for the factory owners to cover this risk by taking out insurance cover.

- Under s. 11(2), in the case of exemptions of implied terms in the sale or supply of goods (UCTA 1977, ss. 6 and 7: see **7.5.3.1**), the court is referred to a set of guidelines on reasonableness, set out in Sch. 2. Among the factors to be taken into account are:

  - the relative strengths of the bargaining positions of the parties;
  - whether, in agreeing to the exemption, a party received an inducement (e.g. a lower price);
  - whether any condition for the enforcement of liability (e.g. claiming within seven days of performance) could practically be complied with; and
  - whether the goods were specially made at the request of the buyer.

Schedule 2(c) also refers to knowledge of the existence and extent of the term by the buyer in question. This refers to the reality of any consent to the term rather than the fact that the test of incorporation has been satisfied: *AEG (UK) Ltd v Logic Resource Ltd* [1996] CLC 265. The clearest evidence of consent to a term will be evidence that it is the result of negotiation: see *Britvic Soft Drinks v Messer UK Ltd* [2002] EWCA Civ 548, [2002] 2 Lloyd's Rep 368.

Although, in theory, this Sch. 2 list of factors applies only in relation to exclusions of implied terms in sale and supply contracts, these factors have been applied more generally by the courts: as confirmed by Stuart Smith LJ in *Stewart Gill Ltd v Horatio Myer & Co. Ltd* [1992] 1 QB 600, at p. 608. Their application has now become a matter of course in case law involving an assessment of reasonableness under UCTA 1977; so much so, in fact, that judgments are frequently structured around an examination of the application of each in turn.

7.5.5.2.2 Factors identified by the courts

Bearing in mind the limitations of decided cases in this area as precedents, all that is possible is to identify recurring factors and themes that may be of assistance in terms of giving advice in the context in which the reasonableness test will now be applied, i.e. commercial contracting.

Adams and Brownsword (1988) 104 LQR 94 identified two different possible approaches to reasonableness in the commercial context:

- the approach in *Photo Production Ltd v Securicor Transport Ltd* [1980] AC 827 of freedom of contract and the ability to allocate risks, bearing in mind the availability of insurance cover—which approach has gained prominence in subsequent decisions, such as *Monarch Airlines Ltd v London Luton Airport Ltd* [1997] CLC 698 and *Watford Electronics Ltd v Sanderson CFL Ltd* [2001] EWCA Civ 317, [2001] 1 All ER (Comm) 696, noted by Peel at (2001) 117 LQR 392; and

- a more interventionist approach, exemplified by *George Mitchell (Chesterhall) Ltd v Finney Lock Seeds Ltd* [1983] 2 AC 803.

In **George Mitchell (Chesterhall) Ltd v Finney Lock Seeds Ltd**, the defendants had supplied cabbage seed at a contract price of approximately £200. The cabbages did not grow properly, causing lost production to the value of £61,000. The contract purported to limit liability for defective seeds to the amount of the contract price. (The 1977 Act did not apply to this contract because it was entered into before 1 February 1978, but it was subject to the reasonableness test applicable under s. 55(3) of the SGA 1979, which for these purposes was essentially similar to the UCTA 1977 test.) The House of Lords considered the clause to be unreasonable on the basis that the suppliers should have insured against the risk that the seeds were defective, it had not been negotiated between the relevant trade bodies, the consequences of any defect could mean complete crop failure, and the clause amounted to the defendants limiting their liability for their own negligence. The context of this case is also important. It was customary at the time, for suppliers of seeds to make ex gratia payment when the wrong seed was delivered (see at p. 209F).

By comparison, in **R. W. Green Ltd v Cade Brothers Farms** [1978] 1 Lloyd's Rep 602, a supply of potatoes had been infected with a virus, but a limitation clause in the contract purported to limit liability to the price (£634), although the actual loss of profit on the crop was around £6,000. This limitation clause was held to be reasonable because the parties were of equal bargaining power, the clause had been negotiated between relevant trade bodies, and it had been in use for many years. Moreover, the buyers could have paid more to obtain a guarantee against the virus.

> ## ! KEY POINT
>
> In the commercial context, the most important factors pointing to the reasonableness of a clause appear to be:
>
> - equality of bargaining position;
> - whether the clause is a generally accepted clause in the industry in question, which was negotiated by the trade bodies concerned; and
> - whether, on this basis, it is essentially a clause allocating a particular risk between two commercial parties, thereby avoiding the risk of duplicate insurance.

These factors were cited in *Monarch Airlines Ltd v London Luton Airport Ltd*, in support of a finding that a clause, excluding the liability of the airport for unintentional damage to aircraft, was reasonable. They were also used for a 'no set-off' clause in a commercial agreement in *Schenkers Ltd v Overland Shoes Ltd* [1998] 1 Lloyd's Rep 498. The clause in question was in common use (having been arrived at following negotiations between the relevant representative bodies). It was also well known in the trade and by these parties, who were in roughly equal bargaining positions. There are numerous other examples, e.g. *AXA Sun Life Services plc v Campbell Martin* [2011] EWCA Civ 133, [2012] Bus LR 203, [2011] 1 CLC 312.

The most significant decision in terms of this approach in the commercial context is a decision of the Court of Appeal.

Watford Electronics Ltd v Sanderson CFL Ltd concerned a claim for damages for breach of a contract to supply a bespoke integrated software system. The contract contained the defendant's standard terms, including a clause purporting to exclude any liability for indirect or consequential losses and a clause limiting liability in a general sense to the price paid under the contract (£104,600). The contract also contained entire agreement clauses (see **6.2.1.4**). The system proved to be faulty and the claimant sought damages amounting to £5.5 million for breach of contract—namely, loss of profits, the increased costs of working, and reimbursement of the cost of replacement.

At first instance—[2000] 2 All ER (Comm) 984—the judge held the exemption clauses to be unreasonable in their entirety. However, the Court of Appeal reversed the judge's decision and held that the clauses were reasonable. *The contract had been negotiated between experienced businessmen of equal bargaining power and skill, who had chosen to allocate the risk in a particular way. It was not for the court to interfere in this allocation of risks between commercial parties by concluding that the clause was unreasonable and could not be relied upon.*

Chadwick LJ stated, at [54]:

> In circumstances in which parties of equal bargaining power negotiate a price for the supply of product under an agreement which provides for the person on whom the risk of loss will fall, it seems to me that the court should be very cautious before reaching the conclusion that the agreement which they have reached is not a fair and reasonable one.

Chadwick LJ continued:

> [E]xperienced businessmen representing substantial companies of equal bargaining power . . . should . . . be taken to be the best judge of the commercial fairness of the agreement which they have made; including

the fairness of each of the terms in that agreement . . . Unless satisfied that one party has, in effect, taken unfair advantage of the other–or that a term is so unreasonable that it cannot properly have been understood or considered–the court should not interfere.

This 'freedom of contract', or 'sanctity of contract', approach for commercial contracts is very much in line with that of the House of Lords in *Photo Production Ltd v Securicor Transport Ltd*.

In *Granville Oil & Chemicals Ltd v Davies Turner & Co. Ltd* [2003] EWCA Civ 570, [2003] 1 All ER (Comm) 819, at [31], Tucker LJ (with whose judgment Potter LJ and Hart J agreed) explained the role of UCTA 1977 in the context of its then application to both commercial and consumer contracts. He stated:

The 1977 Act obviously plays a very important role in protecting vulnerable consumers from the effects of draconian contract terms. But I am less enthusiastic about its intrusion into contracts between commercial parties of equal bargaining strength, who should generally be considered capable of being able to make contracts of their choosing and expect to be bound by their terms.

This non-interventionist approach to clauses in commercial contracts was also evident in *Frans Maas (UK) Ltd v Samsung Electronics (UK) Ltd* [2004] EWHC 1502 (Comm), [2005] 2 All ER (Comm) 783, at [158]–[159], where Gross J explicitly adopted Tucker LJ's comment in *Granville Oil*. In *Sterling Hydraulics Ltd v Dichtomatik Ltd* [2006] EWHC 2004 (QB), [2007] 1 Lloyd's Rep 8 (see **6.3.1.2**), in a commercial supply contract, there were clauses that attempted to exclude all liability (including consequential loss) for defects in the seals supplied, unless there was either intentional or gross negligence by the supplier or prompt reporting of defects, when liability would be limited to price of the goods. However, apart from imposing a one-week limit for reporting claims based on hidden defects, the exclusion and limitation provisions were considered to be reasonable in view of the equal bargaining power. Limitation to the price was reasonable because it was a 'low value high volume contract' and, since the supplier was given no information as to the precise use for the seals, it could not have taken out insurance for the full risks. *Goodlife Foods Ltd v Hall Fire Protection Ltd* [2018] EWCA Civ 1371 (see below) confirms this non-interventionist approach and the reiteration of the importance of party autonomy and freedom of contract, especially where the parties are of equal bargaining power (at [103]), the clause was an 'entirely reasonable allocation of risk' (at [88]).

Further, in *Regus (UK) Ltd v Epcot Solutions Ltd* [2008] EWCA Civ 361, [2009] 1 All ER (Comm) 586, the Court of Appeal held that there was nothing unreasonable in a clause limiting liability for loss of profits and consequential losses in a commercial contract providing for serviced office accommodation, since the parties were of equal bargaining power, had negotiated their contract, and the evidence was that the customer used a similar clause in its own business. Customers were advised to take out insurance to cover their business losses and it was generally more appropriate for the customer to take out this insurance than the service supplier. The particular importance of insurance was again more recently emphasized by the Court of Appeal in a very detailed analysis in *Goodlife Foods Ltd v Hall Fire Protection Ltd* [2018] EWCA Civ 1371. Upholding the High Court's decision (see **7.5.2**), the Court of Appeal found the clause to be reasonable. After reiterating the importance of the agreed terms (at [61]), the court focused on the question of the insurance (at [64]–[83]). Looking at the clause in some detail, Coulson LJ stated that far from being a 'neutral factor', the insurance was 'an important consideration in favour of Hall Fire and the reasonableness of clause 11' for two reasons (at [76]). First was the identity of the party best placed to take out insurance, in this case Goodlife because it was 'conducting (as part of its regular business) a potentially hazardous operation'. Consequently Goodlife, 'with its own unique knowledge of its property and the precise effect on its business if there was a fire which stopped the factory working, was plainly in the best position to place its own insurance to cover those risks in the way most suited to that business' (at [77]). Second, because of the manner in which the clause was drafted, Goodlife was offered an alternative. Indeed, 'the first two parts of clause 11 limit Hall Fire's liability very significantly. But the third part of the clause went on to say that, if Goodlife wanted that liability to be reinstated, it would cost them more, but would give rise to insurance, and therefore protection for losses which would otherwise be excluded' (at [79]). Coulson added that this part of the clause 'was not an empty offer' since it was 'reiterating that Hall Fire did not assume a liability for future events if Goodlife did not put in place the necessary insurance' (at [80]). The case is also important for its analysis of Goodlife's argument that the clause was unreasonable as Hall Fire was attempting to evade its core obligation to provide a proper fire suppression system, relying on *Balmoral v Borealis* (at [84]). Coulson LJ rejected the argument stating that to do so meant ignoring clause 11 altogether (at [84]). He added, 'When looking at the parties' rights and obligations, the contract has to be looked at as a whole. Thus, although Hall Fire had agreed to provide the fire suppression system, they had agreed to do so on the basis that they had severely limited their liability for any future claims. The supply of the system cannot be looked at in isolation from the terms on which Hall Fire were prepared to supply and install it. So clause 11 cannot be left out of account when considering the parties' core obligations' (at [85]). He also added that the situation in the present case was not comparable to that of *Balmoral* and the analysis was therefore inapplicable (at [86]).

The courts also consider the nature of the contract and the extent of the commercial risks involved when concluding that exemption clauses were reasonable. For example, the supply of computer software is a notoriously risky commercial operation and the potential scope of liability is extensive. In light of these facts, the courts are prepared to permit exclusions of consequential (or indirect) losses as long as it is possible to recover for direct losses resulting from the breach. For example, in *SAM Business Systems Ltd v Hedley and Co.* [2002] EWHC 2733 (QB), [2003] 1 All ER (Comm) 465, the judge held that, because there was a money-back guarantee covering the price of the software (i.e. a limitation of liability for direct loss), the exclusion of incidental or consequential losses was reasonable. The clause was also considered to be a common clause in relation to the supply of computer software.

By comparison, in the 'soft drinks' cases—*Britvic Soft Drinks v Messer UK Ltd* [2002] EWCA Civ 548, [2002] 2 Lloyd's Rep 368, and *Bacardi-Martini Beverages Ltd v Thomas Hardy Packaging* [2002] EWCA Civ 549, [2002] 2 Lloyd's Rep 379—exclusion clauses in commercial contracts, which purported to exempt the suppliers from liability for the contamination of the supply of carbon dioxide to be used in the manufacture of soft drinks, were considered to be unreasonable. This decision was based on the lack of negotiation of the clause, the fact that the contamination resulted from the negligence of the supplier, and the fact that this particular event would not have been contemplated as a commercial risk. In *Balmoral Group Ltd v Borealis (UK) Ltd* [2006] EWHC 1900 (Comm) (discussed at **6.3.2**), at [418]–[426], the judge held that since the clause required Balmoral to bear the entire risk of latent defects in Borealis's product, it was unreasonable and an inappropriate allocation of the risk. Balmoral had no choice other than to accept Borealis's terms and Borealis could have covered the risk in relation to its own products with insurance.

However, as *Overseas Medical Supplies Ltd v Orient Transport Services Ltd* [1999] CLC 1243 illustrates, it also remains possible for a clause to be unreasonable in a commercial contract where it undermines a contractual allocation of risk.

The claimant contracted with the defendant freight forwarders for the transportation to Iran and back of equipment for an exhibition. The contract required the defendant to insure the equipment. However, the defendant failed to do so and, in response to a claim by the claimant when the equipment was lost, sought to rely on a limitation clause limiting recovery to an amount per kilo (approximately £600, when the actual loss was £8,590). The judge held that the limitation was reasonable in respect of liability for loss of the goods, but not in relation to liability for breach of the obligation to insure. The Court of Appeal agreed. The failure to insure, when taken with the limitation, would have meant that the customer lost both the goods and the insurance, which would otherwise have provided compensation. Moreover, the claimant had no real choice other than to use the defendant, a specialist firm.

A similar approach can be seen in *Trustees of Ampleforth Abbey Trust v Turner & Townsend Management Ltd* [2012] EWHC 2137 (TCC), [2012] TCLR 8, in which the judge held that a limitation clause in a contract engaging a project management company, which provided that liability for negligence should be limited to the liability covered by the professional indemnity policy but also stated that liability was to be limited to the fees paid (in this case, £111,321), was unreasonable since the company was required by the contract to take out indemnity insurance for £10 million. The clauses were internally incompatible.

Equally, it may be possible to establish that although the contract is made in the commercial context, the positions of the parties are unequal so that the rationale underlying the non-interventionist approach in commercial contracts cannot apply. Thus, in *Motours Ltd v Euroball (West Kent) Ltd* [2003] EWHC 614 (QB), [2003] All ER (D) 165, the judge avoided the non-interventionist approach advocated for commercial contracts and concluded that a clause in standard conditions of a telephone service supplier excluding liability for consequential losses was unreasonable. He concluded that the parties were not of equal bargaining power, taking particularly into consideration the differing financial situation of the parties (the defendant was a large organization with substantial (multi-million pounds) financial resources and capital whereas the claimant was a small company with a turnover of £3 million) and there had been no discussion or negotiations about the terms of the contract. A similar result was achieved in *Kingsway Hall Hotel Ltd v Red Sky IT (Hounslow) Ltd* [2010] EWHC 965 (TCC), (2010) 26 Const LJ 542, because the commercial parties were not of equal bargaining power. This conclusion was reached primarily because the contract was not negotiated, except the price, as it was on Red Sky's terms and Kingsway relied entirely on the defendant's advice that the product would be good for them rather than being a bespoke product (see especially [246] and [255]–[257]). Finally, in *Barclays Bank plc v Grant Thornton* [2015] EWHC 320 (Comm), [2015] 2 BCLC 537, Cooke J at [91] appeared to draw a distinction between the approach in commercial contracts where the contracting parties were both major commercial concerns and the approach where one commercial concern was a small company: 'The court here can be confident of its answer in circumstances where sophisticated business parties are able to protect their own interests and do not require the protection of the 1977 Act in the same way as small companies . . .'. This is likely to become an important distinction in terms of interpretation of UCTA reasonableness post the CRA 2015.

7.5.5.3 The effect and scope of a finding of unreasonableness

Each substantive provision of the 1977 Act that subjects an exemption clause to the requirement of reasonableness is drafted in such a way as to make it clear that, if the requirement of reasonableness is not met, the clause may not be relied upon to exclude or restrict a liability that would otherwise arise under the contract.

Similarly to what was seen for negligence (see **7.5.2**), difficulties may arise, however, where the exemption clause is in a composite form relating to several different possible breaches of the contract in question, or purports to exclude or restrict liability, remedies, or procedural rights in more than one way. In such a case, the question arises whether a failure to satisfy the requirement of reasonableness in respect of one particular dimension of the clause will cause the whole clause to fail, or whether an offending element may be severed from the remainder of the clause where that remainder does satisfy the requirement of reasonableness.

In **Stewart Gill Ltd v Horatio Myer & Co. Ltd** [1992] 1 QB 600, the clause in question purported to prevent the buyer from withholding payment of any amount due to the supplier 'by reason of any payment credit set off counterclaim allegation of incorrect or defective Goods or for any other reason whatsoever which the customer may allege excuses him from performing his obligations'. The claimants claimed the final instalment due under the contract, which the defendants had withheld because of a counterclaim in respect of an alleged breach. The claimants sought to rely upon the set-off and counterclaim element in the exemption clause to show that withholding the sum due was not allowed under the contract, even if the alleged breach by the claimants could be established. The defendants argued that the element in the exemption clause relating to payments and credits was unreasonable, so that the whole clause failed.

Lord Donaldson MR (with whom Balcombe LJ agreed) appears to have been willing to believe that a clause preventing a right of set-off might be reasonable, but was unwilling to believe that it might be reasonable to prevent withholding payment where the claimants owed the defendants money as a result of pre-existing payments or credits. The question therefore was whether the unreasonable part relating to payments and credits could be severed from the remainder of the clause. The court was unanimous that it could not.

- Lord Donaldson relied upon the wording of s. 11(1), which states that the requirement of reasonableness 'is that *the term* shall have been a fair and reasonable one' (emphasis added).

- Stuart-Smith LJ (with whom Balcombe LJ and Lord Donaldson agreed) relied upon the fact that the assessment of whether the clause is reasonable is to be made considering the circumstances known to the parties at the time of contracting. He pointed out that it is impossible to know at the time of contracting which part of a composite and potentially severable exemption clause will be relied upon at some indeterminate time in the future, so that unless the entire clause is the subject of scrutiny, and stands and falls as a whole, the reasonableness test cannot be applied as laid down by the Act.

Nevertheless, in *J. Murphy & Sons Ltd v Johnston Precast Ltd* [2008] EWHC 3024 (TCC), at [137], Coulson J commented that he did not think that *Stewart Gill* was a case concerned with actual severance, but:

> whether the court should look only at part of the clause in question, rather than the entirety of the clause. Moreover, the dispute there came down to the consideration of a few words within a clause, which made severance, for all practical purposes, impossible.

Coulson J therefore concluded that it was perfectly consistent to break down a lengthy contractual term into parts and then assess whether 'those different parts are performing different functions'. Moreover, in *Regus (UK) Ltd v Epcot Solutions Ltd* [2008] EWCA Civ 361, [2009]

1 All ER (Comm) 586, the Court of Appeal commented (*obiter*) that if clauses are seen as independent, i.e. serving a different purpose (in this case, a very specific limitation clause limited to recovery of 125 per cent of the fees or £50,000), they can be severed and enforced.

7.6 Consumer Rights Act 2015, Part 2: unfair terms in B2C contracts

7.6.1 The history

Directive 93/13/EEC on Unfair Terms in Consumer Contracts was originally implemented in English law by the Unfair Terms in Consumer Contracts Regulations 1994, SI 1994/3159 (the 1994 Regulations), which substantially reproduced the wording, if not the order of presentation, of the Directive itself. However, no attempt was made to tackle any clear overlap or potential conflicts between the Directive, the existing legislation (UCTA 1977), and common law rules. One of the frequent criticisms was that the implementation of the Directive had been rushed, and this may explain why there was no attempt to consolidate the Directive and the existing law. Although the 1994 Regulations were subsequently repealed and replaced by the Unfair Terms in Consumer Contract Regulations 1999 Regulations, SI 1999/2083 (the 1999 Regulations), the main difference of substance was confined to so-called pre-emptive challenges to unfair terms by 'qualifying bodies' (see **7.6.8**), and again there was no attempt to rationalize legislative regulation in this area. The potential therefore remained for the English courts to be presented with a series of complex questions about the interplay of the sometimes parallel, sometimes overlapping, and potentially conflicting rules.

In 2005, the Law Commission examined the complex relationship between UCTA 1977 and the 1999 Regulations, and made recommendations in its report *Unfair Terms in Contracts*, Law Com. No. 292 (Cm. 6464, 2005), for reform of the law in this area (discussed in more detail at **7.4.3**). The principal recommendation was for a unified regime for consumer contracts, with the aim of simplifying and clarifying the applicable principles, and altering the burden of proof. These recommendations were put on hold pending the Consumer Rights Directive (CRD) 2011/83/EU. This Directive was originally intended to repeal Directive 93/13; in fact, it made only minor amendments to it. However, the CRD's other provisions offered the opportunity for a single consolidation of consumer law, including the consumer law regime governing exemption clauses and unfair terms, and the proposal to achieve this was published as a Consumer Rights Bill. The Consumer Rights Act 2015 was passed in March 2015 and came into force in October 2015. The Act revokes and replaces the 1999 Regulations. Nevertheless, the case law interpretation of those Regulations remains relevant since the language of Directive 93/13 is largely preserved in the 2015 Act.

7.6.2 When does the Act apply?

7.6.2.1 Consumer contracts

The Consumer Rights Act 2015 applies to contracts between a 'trader' ('a person acting for purposes relating to their trade, business, craft or profession, whether acting personally or through another person acting in the trader's name or on the trader's behalf', CRA 2015 s. 2(2)) and a 'consumer' ('an individual acting for purposes that are wholly or mainly outside that individual's trade, business, craft or profession', CRA s. 2(3)). In Part 2 these expressions have the same meaning as in Part 1 (s. 76(2)).

The definition of 'consumer' as an 'individual' clearly means that a company, limited liability partnerships (LLPs), and general partnerships cannot qualify as a consumer—although, technically, a sole trader is an individual and as such could be covered. However, to gain the protection in CRA 2015 Part 2, the sole trader in question would need to be acting for purposes that are 'wholly or mainly' outside their business purposes (so, the other party—the trader—could counter this by proving that the sole trader was not acting, in their contract, for purposes that were wholly or mainly outside their business, ss. 2(4) and 76(3)).

The definition of consumer in the CRA 2015 requires only that the individual be acting for purposes that are 'wholly or mainly' outside his business rather than exclusively for non-business purposes. This approach derives from the Law Commission's report *Unfair Terms in Contracts*, Law Com. No. 292 (Cm. 6464, 2005) which contained this proposed definition. The inclusion of the words 'wholly or mainly' addresses the classification problems where a contract is partly private and partly for business purposes. The Law Commission had recommended that it should be for the courts to classify a contract as 'consumer' in accordance with what the courts regard as the *predominant purpose* of the contract. The explanatory notes to the CRA 2015 (para. 36) provide that 'a person who works from home one day a week', who buys a kettle to use when working from home, would still be a consumer. 'Conversely, a sole trader operating from a private dwelling who buys a printer of which 95 per cent of the use is for the purposes of the business, is not likely to be held to be a consumer.' These are extreme examples and most issues are likely to appear in the marginal cases, e.g. a 75:25 private-to-business usage ratio of a product.

The courts have addressed this issue and clearly the 'purpose' (or intention) underpinning the contract is all-important. In *Overy v Paypal (Europe) Ltd* [2012] EWHC 2659 (QB), [2013] Bus LR D1, the judge had to consider whether an individual qualified as a 'consumer' within the 1999 Regulations (containing a similar definition of a consumer as a 'natural person' acting for purposes outside their trade, business or profession) when that individual had applied to use Paypal's electronic payment services to collect competition entry fees (the competition prize being his house). He had indicated that the payment service was required for business purposes, because this enabled payments to be made to him directly, but had supplied a mixture of personal details and details of his photography business on the application form. However, it was held that a contract would be treated as having been concluded for a purpose outside the person's business, trade, or profession only if this business purpose were insignificant or negligible and the focus was on satisfying the consumer's needs in terms of private consumption. On these facts, although the claimant's purpose in opening the account was outside his business or profession, he also intended to use the account for payments relating to his photography business and so could not be a consumer under the definition in the 1999 Regulations. The judge also stressed the nature of the representations made when opening the account, which led to the conclusion that the individual was acting for business purposes.

Where a consumer acts as agent for a non-consumer, the contract will not generally be a 'consumer contract'. Nevertheless, it may fall within the consumer legislative regulation where the 'agent' also undertakes personal liabilities in that contract made on behalf of another. *Domsalla (t/a Domsalla Building Services) v Dyason* [2007] EWHC 1174 (TCC), [2007] BLR 348 (also discussed at **7.6.4.4**), concerned a dispute between a builder and a residential occupier under a contract to reinstate a house seriously damaged by fire. The occupier had entered into the contract with the builders as agent for the insurance company dealing with the claim. However, it was held that the 1999 Regulations applied because the contract terms made the occupier liable to the builders both as principal and agent.

7.6.2.2 Terms and notices covered by the Act

CRA 2015 Part 2 applies to contractual terms and notices which relate to obligations between a trader and consumer or which purport to exclude a trader's liability to a consumer (s. 61(4)), whether or not the term or notice expressly applies to a consumer as long as it is reasonable to assume that it is intended to be seen or heard by a consumer (s. 61(6)).

Section 61(2) and (5) make it clear that this Part does not apply to a term or notice relating to obligations or liabilities between an employer and employee. However, there are no other general exclusions. Therefore, the previous law governing the scope of the legislation should continue to apply and the CRA 2015 should apply to guarantee contracts concluded by a consumer in favour of a business, but only where the principal contract to which it relates, and to which it was ancillary, had also been executed by an individual who was not acting wholly or mainly in the course of their trade or profession. In *Barclays Bank plc v Kufner* [2008] EWHC 2319, [2009] 1 All ER (Comm) 1, the defendant guarantor had given a guarantee as security for a loan made by the claimant bank to a company that was beneficially owned by the defendant. The loan agreement had been entered into by a company, which was not a consumer, and the guarantee had also not been executed by a consumer since the defendant had been acting for business purposes in seeking to establish a ship chartering business. It followed that the 1999 Regulations did not apply on the facts.

Contracts relating to land ought also to be covered by CRA 2015 Part 2 on the basis of the previous case law. In *London Borough of Newham v Khatun* [2004] EWCA Civ 55, [2004] 3 WLR 417, the 1999 Regulations applied to local authorities carrying out their statutory duties to house homeless 'consumers'.

7.6.2.3 Mandatory statutory or regulatory provisions to which Part 2 CRA 2015 does not apply

CRA 2015 Part 2 does not apply to contractual terms or contractual notices reflecting mandatory statutory or regulatory provisions' (s. 73(1)(a)), the assumption being that if member states have, by legislative Act, given approval to particular contract terms or notices, those terms cannot by definition be deemed to be unfair (Preamble to Directive 93/13, recital 13). The Preamble envisages that 'default' obligations such as ss. 9 and 10 of the CRA 2015 (satisfactory quality and fitness for purpose: see **6.4.2.4**) would be excluded from the scope of this regulatory regime. It would therefore be odd if they could be assessed for potential unfairness. Indeed, s. 31 CRA 2015 entrenches these 'rights' and provides that these obligations, or liability for them, cannot be excluded or restricted.

Section 73(1)(b) CRA 2015 also expressly excludes 'the provisions or principles of international conventions', such as the Warsaw Convention limitations on liability towards passengers in aircraft.

In *obiter* remarks in *Baybut v Eccle Riggs Country Park Ltd*, The Times, 13 November 2006, the judge considered that all implied terms under statute fell within what is now s. 73(1) as 'mandatory statutory or regulatory provisions'. He went further, at [23], and considered it 'highly unlikely' that the 1999 Regulations were intended to have any application to any implied terms, i.e. implied by the courts, on the basis that such terms could not be implied unless 'reasonable' and so could not be 'unfair'. Moreover, Sch. 2 clearly applies only to express terms. However, terms implied by custom or on the basis of a course of dealing are not subject to the same test for initial reasonableness; it need only be established that they are clearly established and 'notorious' (see **6.4.2.1**), so the scope of this pronouncement must be questionable.

7.6.2.4 Terms can be assessed for fairness but not so-called 'core terms'

Unlike UCTA 1977, which applies only to exemption clauses in B2B contracts (albeit including exemption clauses within the s. 13 extended definition), CRA 2015 Part 2 is broader and regulates 'unfair terms' in 'consumer contracts' or 'unfair consumer notices', providing that they are not binding on the consumer at the consumer's option (s. 62(1)–(3)). For example, since the legislation regulates 'unfair terms' in a general sense, in addition to regulating unfair exemption clauses (see Sch. 2, Part 1, terms 1 and 2 for examples), it also covers unreasonable deposits and penalty clauses (Sch. 2, Part 1, terms 5 and 6) and so overlaps with existing common law control provided by 'the penalty rule' (see **9.6.1**).

However, the CRA 2015 does exclude certain (so-called 'core') terms, potentially within the scope of the Act, from any assessment of their fairness under s. 62, although it is clear that the terms listed in Part 1 of Sch. 2 will always be subject to such an assessment since 'they *may be* regarded as unfair' (s. 63(1), emphasis added). This apart, s. 64(1) excludes from this assessment any term which is transparent and prominent (i.e. not hidden in the small print) and which 'specifies the main subject matter of the contract' (s. 64(1)(a) and (2)). Furthermore, it is not possible to assess the price term where the assessment for fairness would involve assessing 'the appropriateness of the price payable . . . by comparison with the goods, digital content or services supplied under it' (s. 64(1)(b) and (2)). Transparency therefore requires that the term be 'expressed in plain and intelligible language' and written terms must also be legible. Prominence relates to 'notice' in that the term must be 'brought to the consumer's attention in such a way that an average consumer (who is reasonably well-informed, observant and circumspect) would be aware of the term'.

Therefore, the clause in question may be interpreted as a 'core term' because it specifies the main subject of the contract. In this case the legislative regulation will not apply and the term cannot be assessed for fairness.

In **Bankers Insurance Co. Ltd v South** [2003] EWHC 380 (QB), [2004] Lloyd's Rep IR 1, the defendant, South, had purchased holiday insurance for a trip to Cyprus. The policy contained an exclusion of liability for accidents 'involving your ownership or possession of any . . . motorised waterborne craft'. While South was driving a jet ski, he was involved in a collision, and the other person (the second defendant) was seriously injured. The second defendant commenced proceedings against South. The insurer sought a declaration that, because of the exclusion, it was not liable to indemnify South. It was held that the exclusion clause clearly covered the jet-ski accident (its terms were in 'plain and intelligible' language) and that, since it related to the definition of the subject matter of the contract (within the 1999 Regulations, reg. 6(2)), the Regulations did not apply and the term could not be assessed for fairness.

In **Baybut v Eccle Riggs Country Park Ltd**, The Times, 13 November 2006 (see **7.6.2.3**), a term providing for a yearly licence to use a static caravan park was held to be 'a core term' within reg. 6(2), as defining the main subject matter of the contract.

However, when assessing price terms under the 1999 Regulations, reg. 6(2), the courts had drawn a not altogether convincing distinction between 'core' terms relating to the price (which could not be assessed) and 'ancillary' price terms, which could because they fell outside the exclusion from assessment in reg. 6(2). This enabled a 'results-based' approach to be taken to the application of this provision—and hence to the question of whether a term could be assessed for fairness and potentially be considered not binding on the consumer. This distinction is, however, accepted by the ECJ, e.g. in Case C-26/13, *Kásler v OTP Jelzálogbank Zrt* [2014] Bus LR 664, [2014] 2 All ER (Comm) 443, the ECJ considered that terms exempted from consideration for unfairness had to be interpreted strictly and only extended 'to terms laying down the essential obligations of the contract'. The exemption did not extend to 'terms ancillary to those that define the very essence of the contractual relationship'.

In the first case assessing the UTCCR (albeit the 1994 version), *Director General of Fair Trading (DGFT) v First National Bank plc* [2001] UKHL 52, [2002] 1 AC 481, one of the arguments by the bank was that the Regulations could not apply to the contested term, since it was a 'core term' concerning the 'adequacy of the price or remuneration'.

> The term in question in **DGFT v First National Bank plc** was in a consumer loan agreement that provided for interest to be paid after any judgment on the debt. Therefore, in the event of judgment on the debt, contractual interest remained payable despite the fact that the debtor paid the instalments due under the terms of the judgment. The House of Lords held that the term was an incidental term dealing with the consequences of the borrower's default. It did not concern the adequacy of the interest earned by the bank as its remuneration for the loan. Accordingly, this was not a 'core term', the 1994 Regulations applied, and the term could be assessed for fairness.

Lord Bingham (with whose reasons the other members of the House agreed) stated, at [12]:

> The object of the Regulations and the Directive is to protect consumers against the inclusion of unfair and prejudicial terms in standard-form contracts into which they enter, and that object would plainly be frustrated if regulation 3(2)(b) [later the 1999 Regulations, reg. 6(2)] were so broadly interpreted as to cover any terms other than those falling squarely within it.

(The claim that the term was an unfair term under the 1999 Regulations is discussed at **7.6.4.4**.)

Subsequently, in *Bairstow Eves London Central Ltd v Smith* [2004] EWHC 263 (QB), [2004] 2 EGLR 25, it was held that reg. 6(2) of the 1999 Regulations (core terms) was to be interpreted restrictively, thereby allowing more terms to be assessed for unfairness.

> *Bairstow Eves London Central Ltd v Smith* concerned a term in an estate agency contract providing for commission at the rate of 1.5 per cent if paid in full within ten days of completion or an agreed alternative payment date; otherwise, commission was payable at 3 per cent on the sale price, with interest at 3 per cent above base. The judge had concluded that this was not a 'core term' (i.e. did not concern the adequacy of the price or remuneration), and that the 3 per cent term was unfair and so not binding on the vendors. The estate agents appealed on the applicability of the Regulations and, on appeal, it was held that the issue here was whether the core rate was 3 per cent, with an option to pay 1.5 per cent (in which case, reg. 6(2) was applicable), or whether the core rate was 1.5 per cent, with a 'default' provision of 3 per cent. The judge concluded that the 1.5 per cent was contemplated as the price, with a default position of 3 per cent if the vendors failed to pay within ten days. Accordingly, reg. 6(2) did not apply and the Regulations as a whole were applicable. (The issue of unfairness was not appealed.)

Relying on the guidance in *DGFT v First National Bank*, Gross J concluded, at [25]:

> [R]egulation 6(2) must be given a restrictive interpretation; otherwise a coach and horses could be driven through the Regulations. So, while it is not for the Court to re-write the parties' bargain as to the fairness or adequacy of the price itself, regulation 6(2) may be unlikely to shield terms as to price escalation or default provisions from scrutiny under the fairness requirement . . .

The question of the application of reg. 6(2) to exclude the operation of the 1999 Regulations was also considered in *Office of Fair Trading v Foxtons Ltd* [2009] EWHC 1681 (Ch), [2009] 3 EGLR 133, [2009] 29 EG 98 (CS). The case concerned a term in the standard terms of a letting agent, which provided that commission was payable not only when a tenant was first introduced, but also if the tenant renewed, although this was not attributable to anything done by the letting agent. The question was whether this commission was part of the contract price within reg. 6(2). Mann J considered that it was a question of impression and how the term in question would be perceived by the typical consumer landlord, as well as how it was perceived by Foxtons, i.e. was it perceived to be part of the core bargain, or was it perceived to be ancillary? The judge concluded that the term was not core, pointing to the fact that it was hidden away in the document, and was not expressed in plain and intelligible language. This decision has all of the hallmarks of a policy decision to be able to test the commission clauses for unfairness. The commission clearly relates to the key duties of the letting agent and would seem to be the price charged for that service. The decision on this point might therefore differ following the rather different approach subsequently adopted by the Supreme Court in the 'bank charges' case.

In the 'bank charges' litigation, the banks had argued that the terms imposing such charges could not be considered as unfair terms, since they were 'core terms'. (Banking is generally free for those customers who stay in credit, but fixed fees and interest are payable by customers with overdrafts, particularly customers who have unauthorized overdrafts.) In *Office of Fair Trading v Abbey National plc* [2009] UKSC 6, [2010] 1 AC 696, the Supreme Court accepted this argument, and therefore concluded that the 1999 Regulations could not apply to test the fairness, or otherwise, of bank charges levied on personal current account customers for unauthorized overdrafts.

At first instance and before the Court of Appeal in *Office of Fair Trading v Abbey National plc* [2009] EWCA Civ 116, [2009] 2 WLR 1286, the banks had lost the argument on the basis that bank charges were interpreted as ancillary and not part of 'the core terms'. However, in **Office of Fair Trading v Abbey National plc** [2009] UKSC 6, [2010] 1 AC 696, the Supreme Court rejected the distinction between sums that represented the core bargain and ancillary sums. There was no principled basis for treating some terms as more essential than others in this context: *per* Lord Walker at [41]. The question was only whether the charges represented the monetary price for the service provided in exchange under the contract. These charges were part of the customer's package—*per* Lord Mance at [114]—and the price paid for banking services. Their Lordships were aware of the wider implications and Lord Walker noted that these charges amounted to 'over 30 percent' of the revenue stream for banks from personal account customers, which suggested that they must be part of 'the core or essential bargain'. It was also irrelevant that payment of these charges was contingent, so that the majority of customers would not pay them: at [47]. It followed that the 1999 Regulations had no application.

This issue of core and ancillary obligations remained controversial, and in *Office of Fair Trading v Ashbourne Management Services Ltd* [2011] EWHC 1237 (Ch), [2011] ECC 31, the court had to consider whether a term concerning minimum membership periods in a contract for gym membership was a core term within reg. 6(2), or ancillary and so capable of being assessed under the Regulations. It might be thought that the main subject of such an agreement is the membership and right to use the club, and that the period of time for which this applied would be ancillary to this. However, the judge held that the period of membership was a core term. Nevertheless, since reg. 6(2)(b) only precluded the assessment of fairness by reference to the adequacy of the price or remuneration as against the services supplied, the judge thought, at [153], that reg. 6(2)(a) should only preclude an assessment for fairness by reference to the definition of the main subject matter. It was therefore possible to assess this clause for fairness in relation to the consequences for members of early termination of their memberships. This approach enabled the court to give effect to the evident policy of the legislation, e.g. as expressed by Gross J in *Bairstow Eves London Central Ltd v Smith* and by Lord Steyn in *DGFT v First National Bank plc*, at [31].

The intention behind the slightly adapted wording in s. 64(1) CRA 2015 is to reflect the case law and to distinguish between 'the price' and 'aspects of the price other than the amount'. The explanatory notes cite (para. 316) the example of the timing of payment. The terms specifying the amount of the price cannot, however, be assessed since they fall within the exclusion assuming that they are transparent and prominent. Paragraph 317 provides a further example involving a contract to engage a catering company to provide a buffet lunch where the price term is £100 for a three-course meal. The court cannot examine whether paying £100 for the three-course meal is fair. It can, however, evaluate the cancellation rights available to both parties and any term governing when payment is due.

It follows, by looking at previous case law, that the intention is to eliminate the concept of ancillary terms relating to the price amount or any aspect of calculating the price, and so eliminate some of the previous inconsistencies in approach.

7.6.3 Exclusion or restriction of negligence liability

The CRA 2015 Part 2 contains a specific provision which mirrors s. 2(1) UCTA 1977 and provides that (with some exceptions such as an insurance contracts and certain liability of occupiers, s. 66) a term or notice cannot exclude or restrict liability for death or personal injury resulting from negligence (s. 65(1)). Moreover, the consumer cannot be assumed to have accepted any risk simply by agreeing to, or having knowledge of, the existence of such a term (s. 65(2)). This is important because under the previous 1999 Regulations, terms seeking to exclude or restrict liability in negligence for death or personal injury were not barred automatically but subjected to the fairness test.

Where the term seeks to exclude or restrict other loss or damage, e.g. death or personal injury which does not result from negligence, or financial loss resulting from negligence, it is subject to the fairness test.

For qualified obligations and, in particular, breaches of s. 49 CRA 2015 (trader's obligation to supply a service with reasonable care and skill), s. 57 provides that the trader cannot exclude this liability, i.e. the parties cannot agree that the trader will have no responsibility to perform with reasonable care and skill. Such a term will have no effect and therefore some negligence liability resulting from such a breach has to be accepted by the trader. If there is an attempt to limit this liability for breach of s. 49, s. 57 makes it clear that the limitation figure cannot be less than the contract price and any such limitation would also be subject to the fairness test.

7.6.4 Determining unfairness and the meaning of 'good faith'

> **! KEY POINT**
>
> The contractual term shall be regarded as unfair if 'contrary to the requirement of good faith, it causes a significant imbalance in the parties' rights and obligations arising under the contract, to the detriment of the consumer' (CRA 2015, s. 62(4) and (6)).

This provision is the key to the control mechanism adopted by Directive 93/13 and it is significant since it introduced the concept of good faith into English law. The issue of fairness is so critical that a court must consider the issue even if none of the parties have raised it under s. 71(2) CRA 2015. *The critical issue is where the burden of proof with regard to fairness lies.* Under the 1999 Regulations it was clear that the consumer had the burden of proving unfairness. It was equally clear that the Law Commission had proposed the reversal of this burden of proof. However, nothing is stated explicitly in the Act to indicate a reversal of this burden. It is clear that an unfair term is not binding on the consumer and there is a definition of when terms will be 'unfair'. However, this is referred to as 'the fairness test' in the explanatory notes and since the court now has a duty to consider whether a term is fair even if unfairness is not pleaded by the consumer (s. 71 CRA 2015), it might be suggested that the 'fairness test' would now be a determination by the court rather than relying specifically on the consumer to establish the unfairness, i.e. the court would look at all the evidence to determine whether the term was fair and permitted.

One significant change in the CRA 2015 is the existence of 'entrenched consumer rights' (s. 62(8) CRA 2015). This means that the terms providing for the goods in a consumer sale of goods to be of satisfactory quality, fit for purpose, and corresponding to description and sample etc., are essential consumer protections and cannot be excluded or restricted (s. 31 CRA 2015). Such 'rights' cannot be rendered inoperative so that any exclusion or restriction would be of no effect, irrespective of the test of fairness in s. 62. This clarifies one area of uncertainty that used to exist under the 1999 Regulations (i.e. although the old s. 6(2) SGA 1979 stated that it was not possible to exclude or restrict the satisfactory quality term in a consumer contract, the term would still have needed to be shown to be unfair under the 1999 Regulations). This is no longer the case.

7.6.4.1 'To the detriment of the consumer'

It appears that the notion of 'detriment to the consumer' is unlikely to cause great difficulty; it is subordinate to the notion of 'significant imbalance', and its only purpose is to indicate for whose benefit the control is to be exercised. In the unlikely event of an imbalance *in favour* of the consumer, the term would clearly not be 'unfair'.

7.6.4.2 'Contrary to good faith, [the clause or term or notice] causes a significant imbalance in the parties' rights and obligations'

The key notion is a 'significant imbalance in the parties' rights and obligations arising under the contract' that is in some way contrary to the 'requirement of good faith'. These are vague and ill-defined criteria, and the CRA 2015 fails to make clear the relationship between them. In particular, the drafting of s. 62(4) does not make clear whether the requirement of lack of good faith is additional to the condition of imbalance between the parties, or whether imbalance is to be regarded in itself as evidence of a lack of good faith. Neither Directive 93/13 nor the implementing legislation provide clear guidance on this matter, or on what constitutes a significant imbalance. Some assistance towards 'good faith' can be gained by referring to recital 16 of the Preamble to the Directive, which defines compliance with the requirement of good faith as being satisfied by dealing equitably and fairly with the consumer, whose legitimate interests must be taken into account.

The only assistance provided in the 1999 Regulations, and now contained in s. 62(5), is a general provision which refers to unfairness as being assessed:

> taking into account the nature of the subject matter of the contract; and by reference to all the circumstances existing when the term was agreed and to all of the other terms of the contract or of another contract on which it depends.

In summary, therefore, *unfairness is determined following the subject matter, the circumstances surrounding formation, and the other terms of the contract.* As an example of the application of the fairness test, para. 299 of the explanatory notes to the CRA 2015 cites 'a contract to subscribe to a magazine which allows the publisher to cancel the subscription at short notice'. Factors relevant to the assessment of fairness would include 'whether the subscriber can also cancel at short notice or obtain a refund if the publisher cancels the contract'.

This guidance in s. 62 CRA 2015 is very evidently rather general in its nature. Consequently, identification of the criteria for compliance with the terms of the Act is a process of deduction from what is termed, in s. 63(1), an 'indicative and non-exhaustive list of terms . . . that may be regarded as unfair' and which is contained in Sch. 2, Part 1 of the CRA 2015.

7.6.4.3 The Schedule 2, Part 1 list of indicative terms that may be unfair

The list is too long (20 items) to reproduce here, but it is possible to indicate its main themes. Not unexpectedly, terms that are clearly within the scope of UCTA 1977 (e.g. para. 2, inappropriately excluding or restricting the consumer's legal rights in the event of total, partial, or inadequate performance of the trader's obligations) are included. Other items on the list, such as terms 'enabling a trader to terminate a contract of indeterminate duration without reasonable notice except where there are serious grounds for doing so' (para. 8), and terms 'enabling the trader seller or supplier to alter the terms of the contract unilaterally without a valid reason which is specified in the contract' (para. 11). Such terms had not previously been subject to control under English law, although it might be argued that, in some circumstances, they might be classified as terms that modify expected contractual obligations and so to be subject to the reasonableness test under s. 3(2)(b)(i) of the 1977 Act, although only where one party deals on the other's written standard terms of business (see **7.5.3.2**), and some of them fall within the application of the penalty rule (see **9.6.1**).

From this list, it appears possible to deduce that imbalance and lack of good faith are distinct elements in the test. A power to alter terms unilaterally constitutes an imbalance in the rights and obligations of the parties—but that in itself is not deemed to be unfair. There must also be no valid reason specified in the contract for such unilateral alteration, and it appears to be the absence of valid reason that constitutes the lack of good faith.

Nevertheless, although the two-part mechanics of the test appear clearly established, the list also demonstrates the extent to which both imbalance and lack of good faith will always be questions of fact in each particular case, thereby leaving a very considerable element of discretion to the courts.

7.6.4.4 'Good faith': the English reaction

As discussed in **Chapter 1**, English law does not formally recognize any concept of 'good faith' as such, although the Chancery courts, in the exercise of their 'equitable' jurisdiction, have developed principles based on conscience and unconscionability that are closer to the notion of good faith in the civil law than any common law concepts. In that context, it is said that the purpose of the rule is to prevent oppression or unfair surprise. Since we are back to fairness, there is a danger of circularity as well as confining unfairness to procedural matters. Indeed, the reference to 'significant imbalance' would appear to be more closely concerned with substantive unfairness.

Professor Beale, in 'Legislative control of fairness: The Directive on Unfair Terms in Consumer Contracts' in Beatson and Friedmann (eds.), *Good Faith and Fault in Contract Law* (Oxford University Press, 1995), at p. 245, made the following comment concerning the meaning of 'good faith':

> I suspect that good faith has a double operation. First, it has a procedural aspect. It will require the supplier to consider the consumer's interests. However, a clause which might be unfair if it came as a surprise may be upheld if the business took steps to bring it to the consumer's attention and to explain it. Secondly, it has a substantive content: some clauses may cause such an imbalance that they should always be treated as contrary to good faith and therefore unfair.

The first reported decision of the higher courts examining the Regulations (1994 version) was the House of Lords' decision in *Director General of Fair Trading (DGFT) v First National Bank plc* [2001] UKHL 52, [2002] 1 AC 481 (for facts, see **7.6.2.4**).

> The Director General of Fair Trading sought an injunction to prevent the continued use of the term providing for interest to continue to be payable after any judgment on the debt (see **7.6.2.4**), arguing that it was 'unfair' within the Regulations. The Court of Appeal held that the term was unfair because of the imbalance of bargaining power and the fact that the term would create 'unfair surprise', i.e. if the judgment debtor were to comply with that order and pay his debt in instalments, he would then find that he had to pay additional sums to cover the contractual interest, when his attention had not been drawn to this fact.
>
> On appeal, the House of Lords held that the term was not unfair. Although a consumer subject to a judgment debt was clearly affected to his detriment, this was not the result of the application of the challenged term, but followed the applicable legislation and its failure to allow the contractual interest to be covered by the terms of the judgment on the debt. The term itself was a perfectly fair provision, which enabled the lender to recover the principal and interest on the loan amount.

Lord Bingham noted, at [17], that good faith is not 'a concept wholly unfamiliar to British lawyers. It looks to good standards of commercial morality and practice'. He equated good faith with 'fair and open dealing'. Lord Bingham stated, at [17]:

> The requirement of significant imbalance is met if a term is so weighted in favour of the supplier as to tilt the parties' right and obligations under the contract significantly in his favour. This may be by the granting to the supplier of a beneficial option or discretion or power; or by the imposing on the consumer of a disadvantageous burden or risk or duty . . . The requirement of good faith in this context is one of fair and open dealing. Openness requires that the terms should be expressed fully, clearly and legibly, containing no concealed pitfalls or traps. Appropriate prominence should be given to terms which might operate disadvantageously to the customer.

Lord Bingham appears to confine good faith to procedural aspects ('fair and open dealing'), although he referred to the Regulations as laying down a composite test, i.e. the 'significant imbalance' requirement imports considerations of the substantive fairness of the term judged in the context of the contract terms as a whole. However, whilst there was agreement that 'significant imbalance' relates to substantive considerations, it would also appear that good faith may entail both procedural and substantive issues, and Lord Bingham appears to accept this, since the examples he uses refer to issues of unconscionability and taking advantage of a position of vulnerability in bargaining.

Lord Steyn concluded, at [36], that '[a]ny purely procedural or even predominantly procedural interpretation of the requirement of good faith must be rejected', and considered that there was a large area of overlap between 'significant imbalance' and 'contrary to good faith'. This amounts to acceptance that good faith can involve issues relating to substantive fairness.

Thus it seems that 'good faith' in this context is an overarching concept that may be infringed in circumstances either of substantive or procedural unfairness, where this results in significant imbalance in the parties' positions to the detriment of the consumer. References in s. 62(5) to the position surrounding the making of the contract and its substantive fairness add support to such an interpretation.

In *Office of Fair Trading v Foxtons Ltd* [2009] EWHC 1681 (Ch), [2009] 29 EG 98 (CS) (for facts, see **7.6.2.4**), Mann J assessed whether the commission clauses were unfair, and noted a significant imbalance following the term, since the amounts of commission were significant and operated adversely over time, e.g. commission was payable for a renewal when the services given were minimal. The judge then considered procedural questions of 'openness and fairness', and concluded that unless the landlord knew the clause was there, it would operate as an annual 'trap, or a time bomb'. However, it was doubtful that the typical consumer landlord would realize that the clause was there and it was likely that he would not expect it. The clause would therefore have to be clearly presented and drawn to the attention of the consumer landlord.

In *Office of Fair Trading v Ashbourne Management Services Ltd* [2011] EWHC 1237 (Ch), [2011] ECC 31, terms in contracts for gym membership that set minimum membership periods of 12 to 36 months were unfair terms because they were weighted to cause a significant imbalance in the parties' respective positions, which was contrary to good faith. These periods were designed to exploit consumers' overestimation of their use of their gym membership.

Whether an adjudication provision in a standard form used in the construction industry will be unfair in the consumer context appears to turn on whether it has been 'imposed' on the consumer so that the supplier will be unable to satisfy the requirements of fair dealing. However, in *Bryen & Langley Ltd v Boston* [2005] EWCA Civ 973, [2005] BLR 508, the standard form was used at the instigation of the consumer's surveyor. It is, of course, unlikely that the consumer actually knew of, and read, the applicable provisions before submitting them for adoption as the contract terms. However, the relevant question is whether the consumer was able to influence the terms on which the parties contracted. Other cases following this conclusion and reasoning are *Lovell Projects Ltd v Legg* [2003] 1 BLR 452 and *Westminster Building Co. Ltd v Beckingham* [2004] EWHC 138 (TCC), 94 Con LR 107. By comparison, in *Picardi v Cuniberti* [2002] EWHC 2923 (Ch), [2003] BLR 487, the adjudication provisions were held to be unfair terms, having been imposed on the consumer by the supplier's architect.

In *Mylcrist Builders Ltd v Buck* [2008] EWHC 2172 (TCC), [2009] 2 All ER (Comm) 259, [2008] BLR 611, Ramsey J held that an arbitration clause in a consumer contract was unfair because the consumer was forced to submit to arbitration. The judge concluded that a lay person would not necessarily appreciate the significance of an arbitration clause, so that there had not been 'fair and open dealing' as required by the 1999 Regulations. Finally, this was not a case in which the consumer was responsible for instigating the use of the standard form containing this clause.

In *Domsalla (t/a Domsalla Building Services) v Dyason* [2007] EWHC 1174 (TCC), [2007] BLR 348 (see **7.6.2.1**), the occupier withheld payments and the builder therefore submitted the dispute to adjudication before the Joint Contracts Tribunal (JCT).

- Although it was potentially unfair for the builders to rely on the adjudication provisions, since the owner had no control over the contract and was required to enter into it on those terms by the insurers, the adjudication provisions did not substantially alter the balance of the parties' rights and obligations.

- However, since the occupier was not entitled, as is normally the case for an employer, to issue withholding notices (this was a matter for the insurers), and if the notices were not properly issued, the owner would incur liability, the effect of the provisions on withholding notices could substantially affect the owner's rights, so that these withholding provisions were unfair.

An example of an application of both substantive and procedural unfairness is *Spreadex Ltd v Cochrane* [2012] EWHC 1290 (Comm), since the clause in question resulted in the consumer having potential unlimited liability in all circumstances for any unauthorized dealings with its online spread-betting account with the bookmaker, e.g. even if the consumer were able to demonstrate that he had not been negligent. The judge also considered that the manner for giving notice of this clause was inadequate, i.e. the consumer was told that four documents could be viewed elsewhere by clicking on a key. The customer agreement containing the clause was in small print and extended to 49 pages. It was considered most unlikely that it would have been read, thereby suggesting that an argument could have been made to reject the clause altogether under the principle in *Interfoto Picture Library Ltd v Stiletto Visual Programmes Ltd* [1989] QB 433 (see **6.3.1.4**).

A more recent example is *West v Ian Finlay & Associates* [2014] EWCA Civ 316, [2014] BLR 324.

The Court of Appeal had to consider the fairness of a 'net contribution clause' in a contract with a firm of architects to renovate a domestic house. A Net Contribution Clause (NCC) limits a contractor's liability to losses for which it is responsible so as to avoid a contractor being liable for losses caused by others (and in the absence of such a clause all wrongdoers would be jointly and severally liable for all loss suffered irrespective of fault). The particular NCC provided that: 'Our liability for loss or damage will be limited to the amount that it is reasonable for us to pay in relation to the contractual responsibilities of other consultants, contractors and specialists appointed by you.' The main contractor was insolvent and the house-owners sued the architects, who were responsible for coordinating the work done by a series of contractors, seeking damages in respect of defective renovations. The architects argued that their liability was limited by the NCC because the main contractor had also been at fault. Were net contribution clauses inherently unfair and contrary to good faith under the 1999 Regulations (and unreasonable under UCTA 1977)? It was held that such clauses could be fair and reasonable if drafted in clear terms. Although the NCC clearly resulted in an imbalance in the parties' rights and obligations because it limited the householders' ability to recover in full against the architects, this was not 'significant' because net contribution clauses are standard in industry forms and (per Vos LJ at [52]): '[W]e doubt whether any lawyer advising a commercial party to a building contract would be likely to object to such a term.' In any event, the clause was not contrary to good faith since it had been clearly presented and was not a concealed trap, the householders were perfectly able to understand

Thus, NCCs are not unreasonable or unfair simply because they seek to avoid the principle of joint and several liability.

7.6.5 Transparency—plain, intelligible language

A transparency requirement for written terms and consumer notices requires them to 'be expressed in plain and intelligible language' and be 'legible' (s. 68(2)). The need to use 'plain and intelligible language' reflects the language previously used in reg. 7(1) of the 1999 Regulations and the requirements of the Directive.

However, the issue in the past was the apparent absence of any sanction for breach of this duty. The CRA 2015 seeks to address this shortcoming and the explanatory notes to the Act (para. 329) explain that this duty will be capable of being enforced under the enforcement provisions in Sch. 3, e.g. on referral to the Competition and Markets Authority (CMA). Alternatively, public bodies may enforce it under the provisions of Part 8 of the Enterprise Act 2002, e.g. if the term harms the collective interest of consumers (see **7.6.8**). This has the potential to make an impact in terms of clarity of drafting in the consumer context.

Nevertheless, in an individual dispute, the consumer has no effective remedy should the terms be poorly drafted, other than the possibility of being able to test a 'core term' for fairness in accordance with s. 64(2). Section 69(1) will provide the consumer with the benefit of the *contra proferentem* rule in such circumstances, i.e. if there are different meanings of the words used, the meaning that is most favourable to the consumer will prevail (see **7.3.1.2**) but this rule would also apply at common law irrespective of the Act.

7.6.6 Secondary contracts

Unlike the 1999 Regulations, the CRA 2015 contains a provision addressing the application of the 'fairness' regime to secondary contracts that have an effect on the obligations under a main consumer contract (see also **7.5.4** discussing secondary contracts and s. 10 UCTA 1977). The Part 2 regime applies to the terms of the 'secondary contract' as it would if the terms were contained in the main contract, and it makes no difference whether the parties to the secondary contract are the same as the parties to the main contract or even whether the secondary contract is a consumer contract (as long as the main contract is). However, the clause explicitly excludes application of the CRA 2015 Part 2 if the secondary contract is a settlement agreement relating to a claim under the main contract.

7.6.7 The consequences of a term being unfair

Where a term or notice is unfair under the Part 2 regime, it is unenforceable (or not binding) on the consumer (s. 65(1)(2)). However, the consumer can choose to rely on the term or notice

(s. 62(3)). As noted above, this unenforceability sanction does not apply simply because there is a breach of the obligation to use plain, intelligible language (**7.6.5**).

Under s. 67, however, where a term is unfair and so not binding on the consumer, 'the contract continues, so far as practicable, to have effect in every other respect'. This implies that where a term contains an unfair element, the whole term is affected, so that the contract must be read without the whole term. It will be seen later, in relation to illegality, that English law is willing to consider severing the offending parts from terms where that is grammatically possible and consistent with the public policy issues at stake (see **16.5.3**). The severance rule might be thought to contribute to the preservation of contracts; the deletion of whole terms must increase the risk that the commercial balance of the contract will be upset, or that the contract will become too vague to be enforceable. This must be balanced against the overall purpose of consumer protection, which is perhaps more likely to be guaranteed if unfair terms are completely outlawed. (See also **7.5.5.3** for severance in relation to UCTA 1977.) The ECJ has held that where severance of the unfair term has occurred and the contract cannot then continue in existence, the national court could cure this deleted unfair term (and hence the contract) by substituting a supplementary provision of national law which did not fall foul of the unfairness test: Case C-26/13, *Kásler v OTP Jelzálogbank Zrt* [2014] Bus LR 664, [2014] 2 All ER (Comm) 443, [80]–[82]. This might be particularly useful if the effect of the invalidity of the whole contract would be problematic for the consumer, e.g. requiring the consumer to make immediate repayment of a loan.

7.6.8 General challenges to unfair terms

Article 7 of Directive 93/13 requires member states to ensure that adequate and effective means exist to prevent the continued use of unfair terms, including powers under which persons or organizations having a legitimate interest under national law in protecting consumers shall be able to bring representative 'actions' to determine whether contractual terms drawn up for general use are unfair.

The provisions of the Consumer Rights Act 2015 that give effect to Art. 7 of Directive 93/13 (pre-emptive referrals and challenges) are contained in Sch. 3 (and their investigative powers are contained in Sch. 5). Section 70 CRA 2015 refers to the general enforcement of the law on unfair contract terms as being the function of the Competition and Markets Authority (CMA) (which took over the previous functions of the Office of Fair Trading in 2014) and other regulators, as set out in Sch. 3 (e.g. the Financial Conduct Authority, utility regulators and the Consumers' Association).

Schedule 3 provides that a 'regulator' under the Act may consider a complaint covered by CRA 2015 Part 2 (and the CMA is to be informed if it is not the regulator in question in the individual instance). The regulator may apply for an injunction to prevent the use of an existing term or notice, or the proposed use of a future term or notice (*Office of Fair Trading v Foxtons* [2009] EWCA Civ 288, [2010] 1 WLR 663) where the term is purporting to exclude or restrict liability of an entrenched right (e.g. liability mentioned in s. 31) or a barred exclusion (negligence liability for death or personal injury), or the term or notice is unfair to any extent, and this ability exists irrespective of whether the regulator has received a complaint from a member of the public. A regulator may accept an undertaking (usually with agreed conditions attached) from any trader against whom the regulator has applied for an injunction or believes it is entitled to apply for an injunction. In practice, undertakings have staved off action in the majority of instances, although see e.g. *DGFT v First National Bank plc* [2001] UKHL 52, [2002] 1 AC 481 and *Office of Fair Trading v Foxtons Ltd* [2009] EWHC 1681 (Ch), [2009] 3 EGLR 133, [2009] 29 EG 98 (CS). The effectiveness of undertakings explains the limited case law discussing legislative regulation of unfairness in the consumer context.

Schedule 5 sets out the enforcement and investigative powers available to 'enforcers' such as the CMA and 'public designated enforcers' under the Enterprise Act 2002. General enforcement procedures in the consumer context were strengthened by Part 8 of the Enterprise Act 2002 which allow these designated enforcers to apply to the courts for enforcement orders (which are similar to injunctions) against traders who do not comply with their legal obligations to consumers. These powers extend to domestic and European law that impacts on consumers: see *Office of Fair Trading v Ashbourne Management Services Ltd* [2011] EWHC 1237 (Ch), [2011] ECC 31, for a fairly recent example.

The Consumer Protection from Unfair Trading Regulations (CPRs) 2008, SI 2008/1277, implementing the European Unfair Commercial Practices Directive (UCPD) 2005/29/EC, could apply to the use of unfair contract terms if there are terms that implement unfair commercial marketing and selling practices, e.g. misleading consumers about their rights, such as cancellation rights. The CPRs create offences in respect of these unfair commercial practices. It is possible that the use of such terms could give rise to enforcement action under the CPRs in addition to, or in place of, the CRA 2015.

MULTIPLE-CHOICE QUESTIONS

Test your knowledge by trying this chapter's **multiple-choice questions**: www.oup.com/uk/poole

FURTHER READING

General
Lawson, *Exclusion Clauses and Unfair Contract Terms*, 11th edn (Sweet and Maxwell, 2014).

Construction
Adams, 'Fundamental breach: positively last appearance' (1983) 46 MLR 771.
Barendt, 'Exclusion clauses: incorporation and interpretation' (1972) 35 MLR 644.
Gower, 'Exemption clauses: contractual and tortious liability' (1954) 17 MLR 155.
Nicol and Rawlings, 'Substantive fundamental breach burnt out' (1980) 43 MLR 567.
Peel, 'Contract preferentem revisited' (2017) 133 LQR 6.
Shaw-Mellor, 'Negligence construction: does anything remain of Canada Steamship?' the [2017] JBL 610.
White, 'Defining "exclusion clauses" and "defining" clauses: the need to clarify the scope of the UCTA 77' [2016] JBL 373.

Unfair Contract Terms Act 1977
Adams and Brownsword, 'The Unfair Contract Terms Act: a decade of discretion' (1988) 104 LQR 94.
Macdonald, 'Exclusion clauses: the ambit of s. 13(1) of the Unfair Contract Terms Act 1977' (1992) 12 LS 277.
Peel, 'Reasonable exemption clauses' (2001) 117 LQR 545.

Unfair Terms in Consumer Contracts Regulations 1999

Beale, 'Unfair contracts in Britain and Europe' [1989] CLP 197.

Beale, 'Legislative control of fairness: the Directive on Unfair Terms in Consumer Contracts' in Beatson and Friedmann (eds.), *Good Faith and Fault in Contract Law* (Oxford University Press, 1995).

Bright, 'Winning the battle against unfair contract terms' (2000) 20 LS 331.

Macdonald, 'Scope and fairness of the Unfair Terms in Consumer Contracts Regulations: *Director General of Fair Trading v First National Bank*' (2002) 65 MLR 763.

Macmillan, 'Evolution or revolution? Unfair terms in consumer contracts' [2002] CLJ 22.

Morgan, 'Bank charges and the Unfair Terms in Consumer Contracts Regulations 1999: the end of the road for consumers?' [2010] LMCLQ 208.

Law Commission and Consumer Rights Act 2015

Law Commission Consultation Paper No. 166, *Unfair Terms in Contracts* (2002).

Law Commission Report No. 292, *Unfair Terms in Contracts* (Cm. 6464, 2005).

Law Commission Issues Paper, *Unfair Terms in Consumer Contracts: A New Approach?* (July 2012).

Law Commission, *Unfair Consumer Contracts: Advice to Department for Business, Innovation and Skills* (March 2013).

See online at http://lawcommission.justice.gov.uk/areas/unfair_terms_in_contracts.htm

Consumer Rights Act 2015, Part 2, www.legislation.gov.uk/ukpga/2015/15/contents/enacted

Consumer law

Howells, Twigg-Flesner, and Wilhemsson, *Rethinking Consumer Law* (Routledge, 2018).

Chapter 8

Breach of contract

SUMMARY OF THE ISSUES

A contract can be discharged by performance, agreement, frustration (see **Chapter 12**), or breach. This chapter's main focus is breach, and particularly repudiatory breach, i.e. discharge (termination) of the contract for that breach.

- In practice, most contracts are discharged by performance. It is necessary to identify the standard of performance required in relation to each contractual obligation, since a failure to perform to the required standard constitutes a breach. Contractual performance obligations are either strict or qualified.

- Contracts may be discharged by agreement, but such an agreement to discharge must be legally enforceable and so must be supported by consideration, if not contained in a deed.

- A contract breach will occur where, without lawful excuse, a party either fails or refuses to perform a contractual obligation imposed on that party by the terms of the contract or performs a contractual obligation in a defective manner.

- Every breach of contract, however small, gives rise to a right to claim damages. However, unless the breach constitutes a repudiatory breach, the contract will remain in force. If the breach is repudiatory, the non-breaching party will have the option either to accept the breach as terminating the contract (in which case, both parties' future obligations will be discharged) or to affirm the contract (in which event, the contract remains in force for both parties). If the breach is non-repudiatory (such as a breach of warranty), the victim will only be entitled to claim damages for the loss suffered.

- It is crucially important therefore to identify repudiatory breaches and the classification of terms is important for this purpose. Breaches of certain types of term (conditions) are, in the main, repudiatory breaches, and breaches of innominate terms will be repudiatory breaches if the effects of the breach are serious. However, the process of identifying conditions and innominate terms is uncertain, and there are risks for the non-breaching party in deciding to treat a breach as repudiatory, because, if not confirmed as such, this will constitute wrongful repudiation.

- A breach of an entire obligation will also constitute a repudiatory breach, but entire and severable obligations must be distinguished, since breach of a severable obligation does not entitle the non-breaching party to elect to terminate the whole contract. There are recognized circumstances in which it is possible to avoid the usual consequences of the entire obligation rule.

- Breach may be anticipatory, i.e. breach occurs before the time for performance because, for example, one party indicates that he will not be performing on the performance date. The non-breaching party can take the other party at his word and elect to accept this breach by anticipatory repudiation as terminating the contract, in which event he need not wait until the date for performance before claiming damages. Alternatively, the non-breaching party can affirm and

8

»

await the date for performance (i.e. give the breaching party a second chance). If the non-breaching party chooses to affirm, he may, in certain circumstances, continue with his performance and claim the contract price—although this is controversial since it is clear that the performance is not wanted by the party committing the breach. Affirmation also means that both parties are expected to perform their obligations as they fall due, so that there are some risks to the non-breaching party in selecting this route.

8.1 Background: bringing primary obligations to an end

1. The primary obligations of a contract are those that determine the performance obligations of the parties: see Lord Diplock in *Photo Production Ltd v Securicor Transport Ltd* [1980] AC 827.

2. *Discharge of a contract* is the process whereby the primary obligations under a validly formed contract come to an end. Most commonly, the discharge of a contract will occur on *performance* of both parties' primary obligations (see **8.2**). However, a contract may also be *discharged by agreement* of the parties. This chapter will briefly examine both discharge by performance and discharge by agreement, before focusing on *discharge for breach*. A third form of discharge of a contract, is through the operation of the *doctrine of frustration*, which discharges both parties from performance of their future obligations (**Chapter 12**). For discharge by breach, a secondary obligation to pay damages for loss caused (or a secondary obligation to pay the contract price) continues (see **8.4**). However, where the contract is discharged by frustration (see **12.7**), the obligation to pay damages also ends.

> ! KEY POINT
>
> It is crucial to distinguish the process of discharge of valid contracts from situations in which a contract is void or is rescinded.
>   A contract may be invalid (void or voidable) because it is affected by:
>
> - mistake (see **Chapters 3** and **13**);
> - misrepresentation (see **Chapter 14**);
> - duress or undue influence (see **Chapter 15**); or
> - illegality, including restraint of trade (see **Chapter 16**).
>
> *Void*: Since a void contract is automatically of no effect from the very beginning, and hence gives rise to no obligation to perform, the party asserting its invalidity does not need to do anything aside from pleading the invalidity as a defence to a claim for breach.
> *Voidable*: Where a contract is voidable (e.g. for misrepresentation), the contract remains valid until it is set aside by the party with the right to do so, a process known as *rescission*. The process of rescission is very different from the discharge of a contract, because if a voidable contract is rescinded, the contract is then treated as having no effect from the beginning; discharge of the contract, however, does not destroy the contract itself—rather, it merely brings the primary obligations to an end, i.e. only future obligations are discharged.

Part 2

Content, interpretation, performance, and breach

8.2 Discharge by performance or agreement

8.2.1 Discharge by performance

A contract is discharged by the performance by both parties of all of the primary contractual obligations, express and implied. An obligation is performed only where the performance meets the standard of performance required. Consequently, a failure to reach the required standard constitutes breach.

8.2.1.1 The standard of performance

Contractual obligations require one of two standards of performance.

8.2.1.1.1 Strict contractual obligations

Generally, the performance obligation is strict, so that the contractual obligation must be completely and precisely performed. There is no defence for failure to meet this strict obligation (other than an enforceable exemption clause, discussed in **Chapter 7**). The only other exception to this strict contractual liability is for what may be regarded as 'microscopic' deviations (the *de minimis* rule).

For example, if a seller fails to deliver the goods to the buyer on the contractual date set for delivery to occur, he is guilty of a strict contractual breach. It is irrelevant that the seller's breach was due to his own supplier, although the seller may have a remedy against its supplier under the terms of the separate contract with its supplier.

The obligations as to description, fitness for purpose, satisfactory quality, and correspondence with sample in a B2B (business to business) sale of goods contract—under the Sale of Goods Act (SGA) 1979, ss. 13–15 (see **6.4.2.4**)—are strict contractual obligations, i.e. any failure of performance to match the contractual undertaking, however slight, is still breach. In *Arcos Ltd v Ronassen* [1933] AC 470, timber staves of half an inch in thickness were purchased to make into cement barrels. In fact, most of the timber was one-sixteenth thicker than the contractual description, although it was still perfectly useable for the purpose of making cement barrels. Nevertheless, this amounted to a breach of contract. Since it amounted to a breach of condition (SGA 1979, s. 13: see **8.5.3.1** and **8.5.7**), the buyer could reject the timber. This, however, is now subject to the SGA, s. 15A(1) which states that there is no right to reject the goods if the breach is so slight that to do so would be regarded as unreasonable.

For B2C (B2C—'trader' and 'consumer'), these various statutory rights relating to goods in contracts to supply goods and digital content (see Part 1 of the Consumer Rights Act (CRA) 2015, ss. 9–11, 13, and 34–36) are entrenched as 'rights' and hence strict obligations. Consumers are given specific rights of enforcement in the event of breach (CRA 2015, ss. 19 and 42).

8.2.1.1.2 Qualified contractual obligations

If an obligation is qualified, there is no requirement to achieve a guaranteed result; instead, the obligation is only to exercise reasonable care and skill.

An example of a qualified contractual obligation in the B2B context is s. 13 of the Supply of Goods and Services Act (SGSA) 1982 (see **6.4.2.4**). For consumers, s. 13 of the SGSA 1982 is not revoked by Sch. 1 of the Consumer Rights Act 2015, but s. 49 expressly stipulates that there is a term that the trader must perform the service for the consumer with reasonable care and skill (and remedies are provided for in s. 54 CRA 2015). At common law, this standard of performance is regarded as the appropriate standard for professional people such as doctors and lawyers, whose work makes it impossible to guarantee a result. However, it is possible to undertake a strict standard of performance in relation to certain obligations, e.g. in *Platform Funding Ltd v Bank of Scotland plc* [2008] EWCA Civ 930, [2009] QB 426, the majority of the Court of Appeal (Sir Anthony Clarke MR dissenting) accepted that the normal duty owed by a surveyor was a duty of reasonable care and skill in carrying out the survey and checking for defects. It was, however, a strict undertaking that the surveyor would survey the correct property!

Another example of an implied qualified obligation is the House of Lords' decision in *Liverpool City Council v Irwin* [1977] AC 239, involving an obligation to take reasonable care to keep the common parts of a tower block in reasonable repair. On the facts, the local authority had met this standard of performance (see **6.4.2.2**). Any failure to exercise reasonable care and skill (i.e. failing to meet the qualified standard) would amount to breach.

8.2.2 Discharge by agreement

8.2.2.1 General

Discharge by agreement between the parties is possible. Provided discharge occurs with the free consent of both parties and without subsequent change of heart, no particular form of agreement is required. The parties may simply abandon performance. In practice, however, to guard against a change of heart by the other party, it is desirable to adopt some form of legally binding agreement to discharge all future performance obligations.

8.2.2.2 The requirement of consideration

In addition to demonstrating the existence of an agreement to discharge future obligations— *The Hannah Blumenthal* [1983] 1 AC 854—the parties must also demonstrate that this agreement to discharge is legally enforceable. The best way of so doing will be to establish the existence of a second contract to discharge the first, which will require the existence of consideration (see **4.5.2**).

8.2.2.3 Mutual release

Where both parties have performance obligations remaining under the contract, mutual abandonment of those remaining obligations (mutual release) is enough to satisfy the requirement of consideration (i.e. each party agrees to give up its right to receive the other's performance), so that such discharge is legally enforceable (see **4.5.2**).

The position is the same where *both* parties breach obligations under their contract and then agree to discharge it.

8.2.2.4 What is the position if one party's obligations have been performed, but the other owes future performance?

Where one party's obligations have been performed so that only the other party needs to be discharged from further performance, the consideration requirement may not be satisfied by mere abandonment of the contract. The parties may enter into a binding release in a deed, whereby the party whose obligations have been performed agrees to discharge the other from that other's performance obligations. No consideration is required because this agreement to discharge is in a deed (see **4.1**).

8.2.2.4.1 Release and replacement

Agreements that amount to a *release and replacement* are possible. This involves the total discharge of the original contract, followed by the substitution of a new contract between the parties, assuming that the necessary consideration is present: *Morris v Baron and Co.* [1918] AC 1. The Court of Appeal, in *Compagnie Noga D'Importation et D'Exportation v Abacha (No. 4)* [2003] EWCA Civ 1100, [2003] 2 All ER (Comm) 915 (discussed at **4.5.2**), held that there was a mutual release from an earlier agreement, followed by a replacement agreement. The mutual release and the mutual promises in the replacement agreement were construed as the consideration to support that new agreement.

8.2.2.4.2 Binding variation (accord and satisfaction)

Alternatively, there may be a separate agreement supported by new consideration (*accord and satisfaction*) to discharge (or vary) a particular contractual term. For example, one party (A) may agree to release the other (B) from B's liability to pay damages for B's breach as long as B pays A £200 in compensation. However, the 'satisfaction' (i.e. the consideration) cannot be a lesser form of what was due under the contract: *Pinnel's Case* (1602) 5 Co Rep 117a (see **4.6.2.1**). Payment of a smaller sum cannot therefore discharge (or extinguish) the obligation to pay the full amount owed. This remains the position because the principle in *Williams v Roffey Bros. & Nicholls (Contractors) Ltd* [1991] 1 QB 1 which identifies consideration as constituted by a factual (or practical) benefit to the promisor arising from an alteration promise applies only to alteration promises to pay more and does not apply to alteration promises to accept less than the sum owed: *Re Selectmove Ltd* [1995] 1 WLR 474 (see **4.6.2.3**). Therefore, in order for there to be the necessary 'satisfaction' to support the variation in the contract terms, the promisee will need to supply something extra, such as agreeing to pay a smaller sum on an earlier date or at a different place at the creditor's request.

8.2.2.4.3 Estoppel

If the necessary consideration to support a release or variation of a contract term is lacking, a promise to discharge one or more obligations may have some limited effect because of the operation of the doctrine of promissory estoppel. Promissory estoppel operates only to suspend contractual rights and not to extinguish or terminate them (see **4.8.5**). Therefore it might be considered that it has no relevance to the discharge of contracts. Nevertheless, since it may cause individual instalment obligations to be extinguished, e.g. as in *Central London Property Trust Ltd v High Trees House Ltd* [1947] KB 130 (see **4.8.2.1** and **4.8.5**), in this limited sense it can be said that a contract (or at least an obligation under that contract) may be discharged by estoppel.

8.3 Discharge (termination) by occurrence of a condition subsequent

A contract may also be discharged by the occurrence of a condition subsequent stipulated by the parties. A *condition subsequent* is a stipulation of a state of affairs that will cause existing contractual obligations to terminate: *Head v Tattersall* (1871) LR 7 Ex 7. A modern example might be a provision in a long-term supply agreement that the contract should terminate when the price of the goods in question reaches a stated figure. Thus the condition may be an event beyond the control of either of the parties (e.g. attainment of a certain point on a cost-of-living index), or within the control of one of the parties (e.g. giving and serving a stipulated period of notice).

> **! KEY POINT**
>
> A condition subsequent is a 'contingent' condition, and such conditions impose no positive obligation to ensure absolutely that the condition does (or does not) materialize. It is therefore different from a *promissory condition*, whereby one party undertakes (promises) that a certain result will be achieved. For a promissory condition (discussed at **8.5.2.1**), failure to achieve the promised result is a breach. Thus a promissory condition is the type of condition that is used to express a primary obligation of the contract.

Where a contract, on its face, has no provision for termination, then, in the absence of any indication of an intention that the contract be perpetual, the courts will imply a term that the contract is terminable upon reasonable notice: *Staffordshire Area Health Authority v South Staffordshire Waterworks Co.* [1978] 1 WLR 1387.

8.4 Breach and discharge by breach (repudiatory breach)

8.4.1 Identifying breach and remedies available for breach

A breach of contract will occur where, without lawful excuse (e.g. frustration: see **Chapter 12**), a party either fails or refuses to perform a performance obligation undertaken in accordance with the terms of the contract. Alternatively, a party may perform its contractual obligations, but may do so defectively, by failing to meet the required standard of performance (see **8.2.1.1**).

Generally, the non-breaching party is entitled to be compensated for the loss it suffers that was caused by this breach. This is because the failure to perform a primary obligation under the contract gives rise to a secondary obligation to pay damages or to pay the contract price: see Lord Diplock in *Photo Production Ltd v Securicor Transport Ltd* [1980] AC 827, at 849B. However, that right to damages may be effectively excluded or limited by an exemption clause in the contract (see **Chapter 7**). This apart, the secondary obligation to pay damages or the contract price will arise on proof of breach.

Damages aside, the consequences of breach by one party for the other party's performance obligations depend largely upon the nature of the obligation breached (see **8.5.2.1**) and upon whether one party's performance obligation is 'entire', so that it must be completely and precisely performed before the other's obligation arises (see **8.6**).

8.4.2 Repudiatory breach and the election to terminate or affirm

Unless the breach of contract constitutes a repudiatory breach, the contract remains in force and both parties must continue to perform their obligations under it. However, a repudiatory breach allows the non-breaching party to treat the contract as repudiated (or terminated for the future). It is sometimes said that such a breach entitles the non-breaching party to 'rescind' the contract, and this choice of word appears to have been approved by some members of the House of Lords, e.g. Lord Roskill in *Photo Production Ltd v Securicor Transport Ltd* [1980] AC 827 and Lord Diplock in *Gill & Duffus SA v Berger & Co. Inc.* [1984] AC 382. Nevertheless, this meaning of 'rescind' is very different from the meaning of this expression that is applied in relation to misrepresentation (see **14.5.1**), under which a contract is set aside and treated as if it had never existed from the very beginning. The use of 'rescission' in relation to breach was attacked several times by Lord Wilberforce, in both *Johnson v Agnew* [1980] AC 367 and *Photo Production*. To avoid confusion—exemplified in *Howard-Jones v Tate* [2011] EWCA Civ 1330, [2012] 1 P & CR 11, in which the wrong measure of damages was applied in the belief that termination for repudiatory breach resulted in rescission *ab initio*—it is better to restrict the notion of rescission to misrepresentation and, for breach of contract, to refer to termination for repudiatory breach.

Should a repudiatory breach occur, the non-breaching party *may* treat the contract as repudiated, but is not obliged to do so. Thus, in the event of a repudiatory breach of contract, the non-breaching party has the option (or 'election') to treat both parties' future obligations to perform as terminated or to choose instead to affirm the contract: see *Decro-Wall International SA v Practitioners in Marketing Ltd* [1971] 1 WLR 361.

⟳ SUMMARY

Termination: If the non-breaching party elects to accept the breach as terminating the contract, only the parties' future obligations are discharged. The contract itself survives and its terms may be relevant for the purposes of assessing remedies, e.g. any exemption clauses and/or agreed damages clause will remain, and will be relevant to the assessment of damages.

Affirmation: The alternative option to termination is for the non-breaching party to affirm the contract, i.e. to choose not to act upon the breach of the other party. This obliges both parties to continue to perform all remaining obligations due under the contract.

Damages: In addition, irrespective of whether the non-breaching party decides to terminate or affirm, the breach will cause the secondary obligation to pay damages as compensation to arise.

If, after a repudiatory breach, the non-breaching party affirms the contract, effectively the 'slate is wiped clean' as far as future performance is concerned. Consequently, future defective or non-performance by the party electing to affirm the contract will in turn become a breach: e.g. *Motor Oil Hellas (Corinth) Refineries SA v Shipping Corporation of India, The Kanchenjunga* [1990] 1 Lloyd's Rep 391 (HL). It may even be a repudiatory breach entitling the other party, who was originally at fault, to treat the contract as at an end.

8.4.2.1 **Electing to treat the repudiatory breach as terminating the contract**

Until such time as the non-breaching party elects to treat the contract as repudiated, the contract stands. In *Howard v Pickford Tool Co. Ltd* [1951] 1 KB 417, at p. 421, Asquith LJ described an unaccepted repudiation as 'a thing writ in water'. A majority in the Supreme Court in *Geys v Société Générale* [2012] UKSC 63, [2013] 1 AC 523, confirmed that the elective theory (and not the automatic theory, as had been argued) also applies to employment contracts, so that an employer's repudiation of an employment contract did not terminate it immediately, but required the employee's acceptance. The fact that repudiation does not automatically bring the contract to an end (the elective theory) has however been doubted by the Court of Appeal in *MSC Mediterranean Shipping Co. SA v Cottonex Anstalt* [2016] EWCA Civ 789, [2016] 2 Lloyd's Rep 494, [2017] 1 All ER (Comm) 483. Indeed, *Geys* was distinguished by Tomlinson LJ (at [61]) who emphasized the lack of choice on the victim in *MSC* since the contract could no longer be performed. His lordship stated [at 61], 'Geys is broadly speaking . . . a case where the innocent party has a choice between, on the one hand, treating the remaining obligations as discharged or, on the other hand, affirming the contract to wait to see whether the guilty party performs its obligations when the time comes. The present case is different. I do not believe that Lord Wilson in *Geys* had in mind a case where a contract has become repudiated because it is no longer capable of performance as in the classic case of frustrating delay.' After emphasizing that in *MSC* the facts highlighted the classic case of frustrating delay, his lordship concluded (at [61]) that 'as from 2 February 2012, the contract in its agreed form was not capable of performance'.

A difficult question of fact may be to ascertain whether the non-breaching party has elected to accept the repudiation and treat the contract as at an end. A clear and unequivocal communication to that effect will resolve the matter, and an 'unequivocal overt act which is inconsistent with the subsistence of the contract' should be equally effective: *State Trading Corporation of India v M. Golodetz Ltd* [1989] 2 Lloyd's Rep 277. In *Force India Formula One Team Ltd v 1 Malaysia Racing Team Sdn Bhd* [2013] EWCA Civ 780, [2013] RPC 36, F had told X that it was unable to pay the instalments due to X under a contract to provide wind tunnel aerodynamic testing for F's Formula One (F1) racing cars and would discuss the matter after a two-week shutdown. At the start of the shutdown, X disabled F's connections to its servers. The Court of Appeal held that this action was not consistent with an unequivocal communication that the contract was at an end; neither was a demand for future instalments of periodical payments due under a contract. However, there was a sufficient unequivocal communication when F was told that X had stopped working for F and would be working for another F1 team.

? QUESTION

What if the non-breaching party simply does not perform its own contractual obligations? Is this sufficiently unequivocal to constitute acceptance of the repudiatory breach as terminating the contract, particularly bearing in mind that, generally, an 'acceptance' must be unequivocal and that silence will not suffice (see **2.4.5.1**)?

In **Vitol SA v Norelf Ltd, The Santa Clara** [1996] AC 800, the buyers had sent a telex that amounted to a repudiatory breach and the question was whether that repudiation had been accepted by the sellers, who had then not performed any of their own obligations, including tendering the bill of lading (which would be necessary to give rise to the obligation for the buyers to pay the price). In the House of Lords, Lord Steyn, whose speech was unanimously supported by the other members of the House, considered that the question of whether the election to treat the contract as repudiated had been communicated was a question of fact, depending on 'the particular contractual relationship and the particular circumstances of the case'. However, he was prepared to accept, at p. 811F, that 'a failure to perform may sometimes signify to a repudiating party an election by the aggrieved party to treat the contract as at an end'. Lord Steyn then gave two examples of situations in which non-performance could be interpreted as an election to treat the contract as at an end.

1. In his first example, an employer informs a contractor that his services are no longer required and that the contractor need not return the next day. If the contractor never returns, then, in the absence of any other explanation, in Lord Steyn's words, at p. 811F, this would 'convey a decision to treat the contract as at an end'.

2. The second example concerns an overseas sale, with shipment of the goods on a specified vessel sailing on a specified date and where the seller is under a contractual duty to obtain the necessary export licence. If the buyer repudiates the contract before any loading starts and the buyer knows that the seller has not applied for the export licence, 'it may well be that an ordinary businessman . . . would conclude that the seller was treating the contract as at an end': *per* Lord Steyn at p. 811G.

It is clear that general inactivity or acquiescence will not suffice as 'acceptance' of the repudiatory breach. Examples where an acceptance of the repudiatory breach has undoubtedly taken place can be gleaned from the circumstances of a case, especially where a response or an action is required. For instance, in *The Santa Clara*, 'if the contract was still on foot, it was incumbent on the innocent party to perform a positive obligation under the contract', e.g. tendering the bill of lading. Where, however, no response or action is required it would not be possible to spell out the necessary acceptance (*Dubai Islamic Bank PJSC v PSI Energy Holding Co. BSC* [2013] EWHC 3781 (Comm), [164]–[166]).

A more recent illustration of a situation when the non-breaching party's non-performance of its obligations will not amount to an acceptance of a repudiatory breach is *Vitol SA v Beta Renewable Group SA* [2017] EWHC 1734 (Comm). On the facts, a failure to nominate a vessel in accordance with a time period specified in a contract did not amount to a clear and unequivocal act amounting to an acceptance of the other party's repudiatory breach, with the court emphasizing the importance of context (including the 'background of previous consensual variation to the parties' contractual arrangements' and 'ongoing negotiations between the parties' at [45]).

8.4.2.2 Electing to affirm the contract

In order for an affirmation to be valid, the non-breaching party must know of the facts giving rise to its right to accept the repudiatory breach as terminating the contract, and of its right to choose between affirming the contract and treating the contract as discharged.

8.4.2.2.1 Must be unequivocal

The election to affirm must also be unequivocal and must make it clear that the non-breaching party is committing to continuing with performance of the contract: *White Rosebay Shipping SA v Hong Kong Chain Glory Shipping Ltd, The Fortune Plum* [2013] EWHC 1355 (Comm), [2013] 2 CLC 884, [2013] 2 All ER (Comm) 449. In *Yukong Line Ltd of Korea v Rendsburg Investments Corporation of Liberia* [1996] 2 Lloyd's Rep 604, the response to a repudiatory breach indicated that it was 'totally unacceptable' and 'strongly requested' the party in breach 'to honour their contractual obligations' and to confirm that this would occur. This response was held to be insufficient to convey an intention to continue with the contract. Moore-Bick J stated, at p. 608:

Considerations of this kind are perhaps most likely to arise when the injured party's initial response to the renunciation of the contract has been to call on the other to change his mind, accept his obligations and perform the contract. That is often the most natural response and one which, in my view, the court should do nothing to discourage. It would be highly unsatisfactory if, by responding in that way, the injured party was to put himself at risk of being held to have irrevocably affirmed the contract.

Breach of contract

8

The choice between termination and affirmation of the contract is sometimes dictated purely by commercial reasons. If the parties have been involved in commercial contractual relations for years, and it is in the interest of the non-breaching party to keep the contract alive in spite of the breach, it will affirm the contract. If, however, the breach is such that, commercially, the relationship cannot be preserved (because the breach creates a lack of trust), the non-breaching party may well choose termination.

8.4.2.3 In what circumstances will the right to accept the repudiatory breach as terminating the contract be lost?

8.4.2.3.1 Estoppel

There is a danger that a party who has not yet affirmed, but is still deliberating what to do, may lose the right to treat the contract as terminated because of the operation of estoppel: see *Clough v London and North Western Railway Co.* (1871) LR 7 Ex 26. In order for such an estoppel to operate, the position of the party in breach must have been prejudiced in the meantime.

In *Peyman v Lanjani* [1985] Ch 457, at pp. 495–6, May LJ adopted the following passage from the judgment of Sholl J in the Australian decision in *Coastal Estates Pty Ltd v Melevende* [1965] VR 433, at p. 443:

> If the defrauded party does not know that he has a legal right to rescind, he is not bound by acts which on the face of them are referable only to an intention to affirm the contract, unless those acts are 'adverse to' the opposite party, i.e. unless they involve something to the other party's prejudice or detriment . . . This is a form of estoppel, for the other party has in such a case acted upon a representation, made by the defrauded party's conduct, that the latter is going on with the contract.

In **Peyman v Lanjani**, the defendant entered into an agreement for the assignment to him of a lease, expressed to be non-assignable without the true consent of the landlord. The landlord's consent was obtained by deception. The claimant then agreed to purchase the lease from the defendant and, again, an attempt was made to obtain the landlord's consent by deception, although the claimant was not a party to this. On discovering the deception, the claimant consulted the solicitor acting for both parties, who urged him to proceed with the purchase. The claimant therefore paid the first £10,000 of the purchase price. A month later, the claimant consulted new solicitors, who advised him of his right to terminate the agreement on account of the defect in the defendant's title caused by the original deception.

The Court of Appeal held that the claimant had not lost the right to treat the contract as repudiated. The payment of £10,000 was not an irrevocable election because it had been made before the claimant was aware of the full facts, including the fact that he had a right to treat the agreement as at an end; neither did it give rise to an estoppel preventing the claimant from treating the contract as repudiated, most particularly because there was no detriment to the defendant.

8.4.2.3.2 Acceptance of goods in the B2B context

In relation to a commercial sale of goods, the option to terminate the contract for repudiatory breach will be lost once the buyer has accepted the goods (SGA 1979, s. 11(4)). Section 35(1) and (2) of the 1979 Act define this acceptance to include express indication of acceptance or, once the goods have been delivered, any act by the buyer that is inconsistent with the seller's ownership after the buyer has had a reasonable opportunity to inspect the goods to determine their conformity with the contract, or to compare the bulk with the sample. A buyer is also deemed to have accepted the goods after the lapse of a reasonable time during which he has retained the goods without indicating an intention to reject them (s. 35(4)). The availability of a reasonable opportunity to inspect the goods is a material factor in determining whether the 'reasonable' time has passed so as to constitute a lapse of time. However, in accordance with the SGA 1979, the buyer is not deemed to have accepted the goods by asking for or agreeing to repair (s. 35(6)(a)), or delivering the goods to a third party under a sub-sale (s. 35(6)(b)), or by accepting part of a delivery of goods (most probably a part unaffected by the breach) while claiming to be entitled to reject the rest (s. 35A(1)). In *J. H. Ritchie Ltd v Lloyd Ltd* [2007] UKHL 9, [2007] Bus LR 944, [2007] 1 WLR 630, the House of Lords considered that if the commercial buyer agrees to repair—so that, under s. 35(6), there is no acceptance—there is a separate contract that suspends the right to reject. This contract places a duty on the repairer to disclose the nature of the defect so that the buyer can make an informed decision as to whether to reject later.

Consumer protection: the right to reject and the availability of other remedies for consumer buyers

By comparison, in the consumer context (B2C—'trader' and 'consumer'), the Consumer Rights Act 2015 collects the statutory implied terms in relation to goods and services in the sales and supply law into a separate regime of consumer terms as 'rights', and extends this protection to 'digital content' contracts, e.g. that goods will be of satisfactory quality, fit for the particular purpose, etc. These implied terms are presented as 'rights' that cannot be excluded or restricted, and consumers are given various remedies that they can enforce (ss. 19, 42, and 54). The existing law (i.e. the SGA 1979 and the SGSA 1982) will remain applicable to B2B contracts and (for some provisions of the SGA 1979) also to B2C contracts.

In relation to the right to enforce terms concerning goods, the following consumer remedies apply under the CRA 2015, s. 19:

1. There is an immediate short-term right to termination within 30 days (i.e. rejection of the goods or part of the goods) for breaches of terms imposing obligations relating to the goods (e.g. satisfactory quality, fitness for purpose, and correspondence with description, sample, or model seen or examined) and, subject to some qualifications, to receive a refund (ss. 20–22).

2. The consumer may require the trader to repair or replace the goods unless this is impossible or disproportionate (s. 23).

3. There will be a right to a price reduction *or* a final right to reject where repair or replacement is impossible or disproportionate, or the repair or replacement has failed or has not taken place within a reasonable time and without significant inconvenience to the consumer (s. 24). There may be a deduction from any refund for use of the goods by the consumer.

The consumer rights legislation therefore provides for an initial right of rejection to be available to consumer buyers for 'goods breaches' for a period of up to 30 days and that any request for repair and or replacement will act to stop time running. If the repair or replacement does not occur or does not result in the buyer receiving goods conforming to the contract, then the 'waiting period' comes to an end and the final right to reject is available. Therefore, for breaches of the obligations relating to the goods (as opposed to incorrect installation of goods by the trader, s. 15), consumers will not be compelled to seek a repair or replacement in the first instance, but will retain the ability to reject. This is important because the UK reacted strongly to the proposal in the CRD to give primacy to the remedy of repair or replacement.

8.4.2.3.3 Lapse of time in general

Except as described earlier for sale of goods, the right to treat the contract as repudiated is not lost by mere lapse of time. Nevertheless, in limited circumstances, lapse of time might result in prejudice to the party in breach or might be regarded as evidence of an intention to continue with the contract, in which case the right to treat the contract as repudiated would be lost: *per* Fenton Atkinson LJ in *Allen v Robles* [1969] 1 WLR 1193. In *Tele2 International Card Company SA v Post Office Ltd* [2009] EWCA Civ 9, affirmation was held to have occurred by means of a delay of over a year in reacting to a repudiatory breach. As no right to terminate arose, when purporting to so terminate, a repudiatory breach had therefore occurred. By comparison, in *Force India Formula One Team Ltd v Etihad Airways PJSC* [2010] EWCA Civ 1051, [2011] ETMR 10, the Court of Appeal held that Force India had committed repeated breaches of its sponsorship agreement, which had ultimately amounted to a repudiation of the contract since Force India was considered to have adopted an overarching strategy that had ridden roughshod over the sponsors' rights: *per* Rix LJ at [95]. Despite delay, the sponsors had not acquiesced in this repudiation and had not affirmed; rather, they had successfully terminated the agreement.

The courts appear to have permitted some latitude on delay in terminating or affirming in times of economic uncertainty. In *Red River UK Ltd v Sheikh* [2010] EWHC 961 (Ch), in relation to a deliberate sabotage of a property-refinancing transaction, Henderson J held that although it had been over a year before the repudiation had been accepted as terminating the contract, this did not amount to affirmation, but merely 'keeping . . . options open'. In *Stocznia Gdanska SA v Latvian Shipping Co. (No. 3)* [2002] EWCA Civ 889, [2002] 2 All ER (Comm) 768, [2002] 2 Lloyd's Rep 436 (discussed at **8.7.4.1**)—also known as *Stocznia Gdanska SA v Latvian Shipping Co. (Repudiation)*—Rix LJ referred to this period as 'the middle ground'.

Later, in *Force India Formula One Team v Etihad Airways PJSC*, at [122], Rix LJ noted:

In the present case . . . we are not faced with either an urgent situation . . . nor are we faced with some minor and remediable breach where the injured party only has to speak up for the matter to be remedied; or where firm protest is immediately necessary to prevent the party in breach from being misled. The present case concerns a complex and medium term relationship, which a takeover has destabilised, and where it necessarily and legitimately takes time for the consequences to become clearer and for the innocent party to consider his position. That is the middle ground between acceptance of a repudiation and affirmation of a contract which I discussed in the . . . *Stocznia* case . . . In my judgment, the sponsors were always in fact considering their position, and Force India knew or must have known that that was so . . . In my judgment there was no affirmation, waiver or acquiescence which prevented the sponsors from exercising their common law right to accept Force India's repudiation of the contract.

8.5 What constitutes a repudiatory breach of contract?

8.5.1 Renunciation and incapacitation

The party not in breach must be able to identify whether a repudiation has occurred. The repudiation must therefore be—within evidential limits—unequivocal. Clearly, an express statement that no performance will be undertaken will suffice. Where the repudiation is deduced from conduct, it is not enough simply that performance is unlikely to match the contractual undertakings. It must be apparent that, on the balance of probabilities, the party in question either will not (renunciation) or cannot through its own act or default (incapacitation) perform its obligations: *Alfred Toepfer International GmbH v Itex Itagrani Export SA* [1993] 1 Lloyd's Rep 360. As Lord Wilberforce stated, in *Woodar Investment Development Ltd v Wimpey Construction (UK) Ltd* [1980] 1 WLR 277, at p. 280: '[I]n considering whether there has been a repudiation by one party, it is necessary to look at his conduct as a whole. Does this indicate an intention to abandon and to refuse performance of the contract?'

The majority of the House of Lords in *Woodar v Wimpey* (for facts, see **11.7.3.1**) held that there was no renunciation (i.e. repudiation) of the contract on the facts because, instead of the necessary communicated intention to abandon the contract, Wimpey was relying on a contractual term as justifying the right to terminate. This term gave a right to terminate where compulsory purchase had been commenced and that was precisely what had occurred on the facts.

In *Eminence Property Developments Ltd v Heaney* [2010] EWCA Civ 1168, [2011] 2 All ER (Comm) 223, the Court of Appeal held, following *Woodar*, that the test for repudiatory conduct was whether, looking at all of the circumstances objectively (from the perspective of a reasonable person in the non-breaching party's position), the contract-breaker had clearly shown 'an intention to abandon and altogether refuse to perform'. It therefore turned on all of the circumstances of the individual case, including motive (although usually a subjective matter), where that motive threw light on the way in which actions would be viewed by that reasonable person. Nevertheless, as Lord Wilberforce had stated in *Woodar*, the motive for actions, even if relevant, could not of itself be decisive.

8.5.2 Type of term broken determines whether the breach is repudiatory

Outside instances of renunciation and incapacitation, breaches of certain types of term constitute repudiatory breaches, giving rise to the option for the non-breaching party to accept the breach as terminating the contract or to affirm. It is therefore necessary to determine the classification of terms for this purpose, to consider the type of term broken and therefore whether the particular breach is repudiatory.

8.5.2.1 Classification of terms

For this purpose, there are three basic types of promissory term:

- *conditions*;
- *warranties*; and
- *innominate (or intermediate) terms.*

8.5.2.1.1 Different meanings for the term 'condition'

In ordinary language, a 'condition' is a stipulation of something that must be fulfilled before further action will take place or results will be achieved. The law however attributes more specific meanings to the word.

1. Contingent conditions: distinguished from promissory conditions

Conditions precedent and subsequent, which are sometimes collectively called 'contingent' conditions, impose no positive obligation to ensure absolutely that the condition does (or does not) materialize.

- A *condition precedent* is a stipulation of a state of affairs that must be achieved before any contractual liability, or possibly any further contractual liability, will be incurred. In some circumstances, the parties agree that a contract shall come into existence between them upon the occurrence of some event that is uncertain, but remain free to withdraw from that agreement until the event occurs: *Pym v Campbell* (1856) 6 E & B 370. More usually, however, the main contractual obligations do not come into force until the condition is satisfied, but the parties are contractually bound not to withdraw from the conditional agreement: *Smith v Butler* [1900] 1 QB 694. In these circumstances, the parties may be under an obligation not to impede the occurrence of the condition: *Mackay v Dick* (1881) 6 App Cas 251. Sometimes, there may even be an obligation to use reasonable efforts to cause the event upon which the contract is conditioned to occur, and failure to use such efforts will constitute a breach: *Hargreaves Transport Ltd v Lynch* [1969] 1 WLR 215.

- A *condition subsequent* is a stipulation of a state of affairs that will cause existing contractual obligations to terminate (discussed at **8.3**), e.g. that the contract should terminate when the price of the goods in question reaches a stated figure.

These contingent conditions must therefore be distinguished from promissory conditions, under which one party undertakes that a certain result will be achieved and guarantees that undertaking by its promise. Failure to achieve the promised result is a breach. Thus a promissory condition is the type of condition that is used to express a primary obligation of the contract.

Where the word 'condition' is used without qualification, it is almost certainly being used as a promissory condition and it is in that sense that it is being referred to here when discussing breach of contract. The confusion of terminology can arise because these promissory obligations are themselves classified as conditions, warranties, or innominate terms, and the type of term broken determines the remedy available for breach.

2. Promissory conditions (terms): distinguishing conditions, warranties, and innominate terms

- *Conditions* are important terms that are said 'to go to the root of the contract'; if they are broken, the breach is generally regarded as repudiatory, so that the non-breaching party has the option of terminating the contract for the future or affirming it, in addition to the remedy of damages. Conditions can be directly contrasted with warranties.

- *Warranties* are less important terms that do not 'go to the root of the contract'; the breach of which is adequately compensated with a remedy of damages. Accordingly, breach of warranty is not a repudiatory breach and there can be no option for the non-breaching party to terminate or to affirm. The only remedy for the non-breaching party will be damages.

- *Innominate (or intermediate) terms* defy rigid classification, but appear to lie somewhere between a condition and warranty, and might best be described as the type of term that may be broken in a number of different ways, not all of which would be serious. Therefore whether a breach of an innominate term constitutes a repudiatory breach, giving rise to the option to terminate or affirm, will depend upon the effects of the breach and whether these effects are serious. If the effects are serious, the breach is repudiatory (with an option to terminate or affirm); if the effects are not serious, the non-breaching party will be limited to a remedy of damages.

A further classification of obligations relevant in determining if a repudiatory breach has occurred is the distinction between breach of an entire obligation and breach of a severable obligation (discussed at **8.6**).

8.5.3 Is the term a condition?

Breach of a condition (used in the specific sense) entitles the non-breaching party to treat both parties' future obligations under the contract as discharged, so that the contract is brought to an end for the future (see the discussion of discharge for breach at **8.4**). For this reason, not all of the terms of the contract are classed as conditions. The parties rarely intend that breach of relatively unimportant terms should cause the whole agreement to collapse. Equally, the courts will not lightly classify terms as conditions because of the fact that the consequence of breach of such terms is fixed and does not take account of the actual effects of the breach in question.

8.5.3.1 The statutory classification of conditions

In B2B contracts the implied terms as to description, fitness for purpose, satisfactory quality, and correspondence with sample in the sales and supply legislation are classified as conditions in the SGA 1979 (e.g. ss. 13(1A), 14(6), and 15(3), as amended). It should follow that, in the event of a breach, the buyer should be entitled to reject the goods (terminate the contract for repudiatory breach) or to affirm (as by acceptance of the goods: SGA 1979, s. 35). However, SGA 1979, s. 15A(1) in the B2B context provides that, where there is a breach of ss. 13, 14, or 15, such a breach *may* instead be treated as a breach of warranty (so that the only remedy will be damages) if the breach is so slight that it would be unreasonable to reject the goods (i.e. unreasonable to exercise the normal remedy of terminating the contract). This legislative provision, which may be ousted by the terms of the contract (s. 15A(2)), introduces remedial flexibility to allow the courts to take account of the nature of the breach that occurs in the B2B context.

8.5.3.2 Non-statutory classification as a condition

Outside this statutory classification in the B2B context (see e.g. SGA 1979, ss. 14(6) and 15(A), discussed at **6.4.2.4 and 8.5.3.1**), the starting point for identifying conditions, in both commercial and consumer contexts, is the intention of the parties. Generally, description of a term as a condition, or as entitling a party to terminate the contract (or to reject the goods) upon breach, will result in the court following the parties' own classification. In *Lombard North Central plc v Butterworth* [1987] 1 QB 527, at pp. 535–7, the point was considered very carefully by Mustill LJ, who stated:

> A stipulation that time is of the essence, in relation to a particular contractual term, denotes that timely performance is a condition of the contract. The consequence is that delay in performance is treated as going to the root of the contract, without regard to the magnitude of the breach.

Nevertheless, the court may be unwilling to accept the parties' classification if the court considers that a breach of this term could not have been intended by the parties to give rise to the option to terminate the contract.

In **L. Schuler AG v Wickman Machine Tools Sales Ltd** [1974] AC 235, the House of Lords refused to treat as a condition a term that was expressly stated to be 'a condition of this agreement'. The clause went on to provide for weekly visits over a period of four-and-a-half years to six named firms (some 1,400 visits in total). The House of Lords did not believe that the parties can have intended that a single failure to make one of the visits should entitle the other party to bring this long-term distribution contract to an end.

Lord Reid said, at p. 251:

We must remember that we are seeking to discover intention as disclosed by the contract as a whole. Use of the word 'condition' is an indication—even a strong indication—of such an intention but it is by no means conclusive.

The fact that a particular construction leads to a very unreasonable result must be a relevant consideration. The more unreasonable the result the more unlikely it is that the parties can have intended it . . .

Schuler v Wickman may therefore constitute an early example of contractual construction to give effect to the meaning that the parties must reasonably have intended on an objective assessment: *Investors Compensation Scheme Ltd v West Bromwich Building Society* [1998] 1 WLR 896 (see **6.5.2**). Nevertheless, the recent decisions of the Supreme Court in *Arnold v Britton* [2015] UKSC 36, [2015] 2 WLR 1593 (see **6.5.3**), and *Wood v Capita Insurance Services Ltd* [2017] UKSC 24, [2017] 2 WLR 1095, [2017] AC 765 (see **6.5.4**) suggest that departures from the natural meaning of the words used must not be pushed too far. The words used must be judged at the date of the contract and it is not possible for the courts to rewrite a term on the basis that events the parties thought they were providing for had not developed as anticipated.

There is further evidence of this approach to classification in the Court of Appeal in *Rice (t/a The Garden Guardian) v Great Yarmouth Borough Council* [2003] TCLR 1, (2001) 3 LGLR 4, The Times, 26 July 2000, although the problem in this case was that the term in question was not expressly stated to be a condition; rather, the clause referred to a right to terminate.

In *Rice (t/a The Garden Guardian) v Great Yarmouth Borough Council*, a clause of the four-year contract to provide leisure management and grounds maintenance services stated that 'if the contractor committed a breach of any of its obligations . . . the council may . . . terminate the contractor's employment . . . by notice in writing'. The Court of Appeal held that a literal interpretation of this would entitle the council to terminate 'for any breach of any term' and that this 'flies in the face of commercial common sense'. The breach in question would have to constitute a repudiatory breach to justify the ability to terminate.

In light of this decision, it would seem sensible to avoid such open termination provisions and to spell out the status of individual potential breaches. In *Dominion Corporate Trustees Ltd v Debenhams Properties Ltd* [2010] EWHC 1193 (Ch), [2010] 23 EG 106 (CS), [2010] NPC 63, Kitchin J, relying on *Rice*, interpreted a similar 'any breach' clause as requiring a repudiatory breach. The judge considered, at [32], that 'the Agreement contains a multitude of obligations, many of which are of minor importance and which can be broken in many different ways'. He therefore concluded that the construction for which Debenhams contended, i.e. any breach gave rise to a right to terminate, 'flouts business commonsense' and could not have been what the parties intended on an objective evaluation.

8.5.3.2.1 Termination provisions and the relationship with repudiatory breach

Such express termination provisions are common in contracts and the Court of Appeal, in *Stocznia Gdynia SA v Gearbulk Holdings Ltd* [2009] EWCA Civ 75, [2010] QB 27, confirmed that the exercise of an express termination provision in a contract does not prevent the non-breaching party from treating the contract as repudiated at common law (and so recovering contractual damages based on lost expectation), rather than recovering on the basis provided for in the termination provision (in this case, repayment of instalment sums received in anticipation of performance, together with interest). Equally, exercising that termination provision would not constitute accepting a repudiatory breach, because there was no election involved. A termination provision might operate when there was no repudiatory breach, but it would be envisaged that there would come a point at which a breach might be repudiatory, i.e. when the breach went to the root of the contract. Since the delay in delivery on these facts was repudiatory (i.e. it went to the root of the contract), the purchaser could therefore recover the instalment payments (restitution based on total failure of consideration: see **10.5.1**) and damages for repudiation (lost bargain).

Where both rights exist and 'the consequences of contractual termination and termination are identical', either right can be exercised. However, 'where the consequences of exercising the two rights are different, but not inconsistent, it is necessary to make it clear which right is being exercised or that both rights are being exercised; otherwise there will not be the certainty required for an effective termination' (*per* Leggatt J in *Newland Shipping and Forwarding Ltd v Toba Trading FZC* [2014] EWHC 661 (Comm), at [54]).

8.5.3.3 **Assessment of the importance of the term to the contract as a whole**

In *Hongkong Fir Shipping Co. Ltd v Kawasaki Kisen Kaisha Ltd* [1962] 2 QB 26, at p. 69, Diplock LJ suggested that a condition exists for a term only 'where every breach . . . must give rise to an event which will deprive the party not in default of substantially the whole of the benefit which it was intended that he should obtain from the contract'. That definition of a condition was rejected by Megaw LJ in the Court of Appeal in *Bunge Corporation v Tradax Export SA* [1980] 1 Lloyd's Rep 294 and his view was affirmed by the House of Lords: [1981] 1 WLR 711. It is too strict a test to say that every breach must deprive the other party of substantially the whole benefit for a term to qualify as a condition. Nevertheless, the formulation does give a good indication of the nature of terms that are conditions. They are those terms that contain the main obligations and which are central to the existence of the contract. Consequently, the determination of whether a clause is a condition may require the court to make a 'value judgment about the commercial significance of the term in question': *per* Kerr LJ in *State Trading Corporation of India Ltd v Golodetz Ltd* [1989] 2 Lloyd's Rep 277, at p. 283; approved by Lord Ackner in *Compagnie Commerciale Sucres et Denrées v C. Czarnikow Ltd, The Naxos* [1990] 1 WLR 1337, at pp. 1347–8.

In *Bunge Corporation v Tradax Export SA* in the House of Lords, Lord Wilberforce expressly approved the *dictum* of Roskill LJ in *Cehave NV v Bremer Handelsgesellschaft Gmbh, The Hansa Nord* [1976] QB 44, that the courts should not be too ready to interpret contractual clauses as conditions. The usual alternative will be to classify the term as *innominate*, which may be more appropriate if the term is such that breach involves either serious or trivial consequences; for those, the courts are unwilling to treat the breach as repudiatory where the practical consequences of breach are trivial.

In *Barber v NWS Bank plc* [1996] 1 All ER 906, Sir Roger Parker in the Court of Appeal clearly had this distinction in mind when determining whether a term was a condition of the contract.

The term in question related to an assertion by a finance company that it would be the owner of a particular car at the time of its eventual sale to a buyer. In concluding that it was a condition, two tests were used. First, the term was 'fundamental to the transaction'; and secondly, at p. 911:

> This term is not one which admits of different breaches, some of which are trivial, for which damages are an adequate remedy, and others of which are sufficiently serious to warrant rescission. There is here one breach only.

Expressions such as 'fundamental to the transaction' are problematic, because they mean different things to different judges. Clearly in this case, however, the two tests led to the same conclusion.

8.5.3.4 Time stipulations in commercial (mercantile) contracts

Certain terms that are in common use in commercial contracts have acquired, by custom and the operation of the doctrine of precedent, definitive classification as conditions. The main explanation for this is the requirement of commercial certainty: business people need to know the effect of a contractual term and, more particularly, they need to know what the effect of breach will be. Therefore, when words have been interpreted in a certain way by the courts, it is generally desirable that that interpretation be consistently maintained—a principle of commercial certainty reaffirmed by Lord Steyn in the House of Lords' decision in *Jindal Iron & Steel Co. Ltd v Islamic Solidarity Shipping Co. Jordan Inc.* [2004] UKHL 49, [2005] 1 WLR 1363. The certainty requirement is particularly true of time conditions: see *United Scientific Holdings Ltd v Burnley Borough Council* [1978] AC 904. A striking example of the strictness of the approach to time clauses is provided by the decision in *Union Eagle Ltd v Golden Achievement Ltd* [1997] AC 514. A delay of ten minutes caused the contract to be lost and the only real issue before the Privy Council was whether relief could be granted (see further **9.6.4.3**).

Thus, in commercial and particularly mercantile (or shipping) contracts, the normal rule is that stipulations as to time of performance are crucial ('time is of the essence'), so that any breach entitles the other party to treat the contract as repudiated without assessing whether the term in question actually 'goes to the root of the contract'. As explained by Megaw LJ in the Court of Appeal in *Bunge Corporation v Tradax Export SA* [1980] 1 Lloyd's Rep 294, at p. 306:

> I think it can fairly be said that in mercantile contracts stipulations as to time not only may be, but usually are, to be treated as being 'of the essence of the contract', even though this is not expressly stated in the words of the contract. It would follow that in a mercantile contract it cannot be predicated that, for time to be of the essence, any and every breach of the term as to time must necessarily cause the innocent party to be deprived of substantially the whole benefit which it was intended that he should have.

This reasoning was applied by the courts in a series of cases.

> In *The Mihalis Angelos* [1971] 1 QB 164, a charterparty stated that the vessel was 'expected ready to load' on 1 July 1965 at Haiphong. The charterers purported to cancel the charter because their cargo was unavailable after the American bombing of the railway line to Haiphong. Such cancellation was not allowed under the terms of the contract. However, unknown to the charterers when they cancelled, at the time of entering the contract the owners had no reason to believe that the ship would be ready to load on the date stated. The phrase 'expected ready to load' was held to be a condition, breach of which entitled the charterers to treat the contract as repudiated irrespective of the consequences of the breach.

This approach to time clauses was confirmed by the House of Lords in *Compagnie Commerciale Sucres et Denrées v C. Czarnikow Ltd, The Naxos* [1990] 1 WLR 1337, in which Lord Ackner cited, with approval, Lord Wilberforce's statement in *Bunge Corporation v Tradax Export SA* [1981] 1 WLR 711 that time clauses in mercantile contracts should 'usually' be treated as conditions.

Despite the strength of the authorities indicating that time stipulations in commercial or mercantile contracts will be treated as conditions, such a position cannot be regarded as conclusive following the House of Lords' decision in *Torvald Klaveness A/S v Arni Maritime Corporation, The Gregos* [1994] 1 WLR 1465, concerning the obligation to redeliver a vessel on time at the end of a time charterparty. The majority of the House of Lords considered this obligation to be an innominate term, and only Lord Templeman (dissenting) considered that, as a time stipulation, it amounted to a condition and was therefore of the essence of the contract. The majority was clearly concerned to achieve flexibility in terms of remedy in the event of a short delay, whereas Lord Templeman's speech emphasizes the commercial importance of this provision and the need for commercial certainty. This tension between flexibility and commercial certainty is evident throughout this area of law. The underlying basis for this decision appears to be the more general justification for innominate terms—namely, the avoidance of a classification of a term as a condition to prevent a party from using such a breach as justifying escape from the contract for other (normally economic) reasons: see e.g. *Reardon Smith Line Ltd v Hansen-Tangen* [1976] 3 All ER 570. As Lord Mustill stated in *Torvald Klaveness v Arni Maritime, The Gregos*, at p. 1475:

> [A]lthough it is well established that *certain obligations* under charterparties do have the character of conditions I would not . . . wish to enlarge the category unduly, given the opportunity which this provides for a party to rely on an innocuous breach as a means of escaping from an unwelcome bargain [Emphasis added]

In light of this decision of the House of Lords, the courts are unlikely to automatically assume that a time stipulation in a mercantile contract is a condition, irrespective of the consequences of the breach, but will instead assess whether the clause fulfils the criteria to qualify as a condition on the facts. This is therefore a question of contractual interpretation—*Rainy Sky SA v Kookmin Bank* [2011] UKSC 50, [2011] 1 WLR 2900.

In practice, much may turn on the nature of the obligation broken for mercantile contracts. Payment of hire clauses appear to be treated differently from the notice provisions, so that in instances in which there are concurrent 'conditions' so that payment is a condition precedent to the delivery of a vessel in a mercantile contract, full compliance with that payment obligation is likely to be considered as a condition—*PT Berlian Laju Tanker TBK v Nuse Shipping Ltd* [2008] EWHC 1330 (Comm), [2008] 2 Lloyd's Rep 246, [2008] 2 All ER (Comm) 784—since the parties would not contemplate delivery without payment in full. In *Kuwait Rocks Co. v AMN BulkCarriers Inc., The Astra* [2013] EWHC 865 (Comm), [2013] 1 CLC 819, [2013] 2 All ER (Comm) 689, Flaux J challenged the result of *The Gregos* as being 'limited to the particular provisions' and not extending 'to the obligation to make punctual payment of hire' (at [117]). Flaux J therefore considered, on the facts, that where there is an obligation to make punctual payment of hire and the contract makes it clear that there is a right to withdraw the vessel in the event of any breach, it may be that such an obligation will be considered as a 'condition' (making time of the essence) and hence its breach will constitute a repudiatory breach. Flaux J further noted in *Kuwait*, at [117], relying on statements by Lords Wilberforce and Roskill in *Bunge v Tradax*, that 'in the case of so-called time clauses in mercantile contracts . . . the courts should not show any reluctance to find that such provisions are conditions and, indeed, should usually do so'. Subsequently, however, Popplewell J in *Spar Shipping AS v Grand China Logistics Holding (Group) Co. Ltd* [2015] EWHC 718 (Comm), [2015] 1 All ER (Comm) 879, [2015] 2 Lloyd's Rep 407, disagreed with Flaux J's analysis in *The Astra* and held that payment of hire was not a condition of the contract in circumstances where there was a similar right to withdraw provision. The Court of Appeal in *Grand China Logistics Holding (Group) Co. Ltd v Spar Shipping AS* [2016] EWCA Civ 982, [2016] 2 Lloyd's Rep 447, affirmed the High Court's decision on the preference for classifying terms as 'innominate' ([2015] EWHC 718 (Comm), [2015] 1 All ER (Comm) 879). The court also held that the approach of Popplewell J at first instance in that case was to be preferred to the judgment of Flaux J in *Kuwait Rocks Co. v AMN Bulkcarriers Inc., The Astra* [2013] EWHC 865 (Comm), [2013] 2 All ER (Comm) 689, which, on that issue, is now to be considered as overruled.

8.5.4 Is the term a warranty?

A warranty is a term of a contract containing a minor (or less important) primary obligation. Breach of such a term gives rise to a secondary obligation to pay damages, but does not constitute a repudiatory breach. The non-breaching party therefore does not have the additional option of accepting the breach as terminating the contract or affirming.

The distinction between conditions and warranties is traditionally demonstrated by contrasting two cases with similar facts.

1. In *Poussard v Spiers* (1876) 1 QBD 410, a singer, hired to perform during the entire run of an operetta, did not arrive until after one week of the run, when a substitute had been hired. The singer's obligation to appear from the first night was held a condition, the breach of which entitled the show's producer to dispense with her services.

2. However, in *Bettini v Gye* (1876) 1 QBD 183, a singer, hired to perform during an entire season, had agreed to arrive six days in advance for rehearsals, but was three days late. The court did not believe that the clause relating to rehearsals was so central to the main purpose of the contract as to constitute a condition. The singer's breach therefore did not allow the contract to be treated as repudiated, but only allowed recovery of damages for loss.

In the past, the distinction between conditions and warranties was made without considering the actual results of breach, and was determined following the relative importance of the term in relation to the contract as a whole at the date on which it was drafted. Today, it is still true, where the parties have expressly designated a term as a warranty or where the term is classed as a warranty by statute, that the consequences of the actual breach should not be considered. But where there is no express classification of the term by either of these means, the courts are unlikely to classify a term as a warranty without first considering the result of the breach under the innominate term doctrine (see **8.5.5**).

8.5.5 More flexibility at a price: innominate or intermediate terms

8.5.5.1 Introduction of the innominate term

Hongkong Fir Shipping Co. Ltd v Kawasaki Kisen Kaisha Ltd [1962] 2 QB 26, introduced the innominate term. Although a classification of either condition or warranty had the advantage of certainty of remedy in the event of breach, once a term was classified as a condition, it allowed the non-breaching party to rely on a trivial breach of that term to escape from the contract for other reasons, such as the fact that the contract had turned out to be a bad bargain. The certainty was therefore inflexible.

In **Hongkong Fir Shipping**, clause 1 of a contract for the charter of a vessel for a period of two years (commencing in February 1957) described the vessel as 'being in every way fitted for ordinary cargo service' (the seaworthiness clause). When delivered to the charterers, the vessel was unseaworthy, because her engines were old. On her first voyage under the charter, she needed repairs, and the vessel was not properly seaworthy until mid-September 1957. In June, treating the breach as repudiatory, the charterers terminated the contract. The question for the Court of Appeal was whether the breach of clause 1 entitled the charterers to treat the contract as repudiated or only entitled them to damages. The court held that since after the repairs had taken place, there were still 17 of the original 24 months left on the charter, the charterers did not have the right to treat the contract as repudiated by the breach of clause 1.

In reaching this conclusion, Diplock LJ analysed the clause broken and said, at p. 70:

There are, however, many contractual undertakings of a more complex character which cannot be categorised as being 'conditions' or 'warranties'. Of such undertakings all that can be predicated is that some breaches will, and others will not, give rise to an event which will deprive the party not in default of substantially the whole benefit which it was intended that he should obtain from the contract; and the legal consequences of the breach of such an undertaking, unless provided for expressly in the contract, depend on the nature of the event to which the breach gives rise and do not follow automatically from a prior classification of the undertaking as a 'condition' or a 'warranty'.

Such terms were christened 'innominate' (there being no technical name for them) or 'intermediate', since they lay somewhere between conditions and warranties in terms of relative importance. A finding that a term is innominate rather than a condition is said to 'repress sharp practice'—Weir [1976] CLJ 33—since it prevents a trivial breach of the term being used to justify termination and withdrawal from the contract for other reasons: see e.g. *Reardon Smith Line Ltd v Hansen-Tangen* [1976] 1 WLR 989 where the parties had entered into a charterparty for a tanker to be built in Japan. The charterparty referred to the tanker as one to be built in Osaka, hull number 354. The tanker was however built in a different yard and bore a different number, even though throughout the correspondence between the parties, the tanker was referred to as 'Osaka 354'. By the time the tanker was ready for delivery, following the oil crisis of 1974, market prices had collapsed and the charterers were looking for a way out of the contract and consequently argued that, by analogy to contracts for the sale of goods, as the tanker bore a different number than what the contract stated, a breach of description allowed them to terminate the contract. Their argument was rejected unanimously by the House of Lords, the words were not part of the description; see also *Torvald Klaveness A/S v Arni Maritime Corporation, The Gregos* [1994] 1 WLR 1465 (discussed at **8.5.3.4**).

8.5.5.2 Difficulties in identifying innominate terms

Diplock LJ's analysis in *Hongkong Fir Shipping Co. Ltd v Kawasaki Kisen Kaisha Ltd* [1962] 2 QB 26 was welcomed by the courts: see e.g. Lord Wilberforce in *Reardon Smith Line v Hansen-Tangen* [1976] 1 WLR 989, at p. 998. Nevertheless, there was some reaction against the uncertainty that the doctrine introduces into commercial contracts because of the need to wait and see whether the consequences of the breach are sufficiently serious as to render it a repudiatory breach.

> In **Bunge Corporation v Tradax Export SA** [1981] 1 WLR 711, buyers agreed to purchase 15,000 tons of soyabean meal from the sellers. The contract provided for three shipments of 5,000 tons, one to be made during June 1975. Under the contract, the buyers were to provide a vessel at a nominated port and give 15 days' notice of expected readiness of the vessel. For shipment in June, notice had to be given by 13 June. Notice was, in fact, given on 17 June. The Court of Appeal and House of Lords both found the delay in giving notice to be a repudiatory breach. Lord Wilberforce said that certain contractual terms, especially those agreed by the parties to give rise upon any breach to a right to treat the contract as repudiated, were not amenable to being classified as innominate terms. He said, at p. 715F, that the contrary proposition would be 'commercially most undesirable . . . It would fatally remove from a vital provision in the contract that certainty which is the most indispensable quality of mercantile contracts'.

However, as noted at **8.5.3.4**, this did not prevent the majority of the House of Lords in *Torvald Klaveness A/S v Arni Maritime Corporation, The Gregos* [1994] 1 WLR 1465 from determining that an obligation under a time charter to redeliver a vessel on time was only innominate.

Innominate terms are therefore identified through a process of elimination. Hale LJ, in *Rice v Great Yarmouth Borough Council* [2003] TCLR 1, (2001) 3 LGLR 4, The Times, 26 July 2000 (for facts, see **8.5.3.2**), at [26], defined an innominate term as 'one which can be broken in so many different ways and with such varying consequences that the parties cannot be taken to have intended that any breach should entitle the innocent party to terminate the whole contract'.

Upjohn LJ, in *Hongkong Fir Shipping*, at pp. 62–3, explained why the clause in that case constituted an innominate term:

> Why is this basic and underlying condition of seaworthiness not, in fact, treated as a condition? It is for the simple reason that the seaworthiness clause is breached by the slightest failure to be fitted 'in every way' for service. Thus . . . if a nail is missing from one of the timbers of a wooden vessel, or if proper medical supplies or two anchors are not on board at the time of sailing, the owners are in breach of the seaworthiness stipulation. It is contrary to common sense to suppose that, in such circumstances, the parties contemplated that the charterer should at once be entitled to treat the contract as at an end for such trifling breaches.

The distinction between conditions and innominate terms can sometimes be far from obvious. For example, in *BS & N Ltd (BVI) v Micado Shipping Ltd (Malta) No. 1, The Seaflower* [2001] 1 Lloyd's Rep 341, [2001] 1 All ER (Comm) 240, although the judge at first instance—[2000] CLC 795—held that a clause guaranteeing to obtain approval for a vessel was an innominate term, the Court of Appeal considered it to be a condition. This type of uncertainty does little to assist business people in determining their options, especially considering the possible dangers of wrongful repudiation (see **8.5.5.4**).

8.5.5.3 The effect of breach of an innominate term

Where the result of the breach is substantially to deprive the non-breaching party of the benefit that it was intended to obtain under the contract, the breach of the innominate term will be treated as repudiatory: see e.g. *Federal Commerce & Navigation Co. Ltd v Molena Alpha Inc.* [1979] AC 757.

Where, however, the effects of the breach caused loss to the non-breaching party, but were not so serious as to deprive that party of the benefit of the contract, the non-breaching party is limited to the remedy of damages. In *Hongkong Fir Shipping Co. Ltd v Kawasaki Kisen Kaisha Ltd* [1962] 2 QB 26, after the repairs to the ship, 17 months of the original charter of 24 months remained and therefore the effects of the breach did not deprive the non-breaching party of substantially the whole benefit of the contract. In *Wuhan Ocean Economic & Technical Cooperation Company Ltd v Schiffahrts-Gesellschaft 'Hansa Murcia' mbH & Co. KG* [2012] EWHC 3104 (Comm), [2013] 1 All ER (Comm) 1277, [2013] 1 Lloyd's Rep 273, a shipyard's failure to procure a renewal of a refund guarantee provided to the buyers (until two days before its expiry) was a breach of an implied term of the shipbuilding contract that the shipyard must procure an extension within a reasonable time. The shipbuilding contract had become unprofitable and the buyers were looking for an escape route, and so commenced arbitration alleging repudiatory breach. However, this was held to be a breach of an innominate term. To identify breaches of the term that might have gone to the root of the contract was possible, e.g. if the sellers had failed to procure the extension of the refund guarantee for a period of a year or more after the expiry of the guarantee. The term could therefore be broken in ways that could be serious. However, on the facts, there was no repudiatory breach, since the breach of the innominate term did not deprive the buyers of 'substantially the whole benefit of the contract'. The buyers' security was not at risk owing to the fact that the refund guarantee was automatically extended if the buyers commenced arbitration, which they had done, against the shipyard. This also reinforced the term as innominate because breach could have deprived the buyers of substantially the whole benefit of the contract if arbitration had not been commenced.

8.5.5.4 Flexibility, but uncertainty: dilemmas for the non-breaching party

The innominate term is a focal point of the tension that exists in the law of contract between the conflicting interests of certainty and fairness. The essential flexibility, or fatal uncertainty, of innominate terms stems from the fact that it is not possible to predict before the time of the breach what the effect of breach of such a term will be. It is therefore for the parties, if they value certainty so highly, to ensure by careful drafting of their contracts that the consequences of breach of every term are clearly stated, thereby seeking to avoid the possibility of the court treating a term as innominate. However, as noted earlier, it can be difficult to ensure effective classification of a term as a condition—e.g. *Schuler v Wickman Machine Tools* [1974] AC 235 (see **8.5.3.2**)—and the approach of the courts has sometimes been unpredictable, e.g. the approach to time stipulations in mercantile contracts: see *Torvald Klaveness v Arni Maritime Corporation, The Gregos* [1994] 1 WLR 1465 (at **8.5.3.4**).

Whilst there is much to be said in favour of removing the rigidity of the condition/warranty classification, the current uncertainty presents a difficulty for the non-breaching party, who has to decide what action to take and whether to treat the breach as repudiatory.

Weir [1976] CLJ 33 also criticized the innominate term, relying on the decision in *Cehave NV v Bremer Handelsgesellschaft Gmbh, The Hansa Nord* [1976] QB 44, to conclude that classification as an innominate term and the application of the effects of the breach test can operate to 'reward incompetence', i.e. that the party who was originally in breach of contract may terminate in the belief that the term broken is a condition when, in fact, the term broken is only an innominate term and not repudiatory in light of the seriousness of the breach. This action would constitute a wrongful repudiation, entitling the party who committed the original breach to the usual remedies.

Cehave v Bremer concerned the sale of citrus pulp pellets to be used as animal feed at a price of £100,000. Shipment was to be made in good condition. On arrival, it was discovered that some of the pellets were damaged, and the buyers rejected the entire cargo on the basis that this amounted to a breach of condition; it was also the case that the market price for these pellets had fallen since the making of the contract. The sellers then resold the pellets to an importer and the importer resold them on the same day to the original buyers, who used the pellets for the original purpose as animal feed. The Court of Appeal held that the term 'shipment in good condition' was innominate and, since the cargo had been used for its intended purpose, the effects of the breach were not serious. Accordingly, the buyers had wrongfully repudiated because they had made the wrong decision on the applicable remedy. (See **8.7.6** on the risk of overreacting to a breach.)

Similarly, in *Ampurius NU Homes Holdings Ltd v Telford Homes (Creekside) Ltd* [2013] EWCA Civ 577, [2013] 4 All ER 377, [2013] BLR 400, it transpired that the wrong decision had been taken when terminating for an alleged repudiatory breach.

Ampurius NU Homes Holdings Ltd v Telford Homes (Creekside) Ltd concerned an agreement whereby Telford was to build four blocks of flats by a contractual deadline, 'or as soon as reasonably possible' after this date, and to lease these blocks to Ampurius under a 999-year lease. Owing to financial pressures, building work on two of the blocks was suspended while Telford sought additional funding. Ampurius had written to Telford, stating that it considered the suspension to be a repudiatory breach and reserving its right to affirm or terminate at a later stage. A year after its initial letter to Telford, Ampurius sought to terminate on the basis of delay and to claim damages. By this stage, work had resumed on the remaining two blocks. The judge at first instance held that Telford had been in repudiatory breach. The Court of Appeal disagreed and held that the consequences of the breach were not sufficiently serious to entitle Ampurius to terminate the contract.

The Court of Appeal held that the test for finding repudiatory breach involved an assessment of whether the breach had deprived the injured party of substantially the whole benefit of the contract judged at the time when the right to terminate was exercised and not at the date of the breach. This involved assessing the benefits Ampurius was intended to get through performance of the contract (a leasehold interest in the four blocks for a 999-year term) and the effect of Telford's breach (whether Ampurius could be adequately compensated through an award of damages). It was also important to assess whether the breach was likely to be repeated, whether Telford would resume compliance with its contractual obligations, and, in particular, whether the breach had fundamentally changed the value of future performance of the Telford's outstanding obligations. Telford had restarted the work at the date of the purported termination so that, at the date of the purported termination, it was not possible to say that the actual and reasonably foreseeable effects of Telford's breach had deprived Ampurius of substantially the whole benefit of the contract—namely, the eventual leasehold interest in the four blocks. The delay was short in relation to the intended 999-year lease and any loss could be compensated in damages. Ampurius had therefore put itself in repudiatory breach of contract by purporting to terminate when this option was not available.

The Court of Appeal in *Urban I (Blonk Street) Ltd v Ayres* [2013] EWCA Civ 816, [2014] 1 WLR 756 also held that, for a development relating to a 125-year lease of property, a delay of only a month between the earliest possible date for completion and the purported termination of the contract did not deprive the purchasers of substantially the whole benefit of the contract.

The obligation to make monthly payments under the terms of a dental facilities contract was held by a majority of the Court of Appeal in *Valilas v Januzj* [2014] EWCA Civ 436, [2015] 1

All ER (Comm) 1047, 154 Con LR 38 (Arden and Floyd LJJ, Underhill LJ dissenting), to be only an innominate term so that it was necessary to consider the nature and consequences of the breach. Floyd LJ (at [53]) considered that 'a multi-factorial assessment', similar to that employed for frustration (see **12.3.2.1**), was needed in such instances so that the court would need to consider 'the nature of the contract and the relationship it creates, the nature of the term, the kind and degree of the breach and the consequences of the breach for the injured party'. (This was also accepted as the correct approach in *Williams v Leeds United Football Club* [2015] EWHC 376 (QB), [2015] IRLR 383 (at [53]) where, in relation to an employment contract, forwarding a pornographic email to a junior employee was held to constitute a sufficiently serious breach to result in summary dismissal.)

On the facts in *Valilas v Januzaj*, the effect of the breaches did not deprive the practice owner of substantially the whole benefit of the contract since he knew that he would eventually be paid. This was not the same as an outright refusal to pay. The loss therefore related to loss of use of the money in the meantime and that is usually compensated by means of interest. However, since the practice owner had accepted the breaches as terminating the contract, he had wrongfully terminated.

8.5.6 Conditions and non-conditions?

In practice, the essential distinction to be made is that between conditions and non-conditions, the effects of the breach test in *Hongkong Fir Shipping Co. Ltd v Kawasaki Kisen Kaisha Ltd* [1962] 2 QB 26 being applied to all non-conditions. This appears to be because, except for terms expressly designated as warranties, there is little point in distinguishing between innominate terms and warranties. The outcome in terms of remedy is the factor having practical importance and this can be determined by applying the effects of the breach test. This has led to the suggestion that there are two types of contractual term: conditions (repudiatory) and non-conditions (which will be repudiatory only if the effects of breach are serious)—see Reynolds (1981) 97 LQR 541. This also appears to be the approach adopted by Upjohn LJ in the *Hongkong Fir* case. On this approach, the key determinant is whether a term is a condition. If it is not, it is a non-condition to which the *Hongkong Fir* test applies.

The approach of the Court of Appeal in *Ampurius NU Homes Holdings Ltd v Telford Homes (Creekside) Ltd* [2013] EWCA Civ 577, [2013] 4 All ER 377, [2013] BLR 400, appears to indicate support for such an approach, since the focus was on distinguishing repudiatory breach from non-repudiatory breach. The Court of Appeal held that the test for finding repudiatory breach was whether the breach had deprived the injured party of substantially the whole benefit of the contract (the *Hongkong Fir* test applied to innominate terms).

However, in *Urban I (Blonk Street) Ltd v Ayres* [2013] EWCA Civ 816), at [44], Sir Terence Etherton C was clear that it was necessary to distinguish the type of term as a condition, warranty, or innominate term using principles of contractual interpretation—*Investors Compensation Scheme Ltd v West Bromwich Building Society* [1998] 1 WLR 896 (see **6.5.1**)—and Peel, in *Treitel's The Law of Contract*, 14th edn (Sweet and Maxwell, 2015), [18-051], maintains that it remains important to make the classification between conditions, warranties, and innominate terms because a breach of warranty can *never* be a repudiatory breach and so will never give rise to the option to terminate or affirm. However, it is extremely difficult to make classifications of terms and it can be argued that the classification can be achieved through the application of the effects of the breach test in *Hongkong Fir*, i.e. if the effects of the breach are not serious, then the remedy is limited to damages only—and, reasoning backwards, the term is a warranty.

8.5.7 The classification of implied terms as conditions, warranties, or innominate terms

Just as express terms may be classified according to their relative importance (see **8.5.2.1**), so some *implied* terms are more important than others. For B2B contracts, the SGA 1979 employs the expression 'implied term', but it goes on to specify more precisely the type of obligation. So the implied terms of satisfactory quality and fitness for purpose in s. 14 are said to be conditions (s. 14(6)). If s. 15A of the 1979 Act (inserted by the Sale and Supply of Goods Act 1994) applies to the sale, it may follow that the applicable remedy will be damages only, rather than the usual option to terminate or affirm. Under s. 15A(1) where there is a breach of ss. 13, 14, or 15 (so-called breaches of condition), such a breach *may* instead be treated as a breach of warranty (so that the only remedy will be damages) if the breach is so slight that it would be unreasonable to reject the goods (i.e. unreasonable to exercise the normal remedy of terminating the contract). Section 15A can be expressly or impliedly ousted (s. 15A(2)).

This only applies to B2B contracts and not to B2C (consumer) contracts, where the CRA 2015 applies. The CRA 2015 also includes terms of satisfactory quality and fitness for purpose (**6.4.2.4**) and, although the Act does not describe these terms as conditions, it is clear that they are entrenched rights and give rise to an initial option to reject for repudiatory breach if broken.

Not all implied obligations in the SGA 1979 (B2B) are conditions, e.g. the implied term that the goods in question are free of any charge or encumbrance and that the buyer has a right to quiet possession is expressed to be a 'warranty' (SGA 1979, s. 12(5A)). By contrast, the CRA 2015, refers to the corresponding obligations in consumer contracts as 'terms', and s. 19(6) states that breach gives rise to the right to reject in the circumstances covered by s. 20, i.e. initial and final rights to reject (discussed at **8.4.2.3**).

However, SGSA 1982, s. 13, which imposes an obligation of reasonable care and skill in the supply of services, has always referred only to an 'implied term'. It must be assumed that the statutory intention was for this term to be treated by the courts as innominate, on the basis that it is the type of term breach of which may sometimes result in serious damage and sometimes trivial damage. Although s. 49 of the CRA 2015 states that it is a term of the consumer contract that the trader will perform the service for the consumer using reasonable care and skill, the remedies set out for breach of this provision are limited to the right to require repeat performance (s. 55) and the right to a price reduction (s. 56). Nevertheless, s. 54 makes it clear that the consumer buyer can pursue other remedies, if available, instead of or in addition to the remedies in the CRA 2015, including terminating the contract and claiming damages (s. 54(6) and (7)). The usual principle preventing double recovery applies (s. 54(6)). This also suggests that this term may be innominate, since it is implicitly accepted that the right to reject may not always be available.

Except for statutory implied or entrenched terms, there is no reason for prior classification of implied terms, since the terms are not known to the parties until the time of litigation. There is therefore no requirement of certainty or predictability of the effect of breach of such terms, since, being implied, they cannot be relied upon in the course of a party's planning. The court is free simply to indicate the type of term when specifying the term to be implied in any given case. It seems likely that, in practice, the courts will do so only after considering the consequences of the breach that has been found to have occurred (see, generally, **8.5.6**).

8.6 The entire obligation rule and repudiatory breach

8.6.1 Entire obligations

Entire obligations are obligations under which the whole of each party's side of the bargain is the necessary condition for the performance of the other. Failure to perform an entire obligation completely and precisely therefore constitutes a repudiatory breach. The obligation to pay a lump sum on completion for building work or some other service in a domestic setting is an entire obligation: e.g. *Bolton v Mahadeva* [1972] 1 WLR 1009 (lump-sum contract to install central heating in a private house). An advantage of the 'entire obligations' rule in such cases is that it gives the consumer a useful means of ensuring that work is completed, since until it is completed, no payment is due.

The classic case example of an entire obligation, *Cutter v Powell* (1795) 6 TR 320, involved the entire obligation rule operating harshly against an employee.

> In **Cutter v Powell**, a sailor had been hired as mate for the voyage from Jamaica to England. He was to be paid a lump sum on completion of the voyage, and it appears that the payment was considerably in excess of the normal amount for such a voyage. He died before reaching England and his widow sued to recover a reasonable sum as payment, based on the period of the sailor's service before his death. The court refused her claim. Lord Kenyon CJ regarded the contract as 'a kind of insurance', with the result that the sailor's entitlement was 'all or nothing'. Moreover, the court was unwilling to allow the remedy of *quantum meruit* (reasonable sum) where there was an express contract governing relations between the parties.

Ashhurst J said, at p. 325:

> This is a written contract, and it speaks for itself. And as it is entire, and as the defendant's promise depends upon a condition precedent to be performed by the other party, the condition must be performed before the other party is entitled to receive anything under it.

Thus failing to perform an entire obligation completely and precisely may result in depriving the party in breach of any payment for whatever performance there has been. This is why the courts are often unwilling to find that the obligations under a contract are entire.

8.6.2 Avoiding the harshness of the entire obligation rule

8.6.2.1 Construing the contract as comprising a number of separate obligations

Complex commercial contracts, e.g. construction contracts, may be broken down into stages, with stage payments, or long-term sale and supply contracts may involve sale and delivery in instalments, with payment for each instalment. The Court of Appeal in *Smales v Lea* [2011] EWCA Civ 1325, [2012] PNLR 8, [43], regarded it as 'relatively unusual' for the payment obligation in modern construction contracts and contracts of retainer for professional services to be entire.

Instalment payments avoid the entire obligation rule; instead, any individual instalment or stage can be assessed to determine whether any breach of an instalment or stage is sufficiently serious to constitute a repudiatory breach in relation to the contract as a whole. Such a breach will entitle that party to damages and possibly (e.g. subject to *de minimis*) entitle the non-breaching party to avoid performance of an obligation that was dependent upon the obligation breached, i.e. to avoid payment for a stage or instalment. In the B2B sale of goods context, s. 31(2) of the SGA 1979 states that, for delivery by instalments that are to be paid for separately:

> [I]t is a question in each case depending on the terms of the contract and the circumstances of the case whether the breach of contract is a repudiation of the whole contract or whether it is a severable breach giving rise to a claim for compensation.

In practice, the non-delivery of a single instalment or a defective delivery of that instalment may not be sufficient to constitute a repudiatory breach. (Section 31 of the SGA 1979 no longer applies in the consumer context. Instead, s. 26 CRA 2015 sets out the applicable provision covering defective instalment deliveries and s. 28 covers failure to deliver an instalment. Section 26(3) provides that defective deliveries in a consumer contract may give rise to a short-term right to reject the whole contract or to reject the goods in the particular instalment. Section 26(4) further provides that the availability of these remedies will depend on 'the terms of the contract and the circumstances of the case'.)

> In *Regent OHG Aisestadt v Francesco of Jermyn Street Ltd* [1981] 3 All ER 327, the contract called for the supply of 62 suits in a number of instalments. After delivery of several instalments, which had been accepted, one instalment was defective, being one suit short. The buyers claimed to be entitled to treat the whole contract as repudiated on the basis of breach in respect of the single instalment (the shortfall of one suit being outside *de minimis*: see **8.2.1.1**).
>
> Mustill J rejected that argument. The obligation to supply was severable, so that each instalment was a separate delivery. A breach of one instalment did not entitle the non-breaching party to treat the whole contract as repudiated.

The judge did not say, as seemingly he should have, that the breach did, however, entitle the buyers to reject the whole instalment affected by the short delivery: *Jackson v Rotax Motor and Cycle Co.* [1910] 2 KB 937.

Of course, a series of such breaches having a cumulative effect may amount eventually to a repudiation of the whole contract: e.g. *Alexander Corfield v David Grant* (1992) 59 BLR 102. In *Rice (t/a The Garden Guardian) v Great Yarmouth Borough Council* [2003] TCLR 1, (2001) 3 LGLR 4, The Times, 26 July 2000 (for facts, see **8.5.3.2**), involving a long-term contract for leisure services of which no single breach was repudiatory, but there were a number of repeated breaches, the Court of Appeal held that the correct approach to determine whether there was a repudiatory breach would be to look at the contractor's performance over one year (of the four-year contract period) to determine whether the council was substantially deprived of the benefit that it had contracted for in that period. It was possible that there would be some aspects of the contract that were so important 'that the parties would be taken to have intended that any deprivation would be sufficient in itself' to justify termination. However, subject to this, the test required an examination of the cumulative past breaches to see whether they were such as to justify an inference that the contractor would continue to deliver a substandard performance in the future. On the facts, the cumulative effect was considered to be insufficient.

Although the courts sometimes refer to entire or severable *contracts*, it is important to note that it is *obligations* that are either entire or severable, and not the contracts themselves. A contract may well consist of both entire and severable obligations. For example, although *Cutter v Powell* (1795) 6 TR 320 is the classic example of an entire 'contract', the court's reflections on the nature of entire obligations did not suggest that every minor breach of the deceased's duties as a mate during the voyage would have entitled the employer to deny him any payment for his services: *per* Somervell LJ in *Hoenig v Isaacs* [1952] 2 All ER 176.

8.6.2.2 Acceptance of the benefit by the non-breaching party

The party in breach of an entire obligation may be entitled to reasonable payment for the value of its actual performance if the non-breaching party accepts such performance as has been given and determines to keep whatever benefit may have been derived from it. 'Acceptance' in this sense means that the non-breaching party, while regarding the breach of the entire obligation as bringing the original contract to an end, wishes to keep a benefit conferred and is willing to pay the 'going rate' for it. Although the contract may be discharged for the breach of the entire obligation, a new contract to pay a reasonable sum for the benefit that has been accepted will therefore be implied.

This principle was explained in **Sumpter v Hedges** [1898] 1 QB 673, in which the claimant builder had contracted to build two houses on the defendant's land for a lump sum of £565. After completion of just over half the work, the builder abandoned the project. The defendant completed the building work, using materials left on the site by the claimant. At first instance, the claimant was awarded the value of the materials used by the defendant to complete the building, but was awarded nothing for the work done but not finished. The first-instance judgment was upheld on appeal.

Collins LJ said, at p. 676:

There are cases in which, though the plaintiff has abandoned the performance of a contract, it is possible for him to raise the inference of a new contract to pay for the work done on a *quantum meruit* from the defendant's having taken the benefit of that work, but, in order that that may be done the circumstances must be such as to give an option to the defendant to take or not to take the benefit of the work done.

Therefore such payment depends upon finding a new, implied contract, which will not be found where the non-breaching party has no real choice whether to accept the benefit. For a half-finished building erected on the non-breaching party's own land, there is no choice over whether to accept the benefit; the building cannot be knocked down and 'returned' to the builder in any meaningful way. The builder could not recover for his part performance. However, building materials not incorporated into the unfinished building could have been returned, so that a positive choice had been made to keep them. On this basis, the builder in *Sumpter v Hedges* was entitled to payment representing the reasonable value of these building materials.

The Law Commission suggested that the fact that payment for an accepted benefit depends upon the availability to the beneficiary of a real choice of whether to accept it has made this rule too strict and that there should be more general recovery in respect of benefits conferred: Law Commission Report No. 121, *Pecuniary Restitution on Breach of Contract* (1983). *Bolton v Mahadeva* [1972] 1 WLR 1009 is a striking modern example.

The claimant in **Bolton v Mahadeva** had agreed to install central heating for a lump sum of £560. It proved to be defective, but the claimant would not put it right, which would have cost a further £174. The claimant was not allowed any payment for the work done, although he had conferred a net benefit on the defendant of £386.

Nevertheless, as was pointed out in a note of dissent in the Law Commission's Report, the main value of classifying an obligation as entire is that it places powerful means of ensuring proper performance of the obligation—namely, the refusal of payment—in the hands of the other party. Were that possibility to be removed, it might do harm to the interests of a significant number of people who are probably the least likely to be willing to resort to litigation, i.e. since most complex construction contracts are now designed for performance in stages with interim payments, and so are severable, most contracts involving entire obligations will be between small builders and domestic consumers. Therefore entire obligations, which may once have been thought as oppressive to the less powerful in society—see *Cutter v Powell* (1795) 6 TR 320—may now serve a useful purpose for consumer protection. The recommendation in the Law Commission's Report, which would have reversed cases like *Bolton v Mahadeva*, has not been implemented: see Burrows (1984) 47 MLR 76 for discussion of these issues.

8.6.2.3 Substantial performance

The rigours of the 'entire obligation' rule may also be avoided by means of the doctrine of substantial performance. *Where performance is incomplete or defective (the breach), but the extent of the failure to match the contractual undertaking is trivial by comparison with the primary obligations that have been satisfactorily performed, the court may be prepared to find that there has been substantial performance.* The result is to prevent the non-breaching party from treating the contract as repudiated, although that party will still be entitled to damages, or to a set-off against the contract price, for any loss caused by the fact that there has been a breach: *Hoenig v Isaacs* [1952] 2 All ER 176 and *Williams v Roffey Bros. v Nicholls (Contractors) Ltd* [1991] 1 QB 1, in which there had been substantial completion of the eight flats, so that the claimant was entitled to be paid part of the extra £10,300 promised (see **4.4.4** for discussion of the enforceability of the promise to pay extra).

In **Hoenig v Isaacs**, the claimant had agreed to decorate and furnish the defendant's flat for a lump sum of £750. Some progress payments were made, but, upon completion of the work, £350 was outstanding. The defendant claimed that the claimant could not recover this amount, since this was an 'entire contract' and the claimant was in breach in that some of his workmanship was defective. It was found as a fact that some of the work was defective, but that it would cost in total no more than £55 to put it right. It is not surprising, in these circumstances, that the Court of Appeal was unwilling to find that the claimant was not entitled to further payment. This very minor breach would have resulted in a large windfall for the defendant as a result of not having to make full payment under the contract. Therefore the Court of Appeal held that the claimant had substantially performed the contract and could recover, less a deduction to cover the cost of remedying the defects.

The result was not to overlook the claimant's breach, but to limit the consequences of that breach to the creation of a secondary obligation to pay damages rather than to allow it to operate to excuse the defendant from performing his obligations. It is nevertheless difficult to see that this case should have involved the 'entire obligations' rule since the obligation to perform the work with reasonable care and skill is not entire, only the obligation to complete it to be paid. The only explanation therefore must be that the court viewed defective performance as a failure to complete the work.

Furthermore, although the doctrine of substantial performance plays a useful role in mitigating the effects of the entire obligation rule, it is limited to minor failures to match the contractual undertaking. In *Bolton v Mahadeva* [1972] 1 WLR 1009, for example, the breach was far too serious to fall within the substantial performance rule.

There are clear similarities between the doctrine of substantial performance and the category of innominate terms, the consequences of breach of which depend upon how serious the breach was (see **8.5.5**). This similarity is by no means coincidental. In *Hoenig v Isaacs*, Somervell LJ traced the origin of the substantial performance doctrine to the judgment of Lord Mansfield in *Boone v Eyre* (1779) 1 H Bl 273, 126 ER 160, and in *Cehave NV v Bremer Handelsgesellschaft Gmbh, The Hansa Nord* [1976] QB 44, Lord Denning MR traced the origin of the innominate term to the same source.

8.7 Anticipatory breach

8.7.1 Identifying a breach by anticipation and assessing its nature

Thus far, the breach is constituted either by non-performance or by defective (including late) performance once the time for performance stipulated in the contract has arrived. However, where one party indicates in advance of the time for performance, either expressly or by conduct, an intention not to perform, or to perform in a manner inconsistent with the contractual undertaking, special rules apply—or at least the usual rules apply somewhat differently to this particular situation. Such an indication is sometimes called 'anticipatory breach', but should more properly be referred to as 'breach by anticipatory repudiation', since it is the announcement of intention rather than the non-performance that is in advance of the stipulated time.

In *Yukong Line of Korea v Rendsburg Investments Corporation of Liberia* [1996] 2 Lloyd's Rep 604, at p. 607, Moore-Bick J accepted the following clear principle:

> A renunciation of the contract by one party, prior to the time for performance is not itself a breach but it gives the other party, the injured party, the right to treat it as a breach in anticipation and thus to treat the contract as discharged immediately. In other words, if a person says he will not perform, the law allows the other to take him at his word and act accordingly.

The application of this doctrine is well illustrated by the early leading case of *Hochster v De La Tour* (1853) 2 E & B 678, 118 ER 922.

> On 12 April 1852, the defendant had contracted to employ the claimant as a courier for three months as from 1 June 1852. However, on 11 May, the defendant wrote to the claimant stating that he had changed his mind and that the claimant's services were no longer required. On 22 May, the claimant commenced an action for breach of contract, and the defendant argued that there could be no breach of contract before 1 June since, until that time, the claimant could not show that he was ready and willing to perform his side of the contract, and was therefore entitled to a remedy. The court held that the claimant was free to choose whether to await the time for performance, in which case he must then be ready and willing to perform, or to treat the contract as immediately repudiated and claim damages immediately, in which case he did not have to wait until 1 June.

The main justification given for the rule was that it was better for both parties that the claimant should avoid the wasteful expenditure of preparing for a performance that he had already been told would not be accepted. It is clear that the court took the view that the right to an immediate remedy was based on the fact of repudiation and not on any notional 'acceleration' of the contract date for performance. Lord Campbell CJ explained this finding on the basis of an implied term that, between the time of contracting and the due date for performance, neither party would 'do anything to the prejudice of the other inconsistent with' the contractual relationship that had been created.

8.7.2 Identifying a breach by anticipatory repudiation

For a breach by anticipation, it is necessary to decide whether the anticipatory breach is repudiatory to determine whether there is an option to terminate or affirm the contract. Renunciation (declaring an intention not to perform or to perform in a manner inconsistent with the contract) and incapacitation (being unable to perform when due) may both constitute anticipatory repudiatory breaches, but the court will need to determine whether what the breaching party has indicated it will not do at the time set for performance, or cannot now do, would amount to a repudiation at the time fixed for performance in the contract (*Geden Operations Ltd v Dry Bulk Handy Holdings Inc., The Bulk Uruguay* [2014] EWHC 855 (Comm), [2014] 2 All ER (Comm) 196, [2014] 2 Lloyd's Rep 66, [15]). The classification of the term broken is relevant to determine whether the breach would constitute 'a substantial failure to perform'. There needed to be either a breach of condition or a breach of an innominate term which went to the root of the contract or deprived the non-breaching party of substantially the whole benefit of the contract. In *Decro-Wall International SA v Practitioners in Marketing Ltd* [1971] 1 WLR 361, the claimant argued that late payments, which were likely to be repeated, amounted to an anticipatory repudiation of the whole agreement. The Court of Appeal accepted that the late payment was a breach and that there was every likelihood of that breach being repeated in the future, but did not accept that this amounted to an anticipatory repudiatory breach since the practical results of the breach were not sufficiently serious to amount to repudiation justifying bringing the whole contract to an end.

In *Geden Operations Ltd v Dry Bulk Handy Holdings Inc., The Bulk Uruguay* [2014] EWHC 855 (Comm), [2014] 2 All ER (Comm) 196, [2014] 2 Lloyd's Rep 66, Popplewell J considered that where a party makes it clear that its ability to perform is wholly dependent on the actions of a third party, this may not be sufficient to constitute an anticipatory breach by renunciation since it did not necessarily evince an intention not to be bound. It was also necessary to consider the benefit that the non-breaching party might be deprived of if the third party acted so as to prevent the contracting party's performance and whether this constituted 'substantially the whole benefit of the contract'. This determination needed to be made at the time of the alleged anticipatory breach, i.e. prospectively.

For a thorough review of the law and academic views on anticipatory breach, see the judgment of the Singapore Court of Appeal, delivered by Andrew Phang Boon Leong JA in *The 'STX Mumbai'* [2015] SGCA 35, [40] ff.

8.7.3 The election to terminate for anticipatory repudiatory breach or to affirm

If the anticipatory breach is repudiatory, the usual election will apply, so that the non-breaching party can either accept the breach as terminating the contract or affirm and await performance on the contractual date set for that performance to begin: *Fercometal SARL v Mediterranean Shipping Co. SA* [1989] AC 788.

However, there is a limitation on the power of the non-repudiating party to elect to affirm the contract.

8.7.3.1 The limitation on the power of the non-repudiating party to elect to affirm the contract

In *White & Carter (Councils) Ltd v McGregor* [1962] AC 413, the appellants had agreed with the respondents to advertise the respondents' business on litter bins to be supplied to local authorities. On the same day, the respondents repudiated the agreement, but the appellants went ahead, performed their side of the contract for the full three years agreed, and claimed the contract price. The House of Lords (by a majority of three to two) held that they were entitled to recover the contract price. There was no requirement that they minimize (or mitigate) their loss by finding an alternative business or product to advertise on the litter bins.

This decision has proved controversial because of the wastage involved. Nevertheless, in *Reichman v Beveridge* [2006] EWCA Civ 1659, [2007] Bus LR 412, a landlord and tenant case, the tenant argued that, having left the premises three years into a five-year lease, there was a duty placed on the landlord to mitigate in a claim for rent arrears following the abandonment, e.g. by finding a replacement tenant, marketing the premises, and not rejecting offers from prospective tenants. However, the Court of Appeal accepted that there was no such duty to mitigate in an action in debt (i.e. the action for arrears of rent).

Whereas we could assert that the principle deriving from *White & Carter* is that mitigation does not apply to an action in debt, in *MSC Mediterranean Shipping Co. SA v Cottonex Anstalt* [2015] EWHC 283 (Comm), [2015] 2 All ER (Comm) 614, [2015] 1 Lloyd's Rep 359, at [91], Leggatt J considered that mitigation would be relevant only 'once the breach of contract on which the claim is based has occurred' and it was this point that had significance in *White & Carter* rather than the nature of the claim. The judge considered that mitigation had no relevance to the critical question of whether it was possible to affirm and so continue to perform to trigger the payment obligation. Although on appeal ([2016] EWCA Civ 789, [2017] 1 All ER (Comm) 483) it was not necessary to reach a final decision on this particular question, Moore-Bick LJ nevertheless stated that Leggatt J had reached the right decision on this question (at [49]).

Considering the objections to wastage inherent in the *White & Carter* principle, subsequent courts have seized upon statements by Lord Reid to limit the potential scope of the principle—indeed, in *Hounslow v Twickenham* [1971] Ch 233, Megarry J considered them to be part of the *ratio* in *White & Carter*.

! KEY POINT

In *White & Carter*, at p. 431, Lord Reid said that the general power to affirm the contract could not be exercised by a person who had no 'legitimate interest, financial or otherwise, in performing the contract rather than claiming damages'. However, it would not be sufficient that it was merely 'unreasonable' to affirm; something more than this was required.

Thus the breaching party can avoid the operation of the principle in *White & Carter* by establishing that the non-breaching party has no legitimate interest in continuing performance.

Lord Reid's statement was adopted and applied by the Court of Appeal in *Attica Sea Carriers Corporation v Ferrostaal Poseidon Bulk Reederei GmbH, The Puerto Buitrago* [1976] 1 Lloyd's Rep 250 and by Lloyd J in *Clea Shipping Corporation v Bulk Oil International Ltd, The Alaskan*

Trader [1984] 1 All ER 129. The initial approach to 'legitimate interest' in these cases was to consider the reasonableness of the affirmation by the non-breaching party, bearing in mind the availability of damages for the anticipatory breach. If continuation with the contract would be 'wholly unreasonable' given the availability of a remedy in damages (and this tended to relate to the relative costs involved in affirming as compared with termination), then affirmation was unavailable.

> The facts of ***The Puerto Buitrago*** were extreme. The charterers tendered redelivery of the vessel in breach of the repair obligation. The shipowners sought to affirm the premature redelivery and to claim the charter hire until the repairs were completed. In the Court of Appeal, Lord Denning MR rejected this as amounting to enforcing specific performance when damages were an adequate remedy. The cost of repair was double the value of the ship when repaired and four times the scrap value.
>
> In ***The Alaskan Trader***, it was held that the owners had acted 'wholly unreasonably' when, despite the charterers' rejection of a two-year charter after one year of the term when the vessel had to undergo extensive repairs, the owners had carried out repairs, and kept the vessel and the crew ready to receive sailing instructions from the charterers, although it was clear that this was unwanted.

However, the balance was altered in favour of allowing affirmation, in relation to early redelivery by the charterers and the owner's claim to be entitled to affirm and claim the hire, in *Ocean Marine Navigation Ltd v Koch Carbon Inc., The Dynamic* [2003] EWHC 1936 (Comm), [2003] 2 Lloyd's Rep 693. Simon J considered that the rationale for Lord Reid's limitation of 'legitimate interest' was to avoid saddling 'the other party with an additional burden with no benefit to himself'. However, it was accepted that it was serious to 'fetter' the non-breaching party's right of election (by restricting the election to terminating and claiming damages). Therefore the limitation needed to be confined to 'extreme cases' in which damages would be an adequate remedy, and in which an election to affirm and go on with the contract would be 'wholly unreasonable'—the word 'wholly' indicating that this exception applied only in extreme cases.

At [23], the judge considered the following to be the applicable principles governing the exceptional case in which affirmation will be prevented:

> (i) The burden is on the contract-breaker to show that the innocent party has no legitimate interest in performing the contract rather than claiming damages. (ii) This burden is not discharged merely by showing that the benefit to the other party is small in comparison to the loss to the contract-breaker.

Thus the burden of preventing the usual election from operating will be on the contract-breaker and it requires more than simply evidence that the benefit of affirmation to the non-breaching party is relatively small.

For example, in *Isabella Shipowner SA v Shagang Shipping Co. Ltd, The Aquafaith* [2012] EWHC 1077 (Comm), [2012] 2 All ER (Comm) 461, [2012] 1 CLC 899, shipowners refused to accept early delivery of the ship in anticipatory breach of the charterparty and so affirmed. Affirmation meant that the charterers would be liable for the charter hire for the minimum term. Cooke J rejected the charterers' argument that the shipowners had no legitimate interest in affirming rather than claiming damages. The judge held that it was not sufficient to refuse affirmation simply because damages would be an available remedy on the facts. Affirmation had to be 'beyond all reason' or 'perverse' before there was no legitimate interest in maintaining the contract. That involved considering whether there was any benefit to the shipowners, however small, as compared to the loss to the charterers. On the facts, there were 94 days left of a five-year time charter in a market in which finding a substitute time charter would have been very difficult. Maintaining the hire was therefore neither 'unreasonable', nor 'wholly unreasonable', and this was not an 'extreme or unusual' case. (The application of Lord Reid's second limitation on these facts is discussed at **8.7.4.3**.)

The movement towards favouring the ability to affirm (and concluding that there is a legitimate interest in keeping the contract alive) appears to have been limited by the decision in *MSC Mediterranean Shipping Co. SA v Cottonex Anstalt* [2015] EWHC 283 (Comm), [2015] 2 All ER (Comm) 614, [2015] 1 Lloyd's Rep 359, and again on appeal ([2016] EWCA Civ 789, [2017] 1 All ER (Comm) 483). A cargo had been delivered but was never collected by the buyer although ownership of the cargo had been transferred. Consequently the seller could not unpack the containers and return them to the shipper. This constituted a repudiatory breach and, in accordance with the terms of the contract, the shipper was entitled to charge 'container demurrage' for every day that the containers were not returned following delivery of the cargo. In the High Court, Leggatt J was unhappy at the prospect of such an open-ended liability and held that the shipper had no legitimate interest in affirming following that breach and should be forced to accept the repudiatory breach as terminating the contract because it was clear that there was no reasonable prospect of redelivery of the containers and future performance. This is a startling result since it limits the non-breaching party's ability to act in its own commercial interests—and the exercise of the agreed 'container demurrage' provision ought to be seen as a legitimate interest in affirming and continuing with the contract. Leggatt J went further (at [97]), stating that the decision to terminate for repudiatory breach needed to be taken in 'good faith' although the judge recognized that the election for repudiatory breach arose by operation of law. This development represents a cause for concern. Critically, perhaps, the judge felt obliged to conclude that the 'container demurrage' was an unenforceable penalty (but this was due to the circumstances in which it operated). This provided justification for the conclusion that there was no legitimate interest in affirming on these facts. On appeal ([2016] EWCA Civ 789, [2016] 2 Lloyd's Rep 494, [2017] 1 All ER (Comm) 483), Leggatt J's analysis of the relevance of principles of good faith in this context were rejected (at [45]). The court also agreed that the delay by Cottonex in returning the containers was indeed a repudiation of the contract but that, on the facts, this was not a case 'in which the *White and Carter* principle applies' (at [43]). The commercial purpose of the venture had been frustrated on 2 February (namely, when the carrier offered to sell the containers to the shipper) and the shipper was in repudiation of the contract as from that date (at which point demurrage ceased to be payable). Once that had occurred, 'the option of affirming the contract' was closed as 'further performance became impossible' (at [43]). The *White & Carter* principle has a particular application for landlord and tenant contracts.

In **Reichman v Beveridge** [2006] EWCA Civ 1659, [2007] Bus LR 412 (discussed earlier in this section), the argument was that the landlord could not choose to affirm and seek rent due under the contract following the anticipatory breach by the tenant because damages would be an adequate remedy and it was 'wholly unreasonable' (relying on Lord Reid's first limitation) to elect to affirm. However, the Court of Appeal held that: (i) it was not wholly unreasonable for an innocent landlord to refuse to take steps to find a new, replacement tenant; and (ii) damages might not be an adequate remedy because if the landlord was to accept the action as forfeiting (terminating) the lease and re-let, but at a lower market rent than that available under the terms of the lease, damages could not be recovered for loss of that rent, there being no authority in English law allowing a landlord to recover loss of *future* rent (i.e. from forfeiture to expiry of lease) from a former tenant. The landlord would therefore not be acting unreasonably in concluding that he should not terminate the lease because, if the future rent were lower, he might not be able to recover the lost rent as damages.

Thus, while the Court of Appeal stressed the limited nature of the principle in **White & Carter**—namely, affirmation and recovery in debt with no duty to mitigate—it found it to be applicable to this situation involving a relationship of landlord and tenant.

8.7.3.2 Conclusion on the *White and Carter* principle

The impact of the Court of Appeal's decision in *MSC Mediterranean Shipping Co. SA v Cottonex Anstalt* is difficult to assess. Moore-Bick LJ, after reviewing the precedent value of the '*White and Carter* principle' stated (at [35]) that 'the outcome of the debate has been, perhaps inevitably, inconclusive, but the decisions reflect a continuing recognition that the principle has a role to play in appropriate cases'. What that will be, given the lack of discussion on appeal of Leggatt J's approach to the 'legitimate interest' (Morgan, CLJ 2017, at 14) is not entirely clear. The debate goes on.

8.7.4 Affirmation following anticipatory repudiation

An election to affirm the contract means that all of the obligations of both contracting parties remain alive. To constitute an affirmation of the renunciation, there must be evidence of a clear and unequivocal intention to continue with the contract: see the earlier discussion of affirmation in *Yukong Line Ltd of Korea v Rendsburg Investments Corporation of Liberia* [1996] 2 Lloyd's Rep 604 (at **8.4.2.2.1**), which is authority for the fact that a request to the renunciating party to change its mind and honour its obligations on the contractual date will not suffice for affirmation.

8.7.4.1 Is the election irrevocable or can the non-breaching party change its mind before the contractual date set for performance?

One of the reasons for the strict approach to identification of affirmation as requiring clear and unequivocal evidence of an intention to continue with the contract is frequently stated to be that the election is irrevocable, i.e. having affirmed, the non-breaching party cannot change its mind in the period between affirmation and the contractual date for performance—although, following non-performance on the contractual date, there would be a new opportunity to elect to terminate or affirm for that *actual* repudiatory breach. As Lord Ackner explained in *Fercometal v Mediterranean Shipping* [1989] AC 788, at p. 805E:

> [T]here is no third choice . . . to affirm the contract and yet be absolved from tendering further performance unless and until [the breaching party] gives reasonable notice that he is once again able and willing to perform.

Although this represents the general principle, it has long been recognized that where the repudiatory breach is a continuing one (i.e. it continues after affirmation), the fact of the earlier affirmation will not prevent the non-breaching party from choosing to terminate in the period prior to that date set for contractual performance. This was recognized by Thomas J (*obiter*) in *Stocznia Gdanska SA v Latvian Shipping Co.* [2001] 1 Lloyd's Rep 537, at p. 565, when he stated:

> To require an innocent party, who has by pressing for the contract affirmed it, to wait until there is an actual breach by the party in breach before he can bring the contract to an end might well . . . have required that innocent party to engage in performance that is entirely pointless and wasteful as the party in breach would, when he became under an obligation to accept performance, refuse to do so.

This involved a different emphasis (and different result), as Thomas J recognized, from the approach taken by Colman J in the *Stocznia* litigation ([1997] 2 Lloyd's Rep 228 (below)). Colman J considered it important that, following affirmation, the breaching party must be able to rely on the fact that it will have a further opportunity to perform, whereas Thomas J's approach focused on the position of the non-breaching party, who would otherwise be bound to continue performance when it was clear that it continued to be unwanted. The existence of these two differing positions made this a difficult area of law. In policy terms, it was necessary to determine whether the law favoured allowing an unrestricted opportunity for the breaching party to rescue initial non-performance (i.e. the possibility of curing the 'breach') at, or before, the contractual date for performance, or favoured recognizing the realities of the parties' positions in the light of recurrent breach so that wasteful additional expenditure could be avoided. In the latter scenario, in essence, the court is concluding that there is no realistic possibility of cure.

In *Stocznia Gdanska SA v Latvian Shipping Co. (No. 3)* [2002] EWCA Civ 889, [2002] 2 All ER (Comm) 768, [2002] 2 Lloyd's Rep 436, also known as *Stocznia Gdanska SA v Latvian Shipping Co. (Repudiation)*, on appeal from Thomas J's decision, the Court of Appeal recognized (again *obiter*) that once affirmation had occurred, in the event of a continuing anticipatory repudiation in the period prior to the contractual date set for performance, the non-breaching party could terminate despite the earlier affirmation. The Court of Appeal therefore preferred the approach taken by Thomas J (*obiter*) on this issue and considered that affirmation of an anticipatory repudiation related only to past breaches 'leaving open the question of continuing or renewed anticipatory breach': *per* Rix LJ at [99]. Of course, as the Court of Appeal recognized, this does leave open the question of defining a continuing breach, especially the status of silence. It was recognized that, for a continuing duty to perform following affirmation, such silence might be 'a speaking silence'. Rix LJ added, at [96]:

> The difficulty with silence is that it is normally equivocal. Where, however, it is part of a course of consistent conduct it may be silence which not only speaks but does so unequivocally. Where silence speaks, there may be a duty on the silent party in turn to speak to rectify the significance of his silence.

In *White Rosebay Shipping SA v Hong Kong Chain Glory Shipping Ltd, The Fortune Plum* [2013] EWHC 1355 (Comm), [2013] 2 CLC 884, [2013] 2 All ER (Comm) 449, Teare J approved the statements and approach of Rix LJ in the *Stocznia* case for arguments concerning the identification and effect of a continuing renunciation, which followed affirmation of an anticipatory repudiatory breach. Teare J stated, at [53]:

> In a case of renunciation or anticipatory breach (as opposed to repudiation based upon an actual breach) it does not necessarily follow that a termination following an affirmation is a repudiatory breach. For if the renunciating party continues to renounce the contract after the affirmation then the acceptance of that continuing renunciation is not a repudiatory breach but a lawful termination of the contract with a right to damages caused by the renunciation.

On the facts, the owners had affirmed on 11 November, and Teare J noted, at [53], that:

> If the charterers' renunciation of the charterparty continued until 14 November when the owners purported to accept the charterers' renunciation as terminating the charterparty then that termination is likely to be lawful and not repudiatory.

The Court of Appeal in *Stocznia* recognized that there was a period *prior* to the election during which the non-breaching party was making up its mind whether to terminate or affirm. In this period, the contract and the right to terminate were both kept alive. As Rix LJ noted, this period cannot extend indefinitely and inaction over a sufficiently lengthy period may be held to constitute affirmation. In addition, since the contract remains alive until the non-breaching party terminates, the non-breaching party will be subject to the same risks that affect the non-breaching party who formally affirms (see below).

8.7.4.2 Risks to the non-breaching party following the decision to affirm after the other party's anticipatory repudiation

Following affirmation, the non-breaching party bears a number of risks during the period between affirmation and the contractual date for performance, which might seriously affect its position and remedies following the earlier renunciation. The existence of these risks lends support to the position adopted by the Court of Appeal in *Stocznia Gdanska SA v Latvian Shipping Co. (No. 3)* [2002] EWCA Civ 889, [2002] 2 All ER (Comm) 768, [2002] 2 Lloyd's Rep 436, since if the non-breaching party does have to accept these risks, it is arguable that, in this period, the ability to terminate should continue to exist where the renunciation is continuing.

The risks placed on the affirming party in the period between affirmation and the date for performance are not insignificant.

1. If the non-breaching party is itself in breach of contract, for example, that party cannot argue—at least not unless estoppel operates—that the initial renunciation by the other party operates as an excuse for its own subsequent breach.

In *Fercometal SARL v Mediterranean Shipping Co. SA, The Simona* [1989] AC 788, charterers of a ship gave notice of cancellation of the contract that was not in accordance with the terms of the charterparty and amounted to repudiation. The shipowners did not accept the repudiation, but instead gave notice of readiness to load. This notice complied with the charterparty's terms and constituted an affirmation, but as the shipowners were not on the facts ready to load, the notice was false, and itself constituted a breach. The charterers consequently rejected the notice and gave further notice of cancellation, which on this occasion complied with charterparty's terms. The shipowners sued the charterers. The House of Lords rejected this claim. Once the contract was treated as being still in force, it was 'kept alive for the benefit of both parties', and the party affirming could not both keep it alive and seek to justify its own non-performance by reference to the earlier repudiation.

2. Similarly, if the contract is frustrated (see **Chapter 12**) in the period between the affirmation and the due date for performance, the frustration will discharge the contract and the non-breaching party will lose the remedy of damages for the breach.

In *Avery v Bowden* (1855) E & B 714, the master of a ship had been told in advance of the last possible date for loading that there was no cargo available. This may have amounted to repudiation. He elected to affirm the contract and remained in port, hoping that a cargo would eventually be provided. Before the last possible date for performance of the contract, the contract was frustrated by the outbreak of the Crimean War, thus depriving the shipowners of a remedy that they might have had for the failure to provide a cargo, had that repudiation been accepted as terminating the contract.

8.7.4.3 Limitation on the ability to claim the contract price having affirmed

In *White & Carter (Councils) Ltd v McGregor* [1962] AC 413, Lord Reid discussed a further limitation (in addition to the legitimate interest requirement before being able to affirm) on the principle in that case. However, it is a limitation on the ability of the non-breaching party to claim the contract price, rather than a limitation on that party's ability to affirm following a breach by anticipatory repudiation.

> **! KEY POINT**
>
> This second limitation requires that the affirming party must be able to continue with its own performance of the contract without the cooperation of the breaching party to be able to claim the contract price. (Otherwise, the affirming party will be limited to a remedy in damages.)

Cooperation in this context includes both active and passive cooperation of the breaching party, e.g. in *Hounslow London Borough Council v Twickenham Garden Developments Ltd* [1971] Ch 233, following renunciation by the local authority employers, contractors had no right to insist on continuing to perform the contract, because the work was being done on local authority property and they were unable to gain access to the site without the local authority's permission.

For a sale of goods contract, the seller can bring a claim for the price where property in the goods has passed from the seller to the buyer, which is determined by ss. 17 and 18 of the SGA 1979 (see the impact of the Supreme Court decision of *PST Energy 7 Shipping LLC and another v OW Bunker Malta Ltd and another* [2016] UKSC 23, [2016] AC 1034 in this area). If the sale is for specific goods, property passes immediately to the buyer (s. 18, r. 1). Specific goods are 'identified and agreed upon at the time the contract is made' (SGA 1979, s. 61). If the sale is for 'unascertained or future goods by description', property cannot pass until the goods are 'unconditionally appropriated to the contract' with the parties' assent (s. 18, r. 5). Unascertained goods include generic goods, such as 1,000 gallons of diesel. Future goods are defined as 'goods to be manufactured or acquired [by the seller] after the making of the contract of sale' (s. 5(1)), and so would include, for example, a yacht to be manufactured to the buyer's specification. Therefore, for unascertained or future goods, the buyer who has indicated in advance that he does not want the goods can prevent the seller who affirms from being entitled to claim the contract price, because the buyer's assent is required for property in the goods to pass. In a practical sense, the buyer would refuse to accept delivery and therefore prevent property in the goods from passing: *per* Lloyd J in *Clea Shipping Corporation v Bulk Oil International Ltd, The Alaskan Trader* [1984] 1 All ER 129.

However, the restriction in *White & Carter* that a claimant will be limited to a remedy in damages where he is unable to perform without the cooperation of the contract-breaker applies only where the performance that has been prevented by the breach was a precondition to the payment obligation, i.e. the performance obligation was entire. In *Ministry of Sound (Ireland) Ltd v World Online Ltd* [2003] EWHC 2178 (Ch), [2003] 2 All ER (Comm) 823, the non-breaching party could perform only if CDs were supplied by the party in breach. However, since there was no link between the required performance and the right to receive the contractual payment, it did not matter that performance was impossible without cooperation, and since the contract had been affirmed and not terminated for repudiatory breach, in principle the contract term providing for payment could be enforced by a claim in debt (i.e. a claim for the sum due under the contract rather than a claim for damages).

Similarly, in *Isabella Shipowner SA v Shagang Shipping Co. Ltd, The Aquafaith* [2012] EWHC 1077 (Comm), [2012] 2 All ER (Comm) 461, [2012] 1 CLC 899 (for facts see **8.7.3.1**), it was argued that the owners could not claim the remaining hire following early redelivery, since the operation of the charter involved the cooperation of the charterer. This argument was rejected. Cooke J, at [39], considered that: 'the court must focus upon dependent obligations and whether the contract breaker had to do something before the innocent party could do what was required of him to earn the contract sum'. Since the hire was payable in advance, earning the hire was not dependent on any performance by the charterers of their obligations and the owners could hold the ship available without any cooperation.

8.7.5 Accepting the anticipatory repudiatory breach as terminating the contract

As discussed at **8.4.2.1**, it must be clear to the party in breach that the non-breaching party has accepted the conduct as terminating the contract and, although it is possible as a matter of law for this to occur simply by the non-breaching party failing to perform its own contractual obligations, whether it will do so is 'a question of fact depending on the particular contractual relationship and the particular circumstances of the case': see generally *Vitol SA v Norelf Ltd, The Santa Clara* [1996] AC 800, *per* Lord Steyn at p. 811 (discussed at **8.4.2.1**). In practice, however, it would seem to depend on whether the non-breaching party's failure to perform its own contractual obligations is explicable to a reasonable person only on the basis that the non-breaching party has accepted the repudiation as terminating the contract.

If the non-breaching party has terminated following the renunciation, they can claim damages from that time and do not need to wait until the date fixed for performance under the contract: *Hochster v De La Tour* (1853) 2 E & B 678 (for facts, see **8.7.1**). However, the non-breaching party would be under a duty to mitigate its loss as from the date of termination.

8.7.6 The risk of overreacting to a breach

A party faced with what it thinks is an actual or anticipatory repudiation must take careful stock before acting.

The position of a party confronted by conduct that is ambiguous and may amount to a repudiation is improved a little by the common-sense approach of Moore-Bick J in *Yukong Line Ltd v Rendsburg Investments Corporation* [1996] 2 Lloyd's Rep 604. On this approach, a party's legal position should not be adversely affected if the first steps taken are to verify the precise intentions of the other, since this will not necessarily amount to treating the breach as repudiatory and electing to affirm. In addition, the decision in *Stocznia Gdanska SA v Latvian Shipping Co. (No. 3)* [2002] EWCA Civ 889, [2002] 2 All ER (Comm) 768, also assists the position of the non-breaching party faced with the election to terminate or affirm, since it recognizes the existence of a period during which the non-breaching party can make up its mind on the election. Nevertheless, it will not be possible to delay unreasonably without risking a finding of affirmation.

However, if the non-breaching party mistakenly thinks that the other party has repudiated the contract, its own purported election to accept this action as discharging future obligations may itself amount to a repudiation, actual or anticipatory: *Federal Commerce and Navigation Ltd v Molena Alpha Inc.* [1979] AC 757.

It might be thought that there is some protection for the mistaken non-breaching party in the statement by Lord Wilberforce in the House of Lords in *Woodar Investment Development Ltd v Wimpey Construction (UK) Ltd* [1980] 1 WLR 277 that, in the absence of bad faith, the mistake as to its rights would not lead the court to regard a purported termination of the contract as a repudiation. It was accepted in *Vaswani v Italian Motors (Sales and Services) Ltd* [1996] 1 WLR 270 that merely to assert a claim based on an erroneous, but good faith, interpretation of the contract would not amount to a repudiation. However, the court was clear that there would necessarily be a repudiation if the assertion were to go beyond any position consistent with being willing to continue with the contract. In many instances, a party who, believing that a repudiatory breach has occurred, wishes to escape from the contract will make it perfectly clear that it wants no more to do with the contract: see *Hongkong Fir Shipping Co. Ltd v Kawasaki Kisen Kaisha Ltd* [1962] 2 QB 26 and *Cehave NV v Bremer Handelsgesellschaft Gmbh, The Hansa Nord* [1976] QB 44, in which the goods were wrongfully rejected. It is for this reason that this 'good faith' solution would not apply in a large number of cases.

To remove some of the uncertainty from that risk, English law might imitate § 2–609 of the US Uniform Commercial Code (UCC), which enables a party who has reasonable ground for insecurity with respect to the other's performance to demand an assurance of the performance due and, if such is not forthcoming within a reasonable time, then to treat the contract as repudiated. Similar provisions exist in Art. 7.3.4 of the UNIDROIT Principles of International Commercial Contracts (PICC) and Art. 8:105 of the Principles of European Contract Law (PECL).

MULTIPLE-CHOICE QUESTIONS

Test your knowledge by trying this chapter's **multiple-choice questions**:
www.oup.com/uk/poole

FURTHER READING

General

Carter, *Carter's Breach of Contract* (Hart Publishing, 2012).

Classification of terms

Bojczuk, 'When is a condition not a condition?' [1987] JBL 353.

Girvin, 'Time charter overlap: determining legitimacy and the operation of repudiatory breach of contract' [1995] JBL 200.

Treitel, 'Types of contractual terms' in *Some Landmarks of Twentieth Century Contract Law* (Clarendon Press, 2002).

Weir, 'The buyer's right to reject defective goods' [1976] CLJ 33.

Repudiatory breach and the election

Adams and Brownsword, 'Breach and withdrawal' in *Key Issues in Contract* (Butterworths, 1995).

Andrews, 'A breach of contract: a plea for clarity and discipline' (2018) 134 LQR 117.

Brownsword, 'Retrieving reasons, retrieving rationality? A new look at the right to withdraw for breach of contract' (1992) 5 JCL 83.

Carter, Courtney, and Tolhurst, 'An assimilated approach to discharge for breach of contract by delay' (2017) 76 CLJ 6.

Carter, Courtney, and Tolhurst, 'Two models of discharge of a contract by repudiation' (2018) 77 CLJ 97.

Carter and Courtney, 'Breach of condition and express termination right: a distinction with a difference' (2017) 133 LQR 395.

Ezeoke, 'Assessing seriousness in repudiatory breach of innominate terms' [2017] JBL 198.

Hedley, 'Eloquent silences and reasonable people' [1996] CLJ 430.

Morgan, *Great Debates in Contract Law*, 2nd edn (Palgrave Macmillan, 2015), ch. 8, pp. 223–34.

Morgan, 'Repudiatory breach: inability, election and discharge' (2017) 76 CLJ 11.

O'Sullivan, 'Repudiation – keeping the contract alive' in Virgo and Worthington (eds.), *Commercial Remedies – Resolving Controversies* (Cambridge University Press, 2017), ch. 3.

Reynolds, 'Warranty, condition and fundamental term' (1963) 79 LQR 534.

Reynolds, 'Discharge of contract by breach' (1981) 97 LQR 541.

Shea, 'Discharge from performance of contracts by failure of condition' (1979) 42 MLR 623.

Stannard and Capper, *Termination for Breach of Contract* (Oxford University Press, 2014).

Treitel, 'Affirmation after repudiatory breach' (1998) 114 LQR 22.

Wilmot-Smith, 'Termination after breach' (2018) 134 LQR 307.

Breach of entire obligation as repudiatory

Burrows, 'Law Commission report on pecuniary restitution on breach of contract' (1984) 47 MLR 76.

Law Commission Report No. 121, *Pecuniary Restitution on Breach of Contract* (1983).

Anticipatory breach

Carter, Phang, and Phang, 'Performance following repudiation: legal and economic interests' (1999) 15 JCL 97.

Coote, 'Breach, anticipatory breach, or the breach anticipated?' (2007) 123 LQR 503.

Dawson, 'Damages for anticipatory breach' [2016] LMCLQ 6.

Liu, 'Inferring future breach: towards a unifying test of anticipatory breach of contract' [2007] CLJ 574.

Liu, *Anticipatory Breach* (Hart Publishing, 2011).

Liu, 'The *White & Carter* principle: a restatement' (2011) 74 MLR 171.

Enforcement of contractual obligations

Overview of the law on remedies for breach of contract

(a) The notion of enforcement: the compensation principle

The definition of contracts as 'legally enforceable agreements' (see **1.3**) assumes that mechanisms exist for the enforcement of those agreements that are identified by the law as creating legally enforceable performance obligations. The mechanisms of enforcement of contractual obligations are the subject of the next two chapters (**Chapters 9** and **10**). **Chapter 11** examines the question of enforcement by or on behalf of third parties and so is related to the general enforcement question.

Although compulsion and penalty probably represent the popular notion of enforcement, the basic legal means of enforcement of contractual obligations is by compensation for loss caused—in other words, by the payment of damages for breach of contract (see **Chapter 9**). It is enforcement in the sense that the party who should have performed, but did not, is compelled to pay the cost of placing the claimant in the same position as he would have been in if the contract had been performed, so that anticipated profits that would have accrued to the claimant from performance are within the scope of damages. Tort, by contrast, provides compensation to place the claimant as nearly as possible in the same position as he would have been in if the tort had not been committed. Those general principles were reaffirmed by the Supreme Court in *Morris-Garner v One Step (Support) Ltd* [2018] UKSC 20, [2018] 2 WLR 1353.

(b) No punishment for breach of contractual obligations

English law has traditionally denied any role for punishment in the enforcement of contracts. Although theorists have, at times, attributed the binding force of contractual undertakings to the moral obligation to keep one's promises, the law does not seek to punish promise-breakers, just as it is not directly concerned with enforcing morality. Punishment is regarded as an instrument of social control, so that the law punishes criminals and may, in limited circumstances, award punitive (or 'exemplary') damages against those who are particularly callous or deliberate in the commission of torts. However, there is little scope for such social control in English contract law; the focus is rather on enabling private transactions and, in the last resort, on remedying grievances. The notion of 'efficient breach of contract' derived from US scholarship on 'law-and-economics' proposes that the law should not punish a party for breaking a contract if the costs to him of doing so are less than the costs of performance. This theory potentially justifies the refusal of the English courts to recognize an award of exemplary damages in all but exceptional cases. However, it has never featured in English decisions.

In *Devenish Nutrition Ltd v Sanofi-Aventis SA* [2007] EWHC 2394 (Ch), [2009] Ch 390, Longmore LJ explained the position:

> 143 There are also some instances when a claimant can recover more than his loss. The most obvious example is a case in which a claimant is entitled to exemplary damages which are intended to penalise a defendant for tortious conduct, particularly if he has calculated that the profit he is likely to make from his wrongful conduct will exceed any damages for which he is likely to be liable to the claimant within the second category of such damages identified by Lord Devlin in *Rookes v Barnard* [1964] AC 1129, as further explained by the *House of Lords in Kuddus v Chief Constable of Leicestershire Constabulary* [2002] 2 AC 122. In the current state of the law, exemplary damages are not available for breach of contract even if a contract-breaker has made a similarly cynical calculation that it will benefit him more to break a contract than to perform it: see *Occidental Worldwide Investment Corpn v Skibs A/S Avanti (The Siboen and The Sibotre)* [1976] 1 Lloyd's Rep 293.

Where breach occurs, but no loss is sustained, in most circumstances only nominal damages will be awarded: *Surrey County Council v Bredero Homes Ltd* [1993] 1 WLR 1361 (although see **10.6.1** and **10.6.2**). In *Bredero Homes*, the breach was deliberate and made with the intention of increasing the profitability of the transaction, which intention was duly realized. It might be thought that such conduct would invite censure from the courts, but, crucially, the non-breaching party could not be shown to have suffered a loss. The Court of Appeal was unanimous in refusing any award of damages, although the House of Lords in *Attorney-General v Blake* [2001] 1 AC 268 has since held that, in very exceptional circumstances, it may be possible to obtain an order whereby the party in breach has to account for profits made as a result of the breach. The exact scope of the principle in *Attorney-General v Blake* is unclear, but, because of the specific facts of the case, it would appear that it was not intended to have more general application and should be very tightly circumscribed. It has since been confirmed that the account of profits in *Blake* is a compensatory remedy: *World Wide Fund for Nature v World Wrestling Federation Entertainment Inc.* [2007] EWCA Civ 286, [2008] 1 WLR 445 (see **10.7.2.**).

Again, in *Morris-Garner v One Step (Support) Ltd* it was said by Lord Reed (at [82]), speaking for the majority, that '*Blake* decided that in exceptional circumstances an account of profits can be ordered as a remedy for breach of contract'. The point was not in issue in *Morris-Garner*, and the majority chose not to explore the scope of or trigger for the *Blake* exception.

Another aspect of the non-punitive approach to contractual damages is the policy of the courts denying enforcement to contractual clauses purporting to impose penalties for non-performance (see **9.6**).

(c) Substitute performance rather than compelling actual performance

The political and economic liberalisms that were the foundations upon which nineteenth-century contract law was built (see **1.4.1**) were inconsistent with the idea of compelling a person to perform a contract against their will in circumstances in which suitable equivalent alternative performance was available. In the case of contracts for goods or services in which there is an available market, the non-breaching party can obtain substitute performance. The price that the party in breach must pay for not being compelled to perform against that party's will is the extra cost of obtaining that substitute performance.

> **→ EXAMPLE**
>
> If A promises to cut B's hedge on Tuesday for £25, but then arranges to cut C's lawn on the same day for £30, making performance of the contract with B impossible, there is undoubtedly a breach of contract. A will not be punished; neither will A be forced to revoke the contract with C in order to perform the contract with B. B must find someone else to cut the hedge, and if the market price for the services of a hedge-cutter is higher than £25, A must pay the difference.
>
> The contract has been enforced only in the sense that, at the end of the day, B will have received the promised contractual performance at the cost to him agreed in his contract with A.
>
> This result can be justified in terms both of the relationship between the parties and also by the theory of efficient breach.
>
> - No doubt B would not be happy to accept A's services, since B believes A to be unreliable; equally, it may be impossible to force A to perform at A's best if it would amount to performance given against A's will. In these circumstances, substitute performance is probably more acceptable to both.
>
> - Alternatively, if A is to pay B's extra costs, B will be no worse off by allowing A not to perform, while A may be better off if B's extra cost is less than the extra profit A will make on A's contract with C. That is, if B's substitute performance costs £28, then A must pay B £3 for B to be no worse off. A makes an extra profit, by contracting with C for £30, so that—after paying B—A will be £2 better off. For one party to be better off while no party is worse off is, in economic terms, an efficient result. (This simple example assumes that B incurred no costs in finding substitute performance.)

It is therefore only where substitute performance is irrelevant or inadequate that the law will compel actual performance. Substitute performance is irrelevant where the contractual obligation that is unperformed is to pay the price (see **10.1**), since compulsion of payment of the price is no different from compulsion to pay damages of the cost of substitute performance. However, substitute performance will be inadequate where the promised contractual performance is in some way unique, or at least exceedingly rare, so that substitution is impossible.

- For example, a contract to sell the *Mona Lisa* is a contract for a unique item, and if it were breached, the buyer could obtain no substitute. In such circumstances, damages are inappropriate and the court will compel actual performance (see **10.2**).

- Substitute performance may also be inadequate where the contractual undertaking is in the form of a promise to refrain from some activity.

> **→ EXAMPLE**
>
> If A pays £50 to B, A's neighbour, in return for B's promise to refrain from making loud noises during the period while A is revising for an examination, calculating A's loss should B disturb A's work may be impossible. A needs to be able to prevent the disturbance occurring.

Again, in such circumstances, damages are inappropriate and the court will compel actual performance (see **10.3**).

(d) Compensation for losses: the interests to be compensated?

Except in those cases in which substitute performance is irrelevant or inadequate, the method of enforcement of contractual obligations is by compensation for losses caused by the breach.

The claimant may have suffered loss in any of three broad areas of interest, and the interest to be compensated determines the measure of damages payable.

- The *expectation interest* refers to whatever is necessary to put the claimant into the position in which they would have been had the contract been performed. Compensation for lost profit is compensation of an expectation interest, as is payment of damages for the cost of substitute performance.

- The *reliance interest* refers to whatever is necessary to put the claimant into the position in which they were before the contract was made, and this means compensating for expenditure incurred in performance of the contract that has been wasted in consequence of the breach. Recent authority (see **9.2.1.2**) confirms that this is, in fact, an aspect of compensation for lost expectation, since this wasted expenditure would have been recovered if the contract had been performed, e.g. as an integral part of the price. The reliance interest was first identified by the classic article by Fuller and Perdue, 'The reliance interest in contract damages' (1936) 46 Yale LJ 52.

- The *restitutionary interest* refers to the restoration to the claimant of a benefit conferred on the defendant to which the defendant is not entitled. The basis for this recovery is that the defendant would otherwise be unjustly enriched at the claimant's expense. Compensation for work done in anticipation of entering a contract that in fact never materializes is compensation of a restitutionary interest, as is the return of an advance payment under a contract that is void for mistake or discharged by frustration.

Chapter 9

Damages for breach of contract

SUMMARY OF THE ISSUES

Damages are available as of right on proof of breach of contract. This chapter examines the aims of contractual damages and the factors influencing their quantification.

- Contractual damages are compensatory and not punitive, i.e. they are intended to compensate the claimant for losses suffered, rather than to punish the defendant.

- The compensatory aim of contractual damages is to put the claimant in the position in which they would have been had the contract been properly performed and had the breach not occurred. This translates into an aim of seeking to protect the expectation of performance (known as the 'expectation interest' or the 'performance interest'). Compensation for lost expectation may include an award of damages to compensate for expenditure wasted as a result of the breach.

- It is important to identify the expectation interest correctly by reference to the loss suffered by the claimant on breach (since it is this loss that the law seeks to compensate) and to recognize that this loss may extend beyond the financial interest in performance to include purely subjective expectations in performance (the 'consumer surplus'). Whereas lost expectation is normally measured in terms of difference in value between what was expected and what was received, where the claimant had a non-financial interest in performance, such a measure may not properly compensate, and it is therefore important to consider the circumstances in which the courts are prepared to award cost of cure damages. However, because there are dangers in the award of cost of cure (or replacement) damages, the courts have developed principles determining the availability of such an award in an attempt to balance the competing considerations.

- Non-pecuniary losses are generally not recoverable in a claim for breach of contract. However, in some circumstances, a modest sum may be awarded for the disappointment suffered as a result of not receiving the promised performance.

- There are other limitations on the claimant's ability to be fully compensated, such as the 'duty' to take reasonable steps to minimize loss (mitigation), the fact that losses that are too remote a consequence of the breach cannot be recovered (remoteness), and the possibility that a damages award may be apportioned to take account of the claimant's own negligence (contributory negligence).

»

9

- The parties may agree in advance on the damages to be payable in the event of breach (agreed damages clauses). However, in certain circumstances, the courts will strike down these clauses if they are penal. It is necessary to distinguish those clauses operating as penalties from those that constitute enforceable liquidated damages.

9.1 The basis of recovery of damages in a contract claim

In *Photo Production Ltd v Securicor Transport Ltd* [1980] AC 827 (see **7.3.3** and **8.4**), at p. 849, Lord Diplock said:

> Every failure to perform a primary obligation is a breach of contract. The secondary obligation on the part of the contract-breaker to which it gives rise by implication of the common law is to pay monetary compensation to the other party for the loss sustained by him in consequence of the breach . . .

Thus damages for breach of contract are available as of right, on proof of breach. In some circumstances, breach may also give the non-breaching party the option of bringing the outstanding primary obligations to a premature end (see **8.4.2**). In this chapter, however, we shall consider the secondary obligation to pay compensation (damages) for loss caused, which arises whenever there is a breach of contract. Essentially, we will be examining how these damages are quantified.

9.1.1 Compensation for loss suffered

The basic aim of contractual damages is to compensate the claimant for the loss that the claimant has suffered as a result of the breach of contract. Therefore, in calculating these damages, the traditional focus has been placed on the claimant's loss. It is for the innocent party to prove its loss, which in turn requires it to establish that, had the breach not occurred, it would have been able to fulfil its obligations under the contract and to obtain the benefits promised under the contract: *Flame SA v Glory Wealth Shipping Pte Ltd* [2013] EWHC 3153 (Comm), [2014] QB 1080. No damages award can put the innocent party into a better position than that in which they would have been had the contract been performed and, in doing so, provide a windfall. A claimant cannot recover more than its actual loss, and if the claimant suffers no loss, the claimant will be constrained to recovering only nominal damages—although see the discussion concerning the ability to recover for substantial losses suffered by a third party (at **11.7.3**) and the discussion of recovery in instances of no identifiable financial loss (at **10.6.4.**).

9.1.2 Can the profit resulting from a deliberate breach of contract be recovered?

The compensatory principle also means that, since it is not part of the loss suffered by the claimant, the claimant cannot, as a general rule, recover any profit made by the defendant, even if that profit resulted from a deliberate breach of contract by the defendant—*Surrey County Council v Bredero Homes Ltd* [1993] 1 WLR 961—although see the discussion relating to the possible recovery of profits and the decision in *Attorney-General v Blake* [2001] 1 AC 268 (at **10.6.3**). This has since been interpreted as a compensatory remedy, rather than restitutionary: *World Wide Fund for Nature (WWF) v World Wrestling Federation Entertainment Inc.* [2007] EWCA Civ 286, [2008] 1 WLR 445.

9.1.3 Are exemplary or punitive damages recoverable in a contract claim?

Since contractual damages are compensatory rather than punitive, exemplary damages have not been available in a claim in contract: *Addis v Gramophone Co. Ltd* [1909] AC 488. In *Johnson v Unisys Ltd* [2001] UKHL 13, [2003] 1 AC 518, it was stated quite clearly that such damages cannot be awarded in a claim for breach of contract, and the Law Commission, in its report *Aggravated, Exemplary and Restitutionary Damages*, Law Com. No. 247 (1997), did not suggest any reform of the law with respect to recovery in a claim based on breach of contract. In 2009, the Ministry of Justice published a response to its Consultation Paper on this question— *The Law on Damages*, CP 9/07 (May 2007)—rejecting possible legislative intervention, and confirming the government's wish to see no further encroachment on the distinction between punishment and compensation: Ministry of Justice, *Civil Law Reform Bill: Consultation*, CP 53/09 (December 2009). (See also Rowan, 'Reflections on the introduction of punitive damages for breach of contract' (2010) 30 OJLS 495.)

9.2 The aim of compensation

The basic rule of recovery of compensation in the case of breach of contract is that the non-breaching party is to be put into the position in which it would have been had the contract been performed as agreed: Robinson v Harman (1848) 1 Ex 850; see also *Surrey County Council v Bredero Homes Ltd* [1993] 1 WLR 961. This principle was also confirmed as fundamental in *Golden Strait Corporation v Nippon Yusen Kubishika Kaisha, The Golden Victory* [2007] UKHL 12, [2007] 2 AC 353, *per* Lord Bingham at [9], Lord Scott at [29], and Lord Carswell at [57] and again by the Supreme Court in *Morris-Garner v One-Step (Support) Ltd*, *per* Lord Reed at [31].

9.2.1 Compensation for what? Lost expectation

This general measure of loss was described in the opening pages to **Part 3**, under heading **(d)**, as compensating the claimant's expectation interest, i.e. compensation for loss of the benefit of the promised performance (the expected gain under the contract).

9.2.1.1 Loss of profits, reduction in value, or the cost to replace

Lost expectation may therefore comprise loss of a profit that would have been made but for the breach.

> → **EXAMPLE**
>
> If A bought machinery from B with the intention of making goods and selling them at a profit to C, then B's failure to deliver the machines will result in A losing the profit to be made on the sale of the goods.

Subject to certain limitations (see **9.5**), quantification of such a loss should not present great difficulty.

However, lost expectation may also occur without any intention to profit from the contract and, in those circumstances, quantification of the loss is more difficult. It may be measured either by reference to the diminished value to the claimant (see **9.3.2**), or by reference to the cost of achieving the agreed performance (see **9.3.3**).

9.2.1.2 Wasted expenditure

In some cases, the claimant may prefer, or may be obliged (see **9.3.5.1**), to recover compensation for his out-of-pocket expenses arising from his performance of the contract and other expenses that it was expected would have been recovered had the contract been performed. These damages are often termed 'reliance interest' damages, but recent authorities indicate that they are a species of expectation loss compensation: *Omak Maritime Ltd v Mamola Challenger Shipping Co.* [2010] EWHC 2026 (Comm), [2011] Bus LR 212 and more recently *Royal Devon and Exeter NHS Foundation Trust v ATOS IT Services UK Ltd* [2017] EWHC 2197 (TCC), [2018] BLR 90, at [61] *per* O'Farrell J. Had the breach not occurred, ordinarily these expenses would have been recovered as an integral element of the price paid.

There is no reason why lost profit *and* out-of-pocket expenses should not both be recovered, provided that there is no double compensation (see **9.3.5.4**), since both are mechanisms for calculating the lost expectation under the contract.

9.2.2 Securing restitution of benefits conferred

Compensation of the claimant's restitutionary interest, i.e. restoration of a benefit conferred by the claimant on the defendant on the basis that otherwise the defendant would be unjustly enriched at the claimant's expense, is discussed at **10.4**.

9.3 Quantification of loss: lost expectation

As discussed earlier, damages to compensate for expectation loss seek to protect the expectation of performance resulting from the promise by compensating for the loss of that expectation. However, in order to achieve this compensation, it is necessary to identify the lost expectation and then to quantify it. Some of the problems in the case law can be attributed to attempts to achieve the quantification without first identifying the loss.

9.3.1 The scope of the performance interest

The 'performance interest' or contractual expectation is based on identifying and assessing the value of certain 'benefits' that the claimant expected to receive under the contract. These benefits may not be limited to an expectation of financial benefits, but can include anticipated subjective benefits (known as 'the consumer surplus'): see the discussion of *Ruxley Electronics v Forsyth* [1996] AC 344 (at **9.3.3.4**) and *Farley v Skinner (No. 2)* [2001] UKHL 49, [2002] 2 AC 732 (at **9.5.4.4**).

Damages for breach of contract should give effect to this 'performance interest' by awarding damages to compensate for:

- the loss of the expected financial benefit; and
- the loss of 'subjective benefits' or preferences that are considered to be part of the contractual expectation: see *Ruxley Electronics v Forsyth* and discussion in *Farley v Skinner (No. 2)*. (This is an aspect of the larger question of the circumstances in which it is possible to recover for non-pecuniary losses—discussed at **9.5.4.3**—e.g. as part of an expectation of contractual 'enjoyment' or peace of mind and recognition of loss of amenity.)

However, the performance interest may also include the interest in getting the performance itself, which should automatically result in a cost of cure measure of damages (subject to reasonableness) to ensure that the performance is achieved. This can be distinguished from the interest in securing the benefits of the contract. See the discussion of Lord Griffiths's 'broad ground' in *Linden Gardens Trust Ltd v Lenesta Sludge Disposals Ltd* [1994] 1 AC 85, at p. 96 (at **11.7.3.2**). The 'broad ground' argument focuses only on the fact that the contracting party has not received 'the bargain for which he contracted'. For example, Lord Griffiths stated that a husband who contracts for repairs to his wife's house has suffered loss because he does not receive the bargain for which he contracted, although in terms of traditional losses, since the husband has no proprietary interest in the property, he suffers no personal tangible loss as a result of the breach.

The award in *Ruxley Electronics v Forsyth* was a loss of amenity award (loss of enjoyment) for failure to install a swimming pool of the required depth. It seems clear that counsel for Mr Forsyth's primary argument was that Mr Forsyth did not get the performance for which he had contracted so that cost of cure damages were required as the applicable remedy. This is supported by the evidence relating to the fact that Mr Forsyth did not dive and so his personal loss of enjoyment would have been minimal. Although rejecting the availability of this award on the facts, the House of Lords wanted to find some way in which to recognize the non-performance (failure to construct a pool of the depth set out in the contractual specification).

This approach receives some support from the approach taken by Lord Scott in *Farley v Skinner (No. 2)*, since Lord Scott distinguished on the ground that the loss in that case was treated as a loss of the entitlement to performance, so that it involves a 'deprivation of contractual benefit'.

Although there is additional support for this 'broad ground' in the speeches of Lords Goff and Millett in *Alfred McAlpine Construction Ltd v Panatown* [2001] 1 AC 518—and possibly in that of Lord Browne-Wilkinson (discussed at **11.7.3.2**)—the existence of such a performance interest entitling the contracting party to receive damages in the event of non-performance has yet to be fully accepted. Accordingly, the emphasis in this chapter is placed on loss caused to the claimant through the non-fulfilment of the promised expectation (benefits): pecuniary and non-pecuniary losses, i.e. losses flowing from the breach rather than for the *fact* of the breach alone.

- Expectation loss will normally be compensated on the basis of the difference in value measure, i.e. the difference in value between the promised performance and the actual performance. Difference in value damages are often calculated using the 'market price' rule. However, where there is no market, these damages will be calculated as the difference between the value of the performance as contracted for and the actual value of the performance received.

- In some circumstances, it may be possible to recover the cost of achieving the expected performance ('cost of cure').

- Where the claimant has incurred wasted expenses in performing the contract and in reliance on it, these may be recovered as compensation on the basis of ensuring that the claimant is not out-of-pocket as a result of the breach.

9.3.2 Difference in value

9.3.2.1 The market price rule

9.3.2.1.1 Assessment of damages for the seller's breach (non-delivery of goods) in a commercial contract (B2B—business to business) for the sale of goods: Sale of Goods Act (SGA) 1979, s. 51(3)

- Where there is an available market, the law assumes that the commercial buyer will mitigate its loss (see **9.5.3**) by immediately going to the market and buying similar goods from another source.

- The buyer will then suffer a loss only if it has to pay more for the substitute goods on the open market than it had originally contracted to pay.

- The buyer's damages will therefore be assessed as the extra cost, i.e. by subtracting the contract price from the market price at the date of breach (SGA 1979, s. 51(3)).

- Where the buyer had anticipated making a profit on the transaction by reselling the goods at a price higher than the market price, the buyer's damages are nevertheless restricted to the difference between market price and contract price, since the buyer would have been able to make the resale, and thus the profit, by obtaining substitute goods in the market: *Williams v Reynolds* (1865) 6 B & S 495.

Section 51 SGA 1979 has no application to contracts within the scope of the Consumer Rights Act (CRA) 2015 (B2C—contracts between a 'trader and a consumer'). Instead, non-delivery in the context of sale of goods is dealt with in s. 28 of the CRA 2015. It provides that where there is a failure to deliver immediately when immediate delivery was essential (and examples given in the explanatory notes relate to a wedding dress or birthday cake), the consumer may treat the contract as at an end and there is no requirement to provide a further opportunity to deliver. However, in other cases, if the trader fails to deliver the goods to the consumer on the agreed date or within 30 days, the consumer may state a further reasonable time frame within which delivery is to occur. In the event that there is no delivery within this reasonable time frame, the consumer may treat the contract as at an end. Section 28 provides for the trader to reimburse the consumer for 'all payments made under the contract' in the event of non-delivery (s. 28(9)). Section 28(13) provides that the consumer may seek other remedies (presumably a reference to damages for the extra cost of any substitute) where it is open to the consumer to do so. There is no provision dealing with the measure of these damages and it seems that, given the non-applicability of SGA 1979, s. 51, the consumer buyer will have to establish the actual loss on the facts in each instance.

9.3.2.1.2 Assessment of damages for the buyer's breach (non-acceptance of goods) in a contract for the sale of goods: SGA 1979, s. 50(3)

- Where there is an available market, it is assumed that the seller will immediately be able to sell the goods to a substitute buyer, so that the seller will suffer a loss only if the market price is below the price that the seller had originally contracted to receive.

- The seller's damages will therefore be assessed as its loss based on subtracting the market price at the time of the breach from the contract price (SGA 1979, s. 50(3)).

Lost-volume sales

Where the buyer breaches the contract by refusing to accept the goods, the market price rule will often result in no loss to the seller; standard items are frequently sold at standard prices, so that there will be no difference between market price and contract price.

> **→ EXAMPLE**
>
> If A has three sacks of coal to sell and contracts to sell them to B at the standard (market) price of £20 per sack, if B later wrongfully refuses to accept the coal, A will almost certainly be able to sell them to C at the same price. B will assert that it is entitled to benefit from A's mitigation of the loss (see **9.5.3**), so that no damages are payable, while A will assert that it has lost the profit on the sale to B, since it would have been able to sell another three bags of coal to C.
>
> The expectation loss claimed by A is usually referred to as created by 'lost volume'.

Supply greater than demand

The claim will succeed in cases in which supply is greater than demand, i.e. if A has unlimited access to supplies of coal, then it is true that it could have made sales to both B and C, so that there is genuinely one lost sale, and A should recover the profit that it would have made on that sale: *Thompson (W. L.) Ltd v Robinson (Gunmakers) Ltd* [1955] Ch 177, which involved the sale of a new 'Vanguard' car—such cars being readily available, so that supply exceeded demand and the breach resulted in a lost sale.

Demand greater than supply

However, where demand is greater than supply, the claim will not succeed, i.e. if the three sacks of coal were A's last three available sacks and no further supplies were obtainable, A could not have made sales to both B and C, and the sale to C was genuinely a substitute for the sale to B. In such a case, there will be no lost profit: *Charter v Sullivan* [1957] 2 QB 117 (also the sale of a new car).

These rules do not apply in the case of unique goods, since in that case there is no market for such goods and no scope for a substitute sale: *Lazenby Garages Ltd v Wright* [1976] 1 WLR 459, which concerned the sale of a second-hand car—although there is scope for doubting whether every second-hand car is 'unique'.

9.3.2.2 Alternative measures of difference in value

The market price rule will not be used as the measure of loss either:

- where there is no available market; or
- where, in the circumstances, the non-breaching party is not expected to avail itself of the market to mitigate its loss.

9.3.2.2.1 No available market

It is a question of fact in each case whether a market exists. A good example of absence of a market is where goods are specially manufactured to the order of the buyer, so that it is very unlikely that a different buyer would have ordered precisely the same goods. Another is where there is a serious disequilibrium between supply and demand. Thus, in ascertaining a seller's loss, there may be no market price if supply so far outstrips demand that the seller cannot reasonably make an alternative sale. Equally, in ascertaining a buyer's loss, there may be no market price if demand so outstrips supply that the buyer cannot reasonably make an alternative purchase. See *Hughes v Pendragon Sabre Ltd* [2016] EWCA Civ 18, [2016] 1 Lloyd's Rep 311, where the damages claim was in respect of the non-delivery of a Porsche and the evidence showed that only 30 such vehicles had been supplied in the UK.

Where there is no market, the court must seek evidence so that it can put its own estimation of the actual value of the goods in question into the formula in place of the market price. That was the approach adopted in *Hughes v Pendragon Sabre Ltd* [2016] EWCA Civ 18, where there was no available market for a Porsche of the type in question and damages had to be assessed by reference to evidence as to the value of the car at the time and place of breach. Such estimations will sometimes be highly speculative, although the court may have some evidence available from actual contracts of resale of the goods, which was the position in *Hughes*. In some circumstances, measurement of the expectation loss is so uncertain that the claimant may be forced to claim wasted expenditure (see **9.3.5.1**).

9.3.2.2.2 Instances in which the non-breaching party is not expected to go into the market

Defective performance

A claimant buyer will not be expected to avail itself of the market to mitigate a loss when, despite the breach, it is obliged to keep the goods rather than buying substitutes. This will occur when the breach relates only to a warranty (see **8.5.4**), or is a non-serious breach of an innominate term (see **8.5.5**), or where the breach once entitled the buyer to reject the goods, but that right has been lost (see **8.4.2.3**).

Such a buyer will still seek to be compensated for its lost expectation through the defective performance, which in this case will normally be represented by the difference in value of the goods as warranted (promised) in the contract and as actually delivered. Here, again, the estimation of values may be somewhat speculative, although where there is a market, the warranted value will be taken to be the same as the market price.

Late delivery

1. Where the delay in delivery constitutes a repudiatory breach and the buyer rejects the goods for this reason, damages are assessed as if the breach constituted non-delivery (SGA

1979, s. 51(3)): see also the discussion at **9.3.2.1** concerning s. 28 CRA 2015 and damages for non-delivery in a consumer contract.

2. However, where the delay in delivery is affirmed or does not constitute a repudiatory breach, the measure of damages will differ depending upon the intended purpose behind the purchase of goods. Damages will normally be assessed on the basis of the difference in market value in the event of late delivery of goods intended for income-generation (e.g. manufacturing machinery), and the lost expectation will be the profits lost during the period when the machinery should have been in operation: see *Victoria Laundry (Windsor) Ltd v Newman Industries Ltd* [1949] 2 KB 528 (discussed at **9.5.2.2**). However, where the intention was to sell the goods in the market, the loss will be the difference between the market price on the date on which the goods should have been delivered and the market price on the date on which they were delivered.

Cancellation of a contract to supply

The normal measure of damages where a contract to supply is cancelled will be the lost net profit on the contract. (It may be possible, in addition, to recover for wasted expenditure incurred in seeking to perform prior to the date of cancellation: see **9.3.5.4**.) In exceptional circumstances, the supplier may, in addition to net profit, be able to recover an element of the gross profit to cover fixed overheads where it is not possible to defray these overheads by obtaining a substitute contract; e.g. in *Western Webb Offset Printers Ltd v Independent Media Ltd* [1996] CLC 77, it was not possible to obtain a substitute contract due to the economic recession.

9.3.3 Cost of cure

Cost of cure (or repair) is another possible way of calculating expectation loss. In some circumstances, awarding cost of cure may be the only way of ensuring that the claimant's expectation under the contract is fulfilled.

9.3.3.1 Contractual purpose

In a contract for the sale of goods, the buyer will probably want performance in order to put the goods into immediate use, or in order to resell them and make a profit on the sale. The seller's failure to deliver may be cured by the buyer obtaining substitute goods in the market. In such a case, difference in value, as measured by the market price rule (see **9.3.2.1**), and cost of cure are one and the same thing. In other circumstances, the claimant may have wanted performance for other 'subjective' reasons, so that a damages award based on an objective difference in value will not compensate her. Harris, Ogus, and Phillips (1979) 95 LQR 581 refer to these 'subjective' reasons for wanting performance as the 'consumer surplus'.

> **! KEY POINT**
>
> The 'consumer surplus' is defined as 'the excess utility or subjective value over and above the market value of the performance contracted for', and which would have been secured had the contract been properly performed. By way of example, the subjective benefits derived from the purchase of an item of clothing may well, in the mind of the purchaser, exceed the market value.

The measure of cost of cure may be significantly greater than the measure of difference in value. The question therefore is whether the courts should give effect to the consumer surplus and award higher cost of cure damages.

> In the famous American case of **Jacob and Youngs v Kent** 230 NY 239 (1921), the claimants had inserted an express clause in the contract to construct a house stipulating that a particular make of piping was to be used in the plumbing work. A different make of piping of identical quality was, in fact, used. The court refused to allow damages on the basis of cost of cure and allowed only the difference in value, which was purely nominal.

9.3.3.2 Balancing the competing issues

The courts have to balance two competing issues here.

- Awarding cost of cure may appear to be out of all proportion to the consequences of the breach and there is a risk of unjust enrichment if the claimant is awarded cost of cure damages, but then does not use this damages award to achieve the cure.

- On the other hand, if a building owner has specified a particular means of performance, the building contractor may save costs of performing by not complying with the specification, but may have to pay only a small difference in value measure of damages. This might send the wrong signals to the construction industry. In addition, if the cost of cure is not awarded, it can be argued that the building owner's performance interest has not been fulfilled.

In order to seek to achieve a balance between these two competing issues, the courts have imposed some limitations on the ability to recover cost of cure damages in such circumstances, whilst showing a willingness to recognize the 'consumer surplus'.

9.3.3.3 Recognition of 'the consumer surplus'

There has been very clear recognition of this non-financial interest in performance, e.g. in *Radford v De Froberville* [1977] 1 WLR 1262, *Ruxley Electronics and Construction Ltd v Forsyth* [1996] 1 AC 344, and *Attorney-General v Blake* [2001] 1 AC 268. For example, in *Attorney-General v Blake*, at p. 282B, Lord Nicholls stated: 'The law recognises that a party to a contract may have an interest in performance which is not readily measured in terms of money.'

Thus the mere fact that the claimant has stipulated for a particular kind of performance that others would regard as having no value, or as not enhancing the value of the property, will not of itself prevent the recovery of cost of cure damages. In *Ruxley Electronics*, Lord Jauncey, at p. 358, referred to the construction of a folly in a garden, and stated that if the folly were to collapse, it would be irrelevant to the determination of the loss suffered to argue that the construction of the folly, which did not increase the value of the land, 'was a crazy thing to do'.

> In **Radford v De Froberville** [1977] 1 WLR 1262, the defendant had contracted to build a wall on her land to mark the boundary, but failed to perform. The claimant was entitled to the cost of building a wall on his own land to mark the same boundary and it was irrelevant that a less costly structure, such as a fence, would have done the job equally well.

9.3.3.4 When will cost of cure damages be awarded?

Cost of cure damages will be recoverable only where both:

- *it is reasonable to award such damages in the sense that the cost of cure is not out of all proportion to the benefit to be obtained*; and

- *the rebuilding has been completed or it is clear that there is an intention to use the damages award to carry out the rebuilding.* This is because, unless there is an intention to rebuild or cure, cost of cure will not be an actual loss needing to be compensated by a payment in damages.

These limitations were confirmed by the House of Lords in *Ruxley Electronics and Construction Ltd v Forsyth* [1996] 1 AC 344, although they can be traced back to *Radford v De Froberville* [1977] 1 WLR 1262 (reasonable on the facts to award cost of cure) and *Tito v Waddell (No. 2)* [1977] Ch 106 (the court was not convinced that the damages award would be used to cure the breach).

> In *Ruxley Electronics and Construction Ltd v Forsyth*, the defendant employed the claimant to construct a swimming pool in his garden. It was to be of a maximum depth of seven feet, six inches. The finished pool was only six-feet deep at the point at which people dive in. However, at first instance, it was found that the pool, as constructed, was safe for diving and that there was no difference in value between the pool as specified and that actually built. The failure to meet the contractual specification could be remedied only by demolishing the existing pool and starting again, at a cost of £21,560. The judge at first instance refused to award cost of cure and instead awarded £2,500 for lost amenity. On appeal, the Court of Appeal awarded the full cost of curing the defect.
>
> The House of Lords was unanimous in holding that, in the circumstances, the cost of cure was not recoverable, so that the Court of Appeal's decision was reversed and the original first instance award for loss of amenity, which had not been challenged, was allowed to stand. Lord Lloyd referred to the judgment of Cardozo J in *Jacob and Youngs v Kent* in stating that, as a general principle, the cost of cure can be recovered only 'if it is reasonable for the claimant to insist on that course'. In assessing whether it was reasonable to allow the cost of cure, it was appropriate to consider the personal preferences of the buyer in stipulating for a particular performance, because this assisted in identifying the loss suffered. However, personal preferences 'cannot *per se* be determinative of what that loss is': *per* Lord Jauncey, at pp. 358H–359A.

The conclusion is that there is a line to be drawn between circumstances in which cure is reasonable and those in which it is not. In his speech in *Ruxley Electronics*, at p. 358A–B, Lord Bridge gave an example, which was also referred to by Lord Jauncey:

> A man contracts for the building of a house and specifies that one of the lower courses of brick should be blue. The builder uses yellow brick instead. In all other respects the house conforms to the contractual specification. To replace the yellow bricks with blue would involve extensive demolition and reconstruction at a very large cost.

This is an example of a case in which it would clearly be unreasonable to award cost of cure damages. Lord Jauncey contrasted this with the position in which a building is constructed so defectively that it is of no use for its designed purpose; it would clearly be reasonable to award cost of cure in such a case. Of course, these examples are extremes and the majority of cases will fall somewhere in between.

In *Harrison v Shepherd Homes Ltd* [2011] EWHC 1811 (TCC), (2011) 27 Const LJ 709, in the context of defective piles in the foundations of homes built on a former landfill site, Ramsey J applied the *Ruxley* principles to determine whether the proper measure was cost of cure (re-piling) or diminution in value. He concluded that (i) the cracking was aesthetic in nature and the expert evidence was that there was minimal risk of movement so that it was not reasonable to provide entirely new foundations; (ii) if damages were awarded the majority of claimants would use the money to sell their homes and move elsewhere since the main issue here was the fall in value of the house as an asset; and (iii) the cost of new piling would be out of all proportion to the loss suffered since any damage could be made good at an acceptable cost. Accordingly, a damages award based on diminution in value was appropriate compensation.

Ruxley Electronics was applied in ***Birse Construction Ltd v Eastern Telegraph Co. Ltd*** [2004] EWHC 2512 (TCC), [2004] 47 EG 164 (CS).

The claimant in ***Birse Construction Ltd v Eastern Telegraph Co. Ltd*** built a residential college for the defendant. After completion, the defendant complained that there were numerous defects. However, by this time, the defendant had decided to sell the property and so took no steps to rectify these defects. The claimant brought an action to recover retention money that had been held back by the defendant and the defendant counterclaimed for damages. The issue for the court related to the measure and type of damages available. Since the proposed sale of the college had reached an advanced stage at the date of the hearing and it had been negotiated without any discount in the price to take account of the defects, the claimant argued that the defects had not caused the defendant any actual loss, so that damages should be nominal. However, the defendant argued that it was entitled to substantial damages because (i) it had not received what it had contracted for, and (ii) many of the defects had an adverse effect on the general appearance, comfort, and amenity of the college, so that loss of amenity damages should be awarded.

Judge Humphrey Lloyd QC applied *Ruxley* and awarded nominal damages of £2. He concluded as follows.

1. If the college were sold at an undiminished price, any financial loss to the defendant would have been avoided and, in such circumstances, it would be unreasonable to award damages based on the cost of repair, especially because there was no intention to repair the defects. The judge rejected the defendant's argument that it was irrelevant that there was no intention to carry out the remedial work.

2. The argument based on loss of amenity was 'hollow' considering that the defendant had taken no steps to rectify any of the defects in question and loss of amenity damages would therefore be refused. In other words, the judge considered that if the defects were that disturbing, a reasonable owner would have taken steps to rectify the position.

He stated, at [51]:

It is now clear from *Ruxley* . . . that the normal measure of damages for defective works is the cost of reinstatement (i.e. the cost of remedial works) but in every instance it has to be reasonable to apply it. Thus where that measure is out of proportion to the claimant's real loss then some other measure should be used. This is the case where there has been a modest effect on the utility of the works and where it would be reasonable to assess the loss on the basis of diminution in value. A pragmatic approach may have to be applied although the claimant is not to be too readily deprived of the ordinary measure of compensation.

The judge's approach is interesting because the result of this award was that the claimant did not need to pay for the consequences of its breach, since there was no award of any kind, even for loss of amenity. It also suggests that Lord Griffiths's 'broad ground' in *Linden Gardens Trust Ltd v Lenesta Sludge Disposals Ltd* [1994] 1 AC 85 (see **11.7.3.2**) did not even come into the equation on these facts, i.e. damages for the fact of non-performance/defective performance. This appears to be because the judge took the view that the defendant had suffered no loss in benefit terms.

The House of Lords in *Ruxley* confirmed that it is important to take into account the intention to carry out the cure or repair, since otherwise the cost of rebuilding is not a loss actually suffered—and it is this point that appears to have prevailed in *Birse Construction*. (Thus intention is important for the purposes of identifying a loss; however, once a clear loss is identified, it is no concern of the courts to assess what the claimant will do with the damages award: *per* Lord Clyde in *Alfred McAlpine Construction Ltd v Panatown Ltd* [2001] 1 AC 518.)

The same principle of 'no loss' was applied in *Sunrock Aircraft Corporation Ltd v Scandinavian Airlines System Denmark-Norway-Sweden* [2007] EWCA Civ 882, [2007] 2 Lloyd's Rep 612. Two leased aircraft had been returned unrepaired and the normal measure of damages would be the cost of repair. Instead of arranging for a repair, the lessor had sold on the aircraft at a price that reflected the fact that there had been no diminution in the value of the aircraft. Nominal damages were therefore awarded.

9.3.3.4.1 *The remedy of cost of cure must be appropriate to the defendant's liability*

In addition to these general principles, we know that cost of cure will be awarded only where such a remedy is appropriate to the liability assumed by the defendant. For example, if the obligation undertaken is a qualified obligation (reasonable care and skill), awarding cost of cure would amount to treating it as if it were a strict contractual obligation. The House of Lords in *Farley v Skinner (No. 2)* [2001] UKHL 49, [2002] 2 AC 732, disapproved a distinction between strict and qualified obligations, but only in the context of the availability of damages for distress and disappointment. Since the disapproval does not extend to recovery of the basic measure of damages, *Watts v Morrow* [1991] 1 WLR 1421 remains good law on this point.

In **Watts v Morrow**, the purchasers of a house brought an action against a surveyor for breach of a contract to exercise care and skill in preparing a report on the house purchased. Defects were found that were not revealed by the defendant's report. The difference in value, between what the claimants paid and what the house would have been worth had the defects been known, was put at £15,000. The claimant paid nearly £34,000 to remedy the defects and sought that sum in damages for breach of contract.

In the Court of Appeal, at p. 1436, Ralph Gibson LJ said that to award damages of the cost of cure would amount to compensating the claimant for breach of a warranty by the defendant that the condition of the house was correctly described by the surveyor. No such warranty was given in a case such as this. Relying on the judgment of Denning LJ in *Philips v Ward* [1956] 1 WLR 471, Ralph Gibson LJ stated that compensation was limited to the amount that would 'put the claimant into as good a position as if the contract for the survey had been properly fulfilled'. Had the survey been properly carried out, either the claimant would not have bought at all (in which case, there would have been no loss), or he would have bought at the lower value (so that the difference in value was the proper measure of the loss). Accordingly, the claimant was limited to recovering the lower difference in value figure.

9.3.4 Expectation loss: speculative and uncertain

The measurement of expectation loss may be a speculative and uncertain process, especially in cases in which it must be assessed by reference to difference in value and in which the assumed value of the market price is unavailable as a guide. Nevertheless, as a general principle, damages for lost expectation may always be recovered, subject to the various limitations considered at **9.5**. The fact that measurement of the loss is difficult or speculative will not prevent the court from attempting such measurement and awarding damages accordingly.

In *Simpson v London and North Western Railway Co.* (1876) 1 QBD 274, the claimant sent specimens by rail for exhibition at a trade show, clearly indicating the date by which they had to arrive. They arrived after that date, and the claimtant claimed damages for loss of the profits that he would have made had he been able to exhibit his specimens. He was entitled to succeed, despite the speculative nature of his loss.

Thus the court will attempt to put some value on an expectation even when what is lost is no more than an opportunity to take the risk of making a profit, rather than a certain loss of a speculative profit.

In *Chaplin v Hicks* [1911] 2 KB 786, there was an agreement between the defendant, a theatrical manager, and the claimant that, if the claimant would attend for an interview, the defendant would select 12 out of 50 interviewees for employment. He then failed, in breach of contract, to give the claimant a reasonable opportunity to attend. She was able to recover damages for that lost opportunity, although there was no certainty that she would have been successful. In those circumstances, the loss was said to depend upon the chances of her succeeding at interview, which were quantifiable. Fletcher Moulton LJ stated, at p. 796:

> Where by contract a man has a right to belong to a limited class of competitors, he is possessed of something of value, and it is the duty of the jury to estimate the pecuniary value of that advantage if it is taken from him.

In some cases, however, the estimation of the lost expectation may be so speculative that the courts will refuse to award damages on the standard basis and will instead compensate only the claimant's out-of-pocket expenses in attempting to perform the contract. The classic example of this principle is the Australian case of *McRae v Commonwealth Disposals Commission* (1951) 84 CLR 377 (see also **13.2.2**).

In *McRae v Commonwealth Disposals Commission*, the claimants and defendants had contracted for the recovery of a shipwrecked oil tanker, said by the defendants to be lying at a specified place. The claimants mounted an expedition to salvage the tanker, but no tanker could be found, and it became apparent that none had ever existed. The claimants claimed lost profit as the measure of their lost expectation resulting from the defendants' breach. The High Court of Australia considered that recovery of lost profit on the vessel would be too speculative, since no details had been given at the time of contracting about the size of the tanker, or whether it still held its cargo of oil, and it could not be known whether the salvage operation would have been successful. Instead, the court awarded the claimants' wasted cost of mounting the salvage expedition. The claimants also recovered the price that they had paid under the contract, i.e. the restitutionary interest (see discussion at **10.5.1**).

Part 3

Enforcement of contractual obligations

The distinction between *McRae* and *Chaplin v Hicks* is that, in *Chaplin v Hicks*, there was a real or tangible loss of a chance of obtaining the prize, while in *McRae* the claimants could not demonstrate that any profit would have been made, so that the loss was purely speculative. This distinction, between loss of a real chance and purely speculative lost expectation, was confirmed by the Court of Appeal in *Allied Maples Group Ltd v Simmons and Simmons (a firm)* [1995] 1 WLR 1602.

> The loss suffered by the claimant in **Allied Maples Group Ltd v Simmons and Simmons (a firm)** as a result of the defendant's breach depended on the hypothetical action of a third party, in that the claimant argued that, had it been properly advised by the defendant, it would have had the opportunity of negotiating a better deal with third party target companies during an acquisition. The Court of Appeal held that the claimant was entitled to succeed in its action, since it had established on the balance of probabilities that there was a 'substantial chance' of negotiating a better deal and not merely a speculative chance. The claimant did not need to establish that the negotiations would definitely have succeeded.

In *Allied Maples* case, the claimant had lost the opportunity of gaining a benefit which was dependent on a third party acting in a particular way. In such a case, the claimant does not need to prove that the third party would have acted in that way, only that there was a real and substantial chance of obtaining the benefit. This is a question of causation and the quantification of damages will then turn on assessment of the percentage chance of succeeding.

In *Wellesley Partners LLP v Withers LLP* [2015] EWCA Civ 1146 [2016] CILL 3757, (for facts see **9.5.2.8**), the judge had found that if the investing partner had been unable to withdraw its capital, the claimant would have opened a New York office. The claimant sought loss of profits on that US operation but since that would be a claim based on a general loss of an opportunity to make profits (e.g. as in *Parabola Investments Ltd v Browallia Cal Ltd* [2010] EWCA Civ 486, [2011] QB 477, **14.6.2.4**), it was different to the loss of a specific opportunity claim in *Allied Maples* and different principles applied. In the case of a claim for general loss of profits it had to be shown on the balance of probabilities that the US trading would have been profitable before there could be any quantification of that loss. This has nothing to do with loss of chance calculations and no discount would be appropriate. On the facts this general profitability could not be established so that the claim for damages was thrown back onto a claim based on loss of a specific contract opportunity in the US. It followed that this claim based on loss of opportunity of securing a contract was similar to *Allied Maples* because, as a matter of causation, it turned on the hypothetical actions of a third party. It was therefore necessary to determine whether there was a real and substantial chance of securing the contract ahead of the separate discounting exercise which occurred when subsequently quantifying the damages. The Court of Appeal did not disturb the judge's finding that had the claimant opened an office in New York it would have had a real and substantial chance of being awarded some of the contract and his finding that there was a 60 per cent chance of being awarded some part of the contract and that if it had been there was a 25 per cent of being awarded the contract as the sole recruitment agency, and a 75 per cent chance of being appointed with one or more other firms. The overall chance of being awarded the contract as the sole recruitment agency was considered to be 15 per cent and 45 per cent of being awarded half.

9.3.5 Wasted expenditure

Damages may compensate for wasted expenditure, i.e. for money that the claimant expended either in preparation for, or in partial performance of, the contract that is then wasted because of the breach.

9.3.5.1 Wasted expenditure must be claimed where loss of profit is too speculative

Where loss of profits are too speculative to recover because it is impossible to say what the profit on the contract would have been, wasted expenditure will necessarily have to be claimed: see *McRae v Commonwealth Disposals Commission* (1951) 84 CLR 377 (above at **9.3.3**), in which wasted expenditure recovery was imposed by the court. A further example is provided by the facts of *Anglia Television Ltd v Reed* [1972] 1 QB 60, which concerned a claim for wasted expenditure where it was not possible to prove what the profits on the contract would have been.

> In *Anglia Television Ltd v Reed*, the claimant television company had been forced to abandon its project to make a film when the lead actor withdrew from the project in breach of contract. The company was able to recover for wasted expenditure, including expenditure incurred before the contract with the actor had been made.

Thus pre-contractual expenditure that has been lost as a result of the breach will also be recoverable as wasted expenditure, provided that 'it was such as would reasonably be in the contemplation of the parties as likely to be wasted if the contract was broken' (see the remoteness rule at **9.5.2**).

9.3.5.2 The nature of a claim for expenditure wasted as a result of breach

Wasted expenditure damages differ from other contractual damages in that their effect is to compensate 'backwards' and restore the claimant to their pre-contractual position. In *Omak Maritime Ltd v Mamola Challenger Shipping Co.* [2010] EWHC 2026 (Comm), [2011] Bus LR 212, Teare J explained that this was merely the appropriate means of giving effect to the party's expectation of performance and therefore was not different in nature from other expectation losses, although inevitably it is different in terms of the way in which it is calculated.

> In *Omak Maritime Ltd v Mamola Challenger Shipping Co.,* the charterer repudiated the charterparty. The owners were in fact able to earn considerably more post-repudiation, since the market rate of hire was unusually much higher than the rate applicable to this charter. However, the owners sought damages based on the expenditure claimed to have been wasted in preparing the vessel ahead of the charter. Teare J considered that 'the expectation loss principle underpins the award of damages in wasted expenditure cases'. It followed that a claim for wasted expenditure was a 'species of expectation loss' and 'not fundamentally different'. Accordingly, awarding wasted expenditure, when the owners had been able to secure higher rates as a result of the breach and so had suffered no real loss due to the breach, was wrong in principle since it amounted to putting the owners in a better position than that in which they would have been had the contract been properly performed and had the breach not occurred. The point here is that the expenditure had to be made in order to achieve the higher rate, so that the expenditure could not be said to have been 'wasted' and did not constitute a loss.

9.3.5.3 Recovery for wasted expenditure

In some circumstances, the claimant's loss is more accurately reflected by wasted expenditure rather than expectation loss. Although some cases refer to the claimant having the right to elect between seeking to recover either for wasted expenditure or on some other basis, the true principle as again confirmed in *Morris-Garner v One Step (Support) Ltd*, *per* Lord Reed at [36], is not one of election but rather one of identifying the loss, namely the difference between the claimant's actual situation and the situation in which he would have been if the primary contractual obligation had been performed, and then quantifying that loss. As is made clear in *Omak Maritime Ltd v Mamola Challenger Shipping Co.* [2010] EWHC 2026 (Comm), [2011] Bus LR 212, the claimant's right to recover wasted expenditure is subject to one important limitation.

9.3.5.3.1 The limitation

The essence of the limitation is that such a claim must not result in the compensation of a loss that is not the result of the defendant's breach.

! KEY POINT

The claimant cannot claim damages for wasted expenditure if this would amount to compensating the claimant for having made a 'bad bargain'. To award wasted expenditure in these circumstances would amount to putting the claimant in a better position than that in which the claimant would have been had the contract been properly performed. In the case of bad bargains, the loss results from the claimant having made the contract rather than from its breach by the defendant.

Of course, this is just the situation in which the claimant would want to recover for wasted expenditure and the courts will therefore be extremely wary of such claims.

> In ***C and P Haulage v Middleton*** [1983] 1 WLR 1461, the defendant was entitled, under a series of six-month contracts, to the use of a garage for the purposes of his business. He had spent some money on equipping the garage for his needs, but under the contracts the equipment installed became the property of the garage owner once the defendant's use of the garage ceased. Ten weeks before the end of one of the six-month contracts, the garage owner ordered the defendant out of the garage in breach of contract. The local planning authority allowed the defendant to use his own garage for more than ten weeks, with the result that he saved the weekly rental on the garage. His profits were therefore greater than if the contract had not been breached. He brought an action to recover the costs of equipping the garage from which he had been ejected. The Court of Appeal rejected that claim on the ground that the cost of the equipment would have been lost had the contract been performed as agreed and lawfully terminated at the end of a six-month period, because he would still have been required to equip a new garage on the termination of the lease. The loss therefore did not result from the breach, but from the terms of the contract itself, and so was not to be compensated. The defendant could recover only nominal damages for the breach.

In *Omak Maritime Ltd v Mamola Challenger Shipping Co.*, Teare J explained the basis for this principle as resting on the nature of recovery of wasted expenditure as fulfilling the expectation interest in performance. Wasted expenditure cannot be recovered if it would result in a claimant being awarded more than his original expectation under the terms of the contract. It would, however, be difficult to justify this long-established limitation on recovery of wasted expenditure if it were entirely separate and had nothing to do fulfilling the contractual expectation. The judge explained it in the following terms, at [45]–[45]:

> It seems to me that the expectation loss analysis does provide a rational and sensible explanation for the award of damages in wasted expenditure cases. The expenditure which is sought to be recovered is incurred in expectation that the contract will be performed. It therefore appears to me to be rational to have regard to the position that the claimant would have been in had the contract been performed.

> If there were an independent principle pursuant to which expenditure incurred in expectation of the performance of a contract was recoverable without regard to what the position would have been had the contract been performed, the defendant would in effect underwrite the claimant's decision to enter the contract.

Although the wasted expenditure in *Omak Maritime* was caused by the breach, unlike the position in *C & P Haulage v Middleton*, it could not be recovered separately where there was no lost expectation overall, i.e. no loss of hire as a result of the higher re-hire rates.

9.3.5.3.2 *The burden of proof*

Teare J, in *Omak Maritime Ltd v Mamola Challenger Shipping Co.* [2010] EWHC 2026 (Comm), [2011] Bus LR 212, explained the burden of proof on the question of whether the claimant would at least have recovered his expenditure had the contract been properly performed (i.e. that it was not a bad bargain for the claimant), concluding that there was a presumption in favour of the claimant. Thus the burden fell on the defendant to demonstrate its claim that the claimant had made a bad bargain and so avoid the claimant's recovery of its wasted expenditure. This conclusion had been justified in *CCC Films (London) Ltd v Impact Quadrant Films Ltd* [1985] 1 QB 16, in which the contract had been discharged by the defendant's breach, thereby depriving the claimant of the films that, it was anticipated, would have generated sufficient profits to cover the claimant's costs. As a result of the defendant's breach, the claimant would have been unable to prove that he would otherwise have recovered his expenditure. The burden thus rested on the defendant to prove the converse.

Therefore, because it is the defendant's breach that often makes it impossible for the claimant to establish that the expenditure would otherwise have been recouped, this should be presumed and the burden should shift to the defendant to establish that the claimant would not have recouped his expenditure irrespective of the breach.

This burden was not discharged in *Grange v Quinn* [2013] EWCA Civ 24, [2013] P & CR 18. The case concerned the measure of damages following a wrongful eviction of the appellant from business premises after only six months of a six-year lease. The loss of profits claim was abandoned and the appellant instead based her claim on recovery of a £9,950 premium for the goodwill (i.e. the commercial value independently of the assets) of the business carried on at the premises. The majority of the Court of Appeal held that, although the court had to have regard to whether the appellant might wrongly recover more than she would have had the contract been performed, the burden of proof was on the respondent to establish on the balance of probabilities that the appellant would not have recouped her wasted expenditure from the gross returns that would have been generated from the business had the contract run, and that burden had not been discharged. (Arden LJ, dissenting, considered that the premium had been paid in relation to the goodwill of the business and not as rent for the period of the lease. Accordingly, she considered that it did not constitute wasted expenditure.)

In *Yam Seng Pte Ltd v International Trade Corp Ltd* [2013] EWHC 111 (QB), [2013] 1 CLC 662, [2013] 1 All ER (Comm) 1321, Leggatt J stressed that the burden of proof was one of the advantages of a claim to recover wasted expenditure. If the defendant adduced no evidence in rebuttal, then it would be assumed that the claimant had made a good bargain and that these wasted expenses would otherwise have been recovered.

In *Royal Devon and Exeter NHS Foundation Trust v ATOS IT Services UK Ltd* [2017] EWHC 2197 (TCC), [2018] BLR 18, the Trust sought damages representing wasted staff time on trying to operate a software system installed by ATOS that did not operate satisfactorily. Following *Omak*, O'Farrell J held that damages for wasted costs were not recoverable where the claimant had made a bad bargain. The defendant had to show that the sums expended by the claimant would have been incurred even if there had been proper performance. In this case ATOS was unable to show that the incurred costs would been wasted in any event.

9.3.5.4 Quantification of loss: avoiding double compensation

In *Anglia Television Ltd v Reed* [1972] 1 QB 60, Lord Denning MR said that a claimant may elect whether to claim for loss of profits or for wasted expenditure, but that the claimant cannot claim for both. That statement, taken out of context, may be misleading. Lord Denning MR did not indicate whether he was speaking of gross or net profits. It is true that a claimant may not claim both wasted expenditure *and* the gross profit expected under the contract, since the claimant would expect to recover expenditure out of such gross profit and to award both would be double compensation of the expectation loss: *Cullinane v British 'Rema' Manufacturing Co. Ltd* [1954] 1 QB 292. But if it is advantageous to the claimant to divide the claim between expenditure on performance and the lost net profit, there seems to be no good reason why the claimant should not do so, since the net profit is calculated by deducting expenditure from the gross profit: see *Hydraulic Engineering Co. Ltd v McHaffie, Goslett and Co.* (1878) 4 QBD 670, in which such a claim was allowed. To award only net profit and the expenditure wasted would involve no double compensation of expectation loss.

> **➜ EXAMPLE**
>
> Contractor A submits a quotation to B to supply B with a bathroom. The quotation is based on the cost of the bath, etc., and the costs of installation, and includes a profit figure. This would constitute the gross profit figure or price for the contract. Shortly after the work commences to remove the old bathroom suite, B cancels the contract.
>
> Had the contract been completed, A would have expected to incur the cost of the bathroom equipment and the labour cost, and to have defrayed these costs out of the contract price, leaving the net profit on the contract. In the event of breach, it is clear that A can claim the net profit as expectation loss.
>
> Can A also recover for other wasted expenditure? In a situation such as this, in which the breach occurs shortly after performance commences, A will be unable to claim the gross profit figure, since the full labour cost will not have been incurred and it should be possible to mitigate the loss attributable to the purchase of the bathroom suite, e.g. the builders merchant might accept return of the unused bathroom suite, but would charge a restocking fee of between 10 and 25 per cent. Therefore A may wish to claim the actual labour cost and any part of the cost of the bathroom suite that cannot be mitigated (e.g. the restocking charge) as wasted expenditure, i.e. losses incurred in performance of the contract that are now wasted as a result of the cancellation.

9.3.6 Consequential loss

The courts sometimes speak of the award of damages for 'consequential loss' resulting from the breach of the contract. The phrase has no very precise meaning, but it usually indicates loss that does not result directly from the breach, but which is still an inevitable consequence of the breach.

> **→ EXAMPLE**
>
> In a contract for the sale of an animal feed hopper, if the ventilation of the hopper is defective, there is a breach of the contract.

- The loss directly resulting is that the hopper is not worth as much as promised in the contract and that loss may be compensated by an award of damages for the difference in value—assuming that the hopper was not, or could not be, rejected (see **8.4.2**)—or for cost of cure (see **9.3.3**).

- Where, in addition, the livestock became ill and the herd had to be destroyed through eating animal feed that had become mouldy owing to the defective ventilation on the hopper, there is a *consequential* loss of the value of the herd resulting from the breach. In such a case, the difference in value or cost of cure may be minimal, but the consequential loss is considerably greater: see *H. Parsons (Livestock) Ltd v Uttley Ingham & Co. Ltd* [1978] 1 QB 791 (discussed at **9.5.2.5**).

Such loss raises particular questions of causation—namely, 'Did the loss actually result from the breach that occurred?' (see **9.5.1.1**)—and, in particular, of remoteness of damage, relating to the ability to recover for that loss—namely, 'Was this consequence of the breach within the contemplation of the parties at the time of contracting, so that the defendant in promising to perform can be taken to have promised not to cause such loss, or to have assumed responsibility for it?' (see **9.5.2**).

9.4 Time for assessment of loss

The general principle is that damages are to be assessed at the time of breach (or when the loss is suffered), which usually occurs at the time when performance became due: Miliangos v George Frank (Textiles) Ltd [1976] AC 443, at p. 468, and Johnson v Agnew [1980] AC 367, at pp. 400–1. This is because it is the earliest date on which the claimant could be expected to mitigate (i.e. to find the substitute performance) or take other appropriate remedial action.

> **→ EXAMPLE**
>
> The buyer's damages for the seller's non-delivery in a commercial contract for the sale of goods are to be assessed according to the market price for the goods (see **9.3.2.1**) at the time when the goods ought to have been delivered (SGA 1979, s. 51(3)). This rule is based on the obligation placed on the commercial claimant to mitigate its loss (see **9.5.3**) and assumes that the claimant will do so by taking immediate action.

However, it is accepted that the breach date principle may not be appropriate in all cases, e.g. Lord Wilberforce stated, in *Johnson v Agnew* at p. 40: 'But this is not an absolute rule: if to follow it would give rise to injustice, the court has power to fix such other date as may be appropriate in the circumstances.'

9.4.1 *The Golden Victory*: taking account of known events at the date of the hearing

In *Golden Strait Corporation v Nippon Yusen Kubishika Kaisha, The Golden Victory* [2007] UKHL 12, [2007] 2 AC 353, the House of Lords, by a majority of three to two, held that damages may be reduced where subsequent events are known to the court at the date of the court hearing (and assessment of quantum) that *have* reduced the actual loss suffered.

> The charterer had chartered the vessel from the shipowner under a time charterparty commencing in July 1998 and the earliest date for its termination was December 2005. The charter provided (clause 33) that if war were to break out between named countries, then both parties would be entitled to terminate. The charterer repudiated on 14 December 2001 by redelivering the ship and the shipowner accepted that repudiation on 17 December. The shipowner claimed to be entitled to damages measured by reference to the full term of the repudiated time charter (another four years). However, in the meantime, the Second Gulf War broke out in March 2003, which was an event that would have justified the charterer terminating the charter under clause 33. The charterer claimed that a party in breach could rely on subsequent events to reduce the damages so that no damages could be recovered after March 2003 (meaning that the damages would cover a period of 14 months instead of four years), whereas the shipowner alleged that, in the interests of commercial certainty and finality, the loss should be measured at the date of acceptance of the repudiation, and that anything that happened afterwards was irrelevant.
>
> The House of Lords (the majority, Lords Scott, Carswell, and Brown; Lords Bingham and Walker dissenting) held that since contractual principles required the non-breaching party (the shipowner) to be placed in the position in which it would have been had the contract been properly performed, the most important principle was to compensate for actual loss suffered (not for more than was actually suffered), rather than commercial certainty and finality. Although the assessment based on the breach date rule would normally achieve that result, the courts should not apply it where it did not. It followed that the subsequent event, which occurred before the assessment of damages was made, could be taken into account.

This majority view of their Lordships followed the approach taken in the lower courts and is based on the principle that where there is knowledge, speculation is not required. There was indeed knowledge of the fact that the Gulf War had broken out in March 2003, but it had to be assumed that, had the charter continued, the war clause would have been exercised by the charterer in March 2003. It is also rather too convenient to rely on the principle of compensation for actual loss where this operates to constrain recovery, while at the same time supporting principles that constrain the ability of a claimant to be fully compensated for its actual loss (see **9.5**).

The Golden Victory is therefore a difficult decision for commercial lawyers whose primary focus is commercial certainty and who regard breach as crystallizing the loss at that date (see the important dissenting speeches of Lord Bingham and Lord Walker). The normal reaction, and expectation, in such instances would be that the loss would be fixed, subject only to the owner's duty to mitigate, i.e. to recharter the vessel in the market, so that damages would be awarded for any difference between this market rate and the rate under the charter for the remainder of the term. However, *The Golden Victory* has the unfortunate side-effect of implicitly encouraging the delay of the hearing for the assessment of quantum in such cases in the hope that a war clause or similar will be assumed to have been activated. On termination, the loss should have become fixed, subject only to mitigation.

The *Golden Victory* principle is to award damages based on actual loss (what actually happened after breach and before assessment) and this was applied in *Glory Wealth Shipping Pte Ltd v Korea Line Corporation, The Wren* [2011] EWHC 1819, [2011] 2 Lloyd's Rep 370. A time charter was repudiated early (five months into a time charter of at least 36 months) following a collapse in the market. The owners had terminated in consequence of the repudiatory breach and claimed damages. The normal measure where there is an available market would be the difference between the contract rate and market rate for the remainder of the charter. However, at the date of the breach, there was no market for this entire period. Nevertheless, it did not follow that damages could be assessed only on the basis of this rate once the market revived, some two years later, since this would not put the owner in the same position as if the contract had been performed. The owner *had* obtained substitute fixtures in the spot market in the short term, and these were relevant to post-repudiation mitigation and the assessment of actual loss.

The principle in *The Golden Victory* now seems to have a life of its own. At first instance in *Force India Formula One Team Ltd v Etihad Airways PJSC* [2009] EWHC 2768 (QB), [2010] ETMR 14 (reversed on appeal [2010] EWCA Civ 1051, [2011] ETMR 10, but on the repudiation issue only: see **8.4.2.3**), the judge allowed Force India to recover damages for wrongful termination, which included points gained in the championship in subsequent seasons. There was no need to speculate about the contingency of the points arising in subsequent seasons, i.e. to make a claim based on loss of the chance of acquiring a bonus based on those points, since there was evidence that the points had in fact been gained. The judge could see no reason not to apply the principle in *The Golden Victory* in order to assess damages in the light of events subsequent to the breach.

However, in *Ageas (UK) Ltd v Kwik-Fit (GB) Ltd* [2014] EWHC 2178 (QB), [2014] Bus LR 1338, Popplewell J refused to apply *The Golden Victory* principle on the facts because it would have infringed a contractual allocation of the risk of subsequent events. The case concerned a claim for breach of warranty under a share purchase agreement. The defendant's insurer had argued that, in order to give effect to the compensatory principle, the assessment of damages should take into account developments after the valuation date of the target company (so-called 'hindsight'). Popplewell J accepted that where the value of the target company depended on a future contingency, any relevant events after the valuation date relating to this contingency could be taken into account to give effect to the compensatory principle. However, this was subject to the limitation that it must not infringe the parties' own allocation of risk. In other words, the judge accepted that as a general principle hindsight could be taken into account where this was necessary to secure actual compensation. This was on the basis that a judge should 'avail himself of all the information at hand at the time of making his award which may be laid before him' and refuse to 'listen to conjecture on a matter which has become an accomplished fact'. However, on the facts, the share purchase agreement had already allocated the risk of such events occurring—and allocated that risk to the purchaser.

This principle was also reaffirmed by Blair J in *Hut Group v Nobahar-Cookson* [2014] EWHC 382 (QB) at [184] when he stated that '[h]indsight cannot be used to confound the allocation of risk under the bargain.' The court should not deprive a party of the benefit of a contingency from which it was entitled to benefit under the terms of the contract, and in a share purchase agreement the party receiving the shareholding assumes the risks or rewards of its subsequent performance or failure.

In the context of sale of goods the application of the principle in *The Golden Victory* had been quite controversial. At first instance in *Bunge SA v Nidera BV (formerly Nidera Handelscompagnie BV)* [2013] EWHC 84 (Comm), [2013] 1 CLC 325, [2013] 1 Lloyd's Rep 621, Hamblen J had refused to allow it to override a contractually agreed damages scheme. In particular, there was uncertainty as to whether *The Golden Victory* could apply to one-off sale of goods contracts where there was an open market. Any residual uncertainty concerning the application of the principle has been conclusively settled on appeal by the Supreme Court [2015] UKSC 43, [2015] Bus LR 987. The Supreme Court roundly endorsed the decision of the House of Lords in *The Golden Victory* (despite the significant academic criticism directed at it) on the basis that certainty did not justify a substantial damages award where no loss had in fact been suffered. Lord Sumption JSC explained the distinction between the majority and minority opinions in *The Golden Victory*:

21. The reasoning has to some extent been obscured by the focus on the implications of the so-called 'breach-date rule' and on the competing demands of certainty and compensation. The real difference between the majority and the minority turned on the question what was being valued for the purpose assessing damages. The majority were valuing the chartered service that would actually have been performed if the charterparty had not been wrongfully brought to a premature end. On that footing, the notional substitute contract, whenever it was made and at whatever market rate, would have made no difference because it would have been subject to the same war clause as the original contract . . . The minority on the other hand considered that one should value not the chartered service which would actually have been performed, but the charterparty itself, assessed at the time that it was terminated, by reference to the terms of a notional substitute concluded as soon as possible after the termination of the original. That would vary, not according to the actual outcome, but according to the outcomes which were perceived as possible or probable at the time that the notional substitute contract was made. The possibility or probability of war would then be factored into the price agreed in the substitute contract . . . I think that the majority's view on this point was correct. Sections 50 and 51 of the Sale of Goods Act, like the corresponding principles of the common law, are concerned with the price of the goods or services which would have been delivered under the contract. They are not concerned with the value of the contract as an article of commerce in itself. As Lord Brown observed at paras 82–83, even if the charterparty rights could have been sold for a capital sum, this was not a proper basis for assessing loss, and an assessment which proceeded as if it were would 'extend the effect of the available market rule well beyond its proper scope'.

The Supreme Court also overruled the first instance rejection of the application of *The Golden Victory*, concluding that the contractually agreed damages scheme did not deal with subsequent events. It is also now clear that *The Golden Victory* principle applies equally to 'one-off' sales contracts and to instalment contracts. On the facts, had the contract not been terminated for a purported repudiation, the sellers would have cancelled the contract without liability in accordance with a prohibition clause in the contract because the export ban imposed by the Russian government on the export of wheat, which was the subject matter of this contract, became final and would have prevented delivery. Applying *The Golden Victory*, the buyers had lost nothing and should receive only nominal damages.

Damages for breach of contract

9

9.4.2 Other instances where 'the date of breach rule' will not apply

The general breach date 'rule' is only presumptive, so that where it would be reasonable for the claimant to do something other than to take immediate steps to mitigate the loss, the court will postpone the time for assessment of damages until whatever date is more appropriate. For example, the non-breaching party may be allowed time to seek confirmation that no performance will be forthcoming, or that defective performance will be cured, before being expected to mitigate the loss.

> In **Radford v De Froberville** [1977] 1 WLR 1262 (see **9.3.3.3**), it was suggested that when, at first, it seems probable that the defendant will make good his default, damages will be assessed at the time when that probability ceases to exist, since the duty to take steps of mitigation arises at that point.

In *Hooper v Oates* [2013] EWCA Civ 91, [2013] 3 All ER 211, the Court of Appeal held that the date for the assessment of damages following a breach of contract for the sale of land in which the purchaser had either failed or refused to complete was not the date of breach, but the date on which the vendors brought an end to their reasonable attempts to resell the property.

Bear Stearns Bank plc v Forum Global Equity Ltd [2007] EWHC 1576 (Comm) is similar in terms of principle, because the buyers had good reasons for not immediately going into the market to mitigate their loss: they had first sought specific performance of a sale of shares before abandoning that claim on discovering that the sellers had disposed of the shares to another. The judge therefore took the market price at a time later than the contractual date for performance.

Further, when damages are awarded in lieu of specific performance (see **10.2.4**), it is accepted that they are assessed at the time of the hearing.

> In *Wroth v Tyler* [1974] Ch 30, the defendant had repudiated a contract for the sale of a house. The question was whether damages in lieu of specific performance should be assessed on the basis of the market price at the date of the breach (£7,500) or at the date of judgment (£11,500). In the particular circumstances, owing to lack of funds, the claimant could not reasonably have done anything to mitigate the loss by purchasing a different house at the date of breach, so that the date of judgment was chosen as the appropriate date for the assessment of damages.
>
> In *Johnson v Agnew* [1980] AC 367, the vendors agreed to sell a house and land to the purchaser, but the purchaser failed to complete the transaction on the day appointed. The vendors then obtained an order for specific performance, but it was not drawn up for some five months, by which time specific performance had become impossible. The vendors sought discharge of the order for specific performance and to recover damages in its place. The House of Lords found for the vendors, holding that damages were to be assessed at the date on which specific performance became impossible.

In *Johnson v Agnew*, at p. 401, Lord Wilberforce said:

> In cases where a breach of a contract for sale has occurred, and the innocent party reasonably continues to try to have the contract completed, it would to me appear more logical and just rather than tie him to the date of the original breach, to assess damages as at the date when (otherwise than by his default) the contract is lost.

Part 3 — Enforcement of contractual obligations

Finally, in some cases, it may be impossible at the time of performance for the non-breaching party to discover that a breach has occurred, e.g. in instances of latent faults. In such a case, the damages will be assessed at the time when the breach could first reasonably have been discovered: *East Ham Corporation v Bernard Sunley & Sons Ltd* [1966] AC 406.

9.5 Limitations on the ability to obtain compensation

9.5.1 Causation and contributory negligence

9.5.1.1 Causation

Damages will not be awarded to compensate loss that was not caused by the breach. We have already encountered an example of this principle in operation in the case of *C and P Haulage v Middleton* [1983] 1 WLR 1461 (see **9.3.5.3**).

> In *C and P Haulage v Middleton*, the user of a garage claimed his wasted expenditure in equipping the garage when the garage owner wrongfully terminated his contract to use the premises. The Court of Appeal rejected the claim, because ten weeks later the owner could have rightfully terminated the contract, whereupon the equipment would in any case have become the property of the garage owner. Therefore the loss due to wasted expenditure was not *caused* by the breach of contract, but by a term of the contract, which in this respect was inherently disadvantageous to the claimant.

On the same principle, it is not open to a party to rely upon a breach of contract to recover losses when the losses had an entirely separate cause.

> In *Phones 4U Ltd v EE Ltd* [2018] EWHC 49 (Comm) the defendant gave notice to terminate a licensing agreement by reason of the claimant's insolvency. In proceedings commenced by the claimant, the defendant counterclaimed for damages for loss of bargain resulting from the termination of the contract, and relied upon the claimant's alleged breach of contract in failing to perform its obligations. The counterclaim was disallowed. The contract had been terminated by the defendant not for breach but for insolvency, and a claim for damages for loss of bargain would fail if the basis of termination was not repudiation but some other ground. It was not open to a party to recharacterize events after the fact and claim that it had terminated for breach when that was not the case at the time.

9.5.1.1.1 An effective cause of the claimant's loss

In contract claims, the breach must be shown to be an effective cause of the claimant's loss, and it is not sufficient that the breach merely provided the claimant with an opportunity to sustain losses: *Galoo Ltd v Bright Grahame Murray* [1994] 1 WLR 1360, where a claim against auditors for producing inaccurate accounts for a company which allowed it to continue trading, leading to loans to the company by the claimant, was dismissed. In the Court of Appeal's view, the negligence had created the situation in which losses on the loans could be incurred, but it was not the effective cause of the loss.

Whether a loss can be said to have been caused by the breach may depend on the scope of the original obligation or duty and therefore what was being promised.

In ***South Australia Asset Management Corporation (SAAMCO) v York Montague Ltd*** [1997] AC 191, mortgage companies were induced to lend money by a negligent overvaluation of the property that was being purchased and which was the security for the loan. The borrower defaulted and the lender's position was made even worse by a very sharp decline in property values. The essential question was whether the extra loss resulting from the fall in property values could be said to have been caused by the breach in the form of negligent overvaluation and to be recoverable as damages. The additional amounts at stake were sometimes several million pounds. The Court of Appeal said that they were recoverable: but for the negligent valuation, the lender would not have lent the money at all, and it was entitled to be compensated for all of the loss suffered, including that resulting from the fall in the market.

However, the House of Lords disagreed. The most significant element in the reasoning was that Lord Hoffmann did not regard the essential issue as one of causation at all. The issue was the extent of liability, which in turn depended upon what it was that the defendant had undertaken to do. In these cases, the defendants had undertaken only to provide information, not to provide advice about the transactions contemplated. Their liability was therefore limited to the direct consequence of the information being wrong, which was that the lenders had inadequate security, but did not include the disastrous consequences of the fall in the market. At best, that was an indirect consequence of the information being wrong, and the law does not impose liability for such loss unless there are grounds of policy to show strong disapproval, as in fraud.

Compare, however, with *Smith New Court Securities Ltd v Scrimgeour Vickers (Asset Management) Ltd* [1997] AC 254 (discussed at **14.6.2.2**): damages for fraudulent misrepresentation could include subsequent loss in value of shares resulting from other causes on the basis that the purchaser of the shares was locked into the transaction by the fraud.

9.5.1.1.2 *Other contributing causes*

Causation may sometimes present difficulty when it appears that the loss was caused partly by the breach and partly by some other factor. The general rule is that where breach can be shown to be *an* actual cause of the loss, the fact that there is another contributing cause is irrelevant. The breach will entitle the non-breaching party to damages in contract.

For example, in *Wroth v Tyler* [1974] Ch 30 (see **9.4.2),** the claimant's loss was caused partially by the defendant's breach of contract and partially by the fact that the claimant lacked the financial resources to take active steps to mitigate the loss. The loss was nevertheless recoverable.

Similarly, in ***County Ltd v Girozentrale Securities*** [1996] 3 All ER 834, the Court of Appeal said that the trial judge had been wrong, having identified two contributing causes to the loss sustained, to choose which of them was *the* effective cause by inquiring which had been of 'greater efficacy' in causing the loss. The fact that the breach of contract might have had a lesser role in causing the loss did not mean that it was not *a* cause for the purposes of the recovery of damages. It was sufficient in a claim in contract that the cause in question was *an* effective cause of the loss.

9.5.1.1.3 *Intervening acts of third parties*

Where the act of a third party or parties is a factor contributing to the loss, in addition to the breach by the defendant, the question of whether the act by the third party will excuse the breaching party from the obligation to pay damages is largely a question of whether the contract has been frustrated (see **Chapter 12**). The court is likely to be especially concerned to know whether the intervening act was so foreseeable that steps could have been taken to avoid it.

In *The Eugenia* [1964] 2 QB 226 (see **12.3.5.1** and **12.6**), for example, the charterers of a vessel breached their contract by taking the vessel into the Suez Canal at a time when it was a 'dangerous' zone. The effect of that breach was made many times worse by the act of a third party in closing the Canal. Nevertheless, the charterers were not excused the obligation to pay compensation for their breach.

9.5.1.1.4 Intervening act of the claimant

Where the claimant is negligent and that negligence is a *novus actus interveniens* (an independent intervening act) this action provides a complete defence because it breaks the chain of causation.

In **Beoco Ltd v Alfa Laval Co. Ltd** [1995] QB 137, for example, the defendants supplied a defective machine. It was inadequately repaired. The claimants put the machine back into service without carrying out tests and it exploded, causing much more serious damage and a loss of production. The Court of Appeal held that although, at one time, the claimants had a right of recovery for breach of contract against the defendants because of the original defect, any loss resulting from that breach was extinguished by the explosion that destroyed the machine and was not therefore attributable to the defendants.

In the majority of breach of contract cases, causation is not a difficult issue; greater difficulty arises from the question of whether loss, which admittedly results from the breach, is too remote to be compensated (see **9.5.2**).

9.5.1.2 Contributory negligence

Where the claimant has been negligent, but the claimant's negligence is not so great as to break the chain of causation, the position is quite complex. Contributory negligence by a claimant relates to issues of quantum and the possible apportionment of damages. At this stage, liability is established, and there are no issues of causation.

In the law of torts, under the Law Reform (Contributory Negligence) Act 1945, where injury is caused by the negligence of the defendant and by the contributory negligence of the claimant, the damages payable by the defendant to compensate the claimant will be reduced proportionately to the amount by which the claimant's negligence contributed to the injury. *The question is whether the provisions of the Law Reform (Contributory Negligence) Act 1945 cover breach of contract*. The difficulty is the definition of 'fault' in s. 4 of that Act as meaning 'negligence, breach of statutory duty or other act or omission which gives rise to a liability in tort or would, apart from this Act, give rise to the defence of contributory negligence'.

The applicable principles in contractual claims were determined in *Forsikringsaktieselskapet Vesta v Butcher* [1986] 2 All ER 488, a decision of Hobhouse J, which was affirmed by the Court of Appeal: [1989] AC 852. *The availability of apportionment for the claimant's contributory negligence is dependent on the nature of the obligation broken by the defendant, i.e. whether the defendant's breach is strict or qualified.*

In **Forsikringsaktieselskapet Vesta v Butcher**, the claimants were Norwegian insurers of a fish farm in Norway under a policy governed by Norwegian law. They had secured reinsurance of 90 per cent of the risk from London market reinsurers through brokers. The reinsurance was governed by English law. There was a warranty in both the insurance and the reinsurance that the farm was subject to a 24-hour watch. The farm lost 100,000 fish at a time when it had been impossible to mount a watch because of weather conditions. The Norwegian insurers were liable for the loss despite the breach of the warranty, because under Norwegian law a warranty gave a defence only if the breach caused the loss. However, the reinsurers denied liability by reason of breach, in that English law did not at the time require any causal link between breach and loss (a matter now corrected by s. 11 of the Insurance Act 2015). The House of Lords ultimately ruled that the intention of the parties had been that the insurance and reinsurance should be construed consistently, so that the reinsurers were liable. No question of broker liability arose. However, in the lower courts there was a fallback claim against the brokers for failing to secure reinsurance that matched the insurers own liability.

Hobhouse J divided contractual claim into three categories and concluded that, in at least one of these cases, apportionment for contributory negligence was applicable.

9.5.1.2.1 *Category 1: where the contractual obligation is strict*

Many claims for breach of contract depend upon contractual terms imposing a strict standard of performance on the defendant (see **8.2.1.1**), so that performance is guaranteed. Hobhouse J stated that where the defendant has breached a term imposing a strict standard of performance (a 'Category 1' case), there is no scope for the operation of the contributory negligence rule. This is because, since the defendant's negligence, if any, is irrelevant to the defendant's liability for breach of such a term, any negligence by the claimant should also be irrelevant.

The Law Commission's Working Paper *Contributory Negligence as a Defence in Contract* (Law Com. No. 114, 1990) provisionally recommended that contributory negligence should apply to Category 1 cases (breach of strict obligation by the defendant), but this would undoubtedly have been an undesirable development in the law since it would undermine the nature of strict liability. In its final report *Contributory Negligence as a Defence in Contract* (Law Com. No. 219, 1993), the Law Commission abandoned this proposal, and the *Vesta v Butcher* position that there is no apportionment in cases of breaches of strict contractual obligations was reaffirmed by the Court of Appeal in **Barclays Bank plc v Fairclough Building Ltd** [1995] QB 214 and in **Hi-Lite Electrical Ltd v Wolseley UK Ltd** [2011] EWHC 2153 (TCC), [2011] BLR 629: where the defendant had breached SGA 1979, s. 14(2) (a strict contractual obligation: see **6.4.2.4**), there could be no apportionment for any contributory negligence by the claimant.

9.5.1.2.2 *Category 2: qualified contractual obligation to take care, but no independent duty of care in tort*

Where the contract term broken imposes only an obligation to exercise reasonable care and skill, i.e. it is a qualified contractual obligation (see discussion at **8.2.1.1**), but there is no duty of care existing independently of the contract ('Category 2' cases). It has now been confirmed by the Court of Appeal in *Marintrans v Comet Shipping Co. Ltd* [1985] 1 WLR 1270 that there is no apportionment in this situation. Accordingly, even if the defendant owes duties in contract and tort, but the claim does not allege negligence and is brought only in contract, there can be no apportionment: *Raflatac Ltd v Eade Ltd* [1999] BLR 261; *Greenwich Millennium Village Ltd v Essex Services Group plc* [2013] EWHC 3059 (TCC).

9.5.1.2.3 *Category 3: qualified contractual obligation and duty of care owed in tort*

Some contracts impose a duty to exercise reasonable care (qualified contractual obligation), breach of which would in any case amount to an independent tort ('Category 3' cases). *Vesta v Butcher* [1986] 2 All ER 488 belonged to this category, and therefore Hobhouse J found no difficulty in holding that the 1945 Act did apply to such a claim: see also *Platform Home Loans Ltd v Oyston*

Shipways Ltd [2000] 2 AC 190. As Neill LJ remarked in *AB Marintrans v Comet Shipping Co. Ltd, The Shinjitsu Maru No. 5* [1985] 1 WLR 1270, at p. 1288G–H, there is 'great force in the contention that the same rule should apply to claims whether they are based in contract or tort where the act complained of involves the breach of a duty of care'. In *Vesta v Butcher* [1989] AC 852, in the Court of Appeal, Neill LJ accepted that this might be achieved under the analysis offered by Hobhouse J at first instance, although he expressed doubts about whether the wording of s. 4 of the 1945 Act was capable of such an interpretation. This objection might be met by a very minor amendment of the 1945 Act to include a definition of negligence as contained in s. 1(1) of the Unfair Contract Terms Act (UCTA) 1977, which covers 'any obligation, arising from the express or implied terms of a contract, to take reasonable care or exercise reasonable skill in the performance of the contract'.

In its 1993 report, the Law Commission recommended that contributory negligence should apply in all cases of contractual negligence, i.e. where the defendant's breach of contract was a breach of a qualified contractual obligation (Categories 2 and 3). The Law Commission also recommended that the parties should be able to exclude apportionment for contributory negligence if they so wished. It was proposed that this could be achieved expressly or by implication, e.g. using an agreed damages clause would impliedly exclude apportionment for contributory negligence. However, it was proposed to implement these recommendations by means of a separate Bill relating to contributory negligence in contract claims, rather than by amendment to the wording of the 1945 Act.

No progress has since been made with the Law Commission's proposals, although the decision of the Court of Appeal in *Barclays Bank plc v Fairclough Building Ltd* [1995] QB 214 is in line with the recommendations contained in the 1993 report in relation to breaches of strict contractual obligations (i.e. no contributory negligence). The position seems reasonably settled. However, it will be interesting to see whether future courts will be prepared, in the absence of legislation, to treat Category 2 and Category 3 cases in the same way, and how they justify their actions under the 1945 Act.

> ### ⚙ SUMMARY
>
> Apportionment of damages for the claimant's contributory negligence
>
> - Defendant's breach—Category 1: ✗
> - Defendant's breach—Category 2: ✓?
> - Defendant's breach—Category 3: ✓

9.5.2 Remoteness of damage

The defendant is not liable for all losses that result from the breach of contract. Some losses are too remote a consequence of the breach to be recoverable, in the sense that they are regarded as too improbable and so not within the scope of the contractual responsibility undertaken.

The remoteness rule in contract is therefore concerned with recoverability for identified loss and is designed to prevent the defendant having to compensate a loss attendant upon a risk that was not the defendant's to bear because the defendant had not 'assumed responsibility' for it. However, this is a statement of outcome; it does not tell us how we decide for which losses a defendant is to be responsible.

The test

The starting point for any discussion must be the test that determines this question—namely, the statement of principle in *Hadley v Baxendale* (1854) 9 Ex 341, at p. 354, where Alderson B said:

> Where two parties have made a contract which one of them has broken, the damages which the other party ought to receive in respect of such breach of contract should be such as may fairly and reasonably be considered either arising naturally, i.e. according to the usual course of things, from such breach, of contract itself, or such as may reasonably be supposed to have been in the contemplation of both parties, at the time they made the contract, as the probable result of the breach of it.

This rule, which is the test of the remoteness of damage, is intended to ensure that the defendant was aware when making the contract that it had to avoid causing the kind of loss that occurred. The rule can be analysed in economic terms and is concerned with optimizing the allocation of risks between the parties to the contract.

- If a party knows that it must bear the risk of losses occurring naturally ('in the usual course of things'), that party can take preventative action, with the aim of avoiding that loss.

- In addition, if a party knows that it must bear a particular risk, then that party can take out appropriate insurance cover for that risk. Uncertainty over allocation of risk often leads to duplicate insurance, which is economically inefficient.

- The fact that the breaching party will also be responsible for unusual losses, where knowledge of the relevant facts has been disclosed, encourages the parties to address the risks and to give relevant information.

It is important to remember that remoteness is judged on the basis of contemplations (or knowledge) at the time of the contract, rather than at the time of the breach—*Jackson v Royal Bank of Scotland* [2005] UKHL 3, [2005] 1 WLR 377—and that damages are therefore assessed on this basis.

9.5.2.1 Two limbs or a single remoteness rule?

The test of remoteness of damage established in *Hadley v Baxendale* (1854) 9 Ex 341 is frequently described as consisting of two rules, or a single rule with two limbs: *Victoria Laundry (Windsor) Ltd v Newman Industries Ltd* [1949] 2 KB 528. It is often applied on this basis in order to distinguish between the general damage in the first limb (not needing to be specifically pleaded in a breach of contract claim) and the special damage covered by the second limb (which does).

- *Under the first limb, damages may be recovered for loss arising 'according to the usual course of things' from the breach of contract (i.e. normal loss). The intention of this rule may be said to be the identification of those losses that must inevitably have been within the contemplation of the parties as likely to result in the event of breach of contract.* The likelihood of such losses is a reasonable deduction from the nature of the contract. Knowledge of such losses is therefore imputed and, consequently, the loss must have been within the reasonable contemplations of both parties. It might be said that there is an 'assumption of responsibility' for such losses.

- *Under the second limb, damages that result from special circumstances may also be recovered, provided that the defendant knows of those circumstances. Only if there is knowledge of the relevant facts giving rise to the special damage can it be said that the loss was within the reasonable contemplations of both parties*, and only then can it be said that responsibility for such a loss has been 'assumed': see e.g. *Seven Seas Properties Ltd v Al-Essa (No. 2)* [1993] 1 WLR 1083 (no actual knowledge of the sub-sale and so could not recover lost profit on that sub-sale).

In *Hadley v Baxendale*, at pp. 354–5, Alderson B said:

> Now, if the special circumstances under which the contract was actually made were communicated by the claimants to the defendants, and thus known to both parties, the damages resulting from the breach of such a contract, which they would reasonably contemplate, would be the amount of injury which would ordinarily follow from a breach of contract under these special circumstances . . .

It is almost certain that Alderson B did not intend to establish two rules of remoteness of damage. Rather, there is a single test that requires greater knowledge on the part of the defendant as the degree of likelihood of the particular loss resulting from the breach diminishes.

- The single test was applied in *The Heron II* [1969] 1 AC 350, at p. 385.
- In *Kpohraror v Woolwich Building Society* [1996] 4 All ER 119, at pp. 127–8, Evans LJ stated:

> I would prefer to hold the starting point for any application of *Hadley v Baxendale* is the extent of shared knowledge of both parties when the contract was made . . . When that is established it may often be the case that the first and second parts of the rule overlap, or at least that it is unnecessary to draw a clear line of demarcation between them.

- In *Jackson v Royal Bank of Scotland* [2005] UKHL 3, [2005] 1 WLR 377, at [25], Lord Hope referred to the existence of a single principle of 'what was in the contemplation of the parties at the time they made their contract'. However, his Lordship then identified the loss as normal loss, arising naturally from the breach.

Usual (or normal) loss and loss resulting from special circumstances (abnormal loss) are therefore no more than the polar positions of that single shared knowledge test. However, they assist greatly in coming to a determination under that single test of shared knowledge.

9.5.2.2 The operation of the limbs in practice

The operation of the two limbs to determine reasonable contemplations is well illustrated by the decision of the Court of Appeal in *Victoria Laundry (Windsor) Ltd v Newman Industries Ltd* [1949] 2 KB 528.

> The defendant engineering company had contracted to sell a boiler to the claimant laundry company. The boiler was to be delivered on 5 June. The defendants were aware of the nature of the claimants' business and had been informed by letter that the claimants intended to put the boiler to immediate use. The boiler was delivered late. The claimants sought damages for the profit that they would have earned through the use of the boiler in their business during the period of the delay and for the profit on a number of highly lucrative government contracts that they 'could and would have accepted'.
>
> The Court of Appeal held that:
>
> (i) the claimants were not entitled to recover for the loss of profit on the government contracts, since the defendants had no knowledge of these contracts or of their terms;

(ii) however, that did not mean that the claimants could not recover damages for general lost profit from the expansion of their business intended as a result of purchasing the boiler. Once the defendants knew that the boiler was intended for immediate use, they were taken to know that late delivery was likely to lead to loss of business.

These general profits are usually treated as normal loss and it is submitted here that this is the correct conclusion. Every loss depends on *some* fact, and the fact in question was not a special fact, but very common: see e.g. *The Heron II* [1969] 1 AC 350, in a fall in the market price of sugar owing to delay in shipment was normal loss, but on the basis that the shippers *knew* that they were shipping sugar for sugar merchants to a port where there was a sugar market. Arguably, therefore, if a business purchases machinery or equipment, the natural conclusion is that it is intended to be used immediately on receipt. Another view can be adopted—namely, that the loss of profits in this case was dependent on knowledge of the special fact that the claimants intended to put the boiler to immediate use in their business so that this amounted to abnormal loss. If this is the case, had the defendants not known that the boiler was intended for immediate use, the court might have found that even damages for loss of general profits were too remote. This type of distinction may be the approach that was adopted by Lord Rodger and Baroness Hale in *Transfield Shipping Inc. v Mercator Shipping Inc., The Achilleas* [2008] UKHL 48, [2009] 1 AC 61 (see discussion at **9.5.2.7**). It may be that a more contextual basis for determining whether a loss is normal loss should be adopted in future.

9.5.2.3 Loss depending on special facts

By comparison with the position in *The Heron II* [1969] 1 AC 350, recovery on the facts of *Hadley v Baxendale* (1854) 9 Ex 341 was held to turn on a special fact and the lack of knowledge of that special fact.

The claimants in **Hadley v Baxendale**, mill owners in Gloucester, engaged the defendant carriers to take a mill shaft to Greenwich as a pattern for a new shaft. In breach of contract, delivery was delayed, so that the stoppage at the mill was extended. The claimants claimed damages for their loss of profit caused by the delay. It was held that this loss of profit was not recoverable because it was too remote a loss. The loss did not arise naturally since the claimants might have had a spare shaft.

The fact that the mill did not have a spare shaft would not be a natural inference from the circumstances and, on this basis, this case can be distinguished from the loss of general profits in *Victoria Laundry (Windsor) Ltd v Newman Industries Ltd* [1949] 2 KB 528. Thus *Hadley v Baxendale* indicates the importance of informing the other party of circumstances that affect performance and the risk where full recovery is required. It also indicates the importance of identifying a loss as abnormal on the facts and in the context of the particular contract. This may be precisely what the House of Lords was seeking to do in *Transfield Shipping Inc. v Mercator Shipping Inc., The Achilleas* [2008] UKHL 48, [2009] 1 AC 61.

9.5.2.4 Identifying normal and abnormal losses

An examination of the case law reveals that it is often difficult to divide losses into two simple categories of:

- *normal losses* (those arising in the usual course of things); and
- *abnormal losses* (those arising out of special circumstances).

It is significant that the approach evidenced in the case law is generally to restrict normal loss, thereby encouraging greater disclosure of the factual background see e.g. *Balfour Beatty Construction (Scotland) Ltd v Scottish Power plc* (1994) 71 BLR 20 (actual knowledge of the construction process of continuous pour of concrete was required and could not be imputed). That said, if the loss suffered arose from circumstances generally known to apply to contracts of the type in question, such loss can be said to be normal, as in *125 OBS (Nominees1) v Lend Lease Construction (Europe) Ltd* [2017] EWHC 25 (TCC), (2017) 174 Con LR 105 (financing arrangements were inevitably in place for major construction works, and so financing losses were not too remote even though the detail was unknown to the defendant).

However, the approach to 'normal loss' or 'direct loss' may depend on the context in which the distinction arises. In the context of the remoteness rule, there is a strong policy incentive to restrict the scope of normal loss in order to encourage disclosure of facts and risks. In the context of construction of exemption clauses that exclude liability for 'indirect or consequential loss', the policy considerations may suggest limiting the scope of 'indirect loss' in order to limit the scope of the exclusion, so that a more generous interpretation of 'direct loss' is apparent. For example, in *Hotel Services Ltd v Hilton International Hotels (UK) Ltd* [2000] 1 All ER (Comm) 750, the question was whether such a clause exempted the supplier of defective electronic mini-bars from liability for the cost of their removal and the loss of profit on their use suffered by the hotel. The Court of Appeal held that neither of these losses depended on special facts. Both losses were *direct and natural consequences of the breach*, because it was obvious that if the mini-bars were dangerous, they would have to be removed, and it was clear that, when in use, such mini-bars would generate a profit.

9.5.2.5 The test for the likelihood of loss

It remains to be determined what must be the likelihood of a loss resulting in order for it to be recoverable as being within the parties' reasonable contemplations at the time of contracting.

In *Victoria Laundry (Windsor) Ltd v Newman Industries Ltd* [1949] 2 KB 528, at p. 539, Asquith LJ impliedly suggested that the test was the same as the test of foreseeability in the tort of negligence, since he said that the claimant may recover 'such part of the loss actually resulting as was at the time of the contract *reasonably foreseeable* as liable to result from the breach' (emphasis added). However, this formulation was called into question by the House of Lords in *The Heron II* [1969] 1 AC 350. Lord Reid said that the claimant may only recover 'loss arising naturally' or 'in the usual course of things'—echoing Alderson B in *Hadley v Baxendale* (1854) 9 Ex 341—and the claimant may not recover loss that, although a real possibility, was likely to occur only 'in a small minority of cases'. Lord Reid went on to stress that the test of remoteness in contract is stricter than the test of remoteness in tort, for the reason that the communication of special circumstances is irrelevant to many torts, but in contract allows the defendant to modify the contract or performance according to the known risks of the contract. The remoteness test must therefore encourage such communication.

In *H. Parsons (Livestock) Ltd v Uttley Ingham & Co. Ltd* [1978] 1 QB 791, the Court of Appeal was faced with the task of making sense of the very vague tests of remoteness then available.

> The contract was for the sale of an animal feed hopper. The ventilation of the hopper was defective, amounting to breach of the contract. The farmer's livestock became ill through eating animal feed that was mouldy because the ventilation was defective, so that the herd had to be destroyed. The particular

illness and its consequence would have been considered an unlikely result of the breach in question at the time when the contract was made. The farmer claimed the loss of the value of the herd. The Court of Appeal concluded that the farmer could recover.

However, the approaches of the majority (Scarman and Orr LJJ) and Lord Denning MR differed.

9.5.2.5.1 Lord Denning

Lord Denning MR found the various formulations of the test of remoteness confusing and 'a sea of semantic exercises'. He accepted that on some occasions the test is stricter than at others, but rather than distinguishing between contract and tort, he distinguished between:

- claims for economic loss (such as lost profit); and
- claims for physical loss (as in this case).

In the case of physical loss, he considered that the less strict test of remoteness applied. Provided that some physical injury might be envisaged, its precise nature was irrelevant.

9.5.2.5.2 Scarman and Orr LJJ

Scarman LJ (with whom Orr LJ agreed) rejected Lord Denning's distinction between economic and physical loss, and ultimately decided that the remoteness tests in contract and tort were the same. This reasoning must be doubted, however, in view of Lord Reid's clear statement in *The Heron II* [1969] 1 AC 350 that the test in contract is stricter than the test in tort.

This issue has yet to be resolved, although there must be a preservation of the distinction between remoteness in contract and tort.

- In favour of Lord Reid's approach in *The Heron II* is the argument that contracts enable the parties to allocate risks between themselves and that such allocation will work only if the parties have proper information about the risks involved. The strict remoteness test in contract would encourage the provision of such information since, unless the information is provided, the loss will not be recoverable. Contract and tort remoteness tests should be different in degree to reflect the different contexts for the risk and knowledge of that risk.

- The approach advocated by Lord Denning in *H. Parsons (Livestock) Ltd v Uttley Ingham & Co. Ltd* [1978] 1 QB 791 of distinguishing on the basis of loss has the advantage that it would prevent the result of the case from depending upon the alleged 'artificial classification' of the claim as either contractual or tortious. It would also impose a stricter test on those claims that are inherently speculative (lost profits), while allowing a more lenient test for claims in which the loss is more readily measured (physical loss). However, it begs another question—namely, whether it is always possible to make such a clear distinction between financial and physical loss, and whether it is necessarily the case that the remoteness tests for contract and tort should be assimilated.

9.5.2.6 The type/extent principle

Scarman and Orr LJJ decided *H. Parsons (Livestock) Ltd v Uttley Ingham & Co. Ltd* [1978] 1 QB 791 on the basis that, since the type of loss was within the parties' contemplations, the extent of it need not be. This was also the basis for the decision in *Brown v KMR Services Ltd* [1995] 4 All ER 598.

Brown v KMR Services Ltd arose out of the disastrous losses made by investors in the Lloyd's insurance market (then known as Lloyd's 'Names') and was one of several actions brought against those who had encouraged (or not discouraged) such 'Names' to take on excessive liabilities. The losses were, of course, financial, not physical; they were of a type that it could readily be 'foreseen' might be incurred as a result of the breach of contract, but their extent went well beyond that which might, in any year, arise 'in the usual course of things'. The losses were held to be recoverable because, in this context, the *type* of loss fell within the remoteness principle.

This reasoning highlighted some issues in terms of aligning this principle with the outcome in decisions relating to financial loss, in which the courts have differentiated between types of financial loss or profit loss. For example, in *Victoria Laundry (Windsor) Ltd v Newman Industries Ltd* [1949] 2 KB 528, general loss of profits and profits on specific contracts were not treated as part of a generic class of loss of profits. If they had been, since 'loss of profits' fell within remoteness under the type/extent principle, all losses of profits would have been recoverable.

Kpohraror v Woolwich Building Society [1996] 4 All ER 119 concerned the extent of liability for breach of a banking contract where the bank had wrongfully dishonoured the claimant's cheque. Counsel for the claimant sought to rely on *Brown v KMR Services Ltd* to establish that, once the defendant knew that the account would be used in export–import transactions, the particular extent of financial loss in such transactions was of no concern and the full loss should be recoverable. The Court of Appeal baulked at such reasoning—perhaps not surprisingly since the cheque was for £4,550, while the total loss claimed was more than £57,000. In refusing to award such extensive compensation, the court clearly proceeded on the basis that knowledge of the particular risk, or that generic risks of a similar extent might arise, was necessary to avoid the conclusion that such loss was too remote.

9.5.2.7 The decision of the House of Lords in *The Achilleas*

In *Transfield Shipping Inc. v Mercator Shipping Inc., The Achilleas* [2008] UKHL 48, [2009] 1 AC 61, time charterers were nine days late in redelivery of the vessel. The owners had re-chartered the vessel and, when it was not redelivered on time, the owners had agreed an extension of the cancelling date under the new (follow-on) charter, but only on the basis that the new charterers received a reduction in the daily rate of the hire. The question was whether damages were limited by the remoteness principles to the difference between the charter rate and the market rate at the time of redelivery for the nine-day period of the over-run during which the owners did not have the vessel because of the breach (as argued by the charterers), or whether the owners could claim damages based on the loss of hire on the next charter ($8,000 a day for 191 days of the follow-on charter). The owners alleged that the latter measure was the only way in which they could be compensated for their actual loss, but the charterers argued that this was possible only where there was actual knowledge, i.e. the second limb in *Hadley v Baxendale* (1854) 9 Ex 341.

The arbitrator and judge had considered that this situation fell within the first limb (normal loss), so that the actual loss suffered was within reasonable contemplations. The Court of Appeal agreed, on the basis that a time charterer would know that the owner was likely to have entered into a new charter to follow closely on from the redelivery of the vessel and impliedly took the risk of loss in relation to this if they were late in redelivering.

However, the House of Lords disagreed and considered that damages were limited to the lower figure—namely, the difference between the charter rate and the market rate at the time of redelivery for the nine-day period of the overrun. The majority expressed the position in the following terms: the charterers had assumed responsibility for the nine-day delay in returning the vessel, but they had not assumed responsibility for the entirety of the follow-on charter, because they could neither control that loss nor quantify it.

Unfortunately, in terms of clarity of the law, their Lordships did not adopt a single line of reasoning to justify their overall conclusion, and this has led to some regrettable uncertainty of principle in a key area of contract law that subsequent courts, despite precedent, have done their best to temper.

9.5.2.7.1 Lord Hoffmann and Lord Hope

Lords Hoffmann and Hope considered that the key question to ask in terms of remoteness in contract was whether, in objective terms, the charterers had 'assumed responsibility' for the loss in question, i.e. remoteness turned on party intention and agreement. Remoteness on this basis would turn not on questions of normal or abnormal loss, but on whether the loss for which compensation is sought is of a 'kind' or a 'type' for which the contract-breaker ought fairly to be taken to have accepted responsibility.

'Assumption of responsibility' may be envisaged as a way of recognizing what losses ought objectively to be treated as falling within the parties' contemplations, and it is tempting to talk of this being constituted by those losses for which the parties must have intended to assume responsibility, but it does not actually take us to that determination. It might just as effectively be argued that the parties assume responsibility for normal losses because these are expected, whereas abnormal losses would not be assumed without a more express assumption of the risk involved. The question: 'for what losses does a party assume responsibility, and on what basis?', still needs to be addressed.

The real issue in *The Achilleas* was the extent or type of the loss and whether the extent of a loss fell within the parties' reasonable contemplations. The problem appears to have been the finding, in general terms, by the courts below that this follow-on charter was normal loss and therefore that the full extent of that normal loss ought to have been within remoteness. However, neither conclusion need follow. The motivation for this decision was accepted practice and understanding in the shipping industry that 'liability was restricted to the difference between the market rate and the charter rate for the overrun period'. Such an outcome could have been accommodated within the application of existing principles and approaches. How could the full extent of the loss be within the parties' reasonable contemplations when both would have been aware of this restriction and so could not be said to be contracting on a different basis unless there were express evidence of a contrary intention? Despite the accepted market understanding, the House could have concluded that, on the facts, this was abnormal loss, so that an express acceptance of the risk based on knowledge would be required.

The consequence of adopting the Hoffmann 'assumed responsibility' (or agreement) approach is that it invites arguments denying an assumption of responsibility for all and any losses, since this has now become a question of fact in each instance. The clear market understanding in *The Achilleas* is likely to be a rarity. Defendants will need to establish all of the background facts upon which they will rely as denying an assumption of responsibility. The result might well be complex arguments on remoteness—both facts and law. There are also unhelpful references throughout to 'reasonable foreseeability' (tort) and duties of care, which have no place in the contractual context: *The Heron II* [1969] 1 AC 350. The scope of recovery in contract must reflect the fact that the context and knowledge is necessarily tighter.

9.5.2.7.2 *Lord Rodger and Baroness Hale*

The approach of Lord Rodger and Baroness Hale has more to recommend it, with the exception of references to reasonable foreseeability, since it takes existing principles as its context. Lord Rodger concluded that neither party would reasonably have contemplated that an over-run of nine days would, 'in the ordinary course of things', cause the owners the type of loss for which they claimed damages. It followed that this was not normal loss, but the product of the 'extremely volatile market conditions', causing the owners' actions in relation to the discount. The charterers had no specific knowledge of this discount. On this basis, the loss was too remote to be recoverable.

There is an inevitable tension with the type/loss principle—see *H. Parsons (Livestock) Ltd v Uttley Ingham & Co. Ltd* [1978] 1 QB 791 and *Brown v KMR Services Ltd* [1995] 4 All ER 598 (at **9.5.2.6**)—unless certain liberties are taken with the initial definition of the 'type' of loss, as happened with the differing types of profits in *Victoria Laundry (Windsor) Ltd v Newman Industries Ltd* [1949] 2 KB 528. The type/extent principle was not regarded as being incorrect by either Lord Rodger or Baroness Hale, but there are fairly easy ways of avoiding its application through construction where its application delivers a result that does not fit with context or understandings in particular commercial markets.

9.5.2.7.3 *Lord Walker*

Whilst Lord Walker regarded the assumption of responsibility principle as 'helpful' in the tort context, he did not go as far as adopting it for contract. Lord Walker considered that the parties had simply not contracted, on the basis that there should be unlimited recovery for losses associated with the follow-on charter, particularly as the charterers could have no control over the follow-on contract or the terms on which the owners had contracted. Lord Walker's approach is therefore formulated in language similar to that employed by Lords Hoffmann and Hope, but without the express adoption of a test of 'assumption of responsibility', and he also purported to be in agreement with the reasoning of Lord Rodger. In *Sylvia Shipping Co. Ltd v Progress Bulk Carriers Ltd* [2010] EWHC 542 (Comm), [2010] 2 Lloyd's Rep 81, [2010] 1 CLC 470, at [39], Hamblen J concluded that there was a majority for the 'assumption of responsibility' test.

9.5.2.7.4 *Conclusion*

In the initial aftermath of the decision in *The Achilleas*, it was difficult to say where this left the remoteness test for recovery in contract, although the evidence suggested that it was always unlikely that the limbs of *Hadley v Baxendale* (1854) 9 Ex 341—and the use of normal and abnormal loss—would be allowed to disappear by those who use them.

It may be that the type/extent principle ought to be reformulated in the context of reasonable contemplations so as to limit recovery. *The Achilleas* is in line with *Victoria Laundry (Windsor) Ltd v Newman Industries Ltd* [1949] 2 KB 528, although difficult to assimilate with other decisions on the type/loss principle such as *Brown v KMR Services Ltd* [1995] 4 All ER 598. The answer may be to limit the application of the type/loss principle to concurrent claims, i.e. where liability can be established in both contract and tort, and to leave the key principles in *Hadley v Baxendale* unscathed since the rationale for these principles in the contractual setting remains.

Alternatively, a restrictive approach to the definition of what is normal loss, bearing in mind the specific context, can be taken. It is possible to analyse *The Achilleas* as a decision based on the loss falling outside the parties' reasonable contemplations because the contractual context required special knowledge of the facts pertaining to the follow-on contract. In essence, this is the approach adopted by Lord Rodger and Baroness Hale.

In any event, those tasked with applying tests prefer as much guidance as possible. The distinction between normal loss and abnormal loss, whilst imperfect, provides this when identifying losses within 'reasonable contemplations' and can just as easily provide guidance if the test requires that it needs to be shown that responsibility for the type of loss has been assumed.

Subsequently, in *ASM Shipping Ltd of India v TTMI Ltd of England, The Amer Energy* [2009] 1 Lloyd's Rep 293, at [17]–[19], in the context of an attempt to reopen the *Hadley v Baxendale* approach to remoteness, Flaux J stated:

> To the extent that Lord Hoffmann was purporting to lay down some new test as to recoverability of damages in contract, he was in a minority. Although Lord Hope adopts a similar analysis at paras 30 and 36, he does so essentially by way of application of established principles. In any event it is important to note that even Lord Hoffmann acknowledges in paras 9 and 11 of his opinion that departure from the normal principles of foreseeability would be unusual. Although he refers to shipping as a market where limitations on the extent of liability arising out of general expectations in that market might be more common, I do not consider that he was intending to say that in all shipping cases (as opposed to the type of time charter case then under consideration) the rule in *Hadley v Baxendale* as subsequently refined, will no longer apply. If he was saying that, it was not a view shared by the majority and it would be heterodox to say the least.

In *Saipol SA v Inerco Trade SA* [2014] EWHC 2211 (Comm), [2015] 1 Lloyd's Rep 26, at [17], Field J referred to *The Achilleas* as 'a highly exceptional case' since 'there was not only a generalised understanding in the trade or the market that losses for late delivery of a vessel under a time charter were to be assessed simply by reference to the market rate at the time the vessel should have been redelivered, but that was also the considered view of the legal profession'. This restrictive interpretation also received some support from Cooke J in *Classic Maritime Inc. v Lion Diversified Holdings Berhad* [2009] EWHC 1142 (Comm), [2010] 1 Lloyd's Rep 59, [2010] 1 CLC 445, when he noted the disapproval of Flaux J in *The Amer Energy* and commented that it would have been surprising had the House of Lords altered the remoteness test for contract to 'assumption of responsibility'. Cooke J went on to apply the first limb in *Hadley v Baxendale* and approved references to 'reasonable contemplations'. On the basis that the loss in question was within the parties' contemplations, Cooke J considered that none of their Lordships in *The Achilleas* had said that the full extent of such a loss should not be recoverable.

Thus the crucial factor is not that 'assumption of responsibility' and 'reasonable contemplations' are different tests, which Faux J denied in *The Amer Energy*, but whether it is possible post-*The Achilleas* to retain the limbs of normal loss and abnormal loss to assist in reaching a conclusion on this outcome. The comments in *Classic Maritime* and the application in *GB Gas Holdings Ltd v Accenture (UK) Ltd* [2009] EWHC 2734 (Comm) suggest that the limbs are not so easily overturned, because they provide an established and helpful route to a conclusion. (This first instance decision in *GB Gas Holdings* was reversed in part on other grounds by the Court of Appeal—[2010] EWCA Civ 912—but the judge's conclusions on the limbs were incorporated without question.) The application in *Mayhaven Healthcare Ltd v Bothma (t/a DAB Builders)* [2009] EWHC 2634 (TCC), [2010] BLR 154, 127 Con LR 1, also suggests retention of the limbs for the same reasons. In *Mayhaven*, the judge made express reference to the fact that he was not applying Lord Hoffmann's principle. He considered that loss of profits was not to be treated as a single 'type of loss' and concluded that the particular loss of profit in relation to use of a care home for particular occupants was not recoverable under the first limb in *Hadley*, nor was it recoverable under the second limb for lack of actual knowledge.

In *Sylvia Shipping Co. Ltd v Progress Bulk Carriers Ltd* [2010] EWHC 542 (Comm), [2010] 2 Lloyd's Rep 81, [2010] 1 CLC 470, Hamblen J considered that assumption of responsibility would be relevant only in exceptional cases (in which the liability would be contrary to market understanding and in conditions of extreme volatility leading to 'unquantifiable, unpredictable, uncontrollable or disproportionate' loss). However, in general, 'the orthodox approach' would apply and remained the 'standard rule', so that it was not necessary to address 'assumption of responsibility' at all. That said, there would be an assumption of responsibility (i.e. as in an outcome) where the tests of normal loss or abnormal loss indicated that the loss fell within the parties' reasonable contemplations. The loss on the facts (loss on a sub-charter where the owners were late in delivering the vessel) clearly fell within the first limb as normal loss, and the general market understanding was that such loss was recoverable.

The Court of Appeal in *Supershield Ltd v Siemens Building Technologies FE Ltd* [2010] EWCA Civ 7, [2010] 2 All ER (Comm) 1185, [2010] 1 CLC 241, has also endorsed this attempt to confine the scope of the 'assumption of responsibility' principle, Toulson LJ concluding, at [43], that *Hadley v Baxendale* remains a standard rule, on the basis that:

> [I]t reflects the expectation to be imputed to the parties in the ordinary case, i.e. that a contract breaker should ordinarily be liable to the other party for damage resulting from his breach if, but only if, at the time of making the contract a reasonable person in his shoes would have had damage of that kind in mind as not unlikely to result from a breach.

The Achilleas was confined to those cases in which there could be no such imputation on examining the contract and the commercial background.

> The appellant company, consultant engineers, had been late in designing the road and drainage, and obtaining statutory approvals for a proposed development site, leading to considerable delays in completion of the respondent's property development project. The company sought unpaid fees and the developer counterclaimed for damages resulting from the fall in market value of the development owing to the failure to complete the work on time. Was this loss too remote a consequence of the breach? The judge at first instance considered that, since the type of loss (delay to a development and market fluctuations in the value of land) fell within the contemplation of the parties at the time of entering into the contract, the loss was recoverable. The company appealed on the basis that the 'assumption of responsibility' test required the court to consider the commercial background and that this was therefore not a type of loss for which responsibility could be assumed, since the company could have no control over the property market.

The Court of Appeal dismissed the company's appeal and held that the type of loss fell within the parties' reasonable contemplations. The test of reasonable contemplations in *Hadley v Baxendale* was 'the standard rule' and should be departed from only where 'the commercial background' to the agreement indicated that this 'would not reflect the expectation or intention reasonably to be imputed to the parties': *per* Sir David Keene, at [22]. Sir David Keene expressed the approach to be taken, at [24]:

> If there is no express term dealing with what types of losses a party is accepting potential liability for if he breaks the contract, then the law in effect implies a term to determine the answer. Normally, there

is an implied term accepting responsibility for the types of losses which can reasonably be foreseen at the time of contract to be not unlikely to result if the contract is broken. But if there is evidence in a particular case that the nature of the contract and the commercial background, or indeed other relevant special circumstances, render that implied assumption or responsibility inappropriate for a type of loss, then the contract-breaker escapes liability.

Sir David Keene considered *The Achilleas* to be such a case. However, it is by no means clear where the line is to be drawn and when the 'standard approach' will not apply, and it is certainly not clear why a test based on 'knowledge' requires justification as a separate implied term agreeing to accept responsibility for a loss. It seems preferable to return to the *Hadley v Baxendale* approach of assessing actual or presumed knowledge of risk of loss in context and, at that stage, to conclude whether responsibility for it can be accepted on the facts. Unfortunately, if only as an alternative argument, the predicted need to establish an array of background facts that will be relied upon to establish or deny the 'assumption of responsibility' is liable to continue and to make this area of law unnecessarily complex.

There are also clear signs of retrenchment, with suggestions that assumption of responsibility is not to be treated as a separate principle (e.g. it was described as a 'rationalisation of the rule in *Hadley v Baxendale*' in *Supershield v Siemens*), although in ***Borealis AB v Geogas Trading SA*** [2010] EWHC 2879 (Comm), [2011] 1 Lloyd's Rep 482, Gross LJ considered that the loss in question was too remote on *either* test. On other occasions, even the existence of *The Achilleas* goes unnoticed in the High Court, and the case is pleaded and assessed only on the basis of the two limbs in *Hadley v Baxendale*. In the Singapore Court of Appeal, in *MFM Restaurants Pte Ltd v Fish & Co. Restaurants Pte Ltd* [2010] SGCA 36, Andrew Phang Boon Leong JA (delivering the judgment of the court) rejected 'assumption of responsibility' altogether, noting that the fact scenario in *The Achilleas* could be accommodated within the existing scope of *Hadley v Baxendale*. This is a view that this author would endorse.

9.5.2.8 The remoteness tests in contract and tort distinguished

The Court of Appeal in ***Wellesley Partners LLP v Withers LLP*** [2015] EWCA Civ 1146, [2016] CILL 3757, was faced with determining whether the contract 'reasonable contemplations' or tort test 'reasonable foreseeability' applied to recovery where there was concurrent liability. In addressing this question, the Court of Appeal helpfully reiterated the distinction between the tests and the different language to be employed.

The defendant law firm was engaged by the claimant headhunter to draft a partnership agreement to cover new partners. The claimant wanted the partnerships agreement to allow a withdrawal of half of the capital invested by a new partner after 42 months. However, the agreement as drafted allowed this to happen at any time within the first 41 months. The investment bank was a new partner which exercised this option to withdraw its capital. The judge had found that the defendant firm had been negligent in drafting this agreement and it was also clearly a breach of contract, i.e. there was concurrent liability. The appeal concentrated on the measure of damages. Part of the claimant's alleged loss were losses resulting from the loss of a chance to generate more profits by opening an office in New York.

In relation to the applicable remoteness test in instances of concurrent liability, the judge had been strongly attracted to having one test for remoteness of damage on the basis that '[a] rational system of law would give only one answer' to the question of which losses should be recoverable in instances of professional negligence. The judge considered that the correct test should be a contractual one whenever the parties were in a contractual relationship since the contractual context meant that the parties were not strangers and could make an assessment of risk. However, the judge had accepted that he was bound to take the more generous test to the claimant, the tort test of reasonable foreseeability. On this basis the loss of the opportunity in New York fell within remoteness. *Obiter*, the judge was not satisfied that damages for this loss would be recoverable in contract because it was a very particular opportunity that did not exist when the partnership agreement was drafted and it could not reasonably have been contemplated at that time.

The Court of Appeal held that where there was concurrent liability, the remoteness test determining recovery for economic loss should be the same—and it should be the contractual test because the parties to the contract had the opportunity to draw special circumstances to each other's attention when contracting and they were assumed to be contracting on the basis of recovery of only those losses that fell within their reasonable contemplations. That position should not alter simply because there was a concurrent duty of care in tort.

Applying the contractual test, the Court of Appeal disagreed with the judge at first instance, and considered that this loss did fall within the parties' reasonable contemplations because the defendant firm did know that the partnership planned to expand into the US at the time of making the contract to draw up the agreement and this loss (the Nomura contract) was therefore of a 'kind' (or type) that fell within reasonable contemplations. *Victoria Laundry* was distinguished because the sellers of the boilers would have regarded the loss on these contracts as a different and higher form of risk, whereas it would be artificial to suppose that a law firm engaged to draft an agreement preventing the withdrawal of capital from a partnership would have regarded the loss of the specific contract for the US as a different sort of risk. It followed that the losses in respect of the US contract were recoverable.

9.5.3 Mitigation

A claimant is under a 'duty' to mitigate its loss, in the sense that a claimant may not recover damages for losses that it could have avoided by taking reasonable steps.

In **British Westinghouse Electric and Manufacturing Co. Ltd v Underground Electric Railways Co. of London Ltd** [1912] AC 673, at p. 689, Viscount Haldane LC said:

> The fundamental basis is . . . compensation for pecuniary loss naturally flowing from the breach; but this first principle is qualified by a second, which imposes on a claimant the duty of taking all reasonable steps to mitigate the loss consequent upon the breach, and debars him from claiming in respect of any part of the damage which is due to his neglect to take such steps . . . [T]his second principle does not impose on the claimant an obligation to take any step which a reasonable and prudent man would not ordinarily take in the course of his business.

9.5.3.1 Reasonable steps

The duty to mitigate is limited by the fact that a claimant is required to take only *reasonable steps* to minimize its loss. Thus loss will not be recoverable if it could be avoided by taking reasonable steps. The market price rule for quantifying difference in value damages embodies this limitation, in that where there is a market, it is reasonable for the claimant to seek substitute performance via the market and loss greater than that represented by the market price formula cannot be recovered.

What is reasonable will very largely depend upon the facts of individual cases. In *Pilkington v Wood* [1953] Ch 770, it was held that there was no duty to embark on 'a complicated and difficult piece of litigation' in order to attempt to remedy the consequences of the defendant's breach of contract. In *Gul Bottlers (PVT) Ltd v Nichols plc* [2014] EWHC 2173 (Comm), a licensee had not acted unreasonably in refusing an offer for a new licence agreement where the offer was 'a legal stratagem' to protect the breaching party's position in the event of litigation. However, in some circumstances, it may be reasonable to accept the performance offered by the defendant even when that performance amounts to breach of the original contract. If it remains the best substitute performance available, then it will be unreasonable not to go to that source: see *Payzu Ltd v Saunders* [1919] 2 KB 581, where the court thought that a buyer who defaulted on payment for goods, but who was offered further supplies if payment was made in cash, should have accepted that offer rather than treating non-delivery as breach. What is reasonable may also depend upon the circumstances of the claimant. In *Wroth v Tyler* [1974] Ch 30, the claimant was unable to mitigate because he lacked the financial resources to make a substitute purchase. His failure to mitigate was not unreasonable in the circumstances.

A claimant must not, by unreasonable action on its part, increase the loss resulting from the breach, and reasonableness of the action is judged at the time when the need to take such action arises.

- *If the claimant takes reasonable steps in an attempt to minimize the loss, but these reasonable steps result in increased loss, the claimant can recover for that increased loss.*

In **Banco de Portugal v Waterlow** [1932] AC 452, the defendant's breach resulted in large numbers of forged banknotes circulating in Portugal. The claimants undertook to honour the face value of all such notes, although they were able to detect the forgeries. The claimants' action increased the loss resulting from the breach, but was held to be reasonable because to have done otherwise would have caused a crisis of confidence in the paper currency. The assessment of reasonableness must be judged at the time and not with the benefit of hindsight.

As Lord Macmillan stated, at p. 506:

> It is often easy after an emergency has passed to criticize the steps which have been taken to meet it, but such criticism does not come well from those who have themselves created the emergency. The law is satisfied if the party placed in a difficult situation by reason of the breach of a duty owed to him has acted reasonably in the adoption of remedial measures, and he will not be held disentitled to recover the cost of such measures merely because the party in breach can suggest that other measures less burdensome to him might have been taken.

- *Conversely, if the mitigating act has the effect of wiping out the loss resulting from the breach, the claimant will be entitled to nominal damages only for that breach.*

In **British Westinghouse Electric and Manufacturing Co. Ltd v Underground Electric Railways Co. of London Ltd** [1912] AC 673, the appellants were to supply electricity turbines to the respondents' specification. The turbines never met that specification and, after a time, were replaced by the turbines of a different manufacturer. These turbines were much more efficient to run, so that the savings over the original turbines were such that the replacement machines paid for themselves in a short time. The respondents claimed damages for the cost of replacing the original turbines, but the House of Lords refused that

In *Dalwood Marine Co. v Nordana Line AS, The Elbrus* [2009] EWHC 3394 (Comm), [2010] 2 Lloyd's Rep 315, [2010] 2 All ER (Comm) 802, the judge held that it was correct to bring into account the higher rate of hire that the shipowner had secured from a substitute charterparty when the original charterers had terminated their charter before the end of the charter term. Damages would usually be based on the market rate of a substitute charter for the remainder of the term. However, the principle in *Golden Strait Corporation v Nippon Yusen Kubishika Kaisha, The Golden Victory* [2007] UKHL 12, [2007] 2 AC 353 (see **9.4**), required the court to take account of the actual compensatory position and it followed that, since this was a benefit that could not have been secured but for the breach, it should be brought into account. Nevertheless, the rule that benefits from actions taken in mitigation of the loss must be set off against the loss, even to the point of eliminating it, applies only where there is a demonstrable link between the original breach, the mitigating steps, and the benefit accruing. A merely collateral benefit accruing as a result of a new contract entered into in an effort to mitigate would not be set off against loss claimed as a result of the breach: *Famosa Shipping Co. Ltd v Armada Bulk Carriers Ltd* [1994] 1 Lloyd's Rep 633.

The principles applicable to avoided loss and when a benefit received following the other's breach must be brought into account were considered by the Supreme Court in *Globalia Business Travel SAU of Spain v Fulton Shipping Inc of Panama* [2017] UKSC 43, [2017] 1 WLR 2581.

The case concerned an early redelivery in November 2007 in breach of a time charter that was due to expire in November 2009. The owners immediately sold the vessel for a sum in excess of US$23.7 million. The evidence showed that if the vessel had been redelivered on the agreed date in 2009 the effect of the Global Financial Crisis would have reduced its value to only US$7 million. Were the owners obliged to give credit for this substantially higher value in their damages claim for net loss of profits in the remaining two years of the charter? This would have extinguished the owners' claim. Popplewell J held that the owners' decision to sell the vessel was independent of the charterers' breach in redelivering the vessel two years early. The Court of Appeal disagreed, and held that if the claimant secured a benefit through actions in mitigation which had been caused by a breach of contract and if this action was taken 'in the ordinary course of business', the benefit would need to be brought into account when assessing the claimant's loss. The Supreme Court reinstated Popplewell J's conclusion, and held that the test was whether there was a causal link between the breach and the benefit to be brought into account. That was plainly not the case on the facts, in that the sale of the vessel could not of itself mitigate the loss of income following the breach of the charterparty.

These principles had earlier been applied by Leggatt J in *Thai Airways International Public Company Ltd v KI Holdings Co. Ltd* [2015] EWHC 1250 (Comm) so that the claimant had to account for benefits received in mitigation. The breach involved a failure to deliver aircraft seats. Thai Airways sought to recover its expenses in mitigation, including the cost of leasing a third party aircraft (circa $162 million) and the cost of purchasing alternative, more expensive, seats. Koito argued that Thai Airways' costs in mitigation should be offset against the financial benefits it had derived in the process, i.e. the profits made from operating the additional leased aircraft as well as fuel savings following from the lighter seats it had purchased, and that these eliminated the airline's losses. Leggatt J accepted that any increased profits or savings had to be deducted from the airline's losses despite the fact that this profitability resulted from acts of mitigation. He also considered that since a lease for two years would have been sufficient to mitigate, taking the lease for three years was commercially motivated and the airline could not recover the lease costs for the extra year.

Perhaps the most interesting aspect of the decision is the formulation of the burden with regard to identifying the benefits of mitigation to the non-breaching party. This burden was held to lie on the party in breach by analogy with the burden of proof in wasted expenditure cases (*Omak Maritime Ltd v Mamola Challenger Shipping Co.* [2010] EWHC 2026 (Comm), [2011] Bus LR 212 and *Yam Seng Pte Ltd v International Trade Corp Ltd* [2013] EWHC 111 (QB), [2013] 1 CLC 662, [2013] 1 All ER (Comm) 1321, see **9.3.5.3**). Since Koito had failed to show that the increased profits covered the cost of the two-year lease, Thai Airways was awarded the full cost of $107 million. Koito had also failed to adequately demonstrate fuel savings in relation to some of the alternative seats so that in addition these savings could not be offset.

9.5.3.2 Mitigation and anticipatory breach

The mitigation principle applies to breach by anticipatory repudiation (see **8.7**) as it applies to ordinary breach, but in some instances the effect of its application is rather different.

- Where the non-breaching party accepts the repudiation as terminating the contract, loss sustained is subject to the mitigation principle from the moment of that acceptance and it is not possible to wait until the date for performance due under the contract before mitigating.

- However, where the non-breaching party affirms the contract following an anticipatory breach, the rule that the loss must not be increased by taking unreasonable steps is reflected in the rule that a party may not affirm the contract and continue performance in the face of a repudiation unless that party has a legitimate interest in so doing (see **8.7.3.1**). Where the contract is affirmed, the obligation to take steps to reduce the loss that will be sustained when the time for performance comes arises only at the time for performance.

This rule is conceptually logical, in that the mitigation principle expects the claimant to take steps to reduce the loss resulting from breach. If the contract is affirmed, there will be no breach until non-performance on the due date and, until then, both breach and loss are only potential, so that there is no scope for the mitigation principle to apply.

9.5.4 Non-pecuniary loss

9.5.4.1 General limitation

As a general rule, damages cannot be recovered in contract for losses that do not affect a pecuniary interest of the claimant and, to this extent, contractual damages may under-compensate that claimant.

> **! KEY POINT**
>
> In addition to financial loss, a claimant might suffer disappointment, hurt feelings, or distress as a result of breach, but damages for such non-pecuniary losses are generally not recoverable in contract.

This general rule is said to stem from the decision of the House of Lords in *Addis v Gramophone Co. Ltd* [1909] AC 488, in which it was held that it was not possible to recover damages for the distress caused by the nature of a dismissal from employment (i.e. caused by the *manner of the breach*), as opposed to directly caused by the breach itself. This general principle was approved by the House of Lords in *Johnson v Gore Wood and Co. (a firm)* [2002] 2 AC 1.

In *Watts v Morrow* [1991] 1 WLR 1421, Bingham LJ explained that the general denial of liability for non-pecuniary loss was based 'on considerations of policy' rather than because such loss was not considered to be a foreseeable consequence of the breach.

9.5.4.2 Distress consequent on physical inconvenience

Damages for distress *are* recoverable where that distress is directly consequent on physical inconvenience caused by the breach. In *Perry v Sidney Phillips and Son* [1982] 1 WLR 1297, the Court of Appeal held that damages for distress caused by repairs necessitated following a negligent property survey were recoverable. This loss was foreseeable. This principle was also applied in *Watts v Morrow* [1991] 1 WLR 1421, to allow recovery for distress caused by the physical inconvenience of living in a property while repairs were carried out.

Distress consequent on physical inconvenience also appears to be the basis for recovery in *Hobbs v London and South Western Railway Co.* (1875) LR 10 QB 111.

> The claimant and his family were taken to the wrong station by the railway company, necessitating a walk of several miles on a wet night. The claimant recovered damages for that inconvenience.

Had the claimant mitigated his loss by hiring a cab (which, assuming that one could be found, would have been reasonable), his expenditure would clearly have been recoverable. Thus, although the loss was in fact not financial as events transpired, it was quantifiable in financial terms.

The House of Lords in *Farley v Skinner (No. 2)* [2001] UKHL 49, [2002] 2 AC 732, considered, as an alternative basis for the award of damages on the facts in that case, that the claimant could have recovered damages for distress consequent on the physical inconvenience caused by the breach of contract.

> *Farley v Skinner (No. 2)* involved a negligent survey report in relation to a house in the vicinity of Gatwick Airport. The claimant had specifically requested that the defendant investigate whether the house would be affected by aircraft noise and the surveyor had negligently reported that this noise would not be a problem. The claimant purchased the house and spent money on modernization, but, on moving in, discovered that the house was close to a navigation beacon where aircraft were stacked prior to landing and, as a result, was badly affected by aircraft noise at such times. The claimant decided not to sell, but sought damages for the breach of contract. It was found as a fact that there was no difference in value between the price paid for the house and its market value. However, the judge at first instance awarded £10,000 damages for distress consequent upon the claimant's physical discomfort caused by the aircraft noise. The majority of the Court of Appeal allowed the defendant's appeal on the basis that the distress involved no physical inconvenience. (This would appear to miss the point, since, in accordance with the terms of this exception, the distress must be *consequent on physical inconvenience caused by the breach*; it is not the case that the distress itself needs to be classified as physical.)
>
> Although the House of Lords considered that the case fell within one of the exceptional situations in which it was possible to recover damages for distress, their Lordships also considered (*obiter*) that the claimant might have recovered damages for distress consequent on physical inconvenience.

Lord Scott treated the *physical discomfort* suffered by the claimant as consequential loss, so that the distress that followed was recoverable as being within the reasonable contemplations of the parties as liable to result from this breach. He stressed that it was the *cause* of the inconvenience or discomfort that was vital, rather than assessing whether the distress itself was physical or non-physical, and this must be the correct approach. By comparison, distress or disappointment attributable only to the fact that the breach of contract has occurred is not recoverable, whereas if the breach leads to physical consequences and inconvenience, damages can be awarded to compensate for the distress that follows from those physical consequences.

9.5.4.3 Where the major or important object of the contract is to provide pleasure, relaxation, peace of mind, or freedom from molestation

In addition to distress consequent on physical inconvenience, there are other recognized instances in which damages for distress may be recovered. These exceptions were recognized by the Court of Appeal in *Bliss v South East Thames Regional Health Authority* [1987] ICR 700, which also reinforced the authority of *Addis v Gramophone Co. Ltd* [1909] AC 488 as the central principle.

Dillon LJ stated, in *Bliss* at p. 718B–C, that there were exceptions 'where the contract which has been broken was itself a contract to provide peace of mind or freedom from distress': see *Jarvis v Swans Tours Ltd* [1973] QB 233, *Hamilton-Jones v David and Snape (a firm)* [2003] EWHC 3147 (Ch), [2004] 1 WLR 924, and *Heywood v Wellers* [1976] QB 466.

In *Watts v Morrow* [1991] 1 WLR 1421, at p. 1445, Bingham LJ explained the exceptional cases in the following statement, which has subsequently been accepted as the authoritative statement of the scope of these exceptions:

> But the rule is not absolute. Where the very object of a contract is to provide pleasure, relaxation, peace of mind or freedom from molestation, damages will be awarded if the fruit of the contract is not provided or if the contrary result is procured instead.

9.5.4.3.1 Loss of expectation of pleasure or of freedom from molestation

In these exceptional situations, where the contract is intended to confer a benefit other than a pecuniary gain, damages for disappointment can be justified on the basis of compensating for the loss of expectation of that benefit (or, to put it another way, protection of the 'performance interest'). Again, these exceptions can be seen as covering distress caused by the breach rather than the manner of the breach. In *Johnson v Unisys Ltd* [2001] UKHL 9, [2003] 1 AC 518 (see **9.5.4.5**), Lord Millett explained the 'exceptional' cases such as *Jarvis v Swans Tours Ltd* [1973] QB 233 (below) not as exceptions, but as falling outside the principle in *Addis v Gramophone Co. Ltd* [1909] AC 488 altogether, because the loss (distress and disappointment) in such cases is the direct result of the breach itself, rather than the manner of the breach.

In *Jarvis v Swans Tours Ltd*, the claimant booked a winter holiday, which the defendants promised in their brochure would be like a 'house party', with special entertainment and proper facilities for skiing. The skiing facilities were in fact inadequate, the entertainment was far from special, and in the second week the 'house party' consisted of the claimant alone. The Court of Appeal held that he was entitled to recover not merely the cost of the holiday, but a similar amount again as general damages for the disappointment suffered and the loss of the entertainment that he had been promised in the brochure. Lord Denning MR pointed out that the claimant had entered the contract not merely to purchase the travel facilities and the board and lodging, but also in order to enjoy himself, and that he was entitled to compensation for the loss of that part of his expectation.

Heywood v Wellers [1976] QB 446 concerned a contract employing a solicitor for the express purpose of obtaining a non-molestation injunction against a former male friend of the claimant. The solicitor was negligent, so that no effective protection was achieved. The damages award included a sum to compensate the claimant for the distress consequent on this failure to ensure the peace of mind and freedom from molestation, which it was the purpose of the contractual duty to achieve.

Similarly, in *Demarco v Perkins* [2006] EWCA Civ 188, [2006] PNLR 27, the claimant had lost a substantial chance of obtaining an annulment of his bankruptcy through the negligence of the defendant accountants and was able to recover for the distress suffered as 'a material element in a retainer was the provision of peace of mind and the avoidance of distress'.

In *Yearworth v North Bristol NHS Trust* [2009] EWCA Civ 37, [2009] 3 WLR 118, the Court of Appeal held that contractual arrangements for the storage of sperm amounted to a contract for the provision of peace of mind, in that the purpose of the contract was to preserve the ability for the men involved to become fathers when they were about to undergo cancer treatment that would impact their fertility. It followed that modest recovery of damages for distress was possible when the storage equipment failed.

In *Halcyon House Ltd v Baines* [2014] EWHC 2216 (QB) an important purpose of a clause in a compromise agreement, by which the parties agreed not to make any disparaging or derogatory comments about each other, was interpreted as intended to provide peace of mind.

9.5.4.3.2 *Loss of amenity as a loss of expectation*

A similar rationale appears to underlie those cases in which the court awards damages in instances in which there is no difference in value and an award based on cost of cure would be out of proportion, in order to meet the claimant's particular expectation or 'consumer surplus': e.g. *Radford v De Froberville* [1977] 1 WLR 1262 (see **9.3.3.3**).

In *Ruxley Electronics and Construction Ltd v Forsyth* [1996] 1 AC 344, at p. 360H, Lord Mustill recognized the need to 'cater for those occasions where the value of the promise to the promisee exceeds the financial enhancement of his position which full performance will secure' (see **9.3.3.1** for the earlier discussion of the 'consumer surplus'). Lord Lloyd believed that, in this case, the owner's subjective appreciation of the benefit of the contract could be catered for by making a modest award (for loss of amenity) expressly in reliance on *Jarvis v Swans Tours Ltd* [1973] QB 233: see also *Jackson v Horizon Holidays Ltd* [1975] 1 WLR 1468. Lord Lloyd stated that he could live with this conclusion as 'a further inroad on the rule in *Addis'—Addis v Gramophone Co. Ltd* [1909] AC 488—although he preferred to regard it as 'a logical application or adaptation of the existing exception to a new situation'. The argument was that Mr Forsyth had contracted for a swimming pool for reasons of pleasure and, in this sense, his expectation had not been fulfilled. However, the amount awarded as damages for loss of amenity was relatively small and significantly less than the cost of cure being claimed.

The award of damages for loss of amenity was considered by Lord Steyn in *Farley v Skinner (No. 2)* [2001] UKHL 49, [2002] 2 AC 732, at [21], to 'have been authoritatively established', although in *Johnson v Gore Wood and Co. (a firm)* [2002] 2 AC 1, when the House of Lords commented on this aspect of the decision in *Ruxley*, Lord Bingham made it clear that he did not consider that it affected the general applicability of *Addis* on the facts before him (a claim for distress damages by a company shareholder in relation to the management of the company).

Despite having been 'authoritatively established', it is difficult to justify any conclusion that the award of loss of amenity is generally available outside the context of the 'pleasure' exception to *Addis*—see Poole (1996) 59 MLR 272—so that if the main purpose of the contract is not the provision of pleasure, e.g. commercial contracts, *Ruxley* cannot permit a loss of amenity award. This was confirmed explicitly in ***Regus (UK) Ltd v Epcot Solutions Ltd*** [2007] EWHC 938 (Comm), [2007] 2 All ER (Comm) 766. (The decision of the Court of Appeal—[2008] EWCA Civ 361—related to reasonableness of the exemption clause under UCTA 1977.)

> **Regus (UK) Ltd v Epcot Solutions Ltd** concerned a contract for serviced office accommodation. The air-conditioning system was defective and an inspector had recommended urgent remedial work, costing £23,500, but this was not carried out. In its claim for damages for breach of contract, the accommodation user had sought, along with damages for loss of profits, damages for distress, inconvenience, and loss of amenity in connection with the defective air-conditioning system. However, the judge held that there was no authority permitting recovery for loss of amenity where the purpose of the contract was not to provide pleasure and that **Ruxley** could not apply here. In relation to **Ruxley**, he stated, at [48]:
>
> > As I read the decision . . . the House of Lords . . . upheld, for the most part in passing, an award of damages of £2,500 for loss of pleasurable amenity [i.e. fun] of a swimming pool. This was on the basis that the contract was one to provide pleasure and amenity analogous to *Jarvis* and the holiday cases, and thus very different from the business purpose of the contract in this case. Epcot does not however appear to claim damages for loss of any subjective or idiosyncratic pleasure or amenity and it would be unusual, if not impossible for a company to do so. For the most part a company's advances and setbacks are measured in financial terms. I emphasise that I was taken to no authority on this issue.

Subsequently, in *Harrison v Shepherd Homes Ltd* [2011] EWHC 1811 (TCC), (2011) 27 Const LJ 709 (for facts see **9.3.3.4**), the judge made a clear link between loss of amenity and the need to demonstrate that one of the exceptions in *Bliss* applied. Having awarded diminution in value because the costs of cure was unreasonable, Ramsey J held that loss of amenity would usually be appropriate only where the cost of cure was unreasonable and there was no diminution in value. Nevertheless, he considered, at [264], that 'there may be a case where lesser remedial works will leave an element of loss of amenity', and that this would not involve any double recovery. On the facts the judge held that such damages were not appropriate in any event because the contract for the sale of the new homes did not contain a term to the effect that the object of the contract was to give 'pleasure, relaxation or peace of mind' and such a term should not be implied. (However, the judge did award £150 per year as damages for distress and physical inconvenience to cover 'sensory aspects' arising from the defects, such as visible defects and problems with the levels to the paths and driveways.)

9.5.4.4 The scope of the exceptions and refusal to allow distress damages in commercial claims

With the exception of these situations, the courts have refused to award damages for non-pecuniary loss, and they have consistently refused to extend the recognized scope of these exceptions despite encouragement to do so from counsel in a number of cases. This may be explained in part by the difficulty of quantification of such losses, in part by the fear of unfounded claims (since such feelings are hard to prove or disprove), and in part by the fear of double compensation (in that disappointment, etc., may be adequately compensated by an award of damages for any pecuniary interest injured by the breach).

The scope of the exceptions was believed to be limited by the need to show that the object of pleasure, peace of mind, or freedom from distress was the **very object** of the contract, i.e. the fundamental purpose of the contract: see Macdonald (1994) 7 JCL 94 and Capper (2000) 116 LQR 553.

In *Watts v Morrow* [1991] 1 WLR 1421, the Court of Appeal, placing considerable reliance on the decision in *Hayes v James and Charles Dodd* [1990] 2 All ER 815, declined to give more than a very narrow scope to the category of contracts 'to provide peace of mind or freedom from distress', and refused to regard a surveyor as having any such contractual obligation towards the purchaser of a house for whom he had prepared a report on the basis that providing 'peace of mind' was not the subject matter of a survey contract. A further example is provided by *Alexander v Rolls Royce Motor Cars* [1996] RTR 95, in which it was held that a contract for car repair was not a contract to provide freedom from worry and anxiety, since this was not the subject matter of the contract.

This restrictive interpretation enabled the courts to discount the possibility of recovery of distress damages in the case of breaches of commercial contracts, since the essential object of such contracts is not the provision of pleasure or peace of mind. Of course, as a matter of policy, there is much to be said in favour of not permitting any extension of distress damages to commercial cases.

In *Hayes v James and Charles Dodd*, Staughton LJ was very robust in dismissing such a claim for distress damages (in the context of a claim against solicitors dealing with a commercial conveyance where there had been a failure to advise that the business purchased would be landlocked). He referred to the dangers of allowing recovery of distress damages in commercial cases when he stated, at p. 823e:

> I would not view with enthusiasm the prospect that every shipowner in the Commercial Court, having successfully claimed for unpaid freight or demurrage, would be able to add a claim for mental distress suffered while he was waiting for his money.

In Staughton LJ's view, the reason for disallowing the claim was not merely a question of remoteness of damage, but one of policy. The policy was to limit recovery for mental distress to 'certain classes of case': see, more recently, *Johnson v Gore Wood and Co.* [2002] 2 AC 1, confirming this position, and Lord Scott in *Farley v Skinner (No. 2)* [2001] UKHL 49, [2002] 2 AC 732, at [82] (if the only disappointment relates to a failure to perform the contractual obligations and nothing more, then recovery is ruled out on policy grounds).

9.5.4.4.1 *More liberal interpretation of the 'objects' exception*

In light of this general approach, the decision of the House of Lords in *Farley v Skinner (No. 2)* [2001] UKHL 49, [2002] 2 AC 732, represents a more liberal interpretation of the scope of the 'objects' exception, since the House awarded distress damages on the basis that the *major or important object* of the contract was to provide pleasure, relaxation, or peace of mind. *This object no longer needs to be the sole or 'very' object of the contract.*

The crucial fact in **Farley v Skinner** (for full facts, see **9.5.4.2**) was that the claimant had specifically requested the surveyor to report on the impact of aircraft noise, so that the case could be distinguished from a general survey contract. As an alternative to the argument that damages were recoverable for distress consequent on physical inconvenience, the claimant argued that the 'objects' exception applied. However, the majority of the Court of Appeal had rejected this argument on the basis that 'the very object' of the contract was to undertake the survey with reasonable care and skill, and not to provide peace of mind. The obligation to investigate the aircraft noise was not 'the very object', but a minor aspect of the overall contractual purpose.

On appeal, the House of Lords held that because the claimant had specifically asked for confirmation on this matter, it was sufficient that the obligation to investigate the aircraft noise was a major or important part of this contract.

In practical terms, this relaxation was thought unlikely to have much impact in the absence of some specific request to give an undertaking, such as occurred on the facts in *Farley v Skinner (No. 2)*.

In addition, Lord Scott considered that such an award of damages for distress would not arise at all if there were a difference in value as a result of the breach. Lord Scott justified this conclusion by stating that any other conclusion would involve double recovery. With respect, it is difficult to see that this necessarily follows, since a claimant may suffer a reduction in the value of property *and* additional loss of satisfaction with the end product. In *Hamilton-Jones v David and Snape (a firm)* [2003] EWHC 3147 (Ch), [2004] 1 WLR 924, the court awarded damages for distress as an additional element of the damages award. In addition, in the context of a holiday contract in *Milner v Carnival plc (t/a Cunard)* [2010] EWCA Civ 389, [2010] 3 All ER 701, the Court of Appeal considered that it would technically be possible to award damages for diminution of value in the promised holiday, consequential loss, physical inconvenience and discomfort, and damages for distress, although noted the importance of ensuring that there was no duplication in relation to the different heads of loss, particularly the discomfort (physical) and distress (not turning on physical inconvenience). This was also a matter of concern in *Herrmann v Withers LLP* [2012] EWHC 1492 (Ch), [2012] PNLR 28 (facts at **9.5.4.4.3**), since it was argued that the difference in value damages relating to the house would reflect the absence of access to a garden. However, the judge considered the pecuniary and non-pecuniary losses to be distinct, and the non-pecuniary loss was suffered because the property had been purchased to live in. The purchasers would not have suffered this distress as an additional loss if the property had been purchased as an investment.

In *Farley v Skinner*, it had also been argued that damages for distress could not be awarded in relation to a breach of a qualified contractual obligation, such as the duty to exercise reasonable care and skill in carrying out a survey: *Watts v Morrow* [1991] 1 WLR 1421. The House of Lords rejected such a restriction on the basis that it should not make any difference to the recovery of distress damages whether the claimant had negotiated for a guarantee or only a qualified contractual obligation.

Finally, their Lordships rejected the argument that the claimant had forfeited any right to claim non-pecuniary damages by failing to move out of the house; such action was reasonable in the circumstances, so that the claimant had not failed in the duty to mitigate his loss.

9.5.4.4.2 Differences in approach in Farley v Skinner

There is a considerable divergence in approach, if not in outcome, between Lord Steyn (with whose reasons Lord Browne-Wilkinson agreed) and Lord Scott (who expressed the belief that he was agreeing with the reasoning of Lord Steyn).

Lord Scott appears to have been advocating a broader approach to the assessment of distress damages as part of the performance interest debate (see **9.3**). Indeed, his approach is not linked expressly to the 'objects' exception. The loss of amenity award in *Ruxley Electronics and Construction Ltd v Forsyth* [1996] 1 AC 344 was treated as a direct consequence of the failure to fulfil the performance interest (referred to as 'deprivation of a contractual benefit') and compensable on the normal basis. Lord Scott distinguished this case from a true distress damages case, in which distress is treated as a consequential loss. He then proceeded to analyse many of the damages for distress cases as being examples of 'deprivation of contractual benefit' to which normal principles for determining the measure of damages applied. This analysis also applied on the facts of *Farley v Skinner (No. 2)* [2001] UKHL 49, [2002] 2 AC 73 because of the specific request and report on the aircraft noise.

This moves determination of recovery away from the 'objects' exception and back towards general principles of recovery. It ought to follow, therefore, that recovery for distress would be more generous on the 'deprivation of contractual benefit' analysis, since the main limitation will be remoteness and not the scope of the contractual object.

9.5.4.4.3 *The subsequent application of Farley v Skinner*

In **Hamilton-Jones v David and Snape (a firm)** [2003] EWHC 3147 (Ch), [2004] 1 WLR 924, in addition to an award for her financial loss, the claimant was awarded £20,000 as damages for mental distress, on the basis that 'a major or important object of the contract' was to ensure the claimant's peace of mind through the actions of the defendant solicitors, with a view to preventing her estranged husband from removing their children from the country. The defendant failed in this duty and two of the children were removed from the jurisdiction. The claimant's peace of mind could not be the sole purpose of the contract because, under the applicable legislation, that was the protection of the child. However, Neuberger J referred to this peace of mind purpose as 'a significant reason for the claimant instructing the defendants' and concluded therefore that it 'was at least "an important" object of the contract and part of the reason for contracting', which satisfied the test for recovery stipulated in **Farley v Skinner.**

The judge made no attempt to apply Lord Scott's approach to the determination of recovery, but relied on the traditional exceptions, as interpreted and extended in *Farley v Skinner (No. 2)* [2001] UKHL 49, [2002] 2 AC 73. *Hamilton-Jones* has therefore entrenched the approach in *Farley v Skinner*, but its real significance may lie in the size of the award of damages for distress, since the usual figures awarded are on the low side, e.g. £2,500 in *Ruxley Electronics and Construction Ltd v Forsyth* [1996] 1 AC 344 (not challenged or debated as to figure on appeal) and £10,000 in *Farley v Skinner*. Lord Steyn noted that such awards 'should be restrained and modest', and Lord Scott considered £10,000 to be 'on the high side'. *Gemma Ltd v Gimson* [2004] EWHC 1982 (TCC), 97 Con LR 165, may represent a high point of likely recovery, and is based on extreme inconvenience and distress over a 90-week period. The couple (the building owners) were awarded £4,500 each, with £250 to each of their four children, totalling £10,000. Even the holiday of a lifetime in *Milner v Carnival plc (t/a Cunard)* [2010] EWCA Civ 389, [2010] 3 All ER 701, resulted in distress damages of only £8,500 for the couple affected, the Court of Appeal noting that such damages in 'honeymoon' cases seldom reached £2,000.

Recent examples demonstrating the liberality of the 'peace of mind' exception post-*Farley v Skinner* in consumer cases are provided by *Haysman v Mrs Rogers Films Ltd* [2008] EWHC 2494 (QB) and *Herrmann v Withers LLP* [2012] EWHC 1492 (Ch), [2012] PNLR 28. In *Haysman v Mrs Rogers Films Ltd*, the judge considered that one of the important objects of the contract to use the claimant's house for filming was the peace of mind to the homeowner who was permitting this activity to take place in his home. On the facts, the film company had expressly promised to indemnify against damage to the property and to restore it to its original condition, so that there may be an obligation to protect that could be seen as similar to the express undertaking to investigate the noise in *Farley v Skinner*. It followed that the case fell within the extended scope of the exception and that damages for distress were recoverable. In *Herrmann v Withers LLP*, solicitors acting for a couple in relation to a property purchase had incorrectly advised the couple that the property included a right to use the garden in the nearby square. Newey J considered that, because the garden was important to the couple when purchasing a house near a garden square, 'a major or important object' of the contract with the solicitors was 'to give pleasure, relaxation or peace of mind', and the couple would have suffered disappointment on discovering the truth.

9.5.4.5 Damages for loss of reputation

Traditionally, it has not been possible, as a general rule, to recover contractual damages for loss of reputation. Quite apart from the inevitable difficulties of causation, the problem is that such a loss could not be formulated in terms of financial interests.

Addis v Gramophone Co. [1909] AC 488 has been interpreted as authority for the fact that a claimant wrongfully dismissed in a particularly abrupt way could not recover damages for injury to his reputation by the manner of his dismissal. Lord Loreburn went on to suggest that damages were not recoverable for the increased difficulty of obtaining alternative employment and this has also been interpreted as part of the *ratio* in the case, although in *Johnson v Unisys Ltd* [2001] UKHL 9, [2003] 1 AC 518, Lord Steyn regarded the headnote as 'arguably wrong' in so far as it states that it is never possible to sue for loss of employment prospects resulting from the manner of a dismissal. In a general sense, it is possible to distinguish this type of loss relating to future employment, since it can be identified as financial loss and, in general, the law will allow damages for lost expectation (see **9.2.1**); loss of this kind is sufficiently similar for it to be difficult to justify any distinction being made. It is on this question that there has been a radical re-evaluation.

9.5.4.5.1 *Stigma compensation*

Such damages for financial loss caused by difficulty in obtaining alternative employment (so-called 'stigma compensation') were awarded by the House of Lords in *Mahmud v Bank of Credit and Commerce International SA (in liquidation)* [1998] AC 20 (also known as *Malik v BCCI*) on the basis that the employer in the case was in breach of an implied term not to conduct the business in a dishonest and corrupt way. Exceptionally, because the employee was tainted by being associated with a fraudulent business, it was reasonably foreseeable that such a breach would prejudice the future employment prospects of these employees. This was seen as an extremely limited decision, because the claim in *Mahmud* was not a claim for true distress damages and it was not based on wrongful dismissal. It was limited to a claim for continuing financial loss ('special damage') owing to an inability to obtain alternative employment resulting from breach of this particular implied term in the operation of the business.

In *Johnson v Unisys Ltd* [2001] UKHL 9, [2003] 1 AC 518, the claimant tried to use the principle in *Mahmud*, but to extend it to such damages resulting from the *manner* of a wrongful dismissal. The Court of Appeal—[1999] 1 All ER 854—had considered that such a claim was precluded by *Addis v Gramophone Co.* [1909] AC 488 and that *Mahmud* could not apply to a claim based on the *manner of dismissal*. There is also a legislative regime for compensation for unfair dismissal under which compensation is capped at a maximum amount.

In *Johnson v Unisys Ltd*, the claimant had been summarily dismissed from his employment and had obtained the statutory maximum for unfair dismissal from an employment tribunal (at the time, this was just under £11,700). He claimed that, as a result of the manner of the dismissal, he had suffered psychiatric illness and considerable distress, and had been unable to obtain employment. Accordingly, he sought to recover £400,000 in lost earnings, relying on the *Mahmud* argument, i.e. that, by dismissing him in this way, his employers had breached the implied term not to conduct themselves so as to damage the relationship of trust and confidence.

The majority of the House of Lords considered that the implied term of trust and confidence was an obligation in a continuing relationship rather than one relating to the termination of that relationship. However, the principal difficulty for the majority in accepting any common law right to such damages lay in the fact that Parliament had already put in place a statutory regime governing this compensation. Only Lord Steyn did not consider this a difficulty, but he agreed with the majority that the claimant could not recover at common law by citing the difficulties of establishing that the loss was not too remote and that it had actually been caused by the manner of the dismissal rather than the fact of dismissal.

It is unlikely, therefore, that an argument such as that in *Johnson v Unisys Ltd*, in relation to the dismissal process itself, will ever get very far because of these practical difficulties of proof: see *Bank of Credit and Commerce International SA (in liquidation) v Ali (No. 3)* [2002] EWCA Civ 82, [2002] 3 All ER 750, for evidence of the difficulties of causation even where the claim falls within *Mahmud*. The House of Lords has also made it clear that it is not possible to argue that the statutory unfair dismissal legislation permits any award for injured feelings: *Dunnachie v Kingston upon Hull City Council* [2004] UKHL 36, [2005] 1 AC 226.

The principle in *Mahmud* is therefore limited in its operation and cannot apply to losses claimed to result from the manner of a wrongful dismissal. Nevertheless, in *Eastwood v Magnox Electric plc* [2004] UKHL 35, [2005] 1 AC 503, the House of Lords was able to distinguish *Johnson v Unisys Ltd*, since the breach causing loss (financial loss owing to the psychiatric illness caused by the breach) had occurred prior to the dismissal process and so could be seen as independent of the subsequent unfair dismissal. This enabled a separate award of common law damages to be made in respect of this breach under the principle in *Mahmud* despite the existence of an award for the later unfair dismissal under the statutory scheme. In addition, in *Edwards v Chesterfield Royal Hospital NHS Foundation Trust* [2011] UKSC 58, [2012] 2 WLR 55, it was necessary to consider whether the reasoning in *Johnson* applied so as to preclude recovery of damages for loss arising from the unfair manner of a dismissal in breach of an *express* term of an employment contract. The Supreme Court held that the reasoning in *Johnson v Unisys* applied and precluded such recovery. Lord Dyson noted, at [39]:

> It is necessarily to be inferred from this statutory background that, unless they otherwise expressly agree, the parties to an employment contract do not intend that a failure to comply with contractually binding disciplinary procedures will give rise to a common law claim for damages.

Lord Dyson considered, at [51], that, in determining the application of *Johnson*:

> The question in each case is, therefore, whether or not the loss founding the cause of action flows directly from the employer's 'failure to act fairly when taking steps leading to dismissal' and 'precedes and is independent of' the dismissal process . . . In other words, the court must decide whether 'earlier events do or do not form part of the dismissal process'. This is a fact-specific question.

Although the actual decision in *Johnson v Unisys Ltd* is restrictive, it is clear that the House of Lords wished to see further movement away from *Addis*, on the basis that the employer–employee relationship had moved on in the intervening 90 years (see Lord Steyn's speech), and Lord Hoffmann's suggestion of a willingness to get around *Addis* in the context of distress damages indicates that we may yet see further relaxation of the principle where the circumstances permit. Nevertheless, the House of Lords has also applied *Addis* in the context of a claim by company shareholders in *Johnson v Gore Wood and Co. (a firm)* [2002] 2 AC 1—although, even in this decision, Lord Cooke, at p. 109, suggested that *Addis* may not be a permanent feature of English law.

9.5.4.5.2 *Instances in which damages for loss of existing reputation are recoverable*

There are a number of recognized instances of damage to an *existing* reputation.

- One such instance applies in the case of breach of a banking contract by the wrongful dishonouring of a cheque, which traditionally was limited to dishonouring the cheques of traders: *Wilson v United Counties Bank Ltd* [1920] AC 102.

In **Kpohraror v Woolwich Building Society** [1996] 4 All ER 119, the Court of Appeal extended this to non-trader clients of banks on the basis that the exception existed to protect the reputation for creditworthiness of the client. A reputation for creditworthiness is 'as important for their personal transactions' for individuals as it is for traders given the existence of central registers of credit ratings. The Court of Appeal held that since individuals might also suffer loss if their reputations were damaged by the wrongful dishonouring of cheques, there was no good reason for limiting this recovery of such damages to traders.

- Damages for loss of reputation may also be recoverable for breach of an advertising or publicity contract, where the main purpose of the contract is to promote and publicize. If the breach has the opposite effect, there is a failure of the main purpose of the contract. A good illustration of this is *Aerial Advertising Co. v Batchelors Peas Ltd (Manchester)* [1938] 2 All ER 788 (the 'one' contract law case that every law student seems to remember!).

The claimants in **Aerial Advertising Co. v Batchelors Peas Ltd (Manchester)** were to advertise the defendants' peas by flying over towns trailing a banner reading: 'Eat Batchelors' peas!' In breach of contract, the pilot flew over the main square of Salford during the two minutes' silence on Armistice Day. This caused great upset and the defendants' products were boycotted, leading to a fall in sales.

9.6 Agreed payment provisions

As in many other areas of contract law, the nineteenth-century view that contractual obligations were founded in the will of the parties resulted in the rule that the common law provisions as to the award of damages might be displaced by express agreement. The *prima facie* rule is that if the parties provide in their contract for the amount of damages to be paid upon breach, that term of the contract will be enforced to the exclusion of whatever might be the common law measure of damages. Such clauses are common in commercial contracts, especially to deal with delay in performance.

There are advantages for both parties in the use of such clauses:

- the non-breaching party is spared the effort and possible expense of proving its loss, together with the added complexities of remoteness and mitigation, so that a claim for compensation will be relatively straightforward;

- in addition, the party who must perform has clear notice of the extent of the risk in the event of non-performance; and

- the existence of such contractually agreed damages should avoid much of the disruption to the continuing relationship between the parties and the associated costs of a dispute on quantum, so that such clauses are generally regarded as efficient and desirable.

The courts have nevertheless been unwilling to allow their unfettered use on the basis that there is a danger that, where the damages payable are set too high, the clause will have a punitive effect, which would be contrary to the essential purpose of enforcement of contractual obligations (see the opening pages to **Part 3**, under heading **(b)**). Further, there is a danger that disadvantageous terms as to damages might be forced by the stronger party on the other, rather than be freely negotiated.

> **! KEY POINT**
>
> The distinction between clauses that will be enforced and those that will not is expressed as a distinction between *liquidated damages clauses* (enforceable) and *penalty clauses* (unenforceable).

A penalty has traditionally been defined as a clause designed as a threat to compel performance by penalizing the other for non-performance and as not amounting to genuine compensation because it was unrelated to the amount of the likely loss, i.e. not being a genuine pre-estimate of the likely loss or being 'an exorbitant alternative to common law damages'. It followed that a liquidated damages clause was generally defined as a clause which represented a genuine attempt to pre-estimate the loss so that it was in line with the compensatory principle.

The Supreme Court in the conjoined appeals in *Cavendish Square Holding BV v Makdessi* (the '*Makdessi* appeal', see **9.6.1.3**) and *Parking Eye Ltd v Beavis* (the '*Beavis* appeal', see **9.6.1.4**) [2015] UKSC 67, [2015] 3 WLR 1373, has now reformulated the test for a penalty. The penalty rule was concerned with two questions.

The first was the circumstances in which the rule was engaged. The Supreme Court considered that a provision could not be a penalty unless it provided an exorbitant alternative to common law damages. It followed that it had to be a provision operating on breach (see **9.6.3** for the criticisms of the implications of this which are now explained by the Supreme Court's statement of the scope of the rule). The penalty rule only regulated the remedy for breach of a primary obligation under the contract; it did not amount to a licence to review the fairness of primary contractual obligations. (In the consumer context, there is no such distinction in the regulation of obligations under the 'unfair terms' regime in Part 2 of the Consumer Rights Act 2015.) It follows that in so far as the penalty rule represents a control on contractual substance, that control is restricted to remedial provisions only and this will reduce the scope of its operation. Where there was a contractual obligation to perform an act coupled with an obligation to pay a specified sum of money if the act was not performed, the obligation to pay money was a secondary obligation capable of amounting to a penalty. By contrast if there was no obligation to perform an act but merely an obligation to a specified sum of money if the act was not performed, the payment was a conditional primary obligation and thus could not be a penalty. In order to determine into which category a payment obligation fell, it was necessary to evaluate provisions in terms of their substance rather than their form to determine whether in substance they amounted to a conditional primary obligation or a secondary obligation providing a contractual alternative to damages at common law. Although payment of money was the classic manifestation of a penalty clause, the Supreme Court recognized that other terms providing for forfeiture of property in the event of breach could also amount to penalty clauses, e.g. an obligation to transfer assets at an undervalue, forfeiture of a prepaid deposit, or, as in *Makdessi* itself, a loss of payments otherwise due. However, that depended upon whether they were primary or secondary obligations, In *Vivienne Westwood Ltd v Conduit Street Development Ltd* [2017] EWHC 350 (Ch) it was held that an agreement conferring a discount on rent payable under a lease so long as the terms of the lease were complied with was capable of being a penalty clause.

The second question was concerned with the central issue of what made a remedial contractual provision penal. The test had become too closely tied to whether the clause represented a genuine pre-estimate of loss or a penalty/deterrent to secure performance. Instead, the real question was whether the clause was penal, not whether it was a pre-estimate of loss. The fact that the clause was not a pre-estimate of loss did not, without more, mean that it was penal. To describe it as a deterrent did not add anything since a deterrent provision in a contract was only an example of a provision designed to influence conduct and was therefore no different from a contractual inducement. Neither was inherently penal or contrary to the policy of the law. The real test of a penal clause turned on whether the means by which the contracting party's conduct was to be influenced were unconscionable or extravagant and this was formulated (at [32]) as a test of whether the clause 'amounts to a secondary obligation which imposes a detriment on the contract-breaker out of all proportion to the non-breaching party's legitimate interest in the enforcement of the primary obligation'. Thus the emphasis is placed on the performance interest of the non-breaching party and the Supreme Court accepted that compensation was not necessarily the only legitimate interest that the innocent party might have in ensuring the other's performance of its primary obligations. The interest might be securing compensation for breach but there could be wider interests.

In particular, the court rejected the argument in the *Makdessi* appeal (see **9.6.1.4**) that the penalty rule should be either confined to commercial cases or abolished. The Supreme Court here held that the rule should apply in all circumstances, and that a distinction could not sensibly be drawn between consumer and commercial cases given that there could be significant imbalances in bargaining strength even in business to business contracts. The strength of the parties' bargaining positions was nevertheless a relevant consideration in determining whether a clause was in fact penal.

Alternatively, it had been argued that it should be extended (on the basis of the decision of the High Court of Australia in *Andrews v Australia and New Zealand Banking Group Ltd* (2012) 247 CLR 205) to apply when the clause was triggered by a non-breach event. However, the Supreme Court also rejected this argument as being inconsistent with English authority and was satisfied that the rule against penalties did not prevent the parties to a consumer or commercial transaction from reaching sensible arrangements for determining the consequences of a breach of contract.

Since the Supreme Court has rejected abolition but limited the scope of the rule to true remedial provisions for breach of primary contractual obligations, it is necessary to consider how future courts will approach the central question of determining whether a clause is penal.

9.6.1 Determining whether the clause is penal

It would appear that the starting point is the determination of whether the clause is penal. If it is not it will be enforceable as a liquidated damages clause. It was confirmed in *Makdessi* that a secondary obligation was valid if it constituted a genuine pre-estimate of damages likely to be suffered in the event of breach of contract, that question to be determined as a matter of construction as at the time that the clause was agreed.

Some guidelines to assist in determining this intention, set out below, were laid down by Lord Dunedin in *Dunlop Pneumatic Tyre Co. Ltd v New Garage and Motor Co. Ltd* [1915] AC 79. In this case tyres were supplied by the claimant manufacturers to dealers, and the contract of sale imposed a variety of different restrictions on the resale of the tyres. £5 per tyre compensation was payable for any breach. The House of Lords upheld the clause as a genuine pre-estimate of loss. The guidelines were endorsed by the Privy Council in *Philips Hong Kong Ltd v Attorney-General of Hong Kong* (1993) 61 BLR 49, although recognizing that they were probably easier to apply in the consumer than the commercial context. They are, however, formulated around the traditional test of whether the clause is a genuine pre-estimate of the loss. The Supreme Court in *Makdessi* considered that these guidelines had developed 'the status of a quasi-statutory code' and regretted their general applicability when compared to their preferred approach, namely that of Lord Atkinson in *Dunlop* who had concentrated more on the legitimate interest driving the provision in question—and specifically on the facts in *Dunlop*, the interest that Dunlop had in preventing undercutting of their listed price. The test laid down by the Supreme Court in *Makdessi* was whether the secondary obligation in question imposed a detriment out of all proportion to the innocent party's 'legitimate interest' in the enforcement of the primary obligation. If the clause had a purpose other than a desire to recover compensation, e.g. to secure the innocent party's interest in the due performance of the contract, and the sum was not exorbitant or unconscionable, then it would not be construed as a penalty.

9.6.1.1 Lord Dunedin's guidelines in *Dunlop Pneumatic Tyre v New Garage and Motor*

- *The clause will be a penalty if the sum payable is 'extravagant and unconscionable' by comparison with the greatest loss that might be caused by the breach.*

In many cases, this rule will be simple to apply but it is significant that *Makdessi* requires a rejection of the language of pre-estimates of loss in favour of the language of extravagance as compared with a norm. In *Philips Hong Kong Ltd v Attorney-General of Hong Kong*, it was held that comparisons must be made in respect of reasonably likely eventualities, and it would not be adequate proof that a clause amounts to a penalty to show a serious disparity between amounts recoverable and loss actually sustained in wholly unlikely, hypothetical situations. The Privy Council accepted that it would be very difficult to draft a clause that would never operate in a penal way. Lord Woolf also stressed that in a commercial contract, in the absence of blatant domination by one party over the other, the courts should not be as ready to conclude that a clause is penal because of the need for certainty in the commercial context. A test of extravagance adopts a more 'broad brush' evaluation of the sum stated in the clause, in line with the *Philips Hong Kong* approach.

The *Philips Hong Kong* principle was subsequently confirmed in *McAlpine Capital Projects Ltd v Tilebox Ltd* [2005] EWHC 281 (TCC), [2005] BLR 271. The judge noted that, since a penalty clause is an anomaly, the courts were predisposed to enforce agreed damages clauses as liquidated damages, particularly where the agreement was made in a commercial context between two parties of equal bargaining power. In *Cenargo Ltd v Izar Construcciones Navales SA* [2002] EWCA Civ 524, [2002] CLC 1151, the Court of Appeal (*obiter*) also adopted the approach in *Philips* and considered that, in the commercial context, an agreed damages clause should not be tested against trifling breaches causing trifling loss. The clause in question therefore needed to be construed as applying only to major breaches, for which it would be a genuine pre-estimate of the loss.

- *Where the breach consists of not paying a sum of money and the amount payable under the clause upon breach is greater than the sum owed, the clause will be a penalty.*

- *Where the contract provides for the same amount to be payable as damages in the event of several different types of breach, some of which may result in serious and others only trifling damage, it is presumed that the clause is a penalty.*

The rationale of this presumption is simply that it is unlikely that each type of breach will result in exactly the same degree of loss, so that a clause with multiple applications and single sum is unlikely to represent a genuine attempt to pre-estimate the loss. It might also be argued that there would be different interests in performance so that different forms of protecting the interest would be expected.

- *Finally, Lord Dunedin pointed out that the fact that the loss is difficult or impossible to pre-estimate does not of itself turn every liquidated damages clause into a penalty.*

In **Dunlop Pneumatic Tyre Co. Ltd v New Garage and Motor Co. Ltd**, the contract contained a provision providing for a payment of £5 per tyre in 'liquidated damages' if any tyre was sold at below the list price. The House of Lords held that this was a liquidated damages clause despite the fact that precise quantification of Dunlop's loss in these circumstances would have been difficult, and the £5 figure was only a rough and ready way of estimating it. The £5 figure was reasonable in the circumstances and represented 'the true bargain between the parties'. Lord Atkinson had looked behind the clause to the underlying rationale for its inclusion and considered that it was Dunlop's attempt to prevent undercutting and this legitimate interest was not out of line with the sum agreed to be paid.

The decision of Jackson J in *McAlpine Capital Projects Ltd v Tilebox Ltd* confirms that an objective test is applied when determining whether an agreed damages clause is penal. The test does not turn on the question of bona fides and the honesty of the party in question. In addition, it was important to stress that the genuine pre-estimate of loss did not have to coincide with the actual loss suffered in order to confirm the clause as liquidated damages, i.e. the estimate did not need to be correct. The clause would fail to be a genuine pre-estimate of the loss only if there is an unacceptable difference between the estimate and the likely damages. The unacceptable difference could be put more succinctly as 'extravagance'.

9.6.1.2 The relationship with commercial justification in the commercial context

After *Philips Hong Kong*, subsequent case law clarified the position in the commercial context with the case law applying a two-stage approach before concluding that any clause in the commercial context was a penalty:

1. Was the clause extravagant or unconscionable by comparison with the actual loss so that its function was to deter breach?

2. Could the clause be rescued from being a penalty as fulfilling a commercial or economic function, i.e. on an assessment of the contract as a whole were there balancing advantages in the form of obligations placed on the other party which counter-balanced the clause?

In *Murray v Leisureplay plc* [2005] EWCA Civ 963, [2005] IRLR 946, the Court of Appeal had to consider whether a clause in a service agreement, providing for the payment of one year's gross salary in the event of termination of the employment without a year's notice, constituted an unenforceable penalty clause. The conclusions of the Court of Appeal reinforce the position that, in a commercial contract, it will be difficult to argue that a clause is penal. The Court of Appeal held that the employee would have to mitigate by giving credit for any salary that he could reasonably have earned in the remainder of the one-year period, but the comparison between that figure and the one-year gross salary was not conclusive on the question of whether the clause was imposed as a deterrent. Instead, it was clear that the context for the agreement was commercial and the employee had been able to negotiate its terms. There were balancing advantages to the employer and balancing disadvantages to the employee, and the employer had freely agreed to this figure as compensation without any discount for mitigation. Therefore the Court of Appeal concluded that, in all of the circumstances, the employer had not discharged the burden of showing that the clause was not a genuine pre-estimate of the loss and the clause was enforceable.

The principles advanced in *Murray v Leisureplay* were applied in *Azimut-Benetti SpA v Healey* [2010] EWHC 2234 (Comm), [2011] 1 Lloyd's Rep 473. The clause in a commercial contract to build a yacht enabled the builder to terminate the contract and recover 20 per cent of the contract price if the employer were to fail to make regular payments. It was clear that the contract placed obligations on both parties and had been freely entered after the benefit of expert representation. Accordingly, it was not the role of the courts to strike out a clause, the dominant purpose of which was not to deter the other from breach and which was commercially justifiable on a reading of the contract as a whole.

In *M. & J. Polymers Ltd v Imerys Minerals Ltd* [2008] EWHC 344 (Comm), [2008] 1 Lloyd's Rep 541, [2008] 1 All ER (Comm) 893, on the evidence it was clear that the 'take or pay' clause was commercially justifiable, did not amount to oppression, was negotiated and freely entered into between parties of comparable bargaining power, and did not have the predominant purpose of deterring a breach of contract or acting as a provision '*in terrorem*'.

The same policy prevailed in *Meretz Investments NV v ACP Ltd* [2006] EWHC 74 (Ch), [2007] Ch 197. The question was whether a leaseback option clause (providing for the transfer of the property from one party to another in the event of breach through failure to develop in time) in an agreement for the sale of a development lease amounted to a penalty. It was capable in principle of being a penalty since it was not intended to compensate for loss and could be seen as an attempt to penalize the other for breach. However, Lewison J stated, at [349]:

But that is only the starting point for the inquiry whether it is a penalty. To characterise a clause as a penalty, with the consequence that the court will refuse to enforce it, is a blatant interference with freedom of contract, and should normally be reserved for cases of oppression. There is, in my judgment, nothing inherently oppressive in a contractual term which has the effect of precluding one party to the contract from continuing to enjoy benefits under the contract at a time when he is not adhering to his own obligations. That, as it seems to me, is the substance of the lease-back option.

In addition, there were other factors that favoured the clause not being a penalty, including the fact that it is common for a development lease to be capable of termination if the developer does not develop, the fact that only a small initial consideration had been given so that the best hope of a return was completion of the development, and the fact that the time limit on development was subject to various extension possibilities.

However, it is clear that there are limits even in the commercial context and, in *Jeancharm Ltd v Barnet Football Club* [2003] EWCA Civ 58, 92 Con LR 26, the Court of Appeal held that where a clause in a commercial contract was very clearly not a genuine pre-estimate of the likely loss, it could not be rescued.

> The clause in question provided for interest at 260 per cent per annum for late payment to the supplier. The supplier sought to argue that it was necessary to assess this clause as one of several clauses allocating risks between the parties in a commercial contract and was balanced by the existence of a clause whereby it had to pay 20p per garment per day if the goods (football kits) were delivered late, i.e. this was not a situation of dominance by one commercial party over another. The Court of Appeal refused to accept that this made any difference to the fundamental principle that if a clause was very obviously not a genuine pre-estimate of loss, then it was an invalid penalty. This is a clear example of extravagance that was not rescued by the alleged commercial justification.

9.6.1.3 Protecting legitimate interests in performance

The Supreme Court in *Cavendish Square Holding BV v Makdessi* [2015] UKSC 67, [2015] 3 WLR 1373 recognized the broader contractual interests and the objectives underpinning the inclusion of the particular clauses but considered that the clauses did not fall within the scope of the penalty rule because they concerned primary contractual obligations. However, views were expressed to the effect that the clauses were, even if secondary obligations, not penal.

> In *Cavendish Square Holding BV v Makdessi* (the '*Makdessi* appeal') [2015] UKSC 67, [2015] 3 WLR 1373, Makdessi entered into an agreement with Cavendish whereby, following extensive negotiations over a six-month period that had been conducted through highly experienced lawyers, Makdessi agreed to sell a controlling stake in his marketing and communications company. The price was payable in instalments and reflected, to a large extent, the existing goodwill in this business. The terms of the agreement between the parties sought to protect this goodwill. In particular, breaches of the non-competition clause by Makdessi would mean that he would not be entitled to receive the interim and/or the final instalment payments (clause 5.1) and that he granted Cavendish an option to purchase his remaining shares at their net asset value price, i.e. at a price excluding any value for the goodwill (clause 5.6).
>
> Makdessi admitted that he had committed a breach through his ongoing, although unpaid, involvement in a company called Carat. This invoked clauses 5.1 and 5.6 but he argued that both clauses were unenforceable penalties because the consequence of their application was extreme financial loss for him, e.g. the operation of clause 5.1 would cost him over $40 million and the price for the shares in the compulsory sale would be greatly reduced if no account was taken of the value of the goodwill. Cavendish, on the other hand, denied that the clauses were penal on the basis that the contract as a whole represented a negotiated, and freely entered into, commercial bargain and that the purpose of these clauses was to protect the goodwill in the marketing business being purchased which, as a major part of the price, would have been negatively impacted by any breach of covenant of the type contemplated.

The Supreme Court held that clause 5.1 was a price adjustment clause so that it constituted a primary obligation, rather than a secondary provision. Even if it was a secondary obligation, it would not have been void: Cavendish had a legitimate interest in the observance of the restrictive covenants which extended beyond the recovery of its loss and since the clause amounted to a carefully negotiated agreement between informed and legally advised parties at arm's length, the clause could not be regarded as extravagant, exorbitant, or unconscionable. Clause 5.6, which contained a price formula for the sale of retained shares, was also a primary obligation. It did not represent the estimated loss attributable to the breach but it did reflect the reduced price with Cavendish would have been prepared to pay for the business in the event of competitive behaviour of the type undertaken by Makdessi. It was therefore not a penalty clause.

The ruling thus turned on the finding that the clause was not a penalty clause at all. *Makdessi* was distinguished in *Vivienne Westwood Ltd v Conduit Street Development Ltd* [2017] EWHC 350 (Ch), where a clause giving the tenant a discounted rent if the terms of the lease were complied with was held to be penal in nature. Unlike the provisions in *Makdessi*, the clause did not constitute a price variation clause designed to protect the landlord's interests, but rather was a secondary obligation. It was also a penalty in that the discount was removed for any breach, trivial or otherwise, and with retrospective effect back to the date on which the lease commenced.

The language of legitimate interest has therefore replaced that of commercial justification. These are not the same since the emphasis has now altered to focusing on the position and perspective of the non-breaching party rather than analysing the clause in the context of other provisions which may alter the initial interpretation of extravagance. Although the Supreme Court is correct to conclude that the penalty rule regulates only the contractual remedy, that remedy is best understood in the context of the other contractual provisions rather than as a provision in the abstract.

9.6.1.4 The penalty rule in the consumer context

In **ParkingEye Ltd v Beavis** (The '*Beavis* appeal') [2015] UK SC 67, [2015] 3 WLR 1373, Mr Beavis parked at a retail park. The car park operator for this retail park was paid a fixed weekly amount to oversee the car park and was obliged by the terms of its contract to keep it as a free parking facility. It was allowed to retain any parking charges collected for breaches of the car parking rules. Notices in the car park were clear about the charge imposed if the period of free parking was exceeded. Mr Beavis left his car in the car park for longer than the permitted two hours of free parking and was subject to the charge—£85, reduced to £50 for prompt payment. He refused to pay this sum and was sued by the parking company, ParkingEye, for breach of the parking contract. Mr Beavis argued that he did not need to pay the charge because it was an unenforceable penalty on the basis that car park operator had suffered no financial loss and therefore the £85 could not be a genuine pre-estimate of the likely loss due to his breach in overstaying, and in any event it was not binding on him as an unfair contract term within the relevant consumer legislation (then the UTCCR 1999).

It was held that while the penalty rule was plainly engaged, the £85 charge was not a penalty. Although the claimant was not liable to suffer loss as a result of overstaying motorists, it had a legitimate interest in charging them which extended beyond the recovery of any loss. There was no reason to suppose that £85 was out of all proportion to the claimant's interests. The charge was neither extravagant nor unconscionable.

The Supreme Court again looked at the purpose underpinning the imposition of the charge and concluded that there were two main objectives which the court considered to be perfectly reasonable: (i) to manage the efficient use of parking space in the interests of the nearby retail outlets and of their customers, and (ii) to provide an income stream to enable ParkingEye to meet the costs of operating the scheme and make a profit. ParkingEye therefore had a legitimate interest in charging overstaying motorists which extended beyond the recovery of any loss and there was no reason to suppose that £85 was out of all proportion to ParkingEye's interests. The court noted the fact that consumer motorists regularly used the car park knowing of the charge and took the risk that they would need to pay £85 if they overstayed. It was also the case that similar parking charges applied elsewhere. The charge was therefore no higher than was necessary to achieve the objectives and was not a penalty.

Six of the seven Justices also considered that the charge did not infringe the UTCCR 1999 as being an unfair term because any imbalance in the parties' positions was not 'contrary to the requirements of good faith' given Parking Eye's legitimate interest in managing the car park for the benefit of all users and the fact that the charge was not higher than was necessary to protect that interest.

9.6.2 The effect of a finding that the clause is penal

9.6.2.1 Clauses which are penal

If a clause is penal it will be unenforceable. Until *Jobson v Johnson* [1989] 1 WLR 1026, it had largely been assumed that classification of a term as a penalty resulted in the clause being wholly unenforceable and the non-breaching party being left to recover unliquidated damages at common law to compensate for its actual loss. However, in *Jobson v Johnson*, the Court of Appeal held that it is for the court, in the exercise of its equitable jurisdiction against penalties, to enforce the penal clause only to an extent commensurate with the actual loss sustained by the non-breaching party, i.e. the penalty is unenforceable beyond the actual loss suffered: *per* Nicholls LJ at p. 1040. Of course, in many cases, the distinction is of no relevance, for the quantification of damages payable would be the same in each case. But, in *Jobson v Johnson*, the Court of Appeal relied on the exact nature of this equitable jurisdiction to impose complex terms on the claimant's right to a remedy, involving an election between alternative modes of proceeding, which went way beyond the mere recovery of damages.

To summarize the position:

- *If the actual loss is lower than the penalty amount, only the actual loss can be recovered because the penalty is invalid.*

- *It should follow that if the actual loss is greater than the penalty amount, the non-breaching party should be able to claim its higher actual loss.*

This conclusion was given some support by the decision in *Wall v Rederiaktiebolaget Luggude* [1915] 3 KB 66, but provoked some considerable academic debate: see Hudson (1974) 90 LQR 31 and (1975) 91 LQR 25, Gordon (1974) 90 LQR 296, and Barton (1976) 92 LQR 20. Such a conclusion encourages the non-breaching party whose actual loss is higher than the penalty amount to argue that an agreed damages clause is an unenforceable penalty: see e.g. the argument in *Cellulose Acetate Silk Co. Ltd v Widnes Foundry (1925) Ltd* [1933] AC 20.

In the context of consumer contracts (see **7.6**), penalties may additionally be unenforceable as 'unfair' terms. The CRA 2015 contains a list of terms which may be regarded as unfair (Sch. 2,

Part 1), including para. 6 which requires 'a consumer who fails to fulfil his obligations under the contract to pay a disproportionately high sum in compensation'.

In **Munkenbeck and Marshall v Harold** [2005] EWHC 356 (TCC), a term providing for interest to be payable at 8 per cent over base in the event of late payment was held to be unfair within the Unfair Terms in Consumer Contracts Regulations (UTCCR) 1999 (the previous legislative regulation which was revoked and replaced by Part 2 of the CRA 2015). It was considered to be onerous and unusual, and to cause an imbalance contrary to the good faith requirement since there was no similar term in respect of monies that might fall due to the consumer. However, the interest clause did not constitute a penalty because, in the light of the relevant rate of interest under the late-payment legislation, it could not be said that the figure in question did not represent a genuine pre-estimate of the damage likely to be suffered by the claimant architects in the event of non-payment by a client. Thus, on the facts, a liquidated damages clause was held to be an unfair term within the applicable consumer unfair terms legislation even though it was not a penalty in the common law sense (see **7.6**).

9.6.2.2 Liquidated damages

An agreed damages clause will be enforced by the courts unless it falls foul of the rule against penalties (see **9.6**). A remedial clause which does not fall foul of the penalty rule will therefore be enforceable by default as liquidated damages. One of the main values of liquidated damages clauses is that they encourage consideration of the contractual risks and the formulation of an attempt to protect legitimate interests in performance through an agreed figure or formula. The courts should therefore give effect to this and *the liquidated sum will be payable whether the actual loss is greater or smaller than this stipulated sum*.

In **Cellulose Acetate Silk Co. Ltd v Widnes Foundry (1925) Ltd** [1933] AC 20, the contract contained a term providing for damages for late performance to be paid 'by way of penalty' at a rate of £20 per week. The actual loss for a delay of 30 weeks was £5,850. The House of Lords held that, despite the designation of this clause as a penalty, it was in fact a genuine pre-estimate of the likely loss resulting from delay and so was a liquidated damages clause. It therefore followed that the non-breaching party could recover only £600 (£20 × 30).

9.6.2.3 Distinguishing liquidated damages and limitation clauses

One function of a liquidated damages clause may be to keep the compensation payable upon breach below the amount of the loss actually sustained. For the party who must perform, the advantage of knowing the precise extent of the risk of non-performance usually lies in knowing that the risk is limited. Thus, in *Cellulose Acetate Silk Co. Ltd v Widnes Foundry (1925) Ltd* [1933] AC 20, damages payable under the clause amounted to £600, while the actual loss was £5,850. Ironically, it was the non-breaching party who sought to avoid the clause on the ground that it was a 'penalty', a threat to compel him to perform, so that he could recover his actual loss.

Cases of this kind raise the question of whether liquidated damages clauses are a class of exemption clause, subject to the legislative controls that apply to such clauses (see generally **7.4**). In *Suisse Atlantique Société d'Armement Maritime SA v NV Rotterdamsche Kolen Centrale* [1967] 1 AC 361 (see **7.3.3**), it was suggested that such a liquidated damages clause was not a limitation clause, since it fixed the amount payable irrespective of loss, so that the sum would be payable even if the loss were less than the amount stipulated. A limitation clause simply puts a ceiling (or upper limit) on the loss recoverable, and if the loss is below that amount, only the actual loss is recoverable. Nevertheless, a liquidated damages clause, such as that in *Cellulose Acetate Silk*, may operate in practice as a limitation clause. Thus the area of overlap between limitation clauses and liquidated damages clauses may require further examination, and perhaps reform (see **9.6.3**). (Of course, in the consumer context, a liquidated damages clause can be assessed as an unfair term under Part 2 of the CRA 2015.)

9.6.3 A critique of the scope of the penalty rule: the penalty rule applies to sums payable on breach

The Supreme Court in *Makdessi v Cavendish Square Holding BV v Makdessi* [2015] UKSC 67, [2015] 3 WLR 1373, has confirmed that the penalty rule applies only where the sum specified as agreed damages is payable on breach. This can be justified in light of the Supreme Court's assessment of the scope of application of the penalty rule and the fact that it applies only to agreed damages clauses which are remedial in nature and as an alternative to common law damages on breach.

Therefore if an agreed sum is penal in nature, but payable on some event other than breach, it will remain payable: see *Export Credit Guarantee Department v Universal Oil Products Co.* [1983] 1 WLR 399 (HL); *UK Housing Alliance Ltd v Francis* [2010] EWCA Civ 117, [2010] Bus LR 1034, [2010] 3 All ER 519, involving a sale and leaseback contract under which final payment was not payable on breach, but on exercise of a right to terminate a tenancy after obtaining a possession order; and *Lehman Brothers Special Financing Inc. v Carlton Communications Ltd* [2011] EWHC 718 (Ch), in which a clause applying to events of default where the triggering event was bankruptcy and not breach of contract was not penal or oppressive. This position was also accepted in *Berg v Blackburn Rovers Football Club & Athletic plc* [2013] EWHC 1070 (Ch), [2013] IRLR 537, in the context of a sum payable under the provisions of a termination clause to a dismissed manager of a football club. Dismissal in accordance with the provisions of the termination clause was not a breach of contract.

This is unsatisfactory and leads to all sorts of fine distinctions in practice, e.g. *Alder v Moore* [1961] 2 QB 57, in which the promise was interpreted as a promise to repay £500 if the defendant played football again, rather than a promise not to play with a £500 penalty if the promise was breached. This is little more than an exercise in semantics, although the outcome was that the penalty rule did not apply and the £500 had to be repaid. The exercise of construction can also operate to avoid the penalty rule, e.g. in *Euro London Appointments Ltd v Claessens International Ltd* [2006] EWCA Civ 385, [2006] 2 Lloyd's Rep 436, in which a clause in an employment agency contract provided that payment had to be made within seven days of the date of the invoice and that there would be no refund of fees (available on a sliding scale) if arranged employment were to end prematurely, unless the payment term had been complied with. The invoice was not paid, but the client sought a refund. The judge had considered that the refund clause was a disguised penalty clause, but the Court of Appeal held that the seven-day requirement was not an obligation (i.e. it required no payment of money in itself); it was merely a condition precedent to the ability to secure a refund. In addition, if the client failed to pay within the seven days, there was no breach of any obligation in the refund clause. It followed that the refund clause could not be a penalty payable on breach.

These artificial constructions may cease after *Makdessi* and the emphasis on substance over form in identifying those terms which are remedial rather than primary obligations.

The fact that the penalty rule applies only on breach also has the potential to cause particular difficulties in the context of minimum payment clauses in the event of termination of hire purchase agreements.

- If the customer gives notice to terminate the agreement early, the contract may provide for the customer to make payment of a minimum sum as compensation for loss of the agreement. Since this is a non-breach event, the penalty rule will not apply to this payment.

- However, if the customer were to default on the payments under the agreement, the penalty rule would apply to this breach and render the minimum payment clause unenforceable.

This was criticized in *Bridge v Campbell Discount Co. Ltd* [1962] AC 600, Harman LJ referring to it as a 'paradox'. In the Law Commission's Working Paper *Penalty Clauses and Forfeiture of Monies Paid*, Law Com. No. 61 (1975), para. 26, the Commission recommended the abolition of this arbitrary distinction, so that the penalty rule 'should be applied wherever the object of the disputed contractual obligation is to secure the act or result which is the true purpose of the contract'. However, no action was taken on this recommendation and the House of Lords, in *Export Credit Guarantee Department v Universal Oil Products Co.* [1983] 1 WLR 399, confirmed the restriction on the application of the penalty rule to breaches of contractual obligations.

Schedule 2, Part 1, para. 6, of the CRA 2015 provides that, in consumer contracts, a term may be unfair if it requires any consumer 'who *fails to fulfil his obligations* under the contract to pay a disproportionately high sum in compensation' (emphasis added). It therefore appears that the same restriction applies in the consumer context.

9.6.3.1 Bank charges

The body previously charged with monitoring unfair terms in consumer contracts (i.e. the forerunner of the Competition and Markets Authority (CMA)), the Office of Fair Trading (OFT), had argued that since the amount of bank charges levied by banks on customers was not a genuine pre-estimate of the likely loss (i.e. administrative costs, etc.) to the bank in the event that the customer's account was overdrawn, such charges amounted to an unenforceable penalty payable on breach. However, the banks argued that since customers were not prohibited from becoming overdrawn, payment of this charge did not arise through breach.

In *Office of Fair Trading v Abbey National plc* [2008] EWHC 2325 (Comm), [2009] 1 All ER (Comm) 717, the OFT had argued that a term governing a bank account whereby the customer was prohibited from giving an instruction for payment when the customer did not have the funds to cover the payment in the account and had no agreed overdraft was penal in nature and imposed a charge upon breach. The banks argued that any charge would be payable when the overdraft was provided to cover this payment instruction and not on the breach itself. Accordingly, they did not consider that it could be penal. Andrew Smith J held that it did not follow that the penalty rule had no application to benefits received from wrongdoing short of a breach, e.g. obtaining an overdraft through the use of a cheque backed by a cheque guarantee card. The judge also considered that a sum could be penal if payable on an event that might not be a breach of contract, if the reality was that it became payable upon a breach. Nevertheless, he considered that the OFT's arguments involved strained constructions of wording and held that the banks were entitled to declarations that the terms, and charges imposed under the terms, were not capable of amounting to penalties at common law. The judge had already rejected a claim in previous proceedings that the legislation regulating unfair terms in consumer contracts at the time (the UTCCR 1999) had removed the application of the common law penalty doctrine in the context of consumer contracts: [2008] EWHC 875 (Comm), [2008] 2 All ER (Comm) 625. See also [2009] EWHC 36 (Comm) for declarations and, in some instances, refusal of declarations that conditions were not penal. (For arguments relating to unfair terms and the current legislation controlling the use of unfair terms, see Part 2 of the CRA 2015, see **7.6**.)

However, the need for the bank charges to be payable on breach in order to invoke the penalty rule no longer seems to apply in Australia, since the High Court of Australia in *Andrews v Australia and New Zealand Banking Group Ltd* [2012] HCA 30, (2012) 290 ALR 595, considered that such a restriction had no historical basis. Equity had granted relief against penalties on the failure of conditions in bonds that did not constitute breaches of contract. Nevertheless, although the High Court of Australia decided that the rule against penalties could apply to these bank fees, it did not hold that the bank fees were penalties. The Supreme Court in *Cavendish Square Holding BV v Makdessi* refused to extend the operation of the penalty rule to non-breach events given the weight of authority in England supporting its application to breach events and the court's own explanation of such clauses as providing an alternative to common law damages.

9.6.4 Deposits, prepayments, and relief from forfeiture

Closely related to the rule against penalty clauses and the rules governing restitution of sums paid under contracts (see **10.5**) are those rules that govern claims to recover various forms of advance payment made in respect of a contract. The law in this area, like the law relating to penalty clauses, is not always logically defensible.

9.6.4.1 Deposits

Money paid in advance that is expressly designated as a deposit is not normally recoverable in the event of breach of the contract by the paying party even if the payee has not suffered any loss as a result of the breach. Authority for this rule is well established: in *Howe v Smith* (1884) 27 Ch D 89, the element of penalty embodied in the rule was invoked as a desirable incentive to performance, 'an earnest to bind the bargain'. In *Damon Compania Naviera SA v Hapag-Lloyd International SA, The Blankenstein* [1985] 1 WLR 435, the Court of Appeal, confirming the rule, also held that if the deposit remained unpaid at the time of the breach, the non-breaching party was entitled to bring an action to recover payment (see also *Griffon Shipping LLC v Firodi Shipping Ltd, The Griffon* [2013] EWCA Civ 1567, [2014] 1 All ER (Comm) 593, [2014] 1 CLC 1).

The main form of potential relief against loss of a deposit applies to contracts for the sale or exchange of interests in land since, by s. 49(2) of the Law of Property Act 1925, the court may, if it thinks fit, order the repayment of any deposit. There are clear differences between deposits and penalties, in that a deposit is payable before breach, whereas a penalty is a sum payable on breach. However, their purpose is similar, in that they are aimed at guaranteeing performance of the contract. Nevertheless, although the rule against recovery of deposits may be equivalent to the enforcement of penalty clauses, in that the amount of the deposit may far exceed the actual loss to the party entitled to retain it, it had been thought—subject only to an *obiter* statement of Denning LJ in *Stockloser v Johnson* [1954] 1 QB 476, at p. 491—that the rule against penalties could not apply to deposits. The Law Commission's Working Paper on

Penalty Clauses, Law Com. No. 61 (see **9.6.3**) had made a recommendation that the penalty rule should apply to all deposits, but that came to nothing.

However, in *Workers Trust and Merchant Bank Ltd v Dojap Investments Ltd* [1993] AC 573, the Privy Council imposed an important limitation on the general principle. Lord Browne-Wilkinson accepted that a deposit is not normally recoverable, because it is given in earnest of performance. Nevertheless, he went on to say, at p. 579G, that 'it is not possible for the parties to attach the incidents of a deposit to the payment of a sum of money unless such sum is reasonable as earnest money'. In the particular case, a deposit of 25 per cent had been demanded when the prevailing local rate was 10 per cent. The Privy Council advised that the deposit was unreasonable and that the deposit should be repaid subject to a set-off for any loss actually sustained.

9.6.4.2 Prepayments not expressed to be deposits

Where part of the contract price has been paid in advance, *without that payment being expressed to be in the nature of a deposit or subject to express forfeiture*, the payment may be recovered upon termination of the contract, subject to any set-off that there may be for performance rendered before the time of discharge: *Dies v British & International Mining & Finance Corporation Ltd* [1939] 1 KB 724 and *Rover International Ltd v Cannon Film Sales Ltd (No. 3)* [1989] 1 WLR 912). It is therefore vital to be able to distinguish between deposits (above) and mere prepayments, although *Dies v British & International Mining & Finance Corporation Ltd* is also authority for the proposition that, in the event of doubt, the payment will be treated as a prepayment rather than as a deposit to be forfeited on breach.

9.6.4.3 Relief from forfeiture

Where breach results in the breaching party losing the benefit of all payments or rights under the contract in a manner that is disproportionate to the actual breach or the loss caused by it, the law may provide relief from that forfeiture, e.g. preventing payments made by a defaulting party from being lost. Such relief is closely related to the rule against penalties, although the technical requirements for its application are very different.

There is an equitable jurisdiction in the court to provide relief from forfeiture in some circumstances, but the courts have taken take a very restrictive view of their powers in this area. Consequently, there are considerable advantages in being able to characterize a clause as amounting to a penalty, rather than merely leading to forfeiture, since relief of some kind is then immediately available: *Jobson v Johnson* [1989] 1 WLR 1026 (see **9.6.2.1**). There would seem to be no functional difference between a deposit (as described in **9.6.4.1**) and an express clause allowing forfeiture of prepayments. However, it appears that the jurisdiction to relieve against forfeiture does not extend to deposits as such—although Lord Browne-Wilkinson in *Workers Trust and Merchant Bank Ltd v Dojap Investments Ltd* [1993] AC 573 clearly indicates that it does apply to forfeiture of 'unreasonable deposits'. The modern foundation for the equitable jurisdiction is *Stockloser v Johnson* [1954] 1 QB 476. The Court of Appeal held that a clause providing for forfeiture of prepayments would not be enforced if it were penal, and if to enforce it would be oppressive and unconscionable. Denning LJ had suggested, at p. 491, that a buyer who has already paid 90 per cent of the purchase price by nine equal payments, but lacks the means to pay the last instalment, deserves relief 'against forfeiture of the money on such terms as may be just'. However, relief against forfeiture of advance instalments paid for the purchase of plants was refused in *Cadogan Petroleum Holdings Ltd v Global Process Systems LLC* [2013] EWHC 214 (Comm), [2013] 1 CLC 721, [2013] 2 Lloyd's Rep 26. Eder J noted that such a claim was very difficult to make in a commercial context and would generally be limited to providing more time to pay. Assuming that there was a discretion to order relief against forfeiture in the form of repayment, this was not a case in which justice demanded it given that the plants had not been resold and the price that might be achieved was uncertain.

Relief will not be granted if the primary object of the transaction would thereby be defeated: *Shiloh Spinners Ltd v Harding* [1973] AC 691, at p. 723. However, more significantly, the House of Lords has ruled that the power to provide relief from forfeiture may be exercised only in relation to possessory or proprietary rights: *Scandinavian Trading Tanker Co. AB v Flota Petrolera Ecuatoriana* [1983] 2 All ER 763. It seems that this restriction is part of a more general policy of limiting the scope of relief from forfeiture, largely for reasons of commercial certainty. The decision of the Privy Council in *Union Eagle Ltd v Golden Achievement Ltd* [1997] AC 514 provides a good illustration of this principle.

In **Union Eagle Ltd v Golden Achievement Ltd**, time was of the essence in relation to completion of the purchase of a flat and there was a provision allowing for forfeiture of the deposit in the event of any failure to comply with the contract terms. The purchaser was ten minutes late in tendering the purchase price and sought relief against forfeiture in the form of an extension of the time for completion. The Privy Council refused this relief, citing the need for certainty.

In essence, the Privy Council was being asked to relieve against the immediate right to terminate the contract for failure to comply with the essential time condition when it was important, for reasons of certainty, for the vendor to know whether he could resell the flat. However, it would seem questionable whether that relief should also mean that the vendor can keep a reasonable deposit.

MULTIPLE-CHOICE QUESTIONS

Test your knowledge by trying this chapter's **multiple-choice questions**:
www.oup.com/uk/poole

FURTHER READING

General principles determining recovery of damages

Blackburn, 'Damaging revelations and giving credit where credit is due' [2017] LMCLQ 482.

Burrows, *Remedies for Torts and Breach of Contract*, 3rd edn (Oxford University Press, 2004).

Carter and Peden, 'Damages following termination for repudiation: taking account of later events' (2008) 24 JCL 145.

Carter and Tolhurst, 'Contract damages following discharge for repudiation revisiting later events' (2016) 132 LQR 1.

Cartwright, 'Compensatory damages: some central issues of assessment' in Burrows and Peel (eds.), *Commercial Remedies: Current Issues and Problems* (Oxford University Press, 2003).

Coote, 'Breach, anticipatory breach, or the breach anticipated?' (2007) 123 LQR 503.

Friedmann, 'The performance interest in contract damages' (1995) 111 LQR 628.

Harris, Ogus, and Phillips, 'Contract remedies and the consumer surplus' (1979) 95 LQR 581.

Hooper, 'Breach, benefit and the lost cause' (2016) 132 LQR 547.

Kramer, *The Law of Contract Damages* (Hart Publishing, 2014).

Law Commission Report No. 247, *Aggravated, Exemplary and Restitutionary Damages* (1997).

Liu, 'The date for assessing damages for loss of prospective performance under a contract' [2007] LMCLQ 273.

Loke, 'Cost of cure or difference in market value? Toward a sound choice in the basis for quantifying expectation damages' (1996) 10 JCL 189.

McLauchlan, 'The redundant reliance interest in contract damages' (2011) 127 LQR 23.

McLaughlan, 'Repudiatory breach, prospective liability, and The Golden Victory' [2015] JBL 530.

McKendrick, 'Breach of contract and the meaning of loss' [1999] CLP 37.

Morgan, 'The penalty clause doctrine: unloveable but untouchable' (2016) 75 CLJ 18.

Mustill, '*The Golden Victory*: some reflections' (2008) 124 LQR 569.

O'Sullivan, 'Loss and gain at greater depth: the implications of the Ruxley decision' in Rose (ed.), *Failure of Contracts: Contractual, Restitutionary and Proprietary Consequences* (Hart Publishing, 1997).

Phang, 'Subjectivity, objectivity and policy: contractual damages in the House of Lords' [1996] JBL 362.

Poole, 'Damages for breach of contract: compensation and "personal preferences"' (1996) 59 MLR 272.

Rowan, 'Reflections on the introduction of punitive damages for breach of contract' (2010) 30 OJLS 495.

Rowan, 'Cost of cure damage and the relevant of the injured promisee's intention to cure' (2017) 76 CLJ 616.

Summers, 'Unresolved issues on the law of penalties' [2017] LMCLQ 95.

Webb, 'Performance and compensation: an analysis of contract damages and contractual obligation' (2006) 26 OJLS 41.

Yip and Goh, 'The compensatory principle: a golden victory for a new certainty?' [2016] JBL 335.

Limitations on the compensation principle

Bridge, 'Mitigation of damages in contract and the meaning of avoidable loss' (1989) 99 LQR 398.

Burrows, 'Contributory negligence in contract: ammunition for the Law Commission' (1993) 109 LQR 175.

Burrows, 'Lord Hoffmann and remoteness in contract' in Davies and Pila (eds.), *The Jurisprudence of Lord Hoffmann: A Festschrift* (Hart Publishing, 2015).

Capper, 'Damages for distress and disappointment: the limits of *Watts v Morrow*' (2000) 116 LQR 553.

Capper, 'Damages for distress and disappointment: problem solved' (2002) 118 LQR 193.

Cartwright, 'Remoteness of damage in contract and tort: a reconsideration' (1996) 55 CLJ 488.

Dyson, 'Choice, benefits and the basis of the market rule' [2016] LMCLQ 202.

Enonchong, 'Breach of contract and damages for mental distress' (1996) 16 OJLS 617.

Goh and Yip, 'Unpacking the compensatory principle' [2016] LMCLQ 33.

Hoffmann, '*The Achilleas*: custom and practice or foreseeability?' [2010] Edin LR 47.

Hunter, 'Has *The Achilleas* sunk?' (2014) 31 JCL 120.

Kramer, 'The new test of remoteness in contract' (2009) 125 LQR 408.

Law Commission Working Paper No. 114, *Contributory Negligence as a Defence in Contract* (1990).

Law Commission Report No. 219, *Contributory Negligence as a Defence in Contract* (1993).

Lee, 'Contractual interpretation and remoteness' [2010] LMCLQ 150.

Macdonald, 'Contractual damages for mental distress' (1994) 7 JCL 94.

McKendrick and Graham, 'The sky's the limit: contractual damages for non-pecuniary loss' [2002] LMCLQ 161.

McLaughlan and Summers, 'Mitigation and causation of benefits' [2018] LMCLQ 172.

Pearce, 'Of ceiling and flaws: a critical evaluation of the minimum performance rule in contract damages' (2016) 36 OJLS 781.

Peel, 'Remoteness re-visited' (2009) 125 LQR 6.

Phang, 'The crumbling edifice? The award of contractual damages for mental distress' [2003] JBL 341.

Robertson, 'The basis of the remoteness rule in contract' (2008) 28 LS 172.

Agreed damages clauses

Barton, 'Penalties and damages' (1976) 92 LQR 20.

Beale, 'Unreasonable deposits' (1993) 109 LQR 524.

Comte, 'The penalty rule revisited' (2016) 132 LQR 382.

Day, 'A pyrrhic victory for the doctrine of penalties' [2016] JBL 115.

Gordon, 'Penalties limiting damages' (1974) 90 LQR 296.

Harpum, 'Equitable relief: penalties and forfeitures' [1989] CLJ 370.

Hudson, 'Penalties limiting damages' (1974) 90 LQR 31 and (1975) 91 LQR 25.

Law Commission Working Paper No. 61, *Penalty Clauses and Forfeiture of Monies Paid* (1975).

Morgan, *Great Debates in Contract Law*, 2nd edn (Palgrave Macmillan, 2015), ch. 8, pp. 234–42.

Chapter 10

Remedies providing for specific relief and restitutionary remedies

SUMMARY OF THE ISSUES

This chapter is divided into two parts. The first part of the chapter considers those equitable remedies that provide for *specific relief*. Specific relief is the general name for those remedies for breach of contract that compel actual performance rather than providing compensation for loss caused by breach.

Compulsion of performance may take the form of claiming an agreed sum (see **10.1**), or a claim seeking specific performance (see **10.2**), or a claim seeking an injunction (see **10.3**).

- The claim or action for an agreed sum gives effect to the claimant's performance interest by ordering that the party in breach pays the liquidated sum (debt), which was the claimant's agreed performance under the contract. The claimant can seek this remedy only where the claimant has performed the obligations that caused the debt obligation to arise.

- Specific performance is a court order compelling actual performance of agreed obligations (other than payment of the price). Because it is an equitable remedy, it is available at the discretion of the court and, since English law regards damages as the primary remedy for breach, specific performance is available only when damages would be an inadequate remedy. There are a number of other restrictions on the court's ability to order specific performance.

- An injunction is a court order restraining the defendant from a specified activity, e.g. breach of a negative stipulation in the contract such as a restraint of trade clause.

- Until the passing of the Chancery Amendment Act 1858 (often referred to as Lord Cairns' Act), equitable remedies could be obtained only from the Court of Chancery and damages could be obtained only from the common law courts. The 1858 Act, now re-enacted as s. 50 of the Senior Courts Act 1981, remedied this procedural difficulty by providing that, where the Court of Chancery had jurisdiction to grant an equitable remedy, it could award damages in addition to or in substitution for that remedy. The fusion of law and equity by the Judicature Acts 1873 and 1875 has removed jurisdictional questions, but power to award such damages remains in place.

The second part of the chapter contains a brief introduction to restitutionary remedies—namely, recovery based on failure of consideration and *quantum meruit* (see **10.5**). These are situations in which one party has received a benefit at the expense of the other. This is sometimes referred to as 'unjust enrichment by subtraction'.

The controversial question of the availability of 'restitutionary damages for breach of contract', which focuses on whether the claimant can obtain restitution of a gain made by the defendant (in excess of any loss made by the claimant) as a result of a breach of contract, is discussed at **10.6**.

- Restitutionary remedies seek to restore money paid or the value of a benefit conferred in circumstances in which it would be unfair for the recipient to retain that benefit. These remedies can apply in circumstances in which no contract exists and, accordingly, are not limited to instances of breach of contract.

- Money paid in advance may be recovered where there has been a total failure of consideration. This may occur because an anticipated contract fails to materialize, or because the contract has become frustrated or is affected by a fundamental initial mistake. Restitution may also be sought in cases of illegality (see **Chapter 16**).

- In certain circumstances, it may be possible to recover the reasonable value of a performance as a *quantum meruit* claim on the basis that a benefit has been conferred on the other party for which no payment under a contract can be made.

- In very exceptional circumstances, the court may order a defendant to account for a gain resulting from a breach of contract in the form of an account of profits where the claimant has suffered no loss. This head of damages was at one time thought to encompass cases where the defendant exploited an opportunity otherwise open to the claimant, but recent authority suggests that in that situation the claimant's damages are based on the loss of the value of exploiting the opportunity (often, the notional cost of a licence, i.e. 'negotiating damages'), and the possibility of an account of profits is relevant only in the very exceptional situation where the opportunity was one incapable of being exploited by the claimant or licensed for a fee.

- The court may award 'negotiating damages', representing the sum that the claimant could hypothetically have received in return for releasing the defendant from the obligation which he failed to perform. As just noted, such cases were at one time regarded as giving rise to an account of profits on the basis that the claimant could not demonstrate any loss. Recognition had been afforded to damages of that class by a series of decisions flowing from *Wrotham Park Estate Co. Ltd v Parkside Homes Ltd* [1974] 1 WLR 798. In *Morris-Garner v One Step (Support) Ltd* [2018] UKSC 20, the Supreme Court laid down definitive principles for the award and assessment of such damages, and confirmed that the measure is the claimant's loss rather than the defendant's profit; that will very often be a notional licensing fee. In so doing the Supreme Court adopted the description 'negotiating damages' in place of the previous widely used epithet '*Wrotham Park* damages'.

10.1 Claiming an agreed sum

The most common form of claim for an agreed sum is a claim for the price. The purpose of the claim is to enforce the defendant's contractual obligation (the promise to pay). It rests on the fact that the claimant has performed those obligations that gave rise to the obligation to make payment, i.e. the money must be due to the claimant. It is therefore a claim in debt, rather than a claim for damages.

There are many advantages of such a claim, since the amount claimed is known from the beginning (a 'liquidated sum').

- Many of the difficulties relating to actions for damages—notably, remoteness of damage (see **9.5.2**) and mitigation (see **9.5.3**)—are avoided. In a debt claim, the amount of the debt is the amount recovered.

- In addition, because the issues at trial are frequently uncomplicated, there is a streamlined procedure for claims for unpaid debts (i.e. summary judgment under the Civil Procedure Rules, r. 24).

In most cases, the only difficulties, if there are any, are (i) questions of fact and (ii) problems of enforcement. Questions of fact (i) arise where the defence offered is that the obligation to pay has been discharged by a defective performance by the claimant (see **8.4**). Enforcement problems (ii) arise where the defendant has not paid because they lack the means to pay.

Greater difficulties occur where the party in breach will not allow the other party to complete performance, which has the effect of preventing the latter from bringing a claim for the price. The performing party will be confined to a claim for damages for its actual loss and will be subject to a duty to mitigate that loss.

10.1.1 Breach by anticipatory repudiation and claiming the agreed sum

In **White & Carter (Councils) Ltd v McGregor** [1962] AC 413, before the appellants had commenced performance of the contract, the respondents had announced that they no longer wanted them to do so. The appellants nevertheless elected to affirm the contract (which they were held to be entitled to do: see the facts at **8.7.3.1**) and continued their performance, claiming thereby to be entitled to the price. On the facts of this case, they were able to perform without the need for the other party's cooperation, so that there was nothing to prevent them from performing despite the respondents' protestations that it was pointless. A majority of the House of Lords upheld the appellants' claim to recover the price despite the absence of any attempt to minimize the loss (see **9.5.3**). Unlike the position in relation to a claim for unliquidated damages, there is no obligation to mitigate when claiming only for an agreed sum.

This decision raised the possibility that a party might be able to elect to continue performance without any substantive reason. If the performance were to remain unwanted by the other party, then the cost of performance would be wasted. *For this reason, the right to elect to affirm the contract is limited to those cases in which the party wishing to affirm has a legitimate interest in so doing* (see **8.7.3.1**) *and recovery of the price turns on the affirming party's ability to perform without the cooperation of the party in breach.* However, as discussed at **8.7.3.1**, the courts have been reluctant to deny the injured party the option to affirm in all but exceptional cases. Therefore the practical issue restricting the ability to claim the price (as an action for an agreed sum) is the ability of the injured party to carry on with the contractual performance required as a precondition to the payment obligation—*Ministry of Sound (Ireland) Ltd v World Online Ltd* [2003] EWHC 2178 (Ch), [2003] 2 All ER (Comm) 823—without the cooperation of the party in breach. Where there is no legitimate interest in continuing to perform the contract rather than claiming damages (and assuming that the right to claim the price has not yet arisen because the necessary performance has not yet taken place), the non-breaching party will be forced to mitigate its loss and claim damages. However, mitigation can have no relevance where the claim for the price has already arisen.

Remedies providing for specific relief and restitutionary remedies

10

10.1.2 The sale of goods

A particular problem may arise in the sale of goods when legal performance, which is constituted by the passing of property, is separated from the physical delivery of the goods, which may take place at a later date. This is because s. 49 of the Sale of Goods Act (SGA) 1979 provides that the seller can bring a claim for the price if the property in the goods has passed to the buyer.

> **→ EXAMPLE**
>
> A sells his cow 'Rose' to B for £500, promising to deliver her to B's farm five days later. Since this is a contract for the sale of specific goods, property passes immediately to B (SGA 1979, s. 18, r. 1), with the result that A has performed everything necessary to bring a claim for the price (SGA 1979, s. 49(1)).
>
> If B informs A before the time for delivery that he no longer wishes to buy 'Rose', it seems that A may still claim the price, obliging B to take on the responsibility of disposing of the cow. If B is a dealer, then he may well be better able to dispose of the cow, in which case this rule is justified. However, in a similar case in which A is a dealer and B is only a consumer, it makes little sense to leave disposal of the unwanted goods to the party less likely to be able to sell them without difficulty.

Section 49(2) of the SGA 1979 provides that where the price is payable on a fixed date, irrespective of delivery, and the buyer fails to pay, the seller can claim the price, although the property in the goods has not passed and the goods have not been appropriated to the contract.

In *Caterpillar (NI) Ltd (formerly FG Wilson (Engineering) Ltd) v John Holt & Co. (Liverpool) Ltd* [2013] EWCA Civ 1232, [2014] 1 WLR 2365, there was a retention of title clause in the claimant's standard terms for sales (providing that ownership in the goods did not pass until payment in full). The Court of Appeal therefore held that property in the goods had not passed to the defendant buyer, s. 49(1) did not apply and there could be no action to claim the price. This might suggest that there are dangers in the use of retention clauses. However, due to s. 49(2), irrespective of the existence of a retention clause, any standard terms need only provide for payment on a fixed date for the claim to fall within s. 49.

10.2 Specific performance

An order of specific performance is a court order compelling actual performance of the substantive primary obligations under the contract (i.e. the obligations to perform rather than those merely to pay the price: see **10.1**). The court ensures compliance with its order by deterring non-compliance with threats of punitive measures against the person to whom the order is addressed. These measures include committal to prison for contempt of court, sequestration of property, and fines.

At common law, the only remedy for breach of contract was by way of damages to compensate for loss caused. The Chancery Court made specific performance available, by way of exception. It remains an exceptional remedy even after the amalgamation of law and equity, in that damages are available as of right upon breach if loss can be proved, while the availability of specific performance is subject to a number of restrictions, including that damages be an inadequate remedy.

This position, in theory at least, can be compared to that in civil law systems, under which specific enforcement of the contract may be considered the primary remedy for breach of contract.

10.2.1 Inadequacy of damages

The principle whereby damages may compensate the non-breaching party's cost of obtaining substitute performance has already been explained (see the opening pages to **Part 3**, under heading **(c)**). In such circumstances, damages may be said to be an adequate remedy and it is for this reason that, in the ordinary run of cases, specific performance will not be awarded.

> ⇢ **EXAMPLE**
>
> In many contracts for the sale of goods, it is possible to purchase substitute goods in the market, and therefore damages, to cover the cost of obtaining substitute performance, will be an adequate remedy: *Société des Industries Metallurgiques SA v The Bronx Engineering Co. Ltd* [1975] 1 Lloyd's Rep 465.

Nevertheless, it is open to a party to demonstrate that, for some reason, damages would be an inadequate remedy—the important point being that this burden is placed on the non-breaching party.

It is impossible to list every eventuality allowing specific performance, but the more common situations in which the remedy will be available can be identified as follows.

- *The most obvious case is where substitute performance is unavailable.* Thus, where goods are in some way unique, no substitute for them will satisfy the buyer and, in such circumstances, specific performance is the better remedy (SGA 1979, s. 52). The example of a valuable painting has already been suggested (see the opening pages to **Part 3**, under heading **(c)**); another example of a unique good might be a family heirloom.

Perhaps more significantly, it appears that the courts may be willing to accept a commercial definition of the unavailability of substitute goods. In such circumstances, rarity in absolute terms may not be necessary if, within the relevant time limits of the particular contract, substitute performance cannot be obtained.

In *Sky Petroleum Ltd v VIP Petroleum Ltd* [1974] 1 WLR 576, the claimant company had contracted to purchase all of its requirements of petrol and diesel fuel from the defendant at fixed prices for a ten-year period. During a time of worldwide shortages of petroleum products, the defendant purported to terminate the contract, leaving the claimant with no realistic prospect of obtaining alternative supplies. The claimant sought an injunction to prevent termination of the contract. Goulding J accepted that, by granting an injunction, he would be specifically enforcing the contract, and that petrol and diesel fuel were not of themselves unique. Nevertheless, he granted the injunction because, in the particular circumstances, damages were an inadequate remedy, since 'for all practical purposes' substitute performance would not be available in time to prevent the claimant going out of business.

- Contracts for the sale of land merit separate attention. As a matter of law, all land is unique, so that specific performance is available upon breach of a contract for the sale of land. This rule does not vary according to the facts of each case, so that even a contract to purchase a modest house, of a kind that may be duplicated several times in a single development, is regarded as subject to the remedy of specific performance. The rule extends not only to purchasers of land, but also to vendors. It is not clear that the purchaser's obligations to pay the purchase price and to take conveyance of the land are in every case unique, and it seems likely that the extension of specific performance to claims brought by the vendor is based in the principle of mutuality (see **10.2.3.2**).

- *Specific performance may also be granted when the quantification of damages is difficult for some reason and matters can be resolved by requiring the contract to be performed.* For example, it was accepted in *Co-operative Insurance Society Ltd v Argyll Stores (Holdings) Ltd* [1998] AC 1 that damages would not be adequate because of difficulties in quantifying the claimant's loss over the full term of the lease (although the House of Lords refused specific performance for other reasons: see **10.2.2.1**).

- *Specific performance will also be available where there is a risk that the claimant will not be properly compensated if restricted to the remedy of damages, such as where, for technical reasons, damages would be nominal only, so that the sole means of protecting the claimant's expectation is by compelling performance.*

In **Beswick v Beswick** [1968] AC 58, a contract between uncle and nephew provided for the sale of the uncle's business to the nephew in return for payment of a pension to the uncle, which was to continue after the uncle's death as payment to his widow. After the uncle's death, the nephew ceased making the payments. The widow was prevented from suing in her own right because of the application of the doctrine of privity (see **11.7.1**, although compare with the position now under the Contracts (Rights of Third Parties) Act 1999). However, she could succeed in an action as administratrix of her husband's estate. The difficulty was that the estate had suffered no loss as a result of the breach of contract, since Mr Beswick's interest—and so the estate's—ceased upon his death. The widow had suffered the loss in her personal capacity. However, her husband's estate could not recover damages on behalf of someone who was not a party to the contract (discussed at **11.7.3**). Nevertheless, the House of Lords was able to avoid the obvious injustice of allowing the nephew to break his promise by awarding specific performance of the contract. On the facts, specific performance was the most appropriate remedy.

- In *AB v CD* [2014] EWCA Civ 229, [2015] 1 WLR 771, the Court of Appeal granted an interim injunction requiring continued performance of obligations under a licence (representing the claimant's only business) and preventing immediate termination or suspension on the basis that damages would be an inadequate remedy on the facts due to the existence of a broadly drafted exemption clause in the parties' agreement. Law LJ noted (at 33]): 'Where a party to a contract stipulates that if he breaches his obligations his liability will be limited or the damages he must pay will be capped, that is a circumstance which in justice tends to favour the grant of an injunction to prohibit the breach in the first place.' It follows that this will be a factor to take into account in deciding whether to grant such an interim injunction—and compel performance of the contract.

- In some circumstances, specific performance may even be awarded simply because the defendant is unlikely to be able to come up with the money to pay damages: *Evans Marshall and Co. Ltd v Bertola SA* [1973] 1 WLR 349.

10.2.2 Contracts not specifically enforceable

Certain contracts, which might otherwise satisfy the tests for the availability of specific performance, cannot be enforced in this way because of the nature of the obligations undertaken.

10.2.2.1 Difficulties in supervision

It was once thought that contracts requiring considerable supervision of performance would never qualify for specific performance.

> In **Ryan v Mutual Tontine Westminster Chambers Association** [1893] 1 Ch 116, for example, a lease contained a term by which the landlords undertook to provide a resident porter in constant attendance at a block of flats. The person appointed had other employment and so was often absent from the flats. The court refused specific performance of this term of the lease, because it would require a level of constant supervision beyond that which the court was able to provide.

This principle has been invoked in a number of different situations, including building contracts. Nevertheless, it may well be that the unavailability of specific performance on this ground can always be avoided by careful drafting. The decision in *Ryan* was effectively distinguished in the similar case of *Posner v Scott-Lewis* [1987] Ch 25, on the ground that, in the particular circumstances, what was necessary to comply with the contract could easily be defined and did not require excessive supervision. Thus it is not that the court lacks the power to ensure that the terms of the contract are being carried into effect properly; rather, the difficulty usually stems from the fact that the contract does not state the performance intended by the parties with sufficient precision. Equally, building contracts can be specifically enforced provided that 'the particulars of the work are so far definitely ascertained that the court can sufficiently see what is the exact nature of the work': *per* Romer LJ in *Wolverhampton Corporation v Emmons* [1901] 1 QB 515, at p. 525.

In addition, in *C. H. Giles & Co. Ltd v Morris* [1972] 1 WLR 307, Megarry J expressed dissatisfaction with any absolute restriction based on the difficulty of supervision, because clearly much will depend upon the drafting of the term in question and the background circumstances. These surrounding circumstances appear to have been crucial in the decision of the House of Lords in *Co-operative Insurance Society Ltd v Argyll Stores (Holdings) Ltd* [1998] AC 1 to refuse specific performance because of difficulties in supervising compliance.

> In **Co-operative Insurance Society Ltd v Argyll Stores (Holdings) Ltd**, the defendant, a supermarket chain, had a lease of a unit in the claimant's shopping centre. It was a term of the lease that the defendant covenanted to keep the premises open for retail trade during the usual hours of business. Although the lease was for a 35-year term, after less than six years the defendant closed the supermarket and moved out of the centre. The claimant sought specific performance of the covenant to compel the defendant to continue to operate the supermarket. Despite the fact that damages would clearly have been an inadequate remedy on the facts (see **10.2.1**), the House of Lords refused to order specific performance on the basis that its effect would be to order the carrying on of an uneconomic business. Thus the loss that might then be suffered by the claimant would be out of all proportion to the loss suffered owing to the breach of the covenant. In addition, it would be difficult both to formulate a suitable order and to supervise it.

A further example is provided by *Vertex Data Science Ltd v Powergen Retail Ltd* [2006] EWHC 1340 (Comm), [2006] 2 Lloyd's Rep 591.

> V had agreed to supply P, the electricity supply company, with outsourcing services. The parties' relationship was a difficult one and, when P issued a notice of termination alleging a number of persistent and material breaches, V sought an injunction to prevent P from acting on its notice, which would be equivalent to an order for specific performance. Tomlinson J held that it would not be appropriate to grant this relief since the agreement required extensive mutual cooperation and the injunction would have the effect of compelling parties whose relationship had broken down to continue in a contractual relationship. In addition, the court would struggle to enforce such an order given that the contract did not indicate precisely the action required if P was to avoid preventing or hindering V from performing its contractual obligations: *Co-operative Insurance Society v Argyll*.

These decisions may be compared with that in *Rainbow Estates Ltd v Tokenhold Ltd* [1999] Ch 64, which concerned breach of a tenant's covenant to repair. This could be specifically enforceable because it would be an order to achieve a specified result (which was capable of supervision), rather than an order to carry on an activity (as in *Co-operative v Argyll*). Similarly, in *Sparks v Biden* [2017] EWHC 1994 (Ch) specific performance of an option over land was granted despite the inability of the court to lay down in detail exactly how the order could be implemented, the court referring to 'the well-established practice of the trial Judge making a decree for specific performance and then adjourning the working out of the order to the Master'.

10.2.2.2 Contracts of personal service

More clearly excepted from the scope of the remedy of specific performance are contracts of personal service. The reason is usually said to be that it would be an infringement of liberty to oblige one party to work in a personal capacity for the other—*De Francesco v Barnum* (1890) 45 Ch D 430 (facts given at **5.5.1.2**)—or to have to employ a particular person.

> In *Page One Records Ltd v Britton* [1968] 1 WLR 157, pop group The Troggs appointed the claimants as their sole agent and manager for a period of five years. The contract contained an express negative covenant whereby the group agreed not to engage anyone else to act as their manager during that period. The judge refused to enforce this covenant by means of an injunction because such a group could not work at all without a manager. An injunction would therefore have had the same effect as an order of specific performance of the management contract. It would be wrong to force the group to continue to employ as their manager and agent any person in whom they had lost confidence.

See also *Warren v Mendy* [1989] 1 WLR 853, in which no injunction would be granted to compel a boxer to use the exclusive services of a particular manager. The position in question necessitated mutual trust and confidence, and it would therefore be wrong to force the boxer to employ as a manager a person in whom he had lost confidence.

There is now a statutory provision preventing specific performance (or a compelling injunction) against an employee in relation to the general obligation to work for an employer (Trade Union and Labour Relations (Consolidation) Act 1992, s. 236). *Thus an injunction is extremely unlikely to be issued to force one person to employ another where the relationship is based on the maintenance of confidence.* A recent example is provided by the decision in *Ashworth v Royal National Theatre* [2014] EWHC 1176 (QB), [2014] 4 All ER 238. Referring to the loss of confidence argument (at [23]), Cranston J refused an application by musicians for specific performance (or a mandatory injunction) which would require the theatre to re-engage them after the theatre had decided to use recorded music and dispense with live music for the production.

Although, in general, an injunction will not be issued to prevent a person from working for any other person in breach of covenant, it may be granted where there is an express term of the contract preventing the party in question from taking up *specified* alternative employment.

> For example, in ***Lumley v Wagner*** (1852) 1 De GM & G 604, 42 ER 607, the claimant engaged the defendant to sing at his theatre, and the contract contained an express clause forbidding the defendant from singing anywhere else for the period of the contract. The defendant then entered another contract to sing elsewhere and refused to perform under her contract with the claimant. Specific performance was not available to the claimant because the contract was for personal service, but the express negative covenant could be enforced by injunction, thereby preventing the defendant from singing elsewhere.
>
> Similarly, in ***Warner Brothers Pictures Inc. v Nelson*** [1937] 1 KB 209, an injunction was granted to prevent the film actress Bette Davis from appearing in any film or stage production for anyone other than Warner Brothers without their consent. The important point was that Warner Brothers did not seek enforcement of a positive performance obligation, which would have been refused. Counsel for Miss Davis had argued that if the injunction were granted, she would effectively be placed in the position of having to work for Warner Brothers or starve. The judge rejected this argument on the basis that Miss Davis could earn money in other ways.

There is an evident tension here between avoiding forcing a person to work for a particular employer and yet giving effect to stipulations in the contract to which they freely agreed and which have significant financial implications for the employer. In practice, the courts are unlikely to apply the test in *Warner Bros.* when considering whether to grant an injunction. It is far more likely that they will have regard to the circumstances in which the restraint is asked for, including matters such as the duration and likely effect on the reputation, and the general prospects of the person being restrained (see the discussion of restraint of trade clauses at **16.4.6**). In *Araci v Fallon* [2011] EWCA Civ 668, [2011] LLR 440, the Court of Appeal granted an interim injunction to prevent the jockey Kieren Fallon from breaching a positive obligation in a services agreement (i.e. not an employment contract), requiring him to ride a particular owner's horse in the Epsom Derby, by riding a rival horse. Fallon was also under a negative obligation in the contract, which prevented him from riding any rival horse, and these promises had clearly been broken.

As *Vertex Data Science Ltd v Powergen Retail Ltd* [2006] EWHC 1340 (Comm), [2006] 2 Lloyd's Rep 591 (see **10.2.2.1**) illustrates, even where the parties are in a commercial and not a personal relationship, the courts are unlikely to order specific performance where the mutual confidence in the relationship has broken down.

10.2.3 Equitable limits: discretion, mutuality, and volunteers

10.2.3.1 Discretion

Specific performance is an equitable remedy. This fact is significant in that equitable remedies are not available as of right, unlike the common law remedy of damages. Even where the claimant can demonstrate that its claim satisfies the conditions of availability of the remedy, the court has a discretion to refuse specific performance. Of course, the discretion is not entirely arbitrary. The extent of the discretion is that if the claim falls within certain loosely defined categories, the court may refuse to award specific performance if, in the circumstances, it believes that would be the right thing to do.

- *The court may consider the conduct of the claimant, and if the claimant has not behaved entirely properly, it may refuse specific performance.* The claimant's conduct need not amount to a legal wrong; mere 'trickery' will suffice to allow the court to consider exercise of the discretion—*Quadrant Visual Communications Ltd v Hutchison Telephone (UK) Ltd* [1993] 1 BCLC 442—and specific performance will be refused where the claimant has been guilty of some unfairness or sharp practice: *Pateman v Pay* (1974) 232 EG 457. This principle is sometimes colourfully stated in the maxim 'He who comes to equity must come with clean hands'. Any provision of the contract that purports to prevent the application of the 'clean hands' rule will be ineffective, i.e. the parties cannot fetter the discretion of the court: *Quadrant Visual Communications Ltd v Hutchison Telephone (UK) Ltd.*

- *The remedy may also be refused where it would be unfair to the defendant or would result in personal hardship*: e.g. *Patel v Ali* [1984] Ch 283. In *Shell UK Ltd v Lostock Garage Ltd* [1976] 1 WLR 1187, an injunction to prevent a tied garage from obtaining petrol from another supplier was refused on the ground that the claimant supplier had granted discounts to all garages in the area other than the defendant's, so that it had become impossible for the garage to compete. No injunction could therefore be granted while this discount scheme for other garages was in place.

10.2.3.2 Mutuality

Specific performance may also be refused where there is no mutuality of remedy between the parties. It was once thought that this requirement meant that specific performance would not be available if, at the time of contracting, it could not also have been available to the other party. There was little sense in such a strict rule and there were a number of exceptions to it.

The rule was subsequently clarified by the Court of Appeal in *Price v Strange* [1978] Ch 337, which considered that the crucial time at which mutuality must be tested is the time of the trial. At that point, the claimant must have performed all of its obligations, or these obligations must themselves be capable of specific performance, or non-performance of those obligations must be adequately compensable by an award of damages (see **10.2.1**).

The purpose of the rule is to protect a defendant from the risk of being obliged to perform the actual contractual undertakings only to find that it will be inadequately compensated for the claimant's own non-performance. As such, it may be no more than a particular application of the undue hardship principle.

10.2.3.3 Volunteers

It is a general principle of equity that it will not 'assist a volunteer', i.e. *equitable rules and remedies will not be applied in the case of a person who has not given real consideration for a promise.* Thus a promise that is binding under the common law because it was made under in a deed (see **4.1**), or which was given for a nominal and symbolic consideration such as a peppercorn (see **4.3.1**), cannot be specifically enforced: *Re Parkin* [1892] 3 Ch 510. However, there are signs that this principle may have been relaxed. Under the Contracts (Rights of Third Parties) Act 1999, a third party who satisfies the test of enforceability will be able to enforce a contractual term even where they have not provided any consideration to support it, assuming that the promise is supported by consideration provided by the promisee so that it is not a gratuitous promise. The third party will have any remedy that 'would have been available to him in an action for breach of the contract if he had been a party to the contract' (s. 1(5)). This would, in principle, include the remedy of specific performance, although the third party would technically be a volunteer in equity.

10.2.4 Damages in lieu of specific performance

Under the Senior Courts Act 1981, s. 50, the successor to the Chancery Amendment Act 1858 (Lord Cairns' Act) the High Court is empowered to award damages in lieu of specific performance. In the majority of cases, the claimant will be unlikely to invite the court to exercise its power, since it is possible to claim damages and specific performance at the same time (for an example of specific statutory provisions setting out the court's powers to award specific performance and damages, see s. 52 SGA 1979 and s. 58 Consumer Rights Act (CRA) 2015). However, damages in lieu of specific performance may be awarded in circumstances in which common law damages would not be, although instances are likely to be rare. It was suggested by Lord Wilberforce in *Johnson v Agnew* [1980] AC 367 that damages under s. 50 of the 1981 Act were the same as at common law, but it was pointed out by Lord Reed in *Morris-Garner v One Step (Support) Ltd* [2018] UKSC 20, at [47] that that was not necessarily the case, given that common law damages are designed to put the claimant into the position that he would have been in had the contract been performed whereas one of the purposes of statutory damages was to compensate the claimaint for his inability to prevent future loss from any existing or subsequent breach of contract.

10.3 Injunction

An injunction is a court order restraining the defendant from a specified activity. Its use extends far beyond the law of contract but, in this context, it may be used to prevent the breach of a negative stipulation in the contract. The example given earlier of such a stipulation was a promise in the form of a contract not to make loud noises during the period when the promisee was revising for an exam (see the opening pages to **Part 3**, under heading **(c)** and see also discussion of restraint of trade provisions at **16.4.6**). Such promises may be enforced by means of an injunction.

The requirement that damages need to be shown to be inadequate before specific relief will be granted does not apply strictly to ordinary injunctions. Nevertheless, in most circumstances, the courts will not allow the claimant to exploit this difference to achieve by injunction what cannot be achieved by specific performance. We have already seen how this principle applies in the case of contracts of employment (see **10.2.2.2**). In other contracts, the courts will be unwilling to enforce by injunction an express term that does no more than broadly prohibit breach of the positive stipulations in the contract where that contract would not otherwise qualify for specific performance. Thus injunctions are limited to specific restraints.

Normally, the activity to be restrained will be stipulated expressly in the contract and the courts will be unwilling to imply a negative stipulation from the positive terms of the agreement. Such implication will occur, however, where the circumstances justify it. For example, where an exclusive dealing agreement is found not to be in restraint of trade (see **16.4.6.4**), the court may imply a negative term preventing conduct that is inconsistent with the purpose of such a contract: *Evans Marshall and Co. v Bertola SA* [1973] 1 WLR 349. Nevertheless, it is usual for such contracts to contain explicit negative stipulations.

10.3.1 Types of injunction

- *Prohibitory injunctions* are granted to prevent future breach of contract. Such injunctions are particularly useful where a potential future breach will lead to difficulty and expense for the claimant. One common form of injunction is the 'anti-suit' injunction, available where the parties have agreed that they will resolve their disputes in the English courts or in arbitration but one of them commences proceedings in an overseas court: the English court may grant an injunction to prevent the defaulting party from maintaining the foreign action.

- However, if the claimant wishes to compel the defendant to remedy an injury caused by a breach that has already occurred, that claimant must obtain a *mandatory injunction*. The effect of such an injunction is to compel the defendant to undo work that has been done in breach of a negative stipulation in the contract.

> → **EXAMPLE**
>
> A mandatory injunction might be granted to compel the defendant to cut down trees that had been planted in breach of a covenant not to restrict the claimant's view: *Wakeham v Wood* (1982) 43 P & CR 40.

Mandatory injunctions are subject to the same rules as specific performance. Damages must be an inadequate remedy and grant of the injunction must not cause undue hardship to the defendant. This latter requirement may be waived where the breach was deliberately and knowingly committed: *Wakeham v Wood*. In practice, mandatory injunctions are rarely granted.

10.4 Restitution

The modern law of restitution is firmly based in the notion of unjust enrichment: *Lipkin Gorman v Karpnale Ltd* [1991] 2 AC 548.

10.4.1 Enrichment by subtraction

In the general field of contracts, unjust enrichment will usually take the form of a benefit accruing to one party that for some reason may be regarded as 'belonging' to another, and the purpose of a restitutionary remedy would be to restore the benefit to its 'rightful owner'—either on the basis that there has been a total failure of consideration or via a *quantum meruit* payment for the reasonable value of the performance. *Such cases are often referred to as instances of 'enrichment by subtraction from the claimant'.*

A classic example would be the rendering of some performance, in anticipation of a contract being made, only to have that expectation come to nothing because of a failure to agree terms. The recipient of the performance has received a benefit that must have cost the other party something to provide and it would be unjust to allow the benefit to be retained without payment of some kind.

In this context, restitutionary remedies do not provide a response to one party's failure to satisfy the other party's expectation under the contract; *rather, they seek to restore money paid or the value of a benefit conferred in circumstances in which no contract exists, or in which there is no longer any obligation to perform under an admitted contract.* Thus their availability is not solely dependent upon the existence of a breach of contract, although where there has been breach the non-breaching party may have to decide whether a claim for expectation loss or a restitutionary remedy would provide a better remedy.

10.4.2 Enrichment without subtraction

There may also be an enrichment, which in some circumstances might be considered unjust, where one party receives a benefit as a result of a wrong done to the other party, without there being any 'subtraction' from that party (or measurable loss suffered by the non-breaching party). The question then posed is whether a remedy should be available in such a case (and the nature of such a remedy). This question is considered at **10.6**.

10.5 Enrichment by subtraction

10.5.1 Total failure of consideration

Even in the absence of breach, a party may recover money paid in anticipation of a contractual performance that the other party has failed to provide where there has been a total failure of consideration.

Performance may be impossible because the contract has been frustrated (see **Chapter 12**), or because, unknown to the parties, the subject matter of the contract had been destroyed before the time of contracting (see **13.3.1**). In each case, the promisee may recover money paid in advance despite the fact that the failure of performance does not amount to breach. Indeed, most claims for total failure of consideration do not arise out of breach by the other party. In the event of breach, the normal reaction will be to claim damages for lost expectation, but the restitutionary remedy is available as an alternative (see **10.5.3**).

10.5.1.1 Relationship to consideration as 'promise'

In relation to the formation of contracts, 'consideration' was described as constituted not merely by an exchange of performances, but also by an exchange of promises. It might be thought, therefore, that where it is possible to show agreement, there can never be a failure of consideration. However, where 'consideration' is used in the technical sense of giving rise to a restitutionary remedy upon total failure, it must be understood as referring to *performance* of whatever was promised in the agreement.

In *Fibrosa SA v Fairbairn Lawson Combe Barbour Ltd* [1943] AC 32 (see **12.7.1.1**), at p. 48, Viscount Simon LC explained:

> [I]n the law relating to the formation of contract, the promise to do a thing may often be the consideration; but, when one is considering the law of failure of consideration and of the quasi-contractual right to recover money on that ground, it is, generally speaking, not the promise which is referred to as the consideration, but the performance of the promise. The money was paid to secure performance and, if performance fails, the inducement which brought about the payment is not fulfilled. If this were not so, there could never be any recovery of money, for failure of consideration, by the payer of the money in return for a promise of future performance.

This standard explanation of the doctrine of total failure of consideration was affirmed by the Privy Council in *Goss v Chilcott* [1996] AC 788, at p. 797.

In ***Fibrosa SA v Fairbairn Lawson Combe Barbour Ltd***, the seller was prevented from completing performance of a contract by the outbreak of war, since the buyer was in enemy-occupied territory. The buyer had paid part of the price in advance and, since it had received none of the promised performance, it was entitled to repayment of that money because there had been a total failure of consideration.

In ***Rover International Ltd v Cannon Film Sales Ltd*** [1989] 1 WLR 912, Rover paid advances in the nature of royalties to Cannon, for which Rover was to distribute Cannon's films in Italy after dubbing them into Italian. The contract was void because Rover had not at the time been registered as a company. The Court of Appeal held that there had been a total failure of consideration despite the fact that Rover had received the films in question. The total failure of consideration related to the fact that the promised performance for which it had contracted was the securing of a profit and this had been prevented.

It will therefore be a matter of determining what performance is owed under the terms of the contract. This was again confirmed by the House of Lords in *Stocznia Gdanska SA v Latvian Shipping Co.* [1998] 1 WLR 574. The House of Lords explained that, for there to be a total failure of consideration, it did not need to be established that the promisee had received nothing under the contract; the issue was whether the other party had performed any part of its contractual duties in respect of which payment was due.

The argument on the facts of ***Stocznia Gdanska SA v Latvian Shipping Co.*** was that, because the defendants had not received the vessels being constructed under the contract, there was a total failure of consideration. The House of Lords considered that the contractual obligations, for which payment was to be made, extended beyond delivery of the vessels, and included design and construction. Accordingly, since some of this work had been completed, there was no total failure of consideration. This was reinforced by the fact that payment was to be made in instalments.

In *Giedo Van der Garde BV v Force India Formula One Team Ltd (formerly Spyker F1 Team Ltd (England))* [2010] EWHC 2373 (QB), the judge followed the decisions in *Stocznia* and *Rover International v Cannon Film Sales,* and held that although the receipt of benefits that were merely incidental to the performance of the contract would not be inconsistent with a finding of total failure of consideration, the benefit on the facts went beyond this—namely, a contingent right (subject to the driver obtaining the necessary licence) to drive in the Grand Prix Friday morning test sessions. It followed that there had been no total failure of consideration.

10.5.2 Partial failure of performance

The general rule is that where the promisee has received some of the performance to which the promisee is entitled under the contract, so that the failure is only partial, the promisee is not able to recover money paid in advance: *Whincup v Hughes* (1871) LR 6 CP 78.

The explanation for this rule is usually said to be that it is impossible to apportion the consideration between the performed and unperformed parts of the contract. For this reason, where performance is severable (or divisible) (see **8.6.2.1**), so that the money paid can easily be split pro rata among the several parts, recovery of part of the money for partial failure of consideration will be allowed: *Ebrahim Dawood Ltd v Heath (Est. 1927) Ltd* [1961] Lloyd's Rep 512.

This rule was applied to slightly surprising effect in *Goss v Chilcott* [1996] AC 788.

> The appellants had borrowed a sum of money, but had been unable to repay any of the capital and, in fact, paid only two instalments of interest. The contract was void because the respondents had altered the loan documents without the appellants' consent. In the absence of a contractual claim, the question was whether the capital was recoverable for total failure of consideration. The Privy Council rejected the argument that there was no failure of consideration because of the reciprocal exchange of promises at the time of making the contract. For these purposes, the existence of consideration required actual performance of some part of what had been promised (see **10.5.1**). More difficulty was presented by the fact that two instalments of interest payments were made. In the light of these payments, it could be argued that there had been *some* performance, so that there had not been a *total* failure of consideration. However, the contract did not provide, as would usually be the case with a long-term loan, for the scheduled payments to combine both interest and some repayment of capital; these were only payments of interest due. As a result, Lord Goff said, it was possible to separate the elements of the contract; since there was no performance in respect of the capital, it could be recovered.

It may also be possible for a promisee to convert a partial failure of consideration into a total failure of consideration by returning any benefit received by such performance as has taken place. This may be a particularly desirable course of action if the promisee is of the opinion that a restitutionary remedy would be preferable to a claim for damages (see **10.5.3**). In some circumstances, of course, restoration of the benefit will be impossible. Where building work has been done on the promisee's land, but not completed, the promisee cannot return the work done: *Sumpter v Hedges* [1898] 1 QB 673 (see **8.6.2.2**). If, however, it is impossible to return the performance received for some reason connected with the other party's breach, there will be no obstacle to recovery of payment on the basis of total failure of consideration.

The Law Commission, in its Working Paper *Pecuniary Restitution on Breach of Contract*, WP No. 65 (1975), had provisionally recommended that restitutionary recovery ought to be available in cases of partial failure of the consideration. However, the Law Commission changed its mind in its report *Law of Contract: Pecuniary Restitution on Breach of Contract*, Law Com. No. 121 (1983). This may be explicable in the light of the inventiveness of the courts in enabling recovery, despite what appears to be only a partial failure of consideration.

10.5.3 Restitution versus damages

Where the total failure of consideration is the result of breach by the other party, the promisee will normally claim damages for loss of expectation, since the promisee will probably wish to recover the cost of mitigating its loss by resort to the market and may wish to recover damages for lost profits. If the contract was an advantageous one, then the expectation measure of damages will almost certainly be more attractive than recovering money paid. If, however, the claimant had made a bad bargain, so that a loss would have been made on the contract had it been performed, the claimant may be glad of the opportunity provided by the total failure of consideration to retrieve intact the investment made.

10.5.4 *Quantum meruit*

Quantum meruit *is a remedy under which a party who has provided a benefit, and who for some reason cannot obtain payment under a contract, may recover the reasonable value of the benefit provided.* It may apply where there is no contract, or where the contractual provisions as to remuneration are inapplicable. This is an objective evaluation of a 'reasonable sum'—namely, the price that a reasonable person in the defendant's position would have had to pay for the services. In *Benedetti v Sawiris* [2013] UKSC 50, [2014] AC 938, the Supreme Court confirmed that, where a benefit received has an objective market value, the court should not permit the claimant to succeed in an argument that the *quantum meruit* must be a higher sum because the defendant placed a higher subjective value on the benefit.

10.5.4.1 *Quantum meruit* in the absence of contract

Where one party confers a benefit on another with the intention on both sides that this benefit will be paid for, then, in the absence of any contract between the parties, the party conferring the benefit will be able to recover reasonable remuneration from the recipient under the restitutionary remedy of *quantum meruit*: *Planche v Colburn* (1831) 8 Bing 14, 131 ER 305. This is a sum that is not based on any contract price, because there is no agreed contract price. It will need to be calculated by reference to market rates.

British Steel Corporation v Cleveland Bridge & Engineering Co. Ltd [1984] 1 All ER 504 (see **3.1.4.1**) is an example of the operation of this principle.

> The claimants in *British Steel Corporation v Cleveland Bridge & Engineering Co. Ltd* had begun work on the manufacture of steel nodes at the request of the defendants, despite the fact that the parties had yet to reach agreement on all of the elements of the contract. Final agreement was never reached. The claimants had delivered all but one of the nodes and claimed a *quantum meruit* for the work that they had done. Their claim succeeded.

The *Cleveland Bridge* decision was rightly distinguished by Rattee J in *Regalian Properties plc v London Dockland Development Corporation* [1995] 1 WLR 212. In *Regalian* (unlike the *Cleveland Bridge* case), the claimants had not carried out the work at the request of the defendants; rather, they had done it in order to be able to win the contract from the defendants. In addition, the negotiations had been conducted on a 'subject to contract' basis, so that such expenditure was at the claimants' own risk, conferred no benefit on the defendants, and was not recoverable when they failed to obtain the anticipated contract.

Remuneration on the basis of *quantum meruit* may also be recoverable where performance is rendered under a contract that, unknown to both parties, is void.

> In *Craven-Ellis v Canons Ltd* [1936] 2 KB 403, the claimant had worked as managing director of a company without being appointed in the manner required by law. His contract was therefore void, but he was able to recover the reasonable value of his work.

Similar rules apply in the case of work done by companies under contracts that are void because, at the time at which the contract was made, the company had not been incorporated and so had no legal existence: *Rover International Ltd v Cannon Film Sales Ltd* [1989] 1 WLR 912.

10.5.4.2 *Quantum meruit* despite the contract

Where there is a contract between the parties, it is fundamental to the law of contract that payment is to be determined according to the terms of the contract. The courts must not interfere with the parties' agreement. In *Macdonald Dickens & Mackin (a firm) v Costello* [2011] EWCA Civ 930, [2012] QB 244, the Costellos were the only shareholders and directors of a company, Oakwood. They obtained bank finance to build houses, and, for tax reasons, the funds were routed through this company and it was the company that contracted with the builders. The builders knew about the arrangement. Disputes arose. The company failed to pay, and the builders pursued a claim in unjust enrichment against the company and the Costellos. However, the Court of Appeal held that the contractual obligation to pay for the building work was confined to the company. The unjust enrichment claim against the Costellos had to fail because it would otherwise undermine the contractual position. Thus, even where the Costellos had benefited from the builders' services, they were not liable in restitution because of the existence of the contract. Etherton LJ stated, at [23]:

> The general rule should be to uphold contractual arrangements by which parties have defined and allocated and, to that extent, restricted their mutual obligations, and, in so doing, have similarly allocated and circumscribed the consequences of non-performance. That general rule reflects a sound legal policy, which acknowledges the parties' autonomy to configure the legal relations between them and provides certainty and so limits disputes and litigation.

However, in limited circumstances, that general rule is displaced and the court will allow a *quantum meruit* remedy despite the existence of a contract.

- Where the contract fails to provide for the payment to be made, a reasonable price is payable. This rule has been embodied in statute (SGA 1979, s. 8; Supply of Goods and Services Act 1982, s. 15 (B2B—business to business) and the CRA 2015, s. 51 (B2C—'trader' to 'consumer')). The same rule may also apply where the contract provides a price-fixing mechanism that is regarded as a mechanism for fixing a fair price rather than an essential factor in its determination and, for some unforeseen reason, this mechanism fails to work: *Sudbrook Trading Estate Ltd v Eggleton* [1983] 1 AC 444 (see **3.1.4.4.2**).

- In the case of an entire obligation, partial performance does not entitle the party who breaches by abandoning performance before completion to any payment under the contract (see **8.6.1**). Where, however, the non-breaching party voluntarily accepts a benefit conferred by partial performance before the contract has been abandoned, the party who has breached may recover the reasonable value of the benefit conferred.

- Conversely, where the non-breaching party confers a benefit on the other party before the latter's breach, the non-breaching party may recover the value of that benefit under a *quantum meruit* rather than bringing a claim for damages: *Slowey v Lodder* (1901) 20 NZLR 321, affirmed by the Privy Council *sub nom Lodder v Slowey* [1904] AC 442. By so doing, the non-breaching party may be able to avoid the consequences of having made a bad bargain. In *Lodder v Slowey* a contractor had partially performed his contract before the breach which meant that the contractor was wrongfully excluded from the land on which the work was taking place and therefore unable to complete the contract. The Privy Council upheld the right of the non-breaching party to sue for the work done on a *quantum meruit* instead of suing for damages for breach of contract.

10.6 Enrichment without subtraction from the claimant: the remedy of the account of profits

In this context, the question is whether the claimant can recover where the defendant has been unjustly enriched as a result of a breach of contract, but there is no measurable loss suffered by the claimant (i.e. no subtraction from the claimant). As explained at **9.1.2**, the difficulty is that a transfer (disgorgement) of the defendant's profit, where the claimant has suffered no loss, would appear to constitute punishment for a breach, whereas the contractual remedy of damages is compensatory.

10.6.1 Rejection of such a general remedy

In **Surrey County Council v Bredero Homes Ltd** [1993] 1 WLR 1361, the council sold land to the defendant property developer, who covenanted not to build more than 72 houses on it. Without seeking a variation of the covenant (for which it would certainly have had to pay), the developer built an additional five houses. The council claimed damages based on its estimate of what the defendant would have been required to pay as the 'price' for variation of the covenant. Inevitably, there was some sympathy for the council's case: the developer had deliberately breached the covenant in order to make a greater profit. On the other hand, the council could not be shown to have suffered a loss. Thus there was an enrichment of the defendant without there being any subtraction from the claimant in this case. Normal contract damages were not recoverable, because the claimant was already in the position in which it would have been had the contract not been breached. The question was simply whether the deliberate breach of the contract should in some way be sanctioned by making the defendant disgorge a part of its profit. The Court of Appeal did not think that it should. Case law rejected this possibility. For example, in *Tito v Waddell (No. 2)* [1977] Ch 106, 332, at p. 332. Megarry VC stated: 'The question is not one of making the defendant disgorge what he has saved by committing the wrong, but one of compensating the claimant.' The Court of Appeal in *Surrey v Bredero* was also concerned in policy terms about the potential extension to permit a general right to damages based on disgorging the defendant's profit.

10.6.2 Arguments in favour of a more general ability to disgorge profits

It has been argued that a more general right to 'restitutionary damages' could solve many of the existing dilemmas in the application of principles governing breach of contract. For example, it has been suggested—see Poole (1996) 59 MLR 272, in the context of *Ruxley Electronics v Forsyth* [1996] 1 AC 344 (see **9.3.3.4**)—that in cases in which there is no difference in value, but cost of cure damages would be disproportionate (cases of 'skimped performance'), a suitable remedy would be to require the defendant contractor (say) to disgorge its savings in costs through constructing the swimming pool at less than the required depth. This would send a more appropriate signal to the construction industry and achieve a better balance of the respective interests.

In its report *Aggravated, Exemplary and Restitutionary Damages*, Law Com. No. 247 (1997), at paras 3.38–3.47, the Law Commission rejected suggestions advocating a legislative formulation for such 'restitutionary' damages on the basis that this would 'freeze' the position. Instead, the Law Commission recommended that the availability of such damages should be left to common law development. The conclusion that legislation is not considered necessary was reaffirmed when in 2009 the Ministry of Justice published a response to its 2007 Consultation Paper on this question—*The Law on Damages*, CP 9/07 *Civil Law Reform Bill: Consultation*, CP 53/09 (December 2009).

10.6.3 The decision in *Attorney-General v Blake*: account of profits in very limited circumstances

The question was discussed again in *Attorney-General v Blake* [2001] 1 AC 268 and some common law development occurred, although the exact scope of this development was uncertain. At first sight, this development appeared to be very limited, but, almost inevitably, the decision was initially seized upon by counsel as supporting a broader principle. *The majority of the House of Lords considered that, in 'exceptional circumstances', the non-breaching party could recover the profits made as a result of the other's breach of contract (by way of an account of profits) even where the breach of contract did not involve the use of, or interference with, a property interest of the claimant.*

Lord Nicholls (with whom Lords Goff, Browne-Wilkinson, and Steyn agreed) put the position as follows, at pp. 284H–285B:

> When, exceptionally, a just response to a breach of contract so requires, the court should be able to grant the discretionary remedy of requiring the defendant to account to the claimant for the benefits he has received from his breach of contract. In the same way as a *claimant's interest in performance* may make it just and equitable for the court to make an order for specific performance or grant an injunction, so the *claimant's interest in performance* may make it just and equitable that the defendant should retain no benefit from his breach of contract. [Emphasis added]

In other words, it was considered that such a remedy would give effect to the claimant's 'interest in performance', which subsequently has been interpreted to mean that such damages are compensatory in nature (see discussion at **10.6.4**).

In *Attorney-General v Blake*, Blake had worked for the intelligence services, but had become an agent for the Soviet Union. He had been tried and imprisoned for treason, but had escaped from prison to Moscow, where he had written his autobiography. This book had been published in England and (although by this time none of the material that it contained was confidential) publication was in breach of a term of Blake's former employment contract that he would not divulge official information. The Attorney-General wanted to prevent payment of the royalties to Blake.

The facts of *Blake* were exceptional because of the nature of the wrong involved (which may be analogous to breach of fiduciary duty) and the majority considered that it justified an order that the Attorney-General was entitled to an account of these profits.

Lord Nicholls expressly approved the reasoning in *Wrotham Park Estate Co. Ltd v Parkside Homes Ltd* [1974] 1 WLR 798 and stated that, 'in so far as the *Bredero* [*Surrey County Council v Bredero Homes Ltd* [1993] 1 WLR 1361] decision is inconsistent with the approach adopted in the *Wrotham Park* case, the latter approach is to be preferred'.

10.6.4 What will constitute 'an exceptional case'?

This left open the question of precisely what would constitute an 'exceptional case'. The House of Lords laid down no detailed guidance and stated that 'no fixed rules can be prescribed': *per* Lord Nicholls. The only real comments are the following statements by Lord Nicholls, at p. 285G–H:

> The court will have regarded to all the circumstances, including the subject-matter of the contract, the purpose of the contractual provision which has been breached, the circumstances in which the breach occurred, the consequences of the breach and the circumstances in which relief is being sought.

This is not terribly helpful, because it is far too general. Lord Nicholls added the following as a possible qualifying condition, at p. 285H:

> A useful general guide, although not exhaustive, is whether the claimant has a legitimate interest in preventing the defendant's profit-making activity and, hence, in depriving him of his profit.

In his speech, Lord Nicholls examined the two instances that had been suggested by the Court of Appeal as justifying restitutionary intervention: (i) 'skimped performance'; and (ii) instances in which the profit was made by the defendant doing the very thing that the defendant had contracted not to do. Lord Nicholls considered that neither instance could be covered by an account of profits—implying that instances of skimped performance might be addressed in other ways and that the second possibility was far too wide because it extended to all negative stipulations. It therefore seems that the possibility of recovering account of profit damages for skimped performance has been ruled out.

Lord Nicholls did, however, agree with Lord Woolf in the Court of Appeal that the following factors would *not* be a sufficient basis to justify the award of an account of profits:

- the existence of a cynical and deliberate breach;
- the fact that the breach enabled the defendant to enter into a more profitable contract elsewhere;
- that the defendant had put it out of his power to perform his contract with the claimant.

Thus, although *Attorney-General v Blake* [2001] 1 AC 268 is an important decision in recognizing the possibility of disgorgement of a defendant's profit (in the limited sense of an account of profits), the circumstances in which this remedy might operate are uncertain. The majority clearly considered the practical scope of such a remedy to be extremely limited. Only Lord Hobhouse warned against the potential consequences of this apparent recognition of non-compensatory damages for breach of contract if applied to commercial contracts, arguing that such a step would require 'very careful consideration before it is acceded to'. In particular, Lord Hobhouse stressed the fact that such an award would bypass the usual duty to mitigate in this context. However, this was always unlikely to deter the making of commercial claims including an account for profits, and this proved to be the case.

10.6.5 Claims for an account of profits in subsequent case law

In *Esso Petroleum Co. Ltd v Niad Ltd*, unreported, 22 November 2001—noted by Beatson (2002) 118 LQR 377—Morritt VC concluded that an account of profits was an available remedy on the facts, involving a breach of a commercial contract.

> In return for a discount on the price of petrol received from the claimant, the defendant, the owner of a petrol service station, had agreed to report the petrol prices of local competitors and to charge the price recommended by the claimant oil company. The defendant kept the discount he received, but deliberately failed to implement the scheme. The claimant wanted to know whether it was possible to secure an account of profits obliging the defendant to return the amount charged for petrol over and above the price recommended by the claimant. Morritt VC discussed the decision in *Attorney-General v Blake* [2001] 1 AC 268 and concluded that an account of profits would be an available remedy only in exceptional circumstances in which:
>
> (i) the usual remedies for breach of contract would be inadequate; and
>
> (ii) the claimant had a legitimate interest in preventing the defendant from profiting from the breach
>
> On the facts, and applying these criteria, Morritt VC concluded that this was an exceptional case within the decision in *Blake* because (i) the claimant could not establish the lost sales that were attributable to the defendant's failure to implement the scheme and so damages for breach would have been limited to nominal damages only, and (ii) the claimant had the necessary legitimate interest because the defendant's deliberate breach of the terms of the scheme threatened to undermine that scheme.

It can be argued that one of the difficulties with an account of profits—and a fact that should limit its application—is the need to establish a causal link between the breach and the profit/sales. However, in *Esso v Niad*, the absence of this link is used as a ground justifying the availability of this remedy on the basis that damages were unavailable owing to the very same causal difficulties. Nevertheless, an alternative remedy was considered to exist on the facts—namely, restitutionary recovery on the basis of unjust enrichment. This would allow recovery in full of the excess amount (the difference between the price charged and the recommended prices) and was clearly considered to be the more appropriate remedy by Morritt VC.

The worrying aspect of the decision relates to the liberal interpretation of the *Blake* principles said to govern the circumstances in which the remedy of an account of profits was to be available.

The Court of Appeal was then called upon to determine whether an account of profits could be ordered in a commercial context.

> In *Experience Hendrix LLC v PPX Enterprises Inc.* [2003] EWCA Civ 323, [2003] 1 All ER (Comm) 830, [2003] EMLR 25, PPX owned the copyright in a series of recordings made by Jimi Hendrix before he had become an established artist. By an agreement with the artist's estate, PPX's rights to exploit the copyright were limited and royalty payments were required. PPX granted licences to third parties in terms contravening the agreement. The estate secured an injunction against further breaches, but also sought damages for the earlier breaches. However, the estate could not demonstrate financial loss, and the claim was therefore based on an account of PPX's profits.

The Court of Appeal awarded damages based upon the royalties that the claimant would have charged had a licence been sought and obtained. Mance LJ explained the scope of the *Blake* decision using factors referred to by Lord Nicholls in the House of Lords in *Blake*, emphasizing its exceptional (if not extreme) nature as justifying the account of profits. Mance LJ said, at [29]:

> The exceptional nature of *Blake's* case lay first of all, in its context—employment in the security and intelligence service, of which secret information was the lifeblood, its disclosure being a criminal offence . . . Blake had furthermore committed deliberate and repeated breaches causing untold damage, from which breaches most of the profits indirectly derived in the sense that his notoriety as a spy explained his ability to command the sums for publication which he had done . . . Thirdly, although the argument that Blake was a fiduciary was not pursued beyond first instance, the contractual undertaking he had given was 'closely akin to a fiduciary obligation, where an account of profits is a standard remedy in the event of breach'.

Peter Gibson LJ at [58] expressed his own reasons for agreeing with the outcome:

> In my judgment, because (1) there has been a deliberate breach by PPX of its contractual obligations for its own reward, (2) the claimant would have difficulty in establishing financial loss therefrom, and (3) the claimant has a legitimate interest in preventing PPX's profit-making activity carried out in breach of PPX's contractual obligations, the present case is a suitable one . . . in which damages for breach of contract may be measured by the benefits gained by the wrongdoer from the breach. To avoid injustice I would require PPX to make a reasonable payment in respect of the benefit it has gained.

Similar views were expressed by Hildyard J in *CF Partners (UK) LLP v Barclays Bank plc* [2014] EWHC 3049 (Ch). The correctness of the approach in *Experience Hendrix* was considered by the Supreme Court in *Morris-Garner v One Step (Support) Ltd* [2018] UKSC 20. This case did not involve a claim for loss of profits and so the discussion was *obiter*. The majority of the Supreme Court held that *Experience Hendrix* could be supported on the orthodox basis that 'The agreement gave the claimant a valuable right to control the use made of PPX's copyright. When the copyright was wrongfully used, the claimant was prevented from exercising that right, and consequently suffered a loss equivalent to the amount which could have been obtained by exercising it' (*per* Lord Reed at [89]). However, *Experience Hendrix* was not to be taken as authority for the propositions that 'the fact that loss or damage may be difficult to measure renders it unnecessary to identify such loss or damage, or that it is relevant to an award of damages that the breach of contract was deliberate or the party in breach benefited from his conduct, or that it is relevant to an award of damages that the claimant has a "legitimate interest" in preventing an activity carried out in breach of contract, or that damages for breach of contract and an account of profits are similar remedies at different points along a continuum' (*per* Lord Reed at [90]). The judgment of Peter Gibson LJ is accordingly no longer authoritative.

10.6.6 Assessment

Morris-Garner v One Step (Support) Ltd makes it clear that, other than in exceptional circumstances the criteria for which were not identified, damages are based on the claimant's loss and not on the defendant's profit. In the vast majority of cases, the profits made by the defendant will reflect the opportunity lost by the claimant to make those profits itself. However, the valuation of the claimant's lost opportunity cannot automatically be said to be equal to the defendant's profits, because such profits might not have been open to the claimant. *Blake* is the obvious example, in that the British Government plainly could not assert that it could have made profits from publishing its own secret material on a commercial basis. Again, the claimant may not have had the capacity or finance to exploit the subject matter.

The approach after *Morris-Garner* is that damages are available for the loss of the claimant's opportunity to exploit its right, and the fact that it may be difficult to assess the value of the right does not mean that the claimant can automatically seek an account of profits; it must prove its loss. Perhaps the best means of valuing the right is the amount that the claimant would have charged by way of licence for its exploitation. As will be seen at **10.7**, *Morris-Garner* has adopted this approach, in the form of 'negotiation damages'. *Experience Hendrix* would now be decided on that basis.

The Supreme Court did not refer to *Esso Petroleum v Niad*. In the thirteenth edition of this work, published before the decision in *Morris-Garner*, Professor Poole suggested that the criteria adopted in *Niad*—that damages would not be easy to assess and that the claimant had a legitimate interest in preventing future breaches—'hardly seem appropriate criteria to limit recovery to exceptional cases and may well apply in many commercial cases. In particular, it is difficult to identify circumstances in which a claimant who is owed a contractual performance would not have the necessary legitimate interest in securing that performance and preventing the defendant from profiting from the breach.' Her instincts have proved to be entirely correct. The issue in *Niad* was not preventing future breaches, but rather the quantification of loss from previous breaches, and such loss—although not easy to prove—would have been in the form of sales lost by the claimant as a result of failure to adhere to its pricing requirements. In *Vercoe v Rutland Fund Management Ltd* [2010] EWHC 424 (Ch), [2010] Bus LR D141, Sales J had stated that where the case did not involve an infringement of a proprietary right and where 'there is nothing exceptional to indicate that the defendant should not be entitled to adopt a commercial approach in deciding how to behave in relation to that right, the appropriate remedy is likely to be an award of damages . . . rather than an account of profits'.

10.7 'Negotiating damages'

'Negotiating damages' are appropriate where the defendant has infringed a right belonging to the claimant. It is only where the claimant itself could not have exploited that right that the question of whether the claimant can seek an account of the defendant's profits becomes relevant: that was discussed at **10.6**. The issue here is the assessment of damages where the claimant could itself have exploited that right. In some cases the measure of damages may simply reflect the defendant's profit, because that profit could have been made by the claimant. In many cases, however, the correct measure of damages is the amount that the claimant would have charged for authorized use by the defendant. Damages assessed by way of a notional licence has long been the measure used in proceedings brought for the infringement of intellectual property rights (notably patents, trademarks, copyright, and rights in designs). The majority of the Supreme Court in *Morris-Garner v One Step (Support) Ltd* has now extended the notional licence concept—under the description 'negotiating damages'—to the law of contract generally, but confined to the situation where the claimant has been deprived of his right to enjoy an asset and is to be compensated for loss of that right by reference to its value.

10.7.1 The background: *Wrotham Park* damages

The modern development of the law begins with the *Wrotham Park* decision.

> In *Wrotham Park Estate Co. Ltd v Parkside Homes Ltd* [1974] 1 WLR 798 the defendant had built houses on his land in breach of a restrictive covenant in favour of an adjoining estate. The estate owners sought an injunction, but were unsuccessful. However, they were awarded damages based on the profit that the defendant made from the breach of covenant on the basis that this related to the sum that the estate owners might reasonably have required to relax the covenant. Brightman J clearly considered that the price of the release as damages was essentially compensatory, i.e. compensation for lost expectation, since the position where there is a negative stipulation in a contract is to raise an expectation that the activity in question will not take place, e.g. building more houses than the planning permission permits, or publishing an autobiography that breaches a contractual undertaking not to divulge official secrets. However, there is also an expectation that it is possible to negotiate a release from the negative stipulation at a price. Therefore, assuming that the breach prevents the negotiation of a release, it defeats the claimant's expectation that it will be possible to receive payment to agree to a release.

Quite what had been decided in *Wrotham Park* gave rise to prolonged academic and judicial debate.

10.7.2 Acceptance of *Wrotham Park*

The Court of Appeal in *World Wide Fund for Nature (WWF) v World Wrestling Federation Entertainment Inc.* [2007] EWCA Civ 286, [2008] 1 WLR 445, [2007] Bus LR 1252, at [59] stated that both the *Wrotham Park* award *and* the account of profits in *Attorney-General v Blake* [2001] 1 AC 268 were not 'gains-based'.

> In *World Wide Fund for Nature (WWF) v World Wrestling Federation Entertainment Inc.*, a dispute had arisen between the parties concerning the initials 'WWF', which were used by the Wrestling Federation, but had long been associated with the Fund for Nature. The parties had entered into an agreement to compromise their litigation and to regulate the future use of these initials. This agreement restricted the use that could be made of the initials by the Wrestling Federation. However, the Fund for Nature later alleged various breaches of this agreement and, although it had been refused an account of profits in earlier proceedings, the High Court had later concluded that, in appropriate circumstances, a claimant might be entitled to damages on the *Wrotham Park* basis (accepted to be compensatory), i.e. on the basis of the price to release the negative stipulation. The Wrestling Federation had appealed, claiming that the *Wrotham Park* remedy was a juridically similar remedy to the account of profits, which had been refused earlier in the proceedings. If this was the case, it followed that the matter of the remedy had already been decided and was *res judicata*. The argument was that both were 'gains-based awards'.
>
> The Court of Appeal held that, since the account of profits had been refused, it would be an abuse of process to give permission to seek damages on the *Wrotham Park* basis because these claims were juridically 'highly similar', although this was because they were both compensatory in nature (albeit compensation where there was no identifiable financial loss) and not because they were both restitutionary (or gains-based) remedies.

Thus, although the *Wrotham Park* award was unavailable in this case, the Court of Appeal made it clear that, in a claim relating to a breach of restrictive covenant for an injunction and damages for past breaches, the court might award damages of the price for the release of the negative covenant (as the sum that the court considered would be reasonable for the covenantor to pay and the covenantee to accept for the hypothetical release of the covenant), in addition to an injunction, or *Wrotham Park* damages alone, despite the fact that the claimant (covenantee) was unable to establish any identifiable financial loss. This sum was to be assessed as at the date immediately before the breaches occurred and would cover the period until the injunction (covering future breaches) began to operate.

In *Vercoe v Rutland Fund Management Ltd* [2010] EWHC 424 (Ch), [2010] Bus LR D141, the defendants were parties to a joint venture agreement and used for their own profit information provided by the claimant that should have been used for the parties' joint benefit. Sales J held that damages should be assessed on the basis of a notional release fee.

In *Giedo Van der Garde BV v Force India Formula One Team Ltd (formerly Spyker F1 Team Ltd (England))* [2010] EWHC 2373 (QB), Stadlen J stated that *Wrotham Park* damages were available 'in any suitable case where recoupment of financial loss may not provide an adequate answer' and in *Arroyo v Equion Energia Ltd* [2013] EWHC 3150 (TCC), Stuart-Smith J explained that the basis for the award of *Wrotham Park* damages had been to achieve justice by ensuring that the claimants received some compensation and avoiding leaving the defendants with 'the fruits of their wrongdoing'. Stuart-Smith J therefore sought (at [65]) to extend the remedy to instances 'when the application of the conventional measures of damage cannot provide adequate compensation'; it was not limited to instances where there was no identifiable loss to measure. This accords with the statement made by Chadwick LJ in *WWF* (at [59]) that such damages might be awarded as 'a just response to circumstances in which compensation which is the claimant's due cannot be measured (*or cannot be measured solely*) by reference to identifiable financial loss' (emphasis added).

10.7.3 *Wrotham Park* doubted

Wrotham Park was distinguished in *Surrey County Council v Bredero Homes Ltd* [1993] 1 WLR 1361, and the principle was treated as being of limited application and relevance. It was interpreted by Dillon and Steyn LJJ as resting on wrongful interference with property rights— seemingly by analogy with tort cases of trespass, under which a person who uses land without permission must pay for that use even if no harm has been done to the land (e.g. *Whitwham v Westminster Brymbo Coal and Coke Co.* [1896] 2 Ch 538). In addition, *Wrotham Park* was seen as a decision to award damages in lieu of an injunction, whereas in *Surrey v Bredero* the council had not sought specific enforcement.

In *Marathon Asset Management LLP v Seddon* [2017] EWHC 300 (Comm) there was a primary claim against ex-employees for damages for breach of confidence in taking documents belonging to the employer, and a secondary claim for damages for breach of contract against one of the defendants for failing to report the activities of the others. The difficulty was that there was no evidence that the documents had been used, so the claimant had suffered no loss and the defendants had made no gain. Nevertheless, damages were sought on the basis of the notional fee that would have been charged for a licence of the documents. The *Wrotham Park* claim for breach of contract was dismissed on the ground that there was no implied reporting duty, but Leggatt J noted the exceptional nature of *Wrotham* damages and held that they were available only where the claimant had a legitimate interest in preventing the defendant's profit-making activity, e.g. the protection of a proprietary right. In the present case the employer had no legitimate interest in the performance of a duty to report copying, given that the employee did not himself stand to make any financial gain. Leggatt J expressed the view that *Wrotham* damages could not accurately be described as compensatory because there was no loss, nor could they be described as restitutionary because there was nothing to restore. The description of *Wrotham* damages as restitutionary was accurate only if the word was understood broadly to denote a remedy.

10.7.4 *Morris-Garner* and 'negotiation damages'

In *Morris-Garner v One Step (Support) Ltd* [2018] UKSC 20 the claimant company, which provided supported-living services to those needing care, alleged that the defendants (a former director and manager) had breached restrictive covenants not to compete, not to solicit clients, and not to use the company's confidential information once they left the company. The claimant sought damages for loss, and also an account of profits based upon the sum that would reasonably have been charged to the defendants as the price of releasing them from their covenants. Phillips J ordered an inquiry into damages based upon *Wrotham Park*, in that financial loss was not readily identifiable and that it was just for the claimant to recover damages based upon a notional licence fee or, in the alternative, compensatory damages. That outcome was upheld by the Court of Appeal. The Supreme Court rejected the reasoning of the lower courts. In the words of Lord Reed (at [96]–[97]).

> The judge was mistaken in considering that the claimant had a right to elect how its damages should be assessed. He was mistaken in supposing that the difficulty of quantifying its financial loss, such as it was, justified the abandonment of any attempt to quantify it, and the award instead of a remedy which could not be regarded as compensatory in any meaningful sense. The Court of Appeal was mistaken in treating the deliberate nature of the breach, or the difficulty of establishing precisely the consequent financial loss, or the claimant's interest in preventing the defendants' profit-making activities, as justifying the award of a monetary remedy which was not compensatory. The idea that damages based on a hypothetical release fee are available whenever that is a just response, that being a matter to be decided by the judge on a broad brush basis, is also mistaken. The basis on which damages are awarded cannot be a matter for the discretion of the primary judge.

The Supreme Court's conclusion was that this was not a claim for the loss of a valuable asset but rather one for financial loss suffered for damage to business and that case should be remitted to the judge for quantification of loss: that might not be easy, but difficulty did not mean that there was an automatic right to 'negotiating damages'. The award of 'negotiating damages' was generally to be limited to the situation 'where the breach of contract results in the loss of a valuable asset created or protected by the right which was infringed, as for example in cases concerned with the breach of a restrictive covenant over land, an intellectual property agreement or a confidentiality agreement . . . The claimant has in substance been deprived of a valuable asset, and his loss can therefore be measured by determining the economic value of the asset in question. The defendant has taken something for nothing, for which the claimant was entitled to require payment' (*per* Lord Reed at [92]).

10.8 Summary

In *Morris-Garner* the Supreme Court laid down (at [95]) the principles governing the award of damages, particularly where there is no obvious means of assessment. This analysis reflects the issues discussed in the present chapter:

1. Damages assessed by reference to the value of the use wrongfully made of property (sometimes termed 'user damages') are readily awarded at common law for the invasion of rights to tangible moveable or immoveable property (by detinue, conversion, or trespass). The rationale of such awards is that the person who makes wrongful use of property, where its use is commercially valuable, prevents the owner from exercising a valuable right to control its use, and should therefore compensate him for the loss of the value of the exercise of that right. He takes something for nothing, for which the owner was entitled to require payment.

2. Damages are also available on a similar basis for patent infringement and breaches of other intellectual property rights.

3. Damages can be awarded under Lord Cairns' Act in substitution for specific performance or an injunction, where the court had jurisdiction to entertain an application for such relief at the time when the proceedings were commenced. Such damages are a monetary substitute for what is lost by the withholding of such relief.

4. One possible method of quantifying damages under this head is on the basis of the economic value of the right which the court has declined to enforce, and which it has consequently rendered worthless. Such a valuation can be arrived at by reference to the amount which the claimant might reasonably have demanded as a quid pro quo for the relaxation of the obligation in question. The rationale is that, since the withholding of specific relief has the same practical effect as requiring the claimant to permit the infringement of his rights, his loss can be measured by reference to the economic value of such permission.

5. That is not, however, the only approach to assessing damages under Lord Cairns' Act. It is for the court to judge what method of quantification, in the circumstances of the case before it, will give a fair equivalent for what is lost by the refusal of the injunction.

6. Common law damages for breach of contract are intended to compensate the claimant for loss or damage resulting from the non-performance of the obligation in question. They are therefore normally based on the difference between the effect of performance and non-performance upon the claimant's situation.

7. Where damages are sought at common law for breach of contract, it is for the claimant to establish that a loss has been incurred, in the sense that he is in a less favourable situation, either economically or in some other respect, than he would have been in if the contract had been performed.

8. Where the breach of a contractual obligation has caused the claimant to suffer economic loss, that loss should be measured or estimated as accurately and reliably as the nature of the case permits. The law is tolerant of imprecision where the loss is incapable of precise measurement, and there are also a variety of legal principles which can assist the claimant in cases where there is a paucity of evidence.

Remedies providing for specific relief and restitutionary remedies

10

9. Where the claimant's interest in the performance of a contract is purely economic, and he cannot establish that any economic loss has resulted from its breach, the normal inference is that he has not suffered any loss. In that event, he cannot be awarded more than nominal damages.

10. 'Negotiating damages' can be awarded for breach of contract where the loss suffered by the claimant is appropriately measured by reference to the economic value of the right which has been breached, considered as an asset. That may be the position where the breach of contract results in the loss of a valuable asset created or protected by the right which was infringed. The rationale is that the claimant has in substance been deprived of a valuable asset, and his loss can therefore be measured by determining the economic value of the right in question, considered as an asset. The defendant has taken something for nothing, for which the claimant was entitled to require payment.

11. Common law damages for breach of contract cannot be awarded merely for the purpose of depriving the defendant of profits made as a result of the breach, other than in exceptional circumstances, following *Attorney General v Blake*.

12. Common law damages for breach of contract are not a matter of discretion. They are claimed as of right, and they are awarded or refused on the basis of legal principle.

MULTIPLE-CHOICE QUESTIONS

 Test your knowledge by trying this chapter's **multiple-choice questions**:
www.oup.com/uk/poole

FURTHER READING

General

Burrows, *Remedies for Torts and Breach of Contract*, 3rd edn (Oxford University Press, 2004).

Penalty clauses

Dawson, 'Determining penalties as a matter of construction' [2016] LMCLQ 207.

Fisher, 'Rearticulating the rules against penalty clause' [2016] LMCLQ 70.

Restraint of trade

Lucey, 'Restraint of trade doctrine: a traditional tool fit for the modern economy?' in Merkin and Devenney (eds.), *Essays in Memory of Professor Jill Poole* (Informa Law, 2018), ch. 11.

Specific performance

Burrows, 'Specific performance at the crossroads' (1984) 4 LS 102.

Jones, 'Specific performance: a lessee's covenant to keep open a retail store' [1997] CLJ 488.

Kronman, 'Specific performance' (1978) 45 U Chi L Rev 351.

Phang, 'Specific performance: exploring the roots of "settled practice"' (1998) 61 MLR 421.

Schwartz, 'The case for specific performance' (1979) 89 Yale LJ 271.

Enrichment by subtraction: total failure of consideration and quantum meruit

Carter and Tolhurst, 'Restitution for failure of consideration' (1997) 11 JCL 162.

Law Commission Working Paper No. 65, *Pecuniary Restitution on Breach of Contract* (1975).

Law Commission Report No. 121, *Pecuniary Restitution on Breach of Contract* (1983).

Blake and Wrotham Park

Beatson, 'Courts, arbitrators and restitutionary liability for breach of contract' (2002) 118 LQR 377.

Birks, 'Profits of breach of contract' (1993) 109 LQR 518.

Burrows, 'No restitutionary damages for breach of contract' [1993] LMCLQ 453.

Campbell, 'The treatment of *Teacher v Calder* in *A-G v Blake*' (2002) 65 MLR 256.

Campbell, 'The extinguishing of contract' (2004) 67 MLR 817.

Cunnington, 'Changing conceptions of compensation' (2007) 66 CLJ 507.

Cunnington, 'The assessment of gain-based damages for breach of contract' (2008) 71 MLR 559.

Davies, 'One step forwards: the availability of *Wrotham Park* damages for breach of contract' [2017] LMCLQ 202.

Edelman, *Gain-Based Damages: Contract, Tort, Equity and Intellectual Property* (Hart Publishing, 2002).

Goodhart, 'Restitutionary damages for breach of contract' [1995] RLR 3.

Hedley, 'Very much the wrong people: the House of Lords and publication of spy memoirs' (2000) 4 Web JCLI.

Law Commission Report No. 247, *Aggravated, Exemplary and Restitutionary Damages* (1997).

McKendrick, 'Breach of contract, restitution for wrongs and punishment' in Burrows and Peel (eds.), *Commercial Remedies* (Oxford University Press, 2003).

Morgan, Great *Debates in Contract Law*, 2nd edn (Palgrave Macmillan, 2015), ch. 9.

Rotheram, 'Subjective valuation of unjustment in restitution for wrong' [2017] LMCLQ 412.

Chapter 11

Privity of contract and third party rights

SUMMARY OF THE ISSUES

- The doctrine of privity of contract provides that a person who is not a party to a contract cannot acquire any rights under that contract or be subject to any of its burdens. This doctrine remains the general rule in English law.

- The fact that a third party beneficiary of a contract could not enforce the contractual benefits in its favour was generally regarded as unsatisfactory and a number of devices were developed in order to circumvent this aspect of the privity doctrine. In addition, a number of exceptions were developed whereby third party rights were recognized. These devices and exceptions can be artificial and complex, so that there were calls for reform of the third party beneficiary rule. However, these devices and exceptions remain, despite legislative reform.

- The Contracts (Rights of Third Parties) Act 1999 allows the parties to a contract to grant enforceable rights (such as the ability to rely on an exemption or limitation) to third parties. It is not every third party who will be able to enforce a contractual provision in its favour, only those third parties who satisfy the test of enforceability in s. 1 of the Act. Part of this test requires that the third party be expressly identified in the contract by name, description, or as falling within a particular class, e.g. independent contractors.

- Where the s. 1 test is satisfied, it will not matter that the third party may not have provided consideration for the promise that it is seeking to enforce, as long as the promise is not gratuitous (i.e. as long as it is supported by consideration supplied by another).

- The 1999 Act includes provisions dealing with the effect on third parties of variations and cancellations of the original contract terms and the question of enforcement by both the promisee and third party.

- If the third party has not been given an enforceable right under the 1999 Act, it is still possible for the promisee to enforce the promise and seek to obtain a remedy on behalf of the third party beneficiary, e.g. specific performance requiring that the promisor perform the promise for the benefit of the third party. The difficulty in a promisee seeking to recover damages on behalf of a third party is that a party is generally restricted to recovering damages for their own loss. In some circumstances, it is possible for a promisee to recover substantial damages to compensate for a loss suffered by a third party. One argument, giving a broad interpretation to the scope of the promisee's performance interest, has been the subject of much academic debate and has wider potential implications for damages for breach of contract. However, there is no judicial consensus as to its merits.

- The 1999 Act does not affect the rule that a contract cannot impose an obligation (or burden) on a person who is not a party to the contract. Nevertheless, some specific exceptions exist at common law.

11.1 Background: who can enforce the contract?

The examination of the law of contract in the preceding chapters of this book almost always assumed that the type of contract under consideration involved two parties who were each to perform a stipulated obligation towards the other. From that assumption, it followed that the enforcement of the obligations promised in the contract was a principal concern of the contracting parties themselves and the question of whether any other person might be entitled to enforce performance of the contract did not arise. This concentration on the effect of bilateral contracts between the contracting parties is inevitable, since that is the area in which most contractual disputes occur. Nevertheless, it is easy to imagine situations in which one party has stipulated in the contract that performance be made towards some other person, and examples of this type of contract have been noted in passing (e.g. at **4.4.2** and **10.2.1**).

This chapter considers the rules of the law of contract, and related rules, applicable to contracts that stipulate a benefit for a third party. This type of contract may most easily be described in terms of a triangular relationship (see **Figure 11.1**).

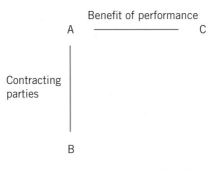

FIGURE 11.1 Triangular relationship

The contract is negotiated and made between A and B, but B stipulates that A's performance should be made to C (the third party). Thus, A may agree with B that goods or services are to be supplied to C. Alternatively, A may agree to provide services to B (e.g. carrying goods) but the carriage is delegated to C, and B agrees that it will not bring proceedings against C if the goods are damaged. The questions that arise are:

- whether C may enforce A's promise to perform for C's benefit; and
- whether B may enforce A's promise for the benefit of C.

Related problems arise when B purports to stipulate not for a benefit to accrue to C from A's performance, but for C to perform B's obligations under the contract (so-called 'burdens' under the contract).

The general principle is that only the parties to the contract are bound by, or are entitled to a remedy for enforcement of the obligations under, the contract. This rule is known as the *doctrine of privity of contract*. The effect of the doctrine may be demonstrated by reference to a classic case from the law of torts.

In ***Donoghue v Stevenson*** [1932] AC 562, the appellant and a friend went into a cafe, where the friend ordered a bottle of ginger beer for the appellant. The drink came in an opaque bottle. Part of the contents was poured out and the appellant consumed it. When the rest was poured out, a partly decomposed snail was found. The appellant suffered nervous shock and illness, and wished to recover compensation. She was unable to proceed against the cafe owner in contract because the contract to purchase the ginger beer was made with her friend and the appellant was not a party to it. Accordingly, she chose to proceed against the manufacturer of the ginger beer and established a breach of a duty of care in tort.

The unavailability of an action in contract against either manufacturer or retailer led to the development, in *Donoghue v Stevenson*, of the modern tort of negligence, under which the claimant may recover compensation for loss suffered as a result of the defendant's breach of a duty of care.

11.2 The doctrine of privity of contract and its relationship with the consideration requirement

The doctrine of privity of contract states that a person may not enforce a contractual promise and obtain remedies for its breach, even when the promise was expressly made for that person's benefit, if they are not a party to the contract. The corollary of this is that persons who are not party to a contract may not have their rights diminished by that contract.

Both aspects of the doctrine have been subject to certain exceptions, although the exceptions to the latter rule (the 'burden' rule) are limited. Indeed, the rationale of the burden rule is easy to understand, since any other rule would be an infringement of individual liberty. However, the benefit rule is less readily explained (although **see 11.3**). It was confirmed in English law in the early nineteenth century: *Price v Easton* (1833) 4 B & Ad 433 and by the House of Lords in *Dunlop Pneumatic Tyre Co. Ltd v Selfridge & Co. Ltd* [1915] AC 847.

In **_Dunlop Pneumatic Tyre Co. Ltd v Selfridge & Co. Ltd_**, Dunlop, the appellant, had sold tyres to a distributor (Dew & Co.) on terms that the distributor would not resell them at a price lower than the appellant's list price and on terms requiring that if tyres were sold to a trade buyer, the distributor would obtain a similar undertaking from that buyer. The distributor resold some tyres to the respondent, Selfridge, who gave the required undertaking, agreeing to pay £5 liquidated damages to the appellant for each tyre sold in breach of that undertaking. The respondent sold tyres below the list price and the appellant sued to recover the agreed damages. The scenario was, accordingly, one in which the distributor, A, sold goods to trade buyers, B, on terms that B would not resell below manufacturer C's list price and if B did so then compensation would be paid to C.

In a much-quoted passage, Viscount Haldane LC said, at p. 853:

My Lords, in the Law of England certain principles are fundamental. One is that only a person who is a party to a contract can sue on it. Our law knows nothing of a *jus quaesitum tertio* arising by way of contract. Such a right may be conferred by way of property, as, for example, under a trust, but it cannot be conferred on a stranger to a contract as a right to enforce the contract *in personam*. A second principle is that if a person with whom a contract not under seal has been made is to be able to enforce it consideration must have been given by him to the promisor or to some other person at the promisor's request.

Viscount Haldane's statement of the privity doctrine has been taken as comprising two elements: the need to be a party to the contract in order to enforce it; and the need to provide consideration for the promise being enforced.

11.2.1 Consideration must move from the promisee

The rule that consideration must move from the promisee appears to originate in an early privity case: *Tweddle v Atkinson* (1861) 1 B & S 393.

> In **Tweddle v Atkinson**, after a marriage, the partners' respective fathers entered into an agreement whereby each would pay a sum of money to the husband and, by that agreement, the husband was to have the power to sue for the sums of money promised. After the death of his wife's father, the husband sued his father-in-law's estate to recover the sum promised. However, the action failed because the husband had given no consideration for the promise (although he was also not a party to the contract).

The rule that consideration must move from the promisee also appears to have been the *ratio* of the decision of the House of Lords in *Dunlop Pneumatic Tyre Co. Ltd v Selfridge & Co. Ltd* [1915] AC 847 (see **11.2**). The need to establish consideration has resulted in all kinds of complexities in devices designed to avoid the application of the privity doctrine, e.g. agency (see e.g. **11.5.2.2**).

The rule that consideration must move from the promisee was traditionally explained on the basis that a party not providing consideration is not part of the axis of inducement or mutual exchange, which is central to the enforceability of agreements. However, it is clear from an examination of *Tweddle v Atkinson* that this was not how this rule was interpreted in the context of third party enforcement. Instead, it was interpreted as 'consideration must move from the *plaintiff* [*claimant*]' or person seeking to enforce the promise. The promisee (the groom's father in relation to the promise of the bride's father that the husband—son and son-in-law— was seeking to enforce) had clearly provided consideration for the promise in the form of his reciprocal promise of payment, so that the promise was not gratuitous. The difficulty was that no consideration had been provided by the person who was seeking to enforce the promise (the claimant husband).

This matter had to be addressed by the Law Commission, when it proposed legislation to permit enforcement by third party beneficiaries in some instances. Clearly, the entire reform would be ineffectual if the third party could be prevented from enforcing the contract on the basis that it had not provided consideration. In its report *Privity of Contracts: Contracts for the benefit of third parties*, Law Com. No. 242 (Cm. 3329, 1996)—see Part VI, pp. 68–73—the Law Commission concluded that the third party beneficiary of a promise need not provide consideration if consideration had been provided by the *promisee*. It did not follow that consideration had to be supplied by the claimant third party.

There is no provision in the applicable legislation, the Contracts (Rights of Third Parties) Act 1999, spelling out the position on consideration, but the case law indicates that the fact that consideration does not move from the third party claimant will not defeat the legislative purpose.

⚙ **SUMMARY**

Since the introduction of this legislation, a third party seeking to enforce a contractual provision using the 1999 Act cannot be defeated by a claim that the third party has not provided consideration to support the promise, as long as the promise is not gratuitous (i.e. as long as the promisee has supplied consideration).

11.3 Criticisms and calls for reform

The reasons for the privity doctrine are unclear. In *Trident General Insurance Co. Ltd v McNiece Brothers Proprietary Ltd* (1988) 165 CLR 107, in the High Court of Australia, Toohey J considered that the privity doctrine 'lacks a sound foundation in jurisprudence and logic'.

11.3.1 Justifications of the privity doctrine

1. It has sometimes been suggested that the doctrine rests on a principle of mutuality, to the effect that it would be unfair to allow a person to sue on a contract where that person cannot be sued by the other party: *Tweddle v Atkinson* (1861) 1 B & S 393.

2. It has also sometimes been suggested that it would be undesirable to allow third party rights to be created by contract, since that would restrict the freedom of the parties subsequently to amend or rescind their agreement: *Re Schebsman* [1944] Ch 83.

3. Alternatively, it was suggested that third party beneficiaries were frequently gratuitous recipients of the benefit in their favour and so the rule was closely related to the doctrine of consideration.

Each of these explanations is open to objection, either on the ground that, provided that the contract is freely negotiated, there is no particular reason why contracting parties should not undertake obligations that lack mutuality or which restrict their future freedom to act, or on the ground that the explanation does not account for the full extent of the rule.

11.3.2 Criticism in the context of the intended third party beneficiary

Whatever the explanation of the rule may be, it has been strongly and consistently criticized, at least in the context of contractual provisions in favour of third parties: see e.g. Flannigan (1987) 103 LQR 564. Thus whereas it has generally been accepted that there must be a privity doctrine to prevent total strangers from seeking to enforce a contract, it is more difficult to justify why, in situations in which a contract is expressly made for the benefit of a third party—such as the husband in *Tweddle v Atkinson* (1861) 1 B & S 393—that third party should not be able to enforce this benefit. It is essentially in the context of enforcement by these third party intended beneficiaries that exceptions to privity have been recognized and various devices have been invented to avoid the operation of the doctrine.

In *Dunlop Pneumatic Tyre Co. Ltd v Selfridge & Co. Ltd* [1915] AC 847, at p. 855, Lord Dunedin, who felt compelled to agree with Viscount Haldane in finding against the appellants, said:

> I confess that this case is to my mind apt to nip any budding affection which one might have had for the doctrine of consideration. For the effect of that doctrine in the present case is to make it possible for a person to snap his fingers at a bargain deliberately made, a bargain not in itself unfair, and which the person seeking to enforce it has a legitimate interest to enforce.

As long ago as 1937, the Law Revision Committee, in its Sixth Interim Report (Cmnd 5449, 1937), at p. 31, proposed that a third party should be able to enforce a contract where the contract expressly conferred a benefit on that third party. In *Beswick v Beswick* [1968] AC 58, at p. 72C, Lord Reid referred to this proposal and said that 'if one had to contemplate a further long period of Parliamentary procrastination, this House might find it necessary to deal with this matter'. In *Woodar Investment Development Ltd v Wimpey Construction (UK) Ltd* [1980] 1 WLR 277, Lord Scarman regretted that nothing had been done about this 'unjust rule', and he was not alone in his criticism. Lord Goff in *White v Jones* [1995] 2 AC 207, at pp. 262H–263A, commented that:

> [O]ur law of contract is widely seen as deficient in the sense that it is perceived to be hampered by the presence of an unnecessary doctrine of consideration and (through a strict doctrine of privity of contract) stunted through a failure to recognise a *jus quaesitum tertio*.

The justifications for reform of the third party beneficiary rule are well rehearsed, and were set out and explained by the Law Commission in its 1996 report, at pp. 39–50. The fundamental justifications for reform were also set out by Steyn LJ in *Darlington Borough Council v Wiltshier Northern Ltd* [1995] 1 WLR 68, at p. 76:

> The case for recognising a contract for the benefit of a third party is simple and straightforward. The autonomy of the will of the parties should be respected. The law of contract should give effect to the reasonable expectations of contracting parties . . . there is no doctrinal, logical, or policy reason why the law should deny effectiveness to a contract for the benefit of a third party where that is the expressed intention of the parties. Moreover, often the parties, and particularly third parties, organise their affairs on the faith of the contract. They rely on the contract. It is therefore unjust to deny effectiveness to such a contract. I will not struggle with the point further since nobody seriously asserts the contrary.

- *Intention* Whereas the intentions of the parties are usually given prominence in English contract law (see the discussion of classical contract law, at **1.4.1**), in respect of the operation of the privity doctrine, those expressed intentions were ignored.

- *Reliance by third party beneficiary* Not unreasonably, a third party intended beneficiary may have relied upon the promise.

- *Attempts to avoid privity: complex, artificial, and uncertain* It is also the case that the various attempts to avoid the operation of privity in this context (see **11.6**) have resulted in legal principles that are complex, artificial, and uncertain.

- *European position* Perhaps most significant is the fact that many of the jurisdictions in the European single market provide for the enforceability of stipulations for the benefit of third parties and the English position would cause harmonization difficulties for the European Union: see e.g. Art. 6:110 of the Principles of European Contract Law (PECL), by which a third party's right to enforce may be expressly or impliedly agreed by the parties, and the Draft Common Frame of Reference (DCFR) II-9:301, under which the parties to a contract may, by the contract, confer a right or other benefit on a third party.

- *Commonwealth position* Significantly, the doctrine has also either been rejected or abrogated in many Commonwealth and common law jurisdictions—a good example is the New Zealand Contracts (Privity) Act 1982 (re-enacted in the Contracts and Commercial Law Act 2017)—so that the English position appeared to be out of line.

- *Commercial difficulties* However, perhaps the greatest impetus for reform stemmed from the fact that the third party rule led to difficulties in commercial life. The Law Commission specifically cited and explained the problems in relation to construction contracts and insurance contracts. (Unfortunately, it appears that the legislative reform, with its associated uncertainties, has had the opposite effect to that intended—see also **11.4.2**—because parties to such agreements are contracting out of the application of the legislation designed to enable third party beneficiaries to rely on contractual provisions in their favour.)

11.3.3 The debate concerning the format for reform

The debate in the early to mid-1990s focused on the format for reform and, in particular, whether reform should be achieved judicially on a case-by-case basis or by means of legislation.

The Supreme Court of Canada in *London Drugs Ltd v Kuehne & Nagel International Ltd* (1993) 97 DLR (4th) 261, when faced with a situation that did not fall within the technical requirements of an existing exception—*New Zealand Shipping Co. Ltd v A. M. Satterthwaite & Co. Ltd, The Eurymedon* [1975] AC 154 (see **11.6.4**)—created a new exception in order to give effect to the 'true intentions of the contracting parties and commercial reality'. Iacobucci J advocated this 'incremental approach' to change in appropriate circumstances.

A further example of this approach can be seen in *Fraser River Pile & Dredge Ltd v Can-Dive Services Ltd* [2000] 1 Lloyd's Rep 199. The Supreme Court of Canada continued its 'incremental changes' and held that a third party who fell within the class of 'charterers' could rely on a 'waiver of subrogation clause' in an insurance policy notwithstanding the doctrine of privity of contract.

However, as Iacobucci J made clear in his judgment in *London Drugs*, 'major reforms . . . must come from the legislature' and, in *Fraser River*, at [43], he again stated:

> Wholesale abolition of the doctrine would result in complex repercussions that exceed the ability of the Courts to anticipate and address. It is now a well-established principle that the Courts will not undertake judicial reform of this magnitude, recognizing instead that the legislature is better placed to appreciate and accommodate the economic and policy issues involved in introducing sweeping legal reforms.

There are also distinct problems posed by judicial reform of the privity rule, such as having to wait for an 'appropriate' case to arise and for the question of reform to be fully argued: *per* Lord Goff in *The Mahkutai* [1996] 3 All ER 502. However, the greatest danger of judicial reform is the uncertainty that it would generate (a particular problem in the commercial context), and the

Law Commission cited this uncertainty as a reason in favour of its proposed legislative reform on the question of enforcement by third party beneficiaries.

11.3.4 The scope of the legislative reform

> **! KEY POINT**
>
> The Law Commission's proposed legislative reform was broadly adopted as the Contracts (Rights of Third Parties) Act 1999, a lead followed in Scotland by the Contracts (Third Party Rights) (Scotland) Act 2017. However, it is important to appreciate that the 1999 Act does not abolish privity.

There are a number of reasons why the scope of the 1999 Act is limited.

1. Burdens were excluded from the scope of the Law Commission's reform and the Act does not therefore allow enforcement of burdens imposed on third parties. The exceptional situations in which a 'burden' may be imposed on a third party are discussed briefly at **11.8**.

2. It is not every third party who can enforce a contractual provision. The test of enforceability in s. 1 of the Act must be satisfied before a third party will have rights of enforcement. This test of enforceability is vital to the scope of the legislation and, as we will see, many of the existing decisions would be unaffected if the Act were to apply to the same set of facts. However, s. 7(1) of the Act makes it clear that the existing exceptions to privity and devices to avoid privity will continue to operate in this situation.

3. It is possible—and, in fact, common in practice—for the contract to opt out of the legislation, e.g. a common third party rights clause will provide: 'A person who is not a party to this Contract shall have no right under the Contracts (Rights of Third Parties) Act 1999 to enforce any term of this Contract. This clause does not affect any right or remedy of any person which exists or is available otherwise than pursuant to that Act.'

It is therefore necessary to approach this topic by first examining the Act and its scope, and then examining what are now residual common law exceptions, which may still be relevant in some situations falling outside the Act. It was envisaged that the existence of the Act would not curtail judicial developments outside the scope of the Act, although it was always likely that the Act would have some effect on interpretation of common law devices falling outside its remit. It is also the case that the existing rights of promisees to secure remedies for the benefit of third parties are unaffected by the legislation. The Law Commission specifically left this question for judicial reform. The scope for the promisee to recover on behalf of the third party, and the limitations on this ability, are discussed at **11.7**.

11.4 The Contracts (Rights of Third Parties) Act 1999

11.4.1 Third party enforcement

In its 1996 report, the Law Commission had recommended that the privity doctrine be reformed by legislation in order to 'enable contracting parties to confer a right to enforce the contract on a third party', i.e. the right to enforce remedies for breach of contract that would have been available had the third party been a contracting party and the right to enforce an exemption clause as if the third party had been a party to the contract.

- This basic right is contained in s. 1(1) of the 1999 Act, which states that a person who is not a party to the contract may enforce a term of the contract in his own right if the test of enforceability in s. 1(1)–(3) is satisfied.

- Section 1(5) provides that, for this purpose, the third party will have:

> any remedy that would have been available to him in an action for breach of contract if he had been a party to the contract (and the rules relating to damages, injunctions, specific performance and other relief shall apply accordingly).

- For the avoidance of doubt, s. 1(6) provides for a third party to be able to enforce— either as a right of action or a contractual defence: *Fortress Value Recovery Fund I LLC v Blue Skye Special Opportunities Fund LP* [2013] EWCA Civ 367, [2013] 1 CLC 752, at [28]—an exemption or limitation clause in a contract (where the test of enforceability is satisfied). This is important to the reform, because many of the difficult cases have concerned enforcement of these clauses by third parties and one of much criticized technical common law exceptions to privity was developed to deal with the situation in which a third party beneficiary seeks to rely on an exemption clause in a contract (see **11.6.4**).

- The fact that the third party has not provided consideration to support the promise will not prevent that third party from enforcing the term (assuming that the promise is not gratuitous). This is not contained in the Act, but the entire reform would fail if the position were otherwise, and the Law Commission made this clear in its report.

- By s. 3, the promisor will have the same defences and rights of set-off in a claim for enforcement brought by the third party as in a claim brought by the promisee. Section 3(6) specifically states that a third party seeking to enforce an exemption clause will be subject to the same controls on enforcement as would exist in the case of enforcement by a contracting party. This is subject to any express clause in the contract giving additional or reduced defences in an enforcement claim by a third party.

11.4.2 The test for third party enforceability

As discussed earlier (at **11.3.2**), it was never intended that complete strangers should be able to enforce contractual provisions; only third parties who were intended to benefit under the relevant term of the contract. Accordingly, the test of enforceability must achieve this objective. Formulating such a test proved to be difficult and the proposed test contained in the Report was altered from that which had originally been proposed in the Consultation Paper on the basis that the original test was too restrictive, since it required not only that there be an intention that the terms should confer a benefit on the third party, but also that there was an intention that it should create a legal obligation enforceable by that third party (the so-called 'dual intention test'). This dual intention test was rejected and replaced with the test now contained in s. 1(1)–(3) of the 1999 Act.

There are two ways in which a third party may satisfy the test of enforceability and be able to enforce contractual terms under the Act. These are:

1. *The contract may expressly state that the third party is to have a right to enforce the provision (s. 1(1)(a)).* Under s. 1(3), the third party 'must be expressly identified in the contract by name, as a member of a class or as answering a particular description', although the third party need not be in existence at the time the contract is made. On the basis of current drafting practice, it will be rare that the s. 1(1)(a) test of enforceability will be satisfied. It requires a particular form of drafting, which, if used in the past, did not achieve its objective. Ironically, there was such a provision on the facts in *Tweddle v Atkinson* (1861) 1 B & S 847, so that if this set of case facts were to arise again, the husband ought to be able to enforce the promise in his favour. Section 1(1)(a) does, however, indicate the most straightforward method for conferring a right of enforcement on third parties, where this is desired, and ought therefore to have affected **future** drafting practice. Nevertheless, the evidence to date is that, rather than contracting to fall within the Act, many commercial parties are contracting to avoid its operation because of the uncertainties over some of its other provisions. Contracting so that the Act will not operate can be achieved by stating that the third party will not receive an enforceable right (see **11.3.4** for an example of such a clause).

2. *As an alternative to the s. 1(1)(a) test, third parties will also fall within the Act and be able to enforce contractual provisions in their own right where they are expressly identified in the contract and 'the term purports to confer a benefit' on that third party (s. 1(1)(b)).* For s. 1(1)(b) to apply, it is vital to establish that the clause or agreement in question was 'intended to confer a benefit' on a 'third' party. It is not enough that an incidental benefit is conferred upon a third party by reason of the necessary operation of the term. Christopher Clarke J made this clear in his application in *Dolphin & Maritime & Aviation Services Ltd v Sveriges Angfartygs Assurans Forening, The Swedish Club* [2009] EWHC 716 (Comm), [2009] 1 CLC 460, [2009] 2 Lloyd's Rep 123.

In **The Swedish Club**, the claimant (Dolphin) was a recovery agent acting on behalf of the insurers in relation to a vessel entered with the Swedish Club, which had been involved in a collision. Acting on behalf of the insurers, Dolphin had entered into an agreement with the Club whereby sums recoverable from the owner of the vessel that had caused the collision were to be paid to Dolphin. However, the insurers had settled directly with the Club and had refused to pay Dolphin's commission. Dolphin had therefore sought to enforce the terms of its agreement with the Club. The judge held that the agreement with the Club related only to the means by which payment was to be made to the insurers. The intended beneficiaries of the agreement were the insurers, on whose behalf the payment was to be received, and not Dolphin, albeit that Dolphin's position would have been improved had the Club paid Dolphin (since the commission could have been deducted from this sum). This was not 'an agreement by A and B that A will pay C (C not being A's agent or trustee)', but a 'provision for payment of a sum to an agent on his principal's behalf', and so not covered by s. 1(1)(b)).

Dolphin was distinguished in *Cavanagh v Secretary of State for Work and Pensions* [2016] EWHC 1136 (QB), [2016] ICR 826. Two employees opted in their contracts of employment to have their subscriptions to the Public and Commercial Services Union deducted from their salaries. The Secretary of State discontinued these check-off arrangements. It was held that the employees and also the Union had the right to enforce the arrangements. A contract term was perfectly capable of conferring benefits upon both the promisee and a third party, and this was not a case of incidental benefit: the very purpose of the provision was to permit the Union to be paid subscriptions directly from salaries.

11.4.2.1 The proviso to s. 1(1)(b): s. 1(2)

By s. 1(2) of the 1999 Act: 'Subsection (1)(b) does not apply if on a proper construction of the contract it appears that the parties did not intend the term to be enforceable by the third party.'

This would appear to be the case in most construction contracts, so that s. 1(1)(b) will not enable a building owner (a third party to the contract between main contractor and subcontractor) to sue a subcontractor directly, since the intention is that the building owner should sue the main contractor.

The literal interpretation of the s. 1(2) proviso to s. 1(1)(b) indicates that it will defeat the test of enforceability in s. 1(1)(b) only where there is something in the contract that indicates that the parties had no intention to confer an enforceable benefit on the third party on whom the contract terms purport to confer a benefit. It follows logically that the third party does not need to prove a negative. If the contract is silent on the matter, the s. 1(1)(b) test of enforceability will be satisfied.

The operation of the test of enforceability was considered in *Nisshin Shipping Co. Ltd v Cleaves & Co. Ltd* [2003] EWHC 2602 (Comm), [2004] 1 Lloyd's Rep 38.

In *Nisshin Shipping Co. Ltd v Cleaves & Co. Ltd*, Cleaves (C) had negotiated a number of time charters on behalf of the owners (N). Each charter contract provided for the payment of commission to C and contained an arbitration clause. N claimed that C was not entitled to the commission because it was in repudiatory breach of the agency agreement. C purported to refer the commission issue to arbitration and claimed to have the standing to be able to enforce the commission clause as a result of the application of s. 1(1)(b) of the 1999 Act, although it was not a party to the charter contracts. (It was accepted that the clauses did not expressly provide that Cleaves could enforce the commission clause directly against Nisshin.)

Colman J held:

1. The clause purported to confer a benefit on Cleaves.

2. Section 1(2) did not require that, for s. 1(1)(b) to apply, it had to be shown that the parties positively intended that the benefit should be enforceable by the third party; rather, it stated that s. 1(1)(b) could not apply if it appeared that the parties did *not* intend the third party to have a right of enforcement. Thus, since the contract was silent on the matter, there was nothing to indicate that the parties did not intend C to have the right of enforcement and the s. 1(1)(b) test of enforceability was satisfied.

This decision therefore confirms the literal interpretation of the s. 1(2) proviso and the analysis was subsequently confirmed by the Court of Appeal in *Laemthong International Lines Co. Ltd v Artis, The Laemthong Glory (No. 2)* [2005] EWCA Civ 519, [2005] 1 CLC 739, [2005] 2 All ER (Comm) 167.

In *The Laemthong Glory (No. 2)*, a problem had arisen concerning the delivery of goods at the end of a voyage charter, since delivery was to be on presentation of the bills of lading, but these documents had not reached the receivers of the cargo prior to the arrival of the ship at the port of destination. Where the bills of lading were unavailable, the goods could be delivered to the receivers if a letter of indemnity

(LOI) were provided by the receivers. The parties to the LOI were the charterers and receivers, so that it amounted to a contract between the charters and the receivers. The LOI contained a promise by the receivers to indemnify the charterers, its servants, or agents in respect of any liability resulting from the delivery of the goods at the receivers' request without production of the bill of lading. On the arrest of the vessel and production of the original bills of lading by the Yemen Bank and its claim to the value of the goods discharged, the question arose of whether the shipowners were covered by this LOI (between charterers and receivers) because the shipowners were not a party to it, but had delivered the cargo to the receivers. The shipowners sought to rely on s. 1 of the 1999 Act.

The Court of Appeal held that the shipowners were to be regarded as the 'agent' of the charterers for the purpose of delivery of the goods to the receivers. The terms of the LOI amounted to a promise to confer a benefit on the shipowners, acting as 'agent' and the receivers had failed to discharge the burden imposed by s. 1(2) of proving that this LOI was not intended by the parties (receivers and charterers) to be enforceable by the shipowners. As a result, the indemnity promise in the LOI was enforceable.

A further example of the application of s. 1(1)(b) and its relationship with the s. 1(2) proviso is provided by the next case.

In **Prudential Assurance Co. Ltd v Ayres** [2007] EWHC 775 (Ch), [2007] 3 All ER 946, the tenant had assigned the lease and provided a guarantee to the landlord for payment of the rent in the event that the new tenant (the assignee), a partnership, failed to pay. However, the landlord and the new tenant (the assignee partnership) had then entered into a separate deed agreeing that the liability under the lease should be limited and that the same limitation should apply in relation to 'any previous tenant' on a guarantee. When the partnership became insolvent, the landlord sought the unpaid rent from the original tenant in accordance with the guarantee. The original tenant sought to rely on the limitation in the deed to which it was not a party. Lindsay J held that the tenant could enforce the deed through the application of s. 1(1)(b) of the 1999 Act. He considered that the tenant fell within the expression 'any previous tenant' used in that deed and that the deed purported to confer a benefit on that tenant. The judge noted, at [28], that:

> There is within s. 1(1)(b) no requirement that the benefit on the third party shall be the predominant purpose or intent behind the term or that it denies the applicability of section 1(1)(b) if a benefit is conferred on someone other than the third party.

In addition, there was nothing to indicate that the tenant was not intended to be able to enforce this protection directly, although the judge pointed out, at [27], that: 'It would have been easy enough (but somewhat destructive of the overall purpose of [the deed]) so to provide had that been intended but nothing to that effect appears.' It followed that the original tenant could rely on the deed's limitation clause when sued under the guarantee.

Although this decision was overturned by the Court of Appeal—[2008] EWCA Civ 52, [2008] 1 All ER 1266—this was on the construction of the deed, which it was held did not purport to convey any benefit on the original tenant in relation to the guarantee relationship between the landlord and the original tenant. Accordingly, no application of the 1999 Act arose. Nevertheless, it is clear that the first instance comments of Lindsay J concerning the construction of s. 1(1)(b) of the Act remain valid and they were cited by Christopher Clarke J in the subsequent decision of *Dolphin & Maritime & Aviation Services Ltd v Sveriges Angfartygs Assurans Forening, The Swedish Club* [2009] EWHC 716 (Comm), [2009] 1 CLC 460, [2009] 2 Lloyd's Rep 123 (discussed above).

11.4.2.2 Section 1(3)

In a practical sense, the s. 1(1)(b) test will also be limiting because of the s. 1(3) requirement that applies to both limbs of s. 1(1) and requires that the third party be '*expressly* identified in the contract by name, as a member of a class or as answering a particular description' (emphasis added), although the third party need not be in existence at the time the contract is made. An analysis of existing case law will illustrate the limitations this imposes and the fact that it restricts the operation of the Act (see e.g. **11.6.4.4**). This limitation operated to significant commercial effect in *Avraamides v Colwill* [2006] EWCA Civ 1533, [2007] BLR 76.

In *Avraamides v Colwill*, A had employed C to refurbish A's bathroom. C's performance was defective and C was therefore liable to A. However, C then sold his business to B on terms whereby B agreed 'to complete outstanding customer orders taking into account any deposits paid by customers as at 31 March 2003, and to pay in the normal course of time any liabilities properly incurred by the company [C] as at 31 March 2003'. Did this mean that A as a third party beneficiary had the ability to enforce this agreement (between B and C) against B?

The Court of Appeal held that, since A as third party was not *expressly* identified in the contract B/C by name, it could not be said that the intention and effect of the agreement was that persons with rights against C could enforce those rights directly against B. Waller LJ considered that it was simply not possible, however attractive the solution, to construe the terms of the commitment in a way which would allow an extended definition of 'liabilities', e.g. to mean the identified class of 'customers'. He stated:

> 19. The answer I am afraid is that section 1(3), by use of the word 'express', simply does not allow a process of construction or implication. I considered whether it would be possible for [counsel for Avraamides] to rely on the fact that 'customers' are identified in the contract as beneficiaries of the first part of paragraph 3, even if liabilities in the second part includes persons other than customers. Could [counsel] submit that even though others are included within the liabilities under the second part, 'customers' as a class are identified and that is sufficient. The difficulty is that the section is concerned with the benefit conferred on a third party, and with the identification of that person. The benefit from the obligation to pay liabilities properly incurred would benefit third parties but of a large number of unidentified classes.

This is a major limitation on the ability of the Act to give third parties enforceable rights. There are some signs of a willingness to seek to avoid this conclusion. In *Laemthong International Lines Co. Ltd v Artis, The Laemthong Glory (No. 2)* [2005] EWCA Civ 519, [2005] 1 Lloyd's Rep 632 (for facts see **11.4.2.1**), it was argued that the LOI did not expressly identify the owners by name, but the Court of Appeal held that they must fall within the expression 'agents' of the charterer in the light of the rest of the wording of the LOI and the fact that they were instructed to deliver the cargo on behalf of the charterers. This appears to involve some contextual construction although this option had been rejected by the Court of Appeal in *Avraamides*. In *Starlight Shipping Co. v Allianz Marine & Aviation Versicherungs AG* [2014] EWHC 3068 (Comm), [2014] 2 Lloyd's Rep 579, [2014] 2 CLC 503, having construed 'underwriters' to include their servants and agents, specifically lawyers who had acted for the insurers and the adjuster which had investigated the insurance claim, Flaux J considered that these third parties were entitled to enforce the terms of a 'full and final' settlement agreement of claims against the underwriters on the basis that they were third parties who were expressly identified (within s. 1(3)) as intended to be protected by the settlement terms. The judge reasoned that counsel faced a difficulty because of the s. 1(3) requirement that these parties 'must be expressly identified in the contract by name or as [members of] a class'.

> 88 . . . [Counsel's] primary position is that, on the basis of my decision that on the true construction of the CMI and LMI settlement agreements, 'Underwriters' in the settlement provisions encompasses the servants or agents of the insurers, then the HD parties are expressly identified by the use of that word in those clauses. Although my initial reaction was that this was not sufficient for express identification, having considered the matter further I have concluded that because 'Underwriters' in clause 2 of the CMI settlement agreement and clause 3 of the LMI settlement agreement encompasses servants or agents, that word expressly identifies a class of third party intended to have a benefit conferred on them by the settlement agreements. Accordingly, I consider that the HD parties do have a claim to damages for breach of those settlement agreements under the 1999 Act.

This appears similar to the principled exception approach in the Canadian case of *Fraser River Pile & Dredge Ltd v Can-Dive Services* [2000] 1 Lloyd's Rep 199 (**11.6.4.4**). It appears that these facts would fall within the scope of third party enforcement in the 1999 Act.

The s. 1(3) requirement is the pivotal provision in relation to the scope of the legislation and it will be interesting to see whether the *Starlight Shipping* construction approach to this provision becomes standard practice since it has the potential to extend the enforcement potential of the 1999 Act.

11.4.2.3 Innovative (but unsuccessful) arguments

There have been some innovative arguments seeking to rely upon the 1999 Act. One example is *Petrologic Capital SA v Banque Cantonale de Geneve* [2012] EWHC 453 (Comm), [2012] ILPr 20, in which Petrologic tried to prevent its bank from making payment under a standby letter of credit to the seller of goods. (A standby letter of credit is a guarantee of payment issued by a bank on behalf of a client that is used as 'payment of last resort' should the client fail to fulfil a contractual commitment with a third party.) Petrologic, as buyer, had been a victim of fraud and did not have the goods in question. However, the conditions for the letter of credit were satisfied and the bank should have made payment. Petrologic sought an injunction to prevent payment occurring, claiming to have the benefit of an English jurisdiction clause in the letter of credit. However, it was held, at [53]–[56], that the clause did not expressly confer any benefit on Petrologic as the initiator of the letter of credit (s. 1(1)(b)) and it was not intended that Petrologic, as the applicant for the letter of credit, should be entitled to avail itself of the terms of that credit (s. 1(2)); rather, the seller was the beneficiary. Petrologic was also expressly identified in the credit (s. 1(3)) only because it was initiating the credit. In any event, Petrologic was not seeking to enforce the jurisdiction clause to ensure that a dispute between the bank and the seller was litigated in the forum agreed in the letter of credit (England), which at least would have met the objectives of the 1999 Act. There was no dispute between the bank and the seller; instead, Petrologic was trying to take the benefit of the clause itself to prevent the bank from making payment, and in order to avoid the Swiss jurisdiction clause in the contract between Petrologic and the bank. It is not surprising that the judge rejected this, holding that the English courts had no jurisdiction in relation to the relationship between Petrologic and the bank.

11.4.3 Variation or cancellation

One of the most controversial and difficult issues to be resolved when formulating such a legislative reform is the crucial question of whether the original parties should be able to vary or cancel the third party's benefit under the contract. This is a particular problem where the third party has relied on the rights in the contract.

- Section 2(1) provides that the contracting parties cannot vary or cancel the third party's rights without that third party's consent where the third party had communicated its assent to the term to the promisor (s. 2(2) explains this assent and ousts the postal rule in the case of assent by post), or the third party had relied on the term and the promisor knew this (or ought reasonably to have foreseen this).

It appears that any reliance will suffice for this purpose. Thus this section appears to offer generous and effective protection for third parties in this situation—or at least it would offer protection but for s. 2(3).

- Section 2(3) expressly allows contracting parties to opt out of this provision by stipulating for a different crystallization test (other than assent or reliance), or by reserving the right to vary or cancel the third party's right irrespective of reliance or acceptance by the third party.

- In accordance with the recommendations of the Law Commission in its 1996 report, there is also a specific judicial discretion to vary or cancel irrespective of reliance or acceptance by the third party in certain circumstances (s. 2(4)–(7) of the Act).

These provisions shift control, and hence the balance, back in favour of the contracting parties.

11.4.4 Overlapping claims

Another potential difficulty posed by third party reform concerns the question of overlap with remedies of the promisee against the promisor. *In other words, should the promisee lose the right of enforcement where the third party has such a right?* This would require an extremely complex piece of drafting, and arguably would be undesirable and impossible to achieve. *On the other hand, if both retain a right of action, who has priority?*

The Law Commission recommended that the promisor's duty to perform should be owed to both promisee and the third party, so that (unless otherwise agreed between the parties) the promisee should retain the right to enforce a contract even if it was also enforceable by the third party. Since each has a separate right of action, there should be no priority rule (although the appropriate course would be to join the third party if the promisee were to sue). In addition, although it did not require legislation to say so, if the promisor fulfilled its duty to the third party, the promisor was, to that extent, to be discharged from its duty to the promisee.

The legislation is minimalist and to the point;

- s. 4 preserves the promisee's right to enforce the promise; and

- s. 5 expressly seeks to avoid double liability by explaining that, where the promisee has recovered substantial damages (or agreed sum) for the third party's loss, the third party will not be entitled to a duplicate damages sum because 'the court . . . shall reduce any award to the third party to such extent as it thinks appropriate to take account of the sum recovered by the promisee'.

This situation appears to be of great concern to students, who point out that if the promisee does recover damages for the third party, there is no provision of the Act requiring the promisee to pass those damages to the third party. The absence of a provision is explicable because this is a question of remedies of the promisee and therefore outside the scope of the legislation. The question of liability to account to the third party should therefore be dealt with at common law (see the discussion at **11.7.4**).

11.4.5 The application of the Unfair Contract Terms Act 1977

The drafters of the 1999 Act appear to have been concerned to avoid making it complex or providing provisions on matters that might become too prescriptive. However, they did include one particularly controversial provision.

? QUESTION

To what extent does the Unfair Contract Terms Act (UCTA) 1977 protect a third party who acquires rights under this Act?

By s. 7(2) of the 1999 Act, s. 2(2) of UCTA 1977 shall not apply to the breach of a qualified contractual obligation where the person seeking to challenge the contractual provision is a third party relying on s. 1 of the 1999 Act. It follows that a contractual term excluding or limiting this liability will not be subject to the reasonableness test in UCTA where the claim is brought by a third party relying on s. 1 of the 1999 Act. However, s. 2(1) of UCTA 1977 will apply (as an existing right or remedy), so that any contractual provisions excluding liability for death or personal injury will remain ineffective when utilized by a third party. This was stated in the debate in the House of Lords to be 'consistent with the underlying policy of the Bill which is to enable contracting parties to confer rights on third parties but to allow them to retain control over the nature and extent of those newly conferred rights': *per* Lord Irvine, 11 January 1999. Nevertheless, it is questionable whether UCTA 1977 should be restricted in this way so as to exclude its protection in the context of third parties.

It is also made clear by s. 7(4) that s. 1 of the 1999 Act will not allow a third party to be treated as a contracting party for the purposes of any other enactment. Specifically, s. 3 of UCTA 1977 applies '*as between contracting parties* where one of them deals on the other's written standard terms of business' (emphasis added). Thus if an exclusion clause were to operate to exclude or limit a third party right, it would not be subject to regulation under s. 3 of UCTA 1977. It also follows that the Part 2 provisions of the Consumer Rights Act (CRA) 2015, which apply only to contracts between a trader and a consumer and to notices relating to rights, obligations, or liabilities as between a trader and a consumer, cannot apply in the context of a third party. In this sense, the third party is not treated in the same way as the promisee, and it will be easier for contracting parties to exclude third parties' rights. This appears to be in conflict with the apparent purpose of the 1999 Act.

11.4.6 Miscellaneous matters

Section 6 of the 1999 Act contains an extensive list of exceptions under which this Act will not apply, e.g. contracts of employment, negotiable instruments (see **11.5.4**), contracts for the carriage of goods by sea (other than in relation to the benefit of exemption clauses: **see 11.6.3**), and the s. 33 contract (Companies Act 2006).

Finally, it is important to remember that the existing exceptions to privity are expressly preserved by s. 7(1) of the Act. Thus, although the Law Commission's 1996 report envisaged that the reform would avoid the 'complexities of the devices presently used to circumvent the privity doctrine', these complexities will remain, at least where the device has not been overtaken by the availability of a direct right of enforcement in the legislation. In *Nisshin Shipping Co. Ltd v Cleaves & Co. Ltd* [2003] EWHC 2602 (Comm), [2004] 1 Lloyd's Rep 38 (for facts, see **11.4.2**), the terms of the charter contracts had created an express trust of the promise to pay commission to C and this was enforceable by the charterers as trustees. However, the existence of this trust did not mean that C was therefore denied its direct right of enforcement under s. 1(1)(b) of the 1999 Act.

It is important, therefore, to consider these common law exceptions and their potential usefulness in light of the new legislation. Some of these 'exceptions' are merely means of circumventing the application of the privity doctrine using other legal concepts (see **11.5**). Others are true exceptions to privity that exist within the law of contract. These are considered at **11.6**.

11.5 Means of circumventing the privity doctrine

This section examines those mechanisms that exist as independent legal concepts and enable a benefit to be conferred on a third party who was not apparently a party to the making of the contract. Tort claims are clearly outside the law of contract. The other mechanisms are related to contract, but represent independent concepts.

11.5.1 Claims in tort

The appellant in *Donoghue v Stevenson* [1932] AC 562 (discussed at **11.1**) was able to avoid the effect of the privity doctrine by framing her action in tort. This may be possible as a means of avoiding the privity doctrine, but only where the loss in question is personal injury or physical damage. Further, a third party may be permitted to enforce the terms of a contract by bringing an action in tort only where it can be shown that the promisor owed a duty of care to the third party claimant. In *White v Jones* [1995] 2 AC 207, for example, a claim based on negligence was brought by intended beneficiaries of a will where the solicitor preparing the will had been negligent. The majority of the House of Lords considered that its conclusion that a duty of care was owed was necessary to ensure that the beneficiaries were not deprived of a claim, albeit that this amounted to circumventing privity by giving the intended beneficiaries the benefit of a contract to which they were not parties. On the facts, it was not possible for the estate to bring a claim.

However, it is by no means always possible to avoid the doctrine in this way because the promisor may not owe the necessary duty of care to the third party. This turns on the relationship and dealings between the 'parties', so that it can be said that there has been an assumption of responsibility: *Robinson v P E Jones (Contractors) Ltd* [2011] EWCA Civ 9, [2011] 3 WLR 815 (see **1.5** and **7.5.2**). In any event, a claim in tort will not normally result in the award of compensation for expectation loss (see **6.1.2.2**). The facts in *White v Jones* were unusual because the measure of damages, where there has been negligence in preparing a will, is the value of the benefit not received (expectation loss). Normally, the tort measure will ensure that recovery is limited to reliance losses.

In addition, the practical viability of a tort claim as a means of avoiding the privity doctrine is dependent upon it being possible to recover for economic loss in tort, e.g. the diminished value of the work done. However, the law has placed some constraints on the recognition of a duty of care in such cases. In *Junior Books Ltd v Veitchi Co. Ltd* [1983] 1 AC 520, English law appeared to accept the idea of permitting third party recovery for economic losses in a negligence claim, although this availability would appear to turn on the specific facts and the specific 'assumption of responsibility'.

> In *Junior Books Ltd v Veitchi Co. Ltd*, JB had engaged a main contractor to build a factory. The laying of the floor was subcontracted out to V Ltd on the instructions of JB's architect. The floor was laid defectively, began to crack up, and had to be replaced. JB sued V Ltd in negligence to recover the cost of the new floor. This was dependent on JB establishing that V Ltd owed a duty to JB to lay the floor with reasonable care and skill. The House of Lords accepted the existence of such a duty and, although this amounted to circumventing the contractual duty owed to the main contractor, it has been justified subsequently as turning on the fact that V Ltd had indicated to JB, via its architect, that it could be relied upon to lay the floor with reasonable care and skill, and this had been relied upon by JB in nominating V Ltd as the subcontractor.

This position can be compared with that in *Simaan General Contracting Co. v Pilkington Glass Ltd (No. 2)* [1988] QB 758, in which there was no such indication that the contractor could be relied upon to meet this standard of performance and no such duty of care was recognized.

This interpretation of the principle in *Junior Books Ltd v Veitchi Co. Ltd* was also applied in *Henderson v Merrett Syndicates Ltd* [1995] 2 AC 145, in which the House of Lords accepted that the existence of a contractual relationship did not prevent the recognition of a duty of care in tort based on the fact that there had been a clear indication by the managing agent to the Lloyd's 'Name' through the underwriting agent that the 'Name' could safely rely on the managing agent to manage the affairs of the Lloyd's syndicate with care and skill.

11.5.2 Assignment and agency

Both assignment and agency make important contributions to the commercial world. Although not strictly exceptions to the privity doctrine, they are contrary to the spirit of that rule and were developed to meet the practical needs of those in business, for whom the privity doctrine proved unduly restrictive.

11.5.2.1 Assignment (or transfer) of contractual rights

Assignment is a legal device that enables one party (the assignor) to transfer the benefit of a performance, which that party has contracted to receive, to another person in such a way that the assignee (to whom the benefit is transferred) may enforce performance (see **Figure 11.2**).

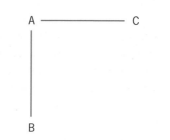

FIGURE 11.2 Transfer of contractual rights

B (the assignor) transfers the benefit of the performance owed by A to B (e.g. payment of a debt of £50) to C (the assignee). A typical illustration of this scenario is where A, a car park operator, assigns unpaid parking charges owed by B to a debt collection agency, C. C will pay a discounted sum to A, so that A gets much of what it was owed by B but the risk of non-recovery is borne by C. In this situation C can enforce the performance (debt) against A (the debtor). In this situation, the original contract does not stipulate that the benefit of performance should go to a third party. Instead, after the contract A/B is made, B (the assignor/creditor) assigns the right to enforce the contract to C (as assignee). C then has a direct right of action against A (the debtor).

However, some rights cannot be assigned (e.g. if the contract that contains them is of personal nature or is a relationship of confidence) and some contracts contain prohibitions on assignment without consent. For example, in ***Linden Gardens Trust Ltd v Lenesta Sludge Disposals Ltd*** [1994] 1 AC 85 (known as the '***St Martins Property appeal***'), the ability to assign without consent was prohibited. Similarly, in *National Bank of Abu Dhabi PJSC v BP Oil International Ltd* [2016] EWHC 2892 (Comm) the parties to a series of sales contracts agreed that neither party could assign its rights to a third party without the consent of the other, subject to the very common limitation that consent was not unreasonably to be withheld. It was held that the prohibition applied to both assignment of the rights themselves and also assignment of claims arising from breach of those rights.

The drawback of assignment is that the assignee takes the benefit of performance 'subject to equities', i.e. the assignee cannot recover more from the debtor than the assignor might have recovered. Thus defences available to the debtor against the assignor are equally valid against the assignee.

11.5.2.2 Agency

Agency is the legal device by which one person (the agent, or A) may act on behalf of another (the principal, or P) in the formation of a contract between that other and a third party. The agency doctrine, in its standard form, is not really an exception to the privity doctrine, since the principal is a party to the contract with the third party.

The agency argument was attempted—unsuccessfully—in ***Dunlop Pneumatic Tyre Co. Ltd v Selfridge & Co. Ltd*** [1915] AC 847 (for facts, see **11.2**).

In ***Dunlop Pneumatic Tyre Co. Ltd v Selfridge & Co. Ltd,*** the claimant argued that, since Dew and Co. had acted as Dunlop's agent for the purposes of obtaining the undertaking from Selfridge that it would not sell tyres to trade buyers at less than the list price, Dunlop could sue Selfridge on this promise. However, Dunlop was unable to rely on the agency argument, because it was unable to show that it had supplied any consideration to support such a promise.

Thus, in order to be able to enforce a third party promise, the principal needs to show that it, rather than the agent, has supplied the consideration for that promise.

Nevertheless, agency has sometimes been used successfully as a means of avoiding the impact of the privity doctrine: see the device in *New Zealand Shipping Co. Ltd v A. M. Satterthwaite & Co. Ltd, The Eurymedon* [1975] AC 154, which was designed to enable a third party to rely on an exemption clause in a contract to which it was not a party (see **11.6.4**) and where the necessary consideration for the promise was identified.

11.5.3 Trusts

The trust is a device developed by the Court of Chancery long before the Judicature Act 1875. It allows one party to pass property to a second party, while stipulating that the second party must hold the property for the benefit of a third. This arrangement is typically adopted for tax reasons or in situations where the third party is under some incapacity making the third party unfit or unable to manage the property. Such a stipulation is enforceable by the third party. In terms of the triangular relationship outlined in **Figure 11.1**, A (the trustee) receives property from B over which B has declared a trust in favour of C (the beneficiary, or *cestui que trust*). C is then able to enforce the terms of the trust to prevent A from dealing with the property other than in a manner that is to C's benefit. Although the relationship between the party declaring the trust (B) and the trustee (A) is not necessarily contractual, where it is, the device is inconsistent with the privity doctrine.

The Court of Chancery had developed the trust in response to issues of property and conscience arising out of such cases. Chancery took the view that a properly constituted trust had the effect of actually transferring and splitting the ownership of the property in question. The legal owner (i.e. under the common law rules) was the trustee, but the effect of the constitution of the trust was to make the third party the beneficial owner of the property. To allow the third party to enforce the trust was not, therefore, to allow the enforcement of a contractual right to acquire the property. The property belonged to the third party from the moment of constitution of the trust, and enforcement of the trust by the third party was necessary to prevent improper interference with that third party's right, which was similar in nature to a property right. In turn, the trustee could not, as a matter of good conscience, interfere with that right.

In order for there to be a properly constituted trust, there must be property that is capable of being subjected to a trust. Property includes not only land and goods, but also rights, such as a right under a contract, which are known as *choses in action*. There must be a declaration of, or disposition on, trust by a competent person, which demonstrates a certain intention that a trust be created. There must also be certainty of property and of object, i.e. it must be possible to determine the property to which the trust attaches and the purposes for which the trust was created. The most significant aspect of the trust as an exception to the privity doctrine arises where one party declares itself to be a trustee on behalf of a third party of a right to performance owed to the third party by the other contracting party, i.e. in terms of the triangular relationship outlined at **Figure 11.1**, where B declares *himself* to be trustee on behalf of C of the performance due to C under the contract from A. (This situation is considered at **11.6.1**.)

11.5.4 Negotiable instruments

The negotiable instrument is a device originally developed by the law merchant to overcome the privity doctrine and certain commercial disadvantages inherent in the device of assignment. Negotiable instruments are expressly excluded from the application of the 1999 Act by s. 6(1).

In the case of assignment (**see 11.5.2.1**), the assignee of a contractual right is at the very least inadequately protected unless notice of the assignment is given to the original debtor each time the right is assigned. Moreover, the assignee takes the right that has been assigned 'subject to equities', which means that any defences enjoyed by the original debtor against the assignor are equally valid against the assignee. Thus an assigned right may not be worth its face value if the original debtor has a separate claim against the assignor the amount of which can be deducted ('set off') from the sums due to the assignor.

> **→ EXAMPLE**
>
> Returning to the triangular relationship outlined in **Figure 11.1**, if B agrees to sell goods to A for £100, but the goods delivered are reduced in value to £80 by a breach of the quality term, the fact that B has assigned to C the right to recover payment from A will not entitle C to recover any more than the £80 that B could have recovered in his own right.

If, however, A's obligation to pay is recorded in a document ('instrument') that is recognized by the law as 'negotiable', B may transfer the right to recover the amount recorded in the instrument to C by simple delivery (i.e. by handing it over), or perhaps by indorsement and delivery (e.g. by signing it and then handing it over). There is no need to give notice of the transfer to the original debtor (A), and it may be transferred several times before the debt that it represents is collected from A. Moreover, the particular advantage of the negotiable instrument is that the transferee(s) do not take 'subject to equities', provided that they receive the instrument for value and without notice of any defect in title that may have arisen before they became 'holder in due course' of the instrument.

Common forms of negotiable instrument are bills of exchange (of which the most familiar example is the cheque) and promissory notes (of which the most familiar example is the banknote). These are regulated by the Bills of Exchange Act 1882. It is beyond the scope of this book to list all other forms of negotiable instrument, but they include certain forms of bonds and share certificates.

11.5.4.1 The requirements of negotiability

It is sometimes said that there are four requirements of negotiability:

1. that the right expressed in the instrument is to be transferable upon delivery (with indorsement where necessary);

2. that the holder of the instrument for the time being has the right to collect payment from the original debtor;

3. that the holder for the time being, if taking for value and without notice, does not take subject to equities; and

4. that the instrument is of a type recognized by the law as negotiable.

However, the first three elements are not requirements, but statements of the legal effect of the recognition that the instrument is negotiable. There is really only one requirement of negotiability, which is that the instrument is recognized as negotiable. But the mere fact that an instrument falls within a category of instruments generally regarded as negotiable does not prevent a particular instrument from being denied negotiability by express words (Bills of Exchange Act 1882, s. 8(1)). For example, cheques may be crossed 'not negotiable'. If they are crossed 'account payee' or 'account payee only', they are not negotiable and are not even transferable.

11.5.4.2 The position of the holder in due course

Negotiable instruments provide a means of circumventing the privity doctrine because the original contract debt is enforceable not only by the other contracting party, but also by any other person for the time being holding the instrument who has been constituted holder in due course. The position of the holder in due course is strengthened still further by the fact that if the party primarily liable on the instrument fails to pay, the holder in due course may, if necessary, bring a claim against all previous signatories of the instrument (Bills of Exchange Act 1882, s. 38(2)).

A party is a holder in due course if that party receives the instrument for value and in good faith, provided that it is complete and regular on its face (Bills of Exchange Act 1882, s. 29(1)), and is in a deliverable state (s. 31(3)–(4)). The requirement that the transfer be made for value is considerably more relaxed than the requirement of consideration in contracts generally.

- Provided that value has been given at some time, the holder for the time being is deemed to have given value (s. 27(2) of the 1882 Act).
- Moreover, negotiable instruments are an exception to the general rule against past consideration (s. 27(1)(b): see **4.3.3.4**).

The requirement of good faith is the same as that in other parts of the law: the transferee must not have acquired the instrument by means of fraud, duress, undue influence, or other unacceptable behaviour; neither must the transferee have acquired it in the knowledge that it was already tainted with such defects before it came into the transferee's hands (s. 30(2) of the 1882 Act). The requirement that the instrument be complete and regular on its face poses little difficulty. It covers such defects as omission on the instrument of a payee or the amount payable. The requirement that the instrument be in a deliverable state is more complex. It relates to the need, in certain circumstances, for the instrument to be indorsed for the delivery to be effective. An instrument made payable to the bearer (a 'bearer bill') does not require indorsement in order to be negotiated and so is always in a deliverable state. But an instrument made payable to a named person, or to a named person 'or order' (an 'order bill'), cannot be negotiated unless indorsed, and the fact of indorsement puts the bill in a deliverable state. Transfer of an order bill without indorsement would remove one of the essential characteristics of negotiability, i.e. that the holder acquires the instrument free from equities.

11.5.5 Collateral contract

The privity doctrine may be avoided by the collateral contract device, which gives a third party a right to enforce promises under a separate contract with the promisor.

In ***Shanklin Pier Ltd v Detel Products Ltd*** [1951] 2 KB 854, the claimants had hired a firm to paint their pier and, on the strength of a representation made by the defendants, had instructed the firm to use the defendants' paint. The paint did not last anywhere near as long as the defendants had represented, but the contract for the purchase of the paint was between the firm of painters and the defendants, and so could not afford the claimants a remedy. The court held that there was a collateral contract between the claimants and the defendants to the effect that the paint would last for seven years. In this case, the claimants had furnished consideration for the defendants' undertaking by instructing the firm of painters to use the defendants' paint.

The collateral contract is of considerable practical significance in relation to commercial contracts as a means of avoiding the operation of the privity doctrine: see e.g. *Andrews v Hopkinson* [1957] 1 QB 229, in which a promise by a car dealer was enforced as a collateral contract with the customer when the dealer's promise had induced the making of the separate contract of hire purchase between the customer and the finance company. However, the concept is an artificial one, and is a means of overcoming the privity rule to be pressed into use to avoid obvious injustice.

11.6 Exceptions to the privity doctrine

We have already considered devices, some of which may have had their origin in contract but all of which must now be regarded as conceptually independent, that may be used to circumvent the privity doctrine (see **11.5**). In this section, we consider genuine exceptions to the privity doctrine.

11.6.1 Trusts of rights created by contract

We saw at **11.5.3** that the concept of privity is restricted to contracts and does not extend to trusts. A trust may attach to property of any kind, including a *chose in action*, which is a form of intangible property such as a right to enforce an obligation. It follows from that definition that a right under a contract is a chose in action and thus may be subject to a trust.

The possibility is therefore raised that the promisee under a contract might declare herself trustee of the benefit of the promise in question on behalf of a third party and, by that means, avoid the privity doctrine.

This device was used successfully during the nineteenth century, e.g. in *Lloyd's v Harper* (1880) 16 Ch D 290, and its existence as a means of avoiding the privity doctrine was acknowledged by Viscount Haldane LC in ***Dunlop Pneumatic Tyre Co. Ltd v Selfridge & Co. Ltd*** [1915] AC 847, in the passage previously quoted (see **11.2**).

11.6.1.1 The effect of a trust of a contractual right

Where a trust of a contractual right is found to have been created, the principal effect is to permit the third party to enforce the benefit.

In ***Les Affréteurs Réunis SA v Leopold Walford (London) Ltd*** [1919] AC 801, for example, a charterparty between the shipowner and the charterer provided that the shipowner would pay a commission of 3 per cent to the broker who had negotiated the contract for the parties. When the shipowner failed to pay, the broker brought an action to recover the commission, although he was not a party to the contract. The

House of Lords accepted that it was the practice of the shipping trade in such cases for the charterer to sue to enforce the promise of commission as trustee for the broker. Since the shipowner was willing to allow the case to be treated as having been brought upon such an action, the broker succeeded in recovering the commission.

The third party's claim to enforce the contract would normally need to be brought in the name of the trustee, but as *Les Affréteurs Réunis SA v Leopold Walford (London) Ltd* shows, the promisor may waive that requirement, in which case the third party may bring the claim in the third party's own name. Equally, if the trustee is unwilling to cooperate in bringing a claim to enforce the promise, the third party may start proceedings in their own name and join the trustee as co-defendant: *Vandepitte v Preferred Accident Insurance Corporation of New York* [1933] AC 70, at p. 79.

A further effect of the creation of a trust of a contractual right is to prevent the contracting parties from varying or rescinding the contract, since to do so would be an improper interference with the beneficiary's rights. An intention to reserve the right to vary in the future if so desired has been regarded as evidence contradicting the alleged intention to create a trust: *Re Schebsman* [1944] Ch 83.

11.6.1.2 The limits of the trust exception

Despite the apparent utility of the trust device as a means for avoiding the privity doctrine, it has largely fallen into disuse. *The reason is to be found in the requirements for the constitution of a trust (see 11.5.3) and especially in the requirement that there be a certain intention on the part of the person allegedly declaring the trust that a trust be created: Vandepitte v Preferred Accident Insurance Corporation of New York* [1933] AC 70 and see *Nisshin Shipping Co. Ltd v Cleaves & Co. Ltd* [2003] EWHC 2602 (Comm), [2004] 1 Lloyd's Rep 38 (discussed at **11.4.2** and **11.4.6**), in which the express trust did not displace a direct right of enforcement under the 1999 Act.

The usual difficulty is that at the time of making the contract—and, indeed, at all times until the particular problem arises—the promisee has not thought at all about how the third party will enforce the benefit to be conferred.

In ***Vandepitte v Preferred Accident Insurance Corporation of New York***, the claimant's action against an insurance company depended upon whether the insured held the promised cover under a policy of motor insurance on trust for his daughter, who was a minor. Under the law of British Columbia, the father was civilly liable for the torts of his minor children, so that it was almost inconceivable that he should feel it necessary to hold the benefit of insurance on his daughter's behalf, since he was the person most likely to be sued, not his daughter. On that ground, the Privy Council considered there to be no trust.

For some time, the English courts have been unwilling to *imply* an intention to create a trust. In *Re Schebsman* [1944] Ch 83, at p. 104, Du Parcq LJ said: '[U]nless an intention to create a trust is clearly to be collected from the language used and the circumstances of the case, I think that the Court ought not to be astute to discover indications of such an intention.'

Further, in *Rolls-Royce Power Engineering plc v Ricardo Consulting Engineers Ltd* [2003] EWHC 2871 (TCC), [2004] 2 All ER (Comm) 129, it was held that a trust of a promise will be effective only if the party whose promise is held on trust either knew, or had reason to know, that the other contracting party was contracting as trustee. Therefore the argument on these facts that the subsidiary had contracted as agent for the parent company could not succeed because there was no such knowledge of the parent company's interest in the contract.

In practice, therefore, unless there is an express declaration of the intention to create a trust, it seems that the device of a trust of a contractual right will fail. In any event, it is likely that the 1999 Act would apply in circumstances in which an express declaration of the trust of the benefit of a contractual promise arose: Nisshin Shipping Co. Ltd v Cleaves & Co. Ltd. The potential benefit for the beneficiary of reliance on the express trust argument is that the beneficiary's rights are irrevocable, whereas a third party's rights are capable of being varied or rescinded by the contracting parties under the 1999 Act (s. 2).

11.6.2 Insurance

In principle, the privity doctrine applies to contracts of insurance, but there are several statutory exceptions to the doctrine in the case of common contracts that provide for benefits to be payable to third parties.

- The compulsory motor insurance regime sets out two alternative means by which the victim of a driver required to be insured for the use of a motor vehicle in the UK has access to the driver's insurers. Under s. 151 of the Road Traffic Act 1988, a third party suffering injury or loss at the hands of an insured driver may recover compensation from the insurance company once the injured third party has obtained judgment against the insured. A more straightforward procedure was introduced by the European Communities (Rights against Insurers) Regulations 2002, SI 2002/3061, implementing the rather more generous EU approach. Under the 2002 Regulations, the third party can, in the case of an accident occurring in the UK, simply bring an action against the insurers without needing first to obtain judgment against the insured.

- Under the Third Parties (Rights against Insurers) Act 2010, where the holder of a liability policy has become insolvent, a person with a claim against that insured may bring a direct claim against the insurers. This Act applies to liability policies of all types. Unlike the specific motor insurance regime which governs all claims that could be made against the assured, the right of direct action under the 2010 Act is triggered only by the insured's insolvency.

- Under s. 11 of the Married Women's Property Act 1882, a spouse has an enforceable right to recover sums due on a policy of life insurance taken out by the other spouse on their own life.

11.6.3 Carriage of goods by sea

It is common in commercial transactions for one party (the shipper) to enter into a contract with another (the carrier) for goods to be taken and delivered to a third party (the consignee). The doctrine of privity of contract would prevent the consignee from suing the carrier for damage caused to the goods in transit, since the consignee was not a party to the contract. In the nineteenth century, Parliament attempted to solve this problem by attaching the right to sue the carrier (originating in the shipper as a party to the contract of carriage) to the ownership in the goods, so that when the consignee became owner of the goods, it acquired the right to sue the carrier for damage in transit (see the Bills of Lading Act 1855). More recently, the complex nature of commercial transactions exposed weaknesses in this solution in the 1855 Act, especially where the consignee was, for some reason, regarded by law as exposed to the risk of loss in respect of the goods, but had not acquired ownership: e.g. *Leigh and Sillavan Ltd v Aliakmon Shipping Co. Ltd* [1986] AC 785. By the Carriage of Goods by Sea Act 1992, Parliament attempted to remedy the situation. The 1855 Act was repealed and, under the 1992 Act, the right to sue the carrier passed from shipper to consignee or lawful holder of a bill of lading (as defined by ss 2 and 5) by operation of law, and independently of the passing of ownership. This statutory exception to the doctrine of privity of contract is said to be justified as a matter of commercial necessity.

The Contracts (Rights of Third Parties) Act 1999 does not apply to contracts for the carriage of goods by sea, which are expressly excluded from its application by s. 6(5)–(7).

11.6.4 The *Eurymedon* device: the ability of a third party to rely on an exemption clause

11.6.4.1 The scope of the exception: background

An exemption clause is a clause that purports to exclude or to limit liability for breach of contract. We have already examined the law relating to exemption clauses in two-party contract situations (see **Chapter 7**). However, some commercial transactions, especially those involving international trade and shipping, cannot easily be analysed in terms of the traditional bilateral contract. Since, in the commercial field, the attitude of the English courts has always been that contract law must be the servant, and not the master, of the needs and practices of those engaged in business (see **1.2**), the law must accommodate those needs and practices as best it can without over-insisting on the purity of the conceptual framework. It was precisely in the context of an attempt to protect a third party by means of an exemption clause that Lord Wilberforce, in *New Zealand Shipping Co. Ltd v A. M. Satterthwaite & Co. Ltd, The Eurymedon* [1975] AC 154 (see **2.1.3**), at p. 167E, made his now well-known statement about the occasional difficulty of 'forcing the facts to fit uneasily into the marked slots of offer, acceptance and consideration'.

The ability to afford protection to third parties through exemption clauses has been accepted as commercially efficient since, in the commercial context, such clauses are generally freely negotiated and operate as risk allocation devices. Nevertheless, even if a third party is able to show that it is protected by the exemption clause, that clause must satisfy any other requirements for its validity that apply (see generally **7.4**).

In **Elder, Dempster and Co. v Paterson, Zochonis & Co. Ltd** [1924] AC 522, shipowners who were not parties to a contract between the shippers of goods and the charterers of the vessel, which was evidenced by a bill of lading, nevertheless claimed to be protected by an exemption clause contained therein. The House of Lords upheld that claim. No reasons for the decision were given, other than that such a decision was consistent with the commercial realities of the situation and that the alternative proposition—that the charterer was protected by the clause, but the shipowners were not—was 'absurd'.

The difficulty of this decision was that it was clearly inconsistent with the privity doctrine, but did not explain how the doctrine had been avoided.

A very similar situation arose for consideration by the House of Lords in *Scruttons Ltd v Midland Silicones Ltd* [1962] AC 446. It was apparent that such purported extensions of exemption clauses to third parties, and especially to stevedores employed to load and unload cargoes, were commonplace in the commercial world and that the particular action was regarded as a test case. The majority of the House of Lords confirmed that commercial contracts were not, as a category, exempt from the requirement in the general law of contract of privity between parties. However, it was accepted that the privity doctrine might be avoided by means of a separate contract between the third party and the shipper of the goods, and that such a contract might arise by way of agency. Nevertheless, their Lordships would not find such a contract on this ground unless the requirements for a finding of agency were present—namely, there had to be authority to act as agent and consideration for the promise would need to be given by the third party (as principal in the agency relationship).

Lord Reid, at p. 474, spelt out four conditions that would need to be satisfied before a third party could rely on an exemption clause in a contract to which that third party was not a party:

> I can see a possibility of success of the agency argument if (first) the bill of lading makes it clear that the stevedore is intended to be protected by the provisions in it which limit liability, (secondly) that the bill of lading makes it clear that the carrier, in addition to contracting for these provisions on his own behalf, is also contracting as agent for the stevedore that these provisions should apply to the stevedore, (thirdly) the carrier has authority from the stevedore to do that, or perhaps later ratification by the stevedore would suffice, and (fourthly) that any difficulties about consideration moving from the stevedore were overcome.

In this particular case, there was nothing in the bill of lading to suggest that the exemption clause was intended to benefit the stevedores and nothing to indicate that the carrier was contracting as agent for the stevedore to obtain the benefit of the clause. Nevertheless, the statement by Lord Reid provided a glimmer of hope to the business community, which considered it commercially necessary to afford this protection to third parties involved in the performance of commercial contracts. As a result, attempts were made to draft contractual exemption clauses that would meet the requirements set out by Lord Reid.

One such clause (known as a 'Himalaya clause') fell to be considered by the Privy Council in *New Zealand Shipping Co. Ltd v A. M. Satterthwaite & Co. Ltd, The Eurymedon* [1975] AC 154. Because it was aimed at fulfilling Lord Reid's criteria, the clause is particularly long and complex, but its essential ingredients are that the clause expressly grants protection to a category of persons ('servants, agents and independent contractors') in a wide range of circumstances and expressly states that, for the purposes of obtaining this protection, the carrier is acting as agent or trustee on behalf of these persons, who, to this extent, are to be regarded as parties to the contract.

It was established without difficulty that the clause satisfied the first three requirements of the agency argument put forward by Lord Reid.

11.6.4.2 Difficulties with Lord Reid's fourth criterion: consideration to support the promise

The issue in *New Zealand Shipping Co. Ltd v A. M. Satterthwaite & Co. Ltd, The Eurymedon* [1975] AC 154 was whether there was any consideration for the contract between the stevedores and the shippers arranged through the agency of the carriers. The stevedores were already under a duty, by virtue of their contract with the carriers, to unload the cargo with due care, and the performance of that duty could also be consideration for the separate contract exempting the stevedores from liability to the shippers (see **4.4.2**).

Although it was possible in *The Eurymedon* to find a contract between the shippers and the stevedores by virtue of the doctrine of agency, there was some difficulty about describing that contract as 'bilateral' since, at the time that the carrier made the principal contract with the shipper, the intended stevedore might be unaware of the actual contract envisaged (this would not affect the carrier's authority to act for the stevedore, which would have been given in general terms). The Privy Council overcame the difficulty by finding that the principal contract resulted in the shipper making an offer in the form of a unilateral contract whereby it would exempt from liability anybody undertaking to unload the cargo. This '*Eurymedon* device' was criticized because of its artificiality and complexity rather than because of its result.

11.6.4.3 Difficulties with Lord Reid's third criterion: authority to act as agent

One reason why it was relatively easy in *New Zealand Shipping Co. Ltd v A. M. Satterthwaite & Co. Ltd, The Eurymedon* [1975] AC 154 to find that the carriers were acting as duly authorized agents for the stevedores was that the carriers and stevedores were part of the same group of companies. It was suggested—see *The Suleyman Stalskiy* [1976] 2 Lloyd's Rep 609—that, where there was no previous relationship between the stevedore and the carrier, the agency argument would not prevail over the privity doctrine. However, that suggestion was disapproved by Lord Wilberforce in a further Privy Council case: *Port Jackson Stevedoring Pty Ltd v Salmond & Spraggon (Australia) Pty Ltd, The New York Star* [1981] 1 WLR 138. Lord Wilberforce thought that the *Eurymedon* device should be regarded as being of general application, and should not depend upon fine distinctions based upon the nature of the relationship between carrier and stevedore.

Nevertheless, in the context of attempts by subcontractors to rely on clauses in the contract between the employer and main contractor, the English courts failed to take this lead on the need to avoid fine distinctions. Instead, they took the view that there could be no authority to act as agent for a person who had not been identified to that contract at the time it was entered into. Subcontractors would not generally be appointed until after the main contract was entered into and so could not have authorized the main contractor to contract on their behalf: *Southern Water Authority v Carey* [1985] 2 All ER 1077 and *Norwich City Council v Harvey* [1989] 1 All ER 1180 (although, in both cases, the subcontractor was protected because the clause was interpreted as a risk allocation provision and as restricting the scope of the duty of care in tort).

This difficulty of 'non-existence' in relation to the main contract was avoided by the High Court of Australia in *Trident General Insurance Co. Ltd v McNiece Brothers Proprietary Ltd* (1988) 165 CLR 107. The court allowed McNiece to obtain the protection of an insurance policy on the basis that it was a subcontractor of the insured and the policy purported to extend to cover subcontractors, even though McNiece was not a subcontractor at the time the policy contract was entered into. The court considered that commercial difficulties would arise unless such a broad interpretation were adopted, because third parties might well rely on the fact that they were covered by insurance and neglect to take out their own cover. Equally, if they did take out their own cover, it might result in double cover, which would be inefficient.

More recently, presumably in light of the position under the 1999 Act, the English courts have shown a greater willingness in the shipping context to interpret the *Eurymedon* principles in a manner that gives effect to the commercial expectations of the parties.

In **Owners of the Ship 'Borvigilant' v Owners of the 'Romina C'** [2003] EWCA Civ 935, [2004] 1 CLC 41, for example, the Court of Appeal upheld the first-instance decision of David Steel J—[2002] EWHC 1 759 (Admlty), [2002] 2 Lloyd's Rep 631—to the effect that National Iranian Oil Company (NIOC) had implied authority to contract with shipowners on behalf of other tug owners, since the language of the tug requisition form referred to the fact that NIOC was contracting on behalf of such owners. It was not necessary for the form to expressly state that NIOC was contracting as agent, and the language used indicated that NIOC must have had the authority of other tug owners to act in this way.

In the Court of Appeal, Clarke LJ referred to Lord Reid's speech in *Scruttons Ltd v Midland Silicones Ltd* [1962] AC 446 and added, at [17] and [19]:

> Lord Reid did not say that the clause must expressly state that the carrier is contracting as agent for the stevedores. He simply said that the contract must make that clear . . . The question remains whether, construed as a whole, the contract provides that NIOC was entering into the contract, at least in part as the agent of the owner of any tug supplied by NIOC but not owned by NIOC. In my view, commercial good sense requires only one answer to that question, namely yes.

Clarke LJ (with whose judgment Dyson and Peter Gibson LJJ agreed) referred to the need (identified in *The New York Star*) to avoid 'a search for fine distinctions which would diminish the general applicability' of the *Eurymedon* principle.

The scope of the *Eurymedon* device was—and is—nevertheless quite limited. In *The Mahkutai* [1996] 3 All ER 502, the Privy Council refused to extend its scope to jurisdiction clauses on the basis that, unlike exemption clauses, which benefit one party only, jurisdiction clauses create mutual rights and obligations. A jurisdiction clause was a neutral clause and not one included simply 'for the benefit' of one party.

11.6.4.4 The first requirement is key: it must be clear that the third party was intended to be protected by the clause

The most fundamental difficulty that could be faced in seeking to rely on *New Zealand Shipping Co. Ltd v A. M. Satterthwaite & Co. Ltd, The Eurymedon* [1975] AC 154 was experienced in *London Drugs Ltd v Kuehne & Nagel International Ltd* (1993) 97 DLR (4th) 261.

> In *London Drugs Ltd v Kuehne & Nagel International Ltd,* there was a limitation clause in a storage contract, which limited 'the warehouseman's liability'. However, the clause did not expressly cover the employees who, in fact, damaged the goods in storage. The Canadian Court of Appeal held that it covered the employees by impliedly extending the meaning of the clause, although this amounted to extending Lord Reid's criteria in *Scruttons Ltd v Midland Silicones Ltd* [1962] AC 446. On appeal, the Supreme Court of Canada considered that it was not possible to extend *The Eurymedon* in this way and instead created a new exception to the privity doctrine in Canada. This exception was outside the scope of *The Eurymedon* and is limited to employees. It would apply where the clause expressly or impliedly extended the benefit of the clause to employees and the employees caused the loss in performing the very services provided for in the contract.

In *Fraser River Pile & Dredge Ltd v Can-Dive Services* [2000] 1 Lloyd's Rep 199, the *London Drugs* exception was put in broader terms—namely, that the parties must have intended to extend the benefit to the third party, and the activities performed by the third party must have been the very activities contemplated as coming within the scope of the contract or the contractual provision that was being relied upon. Thus the only means of avoiding the limitation imposed by Lord Reid's first criterion was to create a specific exception applicable in Canada. This principled exception was applied more recently by the Ontario Court of Appeal in *Sanofi Pasteur Ltd v UPS SCS Inc.* (2015) ONCA 88 by a process of implication in relation to the intention to extend the benefit to the third party. The court referred (at [58] and [60]) to the need to make the implication in order to give business efficacy to the transaction and to preserve the parties' allocation of the risk.

11.6.4.5 The effect of the 1999 Act on the ability of a third party to enforce an exemption clause

The ability of a third party to enforce a contract term (including an exemption clause: 1999 Act, s. 1(6)) is determined by the test of enforceability. Therefore if the clause in question expressly provides that the third party, who is expressly identified in the contract by name or as a member of a class, is to have the right to enforce the exemption clause, the third party will clearly have that right (s. 1(1)(a)). However, the Himalaya clause in *New Zealand Shipping Co. Ltd v A. M. Satterthwaite & Co. Ltd, The Eurymedon* [1975] AC 154 (see **11.6.4.1**) does not expressly give this right. Instead, it states that the stevedore (as a member of the class of independent contractors) is to have the benefit of the clause and that the carrier is acting as his agent for this purpose. Section 1(1)(b) ought therefore to apply to this clause and factual context unless 'on a proper construction of the contract it appears that the parties did not intend the term to be enforceable by the third party'. This will depend on the wording of the contract as a whole. Accordingly, and on the basis that there is nothing to indicate that the parties did *not* intend the term to be enforceable by the third party (as to which, see **11.4.2**), under the 1999 Act there should be a direct right of enforcement of the Himalaya clause in *The Eurymedon*. This should have reduced much of the complexity of the law governing third party enforcement of exemption clauses.

The 1999 Act may also provide a direct right of enforcement in situations such as those in *Southern Water Authority v Carey* [1985] 2 All ER 1077 and *Norwich City Council v Harvey* [1989] 1 All ER 1180 (see **11.6.4.3**), because of the clarity of the risk allocation clauses and because the Act specifically states that the third party (i.e. the subcontractor) 'need not be in existence when the contract is entered into' (s. 1(3)).

However, the Act would not be available in factual situations such as *Scruttons Ltd v Midland Silicones Ltd* [1962] AC 446 because of the absence of an *express* identification of the third party as an intended beneficiary of the clause. The same problem would exist on the facts in *London Drugs Ltd v Kuehne & Nagel International Ltd* (1993) 97 DLR (4th) 261—namely, the fact that the clause does not *expressly* confer a benefit on the employees unless they can be said to be *expressly* identified as members of a class of 'warehouseman', when the reality is that this can be achieved only by fairly generous implication. *The Eurymedon* could not operate in either of these cases, because the first criterion specified by Lord Reid is not satisfied. The 1999 Act effectively keeps this first requirement and dispenses with the remaining three, thereby eliminating the complexity. To illustrate this point, *London Drugs* can usefully be compared with *Fraser River Pile & Dredge Ltd v Can-Dive Ltd* [2000] 1 Lloyd's Rep 199, which *would* satisfy the s. 1(1)(b) test of enforceability in the 1999 Act. On the facts, the clause extended to third party beneficiaries coming within the class of 'charterers', so that this constituted express identification in the waiver of subrogation clause.

11.7 Remedies available to the promisee

It would be possible to avoid the consequences of the privity doctrine if the promisee were able to bring a claim and recover remedies that enforced the third party's rights or compensated for the third party's loss.

The fundamental weakness in relying on this means of enforcement is that the third party will be dependent on the willingness of the promisee to bring a claim. In addition, this method of avoiding the consequences of privity will be less relevant as a result of the 1999 Act if the third party can achieve a remedy directly—although the promisee's right to enforce and recover on behalf of the third party is expressly retained (s. 5). Nevertheless, as we have seen, the 1999 Act does not provide third parties with rights of enforcement in all circumstances, so that the remedies available to the promisee are still relevant to this discussion.

11.7.1 Specific performance

Specific performance is an order that would compel the promisor to carry out the promise so that the third party obtains the intended benefit under the contract. However, as discussed at **10.2.1**, this remedy is discretionary and will not be granted where damages would be an adequate remedy. In *Beswick v Beswick* [1968] AC 58, the fact that the loss suffered by the promisee was negligible, so that damages would be purely nominal, was said to be good reason for awarding the discretionary remedy of specific performance (for the facts of this case, see **10.2.1**). Mrs Beswick would now be able to enforce the nephew's promise directly under s. 1(1)(b) of the 1999 Act since the contract clearly purported to confer a benefit on her as a named individual (although it did not give her an express right to enforce the promise against the nephew). There also seems to be no evidence 'on the proper construction of the contract' that she was not intended to be able to enforce the term.

This remedy of specific performance is undoubtedly the best suited to achieving the promisee's original contractual intention of conferring a benefit on the third party, but it is not without limitations.

1. As a general remedy, specific performance is subject to restrictions, such as the fact that damages must not be an adequate remedy (see also **10.2.1**).

2. Moreover, in *Beswick v Beswick*, it was a happy coincidence that the widow had been appointed administratrix of the husband's estate, since she then had no problem in persuading the 'promisee' to bring the action for specific performance. Since it appears that the third party cannot compel the promisee to act (see **11.7.4**), the remedy of specific performance will be available only when it suits the promisee to enforce the contract.

3. In addition, it is suitable as a remedy only where the performance has yet to take place (or has yet to take place fully). It will not be appropriate where the contract has been performed, albeit defectively, and the third party seeks a remedy.

11.7.2 Enforcement of negative undertakings

Where the contractual term breached is in the form of a negative undertaking (a promise to refrain from doing something), the obvious remedy is an injunction (see **10.3**), which is a form of specific relief similar to specific performance designed to prevent actions rather than to enforce performance. It would appear to be consistent with the reasoning in *Beswick v Beswick* [1968] AC 58 for an injunction to be available to a promisee in appropriate circumstances in the same way as was specific performance in that case.

Where the negative undertaking is a promise not to sue the third party, the correct procedure is not to seek an injunction, but to ask the court to stay the proceedings that have been brought in contravention of the promise. In *Gore v Van der Lann* [1967] 2 QB 31, the Court of Appeal said that, even where there was a definite promise not to sue the third party, the promisee would be granted a stay of proceedings only if he had a sufficient interest in the enforcement of the promise. Such an interest would arise only if, for example, the promisee were under a legal obligation to reimburse the third party (the defendant to the action) in respect of any damages that the third party had to pay to the claimant. However, in the subsequent case of *Snelling v John G. Snelling Ltd* [1973] 1 QB 87, the requirement of sufficient interest appears to have been ignored by the court.

In **Snelling v John G. Snelling Ltd**, three brothers each loaned money to the family company and subsequently the brothers agreed not to seek to recover such loans should any one of them resign his directorship of the company. The claimant resigned and brought an action against the company to recover money loaned to it. The other brothers applied to be joined as defendants to the action and then counterclaimed for a declaration that the claimant was not entitled to recover the sums in question. In theory, the claimant should have succeeded against the company, since the company could not enforce the stipulation made on its behalf, but it was clear that the brothers were entitled to succeed on their counterclaim. Ormrod J resolved this apparent impasse by staying the proceedings, since in reality the claimant had lost his action.

The two brothers were under no legal liability to the company should the third fail to keep his promise to refrain from recovering the money owing to him, so that it is not easy to see what was the sufficient interest that they had in seeking enforcement of the promise. The decision in *Snelling* would therefore appear to be more in line with the approach in *Beswick v Beswick*, i.e. that the nephew could not be allowed to ignore his express promise to pay Mrs Beswick on Mr Beswick's death. The brother in *Snelling* could not be permitted to do the very thing that he had contracted not to do.

It may be that the sufficient interest requirement is either an alternative (where there is no express promise not to sue), or of no effect at all (given that discussion of this issue in *Gore v Van der Lann* was strictly *obiter*).

11.7.3 Promisee's claim for damages

The difficulty with a claim for damages in relation to breach of a contract providing for a third party benefit is that the promisee may usually recover damages only for the promisee's own loss. If the performance to be provided by the other party was intended entirely for the benefit of the third party, the law takes the view that there is no loss to the promisee resulting from the breach, so that damages will be purely nominal: *Beswick v Beswick* [1968] AC 58—although compare the opinion of Lord Pearce. Of course, if the promisee were to receive some benefit from the other party's performance in addition to the benefit intended for the third party, then that loss would be recoverable under the normal rules, but the promisee would still be unable to recover for the third party's loss. It seems, however, that if the promisee were to be under a legal obligation to compensate the third party in the event of non-performance by the other contracting party (e.g. as a result of a contract between promisee and third party), then that obligation would amount to a real loss to the promisee and substantial damages would be recoverable on that account. It is open to question whether payment to the third party by the promisee on the strength of a perceived moral obligation to provide compensation would also be a recoverable loss.

11.7.3.1 Contracts made on behalf of a group for reasons of convenience

If the promisee is able to recover damages for the loss suffered by the third party and if the third party were then able to compel the promisee to hand over the damages recovered (see **11.7.4**), such a remedy would effectively sidestep any privity problems (assuming that the promisee can be persuaded to bring the claim for damages in the first place). Such a claim by the promisee appeared to have been allowed by the Court of Appeal in *Jackson v Horizon Holidays Ltd* [1975] 1 WLR 1468.

> In *Jackson v Horizon Holidays Ltd*, the claimant had booked a package holiday for himself and his family. The holiday fell well short of the standard promised. The claimant brought an action for breach of contract. The defendant holiday company challenged the trial judge's award of damages of £1,100, which was just less than the full cost of the holiday.
>
> In the Court of Appeal, the award was upheld. Lord Denning MR said that the award was excessive as compensation for the claimant's loss alone, but was a correct assessment of the aggregate loss suffered by the whole family. The claimant was entitled to recover damages for loss suffered by the family members because he had contracted on their behalf. The other members of the Court of Appeal, although upholding the award, did not openly state that it represented compensation for loss suffered by the other members of the family as well as by the claimant.

Lord Denning MR regarded *Jackson v Horizon Holidays Ltd* as an example of a general principle allowing the promisee to recover damages on behalf of third party beneficiaries. He claimed that it fell within the principle contained in an *obiter* statement by Lush LJ in *Lloyd's v Harper* (1880) 16 Ch D 290, at p. 321:

> I consider it to be an established rule of law that where a contract is made with A for the benefit of B, A can sue on the contract for the benefit of B, and recover all that B could have recovered if the contract had been made with B himself.

This reasoning and the width of this principle was disapproved (*obiter*) in *Woodar Investment Development Ltd v Wimpey Construction (UK) Ltd* [1980] 1 WLR 277.

> In *Woodar Investments*, the claimants agreed to sell some land to the defendants for £850,000. It was a term of the contract that the defendants should pay £150,000 of the price to a third party. The defendants failed to go ahead with the purchase and the claimants claimed damages for what they said was a repudiatory breach. The House of Lords found that the defendants had not repudiated the contract, but went on to discuss the privity issue. While being far from satisfied with the privity doctrine (see **11.3.2**), their Lordships denied the existence of a general principle allowing the promisee to recover damages for loss suffered by the third party beneficiary and claimed that Lord Denning MR had taken the statement of Lush LJ out of its proper context, which limited this principle to situations of agency or trust. They did not, however, overrule the actual decision on the facts in *Jackson v Horizon Holidays Ltd.*

Lord Wilberforce thought that the decision in *Jackson* probably belonged to a special category of cases 'calling for special treatment' in which one party contracts for the benefit of a group for reasons of convenience. Transactions that may fall within this special category are 'contracting for family holidays, ordering meals in restaurants for a party, hiring a taxi for a group'.

It appears from this that the person contracting on behalf of the group would also need to suffer some loss in order to be able to recover for the members of the party. This would have been of no assistance on the facts in *Woodar Investments* because it was not a contract made on behalf of a group and there was no evidence that Woodar had suffered any loss as a result of the non-payment to the third party. In his speech, Lord Scarman suggested that, had Woodar been under an obligation to pay compensation to the third party following the non-payment, this might have been included within Woodar's loss (as promisee).

11.7.3.2 The *St Martins Property* exception

Another exception to the general rule has been recognized in the commercial context. This exception allows the promisee to recover substantial damages on behalf of a third party even though the promisee has not suffered any loss.

> In *Linden Gardens Trust Ltd v Lenesta Sludge Disposals Ltd* [1994] 1 AC 85 (known as the *'St Martins Property'* appeal) the question arose of what compensation was recoverable where party A engaged party B to carry out work on his property, in circumstances under which both understood that A was very likely to transfer the property to party C. This transfer took place. B performed the work defectively and in breach of contract. In the absence of an assignment (which was contractually excluded), C could not sue, and it was argued that, since A no longer had any interest in the property, its damages would be purely nominal. The House of Lords did not agree. Their Lordships' motivation appears to have been the desire to avoid the conclusion that the building contractor (B) would not have to pay substantial damages for the breach.

Relying on Lord Diplock's explanation in *The Albazero* [1977] AC 774 of the decision in *Dunlop v Lambert* (1839) 6 Cl & F 600, Lord Browne-Wilkinson said, in *Linden Gardens*, at pp. 114–15:

> The contract was for a large development of property which, to the knowledge of both [parties], was going to be occupied and possibly purchased by third parties . . . Therefore, it could be foreseen that damage caused by a breach would cause loss to a later owner and not merely to the original contracting party . . . In such a case, it seems to me proper, as in the case of the carriage of goods by land, to treat the parties as having entered into the contract on the footing that [the original owner] would be entitled to enforce the contractual rights for the benefit of those who suffered from defective performance . . .

11.7.3.2.1 *The narrow ground in Linden Gardens*

This reasoning is referred to as the 'narrow ground' for the decision in *Linden Gardens Trust Ltd v Lenesta Sludge Disposals Ltd* [1994] 1 AC 85. It is stated to be based on the principle explained by Lord Diplock in *The Albazero* [1977] AC 774, at p. 847:

> [I]n a commercial contract concerning goods, where it is in the contemplation of the parties that the proprietary interests in the goods may be transferred from one owner to another after the contract has been entered into and before the breach which causes the loss or damage to the goods, an original party to the contract, if such be the intention of them both, is to be treated in law as having entered into the contract for the benefit of all persons who have or may acquire an interest in the goods before they are lost or damaged, and is entitled to recover by way of damages for breach of contract the actual loss sustained by those for whose benefit the contract is entered into.

This narrow ground principle therefore allows A to retain the right to sue for substantial damages and to recover for the loss suffered by C, on the basis that it was contemplated that someone other than A would suffer loss in the event of breach of the contract, but be unable to sue.

The narrow ground was applied in *Darlington Borough Council v Wiltshier Northern Ltd* [1995] 1 WLR 68.

In **Darlington Borough Council v Wiltshier Northern Ltd**, the contractor had contracted with Morgan Grenfell (which had become involved because of restrictions on local authority expenditure) to construct a recreation centre for the local authority on land owned by that local authority. Contractual rights had been assigned (transferred) to the local authority and the contractor was aware that the centre was being built for that authority. The local authority wanted to bring an action for defective performance of the construction contract, but could recover substantial damages only if Morgan Grenfell had assigned the right to substantial damages. Therefore the question was the same as that in **Linden Gardens**—namely, could the contracting party recover substantial damages for breach of a contract when it had no property interest and had therefore suffered no loss?

The Court of Appeal applied the narrow ground exception and held that there was a right to recover substantial damages, because it was clear to the contractor that the centre was being constructed for the local authority on local authority land and that the local authority would suffer loss in the event of breach.

This extends the application of the narrow ground to instances in which the promisee has never had any ownership interest in the property affected by the breach. Steyn LJ pointed, at p. 808B, to the need, recognized previously by Lord Diplock and Lord Browne-Wilkinson in *Linden Gardens*, to provide 'a remedy where no other would be available to a person sustaining loss which under a rational legal system ought to be compensated by the person who has caused it'.

Subsequently, in *Offer-Hoar v Larkstore Ltd* [2006] EWCA Civ 1079, [2006] 1 WLR 2926, the Court of Appeal faced a 'black hole' problem because the loss had not taken place until after assignment occurred. The question was whether a soil investigation consultant, employed by the original owner of the site, was liable for a property developer's losses caused by a landslip, and the obvious difficulty was that, since the original site owner did not own the property at the time of the landslip, it had suffered no loss and could not assign more than it had. The Court of Appeal avoided this difficulty by concluding that the owner's cause of action was complete when the consultant carried out the investigation, and it was that cause of action that had been assigned to the purchaser. This reasoning neatly sidestepped the perceived difficulty with assignment that had led to the reliance in *Darlington* on the narrow ground. The Court of Appeal nevertheless made more general comments to the effect that if work is carried out by a supplier for an owner and it is known that the subject matter is to be sold on to a purchaser, then if there is subsequent damage it should not be open to the supplier to plead that the purchaser has suffered no loss, thereby leaving the supplier free of liability: a breach of contract should not be allowed to disappear into a black-hole. The principle in *Offer-Hoar* was applied in *Saga Cruises BDF Ltd v Fincantieri SPA* [2016] EWHC 1875 (Comm), where the defendant shipyard had refitted a cruise vessel for the owners, and the owners then chartered the vessel to charterers at which point defects became apparent. It was held that the charterers, as assignees, could recover damages. The reality of the situation was that the vessel had been refitted for the benefit of the charterers and that they were entitled to sue for their own losses.

However, there is a limitation on the availability of the narrow ground argument. This was explained and applied in *Alfred MacAlpine Construction Ltd v Panatown Ltd* [2001] 1 AC 518.

In **Alfred MacAlpine Construction Ltd v Panatown Ltd**, Panatown had employed McAlpine to build an office block and a multi-storey car park. The construction site was owned throughout by an associate company of Panatown, UIPL. The distinguishing fact in this case was that the contractors (McAlpine) had also entered into a 'duty of care deed' with UIPL (the site owner), which gave UIPL a direct remedy against the contractor for breaches of qualified contractual terms. Panatown claimed damages for defective performance of the construction contract; UIPL did not seek to bring an action under the duty of care deed.

The majority of the House of Lords held that, because of the existence of the duty of care deed, which gave the site owner a direct remedy, the narrow ground exception in **Linden Gardens** could not apply; it was unnecessary because the third party had a direct right of action against the contractor. Accordingly, there was no need to depart from the general rule that substantial damages cannot be claimed by a promisee who has suffered no loss.

The decision in *Panatown* therefore rests on its facts. However, it is a significant decision because the House of Lords modified the narrow ground in *Linden Gardens* and stated that it was a solution imposed by law, rather than a solution based on contractual intention and party contemplations. This approach avoided the difficult questions surrounding the determination of the intentions of the parties; on this basis, it should follow that the narrow ground ought to apply whenever a third party suffers loss as a building owner and the employer's loss is purely nominal, either because he no longer owns the property in question or because he never owned it. It will only be in instances in which there is direct redress (as in *Panatown* itself) that this operation of law will be necessarily excluded. Nevertheless, this approach is not without its critics. For example, in *Rolls-Royce Power Engineering plc v Ricardo Consulting Engineers Ltd* [2003] EWHC 2871 (TCC), [2004] 2 All ER (Comm) 129, the judge did not follow the *McAlpine* interpretation of the narrow ground as being imposed by law. He preferred to base the narrow ground on the traditional explanation of contractual intention and contemplations, and insisted, at [124], that any other interpretation would transform the exception into the general rule because it would mean that:

> a claim for substantial damages could be advanced on behalf of anyone whomsoever who contended that they had suffered loss as a result of a breach of contract, however remote their apparent connection to the performance of the contract. Such a possibility would destroy the general rule.

It is difficult to argue with an analysis and conclusion reached by the House of Lords. Nevertheless, the traditional approach to the narrow ground does have the advantage of putting clear ground between it and the alternative analysis in the *Linden Gardens* decision—namely, the 'broad ground'. If the narrow ground is imposed by law, it becomes a default position, and so is conceptually closer to the result that the broad ground seeks to achieve.

11.7.3.2.2 *The broad ground in Linden Gardens*

Lord Griffiths had advocated 'the broad ground' to support his conclusion that the building owner in a 'black hole' scenario could recover substantial damages, and there was some sympathy with this approach from other members of the House of Lords (Lords Keith and Bridge, although Lord Browne-Wilkinson thought that further academic consideration of this ground was required): see Palmer and Tolhurst (1997) 12 JCL 1, (1997) 12 JCL 97, and (1998) 13 JCL 143 for this academic discussion. If the broad ground is accepted as a means of obtaining substantial damages on behalf of third parties, it has the potential to alter the practical consequences of the application of the privity doctrine to a significant extent because the loss will be suffered by the promisee.

The broad ground argument rests on the premise that, in a contract for the supply of work and materials, it makes no difference whether the promisee has any proprietary interest in the subject matter of the contract; the crucial factor is whether there has been defective performance or non-performance, since the result of the breach is that the promisee does not receive 'the bargain for which he contracted'. That is the promisee's loss and the promisee can recover substantial damages on a cost of cure basis for that loss of expectation: see McKendrick [1999] CLP 37 and Coote (2001) 117 LQR 81 for further discussion of this broad ground argument and recovery for loss of the 'performance interest' (see also **9.3**).

Although there was some support in the judgment of Steyn LJ in *Darlington Borough Council v Wiltshier Northern Ltd* [1995] 1 WLR 68 for the 'broad approach' advocated by Lord Griffiths, the case was decided on the basis of the narrow ground. The House of Lords in *Alfred MacAlpine Construction Ltd v Panatown Ltd* [2001] 1 AC 518 (see above) also focused on the application of the narrow ground.

1. The majority (who decided the case on the basis of the duty of care deed) expressed grave doubts about the broad ground, although they accepted that the promisee would be able to recover in the event of defective performance if he had spent money on repairing the defects, despite the fact that he was under no legal obligation to do so.

2. On the other hand, there was support for the broad ground from the dissenting members of the House of Lords, Lords Goff and Millett. They dissented on the duty of care deed because they considered it irrelevant. Their focus was on the loss suffered by the promisee (Panatown) as a result of the defective performance for which it had contracted, whereas the duty of care deed dealt with the question of third party enforceability.

3. Lord Browne-Wilkinson (who was in the majority in that he considered that the duty of care deed prevented the promisee's recovery) also appeared to accept the broad ground argument because he attempted to link the two. He stated that, because of the duty of care deed, UIPL had a remedy against McAlpine, so that Panatown had not suffered a loss of bargain (i.e. there was no damage to Panatown's performance interest).

By comparison, there was a clear rejection of any reliance on the broad ground argument in *Sabena Technics SA v Singapore Airlines Ltd* [2003] EWHC 1318 (Comm). Colman J stressed the need for commercial certainty and stated at [140] that, in his opinion, this aim of commercial certainty would be best served by adopting the approach of the majority of their Lordships in *Panatown*, i.e. an ability to recover 'damages for the benefit of a third party for whom or on whose property the work was carried out and a parallel right of the third party to recover such damages from the contracting party'. Equally, Judge Seymour QC in *Rolls-Royce Power Engineering plc v Ricardo Consulting Engineers Ltd* [2003] EWHC 2871 (TCC), [2004] 2 All ER (Comm) 129, noted some practical difficulties with the application of the broad ground.

1. It gives rise to possible dangers of double liability for the same wrong, e.g. in tort, to the person who has actually suffered loss, and in contract, as a notional loss to the actual claimant. (However, the courts should be capable of dealing with such a possibility: see generally the discussion of overlapping claims at **11.4.4**.)

2. Although Lord Griffiths's approach might be applied where the damage is damage to, or failure to repair, property, it would be difficult to apply in the context of consequential losses, since the nature and degree of consequential loss would tend to vary depending on the particular circumstances of the owner. Accordingly, it might be difficult to make an assessment of damages without reference to what actually happened to the other contracting party. (The question of recovery of consequential loss would, however, seem to be a separate question to the basic question of whether it is possible to recover substantial damages in principle. The consequential loss would need to be actual loss sustained by reference to an actual party, and it might therefore be preferable to rely on the narrow ground for recovery if there are significant consequential losses suffered by a third party. The 'broad' ground would focus only on the 'performance loss' of the contracting party.)

3. Given the lack of judicial unanimity with regard to the 'broad' ground and its potential scope of application, the judge concluded, at [130]: 'In these treacherous waters I prefer to navigate by already published charts and to seek to apply the law as it has already clearly developed, rather than to speculate as to how it may develop in the future.'

Furthermore, in *DRC Distribution Ltd v Ulva Ltd* [2007] EWHC 1716 (QB), Flaux J discussed the broad ground argument in the context of a sale of goods. First, he considered that it clearly did not represent the law and agreed with the comments of Lord Clyde in *Panatown*, at p. 534, that if the loss of expectation used in this sense were to amount to a breach, it might cause a loss, 'but it is not in itself a loss in any meaningful sense'. Secondly, however, the scope of the broad ground had been limited to contracts for the supply of services, such as building contracts, whereas sale of goods contracts did not fall into that category.

11.7.4 Relations with the promisee

The third party's relations with the promisee are most likely to be an issue where, after the time of contracting, the promisee changes their mind about the intention to confer a benefit on the third party. The result of such a change of mind might be either a refusal to bring a claim against the promisor for specific performance or, if damages were recoverable on behalf of the third party, a refusal to hand over the sum recovered. Lord Denning MR believed that the third party could prevent both such refusals. In the Court of Appeal in *Beswick v Beswick* [1966] Ch 538, he suggested that the third party could compel the promisee to bring the claim by starting proceedings and joining the promisee as co-defendant. However, the majority in the Court of Appeal rejected this procedure, and their view is the more orthodox.

In *Jackson v Horizon Holidays Ltd* [1975] 1 WLR 1468, Lord Denning suggested that when the claimant recovered damages on behalf of the third party beneficiaries under the contract, he held these damages as money had and received for the use of the third parties, who in theory could therefore recover the money from him by legal action if he were to refuse to hand it over. Subject to the proviso that such damages appear rarely to be recoverable (**see 11.7.3**), Lord Denning's suggestion would seem to be correct. In *Darlington Borough Council v Wiltshier Northern Ltd* [1995] 1 WLR 68, Dillon and Waite LJJ would have found, if necessary, that damages obtained by the original contracting party were held on a constructive trust for the true owner of the property.

11.8 Privity and imposing obligations upon third parties

The privity doctrine provides that a third party cannot be made subject to a burden in a contract to which that third party is not a party. There are some recognized exceptions to this principle at common law, although, as noted at **11.3.4**, the Law Commission's 1996 report and the Contracts (Rights of Third Parties) Act 1999 do not extend to this aspect of the doctrine.

11.8.1 Bailment

Bailment involves the delivery of goods under a contract by a bailor to the bailee for some purpose—e.g. dry cleaning, repairing, safe keeping—and their subsequent return to the bailor after that purpose has been fulfilled.

In some circumstances, the bailor will be bound by the terms of a sub-bailment entered into by the bailee, including any exemption clauses in that sub-bailment.

In *Morris v C. W. Martin & Sons Ltd* [1966] 1 QB 716, for example, the owner of a mink stole (the bailor) sent it to a furrier (the bailee) for cleaning. The bailee sent the stole to a sub-bailee for cleaning on terms whereby the goods were 'held at the customer's risk'. Could the sub-bailee rely on this exemption clause when sued by the bailor? Lord Denning (*obiter*) considered that, because the bailor had agreed that the bailee should pass the stole to the sub-bailee for the cleaning, she had impliedly consented to the cleaning taking place on the terms of that sub-bailment.

The bailor will therefore be affected by terms in a contract to which the bailor is not a party where the bailor expressly or impliedly consented to those terms.

In *K. H. Enterprise v Pioneer Container, The Pioneer Container* [1994] 2 AC 324, the claimant cargo owners had contracted for the carriage of their goods. The contract terms entitled the carriers to subcontract the carriage on any terms and carriage had been subcontracted to the defendants. The question was whether the claimants were bound by a clause in the contract between the carriers and the defendants, which provided that any disputes were to be determined in Taiwan. The Privy Council held that the claimants were bound because they had consented to the cargo being sub-bailed on the defendant's terms.

In the Court of Appeal in *Sandeman Coprimar SA v Transitos Transportes Integrales SL* [2003] EWCA Civ 113, [2003] 2 WLR 1496, Lord Phillips MR suggested that, as an alternative analysis, this conclusion could be based on a direct collateral contract between the bailor and sub-bailee.

11.8.2 Restrictions on the use of chattels and knowing interference with contractual rights

Under the doctrine in *Tulk v Moxhay* (1848) 2 Ph 774, third parties can be subject to burdens of restrictive covenants affecting land. The vendor of land can attach restrictive covenants to that land that 'run with the land' and regulate its future use. Such covenants are enforceable by adjacent landowners and bind all subsequent purchasers.

It was suggested by the Privy Council in *Lord Strathcona Steamship Co. Ltd v Dominion Coal Co. Ltd* [1926] AC 108 that this principle also applied to restrictions affecting the use of chattels in contracts that did not concern land if the third party purchased the chattel in question with notice of the restriction. In *Lord Strathcona*, it was held that, since a vessel had been purchased with knowledge of the existence of a charter relating to its use, the charterers could obtain an injunction to prevent the new owners from ignoring that charter. However, in *Port Line Ltd v Ben Line Steamers Ltd* [1958] 2 QB 146, Diplock J refused to follow *Lord Strathcona* on the basis that it was wrongly decided owing to an inappropriate analogy with the land law cases, which required the party enforcing the restriction to have retained an independent proprietary interest that would benefit from the restriction. The charterers in *Lord Strathcona* had no such independent proprietary interest. Diplock J also stated that even if the principle did apply, it could do so only where the remedy sought was an injunction to restrain inconsistent use and where the purchaser took with *actual* notice of the restriction.

Lord Strathcona may be better explained as an application of the tort of knowing interference with contractual rights. It is a tort in which a third party (C) intentionally or recklessly interferes in a contract between contracting parties (A) and (B), seeking to persuade (A) to break that contract: *Lumley v Gye* (1853) 2 E & B 216.

In *Swiss Bank Corporation v Lloyds Bank Ltd* [1979] Ch 548, Browne-Wilkinson J followed *Lord Strathcona* on the basis that it was the equitable counterpart of the tort of knowing interference with contractual rights. Hoffmann J, in *Law Debenture Trust Corporation plc v Ural Caspian Oil Corporation Ltd* [1993] 1 WLR 138, did not resolve the question of the relationship between these claims. However, he specifically rejected a claim based on the principle in *Lord Strathcona* on the ground that the claimants were seeking to use the principle to obtain compliance with a positive covenant (to pay compensation to the original owners of shares in companies, whose assets had been confiscated as a consequence of the Russian Revolution) when the principle could only ever permit the issue of an injunction to ensure compliance with a negative covenant. Hoffmann J stated specifically, at p. 144: '[o]ne thing is beyond doubt: [the principle] does not provide a panacea for outflanking the doctrine of privity of contract.'

Although the decisions failed to resolve the uncertainties surrounding the relationship between the *Lord Strathcona* principle and the tort of knowing interference with contractual rights, it is clear that they cannot be identical in view of the restrictive scope and remedy of the *Lord Strathcona* principle and the fact that they had been pleaded as alternatives.

MULTIPLE-CHOICE QUESTIONS

 Test your knowledge by trying this chapter's **multiple-choice questions**: **www.oup.com/uk/poole**

FURTHER READING

Reform

Adams and Brownsword, 'Privity of contract: That pestilential nuisance' (1993) 56 MLR 722.

Adams, Beyleveld, and Brownsword, 'Privity of contract: the benefits and burdens of law reform' (1997) 60 MLR 238.

Burrows, 'Reforming privity of contract: Law Commission Report No. 242' [1996] LMCLQ 467.

Flannigan, 'Privity: the end of an era (error)' (1987) 103 LQR 564.

Law Commission Consultation Paper No. 121, *Privity of Contracts: Contracts for the Benefit of Third Parties* (1991).

Law Commission Report No. 242, *Privity of Contracts: Contracts for the Benefit of Third Parties*, Cm. 3329 (1996).

Morgan, *Great Debates in Contract Law*, 2nd edn (Palgrave Macmillan, 2015), ch. 10.

Smith, 'Contracts for the benefit of third parties: in defence of the third party rule' (1997) 17 OJLS 643.

Contracts (Rights of Third Parties) Act 1999

Andrews, 'Strangers to justice no longer: the reversal of the privity rule under the Contracts (Rights of Third Parties) Act 1999' [2001] CLJ 353.

Beale, 'A review of the Contracts (Rights of Third Parties) Act 1999' in Burrows and Peel (eds.), *Contract Formation and Parties* (Oxford University Press, 2010).

Burrows, 'The Contracts (Rights of Third Parties) Act and its implications for commercial contracts' [2000] LMCLQ 540.

Macmillan, 'A birthday present for Lord Denning: the Contracts (Rights of Third Parties) Act 1999' (2000) 63 MLR 721.

Phang, 'On justification and method in law reform: the Contracts (Rights of Third Parties) Act 1999' (2002) 18 JCL 32.

Roe, 'Contractual intention under section 1(1)(b) and 1(2) of the Contracts (Rights of Third Parties) Act 1999' (2000) 63 MLR 887.

Saintier and Merkin, 'Privity of contract: statutory developments' in Merkin and Devenney (eds.), *Essays in Memory of Professor Jill Poole* (Informa Law, 2018).

Stevens, 'The Contracts (Rights of Third Parties) Act 1999' (2004) 120 LQR 292.

Treitel, 'The battle over privity' in *Some Landmarks of Twentieth Century Contract Law* (Clarendon Press, 2002).

St Martins Property

Coote, 'The performance interest, *Panatown*, and the problem of loss' (2001) 117 LQR 81.

Duncan Wallace, 'Assignment of rights to sue: half a loaf' (1994) 110 LQR 42.

McKendrick, 'Breach of contract and the meaning of loss' [1999] CLP 37.

Palmer and Tolhurst, 'Compensatory and extra-compensatory damages: the role of the "*Albazero*" in modern damages claims' (1997) 12 JCL 1 and 97.

Palmer and Tolhurst, 'Compensatory and extra-compensatory damages: *Linden Gardens* and the "Lord Griffiths" principle' (1998) 13 JCL 143.

Chapter 12

Discharge by frustration: subsequent impossibility

SUMMARY OF THE ISSUES

- A contract will be discharged by frustration where, after the formation of the contract, an event occurs that renders further performance of the contract impossible, illegal, or something radically different from what was contemplated by the parties when they made the contract. Whether the event is frustratory will be determined by examining that event in light of the terms and context of the contract in order to determine whether the performance has become impossible or fundamentally different from that anticipated by the contract terms.

- However, the frustration doctrine is a residual doctrine. It will 'not lightly be invoked' and will not apply where the parties have made express provision in the contract for the risk event that occurs (*force majeure* clauses). It also appears that the doctrine will not apply to events that were foreseeable, but not provided for in the contract.

- The frustration doctrine cannot be relied upon by a party where the event in question is attributable to the fault of that party. Fault in this context includes breach of contract, but also instances in which the event in question results from the exercise of a choice by that party.

- Where the frustration doctrine applies, a frustratory event will automatically discharge both parties from performance of their future obligations under the contract. The legal position in relation to obligations that have already fallen due for performance, or have been performed, is determined in accordance with the provisions of the Law Reform (Frustrated Contracts) Act 1943.

- The 1943 Act provides for benefits to be dealt with on a restitutionary basis, i.e. advance payments are, in general terms, recoverable, although the court may permit the recipient of the payment to retain some or all of that payment to cover its expenses and, where a valuable benefit has been conferred in performing the contract prior to the frustratory event, the court may award that party a just sum, which cannot exceed the value of the benefit to the recipient. The Act's treatment of the pre-existing rights and obligations of the parties, and the purpose underlying the 1943 Act, are the subject of academic debate.

12

12.1 Introduction

In general, the performance obligation in contracts is strict (see **8.2.1.1**): the promisor guarantees to achieve a stipulated result and any failure to achieve that result constitutes a breach.

Such a conclusion would cause injustice if, through no fault of either party, the promisor were to be prevented from performing.

Nevertheless, until the middle of the nineteenth century, English law had no general doctrine to excuse contractual performance. The leading case denying the existence of a doctrine of excuse for non-performance was *Paradine v Jane* (1647) Al 26, 82 ER 897.

> In an action in debt for rent due on certain land, the defendant in *Paradine v Jane* had argued by way of defence that he had been deprived of possession of the land by the action of an enemy army. The defence failed; the defendant had promised to pay rent, and if he sought to be excused in particular circumstances, he should have made provision for the circumstances in his contract.

This reasoning was somewhat unrealistic, for if contracts were to contain express provision for every possible eventuality that might interfere in the contractual performance, they would become very long documents indeed!

The important change in the law came in *Taylor v Caldwell* (1863) 3 B & S 826.

> In **Taylor v Caldwell**, the defendants had agreed to allow the claimants to use their hall for four concerts for a fee of £100 for each day. After this contract was entered into, but before the day of the first concert, the hall was destroyed by fire. The claimants were without a venue for the concerts, for which preparations were well advanced. The claimants sought to recover for their loss from the defendants, who pleaded the accidental destruction of the hall as an excuse for their non-performance. The contract contained no express provision for such an eventuality. The court found for the defendants.

The principle in cases like *Paradine v Jane* was said to be limited to 'positive and absolute' contracts, which were contracts in which one party had guaranteed performance irrespective of all risks. Not all contracts were of that type. Blackburn J said, at pp. 833–4:

> Where, from the nature of the contract, it appears that the parties must from the beginning have known that it could not be fulfilled unless when the time for fulfilment of the contract arrived some particular specified thing continued to exist, so that, when entering into the contract, they must have contemplated such existence as the foundation of what was to be done; there, in the absence of any express or implied warranty that the thing shall exist, the contract is not to be construed as a positive contract, but as subject to an implied condition that the parties shall be excused in case, before breach, performance becomes impossible from the perishing of the thing without default of the contractor.

Thus English law developed a doctrine of excuse in the form of the frustration doctrine: see generally, Treitel, *Frustration and Force Majeure*, 3rd edn (Sweet and Maxwell, 2014). The doctrine provides default rules governing intervening events, whose effect on further performance of the contract is so emphatic that the contract is automatically brought to an end. However, it is important to appreciate that the frustration doctrine is a residual doctrine and will therefore not apply if the parties have provided in their contract that the contract will terminate upon some contingency, or that the parties will not be liable for loss arising out of an incident that is beyond their control. Such express risk allocation clauses are usually referred to as '*force majeure* clauses'. Where there is a *force majeure* clause in the contract, that clause will usually be enforced by the courts: e.g. *J. Lauritzen AS v Wijsmuller BV, The Super Servant Two* [1990] 1 Lloyd's Rep 1.

In addition, the courts have been clear that, in the absence of a *force majeure* clause, 'the doctrine of frustration operates within narrow confines': *per* Coulson J in *Gold Group Properties Ltd v BDW Trading Ltd (formerly Barratt Homes Ltd)* [2010] EWHC 323 (TCC), [2010] BLR 235, at [68]. It is also 'not to be lightly invoked', since it operates 'to kill the contract': *per* Bingham LJ in *J. Lauritzen AS v Wijsmuller BV, The Super Servant Two*, at p. 8.

12.2 The legal basis of the frustration doctrine

12.2.1 Implied term theory

In *Taylor v Caldwell* (1863) 3 B & S 826, Blackburn J based his finding that performance had been excused upon an implied term of the contract between the parties that the concert hall should continue in existence until the time for performance. It is not particularly surprising that Blackburn J chose to base his reasoning on an implied term, since at that time the courts were adamant that it was not their role to interfere in the contracts of the parties (see **1.4.1**). Reasoning based on an implied term enabled the court to say that it was doing no more than enforcing what was the true agreement (or intentions) of the parties, including such terms as were so obvious that they had not been expressed (see **6.4.2.3**). The implied term basis for the frustration doctrine continued well into the twentieth century: e.g. *Krell v Henry* [1903] 2 KB 740. There is no doubt that, at that time, what was intended was a term implied *in fact* between the parties (see **6.4.2.3**).

12.2.2 The construction theory

The notion of the doctrine resting on a term implied in fact between the parties was soon recognized as something of a fiction. This was acknowledged by the House of Lords in *Davis Contractors Ltd v Fareham Urban District Council* [1956] AC 696, when both Lord Reid and Lord Radcliffe pointed out that, in many circumstances in which it was admitted that the frustration doctrine should apply, the test for the implication of a term in fact would not be satisfied (i.e. such an implied term would not be so obvious that it went without saying: see **6.4.2.3**). In *Great Peace Shipping Ltd v Tsavliris Salvage (International) Ltd* [2002] EWCA Civ 1407, [2003] QB 678 (a common mistake case discussed at **13.4.1.3**), at [73], Lord Phillips MR traced the theoretical basis for the frustration doctrine and concluded that 'the theory of the implied term is as unrealistic when considering common mistake as when considering frustration'.

In *Davis Contractors v Fareham UDC*, Lord Reid had instead concluded, at pp. 720–1, that:

[F]rustration depends, at least in most cases, not on adding any implied term, but on the true construction of the terms which are in the contract read in the light of the nature of the contract and of the relevant surrounding circumstances when the contract was made.

Lord Radcliffe had expressed the doctrine, at pp. 728–9, in the following terms:

[P]erhaps it would be simpler to say at the outset that frustration occurs whenever the law recognises that, without default of either party, a contractual obligation has become incapable of being performed because the circumstances in which performance is called for would render it a thing radically different from that which was undertaken by the contract . . . But, even so, it is not hardship or inconvenience or material loss itself which calls the principle of frustration into play. There must be as well such a change in the significance of the obligation that the thing undertaken would, if performed, be a different thing from that contracted for.

This construction approach rejects the artificiality of the implied term approach and requires an assessment of the events that have occurred in light of the agreed terms of the contract in order to determine whether the agreed performance is now impossible or of a fundamentally different nature.

In *National Carriers Ltd v Panalpina (Northern) Ltd* [1981] AC 675, at p. 700, Lord Simon explained how frustration would occur:

Frustration of a contract takes place when there supervenes an event 'without default of either party and for which the contract makes no sufficient provision' which so significantly changes the nature (not merely the expense or onerousness) of the outstanding contractual rights and/or obligations from what the parties could reasonably have contemplated at the time of its execution that it would be unjust to hold them to the literal sense of its stipulations in the new circumstances; in such case the law declares both parties to be discharged from further performance.

More recently, Moore-Bick LJ in *CTI Group Inc. v Transclear SA, The Mary Nour* [2008] EWCA Civ 856, [2008] Bus LR 1729 (for facts, see **12.5**), at [14], explained the operation of the doctrine in the following words:

[I]t is essential to the doctrine of frustration that the performance of the contract in the new situation should be fundamentally different from that originally contemplated. In deciding whether that is the case it is necessary to have regard to the general nature of the contract as well as its specific terms, the context in which it was made and the contemplation of the parties as to the range of circumstances in which it might come to be performed.

12.3 Frustrating events

It is usually said that the question of whether an event frustrates the contract is a question of law. *Great Peace Shipping Ltd v Tsavliris Salvage (International) Ltd* [2002] EWCA Civ 1407, [2003] QB 678, at [73], Lord Phillips MR stated that, like the doctrine of common mistake, the frustration doctrine rests upon 'a rule of law under which, if it transpires that one or both of the parties have agreed to do something which it is impossible to perform, no obligation arises out of that agreement'. However, in every case, it is largely dependent upon the relevant facts whether or not a contract is frustrated. The question of law is whether the relevant facts render the performance demanded 'radically different' from the performance that was required by the contract terms: *Davis Contractors v Fareham Urban District Council* [1956] AC 696 (see **12.2.2**).

Nevertheless, it is crucial to realize that most frustration cases involve sometimes complex issues of fact that relate to the central question of whether the contractual performance required has been so changed by circumstances beyond the control of the parties that one party should be excused from that performance. It is therefore almost impossible to provide a comprehensive list of the circumstances in which a contract will be held to be frustrated. All that may be attempted is to outline some common categories of frustrating event.

12.3.1 Impossibility

Subject to any express allocation of the risk (see **12.5.1**), the most straightforward examples of frustrating events are those in which performance in accordance with the express terms of the contract has become impossible. However, there must be a case of real 'impossibility', so that in *Melli Bank plc v Holbud Ltd* [2013] EWHC 1506 (Comm) the judge held that there was no frustration of a facility agreement between the bank (a subsidiary of Bank Melli Iran) and the defendant company when the bank had been designated on a sanctions list applied under EU regulations. (A facility agreement allows a customer who has supplied goods and services to a buyer to obtain payment for those goods or services from a bank on payment of a fee, at an earlier time than is possible under the terms of payment instruments issued by the buyer.) The designation had resulted in the freezing of the bank's assets and a prohibition on dealing with bank funds, so that the facility in this case had gone unused. However, HM Treasury was able to grant licences to permit commercial transactions with such banks in certain circumstances, and the company could have sought such a licence, but had failed to do so. A licence would have permitted the bank to make the payments under the facility agreement. It followed that the company was liable for the payment of the facility fee.

12.3.1.1 Physical destruction of the subject matter

In some cases, the impossibility results from physical causes, as in the leading case of *Taylor v Caldwell* (1863) 3 B & S 826, in which the destruction of the concert hall made performance impossible (see **12.1**).

12.3.1.2 Death or permanent illness of a party to a personal contract

The death of one of the parties in a personal contract is similar to the physical destruction of something that is essential to performance of the contract. Many contracts, such as contracts for the sale of goods, do not require that the performance be made by any particular person, so that death does not prevent actual performance. But certain contracts, especially those for the performance of some skilled service, demand performance by a stipulated person, who is usually one of the parties to the contract. In such a case, it is clear that death of that party makes performance of the contract impossible: *Stubbs v Holywell Railway Co.* (1867) LR 2 Ex 311.

If the contract is to be performed by a person known to be a sole trader, and that person is unable to complete the contract because they suffer a major heart attack and have to give up work, is that sole trader in repudiatory breach of contract (see **8.4**), or could they succeed in a claim that the contract was frustrated? This was the question facing the judge in *Atwal v Rochester* [2010] EWHC 2338 (TCC) in relation to a sole trader builder and a contract to carry out building works on a house that could no longer be completed. The answer seems straightforward, since building contracts are not generally considered to be personal contracts, but the judge considered that exceptionally this was a personal contract owing to the pre-existing knowledge of the trader, a personal relationship of trust, and the relatively low price agreed. It followed that the sole trader's permanent illness frustrated the contract. (It seems clear from the judgment that the judge did not want to conclude that the non-continuance resulting from a major heart attack constituted a repudiatory breach by the sole trader. Nevertheless, there are potential ramifications for those dealing with sole traders, particularly because the judge awarded the sole trader the value of the building works pre-frustration.)

12.3.1.3 Temporary impossibility

Temporary impossibility will frustrate the contract if the impossibility is of such a nature and likely duration that the resumed contractual performance would be radically different from that which was envisaged by the terms of the contract. A strike, whether by the other party or by a third party, may render performance impossible for part of the contract term, and if there is no express provision to provide for this eventuality (although unlikely in practice), it will be necessary to assess the impact of the strike on the performance contracted for.

In *Pioneer Shipping Ltd v BTP Tioxide Ltd* [1982] AC 724, for example, a charterparty for six or seven voyages to be made during a nine-month period was reduced to half that number of voyages by a strike at the port where the ship was to be loaded. The contract was held to be frustrated because the performance actually possible bore no relation to the performance contracted for.

12.3.2 Unavailability of the subject matter

In some circumstances, contractual performance is prevented because something essential to performance is unavailable. Performance is not strictly *impossible*, because the thing still exists, but for reasons beyond the control of the parties it may not be put to the use that they had intended. For example, in *Gamerco SA v ICM/Fair Warning (Agency) Ltd* [1995] 1 WLR 1226 (for facts, see **12.7.2.1**), the stadium at which the rock band Guns 'n' Roses was to play in concert was declared unsafe and no other venue could be made available in time, so the contract to promote the concert was frustrated.

Common examples of frustration of this kind arise in shipping contracts. Thus where a ship has been requisitioned so that it will be unavailable to the charterer on the delivery date, the contract is frustrated: *Bank Line Ltd v Arthur Capel & Co.* [1919] AC 435. It will also be the case that an illness will frustrate a personal employment contract where the contract calls for performance on a particular day and, on that day, the party in question is unable to perform.

In *Robinson v Davison* (1871) LR 6 Ex 269, the defendant's wife had been engaged to play the piano at a concert, but was unable to play on the particular day through illness. The defendant was able to plead his wife's illness as a defence to an action for breach of contract.

12.3.2.1 Temporary unavailability

Particular problems are caused when the unavailability of the subject matter of the contract is only temporary. For example, although it is clear that incapacitating illness on the single day for performance of the contract amounts to frustration—see *Robinson v Davison* (1871) LR 6 Ex 269—it is less easy to state with certainty the effect of prolonged illness on a contract of employment, which may call for performance over a period of months or years. It is clear that such illness will excuse the employee's performance for the period of the illness and it may give the employer the possibility of terminating the employment contract upon notice; whether it will immediately frustrate the contract will depend upon the particular circumstances. In

Marshall v Harland & Wolff Ltd [1972] IRLR 90, the relevant considerations were stated to include: the terms of the contract; the length of the contract; the nature of the employment (i.e. whether the employee was the only person employed in that capacity and the need of the employer to fill the post); the nature of the relevant incapacity; the period for which the incapacity had continued; the period of past employment; and the prospects of recovery.

Similarly, if there is an agreed means to perform a charterparty using a particular ship and the ship in question is temporarily unavailable, the question will be whether the contractual performance, when resumed, will constitute performance of a fundamentally different contract.

> In *Jackson v Union Marine Insurance Co. Ltd* (1874) LR 10 CP 125, a ship was chartered to proceed with all possible dispatch from Liverpool to Newport and there to load a cargo to be shipped to San Francisco. The ship ran aground one day out of Liverpool and was not ready to load until eight months later. The contract had imposed no particular time limit for performance but it was held that there was an implied term that the ship should arrive in Newport in time for completion of the contract within a reasonable time. It followed that the contract was frustrated by such a long delay since the resumed performance would have constituted 'a different voyage'.

Nevertheless, where the charter of the ship is expressed to run for a given length of time, the older case law suggested that temporary unavailability would frustrate the contract only if it took up a disproportionate amount of the whole contract period. This involved judging the period of a likely interruption, without knowing when it would end.

> In *F. A. Tamplin Steamship Co. Ltd v Anglo-Mexican Petroleum Products Co. Ltd* [1916] 2 AC 397, for example, in the context of a ship that was under charter until December 1917, the court had to determine whether its requisition in February 1915 had frustrated the contract. The House of Lords, which gave judgment in July 1916, said that it did not frustrate the contract, no doubt in the belief that the war that had occasioned the requisition would be over in time to allow a substantial period of the charter to be used as intended.

With hindsight, it is easy to see that the court was unduly optimistic!

This approach of attempting to judge the period of interruption is similar to the approach adopted when assessing whether the nature of a breach of an innominate term is sufficiently serious to constitute a repudiatory breach of contract—*per* Diplock LJ in *Hongkong Fir Shipping Co. Ltd v Kawasaki Kisen Kaisha Ltd* [1962] 2 QB 26, at pp. 65–6 (see **8.5.5**)—and, as a basic approach, it was applied in relation to assessments of temporary unavailability in many of the older cases: *Bank Line Ltd v Arthur Capel and Co.* [1919] AC 435, *F. A. Tamplin Steamship Co. Ltd v Anglo-Mexican Petroleum Products Co. Ltd*, and *National Carriers Ltd v Panalpina (Northern) Ltd* [1981] AC 675.

However, it is clear that, in recent years, there has been a greater recognition of the fact that the individual circumstances are vital to any decision, and that the test of the likely length of any interruption may not be the sole determining factor and may, on the facts of a case, be outweighed by other features.

> *Edwinton Commercial Corporation v Tsavliris Russ (Worldwide Salvage & Towage) Ltd, The Sea Angel* [2007] EWCA Civ 547, [2007] 1 CLC 876, [2007] 2 Lloyd's Rep 517, concerned a charter for up to 20 days of a salvage vessel to enable the salvage company to remove oil from a stricken vessel. The local port authorities unlawfully detained the chartered vessel (on environmental grounds) for a three-month period towards the end of the 20-day charter term. This detention occurred when the salvage vessel had just unloaded its last shuttle cargo of retrieved oil. The Court of Appeal held that the charter was not frustrated by the unlawful detention.

The test of comparing the probable length of the delay with the unexpired duration of the charter was not the decisive test on these facts, since it was very different from cases of requisition, seizure, and entrapment owing to war or major conflict in which it was not possible to negotiate out of the situation. The timing issue was therefore only one of many factors to consider. In particular, this was very different from a supervening event that postponed or interrupted the purpose of the contract, since this purpose had been largely performed and the only consequences of the detention were financial, i.e. the liability to pay hire continued for longer. Rix LJ, at [111], explained the approach to be taken in such cases:

> [T]he application of the doctrine of frustration requires a multifactorial approach. Among the factors which have to be considered are the terms of the contract itself, its matrix or context, the parties' knowledge, expectations, assumptions and contemplations, in particular as to risk, as at the time of contract, at any rate so far as these can be ascribed mutually and objectively, and then the nature of the supervening event, and the parties' reasonable and objectively ascertainable calculations as to the possibilities of future performance in the new circumstances.

Interestingly, the Court of Appeal also stressed that a relevant factor and underlying rationale for the frustration doctrine was the justice of the outcome and whether, on the facts, it would be just to relieve the salvage company of the consequences of its contract or unjust to maintain the contract (the so-called 'reality check'). (This case is discussed further in relation to foreseeability at 12.5.3.)

This 'multifactorial approach' (involving factors at the time of the making of the contract when assessed in the light of factors affecting subsequent performance) was approved and applied in *Islamic Republic of Iran Shipping Lines v Steamship Mutual Underwriting Association (Bermuda) Ltd* [2010] EWHC 2661 (Comm), [2010] 2 CLC 534, [2011] 1 Lloyd's Rep 195, and at first instance in *ACG Acquisition XX LLC v Olympic Airlines SA (in liquidation)* [2012] EWHC 1070 (Comm), [2012] 2 CLC 48, in which the frustration argument was not appealed and the first instance decision was affirmed at [2013] EWCA Civ 369, [2013] 1 CLC 775.

> *ACG Acquisition XX LLC v Olympic Airlines SA (in liquidation)* concerned an unsuccessful argument that a five-year lease of an aircraft was frustrated a matter of weeks into the lease when the Greek aviation authority suspended the aircraft's airworthiness certificate following the discovery of certain defects. Teare J considered this to be an occurrence for which Olympic (the lessee) had to be taken to have accepted the risk and that the expectation was that, after checks, the certificate would be restored a year later at a time when four years of the lease remained. In addition, Olympic had considered it too costly to arrange for the full compliance check to take place in view of its pending liquidation. It followed that 'the demands of justice', at [184], favoured the conclusion that frustration had not occurred, not least because such a conclusion would have reversed the contractual allocation of risk.

The multi-factorial approach was also accepted as correct by Flaux J at first instance in *Bunge SA v Kyla Shipping Co. Ltd* [2012] EWHC 3522 (Comm), [2012] 2 CLC 998 and by Robin Knowles QC in *Melli Bank plc v Holbud Ltd* [2013] EWHC 1506 (Comm).

12.3.2.2 Unavailability of the agreed means of performance

Where there is an agreed means of performance and this means is unavailable, the contract will be frustrated. For example, in *Nickoll and Knight v Ashton, Edridge and Co.* [1901] 2 KB 126, the unavailability of a particular ship that was specifically named in the contract was held to frustrate the contract. A particular ship was also specified in *Jackson v Union Marine Insurance Co. Ltd* (1874) LR 10 CP 125 (see **12.3.2.1**) and the fact that the vessel (or choice of two vessels) was named in *J. Lauritzen AS v Wijsmuller BV, The Super Servant Two* [1990] 1 Lloyd's Rep 1 (see **12.6**) was at the root of the frustration question in that case.

However, what if, in a contract of sale, the seller's *anticipated* source of supply fails without the fault of the parties? Does this amount to a failure of the agreed means of performance, so that the contract is frustrated? Where that source of supply is in no way a condition of the contract, but merely represents the seller's planned means of meeting its obligations, the contract will not be frustrated by failure of that source: *Blackburn Bobbin Co. Ltd v T. W. Allen & Sons Ltd* [1918] 2 KB 467. The reason is that, unless otherwise agreed, the risk of failure of a source of supply lies with the seller. That seller is expected to arrange alternative supplies if its planned supply is unavailable. There is no reason why the buyer should know of, or be affected by, the seller's planned mode of performance.

It is equally clear that even where *both* parties anticipate a particular performance, unless this can be said to be an 'agreed' means of performance, its unavailability will not render performance in accordance with the contract terms impossible.

> In **Tsakiroglou & Co. Ltd v Noblee Thorl GmbH** [1962] AC 93, although **both** parties envisaged that the shipment from Port Sudan to Hamburg would be made via the Suez Canal, there was no express stipulation naming this route as the agreed means of performance. Accordingly, it was not possible to excuse contractual performance simply because the Suez Canal had been closed.

Thus where the seller is concerned about sources of supply and wishes to commit only in so far as the seller believes it has available sources, the seller should make the source of supply a condition of the contract.

> In **Howell v Coupland** (1876) 1 QBD 258, the seller specified that the crop to be sold (200 tons of potatoes) was to be grown in a particular field. The crop in this field failed, so that the seller was able to deliver only 80 tons. It was held that the seller was not liable for non-delivery of the remainder since it had become impossible to perform in accordance with the contract term.

Given this term of the contract, it would have been a breach of contract to supply from any other source, although the buyer might have agreed to a variation in the contract terms if the seller had proposed it.

The matter is, however, more complicated where the contract envisages **two** possible sources of supply, one of which is destroyed, but only after contract performance has been allocated to it, and where the other source will be exhausted by other contracts. In such circumstances, in the absence of a *force majeure* clause, it would appear that the party's choice of which contract to allocate to the source that was destroyed will operate to prevent the contract from being frustrated: *The Super Servant Two* (see **12.6**).

12.3.3 Supervening illegality

In some cases, although performance may remain physically possible, the contract is frustrated because, since the time of contracting, there has been a change in the law that makes further performance of the contract illegal. The most obvious instance of such illegality is where there has been subsequent legislation: *Denny, Mott and Dickson v James B. Fraser & Co. Ltd* [1944] AC 265.

Where the illegality exists before the time of contracting, there is no scope for the operation of the doctrine of frustration and the case falls to be determined according to the rules relating to illegal contracts (see **Chapter 16**). *However, it is possible for a contract to become illegal after it has been entered into, but before completely performed, and this may amount to frustration.* For example, it is against the law to trade with the enemy (Trading with the Enemy Act 1939). If, at the time of contracting, the other party is not 'the enemy', such a contract is not, of course, illegal—but it may become so by subsequent declaration of war. If war is declared before the time for performance, the contract will be frustrated: this is what occurred in *Fibrosa SA v Fairbairn Lawson Combe Barbour Ltd* [1943] AC 32, discussed at **12.7.1.1**.

A frustration claim based on illegality failed in *Islamic Republic of Iran Shipping Lines v Steamship Mutual Underwriting Association (Bermuda) Ltd* [2010] EWHC 2661 (Comm), [2011] 2 All ER (Comm) 609, [2011] 1 Lloyd's Rep 195, because the illegality was not complete and did not undermine the purpose of the contract. The claim related to an insurance contract under which the defendant insured vessels owned by the claimant, an Iranian shipowner. During the term of the insurance cover, the UK government had issued an Order in Council prohibiting transactions and business relationships with Iranian entities, including the claimant, but had also issued a licence under the counterterrorism legislation permitting the provision of insurance in respect of bunker oil pollution for three months. The defendant terminated the insurance cover despite this licence, alleging frustration. Beatson J applied the 'multifactorial' approach (see discussion at **12.3.2.1**), and held that the Order and licence did not frustrate the contract of insurance. The licence did not render the defendant's obligations radically different so as to frustrate the contract of insurance. The purpose of the contract had been to provide indemnity insurance and part of that purpose remained lawful.

Similar considerations apply to temporary illegality as applied in the cases of temporary impossibility or unavailability. The period of the interruption, or likely interruption, was assessed against the contract term and nature of the contracted performance.

> Thus, in *National Carriers Ltd v Panalpina (Northern) Ltd* [1981] AC 675, vehicular access to a warehouse, leased to the defendants from January 1974 for ten years, was blocked by order of the local authority in May 1979 and it was anticipated that access would be blocked for a further 20 months. The House of Lords held that, in view of the length of the term and the period of the lease that would remain after this interruption, the defendants could not rely on frustration as a defence to an action for unpaid rent.

12.3.4 Frustration of the common purpose of both parties

In some circumstances, performance of the contract may still be possible, but it would be a radically different performance from that originally envisaged by *both* parties. In other words, the event has destroyed the purpose of the contract for both parties, thereby frustrating the contract. The classic examples of this possible failure of the common purpose are the so-called 'coronation cases', in which a series of contracts became devoid of purpose when the celebrations connected with the coronation of King Edward VII were cancelled because of the King's illness. However, this frustratory event is strictly interpreted, since frustration of purpose might otherwise easily become a means to escape from a contract for economic reasons. *Therefore the contract will not be frustrated unless the contract is wholly devoid of purpose for both parties.*

In *Krell v Henry* [1903] 2 KB 740, the claimant sued the defendant for the balance due on a contract for the hire of rooms from which to view the coronation procession. The procession was cancelled after the hire contract was entered into. The Court of Appeal held that the contract was frustrated. Vaughan Williams LJ laid considerable emphasis upon the fact that it was known to both parties that the subject of the contract was not merely the hire of a room, but also the provision of a view of the coronation procession. On this basis, viewing the coronation procession was the 'foundation of the contract' for both parties, so that its cancellation destroyed this common foundation. Vaughan Williams LJ distinguished this situation from a contract hiring a cab to go to Epsom on Derby Day. He stated 'I do not think that . . . the happening of the race would be the foundation of the contract', since, without additional qualification, it is simply a contract to drive to Epsom.

This case is usually compared with the decision in *Herne Bay Steam Boat Co. v Hutton* [1903] 2 KB 683.

The contract in **Herne Bay Steam Boat Co. v Hutton** was for the hire of a boat to observe the King's review of the Navy and for a day's cruise round the fleet. The naval review was cancelled because of the King's illness, but it was still possible to cruise round the fleet. The Court of Appeal held that the contract was not frustrated.

The distinction between the cases appears to be that, in *Herne Bay Steam Boat Co. v Hutton* [1903] 2 KB 683, the particular purpose was not the subject of the contract, i.e. the contract was not intended by the parties to stand or fall upon whether the naval review took place. The distinction is also sometimes explained in terms of the fact that part of the purpose in the latter case (the cruise round the fleet) was not frustrated: *per* Stirling LJ and the entire purpose of both parties must be rendered impossible by the frustration: see also *North Shore Ventures Ltd v Anstead Holdings Inc.* [2010] EWHC 1485 (Ch), [2011] 1 All ER (Comm) 81, at [307]–[316] (reversed, but not on this point, by the Court of Appeal).

The approach of the Court of Appeal in the *Herne Bay* case appears to be consistent with the approach of the courts to impracticability (see **12.3.5**), so that *Krell v Henry* [1903] 2 KB 740 may be an exceptional case. In *Maritime National Fish Ltd v Ocean Trawlers Ltd* [1935] AC 524, at p. 529, Lord Wright had indicated that the decision in *Krell v Henry* was 'certainly not one to be extended'.

12.3.5 Impracticability

Impracticability is the term used to describe circumstances in which, although contractual performance is technically still possible, it would impose a burden on one party quite different from that contemplated at the time of contracting. In the United States, the Uniform Commercial Code (UCC) has adopted a standard of impracticability rather than impossibility for all cases (UCC § 2–615), with the express intention of replacing the absolute test of impossibility with a test of what is 'commercially impossible'. In other words, where performance under the contract is theoretically possible, but commercially out of the question, the contract would be frustrated.

English law has generally been unwilling to accept that impracticability frustrates the contract. In *Blackburn Bobbin Co. Ltd v T. W. Allen & Sons Ltd* [1918] 2 KB 467, for example, the court was unwilling to find the contract frustrated despite the fact that not only had the seller's anticipated supply failed, but it was also effectively impossible to get supplies of the kind of timber required.

The leading authority on impracticability in English law is *Davis Contractors Ltd v Fareham Urban District Council* [1956] AC 696.

The contractors in **Davis Contractors Ltd v Fareham Urban District Council** had agreed to build 78 houses for the council over a period of eight months for a fixed price. A shortage of skilled labour caused the work to take a further 14 months. The contractors argued that the contract had been frustrated by the delay and that they were therefore entitled to payment on the basis of *quantum meruit* (see **10.5.4**), rather than the agreed price. The House of Lords held that the contract was not frustrated.

As has already been noted (see **12.2.2**), Lord Radcliffe said, at p. 729, 'it is not hardship or inconvenience or material loss itself which calls the principle of frustration into play'.

12.3.5.1 The effect of changing economic or market conditions

It is accepted that the fact that performance of the contract will cost more than was originally anticipated is not, of itself, enough to frustrate the contract. This point is aptly illustrated by the facts of, and decision in, *Amalgamated Investment & Property Co. Ltd v John Walker & Sons Ltd* [1977] 1 WLR 164.

Amalgamated Investment & Property Co. Ltd v John Walker & Sons Ltd concerned a contract for the purchase of property that had been advertised as suitable for redevelopment and which had been purchased for that purpose. It was held that the purchase contract had not been frustrated despite the fact that development was more or less impossible because the property had been listed as a building of special architectural or historic interest. Performance of the contract was not radically different from the performance contemplated by the parties, since there was no contractual term that the property should continue to be available for development at the date of completion; it was simply a contract to purchase the specified property. The impact of the listing was economic, i.e. the property was worth £1.5 million less than the purchase price because the listing affected the redevelopment value, but it did not prevent the contract for purchase being carried out in accordance with its terms.

This principle was also demonstrated by cases arising out of the closure of the Suez Canal, after the Anglo-French invasion in 1956.

In **The Eugenia, Ocean Tramp Tankers Corporation v V/O Sovfracht** [1964] 2 QB 226—see also **Tsakiroglou & Co. Ltd v Noblee Thorl GmbH** [1962] AC 93—a charterparty provided for a voyage from Genoa via the Black Sea to India. The contract did not expressly provide, but both parties assumed, that the voyage would be made through the Suez Canal. The charterers claimed that the contract was frustrated by the closure of the Canal. The Court of Appeal held that the contract was not frustrated.

Although the ship was actually trapped in the Canal, the case was argued on the basis that it would have been possible not to enter the Canal and to complete the voyage by going the long way round via the Cape of Good Hope. The court might simply have said that, since performance was not impossible, the contract must stand. Instead, Lord Denning MR compared the total length in days of the voyage via Suez (108 days) with the length via the Cape (138 days), and found that the latter was not entirely disproportionate to the former. He said that the fact that performance was more onerous or more expensive was not enough to frustrate the contract, but that it would be frustrated where it would be 'positively unjust to hold the parties bound'.

In some cases, it is possible to view the increased cost of performance resulting from severe inflation (such as that experienced by most Western economies during the mid-1970s after the oil crisis) or recession and the credit crunch (post-2008) as rendering contractual performance something radically different from that which was originally undertaken. However, frustration is again excluded in the vast majority of such cases, because the contract is merely imprudent in the circumstances, rather than impossible to perform: e.g. *Thames Valley Power Ltd v Total Gas & Power Ltd* [2005] EWHC 2208 (Comm), [2006] 1 Lloyd's Rep 441 and, in the context of the world economic downturn of 2008, the decisions in *Tandrin Aviation Holdings Ltd v Aero Toy Store LLC* [2010] EWHC 40 (Comm), [2010] 2 Lloyd's Rep 668, and *Gold Group Properties Ltd v BDW Trading Ltd (formerly Barratt Homes Ltd)* [2010] EWHC 323 (TCC), [2010] BLR 235 (discussed further at **12.3.5.2**).

> In *Thames Valley Power Ltd v Total Gas & Power Ltd*, gas had been supplied under an agreement that contained a pricing mechanism clause. When the price of gas rose sharply so that supply under the terms of the pricing mechanism was uneconomic, the supplier issued a notice stating that an event outside its control had occurred, with the result that it would cease supplies until the price fell. However, although the rising cost of gas had made it less profitable to perform the supply contract obligations, it had not made it impossible. The court therefore refused to relieve the supplier of its obligations.

Nevertheless, there may be some exceptional circumstances under which the effect is so substantial, and the context so extreme, that impracticability qualifies as impossibility. In *British Movietonews Ltd v London & District Cinemas Ltd* [1952] AC 166, at p. 185, Viscount Simon said:

> The parties to an executory contract are often faced, in the course of carrying it out, with a turn of events which they did not at all anticipate—a wholly abnormal rise or fall in prices, a sudden depreciation of currency, an unexpected obstacle to execution, or the like. Yet this does not in itself affect the bargain they have made. If, on the other hand, a consideration of the terms of the contract, in the light of the circumstances existing when the contract was made, shows that they never agreed to be bound in a fundamentally different situation which has now unexpectedly emerged, the contract ceases to bind at that point.

This statement is illustrative of the policy that advocates using the frustration doctrine 'with great caution' and not allowing it to 'become an escape route whenever there is an unexpected turn of events': Adams and Brownsword, *Understanding Contract Law*, 5th edn (Sweet and Maxwell, 2007), at p. 140.

12.3.5.2 Contracting to cover changing market conditions

A party that is concerned that the cost of performance may, in some circumstances, prove greater than anticipated may protect itself by including an express provision in the contract making performance in a particular way a condition of the contract: see e.g. *CTI Group Inc. v Transclear SA* [2008] EWCA Civ 856, [2008] Bus LR 1729 (discussed at **12.5**). Thus, in a case like *The Eugenia, Ocean Tramp Tankers Corporation v V/O Sovfracht* [1964] 2 QB 226, if the contract had stipulated that performance was to be via the Suez Canal, closure of the Canal would have made performance impossible, rather than impracticable, and the contract would have been frustrated.

Alternatively, that party may include a provision in the *force majeure* clause that expressly covers what is to happen in the event of a specific change in the economic conditions. As discussed in more detail at **12.5.1**, it is then a question of construction of this clause to determine whether it covers the specific events that have occurred and so applies on the facts.

Discharge by frustration: subsequent impossibility

12

In *Gold Group Properties Ltd v BDW Trading Ltd (formerly Barratt Homes Ltd)* [2010] EWHC 323 (TCC), [2010] BLR 235, the claimant alleged that the defendant was in breach of a development contract in failing to commence the building works in accordance with its terms. The defendant claimed that the contract was frustrated owing to the fall in property values, which meant that the minimum prices in the contract could not be achieved. However, the contract made express provision providing for the parties to renegotiate the minimum prices if there was a need to reduce these and, clearly, it followed that both parties had foreseen the possibility of a fall in property values resulting in the minimum prices not being achieved. It followed that the contract could not be frustrated. (In any event, it was difficult to identify a 'supervening event', since the allegation of frustration was based only on a forecast as to minimum prices and the contract remained capable of performance. It was not 'an event' and that meant that it was unclear *when* the frustration could be said to occur.)

The general 'catch-all' words of a typical *force majeure* clause (such as 'any other cause beyond the party's reasonable control') will not enable that party to excuse its non-performance in times of recession or the collapse of the world's financial markets by alleging economic or funding difficulties. Such circumstances would need to be expressly specified in the clause as an instance of *force majeure*. In *Tandrin Aviation Holdings Ltd v Aero Toy Store LLC* [2010] EWHC 40 (Comm), [2010] 2 Lloyd's Rep 668, the defendant refused to accept an aircraft that it had ordered from the claimant, asserting the 'unanticipated, unforeseeable and cataclysmic downward spiral of the world's financial markets' justified such refusal. Hamblen J disagreed, holding that the words 'any other cause beyond the purchaser's control' did not encompass general economic circumstances affecting the defendant.

12.4 Contracts concerning land

It has been a matter of doubt over many years whether the doctrine of frustration applies to contracts relating to interests in land. These doubts were expressed by the House of Lords in *Cricklewood Property and Investment Trust Ltd v Leighton's Investment Trust Ltd* [1945] AC 221 in the context of a lease. Two members of the House of Lords considered that the frustration doctrine could never apply, since a lease created a legal interest in land. It was this interest that constituted the subject matter of the lease contract and the interest would survive even if it were to become impossible to use the leased premises.

The matter was reconsidered by the House of Lords in *National Carriers Ltd v Panalpina (Northern) Ltd* [1981] AC 675.

In **National Carriers Ltd v Panalpina (Northern) Ltd**, a ten-year lease of a warehouse was deprived of its purpose for a period of 20 months by the closure of the only street allowing access by lorries. It was claimed that the lease had been frustrated. The House of Lords rejected that claim on the ground that, after the disruption, there would still be some three years of the lease to run.

A majority of their Lordships, however, accepted that, in 'rare' circumstances, a lease might be frustrated. Such occasions would be very infrequent for two reasons:

1. Since many leases run for terms of several years, it is unlikely that a potentially frustrating event would take a sufficiently significant 'bite' out of the full term for actual frustration to occur.

2. The kind of major disaster that might frustrate even a long-term lease is usually provided for by an express term of the contract (see **12.5.1**).

It appears to be implicit in the reasoning in *Amalgamated Investment & Property Co. Ltd v John Walker & Sons Ltd* [1977] 1 WLR 164 (see **12.3.5.1**) that the doctrine of frustration may apply to contracts for the sale of land. Nevertheless, its operation in this context is subject to the fact that such contracts are affected by risk allocation rules (see **12.5**). Although the normal rule is that risk will pass on exchange of contracts, conveyancers may expressly delay the passing of risk until completion, so that, for example, the risk of destruction of the property between contract and completion remains with the vendor and the vendor needs to ensure appropriate insurance cover. Even where there is no such express provision, this is still a matter of risk allocation and the purchaser would cover the risk from exchange of contracts by taking out appropriate insurance.

12.5 Risk allocation and the foreseeability question

When circumstances intervene to frustrate a contract, it may be said that a potential risk of the contract has materialized. Thus if a party enters into a contract to hire a concert hall in several months' time, there is a risk that the concert hall will be destroyed in the meantime. The court must then decide whether that risk was to be borne by one or other of the parties (see also **12.6**). Thus the mere fact that performance turns out to be impossible will not result in the contract being frustrated where one party took upon itself an obligation to perform in all of the circumstances: see *Eurico SpA v Philipp Brothers* [1987] 2 Lloyd's Rep 215.

In the sale and supply context, the risk of inability to supply will normally rest with the seller of the goods, so that the seller's failure to perform will be treated as breach, rather than frustration, despite the fact that the failure of the supply is down to the seller's own supplier. The seller may seek to transfer or offset that risk by means of an express provision.

In ***CTI Group Inc. v Transclear SA*** [2008] EWCA Civ 856, [2008] Bus LR 1729, C had wanted to break the cartel run by Cemex in the Mexican cement market and therefore sought to acquire a large quantity of cement for shipment into the Mexican market. C entered into contracts with the seller (T), who had in turn intended to secure the supply from an Indonesian supplier and later from a supplier in Taiwan. However, each supplier in turn came under pressure from Cemex not to supply the cement, so that the seller had no source of supply. The arbitrator considered that performance of the supply contracts had become commercially impossible, so that this excused the seller from performance. However, C argued that this was at the seller's risk and so amounted to breach rather than frustration. At first instance, it was held that, although the contract between C and T had become impossible to perform, this was not a case of frustration since, as a matter of law, the risk of inability to supply was the seller's, and it was for the seller to guard against that risk in dealings with the suppliers or by making delivery under the contract with the buyer conditional on the cement being available for delivery. The Court of Appeal agreed and dismissed the appeal. Delivery remained physically and legally possible, albeit that the seller's supplier had chosen not to make the goods available. That could not constitute frustration of the seller's contract.

The answer for such a seller is an express provision to allocate this risk.

12.5.1 Express risk allocation

Where one party is anxious not to have to bear a particular risk, that party may insert an express term into the contract, assuming that the other party agrees, allocating the risk to the other party. For example, where a manufacturer is anxious not to bear the risk of increased costs of performance in a long-term supply contract, the manufacturer may provide that the price to be paid is to vary in proportion to some suitable index, such as an index of raw material costs. Equally, the contract may require one party to obtain an import or export licence. If the licence is refused by the authorities, it is then a question of construction whether the contract was frustrated or whether the party who failed to obtain it is liable for breach: see *Pagnan SpA v Tradax Ocean Transportation SA* [1987] 3 All ER 565.

In *Bangladesh Export Import Co. Ltd v Sucden Kerry SA* [1995] 2 Lloyd's Rep 1, BEI entered into contracts with SK for the import of sugar into Bangladesh. Import licences were required. The contract contained a term stating that licences were to be obtained by BEI, the buyer, and that 'the inability to obtain [an] import licence shall not be justification for declaration of *force majeure*'. BEI took steps to obtain the necessary licences, but without success, and the imports were prohibited. The Court of Appeal treated the express term as placing the risk on BEI, so that the possibility of frustration was excluded.

Furthermore, where the contract contains an express provision for the particular event that is alleged to have frustrated the contract, the courts will not intervene. In *Gold Group Properties Ltd v BDW Trading Ltd (formerly Barratt Homes Ltd)* [2010] EWHC 323 (TCC), [2010] BLR 235 (discussed at **12.3.5.2**), it was foreseeable that property prices might decline so that the minimum prices in the development contract could not be achieved, and the parties had provided for renegotiation of these prices in this eventuality. It was not for the court to disregard this provision and the judge rejected the argument that the contract was frustrated.

Nevertheless, in the absence of a very clear express provision, the courts may be faced with difficult questions of construction of the contract to determine what was undertaken and a *force majeure* clause will be interpreted *contra proferentem* (against the party seeking to rely on it): *Great Elephant Corporation v Trafigura Beheer BV, The Crudesky* [2013] EWCA Civ 905, [2013] 2 All ER (Comm) 992. Thus, as a matter of construction of the express terms of the contract, a court may hold that the provision in question was not intended to apply to a supervening event of the gravity that actually occurred—*Metropolitan Water Board v Dick Kerr & Co. Ltd* [1918] AC 119—or in the circumstances that occurred: *Select Commodities Ltd v Valdo SA, The Florida* [2006] EWHC 1137 (Comm), [2007] 1 Lloyd's Rep 1. As Tomlinson J stated in *The Florida*, at [6]:

[A] clause may give one or other party certain rights or protections in certain circumstances, but those circumstances can still result in frustration of the contract unless all of their effects on the rights and liabilities of both parties are dealt with comprehensively.

On the facts, the clause did not comprehensively deal with the positions of the parties in the event of supervening illegality. It merely dealt with how the cargo should be handled if loaded before an event occurred. Where performance was rendered impossible before this, the clause could have no application and the frustration doctrine applied.

12.5.2 Foreseeable risks, but not provided for in the contract

It follows from the above discussion that frustration applies only to contracts affected by events that have not been foreseen, in the sense that they have not been expressly provided for in the contract. In the law generally, however, the notion of foreseeability embraces not only things that have been provided for, but also those that a reasonable person would have foreseen even if the particular parties did not foresee them (e.g. the test for remoteness of damage: see **9.5.2**). This idea has been extended in some cases to the doctrine of frustration, so that it is said that not only does frustration not apply to contracts in which the parties have made express provision, but it also does not apply to contracts in which the parties *could have made* express provision, in the sense that the risk was foreseeable.

In *Davis Contractors Ltd v Fareham Urban District Council* [1956] AC 696, Lord Radcliffe treated the foreseeability of the risk as one of the main reasons for rejecting the argument that the contract had been frustrated. In such circumstances, it is presumed that failure to allocate the foreseeable risk is evidence of an intention that the risk be allocated to lie where it falls 'naturally'. Thus, in the case of a manufacturer's long-term contract to supply goods and in the absence of indexation of the price, the risk of increased cost of performance falls naturally on the manufacturer, since the contract is for a fixed price. The seller in a sale of goods contract will generally bear the risk of a failure in the source of supply: *CTI Group Inc. v Transclear SA* [2008] EWCA Civ 856, [2008] Bus LR 1729 (for facts, see **12.5**).

Nevertheless, it may be doubted whether the fact that the risk is foreseeable will exclude the operation of the doctrine of frustration in every case.

1. Many risks are 'foreseeable' without the probability of their occurrence being so great that the parties ought to provide for them (see **12.5.3**). Contracts are not planned to provide for every extreme and remote eventuality. If this were the position, it would make contract drafting a very lengthy process and would be commercially very inefficient.

2. Moreover, in some cases, it has been held that the fact that the parties actually foresaw a particular risk, but made no express provision for it, did not prevent the frustration doctrine intervening to stop the risk lying where it fell naturally.

In *The Eugenia, Ocean Tramp Tankers Corporation v V/O Sovfracht* [1964] 2 QB 226 (the facts are given at **12.3.5.1**), at p. 239, Lord Denning MR said:

> It has frequently been said that the doctrine of frustration only applies when the new situation is 'unforeseen' or 'unexpected' or 'uncontemplated', as if that were an essential feature. But it is not so. It is not so much that it is 'unexpected', but rather that the parties have made no provision for it in their contract. The point about it, however, is this: If the parties did not foresee anything of the kind happening, you can readily infer that they have made no provision for it. Whereas, if they did foresee it, you would expect them to make provision for it. But cases have occurred where the parties have foreseen the danger ahead, and yet made no provision for it in the contract . . . see *W. J. Tatem Ltd v Gamboa* [[1939] 1 KB 132].

In *The Eugenia*, the parties knew of the danger that the Suez Canal might be closed, but, unable to agree on what provision should be put in the contract, had agreed to 'leave the problem to the lawyers' should it materialize. If an actually foreseen, but unprovided for, risk may constitute a frustrating event, the same should be true of a risk that was foreseeable, but not actually foreseen by these parties.

12.5.3 Foreseeability as an aid to construction

In light of *The Eugenia, Ocean Tramp Tankers Corporation v V/O Sovfracht* [1964] 2 QB 226, there cannot be a rule of law that frustration will never apply where the risk was foreseeable. The same would appear to be true even where the more qualified test of 'reasonably foreseeable' risk is used. In any case, that test is too vague to provide proper guidance.

Nevertheless, there is no denying the relevance of foreseeability to the question of allocation of risk. The courts are entitled to assess the degree of foreseeability of a risk in determining whether the parties intended the risk to lie where it falls naturally. The greater the probability of the risk materializing, the more likely it is that the parties did intend the inherent risk allocation of their contract. On the other hand, where the degree of probability is close to zero, the difficulty of determining the nature of the risk and of agreeing on its allocation may outweigh the likelihood of the risk maturing. As in *The Eugenia*, the parties may prefer to leave the matter to be sorted out later. In those circumstances, a presumption of allocation of the risk based on foreseeability would defeat the intentions of the parties and it would be preferable to find the contract frustrated.

In *Edwinton Commercial Corporation v Tsavliris Russ (Worldwide Salvage & Towage) Ltd, The Sea Angel* [2007] EWCA Civ 547, [2007] 1 CLC 876, [2007] 2 Lloyd's Rep 517 (for facts, see **12.3.2.1**), it was clear that the risk of government detention of the salvage vessel was foreseeable given the environmental concerns about pollution from the stricken vessel. The Court of Appeal considered that it was essentially a question of using foreseeability as an aid to construction, so that the less foreseeable an event, the more likely it is that the end result will be frustration of the contract. On the facts in *The Sea Angel*, the risk was foreseeable, and the general risk had been covered by a special protection and indemnity clause in the charter. It followed that there could be no frustration.

Rix LJ summarized the position on foreseeable and foreseen events, at [127], as follows:

> In a sense, most events are to a greater or lesser degree foreseeable. That does not mean that they cannot lead to frustration. Even events which are not merely foreseen but made the subject of express contractual provision may lead to frustration: as occurs when an event such as a strike, or a restraint of prices, lasts for so long as to go beyond the risk assumed under the contract and to render performance radically different from that contracted for. However . . . the less that an event, in its type and its impact, is foreseeable, the more likely it is to be a factor which, depending on other factors in the case, may lead on to frustration.

Flying Music Co. Ltd v Theater Entertainment SA [2017] EWHC 3192 (QB) was a case in which the risk of adverse events was not just foreseeable but had more or less come to pass. The claimant produced and toured a show based upon the performances of Michael Jackson, *Thriller Live*. In May 2010 the claimant agreed with the defendant, a Greek theatre promoter, that the defendant would put on *Thriller Live* in Athens and Thessalonica for a series of 24 and 8 performances respectively in June 2010. There was a good deal of civil unrest in Greece at the time the contract was entered into, a result of the austerity measures implemented by the Greek Government in return for EU support, and only 16 performances in Athens and 3 in Thessalonica took place. There was held to be no frustration: the situation in Greece was already bad when the contract was signed, and although trouble continued thereafter it had not got worse and certainly had not escalated to a point where it became completely different in quality or effect from what was happening before.

12.6 Fault

The doctrine of frustration applies only where the supervening event is beyond the control of the parties. It goes without saying that where performance has become impossible because of one party's breach, that party cannot claim that the contract is frustrated and the other party may well be entitled to treat the contract as repudiated (in addition to recovering damages for any loss caused: see 8.4).

> In **The Eugenia, Ocean Tramp Tankers Corporation v V/O Sovfracht** [1964] 2 QB 226 (see **12.3.5.1**), a clause in the contract provided that the chartered vessel was not to be taken into a war zone without the owner's consent. The vessel entered the Suez Canal in breach of this clause and became trapped when the Canal was blocked. Therefore the charterers could not rely on the fact that they were trapped in the Suez Canal as frustrating the contract, because this position was attributable to their own breach of contract.

It also follows that a negligent act that results in impossibility of performance will not frustrate the contract. In *Taylor v Caldwell* (1863) 3 B & S 826, Blackburn J clearly believed that **if** the destruction of the concert hall had been caused by the negligence of the owners, then they could not have been excused.

In many cases, the issue of frustration or fault may be decided simply on the basis of the burden of proof, since a party alleging that a contract is not frustrated because the impossibility is caused by the breach or negligence of the other party must prove that default: *Joseph Constantine Steamship Line Ltd v Imperial Smelting Corporation Ltd* [1942] AC 154.

> In **Joseph Constantine Steamship Line Ltd v Imperial Smelting Corporation Ltd**, the appellants chartered a ship to the respondents, with the intention that the ship should proceed to Australia to load. Before the ship could sail, its boiler exploded, causing such a delay that there could be no doubt that the contract was discharged. The reason for the explosion was never discovered, although the respondents suspected that the appellants had been negligent and sought to argue that the frustration doctrine should not apply unless the appellants could prove that they had not been negligent.
>
> The House of Lords rejected this argument. On the contrary, the burden of proving a negligent breach of the contract lay on the respondents and, in the absence of proof, the contract was discharged by frustration.

The law goes further, however, and says that even in the absence of breach of contract or negligence, a party may not rely on the frustration doctrine when the supervening event is self-induced, in the sense that it results from some positive action of that party or persons for whom they are responsible: *DGM Commodities Corporation v Sea Metropolitan SA* [2012] EWHC 1984 (Comm), [2012] 2 Lloyd's Rep 587. In *DGM*, the alleged frustrating event—namely, the continuation of an order from the veterinary authority suspending movement of a cargo of frozen chicken—was caused by the conduct of receivers who had failed to discharge the cargo pending receipt of a substantial cash payment for damage to it. This prevented the charterers, who remained responsible for the discharge of the cargo, from relying on the effects of the veterinary order.

The leading authority on self-induced frustration is *Maritime National Fish Ltd v Ocean Trawlers Ltd* [1935] AC 524, a decision of the Privy Council on appeal from Canada.

> *Maritime National Fish Ltd v Ocean Trawlers Ltd* concerned fishing boats using 'otter trawls' that required a licence from the Minister of Fisheries. The defendants wished to operate five such boats, one of which was chartered from the claimants. They duly applied for five licences, but were granted only three. They were invited by the minister to nominate the boats to which the licences would apply and did not nominate the boat chartered from the claimants. They then claimed that the charter of that boat was frustrated. Their claim was rejected. They could have applied one of their three licences to the boat in question, so that it was their choice rather than the action of the minister that deprived the charter of the boat of its purpose. The supervening event was not beyond their control and so did not frustrate the contract.

It might be assumed that if the defendants had chartered all of their boats, so that two charters would have been without purpose whichever boats were nominated, the court might have been more willing to find that the two had been frustrated. However, in *J. Lauritzen AS v Wijsmuller BV, The Super Servant Two* [1990] 1 Lloyd's Rep 1—discussed by McKendrick [1990] LMCLQ 153 and Hedley [1990] CLJ 209, and see the discussion in Peel, *Treitel's The Law of Contract*, 14th edn (Sweet and Maxwell, 2015), [19-088]—the Court of Appeal took a very strict line, and indicated that any act of choice by one of the parties would prevent the supervening event from being beyond that party's control and so prevent the contract being frustrated. Once the impossibility of performance was attributable to the decision of one of the parties, whether or not amounting to breach of contract or negligence, it would be self-induced and so not frustration.

> In *The Super Servant Two*, the defendants agreed to transport the claimants' oil rig on one of two named barges. As an internal management decision, not communicated to the claimants, the defendants allocated the task to *The Super Servant Two* and allocated other tasks to the other named vessel. *The Super Servant Two* then sank and the defendants claimed that the contract was frustrated, while the claimants claimed that the contract was still physically capable of being performed but for the defendants' choice of vessel. The Court of Appeal held that there was an alternative vessel, so that the sinking of *The Super Servant Two* did not automatically bring the contract to an end. It was the defendants' choice or election to allocate the other vessel to another contract. Accordingly, the defendants remained liable even though the loss was not owing to any breach of contract or negligence.

The court does not appear to have considered whether that would be the case where the choice between the modes of performance lay entirely with the defendants, and the choice was made and communicated to the claimants before the time of the allegedly frustrating event. The court also indicated that the defendants could have altered their risk by including a *force majeure* clause to provide for what was to happen in these circumstances, but had not done so. Therefore the risk of being unable to perform and having no excuse rested on the defendants. This decision illustrates the courts' preference for the use of an express provision rather than reliance on the frustration doctrine and its associated consequences.

12.7 The legal effects of frustration

> **! KEY POINT**
>
> The basic effect of frustration is *automatically* to bring the contract to an end for the future, irrespective of the wishes of the parties: *Hirji Mulji v Cheong Yue Steamship Co. Ltd* [1926] AC 497. In this respect, discharge by frustration is significantly different from discharge by breach, where the non-breaching party may elect whether or not to treat the contract as repudiated (see **8.4.2**).

In **Hirji Mulji v Cheong Yue Steamship Co. Ltd**, a ship, the subject of a charterparty, was requisitioned, but the owners asked the charterers if they were willing to wait a little longer, because they believed that the ship would soon be released. The charterers agreed, but when release eventually came, later than anticipated, they refused to take the vessel. The owners argued that the charterers had elected to affirm the contract, despite the potentially frustrating event. The House of Lords held that there was no scope for such an election. If the event were sufficiently serious to frustrate the contract, the effect would be automatic discharge of all further obligations.

12.7.1 The financial implications of the common law rule

The original common law rule was that frustration caused all primary obligations (to perform) and secondary obligations (to pay damages) that had not already accrued to terminate as from the time of the frustrating event, while obligations that had matured before the time of the frustrating event remained to be performed. Under this rule, the distribution of loss resulting from frustration might appear quite arbitrary, since the loss is said to 'lie where it falls'.

12.7.1.1 Money paid or payable in advance

Where the contract provided for a payment (not necessarily full payment) in advance of performance, the original common law rule was that money paid could not be recovered in the event of frustration and, if not actually paid, would remain payable despite the frustration: *Chandler v Webster* [1904] 1 KB 493.

However, the House of Lords in *Fibrosa SA v Fairbairn Lawson Combe Barber Ltd* [1943] AC 32 held that an advance payment could be recovered where there had been a total failure of consideration (see **10.5.1.1**).

The appellants in **Fibrosa SA v Fairbairn Lawson Combe Barber Ltd** ordered machinery from the respondents to be delivered to the appellants' factory in Poland. The appellants paid £1,000 in advance under the contract. The contract provided that 'Should dispatch be hindered or delayed . . . by any cause whatsoever beyond our reasonable control, including . . . war . . . a reasonable extension of time shall be granted.' The contract was frustrated by the German invasion of Poland, and the clause did not affect that position because there was no possibilty of a reasonable extension of time in the circumstances. The appellants sought the return of the £1,000. The respondents resisted the request, because they had already expended large sums in partial performance of the contract. The appellants were successful in recovering their advance payment. There had been a total failure of consideration in the sense that the appellants had received none of the performance for which they had contracted and, on that basis, they were entitled to a restitutionary remedy to recover the money paid.

The problem with this analysis was that, in remedying the hardship that would otherwise have fallen on the party making the advance payment, the House of Lords imposed as great a hardship on the recipient of the advance payment, who had incurred expenses in part performance. It was very likely that the contract had provided for advance payment as a form of insurance against precisely the kind of risk that materialized, so that the court had interfered in the allocation of risk agreed between the parties, depriving the manufacturers of that insurance.

12.7.1.2 Payment on completion situations

Where the contract called for full performance on one side before payment by the other, the result of frustration was to leave the party who had partially performed before the time of the frustrating event without any payment for the work done.

> In ***Appleby v Myers*** (1867) LR 2 CP 651, the claimants had contracted to install and maintain all machinery in the defendant's factory, payment to be made upon completion. Before the task of installation had been completed, the factory and machinery were destroyed by fire, so that the contract was frustrated. Because the payment obligation was not due to be performed prior to the time of the frustrating event, the claimants were not entitled to any payment for the work done.

In this case, the defendant received no lasting benefit from the claimants' performance, since the machinery was destroyed, but the same result would apply at common law where a lasting benefit was conferred. In *Cutter v Powell* (1795) 6 TR 320 (see **8.6.1**), the contract was frustrated by the seaman's death before completion of the voyage. His services before death were a benefit to his employer, but his estate was still unable to recover any payment, since the contract provided for payment only on completion.

12.7.1.3 The need for reform

The common law rule on the effect of frustration was regarded as unsatisfactory for the above reasons and changes were made to the parties' pre-frustration obligations by the Law Reform (Frustrated Contracts) Act (LR(FC)A) 1943. Nevertheless, it is still important to understand the common law background, since it will apply where the 1943 Act does not, and to remember that the Act has no impact on the issue of whether a contract has been frustrated. It is also important to remember that *the automatic discharge of future obligations when frustration does occur is a common law principle.*

12.7.2 The Law Reform (Frustrated Contracts) Act 1943

12.7.2.1 Money paid or payable in advance: s. 1(2)

Where the contract provides that all or part of the price shall be payable in advance then, by s. 1(2) of the LR(FC)A 1943, money actually paid is recoverable and money payable, but not yet paid at the time of the frustrating event, need not be paid. It is not necessary to demonstrate a total failure of consideration for this rule to operate.

The effect, therefore, is that sums paid before the frustrating event are to be repaid, and sums owing but not paid cease to be payable. Section 1(2) is, however, subject to an important proviso intended to meet the objection to *Fibrosa SA v Fairbairn Lawson Combe Barber Ltd* [1943] AC 32, noted at **12.7.1.1**.

> **! KEY POINT**
>
> Where the person entitled to the advance payment under the contract has incurred expenses directly related to the performance of the contract before the frustrating event occurs, the court has a discretion to allow the recipient of the advance payment to retain or recover such part of the advance payment as the court considers just, having regard to all of the circumstances.

The court's discretion is limited in two ways:

1. *The expenses that the court may determine that the recipient is entitled to retain from the advance payment cannot exceed the total amount payable in advance under the contract.* If the parties are to be assumed to have agreed to the advance payment as insurance for the party who has the substantial performance obligation, their estimate of the necessary insurance cover should be adhered to.

2. *In addition, the sum permitted by the court to cover these expenses may not exceed the value of the actual expenses incurred.*

The need for such provision is unclear, since it seems unlikely that a court should find it just to allow retention or recovery of a sum greater than the actual expenses incurred. The limitation appears to be intended to prevent the advance payment from being regarded as automatically forfeit upon frustration and may also be intended to prevent recovery of any allowance for profit as opposed to actual cost of performance, although in practice the distinction may be hard to draw (see LR(FC)A 1943, s. 1(4)). Thus s. 1(2) is not intended to allow the court a general discretion to permit recovery of expenses. In particular, it cannot be used at all, because it will not apply, to allow for the recovery of expenses where there is no advance payment.

One factor likely to affect the court's assessment of what is just in the circumstances is whether the expenses incurred may be recovered in some other way. For example, in the *Fibrosa* case, it may be that the machinery was not so peculiar to the appellants' needs that it could not be sold to an alternative buyer. Such a sale would 'mitigate' the loss caused by frustration (see **9.5.3**), so that the expenses should not be allowed to be retained or recovered out of the advance payment.

It has been suggested—see e.g. Haycroft and Waksman [1984] JBL 207 and McKendrick, 'Frustration, restitution and loss apportionment' in Burrows (ed.), *Essays on the Law of Restitution* (Oxford University Press, 1991)—that it might, in many circumstances, be 'just' to divide the loss between the parties, allowing retention or recovery of half of the expenses incurred. However, where the advance payment is a genuine form of insurance for one of the parties, freely negotiated between the parties, such an approach would seem to involve undue interference in the parties' contract.

Until comparatively recently, there was no reported decision on the operation of s. 1(2) and its proviso. However, the issue arose in *Gamerco SA v ICM/Fair Warning (Agency) Ltd* [1995] 1 WLR 1226.

> In *Gamerco SA v ICM/Fair Warning (Agency) Ltd*, a contract to promote a rock concert was frustrated by the closure of the stadium on safety grounds. Some US$412,000 had been paid in advance to the defendants, who were assumed, for want of concrete evidence, to have had preparatory expenses of $50,000. The claimant promoters had themselves incurred expenses of around $450,000. The only issue for Garland J was how to apply the proviso. He considered the suggestions that had been put forward concerning how this discretion should be exercised—namely, 'total retention' and 'equal division'—before coming to the

Garland J was reluctant to believe that the advance payment stipulated for was intended to be a form of insurance against loss under the contract. Consequently, the judge did not believe he was depriving the defendants of a bargained-for advantage under the contract. It is possible to imagine that the judge was influenced in part by the failure of the defendants to prove in detail the exact extent of their lost expenditure.

This result has, however, been criticized: see Carter and Tolhurst (1996) 10 JCL 264, who argued that there is no discretion to award a nil-expenses sum once expenses are proved.

12.7.2.2 Performance conferring a valuable benefit and the award of a just sum: s. 1(3)

Where no advance payment is provided for under the contract, there is no entitlement to compensation for expenses incurred in performance of a contract that has been frustrated.

However, by s. 1(3) of the LR(FC)A 1943, if performance confers a valuable benefit on the other party before the frustrating event occurs, the court may award the performing party such sum as it considers just in the circumstances.

1. The sum may not exceed the value of the benefit to the party receiving it.

2. In assessing what would be just, the court must consider expenses incurred by the party receiving the benefit (including the question of whether an advance payment was made and whether the performing party was allowed to retain some or all of this to cover its expenses under the proviso to s. 1(2))—s. 1(3)(a).

3. The court must also consider the effect of the frustrating event on the benefit received—s. 1(3)(b).

Thus, if a builder commences work for a client, and the contract is subsequently frustrated, e.g. because of the builder's illness, he may be entitled to payment for the work done if it is of benefit to the customer. The practical relevance of this provision is nevertheless limited by the fact that the performance must have conferred a valuable benefit, in the sense of a tangible or long-term benefit. For example, there could be no s. 1(3) claim in *Gamerco SA v ICM/Fair Warning (Agency) Ltd* [1995] 1 WLR 1226 in respect of the claimants' expenditure incurred in preparing the stadium for the concert, because that expenditure had not resulted in any tangible benefit to the defendants at the time of discharge for frustration.

In addition, the drafting of s. 1(3) is complex, to say the least. Its operation was considered in *BP Exploration Co. (Libya) Ltd v Hunt (No. 2)* [1979] 1 WLR 783. The important judgment is that of Robert Goff J at first instance, which was subsequently affirmed by the House of Lords at [1983] 2 AC 352.

Robert Goff J said, at p. 801:

> First, it has to be shown that the defendant has, by reason of something done by the claimant in, or for the purpose of, the performance of the contract, obtained a valuable benefit (other than a payment of money [to which s. 1(2) applies]) before the time of discharge. That benefit has to be identified, and valued, and such value forms the upper limit of the award. Secondly, the court may award to the claimant such sum, not greater than the value of such benefit, as it considers just having regard to all the circumstances of the case.

According to Robert Goff J, the correct approach is therefore for the court:

1. to identify and value the benefit to the party receiving it (this value forms the upper limit of any award under s. 1(3)); and

2. to decide what just sum, up to that limit, to award to the party conferring that benefit.

12.7.2.2.1 *What is the position if the frustration destroys the 'benefit'?*

A key matter not entirely clear under s. 1(3) was whether the destruction of the benefit by the frustrating event, as in *Appleby v Myers* (1867) LR 2 CP 651 (see **12.7.1.2**), was relevant to the valuation of the benefit or to the assessment of the just sum. Robert Goff J said that the purpose underpinning the 1943 Act was the prevention of unjust enrichment, and he identified the benefit as being the end product of services rather than the services themselves. Therefore, he considered that if the end product were destroyed by the frustrating event, there would be no valuable benefit and there could be no award under s. 1(3), because there would be no unjust enrichment to remedy. Accordingly, in a case like *Appleby v Myers*, there would be no mechanism for recovery (in the absence of an advance payment under s. 1(2) and the exercise of the discretion under the proviso to allow retention of some or all of the advance payment to cover expenses). Thus *Appleby v Myers* would be decided the same way under the 1943 Act.

It can be argued, however, that Robert Goff J's approach does not coincide with the true construction of the Act, since s. 1(3) speaks of a valuable benefit obtained before the time of discharge, which suggests that the valuation is to be made on the basis of circumstances existing immediately *prior* to the frustrating event. Moreover, s. 1(3)(b) provides that the effect of the frustrating event on the benefit is to be considered in assessing what 'the court considers just'. As Peel points out in *Treitel's Law of Contract*, 14th edn (Sweet and Maxwell, 2015), at [19-103], this alternative reading of the section leaves a wider discretion to the court without eliminating the possibility of following the narrower construction in appropriate circumstances. The court might award no sum at all if, in its view, that was what was just; in other circumstances, it would be able to award a just sum if justified. By linking destruction of the benefit to the setting of the upper limit to any award, rather than to the discretion to fix the sum payable, Robert Goff J perhaps unduly restricted that discretion.

12.7.2.3 **Excepted contracts**

The LR(FC)A 1943 does not apply to all contracts.

1. It does not apply where the parties have made express provision for the consequences of frustration (s. 2(3)).

2. Neither does it apply to wholly performed contractual obligations, which may be severed from those that are affected by the frustrating event (s. 2(4)).

3. Certain types of contract for the carriage of goods by sea (s. 2(5)(a)) and contracts of insurance (s. 2(5)(b)) are excepted from the scope of the Act, since such contracts are themselves largely concerned with the allocation of risk and it was not intended that the courts should interfere with such allocations.

4. Contracts for the sale of specific goods, which are frustrated by the goods perishing, are outside the terms of the Act (s. 2(5)(c)). Section 7 of the Sale of Goods (SGA) Act 1979 is specifically mentioned and provides for an agreement to sell specific goods to be avoided where the goods perish before the risk passes to the buyer. It is difficult to see how frustration could occur in other instances involving the perishing of specific goods and the confusing wording of this final exception appears to reflect excessive caution on the part of the draftsman: see Atiyah, Adams, and MacQueen, *The Sale of Goods*, 12th edn (Pearson Longman, 2010), pp. 354–7.

MULTIPLE-CHOICE QUESTIONS

 Test your knowledge by trying this chapter's **multiple-choice questions**: www.oup.com/uk/poole

FURTHER READING

Lewins, 'Maritime arbitration, maritime cases and the common law: the early development of frustration' [2016] JBL 598.

Morgan, *Great Debates in Contract Law*, 2nd edn (Palgrave Macmillan, 2015), ch. 5.

Peel, *Treitel's The Law of Contract*, 14th edn (Sweet and Maxwell, 2015), ch. 19.

Shaw-Mellor and Poole, 'Recession, changed circumstances and renegotiations: the inadequacy of principle of English law' [2018] JBL 101.

Treitel, *Frustration and Force Majeure*, 3rd edn (Sweet and Maxwell, 2014).

The Coronation cases

Brownsword, 'Henry's lost spectacle and Hutton's lost speculation: a classic riddle solved?' (1985) 129 SJ 860.

McElroy and Williams, 'The Coronation cases' (1941) 4 MLR 241 and 5 MLR 1.

Self-induced frustration and the Super Servant Two

Hedley, 'Carriage by sea: frustration and *force majeure*' [1990] CLJ 209.

McKendrick, 'The construction of *force majeure* clauses and self-induced frustration' [1990] LMCLQ 153.

Swanton, 'The concept of self-induced frustration' (1990) 2 JCL 206.

Law Reform (Frustrated Contracts) Act 1943

Baker, 'Frustration and unjust enrichment' [1979] CLJ 266.

Carter and Tolhurst, 'Gigs 'n' restitution: frustration and the statutory adjustment of payments and expenses' (1996) 10 JCL 264.

Clark, 'Frustration, restitution and the Law Reform (Frustrated Contracts) Act 1943' [1996] LMCLQ 170.

Haycroft and Waksman, 'Frustration and restitution' [1984] JBL 207.

McKendrick, 'Frustration, restitution and loss apportionment' in Burrows (ed.), *Essays on the Law of Restitution* (Oxford University Press, 1991).

McKendrick, 'The consequences of frustration: the Law Reform (Frustrated Contracts) Act 1943' in McKendrick (ed.), *Force Majeure and Frustration of Contract*, 2nd edn (Lloyd's of London, 1995).

Stewart and Carter, 'Frustrated contracts and statutory adjustment: the case for a reappraisal' [1992] CLJ 66.

Williams, *The Law Reform (Frustrated Contracts) Act 1943* (Stevens, 1944).

Methods of policing the making of the contract

This part considers those principles of the law of contract that prevent a contract apparently validly made from being enforced. Much of this policing has the effect of rendering the contract either void or voidable (see **3.2.2** and **8.1**), so that these doctrines are 'vitiating factors'. By comparison, illegality (see **Chapter 16**) means that the contract is unenforceable.

Chapter 13 examines non-agreement or 'common' mistake (initial impossibility), which, if the contract has made no provision for the risk in question and if it is a fundamental common mistake, will render the contract void at common law. In the case of such mistakes, the parties are not denying that they reached agreement, but allege that the contract was impossible from the outset, so that any apparent consent or agreement is nullified. This is linked to subsequent impossibility (frustration), discussed in **Chapter 12**. Frustration discharges the parties' future obligations under the contract, and is therefore similar in its effect to discharge for breach (see **Chapter 8**), but it is dealt with immediately prior to common mistake, because both doctrines deal with the effect of impossibility in the absence of a contractual allocation of that risk. The legal treatment of initial and subsequent impossibility is very different.

Until comparatively recently, it was considered that a contract that was not void at common law for fundamental common mistake might nevertheless be voidable in equity. However, the Court of Appeal has stated that there is no such jurisdiction, thereby removing the previous remedial flexibility.

Chapter 14 examines the law of misrepresentation, which renders contracts voidable if false statements (short of contractual promises) were made in order to induce the contract. **Chapter 15** examines the doctrines of duress and undue influence. These have similarities with misrepresentation since they also regulate unfairness in the way in which the contract was made ('procedural unfairness'). These doctrines

Part 4

will also render the contract voidable if established. The related concept of whether there is a general doctrine of unfairness in bargaining (unconscionable bargaining) is also discussed in this chapter. These chapters also discuss the consumer law regime (B2C—'trader' and 'consumer') in the Consumer Protection from Unfair Terms Regulations 2008, SI 2008/1277 (CPRs 2008), as amended by the Consumer Protection (Amendment) Regulations 2014, SI 2014/870. The CPRs impose criminal offences in relation to unfair commercial practices and provides for a regime of rights which, in certain circumstances, is aimed at providing civil redress for individuals affected by misleading actions and aggressive commercial practices. **Chapter 16** examines those instances in which the law will regard the contract as tainted with illegality and therefore unenforceable. It also examines the effect of that illegality on the parties' positions—in particular, the question of whether money or property passing under an illegal contract can be recovered, the Law Commission's recommendations for reform and the effect of a number of recent decisions.

Chapter 13

Non-agreement mistake

SUMMARY OF THE ISSUES

This chapter examines the legal treatment of those mistakes that are claimed to nullify consent on the basis that, although the parties have reached agreement, both parties entered into the contract under the same fundamental mistake.

- In order to protect the interests of third parties and to ensure certainty in transactions, the doctrine of common mistake in English law has traditionally been very narrowly defined. In any event, like the frustration doctrine, if the parties have allocated the risk of the event in the terms of their contract, that risk allocation clause will govern.

- There will be a fundamental common mistake in instances of true impossibility or failure of consideration, i.e. where both parties contract on the basis of a mistake as to the existence of the subject matter or as to ownership of the subject matter of the contract. However, a more restrictive approach has been taken to mistakes as to a quality of that subject matter, since it is still technically possible to perform such a contract in accordance with its terms, despite the fact that the subject matter does not possess a quality that both parties believed it to have.

- There is authority of the House of Lords (*Bell v Lever Bros. Ltd*) confirming that such quality mistakes will be treated as being fundamental (at common law) only where the mistake is such as to render the subject matter 'essentially different', but this term is very narrowly defined and it is difficult to identify any instances in which it would be satisfied.

- If a common mistake is sufficiently fundamental, it renders the contract automatically void, so that any money or property transferred has to be returned. However, mistakes as to quality will generally not affect validity. This fact led Lord Denning to recognize an equitable jurisdiction to set aside a contract 'on terms' on the basis of a common mistake that was recognized as being sufficiently 'fundamental' in equity, even if it was not sufficiently fundamental in law. Whilst this generated remedial flexibility in many cases of mistakes as to quality, it was difficult to reconcile with authority and to explain why a mistake could be fundamental in equity, but not at common law. Fifty years later, the equitable jurisdiction was denied by the Court of Appeal in *Great Peace Shipping*.

- The result is that the doctrine of common mistake in English law is even narrower than previously supposed, and many instances in which the parties consider the contract is affected by mistake are not recognized by law as being mistakes having legal consequences.

- Fine distinctions can arise in terms of the legal treatment of impossibility depending upon whether the impossibility is initial (common mistake) or subsequent (frustration doctrine). Common mistake renders the contract void, whereas frustration discharges future obligations and the Law

13

»

Reform (Frustrated Contracts) Act 1943 provides for an adjustment of the parties' positions with regard to pre-existing obligations. However, in some instances, it will be a matter of pure chance whether the impossibility is initial (already existing before the contract) or subsequent (occurring after it has been made).

13.1 Introduction

As discussed at **3.2.1**, there is no single coherent doctrine of mistake. This reflects the different contexts in which mistake may be said to exist. There are, however, recognized categories of mistake:

1. *mistakes that negative consent* (i.e. mistakes that prevent agreement), including:
   - cross-purposes (mutual) mistake (see **3.3.1**); and
   - unilateral mistake as to term (see **3.3.2** and **3.3.3**); and

2. *mistakes that are said to nullify consent (or common mistake).*

The only type of mistake discussed in this chapter is a non-agreement mistake, i.e. the parties are not denying that they reached agreement, but instead seek to 'nullify' that consent. It can be termed a 'common' mistake because it is claimed that, in entering into the agreement, both parties made the *same mistake* and the true state of affairs was discovered only after objective agreement had apparently been reached. An example might be where A and B are in a cafe and A agrees to sell her car to B, both parties unaware that ten minutes earlier the car had been destroyed by fire. (Historically, the courts sometimes referred to such mistakes as 'mutual mistakes'. This type of mistake should not, however, be confused with agreement cross-purposes mistakes, which were termed 'mutual mistake' in **Chapter 3**.)

(a) The common 'mistake' must have related to a matter that was 'fundamental' to the parties' decisions to enter into the agreement.

(b) Any party who is seeking to rely on common mistake must have reasonable grounds for their belief: *per* Steyn J in *Associated Japanese Bank (International) Ltd v Credit du Nord* [1989] 1 WLR 255.

The existence and consequences of this type of mistake will arise for court decision where one of the parties (A) wishes to withdraw from the agreement (A/B) on this ground, but the other (B) denies the existence of such a 'fundamental' common mistake, perhaps because the contract has proved advantageous to B.

Traditionally, the definition of 'fundamental mistake' for these purposes has been narrow, so that the operation of the common mistake doctrine at common law has been very limited. Such a mistake renders the contract void and therefore of no effect from the very beginning. Accordingly, because there is no contract, the parties are excused all performance. Not surprisingly, therefore, the courts have been anxious not to extend the operation of such a doctrine because of the effect of such a finding on the positions of the parties and, in particular, on the position of innocent third parties (see the discussion at **3.2.2**).

Although some decisions of the Court of Appeal had determined that equity provided a more extended and flexible remedy in some circumstances (see **13.5**), this has now been denied by the Court of Appeal in *Great Peace Shipping Ltd v Tsavliris Salvage (International) Ltd* [2002] EWCA Civ 1407, [2003] QB 679.

In addition, there is a further limitation on the operation of the doctrine of common mistake, since it cannot operate if one party has assumed the risk of the event in question (e.g. the non-existence of the subject matter) or if the contract was subject to a condition precedent, i.e. a contract shall not take effect unless either the subject matter is in existence at the time of the agreement or a particular state of affairs exists (see **8.5.2.1**).

13.2 The contractual allocation of risk

The risk that the assumed state of facts will not materialize may be allocated explicitly, or impliedly, to one of the parties. Whether such an allocation of the risk of the relevant mistake has taken place must be determined *before* considering the possible operation of the doctrine of common mistake. As Steyn J stated in *Associated Japanese Bank (International) Ltd v Credit du Nord SA* [1989] 1 WLR 255, at p. 268:

> Logically, before one can turn to the rules as to mistake . . . one must first determine whether the contract itself, by express or implied condition precedent or otherwise, provides who bears the risk of the relevant mistake. It is at this hurdle that many pleas of mistake will either fail or prove to be unnecessary. Only if the contract is silent on the point is there scope for invoking mistake.

The fact that the doctrine cannot apply where the contract already allocates the risk of the event was made clear in the judgment of Lord Phillips MR in *Great Peace Shipping Ltd v Tsavliris Salvage (International) Ltd* [2002] EWCA Civ 1407, [2003] QB 679. Lord Phillips stated, at [76]:

> [T]he following elements must be present if common mistake is to avoid a contract: (i) there must be a common assumption as to the existence of a state of affairs; (ii) there must be no warranty by either party that that state of affairs exists; (iii) the non-existence of the state of affairs must not be attributable to the fault of either party; (iv) the non-existence of the state of affairs must render performance of the contract impossible; (v) the state of affairs may be the existence, or a vital attribute of the consideration to be provided or circumstances which must subsist if performance of the contractual adventure is to be possible.

Elements (ii) and (iii) identify instances of risk allocation, i.e. an assumption of responsibility by one of the parties.

13.2.1 Express allocation of the risk

The risk may be *expressly* assumed by one party.

In ***William Sindall plc v Cambridgeshire County Council*** [1994] 1 WLR 1016, the contract to purchase land contained an express term stating that the land was sold 'subject to easements, liabilities and public rights affecting it'. The purchaser later discovered that, unknown to the parties, there was a foul sewer buried under the land. It sought to argue common mistake (for the argument relating to misrepresentation, see **14.6.5**). The Court of Appeal held that the contract term allocated the risk of such incumbrances to the purchaser, in that the purchaser had agreed to the buy the land irrespective of what rights might exist in favour of third parties, so that the operation of the doctrine of mistake was excluded.

It follows that where an allocation of the risk has occurred, the fact that the contract as agreed cannot be performed may simply be something that the claimant purchaser has to accept as not being within the promise made by the other party (seller), so that no remedy is available (as in *William Sindall*). Alternatively, if the risk of non-performance has been allocated to the seller, then the fact of non-performance will constitute a breach of the promise as to the existence of the subject matter and will amount to a breach of contract by that party, as in *McRae v Commonwealth Disposals Commission* (1951) 84 CLR 377 (discussed at **13.2.2** and at **13.3.1.2**, and, as to the measure of damages, at **9.3.4**). In *Dany Lions Ltd v Bristol Cars Ltd* [2013] EWHC 2997 (QB), [2014] 1 Lloyd's Rep 281, the terms of the contract indicated that the defendant, BC Ltd, had taken on the risk of performance. The parties had reached agreement concerning radical works to a very rare vintage car, including the fitting of an automatic gearbox by BC Ltd. However, BC Ltd did not perform the work and the claimant alleged breach of contract. The defendant claimed, however, that the contract was void because the claimant had not realized that it was not possible to convert the car in this way without it impacting adversely on the car's performance. The judge had to determine whether BC Ltd could avoid its contractual obligations by arguing common mistake (or indeed frustration). He held that BC Ltd had committed to carry out the works (and so achieve the contracted-for result). In any event, even if this work would have affected the car's functionality, that did not relieve BC Ltd of the obligations it had assumed in accordance with the contract terms, since this element of the works, whilst important, did not render performance of the contract impossible.

The same conclusion was reached in *Dana Gas PJSC v Dana Gas Sukuk Ltd* [2017] EWHC 2928 (Comm), [2018] 1 Lloyd's Rep 177, see esp. [61]–[64], per Leggatt J.

> The claimant, an Abu Dhabi company, issued certificates to the value of US$1 billion. The defendant, a trustee, held the proceeds of the certificates on trust for the holders of the certificates. To overcome the prohibition on interest imposed by sharia law, a Mudarabah Agreement governed by UAE law was entered into by the parties. Such an agreement is framed as a shared investment rather than a loan. Thus the claimant invested skill and labour and the defendant invested capital, and profits were to be shared between them. To protect the defendant and the investors against any shortfall in repayment by the claimant, a Purchase Undertaking governed by English law was entered into, under which the claimant granted to the defendant the right to require the claimant to purchase the entirety of the defendant's interest in the event of default. The claimant sought a declaration to the effect that the Purchase Undertaking was void on the basis that the Mudarabah Agreement failed to comply with sharia law, and that the parties had shared a mistake on that point, The argument was rejected: the Purchase Undertaking specifically stated that the Purchase Undertaking was to remain valid, legal, binding, and enforceable if it was or became unlawful to perform the Mudarabah Agreement.

A similar focus on whether the contract allocated the risk can be seen in *Triple Seven MSN 27251 Ltd v Azman Air Services Ltd* [2018] EWHC 1348 (Comm). Under two agreements reached on 20 June 2016, the claimants leased two aircraft to the defendant for five years. The defendant was to use the aircraft to transport pilgrims from West Africa to the Kingdom of Saudi Araba for the Hajj and Umrah pilgrimages. To do so, the defendant required approval from the National Hajj Commission of Nigeria (NAHCON), which they obtained prior to the two contracts being signed. They also required approval from the Saudi authorities which they did not obtain. Although the decision to refuse to grant approval was reached by the Saudi authorities on 15 June 2016, the letter informing the defendant of the refusal did not reach them until they had signed the two leases. After attempts by the claimant to deliver the aircrafts, the defendants informed them that they could no longer take the delivery of the aircraft, mentioning their inability to participate in the 2016 Hajj airlift, which was the major reason or one of the major reasons for leasing the aircraft. On 12 August, the claimants purported to terminate the agreements following the defendant's failure to accept delivery. The defendant argued that the contract was void for common mistake (the assumption that the approval of the Saudi authorities would be granted). Peter MacDonald Eggers QC, sitting as a Deputy Judge of the High Court, disagreed. Aside from the fact that the mistake was not sufficiently fundamental to the lease agreement, since the Hajj airlift only represented a short period of the entire agreement (at [89]), the risk of not obtaining approval by the Saudi authorities was on the defendant, and the leases were therefore not void (at [91]). The importance of the allocation of the risk was so crucial to the decision that in refining the test as to whether a mistake will render the contract void or not, Peter MacDonald Eggers QC added as a specific condition the fact that there was no provision of allocation of risk in the event of the common assumption being mistaken (at [76]).

13.2.2 Implied allocation of the risk

McRae v Commonwealth Disposals Commission (1951) 84 CLR 377 is a significant decision because the court implied a promise that the tanker was in the position specified and this implied promise was therefore the basis for the allocation of the risk of the tanker's non-existence.

> In **McRae v Commonwealth Disposals Commission**, the Commission had invited tenders for a shipwrecked oil tanker, which was said by the Commission to contain oil and to be lying at a particular location. The claimants' tender was accepted, and they went to considerable expense in equipping a salvage expedition and sailing to the specified location. However, no tanker could be found and it became apparent that none had ever existed. The Commission sought to resist the claimants' claim for damages by arguing that, since the subject matter did not exist, the contract was void for mistake and they were not liable. The High Court of Australia rejected this argument and instead held the Commission to be in breach of contract. The Commission had assumed contractual responsibility for the existence of the tanker and was in breach since the tanker did not exist.

The existence of the tanker was not *expressly* promised by the Commission, but the court was prepared to *imply* such a promise by attributing fault to the Commission in terms of the manner and context in which the assertion of the existence of the tanker had been made—namely, 'recklessly and without any reasonable ground'. Having found there to be a contract, the court was able to award damages to the claimants to compensate them for their expenses in conducting the salvage expedition. The claimants were also able to recover the price paid (see **9.3.4**).

13.2.3 Implied term as the basis for the doctrine of fundamental common mistake

The implied term was also used to explain the law's interference in the validity of apparent contracts, i.e. through the implication of a term that the goods were in existence at the time the contract was made. *Associated Japanese Bank (International) Ltd v Credit du Nord* [1989]

1 WLR 255 is an example of this approach. However, this is not the same as allocating a risk to *one of the parties*, rather it is an allocation of responsibility for the validity of the contract, which is at the root of the law's interference on the basis of mistake.

In **Associated Japanese Bank (International) Ltd v Credit du Nord**, funds were raised against the security of certain non-existent machines on a 'sale and lease back', i.e. the non-existent machines were sold to the claimant bank for more than £1 million and then immediately leased back. The defendant bank had guaranteed the payments due under this lease. When the perpetrator of the fraud defaulted on the lease payments and disappeared with the £1 million, the claimant bank sought to enforce the guarantee given by the defendant.

However, it was held that the guarantee was subject to either an express or an implied condition precedent that the machines existed. Steyn J accepted that, in order for the condition precedent to be implied, the officious bystander test would need to be applied (see **6.4.2.3**). Although this would be relevant only 'in comparatively rare cases', on these facts he considered that such an implied condition precedent existed. Since the machines did not exist, the guarantee did not become effective and the defendant could not be liable under it.

Similarly, the Court of Appeal in *Graves v Graves* [2007] EWCA Civ 660, [2007] 3 FCR 26, [2008] HLR 10 (discussed further at **13.4.1.4**), implied a condition into a tenancy agreement whereby the tenancy would end if Housing Benefit were not payable to the tenant. Once it had become clear that Housing Benefit was not payable, the contract was terminated as to future performance.

The difficulty with this 'implied term' approach is that it appears to fail to separate the issue of 'risk allocation' to one of the parties (outside the law of mistake) from the separate question of 'impossibility' on the facts (inside the law of mistake). Since the decision in *Great Peace* [2002] EWCA Civ 1407, [2003] QB 679 (discussed at **13.3.1.4**), the implied term theory has been replaced with a construction approach in relation to both common mistake and frustration (**12.2.2**) and therefore it may not be the best explanation of the law's interference to declare a contract void for common mistake. The Court of Appeal in *The Great Peace* accepted that the correct approach, outside the issue of the contractual risk allocation to one of the parties, was to conclude that as a matter of law no obligation could arise out of an agreement to do what is impossible (see Lord Phillips MR at [73]).

13.3 Categories of common mistake at common law

The categories of common mistake at common law are based on a restrictive interpretation of mistakes that can be classified as 'fundamental' for this purpose.

These categories equate with situations that are so acute that they constitute 'initial impossibility', i.e. unknown to the parties, the contract (as agreed) is impossible to perform. Usually, this will be because the subject matter has ceased to exist at the time at which the contract was entered into (res extincta).

13.3.1 Mistake as to subject matter (*res extincta*)

In *Strickland v Turner* (1852) 7 Ex 208, a contract of annuity was void because, unknown to the parties, the annuity related to the life of a person who was already dead at the time that the contract was entered into. A further example of this type of impossibility is provided by *Galloway v Galloway* (1914) 30 TLR 531. In this case, a separation agreement was void because it was entered into in the mistaken belief that the parties were married to each other and therefore needed a formal separation. It transpired after the making of the separation agreement that the husband's previous spouse was still alive so that the marriage between the parties was a nullity from the outset.

13.3.1.1 Perishing of specific goods

In the context of contracts for the sale of goods, the starting point for discussion is s. 6 of the Sale of Goods Act (SGA) 1979. Section 6 provides that 'where the contract is for the sale of specific goods' that have 'perished' by the time the contract is made, the contract is void. This section, as originally drafted in the SGA 1893, was said to be based on *Couturier v Hastie* (1856) 5 HL Cas 673. However, it is doubtful that such a wide interpretation can be given to this decision.

> In *Couturier v Hastie*, a cargo of corn was shipped from a Mediterranean port to England. The cargo owner sold the cargo to the buyer at a time when he believed the corn to be in transit. It later emerged that, because the cargo had begun to deteriorate, the master of the ship had sold it at a port en route *before* this contract of sale had been entered into. Neither party was aware of this position at the time of contracting. The seller argued that the buyer was liable to pay the price for the cargo on the basis that the buyer had purchased the cargo and all inherent risks. The House of Lords held that there was no such liability, because the contract was for the sale of *existing* goods, but the seller no longer had the corn to sell at the time when the contract of sale was made.

It might be thought that this would mean that, if there were an implied term that the goods existed, the seller would be in breach. However, if the basis of the decision is that the contract was void for common mistake, then there is no contract to breach. It has been assumed by subsequent commentators that the basis of the decision is common mistake, but the alternative interpretation (placing the risk of non-existence on the seller) is equally consistent with the decision in *Couturier v Hastie*, i.e. that the buyer was not liable to pay the price.

The other problem with s. 6 is that it appears to require the goods to have existed at one time, but to have subsequently 'perished' or ceased to exist. It is arguable, therefore, that s. 6 will not apply to situations in which the goods have *never* existed: for further discussion, see Atiyah (1957) 73 LQR 340. At common law, it should equally be the case that a contract to purchase non-existent goods should be void for common mistake because there is no logical reason to distinguish it from goods that have perished. The shared misconception will be the same and it must surely be a fundamental misconception if the goods have *never* existed.

The case of *Associated Japanese Bank (International) Ltd v Credit du Nord* [1989] 1 WLR 255 (for facts, see **13.2.3**) might appear to be a further example of *res extincta*. In addition to the finding of an express or implied condition precedent which ought to have resolved the issue, Steyn J considered that, in any event, the existence of the machines was of fundamental importance to the guarantee contract, so that the guarantee contract was essentially different from what the parties believed it to be. The guarantee contract was therefore void for common mistake at common law. In fact, it can be argued, by analogy with *Bell v Lever Bros. Ltd* [1932] AC 161, that the mistake was a mistake as to quality, i.e. that the lease related to machines that existed (see discussion of mistake as to quality, at **13.4**). In any event, the difficulty with a *res extincta* conclusion is that it is the guarantee contract that was void, and the subject matter of the guarantee was not the machines, but the lease and its obligations.

13.3.1.2 Assumption of contractual responsibility for the existence of the subject matter

The decision of the High Court of Australia in *McRae v Commonwealth Disposals Commission* (1951) 84 CLR 377 (for facts, see **13.2.2**) concerned the sale of property that had never existed. However, the decision can be distinguished on the basis that the contractual risk of the non-existence was placed on the seller, so that the non-existence constituted a breach of contract.

It is therefore important not to jump to the conclusion that, in a sale of goods contract, in the event of either non-existence or perishing of the subject matter, the contract will always be void. It may be that the risk of existence has been placed on one of the parties so that there is a contract and the non-delivery of these goods will amount to a breach. A contractual assumption of risk excludes the operation of the doctrine of common mistake, in the same way as an applicable *force majeure* clause excludes the operation of the frustration doctrine.

13.3.1.3 Impossibility: common mistake and frustration

In a sense, therefore, this type of impossibility mistake has similarities with the factual context for frustration, because both doctrines apply, in the absence of a contractual allocation of the risk in question, to instances of contractual impossibility (destruction of the subject matter: see **12.3.1**). However, whereas the frustration doctrine applies where the impossibility occurs *after* the contract was entered into, common mistake will apply where the impossibility is initial (i.e. unknown to the parties, the contract was impossible to perform at the time that it was entered into). This can lead to some fine distinctions of fact that result in significantly different consequences.

> In *Amalgamated Investment & Property Co. Ltd v John Walker & Sons Ltd* [1977]1 WLR 164, the claimants had agreed to purchase property from the defendants, which had been advertised as suitable for redevelopment. Unknown to both parties, a decision had already been taken to list the property as a building of special architectural or historical interest, although the actual listing did not take place until after the purchase contract had been signed. The listing seriously affected the value of the property and the claimants sought to have the contract set aside on the basis of mistake or, alternatively, to claim that the contract had been frustrated. It was held that this was not a case involving a common mistake because the listing had not taken place until **after** the contract was made. In addition, the doctrine of frustration did not apply on the facts because this was a risk that was to be borne by the purchaser.

The fine distinction between circumstances requiring the operation of the doctrine of common mistake or the frustration doctrine can also be illustrated by comparing two cases involving very similar facts.

> In *Griffith v Brymer* (1903) 19 TLR 434, the contract was void for common mistake, so that the deposit had to be repaid. The contract in question was to hire a room to view the coronation procession of Edward VII. The contract was made at 11 a.m. on 24 June 1902, but, unknown to the parties, the decision to cancel the procession had been taken at 10 a.m. that morning.
>
> This can be compared with *Krell v Henry* [1903] 2 KB 740, involving a similar contract to hire a room to view the coronation procession, but this contract was entered into on 20 June, so that the cancellation of the procession amounted to frustration. Since *Krell v Henry* was a case based on frustration, at common law the loss lay where it fell and the deposit could not be recovered. (For a discussion of how the position would differ under the Law Reform (Frustrated Contracts) Act 1943, see **12.7.2.1**.)

It is worth noting that *Griffith v Brymer* is not a case of impossibility owing to the non-existence of the subject matter unless the contract purpose was specifically to hire rooms to view the procession. If it were merely to hire rooms, the contract would still be physically possible. However, the purpose of the parties had clearly become impossible in both cases given that the rooms were advertised for this purpose (see **12.3.4**).

13.3.1.4 Common theoretical basis: common mistake and frustration

The basis for *res extincta* has similarities with the origins of the frustration doctrine, which, as we saw in **Chapter 12**, was based originally on the implication of a term ('a condition') that the subject matter should continue to exist: e.g. *Taylor v Caldwell* (1863) 3 B & S 826 (see **12.1**). In other words, the existence of the subject matter at the time of the contract was interpreted as a condition precedent to the other party's obligation to perform: see *Associated Japanese Bank (International) Ltd v Credit du Nord* [1989] 1 WLR 255 and Smith (1994) 110 LQR 400. However, the theoretical basis for the frustration doctrine evolved in the twentieth century so that it is now based on a rule of law dependent upon the construction of the terms of the contract to determine whether the event that has occurred renders performance in accordance with those terms impossible: *Davis Contractors Ltd v Fareham Urban District Council* [1956] AC 696 (see **12.2.2** and **13.3.5**).

In *Great Peace Shipping Ltd v Tsavliris Salvage (International) Ltd* [2002] EWCA Civ 1407, [2003] QB 679, at [61], Lord Phillips MR (giving the judgment of the Court of Appeal) stated that the two doctrines had developed in parallel, so that 'consideration of the development of the law of frustration assists with the analysis of the law of common mistake'. After reviewing the development of frustration, Lord Phillips concluded, at [73]:

> [T]he theory of the implied term is as unrealistic when considering common mistake as when considering frustration. Where a fundamental assumption upon which an agreement is founded proves to be mistaken, it is not realistic to ask whether the parties impliedly agreed that in those circumstances the contract would not be binding. The avoidance of a contract on the ground of common mistake results from a rule of law under which, if it transpires that one or both of the parties have agreed to do something which it is impossible to perform, no obligation arises out of that agreement.

In other words, if performance is impossible, then, as a matter of law, the contract will be void for common mistake. However, in determining whether the contract is 'impossible' to perform, it is necessary to construe the express contract terms and any implications arising from the surrounding circumstances, which Lord Phillips referred to as the 'contractual adventure'.

13.3.2 Mistake as to ownership (*res sua*)

In addition to res extincta, *there is another category of fundamental common mistake at common law—namely, mistakes concerning the ownership of property (res sua). Such a mistake occurs, for example, where a person contracts to purchase property that, unknown to both parties, the purchaser already owns.*

In **Cooper v Phibbs** (1867) LR 2 HL 149, Cooper agreed to lease a salmon fishery from Phibbs, both parties believing that the fishery belonged to Phibbs. In fact, Cooper was already entitled to enjoyment of the fishery as a life tenant, i.e. although not absolute owner so that he could not dispose of the fishery, Cooper was effectively owner during his lifetime. He had no need to take the lease and Phibbs had no power to grant it. It was held that the contract could be set aside (i.e. it was voidable), but the court allowed Phibbs compensation for money mistakenly spent on the fishery.

In *Bell v Lever Bros. Ltd* [1932] AC 161, Lord Atkin relied on this decision of the House of Lords as an example of mistake operating to nullify a contract, and he expressly stated that the effect of such a mistake was to render the contract *void* and not merely voidable.

13.4 Mistake as to quality at common law

13.4.1 Is it sufficiently fundamental?

A mistake as to quality made by both parties will not generally be sufficiently fundamental to render the contract void at common law, since such a mistake does not render performance, as originally agreed, impossible. The emphasis at common law is placed on the sanctity of contract in the absence of clear impossibility.

13.4.1.1 Distinguishing mistakes as to quality and breaches of the satisfactory quality term: identifying the context for a claim based on mistake

It is important at the outset to explain the distinction between mistakes as to quality and promises as to satisfactory quality that are implied in B2B (business to business) sales contracts (SGA 1979, s. 14(2)) or, in the consumer context (B2C contract—between a 'trader' and 'a consumer'), the term that the quality of goods supplied is satisfactory (Consumer Rights Act (CRA) 2015, s. 9). 'Quality', in the context of mistake, refers to some special quality as opposed to the basic overall minimum quality of the goods that is implied by s. 14(2) SGA 1979 or by s. 9 CRA 2015. For example, mistakenly believing that the contract relates to a high grade of tea or to a particular manufacturer's pottery would not involve any breach of the satisfactory quality term.

13.4.1.2 *Bell v Lever Bros. Ltd*

The leading case on mistake as to quality is *Bell v Lever Bros. Ltd* [1932] AC 161.

In *Bell v Lever Bros. Ltd*, Bell and another were made executive officers of a subsidiary of Lever Bros. Subsequently, the subsidiary was closed down, and a further contract made between Lever Bros. and the executive officers, terminating their appointments in return for substantial compensation. It was then discovered that the officers had earlier engaged in private dealings in breach of their service contracts (which the officers themselves had forgotten about). Therefore, at the time of the contracts to terminate their appointments, Lever Bros. could have terminated the service contracts for these breaches without having to pay any compensation. Accordingly, Lever Bros. claimed that the termination contracts were void for mistake and the compensation repayable.

The House of Lords (by a majority of three to two) refused this claim. The mistake was merely as to a quality of the service contracts—namely, whether they needed to be terminated by the payment of compensation—and did not render the contract void. (The consequence was that the compensation paid was not recoverable because the agreement under which the compensation was payable remained valid.)

Therefore such mistakes will not generally be sufficiently fundamental in nature to render the contract void. Lord Atkin (giving what is generally acknowledged to be the leading speech for the majority) stated, at p. 218, that *a mistake as to quality*:

> will not affect assent unless it is the mistake of both parties, and is as to the existence of some quality which makes the thing without the quality essentially different from the thing as it was believed to be.

In *Associated Japanese Bank (International) Ltd v Credit du Nord SA* [1989] 1 WLR 255, Steyn J regarded this statement by Lord Atkin as forming the *ratio* of the case, and it was regarded as the determinative test by the Court of Appeal in *Great Peace Shipping Ltd v Tsavliris Salvage (International) Ltd* [2002] EWCA Civ 1407, [2003] QB 679 (for facts, see **13.4.1.3**). Lord Phillips MR, giving the judgment of the court, stated that the issue on the facts was whether the mistake as to the distance between the two vessels meant that the services to be provided would be 'something essentially different' from what the parties had agreed.

13.4.1.3 The test of 'essential difference'

As a broad test, it might be considered that this test of essential difference would provide great scope for judicial discretion in evaluating the facts in mistake cases and that, in many instances, a mistake as to quality would render 'the thing without the quality essentially different from the thing as it was believed to be'. However, it would be wrong to jump to this conclusion and the case law does not support such an interpretation.

Kennedy v Panama, New Zealand and Australian Royal Mail Co. (1867) LR 2 QB 580 was one of the cases on which Lord Atkin relied in *Bell v Lever Bros. Ltd* [1932] AC 161.

> In ***Kennedy v Panama, New Zealand and Australian Royal Mail Co.***, the claimant had bought shares in a company in the belief, also held by the company, that the company had recently won a contract from the New Zealand government for the delivery of mail. However, the New Zealand government failed to ratify the agreement and the company shares were therefore worth much less. The court said that there was nevertheless a contract for the purchase of the shares. Such a difference in quality, however severe, did not destroy the agreement. Nevertheless, it is difficult to accept that there was no essential difference in this case.

In addition, despite the existence of this broad principle of 'essential difference', Lord Atkin himself gave a number of examples—see *Bell*, at p. 224—of mistakes that would not be sufficiently fundamental. These examples indicate that 'essential difference' will be very narrowly construed. Lord Atkin's examples included the following.

> **→ EXAMPLE**
>
> A buys a picture from B. Both A and B believe it to be the work of an Old Master, and a high price is paid. The picture turns out to be a modern copy. A has no remedy in the absence of representation or warranty.

In essence, Lord Atkin was saying that it will not suffice to state: 'If I had known the true facts I would not have entered into this contract.' If a quality is important to one of the parties, that party should ensure that its existence becomes a contractual promise or can form the basis for a claim in misrepresentation (a false statement of fact: see **13.4.2**). Lord Atkin justified this position, in *Bell* at p. 224, by stating that:

> [I]t is of paramount importance that contracts should be observed, and that if parties honestly comply with the essentials of the formation of contracts—i.e. agree in the same terms on the same subject matter—they are bound, and must rely on the stipulations of the contract for protection from the effect of facts unknown to them.

Lord Atkin put forward another formulation for the test: 'Does the state of the new facts destroy the identity of the subject matter as it was in the original state of facts?' In Lord Atkin's example, the subject matter was the painting, and that would still be identified as 'the Old Master'. It is interesting, however, to compare this with the suggested approach in Peel, *Treitel's The Law of Contract*, 14th edn (Sweet and Maxwell, 2015), at [8-019]. Peel argues that, in this instance, the test should be whether the particular quality is so important to the parties that they actually use this quality in order to identify the subject matter, e.g. if in the example of the sale of the Old Master, the parties had used the name of the artist to describe the subject matter itself. Of course, this can be explained, depending on the facts, as taking the case outside the context of mistake and into the realms of express terms as to description.

Indeed, this argument was rejected by the Court of Appeal (*obiter*) in *Leaf v International Galleries* [1950] 2 KB 86 on the basis that there was no express term to this effect on the facts.

> In *Leaf v International Galleries*, the claimant had bought a painting believed to be by Constable, and it had also been represented by the seller as having been painted by Constable. Five years later, when the claimant tried to sell the painting, it was discovered that the painting was not by Constable. The claimant therefore argued that the original contract of sale should be set aside. His action for misrepresentation failed because of the lapse of time (see **14.5.2.2**) and, in passing, the Court of Appeal reiterated that no alternative remedy for mistake would be available because this was a mistake as to quality only. The fact that the mistake could be described as essential or fundamental did not change the fact that the contract, as originally agreed, continued to be capable of performance (and indeed had been performed).

Lord Evershed MR rejected the argument that the claimant had 'contracted to buy a Constable' by stating, at p. 93, that '[w]hat he contracted to buy and what he bought was a specific chattel, namely, an oil painting of Salisbury Cathedral' and 'it remains true to say that the claimant still has the article which he contracted to buy'.

Similarly, in *Frederick E. Rose Ltd v William H. Pim Junior & Co. Ltd* [1953] 2 QB 450 (the full facts are given at **3.4.1.1.2**), the contract was for the sale and delivery of horse beans, although both parties were operating under a mistake as to whether horse beans were suitable for the claimants' purposes in fulfilling a contract for the supply of 'feveroles'. It turned out that they were not suitable, but the parties had agreed on the sale and purchase of horse beans, so that the contract as agreed was capable of performance and therefore was not void.

Lord Atkin's test in *Bell v Lever Bros.* has generated a good deal of discussion concerning the meaning of 'essential difference'. There is one *obiter* statement in an English case that applies Lord Atkin's test more literally and suggests that the mistake as to a quality would have rendered the contract void. This is a statement by Hallett J in *Nicholson and Venn v Smith-Marriott* (1947) 177 LT 189, in the context of a sale of napkins and tablecloths described as the 'authentic property' of Charles I. In fact, the linen was Georgian, and it was held that there was a breach of contract since this was a sale by description for Charles I linen. Hallett J stated, at p. 192, that 'a Georgian relic . . . is an "essentially different" thing from a Carolean relic', so that the goods purchased were 'different things in substance from those which the claimants sought to buy and believed they had bought'. This view was subsequently doubted by Denning LJ in *Solle v Butcher* [1950] 1 KB 671 and is generally regarded as weak support for arguing that a contract can be void for mistake as to quality in the light of the decision in the case that the description amounted to a contractual term, which would undoubtedly have influenced the finding of 'essential difference'.

The English approach can be compared with the approach exemplified by the decision of the Supreme Court of the US state of Michigan in *Sherwood v Walker* 33 NW 919 (1887), in which the mistake, relating to whether the cow being sold was barren at the time of the sale, was held to relate to 'the very nature of the thing', i.e. it was held to relate to the subject matter being sold and not merely to a quality possessed by that subject matter. This case also illustrates the difficulties of divorcing the question of value from the determination of 'essential difference', e.g. one would undoubtedly pay a higher price for a painting by a famous artist. In *Sherwood v Walker*, the essential difference was that a cow in calf was worth considerably more than a barren cow, which would be sold for its meat. Therefore a buyer would expect to pay a higher price for a cow in calf. Nevertheless, the English courts have not shown the same willingness to take account of price paid as indicating the existence of 'essential difference' in the subject matter: see e.g. *Bell v Lever Bros. Ltd*, in which the compensation paid could not be recovered, and more recently *Kyle Bay Ltd (T/A Astons Nightclub) v Underwriters Subscribing Under Policy Number 019057/08/01* [2007] EWCA Civ 57, [2007] 1 CLC 164, in which there was a significant difference in amount paid out under an insurance policy owing to a mistake as to a quality of that policy, but the difference could not be recovered.

It seems that Lord Denning's resort to equity was prompted by a desire to allow the court to intervene and set aside a contract (subject to the imposition of terms on such avoidance) in cases where the strict requirements of common law mistake had not been satisfied. However, the lack of any basis in precedent for such a jurisdiction in equity has since been confirmed by the Court of Appeal in *Great Peace Shipping Ltd v Tsavliris Salvage (International) Ltd* [2002] EWCA Civ 1407, [2003] QB 679 (see discussion at **13.5**).

The decision in *Great Peace Shipping Ltd* also confirmed the restrictive interpretation of Lord Atkin's statement of principle in *Bell v Lever Bros.* and therefore the limited category of mistakes that will be sufficiently fundamental mistakes to render the contract void.

The contract in **Great Peace Shipping Ltd v Tsavliris Salvage (International) Ltd** alleged to be affected by a common mistake was a contract whereby the vessel, *Great Peace*, was engaged for a minimum hire period of five days to sail towards the *Cape Providence* (another vessel), which had suffered structural damage, and to stand by in case it was required for the purpose of saving life. At the time of entering into the contract, both parties were mistaken about the distance between these vessels (and therefore how long it would take for the *Great Peace* to rendezvous with the damaged vessel). Both parties thought that the vessels were only about 35 miles apart, when the true distance was nearer 410 miles. On discovering the true position, the salvage company that had engaged the *Great Peace* secured the services of an alternate vessel and cancelled the contract hiring the *Great Peace*. The owners of the *Great Peace* sought the minimum five-day hire payable under the terms of the contract, but the salvage company alleged that the contract was either void for common mistake or voidable in equity.

The Court of Appeal held that the crucial test to determine if the contract was void was whether the common mistaken assumption of fact, relating to the proximity of the two vessels, meant that performance of the contract in accordance with its terms would be essentially different from the performance contemplated by the parties, i.e. were the services that the vessel could provide essentially different from those agreed upon? Since the *Great Peace* would have arrived in time to provide the intended service for a number of days and given that the salvage company had not immediately cancelled the contract on discovering the true position, *performance of the contractual adventure was not impossible*. Accordingly, the contract was not void for common mistake and the salvage company was liable to pay the five-day hire charge.

Thus 'essential difference' in *Great Peace Shipping* was equated with impossibility and it must follow that it will therefore be extremely difficult to identify a common mistake as to quality that will be sufficiently fundamental to render the contract void, albeit that the impossibility is not limited to strict compliance with the contractual terms, but extends to whether the contractual adventure is impossible. Some of these difficulties in identifying fundamental common mistakes based on 'impossibility' are apparent in the post-*Great Peace* case law.

In *Brennan v Bolt Burdon* [2004] EWCA Civ 1017, [2005] QB 303, the key question was the effect of mistakes as to law, since it was argued that a compromise agreement had been made under such a common mistake of law. The Court of Appeal accepted that, in principle, a mistake as to law could render a contract void for common mistake, but there was no true mistake of law on these facts, since at the time of the compromise the law was merely *in doubt*, rather than clearly wrong. When entering into compromise agreements, each party accepted the risk that their view of the law might turn out to be mistaken, and Sedley LJ stressed the need for certainty of compromise agreements and the ability to rely on their terms. He said, at [64], that a shift in the law 'cannot be allowed to undo a compromise of litigation entered into in the knowledge both of how the law now stood and of the fact—for it is always a fact—that it might not remain so'.

Although the Court of Appeal did not completely rule out the possibility that compromise agreements could be void for mistake as to law, it was difficult to envisage how a mistake of law would ever render performance impossible (as required by the test in *Great Peace Shipping*). On the facts, this compromise was at all times capable of being performed. Sedley LJ expressed some difficulty with the *Great Peace* test in the context of mistakes of law and concluded that 'a different test may be necessary'. He considered, at [60], that a more appropriate test might be whether 'had the parties appreciated that the law was what it is now known to be, there would still have been an intelligible basis for their agreement'.

In *Kyle Bay Ltd (T/A Astons Nightclub) v Underwriters Subscribing Under Policy Number 019057/08/01*, [2007] EWCA Civ 57, [2007] 1 CLC 164, the issue again concerned the validity of a compromise agreement that had been entered into with the respondent insurance underwriters.

The mistake in **Kyle Bay Ltd (T/A Astons Nightclub) v Underwriters Subscribing Under Policy Number 019057/08/01** related to the type of insurance cover believed to be in place for a nightclub. When the nightclub was destroyed by fire, it became clear to the appellants that a different type of cover was in place from that requested by them and they were advised to agree to compromise the claim for £205,000—about a third less than they would have been entitled to had the cover for which they had, in fact, applied been in place. However, it later transpired that the policy had been of the type that they had requested, so that a larger sum should have been payable under the claim and the settlement had been entered into on the basis of a mistake. Nevertheless, the judge had held that the mistake was not sufficient to render the compromise agreement void, and the Court of Appeal agreed, on the basis that the subject matter was not rendered 'essentially and radically different', since the settlement compromise remained capable of performance at all times.

The only mistake related to the fact that the nature of the cover was assumed to be on one basis rather than another. However, this was a detail of the basis on which the policy was written and 'did not go to the validity of the policy, the parties, the property, the nature of the business or the risks covered'. Neuberger LJ stated, at [26]: 'The difference between the actual and assumed subject matter of the settlement can in my view certainly be characterised as significant, but it is not an "essential . . . and radical . . ." difference.'

In particular, the fact that the appellants received about a third less than they should have done, although 'a significant, even a substantial, reduction', was not an 'essentially or radically different sum from its entitlement'.

13.4.1.4 Are the 'essential difference' and impossibility tests to be equated?

In *Champion Investments Ltd v Ahmed* [2004] EWHC 1956 (QB), the judge concluded that a mistake concerning the applicable rate of interest (i) was not essentially different from what the parties believed *and* (ii) did not render performance of the contract impossible. The implication therefore is that there may be two hurdles in the path of a claimant alleging common mistake as to quality. Alternatively, this may be equating essential difference and impossibility, and so applying one test.

In *Kyle Bay Ltd (T/A Astons Nightclub) v Underwriters Subscribing Under Policy Number 019057/08/01* [2007] EWCA Civ 57, [2007] 1 CLC 164, the Court of Appeal had first raised the question of whether the mistake concerning the insurance settlement agreement would satisfy the test in *Great Peace Shipping Ltd v Tsavliris Salvage (International) Ltd* [2002] EWCA Civ 1407, [2003] QB 679, of rendering performance of the settlement impossible and, of course, concluded that it would not. (It is difficult to envisage a situation in which a compromise or settlement agreement would be *impossible to perform*, but it could have been entered into on a very different basis from the actual position between the parties.) Neuberger LJ referred to the fact that Sedley LJ, in *Brennan v Bolt Burdon* [2004] EWCA Civ 1017, [2005] QB 303, had considered that the impossibility test might therefore be inappropriate in this context, although recognizing that it was essentially down to how the mistake was defined. Neuberger LJ went on to add that, if these doubts were justified, the right test was that in *Bell v Lever Bros. Ltd* [1932] AC 161 and *Associated Japanese Bank (International) Ltd v Credit du Nord SA* [1989] 1 WLR 255, i.e. the test of 'essentially and radically different'. Although this may suggest that the tests may have different spheres of application, Neuberger LJ helpfully pointed to the fact that *Great Peace* had appeared to equate the tests. It may be that the most appropriate test will be applied in the particular context, assuming that the tests will not produce different results. It should not be necessary, however, to have to establish both tests as separate and independent requirements, as the judge at first instance had assumed was necessary in *Kyle Bay* [2006] EWHC 607 (Comm), at [43].

Unfortunately, different results would have followed from the application of the tests in *Graves v Graves* [2007] EWCA Civ 660, [2007] 3 FCR 26, [2008] HLR 10.

In **Graves v Graves**, an ex-husband had agreed to let his ex-wife live as a tenant in a property that he owned. Both parties mistakenly, but justifiably, thought that 90 per cent of the rent would be paid through Housing Benefit. However, this was not the case, since the couple's child also lived with the ex-wife. The ex-wife was unable to pay the rent and the ex-husband brought proceedings for possession. The Court of Appeal relied on the statement of Steyn J in **Associated Japanese Bank** and stated, at [27], that the preliminary hurdle was to determine 'whether the contract itself, by express or implied condition precedent . . . provides who bears the risk of the relevant mistake'. However, Thomas LJ (giving a judgment agreed by Hughes and Coleridge LJJ) concluded that, in order to establish an implied condition precedent that the tenancy contract would end if Housing Benefit were not payable, it needed to be shown that the tenancy was impossible to perform (obviously not the case) **or** 'essentially and radically different' in kind as a result of the non-availability of the benefit. The Court of Appeal concluded that the agreement was different in kind from that originally contemplated, so that the condition could be implied. Therefore the agreement came to an end. The court then went on to adjust the parties' positions in relation to the deposit and the rent paid for occupation in the interim.

The Court of Appeal therefore applied a test applicable to a determination of whether a contract was void for common mistake in order to decide whether there was an implied condition precedent. The applicable test for the implication of such a term ought to have been the officious bystander test (see **6.4.2.3**), a point made clear in *Butters v BBC Worldwide Ltd* [2009] EWHC 1954 (Ch), [2009] BPIR 1315: see also Capper [2008] LMCLQ 264. As a result of the implication of a condition precedent that had failed, rather than an argument based on mistake as to quality that would have been doomed to failure, the outcome was that the tenancy came to an end from the moment at which the position on Housing Benefit came to light. The wife could not therefore recover all of her deposit and rent paid (which would have followed had the contract been void for mistake).

This decision may indicate a shift from arguments based on common mistake (as to quality) post-*Great Peace*, which may be considered doomed to failure, to an argument based on the implication of an implied condition precedent.

There is much scope for arguments of overlap between the factual context in *Bell v Lever Bros.* and that in *Graves v Graves*, i.e. although both parties in *Graves v Graves* mistakenly thought that Housing Benefit was available in relation to the tenancy, its non-availability did not make performance of the contract (or the adventure) impossible unless a very generous interpretation is taken of the context for the agreement. The reliance on the implied condition precedent could well be the result of a need to do justice on the facts that is not possible in cases of mistakes as to quality, but was possible using the Court of Appeal's analysis. Interestingly, Leggatt J in *Dana Gas PJSC* (**13.2.1**) equated the 'impossibility of performance' test with the 'essential and radical difference' test arguing that 'the two approaches may essentially amount to the same thing' (at [65]). Building on this, Peter MacDonald Eggers QC in *Triple Seven MSN 27251 Ltd* (**13.2.1**) appears to indeed consider them as alternatives when stating (at [76]), 'by reason of the assumption being wrong, the contract or its performance would be essentially and radically different from what the parties believed to be the case at the time of the conclusion of the contract; alternatively, the contract must be impossible to perform having regard to or in accordance with the common assumption. In other words, there must be a fundamental different between the assumed state and actual states of affairs.'

13.4.1.5 Overall conclusion

In practical terms, it is likely that cases of common mistake will be limited to instances involving a total failure of consideration (in which one party is unable to deliver what the other party has contracted to receive), such as res extincta *or* res sua. This seems clear from the decision in *EIC Services Ltd v Phipps* [2004] EWCA Civ 1069, [2005] 1 WLR 1377, in which the Court of Appeal held that a bonus issue of shares was void because the absence of the applicable shareholder approval meant that any bonus shares would have to be nil paid. However, the fundamental premise on which bonus shares were issued was that the company had profits available for distribution, which would extend in amount to pay up the bonus shares.

The fact that, in *Great Peace Shipping Ltd v Tsavliris Salvage (International) Ltd* [2002] EWCA Civ 1407, [2003] QB 679, Lord Phillips chose to extend impossibility to 'the contractual adventure' allows for some possibility of leeway in interpretation. In *Apvodedo NV v Collins* [2008] EWHC 775 (Ch), at [43], Henderson J considered that, if literally interpreted, impossibility may be too strict a test and that 'the true test may rather be whether the non-existence of the state of affairs renders performance of the contract *in accordance with the common assumption* impossible' (emphasis original), adding that 'much would depend on precisely how the "contractual adventure" was identified'. The judge relied heavily on the decision in *Associated Japanese Bank (International) Ltd v Credit du Nord SA* [1989] 1 WLR 255, which turned on the conclusion that the existence of the machines was an express or implied condition precedent to the guarantee contract. Steyn J had also considered that the existence of the machines was of fundamental importance to the guarantee contract, so that the guarantee contract was essentially different from what the parties believed it to be. The guarantee contract could therefore be void for common mistake at common law.

Future claims may show a greater willingness to rely on the decision in *Associated Japanese Bank* as justifying alternative claims based on an implied condition precedent (although see the discussion at **13.2.3**) and an allegation that the contract is void for common mistake, involving an interpretation of 'contractual adventure' as including an assumption about the existence of a state of affairs.

In *Golden Ocean Group Ltd v Humpuss Intermoda Transportasi Tbk Ltd* [2013] EWHC 1240 (Comm), [2013] 1 CLC 929, alternative arguments of failure of an implied condition precedent and mistake were submitted. The case concerned a dispute relating to an addendum to a charterparty entered into between Genuine Maritime and Golden Ocean. Clause 1 of this addendum referred all disputes to arbitration in Singapore. However, the original charterparty to which this addendum related was alleged to be made between another company in the Genuine Maritime group, HIT, and Golden Ocean. Counsel for Golden Ocean therefore claimed that clause 1 was ineffective as an agreement to submit disputes to arbitration in Singapore because, relying on *Associated Japanese Bank* and *Graves v Graves* [2007] EWCA Civ 660, [2007] 3 FCR 26, [2008] HLR 10, it was an implied condition of clause 1 of the addendum that the charterparty to which it related had been entered into between Golden Ocean and Genuine (parties to the addendum). This condition failed because HIT was party to the existing charterparty and its arbitration clause. The alternative argument was that clause 1 was void for mistake, since both parties to the addendum mistakenly believed that the charterparty had been entered into between Genuine and Golden Ocean, and that this amounted to a fundamental mistake as to the subject matter of the addendum. The judge, Popplewell J noted, at [45], that 'an implied condition may arise independently of the operation of the doctrine of mistake' (although see the discussion at **13.2.3** which challenges this position). He concluded that this argument had a real prospect of success and issued a stay to prevent any arbitration of the charterparty disputes in Singapore.

13.4.2 The relationship with other possible claims

It is important to make clear the relationship between mistake and the express undertakings or statements of the parties. The fact that a mistake as to quality does not result in the contract being a nullity means, as Lord Atkin made clear in *Bell v Lever Bros. Ltd* [1932] AC 161, that the claimant's only remedies lie in establishing either an express term of the contract by which the promisor undertakes to guarantee that the quality in question is present or a pre-contractual representation that the desired quality is present. In these cases, absence of the desired quality will provide a remedy, respectively, for breach of contract or for misrepresentation. In other words, in these situations, either by means of their contract or as a result of the pre-contractual negotiations, the parties have allocated the risk that the quality will not be present to one or to the other: see e.g. *Nicholson and Venn v Smith-Marriott* (1947) 177 LT 189 (sale by description within s. 13 of the SGA 1979) and *Leaf v International Galleries* [1950] 2 KB 86.

In these instances, it would be inappropriate for the courts to intervene by means of the doctrine of common mistake, and it must be remembered that common mistake may be very much a last-ditch argument—especially because the equitable jurisdiction to set aside on terms has now been denied by the Court of Appeal in *Great Peace Shipping Ltd v Tsavliris Salvage (International) Ltd* [2002] EWCA Civ 1407, [2003] QB 679—since more effective remedies may be obtainable for breach of contract or for the misrepresentation. This principle is sometimes expressed in terms of the rule that mistake must not be the 'fault' of either party.

Common mistake as a last-ditch argument may need to be attempted, however, where there is no contractual promise or pre-contractual statement relating to the quality.

13.5 Is there an equitable jurisdiction to set aside a contract for a common mistake as to quality although the mistake does not render the contract void at common law?

There has been some dissatisfaction with the rule that common mistakes, falling short of those that make performance of the contract as agreed impossible, do not render the contract void. Common mistakes as to quality might be considered to be fundamental in the sense that, in the absence of the mistake, the parties would not have entered into the contract. Thus a mistake over the authenticity of a painting is no doubt one that is central to the contract. It can be argued that it involves a very narrow interpretation to say that the contract (for the sale of a specific painting) can still be performed and is therefore not void.

As suggested at 3.2.2, the explanation for the narrow interpretation is that any other rule would leave third party interests unduly exposed to disputes between parties to transactions over which the third party has no control. Nevertheless, this explanation raised the possibility that a remedy for common mistake as to quality might be acceptable if it were to operate between the original parties to a transaction, but not to defeat third party interests. This effect would be achieved if the impact of mistake on the contract were to make it merely voidable rather than void (see 3.2.2). Lord Denning had sought to achieve just such a rule and it is necessary to trace that development, albeit briefly, before assessing the decision of the Court of Appeal in *Great Peace Shipping Ltd v Tsavliris Salvage (International) Ltd* [2002] EWCA Civ 1407, [2003] QB 679, which, on the basis of *Bell v Lever Bros. Ltd* [1932] AC 161, has since denied the existence of such a jurisdiction in equity.

13.5.1 Lord Denning's attempts to introduce the equitable jurisdiction

Denning LJ (as he then was) first reformulated the law relating to common mistake in *Solle v Butcher* [1950] 1 KB 671.

> The defendant in **Solle v Butcher** had agreed to lease a flat to the claimant for seven years at £250 per annum. The parties arrived at this figure for the rent only because both believed that the property was not subject to rent control under the Rent Acts. The claimant subsequently discovered that the property was subject to rent control and that the rent payable would have been only £140 per annum. Nevertheless, had the defendant served the necessary statutory notices, the basic rent could have been increased to approximately £250 to take account of repairs and improvements to the property. The claimant sought to recover the overpaid rent over a two-year period and sought a declaration that he was entitled to continue in occupation for the rest of the lease at an annual rent of £140. The defendant counterclaimed for the lease to be set aside for mistake. The Court of Appeal gave the claimant the choice between surrendering the lease and continuing in possession, but paying the full amount of rent allowable (i.e. about £250) once the necessary statutory notices had been served.

In effect, these terms amounted to enforcement of the original contract term and, arguably, this may have been because it was the claimant (surveyor) who had supplied the defendant with the information on the rent that he could charge.

In *Solle v Butcher*, Denning LJ began his analysis of the law of mistake by referring to the statement of the law by Lord Atkin in *Bell v Lever Bros. Ltd* [1932] AC 161 and by accepting the orthodox interpretation of what Lord Atkin said (see **13.4.1.2**). He went on to suggest, however, that *Bell v Lever Bros. Ltd* is not the whole law on common mistake and said that there was a doctrine of equity, not referred to in the House of Lords in that case, by which a contract may be set aside on terms on the basis of common mistake, including in circumstances under which the mistake is only one of quality. (Subsequent commentators have expressed surprise that such a talented House of Lords, addressed by such eminent counsel, should in *Bell* have failed to take account of this equitable doctrine if such existed. The most likely explanation is that the doctrine was Denning LJ's own creation and the evidence suggests that this was the case.)

13.5.2 Post-*Solle v Butcher*

The supposed equitable doctrine was applied or accepted in a number of judicial decisions after *Solle v Butcher* [1950] 1 KB 671.

> In **Grist v Bailey** [1967] Ch 532, for example, Goff J set aside a contract for the purchase of a house believed to be subject to a protected tenancy, whereas in fact it was available with vacant possession, making a difference of some £1,400 to the value of the property. The contract was set aside because the mistake was regarded as being sufficiently fundamental in equity, and it was set aside on terms whereby the vendor undertook to give the purchaser the chance to buy the property at the true value.
>
> Similarly, in **Magee v Pennine Insurance Co. Ltd** [1969] 2QB 507, the majority of the Court of Appeal set aside a contract of settlement of an insurance claim on the ground that the parties had been mistaken about the insured's entitlement to claim as a result of material misstatements in the original

insurance proposal. (It is interesting that the terms in this case did not require the insurance company to return the insurance premium.) In this case, there was a spirited dissenting judgment from Winn LJ, who considered the case indistinguishable on its facts from **Bell v Lever Bros. Ltd** [1932] AC 161.

Perhaps most significantly, there was clear recognition of the equitable jurisdiction in the judgment of Steyn J (as he then was) in *Associated Japanese Bank (International) Ltd v Credit du Nord* [1989] 1 WLR 255, although Steyn J clearly recognized that Lord Denning's interpretation of the majority judgments in *Bell v Lever Bros. Ltd* was rather selective. Steyn J stated, at pp. 267–8:

> No one could fairly suggest that in this difficult area of the law there is only one correct approach or solution. But a narrow doctrine of common law mistake (as enunciated in *Bell v Lever Bros Ltd*), supplemented by the more flexible doctrine of mistake in equity (as developed in *Solle v Butcher* and later cases), seems to me to be an entirely sensible and satisfactory state of the law.

Recognizing the tension that had appeared between the common law and equitable approaches to common mistake, Steyn J had sought to clarify the relationship, and had concluded that the equitable jurisdiction was intended to mitigate the harshness of the strict approach at common law and would be relevant only where the mistake was not sufficiently fundamental to set aside the contract at common law. Although he did not need to clarify the circumstances in which the equitable jurisdiction would apply (the contract on these facts being void for mistake), Steyn J appears to have regarded the doctrine in a positive light, e.g. in terms of flexibility and achieving a balance between fairness between the parties and protection of subsequently created third party rights.

However, a number of obvious discrepancies remained:

1. It was difficult to see why, if there was an equitable jurisdiction to set aside on terms, that jurisdiction had not been exercised (or even mentioned) in *Bell v Lever Bros*, in which fairness between the parties might have suggested the return of all or part of the compensation payment.

2. How could a mistake be *insufficiently fundamental* at common law to render the contract void, but *sufficiently fundamental* in equity for it to be set aside on terms?

The only possible conclusion was that 'fundamental' was being used in different senses. In *William Sindall v Cambridgeshire County Council* [1994] 1 WLR 1016, at p. 1042, Evans LJ (*obiter*) attempted to explain this distinction:

> It must be assumed, I think, that there is a category of mistake which is 'fundamental' so as to permit the equitable remedy of rescission, which is wider than the kind of 'serious and radical' mistake which means that the agreement is void and of no effect in law . . . The difference may be that the common law rule is limited to mistakes with regard to the subject matter of the contract, whilst equity can have regard to a wider and perhaps unlimited category of 'fundamental' mistake.

The suggestion therefore was that a 'fundamental' common mistake in equity required only that the mistake be material to the parties' positions. In any event, this explanation was hardly convincing, although a reasonable attempt at justifying a position already arrived at.

13.5.3 The denial of the equitable jurisdiction to set aside on terms: *Great Peace Shipping*

In *Great Peace Shipping Ltd v Tsavliris Salvage (International) Ltd* [2002] EWCA Civ 1407, [2003] QB 679 (for facts, see **13.4.1.3**), the alternative argument for the salvage company was that even if the mistake was not such as to render the contract void at common law, it was voidable in equity. However, both the judge at first instance, Toulson J, and the Court of Appeal denied the existence of any such equitable jurisdiction. Lord Phillips concluded, at [118]:

> [T]he House of Lords in *Bell v Lever Bros Ltd* . . . considered that the intervention of equity, as demonstrated in *Cooper v Phibbs* . . . , took place in circumstances where the common law would have ruled the contract void for mistake. We do not find it conceivable that the House of Lords overlooked an equitable right in *Lever Bros* to rescind the agreement, notwithstanding that the agreement was not void for mistake at common law. The jurisprudence established no such right. Lord Atkin's test for common mistake that avoided a contract, while narrow, broadly reflected the circumstances where equity had intervened to excuse performance of a contract assumed to be binding in law.

The Court of Appeal also agreed with Toulson J that Lord Denning's approach in *Solle v Butcher* [1950] 1 KB 671 'is not to supplement or mitigate the common law: it is to say that *Bell v Lever Bros Ltd* was wrongly decided'. Lord Denning had been wrong to rely on *Cooper v Phibbs* (1867) LR 2 HL 149 as supporting his position, since the nature of the mistake in that case was to render the contract void at law. In addition, there could be no solid jurisprudential basis for recognition of a category of equitable mistake of the kind alleged, since it had not proved possible in the subsequent case law to identify a test for distinguishing mistakes at law and in equity: *per* Lord Phillips at [153]. (For evidence of an attempt to make this distinction, see Evans LJ in *William Sindall v Cambridgeshire County Council* [1994] 1 WLR 1016, at p. 1042 (see **13.5.2**).) Lord Phillips therefore concluded, in *Great Peace* at [154], that there was only one category of 'fundamental' mistake:

> We do not find it possible to distinguish, by a process of definition, a mistake which is 'fundamental' from Lord Atkin's mistake as to quality which 'makes the thing [contracted for] essentially different from the thing [that] it was believed to be'.

On this basis, it was impossible to reconcile *Bell v Lever Bros. Ltd* [1932] AC 161 and *Solle v Butcher*.

Subsequently, in *Statoil ASA v Louis Dreyfus Energy Service LP, The Harriette N* [2008] EWHC 2257 (Comm), [2008] 2 Lloyd's Rep 685, [2009] 1 All ER (Comm) 1035 (see also **2.1.2** and **3.3.2.1**), Aikens J reviewed the authorities before denying the existence of any equitable jurisdiction to rescind for unilateral mistake relating to a settlement contract. He stated, at [105]:

> If there is no such jurisdiction in the case of a common mistake, I fear I am unable to see how, in logic, one can devise a rationale for an equitable jurisdiction in the case of a unilateral mistake, at least where there has been no misrepresentation by the other party.

More significantly, the Supreme Court in *Pitt v Holt* [2013] UKSC 26, [2013] 2 AC 108, at [115], also appeared to accept (*obiter*) that *Great Peace Shipping* had overruled *Solle v Butcher* (and hence the equitable jurisdiction).

13.5.4 The consequences of the denial of the equitable jurisdiction

While this conclusion may have the advantage of producing a neat and conceptually sound result, and is one that must be correct in terms of legal analysis, it does mean that the common mistake doctrine is extremely limited. In addition, the outcome would appear to be based on 'all or nothing', i.e. either the contract is void and of no effect at all, or it remains valid. There is no remedial flexibility.

Lord Phillips recognized this position when he stated, at [161]:

> We can understand why the decision in *Bell v Lever Bros Ltd* did not find favour with Lord Denning MR. An equitable jurisdiction to grant rescission on terms where a common fundamental mistake has induced a contract gives greater flexibility than a doctrine of common law which holds the contract void in such circumstances.

Lord Phillips did suggest that legislative intervention might be called for 'to give greater flexibility to our law of mistake than the common law allows', but he seems to have confined this comment to instances in which the contract is void at common law. The New Zealand legislation provides a possible model for legislation that provides for a more flexible doctrine of mistake with flexibility of remedy: see Chandler, Devenney, and Poole [2004] JBL 34. In addition, the Singapore Court of Appeal, in *Chwee Kin Keong v Digilandmall.com Pte Ltd* [2005] 1 SLR(R) 502, albeit in the context of a unilateral mistake, criticized that part of the decision in *Great Peace Shipping Ltd v Tsavliris Salvage (International) Ltd* [2002] EWCA Civ 1407, [2003] QB 679, which denied the existence of the equitable jurisdiction. The court considered, at [68], that the reason for this denial was 'the absence of any test to determine how the equitable jurisdiction should be applied to rescind a contract which was distinct from that which rendered a contract void in law', but concluded, at [74], that '[b]y its very nature, the manner in which equity should be applied must depend on the facts of each case and the dictates of justice'.

It will be interesting to see how the courts react to the denial in *Great Peace Shipping* of the equitable jurisdiction, because it will undoubtedly leave less room for manoeuvre. It is likely that other legal principles will be increasingly relied upon to introduce the necessary degree of flexibility, e.g. implied condition precedent—see *Graves v Graves* [2007] EWCA Civ 660, [2007] 3 FCR 26, [2008] HLR 10 and *Butters v BBC Worldwide Ltd* [2009] EWHC 1954 (Ch), [2009] BPIR 1315—or misrepresentation. The difficulties that might arise are well illustrated by the factual scenario in *Nutt v Read* (2000) 32 HLR 761, The Times, 3 December 1999: see also (1999) 96 (42) LSG 44.

The claimants in *Nutt v Read* had agreed to sell a chalet on a caravan park to the defendants. It was also agreed that the defendants were to pay a monthly rent to occupy the pitch (the tenancy agreement). The defendants failed to pay this rent and the claimants sought to eject them from the site. The defendants' defence was that the agreement had been entered into under a common mistake—namely, that both parties mistakenly believed that the chalet could be sold separately from the site pitch on which it stood. The position was complicated by the fact that the defendants had made some improvements to the chalet, increasing its value from £12,500 to £28,750.

The two agreements were treated as separate, so that the judge at first instance held the agreement for the sale of the chalet to be void for fundamental mistake, i.e. the common fundamental mistaken assumption that the chalet could be sold separately from the pitch it occupied. Accordingly, the purchase price had to be returned to the defendant, because the agreement was impossible in law. However, as the Court of Appeal made clear, since the contract was void for mistake, there was no entitlement to compensation for the money spent on improvements.

At the time of this decision, the courts recognized the existence of an equitable jurisdiction to set aside a contract on terms, and the judge at first instance had rescinded the separate tenancy agreement. On appeal, the Court of Appeal confirmed that the tenancy agreement could be rescinded, since the parties were under the common misapprehension that the pitch could be used independently of the chalet upon it. However, the issue of rescission on terms had not been appealed, so that, although the Court of Appeal accepted that the claimants might have been ordered to pay compensation to the defendants for the improvements, it did not make such an order.

If similar facts were to arise post-*Great Peace Shipping*, the possibility of rescinding in equity would not exist, so that it is likely that the court would treat this arrangement as a single agreement that was void at common law. This would allow the return of the purchase price, but would not allow for any flexibility in terms of compensation for the improvements to the property returned. It might therefore be necessary to search for evidence of misrepresentation in order to achieve what the court might consider to be an acceptable result on the facts, or to use the common belief that the chalet could be sold separately to the pitch so that the separate tenancy of the pitch was required, in order to justify an argument that the continuation of this state of affairs was an implied condition precedent of the sale contract.

13.6 The Draft Common Frame of Reference, the Common European Sales Law, and cases of initial mistake

Fundamental common mistake will render the contract voidable, rather than void, under the Draft Common Frame of Reference (DCFR) provisions and, more generally, the DCFR provides for greater flexibility in terms of the treatment of such mistakes. DCFR II-7:201 provides for either party to a common mistake to avoid the contract where the mistake is 'fundamental'; this is regarded as established where the party seeking avoidance alleges either that 'but for the mistake' it would not have made the contract, or it would have done so only on fundamentally different terms. Article 48 of the Common European Sales Law (CESL) appears to be in similar terms.

The DCFR provides, however, that avoidance is not possible if there is fault, i.e. if the mistake was inexcusable in the circumstances or the risk of the mistake was assumed, or should have been assumed, by the party seeking avoidance. Article 48(2) CESL is similar, in that avoidance is not possible where the risk either had been assumed or 'in the circumstances should be borne by' the party who is seeking avoidance.

In cases of common mistake, DCFR II-7:203(3) provides for a discretion in the court to seek to rescue the contract in some form through an ability to respond to a request by either party to adapt the contract in order 'to bring the contract into accordance with what might reasonably have been agreed had the mistake not occurred'. By comparison, the CESL provision is limited to a particular context. Article 89 CESL provides for adaptation or termination by negotiation or order of the court in instances in which performance has become more onerous, but only where the change of circumstances occurred '*after* the time when the contract was concluded' (emphasis added), and this risk was not assumed at the time and could not have been take into account (see **Chapter 12**).

MULTIPLE-CHOICE QUESTIONS

 Test your knowledge by trying this chapter's **multiple-choice questions**:
www.oup.com/uk/poole

FURTHER READING

Atiyah, '*Couturier v Hastie* and the sale of non-existent goods' (1957) 73 LQR 340.

Capper, 'More muddle on mistake: *Graves v Graves*' [2008] LMCLQ 264.

Cartwright, '*Associated Japanese Bank v Credit du Nord*' [1988] LMCLQ 300.

Cartwright, *Misrepresentation, Mistake and Non-Disclosure*, 3rd edn (Sweet and Maxwell, 2012).

Chandler, Devenney, and Poole, 'Common mistake: theoretical justification and remedial inflexibility' [2004] JBL 34.

Macmillan, 'How temptation led to mistake: an explanation of *Bell v Lever Bros Ltd*' (2003) 119 LQR 625.

Macmillan, *Mistakes in Contract Law* (Hart Publishing, 2010).

Smith, 'Contracts: mistake, frustration and implied terms' (1994) 110 LQR 400.

Spark, *Vitiation of Contracts: International Contractual Principles and English Law* (Cambridge University Press, 2013).

Tettenborn, 'Agreements, common mistake and the purpose of contract' (2011) 27 JCL 91.

Treitel, 'Mistake in contract' (1988) 104 LQR 501.

Chapter 14

Misrepresentation

SUMMARY OF THE ISSUES

This chapter examines the legal remedies for actionable misrepresentations, i.e. false statements of fact that induce the contract. A misrepresentation gives rise to different remedies to breaches of contract (i.e. breaches of contractual terms). In particular, the measure of damages is determined using different principles and, whereas a misrepresentation renders the contract voidable so that the contract will be treated as if it had never been made, a breach of contract will not affect the existence of the contract (in the absence of a repudiatory breach that has been accepted as terminating the contract, in which case *future* contractual obligations will be discharged: see **8.4.2**).

• An actionable misrepresentation is an unambiguous false statement of fact made to the claimant, which induces the claimant to enter into the contract with the statement maker. In certain situations, conduct can amount to a misrepresentation.

• There is generally no duty of disclosure in English law, so that silence will not generally give rise to a claim in misrepresentation, in the absence of deliberate concealment. However, there are some recognized exceptions to this position in which a duty of disclosure will arise and the failure to disclose will constitute a misrepresentation.

• The false statement must be a false statement of fact as opposed to a statement of opinion or future intention but, in some circumstances, what appear to be opinions or statements of intention are, in fact, statements of fact.

• The false statement of fact must have induced the contract in the sense that it must be material to the decision to contract, be known to the representee, be intended to be acted upon, and have been acted upon.

• If such an actionable misrepresentation has been established, the contract is voidable, so that, in principle, the remedy of rescission is available to the claimant, i.e. if rescinded, the contract is treated as if it had never been made. However, there are a number of bars to rescission.

• Damages may be available for misrepresentation in order to put the claimant into the position in which it would have been had the misrepresentation not been made. There are three types of misrepresentation (depending upon the state of mind of the statement maker): fraudulent misrepresentation, negligent misrepresentation, and innocent misrepresentation. If the misrepresentation is fraudulent, damages are in the tort of deceit, whereas the possibility of recovering damages for negligent misrepresentation was not recognized until the mid-1960s. However, it is now possible to recover damages for negligent misstatement at common law (i.e. in tort), or under s. 2(1) of the Misrepresentation Act (MA) 1967, which provides a statutory *claim* to damages where the burden of proving negligence is reversed. It is not possible to claim damages for innocent misrepresentation, but damages may be awarded by

14

»

the court instead of the remedy of rescission under s. 2(2) MA 1967.

• By s. 3 MA 1967, clauses attempting to exclude or limit liability for misrepresentation are subject to the reasonableness requirement. There is some debate, however, about which types of clause fall within the scope of s. 3.

• The law governing misrepresentations in business-to-consumer (B2C) contracts has recently undergone a radical transformation with the introduction of the Consumer Protection (Amendment) Regulations 2014, SI 2014/870. These Regulations provide a new regime of civil remedies for misleading actions and aggressive commercial practices that induced the making of a consumer contract. Regulation 27L explains that the consumer can choose to avoid this regime when seeking redress and instead rely upon the general law, e.g. the law of misrepresentation contained in this chapter, and one reason to do so might be the scope of the remedy in damages available outside the CPR regime (Consumer Protection from Unfair Trading Regulations 2008, SI 2008/1277) in accordance with s. 2 MA 1967. However, reg. 5 of the Consumer Protection (Amendment) Regulations 2014 amends s. 2 MA 1967 to provide that where a consumer has a right to redress under Part 4A of the CPRs 2008, e.g. for misleading actions (as opposed to omissions), that consumer may not recover damages for misrepresentation under s. 2 (MA 1967, s. 2(4)). This represents a serious limitation on the usefulness of a B2C misrepresentation claim outside the CPRs.

14.1 Introduction

14.1.1 Misrepresentation and its effect on the parties' positions

Misrepresentation comprises the law relating to the effect on a contract (and hence the parties' positions) where that contract was entered into on the basis of a false statement made during the course of contractual negotiations. A contract made as the result of a misleading representation is, subject to the limitations described in this chapter, voidable at the instance of the person to whom the misrepresentation was made (the misrepresentee). In other words, the primary remedy for misrepresentation will be for the misrepresentee to rescind the contract (to set it aside). That person may also (or in the alternative) be able to recover damages as compensation for loss sustained.

Once the essential conditions for recovery for misrepresentation have been established (see **14.2**), the combination of remedies available (see **14.5** and **14.6**) depends upon the type of misrepresentation in question, whether fraudulent, negligent, or innocent (see **14.4**). The law applicable is a complex blend of common law, equity, and statute. The changes to the Consumer Protection from Unfair Trading Regulations 2008 (CPRs), SI 2008/1277, in the context of consumer contracts and misleading actions ('prohibited practices') present consumers with a separate regime of remedies which they can choose to rely upon rather than seeking redress using the general law (common law, equity and the Misrepresentation Act (MA) 1967). Indeed, consumers are precluded from securing damages for misrepresentation under s. 2 MA 1967 when they have a right to redress under Part 4A of the CPRs regime. The definitions of 'prohibited practices' within the CPRs, and their interpretation by the courts, are also likely to influence the substantive law identifying actionable misrepresentations more generally (see **14.1.2**).

14.1.2 The relationship between misrepresentation and other areas of law

It is important to be able to place misrepresentation in the wider context of regulation of contracts. Misrepresentation is an example of a doctrine designed to police the formation process (i.e. the circumstances surrounding the making of the contract), and to achieve 'procedural fairness' by providing remedies for fraudulent and negligent misrepresentation. Other examples of doctrines aimed at achieving procedural fairness are the doctrines of duress and undue influence (discussed in **Chapter 15**). These can be compared with controls on substantive fairness, which relate to fairness in terms of the content of the contract: see e.g. regulation of unfair terms (**Chapter 7**) and the penalty rule (**9.6.2**).

In addition, although misrepresentation is a separate body of law requiring individual treatment, it enjoys close relations with, and indeed sometimes overlaps with, several other important areas of contract law. When confronted with a factual scenario that, at first sight, appears to raise issues of misrepresentation, it is important to consider whether any other principles of law are also relevant and especially to consider whether the application of those other principles of law might provide a better remedy for the party affected.

14.1.2.1 Misrepresentations that are also terms

Since misrepresentation relates to misleading statements made in the course of contractual negotiations, it is possible for such a statement to take on even greater significance and, by operation of the rules of offer and acceptance, and incorporation of terms (see generally Chapter 6), to become an express term of the contract (see **6.1.4** and **6.3**). The consequences of a statement being classified as a term are explained later in this chapter (see 14.3), but the most obvious is that the falsity of the statement will result in a breach of the contract, giving rise to remedies quite different from those available for misrepresentation (see generally **Chapter 6** and especially at **6.1.2**). While some misrepresentations may subsequently be incorporated as contract terms, it is not the case that pure contract terms take effect as misrepresentations: see *Idemitsu Kosan Co. Ltd v Sumitomo Corporation* [2016] EWHC 1909 (Comm), where the court held that warranties relating to shares in a share sale and purchase agreement were not actionable representations but were contractual in nature.

Section 50 of the Consumer Rights Act (CRA) 2015 provides that, in a consumer contract to supply a service, any statements made to the consumer by or on behalf of the trader that relate either to the trader or the service, and which are either taken into account by the consumer in deciding to contract or taken into account when making any decision about the service after entering into the contract, are treated as terms of the contract. In particular, information provided by the trader in accordance with the requirements of the Consumer Contracts (Information, Cancellation and Additional Charges) Regulations 2013, SI 2013/3134, is treated as a term. This has considerable potential to eliminate the need to identify and rely on actionable misrepresentations in the consumer context, since the misstatement will constitute a breach of contract and remedies will be those specified in s. 54 of the CRA 2015. These remedies differ depending on whether the information supplied by the trader related to the service or to other matters.

14.1.2.2 Claim based on mistake

The circumstances giving rise to a claim of misrepresentation may also substantiate a claim of mistake (**Chapter 13**). For example, to enter a contract masquerading as some other person is a fraudulent misrepresentation, while it may also give rise to relief on grounds of a (unilateral) mistake of identity (see **3.3.3**). The advantage of mistake over misrepresentation in the majority of situations is that, if established, mistake renders the contract void and not merely voidable (see **3.2.2**), so that the party seeking relief may be able to recover property even after it has passed into the hands of a third party.

14.1.2.3 Negligent misstatement in the law of tort

Contractual misrepresentation is very closely linked to negligent misstatements in the law of tort, and a set of facts may raise the possibility of claims for both negligent misstatement in tort and negligent misrepresentation in contract: see e.g. *Esso Petroleum Co. Ltd v Mardon* [1976] QB 801 (discussed at **14.4.3.1**). It is therefore important, in order to give the most appropriate advice, to be fully aware of the differences between these claims and the remedies available in each case. This matter is addressed at various points in this chapter.

14.1.2.4 The consumer regime: the Consumer Protection from Unfair Trading Regulations 2008

The Consumer Protection from Unfair Trading Regulations 2008 (CPRs), SI 2008/1277, implementing the EU Unfair Commercial Practices Directive (UCPD) 2005/29/EC (see also discussion at **1.6.2.2** and **15.3.2**), prohibit the making of false or misleading statements, i.e. such practices constitute a criminal offence in the context of B2C contracts. In this consumer context, the CPRs prohibit unfair commercial practices (marketing and selling practices) and specifically misleading actions, including false or deceptive information (reg. 5), and misleading material omissions (reg. 6). It follows that the CPRs can cover misrepresentations, but also cover aggressive commercial practices (reg. 7) that may be addressed by doctrines such as duress and undue influence (see **Chapter 15**). As originally introduced, the CPRs did not provide for any civil redress for consumers who were on the receiving end of these unfair commercial practices. However, in 2012, the Law Commission recommended reform of the CPRs—in its report *Consumer Redress for Misrepresentation and Aggressive Practices*, Law Com. No. 332 (Cm. 8323, March 2012)—in order to implement Art. 27 of the EU Consumer Rights Directive (CRD) 2011/83/EU by including civil liability as protection for consumers in instances that fall within the scope of the CPRs. The Law Commission highlighted particular concerns with the existing law in relation to the availability of the remedy of rescission (see **14.5** and **15.2.5**), but also the quantification of damages, where damages are available.

The Consumer Protection (Amendment) Regulations 2014, SI 2014/870, amended the CPRs 2008 so as to provide that, where a trader has engaged in a 'prohibited practice' in relation to the product that forms the subject matter of a contract between a trader and a consumer, the consumer has a range of possible civil rights to redress (reg. 27A). However, this extension will not allow civil liability across the entire scope of the CPRs, since misleading omissions are not covered. Under the CPRs the consumer has the burden of establishing causation, i.e. that the prohibited practice was a significant factor in their decision to contract or make payment (reg. 27A(6)), but will then be entitled to a remedy to restore the consumer to the position in which they would have been had the practice not happened (i.e. the right to unwind within a period of 90 days) (reg. 27E). There is also a right to a discount (although not to both unwind and secure a discount), the level of which is determined by the seriousness of the trader's conduct, the impact that it had on the consumer, and the time that has elapsed (reg. 27I). Regulation 27J of the CPRs, as amended, now provides for a right to damages (although the trader has due diligence defence) in instances in which there is financial loss or non-pecuniary loss, such as distress, discomfort, or inconvenience, where a significant purpose of the contract was to provide pleasure, relaxation, or peace of mind to the consumer (compare such damages for breach of contract, discussed at **9.5.4.3**). These Regulations make it clear that these new consumer rights are additional to any common law claims available to the consumer for the prohibited practice, but there can be no double recovery. However, it is also clear that the existing statutory damages claims and discretions (under s. 2 MA 1967) will no longer be available to a consumer who has a right to redress under the CPRs (s. 2(4) MA 1967). This is significant, and is liable to entrench a separation between remedies for misrepresentation available for consumers in the B2C context and those remedies available in B2B contracts induced by misrepresentation.

It is also important to be aware that this more comprehensive regime will elevate the use and importance of the CPRs. However, it may also lead to the use of current common law interpretations when establishing the existence of the 'prohibited practices'.

14.1.2.5 Other statutory measures relating to misrepresentations

There are other measures that apply outside the consumer context in B2B (business to business) contracts, e.g. the Business Protection from Misleading Marketing Regulations 2008, SI 2008/1276, implementing Directive 2006/114/EC concerning misleading and comparative advertising, which prohibit advertising that misleads traders or is likely to injure a competitor. These Regulations also create criminal offences, but do not impose any civil obligations or remedies.

The Fraud Act 2006 contains a general criminal offence of fraud that can be committed in three ways: fraud by false representation (s. 2); fraud by failing to disclose information in circumstances in which there is a duty of disclosure (s. 3; for these circumstances, see the discussion in relation to contract at **14.2.1.2**); and fraud by abuse of position (s. 4).

14.2 Actionable misrepresentations

For a claim based on misrepresentation to succeed, there must have been an unambiguous, false statement of existing fact, which induced the claimant to enter into the contract.

14.2.1 False statement of fact

14.2.1.1 False and unambiguous

It might be assumed that identifying the fact that the statement is true or false would be an easy matter. However, falsity is sometimes a matter of degree. In *Avon Insurance plc v Swire Fraser Ltd* [2000] 1 All ER (Comm) 573, [2000] CLC 665, Rix J held that the test of truth was to see whether the statement is 'substantially correct', so that any difference between what was represented and the correct position would not have been likely to induce a reasonable person to make the contract.

The misrepresentation must also be unambiguous. A party making a representation that, on a reasonable construction, is true will not be liable for misrepresentation simply because the representee has put some other construction on it that is not true. In *McInerny v Lloyds Bank Ltd* [1974] 1 Lloyd's Rep 246, the Court of Appeal held that the defendant bank was not liable for an unreasonable interpretation put on its statement by the claimant seller.

14.2.1.2 Statement

14.2.1.2.1 Conduct

The requirement for a 'statement' has, in one sense, been interpreted fairly broadly, because the courts have shown a willingness to find the existence of a misrepresentation based on conduct without the need for words. For example, in *Curtis v Chemical Cleaning & Dyeing Co. Ltd* [1951] 1 KB 805 (see **7.3.2**), at p. 808, Denning LJ stated: '[A]ny behaviour, by words or conduct, is sufficient to be a misrepresentation if it is such as to mislead the other . . . If it conveys a false impression, that is enough.'

In *Gordon v Selico* (1986) 278 EG 53, the claimant purchased the property in question following an inspection. However, the vendor was found to have fraudulently concealed dry rot and this was held to constitute a representation that the property did not suffer from dry rot. Nothing was actually said, but the manner in which the concealment took place effectively amounted to a statement that all was well.

A more recent example of a misrepresentation by conduct is provided by the facts in *Spice Girls Ltd v Aprilia World Service BV* [2002] EWCA Civ 15, [2002] EMLR 27.

The defendant, a motor scooter manufacturer, had agreed to sponsor the tour of the pop group the Spice Girls. The group had participated in a photo shoot and other promotional material before the agreement was signed at a time when it was found that they knew that one member of the band had declared an intention to leave the group before the expiry of the term of the sponsorship agreement. The claimant sought payment of an instalment payment due under the sponsorship agreement and the defendant counterclaimed for damages for misrepresentation. The Court of Appeal upheld the judgment of Arden J at first instance—[2000] EMLR 478—that taking part in the promotions amounted to a misrepresentation by conduct—namely, a misrepresentation that the group did not know and had no reasonable grounds to believe that any member of the group had the intention to leave before the end of the agreement.

This case authority was relied upon in *Crystal Palace Football Club (2000) Ltd v Dowie* [2007] EWHC 1392 (QB), [2007] IRLR 682.

In *Crystal Palace Football Club (2000) Ltd v Dowie*, the defendant football manager's contract contained a provision requiring compensation of £1 million to be paid if he left Crystal Palace Football Club before the end of the contract term in order to take up employment at a premiership club. The claimant football club later entered into a compromise agreement with the defendant whereby the club agreed to release him without compensation and, eight days later, the defendant was appointed as the manager of a premiership club in London, Charlton Athletic. The claimant alleged that the defendant had deceived it into releasing him without compensation by falsely representing that he wanted to leave to move north of London for family reasons and had had no contact with Charlton Athletic.

It was held that the defendant had represented that he had no contact from Charlton at the relevant time and so was impliedly representing that he had no present intention to join Charlton, whereas he did have such an intention. He therefore knew the representations to be false and these misrepresentations had induced the making of the compromise agreement to forgo the compensation payment.

14.2.1.2.2 Silence or non-disclosure

In another sense, the requirement that there be a false 'statement' has been strictly interpreted. In most situations, because of the principle of *caveat emptor* ('let the buyer beware'), mere silence or non-disclosure does not amount to an unambiguous, false representation and therefore will not give rise to a claim for misrepresentation. Of course, as can be seen from the discussion at **14.2.1.2**, where the non-disclosure goes beyond merely remaining silent and involves taking active steps to conceal a defect, it may amount to misrepresentation: see *Gordon v Selico* (1986) 278 EG 53.

The general rule is usually said to be that there is no duty to disclose facts that, if known, might affect the other party's decision to enter the contract: *Keates v The Earl of Cadogan* (1851) 10 CB 591. The rule reflects the attitude of classical contract law that the parties must look after their own interests in making contracts. It may also be justified by saying that a general duty of disclosure would be too vague, since it would be impossible to specify precisely what should be disclosed. For example, in *Sykes v Taylor-Rose* [2004] EWCA Civ 299, [2004] 2 P & CR 30, in preliminary inquiries, the vendor of a house was required to disclose 'any other information that you think the buyer might have a right to know'. This was held not to extend to include the fact that a child murder had been committed in the house some years earlier. The question of what should be disclosed was to be judged subjectively and the vendor honestly believed that the purchaser had no right to be told.

Nevertheless, the general rule is subject to certain exceptions.

1. Half-truths

It is a misrepresentation to make statements that are true, but which are misleading because they do not reveal all of the relevant facts. Thus to describe property that is the subject of negotiations for sale as fully let, without disclosing that the tenants have given notice to quit, is a misrepresentation: *Dimmock v Hallett* (1866) LR 2 Ch App 21.

2. Change of circumstances

Where a truthful statement of fact is made, but is subsequently rendered misleading by a change of circumstances, there is a duty to correct what has become a false impression.

In **With v O'Flanagan** [1936] Ch 575, the defendant wished to sell his medical practice and gave information to the claimant about the income to be derived from the practice. This information was true at the time that it was given. The defendant then fell ill and the income from the practice fell away to almost nothing. The sale took place five months after the original information had been given and without the defendant disclosing that the income had fallen dramatically. On discovering the state of the practice, the claimant successfully sought rescission of the contract of sale. He was entitled to continue to believe the truth of the statement made until the time of the sale or until it was corrected, so that failure to correct it amounted to a misrepresentation.

In **Spice Girls Ltd v Aprilia World Service BV** [2002] EWCA Civ 15, [2002] EMLR 27, it was held that there was a duty to correct the representation by conduct—namely, that the group did not know of the intention of one member to leave before the period of the sponsorship agreement ended. Nothing had been done to correct this continuing representation.

It is less clear whether a change of circumstances causing a person to amend an opinion voiced in the course of negotiations imposes a duty to disclose the change of opinion. It might be thought that since, in some circumstances, an opinion is treated as a statement of fact (see **14.2.1.3**), in those same circumstances at least there would be a duty of disclosure were the opinion to change. Indeed, an argument could be made for extending the duty further, since an opinion will be treated as a statement of fact where there are no reasonable grounds for the opinion held. A change of circumstances would bring a once honestly held opinion into that category and would appear to justify a duty of disclosure.

The same argument appears to apply to statements of future intention when the intention changes, but is not disclosed before the time of contracting. It has traditionally been considered that there is no duty to disclose a change of intention.

In **Wales v Wadham** [1977] 1 WLR 199, the claimant and the defendant—formerly husband and wife—agreed in the course of divorce proceedings that the claimant would pay the defendant £13,000 from his share of the sale of their house in return for her promise not to seek a maintenance award. The defendant had stated several times that she would not remarry. By the time of this agreement, she had changed that intention, but did not reveal the fact to the claimant, who subsequently claimed that he would not have entered into the agreement had he known she was to remarry. His action for rescission failed. The defendant was under no obligation to communicate her subsequent change of intention since her original statement of intention was honestly held at that time and did not amount to a representation of fact (see **14.2.1.3** for a discussion of the effect of statements of intention).

3. Fiduciary or confidential relationship

A fiduciary relationship is a relationship of special confidence between certain classes of people, imposing particular duties of care on those to whom confidence is entrusted. Typical examples of such relationships are solicitor and client, agent and principal, and partners in a partnership. In such a relationship, there is a duty of disclosure of all material facts. There is a close relationship between this duty of disclosure and the doctrine of undue influence, as can be seen from the case of *Tate v Williamson* (1866) LR 2 Ch App 55 (see **15.2**).

4. Contracts of utmost good faith

Certain types of contract impose a duty of disclosure irrespective of the nature of the relationship between the parties. They are called contracts *uberrimae fidei* (of utmost good faith) and the most common example has been the contract of insurance. Traditionally the insured has been placed under a duty to disclose all material facts at the time of making the contract of insurance and failure to disclose such facts entitles the insurer to refuse to pay when a claim is made (i.e. the insurance contract is voidable at the option of the insurers). The rule may be explained as necessary to enable the insurer to make a proper assessment of the risk that it is to underwrite, and the duty is placed on the insured because it is claimed that the insured is the person in possession of the relevant information. However, it also followed that a person seeking insurance would be placed in a difficult position, because of the need to identify correctly those facts that are material and therefore to be disclosed, and the underlying rationale for the duty—the absence of information available to the insurer other than by disclosure—has long been undermined. It is for those reasons that, in the consumer context, the Consumer Insurance (Disclosure and Representations) Act 2012 replaces the duty to volunteer material information with a duty on consumers to take reasonable care not to make a misrepresentation during pre-contractual negotiations. There are differing remedies depending on the state of mind of the consumer, i.e. the type of misrepresentation. If a consumer makes a deliberate or reckless misrepresentation, the insurer can treat the contract as if it never existed and refuse all claims. If the consumer's answers to the insurer's questions are careless, the remedy depends on whether the insurer would have entered into the contract, but on different terms (i.e. if the risk assessment would have been different). If the insurer would not have entered into the contract at all, it may refuse all claims, but it must return the premiums paid. However, if the consumer acts with reasonable care in answering questions posed by the insurer, the insurer must now pay the claim in full.

In the context of non-consumer insurance contracts, the Insurance Act 2015 has divorced utmost good faith from the new statutory duty of 'fair presentation'. Section 3 of the Insurance Act 2015 imposes a duty on the insured to 'make a fair presentation of the risk' and this duty of fair presentation involves making the disclosure required by s. 3(4) in a manner which would be reasonably clear and accessible to a prudent insurer. This involves (i) full disclosure of every material circumstance which the insured knows or ought to know, or (ii) failing that, partial disclosure which gives the insurer sufficient information to put a prudent insurer on notice that it needs to make further enquiries for the purpose of revealing those material circumstances. A circumstance is 'material' if it would influence the judgement of a prudent insurer in determining whether to take the risk and, if so, on what terms (s. 7(3)). However, in the absence of enquiry, the insured is not required to disclose a circumstance if it diminishes the risk, the insurer knows it, the insurer ought to know it, the insurer is presumed to know it, or it is something as to which the insurer waives information. Section 8 sets out the circumstances in which the insurer has a remedy against the insured for breach of this duty of fair presentation. There is a remedy only if the insurer shows that, but for the breach, the insurer either would not have entered into the contract of insurance at all, or would have done so only on different terms. Such a breach is known as a 'qualifying breach' and is classified as either (a) deliberate or reckless, or (b) neither deliberate nor reckless. The insurer has the burden of establishing that a qualifying breach was deliberate or reckless, and if that can be done then the contract may be avoided. In the absence of deliberate or reckless behaviour, the remedy available to the insurer reflects what would have happened had there been full disclosure: if the insurer would not have insured at all, it may avoid; if it would have insured on different terms, it can rewrite the policy retroactively to reflect those terms; and if it would have insured but only on a higher premium, the insured can recover that proportion of his loss as the premium paid bears to the premium that would have been charged.

14.2.1.2.3 Criminal liability for fraudulent failures to disclose
Where there is a duty of disclosure and a fraudulent failure to disclose the information, a criminal offence may be committed (Fraud Act 2006, s. 3) if there was an intention to make a gain or cause a loss to another.

14.2.1.3 Statements of fact
A false statement must be a false statement of fact as opposed to a statement of belief or opinion or a statement of future conduct or intention. This is because a fact can be true or false and because a representee is only justified in relying on facts. However, it is worth noting at the outset of this discussion that if a statement is made fraudulently (see **14.4.1.1**), it is likely to be treated as a statement of fact.

Statements of law will usually constitute statements of fact because they are rarely abstract statements and are usually statements concerning the application of the law to certain facts (see the discussion at **14.2.1.3.3**).

14.2.1.3.1 Statements of opinion or belief

As a general rule, a statement of opinion is not a statement of fact.

> In **Bisset v Wilkinson** [1927] AC 177, the owner of land told a prospective purchaser that, in his opinion, if properly worked, the land would support 2,000 sheep. However, to the knowledge of the purchaser, the owner had not worked the land himself as a sheep farmer and the statement was no more than an honest estimate, made without particular expertise, as to the capacity of the land. The fact that the land did not have such a capacity did not therefore result in the owner's statement constituting a misrepresentation.

The significant factor in this case was that the statement maker was in no better position to know the facts than the purchaser—and the purchaser knew this.

> In *Economides v Commercial Union Assurance Co. plc* [1997] 3 WLR 1066, it was held that there was no misrepresentation when a son incorrectly stated the value of his parents' belongings for the purposes of a contents insurance policy. They were not his belongings, so that he was not in any better position than the insurers to know their true value.

Significantly, it was also held that there is no duty imposed upon such a person to carry out inquiries to establish an objectively reasonable basis for that statement of belief, i.e. to obtain independent valuations. To hold otherwise would clearly have been inconsistent with *Bisset v Wilkinson* and with the decision in *Hummingbird Motors Ltd v Hobbs* [1986] RTR 276, to the effect that statements of opinion by a person with no special knowledge of the subject matter will not constitute misrepresentations even if the belief is unreasonable.

However, what of the situation in which the statement maker is in a better position to know the truth? Where the statement maker is in a better position to know the true position, that statement maker is representing that their statement is based on a reasonable belief and that they have reasonable grounds for making it. It follows that if the statement maker had no such reasonable belief or reasonable grounds, the false statement will constitute a misrepresentation.

> In **Smith v Land & House Property Corporation** (1884) 28 Ch D 7, the vendor described the tenant of property sold as 'a most desirable tenant', which was far from being the case. It was argued on the vendor's behalf that his statement had been no more than an expression of opinion, but this argument was rejected by Bowen LJ, who said that *a statement of opinion by a person who is in the best position to know the true position would often be a statement of fact because there is an implicit assertion that the statement maker knows of facts that justify that opinion.*

A similar decision is *BV Nederlandse Industrie Van Eiprodukten v Rembrandt Enterprises Inc.* [2018] EWHC 1857 (Comm), in which the defendant, a US supplier of dried egg products, entered into a contract to purchase egg products from the claimant, a Dutch company. Following a fall in the market, the defendant rejected the claimant's products. By way of defence to a claim for damages, the defendant argued that the claimant had deliberately misstated the cost of compliance with US regulatory requirements. The claimant's response was that the statement was merely an 'estimate'. Teare J disagreed: the question had been raised on a number of occasions, the claimant spoke of its figure being a 'calculation' and the defendant was fully entitled to take the statement seriously.

Whether the necessary implied representation of facts can arise is a question of fact, so that, in *Springwell Navigation Corporation v JP Morgan Chase Bank (formerly Chase Manhattan Bank)* [2010] EWCA Civ 1221, [2010] 2 CLC 705 (see also **14.7.2.2**), the Court of Appeal held that there had been no misrepresentation when a bank employee had allegedly stated that certain investments were 'a conservative and liquid investment and without currency risk'. These statements were not made in absolute terms and had to be seen in context; in particular, the word 'conservative' could not 'be lifted like a fish out of water'. Accordingly, the statements were no more than statements of opinion without any implied representation by the employee that the statements were based on objectively reasonable grounds.

What about forecasts by experts? It may be that the rule that statements of opinion are not generally representations of fact is no more than a particular application of the rule that a representation is not actionable unless made with the intention that it be relied upon by the representee (see **14.2.2.3**). Thus it is common practice to preface a remark by saying, 'It is only my opinion', when it is intended that no reliance should be placed upon it. In some circumstances, a statement will be made that can only be an opinion, in that conclusive proof of its truth is unavailable at the time that the statement is made.

Nevertheless, the courts are prepared to impose liability for misrepresentation if the statement was made negligently, by an apparent 'expert', and with the intention that it be relied upon.

In **Esso Petroleum Co. Ltd v Mardon** [1976] QB 801, a forecast was made by an Esso representative, who possessed many years' experience, and therefore was considered to possess special skill and knowledge in relation to the subject matter of his forecast. This forecast of the potential throughput of a petrol station was intended to be relied upon by the prospective tenant, and therefore amounted to a statement of fact that reasonable care and skill had been used in its preparation.

Although this statement was considered to be a statement of fact, the actual decision in the case is that the forecast amounted to a breach of contract (collateral warranty) or that there had been a breach of the duty of care in tort (negligent misstatement).

14.2.1.3.2 *Statements of future conduct or intention*

A misrepresentation as to the future is not, in general, a representation of existing fact and is therefore not actionable. Thus a person may state an intention at a point in time to follow a certain course of conduct in the future. It is not misrepresentation if that person is prevented from following that course of conduct or later changes their mind.

In *Inntrepreneur Pub Co. v Sweeney* [2002] EWHC 1060 (Ch), [2002] 2 EGLR 132, the defendant, the landlord of a public house, had made a statement predicting that the tenant would be released from a beer tie by the end of March 1998. This statement of intention was honestly made and based on good grounds, since the defendants' policy at that time was to release pubs from the ties in accordance with an undertaking to this effect that had been given to the Secretary of State for Trade and Industry.

Nevertheless, if the representation is a continuing one, the decision in *Inclusive Technology v Williamson* [2009] EWCA Civ 718, [2010] 1 P & CR 2, suggests that there is a duty to correct a change in intention and that a failure to do so may give rise to liability in some circumstances.

In addition, *if at the time of stating the intention the person did not, in fact, have any such intention, that would be treated as misrepresentation, since a present intention is a fact that can be falsely described.*

In **Edgington v Fitzmaurice** (1885) 24 Ch D 459, the directors of a company offered debentures for sale, saying that the purpose of the issue of debentures was to raise money for alterations and additions to premises, and for other purposes, implying an expansion of the company's business. In fact, the money was needed to meet the company's liabilities. Bowen LJ noted that a representation as to the future would not normally form the basis of an action for misrepresentation, but had no hesitation in finding that where the state of a man's mind can be ascertained (although it may well not be easy to prove), it is 'as much a fact as the state of his digestion'. As a result, a misstatement as to the state of a man's mind is an actionable misrepresentation and the directors in *Edgington v Fitzmaurice* were held liable.

In **Abbar v Saudi Economic & Development Co. (SEDCO) Real Estate Ltd** [2013] EWHC 1414 (Ch), the judge considered that it was difficult to see how misstating an intention in this way could be other than a fraudulent misrepresentation.

14.2.1.3.3 Statements of law as applied to particular facts can be a statement of fact

Until recently, it had traditionally been considered that a misstatement of law would not found a claim for misrepresentation. However, the correct position was that an abstract misstatement of law (made without reference to particular facts) could not found an actionable misrepresentation (e.g. 'Rent control does not apply to premises that have been substantially altered so that they are in effect new premises'). It is more common for the representation to combine law and facts, e.g. *Solle v Butcher* [1950] 1 KB 671, so that it is a statement of the *effect* of the law in a given situation (e.g. 'The alterations done to these premises have made them new premises in the eyes of the law, so that rent control will not apply'). Such a statement, if false, is often described as a misrepresentation of private rights and has traditionally been actionable.

In *Pankhania v Hackney London Borough Council* [2002] NPC 123, the alleged representation preceding the purchase of a property used as a car park concerned a statement that the occupier of the car park was a contractual licensee whose occupation could be terminated on three months' notice. This was, in fact, incorrect, and the car park user was protected as a business tenant under the Landlord and Tenant Act 1954. The judge held that the statement was an actionable misrepresentation of law and awarded damages for misrepresentation under s. 2(1) MA 1967. The statement of law related to the application of the law to certain facts and such statements have traditionally been actionable on that basis.

14.2.2 Induces the other party to contract

For the representation to be said to have induced the contract, four conditions must be satisfied:

1. The representation must be material.
2. It must be known to the representee.
3. It must be intended to be acted upon.
4. It must be acted upon.

14.2.2.1 Material representation

A representation will induce a contract only if it is material. It must represent a fact that would positively influence a reasonable person, considering entering the contract, to decide in favour of so doing.

In many circumstances, the requirement of materiality may be something of a formality, serving only to exclude trivial misstatements from actionability or to enable the court to infer actual inducement (see **14.2.2.4**). Thus, where a statement is made with the intention of inducing a contract (see **14.2.2.3**) and is such as would influence a reasonable person to agree (i.e. it is material), it is not difficult to infer actual inducement: *Smith v Chadwick* (1884) 9 App Cas 187, at p. 196, and *Avon Insurance plc v Swire Fraser Ltd* [2000] 1 All ER (Comm) 573, at p. 633. Conversely, if a representee does not act unreasonably in actually being induced to contract by the statement, it may be assumed that the representation was material.

14.2.2.2 Known to the representee

A representation cannot be said to have induced a contract unless it was known to the representee.

> In *Horsfall v Thomas* (1862) 1 H & C 90, concealing a serious defect in a gun by inserting a metal 'plug' amounted to representation by conduct. However, since the purchaser did not inspect the gun before purchase, the misrepresentation never came to his attention and he could not have been induced by the representation. It followed that there was no actionable misrepresentation.
>
> *Horsfall v Thomas* can therefore be contrasted with *Gordon v Selico* (1986) 278 EG 53 (see **14.2.1.2**) in which the flat was inspected and the dry rot was not discovered because it had been actively concealed.

However, a representation made by one party to another that induces a third party to enter a contract is actionable by the third party, provided that the first party knew or ought to have been aware that the representation would be likely to be communicated to the third party: *Pilmore v Hood* (1838) 5 Bing NC 97 and *Yianni v Edwin Evans and Sons* [1981] 3 All ER 593. This principle was applied in *Clef Aquitaine Sarl v Laporte Materials (Barrow) Ltd* [2001] QB 488.

> In *Clef Aquitaine Sarl v Laporte Materials (Barrow) Ltd*, the first claimant company had been induced to enter into distribution agreements by a fraudulent misrepresentation based on the price list. However, the second claimant company had subsequently taken over the agreements, which were amended so that the second claimant became a party in place of the first claimant by transfer (novation). It was held that the second claimants could rely on the misrepresentation because the defendants knew that the first claimants were '[notionally] repeating to the [second claimants] the misrepresentations which [the defendants] had made', but had 'stood by and allowed them to complete the novations without disillusioning them': *per* Simon Brown LJ at p. 503E–F.

In *Cramaso LLP v Ogilvie-Grant* [2014] UKSC 9, [2014] AC 1093, the Supreme Court held that a contracting party may be able to claim damages for a negligent misrepresentation made not to that contracting party, but to a person who subsequently became its agent. The respondents, who owned a grouse moor, were unable to make the investment necessary to increase the grouse population, and entered into discussions with Mr Erskine with a view to him becoming the tenant of the grouse moor. These came to nothing, but subsequently negotiations with Mr Erskine were reopened. An email sent to Mr Erskine in October 2006 gave a misleading impression of the total grouse population on the moor. Thereafter Mr Erskine formed the claimant company for the purpose of taking the lease in November 2006, and the lease was then entered into by the claimant and respondents. The claimant sought to avoid the lease for misrepresentation. The Supreme Court ruled that the representation in October 2006 had been a continuing one, and it sufficed that it had been made to the claimant's agent when the respondents knew that the representation would be relied upon by the claimant once it was incorporated.

14.2.2.3 Intended to be acted upon

To be actionable, a misrepresentation must be intended to be acted upon.

> In *Peek v Gurney* (1873) LR 6 HL 377, the promoters of a company issued a prospectus containing material misstatements. The intention had been to induce people to apply for the allotment of shares on formation of the company. The claimants claimed to have been induced by the statements in the prospectus when they later purchased shares in the market. They were unable to recover their losses, since there had been no intention on the part of those issuing the prospectus that it should be relied upon by those dealing in the shares subsequent to the original allotment.

As noted earlier in the chapter (see **14.2.1.3**), the qualification of a statement as merely an opinion is often taken to indicate that it is not intended that the statement be relied upon.

14.2.2.4 Actually acted upon

To establish that the representation induced the contract, it may not be enough merely to show that it was made and known about, that it was material, and that the representee entered into the contract. It is open to the representor to attempt to prove that the representee did not actually rely on the misrepresentation in deciding to enter the contract, but was persuaded by some other factor.

> In *Peekay Intermark Ltd v Australia and New Zealand Banking Group Ltd* [2006] EWCA Civ 386, [2006] 2 Lloyd's Rep 511, [2006] 1 CLC 582 (for facts, see **6.2.2.1**), the question was whether the claimant had been induced to sign an investment contract by relying on the informal (and incorrect) description of the product given over the telephone. The Court of Appeal held that it had been established that there was no inducement, stressing the fact that the claimant was 'an experienced investor' and the loose terms in which the product was described orally. The claimant had therefore been induced to sign the written contract not as a result of anything that the defendant bank had stated orally, but as a result of his own assumption that the investment product in the written contract corresponded with the oral description. (See also the discussion at **14.7.2.2** in relation to the risk disclosure statement that the claimant had signed.)

It seems, however, that if the misrepresentation is fraudulent and material, it will give rise to a presumption of an intention that the statement should be acted upon and that the statement induced the making of the contract: *Barton v County NatWest Ltd* [1999] Lloyd's Rep Bank 408; *Dadourian Group International Inc. v Simms (Damages)* [2009] EWCA Civ 169, [2009] 1 Lloyd's Rep 601. The matter can be expressed in the alternative manner that there is a weaker test for inducement in the case of fraud: *Raiffeisen Zentralbank Osterreich v Royal Bank of Scotland* [2010] EWHC 1392 (Comm); *BV Nederlandse Industrie Van Eiprodukten v Rembrandt Enterprises Inc.* [2018] EWHC 1857 (Comm).

In addition, the misrepresentation does not have to be the sole inducement for the representee to be able to rely on it.

> In *Edgington v Fitzmaurice* (1885) 24 Ch D 459 (see **14.2.1.3**), the representee entered the contract partly as a result of fraudulent misrepresentations made and partly as a result of his own mistake in thinking that the benefits of the contract were greater than was really the case. Nevertheless, the remedy of rescission was available to the representee.

Similarly, in *Morris v Jones* [2002] EWCA Civ 1790, a fraudulent misrepresentation that a basement flat had been 'tanked' could still be relied upon by the claimant, the prospective purchaser of the leasehold, as a factor inducing the contract despite the fact that the claimant had received three reports identifying problems of dampness in the property.

The test is not whether the misrepresentee relied solely and exclusively on the representations; it is sufficient that the representations played a real and substantial part, albeit not a decisive part, in inducing the representee to act (*Dadourian Group International Inc. v Simms (Damages)* [2009] EWCA Civ 169, [2009] 1 Lloyd's Rep 601).

In cases of fraud, once it is concluded that the misrepresentation was intended to be acted upon and was relied upon by the misrepresentee in deciding to enter into the transaction in question, speculation as to how the representee would have acted had the representee been told the truth is strictly irrelevant—*Downs v Chappell* [1997] 1 WLR 426 and *Dadourian Group International Inc. v Simms (Damages)* [2009] EWCA Civ 169, [2009] 1 Lloyd's Rep 601—as is an argument that the representee would have made the contract even if the representation had not been made.

In *Hayward v Zurich Insurance Co. plc* [2016] UKSC 48 the claimant was injured at work in June 1998 and claimed compensation from his employer. Disputes arose as to liability and quantum, and the employer's liability insurers alleged that there had been a 'lack of candour' by the claimant. Following the commencement of proceedings, the claim was settled in October 2003 under a Tomlin Order (a court order staying legal proceedings on terms agreed by the parties), whereby the employer through its liability insurers agreed to pay £134,973.11 and the claimant in turn agreed to stay judicial proceedings. Two years later, the employer received evidence from the claimant's neighbours that his injuries did not appear to be as serious as he had alleged, and the insurers sought to reopen the settlement for fraud. The claimant asserted that the insurers had been aware at the time that there were suspicious circumstances but had nevertheless chosen to settle, and for that reason there was no inducement. The Supreme Court held that in the case of fraudulent misrepresentation the innocent party did not need to demonstrate actual inducement, in the sense that it believed the statements to be true, in order to avoid the contract. The test was broader: namely, whether the misrepresentation was a material cause of the innocent party entering into the settlement and once the fact was shown to be material a 'presumption of inducement' was raised. That test was readily satisfied on the facts, in that although the claimant's statements as to the extent of his injuries were not the sole reason why the contract was made, they were a material consideration. The decision confirms that a party to whom fraudulent statements are made is under no duty to investigate their truth, and that the only ground upon which a contract will be upheld after fraud is where the innocent party was fully aware of the fraud at the time of contracting but took a deliberate decision to ignore it.

14.2.2.4.1 Is there still inducement where the representee chooses to test the truth of the statement and conducts their own investigations?

With the exception of instances of fraudulent statements—*S. Pearson & Son Ltd v Dublin Corporation* [1907] AC 351—if the representee chooses to test the truth of the statement made by making their own investigations, then the representee may be held to have relied upon their own judgement and not upon the misrepresentation.

In *Attwood v Small* (1838) 6 Cl & F 232, the claimants sought to rescind a contract for the purchase of a mine, citing in evidence false statements made by the defendant seller about the mine's potential. However, the claimants had sought to verify the seller's claims by appointing their own agent to examine the mine and the agent had reported in similar terms. The House of Lords held that the contract could not be rescinded, since the claimants had relied on their own expert and not on the word of the seller. The fact that the expert had failed to discover the truth did not make the seller liable.

It is important not to overstate the scope of this principle since it will not operate if the misrepresentation is fraudulent.

In *Clinicare Ltd v Orchard Homes & Developments Ltd* [2004] EWHC 1694 (QB), for example, a fraudulent statement had been made that the lessor was not aware of the property having been affected by dry rot at any time. The claimant's own surveyor reported that there was evidence of dry rot and further investigation was required, but the claimant subsequently entered into the lease, which had imposed a full repairing obligation. It was held that the decision to ignore the surveyor's advice was in part induced by the misrepresentation.

In addition, as this decision illustrates, in order for *Attwood v Small* to operate, it would appear that the misrepresentee must have relied entirely on the results of their own investigations and *not at all* on the misrepresentor's statement. This is unlikely to be the case.

14.2.2.4.2 Is there still inducement if the representee fails to take advantage of an opportunity to discover the truth?

The mere fact that the representee fails to take advantage of an opportunity to discover the truth, e.g. by inspection of goods or property, does not prevent reliance on the misrepresentation. Such a person will still be induced by the misrepresentation: *Hayward v Zurich Insurance Co. plc* [2016] UKSC 48.

In *Redgrave v Hurd* (1881) 20 Ch D 1, an elderly solicitor wished to sell his house and a share in his practice. He told a prospective younger partner that the income of the practice was about £300 a year, showing him ledgers covering some £200 a year and stating that the balance was made up by income not shown in the ledgers, but derived from other work represented by a bundle of papers, which were available. The prospective partner did not examine the bundle of papers; had he done so, he would have discovered that the income they represented was minimal. At first instance, it was held that failure to take the opportunity of inspecting the papers indicated that there had been no reliance on the misstatement. However, on appeal, that finding was unanimously overturned, and it was held that the contract could be rescinded since it was induced by the misrepresentation.

The decision in *Redgrave v Hurd* must now be read in light of the developing law governing negligent misrepresentation and the application of the doctrine of contributory negligence in that context (see **14.6.7**). Any contributory negligence will affect only the measure of the damages award.

The *Redgrave v Hurd* principle was applied in the analysis of the Court of Appeal in *Peekay Intermark Ltd v Australia and New Zealand Banking Group Ltd* [2006] EWCA Civ 386, [2006] 2 Lloyd's Rep 511, [2006] 1 CLC 582 (see **6.2.2.1** and above), since it was noted that the defendant bank could not argue that the claimant was bound because he *should have* read the final terms and conditions before signing. Constructive notice will not suffice to prevent inducement; the knowledge of the true position must be actual.

14.3 Representations that become terms

*As noted earlier in the chapter (see **14.1.2**), a misrepresentation may, in some circumstances, become a term of the contract. In other words, the representation can be incorporated as a term.* (For detailed consideration of the circumstances in which representations become terms, see **6.1**.) To state the converse, it may be the case that a term can also be a pre-contractual representation, entitling the misrepresentee to seek misrepresentation remedies. There would need to be parallel evidence of an equivalent representation on which the other party has relied in entering into the contract, e.g. a term may confirm a pre-contractual representation (e.g. *Ticket2final OU v Wigan Athletic AFC Ltd* [2015] EWHC 61b (Ch), [2015] All ER (D) 182 (Jan), discussed at **14.4.1.1**). At one time, it was particularly important to attempt to establish that a representation had become a term of the contract because, unless fraud could be established (see **14.4.1.1**), the remedies for misrepresentation compared very unfavourably with the remedies for breach (see **6.1.2**). However, since it has been recognized that damages for negligent misrepresentation are available (see **14.4.3**), identifying the fact that a representation has become a term is not as essential in terms of remedy. Moreover, it is no longer the case that the fact that a representation has become a term extinguishes the right to rescission for misrepresentation (MA 1967, s. 1). Nevertheless, it will still be important to be able to determine whether a representation has become a term of the contract (see the discussion at **6.1.2**) for the following reasons.

- Damages are available for misrepresentation outside the context of the CPRs 2008 only on proof of fault, whereas damages are available as of right for breach of a term.
- A different measure of loss applies to misrepresentation outside the context of the CPRs 2008 from that applying to breach, and the remoteness rules are different in breach of contract and misrepresentation claim.

Where a representation becomes a term, the injured party will have two possible claims: in breach of contract; and in misrepresentation. Outside the context of the CPRs 2008, a skilful lawyer may be able to manipulate the distinctions between remedies for breach of contract and remedies for misrepresentation to their client's advantage (e.g. by formulating a claim for damages under s. 2(1) MA 1967 where there are significant consequential losses, or claiming expectation damages for breach of contract where the contract would have been a 'good bargain'). However, it is not possible both to rescind for misrepresentation and to claim damages in contract (expectation measure: see **9.2.1**), since the effect of rescission is to treat the contract as if it had never been made and it is therefore not possible to obtain damages for its breach.

14.4 Types of misrepresentation

Outside the context of the CPRs 2008, the remedies available for misrepresentation depend upon the type of misrepresentation, i.e. upon the state of mind of the statement maker in making the statement that induced the contract. There are three types of misrepresentation: fraudulent; negligent; and innocent. (This should not be confused with the fact that there are four possible *damages awards* for misrepresentation: in tort for deceit; in tort for negligent misstatement; under MA 1967, s. 2(1); and under MA 1967, s. 2(2).)

The distinction between the three types of misrepresentation is particularly important in determining the damages for misrepresentation, but also has some relevance in the context of the remedy of rescission.

14.4.1 Making the basic distinction

14.4.1.1 Fraud

Fraud was defined by the House of Lords in *Derry v Peek* (1889) 14 App Cas 337, at p. 374, as a false statement, 'made knowingly, or without belief in its truth, or recklessly, careless whether it be true or false'.

The essential ingredient for fraud is the absence of an honest belief that the statement is true. It is on this basis that it is possible to distinguish recklessness (fraud) and mere lack of care (negligence). Lord Herschell, who provided the above definition, went on to say that, in order to constitute fraud, recklessness must amount to an absence of belief in the truth of the statement made. In *Thomas Witter Ltd v TBP Industries Ltd* [1996] 2 All ER 573, at p. 587, Jacob J considered that a statement maker would be reckless if they had no knowledge whether the statement was true or false, but asserted that it was true and thereby took a risk.

In ***Ticket2final OU v Wigan Athletic AFC Ltd*** [2015] EWHC 61b (Ch), [2015] All ER (D) 182 (Jan), Ticket2Final OU (T2F) entered into an agreement with Wigan Athletic AFC Limited by which T2F agreed to pay a fee to Wigan for certain sponsorship and advertising rights. In return, Wigan agreed to supply T2F with Carling Cup and FA Cup tickets. T2F had commenced selling options for FA Cup Final tickets at Wembley but the FA refused to approve the arrangements with T2F. T2F sought damages for breach of contract and for pre-contractual misrepresentation as to Wigan's ability to meet its commitments. Since the contract contained a limitation of liability, T2F claimed fraudulent misrepresentation rather than negligent misrepresentation in an attempt to increase its damages because a limitation clause could not limit liability for fraud (see **14.7.1**). It followed that T2F had to claim that at the time of its representation Wigan had no belief in its truth. However, the judge considered, applying the statement of Lord Steyn in *Smith New Court v Scrimgeour Vickers* [1997] AC 254, 274, that although the standard of proof in relation to allegations of fraud was the usual civil standard of balance of proof,

proof to that standard must necessarily take into account the consideration that the more serious the allegation is, the greater the proof is needed to persuade a court that it can be satisfied that the allegation is established. In other words, the very gravity of an allegation of fraud is a circumstance which has to be weighed in the scale in deciding as to the balance of probabilities.

The judge concluded that he was not satisfied that the burden of proof had been discharged on these facts.

14.4.1.1.1 *Change of circumstances misrepresentation: fraudulent or negligent?*

In *Thomas Witter Ltd v TBP Industries Ltd* [1996] 2 All ER 573, it was alleged that a failure to disclose a change in accounting method amounted to a change of circumstances misrepresentation: see also *With v O'Flanagan* [1936] Ch 575. It is certainly easy to jump to the conclusion that such a failure to disclose a change of circumstances will be deceitful. However, Jacob J explained that the failure to disclose might be attributable to a failure to realize that there is a duty to disclose. It is therefore important to consider whether the failure was, in fact, deliberate or dishonest, in which case it will amount to a fraudulent misrepresentation—as in *Banks v Cox (No. 2)*, unreported, 21 December 2000, in which there had been a deliberate failure to inform prospective purchasers of change in the social services budget, which would impact on the nursing home business, and other factors that had affected the business since the last set of accounts had been prepared—or whether there is no dishonesty and the failure to disclose the change in circumstances is merely negligent. In *Erlson Precision Holdings Ltd (formerly GG132 Ltd) v Hampson Industries Ltd* [2011] EWHC 1137 (Comm) (see also **14.5.2.3**), in negotiations over a ten-month period, various income and customer forecasts had been supplied to the potential buyer of the shares in a company. These forecasts included details of the contracts with the company's second biggest customer, although that customer had terminated its supply arrangement a few months after the initial forecasts had been made available to the buyer. This information would have made the business unsaleable. The chief executive officer (CEO) was aware that these forecasts were being made available to the potential buyer, but decided not to correct them. The buyer relied on these forecasts in purchasing the business. It was held that the CEO ought to have corrected the details about the customer and that the failure to do so constituted a fraudulent misrepresentation.

Such a misrepresentation (involving a failure to disclose change of circumstances) would, it seems, have to be *at least* negligent, because, under s. 2(1) MA 1967, the burden of disproving negligence requires the misrepresentor to prove that the facts represented were true 'up to the time the contract was made'. In instances involving a failure to disclose a change of circumstances, the misrepresentor will be unable to discharge this burden.

14.4.1.2 **Negligent misrepresentation**

Fraud can be distinguished from a negligent statement where the statement maker believes the statement to be true (i.e. the statement maker is honest), but has been careless in reaching that conclusion. In other words, the statement maker is in breach of a duty of reasonable care and skill in making the statement.

14.4.1.3 **Innocent misrepresentation**

If the statement maker honestly believes that the statement is true and has reasonable grounds for that belief, the statement will be classified as an innocent misrepresentation.

14.4.2 **Fraudulent misrepresentation and remedies available**

At one time, being able to establish fraud was crucial, since damages could not otherwise be claimed for misrepresentation. Today, a right to damages also exists in the case of negligent misrepresentation (see **14.4.3**), but the distinction is still important in some cases, since proof of fraud *may* permit a greater measure of recovery (see **14.6.2**) and takes the situation outside the scope of the court's discretion to award damages instead of rescission under s. 2(2) MA 1967 (see **14.4.4**).

Fraud provides the strongest combination of remedies for misrepresentation. Rescission and damages are available and, in the case of fraud, the courts will compensate all loss that is a direct result of the transaction: *Doyle v Olby (Ironmongers) Ltd* [1969] 2 QB 158. (Damages for fraudulent misrepresentation are discussed in detail at **14.6.2**.)

14.4.2.1 A note of caution

Although it was suggested at **14.4.2** that there are still advantages, in terms of the remedies available, to a representee who can establish the existence of fraud rather than mere negligence, against those advantages must be weighed the fact that the courts regard fraud as a very serious allegation, may demand more than the usual civil burden of proof from the party seeking to demonstrate its existence, and may penalize in costs a party failing to make out such a claim. On the other hand, the remedies for negligent misrepresentation are often as good as those for fraud and, under s. 2(1) MA 1967 (damages claim), the burden of proof is reversed, so that it is the representor who has to establish that they were *not* negligent (see **14.4.3.2**). In these circumstances, bringing a claim alleging fraud is not something that should be undertaken lightly.

14.4.3 Negligent misrepresentation: the available remedies

Misrepresentations that were made without due care, but were not reckless in the sense of being fraudulent, were once treated as 'innocent' misrepresentations. As a result, although rescission was available, no damages could be recovered. It was a rule that was regarded by many lawyers and commentators as unsatisfactory, and which led to sometimes artificial interpretations to the effect that a representation had been incorporated in a contract, in order to allow the recovery of damages for what would then be breach (see **6.1.4**). Eventually, the position changed, but as a result of almost simultaneous parallel common law and statutory developments, the law relating to negligent misrepresentation has become unnecessarily complicated. *In addition to the availability of the remedy of rescission (assuming that none of the bars to rescission apply), these developments have resulted in two possible claims for damages being available in many instances to a party to whom a negligent misstatement has been made*:

- a claim in tort for negligent misstatement; or
- a claim for damages under s. 2(1) MA 1967—although note that, under the CPRs, as amended (see **14.1.2**), s. 2 will no longer apply in the B2C context where the misrepresentee has a right to redress under Part 4A of the CPRs 2008 in respect of the misrepresentation (s. 2(4) MA 1967). Regulation 27A CPRs provides that the misrepresentee consumer will have a right to redress if the contract is made with a trader who has engaged in a prohibited practice in relation to the product sold or supplied and this prohibited practice was a significant factor in the misrepresentee consumer's decision to contract. Therefore if the CPR right to redress exists on the facts, s. 2 will not—and the consumer would probably be best advised to seek civil redress under the CPR regime.

14.4.3.1 Negligent misstatement at common law

In *Hedley Byrne & Co. Ltd v Heller & Partners Ltd* [1964] AC 465, the House of Lords extended the common law tort of negligence to the field of negligent statements that cause loss.

The claimants had been asked for credit by a company and had sought advice on the financial standing of the company from its bankers, the defendants. The defendants, who had known the purpose of the claimants' request, had carelessly said that the company was financially sound. The House of Lords stated that the defendants owed a duty of care to the claimants, since there was a 'special relationship' between the parties. However, on these facts, there was a disclaimer indicating that the advice had been given expressly 'without responsibility'. Therefore there was no liability. (Note, however, that any such disclaimer must now avoid regulation under the applicable legislative requirements—the Unfair Contract Terms Act (UCTA) 1977 in a B2B situation such as *Hedley Byrne* or under Part 2 of the CRA 2015 (B2C contracts). In the consumer context, the CRA 2015 will prevent exclusions of the duty to perform a service with reasonable care and skill (CRA 2015, ss. 49 and 57(1) and (5)); see discussion of legislative regulation at **7.4.2** and **7.6.4**.) In *Caparo Industries plc v Dickman* [1990] 2 AC 605, the House of Lords made it clear that the duty of care would be imposed only where a close degree of interrelationship, between the party making the statement and the party subsequently complaining, could be found to exist. In particular, those making statements do not owe a duty of accuracy to the whole world, or to anyone who may happen to have the statement communicated to them. Lord Oliver stated, at p. 638C–E:

> The necessary relationship between the maker of a statement or giver of advice (the adviser) and the recipient who acts in reliance on it (the advisee) may typically be held to exist where (1) the advice is required for a purpose, whether particularly specified or generally described, which is made known, either actually or inferentially, to the adviser when the advice is given, (2) the adviser knows, either actually or inferentially, that his advice will be communicated to the advisee either specifically or as a member of an ascertainable class, in order that it should be used by the advisee for that purpose, (3) it is known, either actually or inferentially, that the advice so communicated is likely to be acted on by the advisee for that purpose without independent inquiry and (4) it is so acted on by the advisee to his detriment.

More recently, the courts have placed this analysis of the duty of care within the broader test of 'assumption of responsibility' for a statement: e.g. *Henderson v Merrett Syndicates Ltd* [1995] 2 AC 145; *White v Jones* [1995] 2 AC 207; *Spring v Guardian Assurance* [1995] 2 AC 296; *Williams v Natural Life Health Foods Ltd* [1998] 1 WLR 830; *Merrett v Babb* [2001] EWCA Civ 214, [2001] QB 1174; and *Robinson v PE Jones (Contractors) Ltd* [2011] EWCA Civ 9, [2011] 3 WLR 815.

It appears that the English courts may be willing to find an assumption of responsibility, and hence a duty of care, wherever the person giving advice holds themselves out as possessing some expertise or special skill, and knows that the other party will rely on the advice given, irrespective of whether the person giving the advice is, in fact, a 'professional' adviser. Liability will then apply if it was reasonable for the other party to rely on the statement of the person giving the advice. This depends on the context, so that statements made in the commercial context are more likely to give rise to a duty of care than those made in an informal social setting.

In **Esso Petroleum Co. Ltd v Mardon** [1976] QB 801 (see **6.1.4**), the Court of Appeal found the duty of care to exist where an expert valuer for the oil company made a representation about the petrol sales potential of a garage to a prospective tenant. The statement maker clearly possessed special skill and knowledge concerning the subject matter of the contract. In addition, since the valuer was experienced and knew much more about the business than did the tenant, he could reasonably foresee that the tenant would rely on his judgement, and it was reasonable for the prospective tenant to rely on his statements.

Misrepresentation

14

As *Esso v Mardon* illustrates, although the common law negligent misstatement doctrine is *not limited to* representations that result in a contract between representor and representee—e.g. *Hedley Byrne & Co. Ltd v Heller & Partners Ltd*, in which the representation resulted in a contract with a third party, its application to representations that induce a contract between representor and representee means that, in some factual situations, there may be two, overlapping, possible damages claims: negligent misstatement in tort and under s. 2(1) MA 1967. However, the real difficulty with the claim for damages for negligent misstatement at common law is that the misrepresentee has the burden of proving both the existence of the duty of care (assumption of responsibility) and that the duty of care has been broken. This is very different if the claim is framed under s. 2(1) MA 1967.

14.4.3.2 MA 1967, s. 2(1): damages claim

Section 2(1) of the 1967 Act provides:

> Where a person has entered into a contract after a misrepresentation has been made to him by another party thereto and as a result thereof he has suffered loss, then, if the person making the misrepresentation would be liable to damages in respect thereof had the misrepresentation been made fraudulently, that person shall be so liable notwithstanding that the misrepresentation was not made fraudulently, unless he proves that he had reasonable ground to believe and did believe up to the time the contract was made that the facts represented were true.

14.4.3.2.1   *The scope of s. 2(1) claims*

This statutory claim applies only where the representee has been induced by the misrepresentation to enter a contract with the representor. Thus a case like **Hedley Byrne & Co. Ltd v Heller & Partners Ltd** [1964] AC 465 (see **14.4.3.1**) does not fall within the ambit of the section, because the negligent misstatement did not result in a contract between the party giving the advice and the party seeking it.

It is potentially narrower than a claim in negligent misrepresentation in another sense, in that it may not apply to the exceptional cases of representation by silence (see **14.2.1.2**) on the ground that such a misrepresentation is not 'made' within the terms of s. 2(1). There are *obiter* statements to that effect in *Banque Financière de la Cité SA v Westgate Insurance Co. Ltd* [1989] 2 All ER 952, at p. 1004, and in *Startwell Ltd v Energie Global Brand Management Ltd* [2015] EWHC 421 (QB) per Warby J at [81], although such an approach appears unduly literal and may be inconsistent with the general purpose of s. 2(1).

Finally, it will not apply if the amended CPR regime does, i.e. it will not apply to contracts where a consumer enters into a contract with a trader within the definition in the CPRs as a result of a misleading action (e.g. misrepresentation) which was a significant cause in the decision to contract (see **14.1.2**).

14.4.3.2.2 *The burden of proof*

Where the representation does fall within the ambit of the section and where the CPR right to redress is not applicable, it is likely that the representee will choose to base the claim on s. 2(1) of the 1967 Act rather than the common law, since the burden of proof is reversed as regards negligence. Once the claimant has established the existence of a false statement that induced him to enter the contract, it is for the defendant to show that, in making the representation, 'he had reasonable ground to believe and did believe up to the time the contract was made that the facts represented were true'. This reversal of the burden of proof is a considerable advantage to the claimant.

It is also not merely a matter of disproving negligence. As a result of the decision of the Court of Appeal in *Howard Marine & Dredging Co. Ltd v A. Ogden & Sons (Excavations) Ltd* [1978] QB 574, the defendant has to prove positively that it had reasonable grounds for its belief.

> In *Howard Marine & Dredging Co. Ltd v Ogden & Sons (Excavations) Ltd*, the defendants wished to hire barges and had been given details of capacity of the barges by the claimants' marine manager. The manager's statement had been based on figures in the Lloyd's Register, but the Register was incorrect and the correct figures were available from documents in the claimants' possession. When the defendants discovered the true capacity, they refused to pay the full hire. The claimants sought the outstanding hire and the defendants claimed damages under s. 2(1) MA 1967. The majority of the Court of Appeal held that the claimants had failed to prove that their marine manager had reasonable grounds to believe that the statement was true, since there was no objectively reasonable ground for relying on the Register rather than the ships' documents. However, Lord Denning MR (dissenting) thought that the burden had been discharged and that negligence had been disproved, since it was reasonable to rely on the Register.
>
> In *Spice Girls Ltd v Aprilia World Service BV* [2002] EWCA Civ 15, [2002] EMLR 27, Aprilia was held to be entitled to receive damages because, under s. 2(1), the onus was on the Spice Girls to show that they had reasonable grounds to believe, and did believe, at the date of the agreement that the representation was true. Since it was found that they knew that one member intended to leave, they were not able to discharge that burden.

Thus, in cases in which it is not clear whether the defendant representor acted reasonably, at common law the claim for damages will fail; in the same circumstances under s. 2(1) of the 1967 Act, the claimant will succeed: *Howard Marine & Dredging Co. Ltd v A. Ogden & Sons (Excavations) Ltd.*

14.4.3.2.3 *The fiction of fraud in s. 2(1)*

Section 2(1) MA 1967 is rather clumsily drafted, being based on what has been described as the 'fiction of fraud': Atiyah and Treitel (1967) 30 MLR 369. Liability is said to exist where it would exist had the misrepresentation been made fraudulently, even though, in the particular case, it was not made fraudulently.

It is far from clear why this formulation was used. It may be that it was intended to indicate that the same measure of damages as for fraud should apply (see **14.6.4**), although this appears unlikely. It is not thought that it is *intended* to import any of the other special rules applying to fraud, e.g. loss of profits recovery in *East v Maurer* (see **14.6.2.3**)— although it was inapplicable on the facts, since there was no continuing misrepresentation or lock-in. Contrast, however, *Pankhania v Hackney London Borough Council (Damages)* [2004] EWHC 323 (Ch), [2004] 1 EGLR 135, in which Geoffrey Vos QC appeared to accept that, in theory, the principle in *Smith New Court Securities Ltd v Scrimgeour Vickers (Asset Management) Ltd* [1997] AC 254 (see **14.6.2.2**) could be applied to a s. 2(1) claim for damages because of the fiction of fraud.

It seems more likely that the intention was to indicate the basic circumstances for liability in damages by no more than an analogy with the established circumstances for the availability of damages for the tort of deceit.

There also seems to be some confusion concerning what needs to be pleaded to claim damages under s. 2(1). It is not a fraud claim; this would need to be pleaded as a separate and alternative claim for damages in the tort of deceit. Equally, it does not follow that if a defendant cannot establish the reasonable grounds for his belief that the statement was true under s. 2(1), the misrepresentation must be fraudulent. In such a case, the defendant has failed to disprove that the statement is negligent. Instead, the fiction of fraud merely means that alleging and proving fraud is not required to recover the *measure of damages* applicable for fraudulent misrepresentation in a s. 2(1) claim.

One reason for seeking recovery in the tort of deceit rather than s. 2(1) is the ability to recover for *all losses resulting from having made that contract*, rather than being limited to *all losses resulting from the fact that the individual representation is false: per* Lord Steyn in *Smith New Court* (see 14.6.2.2). Thus the claims can be distinguished. The potential scope of recovery in fraud is wider.

14.4.4 Innocent misrepresentation: the available remedies

An innocent misrepresentation must today be regarded as a false statement that was made neither fraudulently nor negligently. In fact, as a result of the wording of s. 2(1) MA 1967, it would appear that, for the purposes of a claim for damages, an innocent misrepresentation is restricted to those circumstances in which the representee not only believed the statement to be true, but is also able to prove that he was not negligent, i.e. that he had reasonable grounds for the stated belief (see **14.4.3.2**).

The victim of an innocent misrepresentation is entitled to rescission of the contract, assuming that none of the bars to rescission apply (see **14.5.2**), and to an indemnity intended to help to restore the parties to the position before the contract was made (see **14.6.6**).

There is no right to damages for innocent misrepresentation. However, the court has a discretion, under s. 2(2) MA 1967, to award damages in lieu of (instead of) rescission. The weight of authority supports the view that this discretion is available only where the right to rescission has not been lost—*Floods of Queensferry Ltd v Shand Construction Ltd (No. 3)* [2000] BLR 81, *Government of Zanzibar v British Aerospace (Lancaster House) Ltd* [2000] 1 WLR 2333, [2000] CLC 735, and (*obiter*) in *Pankhania v Hackney London Borough Council* [2002] EWHC 2441 (Ch), [2002] NPC 123, at [74] (see **14.6.5.1**)—although this might result in there being no available remedy in a case of innocent misrepresentation. (Note again that there will be no such discretion where there is a right to redress for the consumer under the regime in the CPRs, as amended, since s. 2 damages are unavailable: see **14.1.2**.)

14.5 Remedies for misrepresentation: rescission

14.5.1 The availability of rescission

In principle, rescission is available for all types of misrepresentation. *The effect of misrepresentation is to make a contract voidable, not void (see **14.1.1**), and a claim for rescission is a claim to have the contract set aside, restoring the parties to the position in which they were before the contract was made.*

Rescission will require the party rescinding the contract to restore to the other any property received under the contract. So, if the claimant buys goods from the defendant on the strength of a false statement as to their qualities, he must return the goods as a condition of recovering the price paid. The converse situation may arise. In *BV Nederlandse Industrie Van Eiprodukten v Rembrandt Enterprises Inc.* [2018] EWHC 1857 (Comm) NIVE agreed to sell dried egg products to Rembrandt at an agreed price, and the price was later increased under an amending agreement. Rembrandt successfully argued that the amending agreement had been induced by a fraudulent misrepresentation by NIVE as to the costs to be incurred by Rembrandt in satisfying the requirements of US safety legislation. Teare J held that Rembrandt was entitled to rescind the amending agreement, leaving the original agreement in place, and as a result Rembrandt could recover the additional sums that it had paid under the amending agreement.

In theory, rescission may be achieved without recourse to legal action, but in practice a party is likely to prefer to have the backing of a court order, especially where it is intended to recover property. The essential requirement of rescission, apart from satisfying the conditions of liability, i.e. establishing the actionable misrepresentation (see **14.2**), is that notice be given to the other party. Where it is impossible to trace the other party, the requirement of giving notice may be waived, provided that all necessary steps have been taken to recover the goods.

In *Car and Universal Finance Co. Ltd v Caldwell* [1961] 1 QB 525, for example, the owner of a car had been fraudulently persuaded to sell it to a rogue, who resold it to the finance company and then disappeared with the proceeds. Once aware of the true facts, the owner notified the police and the Automobile Association, and asked for their help in recovering the car. These actions were found to have been enough to rescind the contract and, since they preceded the sale to the finance company, the finance company had not acquired good title to the car.

This principle and result may be explained in terms of the injustice of denying rescission simply because a rogue perpetrated a deliberate fraud and then absconded, so that notice could not be given. On the other hand, allowing rescission in those circumstances may cause hardship to a third party who has innocently acquired goods if, as here, it is found that the rescission occurred before the third party acquired them.

14.5.2 Loss of the right to rescind

The remedy of rescission may be lost (or barred) if any of the following apply. These bars to rescission (with the exception of s. 2(2) MA 1967) apply to all instances in which the remedy of rescission is available, e.g. for duress or undue influence: see *Halpern v Halpern* [2007] EWCA Civ 291, [2008] QB 195, for the application of *restitutio in integrum* to a case of duress.

14.5.2.1 Affirmation

The right to rescind is lost if the contract is affirmed by the representee after discovering the true state of affairs: *Long v Lloyd* [1958] 1 WLR 753. Affirmation is an indication to the representor that the intention is to continue with the contract, despite the misrepresentation and knowledge of the right to rescind: *Habib Bank v Tufail* [2006] EWCA Civ 374, [2006] 2 P & CR DG14, *per* Lloyd LJ at [20]. Affirmation may be indicated by express words, or by conduct.

In **Long v Lloyd**, the claimant purchased a lorry that had falsely been represented to be in good condition. On its first journey, several serious faults were discovered; they were drawn to the attention of the seller, who offered to pay half the cost of repairs. On a second journey, the lorry broke down again, revealing more serious faults. The claimant was held to have lost the right to rescind the contract. The first journey did not constitute affirmation, since the buyer was entitled to a 'test drive' to check the accuracy of the representation. The second journey, however, was made in the knowledge that the vehicle, when sold, was not in good condition and therefore amounted to affirmation of the contract.

The result on the facts in this case was that the claimant had no remedy at all for misrepresentation, since damages were unavailable at this time for such non-fraudulent misrepresentations.

On the other hand, in *Edwards v Ashik* [2014] EWHC 2454 (Ch), the purchaser of a night-club business had operated it for a short period (six weeks) when he knew of his right to elect to rescind or affirm but was awaiting a response from the seller concerning allegations of fraudulent misrepresentation affecting the purchase. It was held that this did not amount to an unequivocal election to affirm so that the purchaser had not lost the right to rescind for the fraudulent misrepresentation.

14.5.2.2 Lapse of time

In some cases, the right to rescind is lost through lapse of time. This is one instance in which it is relevant to consider the type of misrepresentation when determining the ability to rescind.

- In the case of fraudulent misrepresentations, time will run from the time at which the fraud either was, or with reasonable diligence could have been, discovered.

- However, if the misrepresentation is non-fraudulent (i.e. negligent or innocent), time will run from the date of the contract.

A good illustration of the operation of this principle is provided by the facts and decision in *Leaf v International Galleries* [1950] 2 KB 86 (see **13.4.1.3**).

> A painting, which had been misrepresented as having been painted by Constable, was sold to the claimant. Five years later, the misrepresentation was discovered and the claimant purchaser sought to rescind the contract of sale. His action failed because of the lapse of time since the sale. The misrepresentation in this case was innocent (which at the time embraced both negligent and wholly innocent misrepresentation), so that time ran from the date of the contract.

For a more recent example of the remedy of rescission being lost owing to lapse of time (delay), see *Government of Zanzibar v British Aerospace (Lancaster House)* Ltd [2000] 1 WLR 2333, [2000] CLC 735 (see **14.6.5.1**).

However, in *Salt v Stratstone Specialist Ltd (t/a Stratstone Cadillac Newcastle)* [2015] EWCA Civ 745, [2015] CTLC 206, the Court of Appeal appeared to cast doubt on *Leaf v International Galleries* as a decision prior to the MA 1967, although the rationale employed must be considered suspect.

> In 2007 the claimant had purchased a luxury car from the defendant car dealer on the basis that it was a new car. In 2008 he sought to return the car on the basis that it had many defects and then learnt that the car was in fact two years old and had been involved in a collision. He therefore sought rescission for misrepresentation that the car was new. Before the county court the judge had refused rescission on the basis that the car had been registered after the sale so that *restitutio in integrum* was impossible and that too much time had elapsed since the sale. (The county court instead awarded damages in lieu of rescission under s. 2(2) MA 1967 but this was overturned on appeal by the Court of Appeal, see **14.6.5.1**.)
>
> The High Court overturned the county court decision and this was upheld on appeal so that rescission was permitted. The claimant had brought his claim a reasonable time after learning of the misrepresentation and that was sufficient.

Of course, this is at odds with the principle that, in the absence of fraud, time runs from the date of the contract. However, in any event it was open to the Court of Appeal seeking to preserve the ability to rescind to hold that the delay was not unreasonable on the facts, particularly given the absence of any fault attributable to the claimant for the delay in achieving rescission for the misrepresentation.

14.5.2.3 *Restitutio in integrum*

The right to rescind is lost if *restitutio in integrum* is no longer possible, i.e. if it is no longer possible to restore the parties to the positions in which they were before the contract was made.

Such will be the case where the nature of the subject matter has been changed or it has declined in value, e.g. a contract for the purchase of a bottle of wine, induced by a misrepresentation about its quality, cannot be rescinded once the wine has been opened and drunk. In *Clarke v Dickson* (1858) EB & E 148, 120 ER 463, the misrepresentation induced the purchase of shares in a company that was subsequently wound up so that it was no longer possible to return the shares. However, in *Salt v Stratstone Specialist Ltd (t/a Stratstone Cadillac Newcastle)* [2015] EWCA Civ 745, [2015] CTLC 206 (for facts see **14.5.2.2**), the Court of Appeal considered that registration of a car did not prevent it being returned when a misrepresentation was discovered.

It has been confirmed that this principle applies to rescission for duress: *Halpern v Halpern* [2007] EWCA Civ 291, [2008] QB 195.

> *Halpern v Halpern* concerned a compromise agreement alleged to have been reached between groups of relatives relating to inheritance issues and an arbitration before the Beth Din (a Jewish religious court). One term of the compromise was that all documents produced during the arbitration had to be destroyed or handed over to the appellants. The appellants raised the issue of duress in relation to this compromise agreement when sued for damages for its breach. The respondents claimed that, since the relevant documents had been destroyed, the compromise could not be rescinded, because it would not be possible to make restitution and thereby put the parties back into the position in which they were before the compromise. The appellants contended that an inability to give counter-restitution should not be a bar to a claim based on rescission for duress. The Court of Appeal held that rescission for duress was no different in principle from rescission for other vitiating factors, such as misrepresentation.

The problem with this decision is that the inability to make counter-restitution was directly attributable to a condition of the agreement said to be affected by the duress, which surely calls for some different outcome on the facts, if not in terms of legal principle. The Court of Appeal noted, at [76], that, given this situation, 'it would be surprising if the law could not provide a suitable remedy', although did not specify at this stage (before the full facts were known) what this remedy would be or its basis in law other than securing 'practical justice'. However, it was conceded by the Court of Appeal, at [75], that 'the primary objective may not always need to be to restore *both* parties to their previous positions' (emphasis original).

This position derives support from the principle in *Erlanger v New Sombrero Phosphate Co.* (1878) 3 App Cas 1218, an equitable principle that has long been applied in order to mitigate the strictness of the position on the ability to make counter-restitution. The Chancery Court (equity) did not allow minor imperfections in the restoration of the original position to stand in the way of the remedy. For example, in *Armstrong v Jackson* [1917] 2 KB 822, a major depreciation in value of shares sold under a misrepresentation did not bar rescission, since it was possible to return the shares. In ordering rescission, the court may impose terms, e.g. to account for profits and to allow for deterioration, in order to do what has been described as 'what is practically just': *per* Lord Blackburn in *Erlanger*, at p. 1278. In addition, a court is much more likely to be willing to overlook imperfections in the process of restoring the original positions in the case of fraudulent misrepresentations than in the case of negligent or innocent misrepresentations: *per* Lord Wright in *Spence v Crawford* [1939] 3 All ER 271, at p. 288.

14.5.2.3.1 Rescission as an 'all or nothing' process

Although, in *TSB Bank plc v Camfield* [1995] 1 WLR 430, the Court of Appeal held (in the context of a guarantee) that rescission was total and that partial rescission on terms was not possible, the High Court of Australia in *Vadasz v Pioneer Concrete (SA) Pty Ltd* (1995) 130 ALR 570 preferred a more flexible approach. The guarantee in *Vadasz* covered all monies owing in respect of both existing and future debts, when it had been represented that it would cover only future debts. The High Court of Australia was prepared to rescind the guarantee as regards the existing debt, but to enforce it in relation to future indebtedness. The Privy Council in *Far Eastern Shipping Co. Ltd v Scales Trading Ltd* [2001] 1 All ER (Comm) 319 discussed these cases, but found that, on the facts, it was unnecessary to decide between the competing authorities.

However, in the most recent English authority, *De Molestina v Ponton* [2002] 1 All ER (Comm) 587, Colman J emphatically rejected the concept of partial rescission as being contrary to the very nature of rescission. It might reasonably be argued, as counsel attempted to do in that case, that partial rescission is not too far removed from the instances of equitable intervention to permit rescission on terms (e.g. payment to account for minor deterioration) in cases in which substantial restitution is possible: *per* Lord Blackburn in *Erlanger v New Sombrero Phosphate Co.* (1878) 3 App Cas 1218, at p. 1278 (see **14.5.2.3**). However, Colman J considered this, at [6.3], to be entirely different from partial rescission, since it was concerned with adjustments 'to take account of changes to property or benefits derived from the contract by one side or another during the period between the making of the contract and the proceedings for rescission'. He added, at [6.7]:

> The scope of the equitable discretion in a rescission claim is confined to adjustments to achieve substantial restitution to accommodate events that have occurred after the contract has come into force and does not extend to the general reconstruction of the bargain to achieve an objectively overall fair result.

On the facts in *De Molestina v Ponton*, the problems of partial rescission were avoided because the judge provisionally considered that the three share distribution agreements were distinguishable from various other agreements and therefore could be rescinded without interfering with those other agreements. It has long been accepted that, although it is not possible in English law to rescind part of a contract and affirm the other part, if the parts can be severed so that they form separate and independent contracts, each contract can be separately rescinded. This is essentially what happened in *Barclays Bank v Caplan* [1998] FLR 532 in relation to guarantees that could be cleanly separated from one another (see **15.2.5.1**).

14.5.2.3.2 Rescission of contracts to purchase a business: is restitutio in integrum possible?

It appears from the decision in *Thomas Witter v TBP Industries Ltd* [1996] 2 All ER 573 that rescission of a contract to purchase a business may be particularly difficult to achieve because, in the opinion of Jacob J, it may well not be the same business by the time the question of the availability of rescission comes before the courts. The judge stressed that it was almost inevitable that there would have been changes in personnel and that third party mortgages would be affected. It might reasonably be considered that this approach would prove an encouragement to resist rescission of the sale of a business particularly since, in cases of fraudulent misrepresentations in which the misrepresentee is locked in and cannot easily sell the business, the damages award will, subject to mitigation, take account of any fall in the value of the business down to the date of judgment—*Smith New Court Securities Ltd v Scrimgeour Vickers (Asset Management) Ltd* [1997] AC 254—and so be the more popular remedy.

14.5.2.3.3 *The effective date of rescission*

Whether these factors should impact in this way depends upon whether rescission is regarded as a self-help remedy so that it takes effect from the date of the misrepresentee's election to rescind or whether, as Jacob J assumed in *Thomas Witter v TBP Industries Ltd* [1996] 2 All ER 573, at the date of the hearing. If the operative date is the date of the misrepresentee's election, any transactions between the operative date and the judicial 'declaration' of its validity are in danger of being unravelled. However, if the operative date is the date of the court order, then it is possible to take account of factors occurring in the period between the act of rescission and the trial date. This issue of the operative date was raised by counsel for the appellants at first instance in *Halpern v Halpern* [2006] EWHC 1728 (Comm), [2007] QB 88. However, the judge, Nigel Teare QC, stated, at [26]–[27], that he would not resolve this debate because it was not necessary to do so on the preliminary issue, which was concerned with the need to give counter-restitution. In *Erlson Precision Holdings Ltd (formerly GG132 Ltd) v Hampson Industries Ltd* [2011] EWHC 1137 (Comm) (see **14.4.1.1**), the purchase of shares in a company had been achieved by fraudulent misrepresentation, but the sellers were notified of the rescission only hours after completion and rescission was asserted less than a week later. By the date of the trial, the buyer had been running the company for over nine months, so that changes would have occurred. Nevertheless, the court accepted the relevant date as the date of notification, so that rescission was not barred.

14.5.2.4 **Third party interests**

Rescission is a personal remedy so that the right to rescind will be lost if third party rights intervene (see **3.3.3**). Since a contract affected by misrepresentation is only voidable, not void, a person acquiring goods under such a contract may pass good title at any time before rescission to an innocent third party purchaser who has no notice of the misrepresentation (Sale of Goods Act (SGA) 1979, s. 23, and see **3.2.2.1**).

In *Crystal Palace Football Club (2000) Ltd v Dowie* [2007] EWHC 1392 (QB), [2007] IRLR 682 (for facts, see **14.2.1.2**), rescission was unavailable because of third party interests, since it would have the effect of retrospectively reviving the defendant's employment with the club when both had moved on, i.e. the defendant had since been employed elsewhere (Coventry), and Crystal Palace had a new manager. The defendant could not work for two clubs at the same time and the rights of his new club needed to be taken into account. Instead, it was appropriate to order damages as compensation.

Many of the cases in which wives have sought to avoid contracts in which they have agreed to provide security in the form of the matrimonial home in order to cover their husband's business debts rest as much on misrepresentation as to the nature of the transaction as they do on undue influence on the part of the bank. Consequently, the discussion at **15.2.5.2** relating to undue influence by a third party and the question of notice may be relevant in this context: *Royal Bank of Scotland v Etridge (No. 2)* [2001] UKHL 44, [2002] 2 AC 773.

14.5.2.5 Misrepresentation Act 1967, s. 2(2)

Outside the circumstances in which there is a right to redress under Part 4A of the CPRs 2008, in the case of negligent and innocent misrepresentation, the right to rescind will be lost if the court exercises its discretion to award damages in lieu of (instead of) rescission under s. 2(2) MA 1967 (see **14.6.5**).

14.5.2.6 The CPRs and the 'right to unwind'

The Consumer Protection (Amendment) Regulations 2014, SI 2014/870, provide for a right to unwind or a right to a discount in misrepresentation claims falling within the CPRs 2008. The right to unwind will exist only within the relevant time period (90 days) and only if the product is capable of being rejected at that time (e.g. not fully consumed) (CPRs 2008, reg. 27E). The consumer will then become entitled to a refund (CPRs 2008, reg. 27F). Alternatively, the consumer could exercise the right to receive a discount (CPRs 2008, reg. 27I). The level of the discount turns on matters such as the seriousness of the trader's conduct, the impact that it had on the consumer, and the time that has elapsed. There are separate discount provisions if the value of the product exceeds £5,000. Where the consumer has a right to a discount, either party may also elect to terminate the contract (in the sense of discharging obligations relating to future performance) but cannot also unwind the pre-existing contractual obligations.

14.6 Damages for misrepresentation

14.6.1 Background

The original common law position was that damages for misrepresentation were available only for fraudulent misrepresentation, by way of a tortious action for deceit (see **14.6.2**). A non-fraudulent misrepresentation might be rescinded in equity, but gave rise to no common law right to damages. Instead, as part of the process of rescission, an indemnity might be awarded (see **14.6.6**).

It is still the case that a wholly innocent misrepresentation gives no general *right* to damages—but see the discretion to award damages in lieu of rescission under s. 2(2) MA 1967 (at **14.4.4**). However, as discussed above (see **14.4.3**), the development of the tort of negligence (see **1.5**) eventually gave rise to an action for damages for negligent misstatement, which exists in tandem with the statutory right to damages for negligent misrepresentation (see **14.4.3**).

14.6.1.1 Rescission and damages

With the exception of s. 2(2) MA 1967 (see **14.4.4**), the right to damages is additional to the right to rescission. Provided that there is no double recovery, a representee is entitled to rescission *and* damages. This would be appropriate where, for example, despite rescission the misrepresentee was not restored to its original position because of expenditure incurred as a consequence of entering into the voidable contract. In such a situation, the claimant would *also* need to claim damages for misrepresentation (and the courts would have to consider the application of the relevant remoteness rule to the loss in question).

14.6.1.2 Damages where rescission has been lost

If the remedy of rescission has been lost, it follows that (apart from misrepresentations to which s. 2(2) MA 1967 applies) the remedy of damages will remain and will represent the only mechanism for restoring the misrepresentee to its original position.

14.6.2 The measure of damages in the tort of deceit

Since the claim for damages in respect of fraudulent misrepresentation (see **14.4.1.1**) *is the tortious claim for deceit, the measure of damages is the usual tortious measure of out-of-pocket loss, rather than the contractual measure of expectation loss* (explained at **9.2.1**). Thus the representee is to be put into the position in which it would have been had the representation not been made: *Derry v Peek* (1889) 14 App Cas 337.

14.6.2.1 Remoteness and recovery

The remoteness rule in claims in the tort of deceit allows the misrepresentee to recover for all direct loss incurred as a result of the transaction that was induced by the fraudulent misrepresentation, regardless of foreseeability: Doyle v Olby Ironmongers Ltd [1969] 2 QB 158. In *Doyle v Olby*, the claimant had been fraudulently induced to buy a business and was entitled to recover as damages not only the price paid for the business, but also subsequent investments (as consequential losses), subject only to giving credit for the benefits that he received from the business.

The sum payable as damages is *usually* calculated by reference to the difference between the amount paid and the actual value of the subject matter of the contract judged at the date of the contract: *Smith New Court Securities Ltd v Scrimgeour Vickers (Asset Management) Ltd* [1997] AC 254, *per* Lord Browne-Wilkinson at pp. 265 and 267. So if, as a result of a misrepresentation, £2,500 were to be paid for a car that was actually worth only £1,500 at the date of the contract, damages would be assessed at £1,000. It was accepted in *Smith New Court* that the date of contract rule was flexible and could be disapplied where that rule would not fully compensate the claimant.

In *OMV Petrom SA v Glencore International AG* [2016] EWCA Civ 778, the purchaser had contracted for shipments of crude oil from the defendant which were to be imported through Romania. The contract stipulated that the crude oil would be of Iranian Heavy and GOSM grade. The documents provided with the shipment confirmed that the oil was indeed of these grades. However, some of the shipments consisted of other blends. The claimant sought damages in the tort of deceit alleging that the correct measure of damages should be the difference between the price paid for the shipments and the actual value of the shipments which were delivered—a figure of around $40 million. The defendant argued that the amount payable should be the difference between the less valuable yield derived from refining the blends delivered and the yield which would have been derived from refining the contractually agreed grades of crude oil. It was considered that this would amount to approximately $6 million. The Court of Appeal, affirming the judgment of Flaux J, held, relying on *Smith New Court*, that damages were designed to compensate the claimant for its loss by placing it in the position that it would have been in had the false statement not been made, but taking into account the benefit which the claimant had received, i.e. the price for the oil delivered. Thus the damages should be the price paid, giving credit for the actual value of the oil delivered as at the date of purchase. What the claimant chose to do with the oil was irrelevant. There was no good reason in the present case to depart from the general rule that damages were to be assessed at the date of the contract. Sir Christopher Clarke noted at [39] that the flexibility referred to in *Smith New Court* was for the benefit of the claimant, and not for the benefit of a fraudster: in the case of fraud, the measure should be that least favourable to the defendant.

As noted earlier in this section, in the case of fraud the courts award damages for all loss, including consequential loss such as expenses incurred as a result of entering the contract: *Doyle v Olby.*

14.6.2.2 All losses flowing from the 'transaction'

In *Smith New Court Securities Ltd v Scrimgeour Vickers (Asset Management) Ltd* [1997] AC 254, the defendant's fraudulent misrepresentation induced the claimant to purchase shares in a company. Thereafter, it was discovered that a separate massive fraud against the company had been perpetrated by a third party, causing the value of the shares to plummet. Since the claimant had purchased its shares as a long-term 'market making' investment and had paid more than their market value even at the date of the contract, there was no possibility of immediately reselling the shares.

The question for the House of Lords was whether the claimant could recover the difference between the price paid for the shares and their eventual sale price, which reflected the massive third party fraud (around £11 million), or whether the claimant was limited to recovering the difference between the price paid and the actual value of the shares at the date of the contract (just over £1 million). Put another way, the issue was which of the parties should have to bear the consequences of the third party's fraud. If difference in value at the date of the contract were the correct measure, the actual value of the shares at *the date of the transaction* between claimant and defendant would be assessed without taking account of the third party fraud, which had not then been discovered. However, it was equally persuasively arguable that the catastrophic loss was a direct consequence flowing from the defendant's fraud, since the claimant would not have been exposed to the risk at all but for the inducement that fraud provided.

The House of Lords decided that the risk was the defendant's and allowed the claimant full recovery of its claim. According to Lord Browne-Wilkinson, at p. 267B, *the general rule is that loss is to be assessed at the date of the transaction, but that rule was 'not to be inflexibly applied where to do so would prevent [the misrepresentee] obtaining full compensation for the wrong suffered'.*

Accordingly, the general rule had to give way if 'the claimant is, by reason of the fraud, locked into the property': *Smith New Court*, at p. 267. The same would also be true if the fraudulent misrepresentation were to continue to operate after the date of the contract so that the misrepresentee was 'induced to retain the asset'. Therefore, since the fraud induced the claimant to make a long-term investment without the immediate prospect of reselling the shares, the loss was to be assessed as the actual loss suffered (i.e. the difference between price paid and the price at which the shares were eventually sold).

Lord Steyn adopted a less technical analysis: the only question was what loss did the claimant truly suffer? The 'transaction date valuation' rule generally reveals this, but where, on the facts, it does not, it need not be used.

Thus the policy is that where the statement maker has been fraudulent, the statement maker should be responsible for all of the losses resulting from the other party having made the contract (i.e. losses from the 'transaction'). This greater potential liability might be seen as a deterrent to fraudulent inducements and this was the interpretation placed on the decision in *Doyle v Olby Ironmongers Ltd* [1969] 2 QB 158 by Lord Browne-Wilkinson.

The decision in *East v Maurer* [1991] 1 WLR 461 (for facts see **14.6.2.4**) represents a further application of recovery of the difference between the price paid and the price at which the property was eventually sold, plus consequential sale expenses. However, it is also the case that losses other than capital losses can be recovered on the *Smith New Court* basis if there is a lock-in or continuing misrepresentation after the date of the contract, e.g. the consequential losses arising from running a business purchased as a result of a continuing fraudulent misrepresentation: *Man Nutfahrzeuge AG v Freightliner* [2005] EWHC 2347 (Comm).

14.6.2.3 **Loss of profits**

The Court of Appeal in *East v Maurer* [1991] 1 WLR 461—noted by Marks (1992) 108 LQR 386—held that it was possible, in principle, to recover for loss of profits following a fraudulent misrepresentation on the basis of the formula in *Doyle v Olby Ironmongers Ltd* [1969] 2 QB 158 allowing for recovery of 'all the actual damage directly flowing from the fraudulent inducement', even though loss of profits is normally associated with a claim in contract for expectation loss.

However, the Court of Appeal also held that loss of profits in the context of fraudulent misrepresentation could not be calculated on an expectation basis (i.e. as if the representation were true), because that would amount to converting the representation into a contractual promise (i.e. a term) that the statement was true. Instead, the loss of profits was to be calculated on a tortious basis—namely, the profit that might have been made had the representation not been made at all.

Of course, this raises all sorts of questions relating to calculation of this loss of profits, and it is far too uncertain and speculative without further refinement. The Court of Appeal in *East v Maurer* therefore calculated the loss of profit as the profit that the claimants would probably have made had they purchased another *hypothetical* hair salon at that price (and the Court of Appeal calculated this figure as £10,000).

East v Maurer was approved, in respect of fraud cases, by Lord Steyn in *Smith New Court Securities Ltd v Scrimgeour Vickers (Asset Management) Ltd* [1997] AC 254, at p. 282. On Lord Steyn's analysis, the recovery of *hypothetical lost profit* is 'classic consequential loss' and is to be distinguished from the contractual measure of damage, which would allow recovery of the profit as represented in fact. For a further example of a judgment awarding loss of profits, see *Banks v Cox* [2002] EWHC 2166 (Ch).

If strict rules of evidence are followed, claims based on what the misrepresentee would otherwise have done ought to be based on evidence of those 'hypotheticals' and there ought to be an *actual alternative* in order to establish the loss. The Court of Appeal in *Davis v Churchward*, unreported, 6 May 1993—noted by Chandler (1994) 110 LQR 35—considered the question of recovery of loss of profits for fraudulent misrepresentation relating to the purchase of a public house. In this case, however, the court compared the public house purchased with an *actual* public house and came to the conclusion that, because there was no difference between the actual turnover in both, there could be no recovery for lost profits. The same approach can be seen in *Dadourian Group International Inc. v Simms (Damages)* [2006] EWHC 2973 (Ch). In a claim based on fraudulent misrepresentation, the claimant sought to recover loss of the profits resulting from being deprived of entering into a sale agreement with 'some other purchaser'. The judge rejected this claim on the facts, although not in general terms of the availability of loss of profit damages. He stressed that there would need to be evidence of another purchaser in the market and that the claim would need to take account of the duty to mitigate. (The decision was affirmed by the Court of Appeal—[2009] EWCA Civ 169, [2009] 1 Lloyd's Rep 601 (discussed at **14.2.2.4**)—but the arguments on appeal related to other findings.)

However, this contrasts with the acceptance in *4 Eng Ltd v Harper* [2008] EWHC 915 (Ch), [2009] Ch 91, and *Parabola Investments Ltd v Browallia Cal Ltd* [2010] EWCA Civ 486, [2011] QB 477, that lost profits can be recovered in a deceit claim despite an inability to identify a specific alternative (and profitable) contract that would have been entered into had it not been for the fraudulent misrepresentation. This suggests that the principle in *Davis v Churchward* is incorrect and it seems that the usual rules for establishing loss have no application in the context of fraud.

14.6.2.4 Loss of the opportunity to make a more profitable contract: 'classic consequential loss'

Thus it can be seen from *East v Maurer* [1991] 1 WLR 461 that the misrepresentee in a claim based on fraudulent misrepresentation can recover a profit that the court considers would have been obtained from entering into a different transaction. The courts have adopted an extremely generous approach to the identification and proof of loss in this context. In *East v Maurer*, the claimants had suffered a loss as a result of the fraud. However, the Court of Appeal in *Clef Aquitaine Sarl v Laporte Materials (Barrow) Ltd* [2001] QB 488 held that lost profits can be recovered even where the claimant has not made a loss as a result of the fraud, but is claiming for lost profits based on an argument that, were it not for the fraud, it would otherwise have entered a more profitable identified contract.

> In *Clef Aquitaine Sarl v Laporte Materials (Barrow) Ltd*, the claimant company had agreed to purchase goods from the defendant. The defendant had fraudulently stated that the price list applicable represented the lowest prices at which the defendant's salesmen could sell the goods. The claimant managed to resell the goods at a profit, but wanted damages representing the difference between the price paid and the price that probably could have been negotiated but for the misrepresentation. In essence, the issue was whether 'all the damage (actual loss) directly flowing from the transaction' encompassed this situation. The argument against this was that it represented an attempt to create a contractual (loss of bargain) claim.
>
> The Court of Appeal held that there was no absolute rule to the effect that damages in deceit could be recovered only if the transaction were loss-making. If the claimant could prove that he would have entered into a different and more favourable transaction with the misrepresentor or a third party but for the deceit, he could recover for his loss on that basis.

Simon Brown LJ considered that allowing recovery on these facts gave effect to 'the overriding compensatory rule', i.e. that it represented damages for loss of an opportunity that the claimant would otherwise have had to agree better terms. Thus it appears that, in the case of fraudulent misrepresentation, the misrepresentee can recover for lost alternative contracts as a result of entering this contract. This would include the profits that might have been made by purchasing another similar business at the same price.

Ward LJ noted the difficulties of distinguishing between a tortious approach (putting the misrepresentee into the position in which they would have been had the misrepresentation not been made) and the contractual approach (putting them into the position in which they would have been had a true statement been made). In particular, he noted the difficulties of drawing a line between recovery for loss of bargain (which was contractual and ruled out in this context) and recovery for the loss of a bargain that might have been made *had the truth been known*.

In *Parabola Investments Ltd v Browallia Cal Ltd (formerly Union Cal Ltd)* [2010] EWCA Civ 486, [2011] QB 477, the Court of Appeal agreed with the trial judge that a claim could be made in deceit by the investment company not only for loss of the capital investment induced by the fraudulent misrepresentation and the profits that could have been made in relation to this lost investment, but also for the lost profits that could have been made had the fraud not occurred and had the investment company made *an* alternative investment. This loss fell within the general principle in *Smith New Court Securities Ltd v Scrimgeour Vickers (Asset Management) Ltd* [1997] AC 254 (loss flowing from the transaction and the overriding compensatory principle). There was no principled reason why the discovery of the fraud should be the cut-off point for such losses and the company could recover for the profits lost on investments right down to the date of the trial. If this is applied by analogy in the context of damages under s. 2(1) MA 1967 (fiction of fraud: see **14.6.4.1**), it would be a startling conclusion.

Parabola Investments Ltd v Browallia Cal Ltd was not a loss of chance claim (see the discussion at **9.3.4**) because the judge held that, on a balance of probabilities, some profits would have been made from alternative transactions into which the claimant would have entered but for the fraud, i.e. profitability in a general sense was established. The Court of Appeal accepted that it was conducting an entirely hypothetical exercise in order to quantify loss and that it could only make the best attempt that it could to evaluate the chances of particular alternative investments being made or being profitable.

The case of *4 Eng Ltd v Harper* [2008] EWHC 915 (Ch), [2009] Ch 91, is rather more difficult. The judge accepted that damages for loss of the chance to purchase an alternative company fell within the general principle in *Smith New Court* and therefore could be recovered. This related to loss of a specific opportunity, rather than general loss of profitability and this may explain why the judge applied the loss of a chance principles in *Allied Maples*.

It will be recalled that, in a loss of chance claim, the court requires proof of the loss of a substantial chance before determining quantum: *Allied Maples Group Ltd v Simmons & Simmons* [1995] 1 WLR 1602 (discussed at **9.3.4**). On the evidence in *4 Eng Ltd v Harper*, the claimant had established this and it was decided that there was an 80 per cent chance that the owners of the alternative company would have sold their shares to the claimant. It followed that the claimant was entitled to substantial damages for loss of a chance, representing loss of income and loss of capital profit on the investment. A 20 per cent discount was applied to the profits to account for the fact that there was an element of 'chance'.

In *Yam Seng Pte Ltd v International Trade Corporation Ltd* [2013] EWHC 111 (QB), [2013] 1 CLC 662, [2013] 1 All ER (Comm) 1321, at [218], Leggatt J accepted the position on recovering a profit that would have been obtained from entering into some other transaction, but considered that 'it must in principle be equally relevant to take account of any loss' and so reduce the claimant's recovery, despite the fraud. He added, at [217], that this was because:

> There is no difference in principle between an alternative transaction which would have been more profitable and one which would have been less profitable than the actual transaction such that it can be relevant to take account of the former but not the latter.

However, it would be for the fraudulent misrepresentor to prove that 'if the misrepresentation had not been made the claimant would have incurred a loss' and the actual measure of that loss. This will be really difficult to establish. For example, in *Naughton v O'Callaghan* [1990] 3 All ER 191 (see **14.6.4.1**), the claimant might well have suffered some loss had he not entered into the contract in question but purchased another horse, but this was impossible to establish without use of hypothetical assumptions, and that will not suffice. Equally, it is possible to envisage an argument that a claimant might well have made a loss through the purchase of an alternative investment, but without knowing which one, or entering into speculation, that is impossible to establish.

It follows that there is an advantage held by the misrepresentee since 'hypotheticals' can assist the misrepresentee in establishing the loss suffered, whereas the misrepresentor would need to prove that the claimant would have suffered an *actual* loss. In other words, as Leggatt J noted in *Yam Seng*, at [217]:

[I]f the financial outcome of the alternative transaction is uncertain the court will make reasonable assumptions in [the misrepresentee's] favour (for example by allowing damages to be calculated on a loss of a chance basis) to assist in the proof of loss.

Leggatt J continued: 'In this respect there is a disparity, but a principled one, between hypothetical transactions which would have made the claimant worse off and those which would have made the claimant better off.' Given the reasoning above, however, this seems difficult to justify.

It therefore followed on the facts in *Yam Seng* that there could be no reduction in damages based on an argument that, but for this contract, a loss would have been made on another contract in any event.

14.6.2.5 The duty to mitigate

In *Smith New Court Securities Ltd v Scrimgeour Vickers (Asset Management) Ltd* [1997] AC 254, Lord Browne-Wilkinson also stated that the misrepresentee had a duty to mitigate its loss once it discovered the fraud.

> In *Downs v Chappell* [1997] 1 WLR 461, there was a fraudulent misrepresentation relating to the value of a bookshop business. The business was purchased for £120,000 and eventually sold for less than £60,000. However, the misrepresentee had earlier refused two offers of £76,000. The Court of Appeal held that damages were limited to £44,000—namely, the difference between £120,000 and £76,000. The claimant was entitled to damages for his loss to the date on which he could have avoided further losses. The offer of £76,000 had been unreasonably refused and broke the chain of causation. As a result, the further loss (an extra £16,000) was not direct loss flowing from the fraud.

The test for mitigation is the same as that applicable for breach of contract claims (i.e. a duty to take reasonable steps to minimize the loss: see **9.5.3**): *Standard Chartered Bank v Pakistan National Shipping Corporation* [1999] 1 Lloyd's Rep 747 (if the loss could reasonably have been avoided, it would not be regarded as having been caused by the misrepresentation). In affirming this first-instance decision, the Court of Appeal in *Standard Chartered Bank v Pakistan National Shipping (Assessment of Damages)* [2001] EWCA Civ 55, [2001] 1 All ER (Comm) 822, confirmed that, in the tort of deceit, the concepts of mitigation and causation could not be separated and were 'two sides of the same coin': *per* Potter LJ at [41]. Since mitigation requires only that reasonable steps are taken to minimize the loss, in *Banks v Cox (Costs)* [2002] EWHC 2166 (Ch), the claimants were not required to put the nursing home, for which they had paid £250,000, on the market at the suggested price of £120,000, since even if they were to sell the property at the lower figure, that amount would not have covered their indebtedness to their bank.

14.6.2.6 Profits made by the representee

Where damages are sought for misrepresentation leading to the making of a contract, the question arises as to whether the claimant is required to account for profits made by the claimant from the contract. That is the case where the profit is part and parcel of the original transaction. If the profit arises independently, then it does not diminish the claimant's damages.

In **Hussey v Eels** [1990] 2 QB 227 the claimants purchased a bungalow, unaware that false statements had been made by the vendor about the condition of the bungalow. The claimants sought and obtained planning permission, and sold the bungalow at a substantial profit. They nevertheless sought damages for the loss suffered by them represented by the diminished value of the bungalow when it was purchased. The Court of Appeal held that the misrepresentation was not the cause of the profit and was to be left out of account.

The decision in *Hussey* was followed in *Quilter v Hodson Developments Ltd* [2016] EWCA Civ 1125, where suggestions that *Hussey* was exceptional were rejected. As in *Hussey*, the claimant purchased property which was resold at a substantial profit, but was nevertheless able to recover damages for misrepresentation made when the claimant purchased the property. A defendant should not be entitled to benefit from increases in market value unconnected to the original misrepresentation.

14.6.3 Damages for negligent misrepresentations: damages in tort for negligent misstatement

Clearly, damages for negligent misstatement (tort) at common law under the principle in *Hedley Byrne v Heller* [1964] AC 465 are tortious and the remoteness test is whether the loss is a reasonably foreseeable consequence (albeit foreseeable only as a remote consequence) of the tort: *The Wagon Mound (No. 1)* [1961] AC 388.

Unlike the position with regard to fraudulent misrepresentation, it is clear that liability is limited to the position assessed at the date of the wrong. In *South Australia Asset Management Corporation v York Montague Ltd* [1997] AC 191, in the context of a negligent survey, the House of Lords held that damages had to be assessed as the difference between the price paid and the actual value of the property at the date of the purchase contract. The surveyor was responsible only for the consequences of the information in his survey being inaccurate and could not be made responsible for subsequent falls in property values.

14.6.4 Damages for negligent misrepresentation under the MA 1967, s. 2(1)

Section 2(1) MA 1967 does not expressly state the applicable measure of damages. However, since the section is based on what is known as 'the fiction of fraud' (see **14.4.3.2**), it seems that the statutory right to damages, as the common law right (see **14.4.3.1**), is based in tort and so the tortious (out-of-pocket) measure applies. This point was finally settled by the Court of Appeal decision in *Royscot Trust Ltd v Rogerson* [1991] 2 QB 297. *Royscot Trust* has proved to be a very controversial case, but not in respect of the basic measure of damages being tortious (i.e. out-of-pocket loss), since if the common law and statutory claims for negligent misstatement are truly alternatives, the basic measure of damages should be the same.

14.6.4.1 The 'fiction of fraud' and the remoteness test under s. 2(1): *Royscot Trust Ltd v Rogerson*

Instead, *Royscot Trust Ltd v Rogerson* [1991] 2 QB 297 has proved controversial because of the literal interpretation of s. 2(1) MA 1967 (the 'fiction of fraud') adopted by the Court of Appeal. The Court of Appeal stated that damages under s. 2(1) are to be assessed in the same way as damages for fraudulent misrepresentation, even though the misrepresentation is not fraudulent. In particular, the court refused to go against the express literal words of the statute (this 'fiction of fraud') in the context of the applicable remoteness test in order to apply the general test of foreseeability for negligence, but allowed the more generous test in fraud under *Doyle v Olby Ironmongers Ltd* [1969] 2 QB 15 (all direct loss regardless of foreseeability) to govern.

This aspect of the decision in *Royscot Trust* is easy to criticize because it treats negligent misrepresentations (honest statements) in the same way as fraudulent ones (dishonest statements). It also means that the remoteness tests applicable under the common law claim—*Hedley Byrne v Heller* [1964] AC 465—for negligent misstatement and under s. 2(1) of the 1967 Act for negligent misrepresentation are very different. Taken to its logical conclusion, the 'fiction of fraud' ought also to mean that the principle in *Smith New Court Securities Ltd v Scrimgeour Vickers (Asset Management) Ltd* [1997] AC 254 (see **14.6.2.2**) on the measure of damages, and *East v Maurer* [1991] 1 WLR 461 on loss of profit damages for fraudulent misrepresentation, ought to apply with equal force to the assessment of damages under s. 2(1). This would seem a staggering conclusion, especially when the significance of the fraud to the decision in *Smith New Court* is considered.

It must be doubtful whether the same policy considerations should apply to negligent misrepresentations: see Hooley (1991) 107 LQR 547. Nevertheless, in *Spice Girls Ltd v Aprilia World Service BV (Damages)* [2001] EMLR 8, Arden J had to assess damages under s. 2(1) MA 1967 and held that she was bound to follow *Royscot Trust*. It was accepted that the damages had to be calculated as if the misrepresentation was fraudulent and on the basis of compensating Aprilia for losses flowing from the contract (i.e. the *Smith New Court* approach). Thus all direct loss and consequential loss was recoverable, but not payment of sponsorship fees made to the Spice Girls before the contract was concluded, since this payment had not been induced by the misrepresentation.

The position has become so acute that, in *Avon Insurance plc v Swire Fraser Ltd* [2000] 1 All ER (Comm) 573, Rix J considered that, because of application of the fraud rules to negligent misrepresentations under s. 2(1), a court should not be too willing to find there to be an actionable misrepresentation where the court had some room for the exercise of judgement. The judge continued, at [201]:

> If, on the other hand, the rule in the *Royscot Trust Ltd* case were one day to be found to be a misunderstanding of the 1967 Act, and the way were to become open to treat an innocent misrepresentation under section 2(1) as though it was a case of negligence in *Hedley Byrne*, so that in the typical case of the provision of negligent information it would be possible to tailor the damages to the risk undertaken by the negligent representor . . . then there would be nothing to be said against adopting a more closely focused approach to the proof of misrepresentation.

In *Cheltenham Borough Council v Laird* [2009] EWHC 1253 (QB), [2009] IRLR 621, at [524], Hamblen J considered there to be 'a real possibility of [*Royscot Trust*] being reversed' if the decision were to come before a higher court, citing the reasons discussed above. In *Yam Seng Pte Ltd v International Trade Corporation Ltd* [2013] EWHC 111 (QB), [2013] 1 CLC 662, [2013] 1 All ER (Comm) 1321, at [207], Leggatt J considered that '[u]nless and until *Royscot Trust* is overruled . . . it represents the law; and I must therefore apply it'. There are also clear signs of judicial discontent in those higher courts, although as yet no action.

In *Smith New Court*, at pp. 267 and 283, both Lords Browne-Wilkinson and Steyn noted the serious doubts about the correctness of the decision in *Royscot Trust Ltd v Rogerson*, but did not expressly overrule it, since it was not necessary to the decision in the case. Lord Steyn did, however, make it clear that, in his view, fraud and negligence should be treated differently, in that whereas remoteness for fraudulent misrepresentation allows for the recovery of all losses resulting from having entered into the contract, its application in the context of negligent misrepresentation would be limited to allowing for recovery of losses resulting from that negligent statement (which may be significantly narrower): see the discussion of this distinction in *Man Nutfahrzeuge AG v Freightliner* [2005] EWHC 2347 (Comm), at [193]–[197], concluding that the intention was to impose liability for losses 'arising out of the inaccuracy of any of the representations', 'but not against the entire consequences of entering into the agreement insofar as they could not be said to flow from the inaccuracy of the particular representation'. This may be highly significant where there is more than one misrepresentation.

This area clearly cries out for reform: see Poole and Devenney [2007] JBL 269. The Law Commission might usefully look at this issue concerning the MA 1967: see comments advocating this course of action by Jacob J in *Thomas Witter v TBP Industries Ltd* [1996] 2 All ER 573. The Law Commission Consultation Paper and subsequent report *Consumer Redress for Misrepresentation and Aggressive Practices*, Law Com. No. 332 (Cm 8323, March 2012) (discussed at **14.1.2**), was limited to focusing on the consumer context in order to implement the CRD and introduce a civil regime alongside the existing criminal offences contained in the CPRs. It follows that the generous measure of damages provided for negligence in s. 2(1) of the 1967 Act will not be available in future to consumer contracts falling within the CPRs, because s. 2 will not apply in such instances.

However, in the case of B2B contracts or other contracts falling outside the CPRs, until such time as the position is altered and *Royscot* is overruled, the remoteness test under s. 2(1) will be the test of all direct loss resulting from the misrepresentation, so that essentially the test will be to establish that the loss was *caused by the misrepresentation*. Where there is a causal link between the misrepresentation and the loss, the loss will therefore be recovered. The applicable test for this causal link will involve determining whether any subsequent action was reasonable and to be expected in the circumstances.

> In *Naughton v O'Callaghan* [1990] 3 All ER 191, the judge allowed recovery of the difference between the price paid for a thoroughbred colt, intended to be run as a racehorse, and its actual value after the horse's value had fallen dramatically owing to poor racing performances. The claimant's actions in training and racing the horse were exactly the conduct that would have been expected, and were reasonable in the circumstances, given that the colt had been purchased as a racehorse.

Similarly, if the negligent misrepresentation induces the purchase of a business, it will have to be considered whether any consequential expenditure amounts to a reasonable and expected expense, taking into account the circumstances and, in particular, the nature of the business, or whether it is attributable to the independent whim of the purchaser. Thus if the loss is caused not by the misrepresentation, but by the misrepresentee's independent intervening action, it will not be recoverable. In *Butler-Creagh v Hersham* [2011] EWHC 2525 (QB), Eady J stressed the importance of causation (in a deceit claim concerning the purchase of a property as a result of a fraudulent misrepresentation concerning its value, the cost of development, and the need for urgency in completing). The judge noted, at [113]:

> One cannot simply spend money in a situation of this kind and express it as a loss flowing from the actionable misrepresentations . . . It needs . . . to be demonstrated that it was necessary or reasonable to spend the money, not merely as a matter of choice, but as a result of being placed wrongfully in a particular predicament as a result of the misrepresentation(s) comprising the cause of action.

Therefore the stamp duty on the purchase and the borrowing costs flowed directly from the decision to purchase, as did reasonable maintenance costs to ensure that the property did not deteriorate before it could be sold.

There is perhaps one difference between the common law measure of damages for the tort of deceit and the statutory fiction of fraud under s. 2(1). In *Taberna Europe CDO II plc v Selskabet (formerly Roskilde Bank A/S in Bankruptcy)* [2016] EWCA Civ 1262 Sir Christopher Clarke, with the agreement of the remainder of the court, expressed the view, *obiter*, that s. 2(1) damages are limited to loss resulting from a misrepresentation relating to the contract between the parties, and not to loss suffered by the claimant as a result of entering into a contract with a third party. In that case the Court of Appeal held that the claimant, which had purchased securities from a third party in reliance on a false representation by the defendant bank that only a small part of the third party's loans to the seller were non-performing, could not recover its loss from the defendant under s. 2(1).

14.6.4.2 Mitigation and s. 2(1)

The duty to mitigate loss (discussed at **14.6.2.5** in the context of the fiction of fraud) also applies to claims for damages under s. 2(1) MA 1967: see *Pankhania v Hackney London Borough Council (Damages)* [2004] EWHC 323 (Ch), [2004] 1 EGLR 135 (it is a question of whether the claimant acted reasonably in terms of the steps taken subsequent to discovery of the misrepresentation).

14.6.5 Damages in lieu of rescission

Section 2(2) of the Misrepresentation Act (MA 1967) provides:

> Where a person has entered into a contract after a misrepresentation has been made to him otherwise than fraudulently, and he would be entitled, by reason of the misrepresentation, to rescind the contract, then, if it is claimed, in any proceedings arising out of the contract, that the contract ought to be or has been rescinded, the court or arbitrator may declare the contract subsisting and award damages in lieu of rescission, if of the opinion that it would be equitable to do so, having regard to the nature of the misrepresentation and the loss that would be caused by it if the contract were upheld, as well as to the loss that rescission would cause to the other party.

The aim of this provision is to prevent the use of the remedy of rescission in the case of trivial misrepresentations for which compensation would be an adequate remedy. This is because rescinding a contract has serious consequences, i.e. meaning that the contract has no effect and that any money or property that has changed hands will need to be returned: *William Sindall plc v Cambridgeshire County Council* [1994] 1 WLR 1016, *per* Evans LJ at p. 1045.

Section 2(2) does not apply to fraudulent misrepresentation, since the law never treats fraud as trivial, and in practice it is most likely to be relevant where the misrepresentation is wholly innocent. An example of the kind of situation covered by the section might be an innocent misrepresentation, inaccurate by only one year, concerning the age of second-hand factory equipment. Assuming that the misrepresentation was sufficiently material to have induced the sale, it might be thought that the remedy of rescission would be unduly harsh in these circumstances; but for s. 2(2), it would be the only remedy available.

The s. 2(2) remedy is entirely within the discretion of the court, neither party having the right to insist upon its application. In exercising that discretion, the court must weigh:

- the seriousness of the misrepresentation;
- whether the representee will suffer greatly if not allowed to rescind; and
- whether the representor would suffer unduly if rescission were allowed: *William Sindall, per* Hoffmann LJ at pp. 1036–7.

This exercise was carried out by the trial judge and then affirmed by the Court of Appeal in *UCB Corporate Services Ltd v Thomason* [2005] EWCA Civ 225, [2005] 1 All ER (Comm) 601.

A husband and wife were liable to the bank under two guarantees. As a result of misrepresentation (failure to disclose the full extent of the couple's assets), the bank entered into a waiver agreement releasing the liability under the guarantee. On discovering the misrepresentation, the bank sought to rescind the waiver agreement.

The Court of Appeal considered that the trial judge had been correct to conclude that the loss caused by the misrepresentation was the lost chance of recovering more money had it known the truth and therefore not agreed to the waiver, and not the amount of the guaranteed debt. This might result in little additional loss to the bank (the misrepresentee). On the other hand, if rescission were to have been permitted, it would have exposed the misrepresentors to a large liability—albeit that, in practice, that might not have been enforceable given the financial resources of this couple. The Court of Appeal therefore affirmed the decision of the trial judge to refuse to permit rescission.

In *Harsten Developments Ltd v Bleaken* [2012] EWHC 2704 (Ch), it was alleged that the vendor of a plot with planning permission had misrepresented the boundary with neighbouring land. The developer sought rescission of the contract. Rescission was available in principle and it was held that the developer had not affirmed despite having reapplied for planning permission because it had not then been aware of the ability to rescind. The judge went on to consider whether to exercise the s. 2(2) discretion and award damages in lieu of rescission, but concluded that justice was best served on the facts by not exercising this discretion. This appears to be because the misrepresentation was more serious than the alleged misrepresentation in the *Sindall* case in that the property transferred was substantially different from the property that the developer had been led to expect.

If rescission were refused, the developer would retain the land, which it did not want because of the fall in property values since the sale, and would claim damages from the vendors in accordance with s. 2(3). However, if rescission were allowed, the land would be retransferred to the vendors, and they would have to return the price plus interest and any damages under s. 2(1) of the 1967 Act (covering the sale expenses, etc.). It was recognized that lapse of time might be a factor in the exercise of the s. 2(2) discretion in future, but it had not been argued that this had any effect on the vendors despite the fall in property values. It is possibly more surprising that there was no argument that the lapse of time constituted the affirmation, since time would have started to run from the date of the sale contract in 2007 (see **14.5.2.2**).

14.6.5.1 Must the remedy of rescission still be available if the s. 2(2) discretion is to be exercised?

It has traditionally been considered that the discretion to award damages instead of rescission could be exercised only if the right to rescind had not been lost (or barred), because the section as drafted appears to require that rescission be possible. Section 2(2) clearly refers to the discretion as existing where the injured party would otherwise be entitled to rescind. However, the consequence of the application of such a principle is that no useful remedy will exist, rescission having been lost and there being no discretion to award damages in its place. This interpretation was therefore criticized, but not really doubted, by Atiyah and Treitel (1967) 30 MLR 369 at the time that the Act was passed.

The conventional interpretation was challenged by Jacob J in *Thomas Witter Ltd v TBP Industries Ltd* [1996] 2 All ER 573, at p. 590. The judge clearly found such a limit on the discretion to award damages in lieu of rescission to be unattractive. He suggested that it might have been drafted in this way simply to require that the contract should have been open to rescission *at some point*, without requiring rescission to be a continuing possibility. He was offered support by counsel who had carried out a search of Hansard to discover what Parliament's intention had been. In the House of Commons, the Solicitor General had clearly indicated that the intention was to provide a remedy of damages where the right to rescission had been lost: Hansard HC, 20 February 1967, cols 1388–9. Jacob J needed no further encouragement and he duly found, at p. 5901, that 'the power to award damages under section 2(2) does not depend upon an extant right to rescission—it only depends upon a right having existed in the past'.

However, this approach has not been followed in a number of more recent cases.

1. In *Floods of Queensferry Ltd v Shand Construction Ltd* [2000] BLR 81, at p. 93, Judge Humphrey Lloyd QC considered that, for the discretion to be exercisable, the remedy of rescission had to exist at the date of the hearing.

2. In *Government of Zanzibar v British Aerospace (Lancaster House) Ltd* [2000] 1 WLR 2333, [2000] CLC 735, at pp. 2341–4, Judge Raymond Jack QC, sitting as a High Court judge, adopted the same approach, relying on the express words of the subsection and refusing to follow *Thomas Witter v TBP Industries Ltd* on this point.

3. In *Pankhania v Hackney London Borough Council* [2002] EWHC 2441 (Ch), [2002] NPC 123, Rex Tedd QC (*obiter*) also considered that the s. 2(2) discretion could not apply unless the right to rescind was available at the date of the exercise of the discretion. The judge explained this in light of the overall purpose of s. 2(2), which was to mitigate the harsh effects of rescission where this remedy was out of proportion to the misrepresentation and its effects. It was not intended 'to provide a remedy where there was none' prior to the MA 1967.

More significantly, this approach has now been endorsed as correct by the Court of Appeal in *Salt v Stratstone Specialist Ltd (t/a Stratstone Cadillac Newcastle)* [2015] EWCA Civ 745, [2015] CTLC 206, per Longmore LJ at [17]–[18]. Therefore rescission must have been available at the time of the exercise of the discretion because these are 'damages in lieu of rescission'. Although this may be correct, it does have the unfortunate consequence that, in some circumstances (admittedly limited), a misrepresentee may be left with no effective remedy (i.e. if the remedy of rescission has been lost and damages are not available because the misrepresentor had reasonable grounds to justify the statement made, so that s. 2(1) damages cannot be claimed).

The significant differences of interpretation (and hence of result) in relation to this question of the availability of rescission and the s. 2(2) discretion again highlight the need for some reconsideration of the MA 1967 (see **14.6.4.1**).

14.6.5.2 The measure of damages under s. 2(2)

It may be that the measure of damages awarded in lieu of rescission is more restricted than either the out-of-pocket or lost expectation measures. The inference from s. 2(3) of the 1967 Act is that it is anticipated that damages under s. 2(2) will be lower than damages under s. 2(1), since the former are to be taken into account in assessing the latter, and this much is accepted by Hoffmann LJ (*obiter*) in *William Sindall plc v Cambridgeshire County Council* [1994] 1 WLR 1016, at p. 1037.

However, if the purpose of the damages is to compensate for the loss of the right to rescind, it would seem that that loss is best measured as the difference between the contract price paid (which cannot now be recovered) and the actual value of the thing, which is the tortious measure of damages. This was the approach suggested *obiter* by the Court of Appeal in *William Sindall*. Hoffmann LJ said that s. 2(2) allowed the court to uphold the contract and compensate the claimant for the loss suffered on account of the property not having been what it was represented to be. Section 2(2) damages could not be the difference between the price paid and the market value of the property, on the basis that this was a loss flowing from having entered the contract. That would be the appropriate measure for fraud, but s. 2(2) damages are different and represent the loss caused by the misrepresentation if the contract is upheld. Evans LJ said, at p. 1044, that, under s. 2(2), the loss caused by upholding the contract would be compensated by the award of 'the cost of remedying the defect, or alternatively . . . the reduced market value attributable to the defect'. It will not therefore extend to the loss caused as a result of entering into the contract; only the loss caused by upholding the contract. On the facts in *Sindall* (see **13.2.1**), the Court of Appeal considered (*obiter*) that the loss that would be caused to the misrepresentee if rescission were refused (and the contract were upheld) was not the full extent of the loss resulting from entering into the contract, i.e. taking account of the dramatic fall in the price of land, since that was not a loss caused by the misrepresentation if the contract were upheld. Instead, the misrepresentee's loss on this basis would be the cost of diverting the sewer that had been discovered, the loss of one plot, and interest charges for any consequent delay.

For Hoffmann LJ in *Sindall*, the difference between s. 2(1) and (2) lay in the availability of damages for consequential loss, which would not be awarded under s. 2(2). This view was also supported by Jacob J in *Thomas Witter v TBP Industries Ltd* [1996] 2 All ER 573. It is submitted that this is the correct view of the section in view of the purpose of s. 2(2) damages, although Evans LJ in the *Sindall* case seems to contemplate the award of damages to compensate for consequential losses 'if appropriate'.

14.6.6 Indemnity

As was noted earlier (see **14.4.4**), there is no general right to damages for a wholly innocent misrepresentation. Instead, where rescission is available, it may be possible to recover an indemnity, which falls short of any measure of damages. *An indemnity provides compensation for expenditure occurring as a result of 'obligations which have been created by the contract' into which the representee has been induced to enter*: *Newbigging v Adam* (1886) 34 Ch D 582, *per* Bowen LJ at p. 593.

The difference between an indemnity and damages may be demonstrated by reference to the facts of *Whittington v Seale-Hayne* (1900) 82 LT 49.

The claimants were induced to take a lease of a farm, intending to use it for poultry, by an innocent misrepresentation that the water supply was healthy. This proved not to be the case; a farm manager became ill and the poultry died. The claimants were ordered by the local council to renew the drains, and they lost profits and spent money on medical care, rent, rates, outbuildings, and other business expenses. They sought to recover an 'indemnity' for all of these costs. They were able to recover compensation for rent, rates, and renewing the drains, since these were obligations created by the fact of taking the lease. However, they could not recover the other expenses; these were items of damages, which did not qualify for an indemnity. They were expenses resulting from operating a poultry farm and there was no *obligation* to run a poultry farm *created by* the contract.

14.6.7 Contributory negligence

Now that damages for negligent misrepresentation may be awarded, the question arises whether the misrepresentee's own negligence, which has contributed to their decision to enter the contract, operates to reduce the misrepresentee's damages award.

There is no scope for the application of contributory negligence where the misrepresentations were fraudulently made: *Alliance and Leicester Building Society v Edgestop Ltd* [1994] 2 All ER 38 and *Corporation National del Cobre de Chile v Sogemin Metals Ltd* [1997] 1 WLR 1396. If the statement maker has been fraudulent, it should not be protected against the consequences of its statements by claiming that the misrepresentee was negligent. This point was confirmed by the House of Lords in *Standard Chartered Bank v Pakistan National Shipping Corporation (No. 2)* [2002] UKHL 43, [2003] 1 AC 959.

It was alleged that it was the claimant's own deceit that had partly caused the loss suffered. Payment for goods for export was to be made by means of a letter of credit. However, although the cargo was not shipped on time, the sellers had falsely stated the shipment date in the documents and payment had been authorized against these documents by SCB (the confirming bank), although it knew that the documents were presented after the expiry of the credit. SCB then sought reimbursement from the issuing bank by falsely stating that the documents had been presented in time. The issuing bank refused payment because of unrelated discrepancies in the documents. SCB then sought damages for deceit from the sellers, who claimed that SCB's loss was partly attributable to its own deceit on the issuing bank. The House of Lords rejected this argument on the basis that the Law Reform (Contributory Negligence) Act 1945 did not apply to fraudulent misrepresentations, since the Act was not intended to alter the previous position at common law.

Older authorities suggest that contributory negligence has no effect in the case of non-fraudulent misrepresentation: *Redgrave v Hurd* (1881) 20 Ch D 1 (see **14.2.2.4**). These cases, however, pre-date the establishment of a separate category of negligent misrepresentation and the Law Reform (Contributory Negligence) Act 1945. In the general tort of negligence, s. 1(1) of the 1945 Act provides for apportionment of damages to take account of the claimant's contributory negligence. Common law liability for negligent misstatement is clearly tortious (see **14.6.3**), so that the 1945 Act will apply to claims based on *Hedley Byrne v Heller* [1964] AC 465.

Since negligent misstatement at common law and the statutory claim for damages under s. 2(1) MA 1967 are alternatives, and the basic aim of damages in both cases is tortious, it might be thought that, in the case of a claim for damages under s. 2(1), the misrepresentee's damages should also be reduced to take account of their contributory negligence. However, the 'fiction of fraud' in *Royscot Trust Ltd v Rogerson* [1991] 2 QB 297 would suggest that damages under s. 2(1) should be assessed as if the misrepresentation were fraudulent. On this basis, there should be no apportionment for contributory negligence if the claim is brought solely under s. 2(1), since there is no apportionment for the misrepresentee's contributory negligence where the misrepresentor is fraudulent.

However, this latter interpretation would lead to all sorts of fine distinctions, especially since, in *Gran Gelato Ltd v Richcliff (Group) Ltd* [1992] Ch 560, Nicholls VC stated that, where there are concurrent claims under *Hedley Byrne* and s. 2(1), the claimant's damages could be reduced in respect of both claims where there was contributory negligence by the claimant. He stated, at p. 573:

> It would be very odd if contributory negligence were available as a defence to a claim for damages based on a breach of a duty to take care in and about the making of a particular representation, but not available to a claim for damages under the 1967 Act in respect of the same representation.

It should therefore make no difference to the position if the claim is framed only under s. 2(1). A different interpretation would allow the 1945 Act to be avoided by claiming damages under s. 2(1) only, despite it being the case that the facts might also justify a claim based on *Hedley Byrne*. It appears that this is the correct position, at least where the facts would give rise to a concurrent duty of care in tort. Contributory negligence is not dependent on a specific pleading of the alternative claims.

In *Taberna Europe CDO II plc v Selskabet (formerly Roskilde Bank A/S in Bankruptcy)* [2015] EWHC 871 (Comm), the issue arose of whether damages awarded under a s. 2(1) MA 1967 claim could be reduced on account of the other party's contributory negligence in failing to take specialist market advice, relying on out-of-date advice and information, and failing to make a proper assessment of capital adequacy prior to making the investment. The argument for the investor was that damages could not be reduced under s. 2(1) where the claim was limited to s. 2(1) and there was no alternative claim based on negligent misstatement at common law. The judge rejected this conclusion (at [109]–[110]), deciding that it was not the separate claim that mattered but the existence of a concurrent duty of care in tort. If such a duty existed, in principle contributory negligence should be available in relation to damages claimed and awarded under s. 2(1). Nevertheless, it was not 'just and equitable' under the 1945 Act to reduce the damages on these facts based on the alleged instances of contributory negligence relied upon. The actual decision in this case was reversed by the Court of Appeal, [2016] EWCA Civ 1262, on the ground that the defendant was entitled to rely upon its disclaimer of liability in a situation where the parties were in much the same position to know the facts, but the judge's reasoning on the issues discussed in this paragraph was affirmed.

14.6.8 Damages and the Consumer Protection from Unfair Trading Regulations 2008

The Consumer Protection (Amendment) Regulations 2014, SI 2014/870, introduce a right to damages in consumer contracts falling within the scope of the CPRs, as amended, for certain identified losses which would not have been incurred had the misrepresentation not taken place (CPRs 2008, reg. 27J). The identified losses must be financial loss or non-pecuniary loss, such as distress, discomfort, or inconvenience where a significant purpose of the contract was to provide pleasure, relaxation, or peace of mind to the consumer (compare such damages for breach of contract, at **9.5.4.3**). However, this is a limited ability to recover damages since there is no right to be paid financial loss damages covering the difference between the market price of the product and the amount paid or payable for it under the contract (i.e. it is possible to recover consequential financial losses and these must also have been reasonably foreseeable at the time of the misrepresentation; compare with the scope of recovery under s. 2(1) MA 1967 where the CPRs do not apply to a B2C contract, and in the B2B context). In addition, under the CPRs 2008 the trader is provided with a due diligence defence (reg. 27J(5)). The overall effect therefore is to reduce considerably the potential damages available to a consumer misrepresentee when compared to the damages available in the B2B context for the same misrepresentation.

14.7 Excluding or limiting liability for misrepresentation

It is possible, in some circumstances, to exclude liability for misrepresentations, by means of an express term in the contract that was allegedly induced by the misrepresentation. In many respects, such exclusions are subject to the same constraints as exclusions of contractual liability (see **Chapter 7**). For example, the clause will be interpreted restrictively and will apply only if it covers the representation in question. So, in *Toomey v Eagle Star Insurance Co. Ltd (No. 2)* [1995] 2 Lloyd's Rep 88, Colman J found that a clause that purported to exclude the remedy of rescission, but which did not expressly refer to rescission on the basis of negligent misrepresentation, applied only to wholly innocent misrepresentation and did not apply to negligent misrepresentation in the sense of the 1967 Act. Similarly, a clause that excludes or limits liability for misrepresentation will have no operation to a misrepresentation that has become a term: Jacob J in *Thomas Witter v TBP Industries Ltd* [1996] 2 All ER 573.

In the context of misrepresentation, a clause that excludes or limits liability for misrepresentation in the commercial context falls within s. 3 MA 1967 (as amended by UCTA 1977, s. 8 and the Consumer Rights Act 2015, Sch. 4).

> **Section 3 Avoidance of provision excluding liability for misrepresentation**
>
> (1) If a contract contains a term which would exclude or restrict—
>
> (a) any liability to which a party to a contract may be subject by reason of any misrepresentation made by him before the contract was made; or
>
> (b) any remedy available to another party to the contract by reason of such a misrepresentation,
>
> that term shall be of no effect except in so far as it satisfies the requirement of reasonableness as stated in section 11(1) of the Unfair Contract Terms Act 1977; and it is for those claiming that the term satisfies that requirement to show that it does.

By s. 3(2) MA 1967, s. 3(1) does not apply to an exclusion or limitation of liability in misrepresentation in a B2C (consumer) contract falling within the CRA 2015. Instead, such a term is subject to the test for unfairness in s. 62 CRA 2015 (see discussion at **7.6.4**). The ability of the trader to avoid certain 'commitments' made by others on the trader's behalf may be regarded as an unfair term on the basis that it is contained in the list in Sch. 2, Part 1 (e.g. para. 17).

14.7.1 Clauses that purport to exclude liability for fraudulent misrepresentation

The law will not accept the exclusion of liability for a person's own fraud—*S. Pearson & Son Ltd v Dublin Corporation* [1907] AC 351—although it is possible to exclude liability for the fraud of employees and others, assuming that clear words are used to do so: *HIH Casualty and General Insurance Co. Ltd v Chase Manhattan Bank* [2003] UKHL 6, [2003] 1 All ER (Comm) 349, and *Foodco UK LLP (t/a Muffin Break) v Henry Boot Developments Ltd* [2010] EWHC 358 (Ch), [166].

In *BSkyB Ltd v HP Enterprise Services UK Ltd (formerly Electronic Data Systems Ltd)* [2010] EWHC 86 (TCC), [2010] BLR 267, 129 Con LR 147, EDS had successfully tendered for the design and implementation of a new customer relationship management (CRM) system for BSkyB. BSkyB later sought damages for fraudulent misrepresentation which it alleged had led to EDS being selected in the first place, and also for negligent misrepresentation and breach of contract. However, there was a contractual limitation of liability (capped at £30 million) and only if the misrepresentation could be established to be fraudulent would it have been possible to avoid this. Ramsey J held that BSkyB succeeded in the claim for fraudulent misrepresentation based on the time estimates that had been submitted by EDS to secure the contract. These were considered to be 'dishonest'.

Where s. 3 applies, this raises a general point of construction in relation to the reasonableness requirement, since it *may* follow that, where the clause in question purports to exclude liability in respect of *all* types of misrepresentation (fraudulent, negligent, and innocent), it is unreasonable because it *could* apply to exclude liability for fraud. This was the approach taken by Jacob J in *Thomas Witter v TBP Industries Ltd* [1996] 2 All ER 573. However, subsequent decisions of the High Court have not accepted this position, e.g. the decision of Judge Raymond Jack QC in *Government of Zanzibar v British Aerospace Ltd* [2000] 1 WLR 2333, at pp. 2346–7, and Gloster J in *Six Continent Hotels Inc. v Event Hotels GmbH* [2006] EWHC 2317 (QB), (2006) 150 SJLB 1251. In *Six Continent*, Gloster J noted that since any clauses excluding liability could not, as a matter of construction, cover fraud, it could not be the intention to include it within the scope of a clause that purported to cover *all* liability. It followed that the clause could apply to non-fraudulent misrepresentations and was not therefore automatically unreasonable under s. 3. This approach was also accepted by Lewison J in *Foodco UK LLP (t/a Muffin Break) v Henry Boot Developments Ltd* [2010] EWHC 358 (Ch).

14.7.2 The scope of s. 3

14.7.2.1 'Entire agreement' and 'non-reliance' clauses

Since s. 3 applies only to clauses that exclude or restrict liability or remedies for misrepresentation, it can be argued that clauses that are phrased in terms of defining the basic duty owed are outside its scope and so not subject to the reasonableness test, although it must be doubted that this was the legislative intention.

Contracts frequently contain entire agreement clauses, which typically provide that the written document comprises all of the terms of the contract between the parties and often add a statement, although these come in various forms, that the contractor is not accepting responsibility for the information supplied or that the other party is not to be taken to be relying on the clause. These are, in effect, denials of actionable misrepresentations.

In *Inntrepreneur Pub Co. v East Crown Ltd* [2000] 2 Lloyd's Rep 611 (discussed at **6.2.1.4**), Lightman J distinguished between the first part of the clause, which stated that the agreement represented the 'entire agreement between the parties', and the second part of the clause, providing that the party had 'not relied upon any advice or statement of the Company or its solicitors' before executing the agreement (so called 'non-reliance' clauses). He considered that the 'entire agreement' wording had the purpose of preventing 'a party to a written agreement from threshing through the undergrowth and finding in the course of negotiations some (chance) remark or statement (often long forgotten or difficult to recall or explain) on which to found a claim' (para. 7). It operated to define where the terms of the contract could be found (i.e. in the written document only). An 'entire agreement' clause did not 'preclude a claim in misrepresentation, for the denial of contractual force cannot affect the status of a statement as a misrepresentation'. That part of the clause was thus not an exclusion clause and was not caught by s. 3.

By contrast, Lightman J considered that the second part of the clause purported to exclude the existence of any liability for actionable misrepresentation and was therefore subject to s. 3 of the MA 1967. It had to be shown to be reasonable in order to be relied upon. The same approach was also adopted by Judge Raymond Jack QC in *Government of Zanzibar v British Aerospace (Lancaster House) Ltd* [2000] 1 WLR 2333. The judge distinguished the entire agreement clause [A] from clause [B], which excluded liability for misrepresentation.

A clause which simply provided '12.4 This contract is the entire agreement between the parties' in *Mears Ltd v Shoreline Housing Partnership Ltd* [2013] EWCA Civ 639, [2013] BLR 393, [16], was held not to exclude liability for misrepresentation since this needed to be expressly stated.

14.7.2.2 'No reliance' clauses and s. 3

Lightman J in *Inntrepreneur* made clear that s. 3 applied to a 'no reliance' clause. That was confirmed by the Court of Appeal in *First Tower Trustees Ltd v CDS (Superstores International) Ltd* [2018] EWCA Civ 1396. Here, a tenant of commercial premises sought damages for false statements by the landlord to the effect that there was no problem with asbestos. The lease provided that the tenant acknowledged that the lease had not been entered into in reliance wholly or partly on any statement made by the landlord or its solicitors. The landlord argued that the clause could not be reviewed under s. 3 because it created a contractual estoppel preventing the tenant from arguing that there had been reliance. The Court of Appeal accepted the utility of 'no reliance' clauses and that there was no objection to the parties agreeing to bind themselves by contract to accept a particular state of affairs even though that state of affairs had no truth in reality. In *First Tower* the Court of Appeal relied for this proposition upon its own decision in *Springwell Navigation Corporation v JP Morgan Chase Bank (formerly Chase Manhattan Bank)* [2010] EWCA Civ 1221, [2010] 2 CLC 705, where it was held that a purchaser of securities was bound on the basis of a contractual estoppel by the statement in these securities and in dealing letters that no representation or warranty had been made by Chase Manhattan. Aikens LJ noted, at [144], that 'I see commercial utility in such clauses being enforceable, so that the parties know precisely the basis on which they are entering into their contractual relationship.'

However, the Court of Appeal in *First Tower* went on to hold that the utility of such clauses did not mean that they fell outside s. 3 of the MA 1967. That was to conflate the separate questions of the effect of the clause and its reasonableness. The clause prevented reliance on misrepresentation, but the clause did not mean that there was no misrepresentation in the first place. Leggatt LJ expressed the point with characteristic clarity at [99]:

> Even if, by giving the language of section 3 of the Act a strained interpretation, a distinction could be drawn between a contract term which would exclude liability and a term which would prevent liability from arising, there is no reason to draw such a formalistic distinction and good reason not to interpret section 3 in a way which omits the latter type of term from its scope. The result of doing so would be that a lawyer drafting boilerplate provisions could avoid the application of section 3 purely by the choice of words in which the clause is phrased. A clause stating that a party will have no liability for any representation made or on which the other party has relied on any view falls within section 3 and is subject to the requirement of reasonableness. But on this interpretation, if instead the clause were worded to say that A agrees not to assert that B has made or that A has relied on any representation, section 3 would not apply. No rational legislator could have intended that the need for a contract term to satisfy a test of reasonableness could be avoided simply by felicity in drafting the contract term.

14.7.2.3 Clauses in the consumer context

Non-reliance clauses can also be found in consumer contracts and they have also needed to be evaluated to determine whether they purport to exclude or limit liability for misrepresentation. Until recently, clauses which excluded or restricted liability or remedies for misrepresentation in the consumer context needed to be assessed for reasonableness in accordance with ss. 3 and 11 of UCTA 1977 (*Lloyd v Browning* [2013] EWCA Civ 1637, [2014] 1 P & CR 11, [31] *per* Davis LJ). In *Lloyd v Browning* a term which provided that the buyer entered into the contract solely as a result of his inspection of the property and that no statement by the seller, other than responses to the pre-contract enquiries, had induced him to enter into the contract, was held to be a term that fell within s. 3 and it was assessed as a reasonable term in the context of that contract.

Such terms will no longer be subjected to the s. 3 reasonableness test where the contract falls within the CRA 2015 as a contract between a trader and a consumer. Instead, any term that is not a core term will not be binding on the consumer if it is unfair (CRA 2015, s. 62; discussed at **7.6.4**). This is to be welcomed since it will avoid some of the complexities required to determine whether a particular clause fell within s. 3 as 'excluding or restricting' liability or remedies for misrepresentation. Part 2 of the CRA 2015 applies to 'terms, conditions or notices' in a more general sense.

The difficulties are exemplified in the examples given by Toulson J in *IFE Fund SA v Goldman Sachs International*, at [68]–[69], of statements made by the seller of a car: (a) 'I have serviced the car since it was new, it has had only one owner and the clock reading is accurate but those statements are not representations on which you can rely'; and (b) 'The clock reading is 20,000 miles, but I have no knowledge whether the reading is true or false.' The statements in (a) would be representations and would fall within the statutory control in s. 3, despite the statement that they are not representations. However, the qualifying words in (b) do not amount to an attempt to exclude liability for a false representation as to mileage, but relate to the scope of the statement made.

In *Raiffeisen Zentralbank*, at [306]–[307], Christopher Clarke J took a version of Toulson LJ's example:

> The dealer says '*I have serviced the car since it was new, it has had only one owner and the clock reading is accurate*'. He is not fraudulent but mistaken, carelessly confusing one car for another, in relation to which the statement is true. Relying on his statement the buyer purchases the car. Without it he would not have

done so. The car has had several owners, no known service history, and the clock reading is substantially inaccurate. The contract of sale provides (in one of many paragraphs on the back of the form which the buyer does not read and to which his attention is not directed) that the buyer is entering into the contract on the basis that no representations have been made to, or relied on by, the purchaser. In that example there has been a clear statement of fact, on a matter said to be within the representor's personal knowledge, which was in fact intended to induce the contract, upon which the purchaser in fact relied, which is false. If section 3 has no application in respect of a contractual estoppel there is no further control mechanism on its operation, which does not require detrimental reliance. The seller (and any other similar seller) may, subject to any applicable consumer protection laws, make non-fraudulent misrepresentations of that type with impunity.

The judge therefore considered that the limitations on exclusions of liability in s. 3 should apply in this situation and that this was consistent with the decision in *Cremdean Properties Ltd v Nash* (1977) 244 EG 547 that clauses that purport to deny that there has been any actionable misrepresentation at all fell within s. 3. Such clauses seek to avoid liability for what, absent the clause, would be clear liability in misrepresentation. To permit any other position would undermine the purpose of the legislation.

Clauses that state that there is no acceptance of responsibility may be designed to indicate that what appears to be a statement of fact is no more than opinion, or is based on what the statement maker has been told by others, and so not an actionable representation at all, e.g. 'The clock says 20,000 but I do not know whether that is true.' This clause indicates that the statement maker is not accepting responsibility. Christopher Clarke J in *Raiffeisen* was content to conclude that 'a suitably drafted clause' may be taken as indicating that there are no representations being made or that no representations can be relied upon. However, he added, at [315]:

Per contra, to tell the man in the street that the car you are selling him is perfect and then agree that the basis of your contract is that no representations have been made or relied on, may be nothing more than an attempt retrospectively to alter the character and effect of what has gone before, and in substance an attempt to exclude or restrict liability.

This would now seem to be captured as a term which will be subject to scrutiny on the basis of unfairness by Part 2 of the CRA 2015 and the specific language of s. 3 is no longer relevant in this B2C context.

14.7.2.4 Limiting or excluding the authority of agents

Even in the absence of a non-reliance clause, if the term in question limits or excludes the authority of an agent to make representations that will bind the principal, it amounts to a clause restricting the authority of agents and does not therefore come within the definition of an exclusion or limitation clause under UCTA 1977 and, as a result, will not fall within s. 3 MA 1967: *Overbrook Estates Ltd v Glencombe Properties Ltd* [1974] 1 WLR 1353.

In the context of consumer contracts to which Part 2 of the Consumer Rights Act (CRA) 2015 applies, it may be that a clause 'limiting the trader's obligation to respect commitments undertaken by the trader's agents or making the trader's commitments subject to compliance with a particular formality', such as approval of the principal, may be an unfair term and, as such, not binding on the consumer as an unfair term (CRA 2015, s. 62 and Sch. 2, Part 1, para. 17).

14.7.3 The application of the reasonableness requirement, s. 3 MA 1967 (B2B)

If s. 3 applies, any exclusion clause will be effective only if the party seeking to rely on it to avoid liability can satisfy the burden of proving that, at the time of contracting, it was reasonable, having regard to the circumstances within the contemplation of the parties (UCTA 1977, s. 11(1)). The operation of the reasonableness test is considered in more detail in relation to clauses excluding contractual liability (see **7.5.5**). Unsurprisingly, in this context, the courts use similar factors.

In *Lloyd v Browning* [2013] EWCA Civ 1637, [2014] 1 P & CR 11 (for facts see **14.7.2.3**), the non-reliance clause was considered to be reasonable because it was a term in common use, and used by the regional law society. The parties were in equal negotiating positions and each had instructed legal advisers. In addition, the term could be justified by the fact that a contract for the sale of land was one that required all agreed terms to be in one contractual document to be signed by both parties (see **5.4.2.2.1**).

However, a clause is more likely to be unreasonable where the statement maker is seeking to exclude liability for representations based on facts that are only within the knowledge of the statement maker and not that of the other party: e.g. *Howard Marine & Dredging Co. Ltd v A. Ogden & Sons (Excavations) Ltd* [1978] QB 574. Similarly, a clause is more likely to be unreasonable where it is against standard industry practice. In *First Tower Trustees Ltd v CDS (Superstores International) Ltd* (for facts see **14.7.2.2**), the Court of Appeal held a 'no reliance' clause unreasonable: although the parties were of equal bargaining power, the terms were negotiated, and the parties had retained solicitors, the clause prevented reliance on anything said by the defendant's solicitors whereas in the conveyancing world pre-contractual inquiries were the standard means of protection for those seeking to obtain an interest in land. Lewison LJ stated, at [75]: 'I do not consider that there is any ground in this case for interfering with the judge's overall assessment of the application of the test of reasonableness. Indeed, in my judgment, he was right to stress the importance of pre-contract enquiries in the field of conveyancing; and right in the conclusion to which he came. As the judge said, if clause 5.8 governs the landlords' liability the important function of replies to enquiries before contract becomes worthless.' Lewison LJ added (at [75]) that it was possible to find a case where, 'on exceptional facts, a clause which precludes reliance on replies to enquiries before contract might be held to satisfy the test of reasonableness even where those replies have in fact been relied on, I find it very hard to imagine what those facts might be'. Simply agreeing with Lewison LJ, Leggatt LJ nevertheless echoed the exceptional nature of such clause by reiterating that applying a reasonable test to any exclusion of misrepresentation was a necessary 'control mechanism' by the courts, whose duty was to 'uphold the policy which Parliament had thought right to adopt' (at [104]).

MULTIPLE-CHOICE QUESTIONS

Test your knowledge by trying this chapter's **multiple-choice questions**:
www.oup.com/uk/poole

Misrepresentation

14

FURTHER READING

General

Cartwright, *Misrepresentation, Mistake and Non-Disclosure*, 3rd edn (Sweet and Maxwell, 2012).

Devenney and Howells, 'Integrating remedies for misrepresentation: co-ordinating a coherent and principled framework' in Merkin and Devenney (eds.), *Essays in Memory of Professor Jill Poole* (Informa Law, 2018), ch. 5.

Loi, 'Precontractual misrepresentation: mistaken belief induced by mis-statements' [2017] JBL 598.

Spark, *Vitiation of Contracts: International Contractual Principles and English Law* (Cambridge University Press, 2013).

Rescission

Poole and Keyser, 'Justifying partial rescission in English law' (2005) 121 LQR 273.

Misrepresentation Act 1967

Atiyah and Treitel, 'Misrepresentation Act 1967' (1967) 30 MLR 369.

Beale, 'Damages in lieu of rescission for misrepresentation' (1995) 111 LQR 60.

Beale, 'Points on misrepresentation' (1995) 111 LQR 385.

Brown and Chandler, 'Deceit, damages and the Misrepresentation Act 1967, s. 2(1)' [1992] LMCLQ 40.

Cartwright, 'Damages for misrepresentation' [1987] Conv 423.

Chandler, 'Fraud: damages and opportunity costs' (1994) 110 LQR 35.

Chandler and Higgins, 'Contributory negligence and the Misrepresentation Act 1967, s. 2(1)' [1994] LMCLQ 326.

Davies, 'Rescission for misrepresentation' (2016) 75 CLJ 15.

Halson, 'Damages for the tort of deceit' [1997] LMCLQ 423.

Handley, 'Exclusion clauses for fraud' (2003) 119 LQR 537.

Hooley, 'Damages and the Misrepresentation Act 1967' (1991) 107 LQR 547.

Lee, 'Proof of inducement on the law of misrepresentation' [2017] LMCLQ 150.

Marks, 'Loss of profits in damages for deceit' (1992) 108 LQR 386.

Oakley, 'Measure of damages for misrepresentation' [1992] CLJ 9.

Oakley, 'Contributory negligence of a fraudulent representee' [1994] CLJ 218.

Parker, 'Fraudulent bills of lading and bankers' commercial credits: deceit, contributory negligence and directors' personal liability' [2003] LMCLQ 1.

Poole and Devenney, 'Reforming damages for misrepresentation: the case for coherent aims and principles' [2007] JBL 269.

Turner, 'Rescission and damages in lieu of the MA 1967' (2016) 132 LQR 388.

Wadsley, 'Measures in misrepresentation: recent steps in awarding damages' (1992) 55 MLR 698.

Chapter 15

Duress, undue influence, and unconscionable bargains

SUMMARY OF THE ISSUES

This chapter will examine two recognized doctrines of English law that provide a means for a claimant to avoid a concluded contract on the basis that threats or unfair pressures or influence were exerted to persuade the claimant to contract. In addition, more generally, it assesses the circumstances in which the courts have intervened to prevent one party from taking advantage of another.

- The first of the recognized doctrines is the doctrine of duress that takes the form of some form of coercion or threat to the person, property, or to a person's financial interests (economic duress). The doctrine of economic duress is now seen as the primary mechanism to prevent promises obtained by extortion from being enforceable, but it is a comparatively new doctrine and is still being developed.

- To succeed in a claim (or defence) based on economic duress, it must be established that there is some illegitimate pressure or threat that amounts to a significant cause inducing the claimant to contract because the claimant has no real practical choice other than to agree. In addition, the victim of duress will need to protest at the time or shortly thereafter. However, the exact meaning of these ingredients is unclear—particularly the meaning of 'illegitimate pressure' and the effect of so-called 'lawful act duress'.

- Undue influence is an equitable doctrine that can arise in two ways: actual undue influence (which is similar to duress, because it arises from illegitimate pressure and abuse exerted by one party over the other); and circumstances in which there is an evidential presumption that influence has been exercised, which may become an evidential presumption of undue influence where there is something in the transaction that 'is suspicious or calls for an explanation' (i.e. of such a size, nature, or context as to raise suspicions). In the case of presumptive undue influence, the conclusion of influence may arise automatically in the case of certain types of protected relationship, but needs to be established on the facts in other cases on the basis that there is a relationship of trust and confidence between the particular parties. Where undue influence is established as between the contracting parties, the victim can have the transaction set aside.

- A common situation in which undue influence has been applied is where one of two parties to a relationship (typically, in the decided cases, the wife) gives security in order to support the debts of her husband (i.e. her contract is with the lender—someone other than the person exercising the influence), the lender will be affected by the actions of the person exercising the undue influence (e.g. her husband) where that lender is fixed with constructive notice of the other's undue influence. This will occur where the lender is 'put on inquiry' (and may occur in all cases in which a wife stands surety for her husband's debts and not for any joint purpose). Lenders are required to take precise steps (involving ensuring that the practical implications of the proposed transaction have been explained to the wife) or the lenders risk losing their security.

• The final issue in this chapter notes that although inequality of bargaining power per se will not be sufficient to prompt interference in a transaction in English law, principles do exist to prevent 'an abuse' of a position of strength and to protect those in weaker positions, such as consumers. Parliament has had a role to play in terms of regulating substantive unfairness, including a provision in the Consumer Credit Act 1974 enabling the courts to interfere in 'unfair credit agreements' (ss. 140A–D). There is also considerable existing European-led legislation to protect consumers. The Consumer Protection from Unfair Trading Regulations 2008, SI 2008/1277, implementing the Unfair Commercial Practices Directive 2005/29/EC prohibit certain forms of behaviour that fall within the remit of this chapter and provide civil rights of redress in some circumstances in relation to certain prohibited unfair commercial practices: see the Consumer Protection (Amendment) Regulations 2014, SI 2014/870 (at **15.3.2** and **14.1.2**).

General background

This chapter examines doctrines relating to circumstances surrounding the making of the contract. In the context of consumer contracts, Parliament has stepped in to protect consumers against various high-pressure sales techniques, in particular by allowing consumers a 'cooling-off' period during which time the agreement can be cancelled: see e.g. the Consumer Credit Act (CCA) 1974 and the Consumer Contracts (Information, Cancellation and Additional Payments) Regulations 2013, SI 2013/3134 (regs. 29 and 30 extend the cooling-off period from 7 days to 14 days). There are also recognized general doctrines applying to instances in which unfair and illegitimate pressure or threats have been applied, or unfair advantage has been taken by one party over the other, in order to persuade a party to contract or to agree a variation of the contract on disadvantageous terms. Where this is the case and either the doctrine of duress or undue influence applies, the contract is voidable (i.e. it can be set aside by the victim or complainant). The doctrine of duress, in particular, is likely to be highly relevant in the context of commercial contracts. However, there is a fine line to be drawn here, because some commercial pressure in negotiating is both normal and acceptable.

15.1 Duress

15.1.1 The limited early doctrine

The common law always accepted that some forms of coercion in the making of contracts resulted in the victim of the coercion being afforded a remedy, in that the contract would be set aside and any money paid could be recovered. However, the forms of coercion recognized as having such an effect were very limited. There was no doubt that duress to the person had such an effect, whether it took the form of threatened or actual violence (*Barton v Armstrong* [1976]

1 AC 104), creating a frightening and threatening environment (*Antonio v Antonio* [2010] EWHC 1199 (QB)), or a threat of imprisonment (*Williams v Bayley* (1886) LR 1 HL 200, see **15.2.3**)—although the latter rule arose only after the intervention of equity. As such, the doctrine was of little significance, since the number of cases of duress to the person has always been small.

It is also settled that a threat to seize another's property or to damage it (duress to property) will justify a claim of duress and result in the ensuing contract being set aside: see Lord Goff in *Dimskal Shipping Co. SA v International Transport Workers' Federation, The Evia Luck* [1991] 4 All ER 871, at p. 878.

In addition, in the mid-1960s the courts, led by Lord Denning MR, focused on the fairness of economic pressures leading to a contractual promise. Thus, in *D. & C. Builders v Rees* [1966] 2 QB 617 (see **4.8.4**), Lord Denning refused to apply the promissory estoppel doctrine to enforce a promise to accept a payment in final settlement of a debt, on the express ground that the promise had been extracted by unfair pressure and the creditor had been 'held to ransom', since the debtor knew of the creditor's financial difficulties and had sought to take advantage. The result of these developments has been the emergence of a new and far more significant doctrine of economic duress.

15.1.2 Economic duress

The idea that mere economic duress (threats to a person's financial or business interests) might be a ground upon which a contract could be set aside was first canvassed by Kerr J in *Occidental Worldwide Investment Corporation v Skibs A/S Avanti, The Siboen and The Sibotre* [1976] 1 Lloyd's Rep 293. The typical situation raising the possibility of a claim of economic duress is where one party threatens breach of contract unless the contract is renegotiated and the other agrees, rather than face the disastrous consequences that it is feared will follow from breach. However, the area is fraught with difficulty, since companies which deal with each other on a regular basis will often agree quite voluntarily to renegotiate a contract in a context of cooperation. It would be unfortunate if they were to be threatened by the economic duress doctrine. On the other hand, changes to the law relating to consideration, particularly in the area of alterations to commercial contracts—see *Williams v Roffey Bros. & Nicholls (Contractors) Ltd* [1991] 1 QB 1 (**4.4.4**)—have increased the need for such a clear and recognized doctrine in English law.

In the past, contract changes achieved by means of unfair pressure or extortion could be resisted on the formal ground of absence of consideration: see *Stilk v Myrick* (1809) 2 Camp 317, 6 Esp 129 (**4.4.4**), and *Atlas Express Ltd v Kafco (Importers & Distributors) Ltd* [1989] 1 All ER 641. A restrictive approach to the definition of consideration was required to achieve this (i.e. the performance of an existing duty could not be a good consideration because there was no additional legal benefit or detriment). However, in *Williams v Roffey Bros.*, the Court of Appeal cited the availability of the doctrine of economic duress as the mechanism for preventing the enforceability of promises obtained as a result of extortion in order to justify its more relaxed approach to finding consideration. The result of this development is that the emphasis appears to have shifted from the doctrine of consideration towards the doctrine of economic duress in order to prevent promises obtained by extortion, or improper threats, from being enforceable. It is therefore vital that the doctrine be clearly defined. However, as we shall see, the doctrine is a comparatively recent development in English law and, as such, is still developing.

15.1.2.1 Establishing economic duress

In *Pao On v Lau Yiu Long* [1980] AC 614 (see also **4.3.3.2**), the Privy Council approved the doctrine of economic duress and attempted to identify its essential ingredients. Lord Scarman identified two essential conditions for the operation of the doctrine:

1. 'coercion of the will that vitiates consent'; and

2. that the pressure or threat must be illegitimate.

In *DSND Subsea Ltd v Petroleum Geo Services ASA* [2000] BLR 530, at [131], Dyson J identified the ingredients of actionable duress, as they have subsequently developed:

> [T]here must be pressure, (a) whose practical effect is that there is compulsion on, or lack of practical choice for, the victim, (b) which is illegitimate, and (c) which is a significant cause inducing the claimant to enter into the contract.

15.1.2.2 Coercion of the will that vitiates consent

The question in *Pao On v Lau Yiu Long* [1980] AC 614 was whether there had been the necessary coercion of the will vitiating consent.

> Under the terms of a contract, the claimants were to receive shares in the Fu Chip Company. The defendants, the majority shareholders in the Fu Chip Company, had been concerned that if the claimants were to choose to sell all of these shares at one time, there would be a fall in the value of their shareholdings. The claimants therefore agreed with the company that they would not sell 60 per cent of their shares for one year. The claimants then threatened not to perform this promise unless the defendants agreed to indemnify them against any loss in the value of their shares in this one-year period. Fearing delays and a loss of confidence in the company if the deal were not completed, the defendants signed an indemnity agreeing to compensate the claimants if the value of these shares were to fall below $2.50 a share. The share price fell and the claimants sought to rely on the indemnity. However, the defendants claimed that the indemnity had been obtained as a result of duress.
>
> Lord Scarman, giving the advice of the Privy Council, said that there was nothing wrong in principle in recognizing economic duress as a factor making contracts voidable. The essence of the rule, he said, at pp. 635C and 636C, was that 'there must be a coercion of will such that there was no true consent . . . it must be shown that the contract entered into was not a voluntary act'. It was essential to distinguish between mere commercial pressure, which is an everyday incident of the hard-nosed bargaining that goes on in the business world, and duress. On the facts in *Pao On*, Lord Scarman emphasized the question of whether there was a realistic alternative open to the defendants. It was held that the defendants had coolly analysed the options and had taken a commercial decision that the risk to the company of non-performance was greater than the risk of the need to pay under the indemnity. Accordingly, there was no coercion of the will and no duress.

15.1.2.2.1 No realistic choice other than to agree

Nevertheless, it has long been recognized that it is technically incorrect to argue that duress is based upon consent being vitiated, so that the agreement is not voluntary. Atiyah (1982) 98 LQR 197 strongly criticized this requirement and Lord Goff, in *Dimskal Shipping Co. SA v International Transport Workers' Federation, The Evia Luck* [1991] 4 All ER 871, at p. 878, stated that he doubted whether it was helpful to speak of a person's will being coerced. Victims of duress know exactly what they are doing and submit intentionally. In the criminal law, the House of Lords has been clear in saying that the defence of duress does not depend upon the absence of a voluntary act, but rather depends upon intentional submission in the face of no other practical alternative: *Lynch v DPP for Northern Ireland* [1975] AC 653. The same must be true of contract, so that duress does not negate the existence of consent, but is based upon a finding that the victim had no other realistic option available other than to agree. In *Universe Tankships Inc. of Monrovia v International Transport Workers' Federation, The Universe Sentinel* [1983] 1 AC 366, Lords Diplock and Scarman admitted that duress in contract law does not involve the destruction of will, but intentional submission to the inevitable. This reasoning is borne out by the fact that duress renders a contract voidable and not void.

In light of this debate, the first ingredient for duress in *Pao On v Lau Yiu Long* [1980] AC 614 has been reformulated as 'no realistic choice', rather than in terms of 'coercion of the will vitiating consent': see e.g. the statement of Dyson J in *DSND Subsea Ltd v Petroleum Geo Services ASA* [2000] BLR 530, which refers to compulsion and lack of practical choice.

B. & S. Contracts & Design Ltd v Victor Green Publications Ltd [1984] ICR 419 provides a useful example of a situation in which there was no practical choice other than to agree.

> The claimants were to erect exhibition stands for the defendants, who had let these stands to various exhibitors. However, a week before the date of the exhibition, the claimants' workers refused to work unless a pay demand was met. The defendants therefore paid £4,500 in order to avoid serious losses, which would have resulted from the claims against them by disappointed exhibitors. However, the defendants then deducted this figure from the contract price paid to the claimants. The claimants claimed the balance. The Court of Appeal held that the defendants had been affected by duress, because they had no realistic choice other than to pay. An action for breach of contract against the claimants, although technically possible, was unrealistic because it would have been too damaging.

In *Carillion Construction Ltd v Felix (UK) Ltd* [2001] BLR 1, it was held that threats to withhold deliveries when under a contractual obligation to use best endeavours to prevent delay amounted to illegitimate threats, and it was held to be unrealistic to expect the other party to seek a mandatory injunction to ensure performance. Similarly, in *Atlas Express Ltd v Kafco (Importers & Distributors) Ltd* [1989] 1 All ER 641, the defendant had no realistic choice other than to sign a revised contract for carriage of its goods because it could not, at such short notice, have obtained alternative carriage for the goods; without the ability to deliver, it would have lost the contract to supply its major customer (Woolworth). In *Adam Opel GmbH v Mitras Automotive Ltd* [2007] EWHC 3205 (QB), [2008] Bus LR Digest D55, there was a threat to stop supplies of a component needed in the manufacture of vans unless the increased price and compensation were paid. There was no realistic choice other than to pay because there were no alternatives; production would have halted within 24 hours and there would have been significant consequences for other suppliers of parts for these vans.

15.1.2.3 **Illegitimate pressure or threat**

15.1.2.3.1 *Pressure or threat*

In a claim for economic duress, there must be pressure or a threat. This can lead to fine distinctions of fact. For example, in *Williams v Roffey Bros.* [1991] 1 QB 1, it was vitally important that the impetus for the promise to pay more money came from the main contractor and so had not been obtained as a result of threats of non-performance from the subcontractor. It is less clear, however, what the position would be where one contracting party simply advises the other of difficulties or the possibility of non-performance. It would seem to be a question of fact as to whether this amounts to 'pressure' in all of the circumstances.

15.1.2.3.2 *The pressure or threat must be illegitimate*

The pressure or threat must also be illegitimate. It is unclear where the line between legitimate and illegitimate pressures or threats is to be drawn. In *DSND Subsea Ltd v Petroleum Geo Services ASA* [2000] BLR 530, at [131], Dyson J stated that 'illegitimate pressure must be distinguished from the rough and tumble of the pressures of normal commercial bargaining'. Some pressure is clearly legitimate, and it is vitally important to the scope of the doctrine of economic duress that the line between legitimate and illegitimate pressure should be drawn with some certainty.

In ***R v HM Attorney-General for England and Wales*** [2003] UKPC 22, [2003] EMLR 24, an SAS member alleged that he had been subjected to duress when he signed a confidentiality agreement to cover the period after he left the SAS. It was alleged that he had been threatened with return to his ordinary unit if he did not sign the agreement. However, this threat was considered to be a lawful threat, since the Ministry of Defence had the ability to make such a transfer and the SAS was reasonably entitled to regard anyone unwilling to accept the confidentiality agreement as unsuitable to be a member of the SAS. Therefore there was no duress and the decision to sign was no more than a matter of choice for the individual soldier, albeit one where there was 'overwhelming pressure' to sign.

On the other hand, an example of clear illegitimate pressure is provided by the facts of *Vantage Navigation Corporation v Suhail and Saud Bahwan Building Materials LLC, The Alev* [1989] 1 Lloyd's Rep 138.

The charterers had defaulted on the payment of hire for the vessel, but the claimants, the shipowners, were obliged by the contract to carry the cargo on board the vessel to its destination. Nevertheless, they threatened not to ship the cargo unless the defendants, the cargo owners, paid the claimants the sum demanded. The defendants agreed, but subsequently succeeded in a plea of duress. The pressure exerted by the claimants was illegitimate, since the claimants had no rights over the goods and could not refuse to deliver the cargo.

In *Kolmar Group AG v Traxpo Enterprises Pvt Ltd* [2010] EWHC 113 (Comm), [2011] 1 All ER (Comm) 46, [2010] 1 CLC 256, at [92], Christopher Clarke J noted that 'a threat to break a contract will generally be regarded as illegitimate, particularly where the defendant must know that it would be in breach of contract if the threat were implemented'. A further example involves a threat by a party following that party's own breach. In *Progress Bulk Carriers Ltd v Tube City IMS LLC, The Cenk Kaptanoglu* [2012] EWHC 273 (Comm), [2012] 1 CLC 365, [2012] 2 All ER (Comm) 855, the shipowner had refused to supply an alternative vessel unless the charterer waived its right to full compensation for the shipowner's breach. This amounted to illegitimate pressure.

In *Universe Tankships Inc. of Monrovia v International Transport Workers' Federation, The Universe Sentinel* [1983] 1 AC 366, the issue of the legitimacy of the pressure exerted hinged upon the interpretation of the Trade Union and Labour Relations Act 1974.

The case concerned threats by a trade union to 'black' vessels, in the sense that no tugs would be provided to assist the vessels to leave harbour unless the shipowner made a payment to the trade union. If the vessels were unable to leave the harbour, the losses would have been considerable, so the shipowner paid and then claimed the return of this money. The trade union argued that its actions were protected as actions 'in contemplation of a trade dispute' under the 1974 Act.

The majority of the House of Lords considered that the threats were illegitimate because the trade union was not protected by this legislation. However, the minority (Lords Scarman and Brandon) thought that the trade union was protected by the legislation, so that the threat was *prima facie* lawful. However, a lawful threat would constitute duress if used, as here, to further an illegitimate purpose such as blackmail.

In *R v HM Attorney-General for England and Wales*, the Privy Council cited, with approval, the comments of Lord Scarman in *The Universe Sentinel* on the question of identification of illegitimate pressure. Lord Scarman had stated that it was necessary to examine both the nature of the pressure and the nature of the demand that the pressure is applied to support, so that a threat of unlawful action would generally be regarded as illegitimate pressure, although a threat of lawful action would not necessarily mean that the pressure was legitimate, e.g. blackmail using a lawful threat.

Is there a category of lawful act duress?

In the 1990s, the Court of Appeal had to address the question of whether there is a more general category of lawful act duress, i.e. whether lawful (if ultimately unreasonable) demands can amount to illegitimate pressure.

In *CTN Cash and Carry Ltd v Gallagher Ltd* [1994] 4 All ER 714, the defendants had mistakenly sent a shipment of cigarettes to the wrong place of business for the claimants. The claimants undertook to remedy the situation, but before the cigarettes could be moved, there was a burglary and they were stolen. The defendants genuinely, but mistakenly, believed that the cigarettes were at the claimants' risk and so invoiced them for the price, threatening to withdraw credit facilities if the price was not paid. Under the terms of their arrangement, the credit facilities could lawfully be withdrawn at any time. Faced with a choice between two evils, the claimants opted to pay the price and subsequently reclaimed the money paid on the basis that the payment had been made under duress. In finding for the defendants and concluding that there was no duress on the facts, Steyn LJ pointed to three key elements:

- the arm's-length commercial dealings between two trading companies;
- the lawful nature of the threat; and
- the bona fide belief in their entitlement on the part of the defendants.

To allow a claim based on lawful act duress in such circumstances would inevitably cause uncertainty in commercial dealings, and a commercial concern engaged in apparently arm's-length bargaining will find it very difficult to base a claim on lawful act duress. However, Steyn LJ was reluctant to say that 'lawful act duress' could never be established and the position on whether there can be 'lawful act duress' in the consumer context remains open.

Subsequent case law has followed the approach in *CTN Cash & Carry*, e.g. in *Progress Bulk Carriers Ltd v Tube City IMS LLC, The Cenk Kaptanoglu* [2012] EWHC 273 (Comm), [2012] 1 CLC 365, [2012] 2 All ER (Comm) 855, Cooke J considered that although 'illegitimate pressure' could be constituted by conduct that was not in itself unlawful, it would be an unusual case in which that were so, particularly in the commercial context.

In *GMAC Commercial Credit Ltd v Dearden*, unreported, 28 May 2002, a claim based on lawful act duress was firmly rejected on the basis that the pressure applied was normal commercial pressure. Directors of a company had signed personal guarantees in exchange for further funds being released to the company. They later alleged that these guarantees had been obtained as a result of economic duress, since they had signed the guarantees owing to concern about the company's financial reputation with its customers and suppliers. The judge held that this was not economic duress; the pressure was normal and legitimate in such commercial arrangements, and the lender had acted in good faith.

Equally, a threat to withdraw a company's credit facilities as a result of bad debts when there was no express contract to maintain those facilities is liable to be viewed as perfectly justifiable commercial behaviour. In *Bank of Scotland plc v Cohen*, unreported, 16 January 2013, in the context of a bank's demand for a personal guarantee from a creditworthy borrower in order to secure a company loan to enable completion to take place on a purchase of properties by the company, the court held that there was no prospect of succeeding in an argument that the guarantee was voidable based on economic duress. This was because the Cohens had submitted a signed declaration that they had received independent legal advice and, according to the judge, they had entered into the loan agreements freely and as a result of their poor commercial judgment in exchanging contracts ahead of securing the loan facility. In addition, they had not objected at the time or shortly thereafter, but had waited for the guarantee to be enforced.

A recent example of another unsuccessful economic duress argument in the context of a guarantee is provided by the decision in *Bank of India v Riat* [2014] EWHC 1775 (Ch). The judge held that a requirement to give a personal guarantee was standard practice for this lender, and in commercial lending generally. Legal advice had been obtained and no objections made as a consequence. In addition, other financing options were available. It follows that such a claim is unlikely to succeed because there will tend to be a commercial justification underpinning the giving of personal guarantees and the existence of the solicitor's certificate to the lender (in order for the bank to avoid being fixed with constructive notice of any undue influence) will add to the difficulties in pursuing a claim based on economic duress. In *Flying Music Co. Ltd v Theater Entertainment SA* [2017] EWHC 3192 (QB) it was similarly held that a guarantee had not been entered into under duress. The defendant, a Greek theatre promoter, agreed to stage the claimant's production of the Michael Jackson musical, *Thriller Live*. The claimant threatened to cancel further performances in the light of unrest in Greece, and a personal guarantee of payment was given by the defendant's controller, who was a lawyer. In the event a number of the performances had to be cancelled. The court's view was that no duress had been involved in the making of the guarantee: the threat to cancel future performances was lawful, and indeed justified by previous payment defaults and low box office receipts; and the signatory was a lawyer.

A case where the pressure was found to have crossed the line from legitimate to illegitimate was *Times Travel (UK) Ltd v Pakistan International Airlines Corp.* [2017] EWHC 1367 (Ch). The case is perhaps best viewed as one where the illegitimate conduct was not the threat of terminating the contract (which was lawful) but the imposition on the claimant of the requirement to forego existing legal right, i.e. akin to blackmail of the type identified in *The Universe Sentinel*.

In *Times Travel* the claimant operated a small, family-run travel agency mainly selling airline tickets to the Pakistani community in the Midlands. Under the rules of the International Air Transport Association the claimant was required to enter into agency arrangements with the relevant airlines. The defendant was the national flag carrier airline of Pakistan, and agency agreements were entered into in 2008. Those arrangements were terminable by notice. Other operators commenced proceedings against the defendant in respect of unpaid commission, but the claimant was given notice of termination and was offered renewal on terms that it would not join the proceedings and instead would give up all accrued rights of commission. Warren J held that the elements of economic duress had been made out: the sole purpose of the new agreement was to remove any claim for outstanding commission; the notice of termination and offer of renewal were in the same document, and in effect amounted to a threat to the claimant's future business; no negotiation took place; and the claims given up were all well arguable.

Is the existence of good or bad faith a factor?

Good faith on the part of the person making the threat would certainly appear to be an ingredient in the conclusion that there is no duress where the threat is legitimate. However, the bona fides would seem to be less relevant *where the threat is illegitimate.* Mance J, in *Huyton SA v Peter Cremer GmbH and Co.* [1999] 1 Lloyd's Rep 620, accepted that although the courts would be reluctant to reopen compromises reached in good faith, good faith on the part of a party making an *illegitimate* threat would not always give protection against a claim based on duress, and Christopher Clarke J, in *Kolmar Group AG v Traxpo Enterprises Pvt Ltd* [2010] EWHC 113, [2010] 1 CLC 256, [2011] 1 All ER (Comm) 46, regarded a threat to break a contract as *more likely* to be regarded as illegitimate where the defendant acts in bad faith (and must know that this would be a breach of contract). It therefore appears that bona fides has some relevance when determining the nature of a threat as illegitimate. Thus, whereas we know that state of mind has no application to an actual breach of contract, it is relevant to a threat to breach a contract.

15.1.2.3.3 Causation: the illegitimate pressure must constitute a significant cause inducing the other party to contract

In the context of economic duress, any improper pressure must be 'decisive or clinching': *per* Mance J (*obiter*) in *Huyton SA v Peter Cremer GmbH & Co.* [1999] 1 Lloyd's Rep 620. Thus it must be established that the victim would not otherwise have made such a contract (the 'but for' test), or would not otherwise have contracted on those terms. (Compare with the position on causation for fraudulent misrepresentation: see **14.2.2.4.**) By comparison, if the alleged duress relates to duress to the person—*Barton v Armstrong* [1976] 1 AC 104—it is sufficient if the duress was 'a' reason for entering into the contract.

15.1.2.4 The need to protest at the time or shortly thereafter

The remedy for duress will be lost unless the victim of duress ensures that it takes action to 'protest at the time, or shortly thereafter' and seeks to reopen the issue: Kerr J in *Occidental Worldwide Investment Corporation v Skibs A/S Avanti, The Siboen and the Sibotre* [1976] 1 Lloyd's Rep 293.

The application of this requirement is well demonstrated by the decision in *North Ocean Shipping Co. Ltd v Hyundai Construction Co. Ltd, The Atlantic Baron* [1979] QB 705.

The defendants threatened to breach a contract for the construction of a tanker unless the claimants agreed to pay 10 per cent on top of the contract price. Consideration for this agreement was furnished by the defendants agreeing to provide a corresponding increase in their letter of credit as security for performance. The claimants agreed to make the extra payment because if the tanker had not been available, they would have lost a very valuable charter. Eight months after delivery of the tanker, the claimants attempted to recover the extra payment. Mocatta J held that the defendants' demand would have amounted to economic duress making the contract voidable. However, the failure to protest or reopen the issue for such a long time amounted to constructive affirmation of the contract. Therefore the claimants were no longer entitled to a remedy based on duress.

The courts accept that the economic duress itself will prevent anything but mild protest until performance is complete and, in *Kolmar Group AG v Traxpo Enterprises Pvt Ltd* [2010] EWHC 113, [2010] 1 CLC 256, [2011] 1 All ER (Comm) 46, at [92], in the context of protest at the time rather than protest after performance, Christopher Clarke J considered that: '[T]he presence or absence of protest, may be of some relevance when considering whether the threat had coercive effect. But even the total absence of protest does not mean the payment was voluntary.'

However, once there has been performance, the victim will have to take almost immediate action to avoid constructive affirmation of the contract. In *The Atlantic Baron*, it was considered that, once the claimants had taken possession of the tanker, there was no further danger in registering a protest and therefore waiting for eight months before doing so amounted to the affirmation.

The position will be different if the duress is continuing. In *Antonio v Antonio* [2010] EWHC 1199 (QB), the frightening and intimidating environment had continued for two years after X had transferred half of her shares in a company to Y, so that the fact that she did not act until a violent assault occurred was not considered to constitute affirmation.

15.1.2.5 Application of other bars to rescission in duress claim

A claimant who can succeed in establishing duress may be at risk of losing the ability to rescind on other grounds (see bars to rescission, at **14.5.2**). For example, the Court of Appeal in *Halpern v Halpern* [2007] EWCA Civ 291, [2008] QB 195 (for facts and discussion, see **14.5.2.3**), held that rescission would be lost if the claimant could not make restitution. On the facts, a compromise could not be rescinded because documents had been destroyed, although this action had taken place as a direct result of the terms of the agreement proved to be voidable for duress. Whilst confirming the basic principle, the Court of Appeal seemed troubled by the facts, and noted that 'it would be surprising if the law could not provide a suitable remedy'.

15.1.2.6 Conclusion

Although the number of judicial decisions examining economic duress has grown over recent years, key elements of the doctrine clearly require further elaboration. In *Huyton SA v Peter Cremer GmbH & Co.* [1999] 1 Lloyd's Rep 620, at p. 637, Mance J noted that the ingredients for establishing a claim in economic duress were 'minimum ingredients, not ingredients which, if present, would inevitably lead to liability'. He continued by stating, at p. 637, that:

> The recognition of some degree of flexibility is not . . . fairly open to the reproach that it introduces a judicial 'discretion'. The law frequently has to form judgments regarding inequitability or unconscionability, giving effect in doing so to the reasonable expectations of honest persons.

It is nevertheless helpful to have some recognized and clearly defined ingredients for the operation of the doctrine of duress, especially because, since *Williams v Roffey Bros. & Nicholls (Contractors) Ltd* [1991] 1 QB 1, it now appears to be seen as the primary mechanism in English law preventing the enforceability of alteration promises obtained by extortion: see e.g. *Adam Opel GmbH v Mitras Automotive Ltd* [2007] EWHC 3205 (QB), [2008] Bus LR Digest D55 (reporting the economic duress paragraphs only) (discussed at **4.4.4**).

15.2 Undue influence

15.2.1 The nature of the undue influence doctrine

Undue influence is an equitable doctrine that provides relief from contracts entered into under improper pressure. The courts will intervene where there is some relationship between the parties that has been exploited and abused to gain an unfair advantage. The precise basis of the court's intervention is a matter of debate: see, in particular, Birks and Chin, 'On the nature of undue influence', in Beatson and Friedmann (eds), *Good Faith and Fault in Contract Law* (Oxford University Press, 1995).

Undue influence appears to be based on a taking advantage of a relationship and the focus therefore rests on seeking to explain 'why' the complainant acted in the way they did, e.g. in transferring their property to the other party. The focus should be on the complainant rather than on the motives of the alleged influencer, or even whether the alleged influencer was conscious of any wrongdoing: *Hammond v Osborn* [2002] EWCA Civ 885, [2002] 2 P & CR DG20, [2002] WTLR 1125 (see **15.2.4.5**). What matters is whether the end result involves a taking advantage of the relationship.

Whether a transaction has been brought about by undue influence is a question of fact, so that case law has limited value in terms of precedent. The law governing undue influence is concerned with evidence and burdens of proof.

15.2.2 The classification of undue influence

Lord Browne-Wilkinson, in *Barclays Bank plc v O'Brien* [1994] 1 AC 180, approved a classification of types of undue influence put forward by the Court of Appeal in *Bank of Credit and Commerce International SA v Aboody* [1990] 1 QB 923 in terms of a distinction between actual undue influence (so-called 'Class 1') and presumed undue influence (where undue influence was presumed to have been exerted because of a relationship of trust and confidence between the parties). Presumed undue influence was subdivided into Class 2A cases (certain relationships in which this presumption arose automatically) and Class 2B cases (in which, on the facts, the relationship was such that the presumption applied).

This classification underwent revision in *Royal Bank of Scotland plc v Etridge (No. 2)* [2001] UKHL 44, [2002] 2 AC 773, and, in particular, the House of Lords considered that the law on 'presumed undue influence' had not been stated accurately, in that the 'presumption' is no more than an evidential presumption that *influence* has been exercised in light of the parties' relationship. The evidential presumption did not extend to concluding that the influence was also 'undue'; that was a separate matter and required that there be something suspicious in the transaction or something that called for an explanation on the facts, such as the size or nature of the transaction. Only then would the presumption of *undue* influence arise.

Nevertheless, the basic categories of undue influence remain after *Etridge*, i.e. there are three distinguishable categories:

- *actual undue influence*; and
- *two classes of evidential undue influence (protected relationships and other cases established on the facts)*, as follows:

(a) Where the relationship falls within the recognized category of protected relationships, there is an automatic evidential presumption of *influence*. It is then necessary to establish only that the influence is 'undue', i.e. that the transaction is suspicious or calls for an explanation, before concluding that *undue influence* was exercised.

(b) Outside the class of protected relationships, the evidential presumption of influence may arise where one of the parties can be shown on the facts to have placed trust and confidence in the other. However, the difference in this instance is that this presumption of influence can be rebutted by the other party establishing that no such influence was, in fact, exercised. Again, it would be necessary to establish that the transaction was suspicious or called for an explanation in order to raise the presumption of undue influence (i.e. that advantage had been taken of the relationship of trust and confidence).

This is different from the pre-*Etridge* position, but only in the sense that (i) the presumption arising from the relationship between the parties will establish influence (and not that the influence was undue), and (ii) the presumption of influence is rebuttable if the relationship falls outside the protected class of relationships, but irrebuttable where the relationship is protected.

Finally, the 'manifest disadvantage' requirement was clarified by the House of Lords in *Etridge* (see **15.2.4.4**).

15.2.3 Actual undue influence

Cases of actual undue influence can be equated with the type of pressure required to establish duress. In *Royal Bank of Scotland plc v Etridge (No. 2)* [2001] UKHL 44, [2002] 2 AC 773, at [8], Lord Nicholls described this unacceptable conduct as 'overt acts of improper pressure or coercion such as unlawful threats' and added that 'today there is much overlap with the principle of duress as this principle has subsequently developed'.

In cases within this category, the allegation is that actual influence was in fact exercised to take advantage of the claimant and that it induced the complainant to enter into the transaction. In the past, cases of this type of domination frequently involved dubious spiritual advisers.

In *Morley v Loughnan* [1893] 1 Ch 736, action was brought by executors to recover £140,000 paid by the deceased to a member of a religious sect. Wright J, in finding for the claimants, said, at p. 756, that there was no need to show a special relationship between deceased and defendant, because 'the defendant took possession, so to speak, of the whole life of the deceased, and the gifts were . . . the effect of that influence and domination'.

Williams v Bayley (1866) LR 1 HL 200 (which nowadays would probably be decided on the basis of duress: see **15.1.1**), concerned a mortgage over a colliery that had been executed by the claimant following threats to prosecute the claimant's son for forgery. It was held that the claimant could avoid the mortgage on the basis of undue influence.

CIBC Mortgages plc v Pitt [1994] 1 AC 200 was treated by the House of Lords as a case involving actual undue influence.

The defendant had been induced to agree to a second mortgage on the family home as security for a loan to finance share purchases. She had not wanted to go ahead with the scheme, but had given in to a campaign of sustained pressure. The principal issue for decision in *Pitt* was whether her claim of undue influence could succeed without her being able to prove that the transaction was to her manifest disagreement. The House of Lords held that, in a (Class 1) case of actual undue influence, the transaction need not be one that is disadvantageous to the party affected—overruling **Bank of Credit and Commerce International SA v Aboody** [1990] 1 QB 923 on this point.

Manifest disadvantage had been held to be a necessary ingredient of *presumed* undue influence (Class 2) by the House of Lords in *National Westminster Bank Ltd v Morgan* [1985] AC 686. But it had no relevance in the case of actual undue influence. According to Lord Browne-Wilkinson, in *CIBC v Pitt* at p. 209B, this is because actual undue influence is a 'species of fraud' and:

like any other victim of fraud, a person who has been induced by undue influence to carry out a transaction which he did not freely and knowingly enter into is entitled to have that transaction set aside as of right.

Since actual undue influence is akin to fraud, it follows that it is not a defence, where actual undue influence has been proved, to claim that the person influenced would have entered into the transaction anyway. Thus the causation test is the same as that applicable in cases of duress to the person—*Barton v Armstrong* [1976] AC 104 (see **15.1.1** and **15.1.2.3**)—rather than that applicable to economic duress: *Huyton SA v Peter Cremer GmbH & Co.* [1999] 1 Lloyd's Rep 620 (see **15.1.2.3**).

This position was made clear by the Court of Appeal in *UCB Corporate Services Ltd v Williams* [2002] EWCA Civ 555, [2003] 1 P & CR 12.

The wife was found to have been the victim of fraudulent misrepresentation and actual undue influence by her husband. The judge at first instance had rejected her claim to set aside the charge in favour of the claimant lender on the basis that she would have signed the charge even if she had known the full facts and the risks involved. The Court of Appeal allowed the wife's appeal, since it was not relevant to ask whether the wife would have entered into the transaction in any event. It was sufficient that the actual undue influence was *a* factor inducing her to execute the charge.

15.2.3.1 Conclusion

Thus these cases of actual undue influence, which are sometimes referred to as the 'domination cases', do not require the complainant to show that there was any kind of special relationship or that there was a manifest disadvantage resulting from the transaction. On the other hand, complainants have the difficult task of proving that their free will to enter or to decline a particular contract was in some way overcome by the influence of another. It is clear from the speech of Lord Nicholls in *Royal Bank of Scotland plc v Etridge (No. 2)* [2001] UKHL 44, [2002] 2 AC 773, at [32]–[33], that it will not be easy to establish actual undue influence in the context of husband and wife relationships, but that misrepresentations of fact will suffice as the basis for a claim. Lord Nicholls stated, at [32]–[33]:

Undue influence has a connotation of impropriety. In the eye of the law, undue influence means that influence has been misused. Statements or conduct by a husband, which do not pass beyond the bounds of what may be expected of a reasonable husband in the circumstances, should not, without more, be castigated as undue influence. Similarly, when a husband is forecasting the future of his business, and expressing his hopes or fears, a degree of hyperbole may be only natural. Courts should not too readily treat such exaggerations as misstatements. Inaccurate explanations of a proposed transaction are a different matter.

In *Royal Bank of Scotland v Chandra* [2011] EWCA Civ 192, [2011] NPC 26, [2011] 2 P & CR DG1, the Court of Appeal relied on this statement in finding that the husband had not provided his wife with an inaccurate explanation of the transaction. He could merely be accused of providing 'an over-optimistic assessment of the chances of a future overspend'. There was no undue influence and no misrepresentation.

15.2.4 Evidential undue influence: the requirements

In *Daniel v Drew* [2005] EWCA Civ 507, [2005] 2 FCR 365, the Court of Appeal held that whereas actual undue influence was something that had to be done to twist the mind of the donor, in cases of presumed undue influence it was more a case of what had not been done—namely, ensuring that the transaction was the exercise of the free and independent will of the donor. The decision in *Royal Bank of Scotland plc v Etridge (No. 2)* [2001] UKHL 44, [2002] 2 AC 773, has clarified the nature of the presumption of undue influence. It used to be considered that undue influence would be presumed where the relationship between the parties fell within certain recognized relationships or, on the facts, was shown to be a relationship in which one party placed trust and confidence in the other. However, the House of Lords has now made it clear that it is only the existence of influence that may be presumed in such instances (although irrebuttably in the case of the recognized protected relationships). It is still necessary to establish the existence of the wrong, i.e. abuse or taking advantage of that relationship.

> ### ! KEY POINT
>
> The requirements for the evidential presumption of undue influence after *Etridge* were set out in clear terms by the Court of Appeal in *Turkey v Awadh* [2005] EWCA Civ 382, [2005] 2 P & CR 29, [2005] 2 FCR 7.
>
> 1. It was first necessary to determine whether the facts raised the presumption of undue influence. This involved two stages or two presumptions.
>   (a) It required either the existence of a protected relationship (see **15.2.4.1**), or required facts that would persuade the court that the party in question was in a position to influence the will of the other in relation to the transaction, i.e. establishing a relationship of trust and confidence on the facts (see **15.2.4.2**).
>   (b) The transaction had then to be shown to be one that cannot be explained by reference to the ordinary motives by which people are accustomed to act, i.e. suggesting that it is unlikely that the other would have entered into it unless 'his will was overborne' (see **15.2.4.3**).
> 2. It was finally necessary to consider whether the defendant could rebut the presumption by establishing that there was no abuse of trust.

15.2.4.1 Evidential influence: protected relationships

There are certain relationships that the law regards as special, and as always incorporating elements of trust and confidence, so that *influence* can be automatically assumed. Typical of such relationships are solicitor and client, doctor and patient, and parent and child—although not adult child and elderly parents, in which case a relationship of trust and confidence must be established on the facts: *Avon Finance Co. Ltd v Bridger* [1985] 2 All ER 281. Relations between husband and wife are said not to give rise to a special relationship, and so do not automatically raise any presumption of influence: *Midland Bank plc v Shephard* [1988] 3 All ER 17. The relationship of banker and customer is also outside this class of protected relationships (previously known as Class 2A): *National Westminster Bank Ltd v Morgan* [1985] AC 686.

The result of the decision of the House of Lords in *Royal Bank of Scotland plc v Etridge (No. 2)* [2001] UKHL 44, [2002] 2 AC 773, is that if the relationship in question falls within this category of protected relationships, the presumption of influence is automatic and irrebuttable. However, it will still be necessary to establish that the influence was undue, and evidence of this may include the nature of the transaction in the context of the relationship in question, i.e. the principle in *Allcard v Skinner* (1887) LR 36 Ch D 145. If evidence suggests that the transaction is suspicious and the influence is *undue*, the presumption of undue influence will arise, and it will then be open to the party alleged to have exercised the undue influence to establish that no undue influence was in fact exercised, e.g. by demonstrating that independent advice was received.

15.2.4.2 Evidential influence: other cases established on the facts

Where the relationship does not fall into any of the recognized special categories automatically giving rise to the presumption of *influence*, it is still possible for a complainant to show that the particular relationship was in fact one based on trust and confidence, so that the evidential presumption of influence will arise on the particular facts. However, the other party can seek to rebut the presumption of influence by evidence that no such trust and confidence existed.

In any event, there will be no presumption of undue influence unless the transaction is suspicious and calls for an explanation in light of this relationship of trust and confidence.

15.2.4.2.1 Bank and customer

This method of establishing undue influence has been applied to the relationship between bank and customer. In *National Westminster Bank Ltd v Morgan* [1985] AC 686, Lord Scarman accepted that the relationship between bank and customer may be one of confidence, but held that, in the particular situation, the bank 'had not crossed the line' into the realm of confidence.

However, in *Lloyds Bank Ltd v Bundy* [1975] QB 326, the Court of Appeal held that the facts did justify a presumption of (undue) influence between banker and customer.

- There was a special relationship of confidence, because of the fact that old Mr Bundy had banked at this branch for many years and relied on the bank manager for all of his financial advice.

- The manager was aware of this confidence placed in him.

- In addition, whereas the transaction in *National Westminster Bank Ltd v Morgan* was beneficial to Mrs Morgan because it allowed her to stay in her home, which would otherwise have been repossessed by the then mortgagee, the transaction in *Lloyds Bank Ltd v Bundy* was very evidently not in the interests of old Mr Bundy as default by him would have seen him lose possession of his home.

In light of the different approach adopted in *Royal Bank of Scotland plc v Etridge (No. 2)* [2001] UKHL 44, [2002] 2 AC 773, the relationship in *Lloyds Bank v Bundy* would give rise to a presumption of influence, and the general nature and size of the transaction, assessed in the context of Mr Bundy's position, would be evidence suggesting that 'undue' influence had been exercised and therefore requiring an explanation from the bank. It would then be for the bank to seek to rebut the presumption of undue influence.

Of course, where the relationship between bank and customer is the ordinary commercial one, and not a special relationship of confidence, it must be remembered that the bank may still owe an ordinary duty of care to give accurate advice, which may be the basis of liability towards a customer: see *Cornish v Midland Bank Ltd* [1985] 3 All ER 513 (see also **14.4.3.1**).

15.2.4.2.2 *Husband and wife*

It has also been accepted that such relationships of trust and confidence based on the facts (previously Class 2B) may exist between husbands and wives, and indeed between other cohabitees or persons between whom there is an emotional involvement. In particular, it was recognized by Lord Browne-Wilkinson in *Barclays Bank plc v O'Brien* [1994] 1 AC 180, at pp. 190–1, that:

> In those cases which still occur where the wife relies in all financial matters on her husband and simply does what he suggests, a presumption of undue influence within class 2B can be established solely from proof of such trust and confidence without proof of actual undue influence . . . [T]he sexual and emotional ties between the parties provide a ready weapon for undue influence: a wife's true wishes can easily be overborne because of her fear of destroying or damaging the wider relationship between her and her husband if she opposes his wishes.

Whilst it remains the position that there is no automatic presumption of undue influence in cases of husband and wife, the tone of speech of Lord Nicholls in *Royal Bank of Scotland plc v Etridge (No. 2)* [2001] UKHL 44, [2002] 2 AC 773, may suggest a more restrictive approach to concluding that a presumption of undue influence has arisen in the context of husband and wife. Although the presumption of influence may be shown to arise on the facts, e.g. because the wife (or person in a similar cohabiting relationship) places total trust and confidence in the husband and does as she is told, the transaction must also be shown to raise suspicions that this influence is 'undue'. Therefore there will also need to be some feature of the transaction that calls for explanation so as to provide evidence that the husband has abused the trust. Only in such cases will the presumption of undue influence apply.

Lord Nicholls stated that not all cases in which a wife guarantees her husband's debts on the security of the matrimonial home will give rise to a presumption of undue influence by her husband. He added, at [30]:

> Wives frequently enter into such transactions. There are good and sufficient reasons why they are willing to do so, despite the risks involved for them and their families. They may be enthusiastic. They may not. They may be less optimistic than their husbands about the prospects of the husband's business. They may be anxious, perhaps exceedingly so. But this is a far cry from saying that such transactions as a class are to be regarded as *prima facie* evidence of the exercise of undue influence by husbands.

The real change post-*Etridge* would appear to be in relation to the move away from a requirement of 'manifest disadvantage' towards the broader test in *Allcard v Skinner* (1887) LR 36 Ch D 145, at p. 185 (see **15.2.4.1**). Whereas the manifest disadvantage requirement focuses solely on the claimant's position, and led to unfortunate discussions of whether to distinguish direct and indirect advantages to the claimant wife (see the discussion at **15.2.4.4**), the broader approach in *Allcard v Skinner* focuses on the transaction and the nature of the relationship to determine whether the transaction is suspicious so that an explanation is called for. Whereas evidence that the transaction is clearly not to the claimant's advantage will assist in establishing evidence of that suspicion, it will not be conclusive in itself. The result is that this evidence of undue influence is likely to focus more on the extremes and is therefore likely to reduce the discussions concerning indirect advantages to the claimant. However, in light of the comments made by Lord Nicholls, without evidence of clear disadvantage, it is likely that in future a much broader view will be taken of the wife's position and greater allowance will be made for her emotional motivation, so that a transaction may not be considered unusual or as raising any suspicions.

15.2.4.2.3 *Other cohabitees*

As Lord Browne-Wilkinson recognized in *Barclays Bank plc v O'Brien* [1994] 1 AC 180, at p. 198, this discussion relating to husband and wives is also applicable whenever there is an emotional relationship between cohabitees, whether married or unmarried, heterosexual or homosexual. In *Massey v Midland Bank plc* [1995] 1 All ER 929, Steyn LJ extended the category further by including a couple enjoying a long-term emotional and sexual relationship, who had children, but who did not in fact cohabit. The presumption of influence has also been held to apply between a son and his elderly parents: *Avon Finance Co. Ltd v Bridger* [1985] 2 All ER 281. No such presumption was established between a daughter and her mother in *Thompson v Foy* [2009] EWHC 1076 (Ch), [2010] 1 P & CR 16, since the judge considered that there was no evidence of a complete relationship of trust and confidence, but only the trust that a mother places in her daughter that she would repay money borrowed for a deposit. (The mother had also failed to establish actual undue influence by the daughter.)

In *Evans v Lloyd* [2013] EWHC 1725 (Ch), [2013] WTLR 1137 [2013] 2 P & CR DG21, there was no blood relationship between a farmer, Wynne Evans, and Mr and Mrs Lloyd, the proprietors of the farm but the farmer had lived on this farm from the age of 14 and a close relationship had developed so that he had become accepted as a member of the family. He made a gift to his employers, the Lloyds, of all of his property and his personal representatives sought to have this set aside on the basis of undue influence, and unconscionability (discussed at **15.3.4**). Judge Keyser QC, in rejecting the claim based on undue influence, considered that although the farmer was dependent on the Lloyds for his employment and accommodation and had little education and worldliness, the necessary relationship of trust and confidence had not been established, particularly because Wynne was independently minded and the Lloyds had not managed his finances. In addition, the judge considered that the gift could be explained in accordance with the 'ordinary motives by which people are accustomed to act' since the evidence was that Mr Evans wished the property he owned to remain with fellow farmers and he regarded the Lloyds as family.

15.2.4.2.4 *Army (via commanding officer) and soldier*

In *R v HM Attorney-General for England and Wales* [2003] UKPC 22, [2003] EMLR 24 (for facts, see **15.1.2.3**), the alternative argument to the claim based on duress was that undue influence had been exercised in obtaining the signature to the confidentiality agreement.

It was alleged that the soldier placed trust and confidence in his commanding officer, so that the presumption of influence arose on the facts. However, the Privy Council (Lord Scott dissenting) rejected this argument, and stressed the contradiction between, on the one hand, relying on a relationship of trust and confidence, and yet, on the other, pleading duress in securing the signature. 'People do not usually trust those who coerce them': *per* Lewison J in *Thompson v Foy* [2009] EWHC 1076 (Ch), [2010] 1 P & CR 16, at [101]. In any event, the Privy Council in *R v HM Attorney-General for England and Wales* concluded that any influence would not be *undue*, since, because there was no illegitimate pressure sufficient to constitute duress (discussed at **15.1.2.3**), the transaction could not amount to unfair exploitation of the parties' relationship.

15.2.4.3 **The evidential presumption of *undue* influence**

The second stage for the presumption of undue influence to arise required that there be something suspicious about the transaction in light of the relationship, e.g. its size or nature, which called for an explanation and which could not be explained using ordinary motives.

The size of the transactions is important in providing evidence of suspicion that advantage has been taken.

> In **Watson v Huber** [2005] All ER (D) 156 (Mar), the claimant had transferred a total of £900,000 to her half-sister, with whom she had been living since the death of the claimant's husband. The necessary trust and confidence were established on the facts, because the defendant looked after the claimant's financial affairs and operated an account in joint names. In addition, the number and size of the 'gifts' called for an explanation. The presumption was not rebutted. The judge stated that it would be 'unconscionable' to withhold the relief sought given the circumstances of this case, i.e. complete trust and confidence, and the sheer size of the amount transferred.
>
> In **Hodson v Hodson** [2006] EWHC 2878, the transferor, the frail mother of two adopted sons, had executed an enduring power of attorney (EPA) in favour of these sons, jointly and severally (i.e. they could act independently in her affairs). She lived with one of the sons and his wife, and was wholly dependent on them. Her property was transferred into the name of the daughter-in-law and shares were also transferred out of the mother's name. The judge stressed the scale of these transfers and the fact that they left the mother with no assets. In these circumstances—and given the fact that the money was spent on expensive cars and boats, and in supporting the son's ailing business—a proper explanation was required. In particular, the scale of the transfers could not be explained by the nature of the relationship. There was no evidence to rebut the presumption so raised and the judge made a finding of undue influence.

In *Hart v Burbidge* [2014] EWCA Civ 992, [2014] WTLR 1361, [2015] 1 P & CR DG9, the Court of Appeal upheld a decision that Mr and Mrs Burbidge had unduly influenced Mrs Burbidge's mother into transferring around 90 per cent of her assets to them in the months leading up to the mother's death so that gifts to her sons contained in the mother's will had failed due to the limited nature of the residual estate. There was a relationship of influence based on trust, confidence, and dependence and gifts of this size in the period prior to death called for an explanation. It followed that the presumption of undue influence arose and it had not been rebutted. (A detailed account of the current law of undue influence was given at first instance, [2013] EWHC 1628 (Ch), [2013] WTLR 1191, [2013] 2 P & CR DG20.)

By comparison, *Turkey v Awadh* [2005] EWCA Civ 382, [2005] 2 P & CR 29, [2005] 2 FCR 7, concerned an agreement whereby the claimant's daughter and her husband agreed to transfer a long leasehold interest in their house to the defendant in exchange for him agreeing to clear the mortgage on the property and various other debts. The Court of Appeal held that the presumption of undue influence did not arise because the transaction could be readily explained by the nature of the parties' relationship. Similarly, the transaction (father's removal of son as trustee in family company) in *Hogg v Hogg* [2007] EWHC 2240 (Ch), [2008] 1 P & CR DG7, [2008] WTLR 35, was held to be explicable in accordance with ordinary motives, so that no presumption of undue influence arose.

15.2.4.4 Does the transaction need to be manifestly disadvantageous?

In *National Westminster Bank Ltd v Morgan* [1985] AC 686, it was suggested that it is necessary to show that there was a manifest disadvantage to the complainant on the ground that the presumption of undue influence is based on the premise that a party making an unfettered decision would not freely choose to enter into a manifestly disadvantageous contract. In *CIBC Mortgages plc v Pitt* [1994] 1 AC 200, Lord Browne-Wilkinson appeared to be less than certain that, even in cases resting upon presumed undue influence, there was an absolute requirement to establish manifest disadvantage, but he was not required to rule upon the matter in that case. The requirement of 'manifest disadvantage' in cases of presumed undue influence was reconsidered by the Court of Appeal in *Barclays Bank plc v Coleman* [2001] QB 20, but it was bound to apply it. Nourse LJ (delivering the leading judgment) commented, at [63], that 'a serious question mark' has been put 'over the future of the requirement of manifest disadvantage in cases of presumed undue influence', and the matter needed reconsideration by the House of Lords.

In the Court of Appeal in *Royal Bank of Scotland v Etridge (No. 2)* [1998] 4 All ER 705, Stuart-Smith LJ had made the point that evidence of manifest disadvantage is 'a powerful evidential factor', and in the House of Lords, Lord Nicholls confirmed that manifest disadvantage to the claimant would be evidence that the influence exercised was 'undue' or at least raised suspicions. However, a broader assessment was called for, based on the statement of Lindley LJ in *Allcard v Skinner* (1887) LR 36 Ch D 145, at p. 185:

> Where a gift is made to a person standing in a confidential relation to the donor, the Court will not set aside the gift if of a small amount simply on the ground that the donor had no independent advice. In such a case, some proof of the exercise of the influence of the donee must be given. The mere existence of such influence is not enough in such a case . . . But if the gift is so large as not to be reasonably accounted for on the ground of friendship, relationship, charity, or other ordinary motives on which ordinary men act, the burden is upon the donee to support the gift.

The relationship giving the ability to influence will not suffice. There must also be a wrong, in that the transaction is suspicious and calls for an explanation (as opposed to a transaction that is readily explicable, e.g. the usual gifts that are made to children when they get married). In *Goodchild v Bradbury* [2006] EWCA Civ 1868, [2007] WTLR 463, at [27], Chadwick LJ explained the position as follows:

> A gift which is made without informed consideration by a person vulnerable to influence, and which he could not have been expected to make if he had been acting in accordance with the ordinary motives which lead men's actions, needs to be justified on the basis that the donor knew and understood what he was doing.

It follows from this interpretation that manifest disadvantage is not a 'requirement' and that the courts will need to move away from the previous discussion in the case law, which had centred on identification of advantage and disadvantage of the transaction. Indeed, the Court of Appeal in *Macklin v Dowsett* [2004] EWCA Civ 904, [2004] 2 EGLR 75, subsequently confirmed that there is no longer a manifest disadvantage *requirement*. The Court of Appeal focused instead on whether the transaction was readily explicable by the relationship of the parties or whether it was suspicious and called for an explanation. The court concluded that it did call for an explanation, since it gave Macklin the option to require Dowsett to surrender a life tenancy in property in return for a payment of only £5,000.

There had previously been much confusion between the old manifest disadvantage requirement and the requirements for a lender to be put on inquiry in a situation in which the undue influence had been exercised by a third party (see the discussion at 15.2.5.2). Misunderstanding had arisen in third party surety cases involving wives who had given security over the matrimonial home to guarantee their husband's company overdraft with his bank. Much emphasis had previously been placed in cases of presumed undue influence on whether such a transaction was manifestly disadvantageous to the wife. The courts treated manifest disadvantage as an absolute requirement and there was considerable argument concerning whether the fact that a wife might benefit indirectly, in the sense that the household finances would be stronger if further funds were released to the husband's business, meant that she could not be said to be entirely 'disadvantaged'. In addition, this question of 'advantage in a disadvantage' had been caught up in the entirely separate consideration of whether a lender was affected by constructive notice of the husband's undue influence because the transaction on its face was 'not to the financial advantage of the wife'.

The broader approach in *Allcard v Skinner* focuses on the transaction and the nature of the relationship to determine whether it is suspicious so that an explanation is called for. Whereas evidence that the transaction is clearly not to the claimant's advantage will assist in establishing evidence of that suspicion, it will not be conclusive in itself.

Some confusion appears to remain in terms of explicit reference to 'the manifest disadvantage requirement' in establishing the presumption of undue influence in some of the case law since *Etridge*.

In **Leeder (aka Newey) v Stevens** [2005] EWCA Civ 50, (2005) 149 SJLB 112, The Times, 14 January 2005, for example, the claimant had transferred a property into joint names in exchange for her long-term partner paying the remaining £5,000 on the mortgage. The deed of transfer enabled the defendant partner to force a sale. The Court of Appeal considered that the relationship of trust and confidence had been established on the facts, and that this transaction called for an explanation based on the fact that it was 'manifestly disadvantageous'. Therefore the presumption of undue influence had arisen. It had not been rebutted, since no independent legal advice had been received.

This may be no more than the reference to manifest disadvantage as *evidence* that the transaction is suspicious, but the courts will need to be very careful not to reintroduce manifest disadvantage as a *requirement*. A correct statement of the principle was made by Lewison J in *Thompson v Foy* [2009] EWHC 1076 (Ch), [2010] 1 P & CR 16, at [99]:

Disadvantage to the donor is not a necessary ingredient of undue influence . . . However, it may have an evidential value, because it is relevant to the questions whether any allegation of abuse of confidence can properly be made, and whether any abuse actually occurred.

⟁ SUMMARY

Thus, in *Etridge*, Lord Nicholls was stating that there is no longer a 'requirement' to establish manifest disadvantage. Instead, the emphasis is on whether the nature and size of the transaction can be readily explained by the parties' relationship, or calls for some explanation because it raises suspicions. Lord Nicholls suggested that the fact that the transaction was manifestly disadvantageous to the claimant may be evidence to support a conclusion that the transaction is suspicious, so that the influence was *undue* and the transaction needs to be explained.

Equally, the fact that a transaction is not disadvantageous, but perfectly rational in the circumstances, may support a conclusion that no 'undue' influence has been exercised, and there is nothing in the transaction that is not readily explicable in terms of the parties' relationship and the context for the agreement. For example, in *Dailey v Dailey* [2003] UKPC 65, [2003] 3 FCR 369, a wife was unable to demonstrate that the presumption of influence arose on the facts or that there was anything in the transaction that was not readily explicable in terms of the parties' relationship, since the transaction involved a transfer to the husband for full value as part of proceedings for ancillary relief. Lord Hope explained, at [24]:

> Care needs to be taken to distinguish between cases where the wife has entered into a transaction with her husband which is gratuitous and those where the agreement is for her to receive full value for the property or interest which she is to transfer to him. In the former case, as Lindley LJ explained in *Allcard v Skinner* (1887) 36 Ch D 145, 185, the burden is on the donee to support the gift if it is so large as not to be reasonably accounted for on the ground of the relationship. A transaction which is entered into for full value needs no such explanation. There is no presumption to rebut. That is not to say that a transaction of this type is immune from the exercise of undue influence. But if it is to be set aside on this ground it is for the party who makes the allegation to prove that undue influence was in fact exercised.

In other words, in such circumstances, the donor would need to establish actual undue influence in order to succeed.

15.2.4.5 Rebutting the presumption

In order for the presumption to arise in the first place, there must be both a presumption of influence (automatic or established to have arisen on the facts) and evidence relating to the transaction that suggests that *undue* influence may have been exercised or at least raises such a suspicion: *Royal Bank of Scotland v Etridge (No. 2)* [1998] 4 All ER 705. The result is that the presumption of undue influence will not be assumed simply on the basis of an evidential presumption of influence.

In *Hammond v Osborn* [2002] EWCA Civ 885, [2002] WTLR 1125, the Court of Appeal held that a defendant could not avoid such a finding by establishing the absence of an intention to commit a wrong, i.e. an absence of bad faith.

> In *Hammond v Osborn*, an elderly donor had made a number of sizeable gifts (totalling £300,000) to the defendant, his neighbour, who had been taking care of him. The gifts represented over 90 per cent of his liquid assets and exposed him to a considerable tax liability. The necessary relationship of trust and confidence was shown to exist on the facts, and the presumption of undue influence was established because there was clearly something suspicious about gifts of this size in the circumstances. The presumption was not rebutted, because no advice on the wisdom and implications of these actions had been received. It was not sufficient to avoid this presumption by establishing the absence of bad faith on the part of the defendant.

Rebuttal will require the defendant to show that the complainant was not, in fact, induced to enter the contract through the defendant's improper influence, but rather entered into it quite freely and fully aware of the situation. In many cases, this may be achieved by showing that the complainant chose to go ahead even after receiving independent advice about the true nature of the transaction. In *Howard v Howard-Lawson* [2012] EWHC 3258 (Ch), confirmed by the Court of Appeal at [2013] EWCA Civ 654, for example, independent legal advice had been received before signing the contested deeds. In any event, had undue influence been established, it was now 40 years after the alleged 'influence' and 13 years after the events leading to the claim became known, so the claim of undue influence would have been barred by laches (see **15.2.5.1**).

In *Wadlow v Samuel (PKA Seal)* [2007] EWCA Civ 155, (2007) 151 SJLB 331, the issue was whether a management agreement entitled Seal's former manager to commission covering two albums recorded during the period of this agreement. After the release of the albums, the management agreement had been terminated by a settlement agreement, which had provided that the manager was entitled to the management agreement commission despite the fact that the agreement in question had been terminated. It was alleged that the management agreement was affected by undue influence on the part of the manager and that this meant that the settlement agreement was also voidable. However, the Court of Appeal held that the settlement agreement had been freely entered into by Seal, since he had received independent legal advice and the context for the agreement was fundamentally different from the factual context for the making of the management agreement, e.g. breakdown of trust and confidence, and more balanced contract terms including a number of concessions by the manager.

However, in *Etridge*, at [20], Lord Nicholls suggested that independent advice would not be conclusive:

> But a person may understand fully the implications of a proposed transaction, for instance, a substantial gift, and yet still be acting under the undue influence of another. Proof of outside advice does not, of itself, necessarily show that the subsequent completion of the transaction was free from the exercise of undue influence. Whether it will be proper to infer that outside advice had an emancipating effect, so that the transaction was not brought about by the exercise of undue influence, is a question of fact to be decided having regard to all the evidence in the case.

15.2.5 The effect of undue influence

Contracts affected by undue influence are voidable, not void. As with duress, this consequence seems to support the view that the doctrine is not concerned with the reality of consent, but with the protection of victims of improper behaviour. Since a tainted contract is only voidable, the victim must bring a claim for rescission to avoid it and property passes under it. The effect of undue influence must be considered in more detail according to whether the undue influence is alleged between the contracting parties or whether third party undue influence is involved.

15.2.5.1 The effect of undue influence between the contracting parties
15.2.5.1.1 *Affirmation and acquiescence*

The right to rescission may be lost if the complainant has affirmed the contract in some way after the undue influence has ceased. In particular, failure to act within a fairly short time of the undue influence ceasing may be interpreted as constructive affirmation.

In *Allcard v Skinner* (1887) LR 36 Ch D 145, the claimant, under the influence of her spiritual adviser, joined an order called the 'Sisters of the Poor', to which her spiritual adviser was confessor. During the eight years for which she was a member, the claimant gave some £7,000 to the defendant, who was head of the order. Six years after leaving the order, she sought to recover the balance of that sum remaining unspent (about £1,700). The gift to the defendant was held to have been made under undue influence, because the claimant had not been independently advised. The claimant was nevertheless unable to recover the balance of her money, because she had allowed such a long time to elapse before claiming, during which time she had been unaffected by the undue influence and independent advice was presumably available to her.

An example of acquiescence is provided by the decision in **Wadlow v Samuel (PKA Seal)** [2007] EWCA Civ 155, (2007) 151 SJLB 331 (for facts, see **15.2.4.5**). The claim to rescind for undue influence in relation to the management agreement was made more than 15 years after that contract had been made. Accordingly, it was affected by laches (delay) and acquiescence, and it would be inequitable to set it aside.

15.2.5.1.2 Partial rescission

An interesting question is whether partial rescission is possible, i.e. is it possible to separate parts of the contract affected by either misrepresentation or undue influence and to enforce the remainder, or will the entire contract have to be rescinded?

In **TSB Bank plc v Camfield** [1995] 1 WLR 430, it had been argued that the charge in question should be set aside only to the extent that it provided security for a debt in excess of £15,000, the amount that the wife considered was her maximum liability. However, the Court of Appeal held that it had no power to impose terms and, insisting that rescission had to be total, set aside the charge in its entirety.

By contrast, in **Vadasz v Pioneer Concrete (SA) Pty Ltd** (1995) 130 ALR 570, the High Court of Australia was prepared to enforce the part of a guarantee covering future debt, but not that part covering the existing debt, on the basis that it had been represented that the guarantee would cover only future debt. The High Court regarded this as no more than holding the party in question to what he was prepared to agree to independently of any misrepresentation.

Although this authority may be limited to rescission of guarantees, it is submitted that this approach would be generally preferable, since it allows the court to do justice and recognize the realities of the parties' positions.

The question of which authority was to be preferred was discussed by the Privy Council in *Far Eastern Shipping Co. Public Ltd v Scales Trading Ltd* [2001] 1 All ER (Comm) 319, but determination of this question was not necessary for the Privy Council's decision on the facts before it, and more recent English authority, *De Molestina v Ponton* [2002] 1 All ER (Comm) 587, supports the view that partial rescission is contrary to the very nature of rescission (see further the discussion of this case law at **14.5.2.3**). Nevertheless, on the facts in *De Molestina v Ponton*, the judge had provisionally considered that it was possible to distinguish the various agreements and so to rescind some of them. It is also possible, although regarded as exceptional, to sever objectionable parts of an instrument and to enforce the remainder. However, it is clear from *Barclays Bank plc v Caplan* [1998] FLR 532 that this will be possible only where the parts can be separated cleanly without affecting the substance of the part enforced, i.e. first guarantee separated from later guarantees.

15.2.5.1.3 Restitutionary relief

It is very likely that some form of restitutionary relief will be required in association with rescission of the contract: *Dunbar Bank plc v Nadeem* [1998] 3 All ER 876. Where complete restitution is not possible because, for example, property values have gone down, the net balance is to be divided pro rata between the parties according to their original contributions to the transaction: *Cheese v Thomas* [1994] 1 WLR 129. Where the normal remedy of restoring the parties to their original positions, with an account of profits, is impossible, e.g. because property has passed into the hands of a third party, the court has jurisdiction to impose a 'common-sense and . . . fair remedy' in order 'to achieve practical justice between the parties', at least where the undue influence involves a breach of fiduciary duty: *per* May J in *Mahoney v Purnell* [1996] 3 All ER 61, at p. 88, relying on *O'Sullivan v Management Agency and Music Ltd* [1985] QB 428. In the particular case, practical justice was achieved by 'an award . . . akin to damages' giving to the claimant as compensation a sum equal in value to what had been given up under the tainted transaction, but making an allowance for sums received thereunder.

15.2.5.2 The effect of third party undue influence

It may be alleged that a contract is affected by the undue influence of a third party and that, on that basis, the contract is voidable. If the contracting party has knowledge of the undue influence practised by a third party in order to persuade the victim to contract, that contracting party will be affected by the undue influence.

The doctrine of undue influence has, for example, been invoked by a wife (or other cohabitee) in an attempt to avoid an interest acquired by a bank owing to undue influence (either actual influence or, more usually, old Class 2B presumed undue influence on the facts) exercised by her husband (or co-habiting partner). Where one cohabiting partner has misled or influenced the other into granting rights over the 'matrimonial' home to a bank by way of surety in respect of the first party's business liabilities, the victim will understandably be reluctant to give up the home if the business fails. The courts have had to try to find a balance between the rights of parties who risk being dispossessed and the rights of banks, which have legitimately sought to protect their investments in business ventures and which might be forced to rethink their lending policies in relation to couples if they were always liable to lose their security at a later date.

15.2.5.2.1 *Barclays Bank v O'Brien*

After a number of false starts, in **Barclays Bank plc v O'Brien** [1994] 1 AC 180, Lord Browne-Wilkinson held that the key to determining the position of the bank lay in the doctrine of notice, and the significance of the decision of the House of Lords was that it provided the first attempt at guidance for lenders concerning how they might avoid being fixed with notice of a contracting party's undue influence. *Of course, it would be surprising to find that a bank had actual notice of undue influence; the critical issue therefore is whether the bank has constructive notice (i.e. in the circumstances, the bank ought to have known of the undue influence and so is fixed with notice).* It is important to appreciate that, whatever the position of the bank, if such a claim is to succeed, the husband's undue influence must be established (actual or using the evidential presumption) before any question of the lender being affected can arise: *Davies v AIB Group (UK) plc* [2012] EWHC 2178 (Ch), [2012] 2 P & CR 19 (it was not established that the husband had committed any legal or equitable wrong, i.e. he had not exercised undue influence or misrepresented the position to his wife). This is separate from the question of whether the bank is fixed with constructive notice of that undue influence.

The House of Lords in *Barclays Bank plc v O'Brien* held that the notice question involved two steps:

1. A bank would be put on inquiry if it knew of the relationship and the transaction was not obviously of any financial advantage or benefit to the wife (or other cohabitee), so that there was a 'substantial risk' that a wrong had been committed.

2. Once put on inquiry, the bank was fixed with constructive notice of the undue influence exercised by the contracting party, unless the bank had taken reasonable steps to satisfy itself that the wife had entered into the transaction freely and with knowledge of the true facts.

O'Brien provided that the bank could satisfy this requirement by warning the wife (at a meeting not attended by the husband) of the amount of her potential liability and the risks involved, and by advising the wife to obtain independent legal advice.

15.2.5.2.2 *Royal Bank of Scotland plc v Etridge (No. 2)*

In ***Royal Bank of Scotland plc v Etridge (No. 2)*** [2001] UKHL 44, [2002] 2 AC 773, these principles were reformulated and the House of Lords stressed the need to balance the interests of protecting those giving the security, while ensuring that lenders could rely on that security if they had followed the appropriate procedures. Lord Bingham stated, at [2]:

> The law must afford both parties a measure of protection. It cannot prescribe a code which will be proof against error, misunderstanding or mishap. But it can indicate minimum requirements which, if met, will reduce the risk of error, misunderstanding or mishap to an acceptable level. The paramount need in this important field is that these minimum requirements should be clear, simple and practically operable.

The requirements were merely 'concerned to minimize the risk' that a wife had entered into the transaction as a result of her husband's undue influence. They could not guarantee that undue influence had not occurred.

The wife (or other surety) has the burden of proving that the bank or lender had the necessary constructive notice, and the formulation of any claim will need to make clear the facts upon which the notice argument is based: Barclays Bank plc v Boulter [1999] 4 All ER 513.

1. *Putting the lender on inquiry*

Although the decision in ***Barclays Bank plc v O'Brien*** [1994] 1 AC 180 was clearly intended to clarify the law, it resulted in a lengthy catalogue of decisions interpreting its declared principle.

> In **CIBC Mortgages plc v Pitt** [1994] 1 AC 200, for example, the question was whether the circumstances of the particular case were such as to put the bank on inquiry, so that the necessary steps needed to be taken in order for the bank to avoid being fixed with constructive notice of the husband's undue influence. *The House of Lords decided that the bank was not put on inquiry, because the loan application form indicated that it was a joint loan for the purposes of paying off the outstanding joint mortgage and to purchase a holiday home.* In fact, the loan was to enable the husband to speculate on the stock market and he had pressurized his wife into declaring that it was for these other purposes. However, on the face of the application form, there was some apparent financial benefit to the wife. Accordingly, the bank could not be fixed with constructive notice of the husband's actual undue influence.

This decision made it clear that it is the form of the transaction that governs, and the court will not look behind the form at the substance of the transaction.

What was the position if the loan was used partly for joint purposes and partly to guarantee the husband's business debts? ***Dunbar Bank plc v Nadeem*** [1998] 3 All ER 876 differed from *CIBC v Pitt* because the allegation of actual undue influence failed. It was therefore necessary to rely on presumed undue influence by the husband, which at the time required that the transaction be shown to be manifestly disadvantageous to the wife. On the facts, this was held not to be the case, because the wife obtained a beneficial interest in the matrimonial home as a result of the transaction. This requirement of 'manifest disadvantage', which was required to establish the existence of presumed undue influence, had to be distinguished from the requirement, in the context of third party undue influence and notice, that the transaction on its face was not to the advantage of the complainant (thereby putting the bank on inquiry and in danger of losing its security): *Bank of Cyprus (London) Ltd v Markou* [1999] 2 All ER 707, at p. 717.

The latter question is entirely dependent on how the facts are presented to the bank, e.g. in *CIBC v Pitt* the joint loan was presented as having benefits for both husband and wife. It is therefore unusual for the court to look behind this. The court in *Bank of Cyprus (London) Ltd v Markou* looked beyond the facts on paper to the realities of the situation, i.e. although the wife was a shareholder in the husband's company, the bank knew that the company was wholly controlled by the husband and that the wife had no active role.

One of the complexities may now have been eliminated following the decision of the House of Lords in *Royal Bank of Scotland plc v Etridge (No. 2)* [2001] UKHL 44, [2002] 2 AC 773, which has greatly simplified the so-called 'threshold' when the bank is put on inquiry. In *Etridge*, Lord Nicholls considered that *O'Brien* should be interpreted as providing that 'a bank is put on inquiry whenever a wife offers to stand surety *for her husband's debts*' (emphasis added). He went on to extend this to instances in which husbands stand surety for the debts of their wives and to all unmarried couples, whether or not they were cohabiting.

Such a position would eliminate the need to assess the precise nature of the relationship between the parties, because the only issue would be knowledge of the relationship. Since it refers to standing surety 'for her husband's debts', it is unlikely to eliminate some of the difficulties associated with joint purposes, so that it will still be necessary in some instances to assess the declared purpose for the requested loan. However, in a simple case in which the wife stands surety for the husband's debts, the bank will be automatically put on inquiry and questions concerning indirect benefits to the wife do not arise.

Where funds are advanced jointly, the position will continue to be governed by the decision in *CIBC v Pitt*, i.e. the bank will not be put on inquiry. The only situation in which the bank might be put on inquiry would be where the bank had knowledge that, despite the declared joint purposes, the loan was solely for the husband's purposes. Lord Nicholls described instances of loans to the husband's company in which the wife had a shareholding in that company, e.g. as in *Bank of Cyprus (London) Ltd v Markou*, as being 'less clear cut'. Nevertheless, he considered that the bank would be put on inquiry in all such cases, even where the wife was an officer of the company, since there were obvious dangers in such a situation and, at [49], 'the shareholding interests, and the identity of the directors, are not a reliable guide to the identity of the persons who actually have the conduct of the company's business'. By comparison, in *Mortgage Business plc v Green* [2013] EWHC 4243 (Ch), Morgan J held that the lender was not affected by any undue influence that might have taken place by a son in relation to his mother in the context of a remortgage. This was a joint application by mother and son but there was nothing in the application that would have made the lender aware that the mother was a surety for her son's debts so that the lender was not put on inquiry by anything that had come to its attention. *Etridge* required that a lender be put on inquiry where 'it is aware' that the advance is for the purposes of one borrower so that the other borrower is effectively only a surety, and (at [38]) it was not necessary for a lender 'to play detective and follow up any clue which might have indicated that the information provided was not scrupulously accurate'.

In the context of 'non-sexual relationships', Lord Nicholls also considered that banks should not be required to evaluate the extent of influence of one party over the other and added, at [87], that 'the only practical way forward is to regard banks as put on inquiry in every case where the relationship between the surety and the debtor is non-commercial' (known as the 'wider principle'). In the commercial context, the need for the protection does not exist, since, as Lord Nicholls stated in *Etridge*, at [88]: 'Those engaged in business can be regarded as capable of looking after themselves and understanding the risks involved in the giving of guarantees.'

In summary, whenever security is given in a non-commercial setting, a lender will be put on inquiry and will need to take the appropriate steps to avoid being fixed with constructive notice. Lord Nicholls added that he regarded this as 'a modest burden' and, given the need for certainty, this would appear to be entirely sensible as a course of action. To this extent, *Etridge* both simplifies the law and extends the protection available to such sureties. The decision also goes further in clarifying the steps that a bank needs to take to ensure that it is protected.

2. The steps to be taken to avoid being fixed with constructive notice of third party undue influence

The requirement in *Barclays Bank plc v O'Brien* [1994] 1 AC 180 that the bank should first advise the wife in a private interview proved troublesome, because banks were, not surprisingly, reluctant to give direct advice for fear that this would form the basis for a later claim based, for example, on misrepresentation. In practice therefore, and despite *O'Brien*, the banks omitted this step and simply required the wife to seek legal advice. A body of case law developed that had the effect of shifting the responsibility for the giving of advice to solicitors, enabling the banks to be protected by the issue of a solicitor's certificate stating that the nature and effect of the documents had been explained to the wife: e.g. *Bank of Baroda v Rayarel* [1995] 2 FCR 631. It was also held that the bank was not concerned with matters concerning the solicitor's independence: *Massey v Midland Bank plc* [1995] 1 All ER 929, *Banco Exterior Internacional v Mann* [1995] 1 All ER 936, and *Barclays Bank plc v Thomson* [1997] 4 All ER 816.

The House of Lords in *Royal Bank of Scotland plc v Etridge (No. 2)* [2001] UKHL 44, [2002] 2 AC 773, has now explained, in precise terms, the steps that the bank needs to take. The House of Lords considered that it was neither desirable nor practical to expect banks or solicitors to be satisfied that no undue influence has been exercised; that would involve questioning that was far too intrusive and would prove expensive.

Lord Nicholls said, at [54], that 'the furthest a bank can be expected to go is to take reasonable steps to satisfy itself that the wife had had brought home to her, in a meaningful way, the practical implications of the proposed transaction'. He concluded that the wife would then enter the transaction 'with her eyes open so far as the basic elements of the transaction are concerned'. It was not necessary that the bank itself fulfils this task and, if the bank preferred, it could be undertaken by a solicitor, which has since proved to be the standard practice. The speech of Lord Nicholls is also significant in emphasizing that, in the general sense, it is not for the solicitor to veto the transaction; the decision on whether to proceed must lie with the wife (once the practical implications have been explained to her). However, Lord Hobhouse warned against confusing comprehension of a document (which is all that is required on the approach of Lord Nicholls) with agreement given freely in the knowledge of the true facts (which Lord Hobhouse considered was necessary to negative undue influence). Lord Hobhouse was particularly concerned about situations in which the husband's influence extended to the process whereby the wife received the explanation of the transaction and its implications. In such instances, the wife might well comprehend (and so be informed), but would still not be able to give a 'free consent'.

⏿ SUMMARY

As a result of the decision of the House of Lords in *Etridge*, in general terms, the bank need only take reasonable steps to satisfy itself that the practical implications of the proposed transaction have been explained to the wife and can rely on confirmation from the solicitor that this has been done, unless the bank knows or ought to realize that appropriate advice was not received. The bank is not expected to have any knowledge of the advice given by the solicitor and the solicitor is not accountable to the bank for the advice given to the wife. If the advice given were deficient in any respect, then the wife would need to seek redress from the solicitor, by means of an action based on negligent advice.

Their Lordships also considered that there should be no requirement that the solicitor should be wholly independent, i.e. a different solicitor from that engaged by the husband, on the basis that a requirement for a separate and independent solicitor might prove prohibitively expensive. The solicitor would owe duties directly to the client, and if the solicitor was concerned that there was a real risk of conflict of interest that might inhibit the advice given, the solicitor would need to stop acting for the wife.

3. The 'glaringly obvious' instances of undue influence

In *Royal Bank of Scotland plc v Etridge (No. 2)* [2001] UKHL 44, [2002] 2 AC 773, at [62], Lord Nicholls referred to 'exceptional circumstances where it is glaringly obvious that the wife is being grievously wronged' and stated that, in such cases, 'the solicitor should decline to act further', the implication being that if the bank were then to fail to investigate further, it would be fixed with constructive notice. Although these 'exceptional circumstances' are not explained, the example given is so extreme (a poor man transferring all his property to his solicitor) as to suggest that it is unlikely to apply in many instances. Nevertheless, this principle might apply in less obvious circumstances as long as there is clear evidence that undue influence is *more than likely* as opposed to circumstances that merely raise a suspicion.

In *Barclays Bank plc v O'Brien* [1994] 1 AC 180, Lord Browne-Wilkinson had stated that, where undue influence was *probable* in the circumstances, the bank would need to ensure that independent advice was obtained. It would seem that *Credit Lyonnais Bank Nederland NV v Burch* [1997] 1 All ER 144 may be an example of the type of case of 'glaringly obvious' undue influence to which Lord Nicholls was referring in which the bank is subject to this stricter duty.

In **Credit Lyonnais Bank**, the defendant was a junior employee of a company and was a family friend of the claimant, the company's main shareholder. The claimant asked her to provide security to cover the company's overdraft, which involved charging her flat and giving an unlimited guarantee to the bank. Although the bank had advised her to obtain independent legal advice, she had not done so. When the company went into liquidation, the bank sought possession of the defendant's flat. The bank argued that it had discharged its responsibility by advising the defendant to take legal advice and could not be responsible for her failure to do so. The Court of Appeal held that, because the bank knew the nature of the employment relationship, it should have realized that undue influence was *probable*. Therefore it *should have ensured* that the defendant obtained the independent legal advice and explained the potential extent of her liability. Accordingly, the bank was fixed with notice of the undue influence and the transaction was set aside.

15.3 A doctrine of unconscionable bargaining?

15.3.1 Procedural and substantive unfairness

Duress and undue influence are examples of court intervention on the basis of procedural unfairness, i.e. there was something wrong in the other party's behaviour in the period before the making of the contract. A further example of intervention based on procedural unfairness is the ability to set aside the contract for misrepresentation, i.e. one party made misleading statements to the other that led that other to make the contract. This is not the same thing as saying that the content of the contract that the parties made was unfair in some way, i.e. substantive unfairness, so that their agreed terms should be prevented or restricted by legislation or the courts.

Traditionally, it is easier for a law based on party autonomy to recognize procedural unfairness than substantive unfairness, since intervention on procedural grounds would reflect a lack of contractual freedom on the facts. English law does not interfere, in general terms, with bargains based only on the position that the terms appear unfair to one of the parties (although see discussion, particularly in the consumer context, at **15.3.2** and at **7.6.4**). The principle that 'consideration need not be adequate' (see **4.3.1**) is illustrative of the fact that the courts are not interested in the comparative values of exchanges.

However, there has been less difficulty with parliamentary intervention in regulating content, so that in this sense English law, often through the implementation of European legislation, intervenes to protect consumers and so recognizes the dangers of inequality of bargaining power.

15.3.2 Consumer legislation

The legislation discussed below is merely indicative of the nature and extent of the legislative intervention. It indicates, however, that it is not imbalance in a relationship per se that justifies intervention, but an abuse or taking advantage of that imbalance.

1. In accordance with Part 2 of the Consumer Rights Act 2015, a term in a consumer contract will be unfair if 'contrary to the requirement of good faith', it 'causes a significant imbalance in the parties' rights and obligations under the contract to the detriment of the consumer' (s. 62(4)). Many of the terms that are listed as indicative of unfairness in Sch. 2 Part 1 of the CRA 2015 are based on this imbalance, and in *Director General of Fair Trading v First National Bank plc* [2001] UKHL 52, [2002] 1 AC 481, the House of Lords assessed the unfairness of terms by reference to both procedural and substantive unfairness resulting in the contractual rights being tilted significantly in the supplier's favour or imposing a disadvantageous burden, risk, or duty on the consumer. This unfairness is therefore linked with the concept of inequality of bargaining power and a taking advantage of that position, which represent key ingredients in a wider doctrine of unconscionability. Unfairness on its own (or inequality of bargaining power) is not sufficient; there must also be this element of abuse.

2. The 'unfair relationship' provision in ss. 140A–C of the Consumer Credit Act (CCA) 1974, as amended by the Consumer Credit Act 2006 (the replacement for the largely ineffectual

'grossly' extortionate bargaining provision), enables the court to make an order if it finds that the relationship between creditor and debtor arising out of a credit agreement, or that agreement taken with any related agreement, is unfair to the debtor. This unfairness can result from one or more of the following:

(a) any of the terms of the agreement, e.g. restrictions on termination rights or onerous charges;

(b) the way in which the creditor has exercised or enforced any of its rights; and/or

(c) any other thing done by the creditor, whether occurring before or after the making of the agreement.

The court is also permitted to take into account all sorts of issues, such as the debtor's age and financial circumstances, and any high-pressure selling techniques used by the creditor. When an unfair relationship is established, the creditor may be ordered to repay sums paid, or the debt may be written off, or the terms of the agreement may be varied. This provision clearly addresses both procedural and substantive unfairness.

3. There is also intervention by the criminal law to regulate 'unfair trading' in the consumer context. The Consumer Protection from Unfair Trading Regulations (CPRs) 2008, SI 2008/1277, implementing the Unfair Commercial Practices Directive (UCPD) 2005/29/EC (see **1.6.2.2** and **14.1.2.4**), prohibit unfair commercial practices (reg. 3), and this includes aggressive commercial practices (reg. 7) that cause or are likely to cause the making of a contract where these practices significantly impair or are likely to impair consumer freedom of choice as a result of 'harassment, coercion or undue influence'. Regulation 7(2) provides that when:

> determining whether a commercial practice uses harassment, coercion or undue influence account shall be taken of:
>
> (a) its timing, location, nature or persistence;
>
> (b) the use of threatening or abusive language or behaviour;
>
> (c) the exploitation by the trader of any specific misfortune or circumstance of such gravity as to impair the consumer's judgment, of which the trader is aware, to influence the consumer's decision with regard to the product;
>
> (d) any onerous or disproportionate non-contractual barrier imposed by the trader where a consumer wishes to exercise rights under the contract, including rights to terminate a contract or to switch to another product or another trader; and
>
> (e) any threat to take any action which cannot legally be taken.

'Undue influence' in this context is defined as 'exploiting a position of power in relation to the consumer so as to apply pressure, even without using or threatening to use physical force, in a way which significantly limits the consumer's ability to make an informed choice' (reg. 7(3)(b)). The scope of the CPRs was further extended to provide civil rights to redress in relation to defined 'prohibited practices' within the CPRs—as part of the implementation of the EU Consumer Rights Directive (CRD) 2011/83/EU (see discussion at **14.1.2.4**). The Consumer Protection (Amendment) Regulations 2014, SI 2014/870, introduce a new Part 4A into the CPRs 2008 to achieve this aim. It applies to misleading actions (reg. 5) and aggressive practices (reg. 7).

15.3.3 What is unconscionable bargaining?

Are the courts ever able to intervene in contracts based on the unfairness of the parties' bargaining positions? It appears that there must be more than unfairness; there must also be evidence of abuse of the imbalance in contracting positions, often known as 'unconscionability'. In other words, there must be some exploitation of the weakness of the other party to justify intervention on the basis of the unfairness of the bargain.

Unconscionability has long been recognized in other jurisdictions. The US Uniform Commercial Code (UCC) § 2–302(1) allows for intervention on this ground:

> If the court as a matter of law finds the contract or any clause of the contract to have been unconscionable at the time it was made the court may refuse to enforce the contract, or it may enforce the remainder of the contract without the unconscionable clause, or it may so limit the application of any unconscionable clause as to avoid any unconscionable result.

The UCC itself does not define 'unconscionable', but the commentary published with it says that the section is aimed at preventing 'oppression and unfair surprise', and is not intended to disturb normal allocations of risk resulting from disparities in bargaining power.

Australia also has a recognized doctrine of unconscionability as a ground for intervention. In the High Court of Australia in *Commercial Bank of Australia v Amadio* (1983) 151 CLR 447, at p. 461, Mason J commented that:

> Relief on the ground of 'unconscionable conduct' is usually taken to refer to the class of case in which a party makes an unconscientious use of his superior position or bargaining power to the detriment of a party who suffers from some special disability or is placed in some special situation of disadvantage.

In English law, recognition of 'unconscionability' as a distinct ground for intervention has been more haphazard, but it is clear that there cannot be intervention on this basis without disadvantage on the part of party A and a 'taking advantage' of that disadvantage by party B. Such matters come before the courts because the outcome is a contract that evidences unfairness in its result. In *Greenwood Forest Products (UK) Ltd v Roberts* [2010] Bus LR D146, QBD (Leeds), 12 March 2010, there was a specific claim to set aside the transaction as an unconscionable bargain (in addition to claims based on fraudulent misrepresentation and undue influence), and the judge held, at [269]–[282], that there were three requirements, as follows.

1. One party has to suffer from a disability or serious disadvantage.

2. The transaction is 'overreaching or oppressive', so that it shocks the conscience of the court.

3. The stronger party must have acted unconscionably, in the sense that they acted in a morally reprehensible manner, e.g. if the stronger party knowingly took advantage of the weaker party's disabling condition or circumstances.

Once these three conditions are satisfied, it is for the stronger party to show that, in fact, the transaction was 'fair, just, and reasonable'. Independent legal advice might defeat an allegation of unconscionability, but only if the nature of the disadvantage was fully explained and there was no obligation to go ahead with the transaction. The allegation failed on the facts of the case, because the party alleged to be suffering the disability was an experienced businessman who received advice and the transactions were not at an undervalue or oppressive. Finally, the other party had not 'knowingly taken advantage'. In *Fineland Investments Ltd v Pritchard* [2011] EWHC 113 (Ch), [2011] 6 EG 102 (CS), the judge rejected a claim to set aside a transfer of the defendant's home on the basis that it was an unconscionable bargain, noting, at [81], that 'a bargain which is merely hard or improvident is insufficient to qualify as an oppressive and unconscionable bargain'. More is required in order to 'shock the conscience of the court'.

15.3.4 The principle in *Fry v Lane*

In English law, the recognition of a principle of unconscionability has its origins in *Fry v Lane* (1888) 40 Ch D 312. *This doctrine derives from a right of equity to set aside transactions made at a considerable undervalue and without independent advice against the 'poor and ignorant'.* The presumption of fraud, which arises in these circumstances, may be rebutted by evidence that the bargain was 'fair, just, and reasonable'. This principle has gradually been extended in its scope—e.g. *Cresswell v Potter* [1978] 1 WLR 255—so that 'poor and ignorant' is a matter of relative perspective and old age appears to come within its ambit: *Boustany v Pigot* (1993) 69 P & CR 298. In *Credit Lyonnais Bank v Burch* [1997] 1 All ER 144, Nourse LJ would, it seems, have been prepared to extend the doctrine still further, i.e. to a junior employee influenced by an employer and family friend.

However, the key ingredient of any doctrine of unconscionability, as explained in *Boustany v Pigot*, is not that the transaction is unreasonable or unfair, but that there has been an 'abuse' of position. Millett LJ, in *Credit Lyonnais Bank* at p. 153b, referred to the need for 'some impropriety, both in the conduct of the stronger party and in the terms of the transaction itself'. The conscience of the court should be offended. In *Kalsep Ltd v X-Flow*, The Times, 3 May 2001, it was stressed that a party seeking to set aside an agreement as an unconscionable bargain had to show more than just improvidence. Pumfrey J stated that, although it would be difficult, 'it is necessary to prove impropriety, and that is to say not merely harshness but impropriety, both in the terms of the agreement and in the manner in which the agreement was arrived at'. On the facts, there was no evidence of any coercion or other improper pressure, although the judge accepted that it was an 'exceptionally improvident agreement, ignorantly and foolishly entered into'.

In *Evans v Lloyd* [2013] EWHC 1725 (Ch), [2013] WTLR 1137 [2013] 2 P&CR DG21 (for facts see **15.2.4.2**), it had also been argued that Mr and Mrs Lloyd had knowingly taken advantage of the fact that Wynne Evans had left school at an early age and had little worldly experience so this, coupled with the absence of legal advice, amounted to unconscionability and the gifts should be set aside. The judge accepted the fact that the gifts were disadvantageous to Wynne in a practical sense and that he could be classed as 'poor' and 'ignorant', but rejected the unconscionability claim on the basis that it was not possible to say that Mr and Mrs Lloyd were morally culpable.

It therefore seems that, to succeed in a claim based on unconscionability, there must be procedural and substantive 'impropriety' that extends beyond mere unfairness.

15.3.5 *Portman Building Society v Dusangh*

In *Portman Building Society v Dusangh* [2000] 2 All ER (Comm) 221, the Court of Appeal refused to grant relief based on an argument of unconscionability of the bargain.

The defendant in **Portman Building Society v Dusangh** was aged 72. He was illiterate in English and spoke the language poorly. The claimant building society granted him a mortgage, guaranteed by his son, covering 75 per cent of the value of his property over 25 years in order to release the equity in the property. The money was given to the defendant's son to enable him to purchase a supermarket. The son was later declared bankrupt, so that the guarantee was worthless. The building society sought to enforce its security, but the defendant claimed that, because of the nature of the agreement, it could be set aside as an unconscionable bargain, both in respect of unconscionable conduct by the son exploiting his father's weakness, which affected the building society, and in respect of unconscionable conduct by the building society itself based on the principle in **Fry v Lane** (1888) 40 Ch D 312.

The Court of Appeal rejected the argument based on the son's unconscionable conduct, distinguishing *Credit Lyonnais Bank v Burch* [1997] 1 All ER 144, because the building society had not exploited the situation and had not acted in a 'morally reprehensible manner': *per* Simon Brown LJ in **Portman.** The father had merely sought to assist his son in what he hoped would be a profitable venture. Ward LJ stated at p. 232j, that:

> [I]t may be that the son gained all the advantage and the father took all the risk, but this cannot be stigmatised as impropriety. There was no exploitation of father by son such as would prick the conscience and tell the son that in all honour it was morally wrong and reprehensible.

There was also no undue influence on the facts, the transaction was not manifestly disadvantageous, and legal advice had been received.

In addition, although the defendant in the case fell within the 'poor and ignorant' requirement for the operation of the principle in *Fry v Lane* and the transaction was an improvident one, Simon Brown LJ stated that building societies were not required to police transactions to ensure the wisdom of parents' actions in seeking to assist their children.

15.3.6 The link between unconscionability and undue influence

There have also been increasing references in cases involving allegations of undue influence to a link between unconscionability and undue influence: *Credit Lyonnais Bank v Burch* [1997] 1 All ER 144 and *Dunbar Bank plc v Nadeem* [1998] 3 All ER 876. However, other cases have given them a separate identity on the basis that 'unconscionability' turns on abuse of position by the defendant, whereas undue influence focuses on the reason why the claimant made that contract and the context of the parties' relationship. Unconscionability does not require a relationship of trust and confidence.

In *Portman Building Society v Dusangh* [2000] 2 All ER (Comm) 221, at p. 233f–g, Ward LJ cited the following statement of Mason J in the High Court of Australia in *Commercial Bank of Australia v Amadio* (1983) 151 CLR 447, at p. 461:

> Although unconscionable conduct in this narrow sense bears some resemblance to the doctrine of undue influence, there is a difference between the two. In the latter the will of the innocent party is not independent and voluntary because it is overborne. In the former, the will of the innocent party, even if independent and voluntary, is the result of the disadvantageous position in which he is placed and of the other party unconscientiously taking advantage of that position.

Nevertheless, Mason J also stated that he considered that all of the reasons for setting aside contracts on equitable grounds 'constitute species of unconscionable conduct'. It is likely therefore that 'unconscionability' can be used in both a general and a specific context. In addition, of course, unconscionability does not require a pre-existing relationship between the parties.

15.3.7 Conclusion

The development of a doctrine of unconscionability is therefore likely to be hampered by the practical reality that few cases will justify intervention by the courts; where they do so, they are also likely to give rise to a claim based on undue influence that may be conceptually more certain and therefore easier to satisfy. For example, in *Credit Lyonnais Bank v Burch* [1997] 1 All ER 144, there was no plea of unconscionable bargain, although the Court of Appeal considered there to be a sufficient basis for intervention on this ground. On the facts in *Portman Building Society v Dusangh* [2000] 2 All ER (Comm) 221, there was no evidence of undue influence and the required unconscionable conduct was also missing. In *Evans v Lloyd* [2013] EWHC 1725 (Ch), [2013] WTLR 1137, [2013] 2 P & CR DG21, discussed at **15.2.4.2** and **15.3.4**, the judge concluded that if the alternative argument of undue influence failed then the claim based on unconscionability would also fail.

15.4 The Draft Common Frame of Reference, UNIDROIT, and the Common European Sales Law

The Draft Common Frame of Reference (DCFR) has provisions covering duress and abuse of trust/unfair exploitation. DCFR II-7:206 provides for avoidance of a contract induced by 'coercion or by the threat of an imminent and serious harm which it is wrongful to inflict, or wrongful to use as a means to obtain the conclusion of the contract'. However, in order to act as the inducement, the threatened party must have had no reasonable alternative in the circumstances. (The provisions in the Common European Sales Law, or CESL, are clearly based on the DCFR. Article 50 has a similar avoidance provision for threats, although there is no sign of any requirement that there needs to be a reasonable alternative.) DCFR II-7:207 provides for avoidance where that party was either dependent on the other or had a relationship of trust with the other, 'was in economic distress or had urgent needs, was improvident, ignorant, inexperienced or lacking in bargaining skill'. The other party must have had actual or constructive knowledge of these circumstances, and must have exploited or taken advantage of the position 'by taking an excessive benefit or grossly unfair advantage'. (Article 51 CESL, on unfair exploitation, is similar.)

The DCFR does allow for flexibility in terms of remedy by giving the court power to adapt the contract and also (under DCFR II-7:213) allowing for recognition of partial avoidance (see the discussion of partial rescission in English law at **14.5.2.3**). There is also provision for damages for loss in instances in which the contract can be avoided (DCFR II-7:214). (Article 54 CESL allows for partial avoidance, but makes no mention of adaptation in the context of matters affecting the validity of the formation process. Again, there is a provision allowing for damages for loss, possibly in addition to avoidance: Art. 55 CESL.)

These DCFR provisions are based on the virtually identical provisions in the Principles of European Contract Law (PECL), Arts. 4:108, 4:109, 4:116, and 4:117. There are also provisions with different wording, but similar effect in UNIDROIT's Principles of International Commercial Contracts (PICC), Arts. 3.2.6 (threat), 3.2.7 (gross disparity/taking excessive or unjustifiable advantage), 3.2.13 (partial avoidance), and 3.2.16 (damages in instances in which there is the right of avoidance).

MULTIPLE-CHOICE QUESTIONS

 Test your knowledge by trying this chapter's **multiple-choice questions**: www.oup.com/uk/poole

FURTHER READING

General and unconscionability

Atiyah, 'Contract and fair exchange' in *Essays on Contract* (Oxford University Press, 1986).

Brownsword, *Contract Law: Themes for the Twenty-First Century*, 2nd edn (Oxford University Press, 2006), ch. 4.

Enonchong, *Duress, Undue Influence and Unconscionable Dealing*, 2nd edn (Sweet and Maxwell, 2012).

Morgan, *Great Debates in Contract Law*, 2nd edn (Palgrave Macmillan, 2015), ch. 7.

Spark, *Vitiation of Contracts: International Contractual Principles and English Law* (Cambridge University Press, 2013).

Televantos, 'Unconscionable bargains, overreaching and overriding interests' (2016) 75 CLJ 458.

Tiplady, 'The judicial control of contractual unfairness' (1983) 46 MLR 601.

Waddams, 'Unconscionability in contracts' (1976) 39 MLR 369.

Duress

Atiyah, 'Economic duress and the overborne will' (1982) 98 LQR 197.

Beatson, 'Duress as a vitiating factor in contract' (1974) 33 CLJ 97.

Davies and Day, 'Lawful act duress' (2018) 134 LQR 5.

Eldridge, 'Lawful acts duress and marital agreements' (2018) 77 CLJ 32.

Macdonald, 'Duress by threatened breach of contract' [1989] JBL 460.

Moore, 'Why does Lord Denning's lead balloon intrigue us still?' (2018) 134 LQR 257.

Smith, 'Contracting under pressure: a theory of duress' (1997) 56 CLJ 343.

Tamblyn, 'Causation and bad faith in economic duress' (2011) 27 JCL 140.

Undue influence (including relationship with unconscionability)

Bamforth, 'Unconscionability as a vitiating factor' [1995] LMCLQ 538.

Bigwood, 'Undue influence in the House of Lords: principles and proof' (2002) 65 MLR 435.

Birks and Chin, 'On the nature of undue influence' in Beatson and Friedmann (eds.), *Good Faith and Fault in Contract Law* (Oxford University Press, 1995).

Capper, 'Undue influence and unconscionability: a rationalisation' (1998) 114 LQR 479.

Capper, 'Banks, borrowers, sureties and undue influence: a half-baked solution to a thoroughly cooked problem' [2002] RLR 100.

McMurty, 'Unconscionability and undue influence: an interaction?' [2000] Conv 573.

Phang and Tijo, 'The uncertain boundaries of undue influence' [2002] LMCLQ 231.

Chapter 16

Illegality

SUMMARY OF THE ISSUES

This chapter provides an introduction to two issues: (i) identifying contracts that are tainted by illegality or otherwise contrary to public policy; and (ii) examining the effect on the parties' positions of this illegality.

- A contract may be illegal from the outset (illegal as formed) or the illegality may arise in the course of performance of what would otherwise be a valid contract (illegal as performed). A contract illegal as formed is an agreement to perform an act illegally. By contrast, where one party performs an illegal act in the course of carrying out a contract, that act may have nothing to do with what was intended when the contract was made.

- Contracts may be illegal as a result of statute or at common law. Legislation may prohibit particular classes of contract. In addition, at common law, the courts have declared a wide range of contracts to be illegal or contrary to public policy, such as contracts to commit crimes or contracts prejudicial to sexual morality. Furthermore, the courts have struck down restraints of trade where they infringe the public interest in promoting free competition and where they are unreasonable as between the parties.

- The enforceability of illegal contracts and the recovery of benefits conferred in the performance of illegal contracts rest upon a range of factors rather than a single rule. At one time the courts adopted a rigid approach, refusing to enforce contracts illegal as formed and denying any rights to a party who performed an illegal act when fulfilling the contract. That was the effect of the decision of the House of Lords in *Tinsley v Milligan*, where the test was whether the claimant had to rely upon illegality to make good his case. That test was much criticized so that, in 1999, the Law Commission made a series of provisional recommendations for reform. Nevertheless, when the Law Commission published its consultative report on the illegality defence in January 2009, and a final report in March 2010, it recommended that any improvement to the law 'can best be left to development through the case law' based on the application of the policy factors that underpin the illegality defence. In recent years, the courts began to follow the Law Commission's suggestion, and demonstrated a willingness to evaluate and give effect to policy, and to reflect the positions of the parties on the facts, when making determinations on the illegality defence. However, the result was that it became difficult to identify definite principles of law and the volume of case law grew as a consequence.

- A series of contradictory Supreme Court decisions left the law in a state of uncertainty. In *Hounga v Allan* it was suggested that illegality should bar relief only where it was inextricably linked to the claim. By contrast, shortly afterwards in **Les Laboratoires Servier v Apotex Inc.**, the Supreme Court was of the view that illegality is a rule of law based on public policy and not an area in which the courts exercise a discretion based on the facts and circumstances of individual parties. The urgent need for clarity led to the appointment of a nine-member Supreme Court to hear the appeal in *Patel v Mirza*. A majority of 6:3 supported a more flexible approach to the enforceability of illegal contracts.

»

- Benefits transferred under an illegal contract may be recoverable. Before *Patel v Mirza* the courts had established a series of complex exceptions where money or property paid under an illegal contract could be recovered despite the illegality. Those exceptions were, most importantly: where the parties were not equally guilty (not *in pari delicto*), e.g. where one of the parties was aware of the illegality; where the illegal purpose had not been put into effect so that withdrawal was possible (the doctrine of *locus poenitentiae*); and where the claimant could establish title independently of any illegality. After the adoption of the more flexible approach in *Patel v Mirza*, these exceptions have lost their significance.

16.1 Introduction: public policy and illegality

There are three basic questions to consider:

- what constitutes an illegal contract;
- what is the effect of that illegality on the ability to enforce it; and
- does the illegality operate as a defence to a contractual claim, or to a claim in restitution to recover money paid or other benefit conferred under the contract?

The type and degree of illegality will inevitably influence the attitude of the courts to the question of whether relief is possible.

16.1.1 Differences of opinion over the correct approach and the scope of the defence

As a general principle, the courts will not enforce contracts that are tainted with illegality, i.e. *ex turpi causa non oritur actio* (no action can arise from a bad cause), and will not permit the recovery of benefits conferred by such a contract. In *Gray v Thames Trains Ltd* [2009] UKHL 33, [2009] 1 AC 1339, at [30], Lord Hoffmann stated that 'the maxim *ex turpi causa* expresses not so much a principle as a policy . . . not based on a single justification but on a group of reasons, which vary in different circumstances'. Some cases adopted a flexible approach, as may be seen from the judgment of Bingham LJ in *Saunders v Edwards* [1987] 1 WLR 1116, at p 1134:

> Where issues of illegality are raised, the courts have (as it seems to me) to steer a middle course between two unacceptable positions. On the one hand it is unacceptable that any court of law should aid or lend its authority to a party seeking to pursue or enforce an object or agreement which the law prohibits. On the other hand, it is unacceptable that the court should, on the first indication of unlawfulness affecting any aspect of a transaction, draw up its skirts and refuse all assistance to the claimant, no matter how serious his loss or how disproportionate his loss to the unlawfulness of his conduct.

Nevertheless, in *Tinsley v Milligan* [1994] 1 AC 340, the House of Lords decided that the questions of enforceability and recovery of benefits rested upon whether the claimant had to rely upon his own illegal act to make out his case, and that there was no room for a 'public conscience' test whereby the court weighed the various public policy considerations that related to the claim. In that case the parties jointly contributed to the purchase of a home but in the name of Miss Tinsley only, so that Miss Milligan could make false claims for state benefits. Miss Milligan succeeded by a 3:2 majority in the House of Lords in claiming a share in the home, on the basis that in order to make good her claim she was not required to demonstrate why the home had been conveyed to Miss Tinsley. She had contributed to the price and there was a common understanding that they would share the property, so that she had an equitable interest in the property, and there was no need to resort to the illegal nature of the arrangement to establish that interest.

In its Consultation Paper *Illegal Transactions: The Effect of Illegality on Contracts and Trusts*, LCCP No. 154 (1999), at para. 7.70, the Law Commission used a wide definition of illegal contracts as including 'any contract which involves (in its formation, purpose or performance) a legal wrong (other than the mere breach of the contract in question) or conduct otherwise contrary to public policy'. It should follow that the law should not recognize such behaviour and should refuse to intervene to enforce it on public policy grounds even if it is what the parties have freely agreed to.

There is thus a balance to be struck between:

- the freedom of the parties to contract as they wish, which implies being able to enforce a contract freely entered into and, being able to ensure that no party is unjustly enriched through the receipt of benefits under a contract whilst not having to pay for them because the contract is considered illegal; and

- recognizing society's objections to certain types of contract or performance, i.e. 'an element of moral turpitude or moral reprehensibility in the relevant conduct', *per* Flaux J at first instance in *Safeway Stores Ltd v Twigger* [2010] EWHC 11 (Comm), [2010] Bus LR 974, at [26], whilst also taking notice of the fact that one party to such a contract may be entirely innocent of the illegality.

In its 2009 consultative report *The Illegality Defence*, Law Com. No. 189 (2009), at Part 2, para. 2.35, the Law Commission stated:

> The illegality defence should be allowed where its application can be firmly justified by the policies that underlie its existence. These include: (a) furthering the purpose of the rule which the illegal conduct has infringed; (b) consistency; (c) that the claimant should not profit from their own wrong; (d) deterrence; and (e) maintaining the integrity of the legal system.

This approach was expressly commended as the correct approach by the Court of Appeal in *ParkingEye Ltd v Somerfield Stores Ltd* [2012] EWCA Civ 1338, [2013] QB 840 (see also **16.2.2**), so that, in the judgment of Toulson LJ, the role of the court was to examine this policy and reach a balanced judgment, whilst asking whether the particular claimant, in the circumstances of this claim, should be denied the usual rights and remedies associated with that claim. This approach of balancing policy, and examining the parties' positions and circumstances, has the advantage of introducing some flexibility on the facts but, as always, the price for such a process is greater uncertainty.

However, while this approach was accepted by the Supreme Court in *Hounga v Allen* [2014] UKSC 47, [2014] 1 WLR 2889, relying upon the public policy principle of preserving the integrity of the legal system and balancing competing policy considerations on the facts, it was forcefully rejected by a differently constituted Supreme Court in *Les Laboratoires Servier v*

Apotex Inc. [2014] UKSC 55, [2015] AC 430. In *Les Laboratoires* the Supreme Court considered that illegality was a rule of law based on public policy rather than involving the exercise of a discretionary power and expressly rejected the approach and definition of illegality adopted by the Law Commission in its 2009 Consultation Paper. The disagreement was acknowledged but left unresolved by a larger panel of Justices in *Bilta (UK) Ltd (in Liquidation) v Nazir* [2015] UKSC 23, [2015] 2 WLR 1168.

The matter was given detailed consideration by the Supreme Court in *Patel v Mirza* [2016] UKSC 42, [2017] AC 467. This was a claim by Mr Patel to recover £620,000 paid to Mr Mirza and to be used by him to bet on the value of shares using inside information. The betting did not take place and Mr Patel sought to recover his payment. The agreement was illegal as a conspiracy to commit the offence of insider dealing. Although the issue was the recoverability of the sum paid, the Supreme Court chose to set out wider principles of the effect of illegality. Speaking for the majority, Lord Toulson (at [99], [107], and [109]) identified the policy reasons behind the defence of illegality and then the correct approach to dealing with them:

> Looking behind the maxims, there are two broad discernible policy reasons for the common law doctrine of illegality as a defence to a civil claim. One is that a person should not be allowed to profit from his own wrongdoing. The other, linked, consideration is that the law should be coherent and not self-defeating, condoning illegality by giving with the left hand what it takes with the right hand . . . Potentially relevant factors include the seriousness of the conduct, its centrality to the contract, whether it was intentional and whether there was marked disparity in the parties' respective culpability . . . [I]t is right for a court which is considering the application of the common law doctrine of illegality to have regard to the policy factors involved and to the nature and circumstances of the illegal conduct in determining whether the public interest in preserving the integrity of the justice system should result in denial of the relief claimed.

Lord Toulson summarized the new approach in the following way (at [120]):

> The essential rationale of the illegality doctrine is that it would be contrary to the public interest to enforce a claim if to do so would be harmful to the integrity of the legal system . . . In assessing whether the public interest would be harmed in that way, it is necessary a) to consider the underlying purpose of the prohibition which has been transgressed and whether that purpose will be enhanced by denial of the claim, b) to consider any other relevant public policy on which the denial of the claim may have an impact and c) to consider whether denial of the claim would be a proportionate response to the illegality, bearing in mind that punishment is a matter for the criminal courts. Within that framework, various factors may be relevant, but it would be a mistake to suggest that the court is free to decide a case in an undisciplined way. The public interest is best served by a principled and transparent assessment of the considerations identified, rather by than the application of a formal approach capable of producing results which may appear arbitrary, unjust or disproportionate.

The 'range of factors' identified by Lord Toulson (as at [120] mentioned above) was objected to by the minority on the basis that 'it converts a legal principle into an exercise of judicial discretion, in the process exhibiting all the vices of complexity, uncertainty, arbitrariness and lack of transparency' (see esp. at [206], [217], and [262]). The concerns of the minority were adopted by the Singapore Court of Appeal in *Orchid Trading Ltd v Chua Siok Liu* [2018] SGCA 5. However, as far as English law is concerned, the 'range of factors' now determine whether a party to an illegal contract has any rights under that contract and also whether benefits transferred under an illegal contract are recoverable.

Illegality

16

16.2 Statutory illegality

The role of the courts is to seek to identify the purpose behind the relevant statute and the impact that ignoring the prohibition has on the contract.

16.2.1 Express prohibition

Sometimes, statute expressly prohibits the type of contract in question, in which case it is clear that neither party can enforce the contract, even if one of them is innocent.

In *Re Mahmoud and Ispahani* [1921] 2 KB 716, the Seeds, Oils and Fats Order 1919, made under the Defence of the Realm Regulations, prohibited unlicensed dealing in linseed oil. The defendant misrepresented to the claimant that he had a licence, but subsequently refused to accept delivery, arguing that the contract was illegal because he did not possess the required licence. Despite the claimant's innocence, the contract could not be enforced, because to do so would undermine the purpose of the statutory prohibition.

This principle was also applied by the Court of Appeal in *Mohamed v Alaga and Co. (a firm)* [2000] 1 WLR 1815.

The agreement (whereby a firm of solicitors would pay an introduction fee from its legal aid fees to a person introducing refugees requiring legal services) was expressly prohibited by subordinate legislation. Public policy barred relief under the contract or by means of a claim in restitution for the services of introduction. However, the Court of Appeal did grant leave for the claim to be amended to a claim for the value of services rendered (*quantum meruit*), because the claimant was blameless (in the sense that he was not aware of the breach of rules) and no public policy was infringed by allowing him to recover for these services.

16.2.2 Contracts not expressly or impliedly prohibited, but performed by one party in an illegal manner

An illegal act committed in the course of the performance of a contract does not convert the contract into an illegal one in its formation unless the parties have expressly agreed that an illegal act is to be carried out. Instead, the innocent party will have full rights under the contract.

In *Archbolds (Freightage) Ltd v Spanglett Ltd* [1961] 1 QB 374, the defendants agreed to carry a cargo of whisky to London for the claimants, who were unaware that the defendants did not have the required licence to use the vehicle that they had selected for the transportation. The whisky was stolen and, when the claimants claimed damages for the loss, the defendants pleaded illegality. The claimants were allowed to sue on the contract for the defendants' loss of the goods en route. The contract was not expressly or impliedly prohibited by statute (i.e. not illegal on its formation). It was performed by the defendants in an illegal manner, but the claimants were not party to that illegal performance and so could enforce it.

However, if the other party either knows of the illegal performance or participates in it, that party will not be able to enforce the contract. In *Ashmore, Benson, Pease & Co. Ltd v A. V. Dawson Ltd* [1973] 1 WLR 828, the defendants had carried tube banks in contravention of legislation specifying the maximum weight of lorries, but since the claimant's representative had been present at loading and had raised no objection, the claimant was unable to recover damages when the tube bank was damaged during the journey.

As far as the guilty party is concerned, it is clear from *Anderson Ltd v Daniel* [1924] 1 KB 138 that the illegal performer cannot enforce the contract because to allow so would undermine the purpose of the statute. However, if the purpose is not undermined, the courts have been more flexible, e.g. *Shaw v Groom* [1970] 2 QB 504, in which a landlord had failed to give the tenant a rent book, but was allowed to recover the rent from the tenant, since the legislation imposed a penalty for this failure, but did not strike at the tenancy agreement itself, i.e. it was not a licence for tenants without a rent book to avoid the payment of rent. Again, in *St John Shipping v Joseph Rank Ltd* [1957] 1 QB 267 the carrier of goods was held to be entitled to recover freight payable by the owner of the goods under the contract of carriage even though the carrier had deliberately overloaded the vessel so that the load line was below the water. Although there had been an infringement of merchant shipping laws, that was held not to affect the enforceability of the contract itself. Devlin J noted that the plethora of modern regulatory legislation made compliance increasingly difficult and that technical infringements of the law should not be given the disproportionate effect of depriving a party of contractual rights.

The Court of Appeal in *ParkingEye Ltd v Somerfield Stores Ltd* [2012] EWCA Civ 1338, [2013] QB 840 adopted a similarly flexible, analysis to illegality in performance.

The parties had entered into a contract for ParkingEye (P) to install a monitoring system in supermarket car parks run by Somerfield (S). Customers were charged for overstaying. P monitored usage and then sent overstayers demands for the overstay charge. P collected and retained the overstay charges recovered. The contract was to run for 15 months, but S terminated it after only six months. When P claimed damages for its loss of revenue as a result of the early termination, S pleaded the defence of illegality—namely, that, contrary to public policy, one of P's pro forma letters was deceptive and used illegal means to induce overstayers to pay. However, the Court of Appeal considered that the law was not static and it was not the case that, once it was shown that *any* illegality in performance was intended at the outset, however partial or peripheral (as was the case on these facts), then unenforceability would follow automatically. This contract was not performed in a *wholly* illegal manner.

When considering the proper scope and application of the principle, the factors that were to be considered were: (i) the object and intent of the party seeking to enforce the contract; (ii) the centrality and gravity of the illegality in the context of the contract and the claim; and (iii) the nature of the illegality. This was a contract involving continuous performance over a period of time and any intention to act unlawfully was not fixed, but could change at any time. Weighing in the balance was the fact that providing S with a defence to its (wrongful) repudiation would be to give it a windfall reward when S had approved the pro forma letters ahead of the contract, whereas P would be left with no income and no remedy for the repudiation. In short, the court thought that the repudiation was an overreaction. The proper course would have been for S to have drawn the unlawful letter to P's attention and honoured the contract, on the basis that it be performed lawfully.

This decision, weighing a series of policy considerations rather than applying a rigid rule, is clearly consistent with the approach to illegality approved by the Supreme Court in *Patel v Mirza*.

16.2.3 The penalty provided by the statute is considered sufficient sanction

In some cases, the penalty provided for by the statute is thought to be sufficient sanction for the infringement in question, so that the contract may be enforced by both innocent and guilty parties. Such a case was *St John Shipping Corporation v Joseph Rank Ltd* [1957] 1 QB 267 (see **16.2.2**) where the offence of overloading was punishable by the payment of a fine. Devlin J held that the fine was the only sanction specified by the legislation.

A similar conclusion was reached in *Hughes v Asset Managers plc* [1995] 3 All ER 669, in which penalties were imposed on those dealing with share purchases without the necessary licence, but the purchase contracts made by such persons were not void as illegal contracts and they could be enforced by infringers.

16.3 Gambling contracts: legally enforceable

'Gambling' means gaming, betting, and participating in a lottery (Gambling Act 2005, s. 3) and 'gaming' means participating in a game of chance for a prize (s. 6). The 2005 Act reversed s. 18 of the Gaming Act 1845, which had provided that gambling contracts were null and void, so that there could be no action in the courts relating to recovery of any such bet or winnings. Section 335(1) of the 2005 Act instead provides that, in general terms, 'the fact that a contract relates to gambling shall not prevent its enforcement'. It follows that any money paid or property deposited under a gambling contract is no longer irrecoverable merely on the basis that it is a gambling contract.

16.4 Contracts that are contrary to public policy

It is traditional for judges to disapprove resort to public policy—Burrough J in *Richardson v Mellish* (1824) 2 Bing 229, at p. 252, described public policy as an 'unruly horse' to be ridden with care—and to point to the adverse effect on freedom of contract of allowing public policy arguments to prevail: Jessel MR in *Printing and Numerical Registering Co. v Sampson* (1875) LR 19 Eq 462, at p. 465. Nevertheless, the different heads of public policy under which courts have declared contracts to be unenforceable are numerous, and, despite judicial statements, there is no reason to think that they may not increase still further and change over time. There are also legislative provisions in relation to some of these contracts that are also based on public policy considerations.

16.4.1 Contracts to commit crimes

A contract to commit a crime is self-evidently illegal: see *Bigos v Boustead* [1951] 1 All ER 92 (contract contrary to exchange control regulations). Equally, it is contrary to public policy for a criminal or the criminal's estate to benefit from the crime: *Beresford v Royal Insurance Co. Ltd* [1938] AC 586. (The Proceeds of Crime Act 2002, as amended, as just one example, provides for confiscation orders in relation to the proceeds of crime.) In *Gray v Thames Trains Ltd* [2009] UKHL 33, [2009] 1 AC 1339, the House of Lords applied this principle to preclude a passenger on a train involved in the Ladbroke Grove rail crash from recovering damages from the train operator whose negligence was found to have caused the crash. The passenger's psychological injuries caused by the accident had led him to commit manslaughter while suffering from post-traumatic stress disorder (PTSD). Such damages were contrary to public policy, since they flowed from a criminal act or from a sentence imposed for that criminal act.

There is more debate concerning the illegality defence and civil wrongs. In *Les Laboratoires Servier v Apotex Inc.* [2014] UKSC 55, [2015] AC 430, the Supreme Court drew a distinction between instances of civil liability, such as breaches of contract and torts, which did not contain the necessary moral turpitude since they engaged the private interest rather than the public interest, and instances of criminal or quasi-criminal acts (i.e. dishonesty) which did constitute the turpitude necessary for illegality and engaged the public interest.

Contracts to defraud HM Revenue and Customs (HMRC) have been held to be illegal: *Alexander v Rayson* [1936] 1 KB 169 (contract designed to make the value of property seem less to the rating authority) and *Q v Q* [2008] EWHC 1874 (Fam), [2009] 1 FLR 935, [2009] WTLR 1591 (agreement with illegal purpose of cheating HMRC of inheritance tax). However, a company incorporated to evade the payment of value added tax (VAT) was nevertheless able to enforce a sale of goods contract that was lawful in itself. The fraud in relation to the VAT would be committed only when there was a failure to account for it at the end of the accounting period: *21st Century Logistic Solutions Ltd (in liquidation) v Madysen Ltd* [2004] EWHC 231 (QB), [2004] 2 Lloyd's Rep 92. In *Q v Q*, the judge distinguished *21st Century Logistic* on the basis that the illegality in *Q v Q* was the purpose of the transaction, just as the intention to defraud the trustee in bankruptcy was the central purpose in *Barrett v Barrett* [2008] EWHC 1061 (Ch), [2008] 2 P & CR 17. In *K/S Lincoln v CB Richard Ellis Hotels Ltd* [2009] EWHC 2344 (TCC), [2009] BLR 591, [2010] PNLR 5, a defence to a professional negligence claim raised an allegation of tax evasion. Coulson J considered that the claimant should be given the option as to whether to pursue the relevant part of its claim. The judge noted, at [26], that such a fraud 'did not taint the underlying contract which formed the basis of the [professional negligence] claim', so that the allegation of illegality was likely to fail.

16.4.2 Contracts prejudicial to the administration of justice

Contracts that oust the jurisdiction of the courts are illegal. However, arbitration clauses in contracts are enforceable (*Scott v Avery* (1855) 5 HL Cas 811) and an English court is required to stay its own proceedings where there is an arbitration clause covering the dispute unless the clause is null and void, inoperative, or incapable of being performed (Arbitration Act 1996, s. 9).

Maintenance agreements between husband and wife in which one party agrees not to apply to the court for maintenance have been held to be contrary to public policy—*Hyman v Hyman* [1929] AC 601—but s. 34 of the Matrimonial Causes Act 1973 provides that it is only the provision purporting to restrict the right to apply to the court that is void and not the agreement itself. Therefore it is merely the case that a spouse would not be bound by a promise not to apply to the court.

It had been considered that any post-nuptial agreement that made financial arrangements for a separation that had not yet occurred would be contrary to public policy and void. However, in *MacLeod v MacLeod* [2008] UKPC 64, [2010] 1 AC 298, the Privy Council considered that agreements made after marriage that provide for future separation ('post-nuptial agreements') would be valid and enforceable under s. 34 of the Matrimonial Causes Act 1973, although not a provision that ousted the jurisdiction of the court by preventing further court access on separation or divorce. Pre-nuptial agreements were considered by the Supreme Court in *Granatino v Radmacher* [2010] UKSC 42, [2011] 1 AC 534, and the majority (Baroness Hale dissenting), whilst not concluding that they were to be fully enforceable, stated that effect should be given to such agreements (whether pre- or post-nuptial) where they were freely entered into with a full appreciation of the implications of the agreement, 'unless in the circumstances prevailing it would not be fair to hold the parties to their agreement': *per* Lord Phillips PSC, at [62]. (The Law Commission subsequently recommended that certain agreements of this type should be enforceable given various procedural safeguards (Law Com Report No. 343, *Matrimonial Property, Needs and Agreements*, 2014).)

16.4.3 Contracts prejudicial to the family

There are statutory prohibitions on relinquishing the obligations of a parent (e.g. Children Act 1989, s. 2). A surrogacy agreement (whereby it is agreed that the surrogate mother will relinquish parental responsibility in favour of another) is unenforceable under s. 1A of the Surrogacy Arrangements Act 1985, as amended by s. 36 of the Human Fertilisation and Embryology Act 1990.

16.4.4 Contracts prejudicial to (sexual) morality

It is sometimes said that contracts contrary to public morals are unenforceable. The rule is probably limited to sexual morality and attitudes to this question have been transformed in recent years. In the nineteenth century, a strict approach was taken to sexual morality, so that a promise of payment in order to induce a woman to become a man's mistress was unenforceable—*Benyon v Nettlefold* (1850) 3 Mac & G 94—and contracts ancillary to immoral purposes were also regarded as being contrary to public policy: *Pearce v Brooks* (1866) LR 1 Ex 213 (contract of hire of a carriage for the known purpose of prostitution).

The change in attitudes to sexual morality over recent years is evidenced in a number of cases in which the courts have rejected the public policy argument and held the contracts to be valid, e.g. *Armhouse Lee Ltd v Chappell*, The Times, 7 August 1996 (contract for advertising of telephone 'sex lines' was not contrary to public policy, so that the operator of the lines had to pay for the advertising), and *Sutton v Mischon de Reya* [2003] EWHC 3166 (Ch), [2004] 1 FLR 837 (deed of cohabitation between two people in a master/slave sexual relationship was not contrary to public policy). The fact that the attitude to unmarried cohabitees has been relaxed is further illustrated by the approach of the House of Lords in *Tinsley v Milligan* [1994] 1 AC 340 (the agreement between the couple was not challenged as being contrary to public policy on the basis that they were unmarried cohabitees).

16.4.5 Public corruption

Contracts that further corruption in public life are illegal. The rule is most commonly applied in the case of sales of public offices or honours.

> In *Parkinson v College of Ambulance Ltd* [1925] 2 KB 1, the claimant was encouraged to believe that, if he were to make a substantial donation to a certain charity, the officers of the charity would be able to obtain a knighthood for him. The sum of £3,000 was agreed and paid, but no knighthood was forthcoming. The claimant sued to recover the amount paid, but was unable to succeed because the contract was found to be illegal: see also the Honours (Prevention of Abuses) Act 1925.

16.4.6 Contracts in restraint of trade

Contracts in restraint of trade are contracts whereby one or both parties agree to limit their individual freedom to contract. The most important contexts in which restraint of trade clauses will be used are where the seller or a business agrees not to compete with that business for a given time and in a given geographical area, and where an ex-employee agrees not to enter the employ of a competitor for a given time or within a given geographical area. The common law will not tolerate such limitations if the public interest in free competition is adversely affected, or if the limitation is deemed contrary to public policy in terms of maintaining fairness between the parties. Any intervention in such clauses takes place precisely to protect the public interest in freedom of contract.

16.4.6.1 General principles

During the nineteenth century, the restraint of trade doctrine barely existed since freedom of contract was considered the more important policy to pursue: *Printing and Numerical Registering Co. v Sampson* (1875) LR 19 Eq 462. However, the law gradually caught up with the changes associated with industrialization, and the foundation of the modern law can be traced back to the decision of the House of Lords in *Nordenfelt v Maxim Nordenfelt Guns and Ammunition Co. Ltd* [1894] AC 535. This case concerned a restraint upon the seller of an ammunition and arms manufacturing company, which prevented him from engaging in such business anywhere in the world for 25 years.

The leading speech is that of Lord Macnaghten. His statement of the law may be summarized as follows.

> **! KEY POINT**
>
> There is an initial presumption that contracts in restraint of trade are void. The courts may of their own motion refuse to enforce such a contract. The presumption may be rebutted only by showing special justifying circumstances. Whether the circumstances alleged to justify the restraint do so, is a question of law for the court. For a restraint to be justified it must be reasonable both in the interests of the parties and in the public interest. Generally, the burden of proof in relation to what is reasonable between the parties rests on the party seeking to enforce the contract. If that burden is sustained, the party resisting enforcement has the burden of showing that the restraint is contrary to the public interest.

Illegality

16

Lord Macnaghten stressed, at p. 565, that the public has 'an interest in every person's carrying on his trade freely' and that restraints that are fair between the parties must not be 'injurious to the public'.

Of the two streams of public policy in relation to contracts in restraint of trade, fairness between the parties is predominant, since once that has been established the presumption switches to one of validity.

16.4.6.2 Reasonable between the parties

What is reasonable between the parties must be determined in each individual case, but guidance is provided by the decision in *Herbert Morris Ltd v Saxelby* [1916] AC 688. In this case, the defendant's contract of employment as an engineer contained a seven-year restraint on carrying on a wide range of related trades anywhere in the United Kingdom should he leave the claimants' employment. The claimants sought to enforce the clause and failed. The House of Lords identified two different types of contract in restraint of trade in which different policy considerations apply:

- in contracts of employment, it would not normally be reasonable to prevent a former employee from working in any capacity for a competitor, but restraints to prevent the loss of trade secrets or the poaching of customers to whom the employee had access are permitted; and

- in the sale of a business, restraints are permitted that seek to preserve the value of the 'goodwill' of the business by preventing the vendor from setting up in competition with the purchaser.

Thus, the common legitimate interests that may be protected in contracts of employment are trade secrets and clients or customers to whom the employee may have had access during the course of the employment. In each case, the identification of a legitimate interest to be protected is only the first stage in the process of justification. It must also be shown that the duration and geographical extent of the restraint are not out of proportion to the interest identified, and the restraint must not go beyond the scope of the type of activity carried on by the particular employee.

> In *Home Counties Dairies Ltd v Skilton* [1970] 1 WLR 526, a milk roundsman agreed not to sell milk or dairy produce to his former employer's customers. The restraint was found reasonable only upon an interpretation of 'dairy produce' limiting it to the kind of products with which he had dealt during the course of his employment.
>
> In *Mason v Provident Clothing & Supply Co. Ltd* [1913] AC 724, the restraint purported to prevent the employee from entering into a similar business within 25 miles of London. His employment had been in a small shop in Islington and, for that reason, the restraint was too wide to be reasonable.

In the case of sale of a business, equality of bargaining power is more likely to exist between the parties, and so fairness between the parties might be thought to be a less crucial, and the public interest a more prominent, concern. The classic case is *Nordenfelt v Maxim Nordenfelt Guns and Ammunition Co. Ltd* [1894] AC 535. The House of Lords identified the goodwill of the business as the interest entitled to protection by a clause that prevented the defendant from engaging in the business of a manufacturer of guns or ammunition for a period of 25 years. Although this was a worldwide restriction, it was no wider than necessary to protect the purchaser of the business, given the limited number of customers worldwide, and it was not injurious to the public interest.

16.4.6.3 Reasonable in the public interest

Although it would be rare for any restraint to have any perceptible effect on the competitive structure of the market as a whole, the public interest is an important consideration, especially in those cases falling outside the employment contract and the sale of the business type of restraint identified in *Herbert Morris Ltd v Saxelby* [1916] AC 688. When two companies, as a result of arm's-length bargaining, agree not to compete with each other, it may be assumed that both think that the contract is reasonable. In such a case, it is the public that is likely to suffer and control by the courts in the public interest is essential.

16.4.6.4 Exclusive dealing and exclusive service agreements

Exclusive dealing agreements are agreements between undertakings at different stages in the commercial chain that provide for a closer tie between the undertakings than a mere contract of supply. They are sometimes known as 'vertical agreements' (or 'tie agreements'). In principle, it is easy to see how such agreements might appear to be contrary to the public interest as anti-competitive.

> In *Esso Petroleum Co. Ltd v Harper's Garage (Stourport) Ltd* [1968] AC 269, the parties made a contract, known as a 'solus agreement', under which the garage owners agreed to purchase petrol only from the company. In the case of one garage, the tie was to last for four years and five months; in return, the garage owners received a discount on the price of petrol supplied to them. In the case of a second garage, the tie was to last for 21 years; in return, the garage owners received a mortgage loan of £7,000.
>
> The House of Lords made it clear that there is no overall ban on such contracts. An investigation must be made in every case into whether there is a legitimate interest to be protected, and if so, whether the restraints imposed are reasonable to protect the interests in question. On the particular facts, their Lordships found the shorter restraint to be reasonable, but the 21-year restraint was unreasonable and unenforceable.

In some circumstances, restraints are imposed to ensure that a person provides services for only one recipient. Such contracts are common in the world of professional sport and entertainment. The individual who is restricted may not have a contract of employment with the beneficiary of the restriction, but the individual is nevertheless unable to supply their services to anybody else. Such agreements are often referred to as 'exclusive service agreements'. This category includes those agreements under which employers agree to regulate employment in a particular sector and especially agree not to employ those who have previously worked for other parties to the agreement. Such agreements may be equivalent in effect to the restraints contained in contracts of employment (see **16.4.6.2**), and for that reason they are within the restraint of trade doctrine.

> In *Greig v Insole* [1978] 1 WLR 302, the organizers of international and English county cricket sought to exclude from their matches those players who participated in games promoted by a private cricketing 'circus' established in a battle over television rights. The claimant, who until this time had been captain of the England team, successfully challenged the ban imposed on the ground that it interfered with freedom of employment.

Illegality

16

The most striking cases are those in which the bodies responsible for the organization of professional sport impose a rule upon their members intended to prevent large clubs from poaching the best players from small clubs. Often, such rules are alleged to be justified in the interests of the sport-watching public. The employees of the clubs can find that they are unable to make the best commercial exploitation of their skills. The cases make it clear that such rules are in restraint of trade and thus invalid: *Eastham v Newcastle United Football Club Ltd* [1964] Ch 413.

In *Proactive Sports Management Ltd v Rooney* [2011] EWCA Civ 1444, [2012] 2 All ER (Comm) 815, the restraint related to exclusivity in relation to the 'image rights' of a sportsman. At the age of 17, Wayne Rooney had entered into a contract giving exclusive control of his 'image rights' for eight years. This meant that Proactive had exclusive use of Rooney's name in connection with any on- or off-field promotional activity. Commission was payable at a flat rate of 20 per cent of Rooney's earnings. The court applied the restraint of trade doctrine to strike down the restraint in view of Rooney's age, the duration of the contract, and the flat-rate commission, with no tapering arrangements. In addition, Rooney had received no independent legal advice and the court considered that the contract had been effectively 'dictated to him'.

There have also been a number of cases concerning exclusive service agreements between musicians or pop groups and their management.

In **Schroeder Music Publishing Co. Ltd v Macaulay** [1974] 1 WLR 1308, an unknown songwriter entered into a contract with a music publisher whereby the publisher engaged his exclusive services for five years; if royalties exceeded £5,000, the contract was to be automatically extended for a further five years. The contract was terminable at the option of the music publisher (who had copyright in all compositions), but not at the option of the songwriter. The publisher was not obliged to publish any songs. The songwriter sought to escape the confines of the contract after achieving considerable popular success, alleging that the agreement was contrary to public policy. The House of Lords held that such agreements fell within the restraint of trade doctrine. The restrictions in this agreement were one-sided and removed all incentive to creativity. Accordingly, the agreement was an unreasonable restraint of trade.

16.5 The effect of illegality

The general principle is that illegal contracts are unenforceable: *Holman v Johnson* (1775) 1 Cowp 341, at 343 ('No court will lend its aid to a man who founds his cause of action upon an illegal or immoral act'). That principle was reaffirmed by Lord Goff and Lord Browne-Wilkinson in *Tinsley v Milligan* [1994] 1 AC 340, at pp. 355 and 363, with the majority adopting a reliance test. However, the principle does not survive the majority decision in *Patel v Mirza* [2016] UKSC 42. The enforceability of an illegal contract depends upon the operation of the 'range of factors' identified by Lord Toulson in *Patel v Mirza* (see **16.1.1**) and not simply upon whether the claimant has to rely upon illegality.

16.5.1 Collateral contracts

The courts may allow recovery on a collateral contract, but only exceptionally, and this is of limited utility since a remedy under a collateral contract must not be the equivalent of enforcing the illegal contract. The device of collateral contract was developed as a means of overcoming the strict rule that illegal contracts could not be enforced. After *Patel v Mirza* it will rarely be necessary to resort to this fiction. Its operation can be illustrated by the following case.

> In **Strongman (1945) Ltd v Sincock** [1955] 2 QB 525, a builder was informed by his client that the client would obtain the necessary licences, which the client then failed to do. A contract to build without a licence was absolutely prohibited by statute. Although the builder could not recover the contract price because the contract was prohibited, the assurance that the client would obtain the necessary licences was considered to constitute an enforceable collateral contract to obtain them. The Court of Appeal held the client liable for breach of this collateral contract, which was not an illegal contract.

This (fictitious) kind of enforceable collateral contract enabled a court to protect an innocent party to whom a promise or misrepresentation has been made, but it must be distinguished from other transactions collateral to illegal contracts. For example, security given in respect of payment for, or performance of, an illegal contract is tainted by the illegality of the main transaction: *Fisher v Bridges* (1854) 3 El & Bl 642.

16.5.2 Reliance on the illegality of the contract

Tinsley v Milligan rested upon the principle that where a party was required to rely on his own illegal conduct in the performance of a contract in order to found a cause of action, the claim would fail. As seen at **16.1.1**, *Tinsley v Milligan* did not prevent the claimant from relying upon a property right if there was no need to plead illegality to establish that right. It was uncertain whether *Tinsley v Milligan* was confined to contracts illegal as formed or whether it extended to the case where one party had committed an unlawful act in the course of performance. If it did, then the effect of *Patel v Mirza* is to remove that possibility and to allow recovery even if reliance is required as long as the other 'range of factors' points towards recovery. It would seem that if the claimant does not need to rely upon illegality, then there is no need to go further and consider the 'range of factors' identified in *Patel*.

16.5.3 A claimant may be able to sever the offending parts

In some circumstances, illegal contracts remain enforceable by both parties provided that changes are made by removing the offending parts. Severance is allowed only if it is consistent with the public policy that made the contract containing the offending part illegal. If the whole contract is tainted by the illegality, severance cannot save it.

The applicable principles were explained in *Sadler v Imperial Life Assurance Co. of Canada Ltd* (1988) IRLR 388, as approved in *Beckett Investment Management Group Ltd v Hall* [2007] EWCA Civ 613, [2007] ICR 1539.

1. The unenforceable provision is capable of being removed without the necessity of adding to or modifying the wording of what remains, i.e. the illegal portion of the contract must be capable of being verbally and grammatically separated from the rest. *This principle is usually called the 'blue pencil' test.*

Illegality

16

In *Goldsoll v Goldman* [1915] 1 Ch 292, the claimants were dealers in imitation jewellery and entered into an agreement with the defendant, a competitor, to the effect that the defendant would no longer compete with them in any capacity, either in his own right, or as an agent or employee of others, for a period of two years. The clause purported to cover 'the county of London, England, Scotland, Ireland, Wales, or any part of the United Kingdom of Great Britain and Ireland and the Isle of Man or France, the United States of America, Russia or Spain, or within 25 miles of Potsdamerstrasse, Berlin, or St Stefans Kirche, Vienna'. The Court of Appeal was willing to enforce the contract, but for the unreasonable geographical extent of the restraint, and did so after severing the words from 'or France' to the end of the clause.

2. The remaining terms must continue to be supported by consideration.

3. The removal of the unenforceable part must not change the character of the contract to the extent that it becomes 'not the sort of contract that the parties entered into at all'. Whether, in any particular case, the scope and intention of an agreement will be so altered by severance is a question of fact.

In *Attwood v Lamont* [1920] 3 KB 571, the respondent was the owner of a department store, which carried out tailoring and general outfitting. The appellant was employed as a cutter in the tailoring department and his contract of employment contained a clause restraining him from working at any time in the future within 10 miles of the store in the 'business of a tailor, dressmaker, general draper, milliner, hatter, haberdasher, gentlemen's, ladies' or children's outfitter'. The restraint was found to be too wide, since the appellant's only significant skill was as a tailor, and the question arose whether the other functions on the list might be severed. The Court of Appeal held that the rest of the clause could not be severed and that this was a covenant that 'must stand or fall in its unaltered form'.

In *Bennett v Bennett* [1952] 1 KB 249, a husband and wife separated, and the wife commenced divorce proceedings in which she applied for a maintenance order against her husband. Before the trial, she entered into an agreement with the husband by which he undertook to pay her an annuity and to convey property to her, in return for which she promised not to pursue any claim for maintenance in the courts. The husband did not keep his side of the bargain. The promise not to seek maintenance was illegal, so that the whole of the consideration to be furnished by the wife failed, i.e. the various covenants.

16.6 Recovery of money or property

16.6.1 The effect of illegality

Before the decision in *Patel v Mirza* the common law had become complex and labyrinthine. The starting point was that the general rule in *Holman v Johnson* (1775) 1 Cowp 341, that a party who had to rely upon his own illegality could not enforce the contract, applied equally to claims brought to recover money or property passing as a result of an illegal contract as it does to enforcement of the contract itself. The rigidity of this rule led to the development of a series of exceptions under which the claimant would not be deprived of property rights because of illegality. In the light of *Patel v Mirza* there is no longer any need to consider these exceptions; those interested in them may refer to the previous edition of this work.

16.6.2 Reform

16.6.2.1 Proposals for legislative reform

In *Tinsley v Milligan* [1994] 1 AC 340, at pp. 363–4, Lord Goff advocated reform of this area of the law on the basis that the present rules are 'indiscriminate in their effect, and are capable therefore of producing injustice'. The Law Commission examined this issue in its Consultation Paper *Illegal Transactions: The effect of illegality on contracts and trusts*, LCCP No. 154 (1999), and also concluded that the law was 'unnecessarily complex', 'uncertain', and 'may give rise to unjust decisions'. It therefore recommended that the rules (reliance principle, presumption of advancement, and the withdrawal exception) be replaced by giving the courts a discretion to decide whether to enforce the illegal contract or to permit a claim in restitution, or to recognize property rights either created or transferred under an illegal contract. The discretion was to be circumscribed, in the broadest sense, by requiring the courts to consider a number of factors: the seriousness of the illegality involved; the knowledge and intention of the party claiming relief; whether denying the claim would deter the illegality; whether denying the claim would further the purpose of the rule that rendered the transaction illegal; and whether denying the claim would be proportionate to the illegality involved (para. 7.43).

It was also proposed that this discretion should not exist for contracts that do not involve any legal wrong, but are illegal because they are otherwise contrary to public policy.

In its consultative report *The Illegality Defence*, LCCP No. 189 (2009), the Law Commission abandoned any thoughts of a general discretion and re-emphasized the importance of meeting policy objectives when responding to illegality, considering that it was not possible to devise a workable system of rules to determine when the illegality defence should operate in this context. The preferred approach was to assess each case to see whether 'the application of the illegality defence can be justified on the basis of the policies that underlie that defence'. It followed that a balancing exercise was called for that weighed up the policies and assessed whether depriving a claimant of its rights was a proportionate response to meet those policy objectives.

The Law Commission did, however, make a specific recommendation for a statutory discretion to determine the effect of illegality on some trusts, on the basis that the principle in *Tinsley v Milligan* and associated principles were capable of operating in a way that was arbitrary, potentially unfair, and uncertain in terms of its operation. In March 2010, the Law Commission published its final report *The Illegality Defence*, Law Com. No. 320, which included a draft Trusts (Concealment of Interests) Bill. In this report, the Law Commission recommended that, where a trust has been set up to conceal the beneficiary's interest in order to commit a criminal offence, there should be legislative intervention to provide the courts with a discretion to deprive the beneficiary of its interest in limited circumstances. The short draft Bill was intended to implement the recommendation. However, the government announced that this reform was not a pressing legislative priority at the time and that it was 'minded not to implement the . . . proposals': Ministry of Justice, *Report on the Implementation of Law Commission Proposals*, HC 1900 (March 2012), para. 52.

The Law Commission had also been concerned about the interaction of the presumption of advancement and the illegality principles. It recommended abolition of the rule as discriminatory, and the Equality Act 2010 contains a provision to this effect in s. 199—although, at the time of writing, it has yet to be brought into force. In the meantime, even the Law Commission considers that intervening developments in trusts case law mean that this section might not achieve its objectives in any event.

On a more positive note, the Law Commission report had recommended that any improvement to the law 'can best be left to development through the case law', which focused on the application of the policy factors underpinning the illegality defence. In *Stone & Rolls Ltd (in Liquidation) v Moore Stephens (a firm)* [2009] UKHL 39, [2009] 1 AC 1391, a company brought an action against its auditors for negligence in auditing the company accounts. The alleged negligence consisted of a failure to identify massive fraud by the company's sole director in circumstances in which the company's creditors had suffered significant losses. (The key issue was one of corporate attribution, i.e. could the fraud of the director be attributed to the company? If the fraud were the company's, the question arose of whether the company could rely on its own illegality, i.e. the *Tinsley v Milligan* principle.) The majority of the House of Lords (3:2, Lords Phillips, Walker, and Brown in the majority) considered that the company's claim was barred by illegality. However, Lords Scott and Mance (dissenting) looked beyond the company, which was insolvent, to the creditors and noted that any damages would benefit them. The company itself was securing 'no benefit' and therefore there was nothing to offend considerations of public policy. Lord Mance, at [226], rejected a 'mechanistic approach' to the application of *ex turpi causa*, considering that its purpose was 'to preserve the integrity of the justice system' by preventing a person from benefiting from their crime or other illegal conduct. Lord Phillips, in the majority, also considered the 'no benefit' principle to be an important motivation in illegality cases. His approach was dictated by the fact that the duty of care was owed to the company, but not to the creditors—and the company was affected by the illegality.

16.6.2.2 Judicial resolution

As predicted by the Law Commission, the deficiencies in the law were capable of being corrected by the courts without legislative assistance. The 'range of factors' analysis of the majority of the Supreme Court in *Patel v Mirza* (see **16.1.1**) has replaced the earlier rigid principle and the complex set of exceptions that were necessary to overcome what were regarded by the courts as disproportionate or unfair consequences of illegality.

Patel was considered briefly in *Singularis Holdings Ltd v Daiwa Capital Markets Europe Ltd* [2018] EWCA Civ 84. This was a claim by the liquidators of the claimant against the defendant stockbroker who had held funds belonging to the claimant and had paid them over to other companies owned by the claimant's controller. One of the defences raised by the defendant was that the conduct of the controller was imputed to the claimant so that the claimant was relying upon its own wrongful acts in bringing the proceedings. The defence was dismissed on the ground that the claimant had a legal personality distinct from its controller, but that had the question of illegality arisen then the approach was one that involved 'balancing multiple policy considerations and applying a proportionality approach'. The Court of Appeal agreed with the trial judge that *Patel v Mirza* pointed away from a defence based on illegality: the purpose of the prohibition on breach of fiduciary duty was to prevent the company from becoming a victim of fraud, and that purpose would not be enhanced by denying the company a remedy.

MULTIPLE-CHOICE QUESTIONS

Test your knowledge by trying this chapter's **multiple-choice questions**:
www.oup.com/uk/poole

FURTHER READING

Beatson, 'Repudiation of illegal purpose as a ground for restitution' (1975) 91 LQR 313.

Berg, 'Illegality and equitable interests' [1993] JBL 513.

Buckley, 'Illegal transaction: chaos or discretion?' (2000) 20 LS 155.

Buckley, *Illegality and Public Policy*, 3rd edn (Sweet and Maxwell, 2013).

Coote, 'Another look at *Bowmakers v Barnet Instruments*' (1972) 34 MLR 38.

Creighton, 'The recovery of property transferred for illegal purposes' (1997) 60 MLR 102.

Davies, 'The illegality defence: two steps forward, one step back?' [2009] Conv 182.

Dickson, 'Restitution and illegal transactions' in Burrows (ed.), *Essays on the Law of Restitution* (Clarendon Press, 1991).

Enonchong, 'Title claims and illegal transactions' (1995) 111 LQR 135.

Enonchong, 'Illegal transactions: the future? (LCCP No. 154)' [2000] RLR 82.

Furmston, 'Recent developments in illegal contracts' in Merkin and Devenney (eds.), *Essays in Memory of Professor Jill Poole* (Informa Law, 2018), ch. 10.

Goudkamp, 'The end of an era? Illegality in private law in the Supreme Court' (2017) 133 LQR 14.

Grabiner, 'Illegality and restitution explained by the Supreme Court' (2017) 76 CLJ 18.

Law Commission Consultation Paper No. 154, *Illegal Transactions: The Effect of Illegality on Contracts and Trusts* (1999).

Law Commission Consultative Report No. 189, *The Illegality Defence* (2009).

Lim, 'Ex turpi causa, reformation not retribution' [2017] MLR 927.

Phang, 'The intractable problems of illegality and public policy in the law of contract: a comparative perspective' in Merkin and Devenney (eds.), *Essays in Memory of Professor Jill Poole* (Informa Law, 2018), ch. 12.

Rose, 'Reconsidering illegality' (1996) 10 JCL 271.

Sumption, 'Reflections on the law of illegality', Chancery Bar Association, April 2012.

Turner, 'Rescission of the doctrine of rescission for fraud' (2016) 75 CLJ 206.

Virgo, 'Withdrawal from illegal transactions: a matter for consideration' [1996] CLJ 23.

Worthington, 'Corporate attribution and agency, back to basics' (2017) 133 LQR 118–43.

INDEX